A Social and Economic History of the Theatre to 300 BC

Volume II: Theatre beyond Athens

This is the second volume of *A Social and Economic History of the Theatre to 300 BC* and focuses exclusively on theatre culture in Attica (Rural Dionysia) and the rest of the Greek world. It presents and discusses in detail all the documentary and material evidence for theatre culture and dramatic production from the first two centuries of theatre history, namely the period ca. 500 to ca. 300 BC. The traditional assumption is laid to rest that theatre was an exclusively or primarily Athenian institution, with the inclusion of all sources of information for theatrical performances in twenty-three deme sites and over one hundred and twenty independent Greek (and some non-Greek) cities. All texts are translated and made accessible to non-specialists and specialists alike. The volume will be a fundamental work of reference for all classicists and theatre historians interested in ancient theatre and its wider historical contexts.

Eric Csapo is Professor of Classics and **Peter Wilson** is William Ritchie Professor of Classics in the Department of Classics and Ancient History at the University of Sydney. They are leading experts on the early history of the theatre. Since 2005 they have collaborated closely on a three-volume work, *A Social and Economic History of the Theatre to 300 BC,* which will substantially alter our understanding of the ancient theatre from its origin to the Early Hellenistic period. Volume 2, *Theatre Beyond Athens,* is the first to be published, with two further volumes soon to follow. They co-edited *Greek Theatre in the Fourth Century BC* (2014) and are authors of *Actors and Icons of the Ancient Theatre* (Csapo, 2010) and *The Athenian Institution of the Khoregia* (Wilson, Cambridge 2000).

A Social and Economic History of the Theatre to 300 BC

VOLUME II

Theatre beyond Athens: Documents with
Translation and Commentary

ERIC CSAPO
University of Sydney

PETER WILSON
University of Sydney

CAMBRIDGE
UNIVERSITY PRESS

University Printing House, Cambridge CB2 8BS, United Kingdom

One Liberty Plaza, 20th Floor, New York, NY 10006, USA

477 Williamstown Road, Port Melbourne, VIC 3207, Australia

314–321, 3rd Floor, Plot 3, Splendor Forum, Jasola District Centre, New Delhi – 110025, India

79 Anson Road, #06–04/06, Singapore 079906

Cambridge University Press is part of the University of Cambridge.

It furthers the University's mission by disseminating knowledge in the pursuit of education, learning, and research at the highest international levels of excellence.

www.cambridge.org
Information on this title: www.cambridge.org/9780521765572
DOI: 10.1017/9781139023931

© Eric Csapo and Peter Wilson 2020

First published 2020

Printed in the United Kingdom by TJ International Ltd, Padstow Cornwall

A catalogue record for this publication is available from the British Library.

Library of Congress Cataloging-in-Publication Data
Names: Csapo, Eric, author. | Wilson, Peter, 1964– author.
Title: A social and economic history of the theatre to 300 BC.
Description: Cambridge, United Kingdom ; New York, NY : Cambridge University Press, [2019] | Includes bibliographical references and index. Contents: – v. 2. Theatre beyond Athens: documents with translation and commentary / Eric Csapo, University of Sydney ; Peter Wilson, University of Sydney.
Identifiers: LCCN 2019020561 | ISBN 9780521765572 (alk. paper)
Subjects: LCSH: Theater – Greece – History – To 500. | Greek drama – History and criticism.
Classification: LCC PA3201.A2 S63 2019 | DDC 792.0938–dc23
LC record available at https://lccn.loc.gov/2019020561

ISBN 978-0-521-76557-2 Hardback

To MM and JSS

Contents

A plate section can be found between pages 492 and 493

Illustrations

III

IV

Preface

Theatre beyond Athens is the second volume of *A Social and Economic History of the Theatre to 300 BC* and the first to be published. Volume 1 collects the evidence for the Athenian theatre festivals. Volume 3 deals with the people who participated in or patronised theatre. *Theatre beyond Athens* for the first time systematically collects and discusses the evidence for theatre outside the city of Athens from the Late Archaic to the Early Hellenistic period (ca. 500–ca. 300). Part III presents what is known of theatre culture in Attica and Part IV examines theatre culture in the central and eastern Mediterranean and Black Sea.

For Volumes 1 and 3 we were able to build on a substratum of scholarly research reaching back to the early nineteenth century. By contrast, until recently the contents of this volume were a matter of general disinterest and neglect. The Rural Dionysia attracted some attention from religious and regional histories, but virtually none from historians of literature, drama or theatre, except perhaps in the search for fossilised clues about the origins of drama in the Dionysian 'vegetation rites' of the Attic countryside. If rural Attica was pictured as theatre's remote past, theatre outside of Athens was its remote future. A great deal of evidence was ignored, suppressed or otherwise dismissed to preserve the vision that theatre for most of the fifth and fourth century was purely or essentially Athenian. The purpose of this volume is to make that evidence known and explore its implications.

In this volume there is little connection with the great tradition of ancient theatre history that leads from Wilhelm Becker's *Charicles* of 1840, through Albert Müller's magisterial *Lehrbuch der griechischen Bühnenalterthümer* of 1886, up to the second edition of Arthur Pickard-Cambridge's *Dramatic Festivals of Athens* of 1968. This tradition practised and promulgated the extreme Athenocentrism that marks theatre history up to the very end of the twentieth century. The idea of writing Classical theatre history outside Athens was a provocative idea up to and even long after Pat Easterling's seminal study of 1994 'Euripides Outside Athens: A Speculative Note', which in turn inspired Oliver Taplin's groundbreaking 1999 essay 'Spreading the Word through Performance'. The major landmarks are all much more recent: David Carter's collection of 2010, *Why Athens?*, challenged traditional Athenocentricity in the study of tragedy; Kate Bosher's *Theater Outside Athens* of 2012 was the first ever collection of essays on Archaic and Classical theatre in the Greek West. Since 2014 the spread of theatre has become a major focus of scholarly research: that year saw the publication of Vahtikhari's *Tragedy Performances Outside Athens in the Late Fifth and Fourth Centuries*, and important essays by Moloney on theatre in Macedon, by Braund and Hall on theatre in the Black Sea, and by Robinson on theatre in native Peucetia, all collected in the volume *Greek Theatre in the Fourth Century BC*. Without attempting to give an exhaustive scholarly background (for which see the introduction to *Greek Theatre in the Fourth Century BC*, and Csapo and Wilson 2015), but only to give an impression of how rapidly this field is developing, we should note that as we write this Edmund Stewart's *Greek Tragedy on the Move* has just been published, Hans Peter Isler's *Antike Theaterbauten: Ein Handbuch* and Anne Duncan's *Tyranny and Theater in the Ancient World* are in press, and David Braund, Edith Hall and Rosie Wyles' *Greek Theatre and Performance Culture around the Ancient Black Sea* is in preparation. Scholarship in this area is evolving so quickly that we found it a full-time occupation just to keep up with developments related to our topic.

This volume differs from the above-mentioned in scope and comprehensiveness. With the exception of the survey in Csapo and Wilson 2015, those books and essays were confined to specific regions, to the history of tragic production, or to the history of theatre architecture. This volume includes all regions that have produced certain or plausible evidence for theatre culture within our timeframe. Our definition of theatre culture is also broad. We include evidence not only of all genres of dramatic performance, but also the lyric choral genres that were known officially as 'men's' and 'boys'' choruses, and more popularly as 'circular choruses' and 'dithyrambs'. In order to avoid adopting and perpetuating an Athenocentric model of theatre culture, we have also investigated and discussed all known theatres for which there is evidence of any kind of musical, choral or representational performance of any sort. We attempt to give a full account of the character of theatre culture in each region, so far as the evidence permits. At the same time we have tried to identify broader regional and transregional trends. Though we hope we do this well enough, our aim in this volume is not just to prove that Classical theatre, so far from being exclusively Athenian, cannot even be said to be securely Greek. Our more ambitious goal is to lay a foundation for the institutional history of theatre in its own right. The lodestar of this project was always the larger question of the how, when, what and why of theatre's first spread through the Mediterranean and beyond. The received account struggles with the contradiction of a Classical theatre exclusively in, by and for Athens, instantly replaced by an equally static vision of a Hellenistic theatre that is ubiquitously Greek. We hope to replace that with an account of a much more nuanced and fluid process. Without it, we feel, theatre history is not really possible.

If this second volume owes less than the others to Pickard-Cambridge, it adheres no less than they to his guiding principle 'to keep as closely as possible to the evidence, and to state the evidence fully enough to enable the reader to judge for himself the value of the conclusions drawn from it' (Preface, First Edition of *Dramatic Festivals of Athens*). We aspire not only to allow our readers to give informed consent, but to give them the wherewithal to disagree with our conclusions. We have therefore been more scrupulous even than Pickard-Cambridge in presenting the evidence. While Pickard-Cambridge often included the Greek or Latin texts only in brief footnotes or appendices, we place them in full citation (with relevant context) at the very beginning of each discussion. This is true not only of texts but, as far as cost permitted, we have included in the same sections images of important artefacts or site plans. In the case of texts we have taken care to make use of the newest or most reliable editions, but in many cases we have also exercised editorial judgement, and provided in a critical apparatus any alternative readings that might be of theatre-historical consequence. In many cases, we have been able to view by autopsy inscriptions, artefacts or important sites. Unlike Pickard-Cambridge we offer a full translation, not only to make ancient theatre history available to a much broader audience, but also to draw attention to nuances of language, arrangement or punctuation that may affect interpretation. At times we have included evidence that we believe wrongly contributed to conclusions absorbed by the scholarly tradition, so that our readership can pass its own judgement on the evidence's irrelevance. In this way we attempt to give as close an impression as possible of the nature and limitations of the evidence itself before embarking on a discussion of its historical value.

In the twelve years we have spent on this volume we have acquired an enormous intellectual debt to colleagues for advice, information and help acquiring resources of all kinds. We are grateful to Delphine Ackermann, Sophie Agelidis, Emmanuela Bakola, Anna Banfi, Kirsten Bedigan, Alastair Blanshard, Maria Grazia Branciforti, Alexander Cambitoglou, Tom Carpenter, John Colarusso, Thomas Coward, Jaime Curbera, Alessia Dimartino, Amanda Dusting, Federico Favi, Patrick Finglass, Rune Frederiksen, Daniele Fusi, Vincent Gabrielsen, Marco Germani, Laura Gianvittorio, Francesco Guizzi, Elisabeth Günther, Klaus Hallof, Johanna Hanink, Sally Humphreys, Richard Hunter, Lucy Jackson, Fotini Karassava-Tsilingiri, Annette Kelaher, Denis Knoepfler, Anna Lamari, Stephen Lambert, Angelike Lampaki, Robin Lane Fox, Brigitte Le Guen, John Ma, Alessandra Manieri, Clemente Marconi, Giovanni Marginesu, Hallie Marshall, Toph Marshall, Maria Martinelli, Angelos Matthaiou, Bernadette McCall, Archibald McKenzie, Beatrice McLoughlin, Ian McPhee, Raimund Merker, Silvia Milanezi, Benjamin Millis, Giuseppina Monterosso, Jean-Charles Moretti, Glenn Most, Yannis Nakas, Sebastiana Nervegna, Douglas Olson, Massimiliano Ornaghi, Robin Osborne, Alessandro Pagliara, Elodie Paillard, Giorgos Papadopoulos, Zozi Papadopoulou, Nikolaos Papazarkadas, Robert Parker, Stavros Paspalas, Spyros Petrounakos, Alexa Piqueux, Maria Platonos-Yiota, David Pritchard, Bodil Rasmussen, Ted Robinson, David Roselli, Jeffery Rusten, Maria Salta, Gerry Schaus, Scott Scullion, David Sider, Michael Silk, William Slater, George Steinhauer, Edmund Stewart, Jelle Stoop, Daniela Summa, Kazuhiro Takeuchi, Davide Tanasi, Oliver Taplin, Mario Telò, Stephen Tracy, Monique Trédé, Vesa Vahtikari, John Whitehouse, Hector Williams, Bill Zewadski, Denis Zhuralev and Bernhard Zimmermann. Very special thanks for constant and unfailing advice and support are owed to Hans Goette, Dick Green, Andrew Hartwig and Meg Miller. We would like to acknowledge the aid of the following institutions for material resources and support: Australian Research Council, Centre for Classical and Near Eastern Studies of Australia, Australian Archaeological Institute at Athens, Deutsches Archäologische Institut both in Berlin and Athens, Loeb Classical Library Foundation, Alexander S. Onassis Public Benefit Foundation, Ian Potter Foundation, Nicholas Anthony Aroney Research Fund, Faculty of Arts and Social Sciences of the University of Sydney, School of Philosophical and Historical Inquiry of the University of Sydney, Inscriptiones Graecae, Clare Hall College and Pembroke College in Cambridge, Institute of Classical Studies in London, All Souls College, Corpus Christi College, New College, Worcester College in Oxford, the Institute of Advanced Studies of the University of Freiburg (FRIAS), and the directors and staff of the National Museum and the Epigraphical Museum in Athens. We thank Michael Sharp for his patient support throughout this process, and Sarah Starkey and Malcolm Todd for the care they took converting our typescript into a book.

Cross-References and Conventions

Cross-References

The internal cross-references are always given in boldface and follow the sequence: **I Ai 1a**, i.e. roman numeral in upper case > capital letter > roman numeral in lower case > numeral > lower case letter. These elements refer to: Part, Section, Segment (where appropriate), Subsegment (where appropriate) and Document. While all elements follow the same sequence not all parts of the sequence appear in every reference. To avoid such lengthy cross-references as much as possible, we abbreviate where the cross-referenced item is in the same Part and abbreviate more radically where the cross-reference is in the same Segment or Subsegment.

The roman numeral in upper case refers to the major divisions of the work: they are the six Parts, two Parts per each Volume.

Volume 1:	**I** Dionysia	**II**	Other Theatre Festivals
Volume 2:	**III** Attica	**IV**	Beyond Attica
Volume 3:	**V** Performers	**VI**	Political Patrons

As mentioned, this first element is only given if the reference is to a different Part. If, therefore, the reference begins with a capital letter it is to a different Section of the same Part. The Sections are deme locations in Part **III**, but larger regions in Part **IV**. The last three elements of the cross-reference are used only as required. Thus **III X** refers to the one document that we have from Sphettos, but **III Yi** is the first of several documents from Thorikos. Within Part **III** these documents will be referenced simply as **X** and **Yi**. Where there is only one document as at Sphettos, **X** may refer also to the commentary.

The Sections of Part **IV** are regional subdivisions.

- **A** West Greece (Italy and Sicily)
- **B** Megarid, Isthmus and Peloponnese
- **C** Central Greece (Mainland, Ionian Islands, Macedon, Thrace)
- **D** Aegean Islands
- **E** Asia Minor (including Cyprus)
- **F** Black Sea (including Hellespont, Propontis, Bosporus)
- **G** Africa

A reference to **IV D** is to the Section Introduction or the whole Section. The lower case roman numeral marks a Segment that is usually a specific location (though one location can sometimes be broken into several Segments). As above we have used further subdivision only where necessary. **IV Div** takes you immediately to the one document we have for theatre in Cos, but the first document for the more amply attested Rhodes is **IV Dxi**

1. As above the **IV** is omitted where the cross-reference is to the same Part. Within each subsection (e.g. **Dxi**) the documents are internally referenced by the numeral. In this volume further subdivision by lower case letter almost never occurs. The system is easier in practice than this detailed explanation makes it sound.

The abbreviations we use for Greek authors are those found in *A Greek–English Lexicon* by G. Liddell and R. Scott, revised by H. S. Jones (Oxford 1996). Exceptions were made for the plays of Aristophanes that can be translated with an English monosyllable (*Knights*, *Wasps*, *Clouds*, *Peace*, *Birds*, *Wealth*) and the *Laws* and *Republic* (abbreviated *Rep.*) of Plato. For Latin authors we use the abbreviations in *Der Kleine Pauly, Lexikon der Antike* (Stuttgart 1964). Journal abbreviations are those used by the *American Journal of Archaeology* 104 (2000) 10–24, supplemented where necessary by the abbreviations used in *L'Année Philologique*. Other abbreviations are given at the beginning of the Bibliography at the back of this volume.

Conventions

All dates are BC except where indicated otherwise or where blatantly obvious. We have only added BC for dates in the last decade of the ancient era (9–1 BC) in the belief that such redundancy is helpful for signalling that the single digits stand for year-dates.

The names of ancient Greek persons and places well enough known to receive a heading in the *Oxford Classical Dictionary*, 3rd edn by S. Hornblower and A. Spawforth (Oxford 1996), are spelled as they appear in that work. Less well known names are transliterated according to more standard modern conventions (κ = k, χ = ch, υ = y). Thus 'Socrates' is the famous philosopher, but 'Sokrates' is a less famous man of the same name. There are a very few exceptions to this rule: Odeion (not Odeum), Thorikos (not Thoricus), and Taras (not Tarentum).

We capitalise the first letter of some words to indicate their use as a proper name referring to a famous location, practice or institution in Athens, but use lower case elsewhere. This will prove more helpful in Volumes 1 and 3, but we felt bound to be consistent with this practice even in this volume. Thus 'Theatre (of Dionysus)' is the theatre building in Athens, but 'theatre' is a building elsewhere; 'Sanctuary (of Dionysus)' is the sanctuary of Dionysus Eleuthereus in Athens, but 'sanctuary' is any other sacred precinct; 'Proagon' is the ceremony in Athens, but 'proagon' is the equivalent elsewhere; 'Parade' is the Dionysian *pompe* in Athens, but 'parade' is the equivalent elsewhere.

PART III

ATTICA

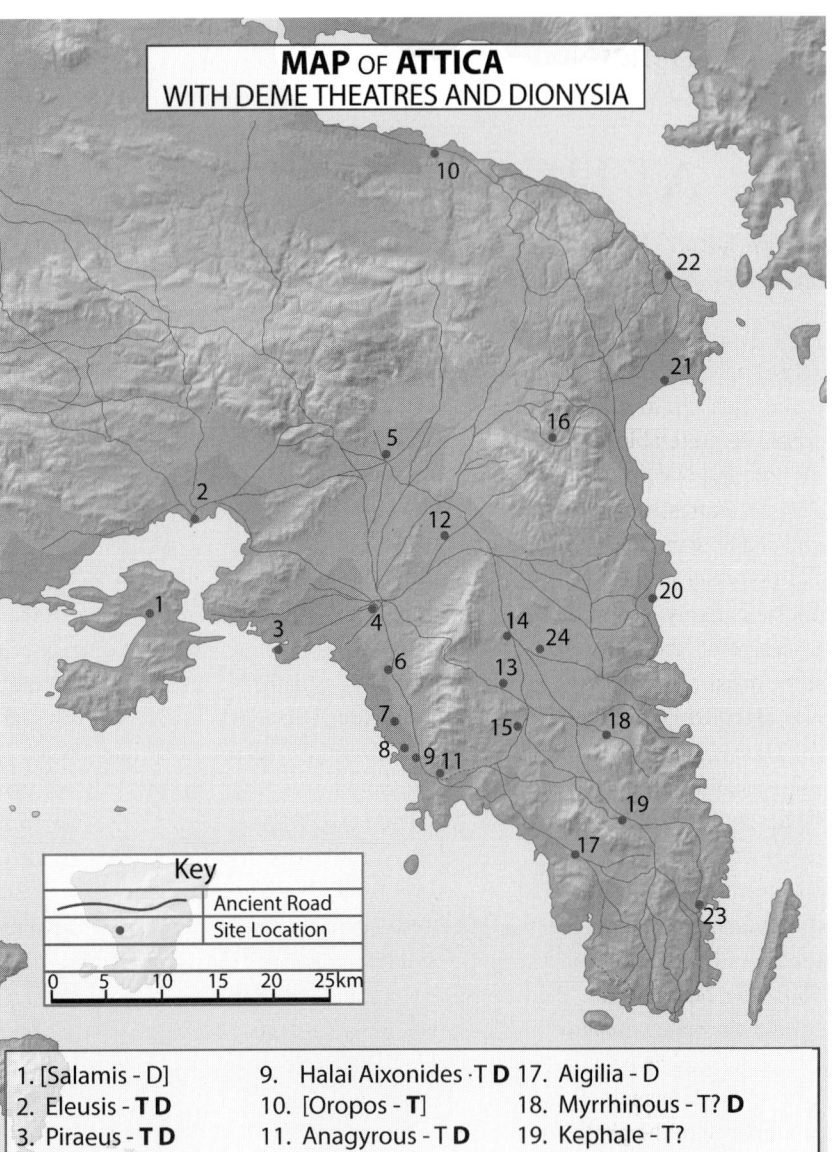

MAP OF ATTICA
WITH DEME THEATRES AND DIONYSIA

Key

Ancient Road

Site Location

0   5   10   15   20   25km

1. [Salamis - D]
2. Eleusis - **T D**
3. Piraeus - **T D**
4. Kollytos - **D**
5. Acharnae- **T D**
6. Euonymon - **T** D
7. Halimous -**T** D
8: Aixone - **T D**

9. Halai Aixonides ·**T D**
10. [Oropos - **T**]
11. Anagyrous - **T D**
12. Phlya - T? D?
13. Sphettos - **T D**
14. Paiania - D
15. Lamptrai T?D
16. Ikarion - **T D**

17. Aigilia - D
18. Myrrhinous - T? **D**
19. Kephale - T?
20. Halai Araphenides - T D
21. Marathon - T? D?
22. Rhamnus - **T D**
23. Thorikos **T D**
24. Oa - D?

D - Certain Dionysia in the deme
D - Likely Dionysia in the deme
T - A theatre attested in the deme
T - A theatre likely in the deme

N

A | General

Introduction

The festivals for Dionysus held by the Attic demes in the month of Posideon (late December: **Aiii**; **Rii**; **Y Introduction**) are known generally to modern scholarship and some ancient observers as the Rural Dionysia, τὰ κατ' ἀγροὺς Διονύσια (**Ai**; **Aiv**; **Oi**; **I Ai 1a**; Sch. Pl. *Rep.* 475d; Sch. Aeschin. 1.43, 95 Dilts; *AB* 1.235.6–8; Hsch. δ 1887). It would be preferable to call these festivals deme Dionysia, or Attic Dionysia. The qualifier τὰ κατ' ἀγρούς 'in the fields' first appears in 425 (**Ai**) and it has been plausibly suggested that the expression, along with the perception it embodies of a sharp antithesis between city and countryside, were products of the mass displacement of Athenians from the latter to the former in the early years of the Peloponnesian War (Polinskaya 2006, 72–3). The phrase is likely also to have depended to some extent on a distinction with the pre-existing name of 'the Dionysia in the City' τὰ Διονύσια τὰ ἐν ἄστει, but it never achieved the same quasi-official status. The demes themselves call their festival simply 'the Dionysia' (e.g. **Bvii**; **Diii**; **Div**; **Eii**; **Hx**; **Mx**; **Rii**; **Vv**; **Wv**; *SEG* 33, 147, l. 31; 'the festival and agon for Dionysus' τῶι Διο|νύσωι τὴν ἑορτὴν ἐποίησεν καὶ τὸν ἀγῶ|να in **Mvi**). The 'rural' sobriquet did however stick (**Oi**; cf. **Aiv**), but always reflects a vantage point from the city (Henrichs 1990, 272; Jones 2004, 127) and never appears in any document emanating directly from a deme. It cannot of itself sustain the view that the Dionysus of these festivals was much more closely tied than the god from Eleutherae to the productive life cycle of the land and to notions of fertility, his festival designed to promote vegetative fertility at a time – mid-winter – when it seems most absent (*DTC*[2] 42–3; Henrichs 1990; Habash 1995, 560, 567), but there are all the same some grounds for such an interpretation. It rests heavily on the nostalgic image of the lost ways and pleasures of a settled country life enjoyed by Dikaiopolis as he celebrates his private Dionysia 'in the fields' during the Peloponnesian War in Aristophanes' *Acharnians* (**Ai**, note also *Peace* 530, discussed there) and on the prominence of the phallic icon in the celebration of the god. It may find further support in an inscription from fourth-century Ikarion that, according to a recent analysis, associated the successful conduct of the Dionysia in that deme with an abundance of crops 'by means of the Ikarian *komos*' (**Mx**).

The Dionysus of the deme Dionysia is remarkably bare of any of the idiosyncrasy in epithet or cult practice more generally characteristic of the demes and well attested by their calendars and regulations (see for instance Parker 2010b, 197–200 in connection with the sacred law from Aixone; **Av** for the possible relevance of Dionysus Theoinos). We do find particularised cults of Dionysus in the demes – for instance Dionysus Anthios in Aixone (**D**), Myrrhinous (**R**) and Phlya (**U**), Melpomenos and Kissos in Acharnae (**B**) – but in no case is there any attested connection to the deme's Dionysia. There is a possibility that the god of the Rhamnus Dionysia was Lenaios, god of the wine press (**W Introduction**;

Wiv), but this limited evidence sets into relief the general lack of precision as to just who the Dionysus of these deme Dionysia was. We find no indication of an attempt to identify him with Dionysus Eleuthereus (god of the City Dionysia: **I Aiii 4**) and some suggestive of the opposite. A tradition of uncertain date relating to Ikarion pointedly places the visit of Dionysus to Icarius earlier in time than the introduction of the image of Dionysus from Eleutherae to Athens by Pegasos (**M Introduction**; **I Aiv 2**). That implies an effort to claim a greater antiquity for the Ikarian cult over that of Dionysus Eleuthereus in the City, and certainly need not represent a response to a pre-existing assimilation between the god of the deme and of the City festivals (note however Lambert's 2003, 66 suggestion that the polis priesthood of Dionysus in Piraeus was held along with that of Dionysus Eleuthereus in the Athenian cult: **Viii**; and the likelihood that the icon brought to Piraeus was in fact the same Dionysus Eleuthereus as resided in the Athenian Sanctuary: **I Aiii 1**). There are also signs that an aetiological account was developed in the fourth century which derived not only the knowledge of viticulture and viniculture but the worship of Dionysus with drama from the missionary journey of Icarius around Attica (**Aiii**; **M Introduction**; **Y Introduction**; **I Aiv 21**; **I Avii 3**).

The lack of cultic specificity attaching to Dionysus of the deme festivals suggests the relatively recent introduction of his cult. It seems likely that demes which did not have a significant (or indeed any) local cult of Dionysus in the sixth century may have decided to introduce one in close association with that of a more prominent, pre-existing local deity or hero, in order that they could hold a Dionysia. Sites where such cultic 'piggy-backing' by Dionysus may have taken place include Eleusis (**H**), Sphettos (**X**) and possibly Halimous (**L**), in the case of all three within the context of pre-existing cults of Demeter. At Halai Araphenides Dionysus may have been woven into the mythical and physical topography of the place long associated with Artemis (**Kii**; see also **G**). We might envisage a similar development in Ikarion, where the sanctuary (and cult) of Dionysus sits close by that of Apollo Pythios, and where the theatre itself was immediately adjacent to the temple of Apollo rather than that of Dionysus (**M Introduction**; **Mi**).

Every deme that held a Dionysia will probably have had a priest who administered the god's cult, although we do find demarchs making sacrifices to Dionysus in the context of the local festival (**Hvii**). Priestesses of Dionysus are as well attested in the demes as their male counterparts (*SEG* 21, 541 Δ, ll. 33–40, Erchia ca. 375–350; *SEG* 54, 214, ll. 9–11, Aixone ca. 400–375; Philoch. *FGrH* 328 F 206, Semachidai), but there is no evidence to suggest the involvement of these priestesses with a theatre or even a Dionysia. As it happens, only in Sphettos (**X**) and Piraeus (**Viii**; **V Introduction**) do we find a priest of Dionysus, and the priest of Dionysus in Piraeus was an appointee of the polis and not required to be a de-mesman. At Sphettos the close connection between the priest of Dionysus and the theatre is guaranteed, for his presence *ex officio* in prohedric seating was evidently the norm.

The issue of the festival's nomenclature is highly relevant to its treatment in modern times. The view long prevalent that everything about the theatre of the Attic Dionysia was irredeemably mediocre (e.g. **Y Introduction**) can ultimately be traced back to a few remarks of Demosthenes (and his nephew Demochares) cast in the face of his political opponent, the ex-actor Aeschines, described as a 'real ape on the tragic stage, a rustic Oenomaus' (**Oiii**) who 'hired yourself to those famous bellowers, the actors Simykkas and Sokrates as a player of third parts' (**Ov**) and 'wandered through the fields' (**Oiv**) 'collect(ing) figs and grapes and olives like a grocer selling stolen fruit, earning more from that than from the contests, in which you competed for your very life' (**Ov**). Demosthenes grossly exaggerates the 'rural' character of the Dionysia at which Aeschines competed. The extent of his misrepresentation is clearest from the fact that the one festival he mentions is the Dionysia of Kollytos. This was held not only within the City walls but quite possibly in the Theatre of Dionysus itself, which will have been no more than a short walk from anywhere in this urban deme (**O**). Demosthenes' casual and polemical insinuation of boorish rusticity has nonetheless stuck. The fact that we possess only one Classical text of any extension relating to the Attic Dionysia, and that this is from an Aristophanic comedy (**Ai**), has also had a distorting effect, further encouraging the view that deme theatre need not be taken seriously as a context for drama of any standing in itself or of significance for the long-term history of the theatre.

A corrective began with the systematic collection by Whitehead (1986a) of the evidence then available within the context of his comprehensive study of deme life. The corpus has since been updated by Jones (2004, 124–58) and Goette (2014) and continues to grow. A number of contributions to a more thorough and sympathetic analysis of the material have appeared in the last decade (Csapo 2004; Spineto 2005, 327–50; Summa 2006; Wilson 2007a; Paga 2010; Csapo 2010, 89–95; Wilson 2010a; Wilson 2011b; Wilson 2013; Wilson 2015; Bultrighini 2015, 349–64; Wilson 2017b). Study of the religious life of the demes more generally has flourished (Mikalson 1977; Henrichs 1990; Humphreys 2004, 130–96; Parker 2005, 50–78; we also draw attention to the doctoral thesis of Kazuhiro Takeuchi 2018 on the epigraphic evidence for the cult of Dionysus in Attica) and monographs devoted to individual demes that take account of important recent archaeological findings have brought a deeper understanding of several relevant communities (Garland 1987 on Piraeus; Petrakos 1999 on Rhamnus; Platonos-Yiota 2004 and Kellogg 2013 on Acharnae; Clinton 2005 on Eleusis; Vivliodetis 2005 on Myrrhinous; Ackermann 2018 on Aixone). A better grasp of the evidence and an attitude to it free of prejudice have led to a more nuanced understanding of the nature and quality of theatre in the demes, and to its significance in the spread of drama, the formation of a canon and the growth of a theatre industry.

If it were not for the haphazard discovery of inscriptions and theatre architecture across Attica, we would hardly know that this energetic theatrical culture existed at all, for it features very little in literary sources, and except in the case of the *Acharnians* passage (**Ai**), where it does, it is late (**Aiv**), not especially informative (**Aii**; **I Ai 1a**), deliberately misleading (Demosthenes on Kollytos, above) or of ambiguous relevance (**Aiii**; **Av**; the Dionysia in Piraeus is a partial exception, but this was a festival significantly sponsored by the city of Athens: **V**). The fact that deme theatres have been discovered by sheer accident as recently as 1993 (Halimous **L**) and 2007 (Acharnae **B**), and that knowledge of the presence of a dramatic festival in a deme can depend on the evidence of a single fragmentary inscription (e.g. **C**; **P**; **T**; cf. **J**; **S**; **X**), means that the figure of twenty-three demes which on present evidence are with certainty or strong likelihood attested as having held theatrical performances is virtually certain to be much lower than the total that actually did so. In the case of some eighteen (see Table) we can be confident the context was a Dionysia. In places where drama is attested but not a Dionysia we can be fairly sure that the context for performance was a Dionysia, as there is no evidence that drama was performed in the demes in any other festival context than for Dionysus.

The evidence for the twenty-three demes with theatrical performances, as also for Brauron (a settlement on the east coast of Attica that was not a deme), is presented and analysed in separate sections below (**B–Y**), following a survey of the limited material from the literary tradition (**A**). This introduction will confine itself to questions of a more general nature. The Table below summarises the material presented fully in the following pages, to capture: the dates at which deme Dionysia are first attested; evidence for the presence of a theatre building; and the first attestation of drama. The last column represents an assessment, on the basis of all the available evidence, of the likely starting date of drama in the deme. Neither Salamis nor Oropus was ever incorporated into the Attic deme system. We therefore consider Salamis, which had a Dionysia from at least ca. 400, in **IV Dxii** and Oropus, which had a theatre by ca. 335, perhaps with a wooden precursor from around 420, in **IV Ci**.

Four other demes are sometimes brought into the discussion of local Dionysia but do not in our opinion warrant inclusion in our list. The first is Cholleidai, with the notably small bouleutic quota of 2. We argue (**Ai**) that the inclusion of this as a deme with attested Dionysia by Jones (2004, 131) is unwarranted. Pallene, Gargettos and Erchia all had cults of Dionysus but none at present has provided explicit evidence for a festival, theatre or drama. A boundary marker from Pallene in the northern Mesogaia (bouleutic quota 6) identifies land belonging to Dionysus, and so points to a cult of the god in that deme by the late fifth century (*SEG* 57, 162; Takeuchi 2010–2013, 101–2). The case of neighbouring Gargettos (bouleutic quota 4) is more suggestive. We know that this inland deme (near modern Gerakas) possessed a temenos of Dionysus, since an honorific decree dated to the second half of the fourth century shows that this was a place where public documents were erected (*SEG* 46, 155, ll. 4–5: ἐν τῶι τοῦ | Διονύσου τεμένει Γαργηττοῖ 'in the temenos of Dionysus at Gargettos'; Goette 1992–1998, 107; Marchiandi 2011, 622). This demonstrates the importance of the cult to the deme. This use of the sanctuary of Dionysus as a place of local civic display, and the fact that Dionysus of Gargettos is unadorned with any further epithet, are consistent with the practice of demes that did hold Dionysia. Humphreys (2004, 180–1) is willing on this basis to deduce the existence of a theatrical Dionysia in Gargettos, but one wants something more.

The case of prosperous Erchia (bouleutic quota 6 or 7), also in the northern Mesogaia (bouleutic quota 7), is similar. The famous fourth-century cult calendar of the deme entitled 'the greater demarchy' (*SEG* 21, 541) shows sacrifice of a goat 'to Dionysus' (Δ, ll. 33–40), and another for Semele 'on the same altar', on Elaphebolion 16 (A, ll. 44–51). The meat is 'to be handed over to the women and to be consumed on the spot'. (The priestess who is to receive the skin in either case doubtless held a single office: Parker 2010b, 197. There is also a young kid for Dionysus on 2 Anthesterion: Γ, ll. 43–7.) These sacrifices to Dionysus and Semele on Elaphebolion 16 were evidently made in some association with the City Dionysia, which finished on Elaphebolion 15. It would be rash however to use this as evidence for the absence of Erchian women from the Theatre (Elaphebolion 16 seems normally to have been the day on which the Pandia fell, and immediately after which the post-Dionysia assembly was held in the city: **I Aix 1**). While this is good evidence for some form of recognition of Dionysus' City festival at the deme level (and something similar may have happened in Marathon: **Q**), there is nothing listed in the calendar for Dionysus in the month of Posideon. On Posideon 16, Zeus is to be given a sheep 'on the rock' (E, ll. 22–7). The latter could conceivably be 'part of the local celebration for the Rural Dionysia' (Humphreys 2004, 180), but aside from the date there is nothing to suggest it was, and one would have to ask why on this theory the calendar ignores the principal deity. Given that one purpose of the Erchian calendar may have been to divide up the deme's sacrificial needs into liturgical-size units (Dow 1965, 193–5; cf. Papazarkadas 2011, 145–6), one might propose that the sacrifices for Dionysus himself at his festival in Erchia did not appear in it because they were provided separately by choregoi. The string of hypotheses is however long and fragile.

	Festival First attested	Earliest Theatre Building	Drama First Attested	Drama Likely Start
Acharnae	Dionysia by early 4th c. (I)	ca. 400–350; partially excavated (A, I)	comedy and possibly tragedy (I)	first half 4th c.
Aigilia	Dionysia by early 4th c. (I)		By early 4th c. (I)	first half 4th c.
Aixone	Dionysia by ca. 330 (I)	Remains noted in 19th c. (A); before ca. 330 (I)	comedy by ca. 320 (I)	mid 4th c.
Anagyrous	Dionysia by ca. 350 (I)	By ca. 325 (I)	tragedy by ca. 440 (I), comedy by ca. 350 (I)	ca. 450
Athmonon	Amarysia or Dionysia by ca. 350 (I)			
Eleusis	Dionysia by first half 4th c. (I)	Seen in 18th c.; no longer visible (A); by ca. 350 (I). Possibly a second theatre under control of Athenians by ca. 355 (I)	tragedy and comedy by late 5th c. (I)	5th c.
Euonymon	Dedication to Dionysus in theatre by ca. 330 (I)	ca. 400, excavated but unpublished (A)	an *agon* by late 4th c. (I)	5th c.
Halai Aixonides	Dionysia tentatively deduced from choregic dedication, mid 5th c. (I)	Unconfirmed reports of remains in 20th c. (A)	comedy and tragedy by ca. 430 (I)	mid 5th c.
Halai Araphenides	Sanctuary of Dionysus by ca. 350 (I); Dionysia likely	By ca. 350 (I)	comedy by ca. 340 (Ic)	first half 4th c.

Halimous		Partially excavated (A)		4th c.
Ikarion	Dionysia by ca. 450 (I)	4th c. (A), with likely earlier phase; not properly excavated	tragedy by ca. 450 (I)	early 5th c.
Kephale		Possibly seen in 17th c.		? 4th c.
Kollytos	Dionysia by ca. 350 (L)		comedy and tragedy by ca. 350 (L)	first half 4th c.
Lamptrai	Dionysia by ca. 325 (I)			mid 4th c.
Marathon	Dionysia by ca. 350 (I)		tragedy by ca. 350 (I)	first half 4th c.
Myrrhinous	Dionysia by ca. 320 (I)			4th c.
Oa	Dionysia tentatively deduced from possible choregic dedication late 4th c. (I)			? 4th c.
Paiania	Dionysia tentatively deduced from choregic dedication ca. 350 (I)		tragedy by ca. 350 (I)	first half 4th c.
Phlya	Dionysia by ca. 400 (L)			? early 4th c.
Piraeus	Dionysia by ca. 350 (I)	By ca. 420 (L); seen in 18th and 19th c. with limited exploration (A)	tragedy by ca. 425 (L), comedy by first half 4th c. (L)	5th c.
Rhamnus	Dionysia by ca. 250 (I)	By mid 4th c. (A)	comedy by ca. 300 (I)	4th c.
Sphettos	Dionysia deduced from existence of priest, theatre and tragedy by ca. 350 (I, Ic)	By ca. 350 (I)	tragedy by ca. 350 (Ic)	first half 4th c.
Thorikos	Dionysia by ca. 425 (I)	ca. 460 (A, S)	tragedy and comedy by ca. 420	early 5th c.

A = Architecture   I = Inscription   Ic = Iconography   L = Literary text   S = Stratigraphy

We can state with some confidence that drama featured at Dionysia in at least seven demes already in the fifth century: Piraeus, Eleusis, Ikarion, Euonymon, Halai Aixonides, Anagyrous and Thorikos. But the idea that it in fact began in rural Attica, and notably in Ikarion, rather than in the City of Athens, is an artefact of late Classical pro-Athenian cultural propaganda, propagated widely in Hellenistic scholarship (**Avi**; **M Introduction**).

The theory appears to have been forged by local Attic historians and publicists such as Phanodemus or Philochorus in accord with a broader Lycurgan policy of cultural and economic regeneration, to which the theatre culture of Athens was central, at a time when theatre was becoming less and less exclusively Athenian in reality (Csapo and Wilson 2014; **VI I**). It is clear that the choice of Ikarion as the 'birthplace' of drama was determined in large part by the existence of a genuinely old tradition of dramatic performance and Dionysiac worship there, the latter certainly dating back to the Pisistratid period and perhaps even to Pisistratid promotion (**M Introduction**). But the earliest evidence for drama in Ikarion places it around 460 (**Miii**). This happens to coincide with the most recent stratigraphic dating of the first phase of the theatre of Thorikos (**Y Introduction**), where direct evidence for drama begins some four decades later.

Although the evidence is insufficient to ask it to bear too much probative weight, it is notable that the demes with drama attested in the fifth century represent a wide geographical spread across Attica – with Ikarion to the north, beyond Mt Pentelikon, Thorikos on the far south-east coast, Eleusis on its bay to the west; Piraeus, Euonymon, Halai Aixonides and Anagyrous at points on or near the western coast and easily accessible to the city and one another by road. The pattern is at least suggestive of a progressive development by which demes introduced drama to meet a demand in their area, or to stimulate one (below). The existence of a 'circuit' of deme theatre in the later fifth century is explicitly noted by Plato (**Aiii 2**). It is noteworthy (always acknowledging the modest evidentiary base and the imprecision of the dates given to many relevant inscriptions) that several other demes are likely to have had drama by the early fourth century, despite its being a time of considerable economic hardship for Athens. It is clear too that more demes added or elaborated theatrical Dionysia over the course of the second half of the fourth century, notably the period of settled prosperity from the time of the financial stewardship of Eubulus (ca. 355). The practical aspects involved in timetabling these many Dionysia in the month of Posideon are considered in **Aiii**.

The demes known to have celebrated a Dionysia with drama are well above the average size of all demes, as judged by their bouleutic quota (Jones 2004, 139). Based on the list above (excluding Kephale and Oa as too uncertain, and calculating the Lamptrais and Paianias as the sum of their Upper and Lower parts), the average figure is 8.15, as compared to an overall average of ca. 3.6. Size and associated material resources were clearly important, if not essential, factors in a deme's capacity to run a festival as complex and costly as a theatrical Dionysia. In general it is probably safe to assume that a theatrical Dionysia was beyond any deme with a bouleutic quota of 1 or 2, representing some nominal 40/60 or 80/120 adult male demesmen (the alternatives depend on whether we assume a citizen population of 20,000 or 30,000: Jones 2004, 140, 296–7). That covers more than half of all demes (and is another argument against Cholleidai: above). Kollytos is the only deme with a bouleutic quota of 3 or less (it was 3) known to have celebrated the festival (**N**). As an intramural deme, the actual resident population of Kollytos will have been far higher than reflected in its bouleutic quota. It will certainly have been able to draw very large audiences from beyond its own members, and that in itself will have yielded significant income. The performances were quite possibly held in the urban Theatre of Dionysus.

The size of some deme theatres – with capacities very much larger than for audiences composed solely of deme members (and their families, including female members and slaves: **Ai**; **Aiv**; **I**; **V**; **Y**) – has prompted the further suggestion that they sought to attract audiences from beyond their membership. This is highly plausible, and is in fact assumed as a norm by Plato, who makes the economic motive of the arrangement explicit (**Aiii 1**). Plato's choice of words indicates that revenue from the sale of seats at deme Dionysia is anticipated (on seat-sales: **Bvi**; **V Introduction**; **Vvi**), and we should probably think in addition of a boost to the local market economy from the influx of visitors (Jones 2004, 152–7; Wilson 2010a). This was a time of year when agricultural activity was at its quietest, and so ideal for the distractions of Dionysia. The creation of a staggered 'circuit' of deme Dionysia no doubt enabled performers to move from one to another during the busy festival season of Posideon; but Plato's emphasis is on the capacity of audience members to do so.

Under these circumstances it is a reasonable hypothesis that smaller demes adjacent to large ones with established theatrical Dionysia would attend – and perhaps participate more fully in – that of the latter (**M Introduction** for possible involvement as performers or worshippers, where a case is made for a significant degree of participation on the part of tiny Plotheia, north of Ikarion, in the latter's Dionysia; Goette 2014, 95–6). But that reasonable assumption needs some modification: the case of Halimous (**L**) most clearly disrupts any neatly systematic theory of regional sharing, and demonstrates the importance of local pride and tradition. Halimous had its own theatre in close proximity to that of its much larger neighbour Euonymon (**I**), which in turn was only some 7 km distant from Aixone (**D**) on the Athens road; the demes of Halai Aixonides (**J**) and Anagyrous (**E**) follow in sequence on the same southerly road. The concentration of Dionysia in the Mesogaia is also noteworthy (**X**). Some have argued that demes possessed of substantial theatres may have made them accessible, perhaps under a leasing arrangement, to others nearby who did not (Lohmann 1993, 288–9; Goette 2014, 96). We regard the interpretation of one relevant item of evidence to this effect as faulty (**R**) and the other as at best unproven (**Q**), but this does not strike the idea down in principle. The city may have sought to maximise the return from its cultural facilities 'out of season', leasing out the Panathenaic stadium for use as pasturage when the festival was not on (*IG* II^2 1035, l. 50, but the date is the Augustan era). Demes that had invested in high-quality cultural infrastructure may have done the same. This high degree of involvement on the part of non-members will have given these Dionysia a somewhat different character from most other local festivals.

Another and not necessarily incompatible explanation for the apparent pattern of spread of demes with large theatres considers local political needs. Some deme theatres were demonstrably multi-functional places. Rhamnus (**W**) is a good example, for its open-plan theatre also served as an agora and place of dedication to multiple deities. The same was doubtless true of others, though one must always be attentive to distinctive local custom suggested by the (limited) evidence: Thorikos for instance possessed a significant commercial agora that was quite separate from its fine theatre (**Y Introduction**). Meetings of the deme assembly are more likely to have taken place in the theatre than in the agora of Thorikos, and in general demes that possessed a theatre are very likely to have used it for their assembly meetings. The fact that these theatres were far larger than required to accommodate the entire population of demesmen has prompted the theory that they also served the needs of political units larger than the deme itself: the Cleisthenic tribes (Ober 2008, 205–10), which needed space for their tribal assemblies and for rehearsals for their choruses competing at the City Dionysia; or, on an alternative view, that elusive entity, the trittys (Paga 2010). The case for both of these propositions is entirely hypothetical and there is no positive evidence for Paga's further suggestion that Dionysia themselves may have been organised on the trittys level, and much tells against it (Goette 2014; Wilson 2017b).

Some of the funds needed to run a costly Dionysia with theatrical performances were as we have seen met by the imposition of seating charges. The fact that some demes, such as Thorikos, continued over the course of the fourth century to increase the capacity of their theatre (**Y Introduction**) suggests a healthy, and growing, demand on the part of the-atregoers. It also probably indicates an assumption that such investment in infrastructure would bring a return. At a fairly conservative calculation, takings from the sale of seats at a Dionysia in Thorikos might have brought in well over 1,000 drachmas, and so constitute a substantial contribution to the running of the festival (assuming an audience of 3,200, each charged 2 obols, the apparent cost of a single day in an 'ordinary' seat at the City Dionysia: **V H**; the Thorikian festival may have had more than a single day of performances).

Choregic systems also played an important part, directing the wealth and energies of members of the local socio-economic élite to the financing of deme Dionysia. Choregia is now known from some twelve demes (**B–E, H, J, K, M, T, V, W, Y**) – thirteen if, as we think highly likely, the relief from Sphettos is choregic (**V F** on Athens NM 2400); and fourteen if the newly published inscription from Oa is properly so restored (**S**). These show signs of remarkable ingenuity and inventiveness: such as the manner in which in Thorikos the right to serve as choregos was 'sold' to the highest bidders (**Yii**). There are signs that deme choregoi tended to be men who chose to devote their abilities and resources to the deme and did not go on to do the same at the urban level. As a group they occupied the economic tier immediately below the level that triggered liturgical obligations in the city. That will still have seen them as possessors of substantial 'three-talent households': the expression κεκτημένος τὸν τριτάλαντον οἶκον 'possessed of a three-talent household' is used by Isaeus 3.80 of a wealthy man named Pyrrhos capable of performing a liturgy in his (unknown) deme, and the figure looks like an acknowledged marker for liability to liturgies in that deme (and probably others) around the middle of the fourth century. These were in other words hardly men of humble means. But more important is their preference for devoting their energies and resources to the local sphere. For it seems that deme theatre finance depended more on voluntarism and enticements than was the case in the city. In fact, it may be that systematic, long-term imposition of choregic obligations was imprac-ticable in many demes, certainly those that were around or below average size – though one should also not underestimate the greater opportunities for shaming that existed in the smaller community of the deme. If an average deme had only some half-dozen families of liturgical status at the urban level, and (say) twice that of more moderate but still consid-erable wealth (say between two to three talents), the pool of those upon whom recurrent local liturgical obligation could be laid will have been small indeed. Little wonder then that the liturgical funding of deme theatre sometimes gives the impression of being bankrolled by a few leading local families, or that already by the 440s Ikarion was taking pains to identify – and devise a special name for – 'men who have not been a choregos before' (ἀχορέγετοι **Miii**, l. 4). And all the more reason to believe that the procedure of antidosis (**I Bi 5**) was initially designed at the local level: the earliest direct reference to the practice comes from fifth-century Ikarion (**Miii**). Its most salient feature is the way it transfers to the rich themselves the delicate business of distinguishing between the current levels of wealth and willingness among the élite in order to identify liturgists. That problem will have been all the more acute in a small community.

Of the twenty-five attested instances of choregia across all demes, a full fourteen were undertaken by singletons (**Bii**; **Ei**; **Eii**; **Hiv**; **Hix**; **J**; **Miv**; **Mv**; **Mviii**; **T**; **Wii**; **Wiii**; **Yi**; including the exceptional **Hii**); six by pairs (**Biii A** twice; **Biii B**; **Hi**; **Miii**; **Mvi**); and five by groups of three men (**Bv**; **C**; **Mvii**; **Mix**; **Yiv**). While a high degree of collaboration among choregoi is a distinctive characteristic of deme choregia, it is thus far from pervasive, with more than half of known choregiai being the work of singletons. The word synchoregia is never used in connection with deme Dionysia in the sources and should be avoided (we prefer 'joint choregia'). We find the technical term synchoregia only at the City Dionysia of 406/5, apparently just for that year and apparently too just for drama, not dithyramb (**I D**). There are good reasons to believe that one of the 'triple' choregiai attested from Thorikos (**Yiv**) reflects a situation in which a group of three men bankrolled all of the performances at the Dionysia (**Y Introduction**; **Yii**; **Yiv**). This is something rather different from the usual understanding of synchoregia – namely a plurality of choregoi preparing a single competitive performance – for in Thorikos a plurality of choregoi join to prepare a plurality of performances in different genres, and moreover they seem not to have confined themselves to the chorus, but dealt with the actors too (note that we also find a singleton choregos at Thorikos in **Yi**). In seven cases a family relation between multiple choregoi is certain or highly likely (**Biii A**, twice; **Biii B**; **C**; **Mvii**; **Mix**; **Yiv**) though the singleton (as we argue, some see a joint choregia here) of **Eii** assumes it as normative that his father should also serve as choregos. In two of these cases a father works with two of his sons (**C**; **Mvii**). Collaboration between members of the same family cannot be explained by economic necessity, nor taken as a sign of the indigent nature of deme funding more generally (*DFA*² 48), since this would not have the effect of introducing additional resources from a second household. The two choregoi honoured in Halai Araphenides by **Ki** are probably the complement for the Dionysia in that deme of 341/0, rather than a joint pair serving together. At Aixone there were it seems ordinarily two choregoi each year (**D Introduction**). We cannot tell whether they worked as singletons or as a pair to fund the comedies favoured by the deme, for we have decrees honouring two choregoi but no dedications that would help resolve the question. The absence of any sign of a contest might hint at collaboration, but does not prove it. Probably it was in general up to an individual who accepted a choregia to decide whether to enlist further partners from or beyond his family to assist and to share the glory. Thus there are likely to be cases where there is a discrepancy between the number of men contributing to choregiai and the number of choregoi formally appointed by the deme. In Ikarion two choregoi seems to have been a long-term norm. But this is a deme that has left examples of dedications by choregic singletons (**Miv**; **Mv**; **Mviii**), pairs (**Miii**; **Mvi**) and triples (**Mvii**; **Mix**). At least one deme – Thorikos – appears to have kept and inscribed in its theatre a public record of its past choregoi (**Yiii**). This creation of an 'honour roll' will doubtless have been designed in part *pour encourager les autres*, and pre-dates the first known attempt to do the same in the city of Athens by nearly a century.

Even granted the highly partial and fragmentary condition of our evidence, there are other signs of the considerable ingenuity applied to ensuring that theatrical festivals were adequately funded. In Ikarion substantial deme funds may have been deployed as interest-bearing loans to provide choregoi with the necessary liquidity to serve (**Mii**). The Eleusinians may have led the way in deploying the honorific decree as an instrument to leverage the great symbolic resources of their locale and attract funds and know-how to their theatre from outsiders (**Hii**). They also developed creative use of fines, such as the 100 drachmas imposed on demarchs who fail to summon an honorand and his descendants to their seat of honour (**Hvii**). Note also the energetic imposition of fines relating to the Dionysia by the Ikarieis (**Miii**). In Acharnae the theatre was leased out to fund an annual sacrifice, and probably more besides (**Bvi**). A leasing arrangement was also important in Piraeus in the fourth century, and the remains of the agreement show how the public authorities involved private enterprise to make sure that the material infrastructure of their theatre – above all, its wooden seating – was constructed and kept in good order (**Vvi**).

The fundamental architecture of a deme Dionysia consisted of parade (*pompe*), sacrifice (**Ai**; **Av**; **Bvii 2**; **Di**; **H Introduction**; **Hvii**; **Mxi**; **V Introduction**; **Viii**; **X**; **Y Introduction**) and agon (**Bvii 2**). The presence of the last is sometimes thought to have been optional, but (admitting the difficulty of proving an absence) we cannot point to a Dionysia that had no theatrical performance. Only the fictive (and interrupted) festival organised by Dikaiopolis in Aristophanes' *Acharnians* (**Ai**) presents itself as a possibility, there being no compelling reason to regard the simple and drama-free 'ancestral festival of the Dionysia of old' (ἡ πάτριος τῶν Διονυσίων ἑορτὴ τὸ παλαιὸν) evoked with intense nostalgia by Plutarch (*Mor.* 527d) as an accurate account of Attic practice of any date (**Ai**). But, as in the city (**I Aiv**), the parade was evidently a (or the) key feature of the festival ('pompam maximi esse momenti': Nilsson 1900, 91–2). As much is clear from Aristophanes (**Ai**) and it is independently attested for the Piraeus (**I Avi 1**; **V Introduction**; **Viv**) and Acharnae (**Bvii 2**; see also **Biv**). Note also the suggestive evidence for Ikarion (**Miii**; **Mx**) and Brauron (**G**). A phallos image (or images) was carried and accompanied by the *phallikon*, the song of the phallos, presumably choral in form (**Ai**; **Miii**). The parade was under the direction of the demarch (**H Introduction** on *IE* 229; cf. **Ai**; **Viv**), who may even have taken part in its phallic chorus (**Aii**). There is abundant evidence showing that responsibility for running the festival as a whole was the job of the demarch, just as the Eponymous Archon in Athens was in overall charge of the City Dionysia (**I Bi**). A man named Nikon from Ikarion is praised for his 'fine and just conduct of the festival for Dionysus and its agon' as demarch around 360 (**Mvi**). This sounds like a summary description of the complex task that faced all demarchs. Other duties for which explicit evidence exists are the appointment of choregoi (**Miii**; **V Introduction**); management of the antidosis process (**Miii**); pre-selection of choreuts (**Miii**); conduct of sacrifices (in one instance at the demarch's own expense: **Hvii**); summoning of choregoi to seats of honour in the theatre (**Ki**); and audited management of relevant funds (**Mii**; **Mx**), including, at Acharnae, income generated by the theatre (**Bvi**). In this last instance the demarch is aided by a treasurer, clearly the norm for

Acharnae (**Bvii**), while the demarchs of Aixone enjoyed the assistance of two treasurers –
suggesting the scale of the operations, or perhaps a belief that spreading the obligation thus
would encourage financial probity (**Di**; **Diii**; **Div**).

It is impossible to describe in any detail the programme of performances at a single deme
Dionysia at any period, but the suggestive snapshots that we do have show that at least
most festivals really did have serious programmes of drama. The presence of choregic systems implies a degree of (desired) predictability and regularity of funding. It is also clear
that there was no single or dominant model. Demes evidently did not try to reproduce the
full suite of events at the City Dionysia (with the possible exception of exceptional Piraeus:
below). There is an overwhelming concentration on the two main dramatic genres, tragedy
and comedy; scarce and dubious evidence of satyr play (**J**; **Mv**); and little of the purely
lyric ('cyclic', 'dithyrambic') choruses of men and boys that featured prominently in the
city (**Bii**; **Biii**; **Hii**; **Vii**): the only certain cases for the latter are Acharnae and Piraeus, and
the large population size of both demes is very likely to be part of the picture. It is also
a possibility (no more) that there was in Acharnae another, distinctive variety of contest
between Dionysiac choruses named *komoi* (**Biv**). Given the great preponderance of tragedy
and comedy, it is probable that when we have evidence for choregia and theatres without
further specification as to the nature of the performances supported, they are most likely to
have been dramatic. We know of some seven demes that staged both tragedy and comedy
(**E**, **H**, **K**, **O**, **V**, **Y**, tragedy less securely attested in **B**) and in at least a few cases, notably
Thorikos, we can be fairly confident both genres appeared concurrently and with some
regularity. On the other hand a number of demes show signs of having specialised in either
tragedy (Ikarion) or comedy – so it seems in Aixone, where comedy is the only genre attested and its special prominence is suggested by the fact that honours are to be proclaimed
'during the Dionysia at the comedies held at Aixone' (**Diii**).

The Dionysia in Piraeus is a revealing but exceptional case, unusual for being part funded and managed by the city. The festival was on a large scale, and not really a festival of
and for the deme alone, since the nominal 320-odd adult male demesmen will have been a
tiny minority in a town with a population estimated as equal to that of the city of Athens.
The Piraeus Dionysia may in effect have been a kind of metic Dionysia for the town of
Piraeus. By the second century at least it reproduced the unusual double processional structure of the City Dionysia (**I Aiii–iv**), for it had its own *eisagoge* or 'Introduction' of the god
at that date, conducted by ephebes, and it formally began with an elaborate parade, like the
City Dionysia. In around 330 Lycurgus added to a programme that already featured tragedy and comedy a contest in the 'circular' chorus, which was to have no fewer than three
contestants. Taken together the evidence suggests an effort to mimic the full programme of
the City Dionysia (**V Introduction**).

We hear of a contest (*agon*) in several demes, and in some of their dedications, choregoi
declare themselves victors (**Bii**; **Bv**; **Bvii 2**; **C**; **Eii**; **H Introduction**; **Hi**; **Hix**; **J**; **Miv**;
Mvii; **Mviii**; **Mix**; **Mx**; **T**; **Vi**; **Vii**; **Vv**). The city's competitive format was thus apparently
reproduced in these places, even if on occasion, as in Ikarion (**M Introduction**; see on
Mx), Halai Araphenides (**Ki**) and Aixone (**D Introduction**), there were apparently only
two choregoi in the race. What if any material prizes were awarded is unclear and was
doubtless open to variation at the wishes of each deme. The fact that some victorious

choregoi dedicated 'infrastructure' items like altars (**C**) suggests that victors sometimes took on the extra burden – and honour – of commissioning permanent objects to celebrate their victory and assist the cult of the god in their deme. The tripods dedicated in the fourth century on a choregic monument for comedy from Eleusis (**Hiv**; cf. **Hix**; **W Introduction**) and on another for tragedy in Ikarion (**Mviii**; cf. **Mvii**) are almost certainly not prizes, but are 'quoting' the symbols of Dionysiac success long established by the award and dedication of tripods at the City Dionysia (note also the ex-voto choregic dedication from Thorikos: **Yi**). A distinctive feature of choregic monuments from the demes is the manner in which they describe themselves as 'dedications' (ἀναθήματα) to Dionysus with a consistency and explicitness equal to that with which the monuments from the city avoid the term (Wilson 2000, 249).

As at all festivals, there were doubtless various other more or less 'fringe' activities alongside the primary contests that have been largely or entirely lost to our vision. One that is sometimes thought to have been especially characteristic of deme Dionysia is a game ('grotesque sport': Whitehead 1986a, 214) of leaping or dancing on greased wineskins, known in later times as *askoliasmos*. A fragment of Eubulus suggests that some such activity may have existed in the early fourth century, but it has no demonstrable connection to deme Dionysia and we believe that the association between *askoliasmos*, the theatre and the origins of drama (found only in Vergil's *Georgics* 2, ll. 380–4) is a product of late Classical or early Hellenistic theory that sought out limited evidence that could scarcely support it (**Avi**).

In Myrrhinous (**R**), and probably also in Ikarion (**Miii**), a meeting of the assembly was held following the Dionysia, as happened in the city (**I Aix**). Other demes probably did likewise. Like its urban equivalent this assembly doubtless dealt with the management of the festival by the demarch and with any alleged wrongdoing committed by those attending it. It was probably here that the various decrees we have honouring choregoi and other supporters of the local festival were proposed and moved. But a post-Dionysia assembly is likely to have served other important functions in the civic life of the deme, not least since it was sure to have been well attended, given the associated attractions of the festival. The agenda of the meeting in Myrrhinous certainly treated more than 'business concerning the Dionysia' (**Rii**, ll. 36–7), and seems to have been one of a small number of statutory annual meetings of that deme's assembly. Demarchs were responsible for making distributions of theoric money for major City festivals, and they evidently did so at meetings of their deme assembly (**I C**; Whitehead 1986a, 110). A meeting that followed the local Dionysia would in many ways have been an ideal occasion for distributing theoric money for the City Dionysia, some two months later.

The entrenched idea that deme theatre was second-rate can be countered at a number of levels. One is to point to the demonstrated ingenuity and inventiveness in the administration and finance of theatre, and to the substantive commitments made to both (above). Another is to consider the quality of the attested performers. Much of the relevant evidence was once ignored or argued away, but it is clear that Sophocles and Aristophanes produced their work in person in the deme of Eleusis (**Hi**; see also **Ai** and **B Introduction** on Sophocles); Euripides down in Anagyrous either very early in or towards the end of his career (**Ei**), as well as in the Piraeus, perhaps regularly (**Vi**); and that one of the greatest tragic actors of all time, Theodoros, probably appeared in Thorikos around 370 (**Yiv**). Despite the slurs of his enemies, Aeschines was clearly a fine actor, working with the greats, Theodoros and Aristodemos (D. 19.246), and he appeared in a reperformance of Sophocles' *Oenomaus* at Kollytos. Another celebrated actor (in this case for comedy) – Parmenon – also performed in Kollytos. Parmenon won a victory in the acting contest at the Lenaea around the middle of the century and was remembered long after for his legendary powers of mimesis (**Oi**). Three of the most illustrious poets of the fifth century produced works in Halai Aixonides: two of the greats of the generation of comic pioneers prior to Aristophanes – Ecphantides and Cratinus – and the tragic poet Sophocles, who moreover produced a full trilogy (or tetralogy) there, the *Telepheia* (**J**). This last fact, known from a lucky survival, is suggestive of a scale and ambition that is likely to have been much more common than our patchy evidence reveals.

The evidence also indicates that there was no deficiency in the chorus of dramatic productions in the demes. Plato (**Aiii**) refers to the Dionysia in general terms using chorocentric language and we can identify an apparent effort on the part of a number of demes to ensure that their tragic choruses had the 'full' complement of fifteen choreuts known from the city (*contra* Sansone 2016). A decree from Ikarion (**Miii**) may suggest that around 440 the deme collectively resolved that their tragic choruses should have fifteen members, and **Mxi** might indicate that that was still a norm a century later. A dedication from Anagyrous of around 440 or the last decade of the fifth century (**Ei**) and a choregic relief from Sphettos (**V F** on Athens NM 2400; **X**) suggest that this norm also prevailed in those demes. The plausible hypothesis that the choruses of deme performances were recruited locally, from members of the deme, is supported by one instance where this was demonstrably so (**Ei**; **Miii** from Ikarion points in the same direction). Performance at deme Dionysia is thus very likely to have represented a significant sphere for the gaining of experience and expertise in dramatic choreia on the part of a fairly wide segment of the citizenry; and to have created a network through which choregoi for city festivals could inform themselves of the best choreuts across Attica. From their experience in running local Dionysia, and given their constitutional responsibility for maintaining a record of the property of demesmen (Arist. *Ath.* 54.8), demarchs will also have been repositories of local knowledge especially valuable to city authorities when appointing choregoi for city festivals.

Given the nature of the evidence, with the theatrical culture of several demes attested by a single epigraphic find or the chance discovery of theatre architecture, it is entirely reasonable to suppose that what we see is the tip of an iceberg. There are grounds for believing that deme theatre is a significant element in understanding the growth of theatre more broadly in the fifth and fourth centuries. Demes were crucial in creating the first relatively stable market to feed the nascent theatrical professions. They were probably also important to the early formation of a dramatic canon. And they are very likely to have been an important venue for dramatic poets in the first half of the fifth century. The hypothesis of a vigorous culture of theatrical production at deme Dionysia is the best way to explain an apparent deficit in performance opportunities in Athens: before dramatic contests were instituted at the Lenaea around the middle of the fifth century (**II A**), the City Dionysia was the only Athenian venue to accommodate the careers of a generation (or more) of early poets, including Magnes, Chionides, Aeschylus, and even Sophocles for the first few decades of his career (Millis 2015, 236). While cities outside Attica offered some scope for these poets, it is very likely – and compatible with the pattern of evidence – that deme theatre played an important role in this early period.

Acknowledging the extent and seriousness of deme theatre also helps explain a phenomenon for which it is otherwise difficult to account – namely the familiarity with the works of Aeschylus and Euripides, long after their deaths, that is assumed by Aristophanes and other comic poets (Mastromarco 2006, 147–9). Circulation in sympotic contexts goes only so far; circulation of written texts, even less far. Opportunities for reperformance at city festivals were constrained (**I Avi**). Plato's 'spectacle-lovers' (*philotheamones* **Aiii 1**) who never miss a deme Dionysia would, broadly speaking, overlap conceptually with those audience members upon whose knowledge of past tragedy the comic poets depended. Deme Dionysia are thus an inherently likely site for extensive reperformance of tragedy (and comedy). There are some grounds for supposing that **Hi**, **J** and **Oii–iv** were repeat rather than first performances. None can be proven, and we should not revert to assumptions that deme theatre was second-rate to argue that works cannot have received their premiere performances there. Probably the most compelling case is the *Oenomaus* in which Aeschines performed at Kollytos, in the title role, which is generally thought to have been the famous play of that name by Sophocles, reperformed some sixty years after its composition (**Oii–iv**). Demosthenes tells us that Aeschines performed as Creon in Sophocles' *Antigone* 'often' (D. 19.246–7); probably also in the title role of the *Kresphontes* of Euripides (**O**). We do not know at which festivals Aeschines made these other appearances in Classic tragedy, but it seems *prima facie* likely that Demosthenes is referring, however loosely, to performances in Athens or Attica with which his audience would have been at least potentially familiar and one may doubt whether the 'old tragedy' slot at the City Dionysia, available from 386 (**I Avi**), would have been sufficient to sustain frequent appearances of Aeschines as the Sophoclean Creon. Nor can it help explain the assumed familiarity on the part of Aristophanes' audience with works by Aeschylus. We tend to credit the evidence that the Athenians made special provision for the reperformance of Aeschylean plays after his death (**I Avi**), but that evidence is far from conclusive and any such reperformances at city festivals are unlikely to have been sufficiently frequent to generate the requisite level of familiarity. This would certainly be established by a custom of reperformance at the many deme Dionysia; and moreover by the high degree of choral participation in such performances by demesmen across Attica (above). Biles (2006–2007, esp. 226–7) may be right to suggest that Dikaiopolis' disappointed expectation to see a performance by Aeschylus at the start of the *Acharnians* (ll. 9–11) serves to characterise him as old-fashioned and wistfully disconnected from more recent cultural developments in urban life. He may also be right to treat the passage as suggestive of a tradition of reperformance of Aeschylus in deme theatres. But to say that '[w]here theatrical production was concerned the Rural Dionysia might have promoted a sense of nostalgia' (Biles 2006–2007, 227) goes too far beyond the evidence.

The prestige derived from producing work at the City Dionysia of course far outshone anything available at the deme level. The very challenge of securing one of the three tragic choruses for the festival was enormous. These considerations encourage another hypothesis about deme drama, what might be called 'preperformance' – the testing out of new work by poets prior to assaying the most challenging competitive venue, in seeking selection for the City Dionysia or Lenaea. This would be especially intelligible for poets early in their career who might thereby build confidence and a reputation that could feed into the process of preselection at the city festivals, for there can be little doubt that an Archon would draw on a network of gossip from the demes to seek out promising new talent. Given the constraints of the city festivals, it is hard to see how new talent could have made itself felt unless in some other venue, especially prior to the establishment of the Lenaean contests. The objection that such 'preperformance' would spoil the dénouement of dramas has limited force, not least since the Athenians appear to have institutionalised foreknowledge of plots through the Proagon of the City Dionysia (**I Aii**).

Evidence for deme Dionysia falls off sharply towards the end of the fourth century, but not entirely. It persists in three demes with powerful identities and appears to stage a reappearance in a fourth – Acharnae – in the Roman period (*SEG* 54, 322; **B Introduction**). In Piraeus, a Dionysia with tragic contest is still going strong, or resurgent once more, after Macedonian occupation shortly after 260 (**Vv**) and a new, second theatre was built in the second century at Zea (**V Introduction**). Eleusis has left evidence for the activity of its festival in the third and second centuries. In the last quarter of the third century a Hierophant is honoured 'at the traditional agon of the Dionysia, in the theatre at Eleusis' (Διονυσίων τῶι πατρίωι ἀγῶνι | Ἐλευσῖνι ἐν τῶι θεάτρωι *IE* 201, ll. 18–19) – traditional indeed, now some two centuries old (further evidence in **V Introduction**). In (probably) 164, another Eleusinian demarch was honoured for the efforts he devoted to what was evidently still the deme's most important festival: '[ap]pointed demarch in the Archon ye[ar] of Pelops he conducted the sacrifices for Dionysus [at the Dionysi]a and arranged the parade and … and conducted the agon in the theatre which [the Eleusinians] ce[lebrate], showing no lack of [energ]y and ambition' ([τοῖς Δι|ονυσί]οις ἔθυσεν τῶι Διονύσωι καὶ τὴν πομπὴν ἔπεμψεν καὶ τ[. . . . 8–9 . . . . | . . . . ca. 8 . . . .]στον, ἔθηκεν δὲ καὶ τὸν ἀγῶνα ἐν τῶι θεάτρωι, ὃν συ[ντελοῦσιν | Ἐλευσίνιοι σπου]δῆς καὶ φιλοτιμίας οὐθὲν ἐλλείπων *IE* 229, ll. 31–4). Rather than declining, the garrison town of Rhamnus gained new prominence in the third century, growing stronger than the demes around it (Parker 1996, 265; Oetjen 2014). Its Dionysia remains active, with its agon in place, mid-century (**Wv**). And it is quite likely that the performances of comedy at it were still being supported by choregoi (**Wiii**).

The effect of the possible abolition of choregia in the demes, shadowing the shift from choregia to agonothesia in the city (which makes its first definitive appearance in 307/6: **V I**), has been overstated as a reason for the decline of the local Dionysia at the end of the fourth century. The change in the city is traditionally thought to be the result of the reforms of Demetrius of Phaleron, who ruled Athens with virtually autocratic power from 317 to 307 (**VI K**), but we have argued that the process may have been more drawn out and that a form of modified choregia may have continued in the city all the way down to 308/7 (Wilson and Csapo 2012). As the case of Rhamnus suggests, the notion that choregia was entirely abolished or abandoned in the demes is open to serious doubt. We have unambiguous evidence that in Aixone choregoi were active still in 317/16 (**Dii**) and quite possibly continued to be so in 312 (**Diii** and **Div**; see also on **Iii**). In 314 the festival in Acharnae shows administrative and financial involvement on the part of the city that may reflect the impact of Demetrius (**Bvii 2**). It is even possible that the city appointed a general overseer (*epimeletes*) of all Athenian Dionysia whose presence may have threatened the independence of the deme's arrangements, and foreshadowed the introduction of the agonothesia in the city. But the picture is far from clear. Perhaps the influence of Demetrius was felt on the scale of choregic monuments in the demes, as it was in the city. While this might help explain the fall-off in choregic dedications at the end of the century, the more general fading out of deme Dionysia from the picture is better explained by the overall conditions of life in the Attic demes in the third century, a period of war, poverty and significant depopulation of the countryside. These factors put enormous strain on the human and material capacities of the demes, and the Dionysia – a key manifestation of the corporate identity and resources of the demes – will have been highly sensitive to them. The numerous sling projectiles found in the Euonymon theatre are a stark testament to the role that war played in its abandonment by the mid third century (**I Introduction**). As Attica declined, other cities prospered. Many of them offered better opportunities for performers at festivals outside Attica.

Ai: Aristophanes, *Acharnians* 237–79. Produced at the Lenaea of 425, in the sixth year of the Peloponnesian War, the *Acharnians* dramatises widespread Athenian frustration at the policy which had seen the countryside of Attica invaded and ravaged by the Spartans each year, its population forced to take refuge within the city walls. The first raid took place in summer 431 (Th. 2.19). Lines 266–7 'after six years I greet you, as I gladly come to my deme' imply that it had been impossible to hold Rural Dionysia since (see Olson 2002, 149 on the apparent use of exclusive rather than the more usual inclusive calculation here, which would require 'seventh'). The reference in l. 270 to 'Lamachuses' is to the general Lamachus, prominent during the Peloponnesian War. He features later in the play (ll. 572ff.) as an aggressive executive of the city's policy. After securing a private thirty-year peace treaty for his family, the play's hero, a farmer named Dikaiopolis, declares 'As for me, freed from war and troubles, I'm going home to celebrate the Rural Dionysia!' ἐγὼ δὲ πολέμου καὶ κακῶν ἀπαλλαγεὶς | ἄξω τὰ κατ' ἀγροὺς εἰσιὼν Διονύσια (ll. 201–2) – εἰσιὼν 'going home', literally 'going inside', indicating that we are to take Dikaiopolis' exit into the stage building at that point to denote departure to his home deme. Dikaiopolis reappears here, pursued by the bellicose old men of the deme Acharnae who make up the chorus, to direct the parade of his private Rural Dionysia. Text: Wilson.

	ΔΙ.	εὐφημεῖτε, εὐφημεῖτε.
	ΧΟ.	σῖγα πᾶς. ἠκούσατ', ἄνδρες, ἆρα τῆς εὐφημίας;
		οὗτος αὐτός ἐστιν ὃν ζητοῦμεν. ἀλλὰ δεῦρο πᾶς
240		ἐκποδών· θύσων γὰρ ἀνήρ, ὡς ἔοικ', ἐξέρχεται.
	ΔΙ.	εὐφημεῖτε, εὐφημεῖτε.
		προΐτω 'ς τὸ πρόσθεν ὀλίγον ἡ κανηφόρος.
		ὁ Ξανθίας τὸν φαλλὸν ὀρθὸν στησάτω.
		κατάθου τὸ κανοῦν, ὦ θύγατερ, ἵν' ἀπαρξώμεθα.
245	ΘΥ.	ὦ μῆτερ, ἀνάδος δεῦρο τὴν ἐτνήρυσιν,
		ἵν' ἔτνος καταχέω τοὐλατῆρος τουτουί.

ΔΙ.   καὶ μὴν καλόν γ᾽ ἔστ᾽. ὦ Διόνυσε δέσποτα,
      κεχαρισμένως σοι τήνδε τὴν πομπὴν ἐμὲ
      πέμψαντα καὶ θύσαντα μετὰ τῶν οἰκετῶν
250   ἀγαγεῖν τυχηρῶς τὰ κατ᾽ ἀγρούς Διονύσια,
      στρατιᾶς ἀπαλλαχθέντα· τὰς σπονδὰς δέ μοι
      καλῶς ξυνενεγκεῖν τὰς τριακοντούτιδας.
      ἄγ᾽, ὦ θύγατερ, ὅπως τὸ κανοῦν καλὴ καλῶς
      οἴσεις, βλέπουσα θυμβροφάγον. ὡς μακάριος
255   ὅστις σ᾽ ὀπύσει κἀκποιήσεται γαλᾶς
      σοῦ μηδὲν ἥττους βδεῖν, ἐπειδὰν ὄρθρος ᾖ.
      πρόβαινε, κἀν τὤχλῳ φυλάττεσθαι σφόδρα
      μή τις λαθών σου περιτράγῃ τὰ χρυσία.
      ὦ Ξανθία, σφῷν δ᾽ ἐστὶν ὀρθὸς ἐκτέος
260   ὁ φαλλὸς ἐξόπισθε τῆς κανηφόρου·
      ἐγὼ δ᾽ ἀκολουθῶν ᾄσομαι τὸ φαλλικόν·
      σὺ δ᾽, ὦ γύναι, θεῶ μ᾽ ἀπὸ τοῦ τέγους. πρόβα.

      Φάλης, ἑταῖρε Βακχίου,
265   ξύγκωμε, νυκτοπεριπλάνητε, μοιχέ, παιδεραστά,
      ἕκτῳ σ᾽ ἔτει προσεῖπον εἰς τὸν δῆμον ἐλθὼν ἄσμενος,
      σπονδὰς ποιησάμενος ἐμαυτῷ, πραγμάτων τε καὶ μαχῶν
270   καὶ Λαμάχων ἀπαλλαγείς.
      πολλῷ γάρ ἐσθ᾽ ἥδιον, ὦ Φάλης Φάλης,
      κλέπτουσαν εὑρόνθ᾽ ὡρικὴν ὑληφόρον,
      τὴν Στρυμοδώρου Θρᾷτταν ἐκ τοῦ φελλέως,
275   μέσην λαβόντ᾽, ἄραντα, καταβαλόντα καταγιγαρτίσαι.
      Φάλης Φάλης,
      ἐὰν μεθ᾽ ἡμῶν ξυμπίῃς, ἐκ κραιπάλης
      ἕωθεν εἰρήνης ῥοφήσει τρύβλιον·
      ἡ δ᾽ ἀσπὶς ἐν τῷ φεψάλῳ κρεμήσεται.

Dikaiopolis: Keep silence! Keep silence! **Chorus**: Quiet, everyone! Didn't you hear the call for silence? This is the very man we're looking for! This way, everyone, [240] out of the way: the man's coming out, so it seems, to make a sacrifice. **Dikaiopolis**: Keep silence! Keep silence! Go forward a little bit, Basket Bearer (*kanephoros*). May Xanthias keep the phallos up straight! Set down the basket, daughter, so we may begin the ceremony. [245] **Daughter**: Mother, hand me up the ladle, so I can pour soup over this cake. **Dikaiopolis**: Why look, that's good! Lord Dionysus, with pleasure for you may I send this parade and make the sacrifice, and with my household [250] may I with good fortune conduct the Rural Dionysia, now that I'm released from military service, and may my thirty-year truce be profitable for me. Come, my pretty daughter, be sure you bear the basket prettily, with a sour-faced look. How blessed is he [255] who marries you and begets weasels as good as you at farting in the early morning! Lead the way! – and when you're in the crowd, be very careful no-one pinches your jewelry. Xanthias, you two must keep [260] the phallos erect from behind the Basket Bearer! I shall follow and sing the phallic song. And you, my wife, watch me from the roof. Forward!

Phales ('Phallos-god'), companion of Bacchus, [265] fellow reveler, night-wanderer, seducer, boy-lover, after six years I greet you, as I gladly come to my deme, with a truce I made for myself, freed from troubles and battles [270] and Lamachuses. Yes, it's much more pleasant, Phales, Phales, to catch a budding girl wood-carrier as she's thieving – Strymodoros' Thracian slave from the rocky land – [275] grab her waist, lift her up, throw her down and take her cherry. Phales, Phales, if you drink with us, after the bout at dawn you will drain a cup of peace; and my shield will be hung by the hearth.

As the only extended Classical text relating to the deme Dionysia, this passage has come to bear great weight in our understanding of the festival (Deubner 1966, 134–8; *DFA*[2] 43–4; Whitehead 1986a, 213–14; Spineto 2005, 330–4). The distorting effects of the comic genre are moderated by the dramatic need for a rapid sketch of the festival that can be readily assimilated by the audience. Comic inversion applies in the idea of a festival held exclusively by a single family, although Dikaiopolis' caution to his daughter to beware of thieves in 'the crowd' (l. 257) is suited to a normal situation in which the festival was held among the whole community. The resulting generic sketch indicates both the complete familiarity of the festival to the audience of the comedy and the likelihood that the scene captures its salient features, while the reduced scale of its eccentric domestic framework will have the effect of making the sketch much more modest and 'homely' than the reality.

This last aspect has been influential in encouraging a view of deme Dionysia as rudimentary and unsophisticated affairs. The tendency (**A Introduction**) is exacerbated by the habit of comparing this passage with one of Plutarch that describes how 'in olden days' 'the traditional festival of the Dionysia was a homely and merry parade' ἡ πάτριος τῶν Διονυσίων ἑορτὴ τὸ παλαιὸν ἐπέμπετο δημοτικῶς καὶ ἱλαρῶς (**I Avii 2h** for the full passage), in which there was 'an amphora of wine and a vine branch, then a celebrant dragged along a goat, another followed carrying a basket of figs, and behind all of them, the phallos'. Nilsson (1900, 91) influentially argued that Plutarch was referring, on the basis of scholarly study (*e litteris ei notis*), to the Classical Attic Rural Dionysia, pointing in particular to the use of the adverb δημοτικῶς to suggest a link to the demes. This interpretation of the adverb is almost certainly untenable (*DFA*[2] 44 n. 4) and Plutarch is drawing, with his own nostalgic and moralising twist, on an evolutionary theory developed by Hellenistic scholars that located the origins of tragedy within a rustic setting in Archaic Attica. Any connection to actual practice at deme festivals in the historical period is highly attenuated at best. Even if some notion of Classical Attic practice does form part of this picture, one effect of Plutarch's distorting and moralising nostalgia is to strip away any sign of theatrical performance, which finds a place in the contrasting image of present-day decline from this imagined, pristine practice of the past: 'masks' feature climactically in the list of 'gold vessels carried past, rich robes, carriages riding by, and masks' (χρυσωμάτων περιφερομένων καὶ ἱματίων πολυτελῶν καὶ ζευγῶν ἐλαυνομένων καὶ προσωπείων).

The centrality of the parade (*pompe*) to deme Dionysia emerges very clearly (Deubner 1966, 135; **A Introduction**). Dikaiopolis has his daughter process as Basket Bearer at the head of the parade, two domestic slaves behind her carrying the phallos-pole, himself at the rear, his wife watching from the roof of the house. His family make up the entirety of the parade's officiants and recipients, his wife notably constituting the festival's participating 'audience'. Despite this extreme anomaly, the arrangement possibly captures something of the way in which the members of a small number of wealthy families dominated the cultic offices at local Dionysia. It is entirely likely that the role of Basket Bearer at deme Dionysia might often have been filled by the daughter of a local worthy. Dikaiopolis has been thought to represent 'a body of revellers' (*DFA*² 43) but, given the way in which he orchestrates the parade, he appears also to evoke the figure of the demarch (Spineto 2005, 333). The participation of slaves (**Aiv**) and women is likely to reflect reality.

Dikaiopolis' parade seems not to have a live sacrificial victim. The only offering, carried and presented by the Basket Bearer, is a cake (l. 246). This is very unlikely to reflect normal practice, and there is evidence for substantial sacrificial activity at the festival (**Av**; **Bvii 2**; **Di**; **H Introduction**; **Hvii**; **Mxi**; **V Introduction**; **Viii**; **Vv**; **X**; **Y Introduction**). Parke (1977, 101) took this to be a parody of the 'proper' consecration of a billy goat. An associated oddity is the fact that the sacrifice apparently precedes the parade, the reverse of the norm. Some editors take the radical step of suggesting that ll. 244–52 have been displaced from a point around l. 276, or argue that the poet's overarching interest in the phallic parade and song, rather than the sacrifice that went along with it, has led him to put the latter first (Olson 2002, 142).

A more likely solution is that the cake is a preliminary offering only (note the verb ἀπαρξώμεθα in l. 244, used often for preliminary offerings) and we are to suppose that, even though no beast is explicitly mentioned, the more usual blood sacrifice (*thysia*) is to be anticipated at the parade's final destination at the sanctuary, which is never reached (Habash 1995, 562). It is probably no more than an intriguing coincidence that the sacrifice is listed before the parade in a decree from Acharnae (**Bvii 2**) that honours officials who have 'in a fine and ambitious manner [super]vised the sacrifice to Dionysus [and the] parade and the contests' τῶν Διονυσίων καλῶ[ς] καὶ φιλοτίμως [ἐπιμ]ε[μ]έ[λ]ηνται τῆς τε θυσίας τ|ῶι Διονύσωι [καὶ τῆς] πομπῆς καὶ τοῦ ἀγῶνο|ς.

Dikaiopolis' parade has a powerfully phallic character from the prominence given the phallos-pole, carried by 'a chorus' of two slaves, and from his 'hymn to the phallos' (ll. 264–79). Phallic song was very probably a prominent feature of the parades of actual deme Dionysia. There are hints of it in Halimous (**L**), and a highly cogent supplement to a mid fifth-century decree from Ikarion shows that it was an essential component of the local festival there (**Miii**, l. 33: [φαλλ]ικὸν ᾆδεν). The fragmentary remains of this decree may also conceal a reference to the involvement of a chorus in its performance and we have aired the possibility (**M Introduction**) that the small neighbouring deme of Plotheia may have sent a phallic chorus to the Dionysia of its larger and more illustrious neighbour. The fact that Dikaiopolis sings his song solo will be a consequence of the eccentric quality of his 'private' festival and a choral form is the likely norm (Parker 1997, 128; Csapo 2013). Or rather, the refrain in Dikaiopolis' song (ll. 271, 277: ὦ Φάλης Φάλης) presumably corresponds to the choral part in a more regular phallic song, while Dikaiopolis plays the role of the *exarchos* or leader, integrating the refrain into his verse.

The refrain is a direct invocation of the personified phallos – as Phales – and this may also be typical of phallic hymn. Semos of Delos (ca. 200) records two fragments of phallic song, *PMG* 851a and b (Ath. 14.622a) that may have been performed at the Dionysia on Delos (Cole 1993) and which offer numerous parallels for Dikaiopolis' performance (extensive discussion in Bierl 2009, ch. 2). In one case (*PMG* 851b) unmasked *phallophoroi* ('Phallos Bearers') sang verses that directly identified the phallos they carry with Bacchus: σοί, Βάκχε, τάνδε μοῦσαν ἀγλαΐζομεν 'For you, Bacchus, we give this bright song'; while as for the other, Semos describes the performance of *ithyphalloi* ('Men with Erections') in a theatre who, masked as drunks, delivered verses such as *PMG* 851a: 'Get back! Make an open space for the god! For the god wants to march through your midst, erect and swollen'. Here the god was evidently equated with the phallos (pole), and the instructions to bystanders to make way find a parallel with the chorus of Acharnians' 'out of the way' (ἐκποδών l. 240). That directive, as well as the one to keep silence (ll. 237, 241), also has parallels in the Dionysiac parade of Euripides' *Bacchae* (ll. 68–70) 'Who's in the way? Who's in the way? Who? Let him get out of the way indoors, and let everyone keep his mouth pure, speaking propitious things' τίς ὁδῷ τίς ὁδῷ; τίς; | μελάθροις ἔκτοπος ἔστω, στόμα τ' εὔφη|μον ἅπας ἐξοσιούσθω (and with the use of third-person imperatives here cf. στησάτω in Dikaiopolis' instruction to 'keep the phallos up straight').

In practice the verses of the leader in the phallic song may have been at least partially improvised. For instance the abusive content that appears in Dikaiopolis' song – with the named targets of Lamachus and Strymodoros – probably reflect improvised abuse. Such *aischrologia* was characteristic of the type of phallic song to which Aristotle ascribed the origins of comedy (*Po.* 1449a11; *DFA*[2] 43; Cole 1993).

Dikaiopolis' song has patent hymnic features, such as the extended initial invocation of the divinity, with a list of quasi-epithets that touch upon his realms of activity (ll. 264–5), but it is hard to judge how much if any of its contents might have featured in a *phallikon* sung at an actual deme festival. The emphasis on the pleasures of illicit sex and peace in rural contexts, while suited to and shaped for the particular comic context, seem entirely at home in the local Dionysiac realm. The situation is similar in a passage of Aristophanes' *Peace* (530–2), performed four years later at the City Dionysia of 421. When Peace and her attendants Fruitfulness (*Opora*) and Holiday (*Theoria*) are finally hauled into view through the efforts of Trygaeus and his fellow farmers, Trygaeus declares that Peace 'smells of fruitfulness, hospitality, Dionysia, pipes, tragedians, Sophoclean songs, thrushes, little passages of Euripidean verse' ταύτης δ' ὀπώρας, ὑποδοχῆς, Διονυσίων, | αὐλῶν, τραγῳδῶν, Σοφοκλέους μελῶν, κιχλῶν, | ἐπυλλίων Εὐριπίδου. While the reference to Dionysia here may to some extent be generic rather than particular (Olson 1998, 185), it was the Dionysia in the extramural demes of Attica that had been interrupted during a full decade of war, and they surely constitute the primary reference – an interpretation seemingly made by the scholia that took the phrase ὑποδοχῆς Διονυσίων as a single unit ('succession of Dionysia') explaining that 'in peace-time the spectacle went on uninterrupted' (ἐν γὰρ εἰρήνῃ συνεχῶς ἦν ἡ θέα. Sch.[RV] Ar. *Peace* 530). Without laying too heavy hands on the light poetic associations made in this passage, it is striking that the things mentioned in closest proximity to these 'Dionysia' are performers of tragedy (τραγῳδῶν probably refers to performers, primarily choral, rather than poets), its music, the lyrics of Sophocles and the elegant verses of Euripides: hardly proof of widespread reperformance of Sophocles at deme Dionysia, but certainly consistent with it (**A Introduction**). And if ὑποδοχῆς means 'hospitality' rather than the scholia's 'succession', the term is suggestive of the arrival and hospitable treatment of guests at local festivals. As Trygaeus goes on to enumerate the further 'scents of Peace', they align very closely with those hailed by Dikaiopolis: 'ivy, a wine strainer, bleating flocks, the bosoms of women running through the fields, a drunken slave-girl, an upturned jug, and a host of other fine things!' (535–8). The deme Dionysia has been plausibly viewed as a festival that promotes vegetative fertility at a time when it seems most absent (**A Introduction**). This dynamic is made to serve the needs of the plot in both comedies, for the fecundity of the Attic countryside has suffered much more than a single winter.

Dikaiopolis is later described as a demesman of Cholleidai (l. 406: Χολλήδης), the location of which is uncertain, though it may have been one of Acharnae's neighbours. Some have treated this as evidence for a Dionysia in Cholleidai (Jones 2004, 131, 146; cf. Goette 2014, 95), but he may be given the demotic for no more than the reason identified by a number of scholia, namely to achieve a pun on 'lame' (*cholos*), with reference – made soon after, l. 411 χωλοὺς ποιεῖς 'you create lame people' – to the lame characters of Euripidean tragedy. With a bouleutic quota of 2, Cholleidai was probably too small to sustain a local Dionysia of any scale, and there is no suggestion in the *Acharnians* of a theatre either as the location for or destination of Dikaiopolis' phallic parade, nor is there any hint that theatrical performances are to form part of his (interrupted) Dionysia.

Aii: Pherecrates *PCG* F 182. Pherecrates was a significant Athenian poet of Old Comedy, somewhat earlier than Aristophanes. He had a victory at the City Dionysia in 437 (*PCG* T 2), possibly his first (*IG* II² 2325C, l. 22 M-O; Olson 2007, 413 thinks a date in the mid 440s likelier); was also successful at the Lenaea (*IG* II² 2325E, l. 7 M-O); and apparently remained active until the mid 410s (Millis and Olson 2012, 167). He is said to have begun his career as an actor (*PCG* T 2). The source for this fragment (play unknown) is a Suda entry (δ 421: Δήμαρχοι 'Demarchs'). It describes the demarchs of Athens as successors to *naukraroi*, in a tradition to which the Aristotelian *Constitution of Athens* (8.3; 21.5 with van Wees 2013, 44–61) belongs; notes their power to seize the property of debtors (οἷς ἐξῆν ἐνεχυράζειν: this is independently attested, including by Ar. *PCG* F 500; Whitehead 1986a, 125–7); and goes on to quote this passage with 'And Pherecrates:' (καὶ Φερεκράτης·). The entry concludes with 'Those [who were] leaders deme by deme. These men used to arrange the festival of the Panathenaea' (οἱ κατὰ δῆμον ἄρχοντες. οὗτοι δὲ διεκόσμουν τὴν ἑορτὴν τῶν Παναθηναίων). The last should be a reference to the procession of the Panathenaea rather than the festival as a whole (Sch. Ar. *Clouds* 37; Whitehead 1986a, 136–7). Text: Kassel and Austin.

> ὑπέλυσε δήμαρχός τις ἐλθὼν ἐς χορόν.

> Some demarch has joined the chorus and undone [? it].

Without context, little certain can be said of this tantalising reference to the actions of a demarch in connection with a chorus. A number of things are however more or less likely. The demarch in question is said to have participated in a choral performance. A metaphorical use of the word 'chorus' here seems unlikely – such as the 'chorus' of sophists at Pl. *Prt.* 314e–315b, or the comparable chorus simile at *Euthd.* 276bc – given the explicit language of performative choral action employed. This is formulaic, and poetic. The combination of a verb of motion (commonly, as here, ἰέναι) with ἐς / εἰς χορόν is widely used for 'joining a chorus' as its performance begins (e.g. Hom. *Od.* 6.65; *h.Ven* 6.13; Pratin. *PMG* F 709; Pi. fr. 94b, l. 39; Sophr. *PCG* F 136; E. *El.* 1198). Thus whatever degree of fiction or reality is in question in the lost context, a demarch is spoken of as having been an active, performing member of a (presumably local) chorus. Given the great preponderance of evidence for dramatic as opposed to any other types of choruses in the demes, the chorus envisaged here is likely to be one such (but see below).

The real difficulty lies with the initial verb, ὑπέλυσε. Whitehead (1986a, 332) offers two possibilities, reflecting two divergent interpretations of the verb: the first is of 'an amiable demarch letting down his official hair, so to speak, and joining in the fun of the dance'. On this scenario ὑπέλυσε would have an assumed (if not expressed, in a lost adjacent line) object, namely 'shoes' or 'sandals'. Choruses did normally dance barefoot so far as we can tell. But while the Middle ὑπολύομαι can be used in the sense of 'take off one's shoes' without the need to express 'shoes' or 'sandals', the same is not evidently true of the Active. In the Active, the object can be personal. Thus in another fragment of Pherecrates (*PCG* F 162.9, from the *Cheiron*) we find οὐχ ὑπολύσεις σαυτόν; 'Won't you take off your shoes?', addressed to a departing dinner guest being encouraged to stay. The absence of an expressed object tells against Whitehead's first interpretation.

Whitehead's second suggestion is that Pherecrates' demarch was said to have 'undone' not his footwear but the dance itself (presumably involving something like the Homeric usage of the verb for 'undoing' an opponent's power and physical capacity, e.g. *Il.* 6.27 ὑπέλυσε μένος καὶ φαίδιμα γυῖα), with the observation that demarchs served as a kind of police force in religious contexts. If the verb ὑπέλυσε is not corrupt (and no compelling emendation has been offered) one would naturally take the chorus to be its object in this way. But this further idea of a killjoy demarch shutting down a rowdy chorus is undermined, if not excluded, by the clear statement that he has just joined it. More likely, perhaps, that the image is one of a demarch less than skilled at or too old for *choreia* whose very entry to the chorus 'undid it'. But a perhaps preferable variant on this line of thinking would be that the demarch had joined the chorus to get at someone in it who had a debt owing which it was his task to secure. This has the major benefit of providing a meaningful connection between the quotation of the line by the Suda and the preceding information about demarchs' powers of seizure for debt, which it would illustrate. The underlying attitude to demarchs would also tally with that of the debt-ridden Strepsiades of Ar. *Clouds* 36 (δάκνει μέ δήμαρχός τις ἐκ τῶν στρωμάτων 'a demarch is biting me from the bedclothes'). The Law of Euegoros (of the first half of the 4th c.; **I Avi 1**) forbade anyone 'either to distrain or to seize property of another person, not even from debtors who are overdue in their payments during those days' at the Piraeus Dionysia, the City Dionysia, the Lenaea and the Thargelia, but it is not known whether the law applied in the context of deme festivals other than the (highly unusual) Piraeus Dionysia (**V Introduction**) or whether it was in force in the fifth century. Perhaps it was not, and Pherecrates is responding to an unpopular phenomenon of deme festival life.

Another line of interpretation is prompted by comparison with **Ai** and **Miii**. In the private deme Dionysia organised by Dikaiopolis in the *Acharnians*, Dikaiopolis seemingly both plays the role of *exarchos* of that festival's phallic chorus and also performs the functions commonly discharged by the demarch in relation to the running of the festival as a whole. In this light, we note an intriguing verbal echo with a phrase from the fragmentary fifth-century deme decree of Ikarion that set out in some detail procedures to be followed by the demarch in organising the Dionysia (**Miii**). In a section to do with the phallic parade of the local Dionysia, we find [...]ες τὸν χορὸ[ν ...] (l. 35). This could be a directive to integrate someone into a performing chorus (rather than, say, to give something to the chorus). A possibility (aired at **Miii**) is that it was a *tragoidos* or *tragoidoi* mentioned in the previous line who were to be made to join the phallic chorus. But perhaps it was the demarch himself, who is the primary addressee of the Ikarian decree as a whole, who was being instructed to join in the phallic chorus in Ikarion. And perhaps it was a more general phenomenon than hitherto supposed for demarchs to take on a role in the phallic parade of the festival he had organised.

Aiii: The Date of Deme Dionysia and the Question of an Attic Theatrical Circuit.

1. **Plato, *Republic* 475d**. Written ca. 380; dramatic date some time in the Peloponnesian War (Boeckh 1874, 448; but see Nails 1998). In the context of an attempt by Socrates to develop a definition of the true lover of wisdom (*philosophos*), Glaukon introduces the ideas of those who love spectacles (*philotheamones*) and those who love to hear new things (*philekooi*) who are eager for all sorts of aesthetic novelty and instruction, but Socrates subsequently (476b) goes on to distinguish such enthusiasts for beautiful appearances from those who are able to apprehend true beauty. Text: Slings.

> καὶ ὁ Γλαύκων ἔφη· πολλοὶ ἄρα καὶ ἄτοποι ἔσονταί σοι τοιοῦτοι. οἵ τε γὰρ φιλοθεάμονες πάντες ἔμοιγε δοκοῦσι τῷ καταμανθάνειν χαίροντες τοιοῦτοι εἶναι, οἵ τε φιλήκοοι ἀτοπώτατοί τινές εἰσιν ὥς γ᾽ ἐν φιλοσόφοις τιθέναι· οἳ πρὸς μὲν λόγους καὶ τοιαύτην διατριβὴν ἑκόντες οὐκ ἂν ἐθέλοιεν ἐλθεῖν, ὥσπερ δὲ ἀπομεμισθωκότες τὰ ὦτα ἐπακοῦσαι πάντων χορῶν περιθέουσι τοῖς Διονυσίοις οὔτε τῶν κατὰ πόλεις οὔτε τῶν κατὰ κώμας ἀπολειπόμενοι.

> Glaukon replied: 'Then according to you they (sc. the *philosophoi*) will be a numerous and strange group. For all spectacle lovers (*philotheamones*) are, it seems to me, what they are because of the pleasure they take in learning, and those who love to hear new things (*philekooi*) are a very strange lot to be ranked among lovers of wisdom (*philosophoi*). They never willingly attend discussions and serious study, but as if they had rented out their ears to listen to every chorus, they run around to the Dionysia, never missing one, either in the cities or in the villages.'

2. **Plato, *Laches* 183a–b**. The *Laches* is generally regarded as an early work, perhaps as early as ca. 405; dramatic date and setting, Athens ca. 420. Laches compares the way in

which an expert in hoplite warfare who had won recognition in Sparta would naturally use that reputation to earn money elsewhere with the practice of tragic poets in relation to Athens. Text: Burnet.

> … καὶ ὅτι παρ᾽ ἐκείνοις ἄν τις τιμηθεὶς εἰς ταῦτα καὶ παρὰ τῶν ἄλλων πλεῖστ᾽ ἂν ἐργάζοιτο χρήματα, ὥσπερ γε καὶ τραγῳδίας ποιητὴς παρ᾽ ἡμῖν τιμηθείς. τοιγάρτοι ὃς ἂν οἴηται τραγῳδίαν καλῶς ποιεῖν, οὐκ ἔξωθεν κύκλῳ περὶ τὴν Ἀττικὴν [183b] κατὰ τὰς ἄλλας πόλεις ἐπιδεικνύμενος περιέρχεται, ἀλλ᾽ εὐθὺς δεῦρο φέρεται καὶ τοῖσδ᾽ ἐπιδείκνυσιν εἰκότως.

Possibly καὶ τὰς ἄλλας πόλεις or καὶ κατὰ τὰς ἄλλας πόλεις Taplin

> … and that anybody who has achieved honour among them (sc. the Spartans) for this activity would earn the most money from others, just like a poet of tragedy does who has achieved honour among us. And so anyone who regards himself as a fine poet of tragedy does not travel around outside in a circuit around Attica ('and' with Taplin's emendation) through the other cities putting on a display, but quite reasonably makes a direct line for this place and puts on a display for our people.

The evidence of contemporary literature (**I Ai 1a**) and inscriptions (below), as of later iconography (**I Avii**) and scholarship (Sch. Pl. *Rep.* 475d; Sch. Aeschin. 1.43; *Lex.Vind.*, *Lex.Rhet.* s.v. Διονύσια = *AB* 1.235.6–8), is unanimous in placing the Attic Dionysia in the month of Posideon. There are some hints from the most direct of these sources – inscriptions published by the demes themselves – that demes scheduled their festivals on different dates within Posideon. In the late fourth century the Dionysia of Myrrhinous fell on or around 17–18 Posideon (**Rii**). The epigraphic evidence relating to mid fifth-century Ikarion is less clear, but one interpretation places it at around the same dates (**Miii**; Wilson 2015, 131–2); while there is reason to believe that the rather grand Piraeus festival, lasting at least four days, fell near the start of the month (**V Introduction**). The fact that, in the sacrificial calendar of Thorikos of ca. 420, the Dionysia (and it alone) is assigned to Posideon without any further specification of date may imply a wish to maintain flexibility in the scheduling of the festival (**Y Introduction**), desirable for meteorological and other reasons (Jones 2004, 153). It is certainly likely that demes which courted outside visitors to their festival will have aimed to hold it before the onset of the worst of the winter weather, and thus earlier in Posideon. But the need to book performers and ensure a large audience speaks against flexibility. Jones (2004, 155) has tentatively aired the possibility of polis involvement in ensuring that the demes, otherwise so idiosyncratic in their cultic arrangements, scheduled this festival in the same month. The polis certainly appears to have taken cognisance of the festival's timetable, for the fact that so few meetings of the Assembly are attested in Posideon is to be explained at least in part by a desire to avoid a clash (Mikalson 1975, 97).

Even when full account is taken of the negative bias in Demochares' talk of Aeschines 'wandering through the fields' as a member of a tragic troupe of actors and in Demosthenes' derogatory accounts of this 'rustic Oenomaus' (**O**), there remains a distinctive image of a

dramatic troupe moving from one rural festival to another. **1** and **2** are important but difficult further evidence for the existence of such a theatrical 'circuit' in Attica. By the highest
date at which the older of them (**2**) was composed – ca. 405 – theatre had spread to other
cities, but perhaps not to so many as to allow this passage to be readily understood as *excluding* the several Attic townships in which it had flourished for a number of decades (the
same is truer *a fortiori* if one considers the dramatic date to exert any control over the issue;
note that e.g. Ghiron-Bistagne 1976, 193 treats the passage as excluding Attica). On the
other hand both the general sentiment and particular expression are not easily compatible
with a view that only a deme circuit is intended, as for instance in the translation of Lamb
(1924): 'does not tour round with his show in a circuit of the outlying Attic towns'. For
one might expect full cities rather than (even large) demes as the realistic potential rival
centres of patronage for aspiring tragic poets – indeed as much is implied by the economic
aspect of the argument here. And one possible interpretation of the expression (rendered
here with clumsy literalness) 'travel around "outside" in a circuit around Attica through the
other cities' ἔξωθεν κύκλῳ περὶ τὴν Ἀττικὴν κατὰ τὰς ἄλλας πόλεις ... περιέρχεται could
suggest a passage not just 'outside' the city centre of Athens but beyond the whole territory
of Attica (note also the repetition of κύκλῳ δὲ περιιόντας in the continued discussion at
183b5, where it seems to mean circling outside a city). However, περί with the accusative
can refer both to movement *round about* an object (LSJ s.v. C.1) and to position 'around'
and so 'throughout' a place (LSJ s.v. C.4; e.g. Th. 6.2.6 ᾤκουν δὲ καὶ Φοίνικες περὶ πᾶσαν
μὲν τὴν Σικελίαν). The evidence of the historical context best suits a text that referred to
a theatrical circuit including cities proper beyond Attica but also the Attic demes. That is
best achieved by Taplin's suggestion (1993, 91) of a lost καὶ before κατὰ: 'travel around
abroad in a circuit around Attica *and* through the other cities'. We thus understand this
expression as speaking from a city perspective: the poet goes about putting on shows in a
circuit outside [Athens] around [= throughout] Attica and the other cities – the point of the
definite article being precisely to specify 'cities other than Athens' (τὰς ἄλλας πόλεις). This
also has the virtue of not requiring πόλεις 'cities' to refer here to the demes, which it cannot
easily do (Taplin 1993, 91; Csapo 2004, 71). One noteworthy consequence of this reading
is that it registers destinations in Attica and cities outside it as of equal standing from the
point of view of theatrical performance.

That solution also makes **2** more compatible with **1**. In this passage we once more find
the notion of a 'circuit' (in the verb περιθέουσι 'run around') of Dionysia so arranged as
to make it possible for the enthusiastic *philotheamon* to miss none (if he hurries). And the
combination' – and contrast – of 'cities' πόλεις and 'villages' κώμας may mirror that implicit in the reading of **2** suggested by Taplin. In that case the 'circuit' envisaged will not
be confined to the Attic month of Posideon, for it is very unlikely that cities outside Attica
chose this time of year for their (single) theatrical Dionysia (that includes even a number
very close by, such as Salamis, Megara and Eretria). In **Aiv** a verb of circumambulation is
used with explicit – and exclusive – reference to the Rural Dionysia (Διονύσια κατ᾽ ἀγρὸν
ἄγωσι περιιόντες).

Other important aspects of **1** have drawn less attention. Plato will not be attempting to
avoid anachronism by having Socrates stress the centrality of choruses (πάντων χορῶν) to
these Dionysia, when he clearly means to refer to theatrical performances. This is then another item of evidence for the continued chorocentric view of drama in the fourth century.

Both passages are also important evidence for the economic dimension of theatre as it spread through and beyond Attica. The roaming spectators of **1** are said to 'rent out' their ears at the various Dionysia. Though a seemingly casual metaphor, the term ἀπομισθοῦν τὰ ὦτα evokes what is virtually a technical term of theatre finance – ἀπομισθοῦν θέαν 'to rent out a seat for the spectacle' (**V A**). From at least the time of Aristophanes, this was used to describe what theatre managers did. And contracts of hire were also used by administrators to engage actors, for which the verb μισθόω 'hire' was used (**I Bi 11**). Plato's language subtly but powerfully ties the spread and timetabling of Dionysia, including deme Dionysia, to commercial forces. Like a troupe of performers wandering from one paying community to another, the theatre audience is itself on tour around Attica, renting out its ears for profit.

It is clear that in **2** Plato has added the reference to teachers of military science making money in other cities after being recognised by the Spartans not because they in fact did so (the whole notion of 'military science' under discussion seems to be entirely hypothetical), but because he is looking forward to the comparison with tragic poets. This amounts to a claim that already by the late fifth century the real money for tragic poets was to be made 'on the circuit' outside Athens, but most effectively by those who had first won the imprimatur of excellence in Athens.

The staggered timetable of deme Dionysia can thus be explained by a range of very practical administrative and economic factors. It will have been essential in order to ensure that performers in high demand and short supply could appear at more than one festival. Although the distances are nothing like those that faced artists in the age of Alexander, travel between distant parts of Attica in wet winter months, even with a reasonable road network (Korres 2009; the map provided by Steinhauer 2009, 35 is especially useful), will have required very careful timetabling. And it is clear that many demes not only opened their Dionysia to outsiders as audience members, but anticipated in doing so the revenue derived from their presence – both as fees for seats and as local consumers – to support their event (Jones 2004, 152–7; Wilson 2010a). The practical dimension of this Attic circuit may have been clothed in an elevating aetiology, for there is reason to believe that the passage of the Dionysiac troupe along the wintry roads of Attica may have been mythologised as retracing the footsteps and the mission of Icarius or of Dionysus himself (**A Introduction**; **I Avii 2**).

Aiv: Slaves at the Deme Dionysia: Plutarch, *That One Cannot Live Pleasantly Following Epicurus* **(*Moralia*) 1098b–c**. Composed 1st c. AD. The dialogue is a Platonist attack on the Epicurean view of pleasure as the highest good. This passage gives an example of the lower bodily pleasures to be abhorred. Text: based on Pohlenz and Westman.

> καὶ γὰρ οἱ θεράποντες ὅταν Κρόνια δειπνῶσιν ἢ Διονύσια κατ᾽ ἀγρὸν ἄγωσι περιιόντες, οὐκ ἂν αὐτῶν τὸν ὀλολυγμὸν ὑπομείναις καὶ τὸν θόρυβον, ὑπὸ χαρμονῆς καὶ ἀπειροκαλίας τοιαῦτα ποιούντων καὶ φθεγγομένων·

> And so too when slaves feast at the Kronia or go around celebrating Rural Dionysia, you could not endure the cries and the uproar, as in their delight and vulgarity they act and speak like this (a call to drinking and revelry follows, generally thought to be a quotation from a 4th-c. comedy: *PCG* adesp. F 745)

The suspicion (Jones 2004, 152) that Plutarch based his remark about slaves celebrating the Rural Dionysia on a passage of Aristophanes' *Acharnians* (**Ai**) is unfounded. There are no verbal echoes and none of the details provided by Aristophanes are included that might have enlivened the account and strengthened its argument (notably the special role of phallos bearer given the domestic slave Xanthias, ll. 259–60). Pickard-Cambridge took the reference to be to Plutarch's own day, while supposing that the same was true centuries earlier (*DFA²* 43). We have little (but not no: *SEG* 54, 322) evidence for the deme Dionysia in the first to second centuries AD, but the reference to the familiar Classical 'circuit' (implied by 'go around' περιιόντες, in which the Platonic Plutarch may recall **Aiii**) may suggest that Plutarch has the Classical period in mind.

Taken literally this phrase may imply that slaves attended various Dionysia around Attica, not just that of their place of residence – whether in the footsteps of their masters (and, in all probability, assisting them on the road) or independently is unclear, though the emphasis of the passage on licence (and the association with the antinomic Kronia: Versnel 1993; Parker 2005, 162, 202, 475) might hint at the latter. This was at any rate the least busy period of the agricultural year. Plutarch stresses their direct participation in the festival (indeed taken literally ἄγωσι implies a degree of agency in conducting the event) and the slaves of Dikaiopolis participate in two key elements of his deme Dionysia: parade (*pompe*) and sacrifice (Ar. *Ach.* 248–50, 259–60). If this reflects reality it would be absurd to suppose that they were excluded from its third key element, the agones.

Plutarch's Platonism may go deeper in this passage. The statement that slaves at a rural Dionysia experience pleasure and show ἀπειροκαλία 'vulgarity' or literally 'inexperience of the beautiful' may draw directly on the anti-theatrical views of Plato, notably the notion of tragedy as a kind of public speech whose proper addressees include slaves (Pl. *Grg.* 502d).

Av: Theoinia and Deme Dionysia: Harpocration, *Lexicon of the Ten Orators* s.v. Θεοίνια ('Theoinia') (= Lycurg. fr. 7.3 Conomis). Harpocration of Alexandria's (1st or 2nd c. AD) *Lexicon of the Ten Orators*, which survives in abridged form, is a gloss of words and phrases, mostly from the Attic orators, that draws on a very wide range of earlier sources. Harpocration or a prior source doubtless had access to the complete speech of the mid fourth-century Athenian politician Lycurgus (**VI I**) delivered for one of the two *gene* that were disputing certain religious roles, possibly in connection with the rites of Eleusis. Dinarchus appears to have spoken for the other side (Harp. s.v. Ἐξούλης; s.v. Ἱεροφάντης). Text: Conomis.

> Θεοίνια· Λυκοῦργος ἐν τῆι διαδικασίαι Κροκωνιδῶν πρὸς Κοιρωνίδας. τὰ κατὰ δήμους Διονύσια Θεοίνια ἐλέγετο, ἐν οἷς οἱ γεννῆται ἐπέθυον· τὸν γὰρ Διόνυσον Θέοινον ἔλεγον, ὡς δηλοῖ Αἰσχύλος καὶ Ἴστρος ἐν α΄ Συναγωγῶν.

> 'Theoinia': Lycurgus in the adjudication of a right (*diadikasia*) of the Krokonidai against the Koironidai. The Dionysia in the demes used to be called Theoinia, at which the members of the *genos* used to sacrifice. For they called Dionysus 'Theoinos', as Aeschylus shows (*TrGF* F 382), as does Istros in the first book of his *Collected Writings* (*FGrH* 334 F 3).

Does this notice have anything to do with the deme Dionysia? Those who say 'no' are forced to translate the phrase τὰ κατὰ δήμους Διονύσια ('The Dionysia in the demes' above) as 'the shrines of Dionysus in rural communities' (Robertson 1993, 232, 237) or simply to dismiss as an error the identification made between deme Dionysia and Theoinia (Parker 2005, 483; cf. 1996, 299). Neither is entirely satisfactory.

The Theoinia appears to be a festival (or at least a ritual: the term ἑορτή 'festival' is not used of it, while θυσία 'sacrifice' is by Hesychius, quoted below) named for an epithet of Dionysus 'Theoinos' ('of the divine wine', or possibly 'of the divine vine'). Aeschylus speaks of 'father Theoinos, master of maenads' (πάτερ Θέοινε, μαινάδων ζευκτήριε *TrGF* F 382). The Theoinia was an event at which members of a *genos* – doubtless the Theoinidai (the phrase is unlikely to mean 'members of *gene* in general') – offered sacrifice, or perhaps 'offered an *additional* sacrifice', one sense of the compound verb ἐπιθύω. The fourteen *Gerarai* or Venerable Women appointed by the Archon Basileus (*EM* 227.35), assistants to the wife of the Archon Basileus at the Anthesteria (**II B**), were required to swear that they would celebrate 'in accordance with tradition and at the appointed times' two other festivals of Dionysus, the Iobaccheia and the Theoinia (Apollod. *Neaer.* 59.78 with Kapparis 1999, 341–4). The Theoinia may have been associated with or even part of the Anthesteria (thus Robertson 1993), but more likely was an entirely separate event (Humphreys 2004, 233–4). The involvement of the Basileus suggests it was in some sense under the aegis of the polis, though the 'at Athens' of Hesychius (θ 274: Θεοίνια· θυσία Διονύσου Ἀθήνησι. καὶ θεὸς Θέοινος Διόνυσος 'Theoinia: a sacrifice for Dionysus at Athens. And the god Theoinos is Dionysus') need not refer to the city of Athens and can be applied equally to all Attica (Nilsson 1900, 106). Most regard the festival as likely to be decentralised (Deubner 1932, 148–9). The prominence of women as important religious ministrants suggests a festival with significant involvement of women (Kapparis 1999, 343). Michael Jameson (*IG* app. crit.) thought that he saw traces compatible with a reference to '[a]t the Theoin[ia]' in the fragmentary inscription from the deme Paiania of ca. 450–430 that deals extensively with the cult of the Eleusinian goddesses (*IG* I³ 250, B l. 23: [ἐ]ν Θεοιν[ίοισι]), but Kazuhiro Takeuchi (*forthcoming*) argues that this reading is impossible, proposing instead the contextually very plausible [το]ῖν θεοῖν 'for the Twain'.

It is true that in the blunt form by which the lemma of Harpocration identifies deme Dionysia with Theoinia, the statement is highly problematic. But no obvious explanation for the supposed error presents itself and Robertson's translation is to say the least forced. The Theoinia can in no sense be identical to or an alternative name for the deme Dionysia. These were fully 'owned and operated' by demes as social and political entities and no evidence suggests that they were controlled by *gene*. That need not however preclude some degree of gentilic involvement, but as *gene* were not systematically associated with demes, any such involvement is likely to have been restricted to one or some local Dionysia, with which the Theoinidai were in some way associated. The alternative – that the Theoinidai went around to all deme Dionysia to make a sacrifice – is so unlikely as to be incredible. The further evidence of Photius (below) suggests the importance of a single sanctuary.

The Theoinidai are long since known (or at least deduced) from Photius (θ 91: Θεοίνιον· ἱερὸν Διονύσου, ἀφ' οὗ καὶ γένος 'Theoinion: a sanctuary of Dionysus, from which also a *genos*') and now more directly attested by a (probably) late Hellenistic decree issued by them in honour of one of their own, a priestess of the *Nymphe* (*SEG* 29, 135). Vanderpool (1979) thinks this may be the Nymphe on the south side of Acropolis, but Kearns (1989, 67) rightly stresses the highly generic nature of the term. She argues for an association with the Κορωνίδες κόραι 'maiden Koronides' known from a fragment of the (undatable) tragedian Dionysios Skymnaios (*TrGF* 208 F 1), who identifies them with 'the daughters of Theoinos', thus revealing a Dionysiac link between the two, as well as suggesting a link between the Theoinia mentioned in Lycurgus' speech and the two *gene* at loggerheads in that legal dispute, the Krokonidai and Koironidai (Parker 1996, 302–4; but see below). Kearns further speculates that the Theoinidai may in fact be the Koironidai, having 're-branded' themselves after the trial, with its dispute over priestly functions, with a new name, Theoinidai, that advertised their Dionysiac associations more forcefully than their old (Kearns also holds that they would in fact have called themselves *Koronidai* to play up the link to the Κορωνίδες κόραι: note that Aeschylus' phrase quoted above is compatible with the notion that the Theonidai/Koironidai were maenads). Perhaps they identified themselves as the daughters of the nymph Koronis (Robertson 1993, 236), whom Pherecydes of Athens (*EGM* fr. 90b) names as one of the nurses of Dionysus who subsequently 'went around with him, giving to mankind the gift of the vine discovered by the god'.

The theory of Humphreys is perhaps the best available on the current evidence: the Theoinia may be associated with the Haloa, a festival particularly known for Eleusis, home of the Krokonidai and Koironidai and celebrated in the month of the deme Dionysia, Posideon (Philoch. *apud* Harp. s.v. Ἁλῶια), more specifically on the 26th according to Photius (α 1080; Deubner 1932, 60–1). 'It is conceivable that the Haloa were (like the Thesmophoria) celebrated locally by women in the demes, and that at least in some demes those celebrations became linked to the Rural Dionysia' (Humphreys 2004, 234; cf. 256; **Q**). Such an interpretation would also make sense of the claim that the sacrifice made at the Dionysia by the Theoinidai was '*additional*'. Dionysus had a prominent place at the Haloa alongside Demeter and Persephone (Deubner 1932, 64; Lowe 1998). Moreover the story of Icarius and his invention of wine at some point became part of the mythology of the Haloa (Sch. Lucian *DMeretr.* 6.1), and this happens also to be the only mythology or aetiology we know of associated with deme Dionysia. A version of this theory was proffered some time ago by Foucart (1904, 83–5), who thought the Theoinia a sacrifice made in addition to those of the festival proper of the deme Dionysia by members of *gene* who claimed some special relation to the god of the vine – like the Semachidai of the deme so named, and (on his view – but see **Mvi**) a special *oikos* of Icarians who claimed descent from the hero, distinct from the members of the constitutional deme.

Avi: *Askos*-Jumping: Eubulus, *Amaltheia*, *PCG* F 7. The Athenian comic poet Eubulus won six times at the Lenaea, probably for the first time in the late 370s or 360s (*IG* II² 2325, l. 144 M-O). The Suda (ε 3386) dates what is presumably his floruit to 376–372 and describes him as 'on the border between Middle Comedy and Old'. This fragment is quoted by the scholia to Aristophanes *Wealth* 1129, the material substantially repeated in Suda α 4177: ἀσκὸς ἐν πάχνῃ 'a wineskin in a frost', and Harpocration's *Lexicon* s.v. ἀσκώλια (Keaney 1967, 210 no. 24). In the *Wealth* passage the verb ἀσκωλιάζειν is used in the sense 'to hop'. The scholia offer a number of glosses: the first gloss speaks of an Athenian festival called the Askolia 'at which they jumped on *askoi* in honour of Dionysus' (ἑορτὴν οἱ Ἀθηναῖοι ἦγον τὰ Ἀσκώλια, ἐν ᾗ ἐνήλλοντο τοῖς ἀσκοῖς εἰς τιμὴν τοῦ Διονύσου), referring in somewhat garbled fashion to the story of the supposed enmity of the goat to Dionysus' vine. Then, apparently in distinction from this Dionysiac meaning ('instead of the other (sc. meaning)' ἀντὶ τοῦ ἄλλου), they continue: 'But they properly used ἀσκωλιάζειν of the act of leaping on wineskins for the sake of a laugh. They used to place inflated and oiled wineskins in the middle of the theatre, onto which they leapt and slipped, as Eubulus says in his *Damaleia* (*Amaltheia* corr. Hemsterhuys):' κυρίως δὲ ἀσκωλιάζειν ἔλεγον τὸ ἐπὶ τῶν ἀσκῶν ἄλλεσθαι ἕνεκα τοῦ γελωτοποιεῖν. ἐν μέσῳ δὲ τοῦ θεάτρου ἐτίθεντο ἀσκοὺς πεφυσημένους καὶ ἀληλιμμένους, εἰς οὓς ἐναλλόμενοι ὠλίσθανον, καθάπερ Εὔβουλος ἐν Δαμαλείᾳ (Ἀμαλθείᾳ Hemsterhuys) φησὶν οὕτως. The quotation is followed by οὕτω καὶ Δίδυμος 'So too Didymus', explicitly naming the authority of 'probably the most prolific of all ancient scholars' (Dickey 2007, 7). Didymus lived in the first century and in his work on comedy 'had a greater interest in history and social context than did his Alexandrian predecessors' and 'consulted a broad range of sources, including fourth-century historians and specialized monographs' (Dobrov 2010, 21). The ascription of the fragment to the attested Eubulan comedy *Amaltheia* rests on the correction of the scholia's Δαμαλείᾳ (the Suda has Δαμαλίᾳ). Text: based on Kassel and Austin.

> καὶ πρός γε τούτοις ἀσκὸν εἰς μέσον < >
> καταθέντες εἰσάλλεσθε καὶ καχάζετε
> ἐπὶ τοῖς καταρρέουσιν ἀπὸ κελεύσματος.

1 <ἄνδρες> ἀσκὸν εἰς μέσον Austin   ἀσκόν <ὑμῶν> or <αὐτῶν> εἰς μέσον Blaydes   ἀσκὸν εἰς μέσον <χαμαὶ> Bentley   <μέγαν> Meineke

then in addition, set down the wineskin in the middle, leap on it and laugh at the signal at those who fall off.

Latte (1957, 390) noted that the verb ἀσκωλιάζειν properly means 'to hop on one leg' (a sense found for instance at Ar. *Wealth* 1129 and Pl. *Smp.* 190d) and Pollux (9.121) describes *askoliasmos* ἀσκωλιασμός as a chasing game with one leg raised that has nothing to do with wineskins. The sense 'to hop or dance (and try to stay) on an inflated and greased wineskin (ἀσκός)' appears to represent a considered attempt to bring the word and activity into the orbit of the Dionysiac through (false) etymologising that derived ἀσκωλιάζειν from ἀσκός 'wineskin', rather than a word describing the raising of a leg *ἄσκωλος < *ἀν(α)-σκωλος (cf. σκέλος and the likely etymological figure used by Plato *Smp.* 190d: ἐφ' ἑνὸς … σκέλους ἀσκωλιάζοντες 'hopping on one leg/*skelos*'). The word ἀσκωλιασμός appears only in the Suda α 4177: ἀσκὸς ἐν πάχνῃ 'a wineskin in a frost', Poll. 9.121 and Suet. Περὶ τῶν παρ᾽ Ἕλλησι παιδιῶν 12.6 and may not be Classical (further sources in Latte 1957).

The only text which connects *askoliasmos* with rural theatre is Vergil's *Georgics* (2.380–4 = **I Avii 2d**). Here we find an explicit association between leaping across greased wineskins in soft meadows (384: *mollibus in pratis unctos saluere per utres*), the sacrifice by 'the sons of Theseus' (383) of a goat for Dionysus 'on all the altars' (380: *Baccho caper* *omnibus altis*), the production of 'old plays' (381: *veteres ineunt proscaenia ludi*) and the award of prizes for talent in rural contexts (382: *praemiaque ingeniis pagos et compita circum*). Around a century later Cornutus follows Vergil in ascribing the activity generically to Attic farmers, but with no connection to theatre (*de nat. deorum* p. 60, 20–4 Lang).

Vergil clearly draws not on any concrete reality or record of it but on tendentious Hellenistic scholarship on the origins of drama in the Attic countryside, notably in Ikarion, which had linked the practice of jumping on a wineskin made from a goat's skin to an aetiological narrative about the killing of a goat for attacking the vine and the invention of both wine and drama. Vergil's aims are also aetiological within the immediate context of Augustan Rome, with the Roman Paganalia (cf. 382: *pagos*), Liberalia and Compitalia (cf. 382: *compita*) festivals and the primitive drama of the *Fescennina carmina* all likely concerns, in addition to the need to adjust the place of Dionysus within the Augustan system of representation after the defeat of Antony, who had adopted a high degree of identification with the god (Mac Góráin 2014; Schiesaro 2016, 32–5). But no other evidence comes as close as Vergil to locating the activity at Classical deme Dionysia. A couple of sources claim that there was an Athenian festival called the Askolia 'at which they jumped on *askoi* in honour of Dionysus' (e.g. Sch. Ar. *Wealth* 1129, quoted above). But this Askolia has long been recognised as a phantom festival (Deubner 1932, 135: 'eine Erfindung der Grammatiker') and the very fact that ancient scholars felt compelled to invent it speaks to a lack of any evidence that put *askoliasmos* at any known Attic festival. The isolated and confused assertion that competitors in the drinking contest at the Choes (the second day of the Anthesteria: **II B**) were required to stand on the wine-filled *askos* that served as the prize 'as they drank, for a contest' ἐφ' οὗ τοὺς πίνοντας πρὸς ἀγῶνα ἑστάναι, Sch. Ar. *Ach.* 1002) tells the same story.

The deliberate linking of *askoliasmos* (in the sense of wineskin jumping) to Dionysiac cult in the Attic countryside was part of – and probably began with – a broader attempt to draft an authorising and comprehensive myth-history for the beginnings of drama in the Attic demes, especially in Ikarion. We believe that that attempt had its origins in the second half of the fourth century, in the work of local Attic historians and publicists such as Phanodemus or Philochorus, but its first identifiable exponent is perhaps Eratosthenes in the third. Some believe that his *Erigone* described the origins of *askoliasmos* in Ikarion as part of an aetiologically abundant account that told of the first appearance of Dionysus, the first wine, first drunkenness, first sacrifice, first festival, first choral song and dance and first drama (**I Avii 2**; Maaß 1883; Solmsen 1947; Rosokoki 1995; Geus 2002, 105; Rozokoki 2017; **M Introduction**). But *askoliasmos* had already acquired a metaphorical significance in the myth-history and cultural polemics of Dionysiac genres as many as three or four decades before Eratosthenes' poem. As much is clear from the fact that Herodas chose to feature it in his autobiographical, academically learned and poetically polemical eighth *Mimiamb* (36–65) of perhaps ca. 270, where it is associated with the sacrifice of the goat that became the wineskin, Dionysiac poetics and victory, a rural setting and choral worship of Dionysus: 'the rustic game of *askoliasmos* will then probably glance at contemporary theories of the origin of drama' (Hunter 1983, 35; Rosen 1992). The word ἀσκός does not appear in the (admittedly fragmentary) work of Herodas, but a number of alternatives to describe the wineskin do (36: λῶπος 'covering'; 47: δορή 'skin'; 74: κώρυκος 'leather wallet'), suggesting that Herodas may have been avoiding the term.

The etymological 'argument' may therefore belong to Eratosthenes, but it could also go back further, to those who in the fourth century were set upon creating an account that determined and over-determined the Attic origin of drama in all its forms, devising a skilful manipulation of traditional practice, legend, etymology and whatever antiquarian lore might be persuasively put together for this end (**I Avii 2**). With what real practice were these Attic publicists working? It is clear that the choice of Ikarion as the 'birthplace' of drama was determined in large part by the existence of a genuinely old tradition of dramatic performance and Dionysiac worship there (**M Introduction**). Perhaps some form of the wineskin game was indeed played in Attic rural contexts such as (wine-producing) Ikarion. It need not have been part of any particular festival, or have had any connection to the theatre; an association with Dionysus, however loose, is guaranteed merely by the centrality to it of the implement used for transporting wine. This view is compatible with the single item of evidence for askos-jumping from the Classical period, this fragment of a comedy by Eubulus from around the second quarter of the fourth century. Despite the efforts of scholars ancient and modern, it cannot be made to prove any connection between the wineskin-leaping *askoliasmos* and theatre or Dionysia. There are no good grounds for seeing the practice as characteristic of deme Dionysia, let alone as constituting a formal contest (*DFA²* 45; Whitehead 1986a, 214–15).

The fragment uses neither the noun ἀσκωλιασμός nor the verb ἀσκωλιάζειν and Latte (1957, 390) was probably right to argue that in Eubulus' day the verb still meant 'to hop on one leg'. Even granted that the scholia cite the considerable authority of Didymus, the grounds for confidence in the information offered are few. The first explanation of *askoliasmos* – as the activity that gave the name to an Athenian festival, the Askolia 'at which they jumped on *askoi* in honour of Dionysus' – is discredited by its patent free fabrication of this unattested festival. The attempt to distinguish this Dionysiac *askoliasmos* from the second explanation – which is the one for which Eubulus is claimed to offer proof, a game held in the middle of the theatre of jumping on greased wineskins 'for the sake of a laugh' – grates with the evident truth that theatre was also a form of Dionysiac worship. But most troubling is the very assertion that the activity took place 'in the middle of the theatre' (ἐν μέσῳ δὲ τοῦ θεάτρου). The text of Eubulus provides no such evidence and the claim very much has the air of a creative extrapolation from the phrase 'in(to) the middle' εἰς μέσον of the incomplete line 1, an extrapolation clearly made in the knowledge of a tradition that had already tied the practice to the Attic theatre. Jones (2004, 143–4) places far too much faith in this reference to the theatre as an anchor to an historical setting at deme Dionysia. The whole account has the air of a scholar in search of a connection between *askoliasmos* and the theatre, with deeply unconvincing results. If this was the best that Didymus could find to contextualise the practice there can have been precious little, if any, evidence for it in the Classical sources available to him.

The little we know or can safely deduce of the *Amaltheia* is of limited help. Even the correction of the scholia's *Damaleia* to *Amaltheia* (above) cannot be regarded as certain. Hunter points out that ἀσκωλιασμός is perhaps 'appropriate to a play which may have concerned a famous goat' (1983, 93), for in one version of the myth this is the name of the goat that suckled baby Zeus or, in some accounts, that of his human nurse (1983, 89). But, because of the certain presence of Heracles in the play (F 6) Hunter himself inclines to the view that it dealt with a version that made Amaltheia the possessor of a cornucopic horn with which Heracles won the hand of Deianeira. A connection with nursling Zeus' goat seems at best highly tenuous.

Setting aside the tendentious context of its transmission, the fragment does appear to provide the earliest evidence for a game of jumping and trying to stay on wineskins. It indicates an activity in which a group of men (presumably, and even without Austin's restored address ἄνδρες 'men') form a circle around the wineskin, jump upon it and laugh at those who fall off. A sense of competition is built into the account without any indication of formality implied (Sifakis 1971, 424; the speaker who enjoins a choral dance/interlude upon the women of Eubulus' *Ankylion PCG* F 6 explicitly establishes a prize for their efforts: θήσω δὲ νικητήριον). The quasi-military order to laugh at those who fall ἀπὸ κελεύσματος 'at the signal' implies a leader of the operations. The phrase evokes the signal given to rowers by a boatswain (the κελευστής), a signal that rhythmically marked the time of their stroke and that was sustained by the music of pipes. A wider network of metaphorical and ritual associations between the two collective spheres of choral and naval activity (e.g. Alcm. *PMG* 1.94; Ar. *Knights* 541–50; Longus 3.21.2) may lie in the background. While our translation follows Hunter and others in taking the phrase ἀπὸ κελεύσματος closely with καχάζετε 'laugh at the signal' (and certainly not with the adjacent τοῖς καταρρέουσιν 'those who fall off'), it may make better sense to see it as referring back to εἰσάλλεσθε, for the leaping / dancing on the wineskin is the activity most in need of rhythmic order. The mockery (καχάζετε) is compatible with a Dionysian environment but does not suggest savage ('iambic') abuse.

Someone is clearly explaining the activity to others in the comedy. Or rather, the instructions are being delivered in a way that implies they are to be implemented forthwith: hence the highly cogent suggestion that they are delivered to the play's chorus and that the dance-game of *askoliasmos* being described in fact served as a choral interlude in the comedy (Sifakis 1971, 424; Hunter 1983, 93; Rothwell 1992, 220; this interpretation would benefit from the rhythmic construal of 'at the signal' ἀπὸ κελεύσματος in relation to the leaping offered above). While this fragment thus offers no evidence that *askoliasmos* was a feature of deme Dionysia, a scenario in which the chorus of a (Dionysiac) comedy played some version of the game would at the very least be suggestive, given that Eratosthenes may have made an aetiology for the first Dionysiac chorus in Ikarion do double service as an aetiology for *askoliasmos* (**I Avii 2**). The suggestiveness is enhanced by what sounds like an echo with the passage of Hyginus that introduces Eratosthenes' telling of Icarius' invention of *askoliasmos*. Hyginus says that after killing the goat in a rage Icarius *ex pelle eius utrem fecisse ac uento plenum praeligasse et in medium proiecisse suosque sodales circum eum saltare coegisse* 'made a wineskin out of his skin and tied it filled with air (or 'wine'?), and placing it in their midst made his fellow farmers dance about it' (**I Avii 2c**): with *in medium proiecisse* compare εἰς μέσον καταθέντες; the commanding tone of ἀπὸ κελεύσματος fits with *coegisse* and, if this was the introduction to a choral interlude, it would inevitably make explicit the latent notion that the 'leaping' of *askoliasmos* was felt to be a form of dance (*saltare*).

B | Acharnae

Introduction

Acharnae was by far the largest of the Attic demes, 'a great part of the polis' of Athens itself (Th. 2.19.2; bouleutic quota 22). Pausanias (1.31.6) cites two cults of Dionysus as among the most prominent in the deme, those of Dionysus Melpomenos and of Dionysus Kissos, 'since they say that the plant of the ivy first appeared there' (for the prominence of myths of Dionysus' sacred ivy in Acharnae in the Hellenistic period see Kellogg 2013, 139–47). Which, if either, was the cult celebrated at the deme's Dionysia is not known. Note also the recent discovery of a small roadside sanctuary of Dionysus in the area now called Kato Kifissia, south of the Cephissus river. A fourth-century inscription records that a sacred official named Dionysios honoured a man for having planted trees in the sanctuary (Platonos-Yiota 2004, 434–5; *SEG* 54, 316. Kellogg 2013, 160 expresses some doubt whether the site is within Acharnian territory; Platonos-Yiota 2013, 145–6 *contra*; reports of a presentation of the inscription by George Steinhauer at a symposium in Athens in May 2014 suggest that the site may have been Pergase rather than Acharnae). Melpomenos 'Dancing and singing' might seem fitting for a god worshipped with theatrical performances, but so too is Kissos 'Ivy' (Kellogg 2013, 159) and an epigram possibly by the late fifth-century Simmias of Thebes claims that 'crooked Acharnian ivy that blooms among the altars and stages' often covered the hair of Sophocles (*AP* 7.21; *TrGF* T 177). The ivy on Sophocles' hair might be 'Acharnian' not only because of the tradition referred to by Pausanias on the origin of the plant (though this is doubtless the principal implication of the term) but because Sophocles himself was known to have had some significant association with the Dionysia held in that deme.

The evidence for the festival is relatively abundant, stretching from around the start of the fourth century (assuming that **Bi** does in fact belong to the deme and refers to the Dionysia) to near its end (**Bvii**, where reference is also made to an unpublished inscription which may indicate its operation in the Roman Imperial period). **Bvii** shows us the festival seemingly flourishing in 314 under the direction of demarch, treasurer (*tamias*) and an 'epimelete of the Dionysia', with full anticipation of a healthy future (**Bvii 2**, ll. 19–22). The administrative and financial involvement of the city in its operation at this date may be of longer standing but is more likely to reflect the reforms of Demetrius of Phaleron (**VI K**).

Theatrical activity probably substantially predates the first surviving epigraphic evidence for it, even if the fifth-century date initially proposed (Pitt 2008) for the theatre discovered in 2007 at no. 21 Salaminos St., near the junction with Liosion St., in the centre of Menidhi, is open to serious doubt. The limited preliminary notices of this important discovery present a somewhat perplexing picture (Platonos-Yiota 2007, 184–6; Platonos in Various Authors 2012, 24–6 with figs. 10–11). A small part of a curved, perhaps semicircular or horseshoe-shaped orchestra (diameter ca. 13.5–15.0 m) was uncovered at a depth of 2.5 m, with a drainage channel between it and the first row of seats. Fragments of worked marble found in this area (some of them arch-shaped) may have come from the prohedria (but see **Bvi** on **Bvii 2**, l. 22). Some eleven rows of low and narrow (0.22–0.4 m) limestone benches were unearthed, built upon a natural slope. The full width of a single kerkis (ranging from 5 m at the bottom to 22 m at the top thus far excavated) was exposed, and small parts of the two others on either side. Above the tenth row were found part of a diazoma and the first step of the upper theatron, where the seating may have been constructed in wood (this area had been badly damaged by ploughing). The capacity of the theatre (without the upper theatron) is estimated at 1,700 to 2,000.

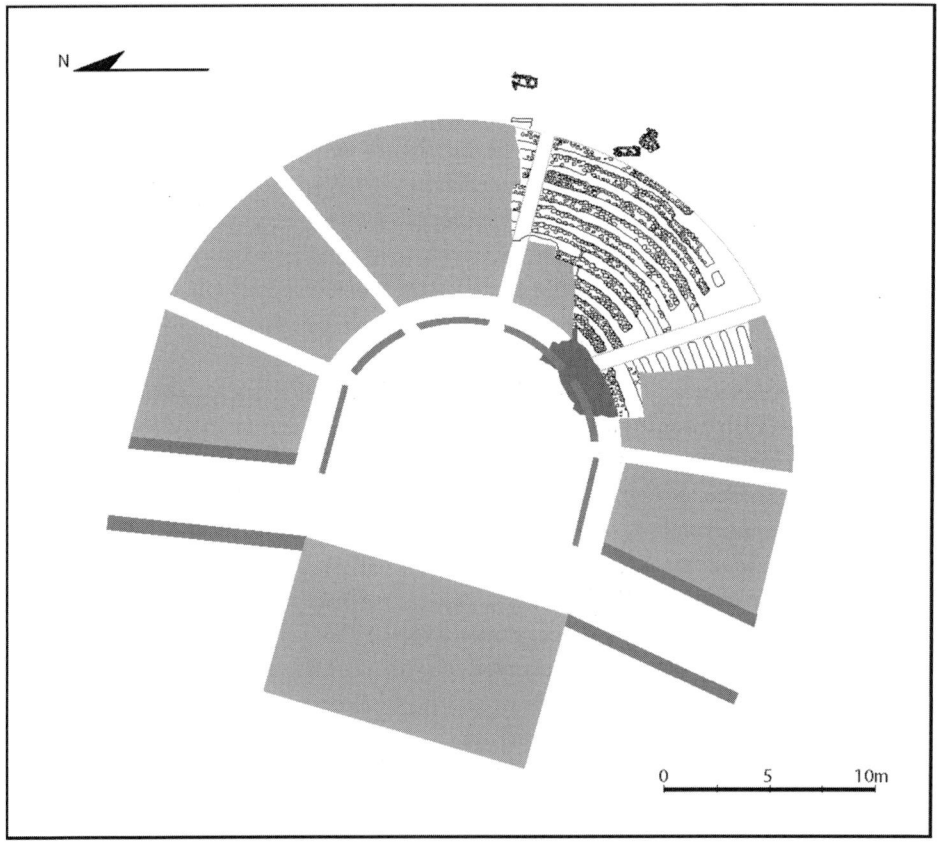

Plan of the Acharnae theatre.

In her most recent brief report, the excavator pronounces this theatre undatable on current knowledge (Platonos in Various Authors 2012, 26) and deduces from the evidence of the inscriptions which refer directly to a theatre in Acharnae that it must have been in existence prior to the middle of the fourth century. Only further excavation will enable more secure conclusions to be drawn as to the date of this theatre. But some have cast doubt as to whether this theatre is in fact 'the' (main) theatre of Acharnae at all. Goette (2014, 84) believes it to be too small for the most populous deme of Athens and supposes that it may have served as a second venue for the assembly of demesmen, perhaps associated with the sanctuary of Athena Hippia and Ares. But two of the inscriptions that deal directly with the operation of the Dionysia of Acharnae and its theatre (**Bvi** and **Bvii**), one of which refers simply to 'the theatre' (**Bvi**, ll. 8–9), were to be erected in the sanctuary of Athena Hippia. Given that the one of these which has a secure findspot (**Bvii**) was found just some 150 m away from the site on Salaminos Street, albeit in secondary (Roman) use, it seems very likely that the excavated theatre is the one intended by that decree, and that the sanctuary of Athena Hippia was close to it (note also *SEG* 54, 322, a Roman Imperial dedication to Athena Hippia and Dionysus). The question of the seemingly modest size of this theatre may be resolved by future excavation, for there may have been a very substantial upper theatron above the diazoma that more than doubled the hypothesised capacity of the partially excavated lower part. It seems very likely that this theatre marks a major municipal centre of the deme (probably one of a number of centres) that extended east from the site of Aghia Saranda towards the centre of Menidhi (Kellogg 2013, 13–19). In recent rescue excavations in a plot to the east of the theatre the foundation level of a strong wall built of large stones was uncovered, which Platonos-Yiota (2013, 148–9) thinks might belong to an ancient temple, possibly that of Dionysus.

The festival saw competitive performances of comedy (**Bii**; **Bv**), with tragedy also likely but not clearly attested (**Biii**). A distinctive feature is the evidence for other performance types – probably the cyclic chorus or dithyramb (**Bii**; **Biii**) and whatever competitive event the komarchs of **Biv** are engaged in (though there is no completely compelling reason to place this at the Dionysia). The presence of these non-dramatic forms may be related to the large size of the deme. Choregoi are found operating as singletons (**Bii**), pairs (**Biii**) and possibly in three (**Bv**) and sometimes recorded the fact with substantial monuments (**Biii**). The deme honoured (with crowns and prohedria: **Bvi**; **Bvii**; see also app. crit. to **Bi**, ll. 13–14) those who helped to run its festival, including its treasurer (*tamias*), who played an important role in its organisation. It was evidently a task for more than one person, and the concern for the festival's finances implicit in the role given to the treasurer is more fully demonstrated in the (virtually certain) employment of a leasing arrangement for the theatre (**Bvi**).

Bi: Decree of a Deme, possibly Acharnae, in Honour of a (?) Demarch and Others, early 4th c. (by letter forms, prosopography and orthography).

Fragment of a marble stele with left-hand side intact, broken at right and bottom. Some remains of moulding on top. Above text (to height of ca. 0.22 m), relief carving of (to left) a young plant and (to right, across the break) nearly half of a well-carved olive crown. Marks of the claw-chisel left in the frieze area may indicate that it was painted.

0.43 × 0.20 × 0.095 m.

No published information on provenance.

Brought by the Danish antiquary and philologist Johan Ussing from Greece to Copenhagen for the royal collection in 1846. Transferred to the National Museum, Copenhagen in 1853–1854 from the Royal Academy of Art, Copenhagen; National Museum Inv. No. ABb255.

IG II 5, 572b; *IG* II² 1173.

Text: based on *IG* II² 1173.

Θ   Ε[Ο   Ι].

Λεοντεὺς εἶπ[ε(ν)· ἐπειδὴ . . 3–4 . . κλῆς ὁ δήμαρχο]-   stoich. ? 34
ς ἐπεμελήθη τ[ῆς ἑορτῆς καὶ τῆς διοικήσεω]-
ς τῶγ κοινῶν [τõ δήμο καλῶς, ἐπαινέσαι . . 4 . .]
5   κλέα Καλλι[. . 5 . . δικαιοσύνης ἕνεκα καὶ σ]-
τεφανῶσαι [αὐτὸν χρυσῶι στεφάνωι ἀπὸ χιλ]-
ίων δραχμ[ῶν, ἐπαινέσαι δὲ καὶ τὸς . . . 6 . . . Λ]-
υκομήδην [. . . . . 26 . . . .]-
μο καὶ τὸ[ν . . . . . 10 . . . . . καὶ στεφανῶσαι θαλ]-
10   λõ στεφά[νωι ἕκαστον, ὅτι καλῶς καὶ φιλοτί]-
μως συν[επεμελήθησαν . . . . . . 15 . . . . τ]-
ὴν ἑορ[τὴν . . . . 18 . . . . τὸν δήμαρ]-
χον τ[ὸν . . . . 28 . . . .]
ΝΚΛ[. . . . . 31 . . . .]

3 τ[ῶν Διονυσίων …] (?) Wilson   6 Wilson   [χρυσῶι στεφάνωι ἀπὸ πεντακοσ]-
Köhler   7 [τὸς χορηγός] Wilamowitz   [τὸς ταμίας] Veligianni-Terzi   9 [ταμίαν (?)
Λύκον] Csapo   12–13 e.g. [τὸν δήμαρ]|χον τ[ὸν ἀεὶ δημαρχοῦντα] or [ἀνειπεῖν τὸν
δήμαρ]|χον τ[οῖς Διονυσίοις] vel sim. Takeuchi   14 Possibly ΝΚΑ Csapo   13–14 e.g.
[εἶναι δὲ τὴν προεδρία]|ν κα[ὶ …] Wilson

G O D S. Leonteus propos[ed: since -kles the demarc]h supervised th[e festival and managemen]t of the common budget [of the deme] in a fine manner, [the deme should praise …-]kles [5] son of Kalli[-… for his honesty and c]rown him [with a gold crown worth one thous]and (*or* [five hun]dred) drachma[s; and also praise the … L]ykomedes [son of … and … son of …-]mos and the [… and to crown them [10] each] with an [o]live crow[n, because they] co-[supervised … t]he festi[val in a fine and ambit]ious manner [… the demar]ch …

Little can be said with certainty about this honorific decree and much of the restoration should be treated with a degree of healthy scepticism. The name Leonteus is very rare. One is known from Acharnae, which has encouraged the assignation to that deme (*APF* 36). His son served on the Council ca. 321 (*Agora* 15, 54, ll. 1–5). Among the few other attested bearers of the name there is a Leonteus son of Antikleides of a deme beginning K[. . . . .], who stood surety for a lease in 343/2 (*Agora* 19, L 6, l. 16). The appearance in 1989 of two Leonteis of Kydantidai in the joint decree of Kydantidai and Ionidai dated to 331/0 (*SEG* 39, 148) should make that deme, despite its tiny size, another contender as the origin of this decree, and Traill inclines thus (*PAA* 602995 'of Kydantidai?'). The first of these Leonteis, son of Antiphanes, was also the proposer of the decree in question, which honours the priest and other officials in the cult of Heracles held jointly by Kydantidai and Ionidai; the second, son of Menestratos, is one of the officials so honoured. The Leonteus who proposed a decree of an association of *Daitaleis* (*IG* II² 1267, late 4th c.) may well be one of these last two men from Kydantidai, given the probable affiliation of that group with the cult of Heracles (Parker 1996, 333–4).

Phraseological similarity with other Acharnian documents offers some support for the assignation to Acharnae (with ll. 3–4 cf. **Bvi**, ll. 12–14; Whitehead 1986a, 149 n. 2). Of the Acharnian treasurer Phanomachos honoured in 314 by **Bvii 1**, l. 5 it is said that he 'supervised the Dionysia' τῶν Διονυσίων ἐπεμελήθη in company with his demarch Oinophilos. We may compare the opening phrase used of the honorand here (as restored by Köhler, but see below) 'he supervised th[e festival]' ἐπεμελήθη τ[ῆς ἑορτῆς] l. 3, though the language is highly generic.

The first and principal honorand receives a gold crown worth 1,000 (or perhaps 500: see apparatus) drachmas. He is praised for supervision of the deme's finances and (very probably) of a festival: [ἑορτῆς] '[festival]' in l. 3 was supplied by Köhler from ἑορ[τὴν] 'festi[val]' in l. 12. This combination of services makes it very likely that he was a demarch (or possibly treasurer: **Bvii 2**, ll. 1–7). Acharnae had many flourishing cults but of its two securely attested major classical festivals, the Dionysia and the Areia for Ares (*SEG* 21, 519, ll. 16–17), the former is the more likely. The logic of the restoration of 'festival' in l. 3 is impeccable. However we should suppose that, at its first mention, the particular festival in question would need to be specified, while subsequently the generalised term ἑορτῆς 'festival' could be used. ἐπεμελήθη τ[ῶν Διονυσίων] 'he supervised the Dionysia' l. 3 is therefore worth consideration, especially in light of the direct parallel from the deme (above; of course such a proposal would have consequences for the other restorations).

A number of others are honoured and crowned, though with a crown of olive only (ll. 9–10). The claim of Kellogg (2013, 159) that these crowns are of ivy is erroneous, but the fact that olive rather than ivy crowns are awarded may not diminish the possibility that the decree has something to do with the Dionysia. For while an ivy crown was awarded to the treasurer, the demarch and the epimelete of the Dionysia of Acharnae for their supervision of the Dionysia and their management 'of the remaining business' in 315 (**Bvii 2**, l. 11), that same treasurer was shortly after awarded an olive (*thallos*) crown (**Bvii 2**, l. 20) for having performed the full suite of sacrifices to the gods and heroes on behalf of the demesmen and, with the demarch, having supervised the Dionysia. It is far from certain that the change in the fabric of the crowns in these two closely related decrees reflects a considered acknowledgement that the duties of the treasurer when honoured alone were somewhat less 'Dionysian'.

A verb describing the activity of the other honorands in l. 11 begins with the prefix 'with' or 'co-' (συν-), indicating that the reason for their praise lies in actions achieved in company with the principal honorand – that is, apparently, ambitious 'co-supervision' of the festival (συν[επεμελήθησαν] in l. 11 restored by reference to the verb ἐπεμελήθη used of the main honorand in l. 3; cf. *IG* II² 1212, ll. 1–6). καὶ τὸ[ν . . .] 'and the [...]' in l. 9 suggests that the third (for there seem to have been three altogether) of the men honoured with the demarch was probably described separately as an officer-holder of a different kind from the preceding two (alternatively this is a third man in the first and only group, whose name begins with To-, e.g. Τολμαῖος or Τολμίδης). Other evidence from Acharnae points to a treasurer (ταμίας) as the most likely candidate for an officer who might co-supervise an important deme festival with the demarch in that deme. In 315/14 we find the treasurer Phanomachos honoured precisely for 'fine and ambitious' supervision of the Dionysia 'in company with the demarch' (**Bvii**). And treasurer and demarch together manage the money generated by the Acharnian theatre in **Bvi**. A treasurer could easily be found a place here (see the apparatus, where however the proposal does not respect the – uncertain – stoichedon 34 pattern).

For the two other men listed in ll. 7–8 Wilamowitz restored before their names the words 'the choregoi' [τὸς χορηγός], suggesting that they helped 'co-supervise' the festival with the demarch. While this can only be an alluring hypothesis (and Wilamowitz' integration of χορηγός in l. 7 has one letter too many for the proposed space) the notion that the appointed official(s) and theatrical sponsors might work and be honoured together in this way is entirely plausible for the deme context. In just this period the demesmen of Ikarion award honours to their demarch for the conduct of their Dionysia and, in addition, to two choregoi, who are to be crowned 'as for the demarch' (**Mvi**, ll. 10–11). Alternatively, and perhaps preferably, we might with Veligianni-Terzi (1997, 129) restore 'treasurers' in the plural to the space in l. 7 and suppose that there were a plurality of these officers, two or three (above).

The claim (Köhler *IG*) that there were two crowns depicted in the relief is almost certainly wrong. The surviving stone preserves between a third and a half of the original width of the stele, and there will only have been sufficient space for the rest of the one single large olive crown, depicted between framing vertical plants growing apparently out of the ground. The notion that there may have been a second crown may be based on a misreading of Ussing (1854, 5), who describes the relief as representing a laurel wreath between two palm branches, only half of which has been preserved ('Det har forestillet en Laurbærkrands imellem 2 Palmegrene; men kun Halvdelen deraf er bevaret'). Ussing misidentifies the foliage of both crown – which is certainly an olive – and of the vertical plant. The latter remains mysterious, but is certainly not a palm and may be intended to represent a young vine shoot – the curving tendrils to the left – propagated on a stiff reed, as advised by Columella 5.5.8. This would be eminently suitable if the decree made special reference to the Dionysia, and moreover the pruning and propagation of young vine cuttings probably took place around the time of the Dionysia.

Bii: (?) Choregic Victory Dedication for (?) Cyclic Chorus and Comedy. Date: first half of 4th c. (by prosopography).

The stone is lost, its dimensions not recorded.
Found in the church of the Holy Virgin 'Anagaliotissa' in Menidhi (ancient Acharnae).
IG II 1283; *IG* II² 3106; *IG* II³ 4, 510.
Text: based on *IG* II³ 4, 510, ultimately dependent on the transcription of Fourmont.

1   - - - - \I/ΟΣΚΡΑΤΙΟΙ νικήσας ἀνέθηκε
           [(?) κυκλίωι] χορῶι καὶ κωμωιδοῖς. Χάρης Θηβαῖος
           [η]ὔλει. Σπευσεάδης Ἀθηναῖος [ἐδίδασκε].

1 - - - - \I/ΟΣΚΡΑΤΙΟΙ Makres   ..\I/ΟΣΚΡΑΠΟΙ Fourmont   [- - - ? Δημ]οσ[τ]ράτο[υ]
Köhler   2 [κυκλίωι] Boeckh   [ἀνδρῶν] Brinck   παίδων also possible; cf. Shear
2003a, 166 n. 9   [(?) κωμικῶι] Wilson   ΧΟΡΙΟΙ ΚΑΙ ΚΟΜΟΔΟΙΣ Fourmont

[...] dedicated this after victory with a [? cyclic] chorus and in comedy. Chares of Thebes [p]layed the pipes. Speuseades of Athens [was the didaskalos].

All knowledge of this inscription from Acharnae rests on the shaky foundations of a transcription made in the eighteenth century by Fourmont (Bibliothèque Nationale de Paris, Suppl. Grec. 854). However it clearly records a dedication (ἀνέθηκε l. 1) following victories in two performances by an individual whose name has not survived. The findspot and the unusual arrangements – one man with two performances, one of them comedy – place it at the local Dionysia. It differs from **Biii** by its reference to victory and the presence of an apparently solo choregos. In fact, no form of the word 'choregos' remains, but it is highly unlikely that the monument belonged to any other, such as a poet or actor.

The first performance was certainly choral (l. 2 'with a chorus', χορῶι). It is difficult to choose between the various restorations offered to qualify the noun. The age- and gender-category terms ἀνδρῶν (men's) and παίδων (boys') might seem the most likely candidates, as they are common in Athenian choregic inscriptions. But they are never used with part of the noun χορός 'chorus' expressed, and there is something to be said for the simple adjective κύκλιος 'cyclic'. This is attested epigraphically in the Classical period, though not directly qualifying 'chorus' (**I D** on *SEG* 25, 177; and once more in Attic inscriptions in the 1st c. AD: *IG* II² 3157, ll. 1–2; see also **V F** on *IG* II³ 4, 435). Along with the other Acharnian choregic inscription (**Biii**), this is a very rare item of evidence for a purely choral performance at a Dionysia outside the city. The enormous size of the deme (bouleutic quota 22) seems to have made possible an ambitious type of choral contest, for the choreuts are all likely to have been local. Perhaps the choruses represented different areas or groups of the deme's population. On the other hand, note the intriguing suggestion of Humphreys (2018, 1021) that the first victory might be the one Nikostratos of Acharnae won with the boys' chorus at the City Dionysia of 330 (*IG* II² 2318, l. 1676 M-O).

The settlement pattern of Acharnae remains something of a mystery, as the deme has to date revealed limited archaeological remains from the Classical period, but as noted above the most likely pattern involves a number of nucleated settlements, with perhaps the major municipal centre extending east from the site of Aghia Saranda towards the centre of modern Menidhi (Kellogg 2013, 13–19), accompanied by a more dispersed population in farmsteads spread over the rest of the territory. While Traill's theory of a split deme has little firm support (Traill 1986, 133–4, 142–8; *contra*: Kellogg 2013, 98–101 with earlier bibliography) there was almost certainly more than one significant population centre. We know that contests took place in the fourth century between *komoi*, led by komarchs (**Biv**). The term *kome* or 'village' was certainly used for local settlements or social groups below and distinct from the level of a deme in Attica (Lambert 1997, 253–7; Ismard 2010, 90–5), but the komarchs of Acharnae appear to be first and foremost leaders of *komoi*, not of *komai*. And while the word *komos* is sometimes associated with dithyramb and may imply Dionysiac activity, there is nothing solid to tie the contest of *komoi* in Acharnae to the chorus in this inscription. That would change if we were to accept Milanezi's proposal that the title [συν]άρχοντ[ας] at **Biv**, ll. 4–5 should be restored as [ἐξ]άρχοντ[ας], in the sense of leaders of the dithyramb or phallic song (Arist. *Po.* 1449a; Milanezi 2004 II, 229).

The relation between the two performances and the two named artists is unclear (Kirchner in *IG* II² assigned the piper to the chorus, the didaskalos to the comedy), and the inscription may have continued beyond the last restored line. Both a chorus and comedy need a piper, though Attic epigraphic practice is much more regular in recording pipers who played for the former. Chares (Stefanis no. 2598) here seems to be given a prominent place before the didaskalos, something that starts to happen in the inscriptions relating to choral contests at the City Dionysia in the 330s (Wilson 2000, 214), but we cannot easily assess the practice of this unusual document by comparison with the larger corpus relating to the city. The placement of Chares the piper before the didaskalos is certainly no reason to date this inscription in the later fourth century. In fact this Chares is very possibly the piper Char- (Χαρ[- - | - - - -] ηὔλει) who played for the successful boys' chorus at the Thargelia in 372/1, as recorded on a recently discovered choregic inscription (Makres and Sakka 2010–2013; *IG* II³ 4, 478, ll. 3–4).

Speuseades is very probably the comic actor known to have performed in Thorikos in the early fourth century, his name spelt on the choregic dedication from the site with the marginally different orthography of Speusiades (**Yiv**). These are the only two occurrences of the name(s). The inclusion of the ethnic *Athenaios* (l. 3) on an Attic document implies he has been granted Athenian citizenship (Guarducci 1987, 282 on Lysiades the didaskalos in **V F** on *IG* II³ 4, 445; see also *IG* II³ 4, 460). The traditional versatility of the poet-actor-producer was not confined to the fifth century, and Speuseades may have served here as one or all of comic protagonist, trainer and even poet. In the fourth century we start to see actors (who were not necessarily also poets) taking responsibility for the full provision of dramatic performances. The evidence that Chares the piper was active in the 370s and Speuseades early in the century makes a date in the first half of the century likely for this inscription.

The alternative restoration aired for l. 2 – 'after victory with a [? comic] chorus and actors' (prompted by **Bv**) – produces a very different picture. The anomaly of the double performance disappears, but is replaced by another, an unparalleled description of a comic performance that carefully distinguishes its two constituent components, chorus and actors.

Given that the event was apparently directed by a comic actor, this unusual emphasis on actors as distinct from chorus may be more explicable than the difficulty of a single choregos commemorating two victories in this way.

The few letters from the patronymic recorded by Fourmont suggest a name ending in -στρατος or perhaps -κράτης. No-one by the name of Demostratos, the patronymic restored by Köhler, is known from Acharnae. For the possibility that it is Nikostratos II, member of a wealthy Acharnian family, see above.

Biii: Choregic Monument, ca. 365 (by prosopography).

Rectangular block of 'Pentelic' marble composed of two joining pieces, broken along back, otherwise intact. Two cavities in the top.
0.17 × 2.09 × 0.21 m.
Found built into the church of Panagia Roiditissa (now demolished) at the foot of the east slope of the Athenian Acropolis: Makres 1992–1998, 68–9.
Athens, EM 10301.
A inscribed on long front side, B on short right-hand side.
A: Pittakys 1835, 113; *IG* II 1280; *IG* II² 3092; *IG* II³ 4, 500.
B: Makres 1992–1998, 65 = *SEG* 46, 250; *IG* II³ 4, 500.
Text: based on *IG* II³ 4, 500.   Photos: Makres 1992–1998, pl. 7–8; *IG* II³ 4,1 tab. LXVII (A).

A

1   Μνησίστρατος Μίσγωνος   Μνησίμαχος ⋮ Μνησιστράτο
     Διοπείθης ⋮ Διοδώρο ἐχορήγον.   5   Θεότιμος ⋮ Διοτίμο ἐχορήγον.
     [Δι]καιογένης ἐδίδασκεν.   Ἀρίφρων ⋮ ἐδίδασκεν.
                                          Πολυχάρης Κώμω[ν]ος ἐ[δί]δασκεν.

B
     Θεότ[ιμος Διοτίμο]
     Μνησί[μαχος Μνησιστράτο ἐχορήγον]
10   Θέρσα[νδρος ἐδίδασκεν]

7 κωμω[ιδ]ὸς Milanezi   9 Μνησί[στρατος Μνησιμάχο ἐχορήγον] Makres (alternative reading)

A Mnesistratos son of Misgon; Diopeithes son of Diodoros were the choregoi. [Di]kaiogenes was didaskalos.

Mnesimachos son of Mnesistratos; [5] Theotimos son of Diotomos were the choregoi. Ariphron was didaskalos. Polychares son of Komo[n] was didaskalos.

B Theot[imos son of Diotimos], Mnesi[machos son of Mnesistratos were the choregoi.] [10] Thersa[ndros] was didaskalos.

This choregic monument presents various puzzles. In the 1830s it was seen by Pittakys built into a church that once stood at the foot of the eastern slope of the Acropolis – that is, close to the Theatre of Dionysus. That it is nonetheless a document of theatrical performances from the deme Acharnae is clear from the fact that all the choregoi mentioned in it are Acharneis; and that they operate in pairs. The modern findspot is perhaps best explained by its usefulness for building construction, making it a 'pierre errante' all the way from Acharnae (on the phenomenon, which extends to itinerant temples, see Alcock 2002, 54–8). The alternative is the otherwise unexampled phenomenon of a memorial erected by demesmen in the vicinity of the city theatre that relates to theatrical events back in the home deme. Family pride might conceivably make such a form of dedication feasible (Wilson 2000, 306–7; Makres in *IG* II³), but it remains less likely. Noting that the performances seem to follow a chronological order, Milanezi (2004 II, 233) has suggested that it formed part of a larger catalogue of deme choregoi, displaced from an original deme setting.

In 1998 Makres identified and published the remains of a third choregic inscription on the right-hand side of the block (B). The restorations necessarily implied by this discovery show that the block was originally at least 2 m². It may have been the epistyle of a small naiskos, making it one of the most substantial surviving theatre monuments from the demes. Three separate pairs of choregoi are listed: Mnesistratos and Diopeithes; Mnesimachos (son of Mnesistratos) and Theotimos; and, very probably, the same pair again in reverse order, Theot[imos] and Mnesi[machos]. The survival of just one more letter in l. 9 would have clarified whether Theotimos served once more with Mnesimachos, or with his father Mnesistratos, or with another son named for him. The same prominent Acharnian family is represented in all three pairs. The extant monument is to a large extent a treasury of their glory. All the more so if, as is very likely, Theotimos son of Diotimos was part of the same family. A Diotimos son of Mnesistratos from Acharnae appears in a mining lease ca. 350 (*Agora* 19, P 13, l. 69) and he too was probably a son of Mnesistratos the choregos. The choregoi of the second set (and probably the third) were thus first cousins, and Diopeithes is the only choregos not known to have belonged to the family (cf. Humphreys 2018, 1016).

It is possible that the joint choregia of Mnesistratos and Diopeithes may date from the late fifth century, especially if the Dicaeogenes in question was a contemporary of Agathon (see below). In that case it will have been included in a monument presumably erected by son and nephew. The lettering of B suggests that it derives from the same period as A (Makres 1992–1998, 65). The best indication of date comes from Kirchner's identification of Mnesimachos as the man of that name who in 325/4 served as an arbitrator (*IG* II³ 4, 35, l. 96). This would put his birth in around 385 and, assuming that he would not have served as choregos until he turned eighteen, set the date of that performance and this monument some time after ca. 367. Makres (1992–1998, 65) would also identify Mnesimachos with the man who was a co-dedicator to Asclepius and Health (*Hygieia*) after the middle of the fourth century (*IG* II³ 4, 713; but cf. Whitehead 1986a, 416). It is an intriguing coincidence that the didaskalos of one of his choregiai may have been the poet Ariphron who was famous for a paean to Health (*Hygieia*).

There is no language or iconography of victory here, though **Bii** makes it clear that performances held at the Acharnian Dionysia were formally competitive at some time in the fourth century. Each pair has an associated didaskalos, except that two appear with the second (l. 7). We may assume that the didaskaloi were poet-directors (but see below on Thersandros and Polychares). Dicaeogenes (l. 3) is possibly the poet known best for tragedy but also as a composer of dithyramb (*TrGF* 52), whom Aristotle praised for the quality of his recognitions, achieved 'through memory': in his *Cypriots* a character wept in recognition at the sight of a painting (Arist. *Po.* 1454b3–7). Another Aristotelian critic judged his lyric composition second to none and compared him, favourably, to Pindar for versatility, though Philodemus took him to task for the claim (*TrGF* 52 T 3). That a scholiast commenting on Aristophanes' *Ecclesiazusae* (l. 1) could wonder whether the opening line of that comedy was a parody of Agathon or of Dicaeogenes suggests they were contemporaries.

Ariphron is a rare name and this may well be the Sicyonian who composed the paean to Health (*TrGF* 53; *PMG* 813). Assuming, as all commentators have, that these choregiai derive from the local festival for Dionysus, dithyramb or some other form of Dionysiac song may be the safest guess for Ariphron's performance (**Bii**). Nothing is known of Polychares. The presence of two didaskaloi with one team of choregoi implies separate performances funded by the same pair. And if only two choregoi regularly served each year, it is perhaps likely that these two performances were of different genres. Less likely is the suggestion that Polychares' performance was a later one, supported by the same pair of choregoi (Köhler). But it is worth considering the possibility that Ariphron and Polychares were co-didaskaloi of the same event, one perhaps the trainer, the other the poet (Vitucci 1939, 222), or (less likely) one stepping into the breach after some misadventure (for the possibility see **V G** on D. 21.17). Milanezi's ingenious suggestion that we should read 'Polychares the *komoidos*' rather than 'Polychares son of Komon' would produce a clear reference to comedy, but such a form of identification is without parallel from Attica. Polychares would on this interpretation be a comic actor-producer, a second probable example of which is found from the deme (Speuseades in **Bii**). κωμωιδός as 'comic actor' is more likely for this date than 'poet' (perhaps first at Pl. *Laws* 935d). Whether it is his role as *komoidos* or his patronymic that has been included in l. 7, its presence is striking and was evidently deemed important, since it disrupts the inscription's neat alignment.

No poet by the name of Thersandros (l. 10) is known but this man may be the piper (Stefanis no. 1193) who died ca. 391 and who is said to have been among the finest of the Ionian artists of his day, hired along with the star actors Kallippides and Nikostratos for a performance in Aeolis (**IV Eiv**). A piper could direct a dithyrambic chorus, as Telephanes did for Demosthenes at the Great Dionysia of 348 (**V G** on D. 21.17). If correct the identification would of necessity push the date of the performance recorded on B back to the late fifth or very early fourth century.

If all or any of these identifications hold, they are clear signs of the high quality of performers appearing at the Acharnae Dionysia in the late fifth and early fourth centuries. And this is one of the very few documents that provide any evidence that dithyramb took place at Dionysia outside the city of Athens (and the Piraeus). See on **Bii**.

Biv: Victory Monument of a Komarch, 340/39 (on prosopographical grounds: Kellogg 2013, 184) or 313/12 (a Theophrastos was Archon in both years; cf. Humphreys 2018, 1016).

Quadrangular marble block, broken on right-hand side, upper surface (damaged) has a round hole in it.
0.17 × 0.365 m.
Found in Menidhi (ancient Acharnae).
Milchhöfer 1888, 340; *IG* II 5, 1306b; *IG* II² 3104; *IG* II³ 4, 234.
Text: based on *IG* II³ 4, 234.

1   [- - - - -] κώμωι Ξ[- - -]
     ἐπὶ Θεοφράστου ἄ[ρχοντος]
     Ἀντιφάνης Ἐπ[- - - - - - - -]
     κωμαρχ[ῶ]ν ἐνίκα [- - - - - -]
5   *vacat* αρχοντ[- - - - - -]

3 [- - - Ἀχαρνεὺς] Kirchner   4–5 [τοὺς συν|]άρχοντ[ας] Köhler   5 [ἐξ]άρχοντ[ας]
Milanezi   ἄρχοντ[ες κωμῶν] Csapo

[…] with a *komos* x[…] in the a[rchonship] of Theophrastos, Antiphanes son of
Ep[-…] was victorious as komarch […] [5] *vacat* (?) archon(s) […]

This intriguing document reveals the existence of a contest among *komoi* in Acharnae.
All that can be said with confidence is that one komarch, Antiphanes, won the contest and
commemorated it in a manner not unlike that adopted by other agonistic victors (note the
formal dating by Eponymous Archon and the use of ἐνίκα + participle, as often in choregic
inscriptions – χορηγῶν ἐνίκα). The possible relevance to the theatre depends on interpretation of the terms κῶμος 'komos' (l. 1) and κωμαρχεῖν 'to be a komarch' (l. 4). A komarch
could be a 'leader of a *kome*/village' or a 'leader of a *komos*/revel'. It is becoming increasingly clear that the term *kome* was used for many local groups below and distinct from the
level of a deme in Attica (Lambert 1997, esp. 253–7), but the latter meaning is assured here
since the word κώμωι in l. 1 must mean 'with a revel/*komos*'.

The *komos* is normally associated with Dionysus in Attica. In Aristophanes' *Acharnians*
(**Ai**), as he initiates his celebration of the Rural Dionysia, Dikaiopolis calls upon the divine personification of the phallos, Phales, as ἑταῖρε Βακχίου, ξύγκωμε, 'companion of
Bakchos, revel-mate' (264–5). The *komos* was a wine-fuelled, boisterous, loosely processional group activity that frequently included music and song and that was often imagined
as taking place in company with Dionysus himself and his companions, satyrs and maenads. Indeed in real-life – as opposed to purely mythic – *komoi*, men may have worn satyr
or silen masks (**I Aiv 23c**). 'Komos' was the second most popular name for satyrs on Attic
vases (only Simos was more common), and it was also given to human boys on such vases,
suggesting the role of the *komos* in initiating young men into the world of Dionysus. These
vases are generally associated with the Anthesteria, because of their form as choes (**II B**),
but a *komos* could be at home at any Dionysia. It may often have been informal, perhaps an
extension of the parade, and so escaped record, but there is evidence for an event so named
at the City Dionysia (**I Avi 1**). In Acharnae too, perhaps because of its great size, it seems
to have taken on a more formal quality. Perhaps it involved some sort of choral contest –
between representative groups from different regional centres of the deme? – within the
context of the parade (for discussion of the probable existence and possible identification
of two or three deme centres see Kellogg 2013, 7–34). If they existed, Acharnian *komai* are
likely to have been spread more widely across the territory of the deme. A contest of *komoi*
drawn from local *komai* is thus an attractive possibility.

The inscription tells us little more. Köhler restored ll. 4–5 to produce a direct object of
Antiphanes' victory – namely, 'Antiphanes … was victorious as komarch over [his fellow]
Archons'. But this requires the difficult assumption that the phrase 'his fellow Archons'

(τοὺς συνάρχοντας) was equivalent to 'the other komarchs' (τοὺς ἄλλους κωμαρχοῦντας) (Kirchner *ad loc.*). A similar difficulty attends Milanezi's proposal [ἐξ]άρχοντ[ας] (2004 II, 229), in the sense of 'leaders of the dithyramb/phallic song' (Arist. *Po.* 1449a11). Another impediment to such reconstructions is that the space before 'Archon(s)' in l. 5 was apparently uninscribed. We may also doubt whether the inclusion of explicit reference to the defeated parties could figure in accepted commemorative practice. An alternative would be to suppose l. 5 has the remains of a heading – 'leaders of *komoi*' ἄρχοντ[ες κωμῶν] *vel sim.* – and that the inscription went on to list the other competing komarchs.

The Dionysiac interpretation of these *komoi* is not beyond all doubt. In the same period (330/29) we know of a contest that apparently took place between four associated Attic demes – Piraeus, Phaleron, Xypete and Thymaitadai, known collectively as the Tetrakomoi (Lauter 1993, 137 would relate this dedication to that contest, on the rather weak basis of a restoration of the demotic Ξ[υπετ-] 'of Xypete' in l. 1). The name implies that the demes had been *komai* prior to the reforms of Cleisthenes, and the Tetrakomoi is generally thought to be a pre-Cleisthenic survival, possibly the missing twelfth 'city of Cecrops' in Philochorus *FGrH* 328 F 94. Their contest involved komarchs, the phrase referring probably not literally to 'leaders of *komai*/villages' but used of a ritual office which alludes to the pre-Cleisthenic social order. But as it also involved *komastai* 'revelers' (*IG* II³ 4, 228; cf. *IG* II³ 4, 227) and as there is reason to associate the event with a festival for Heracles that involved a special dance (Poll. 4.105), we may see here a mingling, deliberate or otherwise, of the two terms *kome* and *komos* (cf. above). Parker (1996, 329) comments: '[a] neat explanation would be that the four demes / *komai* were each represented in the competition by a troupe known (through a popular etymological assimilation) as a *komos* … It is perhaps not inconceivable that the village-chiefs became "*komos*-leaders" on the ritual occasion.'

Kirchner's supplement of Antiphanes' demotic as Ἀχαρνεὺς in l. 3 is redundant if the document was for internal deme consumption only. He (and Köhler) assumed a contest between participating members like that of the Tetrakomoi that drew on groups from beyond the borders of the deme. Given the size of Acharnae such a contest is perhaps more likely to have been among *komai* from within its boundaries.

Bv: Choregic Victory Monument, second half 4th c. (by letter forms).

Fragment of 'Pentelic' marble, broken on all sides.
0.19 × 0.39 × 0.17 m.
Seen on 12 May 1907 by Kirchner in the ruins of the church of Agios Vlassios, Menidhi (ancient Acharnae).
Present whereabouts unknown.
Summa 2004 (= *SEG* 54, 302); *IG* II³ 4, 515.
Text: based on *IG* II³ 4, 515.   Photos: Summa 2004, 147 (photo of Kirchner's transcription); *IG* II³ 4,1 tab. LXIX (squeeze).

- - - - - - - - - - - - - - - - - - - -

1   [νικήσα]ντες κω[μι]κῶι χο[ρῶι]
         [Κλεοφ]ῶν Κλεομέδοντ[ος]

[Θεόδο]τος Δωροθέου
[Θεόπρ]οπος Φειδύλλου

1 Kirchner ΤΕΣΛ........ κωι χο[ρῶι]   2 Peek e.g. [Κλεοφ]ῶν   3 Peek e.g. [Θεόδο]τος
4 Peek e.g. [Θεόπρ]οπος

[…] after [victor]y with a co[mi]c cho[rus, Kleoph]on son of Kleomedon,
[Theodo]tos son of Dorotheos, [Theopr]opos son of Pheidyllos

This inscription was seen in the ruins of the church of Agios Vlassios in Menidhi (ancient
Acharnae) by Kirchner, who made a transcription and squeeze. In the 1940s Peek studied
the squeeze and produced a text. Neither scholar's work was published and the stone is
now lost. In 2004 Summa found the notes of both Kirchner and Peek in the archive of the
BBAW *Inscriptiones Graecae* in Berlin, and published the inscription and notes for the
first time. Peek's squeeze was subsequently located in the BBAW and used by Makres to
produce her text.

The appearance of the squeeze permits a (very approximate) dating to the second half of
the fourth century. The findspot, and the fact that the inscription lists three men (with patronymics) apparently as victorious choregoi, assure the association with the local Dionysia
of Acharnae. The fact that no part of the verb 'to be choregos' is present is no impediment
to the identification of the dedication as choregic. It is also absent from e.g. **Eii** and **Mix**,
which are certainly choregic, and it may in any case have been present in an earlier, lost
line of this inscription. Assuming the three men were choregoi, we find joint choregiai in
Acharnae involving one (**Bii**), two (**Biii**) and three men. The evidence for the competitive
format is not quite beyond doubt ([νικήσα]ντες 'after [victory]' in l. 1 being substantially
restored), but is supported by the comic agon of **Bii**. Makres accepts into her text all three
of Peek's suggested restorations of the names of the three men, noting that Dorotheos,
father of [Theodo]tos, may be the Acharnian who served as prytanis in 360/59 (*IG* II³ 4,
56, l. 50).

The performance type recorded is comedy, but the formulation used is unusual. Peek
noted that the phrase κωμικὸς χορός ('comic chorus') of l. 1 is epigraphically unexampled – κωμωιδοί (*komoidoi*, 'comic-choreuts/performers') being the standard expression –
but Summa points to the literary parallel in Arist. *Pol.* 1276b (χορὸν κωμικόν) and the epigraphic *comparandum* in the choregic epigram from Anagyrous (**Eii**, l.1), which describes
a victory 'with a laughter-loving chorus' (ἡδυγέλωτι χορῶι … ἐν[ίκων]). **Bii** (see on l. 2)
may provide a direct parallel from the very same deme, suggestive of a local idiom. Was
the expression chosen to put special emphasis on the relationship between choregoi and
chorus?

While a choregia for comedy supported by three men is the most likely interpretation of
this monument on the basis of our knowledge of its inscription, it is important to remember
how partial that knowledge is. The stone is said to have been broken on all sides. We would
also draw attention to the reported (and partial) depth of the block – 0.17 m. This rules out
a plaque (*pinax*) or a standard stele and suggests the possibility of a considerably more
substantial construction (perhaps something akin to **Biii**). Earlier lines may have indicated
other performances supported by these three men.

Bvi: Deme Decree Mentioning Funds for an Annual Sacrifice Raised from Leasing the Theatre, ca. 325–300 (by letter forms).

Tapering stele of white 'Pentelic' marble, broken at the top and left; right edge damaged. An area of 0.30 m beneath the text is not inscribed. A circular indentation in this area suggests later reuse. 0.61 × 0.21–0.36 × 0.10 m.

Provenance unknown. Kellogg (2013, 158) writes that the inscription 'has also [like the deme decree *IG* II² 1207] been associated with' the area of the church Aghia Saranda.

Athens EM 7748.

IG II 5, 587b; *IG* II² 1206; Papazarkadas 2007a (= *SEG* 57, 124).

Text: based on *SEG* 57, 124, with improved readings at ll. 16–19 by Takeuchi 2010–2013, 88–9.

Photo: Papazarkadas 2007a, 177 fig. 6.

```
1       [......12......]ΝΤ[......11.....]           stoich. 25
        [......12......]Ο[.]Α[.....10.....]
        [.... διδόνα]ι καὶ αὐτοῖ[ς εἰς τὴ]-
        [ν θυσίαν εἰς] τὸν ἐνιαυτὸν ἔκα[σ]-
5       [τον τὸν ταμί]αν καὶ τὸν δήμαρχ[ο]-
        [ν οἳ ἂν ἀεὶ ἄρ]χωσιν : ΔΔ : δραχμὰς [ἀ]-
        [πὸ τοῦ ἀργυ]ρίου τοῦ ἐγλεγομέ[ν]-
        [ου ἐκ τοῦ θε]άτρου· ἐὰν δὲ τὸ θέα[τ]-
        [ρον ἄπρατο]ν ἦι, διδόναι αὐτοῖ[ς]
10      [τὸν δήμαρχ]ον καὶ τὸν ταμίαν [οἳ]
        [ἂν ἀεὶ ἄρχω]σιν τὸ γεγραμμέν[ον]
        [ἀργύριον ε]ἰς τὴν θυσίαν ἐκ τ[ῆς]
        [κοινῆς διο]ικήσεως τῆς τῶν δη[μ]-
        [οτῶν. ἀναγρά]ψαι δὲ τόδε τὸ ψήφ[ι]-
15      [σμα ἐστήλη]ι λιθίνηι τὸν γραμ[μ]-
        [ατέα μετὰ τ]ῶν δημοτῶν καὶ στῆ-
        [σαι ἐν τῶι ἱε]ρῶι τῆ[ς] Ἀθηνᾶς τῆς
        ['Ιππίας, εἰς δ]ὲ τὴν ἀναγραφὴν τῆ-
        [ς στήλης δο]ῦναι αὐτοῖς τὸν δήμ-
20      [αρχον ....]ένην : ΔΔ : δραχμὰς καὶ
        [λογίσασθα]ι τοῖς δημόταις. vacat
                        vacat
```

1–2 Papazarkadas [......12......]ΝΦΑΝ[....9....|.....11.....]ΑQ.ΑΟΑ[....8....] Nemes   3–4 Papazarkadas   3 [.....10.....]ι καὶ α[ὐ]το[...7...] Köhler   [.....10.....]ι καὶ α[ὐ]τοῖς [..5..] Nemes   [κατατιθένα]ι or [μερίσα]ι Slater   9 [ἄπρατο]ν Csapo, Papazarkadas   [ἐλαττο]ν Wilamowitz [...5..ο]ν Köhler   16 μετὰ Köhler   ὑπὲρ Whitehead 1986a, 140   16–17 στῆ|[σαι] Takeuchi   17–18 Takeuchi   τ[ῆ]ς Ἀθ[η]νᾶς τῆς 'Ι[ππίας] Alipheri and Steinhauer   τ[ῆς] Ἀ[θην]ᾶς τ[ῆ]ς ['Ι]ππίας] Köhler   18–19 Takeuchi   ἀναγραφὴν τῆ[ς | στήλης δοῦ]ναι Köhler   19–20 Takeuchi   δήμ[α|ρχον ....] Köhler   20–1 Takeuchi   κ[α]ὶ [λ]|ογίσασθα]ι Nemes   κ[α]ὶ [λ]|ογίσασθαι] Köhler

[…] and [the treasu]rer (*tamias*) and the demarch in office [from time to time are to giv]e the[m] 20 drachmas [for the sacrifice] each year [from the mon]ey collect[ed from the the]atre. And if the thea[tre] is [not sold, [10] the demarch]

and the treasurer in office [from time to time] are to give them the stipulated [sum f]or the sacrifice from t[he common bu]dget of the de[mesmen.] The secre[tary with t]he demesmen [is to inscri]be this decr[ee on] ¹⁵ a stone [stele] and erec[t it in the sa]nctuary of Ath[e]na Hi[ppia; an]d the dem[arch ...-]enes is to [gi]ve them ²⁰ 20 drachmas for the inscription of the [stele] a[nd to reckon the cost] to the demesmen.

Prior to the discovery of a theatre in Acharnae in February 2007 this was the sole direct testimony to the existence of one in the deme (ll. 8–9). Along with the better-preserved lease of the Piraeus theatre (**Vvi**), it provides an example of the way demes generated income from the leasing of their theatre. The assignation of the decree to Acharnae is now beyond doubt. Improved readings at ll. 17–18 vindicate Köhler's almost total restoration of the reference to a sanctuary of Athena Hippia as the site of erection (cf. *IG* II² 1207; Paus. 1.31.6; *SEG* 54, 322, a Roman Imperial dedication to Athena Hippia and Dionysus). Affinities with a pair of Acharnian honorific decrees (**Bvii**) – in particular the presence of a deme secretary (cf. ll. 15–16) – bring further confirmation. The sanctuary of Athena Hippia was very probably somewhere in the general proximity of the churches of Aghia Saranda and Aghios Ioannis (Makres 2004–2009 places it right at the site of Aghios Ioannis, which is just some 150 m south of the site of the theatre; cf. Kellogg 2013, 158–9).

An unknown quantity of text is lost from the head of this decree, so that its precise nature is unclear. What does survive, however, shows the theatre unambiguously treated as a source of potential revenue. The decree requires future successive Acharnian treasurers and demarchs to fund an annual sacrifice – of a fairly modest scale, at 20 drachmas – '[from the mon]ey collect[ed from the the]atre' ([ἀπὸ τοῦ ἀργυ]ρίου τοῦ ἐγλεγομέ[νου ἐκ τοῦ θε]άτρου ll. 6–8). This probably refers not to money actually taken from spectators at the door, or at least not directly. For the next clause goes on to envisage a situation in which, 'if the thea[tre] is [not sold] [ἄπρατον]', the money for this sacrifice is to be provided directly from the common deme budget (ll. 8–9). The word ἄπρατον – 'unsold' – is a palmary restoration, made independently by Papazarkadas and Csapo (Slater 2011, 277–9 expresses misgivings without providing a viable alternative). 'Sale' of a theatre can only refer to the sale of a theatre lease. The Piraeus lease provides clear parallels for this intermingled language of sale and purchase (**Vvi**), as do the names used for the entrepreneurs who bought the lease – *theatrones* 'theatron-buyer' and *theatropoles* 'theatron-seller' (**V A**; Csapo 2007, 88–90). The money to be 'collected from the theatre' in Acharnae will thus be the money derived from the sale of the theatre lease to such entrepreneurs. This form of second-order 'collection' can be paralleled from the use of ἐκλέγειν of 'collecting' taxes that have in fact been farmed out to a tax collector.

An alternative interpretation would see the reference to money collected from the theatre as indeed the direct receipt of entrance charges on the part of the lessees. The phrase could certainly refer to such 'takings': the cognate noun λόγευμα, used in connection with a *theatrones* in an elegy by Nikarchos (**V A** on *POxy.* 4502, l. 41), offers a good parallel for this sense. The deme would in that case be imposing an additional expense on the lessees quite independently of the money they had paid for the lease. That is to say, the extra 20 drachmas is to be deducted each year from the takings at the door of any future lessees.

The deme of Piraeus clearly kept its hands in the pockets of the lessees with respect to prohedria, which it required the lessees to provide for free to various specified groups, including the rather open clause 'and anyone else to whom the demesmen have granted prohedria' (**Vvi**, ll. 15–16).

The alternative financial arrangements put in place in case the theatre was not leased out show clearly how the practice of leasing took pressure off the ordinary deme budget (the *koine dioikesis* ll. 12–13). And it appears that the money from the lease was not to go into that budget, since the two are treated as separate funds (Papazarkadas 2007a, 169). Its destination was probably a sacred fund of Dionysus, earmarked for the local Dionysia. It is difficult to assess just how likely an eventuality a failure to lease the theatre was deemed to be. Certainly it was taken seriously enough to provoke this precautionary clause.

What is the nature of this sacrifice? And who are the recipients of the funds? Papazarkadas has suggested that the sacrifice is the one for Dionysus mentioned in one of the decrees of 315/14 (**Bvii 2**, ll. 4–5). While such cross-funding of one element of the festival by income generated during the course of it is entirely likely, the recipients of these funds appear to be plural ('them', αὐτοῖς ll. 3, 9) and so cannot be Dionysus himself. Nor are they likely to be his mortal agents, the treasurer and demarch, since this would involve an order to treasurer and demarch to give themselves the funds for the god's sacrifice. Perhaps 'they' are otherwise unattested priests of the god. But the evidence suggests that it was precisely the task of treasurer and demarch to manage the god's rituals in Acharnae (**Bvii**).

Another possibility is that the sacrifice in this decree formed part of a package of honorific gifts for mortal benefactors, and that it is these honorands who are referred to by the 'them' of ll. 3 and 9. In that case, this document would be an honorific decree of which we have just the closing provisions. As here, sums disbursed to honorands for a sacrifice are often specified in such decrees (from the demes, see e.g. **Div**). If it was thought appropriate to fund such a sacrifice – seemingly in perpetuity (ll. 4–5) – from theatre income, it is probable that the meritorious actions that prompted it were somehow related to the Acharnian theatre or its Dionysia – one thinks especially of choregoi or other benefactors, or perhaps even of star performers.

Acharnae may have possessed a stone theatre before the date of this decree (**B Introduction**). If this proves to be true, unlike the people of Piraeus, the Acharnians will have had no need to contract out on lease to have their theatron fully built from wood – the key duty, so it seems, placed upon the lessees in Piraeus. But if the theatre discovered in 2007 is indeed the one mentioned in this decree, while the lower rows of seats are made from stone, its excavator believes that those above the diazoma may have been constructed from wood; and there is in any case no *a priori* reason to assume that the application of a lease to the different theatres around and beyond Attica followed a single pattern. The holders of a theatre lease might have been required to undertake a variety of tasks, depending on the local circumstances. Given the meagre administrative and executive infrastructure maintained by demes, a variety of logistical and financial services for the general management of the theatre would have been essential, including the collection of entrance fees, the organisation of prohedria and the construction of the skene. Organisation of prohedria and some kind of construction work on the skene fall to the lessees in the Piraeus lease (**Vvi**, ll. 1–16). And even if it had a stone substructure, the fourth-century theatre at Acharnae may have needed wooden chairs introduced for prohedria, and possibly benches for the rest (not just those above the diazoma). In 315/14 the deme awarded officials prohedria 'on the first bench/step (*bathron*)' (**Bvii 2**, l. 22: ἐ[πὶ] τοῦ πρώτου βάθρου). In this case *bathron* probably refers to a stone foundation block on which wooden seats were placed.

Bvii: Two Honorific Decrees Relating to the Dionysia of Acharnae. In or soon after 315/14 (Praxiboulos was Archon in 315/14).

Largely intact pedimental stele of white 'Pentelic' marble; inscribed face very worn.
1.0 × 0.45 – 0.37 × 0.075 m.
Found in secondary use in a Roman bath behind the church of Hagios Ioannes in Menidhi (ancient Acharnae).
Athens, Piraeus Museum 5333.

1. Decree in honour of the treasurer (*tamias*) Phanomachos (after summer 314).

Inscribed above **2**.
Steinhauer 1992, 179–80 (= *SEG* 43, 26A); cf. Takeuchi 2010–2013, 85–6.
Text: based on *SEG* 43, 26A with improved readings at ll. 11–15 by Takeuchi 2010–2013.
Photo: Steinhauer 1992, 181.

1	Διογένης Ναυκύδου εἶπεν· ἐπειδὴ Φανόμα-	stoich. 33
	χος ὁ ταμίας ὁ ἐπὶ Πραξιβούλου ἄρχοντος	
	τάς τε θυσίας τέθυκεν τοῖς θεοῖς καὶ τοῖ-	
	ς ἥρωσιν ὑπὲρ τῶν δημοτῶν ἁπάσας [ἐ]ν τ[ῶ]ι ἐ-	
5	[νι]αυτῶι καὶ τῶν Διονυσίων ἐπεμελήθη κα-	
	λῶς [καὶ φιλοτίμως] μετὰ τοῦ δημάρχου Οἰν-	
	ο[φ]ί[λ]ου καὶ [φ]ιάλην πεπόηται μ[ν]ᾶν ἄγουσα-	
	ν ἀργυρίου [κ]ατὰ [τὸν νόμον] καὶ λόγον ἀπεν-	
	ήνοχεν ἁπάντων ὧν δι[ώικησ]εν πρός τε τὴν	
10	πόλιν καὶ πρὸς τοὺς δημότας ἐ[ν] τοῖς χρόν-	
	οις τοῖς ἐκ τῶν [νόμων] τῶν τῆς πόλεως καὶ τ-	
	ῶν δημοτῶν καὶ τὸ περιὸν ἀργύριον παρ᾽ ἑα-	
	υτῶι ἐκ τῆς διοικήσεως καταβέβληκεν Ἀχ-	
	αρνεῦσιν : ΗΗΗΔΔΓⱵⱵⱵⱵ : καὶ τὰς εὐθύνας	
15	δέδωκεν δ[ό]ξας δικαίως τεταμιευκέναι κ-	
	αὶ τῶν [ἄλλων] ἁπάντων [ὧν] αὐτῶι προσέταξα-	
	ν [Ἀ]χαρν[εῖς ἐπιμεμέλη]ται καλῶς καὶ φιλο-	
	τ[ίμ]ως· [ἐψ]ηφ[ίσ]θαι Ἀχαρνεῦσιν ἐπαινέσαι	
	Φανόμαχον Νικοδήμου Ἀχαρνέα καὶ στεφα-	
20	νῶσαι αὐτὸν θαλλοῦ στεφάνωι φιλοτιμία-	
	ς ἔνεκ[α καὶ δι]καιοσύνης τῆς εἰς τοὺς δημ-	
	ότας· ἀναγράψαι δὲ τόδε τὸ ψήφισμα ἐστήλ-	
	ηι λιθίνει τὸν γραμματέα τῶν δημοτῶν κα-	
	ὶ στῆσαι ἐν τῶι ἱερῶι τῆς Ἀθηνᾶς τῆς Ἱππί-	

25   ας, εἰς δὲ τὴν ἀναγραφὴν τῆς στήλης δοῦνα-
      ι τὸν ταμίαν [: ΔΔ :] δραχμὰς καὶ λογίσασθ[α-]
      ι τοῖς δημόται[ς]

14 ΗΗΗΔΔᴨΗΗΗ Takeuchi   ΗΗΗΔΔᴨΙΙΙΙ Steinhauer   22–3 ἐστήλη|ηι *lapis* Humphreys
SEG 44, 57   ἐ στήληι | Steinhauer

Diogenes son of Naukydes proposed: since Phanomachos the treasurer (*tami-as*) during the Archonship of Praxiboulos has performed all the sacrifices to the gods and heroes on behalf of the demesmen in the [5] course of the year; and, with the demarch Oinophilos, supervised the Dionysia in a fine [and ambitious] manner; and has had made a silver [b]owl (*phiale*) weighing one mna (100 dr.) in accord[ance with the law]; and has given full accounts of everything he m[anage]d to both the [10] city and to the demesmen within the times specified by both city and deme [law; and] has paid over to the Acharnians the [ba]lanc[e of] money he had from the budget: 329 dr.; and at his public scrutiny [15] he was deemed to have served justly as treasurer; and has in a fine and ambitious manner [supervise]d everything [else with which] the Acharnians tasked him; the Acharnians [d]ecr[e]ed to praise Phanomachos son of Nikodemos of Acharnae and to [20] crown him with a crown of olive leaves for his ambition [and h]onesty towards his fellow demesmen; and the secretary of the demesmen is to have this decree inscribed on a stone stele and erected in the sanctuary of Athena Hippia, [25] and the treasurer is to give [20] dr. for the inscription of the stele and reckon the expense to the demesmen.

2. Decree in honour of the demarch Oinophilos, the treasurer (*tamias*) Phanomachos and the supervisor (*epimeletes*) of the Dionysia Leon (after mid December 315).

Inscribed below **1**.
Steinhauer 1992, 180 (= *SEG* 43, 26B); cf. Takeuchi 2010–2013, 86–8.
Text: based on *SEG* 43, 26B with improved readings as noted by Takeuchi 2010–2013. Photo: Steinhauer 1992, 181.

1   Διογένης Ναυκύδου εἶπεν· ἐπειδὴ ὁ δήμαρ-   stoich. 33
      χος Οἰνόφιλος καὶ ὁ ταμίας Φανόμαχος κα-
      ὶ ὁ [ἐπι]μελ[η]τὴς τῶν Διονυσίων καλῶ[ς] καὶ φ-
      ιλοτίμως [ἐπιμ]ε[μ]έ[λ]ηνται τῆς τε θυσίας τ-
5   ῶι Διονύσωι [καὶ τῆς] πομπῆς καὶ τοῦ ἀγῶνο-
      ς καὶ τὰ [ἄ]λ[λ]α̣ διοικοῦσιν ὑπὲρ τῶν δημοτ̲-
      ῶν κατὰ τοὺς νόμους· ἐψηφίσθαι Ἀχαρνεῦσ-
      ιν ἐπαινέσαι τὸν δήμαρχον Οἰνόφιλον Οἰ-
      νοφίλου καὶ τὸν ταμίαν Φανόμαχον Νικοδ-
10   ήμου καὶ τὸν ἐπιμελητὴν Λέοντα Δίωνος κ-
      αὶ στεφα[ν]ῶ[σα]ι ἕκαστον αὐτῶν κιττοῦ στε-
      φάνωι καὶ ἀνειπεῖν τὸν δήμαρχον τούσδε

τοὺς στεφάνους Διονυσίων τῶν Ἀχαρνῆσιν τ-
ὦι ἀγῶνι· ἀναγράψαι δὲ τόδε τὸ ψήφισμα εἰ-
15 στήλην λιθίνην τὸν δήμαρχον Οἰνόφιλον
καὶ στ[ῆ]σα[ι] ἐ[ν τῶι ἱερῶι τῆ]ς Ἀθη[νᾶς τῆς] Ἱπ-
πίας. [εἰς δὲ τὴν ἀναγραφὴν τῆς στήλης] δ[οῦ-]
ναι τὸ[ν] τ[αμ]ίαν Φανόμαχον : ΔΔ [:] δραχμὰς κα-
ὶ λογ[ίσασθαι τοῖς δη]μόταις· ε[ἶν]αι δὲ αὐτ-
20 οῖς καὶ π[ρ]οεδ[ρί]α[ν] α[ὐτ]οῖς [καὶ] ἐγγ[ό]νοις
εἰς τὸν ἀεὶ [χρό]νον Διονυσ[ίων] τῶν Ἀχαρν[ῆ-]
σιν τ[ῶ]ι [ἀ]γῶ[νι] ἐ[πὶ] τοῦ πρώτου βάθρου.

6 Takeuchi   -ς καὶ τῶν ἄλλων [διοι]κο[ῦ]σιν ὑπὲρ τῶν δημοτ- Steinhauer   8–9
Takeuchi   O[ἰ|νοφίλου] Steinhauer   9–10 Steinhauer   Νικοδ|ήμου Takeuchi   10
Λέοντα Δίωνος Takeuchi   Λέο[ν]τα [Θέ-?]ωνος Steinhauer   [Δί]ωνος Humphreys
SEG 44, 57   11 Takeuchi   [αἱ στεφανῶσαι ἕκασ]τον Steinhauer   14–15
Takeuchi   ἀ[γῶνι· ἀναγράψαι δὲ τό]δε τὸ ψ[ή]φ[ι]σ[μ]α ἐν | στήλῃ λιθίνει [τὸν δήμαρ]-
χον O[ἰν]όφ[ιλ]ον Steinhauer

Diogenes son of Naukydes proposed: since the demarch Oinophilos and the treasurer (*tamias*) Phanomachos and the [supe]rv[i]sor (*epimeletes*) of the Dionysia
have in a fine and ambitious manner [super]vised the sacrifice to [5] Dionysus
[and the] parade and the contest (*agon*) and manage the remaining business on
behalf of the demesmen according to the laws; the Acharnians decreed to praise
the demarch Oinophilos son of O[inophilos] and the treasurer Phanomachos
son of Nikod[emos] [10] and the supervisor (*epimeletes*) Leon son of Dion and to
cro[w]n each of them with a crown of ivy and to have the demarch announce
these crowns at the co[ntest] of the Dionysia at Acharnae; and [the demar]ch
Oinophilos [is to have th]is decree inscribed on [15] a stone stele and erected i[n the
sanctuary of] Athe[na] Hippia, [and] the treasurer Phanomachos is to give 20 dr.
[for the inscription of the stele] and reck[on the expense to the de]mesmen. Both
they themselves [and] their offspring are [20] also to have p[r]ohed[ri]a for all [ti]
me at the [co]nte[st] of the Dionys[ia] of Acharnae, on the first bench.

This stele was discovered in 1987, excavated in secondary use in a Roman bath. It is inscribed with two honorific decrees, moved by the same man and dated to 315/14, squarely
within the period of rule by Demetrius of Phaleron (**VI K**). It originally stood in the sanctuary of Athena Hippia (**1**, ll. 16–17; so too did **Bvi** and other documents). Though not yet
identified, this important sanctuary was probably close to the theatre, perhaps immediately
adjacent to it. The theatre unearthed in 2007 is on Salaminos Street, near the intersection
with Liosion Street. The Roman bath where the stele was found is on Liosion Street, no
more than 150 m from the theatre. An unpublished dedication of the Roman Imperial period made by one Pompeios, probably for his preparation of the Dionysia, is said to refer to
both Athena Hippia and Dionysus. It too was found built into the church of Hagios Ioannes
(Platonos-Yiota 2004, 265 no. 44; *SEG* 54, 322).

The decree inscribed on the upper part (**1**) honoured the deme treasurer (*tamias*) of 315/14, Phanomachos son of Nikodemos. It was moved some months *after* the one below it (**2**). Phanomachos is also one of the three honorands of that earlier decree, along with the demarch Oinophilos and an 'epimelete of the Dionysia', named Leon (l. 10). They are praised for having successfully supervised the sacrifice, parade and contests of the Dionysia (l. 4), so the festival is over. But they continue to 'manage' (present tense) 'the remaining business on behalf of the demesmen' (ll. 6–7; cf. 14, 18). Thus, their work and the civic year are not yet done. But by the time (**1**) was passed, Phanomachos had rendered his accounts and undergone the scrutiny that followed the end of his tenure as treasurer (ll. 14–15).

The earlier decree (**2**) praises the trio of men for their shared supervision of the Dionysia. It is no surprise to find the demarch and treasurer of Acharnae working together to this end (cf. **Bvi**), though only in Acharnae do we find quite such a prominent role for the treasurer in running the festival. However, the third figure, the 'epimelete of the Dionysia' (ll. 3, 10), was unknown before the discovery of this decree. At its first mention only the title of the office is cited (l. 3), while the personal names of both demarch and treasurer are by contrast included. Leon the epimelete is clearly the odd man out of the trio. It is likely that he was not a deme official at all, but an appointment made by the polis, under Demetrius of Phaleron. Even if we should identify him as a prominent Acharnian, the Leon who was priest of Ares and Athena Areia or a close relative (Humphreys 2004, 190–1; *SEG* 21, 519; Takeuchi 2010–2013, 86–7), this does not rule out his commission from the polis.

Whether or not he was an Acharnian, Leon may not simply have been the 'epimelete of the (Acharnian) Dionysia', but of a number of – possibly all – Attic Dionysia, urban and rural. This new office appears to have been a precursor, dating perhaps from as early as the oligarchy of 321–318 (**I Aix 3e**), of the more familiar office of manager of Athenian festivals known as the 'agonothesia', which makes its first definitive appearance in 307/6 (**V I**). The term 'epimelete', of broad application, had long been used for a number of theatre-related offices, in particular the ten tribally appointed *epimeletai* who assisted the Archon with the organisation of the Parade of the City Dionysia (**I Biii**). But the office in the Acharnian decree is held by a singleton. That brings it in line with the suggestion made by Theophrastus' *Oligarchic Man* (**I B** on Thphr. 26.2) some time around 320 that a single epimelete rather than the usual board of ten be appointed for the Dionysia. That is a fictional suggestion, but the advice is in keeping with the thinking of Theophrastus' own teacher, Aristotle, who recommended for the ideal wealthy community an office of '*epimeleia* for Dionysiac contests' (περὶ ἀγῶνας ἐπιμέλεια … Διονυσιακούς, Arist. *Pol.* 1322b38–23a3) which had powers far greater than those of the traditional Athenian *epimeletai*. The Acharnian decree suggests that these Peripatetic and oligarchic suggestions had become a reality.

The Acharnian Dionysia is described in tripartite form by reference to its three key constituent elements – sacrifice, parade, agon (ll. 4–6). The last term does not of itself imply that there was just one competitive event at the festival, for *agon* can have the collective sense 'agonistic element' (cf. e.g. **I Avi 1**; *IG* II³ 1, 378, ll. 26–7). The 'remaining business' (l. 6) that the three continue to manage must refer to matters arising from the conduct of the festival (outstanding financial and contractual issues are likely). That their behaviour is described as 'according to the laws' (l. 7) implies the existence of laws governing the conduct of the festival, or this may have been part of legislation concerning the demarch's duties (**Rii**).

The three receive appropriately Dionysiac crowns of ivy and, in what looks almost like an afterthought appended to the main body of the decree (ll. 19–22), inheritable prohedria (the honours on this stele are notably inexpensive). The crowns are to be proclaimed by the demarch 'at the contest of the Dionysia at Acharnae' (ll. 13–14). The use of the locatival dative, Ἀχαρνῆσιν 'at Acharnae' (also ll. 21–2), rather than a possessive genitive ('of the Acharnians') finds a parallel from Aixone (**Diii**). The fact that both instances of this usage date to within a year or so of one another (the Aixone decree is probably to be placed in 313/12) might permit us to detect in the phrase another faint indication of the involvement of polis authorities in the festival at this time: it was beyond doubt an event of the deme, but its new organisational circumstances nonetheless meant that it could be described as the Dionysia 'at Acharnae' rather than 'of the Acharnians'.

Although the offer of prohedria extending to offspring can be paralleled (*IG* II² 20, ll. 9–10; **Hvii**, l. 17), the rather grandiose specification εἰς τὸν ἀεὶ [χρό]νον 'for all time' cannot; and we may perhaps detect here a note of bravura, an assertion of the longevity of the festival at a time of change (**Div**). Those honoured are to take their places 'on the first bench (*bathron*)' (l. 22). This detail might suggest that the prohedria of Acharnae consisted of wooden benches rather than separately articulated marble thrones (Csapo 2007, 95); or it could refer to a stone foundation block upon which wooden seats were placed. Either seems consistent with what has thus far emerged from the excavations at Menidhi (**Bvi**; but see **B Introduction** for the suggestion of marble prohedria).

The second document (**2**) is one of only two deme decrees that honour treasurers (the other is from Halai Aixonides: Steinhauer 2004–2009; **J**). The praise extends to all aspects of his – evidently broad – sacral and financial duties on behalf of the deme over the course of the year (ll. 3–5), while singling out for special attention his 'supervision', along with the demarch, of the Dionysia. The verb used (ἐπεμελήθη) is the direct cognate of the word for Leon's office, *epimeletes* 'supervisor', but Leon – who was said to have worked with this pair in the earlier decree – receives no mention here. Phanomachos is praised for having had a silver phiale made (ll. 7–8). This is the first evidence from a deme for a practice known at the urban level from the Lycurgan period – the obligatory, or quasi-obligatory, dedication of a silver phiale, of fixed value, after the performance of a liturgy (**I D** on *SEG* 25, 177). A treasurer was not a liturgist, and we do not know whether this obligation extended to Acharnae's liturgists as well (perhaps unlikely, given the demes' greater dependence on a small number of rich families to fulfil liturgical duties, and thus the difficulty of imposing a further obligation on them). The law that directed this (l. 8) was doubtless an attempt to shore up the deme's finances, and perhaps more specifically, the financial basis of the festival, if the dedication was made not *qua* treasurer but with special reference to his role in the running of the Dionysia (a possibility implied by the order of the clauses).

Lines 8–14, on Phanomachos' accounting, offer an intriguing glimpse into financial relations between deme and city. Phanomachos gave 'full accounts of everything he managed to both the city and to the demesmen within the times specified by both city and deme law' (ll. 8–12). It appears that the treasurer of Acharnae had been handling resources from the city as well as from the deme in organising the festival, and was as a result required to give this form of separate accounting. Was this the normal arrangement for Acharnae, or does it have something to do with the particular historical moment? If the former, Acharnae was somewhat like the Piraeus in receiving funds from the city for its Dionysia (**T**). When the Acharnians constructed altars for Ares and Athena Areia some time after the middle of the century, the cost was split with the polis, since the Athenian demos shared the religious benefit (*SEG* 21, 519 with Robert 1938). But when the author of the *Athenaion Politeia* (54.8) specifies that the demarchs who ran the Dionysia of Piraeus and Salamis were appointed centrally, the implication is that in his day no other deme had a similar arrangement. It is thus more likely that the situation reflects special circumstances, explained by reference to the new office of epimelete, who probably introduced central funds to help run the festival – perhaps at the same time as he suppressed the local tradition of choregic support. For their first editor deduced from the absence of any reference to choregoi in these decrees, and from the presence of the new officer of epimelete, that the choregia had been abolished in both the city and the demes, in conformity with the policy of Demetrius of Phaleron (**VI K**; cf. however Wilson and Csapo 2012, 302–6).

At ll. 12–14, Phanomachos' handling of the funds that remained from this unusual joint budgetary arrangement is singled out for praise, and this may give us an insight into the dynamics of the deme's response to this new situation. Phanomachos 'has paid over to the Acharnians the balance of money he had from the budget: 329 drachmas'. This is not formulaic praise for a standard *paradosis*, the handing over of funds at the end of an official's term to the next incumbent. In this case the money is not divided between its two original sources, city and deme, nor is it said to go to the next treasurer, but simply 'to the Acharnians'. The verb used for Phanomachos' action (καταβάλλω) is not the standard term for handing over a positive budget balance to a successor in office (παραδίδωμι), but suggests some form of special accounting manoeuvre, perhaps with some connotation of returning a profit: at its most neutral, 'he has paid over [the money] to the Acharnians'. The same verb is used to describe the actions for which the deme treasurers of Halai Aixonides are praised, and in that case the issue of returning a profit, or at least a budgetary surplus, is made very explicit: καὶ περιποήσαν[τες ἀπ]|ὸ τῆς προσόδου καταβεβλή[κασιν τοῖ|ς ἱεροποιοῖ]ς (the sum for 388 drachmas follows: Steinhauer 2004–2009, ll. 8–10). Did Phanomachos finesse the books in such a way that all outgoings could be set first against the city's contribution, leaving the remainder sitting on the Acharnian side? And is this part of the reason why he receives separate and fulsome honours from the deme, honours that are offered after the work of the epimelete is over (and that make no reference to him) and that are inscribed above the earlier decree (but apparently at the same time as it: Steinhauer 1992, 182)?

C | Aigilia

Choregic dedication of Timosthenes and his sons, before 350 (by prosopography and letter forms).

Block of 'Pentelic' marble, broken to rear. Top, front, left and right sides are all partly preserved. There is a large ovaloid cutting in centre of top at least 0.42 m wide, to a depth of 0.07 m, probably to receive a statue base.

0.165 × 0.72 × 0.19 (L) – 0.24 (R) m.

Acquired in 1873 from a landowner in the area of Kalyvia Kouvara (today Kalyvia Thorikou): Milchhöfer 1887b, 281.

Athens EM 10670.

IG II 1282; Brinck 1906, no. 13; *IG* II² 3096; *IG* II³ 4, 502.

Text: *IG* II³ 4, 502, with autopsy.   Photos: Agelidis 2009, Taf. 7e; *IG* II³ 4,1 tab. LXVIII.

> [Τιμο]σθένης Μειξωνίδο
> Μειξωνίδης Τιμοσθένος
> Κλεόστρατος Τιμοσθένος
> χορηγοῦντες νικήσαντες ἀνέθεσα[ν]
> τῶι Διονύσωι τἄγαλμα καὶ τὸμ βω[μόν].

> [Timo]sthenes, son of Meixonides; Meixonides, son of Timosthenes; Kleostratos, son of Timosthenes, after victory as choregoi dedicated the statue and al[tar] to Dionysus.

This is the sole testimony to theatrical activity in the south-western coastal deme of Aigilia (bouleutic quota 6). The attribution is suggested by the identification of the choregos Timosthenes with the friend and partner of the banker Phormio, named in [D.] 49.31–2 as an Aigilieus; and of the second son, Kleostratos, with the prytany-secretary of 343/2, likewise named with that demotic (*IG* II³ 1, 306, l. 35; 307, l. 2). Timosthenes seems to have derived his wealth at least in part from trade. We are told that he entrusted some silver Lycian bowls to his friend Phormio before leaving on a business trip ([D.] 49). Only Meixonides, probably the older of the two sons (to judge by his place in the list and the fact that he shares his grandfather's name), is otherwise unknown.

The monument records a dedication to Dionysus by this team of father and sons, following victory as choregoi. There can be little doubt that the victory was won at a local Dionysia (but cf. Agelidis 2009, 198). Group sponsorship of theatrical events by members of the same family is a characteristic of deme Dionysia. At the time of the choregia, the two sons were probably of an age to possess their own properties, and so to contribute independently. As often in deme theatre inscriptions, there is no reference to poet or performers (e.g. **Eii**; **Hiv**; **Mvii**; **Mviii**; **Mix**); nor even to a performance type. All emphasis lies with the local worthies who made the event possible. In addition to their support of the successful theatrical event, the family of Timosthenes contributed to the cultic infrastructure of the deme by commissioning a statue, doubtless of the god. The plausible suggestion that their second gift was an altar goes back to the first editor (Köhler) and improved readings confirm it.

But where exactly was the victory won? The stone was acquired from a landowner who lived in Kalyvia Kouvara, a considerable distance (north and further inland) from the territory of Aigilia. Given the uncertainty over its findspot it is possible that it travelled some way from its original site before being acquired. Goette (2014) airs the possibility that the theatre of Aixone (**D Introduction**) served as the focal point of a large area at the southern tip of Mt. Hymettos comprising the demes of Aixone, Halai Aixonides, Anagyrous – and perhaps even Aigilia. But if this were a dedication made in a sanctuary outside their home deme, we should expect Timosthenes and his sons to have indicated their deme of origin by the inclusion of their demotics.

D | Aixone

Introduction

Five inscribed decrees provide a vivid glimpse into the vibrant theatrical activity of the large and populous southern Attic coastal deme of Aixone (bouleutic quota ? 9–11: Ackermann 2018, 341–2) in the second half of the fourth century (for recent advances in archaeological knowledge of the deme see Giannopoulou-Konsolaki 1990; Papadopoulou 2016). Ackermann (2018) has now given us a comprehensive study of all the available materials relating to the history and life of Aixone. She discusses (2018, 21–59) the topography and identification of the correct location of the deme, now established beyond doubt at the site of modern Glyphada. Its most prominent centre lay in the area around the church of Agios Nikolaos at Pirnari, where there has been found a high concentration of Classical and Hellenistic dwellings (Ackermann 2018, 72) in addition to various other finds. The main ancient road between Athens and Sunium ran through here. Other significant centres of activity were a small but busy port in the bay to the north of cape Exonis (Ackermann 2018, 75–7); the sanctuary of Hebe, to the north of Agios Nikolaos; and possibly an agora and sanctuary complex about 600 m to the north-west of the same church (Ackermann 2018, 93, 272–4).

These five inscriptions show how the deme used its theatre and Dionysia to recognise, reciprocate and further promote the generosity of its benefactors, choregoi (**Di**; **Dii**; **Div**) and others (**Diii**; **Dv**). A further tiny fragment (*SEG* 46, 314) may contain reference to prohedria, otherwise known from **Dv** (but note the reservations of Ackermann 2018, 368). It is relatively clear that the Aixone theatre served as the deme's prime site for the permanent publication in stone of honours, including but not limited to honours earned in connection with the theatre. However it was not the only such site, and the sanctuary of what may have been the deme's principal cult, that of Hebe, was also an important place for the display of public documents. Among these is a decree honouring officials involved directly in the cult of Hebe (Ackermann 2018, 292–305, no. 16 of 320/19), which might encourage one to regard it as only a partial exception, but the sanctuary was also the place for the display of one copy of a rental agreement between the deme and two of its members, accompanied by an associated decree (*IG* II² 2492, Ackermann 2018, 186–216 no. 7). A second copy of these rental documents was to be set up in a *lesche*, on the nature and possible site of which see Ackermann (2018, 213–14). It is generally thought that an important and unique sacred law of the deme that dates to the first half of the fourth century (Ackermann 2018, 271–92 no. 15) was most likely to have been displayed in the sanctuary of Hebe, but Ackermann (2018, 274) has argued, on the basis of the secure findspot of one of its fragments (apparently not in reuse) that it was set up at a site some 600 m to the north-west of Agios Nikolaos. This she believes was the site of the deme's agora, perhaps also the location of the sanctuary for the deme's Founding Hero (mentioned in the sacred law: Ackermann 2018, no. 15, l. 31) and also of the *lesche* mentioned above.

The theatre decrees provide some of the best evidence for a practice energetically espoused by demes (and tribes and city) in the second half of the fourth century, namely of publically rewarding and promoting various civic virtues, above all *philotimia* – 'ambition for honour' – and its associated habit of spending private wealth on behalf of the community (Whitehead 1983; 1986a, 241–52). The valuable crowns awarded to choregoi, by definition the wealthiest members of the community, may have been given in the expectation that they would rededicate them. All the same, the figures – of 100 or more commonly 500 drachmas for each – permit a very rough estimate of how much a deme choregos might have outlaid, for we can be confident that they had spent several times more than that in the first place. The prominent role of the demarch in administrative and financial matters relating to the theatre comes as no surprise. In this rather large deme, he is assisted by (at least two) treasurers (*tamiai* **Di**, **Diii**, **Div**).

Despite having neighbours – in Euonymon, some 7 km away on the Athens road – with an especially well-equipped theatre that could hold several times the local population of demesmen (**I Introduction**), there is no doubt that Aixone possessed a significant theatre of its own (and one should also register the presence of further theatres in the adjacent demes of Halimous to the north, **L**, and Halai Aixonides to the south, **J**). The use of the phrases 'the comedies held at Aixone' (τοῖς κωμωιδοῖς τοῖς Αἰξωνῆσιν) and 'erect [the stele] in the theatre at Aixone' (στῆσαι ἐν τῶι θεάτρωι Αἰξωνῆσιν, **Diii**, ll. 15, 21) create an overwhelming presumption. Goette (2014, 94) argues that this theatre served not only Aixone but a number of neighbouring demes. **Di**, **Diii** and **Dv** explicitly state that they are to be erected in the theatre and **Dii** almost certainly had a similar instruction in its lost final clause.

That theatre is yet to be securely located (Ackermann 2018, 69–71). In 1879 Lolling stated that remains of the theatre of Aixone still stood at Pirnari (also written in his day 'Prinari'), a region stretching from the Pirnari gorge in the north, on the slopes of Mt Hymettos, to at least as far as the church of Agios Nikolaos in the south. Milchhöfer (1883, 29) reported that Lolling had seen the remains of the theatre near the entrance to the Pirnari gorge but various later attempts, including by Milchhöfer himself, failed to locate them (and Milchhöfer 1907, 1157 subsequently concluded that the theatre was more likely to have been near the church of Agios Nikolaos). Ackermann (2018, 70) observes that a location at the mouth of the Pirnari gorge would place the theatre some 4 km from the known centres of the deme, notably the most prominent one at Agios Nikolaos. Having studied Lolling's papers in the DAI archive in Athens, where he makes no mention of seeing a theatre in notes he made during a walking tour of Attica in September 1878, Ackermann (2018, 70) casts doubt on the very idea that Lolling had himself seen the theatre ruins, noting that the expression he used in his publication (1879, 194 'dort noch vorhandene Ruine des Theaters') does not explicitly make a claim about location, but merely reports that ruins were still in existence. Ackermann herself (2018, 71, 111) plausibly suggests that the Aixoneis may have used the natural slopes of Mt Hymettos above Agios Nikolaos for the site of their theatre, perhaps not employing stone in its construction. In his publication of two of the decrees that were originally erected in the Aixone theatre (**Di** and **Diii**) Rousopoulos (1864, 131) comments that the excavations, which had been conducted by the Russian Ambassador to Greece, Count A. D. Bludov (Ackermann 2018, 112), had found in addition 'oltre vari resti di scultura di eccellente lavoro'. This tantalising comment conjures up the possibility of a rich array of material that had once adorned Aixone's theatre.

Three inscriptions present us with pairs of choregoi (**Dii**, ll. 3–6; **Di** and **Div**). The use of the quasi-formulaic phrase 'the choregoi in year X' + two names (e.g. οἱ χορηγοὶ οἱ ἐπὶ Δημογένους ἄρχοντος κτλ.) suggests that there were in fact only two in any year, and in the absence of any sign of formal contest we should not assume it (*pace* Whitehead 1986a, 218). In **Dii** and **Div** both choregoi of the year receive a crown (honorific, not that of a victor). If comedy was the only performance type at the Aixone Dionysia – and it is the only one attested – presumably these two men worked together to produce it (**Diii**, l. 15 and **Div**; Ackermann 2018, 107–8). Unlike some other choregoi we find working together in the demes, these paired choregoi in Aixone seem not to belong to the same family, implying, as Ackermann (2018, 108) notes, that financial factors were in this case probably the dominant force in adopting this form of joint choregia.

A cluster of decrees from Aixone date with greater or lesser certainty from the period during which Demetrius of Phaleron, appointee of Macedonian overlords (the hollow rhetoric of 'election' in *IG* II² 1201, l. 11 notwithstanding), ruled Athens with virtually autocratic power, 317–307 (**VI K**). That makes them rather unusual, since there are virtually no surviving inscribed decrees from the city from that entire decade. The group includes three theatre-related documents, **Dii** from 317/16 and **Diii** and **Div** from (probably) 313/12. Moreover, one of the men honoured by **Diii** in some theatrical connection, Aristokrates, himself proposed the decree with which the deme honoured Demetrius (*IG* II² 1201), early in his rule (Tracy 1995, 45–6). This burst of activity may at some level be a response to major changes afoot, or in the air, in the funding and administration of Athenian theatre. The date at which the choregia was abolished in the city is not known for sure, and there are reasons to doubt that it took place early in Demetrius' stewardship, as was once generally thought likely (Wilson and Csapo 2012; a rejoinder asserting the older view in Ackermann 2018, 134–43). Evidence from the deme of Acharnae suggests that in this very period the city authorities appointed a general overseer (*epimeletes*) of all Athenian Dionysia (**Bvii 2**) whose presence may have threatened the independence of the deme's arrangements, and foreshadowed the introduction of the agonothesia in the city. At a time when the value of choregiai, to the families of choregoi themselves and to the wider community, was under scrutiny and the very institution under threat, the Aixoneis appear to have gone to special lengths to stress the buoyancy of their theatrical culture and to praise and honour the men who funded their own theatre (**Diii**).

A cult of Dionysus Anthios, with a priestess who receives a goatskin as perquisite, is also attested for Aixone by an important and unique sacred law (Ackermann 2018, no. 15, ll. 9–10). Robert Parker (2010b, 204–5) observes that the fact she is not given the remuneration for kindling routinely granted to the other priests and priestesses in the inscription may point to a cult with 'raw meat eating' (*omophagia*). Ackermann (2018, 310) suggests a likely connection with the flowering of the vine and thus a timing of Dionysus Anthios' festival in April or May. If this reasoning holds, there will be no connection with the celebration of the Dionysus of the theatre.

Di: Deme Decree Honouring Two Choregoi, in or soon after 326/5 (Chremes was Archon in 326/5).

> Stele of white marble, made up of two joining fragments; broken at bottom. The rear surface is not carefully worked, suggesting it was displayed against a wall (Ackermann 2018, 113).

0.51 × 0.314 × 0.07 m.

Found (with **Diii**) in February 1864 'in un piccolo scavo impreso in un podere situato a *Trachones* fra l'Imetto ed il mare' (Rousopoulos 1864, 129). By 'Trachones' Rousopoulos doubtless means the region of modern Pirnari (Eliot 1962, 8‒9; Ackermann 2018, 112–13).

Athens EM 139.

Rousopoulos 1864, 131; *IG* II 579; *IG* II² 1198; Ackermann 2018, 112–17 no. 2.

Text: based on Ackermann.   Photos: Giannopoulou-Konsolaki 1990, 101 fig. 81; Ackermann 2018, 548 fig. 16.

[Φιλ]οκτήμων Χρέμητο[ς]   stoich. 19 (18 l.1, 20 l. 2)
εἶπεν· ἐπειδὴ οἱ χορηγ[οὶ]
οἱ ἐπὶ Χρέμητος ἄρχοντ-
ος Δημοκράτης Εὐφιλήτ-
5   ου καὶ Ἡγησίας Λυσιστρ-
άτου καλῶς καὶ φιλοτίμ-
ως ἐχορήγησαν Αἰξωνεῦ-
σιν, ἐπαινέσαι αὐτοὺς κ-
αὶ στεφανῶσαι χρυσῶι σ-
10   τεφάνωι ἀπὸ : [Ⲡ] : δραχμῶ-
ν ἑκάτερον φιλοτιμίας
ἕνεκα καὶ ἐπιμελείας τ-
ῆς εἰς τοὺς δημότας· δοῦ-
ναι δὲ αὐτοῖς καὶ εἰς θυ-
15   σίαν τὸν δήμαρχον Δωρό-
[θε]ον καὶ τοὺς ταμίας : Δ
[δ]ραχμὰς ἀπὸ τῆς προσόδ-
ου τῶν δημοτῶν. ἀναγράψ-
αι δὲ τόδε τὸ ψήφισμα τὸ-
20   ν δήμαρχον Δωρόθεον εἰ-
ς στήλην [λ]ιθίνην καὶ στῆσαι εἰς τ[ὸ] θέατρον, ὅπω-
ς ἂν εἰδῶσιν οἱ ἀεὶ μέλ<λ>-
οντες χορηγεῖν Αἰξωνε-
25   ῦσι ὅτι τιμήσει αὐτοὺς
ὁ δῆμος ὁ Αἰξωνέων τοὺς
εἰς ἑαυτοὺς φιλοτιμου-
[μ]ένους. *vacat*
vacat

2–3 Ackermann   χορηγ|οὶ ἐπὶ Rousopoulos, Köhler   χορηγ|οὶ [οἱ] Kirchner   10 Ackermann   : [.] : Takeuchi   [Ⲏ] Grimes (Stroud) (*SEG* 52, 123)   : [Α]Υ: Tracy (*SEG* 45, 124)   23 ΜΕΛΑ *lapis*   μέλ<λ>- Köhler

[Phil]oktemon son of Chremes proposed: since the choreg[oi] in the Archonship of Chremes, Demokrates son of Euphiletos [5] and Hegesias son of Lysistratos, performed their choregiai in a fine and ambitious manner for the Aixoneis, the deme should confer praise upon them and crown them each with a gold [10] crown worth [500] drachmas for their ambition and for the care they have shown for their fellow demesmen; and furthermore [15] the demarch Dorotheos and the treasurers are to give them 10 drachmas from the deme's income for a sacrifice. The [20] demarch Dorotheos is to inscribe this decree on a stone stele and erect it in the theatre, so that future choregoi for the Aixoneis may know [25] that the deme of the Aixoneis will honour those who are ambitious on their behalf.

This is one of a pair of honorific decrees for choregoi proposed by Philoktemon (the other, moved nine years later, is **Dii**). That he was not motivated solely by a disinterested sense of the communal good is suggested by the fact that this decree advertises itself as having been moved in the year his own father was eponymous Archon in Athens (ll. 3–4). There is no indication of the nature of the performance(s) supported by Demokrates and Hegesias. Hegesias is otherwise unknown (Whitehead 1986a, 419; Humphreys 2018, 1076), but his colleague Demokrates came from an illustrious family, whose best-known member was the general Lysis, eponym of the Platonic dialogue (*APF* 360). In this very period Demokrates is at the receiving end of a curse (Ziebarth 1934, 1023 no. 1A, l. 5).

The honours are substantial. The value of the crowns here is not known for sure, for the letter is damaged, but it is very probably 500 drachmas (Takeuchi 2010–2013, 90), as in the later decree, and we accept Ackermann's restoration in l. 10. It has however been thought that there are indications that the figure for 1,000 was initially inscribed and then erased – whether as the result of second thoughts or a mason's error is unclear. On another interpretation of the traces, the intended sum was a very extravagant 1,400 (Tracy 1995, 100). The 10 drachmas 'for a sacrifice' (the same sum in **Div**) would be enough for a sheep or pig for an informal celebratory party (**I Aviii**), or perhaps for an event in the Dionysion in honour of Dionysus himself. Here it is explicitly budgeted from deme income and is presumably to be shared by the two choregoi. The public praise and crowning probably took place at the next Dionysia: in **Diii** this is made explicit. The permanent record in the Aixone theatre is itself a major honour and the stele, broken at the bottom, in all likelihood depicted the crowns awarded (as in **Diii**, **Div** and **Dv**). In a good example of what has been called a 'manifesto' clause (Whitehead 1986a, 246) this inscription is very explicit about the deme's ulterior motive in erecting the monument: to notify future donors that they will be properly honoured for similar acts of generosity (similarly in **Dv**, ll. 15–21). The formulation used in **Div** (ll. 12–13) achieves the same purpose more obliquely: 'so that the Aixoneis may always conduct as fine a Dionysia as possible'.

The demarch of Aixone is assisted in his duties by multiple treasurers (l. 16; also **Diii**, **Div**, *IG* II² 2492, Ackermann 2018 no. 7), as is also the case in several other demes, although more commonly they serve as singletons (Ackermann 2018, 116–17).

Dii: Deme Decree Honouring Two Choregoi, in or soon after 317/16 (Demogenes was Archon in 317/16).

Pedimental stele of white marble, broken at the bottom. The rear surface is rough-worked, suggesting it was probably erected against a wall (Ackermann 2018, 118).
0.33 × 0.35 × 0.065 m.

Found at Pirnari 'aus den Ruinen des alten Demos Aixone im jetzigen Prinari, halbwegs zwischen Trachones und Vari' (Lolling 1879, 193). Lolling goes on to note that the stones (including **Dv**, *IG* II² 1196 = Ackermann 2018 no. 8 and *IG* II² 2664 = Ackermann 2018 no. 13) had been transported to a small collection in the courtyard of the property Komninos, ex-Louriotis, at Trachones (Eliot 1962, 7–8; Ackermann 2018, 118).

Athens EM 12667.

Lolling 1879, 194; *IG* II 584b; *IG* II² 1200; Ackermann 2018, 117–19 no. 3.

Text: based on Ackermann.   Photos: Giannopoulou-Konsolaki   1990,   103   fig.   8; Ackermann 2018, 548 fig. 17.

Θ   Ε   Ο   Ι.

Φιλοκτήμων Χρέμητος εἶπε-   stoich. 22

ν· δεδόχθαι τοῖς δημόταις, ἐ-

πειδὴ οἱ χορηγοὶ οἱ ἐπὶ Δημ-

5 ογένους ἄρχο[ν]τος Λεόντιο-

ς Δίωνος, Γλαύκων Καλλικρά-

τους καλῶς καὶ φιλοτίμως ἐ-

χορήγησαν Αἰξωνῆσι ἐπαιν-

έσαι αὐτοὺς καὶ στεφανῶσα-

10 ι χρυσῶι στε[φ]άνωι ἀπὸ : Ͷ : δρα-

[χμῶν ἑκάτερον α]ὐτῶν φιλ[οτ-]

[ιμίας ἕνεκα - - -]

1 θεοί on the architrave.

G O D S. Philoktemon son of Chremes proposed; the demesmen made the following decision: since the choregoi in the Archonship of [5] Demogenes, Leontios son of Dion and Glaukon son of Kallikrates, performed their choregi-ai in a fine and ambitious manner for the Aixoneis, the deme is to confer praise upon them and crown them [each] [10] with a gold crown worth 500 dra[chmas for t]heir amb[ition …]

This honorific decree for two local choregoi is the latest securely dated Attic document that shows the choregia in operation (but see on **Diii** and **Div**), excluding the first-century AD 'revival' and a rogue appearance of choregoi at the Thargelia in 129/8 (*SEG* 21, 469, l. 33). It dates to the very first year in the regime of Demetrius of Phaleron. Philoktemon also moved **Di** in honour of choregoi. As with that decree, this one gives no indication of the nature of the performance(s) supported. Leontios and Glaukon are awarded public praise, a perpetual memorial to their service (in the form of this apparently undecorated stele) and gold crowns of high value. Whether this is a sign of buoyancy or bravura in the face of threats is unclear (**D Introduction**). As the stone is broken, there are likely to have been further awards and there can be no doubt that instructions followed to erect the stele in the theatre. Leontios and Glaukon are otherwise unknown, though we can be sure their families were prominent in the deme (Whitehead 1986a, 419; Ackermann 2018, 446, 459). Glaukon's father Kallikrates is honoured in **Diii** for his *philotimia*, as well as his 'virtue and honesty'.

Diii: Deme Decree Honouring Two Demesmen, 313/12 (or 340/39: see on **Div**;
Ackermann 2018, 134–43 makes a robust case for the earlier date).

Stele of white marble, broken at the top and bottom, with relief carving of the lower part of two
figures above the text and two olive crowns below it.
0.66 × 0.31 × 0.058 m (Kirchner).
Found (with **Di**) in February 1864 'in un piccolo scavo impreso in un podere situato a *Trachones*
fra l'Imetto ed il mare' (Rousopoulos 1864, 129). By 'Trachones' Rousopoulos doubtless means
the region of modern Pirnari (Eliot 1962, 8–9; Ackermann 2018, 112–13). The stele was taken
to Russia by the Russian Ambassador to Greece, Count A. D. Bludov, who had conducted the
excavation in 1864 (Ackermann 2018, 126–7).
St Petersburg, Hermitage GR 15520 (A 1105).
Rousopoulos 1864, 130; *IG* II 585; *IG* II² 1202; Ackermann 2018, 126–34 no. 5.
Text: based on Ackermann.   Photos: Lawton 1995, pl. 82; Ackermann 2018, 552 fig. 28.

```
        ἐπὶ Θεοφράστου ἄρχοντος ἐν τεῖ ἀγορᾶι τεῖ κυρ-          stoich. 38
        ίαι· ἔδοξεν Αἰξωνεῦσιν, Γλαυκίδης Σωσίππου Αἰ-
        ξωνεὺς εἶπεν· ἐψηφίσθαι Αἰξωνεῦσιν· ἐπειδή εἰ-
        σιν ἄνδρες ἀγαθοὶ καὶ φιλότιμοι περὶ τὸν δῆμο-
   5    ν τὸν Αἰξωνέων Καλλικράτης Γλαύκωνος Αἰξωνε-
        ὺς καὶ Ἀριστοκράτης Ἀ[ριστοφάνους Αἰξωνεύς, ἐπαινέσαι]
        αὐτοὺς ἀρετῆς ἕνεκα καὶ δικαιοσύνης τῆς εἰς τ-
        ὸν δῆμον τὸν Αἰξωνέων καὶ στεφανῶσαι αὐτοὺς χ-
        ρυσῶι στεφάνωι ἀπὸ πεντακοσίων δραχμῶν ἑκάτ-
  10    ερον, τὸ δὲ ἀργύριον εἶναι τὸ εἰς τοὺς στεφάνου-
        ς ἐκ τῆς διοικήσεως ἐκ τῶν περιόντων χρημάτων
        τῶν ἐπὶ Θεοφράστου ἄρχοντος, δοῦναι δὲ αὐτοῖς
        τὸ ἀργύριον τὸ εἰς τοὺς στεφάνους Ἡγησίλεω τὸ-
        ν δήμαρχον καὶ τοὺς ταμίας· ἀνειπεῖν δὲ καὶ Διο-
  15    νυσίων τοῖς κωμωιδοῖς τοῖς Αἰξωνῆσιν ἐν τῶι θ-
        εάτρωι, ὅτι στεφανοῖ αὐτοὺς ὁ δῆμος ὁ Αἰξωνέων
        ἀρετῆς ἕνεκα καὶ δικαιοσύνης τῆς εἰς τὸν δῆμο-
        ν τὸν Αἰξωνέων καὶ τὰ κοινὰ τὰ Αἰξωνέων. ἀναγρά-
        ψαι δὲ τόδε τὸ ψήφισμα εἰς στήλην λιθίνην τὸν δ-
  20    ήμαρχον Ἡγησίλεω καὶ τοὺς ταμίας καὶ στῆσαι ἐ-
        ν τῶι θεάτρωι Αἰξωνῆσιν.
                crown              crown
```

l. 6 has 46 stoichoi because of an addition in rasura

In the Archonship of Theophrastos, at a principal assembly meeting, the Aixoneis
made the following decision, on the proposal of Glaukides son of Sosippos of
Aixone: since they are fine men and ambitious for the deme [5] of Aixone, the
Aixoneis decree to confer praise upon Kallikrates son of Glaukon of Aixone and
Aristokrates son of Aristophanes of Aixone for their virtue and sense of justice
towards the deme of the Aixoneis, and to crown them each with a gold crown
worth five hundred drachmas; [10] the money for the crowns is to come from the
unspent resources in the operating budget in the Archonship of Theophrastos;

the demarch Hegesileos and the treasurers are to give them the money for the crowns; and the announcement is to be made, [15] during the Dionysia at the comedies held at Aixone in the theatre, that the deme of the Aixoneis is crowning them for their virtue and sense of justice towards the deme of the Aixoneis and its communal activities. The [20] demarch Hegesileos and the treasurers are to inscribe this decree on a stone stele and erect it in the theatre at Aixone.

A Theophrastos was Archon in both 340/39 and 313/12. The date of this decree is thus uncertain, as is that of **Div**, which has the same Archon, demarch and proposer. We incline to the later date (with e.g. *DFA*[2] 49; Whitehead 1986a, 418; Humphreys 2004, 193; Humphreys 2018, 1079; *contra*, Ackermann 2018, 121–6, 134–43). Prosopographical grounds favour it, in particular the fact that Aristokrates himself proposed a decree in or ca. 317 (*IG* II[2] 1201). An active life in deme affairs could extend over a quarter of a century, but the proximate date is more likely. Glaukides had a brother who was a cavalryman in 323 (*IG* II[2] 1955, l. 18), so it is slightly more likely that we should find him proposing a decree ten years later rather than seventeen earlier. Kallikrates' son Glaukon was choregos in 317 (**Dii**). One might expect a father's choregia to precede a son's, but the probability of multiple choregiai over an extended period by wealthy individuals in a deme context weakens the force of this expectation, as does the habit of intergenerational shared choregia in demes. In fact, the very issue of generational priority in choregic performance is directly thematised in an inscription from Anagyrous, where a son's victory is proffered as a spur to emulation for the father (**Eii**). The fact that the Auteas honoured in **Div** held a lease, in company with his father, in 346 (*IG* II[2] 2492), is equivocal. But given that the lease had a term of forty years, Auteas is likely to have been young.

Various stylistic features of the decoration of **Div** suggested to Webster a date closer to 330: the relief sculpture, including the type of the youthful Dionysus and the way the image is framed with flattened anta capitals; and, above all, the masks on the architrave, thought to be closer to those of Middle than of New Comedy (Webster 1951, 222 n. 7; Webster 1953–1954, 192–4; *contra* Lawton 1995, 155). But perhaps the most considerable argument for the earlier date comes from the identification of the mason of this inscription by Tracy (1995, 99–100) as the 'Cutter of *IG* II[2] 244', whose known dates are 338/7– ca. 320. On the other hand, the use of EI rather than morphemic HI (l. 1) is much commoner after ca. 325 (*GAI* I, 374–8).

This decree refers explicitly to the Dionysia of Aixone, and to the performance of comedy at it. Few deme documents specify the particular moment for the proclamation of honours – as had been the practice in the city for the Great Dionysia since at least the late fifth century, where tragedy was the contest of choice (**I Av 4**; Wilson 2009; Wilson and Hartwig 2009). The use of the locatival dative Αἰξωνῆσιν in attributive position – Διονυσίων τοῖς κωμωιδοῖς τοῖς Αἰξωνῆσιν, 'during the Dionysia at the comedies held at Aixone' (l. 15) – may evince a pride in the local comic tradition. If not simply parochial redundancy, perhaps Αἰξωνῆσιν draws a more pointed distinction, presumably with comic performance in the city or elsewhere (**Bvii** for another interpretation). While comedy is the only certainly attested genre at Aixone, it could be argued that the very use of κωμωιδοῖς might suggest that other events were available. But if there were others, comedy served in Aixone, as tragedy did in the city, as the preeminent event (see also on **Div**). So far as a rule can be deduced from the patchy evidence, when the programme of a deme's Dionysia included tragedy, this was the event at which honours were announced (cf. *IE* 99 in **H Introduction**; **Eiii**; **Q**).

The rhetoric of praise remains at too general a level to permit us to say anything about the precise nature of the honorands' services. The demonstration of virtue (*arete*), and especially of justice (*dikaiosyne* l. 7), is suggestive of some sort of official duty discharged with probity, particularly one of a financial character (Whitehead 1993, 67–8; Veligianni-Terzi 1997, 296–8). Observing that this decree was moved in the same year as **Div**, in honour of two choregoi, and by the same man, Whitehead (1986a, 218–19) suggested that Kallikrates and Aristokrates are the defeated choregoi of that year's Dionysia (Kallikrates' son Glaukon had served as a local choregos in 317/16: **Dii**). While this idea has won little support (Lawton 1995, 149; Jones 2004, 110; Ackermann 2018, 129) – the biggest problem being that it entails awarding losers with crowns five times more valuable than those the winners received – it is likely that their service did have some theatrical focus. The crowning relief suggests as much: the figure on the left of the altar is evidently a Papposilenos, dressed for the occasion in a himation, about to pour wine (from an oinochoe: compare the jug held by the satyr in the formally parallel relief on **Div**) into the kantharos held by the figure moving towards him on the right, who is somewhat larger in scale and surely Dionysus (rather than the chorodidaskalos supposed by Picard 1944, 140). The god seems to have held a thyrsos. A large krater stands in the left corner.

The date (assuming it is 313/12) may provide a further clue. This is a time of turmoil in the political and social fabric of Attica and, more specifically, in its theatrical funding (Humphreys 2018, 1080 thinks they 'may have stepped in to avert a financial crisis'). References to the deme or demesmen of Aixone are obsessively repetitive, even by the standards of local officialese, and may hint at an anxiety about 'the communal activities of the Aixoneis' (l. 18). The powers of deme assemblies were no doubt open to question. Note the use of 'the deme of the Aixoneis' (ὁ δῆμος ὁ Αἰξωνέων) twice in ll. 16–18; and especially the use of *kyria* of the assembly in ll. 1–2, unique in the deme context. None of the extensive discussion of this *unicum* sees the relevance of the radically changed political scene. Moreover one of the men honoured, Aristokrates, had himself proposed the deme decree in honour of the individual associated with radical reform in the area of theatre finance, Demetrius of Phaleron (**VI K**). That decree (*IG* II² 1201; Ackermann 2018, 143–56 no. 6) was passed perhaps a few years before this one (Tracy 1995, 43; Ackermann 2018, 156: perhaps 316/15), and suggests an attempt to fall in line with the new realities of power, or to make a show of doing so. It is intriguing that the man who authored it is now himself thanked by his deme, in a 'theatrical' context.

Had Aristokrates secured some understanding for the deme in relation to its festival at a time of change? Another possibility is that he and Kallikrates may have made an advance offer (*epidosis*) to serve as choregoi in the following year, to forfend against its abolition. The year 313/12 is the last for which we have any solid evidence for the choregia in Attica (**Dii**; **Wiii**). Yet in that year Aixone asserts that it will hold comic performances in 312/11, as it speaks of crowning choregoi of 313/12 'at the comedies in the year after Theophrastos was Archon' (**Div**, ll. 6–7). The drafters of this decree are careful to point out that the money for the expensive crowns is to come from unspent funds in the deme budget of the current year, as if to drive home that the deme had enjoyed careful financial management from their demarch, and perhaps to advertise the budget's buoyancy at a time of external involvement in the way demes financed and administered their theatre.

Div: Deme Decree Honouring Two Choregoi, 313/12 (or 340/39: see on **Diii**; Ackermann 2018, 121–6 makes a case for the earlier date).

Pedimental stele of white marble, largely intact (minor breaks at bottom, and at akroteria); relief carving of Dionysus and a satyr above the text, framed by antae supporting a pediment with akroteria; five theatrical masks in low relief and l. 1 inscribed on architrave; two olive crowns in low relief below the text. The rear surface is rough-worked, suggesting it was probably erected against a wall (Ackermann 2018, 119).

0.96 × 0.36–0.40 × 0.05–0.06 m.

Found at Glyphada, the site of ancient Aixone, in 1941.

Athens EM 13262.

Kyparissis and Peek 1941, 218–19 no. 1 (*SEG* 36, 186); Ackermann 2018, 119–26 no. 4.

Text: based on Ackermann.   Photos: *DFA*[2] 49; Lawton 1995, pl. 81; Ackermann 2018, 549–50 fig. 18–21.

```
         Θ              Ε              Ο              I.
```

[Γ]λαυκίδης Σωσίππου εἶπεν· ἐπειδὴ οἱ χορηγοὶ Αὐτ[έα]-   non-stoich
ς Αὐτοκλέους καὶ Φιλοξενίδης Φιλίππου καλῶς [κα]-
[ὶ] φιλοτίμως ἐχορήγησαν· δεδόχθαι τοῖς δημότ[α]-
[ι]ς, στεφανῶσαι αὐτοὺς χρυσῶι στεφάνωι ἑκάτε-
5 [ρ]ον ἀπὸ ἑκατὸν δραχμῶν ἐν τῶι θεάτρωι τοῖς κωμωιδοῖς τοῖς μετὰ Θεόφραστον ἄρχοντα, ὅπως ἂν
[φ]ιλοτιμῶνται καὶ οἱ ἄλλοι χορηγοὶ οἱ μέλλοντες
[χ]ορηγεῖν· δοῦναι δὲ αὐτοῖς καὶ εἰς θυσίαν δέκα δ-
10 ραχμὰς τὸν δήμαρχον Ἡγησίλεων καὶ τοὺς ταμί-
ας· ἀναγράψαι δὲ καὶ τὸ ψήφισμα τόδε τοὺς ταμία-
ς ἐν στήλῃ λιθίνῃ καὶ στῆσαι ἐν τῶι θεάτρωι, ὅπως
ἂν Αἰξωνεῖς ἀεὶ ὡς κάλλιστα <τὰ> Διονύσια ποιῶσιν.
          olive crown   *olive crown*

G O D S. Glaukides son of Sosippos proposed: since the choregoi Auteas son of Autokles and Philoxenides son of Philippos performed their choregiai in a fine and ambitious manner, the demesmen decided [5] to crown each with a gold crown worth one hundred drachmas in the theatre at the comedies in the year after Theophrastos was Archon, so that other choregoi who perform the service in the future might also be ambitious; and furthermore [10] the demarch Hegesileos and the treasurers are to give them ten drachmas for a sacrifice. The treasurers are to inscribe this decree on a stone stele and erect it in the theatre so that the Aixoneis might always hold as fine a Dionysia as possible.

Although little more is known of them, each of the two choregoi was 'no ordinary *demotes*' (Whitehead 1986a, 238; cf. 238–41). Philoxenides was connected by marriage to the family of the statesman Lycurgus. Auteas was, with his father, the holder of a significant deme lease (Ackermann 2018, 186–216 no. 7, 445). This honorific decree follows a similar pattern to **Di** and **Dii**. The instructions for the announcement in the theatre, at the comedies, is closest to **Dii**, but the specification that this is to happen at the next year's festival is unusual and may affect an air of confidence in the face of real uncertainty (on the other hand it is only unusual to the extent that it makes explicit what one would normally take for granted). Similarly, the concern expressed for the festival's future prosperity (ll. 12–13) and the exhortation to future choregoi in the 'manifesto' clause (ll. 7–9) strike a more than formulaic note. It is even possible that the omission of the article before Διονύσια 'Dionysia' (l. 13) is not, as editors assume, a mere mistake but reflects an aspiration for a succession of festivals into the future. 'Other choregoi who perform the service in the future' – οἱ ἄλλοι χορηγοὶ οἱ μέλλοντες χορηγεῖν – here must mean the same as 'future successive choregoi for the Aixoneis' – οἱ ἀεὶ μέλλοντες χορηγεῖν – in **Di**, rather than denoting specifically the choregoi about to perform at the Dionysia of 312/11 itself, immediately after the crowning (Whitehead 1986a, 242).

The relief carving is of high quality, and the addition of such elaborate ornamentation to the stele that carried the deme's decree visually augments the honours it authorises. It may also add a votive or dedicatory character to the monument: as Ackermann (2018, 123) notes, this and comparable reliefs on pedimental stelai often include divinities, and not infrequently scenes of sacrifice; while the architectural frame of the relief itself evokes the form of a naiskos. The five masks in low relief on the architrave are comic, further reinforcing the impression that this was Aixone's favoured (if not only) performance type. Webster preferred the earlier date largely because he found the best parallels for them in the period of Middle Comedy, and most recently Ackermann (2018, 124–5) has endorsed Webster's arguments to this effect (suggesting further a close stylistic parallel in the masks with **Kii**). They are, in Webster's typology (left to right): Old Man (M), Old Woman (R), Young Woman (SS?), Young Man (O), Young Woman (S: Green and Webster in *MMC*³ 118 AS 2). The image below of a young 'real' satyr boy (not a costumed choreut) approaching and about to serve wine to a young Dionysus shows the god of the festival well received in Aixone. Neither this satyr boy nor the Papposilenos in **Diii** are likely to denote the formal performance of satyr play (and tragedy) in Aixone. In fact, this monument draws a clear visual distinction between the explicitly theatrical (masks) and the generally Dionysiac (satyr and god).

Diii, of the same year and proposed by the same man, was the product of a 'principal assembly meeting'. The phrase is not used here. That does not necessarily mean it was passed at another meeting, but this does raise the question as to the nature of the assembly at which the decrees for choregoi were proposed. At least one deme, Myrrhinous, is known to have held a meeting following, and concerning, its Dionysia (**R**) as was the practice in the city (**I Aix**). Ackermann (2018, 119) plausibly suggests that the decision to award these men crowns worth 100 drachmas (l. 6), rather than what looks more like the (generous) Aixonean 'norm' of 500 (as in **Diii** of the same year, **Dii** and probably **Di**), may be because this was a year when a particularly large number of awards were made by the deme.

Dv: Deme Decree Honouring *Syndikoi*, Judicial Assistants to the Demarch, second half of the 4th c. (by letter forms: Ackermann 2018, 103–4).

Stele of white marble, broken at the top and right; rough-worked to the rear, suggesting it was probably erected against a wall (Ackermann 2018, 101).

1.18 × 0.435–0.49 × 0.08–0.095 m.

Found at Pirnari 'aus den Ruinen des alten Demos Aixone im jetzigen Prinari, halbwegs zwischen Trachones und Vari' (Lolling 1879, 193). Lolling goes on to note that the stones (including **Dii**, *IG* II² 1196 = Ackermann 2018 no. 8 and *IG* II² 2664 = Ackermann 2018 no. 13) had been transported to a small collection in the courtyard of the property Komninos, ex-Louriotis, at Trachones. Athens NM Kar. 1205.

Lolling 1879, 195–8 no. 2; *IG* II 584d; *IG* II² 1197 + Add. p. 672; Ackermann 2018, 101–7 no. 1.

Text: based on Ackermann.   Photo: Ackermann 2018, 547 Fig. 15.

```
- - - - - - - - - - - - - - - - - - - - - - -      stoich. 24
      Α[. . . . . . . . . . . . .23 . . . . . . . . . . .]
      ς Γλα?[. . . . . . . . .19 . . . . . . . . . σ]-
      θενην [. . . . . . . . . .19 . . . . . . . .]
      ίδην Κα[. . . . . . . . .18 . . . . . . . .]
5     ν Φιλοθή[ρου τε καὶ τοὺς αὐτοῖ]-
      ς συνακο[λουθοῦντας. . . .7. . .]
      την Ἀντιχ[α . . . . . . .15. . . . . . . .]
      Καλλίου, Γο[ργ. . . . .12. . . . . . Λ]-
```

εωφιλον Εὐδί[κου, καλεῖν δὲ ? αὐτο]-
10   ὺς εἰς τὴν προε[δρίαν τὸν δήμα]-
ρχον τὸν ἀεὶ δημ[αρχοῦντα καὶ]
εἶναι αὐτοῖς τὰς αὐτὰς [δωρεὰ]-
ς ὅσαιπερ καὶ τοῖς συνδίκοι[ς]
τοῖς περὶ Λάχητα ὅσαι κατὰ το-
15   ὺς νόμους δέδονται· ἵνα καὶ οἱ
ἄλλοι φιλοτιμῶνται εἰδότες
ὅτι χάριτας ἀπολήψονται παρ-
ὰ τῶν δημοτῶν, ἀναγράψαι δὲ τόδε τὸ ψήφισμα εἰς στήλην λιθί-
20   νην Φιλόθηρον τὸν δήμαρχον ᵛ
καὶ στῆσαι ἐν τῶι θεάτρωι. ᵛᵛᵛ
       vacat 0.10 m
       ivy crown

[(trace remains of two lines) …]s Glau(?)[-… …-s]thenes [son of …-]ides son of
Ka[-… ⁵ son of] Philothe[ros and thei]r assis[tants …-]tes son of Antich[a … son
of] Kallias, Go[rg-… son of … L]eophilos son of Eudi[kos, and that the dema]rch
in office should [invite th]em ¹⁰ to prohe[dria and] that they should have all
the same [award]s as have been given by ¹⁵ law to the *syndikoi* with Laches. In
order that others might also strive for honour in the knowledge that they will
receive favours from the demesmen, Philotheros the demarch is to have this
decree inscribed on a ²⁰ stone stele and erected in the theatre.

Despite the loss of the start of this decree and most of its long list of eight names, with
patronymics (ll. 1–9), it clearly honoured the listed four men '[and thei]r assis[tants]',
also four in number. From the specification in ll. 12–15 that they are 'to have all the same
[award]s as have been given by law to the *syndikoi* with Laches' (and it is worth noting in
passing that the demes, like the city, could pass laws controlling the nature and extent of
honours that could be publically awarded) it has been unanimously deduced that the present honorands were themselves a group of *syndikoi*. *Syndikoi*, attested in the city of Athens
and at the deme level only here in Aixone (also in *IG* II² 1196, A ll. 17–19, Ackermann
2018, 216–34 no. 8), had a variety of (para-)legal roles (Rubinstein 2000; Ackermann
2018, 105–6). It is highly likely that the son of the current demarch Philotheros was among
those honoured (ll. 4–5, 20; Ackermann 2018, 106), offering a further insight into one of
the motivations for the decree.

What these other awards were we can only guess – public praise is likely, a crown
certain, given the one carved below the text. So far as we can judge it looks as though
only the current *syndikoi* and their assistants are to receive the special grant of prohedria
described in ll. 9–11, notable for its award for life and the extra honour of being invited to
one's place by the demarch each year (as in **Bvii 2**, **Hvii**, **Ki**, **Vv**; see also **Iii**). But even if
it is eight rather than sixteen demesmen who have been so honoured, we can at a minimum
deduce that the prohedria of the Aixone theatre was sufficiently large to accommodate such
a group, in addition to no doubt various others who held prohedria by grant or *ex officio*.

E | Anagyrous

Introduction

The southern coastal deme of Anagyrous (bouleutic quota 6) has been securely identified with the site of the modern town of Vari, situated on a small and fertile plain (Traill 1986, 145; Marchiandi 2011, 615–16; Bultrighini 2015, 27–38). The evidence for a lively theatrical Dionysia, with contests in both tragedy and comedy, consists of three inscriptions, spanning a period of well over a century (ca. 440–300, but note the debate on the dating of **Ei**). The deme probably had its own theatre (below and **Eiii**) and it was there, rather than in the city, that the Anagyrasian choregoi known from two dedications (**Ei**; **Eii**) saw their teams perform – one of them under the direction of Euripides (**Ei**). An unpublished inscription from the area of Anagyrous was announced in 2005 (*Eleftherotypia* 12 August 2005; *AR* 52, 2005–2006, 12) and said to refer to a performance of Euripides, supported by a demarch named Theophilos as choregos. We suspect that this is a garbled combined reference to **Ei** and *IG* II³ 4, 238, the latter a dedication by one Theophilos to commemorate his service as demarch. But if a new inscription as reported does exist and reveals that Theophilos was choregos while serving as demarch, the performance can only have been at the local Dionysia which it was his responsibility to organise. A fourth, nugatory inscription, consisting entirely of the word ἐδίδασκε 'was the didaskalos' (*IG* II³ 4, 517) was assigned by Makres (1994) to Anagyrous, but its findspot in Ano Voula is more consistent with the territory of Halai Aixonides (**J**; Eliot 1962, 31; Goette 2014, 100–1 thinks of Aixone). Goette has made the important point that, in nineteenth-century usage, 'Vari' comprised a much larger region than its modern equivalent, and included an area that is likely to have been within the ancient demes of Halai Aixonides and Aixone. He argues further that the theatre at the Pirnari gorge (**D Introduction**) served a broad region at the southern tip of Mt. Hymettos comprising the demes of Aixone, Halai Aixonides, Anagyrous and perhaps even Aigilia. We consider it more likely that these demes chose to hold their Dionysia in their own territories. And we may possess some evidence for the existence of a theatre in Anagyrous itself (Lauter 1993, 82–4; Bultrighini 2015, 84). In the late nineteenth century Milchhöfer (1888, 361 no. 766) reported finding a marble chair in front of a private home in Korbi, which lies in the eastern zone of the plain of Vari. The chair (the dimensions and present whereabouts of which are unknown) was inscribed as a dedication '[A]rcheneos son of Archemachos dedicated this' [Ἀ]ρχένεως Ἀρχεμάχου | ἀνέθηκεν (*IG* II² 4906). The findspot adds further weight to the identification of the site of the deme Anagyrous, since the dedicant has been securely identified as the 'Archeneos son of Archemachos of Anagyrous' who appears in the tribal dedication *IG* II² 2825, l. 1, dated to around the middle of the fourth century, which is the dating given to the inscribed chair from Anagyrous. Milchhöfer noted that the dedicatory inscription was placed 'between the feet in relief' ('Zwischen den in Relief ausgeführten Füssen'), which further suggests a chair of the type employed as prohedria in deme theatres, and indeed made the object of dedication in the Rhamnus theatre (**W Introduction**; **Wi**) and perhaps elsewhere. As Bultrighini (2015, 50) notes, the most likely place for the theatre and sanctuary of Dionysus in Anagyrous is in the region of the Agioi Pantes church, into the altar of which **Eii**, the dedication to Dionysus following a victory in comedy, was built. Moreover the tragic choregic dedication **Ei**, of substantial size and weight, was found some 200 m distant and is perhaps unlikely to have travelled far from its original home. If this is so, it is noteworthy that there was a major necropolis in the area, affording a parallel for the situation with the Thorikos theatre (**Y Introduction**). A funerary monument from a graveyard in Anagyrous (dated ca. 380–370), which depicts a costumed choreut contemplating a mask (**V E**), advertises the commitment of the deceased to the civic duty of choral performance and the status that it brought. Although the motif is quite widespread, it is striking that we find an example of it in the deme that has also left us a unique testimony to a locally recruited tragic chorus (**Ei**).

Ei: Choregic Dedication, ca. 440–431 or ca. last decade of the 5th c. (by letter forms and prosopography).

Quadrangular marble base, with two fittings (ca. 0.07 m deep) on the upper surface for the feet of a statue (the right with some traces of lead).
0.32 × 0.52 × 0.58 m.
Found in Varkiza in the coastal area known as Ἁλμύρα (very probably ancient Anagyrous: Mitsos 1965, 163; Bultrighini 2015, 42–3).
Athens EM 13180.
Mitsos 1965 (= *SEG* 23, 102); *IG* I³ 969.
Text: *IG* I³ 969 with autopsy.   Photos: Mitsos 1965, pls. 45–6; Wilson 2000, 132.

1	Σωκράτης ἀνέθηκεν	stoich.
	Εὐριπίδης ἐδίδασκε	
	τραγωιδοί	Ἀμφίδημος
	Πύθων	Εὐθύδικος
5	Ἐχεκλῆς	Λυσίας

Μενάλκης	Σῶν
Φιλοκράτης	Κριτόδημος
Ἔχυλλος	Χαρίας
Μέλητος	Φαίδων
10 Ἐμπορίων	*vacat*
vacat	

Sokrates dedicated this. Euripides was the didaskalos. *Tragoidoi*: Python, Echekles, Menalkes, Philokrates, Echyllos, Meletos, Emporion, Amphidemos, Euthydikos, Lysias, Son, Kritodemos, Charias, Phaidon

This monument gives us the only surviving roll-call of a tragic chorus. It was found in the territory of the deme Anagyrous and its dedicator, Sokrates, is probably the prominent Anagyrasian general in the Samian war 441/0 (Androtion *FGrH* 324 F 38) who, alongside Pericles and Thucydides son of Melesias, was a candidate for ostracism in 443 (Thompson 1950, 337). The dedication consisted of a bronze statue, somewhat smaller than (adult) life size. This is perhaps more likely to have been an image of the god Dionysus than, for instance, a member of the performing team. Although lacking any part of the verb 'to be a choregos' (χορηγεῖν), there can be little doubt that Sokrates was the choregos of a production by Euripides (cf. the similar use of the verb ἀνέθηκεν alone of a choregos in the urban dedication from the Thargelia of similar date, *IG* I³ 964). The fact that there is no explicit marker of victory need not preclude an agonistic context (evidenced by **Eii**; **Eiii**).

Dated by Lewis (*IG* I³) to the decade before the Peloponnesian War, this is among the earliest surviving choregic dedications. It is also early in the career of Euripides, the year of whose first entry at the City Dionysia is reported as 455, that of his first victory, 442/1 (*TrGF* T 55–6). This production in Anagyrous may date not long after the latter. While this early date is generally accepted, an alternative view of the letter forms (and prosopography) places it near the end of the fifth century (Mitsos 1965, 164; Matthaiou 1990–1991, 181). Most recently, Millis (2015, 231–2) has made the case that Lewis' dating rested too heavily on the identification of Sokrates as the general in the Samian war and that the lettering places the dedication in the last decade of the fifth century. On this view Sokrates would be the homonymous grandson of the general (*APF* 497) and Euripides is found performing in Anagyrous towards the end rather than the beginning of his career in Athens.

A key point of debate (as also for **Eii**) has been whether the performance commemorated took place locally (Csapo 2004, 60–1; Lewis in *DFA*² 361); or in the city, with the choregos electing to commemorate it back in his home deme (Mitsos 1965, 167; Whitehead 1986a, 220, cf. 234). A local event is much more probable, if not certain. The case for the alternative rests heavily on *a priori* assumptions about the likely – inferior – quality of theatre at deme Dionysia. In her attempt to reconcile a belief that Euripides would not have appeared in Anagyrous with the site of dedication, Ghiron-Bistagne (1976, 120) was led to hypothesise a separate dedication in the city, for which there is no evidence (nor even for the practice of making such double dedications). But there is good reason to believe that Euripides travelled around – and beyond – Attica to produce his work (**Vi**), and the verb ἐδίδασκε 'was the didaskalos' implies that he was present in person at Anagyrous as the director in this case. There is at least no certain instance where it means anything else. The possible evidence of an unpublished inscription may provide a second example of the production of work by Euripides himself in Anagyrous (but see the doubts registered above, **E Introduction**).

In the 430s we might expect the word *tragoidoi* (τραγωιδοί l. 3) to refer to members of a tragic chorus, although there are signs of an idiom developing at least later in the century by which the word could be used to refer to 'tragic performers' or 'performances of tragedy' more generally (**V E**). If the rubric '*Tragoidoi*' refers only to tragic choreuts, the monument apparently omits any reference to the actors. The probable reason is that they were professionals brought into the deme to work with a local chorus. The absence of demotics very strongly suggests that the *tragoidoi* were all locals, and the attestation of a second Anagyrasian with the exceedingly rare name 'Son' (cf. l. 6) guarantees it (*SEG* 41, 191). Note also Milanezi's (2004 II, 265) suggestion that the choreut Euthydikos (l. 4) may be the Anagyrasian who appears early in the fourth century as Εὐθ[ύ...]ος 'Euth[y...]os' on a tribal list (*IG* II² 2366, l. 31), where at l. 29 she would also propose restoring the name of his fellow *tragoidos* (l. 7 above) [Φιλο]κράτης '[Philo]krates' instead of Kirchner's [Πολυ]κράτης '[Poly]krates'. The monument thus becomes a revealing expression of the intimate relationship that existed between a choregos and his chorus, and equally of the divide that separated the more professionalised and mobile actors from the locally recruited choral group.

The question of the meaning of τραγωιδοί is closely tied to that of the number of choreuts we should expect to find in a fifth-century tragic chorus. Doubt has recently been cast on the tradition that reports a 'post-Sophoclean' standard of fifteen choreuts in a tragic chorus (**V E**). Sansone (2016) argues that the increase in the number of actors ascribed to Sophocles from two to three helped to generate a claimed (but poorly motivated) increase in the size of the chorus by the same number (i.e. three), from twelve to fifteen – a confusion fed by the fact that τραγωιδός could refer to both choreuts and actors. Sansone suggests that the increase to fifteen never in fact took place, and that here in Anagyrous the fourteen *tragoidoi* may be three actors plus eleven choreuts, with Sokrates serving as the *koryphaios* (below), or two actors plus twelve choreuts, since plays like Euripides' *Medea* or *Alcestis* only required two (Sansone 2016, 245). In either case, the urban norm (of twelve choreuts) is according to this view observed. Given the virtual certainty that all those listed were demesmen, we would on this scenario find the deme providing the entire cast needed for the production, actors as well as choreuts. This seems somewhat unlikely, and is one reason to doubt Sansone's theory. We tend to think it more likely that the number of tragic choreuts was always fifteen (Taplin 1977, 323; **V E**).

If as we think likely *tragoidoi* here means 'tragic choreuts', we must ask why only fourteen are listed. A few outrider sources claim the number of tragic choreuts as fourteen (**V E**). If not dismissed outright, such evidence could be accommodated with a fifteen-choreut standard by assuming that the leader has been excluded from the tally. It is at any rate unlikely that the city norm was mandatory for a deme festival, so the presence of fourteen names in Anagyrous may require no special pleading. That said, it is also plausible that for reasons of pride and practicality (or perhaps we might say choreographic familiarity) we might expect the familiar norm to have been maintained (**Miii**; **Mxi**; **V F** on Athens

NM 2400). In that case, the absent fifteenth name is likely to be that of the leader of the chorus or *koryphaios*. The leader may have been a paid operative rather than a volunteer, who could sometimes also serve as a specialist choral trainer or *chorodidaskalos* (**V J**). As a result he was not conceptually part of the chorus, at least not to the extent that he featured in the lasting forms of public recognition. Alternative explanations proposed are that Euripides himself may have been the 'missing' fifteenth choreut (his dancing skills are implied by *TrGF* T 33b: Fisher 2003, 208 n. 80); or that the choregos Sokrates served in his own chorus (Wilson 2000, 133).

Eii: Choregic Dedication, after ca. 350 (by letter forms).

Quadrangular block of white marble.
0.15 × 0.71 × 0.40 m.
Found built into altar of the church of Agioi Pantes, near the modern town of Vari (ancient Anagyrous), where it remains.
IG II 1285; *IG* II² 3101; *CEG* II, 773; *IG* II³ 4, 507; Bultrighini 2015, 48–50.
Text: based on *IG* II³ 4, 507 and photograph of squeeze in BBAW. Photo: *IG* II³ 4,1 tab. LXVIII (squeeze).

> [*Name of dedicant and possibly also of his father appeared elsewhere on part of the monument, now lost*]

1   ἡδυγέλωτι χορῶι Διονύσια σύμ ποτε ἐν[ίκα],   non-stoich.
    μνημόσυνον δὲ θεῶι νίκης τόδε δῶρον [ἔθηκεν],
    δήμωι μὲν κόσμον, ζῆλον πατρὶ κισσοφο[ροῦντι]·
    τοῦδε δὲ ἔτι πρότερος στεφανηφόρον [εἷλεν ἀγῶνα].

1 σύμ from squeeze   σ[ύ]μ Keil, Kaibel, Wilamowitz, Hansen   ἐν[ίκα] Keil, Kaibel, Wilamowitz, Hansen   Διονύσια Σ[ῖ]μ[ος ἐνίκα] Keil   ἐν[ίκων] Köhler, Preuner apud Kirchner   2 [ἔθηκεν] Keil, Kaibel, Hansen   [ἔθηκε] Wilamowitz   [ἔθηκαν] Köhler   [ἔθηκα] Preuner apud Kirchner   3 κισσοφορ[οῦντι] Kaibel, Hansen   4 [εἷλεν] Keil, Hansen   [εἷλον] Preuner apud Kirchner   [εἷλετ'] Kaibel, Köhler   [ἦλθ' ἐς] Wilamowitz

> [He] was once vic[torious] at the Dionysia with a chorus of sweet laughter,
> and [he set up] this gift to the god as a memorial of the victory,
> an adornment for the deme, a spur to emulation for his father, wearing ivy.
> Even before him did [he take] the crown-bearing [contest].

The site where this stone was discovered in secondary use, close to an ancient necropolis of the deme, is now generally thought to indicate an origin for the dedication in Anagyrous (rather than Aixone: Papagiannopoulos-Palaios 1929a, 165; cf. Mitsos 1965, 166; Bultrighini 2015, 50). Its four hexameter verses are a rare example of a choregic inscription in poetic form (**Yi**; **V C** on *IG* I³ 833 bis). The loss of the ends of the lines, and with them virtually all of the three main verbs, adds to the puzzles of interpretation. It certainly commemorates a victory (ἐν[ίκα] 'was … vic[torious]' l. 1, the [ἀγῶνα] 'contest' of l. 4 virtually certain) at a Dionysia, in comedy. The currency of the adjective with which it begins – ἡδυγέλως 'of sweet laughter' – as an epithet for the genre is guaranteed by its appearance as a qualifier of κωμωιδία 'comedy' itself on the gravestone of the contemporary comic actor (or poet?) Euthias (**V D**). The victory was doubtless choregic; only choregoi win 'with choruses'. The absence of any reference to actors or poet expresses a similar focus on the chorus in this memorial, as is likely in the older tragic dedication (**Ei**).

The (poetic) placement of the preposition σύν 'with' after the noun it governs, 'a chorus of sweet laughter', has misled some into construing it in tmesis with the following verb, and so to postulate synchoregia: 'he was joint victor' (συνενίκα) or 'they were joint victors' (συνενίκων), rather than 'he was victorious with a comic chorus' (ἐνίκα σὺν ἡδυγέλωτι χορῶι). Despite a cogent rebuttal by Wilamowitz (1930, 242–3) this view has not altogether vanished. And while it remains possible that the verb was a third-person plural (ἐν[ίκων]) rather than a third- (or first-) person singular, and that plural verbs could be restored in ll. 2 and 4 (ἔθηκαν, εἷλον), assuming a team of brothers, on this scenario it is very difficult to produce a cogent interpretation of the last line, and restorations that reflect a singular victor are preferable. And third- rather than first-persons are best throughout – the norm when, as here, the name of the dedicant was given elsewhere on the monument rather than in the epigram itself (Hansen *CEG* II, 185).

With a nice chiastic touch, the monument is conceived both as a record of the victory (μνημόσυνον … νίκης) and as a gift for the god (θεῶι … τόδε δῶρον). This conception of choregic dedications as gifts to the gods is not widespread in Attica, and largely confined to demes (Wilson 2000, 249). The deictic τόδε *'this* gift' makes it clear that the monument included some object, probably a statue (as in **Ei**) or other artwork. Line 3 bears closely and definitively on the argument as to where this victory was won, deme or city. It proceeds to gloss 'this gift' as both 'an adornment for the deme', and 'a spur to emulation for his father'. The monument, with its artwork, is evidently 'an adornment to the deme' by virtue of its very dedication there, probably near the theatre or sanctuary of Dionysus. The view that this phrase shows that the victory was won in the city, because 'such "honor for the deme" … can only have been won outside it' (Whitehead 1986a, 234; also Körte 1935, 634) misconstrues the close grammatical connection between ll. 2 and 3 by making 'adornment' refer loosely back to the victory of l. 1. There is thus no reason to treat this as an urban victory and all presumption points the other way (thus Reisch 1899b, 2419; Brinck 1906, 36). The expression testifies rather to the pride of the man who has thus quite physically 'adorned' his local theatre.

Further puzzles remain. As interpreted in the translation above, the monument is also described as 'a spur to emulation for his father, wearing ivy', implying that the dedicating choregos has won a victory before his own father had done so. The point is worthy of special note since it goes against the grain of all ordinary expectations about the appropriate dynamics of achievement by males of adjacent generations: fathers set the standard for sons. In other words, the son uses the occasion of his victory to take a playful swipe at the father he has outshone (Wilson 2000, 247–8). However the father is himself now 'wearing ivy'. This is very likely to mean 'is wearing the crown of a Dionysiac victor', so it appears that he too has won a victory, subsequent to that of his son (the time necessarily implied by that helping to explain the otherwise unusually vague ποτε 'once' of the son's victory l. 1). The monument in effect commemorates both, though this would entail a slight but entirely acceptable illogicality that sees the monument, envisaged as itself a spur to choregic activity, come into existence only once the father is wearing the victorious choregos' ivy.

But it is also possible to read the inscription as in fact depicting the more normative situation in which the father wins a victory before the son (and for epigraphic parallels see *IG* II³ 4, 545, ll. 4–7; Paus. 6.1.7). This turns on taking the τοῦδε 'him' of l. 4 as referring to the dedicating son, and the sense becomes 'Even before him (= the son) did he (= the father) take the crown-bearing [contest].' On this reading the force of ἔτι is less clear – why stress that the father did it 'even' earlier than the son? This interpretation also requires us to understand ζῆλον (l. 3) in a different, less conflictual sense, though this is less difficult, since it has an inherently ambivalent meaning – 'cause for envy/cause for pride' (LSJ s.v. II for the latter). Further grounds for such a meaning can be found in an inscription of this era on a Macedonian public monument in Delphi, *SEG* 18, 222B, l. 3 (= *CEG* II, 877), which uses, of a father's attitude to his son's agonistic successes, the equivalent verb (ζηλοῦται) not in the sense of 'envy' or 'vie with', but 'admire' or 'praise'.

For the restored phrase in l. 4 'to take the contest' = 'to win a victory' (αἱρεῖν ἀγῶνα), Kirchner compared a third-century inscription from Tanagra, *IG* VII 530, ll. 3–4: ἄλλους τε ἀθλοφόρους πτανοῖς ποσὶν εἷλον ἀγῶνας.

Eiii: Honorific Deme Decree, ca. 325–300 (by letter forms).

> Fragment of 'Hymettan' marble.
> 0.11 × 0.135 × 0.05 m.
> Found in 'Vari' village. Since in nineteenth-century usage 'Vari' encompassed a much larger region than its modern equivalent, this may not refer to the territory of ancient Anagyrous (Matthaiou 1992–1998; Goette 2014, 91).
> *IG* II 576; *IG* II² 1210.
> Text: *IG* II² 1210.

```
        [— — — — — — — — — — — — — ἐπεμελήθη δὲ κ]-    non-stoich. ca. 40
1       αἰ τῆς φυλακ[ῆς — — — — — — — — — — — κα]-
        λῶς καὶ φιλο[τίμως, ἐπαινέσαι — — — — καὶ στεφαν]-
        ῶσαι θαλλοῦ σ[τεφάνωι — — — — — — — — —]
        εἶναι δὲ αὐτῶ[ι καὶ προεδρίαν τραγωιδῶν τῶι ἀγ]-
5       ῶνι ὅταν ποιῶ[σι τὰ Διονύσια καὶ καλείτω αὐτὸν ὁ δή]-
        μαρχος εἰς τὴ[ν προεδρίαν — — — — — — — — —]
        ΝΚΛΗ
```

[… and since he a]lso [supervised] the garris[on … in a f]ine and ambit[ious manner, it was decided to praise him for … and to crow]n him with a cr[own] of olive leaves […]; and to give hi[m prohedria at the con]test [of tragedies] ⁵ whenever they hol[d the Dionysia; and the de]march [is to summon him] to his [prohedria …]

The findspot of this fragmentary decree makes it possible (but no more: see above) that the demesmen awarding honours were Anagyrasioi, and therefore that in the late fourth century this deme held spectacles at which prohedria could be awarded. Though extensive, the restorations of ll. 4–6 are basically secure. The award of prohedria at a contest, with invitation to his place by the demarch, whenever a festival – surely the Dionysia – is held, all seem certain. But one might not quite share Whitehead's confidence (1986a, 220) that the restoration of 'tragedies' τραγωιδῶν in l. 4 is also 'inescapable'. Given that the inscription is non-stoichedon, 'comedies' κωμωιδῶν might at least be a possibility for the type of contest (l. 4). But both comedy and tragedy are otherwise attested for the deme, though the evidence is spread over a long period (**Ei**; **Eii**) and one might suppose that in a case such as this where the programme of a deme's Dionysia is known to have included both dramatic genres, tragedy is the more likely event for the proclamation of honours (**H Introduction**). While the surviving inscription does not specifically mention a theatre, the availability of prohedria implies that Anagyrous had one.

The honorand seems to have performed some service in connection with the garrison (l. 2) in this coastal deme (Whitehead 1986a, 401; for possible remains see Lauter-Bufe 1979). There is no indication that the honours were in any way connected with service to the theatre and Lasagni (2004, 107) reasonably supposes he was a peripolarch or officer in charge of a frontier garrison.

? Choregic Dedication, Possibly Theatrical, ca. mid 4th c. (based on letter forms).

> Fragment of a quadrangular block of white marble, broken at both ends; moulding on upper edge.
> 0.12 × 0.51 × 0.15 m.
> Found built into the Church of Ag. Athanasios, Marousi, where it remains.
> *IG* II² 3057; *SEG* 51, 193; *IG* II³ 4, 511.
> Text: based on *IG* II³ 4, 511.   Photos: Palles 2000–2003, pls. 22–3; Goette 2014 fig. 2.16;
> *IG* II³ 4,1 tab. LXIX.

1   [- - - -]ͅιος ηὔλει.
     [- - - -]: Μειδ[ο]γένης ἐδημάρχει.

1 [- - - -]ͅοιος or [- - - -]ͅθιος Palles   2 ἐ[δίδασκ]ε Curtius

[...-]ios was the piper. [...]. Meidogenes was demarch.

The few surviving words of this inscription constitute the only possible evidence for a theatrical festival in the Attic deme of Athmonon (bouleutic quota 6). It certainly shows that performances were held in the deme that required the services of a piper (l. 1). The fact that his name was recorded in this monumental form shows that the event was of some grandeur and significance. The same is implied by the likely scale of the original monument of which this formed part: it must have been considerably wider than the surviving block, probably well over a metre, and the presence of moulding at the top suggests that it may have formed part of an architrave (faint traces of the bottom of the block may be visible, too, which suggest that its full depth was 0.51 m). The moulding also shows that there cannot have been any lines inscribed above l. 1.

The use of the imperfect ηὔλει 'was the piper' calls to mind the numerous fourth-century choregic dedications relating to victories in dithyramb won at the City Dionysia which record the name of the piper (e.g. *IG* II³ 4, 441; 447; 449; 453; 460; 471). This led Curtius to restore the verb known from such inscriptions ἐ[δίδασκ]ε 'was the trainer' in l. 2, and indeed to classify it as a choregic inscription from the city festival. Following the rediscovery of the stone, the reading ἐδημάρχει 'was demarch' is beyond doubt, and proves that the event in question was at the deme, not the polis, level. Palles (followed by Makres) continues to think that it probably refers to a Dionysia of the deme, organised by its demarch, whose name remains associated with the festival of his year in office. This is certainly possible, but on balance, the festival is perhaps more likely to be the one for which Athmonon was best known, the Amarysia held in honour of Artemis – no less spectacular, according to Pausanias (1.31.5), than the more famous event for Artemis held at Amarynthos near Eretria on the island of Euboea. A contest in pyrrhic dance was the most important event of the Eretrian festival (*IG* XII 9, 237, ll. 21–3) and the agon of the Athmonian Amarysia was evidently the most important cultural event at which the deme gathered, for it was the occasion on which benefactors were honoured (*IG* II² 1203, l. 17). Nothing is directly known of the character of this agon, but it was probably in pyrrhic dance (Ceccarelli 1998, 86), which was often performed to the music of pipes. Indeed the piper doubtless played a significant role in directing the pyrrhiche, in which mimetic dance, rather than lyrics, was paramount. This would be consistent with the presence of the piper's name on this inscription.

Whether Amarysia or Dionysia is meant, the inclusion of the name of the demarch might open the possibility that this was not a single choregic dedication but some sort of public record of past performances (and their choregoi?), of a type possibly seen in Thorikos (**Yiii**).

G | Brauron

Scholion to Aristophanes, *Peace* 874b. Text: Holwerda.

> Βραυρῶναδ᾽· πόρνη γάρ. ἐν Βραυρῶνι δὲ δήμῳ τῆς Ἀττικῆς πολλαὶ πόρναι. ἐκεῖ δὲ καὶ τὰ Διονύσια ἤγετο - ὡς καθ᾽ ἕκαστον δῆμον - ἐν οἷς ἐμέθυον· μεθύοντες δὲ πολλὰς πόρνας ἥρπαζον.

> 'To Brauron': because she is a prostitute. In Brauron, an Attic deme, there were many prostitutes. And a Dionysia was also conducted there – as in every deme – at which people got drunk; and in their drunkenness they picked up many prostitutes.

No theatre, shrine or temple of Dionysus is known in Brauron, but it appears, from the manner in which he was depicted on a circular altar from the site decorated with reliefs, that he had a place there in association with the cult of Artemis (Brauron Museum Inv. NE 1177, ca. 400; *SEG* 54, 330; Despinis 2004a; 2010, 85–103). This shows him arriving in procession at the sanctuary, represented by Artemis, Apollo and Leto. Hermes leads the way, with the Seasons, Charites and Nymphs in attendance, as well as a Silenos (inscribed [Σι]λη[νός], Despinis 2004a, 54). The fact that, among the scores of offerings recorded for Artemis from the Brauronion, a Nikoboule dedicated a new coverlet that depicted Dionysus pouring a libation, also tends in the same direction (*IG* II² 1514, ll. 30–2; *IG* II² 1515, ll. 22–4; *IG* II² 1516, ll. 10–11; **Kii**).

However the existence of a Dionysia in Brauron with theatrical performances must be considered very doubtful. The sole testimony to it inspires no confidence. Nor is it clear who would have organised such a festival. The settlement of Brauron, on the east coast of Attica, a few kilometres south of Halai Araphenides and north of Steiria, was not a deme (as also claimed by Str. 9.1.21). Its important sanctuary of Artemis was under the control of the polis; likewise its festival, the Brauronia, at which Athenian girls 'played the bear' (Ar. *Lys.* 644–5), and which was celebrated with grandeur every fourth year under the direction of a board of Athenian *hieropoioi* (Arist. *Ath.* 54.7). The event included a performance of the *Iliad* by rhapsodes (Hsch. β 1067; West 2010, 6). The community of Brauron is unlikely to have had the infrastructure to hold a theatrical Dionysia and it is extremely unlikely that the polis authorities who ran the sanctuary supported a Dionysia in addition to the Brauronia. Brauron was in the territory of the deme Philaidai, and one might suppose that that deme could have run the Dionysia, in some way using infrastructure in the Brauron area – and thus explaining why the Aristophanic scholion speaks of a Dionysia at Brauron rather than in Philaidai. But if the reference to a Dionysia in this area is more than a pure speculative fiction from the scholiast, a more plausible alternative is to suppose that the Dionysia of the neighbouring deme of Halai Araphenides has been misidentified as held at

Brauron. The fact that Dionysus was associated with Artemis at both sites could have promoted such confusion. And the Dionysia of Halai was evidently held in a theatre that was shared with Artemis and her festival, the Tauropolia (**Ki**; Brulé 1987, 310–13).

The line under comment sees Trygaeus' slave, shown the lovely Theoria, recall how they used to 'bang her all the way to Brauron after a few drinks' (874). He subsequently comments on her 'great quadrennial arse' (876). The note contains a demonstrably false assertion (Brauron was not a deme). The *theoria* upon which the comic *double entendre* rests is the 'journey to a religious spectacle' out to the eastern coast of Attica at the great quadrennial festival of Artemis, the Brauronia, made by Athenian families, especially those with young girls. But the scholiast betrays complete ignorance of this festival. Instead they have been led it seems by the talk of 'festival spectacle' to think only of Dionysia, which certainly had 'spectacles', but of a rather different sort. The fact that the work in hand was a comedy, itself the product of a Dionysia – and one moreover which revels in Dionysiac festive metatheatricality (Hall 2006, ch. 11) – will only have promoted the scholarly misdirection. When, earlier in the play, Trygaeus first caught the scent of Theoria he smelt, among other things, 'harvest-time, entertaining, Dionysia, pipes, tragedies, songs by Sophocles' (529–31). The further comments generated by Theoria's 'quadrennial arse' τὴν πρωκτοπεντετηρίδα (Sch. Ar. *Peace* 876) likewise reveal ignorance of the Brauronia. Sch. Ar. *Peace* 876a weakly glosses: 'because the spectacles (θεωρίαι) of the Dionysia were conducted on a four-yearly cycle'. The quadrennial cycle, never otherwise attested for a Dionysia, is that of the Brauronia.

The phrase 'as in every deme' ὡς καθ' ἕκαστον δῆμον has been added to show the grounds of inference that there was a Dionysia, viz.: Brauron is a deme; all demes had Dionysia; therefore Brauron had a Dionysia. It reveals that the scholiast had no independent information about a Dionysia held at Brauron but was reasoning from false premises. The assertion about prostitutes looks like little more than feeble extrapolation from the comic scene, perhaps fed by references elsewhere in comedy to the attendants of Artemis and, like the Aristophanic image of Theoria herself, fed too by the symbolic association of this coastal region and its cults with burgeoning young female sexuality, and a certain license, sexual and sympotic, at its festivals, with their nocturnal gatherings (the latter more especially true of Halai and its Tauropolia: **Ki**).

While the evidence for a Dionysia with theatrical performances held in Brauron is thus weak, the existence of the altar and dedication from the site suggests that Dionysus did receive sacrifice and some form of cult in Brauron. Perhaps the easiest inference is that Brauron was a stop for, if not the end point of, a Dionysian parade (*pompe*). Perhaps Philaidai did hold a festival for Dionysus, in association with the sanctuary of Artemis, but it consisted of little more than a parade and sacrifice? Given the similarities in the two cults, one could readily imagine a Dionysian parade that processed between Brauron and Halai. Even so (with Despinis 2004b, 311 and Goette 2014; *contra* Vierneisel and Scholl 2002) we suppose it to be most likely that the dedicatory relief in Munich (**Kii**) representing Dionysus and Artemis approached by a family led by a man holding an aulos, and with five comic masks suspended above them, is to be associated with the cult at Halai, rather than Brauron. Similarly, a (lost) plinth fragment with a comic mask from Brauron that has been interpreted as part of a choregic votive statue (Vierneisel and Scholl 2002, 40, fig. 28) is unlikely to be such (Despinis 2004a, 63).

H | Eleusis

Introduction

To judge by the number of attested liturgical-level families, the deme of Eleusis does not appear to have been particularly prosperous (its wealth index is 1.27, below the average for all demes, 1.39: Osborne 1985, 200; cf. 45). The great wealth generated by the sanctuary of the Two Goddesses remained firmly in Athenian hands. There will however have been considerable knock-on economic benefits for the deme. There was for instance a major festival market at Eleusis, primarily built around the huge numbers of pilgrims attending the Mysteries, but no doubt used for other festivals throughout the year, too (Clinton 2008, 23). Locals will have benefited from this. And more generally, the cosmopolitan character of this large deme (bouleutic quota 11), with its own port, will have encouraged economic migration and enterprise (many metics: Whitehead 1986a, 83–4). This was one of the least provincial of all Attic demes.

The great Panhellenic sanctuary thus doubtless loomed large in the lives of those living in Eleusis, but it had little to do, formally and legally, with the deme. The sanctuary and festival of Dionysus, on the other hand, were extremely important to the deme, and the Eleusinian Dionysia was in some sense the deme's principal festival. It has been described as 'the most renowned such festival in Attica' (Clinton 1992, 124), and if Ikarion and the Piraeus might have objected to such a claim, there is no doubt that it was among the most vigorous and important local Dionysia, surely the most significant in west Attica. Easy access by sea will have helped foster attendance, and not only by Athenians. We know that a number of Thebans made a significant contribution to the Eleusinian Dionysia in the fourth century, as sponsors and, very probably, as performers (**Hii**; **Hiii**). The Eleusinians' Dionysus was sufficiently famous to merit evocation by the chorus of the *Antigone* as 'you who hold sway in the all-welcoming folds of Eleusinian Demeter' (S. *Ant.* 1119–21). While the keynote of the relationship between the Goddess' cult and that of Dionysus seems to have been one of neighbourly independence, there were various kinds of interaction and interconnection between the two, the extent of which is a matter of debate (see esp. Mylonas 1960; Graf 1974, 40–66; see further on **Hii** and **Hv**). Choral performances at the Eleusinian Dionysia could be offered to the trio of Demeter, Kore and Dionysus (**Hii**). Evidence of less verifiable authenticity (Sch. Ar. *Frogs* 343) made of Dionysus the *choreutes* and *exarchos* of the *telete* of the Mysteries. The source goes on to note 'and to be sure there is in Eleusis a *hieron* of Dionysus and the mysteries were celebrated at the Dionysia' ἐν Διονυσίοις ἐτελεῖτο τὰ μυστήρια. This is much more than can be deduced or even hypothesised from the *Frogs*, and in any case that comedy suggests that syncretistic identification of Iakchos and Dionysus was uncontroversial. For their part the Eleusinian religious authorities made a greater or smaller contribution to as many as three of the city festivals of Dionysus, the Lenaea (*IG* II² 1496, ll. 74–5; *IE* 177, l. 244; Arist. *Ath.* 57.1); the Anthesteria (*IE* 177, ll. 266–7; [D.] 59.78) and the (quasi-urban) Dionysia in the Piraeus (*IE* 177, l. 168; **V Introduction**). And – from the other side of the border, as it were – Pindar composed his famous 'second' dithyramb for Dionysus of Thebes that included an account of the transference of the Eleusinian mystery cult from Eleusis to Thebes, a city in which Demeter was effectively the poliadic deity.

Another important cult of the deme was that of Heracles on the Akris (the name given the acropolis of Eleusis), whose sanctuary cannot have been far from the theatre and sanctuary of Dionysus (*IE* 85 with Clinton 2008, 94–6; its precise location on the Akris is not known). A Hellenistic votive relief almost certainly from this sanctuary shows a drinking – and drunken – Heracles reclining and listening to a satyr boy playing the pipes. The strong 'dionysische Aura' (Wolf 1998, 84) of this scene indicates some form of interaction between these two gods' cults, an association which may in turn be related to their co-presence in the religion of the Two Goddesses. It is also possible to point to connections between the two at the level of finance. Some of the same demesmen are found investing in and supporting both (**Hvi**).

The Theatre(s) in Eleusis

The precise site of the Eleusinians' sanctuary and theatre of Dionysus is not known and, given the sorry prospects of Eleusinian archaeology, probably never will be. Reports of two early travellers strongly suggest that it was on the south side of the Akris, on the southern side near its western end (Clinton 2008, 4; Travlos 1988, 139), looking out to sea with a view towards the island of Salamis. In 1765 Chandler (1825, 234) observed, from the port of Eleusis: 'About half a mile from the shore is a long hill, which divides the plain. In the side next the sea are traces of a theatre, and on the top are cisterns cut in the rock.' Chandler's evidence was corroborated by Clarke in 1802 who, describing the plain between the Akris and the sea, recorded: 'and upon this side was the *Theatre* … the form of which may be distinctly traced upon the slope of the hill, near the southern [sc. western] wall leading to the sea' (Clarke 1818, 627). This area is also favoured by the information provided by Lenormant and Pittakis on the findspot of an honorific deme decree mentioning the theatre as the place of its erection (**Hiii** with Clinton 2008, 89). Although it was built into a modern wall, this was found at the foot of the Akris, on the side facing the sea – that is, just where Chandler and Clarke saw the remains of a theatre. This encouraged its excavator in the 1860s, Lenormant, to associate some traces of a few steps carved into rock nearby with the koilon of the theatre. The base of a statue (probably of the god) dedicated to Dionysus by four men in recognition of the fact that they had been crowned by the deme was also found on the south side of the Akris (**Hvi**). Another base (0.6 × 0.6 × 0.3 m), carefully worked in white marble and with a quadrangular tenon in its upper surface (0.4 × 0.4 m), was found nearby, along with various other more or less fragmentary items – including three column bases, the base of a pilaster, a fragment of a cornice and a herm on a rectangular base (Papagiannopoulos-Palaios 1929c). From this assemblage of findings Papagiannopoulos-Palaios deduced the presence of a Dionysion adjacent to the theatre (and given that they emerged when major cement-works were being established on the hillside, there is little reason to suppose that they had been moved there from a different original location). This thus seems very likely to have been the site of the deme theatre of Eleusis, though some doubts remain, for as Clinton (2008, 89) notes, most of the inscriptions of known provenance that were to be set up in the theatre were found on the north, rather than the south, side of the hill of Eleusis. Quarrying of the hill for the cement works has radically altered its morphology since the nineteenth century.

What further knowledge we have of the Eleusis theatre comes entirely from inscriptions. There are more than a dozen testifying to a busy life in the Classical period, with rare evidence of renewed activity in the third and second centuries. The majority of them we owe to the enthusiasm with which the Eleusinians used their theatre as a mechanism for the creation and conferral of honour. Nine honorific decrees survive that make reference to the theatre; a tenth from the later third century was (uniquely) issued by the families with hereditary Eleusinian priesthoods, the Kerykes and Eumolpidai, rather than the deme; and an eleventh shows that the practice continued into the second century. It is also very likely that a number of other fragmentary honorific decrees which have lost the relevant clauses were erected there: **Hvii** is one such (Clinton 2008, 109).

The epigraphic evidence raises the strong and remarkable possibility that there may have been a second theatre at Eleusis, under the control of the Athenian authorities of the sanctuary. There is little doubt when reference is being made to the deme theatre. Two inscriptions dating to the middle of the fourth century speak precisely of 'the theatre of the Eleusinians' τὸ θέατρον τὸ Ἐλευσινίων (**Hiii**; **Hv**). This very precision may suggest a desire to make a distinction from another theatre. There is no other example of a deme describing its theatre in this way, as 'the theatre of the *X-demesmen*'. The use of the locatival dative in a decree from Aixone (**Diii**, ll. 15, 21; see also **Bvii**) comes closest – ἐν τῶι θεάτρωι Αἰξωνῆσιν 'in the theatre at Aixone' – but this is no strong parallel, since it fails to register ownership in the way that the genitive Ἐλευσινίων does.

A third decree (*IE* 99), very probably dated to 319/18, a year of the pro-Macedonian oligarchy in Athens, refers to the same theatre when it speaks of proclaiming honours for the general Derkylos 'in the theatre at Eleusis, at the tragic agon' Ἐλευσῖνι ἐν τῶ|ι θεάτρωι τραγωιδῶν τῶι ἀγῶνι ll. 11–12. These honours include 'prohedria in the deme of the Eleusinians' προεδρίαν ἐν τῶι δήμωι τῶι Ἐλευσινίων ll. 17–18 (an unusual formulation), to which 'the demarch from time to time' is to invite him ll. 18–20. At around the same date a man from the deme Phyle was awarded with 'prohedria in the theatre whenever the demos of Eleusis puts on the Dionysia' εἶναι | [δὲ αὐτῶι καὶ π]ροεδρίαν ἐν τῶ[ι θ|εάτρωι ὅταν τὰ Δι]ονύσια ποε[ῖ ὁ | δῆμος ὁ Ἐλευσίνιω]ν· (**Hx**). This theatre is also to be associated with the Dionysion mentioned in a further decree of the mid fourth century, also as a site to erect honorific decrees (**Hii**, ll. 33–4: Clinton 2008, 88). The services for which honours are being awarded in this decree are intimately associated with the Eleusinian Dionysia and its performances.

The deme theatre appears next in a decree in honour of a Hierophant of ca. 225, issued not by the deme but by the Kerykes and Eumolpidai. This has the myrtle crown announced 'at the traditional agon of the Dionysia, in the theatre at Eleusis' Διονυσίων τῶι πατρίωι ἀγῶνι | Ἐλευσῖνι ἐν τῶι θεάτρωι (*IE* 201, ll. 17–19). Clinton (2008, 259) explains the unusual decision to announce this honour for an official of the sanctuary of the Goddesses at the deme festival by reference to the fact that the honorand was a demesman of Eleusis (and, as it happens, the only Eleusinian priest of the Mysteries attested).

The last and latest occasion on which we hear of the theatre is in a decree in honour of a demarch in (probably) 165/4 (*IE* 229). Having been fulsomely praised in an earlier Athenian polis decree on the same stone for his conduct of and personal contributions to a range of Eleusinian festivals that were evidently under the aegis of the polis, his fellow demesmen decide to honour him for his conduct of their own most important festival, the local Dionysia: '[ap]pointed demarch in the Archon ye[ar] of Pelops he conducted the sacrifices for Dionysus [at the Dionysi]a and arranged the parade (*pompe*) and … ca. 18… and conducted the agon in the theatre which [the Eleusinians] ce[lebrate], showing no lack of [energ]y and ambition [. . τοῖς Δι|ονυσί]οις ἔθυσεν τῶι Διονύσωι καὶ τὴν πομπὴν ἔπεμψεν καὶ τ . . . . ca. 9. . . .|. . . . ca. 9. . . . τον, ἔθηκεν δὲ καὶ τὸν ἀγῶνα ἐν τῶι θεάτρωι, ὃν σ[υντελοῦσιν | Ἐλευσίνιοι σπου]δῆς καὶ φιλοτιμίας οὐθὲν ἐλλείπων. The fact that the Athenian Association of Dionysiac *Technitai* makes no mention of the Eleusinian theatre in the substantial remains of their decree of ca. 76 (*IE* 271; cf. *ATD* I, 123–6; II, 87, 93; Mikalson 1998, 258–9), which mentions among other things the fact that the Association had established its own temenos and altar in Eleusis, suggests to Clinton (2008, 290) that the theatre may have ceased to function by that date.

The possibility that there may have been a second theatre in Eleusis, controlled by the Athenians, rests on the interpretation of two inscriptions of a very different nature from the honorific decrees that record the existence of the theatre of the Eleusinians. The first, dated by Clinton to 354/3, is a contract for the construction of a stoa by the south wall of the sanctuary. In rather technical language appropriate to a detailed bill of works, this stipulates that the contractor 'carry out the earth from the sanctuary and place the stones and pliable rocks in the theatre by the stadion' (*IE* 141, ll. 6–8): καὶ ἐκφορήσαντα τὴν γ|ῆν ἔξω τοῦ ἱεροῦ εἰς τὸ θέατρον τὸ ἐπὶ τοῦ σταδίου τιθέναι το|ὺς λίθους τῆς μαλακῆς πέτρας κτλ. This theatre cannot have been the theatre of Dionysus in the deme of Eleusis, which could surely not have been used thus as a temporary works site by an outside body, at least not without prior permission, of which no mention is made in the contract. It will therefore be a structure controlled by the Athenians – either another theatre; or else θέατρον may here be used to refer to the viewing area of the stadium (thus Philios 1894, 181; Lattermann 1906; Arias 1934, 32–4; Clinton 2008, 132). A closer look at the expression is in order. Much depends on which of its various possible senses of place ἐπί has here – 'upon', 'in', 'at', 'on top of', 'in the direction of' or 'near'. Any of the first three meanings encourages the interpretation of θέατρον as the seating that formed part of the stadium. This is, most recently, the view of Clinton, who suggests (2008, 132) that the instruction in ll. 6–8 is to remove the earth to the 'theatre' precisely in order to build up the embankment for the seating area (τὸ θέατρον) of the stadium.

However, the qualifying phrase τὸ θέατρον τὸ ἐπὶ τοῦ σταδίου seems rather to be used here in order to distinguish this theatron from another – no doubt the deme's own theatron, which was quite possibly only some 200 m distant from the site of the works in question. And we incline strongly to the view (shared also by Goette 2014) that ἐπί is used in the sense of 'in the direction of', 'near', or 'next to'. In that case a theatre as an independent structure must be meant – either in the direction of the stadium, viewed from the point at which the stoa is to be built along the south wall of the sanctuary; or simply near to it. Such a theatre will doubtless have housed the musical contests that formed part of the classical (trieteric and penteteric) Eleusinia, just as the stadium was the site for that important festival's famous gymnastic and hippic events.

The second item of evidence dates to some twenty-five years later. At ca. 330, the authorities of the Eleusinian sanctuary directed and paid workmen to dump bricks and earth from an old tower that had collapsed 'into the theatre' and break it down there to form it into new brick (*IE* 177, ll. 44–6; Clinton 2008, 202–3): εἰς τὸ τεῖχος κατὰ ψήφισμ[α βο]υ[λῆ]ς ἀπὸ τοῦ πύργου τοῦ παλαι|οῦ τοῦ πεσόντος μισθωτοῖς τοῖς τὰς πλίνθους καὶ τὸγ χοῦν ἀπο[φ]ο[ρήσ]ασ[ι] εἰς τὸ θέατρον καὶ βωλοκοπή|σασι, ἀνδράσιν : ΔΔΔ :. Dittenberger (*Syll.*[2] 587) concluded that this was the same theatron mentioned in the earlier contract. This remains preferable to the view of Clinton (2008, 202) who, following the identification of this fallen tower by Noack (1927, 211–14) (at H21 on Clinton's Plan), thinks of the deme theatre of Dionysus, on the south side of the Akris. This would however mean that the workers would have had to carry the brick and earth at least half a kilometre. More problematic than the distance of haulage, however, is the issue of ownership. It is just possible that, in the lapidary language of these accounts, all reference to a pre-existing agreement with the deme to use its theatre as a temporary brickworks may have been omitted; more likely however that this theatre was once more one directly controlled by the Athenians themselves. The stadium is much closer to the tower in question, only some 250 m distant. It is therefore much more likely that Dittenberger was right, and this theatre is the same as the one mentioned in the earlier contract. And the fact that this 'theatre' could be used as a place for this kind of work further suggests that it was indeed an independent structure and not simply the seating (or its supporting embankment) of the stadium.

The securely known history of performances in the Eleusinian deme theatre has a spectacular beginning, with evidence of tragedy and comedy by Sophocles (probably but not certainly the elder) and Aristophanes towards the end of the fifth century, supported by multiple choregoi and run on a competitive format (**Hi**). Clinton (1992, 124–5) discusses iconographic evidence that suggests the existence of an Eleusinian Dionysia as early as the Kleophon Painter (440s–420s), in particular an image on a volute krater (Stanford University Museum 70.12) which shows Dionysus with a Papposilenos labelled *Pom[po]s*, a lyre-playing young woman and a satyr (the other side shows Demeter on the Mirthless Rock and the mission of Triptolemos, with clear topographical markers of the sanctuary). Clinton plausibly identifies a reference to the parade (*pompe*) of the Dionysia and its dramatic performances. We can probably place little, if any, weight on the observation that Eleusis was the home of Aeschylus, or on the fact that it was the setting of some eight known tragedies, including at least two by Aeschylus himself (Stewart 2017, 203). Further evidence for comedy appears around the middle of the fourth century (**Hiv**), but tragedy has the higher profile throughout. In one case the tragic agon is mentioned (*IE* 99, l. 11); more commonly the expression used to specify the moment for the proclamation of honorific crowns is simply 'at the tragedies' (**Hii**; **Hv**; *IE* 80, ll. 15–16; *IE* 68, ll. 2–3 [restored]). The variants 'at the agon of the Dionysia' (*IE* 84, l. 10 partly restored: τῶι ἀγ[ῶνι τῶν Διονυσίων]) and 'at the traditional agon of the Dionysia' (*IE* 84, l. 11 partly restored: [τῶι πατρίωι ἀγῶνι τ]ῶν [Δ]ιονυσίων) probably refer, by ellipsis, to tragedy. If Clinton's restoration of this last phrase is correct, it is striking to find the conservative language of the '*patrios agon*' applied to tragedy at the Eleusinian Dionysia in 334/3, as it certainly was over a century later, at a time when this linguistic reflex has become much more generally prevalent (*IE* 201, ll. 17–19 of ca. 225). By the last third of the fourth century, the tragic agon of Eleusis was doubtless felt to be so long-established and venerable as to warrant the title of 'the traditional event'.

List of Inscriptions with Relevance to the Theatre(s) of Eleusis

The first ten (**Hi–Hx**) are discussed below:

Hi, late fifth century: choregic monument commemorating performances of Aristophanes and Sophocles.

Hii, mid fourth century or earlier: decree in honour of Damasias of Thebes for services to the Eleusinian theatre; and another for Phryniskos of Thebes.

Hiii, ca. mid fourth century: decree in honour of a Theban mentioning the theatre of Eleusis.

Hiv, ca. mid fourth century: choregic dedication for comedy.

Hv, ca. mid fourth century: decree in honour of a Hierophant.

Hvi, ca. 340: base for a statue of Dionysus.

Hvii, late fourth century?: decree of the Eleusinians in honour of the demarch Euthydemos son of Moirokles of Eleusis.

Hviii, late fourth century?: dedication to Dionysus by Demonike.

Hix, fourth-century?: choregic dedication of Hieron.

Hx, 321/0: honorary decree of the Eleusinians.

IE **141**, 354/3: contract for the stoa by the south wall of the sanctuary, mentioning the theatre.

IE **68**, ca. mid fourth century: fragment of a decree of the Eleusinians honouring a (?) demarch (l. 1 δ]ή[μαρχ?-]) with an announcement '[at the tragedies of the Dionysia in El]-eus[is]' [τῶν Διονυσίων Ἐλ]ευσ[ῖνι τοῖς | τραγοιδοῖς], ll. 2–3. The award of [prohedria] is a likely restoration, l. 8. This decree is to be erected in the sanctuary of Demeter (ll. 12–13); cf. *IE* 99.

IE **80**, 340–335?: decree of the Eleusinians in honour of Smikythion of Kephale, peripolarch, whose gold crown is to be announced by the next year's demarch at the tragedies of the Dionysia (ll. 14–16) and who is to receive prohedria, announced each year by the demarch 'just like th[e oth]ers to whom prohedria has been awarded' (ll. 21–4).

IE **84**, 334/3: dedication by ephebes of Hippothontis and decree of the Eleusinians honouring them and their *sophronistes* with prohedria and a crown to be announced at the Dionysia (see above).

IE **99**, 319/18?: decree of the Eleusinians in honour of the general Derkylos, the honours to be announced 'in the theatre at Eleusis, at the tragic agon' Ἐλευσῖνι ἐν τῶ|ι θεάτρωι τραγωιδῶν τῶι ἀγῶνι ll. 11–12. These include 'prohedria in the deme of the Eleusinians' προεδρίαν ἐν τῶι δήμωι τῶι Ἐλευσινίων l. 17–18, to which 'the demarch from time to time' is to invite him καὶ καλείτω αὐτὸν ὁ δήμαρχος ὁ ἀεὶ δημαρχῶν εἰς τὴν προεδρίαν· ll. 18–20. This is to be erected not in the deme (theatre) but 'next to the Propylaea of Demeter and Kore' (ll. 25–7) in the sanctuary; cf. *IE* 68.

IE **177**, 329/8: account of the *Epistatai* at Eleusis and Treasurers of the Two Goddesses. Lines 44–6 refer to work on the materials of a tower that had collapsed 'into the theatre' (see above).

IE **201**, ca. 225: decree of the Kerykes and Eumolpidai in honour of a Hierophant. The crown to be announced 'at the traditional agon of the Dionysia, in the theatre at Eleusis' (ll. 17–19).

IE **225**, ca. 170–160: fragment of (probably) a dedication in honour of Nou[menios of Halai] as an epimelete of the *pompe* at the (presumably City) Dionysia. He had probably been honoured for some service in Eleusis and the monument recorded a range of his offices: Clinton 2008, 27.

IE **229**, 165/4: decrees of the Athenians and Eleusinians in honour of a demarch (see above).

Note also **V F** on Eleusis no. 30, marble relief from Eleusis with theatrical mask, ca. 370 that is very probably choregic.

Hi: Choregic Monument Found in Eleusis of Gnathis and Anaxandrides, Commemorating Victorious Performances of Aristophanes and Sophocles, late 5ᵗʰ c. (by letter forms and prosopography).

Quadrangular base of white marble in two fragments, preserved on all sides; a round plinth (H. 0.05 × diam. 0.44 m) centred on top (of a piece with the base, with a dowel hole in centre 0.12 × 0.09 × 0.04 m deep) for an Ionic column; eight small holes in a row in front of the plinth, spaced ca. 0.70 m apart; an additional hole at the same distance behind the extreme left and right holes. 0.31 × 0.66 × 0.60 m.

Found in Eleusis, 'by the Byzantine ruins' – apparently referring to an area 20 m SE of the Lesser Propylaea.

Eleusis, Museum E946 + E254.

IG II² 3090; *IG* I³ 970; *IE* 53.

Text: based on *IE* 53.   Photos: Clinton pl. 25; Goette 2014, 85; drawing of upper surface: Philios 1894, 174.

1   [Γ]νάθις Τιμοκήδος, Ἀναξανδρίδης Τιμαγόρο   non-stoich.
χορηγõντες κωμωιδοῖς ἐνίκων·
Ἀριστοφάνης ἐ[δ]ίδασκεν.
ἑτέρα νίκη τραγωιδοῖς·
5   Σοφοκλῆς ἐδίδασκεν.

[G]nathis, son of Timokedes, Anaxandrides, son of Timagoros, were victorious as choregoi for comedy. Aristophanes was the [d]idaskalos. Another victory, in tragedy: ⁵ Sophocles was the didaskalos.

Two unhelpful obsessions have dogged interpretation of this inscription. The first is a determination to associate known plays by Aristophanes and Sophocles with this hard evidence for performances by them in their own lifetimes; the second, closely related, is the *idée fixe* which insists that these two luminaries of the Classical theatre could not possibly have performed at parochial Eleusis, and that therefore this inscription must refer to victories won in the city.

The monument dedicated by these two Eleusinian choregoi was rather elaborate and, so far as can be judged, of good quality. The surviving base supported a substantial column that in its turn carried another object, probably a statue. The unusual series of small holes on the top of the base probably received metal rods, probably to support further decoration (crowns?) or possibly serving as a protective grille.

This is, by a good half-century, the earliest evidence for theatre in Eleusis. Attempts to date it more precisely rest on unfounded, or at least unprovable, assumptions. Very close similarity in the lettering to a dedication securely dated to 408/7 (*IG* I³ 515; Wilhelm 1906, 177 n. 1) provides the best approximation, and this is supported by the prosopographical evidence. Given the monument's possibly retrospective character in respect of the tragic performance (see below), the Sophoclean victory could have been won at almost any point during the poet's career. It is perhaps slightly more likely to pre-date than to follow the atrocities perpetrated by the oligarchic extremists in Eleusis in 403 and the place's subsequent brief period as an oligarchic enclave.

The significance of this document is manifold: it records performances by two of the most famous names of classical Athenian theatre – and there can be little doubt, given the use of the verb ἐδίδασκεν (ll. 3, 5), that the two poets were involved personally in these productions. Unfortunately the verb is of less use in telling us whether the works in question were performed for the first time or staged as reperformances (**J**). (It is unclear what – if any – the significance may be of the fact that the two lines recording this involvement are inscribed in somewhat smaller letters than the rest. Perhaps the men who funded the events did not want to be entirely overshadowed by these famous names.)

But it is even more important for what it tells us of the status of the Eleusinian Dionysia in the later fifth century. For there can no longer be any doubt that the victories in question were won at the site of the monument's erection (Millis 2015, 229–30). Assuming that that was an unworthy venue for such luminaries, for decades scholarly opinion inclined towards the view that the inscription commemorates victories won at the Great Dionysia on a monument set up in the local theatre of the choregoi's home deme. The most conspicuous obstacle to this view was the clear presence of joint choregoi. The attested introduction of synchoregia under economic pressure caused by the Peloponnesian War long remained the preferred solution to this obstacle. This for instance permitted Foucart (1895) to assert confidently that the tragedy of Sophocles was without doubt the *Oedipus at Colonus*, produced posthumously by his son in 401. (Foucart was also confident – wrongly so – that the inscription could be dated close to 403/2 because of its use of the Eucleidian alphabet and of o for the false diphthong ου.) But in 1943 Capps showed that synchoregia in the city was confined to a single year in the late fifth century – 406/5 – and it was evidently confined to the Great Dionysia, and not extended to the Lenaea (**I D**). In 405 Sophocles was dead and his grandson Sophocles not yet active (Sophocles II *TrGF* 62 T 4).

Despite this virtually conclusive removal of the single item of evidence for an urban origin for these victories, it still has adherents – for instance Mette (1977, 23–4), who goes so far as to restore the names of Gnathis and Anaxandrides as the urban dramatic choregoi in the Victors' List of the Great Dionysia for 405/4, and of Aristophanes and Sophocles as the winning poets. The restriction of urban synchoregia to the Great Dionysia of 406/5 also renders impossible the other favourite identification made à propos of this inscription – namely of Aristophanes' *Frogs*. The many Eleusinian elements of this comedy would certainly have made it a fine choice for performance in that deme, but we cannot gainsay the evidence of the Hypothesis that it was performed at the Lenaea; nor is the attested reperformance accorded (probably) by decree of the Athenian demos likely to have been in Eleusis (Sommerstein 1996a, 21–2; **I Avi**).

If further proof were required, the expression used to introduce the tragic performance – 'Another victory, in tragedy' (l. 4) – implies that the tragic victory was won on a different occasion, and therefore that the inscription deals with victories won in more than one year. That means that they cannot both have been won at the Great Dionysia of 406/5. It is impossible to determine whether the tragic victory was added later to a monument already erected for the Aristophanic performance (Clinton 2008, 83) or whether both were inscribed at the same time. At any event, they were surely won on different occasions.

Nothing else encourages us to assign these performances to the city, and much tells in the other direction. Joint choregia was as common in the demes as it was rare in the city (the term 'synchoregia' is never used in a deme context: **A Introduction**). Another consideration is the known public profile of the families of the choregoi in question, in particular that of the better-documented Gnathis. His family has a record of illustrious service in the deme over a number of generations (see nos. 11, 160, 169, 170 of the prosopography in Whitehead 1986a; Humphreys 2018, 1124–5). Most notably, Gnathis' grandson (or possibly son), also Gnathis, was demarch of Eleusis in the mid fourth century, and we happen to know that under his demarchy the Dionysia was a particularly illustrious occasion (**Hii**). Another likely member of this family, Timokedes son of Timasios (Whitehead 1986a, no. 170), is one of four men who were crowned by their deme ca. 340 and who then made a dedication, evidently of a statue, to Dionysus (**Hvi**). There are many reasons why four men might be crowned by their deme and then choose to make a joint dedication to Dionysus to commemorate it – but service as choregoi or in some other capacity in support of that god's festival must be the most likely. This begins to look like a family tradition of inventive support of the local dramatic festival. Theirs was certainly a family heavily involved in deme politics and life, and this constitutes another argument against the interpretation of this choregic monument as a record of victories won in the city, for it is extremely rare to find men prominent at the deme level going on to a career in the city, and we have no single instance of a man who served as choregos in both deme and city.

Both dramatic genres were presented at the Eleusis Dionysia in this period, despite the physical and economic depredations of the Peloponnesian War. And both were configured in competitive format. As much is *prima facie* implied by the explicit language of victory (ἐνίκων, νίκη ll. 2, 4). In the middle of the fourth century there was still 'a contest of tragedies' (τραγωιδῶν τῶι ἀγῶνι, *IE* 99, l. 11; cf. *IE* 84, ll. 10–11). And some two centuries later, the term *agon* is used of the Eleusinian Dionysia (*IE* 229, l. 33) – no doubt formulaic for 'the performances', but hardly incompatible with actual contests.

Hii: Decree of the Eleusinians in Honour of Damasias of Thebes for Services to the Eleusinian Theatre; and Another for Phryniskos of Thebes, mid 4th c. or earlier (by letter forms, orthography and prosopography: below).

White marble stele, broken at bottom.
0.67 × 0.42 × 0.10 m.

Found 'by the so-called Callichoron well, only a few minutes outside Eleusis and on the road
leading to Thebes and Megara, when a villager was excavating the foundation of his house'
(Tsountas 1884, 69): Clinton 2008, 87 for possible identification of the site.
Eleusis, Museum E176.
Tsountas 1884; *IG* II 5, 547b; *IG* II² 1186; *IE* 70.
Text: based on *IE* 70.   Photo: Clinton pl. 30.

1	[θ] ε ο [ι]	stoich. 30

1   [θ]   ε   ο   [ι]
      [Κα]λ[λί]μαχος Καλλικράτους εἶπεν· ἐπε-   stoich. 30
      [ιδ]ὴ Δαμασίας Διονυσίου Θηβαῖος οἰκ-
      [ήσ]ας Ἐλευσῖνι κόσμιός τε ὢ[ν] διατετ[έ]-
5   [λ]εκε καὶ φιλανθρώπως ἔχει πρὸς πάντ-
      [α]ς τοὺς ἐν τοῖ δήμοι οἰκοῦντας καὶ α[ὐ]-
      [τ]ὸς καὶ οἱ μαθηταὶ αὐτῶ, καὶ Διονύσ[ια]
      ποιούντων Ἐλευσινίων ἐσπούδασε[ν κ]-
      αὶ ἐφιλοτιμήθη πρὸς τοὺς θεοὺς κ[αὶ τ]-
10   ὸν δῆμον τὸν Ἀθηναίων καὶ Ἐλευσιν[ίω]-
      [ν], ὅπως ὡς κάλλιστα γένηται τὰ Διονύσ-
      ια, καὶ παρασκευάσας τοῖς αὐτοῦ <τ>έλε-
      σι χοροὺς δύο, τὸν μὲν παίδων, τὸν δὲ ἀν-
      δρῶν ἐπέδωκεν τεῖ Δήμητρι [κ]αὶ τεῖ Κό-
15   ρει καὶ τοῖ Διονύσωι, δεδόχθαι Ἐλευσ-
      ινίοις, ἐπαινέσαι Δαμασίαν Διονυσί-
      ο Θηβαῖον σωφροσύνης ἕνεκα καὶ εὐσε-
      βείας τῆς πρὸς τὼ θεὼ καὶ στεφανῶσαι
      αὐτὸν χρυσῶι στεφάνωι ἀπὸ Χ δραχμῶν·
20   ἀνειπάτω δὲ αὐτὸν ὁ μετὰ Γνᾶθιν δήμα-
      ρχος Διονυσίων τῶν Ἐ[λ]ευσῖνι τοῖς τρ-
      αγοιδοῖς, ὅτι ὁ δῆμος ὁ Ἐλευσινίων στ-
      εφανοῖ Δαμασίαν Διονυσίου Θηβαῖον
      σωφροσύνης ἕνεκα καὶ εὐσεβείας τῆς
25   πρὸς τὼ θεώ· ἔστω δὲ αὐτῶι προεδρία κα-
      ὶ ἀτέλεια ὧν εἰσιν κύριοι Ἐλευσίν[ι]ο-
      ι καὶ αὐτῶι <καὶ> ἐγγόνοις καὶ ἐὰν τ[ι] ἄλλο β-
      ούληται ἀγαθὸν εὑρέσθαι παρὰ τοῦ δή-
      μου τοῦ Ἐλευσινίων, καὶ ἐπιμελέσθω α-
30   ὐτοῦ ὁ δήμαρχος ὁ ἀεὶ δημαρχῶν ὅτου ἄ-
      ν δέηται· ἑλέσθαι δὲ αὐτίκα μάλα ὅστι-
      ς ἐπιμελήσεται, ὅπως ἂν ἀναγραφεῖ τό-
      δε τὸ ψήφισμα καὶ σταθεῖ ἐν τῶι Διονυ-
      [σ]ίωι, εἰς δὲ τὴν ἀναγραφὴν δοῦναι Δ δρ-
35   [α]χμὰς τὸν δήμαρχον· δοῦναι δὲ εἰς θυσ-
      [ί]αν Δαμασίαι Η δραχμὰς ἀπὸ τοῦ κοινῶ.
      [Κ]αλλίμα[χ]ος Καλλικράτους εἶπ[ε]ν· ἐπε-
      [ι]δὴ Φρυνίσκος Θηβαῖο[ς] οἰκή[σας Ἐλευ]-

[σῖν]ι κό[σμιος -]
- -

1 [θ]εο[ὶ] Nemes   12 <τ>έλε- Pantazides   [μ]έλε- Foucart   ΛΕΛΕ *lapis*

[G]OD[S]. [Ka]l[l]imachos son of Kallikrates proposed: sin[c]e Damasias son
of Dionysios of Thebes, one time resid[en]t in Eleusis, has contin[ue]d to be
orderly [5] and generously disposed towards all those who reside in the deme –
both he h[im]self and his students – and during the Eleusinians' celebration
of the Dionysia, showed commitment and ambition towards the gods, [10] [t]he
demos of Athens, and that of Eleusis, in order that the Dionysia might be as
fine as possible, and having prepared at his own expense two choruses – one of
boys, the other of men – donated them to Demeter [a]nd Kore [15] and Dionysus,
the Eleusinians decided to praise Damasias son of Dionysios of Thebes for his
reverence and piety towards the Two Goddesses, and to crown him with a gold
crown worth 1,000 drachmas; [20] and may the demarch who succeeds Gnathis
proclaim him at the tragedies of the Dionysia in Eleusis, announcing that the
demos of Eleusinians crowns Damasias son of Dionysios of Thebes for his
reverence and piety [25] towards the Two Goddesses; and may he have prohedria
and exemption from those taxes over which the Eleusinians have authority –
both he himself and his descendants – and an[y] other benefit he may wish to
seek from the deme of Eleusis, and may [30] the demarch in office from time to
time take care of whatever he needs; and it was decided to elect immediately
someone to oversee the inscription and erection of this decree in the *Diony[s]-
ion*, and that the demarch should give 10 [35] dr[a]chmas for its inscription; and
to give Damasias 100 drachmas from the public treasury for a sacrif[i]ce.
[K]allim[a]chos son of Kallikrates propos[e]d: si[n]ce Phryniskos of Thebe[s],
one time resid[ent in Eleusi]s, [has continued to be] ord[erly …]

This intriguing inscription offers tantalising insights into the life of the Eleusinian theatre. It
is a member of the familiar category of deme decrees honouring a benefactor, but it is in many
ways a highly unusual example of the type. Or rather, it is the remains of two such decrees:
a second follows the first immediately at l. 37, and may in its original form have been just as
extensive as it. The second was proposed by the same man, doubtless at the same meeting of
the deme assembly. Both decrees honour Thebans and it is a fair guess that the second, like
the first, was prompted by the honorand's service to the Eleusinian theatre (before breaking
off, the initial praise of Phryniskos shows exact parallels with that for Damasias). Phryniskos
is thus very likely also to have rendered special service to the Eleusinian Dionysia.

   Foucart (1893) was surely right to deduce that Damasias of Thebes was a musician.
However he based his argument largely on the somewhat whimsical reading of [μ]έλεσι in
ll. 12–13, which led him to conclude that Damasias had given the Thebans two choruses
furnished 'with his own music'. There is a problem with the engraving of the initial Τ of
τέλεσι, which appears as a Λ on the stone, but this can only be the formulaic 'at his own expense' τοῖς αὐτοῦ τέλεσι (known from e.g. *IG* I[3] 84, l. 14; Schwenk 1985, no. 32, ll. 13–14;
IG II[2] 1678, l. 12). But even in the absence of such specific reference to the compositional

talents of Damasias, there is good reason to suppose that he was in the 'music industry'. The central focus of this decree is on Damasias' services to the Eleusinian Dionysia (ll. 7ff.), in particular its choral performances. Moreover this beneficial behaviour had been shown not just by Damasias himself, but by 'his students' καὶ α[ὐ|τ]ὸς καὶ οἱ μαθηταὶ αὐτõ ll. 6–7. This intriguing detail makes it clear that Damasias was a didaskalos to students who were also based in Eleusis – or perhaps rather, who had been until recently. Whitehead (1977, 32) may be right to point out that the aorist participles οἰκήσας in ll. 3–4 and 38 imply that Damasias and Phryniskos were no longer resident in Eleusis at the time of the award. Alternatively, they are used to refer to the act of resettlement in Eleusis by the Thebans (as e.g. at Th. 2.27; Humphreys 2018, 1119). It is a fairly safe assumption that the field in which Damasias operated as a didaskalos was the (broadly) 'musical'. In this period a didaskalos could be someone who produces plays, trains choreuts, composes music, or lyrics (or both) – or any combination of these. Among the skills of a didaskalos might also be that of the piper (*auletes*). In the same period from which this decree derives, the famous piper Telephanes of Megara took on the direction of a men's chorus at the Dionysia sponsored by Demosthenes when its official didaskalos absconded (**V G** on D. 21.14–18). The likelihood that the particular expertise in which Damasias was a 'teacher' (*didaskalos*) was the very 'Theban' one of *auletike* is high, notwithstanding the fact that he is not explicitly described as an *auletes*. For the fame of Theban pipes in the fifth and fourth centuries was legendary (Wilson 2002), and the demand for and presence of Theban pipers performing in Athens at its urban festivals are amply documented (**V G**; **VI J** on on *IG* II³ 4, 929). For possible evidence that Damasias had performed for a successful chorus in Athens ca. 330–325, see **V F** on *IG* II³ 4, 465.

It is clear that Damasias and his students had been resident in Eleusis for some time (note esp. ll. 4–5 κόσμιός τε ὢ[ν] διατετ[έ|λ]εκε 'and has contin[ue]d to be orderly'). Is this evidence for a Theban musical 'school' operating in Attica? The impression given by ll. 2–7 is that these 'students' are perhaps not local Eleusinian boys learning how to play the pipes or dance and sing for Dionysus so much as Damasias' own group of (perhaps also Theban) apprentices. For they too had been 'orderly and generously disposed towards all those who reside in the deme'. The 'aulos-booming brood of Chairis' who so irritate Dikaiopolis in Aristophanes' *Acharnians* and are 'all pipers from Thebes' (*Ach.* 866, 862) come to mind.

Damasias' father, Dionysios, bore the name of one of Thebes' most celebrated fifth-century melic poets (Stefanis no. 724), and one who took 'students', for he was the teacher of Epaminondas himself. So far as the limited evidence suggests, Dionysios' instrumental expertise was on the kithara rather than the pipes ([Plu.] *Mor.* 1141b; Nep. 2.1), but the example of Meles the kitharode fathering a son, the dithyrambist Cinesias, whose musical expertise will have been on the pipes, serves to show that musical expertise may run in families while at the same time shifting focus between instruments. It is a sufficiently common name to make an identification hazardous, though we might on the other hand deduce that the name of Damasias' father was one to conjure with from the fact that it is repeated three times in this decree (ll. 3, 16–17, 23; **V G** for the habit of mentioning famous musical Theban fathers in inscriptions).

Service at a particular Eleusinian Dionysia is evidently the real focus of the good efforts of Damasias and his students, for which he is being so extravagantly honoured. His central benefaction, motivated by the ambition 'that the Dionysia might be as fine as possible' ll. 11–12, was the preparation at his own expense of two choruses – one of boys, the other of men – given as a voluntary gift to Demeter, Kore and Dionysus, ll. 12–15. 'Giving' choruses is the act of a choregos, and Whitehead (1986a, 151) aptly dubbed Damasias' actions as 'an unofficial choregia'. But this is a very exceptional and unusual variety of choregia. It is probably because of its divergence from the more familiar Attic–Athenian type that the term itself is not used anywhere in this inscription (indeed, it appears to be deliberately avoided). The principle difference from an 'ordinary' Athenian choregia lies in the nature of the conditions under which these choruses were given. This had none of the compulsion, legal or moral, inherent in the Athenian liturgical system and was rather a voluntary gift – an *epidosis* – to public finances (cf. Eudemos of Plataea in **VI I** on *IG* II³ 4, 352, ll. 15–20, who in 330/29 'donated ([ἐπ]ι[δέδ]ωκ[εν]) for construction of the stadium and the Panathenaic theatre a thousand yoke of oxen and has sent them all before the Panathenaea'). Given the likelihood that Damasias was himself 'in the business' (see above), this may to some extent have amounted to a generous contribution in kind (but see further below). The verb παρασκευάσας, l. 12, used of his 'preparation' of these choruses certainly implies direct personal involvement on his part, and, though hardly a technical term, it and cognates are used elsewhere in explicitly choregic contexts (e.g. **I D** on D. 21.11, 106; **I Aiv 25a**; **I Avii**). Whether the choreuts in these donated choruses were locals or recruited from among Damasias' own 'students' we cannot say.

It is generally assumed from this information that 'men's and boys' dithyrambic contests took place at the Eleusinian Dionysia in addition to tragedy and comedy' (Clinton 2008, 88; cf. Ieranò 1997, 278). Caution is however necessary. These certainly look like very special performances, something that on the contrary did not normally feature in the programme. As noted, the verb ἐπέδωκεν implies a special benefaction rather than the fulfilment of an ordinary obligation. There is no talk of a contest. Special too seems to be the intertwining of the Goddesses of the sanctuary with the god of the Dionysia as triple recipients of these choruses.

There can be no doubt however that Damasias took on a number of the key duties of a familiar Athenian choregia. He financed and personally oversaw the training of a chorus, or rather of two. In this connection a phrase used earlier in the decree stands out. While inevitably much in its honorific language is highly generic, the expression φιλανθρώπως ἔχει 'was generously disposed' (l. 5) is not. In fact this is the sole example in the large corpus of classical honorific decrees (Veligianni-Terzi 1997, 216). Presumably – to judge by its later development – generosity of a financial nature is implied.

Another unusual feature of this decree is that the worthy behaviour for which Damasias is honoured is expressed quite explicitly as having been shown to all the residents of Eleusis, not just the demesmen (ll. 5–6 πρὸς πάντ|[α]ς τοὺς ἐν τοῖ δήμοι οἰκοῦντας). Indeed, the good effects of Damasias' actions at the Dionysia had an especially long reach, extending even beyond the residents of the deme, thus broadly defined, to include the Athenian state itself. For the decree goes on to say that this privately funded embellishment of the Eleusinian Dionysia benefited 'the Athenian demos' (l. 10) as well as the Eleusinian. It is probably legitimate to conclude from this inclusive description that the Eleusinian Dionysia was open to all – which we would in any case have expected to be so (**A Introduction**). Perhaps Athenians attended the Eleusinian Dionysia in large numbers – either normatively, or, for some reason, especially in this particular year.

But there may be something more at work here. Perhaps, as Lasagni (2004, 115) suggests, a clue is to be sought in the pan-Attic dimension of Eleusinian cult, though of course strictly speaking Damasias is contributing not to the pan-Attic cult of the Goddesses but rather

to the local cult of Dionysus in Eleusis. This question is closely related to another: the remarkable fact that the choruses were given to Demeter and Kore as well as Dionysus, at the
deme festival for Dionysus, and that Damasias is specifically praised for his piety to the Two
Goddesses (l. 18). Their cult was certainly 'Athenian' rather than 'Eleusinian', and the choruses of Damasias in some irretrievable manner must have linked that cult to the Eleusinian
cult of Dionysus. Clinton (2008, 88) airs the possibility that Demeter and Kore were the
subject of the songs, or that the choruses simply sang in praise of them, perhaps including
the broader Athenian context, while rejecting Foucart's suggestion that the three had a pre-
existing, germane connection in the Mysteries. If the choruses did honour the Goddesses of
the sanctuary in company with Dionysus, the Athenian demos, as the mortal guardians of
their cult, could certainly be said to have benefited. Clinton (2008, 88) explains the reference
to the Athenian demos in l. 10 with the suggestion that Damasias and his pupils may have also
performed in Athens and contributed to the magnificence of the City Dionysia, but it would
be very surprising to find a deme decree registering such an event, and in a manner so oblique
as to be virtually unintelligible. It sounds very much like special pleading designed to keep
apart what this document clearly puts together: the Two Goddesses and Dionysus in Eleusis.

The fact that the demos of Eleusis could honour a benefactor with a crown at the tragedies
of its Dionysia and yet set up the relevant stele not, as here, in the theatre, but 'in the sanctuary of Demeter' (*IE* 68, ll. 12–13) or 'by the Propylaia of Demeter and Kore' (*IE* 99, ll. 25–7)
shows that the jurisdictional difference between these two sanctuaries did not impede such
collaboration and co-ordination between them. So too does the deme's award of a gold crown
(and perhaps prohedria: **H Introduction**) to a Hierophant of the Mysteries, to be announced
by the demarch 'at the Dion[ysia, at the tra]ge[d]ies' (**Hv**, ll. 23–4), while the stele is in this
case to be erected in the Eleusinian theatre (**Hv**, ll. 32–3). The placement of a dedication to
Dionysus within the Sanctuary itself (*IE* 102) tends in the same direction. The cultic association will have been familiar enough to Damasias himself, for in Thebes Dionysus was the
paredros of Demeter on the Kadmeia (Pi. *I.* 7.3–5 with Olivieri 2009; 2011, 149–54). While
this decree does not amount to proof that the cult of Dionysus in Eleusis was integrated into
the rituals of the sanctuary, it points suggestively in that direction. It may also to some extent
represent an overture on the part of the deme toward the sanctuary.

The honours bestowed upon Damasias stand out as quite extraordinary among all the
many deme decrees rewarding benefactors. They are extraordinary for a person of any status,
but quite exceptional for a metic. Damasias is to receive a gold crown worth 1,000 drachmas – the single most valuable crown known from all the demes. It is to be proclaimed by
the demarch at the tragedies of the (no doubt) next Dionysia, the one in the charge of the demarch who succeeds Gnathis (ll. 20–1). (It seems that in Eleusis such tasks of proclamation
fell to the demarch rather than a lesser functionary, at least formally: in **Hvii**, ll. 18–19 the
demarch is also to summon honorands to their seats of honour. The direct involvement of the
deme's highest officer no doubt added to the honour.) Damasias is given prohedria (unqual-
ified, but doubtless referring principally and perhaps solely to the Dionysia); and exemption
from taxes (*ateleia*) over which the Eleusinians have authority. Both privileges are inheritable. The award by the deme of *ateleia* to a metic is paralleled in **Hiii**, where the recipient is
also Theban. *IE* 99 grants the same to the Athenian general Derkylos, certainly a non-demesman property owner, possibly a resident (Whitehead 1986a, 247). Evidently some form of
taxes applied to both metics and resident or landowning Athenian non-members of the deme.

Despite the verbal link between the word used for Damasias' choral gift τέλεσι 'at his own expense' and that used of the tax-exemption ἀτέλεια, the latter is unlikely to refer to liturgies, and so to be evidence that metics in Eleusis were ordinarily called upon as choregoi.

Damasias is also granted the unusual and extremely expansive privilege of 'any other benefit he may wish to seek from the deme of Eleusis' (ll. 27–9), a prerogative protected into the future by the requirement that any demarch from time to time look after any such requests of Damasias (ll. 29–31). The publication formula for this stele has an unusual urgency and an unaccustomed degree of pomp (ll. 31–4), involving as it does the post-haste appointment of a special officer to oversee the process and the allocation by the demarch of ten drachmas for the purpose. Even the selection of the term *Dionysion* (ll. 33–4) – rather than *theatron* – to refer to the site of erection may reflect the choice of the more august term. (*Theatron* seems to be the norm: **Hiii**, ll. 7–8; **Hv**, l. 33; cf. **Hx**, ll. 10–11; *IE* 99, ll. 10–11; this use of *Dionysion* is unique, unless it is restored in the mid fourth-century decree in honour of a Hierophant, **Hv**, l. 33 where *theatron* is equally possible epigraphically.) Finally, another 100 drachmas is to come to Damasias from the Eleusinian public purse 'for a sacrifice' (ll. 35–6). The amount is substantial. It would purchase at least one and possibly two oxen. Presumably Damasias was to bring his 'students', friends and others for the occasion.

Gnathis, the demarch (l. 20) who had overseen this especially magnificent Dionysia, may be the very same man who had co-funded the performances of Aristophanes and Sophocles in Eleusis (**Hi**; cf. Clinton 2008, 88). The decree could date from the first half of the century: note the several instances of older Attic orthography (ο for ω: l. 6; ο for ου: ll. 7, 17, 36; ε for η: ll. 14 × 2, 15, 32, 33; the reversion to Διονυσίο in ll. 16–17 is especially telling). If not the same man, he is almost certainly his son or grandson, in which case we can identify a family with a tradition of significant support for their local theatrical culture.

The second decree, for Phryniskos, was proposed by the same man, and likewise honours a Theban metic. **Hiii** adds a third certain or probable Theban benefactor to the Eleusinian theatre. Eleusis looks to have been good at mobilising support of their theatre from foreigners, no doubt taking advantage of its strategic position and of the cosmopolitan community that passed through. Lasagni (2004, 118) suggests that Phryniskos belonged to the same family as Damasias, perhaps 'una ricca "dinastia" di commercianti che, grazie a un notevole potere economico, era in grado di detenere un ruolo di rilievo all'interno della communità eleusina'. Given the evidence of the decree (see esp. above on ll. 7ff.) we might suppose rather that Damasias' wealth derived from his privileged position in the music industry. But Lasagni is certainly right to see economic forces at work here. This is no 'ordinary' honorific decree for a deme choregos, and the honours are entirely unique for a metic. The closest comparanda are to be found at the polis level. In the last forty years of the fourth century, we find foreigners and metics being honoured for substantial service to the Athenian theatre. In the group of relevant decrees collected and studied by Lambert (2008), which had been passed at the Assembly in the Theatre following the Dionysia, the majority of honorands are certainly or probably foreigners or metics (given the habit of using the ethnic for metics, the difference is often hard to spot). And a significant sub-group of them are, like Damasias, identified as members of the theatre industry – actors, poets, even one piper (**VI I**; **VI J** on *IG* II³ 4, 929). It appears that the deme of Eleusis, like the Athenian polis itself, may have been leveraging its great symbolic resources to attract funds and know-how at a time of need, to secure the viability of theatre production in the rapidly changing economic conditions of the later fourth century. And if, as seems probable, the decrees for Damasias and Phryniskos pre-date the earliest instance of this phenomenon from the city (but see **VI E**), we may have another example of the way in which the demes struck an innovative course in theatre finance that was only later followed by the city itself.

Hiii: Decree of the Eleusinians in Honour of a Theban Mentioning the Theatre of Eleusis, ca. mid 4th c. ? (by letter forms).

Fragment of white marble, preserved on right side and back.
0.31 × 0.295 × 0.120 m.
Found in October 1860 'dans une muraille moderne en pierres sèches au pied du rocher de l'Acropole, du côté de la mer' … 'à quelques pas seulement du point où, sur la pente de l'Acropole, la courbe du terrain et quelques restes de gradins taillés dans le roc nous avaient fait conjecturer que devait avoir existé un théâtre': Lenormant 1862, 271, 274.
Eleusis, Museum 7720.
Pittakis *ArchEph* 1860, 2047–8 no. 4082; Lenormant 1862, 270–8, no. 47; *IG* II 547; *IG* II² 1185; *IE* 71.
Text: based on *IE* 71.   Photo: Clinton pl. 29.

```
- - - - - - - - - - - - - - - - - - - - - - - - - - - -   stoich. 27
1    [- - - - - - - - - - - - - - - - -]_ν ἐπαινέ-
     [σαι . . . . . 11 . . . . . . Θη]βαῖον στε-
     [φανῶσαι θαλλοῦ] στεφάνωι· εἶναι δ-
     [ὲ αὐτῶι καὶ προε]δρίαν καὶ ἀτέλε[ι]-
5    [αν ὧν κύριοί ε]ἰσιν Ἐλευσίνιοι· ἀν-
     [αγράψαι δὲ τό]δε τὸ ψήφισμα εἰς στ-
     [ήλην λιθίνην κ]αὶ στῆσαι εἰς τὸ θέ-
     [ατρον τὸ Ἐλευσ]ινίων τὸν ταμίαν.
     [vacat] vacat 0.009 m
```

3 Possibly [κιττοῦ] Wilson

[it was decided …] to prai[se … of Th]ebes, to cro[wn him] with a crown [of olive leaves (or possibly 'of ivy')]; and that [he should also] have [prohe]dria and exempt[ion ⁵ from those taxes over which] the Eleusinians hav[e authority]; and the treasurer is to ins[cribe th]is decree on a [stone] st[ele a]nd erect it in the th[eatre of the Eleus]inians.

This small fragment of an honorific decree contains a precious reference to 'the theatre of the Eleusinians' (another is restored, by analogy with this, in **Hv**). As in a number of other demes (Acharnae: **Bvii 2**; Anagyrous: **Eiii**; Piraeus: **Vv**; Rhamnus: **Wv**), the Eleusinians used their theatre as an instrument of honour, a place of heavy public exposure in which, at the theatrical performances of the Dionysia, honours like this were announced (e.g. **Hii**, ll. 20–2; **Hv**, ll. 22–4) and their permanent record displayed. The fabric of the crown has not been preserved (l. 3) and has traditionally been restored as θαλλοῦ, 'of olive leaves'; 'ivy' would fit the space just as well (**Bvii 2**, ll. 11–12).

Although it was built into a modern wall, the findspot of this stone is a vital testimony to the likely site of the theatre (**H Introduction**). It was found at the foot of the Eleusinian Acropolis, on the side facing the sea. This encouraged its excavator to associate some traces of a few steps carved into rock nearby with the koilon of the theatre. This theatre should probably be associated with the *Dionysion* mentioned in (**Hii**), also as a site to erect honorific decrees. The services for which honours are being made in that decree are intimately associated with the Dionysia and its performances. It is a reasonable hypothesis that the man honoured by this decree – also a Theban – had similarly rendered service to the theatre in which the decree is to stand: thus already Lenormant (1862, 275), who thought of money to fund performances or to repair the theatre.

Hiv: Choregic Dedication for Comedy, ca. mid 4th c. ? (by letter forms).

> Fragment of a base of white marble preserved on all sides except back and right. On the top, a cutting towards the left front corner, 'probably for a leg of a tripod' (Clinton); and a semicircular hole to the right at the back.
> 0.14 × 0.49 × 0.37 m.
> Eleusis, Museum E174.
> *IG* II² 3100; *IE* 66; *IG* II³ 4, 504.
> Text: based on *IG* II³ 4, 504.
> Photos: Clinton pl. 27; Agelidis Taf. 9a (upper surface); *IG* II³ 4,1 tab. LXVIII.

> Ἀθηνόδωρος Γο - - - -   non-stoich.
> χορηγῶν κωμωιδ[οῖς ἐνίκα].

Athenodoros son of Go[-... was victorious] as choregos in comed[y]

This stone is the surviving left-hand frontal quarter (or a little more) of a substantial rectangular base that will in its original form have been around 1 × 1 m (Agelidis 2009, 219). The cutting on the upper surface to the left was for the foot of a tripod, and the remains of a circular hole to the right and rear of that indicate the presence of a supporting central column for the tripod-lebes. This is in other words another example (to add to **Mviii**; cf. **Mvii**) of the dedication of a tripod by a deme choregos, doubtless for a victory won at the Eleusinian Dionysia. Like the single certain example from Ikarion, this represents the transference of a prize for dithyramb in the city to an object of dedication (and also, perhaps, a prize – there is no way of telling whether or not the tripod was given as a prize in Eleusis) for drama in the deme. It is a unique instance of the dedication of a tripod for a victory in comedy. Comedy is also known to have been performed in Eleusis some decades earlier (**Hi**). Unlike that earlier example – but like the other surviving fourth-century choregic dedication from Eleusis (**Hix**) – this shows a singleton rather than a pair of choregoi (though it may be relevant to the issue that **Hi** is known to have supported both a comic and a tragic performance). The two fourth-century dedications are completely silent about any others who contributed to the performance – poet, trainer, actors or piper (but see on **Hix**).

Hv: Decree of the Eleusinians in Honour of a Hierophant, ca. mid 4th c. (by letter forms and prosopography: Clinton 2008, 89).

Several fragments of a white marble stele.
0.83 × 0.34 × 0.08 m.
Findspot of large piece not recorded; a small piece found not far from Greater Propylaea: Clinton 2005, 81.
Eleusis, Museum E69.
Skias 1897, no. 1; *IG* II² 1188; *IE* 72.
Text: based on *IE* 72.   Photo: Clinton pl. 31.

corona

```
      θ          [ε          ο          ί]
      Ε̣ὐθ[ίας Γνά]θωνος Ἐλευσίνιος ᵛ      stoich. 25 (ll. 1–28)
      εῖπ[ε]ν· ἐπειδὴ ὁ ἱεροφάντης Ἱερ-
      οκλ[είδης Τει]σαμενοῦ Παιανιε-
  5   ὺς ἀ[νὴρ ἀ]γ̣[αθ]ός [ἐ̣]στ[ιν] περὶ τὸν δ-
      [ῆ]μο[ν τ]ὸν Ἐλευ[σιν]ίων καὶ λέγων
      [κ]αὶ [ποι]ῶν ὅτι [δύ]ν̣α̣τ̣α̣ι ἀγαθὸν δ-
      [ι]ατελεῖ καὶ [νῦν] κα̣[ὶ] ἐν τῶι ἔμπρ-
      ο[σ]θ[εν] χρόν̣ῳ[ι, δεδ]ό[χ]θαι Ἐλευσι-
 10   [ν]ίοι[ς κύ]ρια [εἶνα]ι καὶ τὰ ψηφίσ-
      [μα]τα ὅ[σ]α ἐψηφ[ίσα]τ̣ο ὁ δῆμος ὁ Ἐλ-
      [ευσι]νίων τῶι [ἱε]ροφάντηι· ὅπ[ω]ς
      [ἂν εἰδῶσ]ιν κ̣αὶ οἱ ἄλλοι ὅτι [ὁ δ]ῆ-
      [μος ὁ Ἐλε]υσ[]νίων ἐπίστα[ται χ]ά-
 15   [ριτας ἀπ]ο̣δ̣ιδόν̣αι τοῖς εὖ π[ο]ιο-
      [ῦσιν αὐτὸ]ν ἐπαιν[έσ]αι [τ]ὸ[ν] ἱερο-
      [φάντην Ἱεροκλ]εί[δ]ην [Τ]ε[ισ]αμεν-
      [οῦ Παιανιέα καὶ στ]εφαν[ῶσ]αι αὐ-
      [τὸν χρυσῶι στεφάνωι] ἀπὸ 𝈺 ᵛ δρ[α]-
 20   [χμῶν ᵛ εὐσεβείας ἕνε]κ̣α τῆς περ-
      [ὶ τὰ ἱερὰ καὶ φιλοτιμί]ας τῆς ε[ἰ-
      [ς τὸν δῆμον τὸν Ἐλευσιν]ίων· ἀν̣[ε]-
      [ιπεῖν τὸν δήμαρχον τ]οῖ[ς] Διον[υ]-
      [σίοις ᵛ ἐν τοῖς τρα]γωι[δ]οῖς ὅτι
 25   [ὁ δῆμος ὁ Ἐλευσιν]ίων [σ]τε[φ]ανοῖ
      [τὸν ἱεροφάντην εὐσεβεία]ς ἕνε-
      [κα τῆς περὶ τὰ ἱερὰ] κ̣α̣ὶ φιλοτιμ-
      [ίας τῆς εἰς τὸν δῆμο]ν τὸν̣ Ἐλε[υσ]-
      [ινίων· εἶναι αὐτῶι κα]ὶ ἐκγόνοις ἀτέ-   non-stoich.
 30   [λειαν καὶ . . . ca. 7. . . τῶ]ν δημοτῶν· vac.
      [ἀναγράψαι τὸ ψήφισμα τ]όδε τὸν δήμα-
      [ρχον ἐν στήληι λιθί]νηι καὶ στῆσα[ι]
      [εἰς τὸ θέατρον τὸ Ἐλευ]σινίων.
```

vacat

2 Ε̣ὐθ̣[. . . 6 . . .]θωνος Clinton   Ε̣υθ[ίας Γνά]θωνος (?) Clinton, in commentary

Gods. Euth[ias son of Gna]thon of Eleusis made the proposal: since the Hierophant Hierokl[eides] son of [Tei]samenos of Paiania [5] [i]s a g[ood] m[an] to the d[e]me of the Eleu[sin]ians and both in word [a]nd [act]ion continues to [d]o what good he [c]an, both [now] an[d] in form[er] time, the Eleusi[n]ians have [det]er[mi]ned [10] that all the dec[re]es that the deme of the El[eusi]nians pass[e]d for the [Hie]rophant [should b]e [va]lid. In order [that] others [should know] that [the d]e[me of the Ele]us[i]nians know[s how] [15] to [re]pay [f]a[vours] to its b[e]ne[factors], it was decided to pra[is]e [t]he Hiero[phant Hierokl]ei[d]es son of [T]e[is]amen[os of Paiania and to cr]ow[n] hi[m with a gold crown] worth 500 dr[achmas [20] fo]r the [piety] he showed towards [his sa-cred duties and his ambiti]on fo[r the deme of the Eleusin]ians. [The demarch] is to ann[ounce] at [t]he Dion[ysia, at the tra]ge[d]ies, that [25] [the deme of the Eleusin]ians [c]rowns [the Hierophant] for the [piety he showed towards his sacred duties] and his ambiti[on for the dem]e of the Ele[usinians. He an]d his descendants [are to have] [30] exemp[tion from taxes and (?) prohedria of th]e demesmen. The dema[rch is to inscribe t]his [decree on a sto]ne [stele] and erect it [in the theatre of the Eleu]sinians.

The relevance of this decree to the theatrical life of Eleusis was only recently revealed with Clinton's new edition. His much improved readings at ll. 22–4 show that the honours awarded Hierokleides are to be announced at the tragedies of the deme's Dionysia (although one would prefer a restoration that did not require the *vacat* in l. 24). Clinton's restoration of 'the theatre' (l. 33) as the place of erection is also compelling (he airs τὸ Διονύσιον 'the Dionysion' as another possibility, **Hii**). The further suggestion (Clinton 2008, 89) that prohedria was the second benefit awarded (l. 30) is also attractive, especially since the two go together in **Hii**, **Hiii** and *IE* 99, but the resultant expression 'exemp[tion from taxes and (?) prohedria of th]e demesmen' is worryingly harsh (but *IE* 99, ll. 17–18 has προεδρίαν ἐν τῶι δήμωι τῶι Ἐλευσινίων 'prohedria in the deme of the Eleusinians', which is perhaps not that far distant).

The Hierophant was the central officiant at the Mysteries, a member of the Eumolpid *genos* and the embodiment of its sacred tradition. He also needed to be a skilled administrator (Parker 1996, 294–5). The deme evidently had good relations with this particular incumbent, dating back some time (ll. 8–12). Though they were clearly substantial, we know nothing about the nature of the good services Hierokleides had performed for the deme: the religious virtue of 'piety shown towards his sacred duties' is virtually entirely restored (ll. 20–1, 26–7) and only the more mundane quality of 'ambition' (φιλοτιμία ll. 27–8) shown to the deme is certain. The latter is frequently instantiated in benefactions to the theatre itself, but in too many other spheres also to allow any solid deduction here that Hierokleides had done some particular good for the cult of Dionysus in Eleusis. But given other evidence of material contributions made by the Eleusinian authorities to the cult of Dionysus in the city (**H Introduction**; **II A**; **II B**), and of interaction between the deme cult and the Sanctuary of the Goddesses, some more direct contribution to the deme cult of Dionysus by the Hierophant certainly cannot be ruled out. Clinton (2008, 89) plausibly suggests that Hierokleides' success as a hierophant had the effect of benefiting the deme economically.

Hvi: Base for a Statue of Dionysus from Eleusis, Dedicated by Four Men who had been Crowned by the Deme, ca. 340?

Base of grey Eleusinian limestone, preserved on all sides; an oval cutting on top (0.25 m deep) for the plinth of a marble statue; a dowel hole on bottom for attachment to another block.
0.27 × 0.53 × 0.515 m.
Found on the south side of the Akropolis (Akris) of Eleusis: Clinton 2008, 90.
Eleusis, Museum E1139.
Papagiannopoulos-Palaios 1929b, 237; *IG* II² 2845; *IE* 79; *IG* II³ 4, 232.
Text: based on *IE* 79.   Photo: Clinton pl. 33.

Μοιροκλῆς Ε[ὐ]θ[υδ]ήμου
Ἀντίθεος Καλλ[ι]κλέους
Τιμοκήδης Τιμασίου
Ἀντιφάνης Εὐξενίδου
        vacat 0.05 m
5   [ἀνέ]θεσαν τῶι Διονύσωι
    [στεφα]νωθέντες ὑπὸ τῶν δημοτῶν.
        vac.

Moirokles son of E[u]th[yd]emos, Antitheos son of Kall[i]kles, Timokedes son of Timasios, Antiphanes son of Euxenides [5] [ded]icated this to Dionysus having been [crow]ned by their fellow-demesmen.

The block on which this inscription survives formed part of a larger monument that included a statue, almost certainly of Dionysus, dedicated by four men to Dionysus of Eleusis. It was found on the south side of the Akris at Eleusis, and is very likely to have been situated in the theatre or an adjacent sanctuary of Dionysus (**H Introduction**).

The four dedicators were evidently prominent and well-off members of the deme, with demonstrated involvement in its cults, notably that of Dionysus. For instance in 332/1 Moirokles purchased the lease to the quarries of the sanctuary of Heracles on the Akris for a five-year period, donating an extra 100 drachmas on top (*IE* 85, ll. 8–9; Whitehead 1986a, 427–8; Alipheri 2009; Papazarkadas 2011, 151–3). He was himself honoured on that occasion for his efforts in maximising the deme's revenue (ll. 14–17). A decade later he authored the decree that honours the services to the deme by Xenokles of Sphettos, in particular the construction of a new stone bridge over the Kephisos to ensure the safe passage of initiates (*IE* 95). His son Euthydemos served as demarch and in that capacity both demonstrated the family's financial acumen and, like his father before him, paid special attention to the cult of Dionysus (**Hvii**). He may be the same Moirokles who played an active part in urban politics in the later fourth century, and fathered another son, Kallippos, who served as an Athenian ambassador and general (Ampolo 1981). Timokedes is almost certainly a member of the family that includes the Gnathis son of Timokedes who funded performances by Aristophanes and Sophocles in the deme (**Hi**) and another (or possibly the same) (**Hii**) Gnathis who as demarch oversaw an especially elaborate Dionysia. Antiphanes was probably the priest of Heracles on the Akris of that name at the time that Moirokles was investing in its mineral resources (*IE* 85, ll. 48–9).

These four local notables dedicated their statue to Dionysus in commemoration of the fact that they had been earlier crowned by the deme. The service for which they were crowned – surely in the theatre – was doubtless in support of that god's cult. Had the four served as choregoi? Though no example survives, it is likely that Eleusis issued decrees in honour of its choregoi, as commonly in other demes. In **Hi** we find a pair of joint choregoi. Are these four men two such pairs, the victors on two occasions, or in separate genres at the same festival? In **Hiv** and **Hix**, however, choregoi operate as singletons. Whether choregoi or benefactors in some other capacity, there can be no doubt that these four men served that god's festival in some important way. It is possible that their dedication reflects the direct conversion of the value of the crowns the deme had awarded the men into an item of value for Dionysus (and the deme). Such reciprocal generosity was a familiar feature of the economy of cult in Attica and elsewhere (cf. Osborne 2019). The way in which the demesmen had Moirokles immediately hand over the extra 100 drachmas he had donated in addition to his payment for the quarry lease to fund the crown for the man who proposed it in the first place is a not entirely dissimilar form of such honorific economic exchange (*IE* 85).

Hvii: Decree of the Eleusinians in Honour of the Demarch Euthydemos Son of Moirokles of Eleusis, late 4th c. ? (by letter forms and prosopography).

Three fragments of a white marble stele, broken at top and bottom.
0.50 × 0.402 × 0.102 m.
Fr. c (the largest) found in 1887 'in a later (Byzantine) wall by the Propylaea' (Philios).
Eleusis, Museum E461 (a) + 673 (c) + 484 (b).
c: Philios 1887, no. 38; *IG* II 5, 574b; *IG* II² 1194; a: Skias 1896, 28 no. 9; *IG* II² 1274; a+b+c: Threpsiades 1939, 177; *IE* 101.
Text: based on *IE* 101.   Photo: Clinton pl. 45.

1	Θεόβουλος [Θεοβούλ]ου εἶπεν· τύχηι stoich. 28
	ἀγαθῆι τοῦ [δήμου το]ῦ Ἐλευσινίων κ-
	αὶ Ἀθηναίω[ν· δεδόχθ]αι Ἐλευσινίοι-
	ς. ἐπει[δὴ Εὐθύδημος] διατελεῖ εὔνο-
5	υς [ὢν] τῶ[ι] δήμ[ω]ι [τῶι Ἐ]λευσινίων καὶ
	Ἀθηναίων καὶ ἰδ[ία]ι καὶ κοινῆι καὶ
	[λ]αχὼν δήμαρχος κ[αλ]ῶς καὶ δικαίως
	δεδημάρχηκεν καὶ [τ]ὴν θυσίαν τῶι Δ-
	ιονύσωι ὑπὲρ ὑγιε[ί]ας καὶ σωτηρία-
10	ς τῶν δημοτῶν παρ᾽ αὑτοῦ ἔθυσεν καὶ
	εἰς τοὺς δημότας πεφιλοτίμηται κ-
	[-α]ὶ τὴν πρόσοδον πλείω πεποίηκεν κ-
	αὶ τἄλλα τὰ τῶν δημο[τ]ῶν κα[λ]ῶ[ς καὶ κ]-
	ατὰ τοὺς νόμους δι[εχείρισεν, ὑπάρ]-
15	χειν μὲν Εὐθυδήμωι, [δοθείσης καὶ τ]-
	[-ο]ῖς προγόνοις αὐτο[ῦ ταύτης τῆς δω]-
	ρεᾶς, προεδρίαν αὐτ[ῶι καὶ ἐγγόνοι]-
	ς, κα[ὶ] καλείτω αὐτὸν [ὁ δήμαρχος ὁ ἀε]-
	ὶ δημαρχῶν εἰς τὴν π[ροεδρίαν ἢ ὀφε]-

20   ιλέτω ᵛ Η ᵛ δραχμὰς [ἱερὰς τῶι Διον]-
ύσωι· ἐπαινέσαι δὲ [Εὐθύδημον Μοιρ]-
οκλέους Ἐλευσίνιο[ν ἀρετῆς ἕνεκα]
καὶ εὐνοίας τῆς εἰ[ς τὸν δῆμον τὸν Ἐ]-
λευσινίων καὶ στεφ[ανῶσαι αὐτὸν θ]-
25   [αλ]λοῦ στεφάνῳι [- - - - - - - -]

Theoboulos son of [Theouboul]os was the proposer. With good fortune for the demos of the Eleusinians and Athenians, [it was decid]ed by the Eleusinians: sin[ce Euthydemos] has long bee[n] ⁵ well-disposed to th[e] dem[o]s [of the E]leusinians and Athenians, both in the priv[ate] and in the public sphere, and when appointed by lot as demarch he served in that capacity in a f[in]e and honest manner and performed [t]he sacrifice to Dionysus for the heal[t]h and securi-ty ¹⁰ of the demesmen at his own expense, demonstrated his ambition for his fellow demesmen, increased the revenue and ma[naged] all the rest of the deme's affairs in a fi[n]e manner, [and in] conformity with the laws, ¹⁵ Euthydemos [is to h]ave [the same gi]ft that [had also been granted t]o his ancestors – namely prohedria, both he him[self and his descendant]s, an[d the demarch] in office [from time] to time is to summon him to his s[eat of honour or o]we ²⁰ 100 drach-mas [consecrated to Dion]ysus; and to praise [Euthydemos son of Moir]okles of Eleusis [for his virtue] and good-will towards [the demos of the E]leusinians, and to crow[n him] ²⁵ with a crown of [o]live […]

The deme honours a demarch: Euthydemos is a son of the Moirokles who had in his turn served the deme well, including its cult of Dionysus (**Hvi**). It is clear that Euthydemos was on good terms with the authorities of the Sanctuary and of the Athenian military establishment, for he was also honoured by a decree of the Kerykes for his service as *paredros* of the Basileus (*IE* 100), an important administrative role in the festival of the Mysteries; and by another dedication from a general stationed at Eleusis (*IE* 102).

The demarch's sacrifice to Dionysus is singled out as the most significant duty of his office (ll. 8–11). The special attention paid to it may be partly due to the fact that on this occasion he funded it from his own pocket, but the language used of it – 'for the heal[t]h and security of the demesmen' (ll. 9–10) – suggests at the very least that this was, under any circumstances, the single most important sacrifice on the deme's calendar, the cornerstone of the deme's cultic well-being. There can be no doubt that it was performed in the context of the Eleusinian Dionysia. A later decree is more explicit: 'the demarch Pamphilos … sacrificed to Dionysus [at the Di]onysia' (*IE* 229, ll. 31–2).

No further reference is made to Euthydemos' conduct of the festival (its parade, agones etc.: cf. *IE* 229, ll. 32–3), but that entails no doubt over its current vigour, for the elaborate award of prohedria to Euthydemos (ll. 14–21) shows that the festival's theatre was still flourishing late in the fourth century. All the more shame that greater precision in dating it is unattainable. Tracy (1995, 139) assigns it to the cutter of *IG* II² 1262, whose known career extends from ca. 320 to ca. 290 – in other words, across a period of enormous change in the social and political life of Athens, and of the Athenian theatre. It is highly likely that prominent among the 'forebears' (l. 16) of Euthydemos to have been awarded prohedria was his father, Moirokles. He had been crowned by the demos in a Dionysian context (**Hvi**; cf. *IE* 85, ll. 14–17).

Like his father before him, Euthydemos worked to improve the deme's finances (l. 12; cf. *IE* 85, l. 16). In the case of Euthydemos it may be legitimate to hypothesise that his money-wise ways were responsible for the measure, unique in honorific decrees, that requires all future demarchs to summon Euthydemos and his descendants to their seat or suffer the heavy fine of 100 drachmas. The fine is to go to Dionysus, suggesting that the god had a treasury of his own separate from the deme's koinon (ll. 19–21; **Hii**, l. 36). Thus the event at which Euthydemos is to be honoured in perpetuity, and the action through which that honour is to be effected, are themselves made the occasion for potential future income generation for the cult of Dionysus. If this was indeed an invention of Euthydemos himself (or rather an idea he suggested to the proposer of the motion, Theoboulos), through it he secures his own honour against the forgetfulness and envy of future generations (even if one may speculate on its long-term enforceability). Be that as it may, it is a nice example of another potential money-making innovation in Dionysian finances from the demes, however modest in scope. Eleusis is not the only deme that used fines to supplement the running costs of its Dionysia; cf. **Miii** and **Rii**, ll. 38–40 where a demarch is again under threat of a fine for failure to do something in relation to that deme's Dionysia.

The details for the publication and erection of this decree are lost. Clinton (2008, 109) suggests that, despite the fact that the largest fragment found had been built into a later wall by the Propylaea of the Goddesses' Sanctuary, it may have been carried there from an original site in the theatre. But it could equally have been erected, like the decree in honour of the general Derkylos, 'by the Propylaea of Demeter and Kore' (*IE* 99, ll. 25–7), and so be another example of the collaboration between the deme authorities in charge of the theatre and the families of the Kerykes and Eumolpidai who ran the sanctuary for the Athenian polis (**Hii**).

Hviii: Dedication to Dionysus by Demonike, Daughter of Aischraios of Pithos, late 4th c. ? (by letter forms and prosopography: Aischraios may have been a member of the Council ca. 360–340: *Agora* 15, 20, l. 22).

Base of blue-grey 'Hymettan' marble; a rectangular cutting on top (0.08 × 0.36 × 0.3 m) for the dedication.
0.38 × 0.46 × 0.55 m.
Copied by Köhler 'inter rudera fani'.
Currently ca. 15 m in front of the porch of the Telesterion; Eleusis, Museum E987.
IG II 1567; *IG* II² 4604; *IE* 103; *IG* II³ 4, 970.
Text: based on *IE* 103.   Photo: Clinton pl. 46.

Δημονίκη Αἰσχραίου Πιθέως
θυγάτηρ Διονύσωι ἀνέθηκεν.

Demonike, daughter of Aischraios of Pithos, dedicated this to Dionysus.

This dedication to Dionysus has no immediately apparent connection to the theatre. It is however of special interest as one of the very few Classical dedications to the god in Attica made by a woman; and for the fact that it seems to have been erected within the Sanctuary of the Goddesses itself, suggesting once more that there was some form of meaningful interconnection between these two cults in Eleusis (note however that Curbera *IG ad loc.* airs the possibility that it came from the deme's sanctuary of Dionysus). Demonike's family is not from Eleusis, but from the deme of Pithos in the upper plain of Attica. Evidently the Dionysus who is master 'in the all-welcoming folds of Eleusinian Demeter' attracted worship from beyond the borders of his deme.

Hix: Choregic Dedication of Hieron, mid 4th c. ? (by letter forms).

Fragment of a base of grey Eleusinian limestone, broken on all sides except top; a small rectangular cutting on the top near the left front corner, to the right of which another shallow cutting, apparently oval-shaped.

0.17 × 0.36 × 0.32 m.

Eleusis, Museum E866.

IG II² 3107; *IE* 107; *IG* II³ 4, 509.

Text: based on *IG* II³ 4, 509.   Photos: Clinton pl. 48 (photo); *IG* II³ 4,1 tab. LXVIII (squeeze).

χορη[γῶν - - - - - - -]   non-stoich.
Ἱέρων Α[- - - - - - - -]
νι[κήσας ἀνέθηκε].

1 [- ωιδοῖς] Kirchner   3 νι[κήσας] Agelidis   νι[κήσας] Kirchner   ν[ικήσας] Clinton (but writes 'Kirchner')

As chore[gos in ?? …] Hieron son of A[-… dedicated this ? after a] vi[ctory].

This fragment of a choregic dedication is too small to allow any conclusions to be drawn as to the genre commemorated or the nature of the object dedicated, although Makres (in *IG* II³) thinks the cuttings on the top may be compatible with a tripod. Restoration is therefore hazardous, but Hieron, like Athenodoros in **Hiv**, probably served as a sole choregos. Like that inscription, this one also seems to ignore the poet or any other performers. One cannot however entirely exclude a restoration, *exempli gratia*, along these lines:

χορη[γῶν κωμωιδοῖς ἐνίκα]
Ἱέρων Α[(*patronymic*) - - - - - -]
Νι[κόστρατος ἐδίδασκε].

or even:

χορη[γοῦντες κωμωιδοῖς ἐνίκων]
Ἱέρων Α[(*patronymic, name + patronymic*)]
Νι[κόστρατος ἐδίδασκε].

Hx: Honorary Decree of the Eleusinians, 321/0 (an Onetor was demarch in 321/0: *IE* 95, l. 1: Clinton 2008, 106).

Fragment of a white marble stele, preserved only on right side.

0.21 × 0.18 × 0.07 m.

Found near the Greater Propylaea.

Eleusis, Museum E1130.

Philios 1890, 87 no. 53; *IG* II 5, 574f; *IG* II² 1192; *IE* 96.

Text: based on *IE* 96.

Photo: Clinton pl. 42.

[. . . . . 9 . . . . Ὀνήτ]ωρ Αἴσω[νος εἶπ]-   stoich. 25
[ε· ἐπειδὴ . . 4 . . Φ]υλάσιος ἀνὴ[ρ ἀγ]-
[αθός ἐστιν πε]ρὶ τὸν δῆμον τὸν [Ἐ]-
[λευσινίων κα]ὶ ποεῖ ὅτι δύνατα-
5   [ι ἀγαθόν, ἐπαι]νέσαι αὐτ[ὸ]ν καὶ σ-
[τεφανῶσαι χρ]υσῶι στε[φά]νωι ἀπ-
[ὸ πεντακοσίω]ν δραχμῶν ἀρετῆς
[ἕνεκα καὶ φι]λοτιμίας τῆς εἰς τ-
[ὸν δῆμον τὸν Ἐλ]ευσινίων· εἶναι
10   [δὲ αὐτῶι καὶ π]ροεδρίαν ἐν τῶ[ι θ]-
[εάτρωι ὅταν τὰ Δι]ονύσια ποε[ῖ ὁ]
[δῆμος ὁ Ἐλευσίνιω]ν· ἀναγρ[άψαι]
[τόδε τὸ ψήφισμα ἐν στή]λη[ι λιθί]-
[νηι καὶ στῆσαι - - - - - - - - - - - - - -]
15   -

1 [ὁ δήμαρχος Ὀνήτ]ωρ Clinton   [Ὀνήτ]ωρ Kirchner

[(?) The demarch Onet]or son of Aiso[n made the proposal: since … of the deme Ph]yle [is a good] ma[n t]o the deme of the [Eleusinians an]d does whatever ⁵ [good] possibl[e, we should pra]ise h[i]m and c[rown him] with a [go]ld cr[o]wn worth [five hundre]d drachmas [for the] virtue [and am]bition he shows to t[he demos of the El]eusinians. ¹⁰ And [he] is to have [p]rohedria in th[e theatre when the demos of the Eleusinia]ns hold[s the Di]onysia. [This decree is to be] inscrib[ed on a stone ste]le [and erected …]

Clinton's suggestion that the proposer is the Onetor who was demarch in 321/0 is attractive, giving us a decree proposed by the demarch in office for a man from outside the deme (a Thyon of Phyle was a prytanis in 360/59, *Agora* 15, 17, l. 7, and would fit the space in l. 2: Clinton 2008, 107). The nature of the services he had rendered is irrecoverable, but it is worth noting that not only is he to receive his crown in the Eleusinian theatre, but also the more lasting benefit of prohedria (though entirely restored, 'the theatre' in ll. 10–11 is inescapable). Along with **Hii**, **Hiii**, possibly also **Hv**, this is further evidence for the award of prohedria to outsiders, and there can be little doubt that the openness of the Eleusinian theatre extended to those in seats other than the prohedria.

I | Euonymon

Introduction

The large and prosperous deme of Euonymon (bouleutic quota 10) formed part of the city trittys of the tribe Erechtheis. Bordered to the west by the city deme Halimous and to the south by the coastal deme Aixone (both also possessed of theatres **L**; **D**), Euonymon occupied a strategic position on the main ancient road between Athens – only seven kilometers distant – and Sunium. The deme principally derived its wealth in the Classical period from intensive and homogeneous cultivation that produced cash crops traded to a wider market in the city and beyond. The theatre was discovered in 1973, around 200 m to the east of a hill that had long been identified as the likely centre of the deme because of the presence of various funerary inscriptions belonging to Euonymeis (Moreno 2007, 42–3). Its excavation awaits full publication and knowledge of it is dependent on a series of more or less preliminary studies by the excavator, Olga Tzachou-Alexandri.

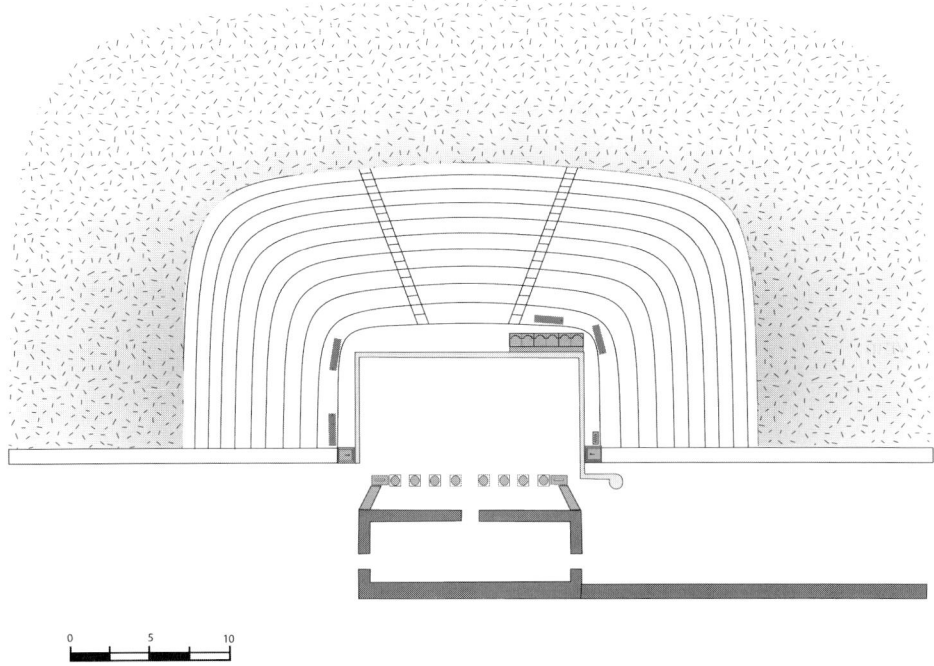

Plan of the theatre at Euonymon.

The seating area was to the north, the stage building to the south. The remains of the seating area show foundations of around eleven rows of stone seats (autopsy; Tzachou-Alexandri 1999, 421, notes six). The full extension of the theatron has been estimated at around twenty-one rows (Lohmann 1998, 195), dug directly into the natural slope. There is no sign of heavy foundations to support an upper extension of the theatron in stone, and it is therefore probable that the upper seats consisted of removable wooden benches, placed directly upon the narrow steps that can be seen cut into the natural rock (there are no traces of postholes of the sort designed to receive *ikria*). Solid retaining walls measuring some 21 m in length and 0.8 m in width supported the spectator area at either side. That on the eastern side is preserved in places to ca. 1 m in height. Their construction is said to show signs of two phases. Some 27.2 m of the northerly section have been dated by the excavator to the first half of the fourth century. The southern extension, which uses larger blocks, appears to belong to a later phase (these two phases may correspond to what can be deduced of the phasing of the theatre from the evidence of the stage buildings and prohedria – below). The theatron was divided by access staircases into three sections. It is said (Slater 2011, 285) that, when first excavated, the earth under the theatron was covered with a thick layer of stucco, designed to prevent erosion or subsidence that seems to have been a characteristic problem of theatres and perhaps especially of those, like Euonymon, that were prone to flooding.

At the end of each retaining wall, right at the point where each parodos enters the orchestra, there stood on stepped plinths a fine, archaising statue of a standing Dionysus, at least one of which held a kantharos that was found nearby. The statues themselves were discovered not far away from their bases (they appear to have been deliberately removed from them and placed in the nearby stage building for protection, perhaps from the fighting that took place in the theatre during the Chremonidean War: below). They are the first statues of the god to be discovered inside a Classical theatre and are evidently not cult statues in a traditional sense, but seem to represent a new direction in the exploitation of the possibilities of theatrical space for display (Lampaki 2015; Lampaki 2012 is a more comprehensive study of the phenomenon). The somewhat better-preserved one measures 1.565 m in height, including its plinth. Archaising in pose and dress, they have been dated on stylistic grounds to around 325 (Tzachou-Alexandri 2007) but there is much scope for disagreement (below). No altar was found near them, nor anywhere else in the theatre. A fragmentary inscription suggests that they may have been dedicated by an illustrious member of the deme, Olympiodorus son of Diotimos (**Ii**), but see below. (The statues are now in the Piraeus museum: Pir. Mus. 18214–15; full publication and discussion in Tzachou-Alexandri 2007).

The orchestra was rectangular in shape, approximately 15.29 m wide and 7.59 m deep, although the first row of seats shows a very slight curvature that is continued and increased in the steps higher up, which become increasingly narrow. The shape has been thought to imply a fifth-century date for either the first phase of which traces survive, or for a predecessor to it (Goette 1995a, 16–17; Tzachou-Alexandri 2007, 37; Tzachou-Alexandri also suggests that the evidence of fifth-century potsherds in the theatron implies that there may have been an earlier phase constructed entirely of wood: 1999, 421). The most economical interpretation of the evidence currently available suggests two phases of construction for the theatre: the first involving a simple rectangular skene and a first set of prohedria (ca. 400); the second, a proskenion extension to the older skene and a second set of prohedria.

Statues of Dionysus found in the theatre of Euonymon.

The presence of two sets of prohedria is a very striking feature of the Euonymon theatre. The older prohedria went around all three edges of the koilon – with gaps for the
two access staircases – and consisted of several slabs of white (probably Hymettan rather
than Pentelic) marble around 1.6 m long (one of them – **c** below – measures 1.59 × 0.42
× 0.13–0.14 m), upon which wooden chairs or benches were presumably placed. There
were probably fifteen or sixteen such slabs in total originally. Four survive (**a–d**). At least
a couple of these were found *in situ* (Lohmann 1998, 221, pl. 6) and it is possible that
the present position (as of September 2013) of all four surviving blocks may reflect their
original placement, although it is clear that **c** has been moved slightly to the east from an
original position adjacent to the eastern staircase in the theatron (it has no clamp to the left).
Each of the surviving blocks is inscribed on its front surface, facing the orchestra, and it is
a safe assumption that the full original extent of the blocks was inscribed. As much is also
implied by the fact that the first inscribed block (**a**) was situated close to the front edge of
the western parodos (it should be stressed however that we do not as yet have an authoritative account of the excavated positions of these blocks).

Base slabs for prohedria, ca. 400 (on the date see below).

a.

Slab of white (probably Hymettan) marble; T-clamp at the right-hand side, none at the left. Inscribed on front surface in widely-spaced letters; average space between letters ca. 0.35 m; L. 1.626 m. Found, probably *in situ*, at the edge of the orchestra on the left-hand side of the theatron, close to the front edge of the western parodos, where it remains.

> ΠΡΟΕ[ΔΡΙΑΝ]

> ΠΡΟΕ[ΔΡΙΑ] Tzachou-Alexandri   ΠΡΟΕ[ΔΡΙΑ ΔΙΟΝΥΣΟ] Pöhlmann   ΠΡΟΕ[ΔΡΙΑΝ] Wilson

> … prohe[dria] …

b.

Slab of white (probably Hymettan) marble; T-clamp at the left-hand side, none at the right. L. 1.636 m.

> ΑΝΑΘΕ[-]

> ΑΝΑΘΕ[ΜΑ] Pöhlmann   ΑΝΑΘΕ[ΙΣ /-ΝΤΕΣ /-ΝΤΟΣ] Wilson

> … having dedicat[ed] (*or* dedica[tion]) …

c.

Slab of white (probably Hymettan) marble; T-clamp at the right-hand side, none at the left. 1.585 × 0.42 × 0.13–0.14 m.
Found probably in or near its original position immediately to the right of the eastern access staircase of the theatron. It is presently slightly to the east of this original position.
SEG 32, 272.

> ΤΟ ΠΡ[-]

> ΤΟ ΠΡ[ΩΤΟΝ + year of dedication] Tzachou-Alexandri

> (?) Fi[rst] …

d.

Slab of white (probably Hymettan) marble; T-clamp at the left-hand side, none at the right. L. 1.43 m.

> ΑΥΤΟ[-]

> αὐτο[ῦ] or Αὐτο[κλῆς] Wilson

> … (?) of it / him … *or* (?) Auto[kles]

These inscriptions have been thought to provide decisive evidence to date the first phase of prohedria to the fifth century. This rests on regarding the *epsilon* of **b** (ΑΝΑΘΕ[-]) as standing for an *eta* in pre-Euclidean official script, thus likely placing it before 403, and on the related assumption that the complete word was ΑΝΑΘΕ[ΜΑ] 'dedication'. The latter is however just as if not rather more likely to have been a verbal form describing the act of dedication itself. An active aorist participle of ἀνατίθημι would produce an *epsilon* in this position: '(*singular or plural subject*) having dedicated'. This removes this criterion for dating and we are left to letter forms. On this basis Tzachou-Alexandri (1999,

421) places it in the middle, Goette (1995a, 16) in the first quarter, of the fourth century. On balance a date ca. 400–375, probably nearer the start than the end of the span, seems most likely.

Based on a calculation of the space between the surviving blocks, and taking account of the interruption of the two access stairs (note the absence of a T-clamp on the left-hand side of **c**), we might propose the following conservative continuous rendering of the entire inscription: ΠΡΟΕ[ΔΡΙΑΝ - - ca. 6 - -]ΑΝΑΘΕ[- - - - - - - ca. 20–25 - - - - - - - -]ΤΟ ΠΡ[- - - ca. 8–9 - - -]ΑΥΤΟ[- - - - ca. 14 - - - -].

Further restoration requires a high degree of speculation. It is however virtually certain that the first part of the inscription records the dedication of the prohedria, and that it does so as the gift of an individual: something like προε[δρίαν τήνδε] ἀναθέ[ντος or ἀναθε[ὶς *name* …], '[*Name* having] dedicated [this] prohe[dria …]'.

Beyond that it is very difficult to go, but we make a number of observations: τὸ πρῶτον (Tzachou-Alexandri) 'in the first place', 'originally' is a possible reconstruction for the ΤΟΠΡ of **c**. That might have served as an adverbial phrase qualifying the initial act of dedication, before going on to refer to a second such: e.g. προε[δρίαν τήνδε] ἀναθε[ὶς *name* + *patronymic* (or Διονύσωι)] τὸ πρ[ῶτον καὶ] αὐτὸ[ς *object* ἔδωκε.] '[*Name* (+ *patronymic*) having] dedicated [this] prohe[dria (*possibly* to Dionysus *instead of patronymic*)] orig[inally also] himsel[f gave *object*].' 'The skene' might even fit the space left available for the *object* on this reconstruction, and the evidence for the date of the stone skene places it reasonably close to the date of inscription (for the possible need to distinguish between the date of inscription and the date of dedication of the prohedria see the next paragraph). The desirability of including Dionysus as the recipient of the dedication is prompted by his presence in **Ii**.

Alternatively, τὸ πρ[ῶτον …] might encourage us to identify a father and son dedication, with the son subsequently – but already, we note, by the late fifth or early fourth century – adding some further object to his father's original benefaction. An immediate difficulty is that such a two-generation dedication might be hard to reconcile with the fact that the earlier act of dedication being described evidently refers to prohedria (**a**), whereas we should naturally expect the inscription on that very prohedria to refer to its dedication. It is however worth mooting the possibility that the inscription was placed some time after the construction of the prohedria. And in fact it seems to sit quite awkwardly on the very rough-chiselled surface of the blocks, perhaps indicating that no inscription was intended when the prohedria was first put in.

A further problem with this line of enquiry is that it probably leaves insufficient space for a clause with a main verb, unless **d**'s ΑΥΤΟ was part of the son's name. That however is a possibility, since Autokles is the name of a known member of the deme's most prominent and wealthy family, 'whose political allegiance was consistent in support of the full democracy and in opposition to Sparta' (*APF* 161), and of which another famous member, Olympiodorus, is securely attested as a substantial benefactor to the theatre of Euonymon in a later generation (below and **Ii**). Autokles is the son of Strombichides, son of Diotimos. Strombichides was general in 412/11 and probably again in 405/4, when he played a leading role in defending the democracy. His son Autokles clearly continued the tradition (*APF* 161–2; Humphreys 2018, 506–7). All three can be found a place on this reconstruction: e.g. προε[δρίαν τήνδε] ἀναθέ[ντος Στρομβιχίδου Διοτίμου (*or* Διονύσωι)] τὸ πρ[ῶτον, ὁ υἱὸς] Αὐτο[κλῆς *object* ἔδωκε.] '[Strombichides son of Diotimos having] dedicated this prohe[dria (*possibly* to Dionysus *instead of* son of Diotimos)] orig[inally, his son] Auto[kles gave *object*]'. This however leaves just some five or so letters for the object given by Autokles and is, needless to say, speculation that verges on free composition.

Other construals of ΤΟΠΡ are certainly possible. Some verb such as πρ[οσέθηκε 'he added' might be a possibility, also in the context of a family double dedication (e.g. προε[δρίαν τήνδε] ἀναθέ[ντος *name, object* τοῦ]το πρ[οσέθηκε ὁ υἱὸς] αὐτο[ῦ *name*]. '[*name* having] dedicated [this] prohe[dria,] his [son *name*] ad[ded th]is [*object*].' Another is πρωτόβαθρον, a word which seems to have been used for the 'first bench' (**V H**), though quite how this might sit with the προεδρία is unclear – perhaps the combination 'the *protobathron* of the prohedria' is not out of the question. (τὸ πρ[οσκήνιον] 'the pr[oskenion]' can probably be ruled out, given that the letter forms speak strongly against a date that might be compatible with the introduction of the proskenion: below.)

The remains of a second and later form of prohedria were found *in situ* in the northeast corner of the orchestra. Three pairs of double throne-like seats made of 'Hymettan' marble, similar to those from the theatre at Ikarion (Biers and Boyd 1982, 15 fig. 16), were discovered under metre-high alluvial layers. It is clear that this prohedria was limited to the central part of the koilon, facing the stage; and that it was placed directly in front of the older, simpler style of prohedria, presumably thus adding another level of priority seating. Jean-Charles Moretti (pers. comm.) compares the situation at Tegea (Vallois 1926, 164–9). Hans Goette (pers. comm.) suggests that this prohedria was confined to the corners of the orchestra, rather than extending all across its front, since the exposed sides of the extant seats are smooth, while the two joins between the three pairs employ careful anathyrosis.

As for the stage building, the first phase identifiable from the remaining foundations shows a simple rectangular skene in stone with a single door facing the orchestra (Plan). For there was evidently no structural connection between the two *antae* of the proskenion stage building whose remains are clearly visible and the rectangular building between them, which will thus have formed the skene of the preceding phase. The masonry of the rectangular skene dates it to some time after ca. 413 (by comparison with the construction style of Attic fortresses built in the Decelean War: this and what follows was communicated by Hans Goette on the basis of personal study of the site). A second phase of construction is to be identified with the addition of the proskenion, equipped with a façade of eight Doric columns (0.5 m diam.) *in antis* (Plan; Tzachou-Alexandri 2007, esp. pls. 1–3). A foundation connects the (northern) ends of the two *antae*, upon which the columns stood. The proskenion thus seems to have been added to the pre-existing simple stone skene. One might assume, on the basis of many other theatres in and beyond Attica, that there was also an earlier wooden phase of the skene building (see above). Autopsy further indicates that there was a stele dock at either end of the proskenion façade, abutting directly to each of the two *antae* (see Plan).

Although its date of construction is not known, this would be a rather early example of a proskenion theatre in the region, much earlier than the Theatre of Dionysus. The earliest examples are known from late fourth-century Epidaurus (**IV Bviii**) and Delos (**IV Dvi**), third-century Priene (for the date see Crowther 1996; **IV Evii**), Dodona and Cassope (**IV C**; cf.

Lohmann 1998, 197 expressing some doubt as to the likelihood of such a form at this date in Euonymon; Moretti 1997 on early proskenion theatres). Whether staircases or ramps associated with the walls were used to reach the upper level from the rear of the stage building is unclear. It is extremely difficult to assess the date of this feature of the stage building in Euonymon – and of the probably associated new phase of prohedria – in the absence of its full publication.

One might be tempted to look to the historical figure of Olympiodorus to provide some sort of chronological anchor. He clearly made a significant votive dedication in the theatre in the closing decades of the fourth century (**Ii**), but of what? The dedicatory stele with his name was found in the orchestra, and the fact that it evidently originally stood immediately beside one of the statues of Dionysus has suggested that his dedication may have consisted of, or at least included, them. But there are difficulties in establishing such a connection: while the statues have been placed by their style around 325 (Tzachou-Alexandri 2007), their archaising style has parallels as early as the 470s, and their somewhat stiff character might be thought to fit better much earlier in the fourth century, around 370 (thus Hans Goette, pers. comm.), in which case they almost certainly have no connection with the dedication of Olympiodorus (excluding as highly implausible the idea of a dedication of statues already some fifty years old), and might in fact be close in date to the dedication of the older prohedria. Perhaps Olympiodorus' dedication consisted rather of the new prohedria and associated proskenion, or of some significant element of one or the other? Recall the two stele docks built in alignment with and at either end of the proskenion, which could have carried the inscription recording their dedication (above). It is also noteworthy that the new prohedria is made of the same 'Hymettan' marble as the bases of the two statues. Whatever its precise nature, a major gift to the community's theatrical life is not implausible, especially at this date when we find many examples of proto-Hellenistic euergetistic gifts in Athenian civic life, and given too the evidence from the older inscribed prohedria of a significant dedication to this theatre many years earlier.

In many ways a date somewhat closer to the end of the fourth century would better suit the involvement of Olympiodorus in his deme's theatre, whatever its nature and extent. In 325 he will have only very recently inherited his family fortune (aged ca. 25; *APF* 164–5) and we might instead look to the period during which nothing is known of the otherwise highly active Olympiodorus, the regime of Demetrius of Phaleron (317–307). All the same, the 'new' theatre at Euonymon presents something of a paradox: the shape of its prohedria and associated orchestra are somewhat old-fashioned, certainly by comparison with the Theatre of Dionysus in Athens; yet the stage building is very modern, even more advanced than that of the city Theatre.

Estimates of the seating capacity of the Euonymon theatre are inevitably approximate, and range from 2,600 to 3,750 adults. As Lohmann (1998, 195) has pointed out, even the lower figure far exceeds the full citizen population of the deme – approximated at around 420; or 2,100 people, including women and children (but not slaves and metics). The theatre's size was evidently not dictated by the need for its use as a political meeting place (or at least not of the deme alone), and attracted an audience from beyond the borders of the deme, probably even from the city. The fact that the small neighbour Halimous (**L**) possessed its own theatre demonstrates that the existence of a well-equipped theatre in close proximity did not extinguish the desire to maintain one's own. Indeed, recent excavation has revealed the existence of a road directly connecting the site of the Halimous theatre on the Ag. Anna hill with the centre of Euonymon (Kaza-Papageorgiou 2005).

The Euonymon theatre was abandoned by the mid third century (**Iii**). Chronic flooding was clearly a significant problem, evidently not solved by the digging of a drainage channel around the edge of the orchestra that fed into a covered storm-water drain, with its own inspection chamber (Kaza-Papageorgiou 2016, 125–7 with plates 204–7), but the effects of the Chremonidean War (267–262) may also have played their part, to judge from the numerous sling projectiles found in the theatre (Tzachou-Alexandri 2007, 37–9).

Ii: **Dedication of Olympiodorus in the Theatre at Euonymon**, ca. 330–300 (by letter forms and prosopography).

Fragment of grey marble from the upper part of a votive plaque, broken at bottom.
0.285–0.165 × 0.40 × 0.08 m.
Found in excavations of the Archaeological Society at Athens in the orchestra of the Euonymon theatre.
Piraeus Museum (no inventory number).
Tzachou-Alexandri 1980, 65–6 (= *SEG* 32, 267); *IG* II³ 4, 968.
Text: based on *SEG* 32, 267.   Photo: Tzachou-Alexandri 2007, 31 pl. 35.

1   [Δ]ιονύσωι [Ὀ]λυμπιόδωρος
        Διοτίμου ἀνέθηκεν.

[O]lympiodorus son of Diotimos made a dedication to [D]ionysus.

This fragment, consisting of the upper part of a marble stele, was found in the orchestra of the Euonymon theatre, 2 m from the tiered statue base of Dionysus that was erected at the end of the eastern parodos (**I Introduction**). Immediately adjacent to this statue base was found another quadrangular marble base, designed to receive a stele – almost certainly the one of which this is the upper part (Tzachou-Alexandri 2007, 33–5, images 38–9, 41; Plan).

The dedicant is a famous member of the most prominent family of the deme, six generations of which are known, with substantial and consistent evidence of democratic commitment (*APF* 164–5). Olympiodorus was born ca. 350 and had inherited his father's liturgical-level wealth (and trierarchic debts) by 325/4 (*IG* II² 1629, ll. 539–41, 622–9). He was best remembered for his recovery of the Mouseion hill from Macedonian control as general in 288/7 and his exceptional double Archonship in 294/3 and 293/2. This dedication in the Euonymon theatre has been dated to ca. 330–320 by letter forms, stratigraphic evidence of Hellenistic sherds, the style of the two statues of Dionysus which seem to have formed part of the dedication and the evidence for his having inherited his father's property. There is however a wide margin of uncertainty, particularly in relation to the use of the stylistic criterion for the statues (**I Introduction**), and the date could well be some two decades or more later. It is worth noting that nothing is known of the otherwise highly active Olympiodorus during the regime of Demetrius of Phaleron (317–307; **VI K**).

Despite the considerable wealth of his family, no liturgy is known for Olympiodorus. He is a rare example of an individual prominent at the polis level who made a substantial contribution to his local theatre, and in a manner much more permanent than through simple choregia. This is the model, becoming more familiar in this period, of the euergetistic gift or special *epidosis*. Just what constitutes his dedication is unclear (**I Introduction**). The likely proximity of the dedicatory stele to one of the statues of Dionysus points in their direction. It is possible that the 'new' prohedria, and perhaps even the new associated proskenion, were (also) donated by this prominent member of the deme, perhaps in company with other family members. The newer prohedria is made of the same 'Hymettan' marble as the bases of the two statues.

Iii: The Deme Euonymon Honours Benefactors in the Theatre, late 4th c. (by letter forms and prosopography); perhaps 313/12? (see on l. 14).

Fragment of a stele of 'Pentelic' marble, broken on all sides.
0.35 × 0.26 × 0.13 m.
Found in excavations of the Archaeological Society at Athens in secondary use built into a wall over the left parodos of the theatre of Euonymon.
Athens EM (provisional).
Steinhauer 2007 (= *SEG* 57, 125).
Text: based on *SEG* 57, 125.   Photos: Steinhauer 2007, 44 (stone); Tzachou-Alexandri 2007, 38 (findspot).

- -

```
1      [. . . . .11. . . . . εἶπ]εν· ἐπ[ειδὴ ? Κτησικλ]-           stoich. ?27–30
       [είδης λαχὼν τῆς] ἀρχῆς [καλῶς καὶ φιλ]-
       [οτίμως ἐπεμε]λήθη τῶν κ[οινῶν καὶ τὰ]-
       [ς θυσίας τέθυκ]εν τοῖς θεο[ῖς καὶ τοῖ]-
5      [ς ἥρωσιν, δεδόχ]θαι Εὐωνυ[μεῦσιν ἐπα]-
       [ινέσαι ν ? Κτησι]κλείδην [τὸν δήμαρχον]
       [καὶ στεφανῶσ]αι αὐτὸ[ν] χ[ρυσῶι στεφά]-
       [νωι ἀπὸ : Χ : δρ]αχμῶν ἀ[ρετῆς ἕνεκα νν ]
       [καὶ δικαιοσ]ύνη[ς] τῆς [εἰς τὸν δῆμον]
10     [τὸν Εὐωνυμέ]ων καὶ δ[ιδόναι αὐτῶι τὸ]-
       [ν δήμαρχον] τὸν ἀε[ὶ δημαρχοῦντα προ]-
       [εδρίαν ἐν τ]ῶι ἀγ[ῶνι . . . . . .11–14. . . . . .]
       [. .2–5. . ἀναγρ]άψα[ι δὲ τὸ ψήφισμα τόδε τ]-
       [ὸν μετὰ Θεόφ]ρας[τον δήμαρχον ἐστήλ]-
15     [ηι λιθίνηι κ]αὶ [στῆσαι εἰς τὸ θέατρον]
       [. . . . . . .]ΤΟ[- - - - - - - - - - - - - - - - - - - -]
```

- -

6 [? τὸν ταμίαν]   12 [ἐν τ]ῶι ἀγ[ῶνι τῶι τῶν τραγωιδῶν·] Hartwig   14–15 δήμαρχον ἐστήλ|ηι λιθίνηι Wilson   ἄρχοντα ἐστήλη|ι λιθίνηι Steinhauer

[... propos]ed: si[nce after being allotted to the] office, [? Ktesikleides super]-
vised the co[mmon resources and has perform]ed [the sacrifices] to the god[s
and heroes in a fine and ambitious manner], ⁵ the Euony[meis deci]ded [to
praise ? Ktesi]kleides [the demarch and to crow]n him with a g[old crown
worth 1,000 dr]achmas [for his] v[irtue and hon]esty towards [the deme ¹⁰ of
the Euonym]eis, and [the demarch] who holds office at any given time ti[me is
to] g[ive him prohedria at t]he con[test ?? of tragedies ... and the demarch in
the year following (sc. the Archonship of) Theoph]ras[tos is to in]scrib[e this
decree on ¹⁵ a stone stele a]nd [erect it in the theatre ...]

This small fragment of an honorific decree from Euonymon was a fortuitous find from filler
used to build a retaining wall over the eastern parodos of the theatre, the construction of
which rendered it useless as an entrance to the acting space, and so helps to date the abandonment of the theatre to the second quarter of the third century (Tzachou-Alexandri 2007,
37). It adds Euonymon to the list of demes that used their theatre to honour benefactors
and shows that in the later fourth century that theatre hosted contests – possibly in tragedy
(below). The restorations are far from certain and it is not possible to determine a secure
number of stoichoi.

The honorand was the holder of a local civic office (l. 2 ἀρχῆς), probably the demarchy
(Steinhauer 2007, 45). Demarchs are often responsible for finances and the conduct of sacrifices (ll. 3–5). Note also the praise for his [δικαιοσ]ύνη '[hon]esty' or 'sense of [jus]tice'
in l. 9, a quality admired in money men (Whitehead 1993, 67–8; **Diii**). We should perhaps
not rule out the possibility that he was a treasurer (*tamias*). They too can be charged with
these duties (**Bvii**).

The name [Ktesi]kleides is not certain, and is restored as the only name known from
Euonymon that fits (Steinhauer 2007, 45). A Ktesikleides of Euonymon (*AM* 110, 1995,
278 col. I, l. 11), a cleruch on Samos (*ISamos* 133, l. 42) and member of the Council ca.
352–347, had a son of the same name who was himself a member of the Council and
would suit the indications by letter forms of a late fourth-century date (*PAA* 586990²). The
honours included a gold crown (l. 7) and very probably (the restorations in ll. 10–12 are in
rough outline fairly secure) prohedria at a contest held in the theatre. In a theatre furnished
at this time with two fine archaising statues of Dionysus, one at the end of each parodos, the
context of this agon must be a Dionysia. The restoration of 'tragedies' in l. 12 can be little
more than a guess, but is epigraphically more likely than 'comedies'.

The meagre traces of the instructions to inscribe and erect this decree (ll. 13–15) may
lay those duties on the demarch in office in the year after the Archonship (in the city) of
Theophrastos. But no adequate restoration has been given. The one printed here lacks a
reference to the status of Theophrastos as Archon – 'in the year following Theophrastos';
that of Steinhauer, more fatally, fails to mention the demarch, the subject of the clause.
However if that dating formula is present, the Archon Theophrastos of 313/12 rather than
that of 340/39 will be intended and this becomes another example of a deme assembly
active during the regime of Demetrius of Phaleron (**Diii**).

J | Halai Aixonides

Choregic Monument, ca. 400–375 (by letter forms, orthography and prosopography).

Fragment of a cylindrical base of 'Pentelic' marble, broken at bottom, with a cavity in the upper surface (0.35 diam. × 0.09 m) to receive the circular tenon of a plinth for a statue or column. 0.31 × 0.535 m diam.

Found in 1929 at Palaiochori (Papagiannopoulos-Palaios 1929a, 162, 171), between Voula and Vari (ancient Halai Aixonides: Eliot 1962, 29–30; Giamalide and Daifa 2013).

Athens EM 12693.

Papagiannopoulos-Palaios 1929a; *IG* II² 3091; *IG* II³ 4, 498.

Text: based on *IG* II³ 4, 498.   Photos: Papagiannopoulos-Palaios 1929a, 162; Goette 2014, fig. 2.14; *IG* II³ 4,1 tab. LXVIII.

Ἐ ιι[. . . . . χορηγῶν ἐνίκα] κωμωιδοῖς·   stoich.
Ἐχφαντίδης ἐδίδασκε [.] Πείρας.
Θρασύβολος χορηγῶν ἐνίκα κωμωιδοῖς·
Κρατῖνος ἐδίδασκε Βουκόλος.
5   Θρασύβολος χορη[γ]ῶν ἐνίκα τραγωιδοῖς·
Τιμόθεος ἐδίδασκε Ἀλκμέωνα, Ἀλφεσίβο[ιαν].
Ἐπιχάρης χορηγῶν ἐνίκα τραγωιδο[ῖς]·
Σοφοκλῆς ἐδίδασκε Τηλέφειαν.
              vacat

1 Start of line Ἐ ιι[- - Makres   Ἐ[. . . . .] Mette   ἘΥ[- - -] Luppe   Ἐ[πιχάρης χορηγῶν ἐνίκα] Papagiannopoulos-Palaios   2 [.] letter deleted by stone-cutter. Possibly [Σ]πείρας Papagiannopoulos-Palaios, Wilamowitz   6 Τιμόθεος ἐδίδασκε Ἀλκμέωνα, Ἀλφεσίβο[ιαν,

<? *name of two more dramas*>] Luppe   8 Σοφοκλῆς ἐδίδασκε Τηλέφειαν, [<? *name of satyr drama*>] Luppe

E[-... was victorious as choregos] in comedy;
Ecphantides was didaskalos of the *Attempts*.
Thrasyboulos was victorious as choregos in comedy;
Cratinus was didaskalos of the *Cowherds*.
5   Thrasyboulos was victorious as chore[g]os in tragedy;
Timotheos was didaskalos of the *Alkmaion*, the *Alphesibo[ia]*.
Epichares was victorious as choregos in tragedy;
Sophocles was didaskalos of the *Telepheia*.

The deme of Halai Aixonides, between Aixone and Anagyrous on the south-western coast of Attica (bouleutic quota 6; 10 after 307/6), is known to have had various scattered farms and small sanctuaries, with (at least) two separate villages rather than a single large con-centrated centre, and a number of very elaborate private houses (Andreou 1994; Schörner and Goette 2004; Giamalide and Daifa 2013). In the fourth century, its political and civic life was dominated by a small group of interconnected, well-off families (doubtless true of many other demes, if less clearly demonstrable: Whitehead 1986a, 239–40). These wor-thies, for instance, tended with their own funds to the fabric and management of an impor-tant shrine of Aphrodite in the north-west (*IG* II² 2820; *SEG* 49, 142) and also to the cult of Apollo Zoster on the southern cape (*ArchDelt* 11, 40, 4, ll. 2–6), both sites used for the display of deme decrees (*SEG* 49, 141–3; Parker 2005, 68).

Halai Aixonides does not usually figure in lists of demes known to have held Dionysia, but we believe the evidence is sufficient to warrant it. The principal item is one of a small set of choregic monuments found in demes whose performances have been assigned to an urban context for little better reason than the fame of the poets named in them. And the likelihood that, from as early as the 450s, Halai Aixonides did support its own theatrical festival, with some of the greatest figures in comic and tragic drama producing at it, is strengthened by the discovery of another, tiny fragment found within its territory (findspot in Ano Voula; Eliot 1962, 31; Andreou 1994, 205). Consisting entirely of the word ἐδίδασκε 'was the didaskalos' (*IG* II³ 4, 517), this almost certainly comes from another choregic monument and, though not found in its original site of erection, the findspot is immediately adjacent to the north of Palaiochori, the findspot of the substantial choregic monument above. Further, a decree in honour of the deme's treasurers of 338/7, discovered only in 2006 (Steinhauer 2004–2009; *SEG* 59, 142), breaks off just before stating where and at what occasion their crowns are to be awarded (l. 16 [κα]ὶ ἀνει[πεῖν]), but a theatrical setting at the local Dionysia is quite likely (Takeuchi 2010–2013, 93–4). Goette (2014, 93–4) considers Halai Aixonides one of a number of demes in this broad area that shared a theatre located on the territory of Aixone. But the absence of identifying demotics in the choregic monument (**C**; **Ei**) tells against the notion that it might have been set up in a theatre not on the territory of its erectors' deme.

There is moreover positive evidence to suggest that Halai Aixonides had a theatre of its own. It is, admittedly, inconclusive and ambiguous. Two apparently distinct sites are in question. The first is in the modern centre of Vouliagmeni, some 3 km to the south of Palaiochori and certainly within the territory of the ancient deme. An unconfirmed report (Koutsogiannis 1984, 38; Ackermann 2018, 55) maintains that, during the construction of a building near a cinema in the modern centre of Vouliagmeni in the 1980s, workers uncovered the stone bench seating of an ancient theatre, which they quickly covered back up to avoid delaying their work. Goette (2014, 94) expresses doubt over the account, not least since the site in question offered no helpful slope, but it is not easy to find a plausible rationale, even in fierce local cultural pride, for the invention of such a story.

The other site is further to the north, on what was once the Kanellopoulos estate, which lay south of a road running east to Vari from a crossroads beyond Ana Voula (marked 'C' on Eliot 1962, 31 fig. 2). In the late 1940s Papagiannopoulos-Palaios saw here a circular structure some 11 m in diameter, bordered by a small wall 0.60 m thick. Next to this were the remains of the foundations of a small quadrangular building which he dated 'probably' (πιθανῶς) to the fourth century (Papagiannopoulos-Palaios 1949–1951). Papagiannopoulos-Palaios identified the circular space as the orchestra of the Aixone theatre (the fact that he was wrong as to the relevant ancient deme hardly undermines the rest of his observations: for the persistent problems in identifying the correct site of Aixone see Ackermann 2018, 32–59) and the foundations as those of a small temple of Dionysus. Though it lacks detail and documentary support, Papagiannopoulos-Palaios' account has been too readily dismissed (Eliot 1962, 32: 'One is tempted to inquire: "Why not a threshing-floor?"') or ignored (but cf. Marchiandi 2011, 623). It would certainly suit the findspot of this choregic monument, on the assumption that it was probably set up in or near the deme's theatre.

The cylindrical marble base was found in the area of Palaiochori, just to the north of Ag. Nikolaos στοὺς Πάλους (Papagiannopoulos-Palaios 1929a, 162, 171). While near the border with Aixone, this is certainly territory of Halai Aixonides, and the earlier assignment of the monument to Aixone is to be rejected (Eliot 1962, 29; Ackermann 2018, 55). This unique and important monument records four choregic victories, two in comedy followed by two in tragedy. Its architectural form is striking – the inscribed cylindrical base carried either a statue (perhaps of Dionysus: Papagiannopoulos-Palaios 1929a, 161) or a column with some further decoration affixed to it. Following the name of each choregos is that of a poet; the standard verb for production ἐδίδασκε 'was the didaskalos/trainer'; and – most unusually – titles of the plays performed. The inclusion of titles on choregic monuments is unparalleled in the demes. Indeed there is only a single urban example, in the inclusion of the phrase 'The song: the *Elpenor* of Timotheus' ᾆσμα· Ἐλπήνωρ Τιμοθέου, on the great monument of Nikias to the western side of the Theatre of Dionysus (**V F** on *IG* II³ 4, 467). The fact that this repeat performance of a work nearly a century old is marked in this way, without the use of the verb ἐδίδασκε, is further reason to believe that the poets listed on the Halai monument produced the plays in person (cf. *DFA*² 55: 'It seems clear that the formula ἐδίδασκε is only used in inscriptions of plays produced by the authors in person'). However, one cannot entirely rule out the possibility that these are repeat performances directed by others.

Three of the most illustrious poets of the fifth century are named – two of the greats of the generation of comic pioneers prior to Aristophanes, Ecphantides and Cratinus. Only a few words of Ecphantides' work survive, and one other title, the *Satyrs*. He won his first victory (of four) at the City Dionysia at some time between 457 and 454 (Bagordo 2014, 72–98). While Cratinus' long career saw him win six Dionysian and three Lenaean victories between ca. 453 and 423 (for the more than five hundred fragments see *PCG* IV; Bakola 2010). He was possibly dead, or at least artistically inactive, by 421 (Ar. *Peace* 700–1). Nothing is known of Ecphantides' *Attempts*. One guess is that the 'attempts' in question are theatrical offerings of rival dramatists. Schmid (1946, 79) compares Cratinus' *Didaskaliai* or *Dramatic Productions* and Aristophanes' *Proagon* or *Prelude to the Contest*. The suggestion that the title was in fact Σπεῖραι ? *Coils* (see app. crit.) is epigraphically weak and provides no improvement in sense. The meagre fragments of Cratinus' *Cowherds* have been speculatively interpreted as an attack on the introduction of foreign cults to Athens in the 430s (Delneri 2006, 43–67). The title, and the reference to the use of dithyramb in the comedy, perhaps the opening entrance of the chorus (**I Bi 9**), make some association with the *boukoloi* who worshipped Dionysus in the form of a bull likely (cf. E. *Antiop.* fr. 203, *Cret.* fr. 472.11; Ar. *Wasps* 10 and Sch.; Arist. *Ath.* 3.5: *Boukoleion*; Jacottet 2003 II, 182–9). A date before 430 has been proposed on the grounds that the play referred to a situation in which an Archon refused Sophocles a chorus (**I Bi 9**), a thing regarded by some as unthinkable in the later part of Sophocles' career (Geissler 1969, 24).

No Timotheos is otherwise attested as a tragic poet, but there is little reason to endorse the view that the Timotheos of this inscription was merely the director of works by the poet Achaios, who is known to have composed an *Alkmaion* (Luppe 1969, 151). Luppe's further suggestion that two more titles may have followed *Alkmaion* and *Alphesiboia* to make up a tragic tetralogy is based on his belief that the performances recorded were won in the city, not the deme (see below), but there is no good reason to reject the possibility of multiple works by a single poet at a deme Dionysia. Those who think the victories are urban tend to view this as a Lenaean victory, for at that festival two tragedies was the norm (Ghiron-Bistagne 1976, 97 following Wilamowitz 1930, 244). Others have suggested that Timotheos is the radical melic composer and friend of Euripides. Poets of dithyramb or other melic forms are certainly known to have turned their hand to tragedy (e.g. Dikaiogenes *TrGF* 52; cf. Polyidos *TrGF* 78). 'The' Timotheos might have been producing drama as early as 420 and would make a good fit on the very plausible assumption that the monument lists events in chronological order. On the other hand the name is common and this may simply be an unattested tragedian.

Since Sophocles died in 406, it has been suggested that this is Sophocles junior (*TrGF* 62), largely because of the belief that his victory should be the latest, and close in date to the time of dedication (Luppe 1974; Snell in *TrGF*). But this argument does not rule out the elder poet, and the lack of a disambiguating patronymic points towards him. This is important evidence that Sophocles chose on occasion to compose connected trilogies or tetralogies, for the title in the form *Telepheia* must refer to a trilogy or tetralogy and it is very improbable that a work so named would be made up of thematically disconnected plays, only one of which dealt with the Telephus myth. This last consideration makes it unlikely that the two fragments of production records found in Rome, which report fourth-century performances at the Athenian Lenaea and Rhodian Dionysia, record a reprise of the Sophoclean *Telepheia*, made up of *Peleus*, *Odysseus*, *Iberians* 'and a satyric *Telephus*' (**IV**

Dxi 7, l. 4: [σατυ]ρικὸν Τήλεφ[ον] with **IV Dxi 1**, ll. 7–8). The physical association of the two fragments required for this reconstruction is in any case not secure (**IV Dxi**). Among the various combinations of known titles that have been proposed to make up the tetralogy (*TrGF* IV, 434–5) perhaps the most likely is *The Sons of Aleus*, *The Mysians*, *Eurypylos* (for which see *TrGF* IV, 195), and a satyric *Telephus*.

What then is the nature of this monument? It has a powerfully retrospective quality, recalling performances that took place as much as seventy years earlier. It is evidently a 'treasury' of theatrical glory, but whose was the glory – the deme of Halai Aixonides? these choregoi? And where was it achieved – at city festivals? in the deme? The current majority view that the plays should be attributed to victories by demesmen at the Lenaea or City Dionysia rests on fragile foundations: 'that so many famous poets of the fifth century should have chosen [the deme] as the place for the production of their plays by themselves ... seems less likely' (*DFA*² 55–6; Csapo 2004, 61–2 *contra*). While at least one deme is known to have taken steps to record performances at its own local Dionysia (**Yiii**), there is no par-allel, in any field of activity, for a deme-sponsored monument that records the successes of its members in the city or anywhere else outside the deme. On the other hand, the fact that Cratinus was apparently (?) initially refused a chorus for the *Cowherds* (**I Bi 9**) cannot be used as evidence of a first production in a deme theatre.

Victories won in the city can be all but ruled out. And, even taking account of its frag-mentary state, the information is too patchy to represent part of an official or systematic attempt to list the victors at the deme's own Dionysia. It is more likely that the monument was erected early in the fourth century by any of its choregoi who were still alive, or by their family or families, rather than as the result of corporate deme action. The three choregoi are likely to have been related to one another, by blood and shared interests, if they were not actually all members of the same family. This group of well-to-do men could look back to illustrious careers of theatrical sponsorship in their deme. If the works they supported look very much like a set of fifth-century classics, that may be because they themselves have made a selection from a larger set of stars made brighter by retrospective light, and are thus to be seen as active agents in a process of theatrical canonisation that was already underway.

The view that there are three rather than two choregoi rests on the most thorough ep-igraphic analyses, which indicate that the second letter of the name of the first choregos is not a Π and may be an Υ, and that the space is probably too short for 'Epichares'. As for the other choregoi, the son of an Epichares of Halai made a dedication on the Acropolis ca. 400–380 (*IG* II³ 4, 1563), which would speak further to the family's wealth.

Ki: Deme Decree Honouring Two Choregoi, Mentioning Prohedria and a Sanctuary of Dionysus, 341/0 (by Archon date, l. 2).

Intact pedimental stele of white marble.
0.915 × 0.30–0.34 × 0.08–0.09 m.
Found ca. 500 m west of the temple of Artemis Tauropolos at Loutsa, site of ancient Halai Araphenides (Traill 1975, 40; Bardane 1992–1998, 58–60).
Brauron Mus. BE 2925.
Bardane 1992–1998 (= *SEG* 46, 153); Kalogeropoulos 2013 I, 142–3.
Text: *SEG* 46, 153.   Photo: Bardane 1992–1998, pl. 4.

```
1        Θ        Ε        Ο        l.
         ἐπὶ Νικομάχο ἄρχοντος, δημα-    stoich. 23
         ρχοῦντος Φόρμου, ἔδοξεν Ἀλα-
         ιεῦσιν· Φιλοκλῆς Φιλοκήδου-
5        ς εἶπεν· ἐπειδὴ οἱ χορηγοὶ κα-
         λῶς καὶ φιλοτίμως ἐχορήγησ-
         αν Ἀντίμαχος Ἀρχεμάχου, Σωι-
         ναύτης Ναυσιστρατίδου, ἐπα-
         ινέσαι αὐτοὺς καὶ στεφανῶσ-
10       αι θαλλοῦ στεφάνωι ἑκάτερο-
         ν αὐτῶν καὶ εἶναι αὐτοῖς προ-
         εδρίαν ἐν τοῖς ἀγῶσι καὶ καλ-
         εῖν αὐτοὺς τὸν δήμαρχον τὸν
         ἀεὶ δημαρχοῦντα εἰς τὴν προ-
15       εδρίαν. ἀναγράψαι δὲ τόδε τὸ
         ψήφισμα τὸν δήμαρχον ἐν στή-
         ληι λιθίνηι καὶ στῆσαι ἐν τῶ-
         ι Διονυσίωι.
```

Σωιναύτης Ἀντίμαχος.

GODS. In the Archonship of Nikomachos, when Phormos was demarch, the Halaieis decided, on the proposal of Philokles son of Philokedes: [5] since Antimachos son of Archemachos and Soinautes son of Nausistratides served as choregoi in a fine and ambitious manner, let us praise them and crown [10] each of them with a crown of olive leaves, and let them have prohedria at the contests and let the demarch in office summon them to their prohedria. [15] And may the demarch inscribe this decree on a stone stele and erect it in the sanctuary of Dionysus. [*Below in larger, rougher letters, probably once inside painted crowns:*] Soinautes – Antimachos.

'A place at the furthest borders of Attica' (E. *IT* 1450), the deme of Halai Araphenides (bouleutic quota 5) was famed for its sanctuary and festival of Artemis Tauropolos – both, according to Euripides, established by Orestes at Athena's command (*IT* 1447–61). The festival drew participants from all over Attica, with its all-night dances (*pannychis*) for young women (Men. *Epit.* 470–519), and contests in pyrrhic dance. Artemis dominated the cultic landscape of this part of the coast (Brulé 1987, 186–95). But in doing so she frequently kept close company with Dionysus (cf. nearby **G**). Indeed the relief from the area now in Munich depicting Artemis and Dionysus, with five suspended theatrical masks, most probably derives from the Dionysion of Halai (**Kii**; Despinis 2004b, 311–12) and is further evidence of theatrical activity there.

No theatre has yet been found, but the existence of one, or at least of a performance space, was already known from two other honorific decrees that were to be erected in the sanctuary of Artemis Tauropolos. One of these (*SEG* 34, 103 ca. 334–314: Tracy 1995, 124; Bathrellou 2012, 158 n. 28; Kalogeropoulos 2013 I, 141–2) honours a choregos named Philoxenos for having sponsored pyrrhic dancers and who is also said to have 'performed all the other liturgies in the deme in a fine and ambitious manner' (*SEG* 34, 103, ll. 5–8). The herald is to announce the 500-drachma crown for Philoxenos at the agon of the Tauropolia for Artemis (ll. 14–16), at which his pyrrhic dancers had doubtless performed (Ceccarelli 2004, 100). And 'he is to have prohedria at all the contests which the Halaieis hold' (ll. 21–5: εἶναι δὲ καὶ προε|δρίαν αὐτῶι ἐν τοῖς ἀγῶσι|ν ἄπασιν, οἷς ἂν ποιῶσιν Ἁλ|αιῆς). The other decree (*ArchEph* 1925–1926, 168–9 mid 4th c. = *SEG* 55, 252; Kalogeropoulos 2013 I, 139–40) is highly fragmentary but evidently honoured two men with, among other things, 'prohedria at the contests [? which the deme organise]s' [εἶναι δὲ κα]ὶ προεδρία|[ν αὐτοῖς ἐν] τοῖς ἀγῶσι|[ν, οἷς τίθησι]ν· (ll. 6–8).

The phrasing used to describe the events at which prohedria is to be awarded at Halai is thus very similar in all three decrees. It is also notably vague – 'at (all) the contests (which the deme holds)'. This shows that the space in which prohedria could be offered witnessed competitions associated with a variety of cults. It follows as likely that the same space was used for the performances at the Tauropolia and those at the local Dionysia. The tantalising 'all the other liturgies in the deme' of the decree for Philoxenos left open the possibility of properly theatrical liturgies, a possibility made virtually certain by the most recently published decree.

The nature of the choregia for which Soinautes and Antimachos are honoured is not specified, but the fact that the stele is to be set up in the sanctuary of Dionysus rightly encouraged its first editor to deduce that they had performed at a local Dionysia (Bardane 1992–1998, 55). The stele was found about half a kilometre to the west of the temple of Artemis (which lay between the ancient salt lake and the sea at Loutsa), among the remains of extensive ancient structures that the excavator supposed to be those of the Dionysion of Halai. These findings were never published, but a very partial report of them notes the discovery of an agonistic dedication possibly to be identified as a choregic monument, due to the fact that its three-sided form suggests it may have been designed to carry a tripod (Bardane 1992–1998, 60). Little more can be said about this choregia – whether for instance the men were joint choregoi (they are not obviously related) or sponsored separate events; or whether they were victors. A Kallimedes son of Archemachos of Halai served as prytanis of the Aigeid tribe in the very same year and was almost certainly the brother of Antimachos (*IG* II² 1749, 53).

As in a number of other demes, the honour of prohedria is here augmented by the special addition of being invited to take one's seat by the demarch of the day (ll. 12–15).

A corrupt fragment of Philochorus may preserve another testimony to the cult of Dionysus at Halai: *FGrH* 328 F 191 (from Sch.ᵀ Hom. *Il.* 6.136, Θέτις δ' ὑπεδέξατο κόλπῳ [*scil.* Διώνυσον])· ἢ ὅτι χρησμὸς ἐδόθη † ἁλιεύειν "ἐν †τόπῳ Διόνυσον ἁλιέα βαπτίζοι τε", ὡς Φιλόχορος. "'And Thetis received [Dionysus] in her bosom": or because an oracle was given † to fish (*halieuein*) "at † the place and may he dip Dionysus the fisher"'. See Jacoby *ad loc.*, who very tentatively airs the possibility of correcting 'the fisher' to Ἁλαιεῖς 'demesmen of Halai' and reading πότῳ instead of τόπῳ, the result being an oracular order about the mixing of wine that would be consonant with the discussion of the invention of wine by Amphiktyon elsewhere in the *Atthis* (*FGrH* 328 F 5).

Kii: Dedication from Halai Araphenides or Brauron, ca. 330 (by style of relief and masks).

Attic dedicatory relief.
0.75 × 1.195 × 0.114 m.
No findspot recorded.
The relief was acquired by the Glyptothek in Munich in 1989. It is somewhat restored. Earlier photographs show a large rectangular gap at the centre of the lower border, presumably where the relief was joined by a tenon to a base. It is rough chiselled at the back.
Munich Glyptothek 552.
Inscription: Vierneisel and Scholl 2002; *IG* II³ 4, 1084.
Text: based on *IG* II³ 4, 1084.   Photos: Vierneisel and Scholl 2002, figs. 1–6; Moraw and Nölle 2002, fig. 137; *IG* II³ 4,2 tab. CXXVI. See also Colour Plate 6.

…]Σ	ΑΘΗΝΑΙΣ
]is	Athenais

The relief is enclosed within an architectural frame with pilasters on either side and an architrave topped by a sima with antefixes. The scene is of an outdoor sanctuary with a group of worshippers approaching two divinities on the left, both carved on a considerably larger scale than the worshippers. The male divinity is seated on a rock and in front of a tree. He wears a crown, is beardless and carries a thyrsus in his left hand, of which the tip and only a trace of the stalk are preserved. He is unquestionably Dionysus. With his right hand he fondles a panther, which turns back to look at the female deity standing behind him. Vierneisel and Scholl read the inscription under the goddess as [ARTEM]IS, but there does not appear to be enough space below the relief for the five letters needed to supplement the name. Moreover, the iota is doubtful. As the figure does not belong to one of the usual iconographic types for Artemis, the identification must depend on the presence of the stag in front of the procession of worshippers. A stag or deer is a common attribute of Artemis in Attic iconography (Jurriaans-Helle 1986).

The stag in this relief (apparently *dama dama:* see Böhr and Böhr 2009) occupies a place normally taken by the sacrificial animal. Though uncommon, cervid sacrifice is particularly associated with Artemis (Stanzel 1991, 157; Felsch 2001, 196–7; Bevan 1986 I, 100–14, II, 389–93). Close parallels are offered by a relief from Aegina of ca. 400 (Athens EAM 1950; Wide 1901, pl. 6; Simon 1985, 279–80 pl. 52.2; van Straten 1995, 85, 293 no. R76), and a fourth-century relief from Delos (Plassart 1928, 302, fig. 253) where deer are led in sacrifice to Artemis. In a thorough study of the topic, Larson (2017) concludes that for Artemis 'sacrificial offerings of deer were considered appropriate on special occasions'. It is however not entirely clear that the stag in this relief is meant to represent a sacrificial animal: here no one appears to be leading the stag. In the relief from Aegina one of the worshippers puts an arm around the body of the deer. Here the appearance of the animal, apparently wandering free in the sanctuary, serves as an attribute for the goddess. Other reliefs from Brauron place the stag beside Artemis and facing the other way (van Straten 1995, R73, fig. 57, R75, fig. 87). Possibly the stag was displaced from this position by Dionysus' panther, a more important attribute, and conceptually the main deity in this scene.

A group of (originally) nine worshippers approaches the deities. There were five adults and four children but one adult (labelled Athenais) and one child were chiselled out of the relief, leaving only their raised right hands and the outlines of their feet. The adult male is portrayed as a man of advanced years, with balding forehead (Vierneisel and Scholl 2002, 11: 'sorgsam als alter Mann characterisiert'). In his left hand he carries a single aulos pipe and it appears that he grasped another with his right, though no trace remains: Scholl concludes that it was originally shown in paint (Vierneisel and Scholl 2002, 36). Pipers are occasionally depicted with one pipe in each hand: in some cases the pose may signify that the performance is over (Taplin 2010, 261). There is no occasion here to go into the detail of the other figures, nor the mystery relating to the erased figures: it is important only to note that this is not a group of performers, but in all likelihood a piper and the members of his family.

J. R. Green (pers. comm.) considers the five comic masks in the upper right to be transitional between Old/Middle and New Comic types. To the right of the thyrsus, we have the mask of a young woman (*MMC*³ Type W rather than SS as reported by Vierneisel and Scholl 2002, 37). Next right is the mask of a slave (N or possibly B and transitional to New Comic masks 21/22: the treatment of the brows is essentially Early Hellenistic). Next, the mask of a middle-aged woman (TT), followed by an old man (E or A, or indeed New Comic mask 3), and old woman (U). The masks serve to mark the scene as a sanctuary sacred to Dionysus, alluding to the practice of choregic dedications of masks as victory offerings (**V F**; note also **Mv** in a deme context). The prominence, number and variety of masks may indicate a specific, not simply generic sign of a sanctuary of Dionysus. The masks constitute a plausible set of characters for a play.

The findspot of the relief is unknown. Vierneisel and Scholl (2002) argue, from the presence of Artemis, that the relief relates to Brauron, where there is only slight evidence from the sanctuary of Artemis for a secondary worship of Dionysus as a 'guest god' (**G**). A fragmentary altar of ca. 400 was decorated with a relief showing a divine parade for Dionysus, including Hermes, Dionysus, the three Seasons, Peace, the Graces, a silen, three nymphs, Apollo, Leto and Artemis (Despinis 2004a; 2010, 57–9, 85–103, plates 5–22). Apart from this there is a fragment of a marble comic mask on a plinth that may have come from a choregic votive (Vierneisel and Scholl 2002, n. 232), but may also, perhaps more easily, have been a motif decorating the statue of a child, a type familiar from Hellenistic times, but possibly attested earlier (Despinis 2004a, 63). Despinis argues that the sanctuary of Halai Araphenides is a likelier spot for a dedication relating to the theatre (2004b; Goette 2014). The relief on the Brauronian altar may indicate that the route of the *pompe* of the Dionysia of Philaidai passed by or through the sanctuary (**G**), but if the presence of comic masks on the Munich relief make a specific local reference to the performance of drama, then Halai Araphenides is a much more likely alternative. In Halai, choregoi, a theatre (prohedria) and competitions are specifically attested, and the sanctuary of Dionysus was located close to the sanctuary of Artemis Tauropolos (**Ki**). An Athenais (the inscribed name of the dedicator or dedicator's wife) made dedications to the sanctuary of Brauronian Artemis sometime before 344 (*IG* II² 1514, l. 48; 1516, l. 26; 1517, l. 155). The name is not common before imperial times but is attested for Halai on a grave stele dated to the second century BC (*IG* II² 5456). Iphigenia, for whom a deer was substituted when she was about to be sacrificed to Artemis, has particularly close connections with both Brauron and Halai (E. *IT* 1449–67).

Vierneisel and Scholl (2002, 37) describe the relief as a dedication by (or for) the piper for a victory at the Dionysia. Pipers did not win victories: they contributed to the choral victory and their role was sometimes acknowledged by choregic dedications (**V G**), but in dramatic competitions in the Classical theatre they won no prizes. Consequently, no victory dedications by pipers are known. Moreover, the representation of family members in a dedication for a dramatic victory is unlikely, though perhaps not unknown (**V F** on Athens NM 1513). This relief is generally supposed to have been dedicated by Athenais, because her name (alone) is inscribed, because women normally made dedications to Artemis at Brauron (we might note that Artemis' name may also have been inscribed, but not Dionysus'), and because it was common at Brauron for women dedicating reliefs to have themselves represented in such 'adoration' scenes modestly following their husbands (Despinis 2002, esp. 162). It is not clear in this case why the husband carries the symbols of his profession. Perhaps the relief was dedicated on a special occasion, such as the piper's retirement from the profession, and is given in thanks to Dionysus and Artemis (for whom there were competitions in pyrrhike at Halai Araphenides) by a local piper and his family who lived partly from the proceeds of the gods' festivals.

L | Halimous

Last of the southern city demes on the western coast of Attica, Halimous (bouleutic quota 3) lay directly south of Phaleron, bordered by Euonymon to the east and Aixone to the south (both with theatres: **I Introduction**; **D Introduction**), with good access in all directions – and to the city beyond – thanks to a well-established road network and easy approach by sea at Cape Kolias (Kaza-Papageorgiou 2006, 62–6). Two candidates have been proposed for the site of the deme's (principal) civic centre, and the question has ramifications for the place of the worship of Dionysus in the lives of the Halimousioi. The first is Cape Kolias itself (Eliot 1962, 137), where a deme decree was discovered in the last century (Hondius 1919–1921 = *SEG* 2, 7, of 330–325; cf. Whitehead 1986a, 146). This revealed the existence of a cult and sanctuary of Dionysus, and showed that this Dionysion was a prominent public site in the deme, used for the display of honorific decrees. The deme honoured one Charisandros for overseeing sacrifices and other religious duties on behalf of a demarch. The decree was to be recorded both 'in the public records' (εἰς τὰ κοινὰ γραμματεῖα ll. 20–1) and on a marble stele, the latter to be erected 'in the Dionysion' (ἐν τῶι Διονυσίωι l. 23). The stele was discovered lying on top of the remains of an ancient wall that Hondius tentatively identified as the Dionysion itself. Lately however Kaza-Papageorgiou (2006, 84–6) has shown that those remains are more consistent with a *peribolos* tomb beside the ancient road linking the hinterland of the deme to the Cape, and that the stele had wandered to the coastal spot from an original site a little further inland, around the hill known as Ag. Anna.

This hill is the second proposed site for the deme's centre (Marchiandi 2011, 624). This area has revealed a considerable density and variety of remains – domestic houses as well as various public structures (Kaza-Papageorgiou 2006, 76–8) and a considerable cemetery (Marchiandi 2011, 407). It is possible that the functions of civic centre were shared between both these places (we know moreover from D. 57.10 that the deme sometimes held its assembly in the city). In fact, the highly unusual stipulation that a copy of the decree should be kept in the deme's office of public records may suggest that this was not only distinct, but also some way distant, from the Dionysion. But the Dionysion was nonetheless evidently itself an important and 'central' public site.

The main reason for disassociating the decree from the site on the Cape is that preliminary and partial excavation on a property on the southern foothills of Ag. Anna (Marinou Antypa St., formerly Hegesipyle St.) in the 1980s brought to light part of the theatron and rectilinear prohedria of a theatre. And it is a reasonable proposition that a deme's Dionysion should be near its theatre. Similarities in the morphology of the theatre, and in particular its prohedria, to those in which drama is known to have been performed elsewhere in Attica, very much suggest that this was a theatre proper, but it has been suggested that this was a structure primarily associated with the important Thesmophoria held by Halimous (Sch.

Ar. *Th.* 80; Plu. *Sol.* 8.4 with Paus. 1.31.1; Whitehead 1986a, 80 n. 59; Clinton 1996). The remains of a Thesmophorion were sighted somewhat higher up this same hill early last century, on or near its top (though reports of excavation by Wrede prior to the Second World War were never published and the site was much changed by German occupation during the war: Kaza-Papageorgiou 2006, 76–82).

On the other hand the recent excavation also found, in an undisturbed layer of the theatron, fragments of what the excavator identified as probably a choregic base, and another large fragment from a base inscribed with olive crowns on three surfaces, likely to be part of an honorific stele, decree or other commemorative monument (Kaza-Papageorgiou 1993, pl. 27d–e; 2006, 84). The slender remains of an inscription on the crowning cornice indicate the involvement of a member of the deme (*SEG* 46, 318: [———]ΛΙΜΟΥ ('-*lim-ou*', doubtless part of *Halimousios*) | [———]ΣΑΥ). These are the sort of objects more likely in a theatre proper than a viewing area associated with a Thesmophorion. Moreover Goette (2014, 98) points to the theatre's high degree of visibility and its situation outside the sanctuary of the Goddesses, making it a less likely place to hold a Thesmophoria. Sherds from the theatre range in date from the late seventh to the third century, attesting to long and continuous use. This has prompted the suggestion that it perhaps began life as a site connected to the Thesmophoria and was later transformed into a theatre and more general place of gathering (Touchais 1999, 655).

That there may in any case have been an interaction of some sort between the cults of Dionysus and that of Demeter and Persephone in Halimous is suggested by the evidence of Arnobius (5.28, 3rd–4th c. AD), who writes of *Alimuntia illa ... mysteria, quibus in Liberi honorem patris phallos subrigit Graecia*. However etiolated this evidence may be, it suggests memory of a tradition of the worship of Dionysus in Halimous that involved phallic procession. This might have been the kind of parade (*pompe*) that seemingly featured as standard in deme Dionysia (**Ai**; **Miii**), or one that somehow linked the two adjacent cults on the Ag. Anna hill, those of the Two Goddesses and of Dionysus.

The theatron followed the gentle inclination of the slope, for an excavated length of ca. 21 m and width of ca. 19.5 m. A wide access passageway cut directly into the rock (at a depth of about 0.40 m) divides the excavated part of the theatron, leading in a SE–NW direction. Its width varies between 0.70 and 0.80 m. It is possible that there was another such parallel passage on the unexcavated, eastern part of the theatron. A number of rough-hewn steps and cavities were found that may have been used by spectators – either directly as seating-positions or with the addition of *ikria*. Fragments of a structure found at the northern extension of the theatron are probably the remains of retaining walls. At the western side was found a narrow and shallow passage or ditch (9.50 × 0.30–40 × 0.10–15 m) that joins the access passageway. Limited excavation in the area south of the prohedria failed to find any clear trace of the orchestra, but it is very probable that this area, of the same even level as the natural rock on which the prohedria sat, was used for the purpose, employing a wooden skene (and in any case the modern road intervenes at this point and no excavation was conducted below it).

The most striking find was three double seats of a type known from various other Attic local theatres (such as Ikarion and Euonymon), here made of limestone. These formed part of the rectilinear prohedria, and there are indications that there may once have been at least one further seat (Kaza-Papageorgiou 1993, pl. 27; 2006, 83, 85 – reconstruction; two pairs were found *in situ*). They were set upon the natural bedrock that had been prepared to fit them. The best-preserved seat (now kept in the Piraeus Museum) measures 1.13 × 0.64 × 0.50 m. A corridor was cut into the rock behind the prohedria, no doubt to permit ease of access for spectators.

M | Ikarion

Introduction

The deme of Ikarion (bouleutic quota 5) lay on the northern foothills of Mt Pentelicon in north-eastern Attica. Though somewhat remote from the city, it was connected by an important road that led to the Marathonian Tetrapolis to the east and, through the mountains, to Kephissia and into the Pedion beyond, to the west. On his way from Kephissia to Marathon on 5 May 1766, near a place named Stamati, Richard Chandler was shown by locals 'a ruined church of St Dionysius, standing on the marble heap of a trophy, or monument, erected for some victory obtained by three persons named Aenias, Xanthippus, and Xanthides. The inscription is on a long stone lying near' (1776, 160; **Mix**). A hundred and twenty years later (in May 1887) Arthur Milchhöfer, walking in the other direction from Marathon to Kephissia, identified the site of the ruined church as the deme of Ikarion (Milchhöfer 1887a; cf. Milchhöfer 1887b, 311). In addition to the inscription reported by Chandler, Milchhöfer saw **Mxii** in the ruined church, whose dedicant identified himself as a member of the deme and whose recipient was Dionysus. The Director of the American School of Classical Studies at Athens, Augustus Merriam, learnt of Milchhöfer's theory and the School undertook work at the site on 30 January 1888, under the direction of Carl Buck. Merriam commented in his report (1889, 10) that 'seldom has work of this kind been so satisfactory, and accomplished so much at so slight expense' (less than $300).

Though highly productive, unearthing numerous sculptural, architectural and inscriptional remains and confirming by the discovery of decrees that the centre of the deme had been found, Buck's excavation was far from systematic and the only subsequent study of the site, that of Biers and Boyd a century later, was largely confined to cleaning and reporting on its current state, although it did also clarify the likely function of a number of important structures. Further light will doubtless be shed by work currently being conducted to document materials at the site by Dr. Fotini Karassava-Tsilingiri and a team of other archaeologists and architects of the Greek Archaeological Service. Buck's campaign had centred on the small Byzantine church. This had been built right in the heart of the religious and administrative centre of Ikarion and, more particularly, in the sanctuary of Dionysus. It had to a large extent been constructed from members of ancient monuments – most notably, its apse was built from the partially reorganised elements of the distinctive large semicircular choregic monument (**Mix**). Where the principal settlement of the deme lay in relation to its religious and civic centre still remains unclear. Most promising are the areas to the south of the sanctuary in the direction of Mt Pentelicon and north-west into the valley through which the road stretches and alongside which a number of grave precincts with some impressive funerary monuments (Valavanis 2007; Marchiandi 2011, 456–8) have been found.

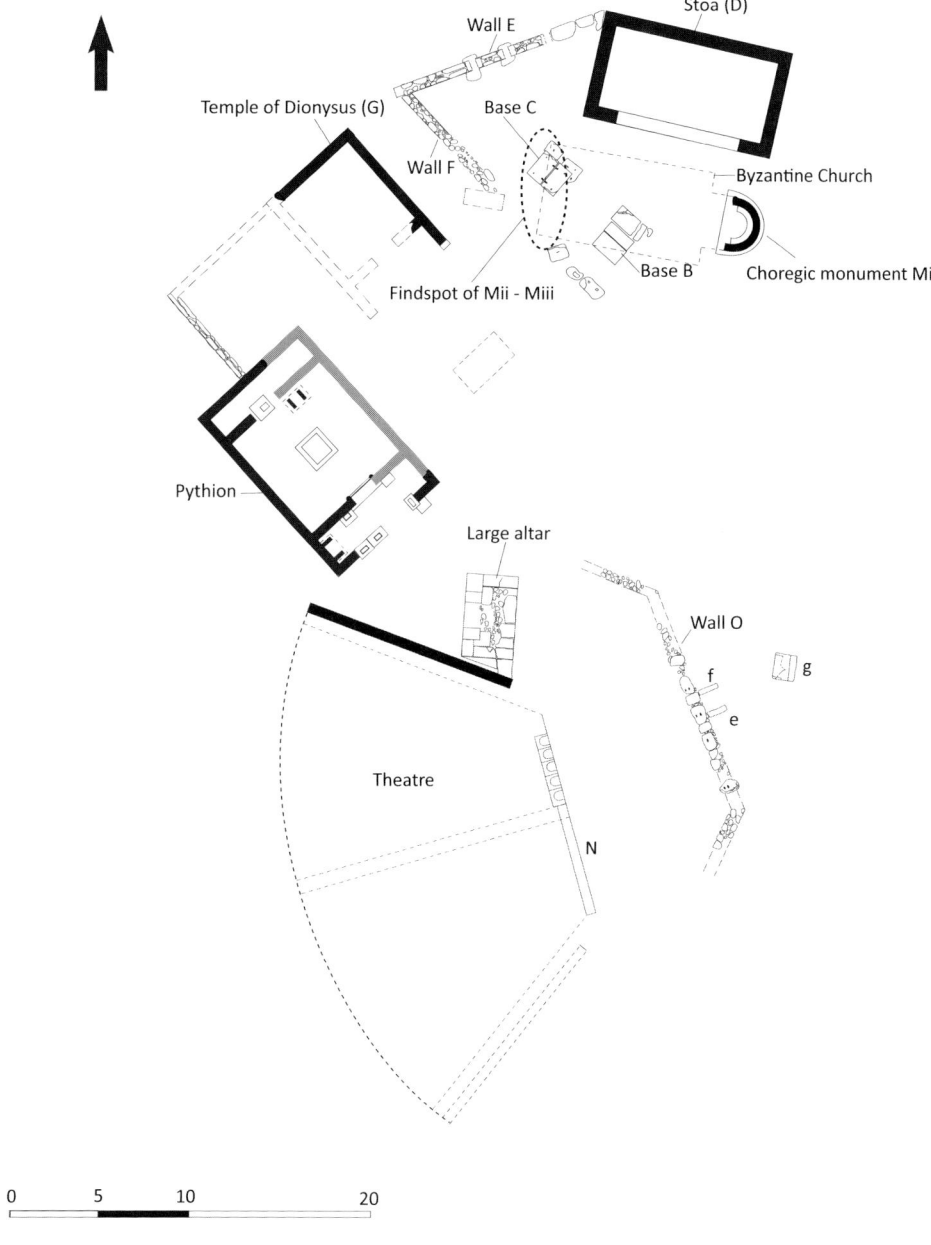

Site plan of Ikarion.

The site slopes down from south to north and east in a series of terraces. On the higher, southern, level are the Pythion, the threshold inscription of which was found *in situ*: Ἰκαριῶν τὸ Πύθιον (*IG* II³ 4, 1866; *SEG* 32, 249c); and the large altar directly in front of it. Slightly to the east, also on the higher ground, is the theatre. Lower down, to the north-east, were found the semicircular monument and various other marble bases in and around the Byzantine church; beyond them and lower still, a wall (E) and, abutting it, a building (D) immediately to the north of the footprint of the church. Biers and Boyd (1982, 9) showed that this building was a stoa, the south side of which evidently opened onto 'a veritable field of monuments'. Some twenty-seven bases of dedications were found in this area, and of the eight of these found *in situ*, all were related to drama and/or Dionysus. Of these, most prominent to view are bases B and C. Despinis (2007, 126–8) has shown that B, previously considered likely to be the foundation of another choregic monument, was the base on which the Archaic statue of Dionysus was reerected under a marble canopy at some time in the fourth century (**Mi**). The god will have looked south-westwards, with a good view of the sacrifices on the altar in front of his temple from his strategic point along what was probably a processional route. For it seems very likely that the poorly preserved and incompletely excavated building (G) to the south-west of the stoa was the temple of Dionysus (Biers and Boyd 1982, 3–6 found evidence that suggested this was likely to be a small temple: the presence of a cross-wall and the same south-east orientation as the Pythion beside it; Romano 1982, 407–8 proposed building D as the temple of Dionysus but its shape would be highly unusual, if not entirely unparalleled, for a temple).

Only the north-eastern corner of the temple of Dionysus (G) is preserved, but it is clear that its eastern wall was parallel to wall F. An important entrance to the site was thus formed by the north-eastern corner of the temple of Dionysus and the meeting place of walls E and F. Wall E appears to have been a peribolos wall, also functioning as a retaining wall (a number of large openings in it may have assisted drainage: Biers and Boyd 1982, 8). Wall F probably extended further to the south-east and helped define a route through the site. The 'Dionysion' mentioned as the place for the erection of **Mx** will have included not just the god's temple but the whole area where the choregic and other dedicatory monuments to Dionysus were erected within the arms of walls E and F, probably also incorporating the stoa (D) that opened onto the dedications (see also on l. 49 of **Miii**). **Mx** is a decree honouring a demarch, and makes wide reference to his religious, financial and civic duties in the deme (without, at least in its surviving part, referring to the Dionysia), which shows that the Dionysion was employed in Ikarion as the site for official public record of important deme documents, indicating that it also served as the deme's civic centre (cf. e.g. **L**, **Y**). A fragment of another decree found in the same area seems to have honoured a demarch for his role in conducting lawsuits (*IG* II^2 1179, recently relocated as Athens NM 4884).

There is considerable uniformity in the style of the surviving architecture, and features such as the use of distinctive 'furrowed' and 'pointed work' on the blocks of the walls and buildings have been thought to imply a late fourth-century date (Biers and Boyd 1982, 7–8). But as we can be certain that earlier temples existed (note especially the Pythion mentioned in **Miii**, ca. 440), it is probable that much of what has been found was a fourth-century rebuild of sixth- and fifth-century structures. The existence of a theatre can also be inferred by ca. 460 from **Miii**. Merriam (in Buck 1892, 70 n. 27) rightly drew attention to the destructive impact the Spartan occupation of Decelea at the end of the fifth century was likely to have had on the deme. A substantial rebuild of the material infrastructure of the sanctuary would also fit with an observable 'boom' in Attic theatre culture in the later fourth century. The revitalisation of the Ikarian theatre and sanctuary might have been part or at least in the spirit of 'Lycurgan' policy. But to judge from the (admittedly somewhat fragile) evidence of the dates of theatre-related inscriptions and dedications from the site, the festival was also in good health, with theatrical performances that left significant choregic monuments to commemorate them, in the first half of the fourth century (**Miv**; **Mv**; **Mvii**; **Mviii**; **Mix**; cf. **Mvi**).

The Theatre

The roughly rectangular space of the orchestra is defined by a row of marble prohedria and the approximately parallel wall O. At each end of the latter the foundations of a wall run off at a ca. 45 degree angle, suggesting that it served as a retaining wall to support the packed-earth floor of the orchestra (Biers and Boyd 1982, 12). Wall O probably defined the front of a stage building. Four of the large, roughly hewn blocks that formed it have cuttings in their smooth upper surfaces: three of these have a pair of dowel holes (each ca. 0.03 × 0.03 × 0.04 m) beside a third pry hole; one, apparently in the centre of the row, has a single elongated cutting (0.02 × 0.06 × 0.03). Biers and Boyd note that the cuttings imply the existence of spaced uprights on a level stylobate, suggestive of a skene, and they air the possibility that the cuttings carried vertical piers of wood or stone, the spaces between the blocks bridged by slabs supported on rubble packing, the whole thus forming a continuous wall. As an alternative they suggest that the row of blocks in O might have supported a more conventional wall of further blocks above it (Biers and Boyd 1982, 12–14 and fig. 5). Telling somewhat against this interpretation is the possibility that there may have been, at around the midpoint of wall O and extending eastward on two parallel blocks (e, f), a dedication or monument of some kind – Buck thought that block g rested on e and f and Biers and Boyd note that g has cuttings on its upper surface to receive some kind of dedication.

There survives what appears originally to have been a continuous set of five marble prohedric seats: two double seats with a single seat between, as implied by the anathyrosis at one end of each pair and both sides of the single. The association of these three separate blocks is suggested by the fact that one of the double seats was originally found *in situ* on a base of marble slabs (Buck 1892, 65–6 with pl. 4). The length of the marble base slabs is 3.55 m; the total length of the two double and one single seat is 3.48 m, leading Buck to deduce that the five seats formed a complete unit on this base. A sixth single seat with rounded back (W. 0.71 m) was found, in line with the others, further towards the large altar (Merriam in Buck 1892, 66 n. 21). It is likely there were also more marble seats further to the south, perhaps beyond a central access stairway. Buck (1892, 66) noted the presence here of a 'rude wall of uncut stones' (N) – no longer visible to Biers and Boyd. That does not sound like a set of stele bases, as Paga (2010, 357) suggests, which would have been perfectly placed to obstruct the view of those behind them. More likely the stones served as a foundation for another set of prohedria.

While many have rightly noted the likely multi-functionality of a structure such as this in a deme, its use as a place of political and other assembly (Biers and Boyd 1982, 14; Paga 2010, 360), there can be no doubt that it was in this theatre that the tragedies attested by several inscriptions were performed in Ikarion. It may be more correct to speak of a precursor to the theatre whose remains were found, as most authorities tend to ascribe them to the fourth century. The only serious study of the archaeological evidence (Biers and Boyd

1982) does not proffer a date for wall O; Travlos (1988, 85) suggests that the first phase probably dates to the end of the sixth century, but notes that all the other buildings in the site are of fourth-century construction. The rest of the seating will have been on the slight natural incline that rises behind the prohedria, which may have been more substantial or artificially built up in antiquity. It is also possible that wooden scaffolded seating (*ikria*) was constructed here. The theatron commanded a view of the plain of Marathon to the left and of the sea between the coast of Attica and Euboea in front.

The earliest evidence for the cult of Dionysus in Ikarion is the late Archaic marble statue of the god from the sanctuary, dated to ca. 525 (**Mi**); of striking size and quality for a relatively small deme. An associated fragmentary inscription confirms the implicit suggestion of the topography of the sanctuary that the cult of Dionysus stood in close relation to that of Pythian Apollo (**Mi**). The cult of Dionysus in Ikarion was evidently vigorous under the Pisistratids and its promotion alongside that of Apollo Pythios may be their work. The head of this statue was once thought to be an entirely separate mask (Angiolillo 1997, 92–3), encouraging the belief that drama was performed in the god's cult from as early as ca. 525. It is now clear that the 'mask' is in fact the damaged head of the statue itself (Despinis 2007) and the earliest evidence for drama from the site itself becomes the decree regulating the festival, which places it around 460 (see on the term ἀχορήγητος used in **Miii**). No terminus for the operation of theatre or cult is available, but after a very energetic life in the fourth century no good evidence for their continuation beyond has been found.

The festival may have taken place on 17 Posideon and following days (**Miii** on ll. 27–9). A diagnostic assembly was held after it (**Miii** on ll. 39–42). Phallic song was prominent in its parade (*pompe*) (**Miii**). A possible part of the route for the parade is from the north, uphill through the entrance to the site by the side of the temple of Dionysus and past the choregic monuments and (at least from some time in the fourth century: **Mi**) the statue of the god seated in their midst, into the heart of the sanctuary. The god's presence in the parade was felt in the form of the phallos, and the emphasis of the mythology of Dionysus and Icarius lies not so much on the arrival of the god but his gift of wine and interaction with the locals. It is likely that Apollo was acknowledged in the parade with some form of (perhaps choral) tribute (**Miii** on ll. 30–2). His temple was right beside the theatre, closer to it than that of Dionysus. The importance of the agon to the festival is clear from the way in which **Mvi** conceives of the whole as 'the festival for Dionysus and the agon'. Tragedy was the preeminent, perhaps the only, event. It is the only one securely attested in the material record (**Mv**). Honours were announced 'at the tragedies of the Dionysia' (**Mx**).

The organisation of the Dionysia fell to the demarch (**Miii**; **Mvi**), and was one of his principal cultic duties. There is no evidence that he was aided by other officers but **Mvi** might imply that he could enlist the help of the year's choregoi to assist him, as may happen elsewhere (**Bi**). The demarchs of Ikarion were also responsible for managing large cultic and public resources, totalling in the region of some five talants around the middle of the fifth century (**Mii**; **Mx**). They very probably invested some, perhaps much, of this money as loans in order to generate further income to support the dramatic festival and perhaps also to offer liquidity to local choregoi.

The Ikarians may have charged a fee to enter their Dionysia already by the middle of the fifth century (**Miii**). The festival is likely to have attracted many visitors. Its evident financial and organisational vigour in the mid fifth century is suggestive, and the fourth century was clearly a period of prosperity too (above). However strong and early its traditions of theatrical performance may have been, the deme is always likely to have looked to draw audiences from outside its own borders. Goette (2014) proposes that the theatre of Ikarion might have done service for the various demes on the north side of Mt Pentelicon, but he thinks primarily in terms of the sharing of the theatrical facilities of Ikarion for their own events by these demes rather than any sort of collaborative celebration.

It is a remote possibility that the Ikarian Dionysia was in some sense celebrated with those neighbours with whom it shared a variety of cult practices, possibly within the religious association known as the Epakreis, a survival of a pre-Cleisthenic trittys. The small demes of Plotheia and Semachidai (both bouleutic quota 1) were members of the Epakreis. Ikarion is a likely third (Papazarkadas 2007c, 27–32; Ismard 2010, 215–18). Semachidai, a little further to the north of Ikarion, is named, like Ikarion, for its Dionysian history. The daughters of Semachos, with their father, were hospitable to Dionysus. The family provided priestesses of his cult (Philoch. *FGrH* 328 F 206). On the other hand, there is no direct evidence that the Dionysia of Ikarion was anything other than a regular deme festival. A different but related possibility, which does have some evidence to support it, is that the deme of Plotheia supported the attendance of its members at the Dionysia of Ikarion, and perhaps some form of direct participation in the festival (Wilson 2017b, 122–7). An inscription of ca. 420 concerning the deme's cult finances indicates that Plotheia provided funds to support the cost of participation of its members at religious events outside the deme (*IG* I³ 258). A Dionysia with theatrical performances of its own will probably have been beyond the means of such a small deme, and that of Ikarion, not 5 km distant, may well have been one event for which such funding was forthcoming (Wilson 2010a, 70–1).

The only possible evidence suggesting that Plotheia itself held a Dionysia consists of Wilamowitz's restoration of [ἐς Διονύσια δὲ] διδασκάλωι κά[δον] '[and] a ja[r] (sc. of wine) for the didaskalos [at the Dionysia]' to this same inscription (*IG* II² 1172, l. 38). Lewis however read an extra iota, leaving insufficient space to restore 'Dionysia': [....7... δὲ τῶ]ι διδασκάλωι κάδο[ν] (*IG* I³ 258, l. 38; Whitehead 1986a, 220). Even this slight whiff of a Plotheian Dionysia thus disappears, but the question remains as to why the Plotheians were making provision for a special distribution of wine to be given to a didaskalos. The context is of 'the other sacred activities' (τὰ ἄλλα ἱερὰ l. 36), distinct from those 'common ones in which the Plotheians feast together' (ll. 34–6). Each Plotheian who attends at such 'other sacred activities' is to receive 'up to a [half-chous] (sc. of wine)' (ll. 36–7), so this could be an instruction to equip a local didaskalos to perform on behalf of the Plotheians at a festival outside the deme, at which fellow members of his deme would be in attendance (and likewise equipped with wine, though rather less than he). The Dionysia of Ikarion remains an intriguing possible venue for this didaskalos. (['Ικαριοῖ δὲ τῶ]ι or [τῶι δὲ Ἰκαριο]ῖ διδασκάλωι κάδο[ν] 'and a ja[r] for [th]e didaskalos [at Ikarion]' would fit the space but is pure speculation in addition to being awkward Greek.) Philochorus (*FGrH* 328 F 187) indicates that a *kados* is the metrical equivalent of an *amphoreus*, and there is a tradition that an *amphoreus* was given to comic poets (**I Avii 3**). It would however be to draw a very long bow indeed to see the didaskalos from Plotheia as providing comedy to Ikarion, outside the agon for tragedy that we know was provided for by decree from **Miii**.

Perhaps a chorus for the phallic parade is more likely. With a little good will, it is possible to detect, in the following two lines of the decree, instructions for the construction and painting of some sort of object – perhaps a phallos, to be carried by a chorus of Plotheians, suitably equipped with wine, in the parade (*pompe*) of the Ikarian Dionysia? (Wilson 2015, 136; 2017b, 127 n. 136).

A choregic system existed from perhaps as early as ca. 460 (see on the term ἀχορήγητος in **Miii**). From at least ca. 440 two choregoi were required (by decree) for the festival (**Miii**), a number that seems to have persisted for as much as a century (**Mvi**). We find choregic dedications by one (**Miv**; **Mv**; **Mviii**) and three (**Mix**; **Mvii**) men. In the case of the latter group, one set (**Mvii**) is certainly, the other (**Mix**) very likely from the same family. Such joint choregoi from the same family probably represent a single choregia of the two mandated by decree. Non-Ikarian residents and/or landowners and possibly metics of sufficient means were liable for choregia (**Miii**), although unfortunately no clear example of a dedication by a non-Ikarian choregos has been found. One should however not automatically infer that the choregoi known from dedications were all Ikarieis. In the case for instance of Mnesilochos (**Mviii**) there is no further evidence suggesting that he was a demesman (as e.g. Whitehead 1986a, 436 and *LGPN* s.v. 4 assume).

The forms adopted by the surviving choregic monuments show considerable variety. Some, like the famous semicircular monument with its covered bench and roof decoration (**Mix**), are of considerable scale. A large marble block (1.68 × 0.34 × 0.22 m) that had been reused as the lintel for the door leading from the narthex to the nave of the Byzantine church was thought by Milchhöfer (1887b, 311) to be the remains of another substantial victory monument. It had been reused in Roman times (Buck 1892, 106 no. 13) but the partial remains of two names in letters of the fourth or third century may be those of two further lost Ikarian choregoi (one of them begins ΑΡΙΣΤΟΜΕ). Other forms include a tripod on a marble base (**Mviii**; cf. **Mvii**); a relief with six dramatic masks (**Mv**); and a large double-sided relief that perhaps served as a fence or altar screen associated with a temple or other sanctuary structure and depicts a number of deities on one side and, on the other, a group of figures that may be a chorus with a goat (the possible choral character of the group being the main reason for supposing it might be choregic: **Mxi**). There was also found a carved mask of a young woman from tragedy, dated by style to ca. 300 (Athens NM 3064; 0.195 × 0.205 × 0.16 m; Buck 1892, 45, 123 no. 20; Zoumpakes 1987, 57 no. 32; Kaltsas 2001, 285 no. 600). This emerged during the clearing of the walls of building D and is likely to have come from one of the many choregic dedications in that area. The hair is parted sharply in the middle of the brow and forms into wavy locks. The wide-opened mouth and broad eyes assure the generic affiliation to tragedy. Two slight mounds on the top of the head were possibly part of a decoration or special hairstyle, but given that on the left-hand side of the head there is a fracture and the marble extends somewhat beyond the natural edge of the hair (Merriam at Buck 1892, 123 n. 49), it is quite likely that this head came from a plaque or relief with multiple masks, as in **Mv**. Unlike **Mv**, however, the female head is sculpted in the round.

Various other bits of Dionysian flotsam might also derive from choregic monuments: the torso of a satyr described by Merriam (1889, 76) as 'of the good period' (Buck 1892, 45, 122 fig. 7); the chest of a Silen, found in building D (Buck 1892, 45, 122 fig. 8); and 'a bronze intaglio of a habited figure holding a thyrsus or sceptre' (Merriam 1889, 76). Merriam also suggested that the fine sculpted relief of a seated female figure found north of the church, her left hand holding up the himation from her breast, the right probably holding a phiale (Buck 1892, 116 esp. n. 22 and fig. 5) is a votive object rather than sepulchral, and proposed that the figure is Erigone, daughter of Icarius. But there is at present no evidence that connects Erigone and Icarius older than the third century (Humphreys 2004, 243, 260–1).

Ikarion is a rare instance of a Cleisthenic deme named after a local hero (Kearns 1989, 94), implying his importance prior to 507. Icarius' association with Dionysus in the area may date as early as the earliest attestation of the god's cult, namely ca. 525 (above). A number of proposed identifications of the hero on Attic black- and red-figure vases from ca. 560–530 (and one of ca. 480–470: Robertson 1986) would, if correct, attest to a wider Attic familiarity with the story, adding the motif of the gift of the vine and wine by Dionysus to Icarius; and some role for the goat (*LIMC* V, s.v. Ikarios 645–7; *LIMC* Suppl. 2009, 291). In the most promising cases, at the centre of the image Dionysus, holding a vine and kantharos, faces the Icarius figure (always unidentified), variously holding a kantharos, staff or spear. A goat is present on a number of occasions. The combination of the giving of the vine and wine to an adult male mortal by Dionysus and the presence of the goat are suggestive but no more (Carpenter 1986, 46–7; Gondicas 1990 notes that the only certain depiction of the story of Icarius in Attic art is in the 2nd c. AD sculpture from the Theatre of Dionysus in Athens that was incorporated in the Phaidros bema, on which Despinis 2003; more accepting: Angiolillo 1981; Robertson 1986; Shapiro 1995, 95–6). Perhaps the most likely candidate for identification is the black-figure panel amphora of ca. 550–540, one side of which possibly depicts Icarius with a cartload of wine pulled by a tumescent mule; the other the (imminent) death of Icarius at the hands of his fellows (Padgett 2004). By the middle of the fifth century Icarius was certainly the object of cult and in possession of a modest fortune, stewarded by demarchs alongside the greater wealth of Dionysus and a very substantial non-cult treasury (**Mii**). This accounting practice implies the intertwining of the fortunes of hero and god in a more general sense; and the collocation of these funds on a stele with a long decree dealing with the running of the Dionysia (**Miii**) further suggests that by ca. 450 Icarius played some part in this.

The question of just how much of the mythology attested from later literary sources that links Icarius, Dionysus, the gift of wine and viticulture, the killing (sacrifice) of the goat (or of Icarius himself: Sch.[vet.[D]] Hom. *Il.* 22.29) and the invention of some form of drama existed already by the date at which we find Icarius involved in the theatrical Dionysia of Ikarion (ca. 450) is intractable. At **I Avii 2** we argue that the earliest surviving accounts of the story of Icarius, dating from the third century (Eratosthenes *Erigone*; Callimachus was also familiar with the story: fr. 178.3–4 Pf.), draw upon local fourth-century Attic historians such as Phanodemus or Philochorus. They are the likely source of a story that was designed to determine and over-determine the Attic origin of drama in all its forms, and they will have mined and massaged pre-existing local tradition to full effect. The theatre and broader sanctuary site of Ikarion underwent substantial renovation in the later fourth century (above), which as we have noted may have been driven in part by a Lycurgan vision of the place and potential of theatre for Athens' social and economic prosperity. It is possible that the leading historian and publicist of the Lycurgan vision, Phanodemus, is the figure primarily responsible for the promotion of the myth of Icarius and the origins of drama in Ikarion.

The relief from Ikarion which has on one side a (possibly tragic) choral group leading a goat beneath a thick vine (**Mxi**) dates to precisely the era in which Phanodemus was most active. There is more direct evidence suggesting that Phanodemus claimed that the first theatrical performances took place in honour of the god of the Anthesteria, Dionysus of the Marshes, rather than Dionysus Melanaigis-Eleuthereus (*FGrH* 325 F 5; **II B**; **VI J**). This might encourage us to look rather to another fourth-century historian propagandist as the promoter of the claims of Ikarion; but we could also imagine that, in the Phanodeman vision, rural beginnings in Ikarion were compatible with first urban performances at the Anthesteria. It may be relevant that the festival in honour of Erigone, the Aiora, was probably connected with, even somehow part of, the Anthesteria (Kearns 1989, 167; Parker 2005, 301, 456; Humphreys 2018, 856). Pausanias (1.2.5; **I Aiv 2**) preserves an Attic tradition, the date of which cannot be determined, that carefully placed the visit of Dionysus to Icarius earlier in time than the introduction of Dionysus from Eleutherae by Pegasos: the Delphic oracle is said to have made mention of the visit the god once made to Icarius. This must reflect a claim that the Dionysia of Ikarion was older, its rites and perhaps also its icon somehow distinct from that of Athens.

Thespis is said to have been the first performer of tragedy (active in the late 530s), and the dominant tradition makes him Ikarian (**I Avii 2**). It might be tempting to treat him as no more than a necessary *protos heuretes* generated by fourth-century propaganda or Hellenistic theory that put the origins of drama in the Attic countryside (his name has given rise to independent scepticism: *DTC*², 72), were it not for the fact he features in the *Wasps* of Aristophanes. In a wine-induced frenzy of pleasure Bdelykleon, to the sound of the aulos, spends the night 'executing those old dances that Thespis competed with, and just now he offered to prove to the modern tragedians, by disputing with them for the dancing prize, that they are nothing but a lot of old dotards' (1478–81: ὀρχούμενος τῆς νυκτὸς οὐδὲν παύεται / τἀρχαῖ᾽ ἐκεῖν᾽ οἷς Θέσπις ἠγωνίζετο· / καὶ τοὺς τραγῳδούς φησιν ἀποδείξειν Κρόνους / τοὺς νῦν διορχησάμενος ὀλίγον ὕστερον). This proves that already by 422 Thespis was thought to be the exponent par excellence of early tragedy. The comment of Sch. *Wasps* 1479 that a kitharode by that name, not the tragic poet, is meant seems a weak attempt to remove Thespis from this context of tragic dances and might conceivably be motivated by some critical *parti pris* on the origins of drama. It seems likely that Thespis was something rather more than a figure of myth-propaganda alone. Aristotle treated him as an historical figure in the early days of tragedy (Them. *Or*. 26, 316d p. 382 Dind. = *TrGF* 1 T 6) and Heraclides of Pontus thought it worth forging plays under his name (D.L. 5.92 = *TrGF* 1 T 24). His connection to Ikarion may be a product of fourth-century propaganda. But it is at least as likely that he did indeed come from Ikarion, which indubitably had a theatrical tradition relatively early in the fifth century, and that his association with the place was later (but already in some form by the later fifth century) much elaborated to fit the rural origins theory.

The situation is precisely parallel with Susarion, said by the *Marmor Parium* (**I Avii 3**) to have invented comedy before 561, 'the people of Ikarion [ha]ving been [fir]st to [per]-for[m] (a comic chorus) when Susarion invented it'. His tradition bears even clearer traces of being influenced, if not entirely fabricated, by the struggle over the origins of comedy between Dorian Megara and Athens. For it is neatly divided between describing him as a Megarian and an Ikarian (**IV Bii**).

Mi: Dedication to Dionysus (a Statue) and Apollo at Ikarion, ca. 525 (by letter forms and style of the statue).

Statue:
Fragments of 'Pentelic' marble of a late Archaic colossal seated statue of Dionysus (torso, right hand with kantharos, feet, face). Original height over 2 m. The floor plan of the base of the marble canopy erected over it in the 4th c. was ca. 1.645 × ca. 1.275 m.
Athens NM 3897 + 3073 + 3074 + 3072 (statue); Marathon Museum Λ 125 + Athens NM 4888 (canopy).
Head found beneath the west wall of the Byzantine church; torso found close to base B at a similar depth; hand found close to and outside the east wall of building D; a large fragment of the beard found in building D, ca. 1.0 m below the lowest course of the wall. The larger fragment of the canopy was found just outside the south wall of building D.   Photos: Despinis 2007, pls. 11–22; pl. 23 (reconstruction).

Inscription:
Fragment of white 'Pentelic' marble. Broken on all sides except the top, which is flat. A small part of the lower right side may be original. The back is rough but flat and seemingly original. Takeuchi (2010–2013, 94) suggests that it was probably a stele or plate, perhaps placed next to the statue, rather than a base. Traces of red colour in the letters and guidelines between the rows were visible to Robinson in 1947. Attic script.
0.16 × 0.26 × 0.082–0.095 m.
Found 'near the altar and the Pythion' in September 1947 (Robinson 1948, 142; see Plan).
Athens NM 12507 (Correction of number given in *IG* I³ thanks to K. Takeuchi).
Robinson 1948, 142 no. 2 (= *SEG* 12, 58); *CEG* I, 303; *IG* I³ 1015; Takeuchi 2010–2013, 94–5 (= *SEG* 63, 48).
Text: based on Takeuchi 2010–2013.   Photo: Robinson 1948, pl. 35.3.

```
1       [- - - - - - τ]õι Διον[ύσοι]           non-stoich.
        [- - - - κ]αλὸν ἄγαλμ[α]
        [- - - - - - -] το τε ηεμιμ
        [- - - - - Ἀ]πόλονι τ[- -]
5       - - - - - - - - - - - - - - - ?
```

0/1–5 [… ca. 7 …. ἀνέθεκ|εν τ]õι Διον[ύσοι τὸ| κ]αλὸν ἄγαλμ[α τοῦτ|ο] τό τε ηεμιμ[ναῖον| Ἀ]πόλονι Π[υθίοι] Robinson   [- - - - - - - - - - | - - - - τ]õι Διον[ύσοι - - - | - - - κ]αλὸν ἄγαλμ[α - - - | - - -] το τε ηεμιμ[- - - | - - - Ἀ]πόλ<λ>ονι τ[- - - | - - - - - - -] Lewis   3 last letter μ or ν Hansen   possibly ηεμῖν Takeuchi   4 Possibly name of dedicator, e.g. Ἀπολλόνιος, Ἀπολλονίδης Takeuchi

[? dedicated] to Dion[ysus … b]eautiful statu[e …] ? and the (?) half-m[na …] to [A]pol<l>o[…]

This late Archaic dedication is the very earliest item of inscriptional evidence for the cult of Dionysus in the demes, dating from a time when the Pisistratid tyrants still dominated Athens (Hippias was Archon in 526/5, the younger Pisistratus in 523/2). Its slender remains tantalise, and attempts at reconstruction are hazardous. Hansen's confidence (*CEG* I, 303) that it is a verse-epigram seems unfounded. Takeuchi's study of the stone has shown that there was no line before l. 1 above (as earlier editors had assumed, on no good grounds) since the upper surface is original. He also suggests that it may be possible to establish the end of the lines, since some of the right-hand edge appears to survive. He argues that we have the upper right-hand corner of a dedicatory stele which probably stood beside the statue. But there can be no doubt that the inscription records the dedication to Dionysus of a 'beautiful statue'. The statue in question is very probably the high-quality colossal cult statue of the seated god, which is independently dated by style to ca. 530–520 (Romano 1982, 401–2).

The second part of the inscription is more difficult. There was also something 'for Apollo'. Even if the pi that Robinson saw in l. 4 as the start of his epithet 'Pythios' cannot be read (the editors of *IG* I³ print a doubtful tau), this is certainly the Pythian Apollo whose sanctuary is identified by an inscription directly on its threshold announcing it as Ἰκαριῶν τὸ Πύ[θιο]ν 'The Pythion of the Ikarians' (*IG* II³ 4, 1866) and which is mentioned in the decree governing the Dionysia (**Miii**) (in ll. 4–5 we might have [τõι Ἀ]πόλονι τ[õι | Πυθίοι]: Takeuchi 2010–2013, 95). The stone was found in close proximity to the Pythion (see Plan). Robinson's 'half mna' (ℎεμιμ[ναῖον] l. 3) was until recently the only proposed restoration that has been offered, but its implications have never been discussed. Dionysus receives a major, costly cult statue; Apollo, a modest cash sum. Rather than reflecting a strictly 'joint' dedication to the pair it seems more likely that the sum represents a form of payment to Apollo relating to the erection of the statue of Dionysus in his sanctuary. This in turn may reflect a situation in which Dionysus was conceived of as the relative newcomer to a place that had long been home to Apollo's cult. Takeuchi (2010–2013, 95) has recently proposed a quite different line of interpretation. He suggests the last letter in l. 3 be read as a nu rather than a mu, making ℎεμῖν 'for us', a possibility. We might compare the ex-voto choregic dedication from Thorikos (**Yi**) that explicitly requests a return from the god (l. 4: σὺ δ' ἀντι[δίδο], where 'to me' is at least implied). Takeuchi also notes that there is no trace of the last letter in l. 4 read by Robinson as a possible pi and by Lewis as a possible tau. He thus suggests that [A]pol<l>oni- might be the start of a personal name, such as Apollonios or Apollonides, and refer not to the god at all but a dedicator.

The evidence for the close cultic association of Dionysus and Apollo in Ikarion is however undoubted and, while familiar enough from Delphi, unique for Attica. It makes sense in the context of the extensive reorganisation and centralisation of the religious life of Attica by the Pisistratids (Ieranò 1992; Shapiro 1989; Angiolillo 1997). Their attention to Apollo is especially well-documented. The elder Pisistratus constructed a temple in the great Pythion in the south-east part of the city (Wilson 2007b, 153). His son Hipparchus made a special dedication to Apollo Ptoios on the Boeotian border (*IG* I³ 1470). He is also said to have demonstrated his concern for the cultural well-being of residents of the Attic countryside by dispensing the moral wisdom of Pythian Apollo with maxims inscribed on herms erected on roadsides thither (Pl. *Hipparch.* 228c–229b; *IG* I³ 1023). The younger Pisistratus continued the tradition by dedicating an altar to Apollo in the urban sanctuary that his grandfather had embellished, in memory of his own Archonship of 522/1. Thucydides describes the altar (6.54.6), which still survives (*IG* I³ 948, with a new fragment published by Charami and Bardani 2011). It is entirely possible that the cult statue of Dionysus in Ikarion, paying, as it appears, due respect to its Apollonian host, and being a dedication of considerable scale and value, was itself the gift not simply of a local worthy, but of a notable and interested outsider – such as a Pisistratid.

The remains of the seated statue of Dionysus were found scattered in the area of building D and the large base B nearby. Its full original height was over 2 m. The god has a full, long beard and down-turned moustache. His hair sits in large snail-like curls around his forehead and falls in long, thick wavy strands behind. His torso is twisted slightly to the right, with the left hand extended a little further forward, probably grasping a branch of ivy or a vine. Romano (1982, 401) rejects the thyrsos later favoured by Despinis (2007) as unknown in Archaic representations of the god. He wears a chiton with a himation thrown over the left shoulder and drawn across the chest down to the waist on the right. His right hand grips a (removable) kantharos and it is noteworthy that Carpenter (1986, 117–23) has argued that the introduction of the kantharos as an attribute of Dionysus in Attica ca. 540 is to be associated with the alliance between the Thebans and Pisistratus that helped to re-store the tyrant to power after his second exile. His feet wear sandals that once had bronze straps. A bronze ivy leaf found by Buck (1892, 110 n. 4) probably came from the wreath that crowned his head.

The association of the fragmentary head with the rest of the remains is not universally accepted, but very likely. Confusion has been generated by the fact that the back of the head was roughly chiselled off into a concave surface in antiquity, giving it a mask-like appearance, and encouraging the belief that drama was performed in the god's cult from as early as ca. 530. But it is clear that the head was originally sculptured in the round and not intended as a 'mask', though it was worked separately and inserted into the body. The chiselling is likely to represent a later repair or reworking of the head. The 'mask' head cannot therefore be corralled as evidence for drama in Ikarion to support the date the Suda and others give for the activities of Thespis.

A certain amount is now known about the life of this statue. There can be little doubt that this is the *agalma* which choregoi (and it seems others) were required to touch as they swore the oath of exemption (**Miii**) in the preparations leading up to the festival. It no doubt played a large part in the rituals of the sanctuary and festival. From some time in the fourth century, it was covered by a marble canopy (or baldachin), with a pyramidal external roof supported by four columns, while the concave internal ceiling was decorated with bunches of grapes in relief. Despinis (2007) made the important identification of the fragments of this canopy, which had presented an insoluble puzzle to Buck (1892, 124), and offers a full reconstruction of the ensemble. The statue was thus not housed in a tem-ple but in the open air, and Despinis (2007, 126–8) has further shown that it stood on the marble base in the sanctuary marked 'B', previously considered likely to be the founda-tion of a choregic monument. The torso was found very close to this base, and at the same depth (Buck 1892, 60). The god will have looked westwards, with a good view of the sacrifices on the altar in front of his temple from his strategic point along the processional route. Given that base B is not as old as the statue, it is quite likely that the statue was reerected, complete with its new covering, on that base at some time in the fourth century. Whether it stood in the same place or elsewhere before that time cannot be determined.

We possibly possess a record of this procedure of protective renovation. An inscription on a substantial base (over 1.0 m high) found in the excavations of Buck (no precise find-spot is given; EM 13317) and dated only broadly to the fourth century records a dedication to Dionysus by a commission of *epimeletai* who had overseen the 're[pair] of the statue'

(*IG* II³ 4, 222: ἐπιμεληταὶ τῆς ἐπ[ισκευῆ]||ς τοῦ ἀγάλματο[ς ἀνέ]|θεσαν τῶι Διον[ύσωι]). 'The statue', without further qualification, shows that a major and well-known item from the sanctuary is meant (Romano 1982, 406–7). A fine ivy crown appears below the inscription, suggesting, as Buck noted (1892, 106), that the team of *epimeletai* were crowned by the deme for their efforts. To have attracted such concerted communal effort and thanks, these repairs probably included, in addition to the physical repair of damage to the Archaic statue noted by archaeologists (in particular, the reworking on the back of the head), the construction of the protective canopy.

Mii: Records of Funds – Including those of Dionysus and Icarius – Passed on between Demarchs of Ikarion, ca. 450 (earliest entries) to ca. 425 (latest entries) (by letter forms, use of Attic and Ionic alphabets and relation to **Miii**: below).

Stele of 'Pentelic' marble inscribed on both sides: **Miii** appears on the other side. The left-hand edge is broken, the right-hand edge virtually intact; broken at bottom and part of the triangular top missing. Only the upper half of the surface is inscribed, the rest rough-worked. Lines 1–10 Ionic script, 11–24 Attic script (but see below). The letter heights vary: 0.010–0.013 m (ll. 1–4); 0.008–0.011 (ll. 5–7); 0.009–0.010 (ll. 8–10); 0.013–0.016 (ll. 11–14); 0.011–0.016 (ll. 15–20); 0.010–0.014 (ll. 21–4).

0.99 × 0.35 (top) – 0.405 (bottom) × 0.153 (top) – 0.165 (bottom) m. Original dimensions ca. 1.12 × 0.54 m.

Found 'under the front wall' of the Byzantine church (Buck 1892, 93): see Plan.

Athens NM 4833 (Face A).

Buck 1892, 93–6 no. 8; *IG* I Suppl. III, 134–7; *IG* I² 186; *IG* I³ 253; Makres 2004, 132–4 (= *SEG* 54, 57); autopsy.

Text: based on Makres 2004, with modifications from autopsy.   Photos: Wilson 2015, figs. 2–3; drawing by Y. Nakas (see **Miii**).

vacat ca. 0.080 m   non-stoich.

1	IV	[- - - - ca. 11 - - - -] δημαρχõν παρέδωκεν
		[- - - - κεφάλαιον] ἀργυρίο Διονύσο ΧΧ[..]
		[? κεφάλαιον Ἰκαρί]ο: ΧΧΗΓΗϹ *vac.*
		[? κεφάλαιον ὁσίο ΤΤΤΤ]ΧΧΓΗΗΗΗΔΔΔΗΗΙΙΙΙ *vac.*
5	V	[- - - ca. 10 - - - δημαρχῶν] παρέδωκε κεφάλαιον ἀργυρίο
		[- - Διονύσο ? ΧΧΧΧ]ΓΗ, Ἰκαρίο κεφάλαιον ΧΧΗΙ[..]
		[- - ὁσίο κεφάλαιον Τ]ΤΤΤΗΗΙΙΙΙ
	VI	[- - - - ca. 11 - - - - δημαρχ]ῶν παρέδωκε κεφάλαιον ἀργυρίο
		[Διονύσο ? ΧΧΧΧ - - ca. 5 - -] Ἰκαρίο ἀργυρίο κεφάλαιον ΧΧΗ[..]
		ΔΔ[..]
10		[κεφάλαιον ὁσίο ἀρ]γυρίο ΤΤΤΤΧΗΔΔΗΗ *vac.*
	I	[- - - - ca. 12 - - - -] δεμαρχõν παρέδοκεν
		[- - - ἀργυρίο κε]φάλαιον τõ Διονύσο
		[? ΧΧΧΧ - ca. 7 -]ΔΓΗΙΙΙ : ἀργυρίο hοσίο
		[- - - κεφάλαι]ον : ΤΤΤΤΧΧΗΗΓΔΔΔΓΗΗΙΙΙ
15	II	[- - - ca. 9 - - - δ]εμαρχõν παρέδοκεν
		[- - - ἀργυρίο κε]φάλαιον τõ Διονύσο

[? ΧΧΧΧ - - -]ⱵΔᴦᴴ⌐⌐⌐⌐ : ἀργυρίο hοσίο

[- - - κεφάλαι]ον : ΤΤΤΤΧΧⱤΗⱵΔΔΔΔᴦ⊦⊦

[- - - ca. 9 - - -]ι : ἀργυρίο : κεφάλαιον

20   [- - - ca. 10 - - -]ΙΙ *vac.*

III   [- - - - ca. 12 - - - -] δημαρχὸν παρέδοκε[ν]

[- - - ἀργυρίο hοσί]ο̣ : κεφάλαιον : ΤΤΤΤΧΧ [?.]

[- - τõ Διονύσο ἀργ]υρίο : κεφάλαιον : ΧΧΧⱤ [?.]

[- - - - - τõ Ἰκα]ρίο : ἀργυρίο : κεφάλαιο[ν]

25   [- - - - - - - - -]

vacat 0.03 m

2 ΧΧ[ΧΧ]ΗΗ Buck   3 [? κεφάλαιον Ἰκαρί]ο: Wilson   [- - - - - -]ο: Makres   3–4
[Ἰκαρί]ου ΧΧΗᴦ⊦⊦C [όσίου ἀργυ|ρίου ΤΤΤΤ] Buck   [ἀργυρίο Καρί]ο ͅ ΧΧΗᴦ⊦⊦C
‖[όσίο ΤΤΤΤ] Hiller   [Ἰκαρ]<ί>ο ͅ ΧΧΗᴦ⊦⊦C ‖[όσίο ΤΤΤΤ] Lewis   6 start [- - Διονύσο
? ΧΧΧΧ]ⱤΗ[- - - - - -] Wilson [- - - - - -] ⱤΗ Makres   end κεφάλαιον ΧΧΗΗ(?)
[· όσίου] Buck   6 [τõ Διονύσο ΧΧΧΧ]ⱤΗΙ : Καρίο κεφάλαιον ΧΧΗΗ Hiller   [τõ
Διονύσο ΧΧΧ]ⱤΗ, Ἰκαρίο κεφάλαιον ΧΧΗΗ Lewis   ΧΧΗ[. .] Makres   7 [ἀργυρίου]
ΤΤΤΤΗΗ[... ὁ δεῖνα] Buck   [όσίο κεφάλαιον ΤΤΤ]ΤΙΙ⊦⌐⌐⌐⌐ Hiller   [όσίο κεφάλαιον
ΤΤ]ΤΤ⊦⊦⌐⌐⌐⌐ Lewis   ΤΤΤ⊦⊦⌐⌐⌐ Makres   ΤΤΤ⊦⊦⌐⌐⌐⌐ Stroud   13 start [ΧΧΧΧ....]
Buck   [ΧΧΧ.....] Hiller, Lewis   14 end ᴦ⊦⊦⌐ Buck, Lewis   ᴦ⌐⌐⌐⌐⌐ Lolling,
Hiller   18 start [κεφάλαι]ον Buck, Lewis   [- κεφάλαιο]ν Makres   [κεφάλαιο]
ν Stroud   end Takeuchi   ΔΔΔ⊦⊦⊦ Buck   ΔΔΔΔᴦ⊦⌐ Lolling, Hiller   ΔΔΔΔᴦ⊦
Lewis   ΔΔΔΔΙ Makres   ΔΔΔΔΙ Stroud   19 [παρέδω?]κ' ἀργυρίο κεφά[λαι]ον
Buck   [Καρ]ί Hiller   Possibly [Ἰκαρί<ο>]ι or [Ἰκαριε]ῖ ?

IV [name] as demarch handed over: [the total] of the money belonging to
Dionysus, 2 (*or more*) thousand (the full sum is more likely to be in the order of
three or four thousand) and [… dr.; the total belonging to Icari]us, 2,107 dr., one-
half ob.; [the total of *hosion* money, (?) 26],933 dr., 4 ob. [5] **V** [name as demarch]
handed over: the total of the money [belonging to Dionysus, (?) three or four
thousand], 600 dr.; the total belonging to Icarius, 2,100 dr. and 1(+) ob.; [the
total of *hosion* money], (probably) 24 (and at least 18) thousand and 2 dr., (?)
4 ob. **VI** [name as dem]arch handed over: the total of the money [belonging to
Dionysus, (?) three or four thousand and ?… dr.]; the total of the money belonging to Icarius, 2 thousand, 1 (or more) hundred and 20 (+?) dr.; [10] [the total of
hosion m]oney, 25,122 dr. **I** [name] as demarch handed over: the [t]otal [of the
money] belonging to Dionysus, [(three or four or possibly more thousand)] and
16 (+?) dr., 3 ob.; [the tot]al of *hosion* money, 26,28(?)8 dr., 3 ob. [15] **II** [name]
as [d]emarch handed over: the [t]otal [of the money] belonging to Dionysus,
[(three or four or possibly more thousand)] and 66 dr., 4 ob.; [the total] of *hosion*
money, 26,697 (?+) dr.; the total of the money [? of *or* for Icariu]s, [20] (??) dr.
and 2 ob. **III** [name] as demarch handed over: the total of *hosi*[on money], 26
thousand (?) and (?) dr.; the total [of the mo]ney [belonging to Dionysus], 3,500
(?) and (?) dr.; the tota[l] of the money belonging to [Ica]rius [25] [*entire sum lost*].

This stele, which has an important decree concerning the Dionysia on its other side (**Miii**),
was originally prepared to record the handover (*paradosis*) of funds in a number of deme
treasuries from one demarch to the next. There are six annual entries. Each begins with

the phrase *name* + δημαρχο̄ν παρέδωκε(ν), '*name* serving as demarch handed over', and goes on to record capital sums of money (κεφάλαιον ἀργυρίο) passed on from the serving demarch to his successor. The successor demarch is never named (as he is in **Mx**, l. 6) which may imply that he was not yet appointed (the present tense δημαρχο̄ν suggests that the handover was made while the named demarch was still in office). The stone is broken in such a way that no single letter of any of the demarchs' names survives.

The order in which they appear on the stone is not the order in which the entries were inscribed. They were made at different times and by a variety of hands. The absolute chronology and even the detail of their relative chronology cannot be established. Nor can we be sure whether all or any represent consecutive years. There is however no doubt as to their general chronological order. The earliest entry (**I**: ll. 11–14) was inscribed at around the vertical mid point of the prepared surface, the area above only coming into use (**IV–VI**: ll. 1–10) once the area below had been filled with two further entries (**II–III**: ll. 15–25). The most likely explanation of this unusual arrangement is that, when the first entry was made, the area above it carried a painting or other impermanent design of some sort that was removed when space was needed for further entries. (Given the evident pressure on space, it is curious that only the upper half of the whole surface was ever prepared for inscription, the rest remaining rough-worked.) **I** may be very approximately dated by its use of Attic script and letter forms to ca. 450 (in addition to the three-bar sigma, indicative letters are the upsilon with curved arms, the phi with large circle and the slanting nu), and **II** (in the same hand) to very soon after. These entries thus predate **Miii**. **I** and **II** were very possibly consecutive years. **III** is in a different hand and its letter forms share more affinities with those of **Miii** than with the earlier entries.

Miii was probably passed very close in time to this entry, either just prior to it – perhaps in the same demarchy – or immediately after (**III** has one instance of Ionic lettering l. 21 δημαρχο̄ν, while **Miii** shows none, but on the other hand **IV** has a single example of Attic o for ω l. 1). It is fairly certain that **Miii** had been passed by the time of **IV**, since **III** had filled the last part of the prepared surface at the bottom and **IV** was placed not on the other side of the stele but on the upper part of the same side, above the older entries (thereby obliterating whatever image had presumably been there before).

The oldest entry (**I**) records sums of money from two funds only – one belonging to Dionysus and the other described as 'the *hosion* money' (ἀργύριον ὅσιον) (in that order). The latter will be 'public' or 'deme' money that did not belong to any particular deity or hero but could be deployed more or less as the deme determined (Blok 2010, with previous bibliography; Papazarkadas 2011, 136, 148–9). The sum of *hosion* money is well preserved, and is a very substantial 26,28(?)8 drachmas, 3 obols. How a small deme like Ikarion came to accrue such significant resources is a matter for speculation (Papazarkadas 2011, 136, 147–50). Only the end of the total for Dionysus survives. The preceding numerals were probably 3,000 or perhaps 4,000 drachmas (Wilson 2015, 141–2). In **II** the *hosion* money has increased by around 400 drachmas (this is one of the few places where totals in physically adjacent years can be compared), though the value of this observation is limited by our complete ignorance as to what the income to and expenditure from this fund (and for that matter, the others) may have been, and uncertainty as to whether the years are consecutive in time. It is impossible to say whether the sum of Dionysus' money in **II** is greater or smaller.

A third fund, that of Icarius, almost certainly makes its first appearance in this year, in ll. 19–20: [- - - ca. 9 - - -]ι ⋮ ἀργυρίο ⋮ κεφάλαιον ‖[- - - ca. 10 - - -]ΙΙ. It is *a priori* most likely that this entry belongs to Icarius, since it follows those for Dionysus and the *hosion* money, and since the local hero certainly has an entry in the next year (**III**: l. 24) and thereafter (ll. 3, 6, 9). The iota at the start of l. 19 is however difficult to accommodate to the inscription's usual accounting style and is possibly an error (for Ἰκαρίο 'of Icarius'); or, less likely, some sort of allocation of a capital sum 'to Icarius', Ἰκαριεῖ. Icarius' presence does not prove but very much increases the likelihood that the hero was associated with the cult and festival of Dionysus in his deme (**M Introduction**).

In **III** the *hosion* money, listed in first place (the order of listing is not fixed, though in the three years **IV**–**VI** it is Dionysus – Icarius – *hosion*) is at least 26,000 drachmas, but probably not that round figure, as other numerals are likely to have been present where the edge of the stone has broken off. Dionysus' money is at least 3,500 drachmas (but less than 4,000), and once again probably not that round figure. The entire sum of Icarius' total has been lost (from the first part of l. 25, lost with the left-hand edge of the stele). The first (and only complete) entry for the hero appears in the next entry (**IV**) at 2,107 drachmas, one-half obol. It remains close to that sum in **V** and **VI**, increasing slightly in the latter at least. In **IV** the *hosion* money is probably just over 26,933 drachmas; in **V**, it seems to have dropped to just over 24,000 drachmas; while in **VI** it has recovered some of that loss, and is (exactly) 25,122 drachmas.

It is highly likely that the two sides of the stele relate to one another, and that they reflect a concerted plan of action centred on the cult and festival of Dionysus in Ikarion. What is most striking about this document from the perspective of theatre history is the fact that the very large fund of *hosion* money was recorded alongside the two sacred funds of the deme's hero and his famous visitor – and of no other deity. That particular combination, as Blok (2010, 86) notes, 'points to a close relation of the *hosion* money with the Dionysian festival'. It strongly suggests that the productive capacity of this well-endowed fund was made available to support the most salient feature of the local cult of Dionysus, and the one that is treated extensively by the decree on the other side of the stone – namely the local Dionysia. That effort may be in response to special historical circumstances, although those suggested by Humphreys (2004, 151) – the plague or the partial depopulation of the deme during the Peloponnesian War – are almost certainly too late. But the cost of a Dionysia with theatrical performances was always unusually high by comparison with all other forms of cult and thus became a stimulus to the creation of novel financial instruments. Blok suggests that this fund was created to cover the costs of the Dionysia that were not met by the choregoi known from the other side of the stone. She thinks of wooden benches needed for the theatre, temporary accommodation, prizes and substantial sacrifices for the large number of locals and visitors that would flock to such a major event (sacrifices for Dionysus and Icarius could be met from their own funds). We may certainly assume that the Dionysia was a feature of the Ikarian economy (as well as its religious community) that was deemed to be worth this level of concerted support, for it no doubt attracted more visitors (and their money) to this distant if august Dionysian enclave than any other event.

It is likely, as Humphreys (2004, 147–51) suggests, that the capital sums in the accounts were put out as loans by the demarch to help generate extra income (cf. **W Introduction** with Blok 2010 for clear evidence of such loans offered by the sanctuary of Nemesis in Rhamnus around the middle of the fifth century). In Ikarion such loans are likely to have been taken up by the well-off (who had the requisite property to secure them) and in particular by choregoi, whose wealth is likely to have been in land and who will have needed the necessary liquidity to meet the cash-intensive costs of choregia. Blok (2010) has argued for a modest interest rate of ca. 2.5% in this and the few similar early deme documents, but a higher rate is perhaps more likely. Attested rates of interest between human agents in Attica are much higher – ranging most commonly between 10% and 30% (Whitehead 1986a, 159; Millet 1991, 104). And the Athenians normally borrowed from Athena – more relevant to the sacred funds here in Ikarion – at a basic rate of 7%, which they permitted themselves to reduce for a brief period of crisis in 427/6 to 1.5%. It is moreover quite likely that we should imagine that, if some of these funds were put out to interest in Ikarion, the loans themselves may have been taken up by 'liturgical borrowers' – wealthy men who took on loans with the aim of supplying new income for the deme and so garnering prestige for themselves within their community (Migeotte 2011; Müller 2011).

The chronological sequence identified above for the account entries and their relation to **Miii** suggests a scenario along these lines: at some point prior to the passing of **Miii** – perhaps a few years earlier – the deme made a decision to place the very large capital sum of its *hosion* money in a close relation to the funds of Dionysus and to advertise the demarch's responsibility for these funds by the erection of a substantial stele. The decision to record the totals belonging to Dionysus and the *hosion* money in **I** does not look like an attempt simply to record all the deme's cultic and other resources on the same stone. Apollo Pythios is absent for one and there will doubtless have been others (the force of this argument is weakened, but only slightly, by the observation that the cult of Apollo Pythios may have been outside the control of the deme: Humphreys 2004, 147). The fact that an entry first appears under Icarius' name only in **II** (and possibly as a special allocation: above on l. 19) points in the same direction. The sums registered under his name are the lowest of the three (where they survive they hover around the 2,100-drachmas mark), and his introduction to the list gives the appearance of an attempt to hunt out all and any resources that might be applied to Dionysian purposes. **Miii** appears to have been passed after this introduction of the funds of Icarius to the list and before **III**. At this point the stele, hitherto used for just two (probably consecutive) years for the sole purpose of recording the performance of these funds, had **Miii** inscribed on its other side. And when it was inscribed, the stele itself was given its special heading, on the face carrying the decree, l. 1: 'The stele [is sacred, (the property) of Dionysus]'. The accounts, by contrast, had no heading. If we take the implications of the header seriously, at this point the entirety of the stele was consigned to Dionysus. It may follow that not only was the stele being placed under the protection of the god, but that in some sense this act of naming also definitively assigned the funds themselves to his overall care or ownership. It thus seems likely that the (two?) years prior to the passing of the decree (**I–II**) were something of an experiment, or a period of preparation. They may represent an attempt to see what sort of funds could be generated (through loans at interest) from the consolidated resources of the treasuries before the deme made formal determinations about the scope of its festival (for a direct parallel for such a procedure see *IG* IX I² 4, 798, from Corcyra, second century with Migeotte 2010; Wilson 2015, 143–4).

Miii: Decree Regulating the Administration of the Dionysia at Ikarion, ca. 440 (by letter forms, use of Attic alphabet and relation to **Mii**; Wilson 2015, 108).

Stele of 'Pentelic' marble, inscribed on both sides (**Mii** appears on the other side). The left-hand side of the surface is broken off obliquely (from the upper left to the lower right), although the left-hand edge of the stele itself is largely preserved. The right-hand edge is not original, but has been cut off clean. The stele is broken at the bottom, not far below where the inscribed text ended. Part of its top, which was of a simple triangular shape, is missing. Attic script.

0.99 × 0.35 (top) – 0.405 (bottom) × 0.153 (top) – 0.165 (bottom) m. Original dimensions ca. 1.12 × 0.54 m.

Found 'under the front wall' of the Byzantine church (Buck 1892, 93): see Plan.

Athens NM 4833 (Face B).

Buck 1892, 96–104 no. 9; *IG* I Suppl. III, 134–7; *IG* I² 187; *IG* I³ 254; Makres 2004, 132–4 (= *SEG* 54, 58); Wilson 2015.

Text: based on Wilson 2015.   Photos: Wilson 2015, figs. 2–3.

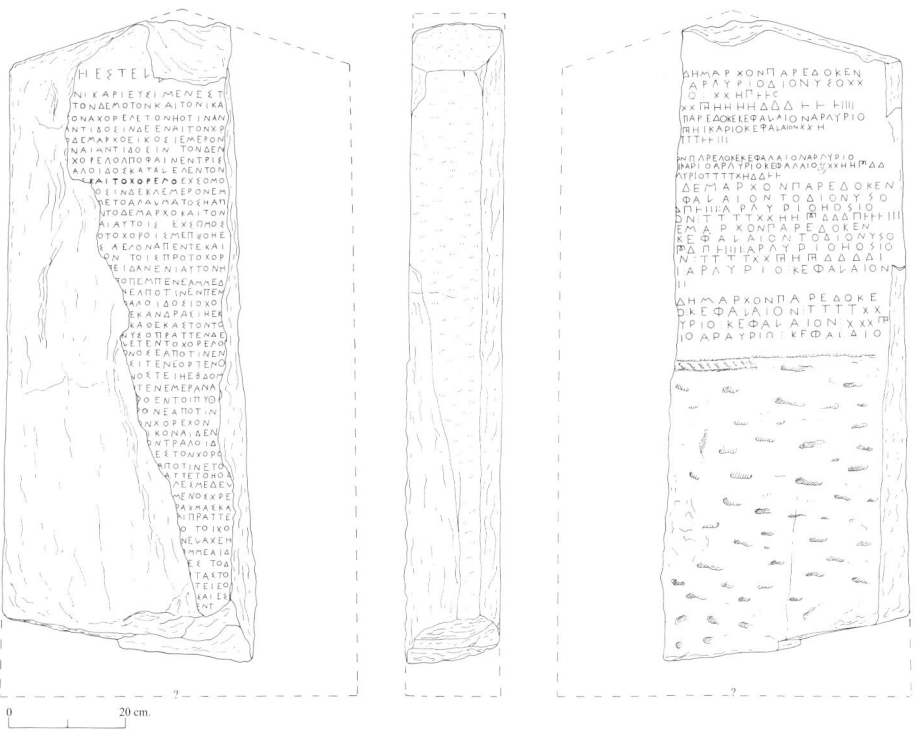

Stele from Ikarion: Left, Face B (**Miii**); centre, side view; right, Face A (**Mii**).

1   [----]ℎε στέλει [-------------------------]
      [ἔδοχσε]ν Ἰκαριεῦσι: Μενέστ[ρατος εἶπε(ν)· ..4(-5)..]   stoich. ? 36
      [...6...]ι τὸν δεμοτὸν καὶ τὸν Ἰκα[ριοῖ οἰκόντον δύο ἄ]-   stoich. ? 42
      [νδρε ἐκ] τὸν ἀχορεγέτον ℎότιν᾽ ἂν [........16........]
5   [...6...]. ἀντίδοσιν δὲ ἔναι τὸν χρ[εμάτον .....10..... ἐνα]-
      [ντίον τ]ō δεμάρχο εἴκοσι ἐμερõν [........16........]

[..3. ε̄̓ μὲ ε̄̓]ναι ἀντίδοσιν. ⱽ τὸν δέμ[αρχον ......11.....]

[...5.. τὸ] χορεγὸ ἀποφαίνεν τρισ[........16........]

[...5.. τρ]αγοιδὸς καταλέγεν τον [........16........]

10   [....7...-]ος καὶ τὸ χορεγὸ ἐχσομό[σα- ....14......]

[.....10..... -]οσιν δέκα ἐμερο̄ν ε̄̓ μ[ὲ̓ ε̄̓ναι ἐχσομοσίαν .]

[.....10.....] δε το̄ ἀγάλματος hαπ[τ-........15.......]

[.....10..... -]ν το̄ δεμάρχο καὶ τοῖ[........16.......]

[.....10..... -]αι αὐτοῖς. ⱽ ἐχσομοσ[-........16.......]

15   [..4.. τοῖς πρ]οτοχόροις μὲ π[ρ]οhε[-........16........]

[.....10..... -]ς. ⱽ ΑΕΓΟΝΑ πέντε καὶ [δέκα ......12......]

[......11..... -]ον. ⱽ τοῖς προτοχόρ[οις ....13......]

[.....10..... ἐ]πειδὰν ἐνιαυτὸν h[-........16.......]

[......11..... ἀ]ποπέμπεν ἐὰμ μὲ δ[-........16.......]

20   [.......13...... -]ν ε̄̓ ἀποτίνεν πεν[τε ....14.......]

[......12...... τ]ρ̣αγοιδο[.] ⱽ τὸ χο[ρεγὸ ......12......]

[...5.. πέντε καὶ δ]έκ' ἀνδράσι hεκ[α-........15........]

[.......14.......] καθ' ἕκαστον τὸ[ν ....15.......]

[.....10..... Διο]νύσο· πράττεν δὲ [........16.......]

25   [......12...... ἑ]ορτὲν τὸ χορεγὸ [........16.......]

[......13....... -]ονος ε̄̓ ἀποτίνεν [........16.......]

[.......14....... -]σι̣ τὲν ἑορτὲν θ[-........16.......]

[......12...... με]νὸς τε̄ι̣ hεβδόμ[ει ....14.......]

[......11..... πέμ]πτεν ἐμέραν ἀπ[-........16.......]

30   [........15....... -]ρο ἐν τῶι Πυθ[ίοι ....14.......]

[.......14....... -]γρον ε̄̓ ἀποτίν[εν ....15.......]

[.......14....... τ]ον χορεγον. ⱽ [.........17........]

[......12...... φαλλ]ικὸν ᾄιδεν [.........17........]

[........15....... τ]ον τραγοιδ[ον ....15.......]

35   [........17........]ες τὸν χορὸ̣[ν ....15.......]

[.........16........ ε̄̓] ἀ̣ποτινέτο [........16.......]

[........16........ πρ]αττέτο hο δ[έμαρχος ....8....]

[..........19.........]γες μεδὲ λ[-........15.......]

[..........19.........]μενὸς χρε[ματίζεν ....8....]

40   [.........18......... δ]ραχμὰς κα[ὶ ....14.......]

[.........18......... κ]α̣ὶ πραττέ[το ....13......]

[..........20.......... -]ο. ⱽ τοι̣ χο[ρ- ....14.......]

[..........20.......... -]ν ἔλαχε h[-........15.......]

[..........20.......... -]ομ μὲ διδ[- ....15.......]

45   [..........20.........]γες. ⱽ τοδ[- ....15.......]

[...........21.......... -]ι τὰς το[........15.......]

[...........21..........]ντελεο[........15.......]

[...........22.......... -]σαι εσ[........15.......]

[...........22..........]εν τ[.........17........]

1 ἡ στήλη [τῆς χορηγίας ?] Buck   [ℎιερὰ] ℎε στέλε [τõ Διονύσο] Hiller   2–3
[ℎε|λέσθα]ι Makres   Possibly ᵛ [καθ|ιστάνα]ι   3 [.....]ι Lolling   Possibly [ἐλέσθα]ι
(Takeuchi)   τõν Ἰκα[ριοῖ οἰκόντον] Wilamowitz in Addenda to *IG* I²   3–4 [δύο
ἄ|νδρε ἐκ] Wilson   4–5 Possibly [δυνατοτάτο χρέμασ|ιν ἔτον.] Wilson   5–6
ἀντίδοσιν δὲ εἶναι τῶν χρ[ημάτων αὐτοῦ ἐν|αντίον τ]οῦ Buck   ἀντίδοσιν δὲ εἶναι τὸν
χρ[όνον] Kirchhoff   7 [μὴ εἶ]ναι ἀντίδοσιν. τὸν δήμ[αρχον] Kirchhoff   8 τρισ[ὶ
μάρτυσι] Buck   τρὶς Lewis   8–9 [τὸ] χορεγὸ ἀποφαίνεν τρὶς [....7... τού|το δὲ τρ]-
αγοιδὸς Lewis   9 τὸν Buck   τõν Lewis   Possibly [δέμαρχον]   9–10 Possibly
[τὸς | τραγοιδ]ὸς   10 [ ]ος καὶ τοῦ χορεγοῦ ἐξομο[σαμένου] Buck   [ ]ος, καὶ τὸ
χορεγὸ ἐχσομο[σα] Lewis   11–12 [ ]οσιν δέκα ἡμερῶν ἐμ [Πυθίοι Ἰκαριῶν - - | - -]
δὲ τõ ἀγάλματος ἅπ[τεσθαι] Buck   [ ]οσιν δέκα ἐμερõν ἒ μ[ἐ ἔναι ἐχσομ|οσίαν ....]
δὲ τõ ἀγάλματος ℎαπ[τ] Lewis   [..4.. ἀντίδ]οσιν δέκα ἐμερõν ΕΜ[.....10.....|....9....]
μὲ τõ ἀγάλματος ℎάπ[τ] Makres   13 τõν [δημοτõν] Buck   τοι- Kirchhoff   τὸν
[δέμαρχον] Lewis   Possibly [ἐναντίο]ν τõ δεμάρχο καὶ τοῖ[ν χορεγοῖν]   14
αὐτοῖσ(ι?) Buck   αὐτοῖς ᵛ Kirchhoff   15 μὴ π[ρ]ὸ ἡ- Buck   μὴ π[ρ]οℎε[γο]
Lewis   14–15 Possibly e.g. ᵛ ἐχσομοσ[ίαν ἐχσέναι διδόνα|ι καὶ τοῖς πρ]οτοχόροις μὲ
π[ρ]οℎε[γε̃σθαι]   16 [ ] ... εγωνα πέντε καὶ [ ] Buck   γεγωνα πέντε καὶ Kirchhoff   [
]σο γεγονάτεν τε καὶ - - Hiller   [ ]ϹΟΛΕΛΟΝΛ πέντε καὶ [δέκα] Lewis   [ ]ς ᵛ ΑΕΓΟΝΑ
πέντε καὶ [ ] Makres   17 ον . τοῖς Buck   ο<ω>ν ἢ τοῖς Kirchhoff   [ ]ον ᵛ τοῖς
Makres   16–17 Possibly e.g. πέντε καὶ [δέκ' ἄνδρας ἔναι ἐς ℎ|εκάτερον χορ]όν. ᵛ
19 Possibly e.g. ἐὰμ μὲ δ[εμότες φαίνεται]   20 Possibly e.g. πεν[τέκοντα δραχμὰς
τõ|ι Διονύσοι.]   21 [τ]ραγωιδοῖ[ς] τοῦ χο[ρ] Buck   [τρ]αγωδοῖ[ς] τοῦ χο[ρ]-
Kirchhoff   [τ]ρ̣αγοιδοῖ[σ]ι ὁ χο[ρε] Lewis   [τ]ραγοιδὸς ᵛ τὸ χο[ρεγὸ] Makres   23
τὸ[ν ἐνιαυτὸν] Buck   τὸ[ν ἄνδρα] Lewis   24 [Διο]νύσου πράττειν δε[ ] Buck   [τοῦ
Διο]νύσου. πράττειν δὲ Kirchhoff   21–4 Possibly e.g. τὸ χο[ρεγὸ τὸ δέον παρέχε|ν
τοῖς πέντε καὶ δ]έκ' ἀνδράσι ℎεκ[ατέρο χορõ καὶ διδό|ναι οἶνο ἀμφορέα] καθ' ἕκαστον
τὸ[ν ἄνδρα ℎόπος καλὸς |ε̃ι ℎο ἀγὸν τõ Διο]νύσο / ℎόπος καλὲ ἒ|ι ℎε ἑορτὲ τõ Διο]-
νύσο·   25 [ἑ]ορτὴν τοῦ χορηγοῦ Buck   [ ]ετεν τὸ χορεγὸ Lewis   [ ]λετεν τὸ χορεγὸ
Makres   26 [ι]õνος Lewis   27 Possibly e.g. [ἐπειδὰν / ℎόταν ἄγο]σι / ποιõ]σι τὲν
ἑορτὲν   θ[εοῦ] Buck   Possibly θ[ύεν]   28 [ ]νὸς τὴν ἑβδόμ[ην] Buck   [ ]νὸς τε̃ι
ℎεβδόμ[ει] Makres   29 [ ]ττειν Buck   [ ]ττεν Hiller   [πέμ]πτεν Lewis   [πέμ]πτεν
Makres   End of line: ἀ[ ] Buck   ΕΜΕΡΑΝΑ⁻ Lolling   α[ ] Makres   28–9 Possibly
e.g. [.2. Ποσιδεõνος με]νὸς τε̃ι ℎεβδόμ[ει ἐπὶ δέκα ....7...|...6... ἐς τὲμ πέμ]πτεν ἑμέραν ἀπ[ὸ
διχομενίας]   30 [ ](ο?)ρο (= ꟼΡΟ) Buck   Possibly [χ]ορο   31 (χ?)ρον Buck   [ ]
ρον Kirchhoff, Lewis   [ ]Λρον Makres   Possibly ἐχς ἀγρõν   33 [ε]ἰκόνα ἰδεῖν Buck,
Kirchhoff   [φαλλ]ικὸν ᾄιδεν Hiller   34 Possibly e.g. [.... τ]õν τραγοιδõν τὸν ἀγõνα
....]   38 Possibly [ἐγλο]γε̃ς   39–40 Possibly [... τõ Ποσιδεõνος] μενὸς χρε[ματίζεν
/ χρε[ματίσαι περὶ τε̃ς ἑ]ορτε̃ς ἒ ἀποτίνεν δέκα δ]ραχμὰς   42 Ο ᵛ ΤΟ ᵛ ΧΟ ([ ]ο το χο[
]) Buck   Ο ᵛ ΤΟ | ΧΟ (ου. τõι χο[ρ]) Kirchhoff   ο ᵛ τοι χο[ ] Makres (τοι Stroud *SEG*
54, 58)   43 [ ]ν ἔλαχε ℎ[ ] Buck, Lolling, Makres   [ ]ν ἔλαχεν Kirchhoff   [ ]ν ἒ λαχε̃ν
[ ] Lewis   42–43 Possibly τõι χο[ρεγõι τõι νικέσαν|τι καὶ τõι διδασκάλοι ℎὸ]ν ἔλαχε
ℎ[ο χορεγὸς δίδοσθα|ι]   44 ΟΜΜΕΔΙΔ/ Buck 1892, 97; cf. Buck 1889, 308   [ἐ]ὰμ
Hiller   Possibly διδα[σκ-]   45 [ ]εσ τοδ[ ] Buck   [ ]ες. ᵛ τὸ δ[ἐ] Hiller   [ ]ες ᵛ τοδ[
] Lewis   [ ]Λες ᵛ τοδ[ ] Makres   46 τοῦ[ ] Buck   τοι - - Hiller   το|[ ] Lewis   το[
] Makres   47 ΝΤΕLΕΟΙ ([ ]ντελεω[ ]) Buck   [ἐ]ντελὲ ὄν[τα] Hiller   [ ]ντελεο⫽[ ]
Lewis   [ℎιερὸ]ν τέλεον Lewis in app. crit.   [ ]υντελεο[ ] Kirchhoff, Makres   48–9
Possibly [..... καὶ ἀναγράφ]σαι ἐσ[τέλει λιθίνει τόδ|ε τὸ φσέφισμα καὶ ἀναθε̃ναι] ἐν τ[õι
Διονυσίοι].   50 -- Lewis, Makres

[…] the stele [? is sacred, (the property) of Dionysus …]. The Ikarians [de-
cid]ed; Menest[ratos proposed: to sele]ct from among the demesmen and the

[residents in] Ika[rion] tw[o men] from those who have not previously been choregoi who [? are the most financially capable ?]. [5] And there is to be an antidosis of properties before t]he demarch within twenty days [… or th]ere is to be [no] antidosis. The dem[arch] is to declare appointed [the] two choregoi […] three times [?? to the Ikarians ?? (Wilson 2015, 120) …?? The demarch is] to make a register of the [*tr*]*agoidoi* [… [10] ?? The *tragoid*]*oi* and the two choregoi are to give excuse under oath […] within ten days or [there is to be] n[o excuse under oath]. And touch[ing] the statue [… ? in the presenc]e of the demarch and the [? …] are to […] to them. [The *pr*]*otochoroi* [15] [?? are also able to give] the oath of exem[ption] from l[ea]d[ing ?? the choruses … ??]. *AEGONA* (error on the stone) five and [ten …] (?? Possibly '[There are to be] fif[teen men for each chor]us'). To the *protocho*[*roi* … w]henever [eac]h year […] to send [a]way if not [… [20] …] (?? Possibly 'to send [him a]way if he [proves] not [to be] a d[emesman …]') or to pay a fine of fiv[e (*or possibly* 'fifteen' *or* 'fifty' drachmas … t]*ragoidos*/*i*). The two cho[regoi … with/to five and t]en men eac[h …] to each [… of Dio]nysus. (?? Lines 21–4 possibly e.g. '[t]he two cho[regoi are to provide what is necessary for the fif]teen men of ea[ch chorus and to give a jar of wine] to each [man so that the festival of Dio]-nysos [is fine].' ??) And [? the demarch] [25] is to see to it [… the f]estival the two choregoi […] or to pay […] the festival (?? Possibly '[When they cond]-uct the festival, make a] sa[crifice …') […] on the sevent[h] of [the m]onth [… fi]fth day fro[m … [30] …] (?? Possibly '… on the sevent[eenth] of [the m]onth [Posideon … to the fif]th day fro[m the middle of the month].') [??… the cho]-rus (?? *or* 'the two [cho]ruses) in the Pyth[ion …?? from the fi]elds or to pay [… t]he choregos. […] to sing the [phall]ic song [… t]he *tragoid*[*os* (*or* 'of t]he *tragoid*[*oi*') (?? Possibly '[the contest] of tragedie[s …]') [… [35] …] (? in)to the choru[s … or] he is to pay […] the d[emarch] is to [s]ee to it […-]*ges* […] (??? Possibly '[of the coll]ection') and not […] of the month busi[ness is to be conducted … [40] … d]rachmas an[d … a]nd is to see to [it …]. (? Lines 39–41 possibly '[… on the x- of the] month [Posideon] busi[ness concerning the fes-tival shall be dealt with or he is to pay ten d]rachmas an[d … a]nd [he] is to see to [it …]') ?? To the cho[r-…] was allotted […] (??? *Possibly something like* '[f]or the [victorious] cho[regos and the didaskalos who]m th[e choregos] was allotted [there is to be given a prize …]') […] not giv[e … [45] …-]*ges*. Thi[s …] the (fem. plur.) […] a mature v[ictim …] to […] ? in th[e ? Dionysion. …] (?? *Lines 48–9 possibly* '[and to inscr]ibe [this decree] on a [stone] s[tele and set it up] in th[e Dionysion.]

This frustratingly damaged deme decree made extensive regulations for the administration of the Dionysia of Ikarion (Makres 2004; Wilson 2015 for full discussion). It dates from not long after the middle of the fifth century (Wilson 2015, 108), making it one of the earliest items of direct evidence for the operation of any dramatic festival. The stele was discovered during the excavation of Ikarion by the American School of Classical Studies in 1888–1889. It was found under the front wall of the Byzantine church and had probably originally stood in the stoa (D) that lay to the north-west of the church. The stoa appears to have served as a place in which to display and protect inscriptions, dedications and other materials relating to the god's cult and to publish important deme decrees on a range of subjects (**M Introduction**; **Mvi**; **Mx**).

The first two lines are in larger letters than the rest, and those of the first (av. 0.014 m H.) are rather larger than those of the second (av. 0.011 m H.). The first line seems to have been a kind of header and probably served to consecrate the stele as a whole to the god: '[----] the stele [? is sacred, (the property) of Dionysus]' (**IV Eiii** offers a parallel). The Menestratos who proposed the decree (l. 2) is not otherwise known (and the name Menestratides, though less common in Attica, cannot be ruled out).

The main body of the decree (ll. 3–49) is inscribed in a neat stoichedon pattern. Wilson (2015) demonstrated that the length of line was ca. 42 letters (rather than 35, as proposed by Lewis *IG* I³). The better-preserved opening lines concern the appointment of choregoi, but close examination of the rest suggests that the decree treated all the major practicalities involved in the planning, funding, administration, and performance of the Ikarian Dionysia under the direction of the demarch (ll. 6, 13). The fact that the decree appears to follow a chronological order of events in the preparation for and conduct of the festival offers some assistance to controlled speculation about the lower, less well preserved lines. What appears to be the use of uninscribed spaces (*vacats*) to organise the text into different sections (there are some eight in this fragmentary text: ll. 7, 14, 16, 17, 32, 42, 45 and possibly 21) is another such aid (Wilson 2015, 99–100).

The decree was inscribed on the reverse side of a stele that had for some time been used for keeping a record of deme funds, including those belonging to Dionysus (**Mii**), and it is extremely likely that the two inscriptions reflect a shared purpose, namely securing the financial viability of the local Dionysia. The surviving provisions of the decree were backed in at least five instances by the threat of fines (those in ll. 20, 26, 31, and 36 are clear; another virtually certain in ll. 40–1: Wilson 2015, 136–7) – further evidence for a concern over finance.

The decree begins with the appointment of choregoi, starting either at the end of l. 2 or – with Takeuchi's neat [ἐλέσθα]ι 'to select' – at the start of l. 3, which is where the main stoichedon pattern begins (Wilson 2015, 114). Two are to be appointed: this is clearest from the use of ὥτινε l. 4, the (rare) dual of the indefinite relative. We should probably construe a number of subsequent noun forms referring to the choregoi as duals rather than genitive singulars (notably ll. 8, 10, 25). Two may have been the standard complement of choregoi at Ikarion over a very long time. Nearly a century later, the deme honours two choregoi of a single year, in company with the demarch (**M Introduction**; **Mvi**).

These two choregoi are to come from a group described as ἀχορέγετοι *achoregetoi* (l. 4), a very rare term that later means 'without resources' (LSJ s.v.) but here clearly must mean 'not having been a choregos'. The aim is to identify men who had not served as choregoi before, implying a likely perception that the duty had not been falling equably (Wilson 2015, 113, 140). The term also shows that, far from setting up a choregic system, this decree is reforming one already in existence – which pushes the date at which choregia is attested in Ikarion to at least ca. 450 or 460. The choregoi are also to come 'from among the demesmen and the [residents in] Ika[rion]'. This imposition of choregia on non-member residents as well as demesmen is striking (Whitehead 1986a, 152) and may be aimed at ensuring that liturgical obligation remains in line with the de facto property possession within the deme (if, as is likely, non-Ikarian – but Athenian – residents and landowners are included). This unusually wide liturgical net looks like a long-term funding strategy for their costly theatre from a deme of only average size, and indifferent wealth. In Osborne's (1985, 45–6, 196–204) 'wealth index', Ikarion comes in at a lowly 0.8, far below the average of 1.39.

The relative clause that goes on to characterise the choregoi more fully (ll. 4–5) is almost entirely lost, but the inherent logic of the decree, plus a good parallel from Thorikos (**Yii**), suggest that it addressed the financial capability of the appointees: 'who [? are the most financially capable ?]'.

The decree goes on to treat the subject of antidosis (ll. 5–7: the *vacat* indicates that a new subject starts around the middle of l. 7), the procedure by which a man nominated for a liturgy could seek to transfer it to another whom he identified as more financially capable of performing it (**I Bi 5**; Wilson 2015, 117–18). In fact, this is the earliest direct reference to antidosis anywhere in Attica: this has led some to suppose a deme origin for the practice (Makres 2004, 140). It is unclear whether the procedures in Ikarion are precisely parallel to those in the city. One point of possible difference is the stated twenty-day period for making a claim (ll. 6–7). In the city, a single day was fixed for the making of an antidosis claim before the relevant officer, but it is not known how long a period was permitted to initiate a claim in the case of any particular liturgy (Arist. *Ath.* 56.3, 61.1; [D.] 42.5; X. *Oec.* 7.3; [*Ath.*] 3.4).

It is difficult to have much confidence about the syntax of the rest of the decree, but the fact that, in what survives from the middle of line 7 to the first part of line 12, four distinct actions are apparent, in the shape of four more or less complete verb forms – ἀποφαίνεν (l. 8); καταλέγεν (l. 9); ἐχσομό[σα-] (l. 10), τõ ἀγάλματος hαπ[τ-] (l. 12) – greatly aids our grasp of the sequence of events after antidosis. We take the first verb (ἀποφαίνεν) to refer to a requirement on the part of the demarch 'to declare formally appointed' the two choregoi (LSJ s.v. A. IV. 2), probably 'three times' (treating the letters in l. 8, with Lewis, as the adverb τρίς). Such an announcement would serve the dual purpose of underpinning the commitment of the choregoi to serve with the knowledge that the public was fully aware of their financial resources, and of advertising and acknowledging the generosity of the community's benefactors.

The next step centres upon the secure phrase [τρ]αγοιδὸς καταλέγεν (l. 9). It is extremely likely that, at this date and in this context, these *tragoidoi* are members of tragic choruses – as may also be true in a (perhaps: see discussion at **Ei**) roughly contemporary dedication from Anagyrous, where the *tragoidoi* listed as such most probably represent the members of a local tragic chorus. Rather than being an (otiose) instruction to choregoi to 'register' the members of their choruses (Wilson 2000, 79) we take this reference to *tragoidoi* to be an instruction to the demarch (thus [… τρ]αγοιδὸς καταλέγεν τὸν [δέμαρχον …]) to prepare a list or register of tragic choreuts (Wilson 2015, 120–1). In a deme as small as Ikarion, it makes sense for the demarch to take on the task of identifying choreuts and allocating them to the competing choruses, especially if, as is likely, membership in a tragic chorus was restricted to demesmen (below on l. 19). Tragedy evidently featured very prominently at the Ikarian Dionysia and the absence of any reference to comedy is probably not a result of the fragmentary nature of the inscription. Although the origins of comedy, as of tragedy, are associated in the literary tradition with Ikarion (**I Avii 2**; **I Avii 3**), the material record from the deme has left no trace of comic performances (**M Introduction**; **Mv**).

The next seven lines (10–16) are much concerned with the subject of *exomosia*. While a lot remains unclear, we are confident that this is a very particular form of oath-taking – that of 'declining or refusing an office by oath that one has not the means or health to perform it' (Humphreys 2004, 150; LSJ s.v. ἐξόμνυμι 2). It appears that the two choregoi who have been chosen (and after any antidosis claims have been made) are now offered the possibility of swearing that they have some grounds for being unable to perform. This is a process known from the city, where it is called *skepsis*, 'excuse-making' (Wilson 2000, 57–61; **I Bi 6**). Grounds known for *skepsis* in the city included being ill, or too young. In Ikarion the process is restricted to a period of ten days (l. 11). With the twenty days allocated for antidosis (l. 6) a full month since the demarch chose choregoi has passed.

At the start of l. 10 it appears that another group is offered the right to 'excuse themselves under oath' from some task. We suggest it is very likely the *tragoidoi* who have just been placed on a list for choral duty: [τὸς | τραγοιδ]ος καὶ τὸ χορεγὸ …. It is entirely plausible that the deme could require of its own members who had been registered to serve as choreuts that those who had some formal grounds for exemption should state them, in person and under oath, in the Dionysion. Line 12 mentions the touching of 'the statue', which must refer to a ritual accompaniment of an oath-taking; and, in combination with l. 13, this looks very much like a stipulation that an oath be sworn while touching the statue in the presence of witnesses. The statue in question is almost certainly the great Archaic seated Dionysus found in the sanctuary (**M Introduction**).

In lines 15 and 17 we find the extremely rare word προτόχορος. Buck (1892, 103–4, followed by Whitehead 1986a, 215) took these *protochoroi* to be 'men with their first chorus', and thus the same as the two appointed choregoi, who – since they were selected from the *achoregetoi* – are now serving for the first time and so could be said never to have had a chorus. But if that were the case we should expect a dual (as used for these two men already), rather than a plural form, and it is moreover hard to imagine how it could be so important or helpful to have a special term for a 'first-timer-with-a-chorus' (Wilson 2015, 124–5 for further detailed arguments against this interpretation). Reisch (1899a, 2393) and Foucart (1904, 82) thought them 'lead members of the chorus', what in later terminology is generally referred to as the *koryphaios*. Reisch offered a further variant on this line of thinking – the 'front-row choreuts' (1899a, 2393: 'in erster Reihe stehenden Choreuten'), but such a meaning would seem to be ruled out by the administrative and practical orientation of the document. Of these approaches the *koryphaios* interpretation has greatest merit (see also **Mxi**), not least since a plausible restoration of ll. 14–16 makes of them an offer to these *protochoroi* of the opportunity for formal excuse under oath (*exomosia*) 'from leading' (ᵛ ἐχσομοσ[ίαν ἐχσῖναι διδόνα]ι καὶ τοῖς πρ]οτοχόροις μὲ π[ρ]οhε[γῖσθαι] '[The *pr*]*otochoroi* [are also able to give] excuse under oa[th] from l[ea]d[ing …]'). There can be little doubt that the *protochoroi* were a group involved in the formation of the choruses for the festival: if not the individual *koryphaioi* of the (presumably two) tragic choruses (in which case we might again have expected a dual rather than a plural form), perhaps a tier of lead choreuts or a first slate of choreuts created by the action of the demarch in l. 9 (Wilson 2015, 126).

We take the subject in the following lines still to be the make-up of the choruses. It is tempting to suppose, as Lewis did, that the number in l. 16 is the same as the one in l. 22. In l. 16 we read, 'five and [. . X . .]'; in l. 22, possibly, '[. . X . . and] te[n]' – so both have been restored as fifteen. In the later passage the reference is to the number of men (ἀνδράσι) who stood in some relation to the two choregoi. That this is the number of choreuts in their choruses is a highly attractive hypothesis. Lines 16–17 could thus be a formal requirement as to the number of choreuts in each chorus, e.g.: '[There are to be] fift[een men for each chor]us' (πέντε καὶ [δέκ' ἄνδρας ἔναι ἐς h|εκάτερον χορ]όν.) This would mean that the number of choreuts in a tragic chorus in mid fifth-century Ikarion was the same as that in tragic choruses at the City Dionysia (but see Sansone 2016; **Ei**; **V F** on Athens NM 2400; **V E**). In this context the verb [ἀ]ποπέμπεν in l. 19 is likely to refer to the 'sending away' of choreuts who do not meet some requirement (with failure to comply triggering a fine, l. 20). A possible restoration of l. 19 that fits with what we know about rules governing participation in choruses in the city (**V E**; MacDowell 1985) is that a *tragoidos* was to be 'sent away' 'if he [proves] not [to be] a d[emesman …]' ἐὰμ μὲ δ[εμότες φαίνεται].

The scant remains of lines 21–4 include snatches of a choral/choregic reference (probably in the dual: τὸ χο[ρεγὸ] l. 21), a number (probably 15) of men in an indirect construction, seemingly distributed to two separate groups ([πέντε καὶ δ]έκ' ἀνδράσι hεκ[ατέρο χορõ] l. 22), with some further form of distributive allocation (καθ' ἕκαστον τὸ[ν ἄνδρα] l. 23) and, lastly, the certain appearance of Dionysus ([Διο]νύσο l. 24). The entirety could be restored *exempli gratia* as an explication in appropriately broad terms of the duties of the two choregoi to the members of their choruses – the two main subjects of the decree thus far brought together: τὸ χο[ρεγὸ τὸ δέον παρέχε|ν τοῖς πέντε καὶ δ]έκ' ἀνδράσι hεκ[ατέρο χορõ καὶ διδό|ναι οἶνο ἀμφορέα] καθ' ἕκαστον τὸ[ν ἄνδρα hόπος καλὲ ἔ|ι hε ἑορτὲ τõ Διο]-νύσο· '[t]he two cho[regoi are to provide what is necessary for the fif]teen men of ea[ch chorus and to give a jar of wine] to each [man so that the festival of Dio]nysus [is fine].'

At the midpoint of the decree, we are no longer treating preliminaries and 'the festival' appears twice in quick succession (ll. 25, 27). Executive action (πράττεν, l. 24) is to be taken in connection with it ([ἑ]ορτὲν, l. 25), probably before a particular date ([-]ονος l. 26 is almost certainly the end of a month name), or another fine will follow. In lines 27–9 we would identify a reference to the conduct of the festival proper, and quite possibly an injunction that '[When they cond]uct the festival, make a sa[crifice, …]' ([hόταν ἄγο]σι τὲν ἑορτὲν, θ[ύεν]). A sacrifice is likely to have featured at the start of the festival proper, and the only other proposal for the word beginning in θ-, Buck's θ[εοῦ] 'of the god', is far from compelling, not least since the article would be expected, if not essential.

Days and dates occupy lines 28–9 : '[…] on the sevent[h] of [the m]onth [… fi]fth day fro[m …]'. It is very likely that two dates are specified, and that they are the start and end dates of the festival (Brinck 1906, 35; Humphreys 2004, 140, 151). The existence of multiple Dionysia across Attica in the same period made it essential for demes to schedule their own event with forethought and precision (**Aiii**), and this seems to be the matter at question here. Our apparatus proposes a supplement which produces a promising result for the first-and-last day theory, and involves a somewhat unusual but not unparalleled expression: [… Ποσιδεõνος με]νὸς τẽι hεβδόμ[ει ἐπὶ δέκα …⁷.... | ...⁶... ἐς τὲμ πέμ]πτεν ἐμέραν ἀπ[ὸ διχομενίας ....] '… on the seven[teenth of the m]onth [Posideon … to the fif]th day fro[m the middle of the month]'. The festival will have lasted three days, from the 17th to the 19th of Posideon (Wilson 2015, 131–2). If tragedy was indeed the only performance type (above), we might suppose that some two full days were devoted to it. Given the evidence of **Mv** it is even possible that we should envisage two tragic-satyric tetralogies.

After establishing the festival dates the decree appears to turn to the event itself. Lines 30–3 seem to have dealt with matters relating to the procession (*pompe*). In l. 30 there is a striking reference to the sanctuary of Apollo Pythios. Something is to take place 'in the Pyth[ion]', or another fine will follow. The fact that a new section is marked by a *vacat* immediately after reference to 'the choregos' in l. 32 encourages us to see him as the one upon whom that obligation was imposed – either upon each individual choregos or upon one who has somehow been singled out. There may well have been a chorus – or two, in the dual – at the start of text in l. 30 '[the cho]rus' (*or* 'the two [cho]ruses) in the Pyth[ion]', [... χο]ρο ἐν τõι Πυθ[ίοι ...]. The Pythion was directly adjacent to the theatre (**M Introduction**). From the unusual sequence of letters that survive at the start of line 31 (-]γρον) we propose that the chorus(es) may have been required to bring a preliminary offering 'from the fields' (ἐχς ἀγρõν) to Pythian Apollo, whose sanctuary will have been overrun throughout the course of the festival by fans and followers of Dionysus (**Mi**); or they may have simply brought themselves thence in formal procession.

This view that we are dealing with the bringing in procession of a preliminary offering to Apollo is strengthened by the virtual certainty that l. 33 concerns the procession (*pompe*) of the festival. For there can be little doubt that it contains an instruction to 'sing the *phallikon*', [φαλλ]ικὸν ἄιδεν. The prominence of phallic song in the procession of deme Dionysia is spectacularly attested by **Ai** (note esp. 261: ἄσομαι τὸ φαλλικόν 'I shall sing the phallic song!'). It is possible that the following lines gave further direction as to the conduct of the phallic song within the context of the procession: we find a *tragoidos* or, perhaps more plausibly, multiple *tragoidoi* (understanding a genitive plural [τ]õν τραγοιδ[õν]) in l. 34 and 'the choru[s]' in l. 35, perhaps even some sort of instruction involving doing something to or 'towards the choru[s]' (with the construal ἐς τὸν χορὸ[ν]; cf. **Aii**). Alternatively, the *tragoido[i]* of l. 34 might have been part of a reference to the '[contest] of traged[ies]' [τ]õν τραγοιδ[õν τὸν ἀγõνα]. The festival's *agon* would naturally find its place after the procession.

Not much can be said about the remainder of the inscription: a possible reference to entrance fees has been detected at l. 38, where the sequence of letters γες that will have formed the end of a word might conceal a reference to a word used for the 'collection' of fees [ἐγλο]γε͂ς (and possible alternative supplements are limited: Wilson 2015, 135). Entrance charges at deme Dionysia in general are implied as normal for the early fourth century by **Aiii**, and are certain for the Piraeus (**Vvi**), very probable for Acharnae (**Bvi**), by the last quarter of the fourth century. Given the close parallels with a decree of the deme Myrrhinous (**Rii**), the suggestion that lines 39–40 mandate that a diagnostic assembly be held after the festival is over (Wilson 2015, 136–7) rests on firmer ground: we propose something along the lines '[on the x- of the] month [Posideon] busi[ness concerning the festival shall be dealt with or he (viz. the demarch) is to pay ten d]rachmas.'

Wilson (2015, 137–9) has made a tentative case that lines 42–5 may have dealt with the subject of prizes and that ll. 42–3 in particular might have been something like τõι χο[ρεγõι τõι νικέσαν|τι καὶ τõι διδασκάλοι hὸ]ν ἔλαχε h[ο χορεγὸς δίδοσθα|ι] '[f]or the [victorious] cho[regos and the didaskalos who]m th[e choregos] was allotted [there is to be given(?) a prize *vel sim*.]', which would offer a way to understand the remarkable appearance of the indicative verb form ἔλαχε (l. 43) in a document that has repeatedly employed infinitives in *oratio obliqua*. The case would be stronger if the letter following διδ[- in l. 44 was in fact an alpha (see app. crit.), making some part of the verb διδάσκειν, and thus a reference to the activity of (theatrical) training, distinct possibilities.

We can be more confident about the closing lines. It seems clear that line 49 was in fact the last line of the decree as inscribed (Wilson 2015, 107, 110). Lines 48–9 almost certainly contained the sort of instructions we would expect to conclude a decree of this sort, directives ensuring its proper publication and presentation in the sanctuary of Dionysus (see app. crit. and translation). Little can be said about what immediately precedes these lines, except that Lewis shrewdly construed the remains of 47 as a reference to 'a mature [sacrificial] victim' [... ℎιερὸ]ν τέλεον [....]. It is easy to imagine that the passing of this important decree might have been solemnised by a sacrifice.

Miv: Choregic Victory Dedication Recording a Performance at the Dionysia, 400–375
(by letter forms).

Base of 'Pentelic' marble, some damage at top, left side and lower front, bottom; three holes in the upper surface to secure the object dedicated, the central (quadrangular) one (0.065 × 0.05 m, depth 0.05 m) somewhat larger than the two (circular) at the sides.
0.53 × 0.47 × 0.24 m.
Found in a wall of the Byzantine church.
Athens EM 13316.
Buck 1892, 86–7 no. 6; *IG* II 5, 1281b; *IG* II² 3094; *IG* II³ 4, 497.
Text: based on *IG* II³ 4, 497; autopsy.   Photos: Agelidis 2009, Taf. 6f–g; Buck 1892, 87 (drawing); *IG* II³ 4,1 tab. LXVII.

1   [Ἄ]ρχιππος Ἀρχεδέ[- - -]   non-stoich.
           [ν]ικήσας ἀνέθηκε [τῶι]
           Διονύσωι.
           Νικόστρατος ἐδίδασ[κε].

1 Ἀρχεδέ[- - -] Buck, Makres   Ἀρχεδέ[μο] Köhler   Ἀρχεδέ[κτο] Kirchner

[A]rchippos son of Archede[-...] dedicated this to Dionysus after a [v]ictory. Nikostratos was the didaskalos.

This stone that emerged from the Byzantine church at Ikarion is the remains of a dedication to Dionysus made to commemorate a victory, no doubt at the local Dionysia. The present shape of the block is likely to reflect a secondary usage, perhaps as the support in a window or part of the templon of the Byzantine church (Hans Goette, pers. comm.). Buck (1892, 88) noted that the three holes on the upper surface were inconsistent with a tripod. They may well be associated with secondary usage in the Byzantine period. Whether Byzantine or original, they might have been designed to fix another block above the extant one, rather than the object dedicated by Archippos (*PAA* 214575). He is not otherwise known, though he is probably a forebear of the Archippos of Ikarion who was the father of the Kleitopolis whose grave monument was found in Piraeus (*IG* II² 6282: redated from the fourth century – *IG* – to the second by Peek: *SEG* 13, 95). The restored name of his father proposed by Buck, Archede[ktes], would be the first occurrence of this (in itself unexceptionable) name and, while the perpendicular stroke of the letter following Ἀρχεδέ- is consistent with a kappa, other names are possible and the possibility aired by Köhler – Archedemos – has the benefit of being attested some forty times in Attica.

Archippos was doubtless a choregos. The inclusion of the name of a didaskalos (l. 4) indicates as much, and the omission of χορηγῶν has parallels (**Mix**). It is a remote possibility that there was another line or lines above the first now extant, whether on the present block that was cut back in the Byzantine period or on another originally affixed above it. This might have included e.g. χορηγῶν τραγωιδοῖς 'As choregos in tragedy, ...'. (For a parallel to this phraseological order, with χορηγῶν and a genre-indicator before the choregos' name: **Hix**.) Against this interpretation however is the extent of the uninscribed space above l. 1. This is one of four items suggesting that choregoi sometimes operated as singletons in Ikarion (**Mv**; **Mviii**; **Mxii**). It is possible that the two cases of triple joint choregoi (**Mvii**; **Mix**) – in both of which the men are apparently close relations – would in fact have been deemed one choregia each, in terms of the official requirements of the deme, as expressed in the fifth-century decree that mandates the appointment of two choregoi (**Miii**). In other words, 'a' choregia might from time to time be undertaken by one, two or three choregoi. There is however also nothing to preclude the further possibility – and probability is in favour of it, given the small size of the deme – that the two choregiai mandated by **Miii** might also have been taken up by a single ambitious family.

Archippos' claim of victory suggests that the *agon* of the Ikarian Dionysia (**Mvi**, ll. 7–8) did indeed involve formal contests, though this does not undermine the possibility that the victory in question in the relatively small-scale *agones* of demes may have been somewhat nominal. Like various other choregic monuments in the demes, and in marked distinction from those in the city of Athens, this explicitly styles itself as a dedication to the god (for ἀνατίθημι and reference to Dionysus: **C**; **Eii**; ἀνατίθημι alone: **Bii**; **Ei**; **Mvii**; **Mix**; **Yiv**; Wilson 2000, 249).

There has been an understandable eagerness to identify Nikostratos (l. 4) with the important fourth-century comic poet (*PCG* VII, 74) who may have been the third and youngest son of Aristophanes (thus e.g. Buck 1892, 89; Wilhelm 1906, 133; *PCG*). But given that the name is extremely common in Attica, and in the absence of any certain evidence for the formal organisation of comic contests in Ikarion (**M Introduction**; **Mv**), there is a high degree of wishful thinking in the identification. Nor is there a compelling reason to identify this Nikostratos with the successful tragic actor of that name at his peak in the early decades of the fourth century (Stefanis no. 1861), though the fact that an actor would in that case be registered as a didaskalos is no impediment, and tragedy is the one genre amply attested at Ikarion. The suggestion that this may be the same Nikostratos who served as didaskalos for a boys' chorus of the tribe Oineis successful at the City Dionysia sometime after 450 (**V F** on *IG* I³ 961; e.g. Bottin 1930, 773) can probably be excluded. The dates (though both very approximate) are somewhat against it, and there is no other evidence that there was a purely choral contest at Ikarion. Indeed there is little evidence for such contests in the demes (**A Introduction**; **Bii**; **Vii**; Wilson 2000, 305–7).

Mv: Choregic Dedication with a Relief Depicting Theatrical Masks, ca. 360 (by style and orthography).

Two joined fragments of a relief of 'Pentelic' marble, broken on left side with damage to surface. The inscription is on a narrow epistyle at the top of the front surface.
0.46 × 0.295 × 0.088 m.
Found in 1958 on property belonging to a Mr Elioupoulos at Dionyso (ancient Ikarion).
Athens NM 4531.
Karouzou 1968, 60–1; Zoumpakes 1987, 44–5 no. 10; *SEG* 44, 131; Kaltsas 2001, 285 no. 600; Kaltsas 2004, 305 no. 181; *IG* II³ 4, 505.
Text: based on *IG* II³ 4, 505.   Photo: *IG* II³ 4,1 tab. LXVIII.

1   [- - -]Ọ ἐχορήγει *vacat*

[…] son of […-]os was choregos.

The precise findspot of this stone is not reported, but there can be no doubt that it records a theatrical performance at the Dionysia of Ikarion. It is a large fragment of a marble relief depicting four masks, all facing to the right, the two on the left in fragmentary state, the one at the lower right much damaged by a fissure and surface abrasions. The inscription on the epistyle above the masks, incised on a special band or *tainia*, proves that this was a choregic monument. Only the verb 'was choregos' survives, plus the last letter of the preceding word, almost certainly an omicron. This will represent the genitive singular ending of the choregos' patronymic, and the fact that it is written -o, rather than -ou, helps to date the monument, suggesting as it does a somewhat higher date. There is however no consensus on the question, and suggestions range from the last decade of the fifth to the third century. While the orthography pulls in the upper direction, aspects of the sculptural style (such as the form of the eyes and the fine facial wrinkles) tend the other way.

The relief is likely to have been originally affixed to a wall or some other architectural member in the sanctuary of Dionysus. Its original size is difficult to assess with precision, but assuming that at least a dozen letters are needed to complete the name and patronymic of the choregos, and that the inscription was centred on the epistyle with a *vacat* to the left, it will have been some 0.65 m wide. This would allow at least six masks in all, a figure which has parallels in the third-century plaque from Amphipolis (Kavala Museum no. 240; *MNC*[3] 34, 1BT 5) and the relief from Brauron (probably Halai Araphenides) of ca. 360 (**Kii**).

It has proved very difficult to reach a consensus on the identity of the masks, to a large degree because of the extensive damage to the carving. Clearest is the upper right-hand mask, which is that of an adult male with long beard, full hair and furrowed brow. He is evidently a figure from tragedy, a king or perhaps a seer. The figure to his left in the upper zone is also male, also bearded, though in a much straighter style. He is not unlike the mask of an old man on the decree from Aixone (**Div**) which Webster and Green identify as an Old Man ('M' in their categorisation) of Middle Comedy, and indeed some regard the entire set of masks as those of Middle Comedy (Scholl 2002, 550; Kaltsas 2004, 305). However Green (1982) was the first to spot the long pointed ear which, in combination with the beard, ensure that he is a Papposilenos (Karouzou 1968, 60 thought him tragic – indeed, she thought all of the masks tragic with the exception of the lower right-hand one, which she identified as comic). The mask in the lower right has attributes that have suggested a comic figure, but the remains of another pointed ear, and of a snub nose (though the damage here is extensive), suggest a satyr (Green 1982). The final mask, in the lower left, is the most difficult of all to assess. The set of the jaw and furrowed ridge of the nose indicate advanced age, as perhaps also the hollowing of the cheeks, if that is not the result of damage. The absence of a beard suggests that the figure may be an old woman, but her generic affiliation is less easy to determine. Tragedy is perhaps the most likely candidate.

Green identifies this as a set of masks from a satyr play. The Pronomos Vase and the fragments of a krater from Samothrace (**V E**) offer parallels for scenes of celebration and the dedication of masks with satyric content. If that identification can stand, and if, as is very likely, we may assume that the masks reflect the genre of the performances being commemorated, this becomes an extremely rare item of evidence for the performance of satyr play in a deme (**J** is the only other possibility). The comedy *Ikarian Satyrs* by Timocles, probably to be dated to the 320s, may or may not be relevant: the spelling (Ἰκάριοι rather than Ἰκαριεῖς) points to the island in the Aegean rather than the Attic deme, but the sense could well have been *Ikarios' Satyrs* (and cf. Phot. s.v. Ἰκαριεύς, ι 86). On the other hand even if the comedy was named from the deme or its hero, that is no evidence that satyr play was staged there. A further, perhaps less likely, possibility is that the masks of satyr play are being employed here not literally but as generic symbols of victory – with the added advantage of perhaps implying that the choregos had funded the full suite of a tragic tetralogy. If however the masks reflect a number of genres – two or more from tragedy, comedy and satyr play – this becomes an even more unusual phenomenon, a monument that mixed genres, presumably commemorating a mixed set of performances under the direction of a single choregos.

The practice of dedicating the actual masks used in a theatrical performance goes back at least to the later fifth century, and probably much earlier. Aristophanes *PCG* F 130 (from *Geras*) takes it back to the 420s. And if as seems likely a fragment of Cratinus' *Seriphioi* (*PCG* F 218) plays a metatheatrical game with the practice of 'petrification' of theatrical masks as a symbol of comic victory within the story of Perseus, equipped with the head of the Medusa, that raises the date further. There may even be an echo of the practice in Aeschylus' satyr play the *Theoroi* (Wilson 2000, 238–40; **V F**). In 402, a choregos for comedy in the city dedicated the *skeue* of his team, and explicitly reckons this as part of the 1,600 drachmas he spent on the production as a whole (**I D** on Lys. 21.4). By *skeue* is probably meant only, and certainly primarily, the masks used by the performers – a fact that provides valuable insight into the way that the mask was conceptualised as central to the theatrical event (Green 1982, 245). It also indicates that they remained the property of the choregos. One would certainly expect that to be true of the masks of choreuts. Actors are another matter. And the masks on the Ikarian relief are clearly those of actors. This might suggest that in Ikarion choregoi were also responsible for the costumes of the actors. But the representation of the masks of actors rather than choreuts in such permanent dedications might also have simply become a conventional variant on choral masks.

It is at any rate clear that a fairly early development in the practice of dedicating the masks in the sanctuary of Dionysus after a successful theatrical performance was for a choregos to have built a permanent stone version of such ephemeral dedicatory practice, as here in Ikarion. When the comic choregos of Lysias 21 said that he spent money on the 'dedication of the *skeue*' he may mean that he too had transformed the fabric to stone.

Mvi: Decree Honouring a Demarch for his Conduct of the Dionysia, and Two Choregoi, ca. 360 (by orthography: variation between o and ου for the spurious diphthong, *GAI* I, 351–2; and letter forms).

Intact gable-top stele of 'Pentelic' marble. The back is roughly worked. The inscription is low on the front surface. The areas above and below, as well as the area where the inscription is placed, have evidently been cut back, indicating reuse. The lettering is rather negligent and uneven.
0.733 (of which the pediment, including geison, is 0.103) × 0.285–0.31 × 0.06–0.08 m.
Found north of the Byzantine church at Ikarion (Buck 1892, 44).
Athens NM 4880.

Buck 1892, 71 no. 1; *IG* II 5, 572c; *IG* II² 1178. See also Colour Plate 7.
Text: based on *IG* II² 1178.

1   Κάλλιππος εἶπεν· ἐψηφίσθαι Ἰκαριεῦσ-   stoich. 31
      ιν ἐπαινέσαι Νίκωνα τὸν δήμαρχον καὶ
      στεφανῶσαι κιττῶ στεφάνωι, καὶ ἀνειπ-
      εῖν τὸν κήρυκα ὅτι στεφανοῦσιν Ἰκαρι-
5   εῖς Νίκωνα καὶ ὁ δῆμος ὁ Ἰκαριέων τὸν δ-
      ήμαρχον, ὅτι καλῶς καὶ δικαίως τῶι Διο-
      νύσωι τὴν ἑορτὴν ἐποίησεν καὶ τὸν ἀγῶ-
      να· ἐπαινέσαι δὲ καὶ τοὺς χορηγὸς Ἐπικ-
      ράτην καὶ Πραξίαν καὶ στεφανῶσαι κιτ-
10   τῶ στεφάνωι καὶ ἀνειπεῖν καθάπερ τὸν
      δήμαρχον.

On the proposal of Kallippos, it was decreed by the Ikarians to praise Nikon the demarch and crown him with an ivy crown; and that the herald announce that the Ikarians crown [5] Nikon, and the demos of Ikarians crown its demarch, for his fine and just conduct of the festival for Dionysus and its agon; and, further, to praise the choregoi Epikrates and Praxias and crown them with [10] an ivy crown, and make an announcement just as for the demarch.

Its excavator was no more explicit about the findspot of this stele than to say that it was found north of the ruined Byzantine church, presumably therefore in or near building 'D' (see Plan), a stoa well-suited to the display of public documents. Unlike a second decree honouring an Ikarian demarch (**Mx**), this does not specify that it was to go 'in the Dionysion', but the findspot implies that it too was erected there, for building 'D' was very probably within the sanctuary of Dionysus. A third, fragmentary, decree that seems to have honoured a demarch for his role in conducting lawsuits (*IG* II² 1179) was found in the same area.

The decree gives clear proof of the demarch's comprehensive responsibility for the organisation of the Dionysia in Ikarion (**Miii**). Lines 6–8 offer an insight into how the event was conceptualised – as 'the festival for Dionysus and the agon': the fact that the agon is picked out for particular attention suggests that it was the most burdensome – and keenly anticipated – element in his care. The detail that Nikon's conduct was 'just' as well as 'fine' doubtless goes to his financial probity. Nikon is to receive a crown of ivy, appropriate to the circumstances of the award, as well as being economical (the economy evidently extended to the public record of the award, since the stele on which the decree is inscribed is a secondary usage and the lettering is not of a high quality). The announcement of the award by the deme's herald (ll. 4–8) was almost certainly to be made at the next festival, though unlike some other deme decrees (**Bvii 2**; **Diii**; **Div**; **Hii**; **Hv**; **Mx**; **Vv**; **Wv**) this one does not specify as much.

The fact that two choregoi, Epikrates and Praxias, are honoured with praise and ivy crowns, likewise publicly proclaimed 'just as for the demarch' (ll. 10–11), indicates that they supported the Dionysia organised by Nikon, rather than (for instance) being two victors from different festivals, or even from different events at the same festival. And the idea that they were victors at a Dionysia at which there were other, unnamed, choregoi supporting other performances (Whitehead 1986a, 218), is improbable. Even in cases (and this is not one) where the language of victory is explicitly used, the victory in question in the relatively small-scale agones of demes is likely to have been somewhat nominal, and it was moreover essential for the life of deme theatre that praise, and the glory of success, be extended as far as possible across the small number of families with sufficient means to support it (Wilson 2010a).

The unusual phraseology used to describe the awarding bodies and their actions in ll. 4–6 – 'the Ikarians crown Nikon, and the demos of Ikarians crown its demarch' – has generated much speculative discussion. Various theories (expounded by Milanezi 2007) have been advanced that see a distinction drawn between two quite separate subjects – one of them the constitutional Cleisthenic deme of Ikarion (ὁ δῆμος ὁ Ἰκαριέων l. 5); the other (simply, if confusingly, 'the Ikarians' οἱ Ἰκαριεῖς ll. 4–5) a pre-Cleisthenic phratry, a *genos* tracing descent to the hero Icarius, an *oikos* with special responsibilities for his cult or the residents of the deme who were not hereditary members of it. Indeed for Jones (1999, 72–3) this is the one key document supporting his theory that a clear conceptual distinction was drawn between territorial and hereditary notions of the deme. The truth is likely to be much simpler. Lambert (1993, 367) and Parker (1996, 325) construe the phrase as implying not two different subjects but one, the ordinary Cleisthenic deme representing itself, with an air of ornate redundancy, in such a way as to reflect honours granted to Nikon as an individual (from the Ἰκαριεῖς) and in his official capacity as demarch (from ὁ δῆμος ὁ Ἰκαριέων).

Mvii: Choregic Dedication for Tragedy by a Father and Two Sons, before 350 (by orthography and letter forms).

Quadrangular marble pillar broken at the bottom. The sides are approximately vertical but there is some gentle widening near the top, which has a moulded crown, cut from the same stone, wider than the main shaft of the pillar and virtually square on top. The top and back show anathyrosis. 1.7 × 0.4 × 0.33 m.
Found by Buck in 1888 lying on wall F, near its junction with wall E (see Plan).
In situ approximately where found by Buck.
Buck 1892, 87 no. 7; *IG* II 5, 1282b; *IG* II² 3095; *IG* II³ 4, 501.
Text: based on *IG* II³ 4, 501.   Photos: Goette 2014, 81 fig. 2.3b; as found by Buck: Biers and Boyd 1982, pl. 2.

1	Ἔργασος Φανομάχο
	Φανόμαχος Ἐργάσο
	Διόγνητος Ἐργάσο
	τραγωιδοῖς χορηγήσαντες
5	νικῶντες ἀνέθεσαν.

Ergasos son of Phanomachos, Phanomachos son of Ergasos and Diognetos son of Ergasos, victorious when they served as choregoi in tragedy, dedicated this.

This substantial marble pillar was found lying on wall F of the sanctuary, near its junction with wall E, a corner that served to define an entrance to the site from the north. However this was clearly not its original place of erection. It evidently abutted another stone at the back. The lower end of the pillar is broken off (not finishing in a tenon, as stated by Biers and Boyd 1982, 8), and will have been set on a stepped base. There will have been a further crowning member above the upper surface. Perhaps the ensemble originally stood directly against wall F, facing into the Dionysion with its other choregic monuments.

This is an especially interesting choregic dedication because of its unusual form. The pillar offers a rather narrow base for a monument that will have been at least two metres high. In view of the high setting for the relatively small object dedicated, Goette (2007, 126) has plausibly proposed that this was a small bronze tripod, rather than a statue, for a statue of such necessarily small dimensions would have been difficult to see at that height. (The torso of a Silen was found near the same angle made by walls E and F – Buck 1892, 122 no. XVIII – but there is no compelling reason to associate it with this monument.) It would thus become a second example of a tripod dedicated by tragic choregoi in Ikarion (**Mviii**).

The monument records a victory in tragedy by Ergasos and two of his sons. It is thus one of a number of examples from the demes where members of the same family jointly fund a choregia (**Mix** is another). The family's wealth may have come from land-owning or trade (or both): the only other Ergasos known from Attica, and also an Ikarian, provided reeds to Eleusis in 329/8 (*IG* II² 1672, ll. 189, 194), and may have been a grandson of this choregos. The language of dedication (l. 5 ἀνέθεσαν), present also in **Miv**, **Mix** (and cf. **Mxii**) but absent from **Mviii**, is unknown in urban choregic monuments.

Mviii: Choregic Dedication for Tragedy, ca. 350 (by letter forms).

> Two joining fragments of a base of 'Pentelic' marble with cuttings in the upper surface (0.055 m deep) designed to receive a tripod.
> No published dimensions.
> Found in 1888 built into the wall of the Byzantine church.
> Current whereabouts of both fragments unknown. The BBAW has a squeeze of the left fragment.
> Buck 1892, 86 no. 5, 90; *IG* II 5, 1285b; *IG* II² 3099; *IG* II³ 4, 508.
> Text: based on *IG* II³ 4, 508.   Photos: Buck 1892, 90 (drawing of upper surface); *IG* II³ 4,1 tab. LXVIII (squeeze of left fragment).

> 1   Μνησίλοχο[ς] Μνησιφίλου
>   τραγωιδοῖς χορηγῶν ἐνίκα.
>
>   1 Μνησι[φίλου] Makres   2 χορηγῶ[ν ἐνίκα] Makres

> Mnesilochos son of Mnesiphilos was victorious as choregos in tragedy.

This is one of a small number of choregic dedications from Attica (city or demes) that explicitly record a victory in tragedy (other deme monuments: **Ei**; **J**; **Mv**; **Mvii**; for practice in the city see **V F** on *IG* II³ 4, 433; **VI B**). Dated only very approximately to the mid fourth century, this base was doubtless erected in the Dionysion of Ikarion, and records a victory by the otherwise unknown Mnesilochos son of Mnesiphilos (but see Humphreys 2018, 860–1), using a familiar formula of choregic dedication: imperfect tense of νικᾶν + participle of χορηγεῖν + dative of performance category. Though its whereabouts are unknown (and Makres airs the doubt as to whether Buck in fact saw the right fragment), its excavator (Buck 1892, 91–2) examined the cuttings in the upper surface in sufficient detail to show that Mnesilochos had dedicated a tripod which had large feet, like those awarded at the

Dionysia and Thargelia. As we have two other victorious choregic dedications for tragedy from Ikarion that evidently did not include a tripod (**Miv**, **Mv**), and another that, according to a plausible hypothesis, may have done so (**Mvii**), it seems unlikely that a tripod was awarded as a prize for tragedy in the deme. Given the apparent similarity in general style between Mnesilochos' tripod and those awarded at the great city festivals, it is likely that Mnesilochos chose to dedicate a tripod on his own initiative, and because the bronze lion's-claw tripod had long since become a powerful symbol of Dionysian victory in Attica by virtue of its use, for well over a century, as the prize for men's and boys' choruses in the city (Wilson 2000, 251). Such a trans-generic deployment of the symbol of victory (from choral to tragic) appears never to have taken place in the commemorative practice of the city festivals.

Mix: Choregic dedication of Hagnias, Xanthippos and Xanthides in the form of a semicircular exedra, ca. 350 (by prosopography and letter forms).

Marble semicircular roofed monument in the form of an exedra, with an interior bench made of three plain blocks set against the curved wall. Two antae – probably originally crowned with small capitals – support the architrave, which carries the inscription. The upper surface of the roof is rough-worked and surrounded by a bevel (0.11 m wide on the curved part, 0.22 m across the front). Cuttings at its centre suggested to Biers and Boyd (1982, 11) that the monument supported on its roof 'a naiskoslike device containing sculpture within'; while an oval cutting near each of the two front corners suggested akroterion figures. Recent analysis by a team of archaeologists and architects of the Greek Archaeological Service led by F. Karassava-Tsilingiri leads them to propose instead that the central cuttings were intended for an enthroned statue, with the Π-shaped groove corresponding to the seat, the central carving for the feet of the seated figure, probably a deity; and the two lateral cuttings for accompanying sculptures: Karassava-Tsilingiri 2007. Full physical description: Biers and Boyd 1982, 9–11.

ca. 3.40 × ca. 3.35 × ca. 2.2 m; length of interior arc: 4.83 m.

Much of the substructure and first course of blocks were found *in situ* by Buck in reuse in the apse of the Byzantine church (see Plan); all the other major members were subsequently identified nearby. The architrave lay behind the apse of the church (Milchhöfer 1887b, 311).

Presently reconstructed on site with the assistance of the local community ca. 2006.

Chandler 1776, 169; *CIG* 237; *IG* II 5, 1317; *IG* II² 3098; *SEG* 58, 188; Takeuchi 2010–2013, 96–7 (= *SEG* 63, 165); *IG* II³ 4, 506.

Text: based on Takeuchi 2010–2013, 96–7.

Ἁγνίας Ξάνθιππος Ξανθίδης νικήσαντες ἀνέθεσαν.

Αἰνίας Chandler, Böckh   Ἁγνίας Buck, Kirchner   Διννίας Köhler (Lolling)   Δεννίας Jordan and Curbera 2008, 138 (*SEG* 58, 188)   ΛΓνίας Makres

Hagnias, Xanthippos and Xanthides dedicated this following a victory.

The remains of this substantial choregic monument are the most striking physical testimony to survive of the life of the Ikarian theatre. Early doubts as to whether, in the absence of part of the verb χορηγεῖν, this is in fact a choregic monument, are quite unnecessary, and were answered by Merriam (in Buck 1892, 60 n. 13). Its place in the precinct is virtually proof enough, while the 'omission' of the verb χορηγεῖν is paralleled in other, indubitably

(a)

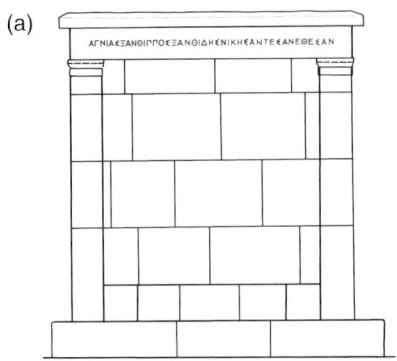
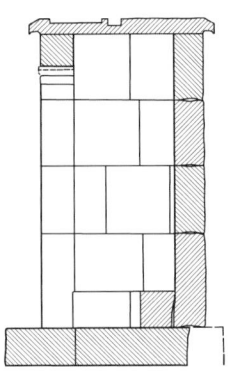

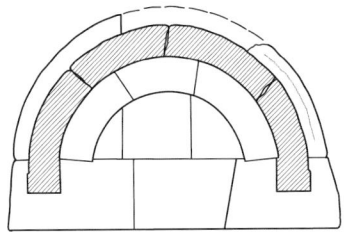
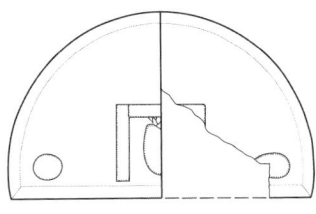

0 ⌞⌟⌟⌟⌟⌟   ⌟   2 m

(b)

Choregic dedication in Ikarion in the form of a semicircular exedra: (a) plan of restored monument;
(b) current reconstructed state.

choregic, inscriptions (e.g. **Miv**). These wealthy notables of the deme will have preferred 'conspicuousness … to exactness' on their architrave (Merriam in Buck 1892, 60), so information was kept to the minimum required by the local community – and that similarly did not include the information that Hagnias was the father of Xanthippos and Xanthides (for which likelihood see *APF* 3–4). Jordan and Curbera (2008, 138; followed in *IG* II³) have proposed, on the basis of the squeeze kept in the BBAW, that the first name should be Denias which, like Lolling's Dinias, is a possible spelling of Deinias, one of whom appears to be attested for Ikarion (*LGPN* II, s.v. 35). We persist with Hagnias, noting Buck's (1892, 59) confidence that 'the second letter of the first name is certainly a *gamma*'. (Full discussion: Takeuchi 2010–2013, 96–7.)

At some point in the Byzantine period, a church, possibly dedicated to a Saint Dionysios, was built directly on top of the monument, with its substructure and many of the blocks being used to form the apse. Its inscription was first recorded by Chandler in 1766 (1776, 169). A hundred and twenty years later Buck produced the first systematic study, and Biers and Boyd returned after another century to report on the state of the monument and produce an improved plan. The original site of erection is beyond doubt, since its lower part remains *in situ*. It lies just south of building D, the stoa whose south side opened 'to a veritable field of monuments' (Biers and Boyd 1982, 9), over which this exedra held a commanding view.

It is an open question whether one should single out the object (or objects) mounted on the roof of the building as the formal dedication, treating the whole marble structure as a kind of elaborate base for them. This distinction is more pertinent to the urban monuments for dithyramb, which for all their architectural elaboration remain bases for the prize tripod awarded by the polis (Wilson 2000, 201–8). In Ikarion there was in all likelihood no such formal prize (as much is suggested by the variety of dedicatory practice), and this shaded stone bench inside the sanctuary should probably be considered as much a part of these men's offering as the (probably) sculptural ornament above it. An intriguing alternative has been proposed by Karassava-Tsilingiri (2007), who airs the possibility that the internal 'bench' was in fact originally intended to be a base for sculptures related to the theatrical performance(s) in question, which for some reason were never included. The case is based on comparison with the best parallel for the Ikarian monument, namely the much larger semicircular monument from Thasos (**IV Dxvi 3**), which also had a semicircular exedra, in that case designed to support a variety of Dionysiac sculpture.

The men in question come from one of the most illustrious families of the deme. There is little doubt that Hagnias is the man who served as syntrierarch in 362/1 and 356 and again as sole trierarch sometime before 323/2 (*APF* 3–4). Although no urban choregia is known for Hagnias, his liturgical status at the city level makes of him the single known case of a man who served as liturgist in both the city and his home deme (but cf. **Ii**; **T**). He thus serves as an exception to the general rule that men who chose to devote their abilities and resources to the deme did not go on to do the same at the urban level. Valavanis (2007) argues that the elaborate funerary monument on the side of the ancient road that leads to the sanctuary belonged to Hagnias and his family. Its peribolos was some 13.65 m wide along the roadside and contained an unusual high columnar monument (over 10 m in height), surmounted by a marble urn decorated with griffin-heads.

This is the most elaborate choregic monument to survive from the demes (cf. **Biii**). It begins to compare in scale and ambition with some of the larger city monuments, even though close analysis of its construction 'suggests … that the dedicators wished to create as large a monument as possible for the sum expended' (Biers and Boyd 1982, 11). Its form is unparalleled among choregic monuments. While various semicircular dedications in sanctuaries outside Attica can be adduced, these are quite different, being generally low and uncovered. The certainly theatrical and possibly choregic monument from the Dionysion of Thasos of the late fourth century (**IV Dxvi 3**), though on a much grander scale, remains the best parallel. It is clear that deme choregoi enjoyed considerable liberty in selecting the form of their dedications, even more than their urban counterparts, although the tradition of choregic dedication in the city had by the mid fourth century evolved in such a way as to produce a wide variety of architectural and artistic possibilities that went far beyond the earlier, narrower economy of form. It was also quite common for deme choregoi to dedicate items that were useful for their local sanctuary (**C**) – as is perhaps the case here – rather than being simply architectural boasts of agonistic success.

There is no way of determining the nature of the performance that gave rise to this monument, but tragedy appears to have been the most prominent and prestigious genre in the Ikarion theatre and is the only one certainly attested (**Mv**). As often in the demes (**Mvii** is another Ikarian example), this is surely a single choregia shared by members of one family.

Mx: Deme Decree of Ikarion Honouring a Demarch, second half of 4th c. (by letter forms and prosopography).

Large quadrangular block of white 'Pentelic' marble. The top surface, which is rough-picked, has a large mortice (ca. 0.20 × ca. 0.17 × ca. 0.045 m deep) at the left-hand end, some 0.15 m from the left-hand edge and ca. 0.11 m from the rear. This will originally have been ca. 0.20 m². (Alipheri 2010–2013, 145 suspects this may be a later addition.) The stone is broken away at the front of the mortice, no doubt by the violent removal of whatever was inserted into it, probably a small column. A large segment of the inscribed front surface of the block was broken away in the process. The letters are roughly carved. Their widths vary considerably, with an average of ca. 0.01 m. Many orthographic slips.
0.545 × 1.02 × 0.38 m.
'found [in September 1947] close to the surface near the altar south of the choregic monument [= **Mix**]' (Robinson 1948, 142).
Athens EM 13319.
Robinson 1948, 142–3 no. 3; Mastrokostas 1961, 23–4 no. 2 (= *SEG* 22, 117); Alipheri 2010–2013 (= *SEG* 63, 105).
Text: based on Alipheri 2010–2013 with autopsy. (The stone has been stored in the outer courtyard of the EM for some time and suffered further wear.)
Photos: Robinson 1948, pl. 36; Alipheri 2010–2013, 153 pl. 1.

non-stoich.

1   [ἔδοξεν τοῖς δημόταις· ἐπειδὴ ὁ δήμαρχος (?) Νεαῖος Σωσ]ιγένους Ἰκαριεὺς τά
          τε ἱερὰ ἔθυσεν ἅπασιν τοῖς θεοῖς
      [καὶ τοῖς ἥρωσιν, κατὰ τὰ πάτρια καὶ τῶν Διονυσίων ἐπεμε]λήθη καλῶς καὶ
          φιλοτίμως, καὶ ἀπήνγειλε<ν> εἶναι καλὰ
      [(?) καὶ σωτήρια - - - - - - - ca. 32 - - - - - - -]ΕΩΝΚΜΩΙ καρπο<ὶ κ>αλοὶ κατὰ
          πᾶσαν τὴν χώρα<ν> γε<γ>όνασιν ΤΑΟ

[- - - - - - - - ca. 36 - - - - - - - - -, ἐπει]δὴ δὲ λόγον ἀπενήνοχεν ἐν τῶι
      Ἑκατονβαιῶνι μηνὶ τεῖ δεκάτει

5   [- - - - - - - - - ca. 38 - - - - - - - - -] ἀπο<φ>αίνει χρήματα περιόντα λογισάμενος
      τὰς προσόδους <κ>αὶ τὰ

ἀν[αλώματα, - - (??) ὥστε δοκεῖν φιλοτίμως τ]ε καὶ δικαίως ἄρξαι, καὶ
      πα<ρ>έδωκεν τῶι μεθ᾽ ἑαυτὸν δημάρχ{ι}ωι Θουκυδί-

δει ΤΩΠΕΗΟΝ[- - - - - ἐπαινέσαι - - - Νε]αῖον καὶ στεφανῶσαι χρυσῶι στεφάνωι
      ἀπὸ Χ δραχμῶ<ν> ἀρετῆς ἕνε-

κα καὶ δικαιοσύνης τῆς πρὸς τοὺς δημότας· ἀναγρά<ψ>αι δὲ τόδε τὸ ψήφισμα
      ἐν τῶι Διονυσίωι· ἀνειπεῖν {ο}δὲ τὸν στέ-

φανον Διονυσίων τοῖς τραγωιδοῖς. *vacat*

1 [ἔδοξεν τοῖς δημόταις· ἐπειδὴ ὁ δήμαρχος Νεαῖος (?) Σωσ]ιγένους Alipheri   [ἔδοξεν
Ἰκαριεῦσιν· ἐπειδὴ . . . . .ca. 11. . . . . -αῖος Σωσ]ιγένους Robinson   2 Alipheri   [οἷς
πάτριον ἦν καὶ τῶν ἄλλων ἁπάντων ἐπεμε]λήθη Robinson   ΑΠΗΝΓΕΙΛΕΗ
lapis   3 [καὶ σωτήρια (?) . . . . .ca. 27. . . . . Ἰκαρι]έων
(?) κ<ώ>μωι (?) καρπο<ὶ κ>αλοὶ Alipheri app. crit. (τὴν δὲ ἑορτὴν ὡς ἄριστα
ἤγαγεν ὥστε Ἰκαρι]έων (?) κ<ώ>μωι (?) καρπο<ὶ κ>αλοὶ Alipheri 2010–2013,
148)   ΚΑΡΠΟΝΙΑΛΟΙ *lapis*   ΩΝ καὶ ὧν καρπὸν διδοῖ Robinson   ΕΩΝΚΜΩΙ καρποὶ
καλοὶ Mastrokostas   ΧΩΡΑΓΕΡΟΝΑΣΙΝ *lapis*   5 ΑΠΟΧΑΙΝΕΙ *lapis*   ΧΑΙ *lapis*   6
ἀν[αλώματα, . . .ca. 7. . . ὥστε δοκεῖν καλῶς τ]ε καὶ δικαίως Alipheri   [ἀναλώματα,
ὥστε δοκεῖν καλῶς τ]ε Robinson   ἀν[αλώματα Mastrokostas   [φιλοτίμως τ]ε
Wilson   ΠΑΙΕΔΩΚΕΝ *lapis*   7 ΙΔΕΙΤΩΠΕΗΟΝ *lapis*   {ι}δει τὸ περιὸν
ἀ[ργύριον] Alipheri   [δηι· ἐπαινέσαι . . . .ca. 9. . . .]ον καὶ Robinson   δει ΤΩΠΕΗΟΝ
Mastrokostas   ΔΡΑΧΜΩΗ *lapis*   8 ΑΝΑΓΡΑΥΑΙ *lapis*

[The demesmen decided; since (?) Ne]aios son of [(?) Sos]igenes of Ikarion
conducted the sacrifices for all the gods [(?) and the heroes in keeping with
tradition, and over]saw [the Dionysia] in a fine and ambitious manner, and
reported that they were fair, [(?) and bringing safety …]*EONKMOI* the crops
have been fair throughout all the land *TAO*[…], and [sin]ce he has rendered accounts on the tenth of Hekatombaion 5 [… and (*or possibly* in which)] he gives
a full record of the remaining funds, reckoning the income and exp[enditure,
so that his ambitious a]nd just conduct in office [is evident], and he has handed
over (?) the balance to his successor as demarch, Thoukydides, [… we should
praise (?) Ne]aios and crown him with a gold crown worth 1,000 drachmas for
his virtue and honesty towards his fellow demesmen; and inscribe this decree
in the Dionysion; and announce the crown at the tragedies of the Dionysia.

This is the remains of a decree of Ikarion honouring a demarch for his cultic, administrative and financial services. It almost certainly made special reference to his conduct of the
Dionysia (below). The decree was inscribed on a substantial base rather than a stele, and
it appears to have been embellished with some significant monumental form (assuming as
we do that the mortice on the upper surface is ancient), perhaps a column with surmounting
statue or pinax. Alipheri (2010–2013, 150) suggests that the inscription might have been
placed directly onto a block that was already part of a dedication in the sanctuary. While
the inclusion of the demotic (l. 1) is unusual in a deme document (but see **Mxii**), there can
be no doubt that this is a decree issued by the deme (cf. *SEG* 57, 128).

Alipheri (2010–2013) has plausibly identified the demarch honoured as a Neaios who was a syntrierarch ca. 356–346/5 (*IG* II² 1622, l. 674). The Thoukydides who succeeded him is probably the Ikarian of that name who served as arbitrator around 330. The restoration of the first part of the honorand's patronymic is far from secure, but Sosigenes is quite a common name in Attica and one of only two names ending in -igenes attested for Ikarion, as the father of one of the Pythaists who made a dedication to Apollo some time before 360 (*IG* II³ 4, 632: Voutiras 1982; Humphreys 2004, 147; the other is Chairigenes son of Agasias known from a fourth-century gravestone from Imbros, *IG* XII 8, 100). These prosopographical indicators point to a date in the second half of the fourth century (consistent with the letter forms), perhaps most likely in the 340s or 330s. Alipheri (2010–2013, 150) suggests the period 331–324 – known for an acute shortage of grain in Athens – since l. 3 seems to refer to the grateful acknowledgement of a bountiful crop (below). While the broad date range is not in doubt, some uncertainty must attend the specific restorations of the personnel, for Alipheri is wrong to suggest that Neaios is the only known Ikarian whose name ends in -aios: a Tolmaios of Ikarion (*PAA* 892830) secured a dowry for his daughter Archestrate in the fourth century (*IG* II² 2661).

This is the only document explicitly to name the sanctuary of Dionysus in Ikarion (l. 8), evidently the prime location for records of honours such as this and other important public documents. The festival for which the demarch had primary responsibility, the Dionysia, was in Ikarion the occasion on which honours were to be proclaimed, a detail not mentioned in the decree for another Ikarian demarch honoured some thirty years earlier (**Mvi**) but doubtless to be assumed in that context. Given its prominence elsewhere in the record, it is no surprise to find the specification 'at the tragedies' (l. 9). While the term 'agon' is not used (i.e. 'at the contest of tragedies'), we should not take the plain phrase to imply that the competitive format in evidence in earlier years (**Mvii, Mviii, Mix**) had been abandoned. One may assume that the festival of Neaios' successor, Thoukydides, is intended.

If we may judge by the surviving inscriptions, the Ikarians were more energetic than most demes in honouring their demarchs (**Mvi**; *IG* II² 1179; Lasagni 2004, 96), whose duties were extensive and, apparently, unsupported by a subordinate officer such as the treasurer (*tamias*) found in a number of other demes. The demarch of Ikarion is responsible not only for regulating the deme's relations with all its gods – and, perhaps, heroes: the restoration καὶ τοῖς ἥρωσιν 'and the heroes' (which we arrived at independently of Alipheri) should be considered likely for the start of l. 2 (see below), especially in a deme like Ikarion with such a prominent eponymous hero. He also has extensive responsibility for managing the deme's finances. His lauded demonstration of 'honesty' (l. 8) suggests he had discharged fiscal duties with probity. And great care is taken to detail his provision of a full account of the income and expenditure made throughout the course of his demarchy (ll. 5–6), with emphasis on his public statement of the remaining funds and his handover of a positive balance to his successor. In l. 7 the unintelligible sequence ΤΩΠΕΗΟΝ might conceal τὸ περιόν 'the balance' (see app. crit.), which in turn is likely to have been followed by a numerical sum or qualifier (Ma 1997, 290 suggests τὰ περιόν[τα χρήματα]; Alipheri 2010–2013 thinks she can see part of an alpha, possibly the start of ἀργύριον 'the balance of money'). Given that there is no doubt about the omega, perhaps it might even be τὼ περιόν[τε] 'the two balances', for two distinct treasuries or types of treasury (common deme funds and sanctuary funds?). The fifth-century record of accounts from the Dionysion, in which several demarchs are recorded as formally handing over sums of money in treasuries to their successors (**Mii**), makes it abundantly clear that the demarchs of Ikarion had for over a century been in effect the Chief Financial as well as Executive Officer of this deme, and that they were familiar with the need to account for a number of separate funds.

The decree takes the trouble to note, with rare detail (cf. **Bvii 1**, ll. 8–12), that the honorand rendered an account of his office a mere ten days after leaving it. Little surprise perhaps that he is awarded the single most valuable gold crown known from all the demes, worth a staggering 1,000 drachmas (l. 7) – a difference from the ivy crown awarded another demarch some thirty years earlier (**Mvi**, l. 3) not to be explained by inflation. The current honorand's exceptional service may have extended, as Lasagni (2004, 98) suggests, to personal monetary contributions. There was in any case probably a tacit expectation that men so honoured would automatically dedicate the valuable crown for the benefit of the deme.

Alipheri (2010–2013) has remedied a problem with previous texts, namely that they offer restorations and proposals for the approximate number of letters missing in ll. 1–6 that are too short (although it must be stressed that the condition of the stone and the absence of a stoichedon pattern make firm estimates difficult). It is also possible that the first line included the name of the proposer (**Miii**; Alipheri 2010–2013, 147). The addition of καὶ τοῖς ἥρωσιν 'and for the heroes' to l. 2 is urged by the common inclusion of heroes alongside gods in such phrases in a deme context (Kollytos: *SEG* 58, 108, ll. 11–12; Rhamnus: *IRhamn.* 6, ll. 8–9; Halai Aixonides: *SEG* 59, 142, 338/7; Acharnae: **Bvii 1**, ll. 3–4; the Mesogeioi: cf. *IG* II² 1247, ll. 5–9). The inscriptions from Acharnae and the Mesogeioi (and see **I Aix 2b**, ll. 10–15) show a pattern in which, after the opening generalities (in Acharnae the official in question 'performed all the sacrifices to the gods and heroes on behalf of the demesmen'; among the Mesogeioi he 'made the sacrifices for the gods and heroes in a fine manner and in keeping with tradition'), specific reference is made to the deme's or association's most significant religious celebration: the Dionysia in Acharnae, the festival of Heracles among the Mesogeioi. It is therefore very likely that a similar pattern featured in l. 2 of this decree, and the Dionysia will surely be the festival in question.

Alipheri (2010–2013, 148) has an intriguing interpretation of l. 3 which divines in the sequence -]ΕΩΝΚΜΩΙ a reference to the 'komos of the Ikarians' (['Ικαρι]έων (?) κ<ώ>μωι), in some such phrase as '[and he conducted the festival in such excellent fashion that] the crops have been good throughout all the countryside by means of the k<o>mos of [the Ikar]-ians'. In other words she sees this as a continuing reference to the demarch's conduct of the festival, and the way in which it led to an abundance of crops in the countryside. This restoration would offer evidence for belief in a direct link between the successful conduct of a Dionysia and the fertility of the land. Difficulties remain with the word *komos*. Given the loose habits of the cutter, the first is relatively minor – the assumption of yet another error in its inscription, with the omission of an omega: κ<ώ>μωι. But while the word has strong associations with Dionysiac revelry, drink, dance and song, even perhaps extending in its possible range to the *pompe* or parade of a Dionysiac festival, there is no direct evidence for its use in connection with a deme Dionysia, as Alipheri acknowledges. The address of Phales at Ar. *Ach.* 264 (**Ai**) as ξύγκωμε 'fellow reveller' (not mentioned by Alipheri) comes closest. The syntax of her proposed restoration is also somewhat (but not impossibly) awkward, requiring as it does that 'the komos of the Ikarians' serves as the instrument (in the dative) of the crops' bounty.

Mxi: Two-Sided Relief Depicting Deities and a (?) Chorus with a Goat, ca. 330 (by style: Agelidis 2009, 49).

Two non-joining fragments (α, β) of a large double-sided relief of 'Pentelic' marble. One side (A) has the remains of six larger figures; the other (B), ten smaller figures in lower relief. The left-hand edge of α (viewed from side A = the right-hand edge of α viewed from side B) is original and the border of the image on both sides at this edge is marked by the stem of a thick vine or tree. There are dowel-holes in the top of each block, the one on α above the first figure's left shoulder (viewed from side A), the one on β above the raised right shoulder of the last preserved figure (again viewed from side A).

0.63 (α, β) × 0.63 m (α); 0.58 (β) × 0.14 m (α, β). The absence of clamp-marks suggests that the relief originally consisted of one block only. The original width of this block will have been at least 1.40 m (see below).

Found at Ikarion by the American School in 1888.

Athens NM 3078 A, B.

Buck 1892, 117–19 no. 10 (fig. 6); Svoronos and Barth 1937, 662–3, no. 423 (Taf. CC-CCI); Agelidis 2009, 194, no. 58 (Taf. 7a-d); autopsy. Photo: Svoronos and Barth 1937, Taf. CC-CCI; Agelidis 2009, Taf. 7a-d.

Buck gives no further context than 'at Ikaria' (1892, 109), but there can be no doubt that this double-sided relief was found in the excavations of the sanctuary site of Dionysus and Apollo in the deme. None of the figures has a preserved head, and chisel-marks (notably on the second, third and fourth figures from the preserved right-hand edge of β, side B) indicate deliberate destruction, almost certainly in the context of reuse of the ancient materials of the sanctuary in the construction of the Christian church that stood on the site of the ancient Dionysion. Potentially of great importance for the study of choral practice and its representation, this relief escaped the notice of all standard accounts prior to the treatment of Agelidis (2009, 46–9, 78–9, 194), who would place it among choregic dedications in Ikarion's cult of Dionysus. It is also, by nearly a century, the earliest evidence for the place of the goat in a cult context in the deme. It is an object that resists easy classification and analysis and is on any interpretation highly unusual (Goette and Wilson *forthcoming* offer a more thorough study).

What survives is broken into two roughly equal, non-joining fragments. Estimation of the original width of the relief depends on a calculation of the distance between the two fragments (made possible by a discovery by Hans Goette: below) and an assessment as to the extent of loss at the right-hand end of β (viewed from side A = the left-hand end of β viewed from side B). The latter operation is considerably more difficult. Different hypotheses result in an original block from around 1.40 to as much as 1.90 m wide. The two dowel-holes in the top suggested to Buck (and Svoronos and Barth 1937, 662) that it was originally affixed to a balustrade or some sort of railing. They certainly show that there was a crowning element above the relief. If this crowning element was simply a block with profiles on both sides it could conceivably have formed part of a (low) balustrade or fence, or perhaps an altar screen associated with a temple or sanctuary. If however this is a choregic dedication, a crowning block – whether a simple profile or a more substantial entablature or cornice – could have had space for an inscription.

The figures on either side are heavily damaged. No single head is preserved. The left-hand end of the (better preserved) side A is original and the border of the image is marked by the stem of a thick vine or tree. So too is the border on the other side (B) at the same end (in this case the right-hand extremity). The absence of such a border-marker at the other end of the relief is one proof that its full extent is not preserved. The figures on side A are much larger, deeper and were it seems generally of higher quality, prompting Agelidis to think of it as the 'front'. The remains of six survive. They are evidently divinities. The second from the right was identified by Buck and all after him as Heracles: a club is visible in his right hand and the garment that drapes over his left arm suggests a lion-skin, rather than a himation or chlamys. His frontal position, seemingly flanked by figures facing him in three-quarter view (but see below on the figure immediately to his right) and with figures approaching him further to his right, has suggested to Agelidis that Heracles was the central figure on this side. She further argues that symmetry would suggest that there were originally three more figures to his left, beyond the one that survives, also facing in towards Heracles from that side (Agelidis 2009, 47). If this argument were sound, it would offer a relatively clear indication of the original width of the block (at a very large 1.80–1.90 m). There are however two problems with it: symmetrical arrangement around a central figure is certainly not a norm in reliefs; secondly, the heavily damaged figure immediately to Heracles' right may also have been presented frontally rather than in three-quarter view, suggesting that Heracles was not the central figure on this side.

Buck identified the four figures to Heracles' right as Muses, though Agelidis has confidence only in the identification as such of the two on the farthest right. But the first figure, at the edge of the scene, in fact appears to be an older female (ruling out a Muse). As much is suggested by the broad form of the body, the posture and the dress, with thick, heavy chiton, large himation and closed shoes. She may have held a sceptre in her left hand, which would be appropriate to an older female deity. The Apollonian triad would not be out of place in Ikarion, and Leto is one possibility for this figure.

The next figure, second from the viewer's left, Buck (1892, 118) thought held 'a musical instrument resembling a mandolin'. A lyre is a more realistic possibility. Her dress is lighter than that of the first figure, suggestive of a younger female deity. The third figure, at the break of the stone, also faced somewhat to its left and may be wearing a himation only. On balance it seems more likely to be male than female (Goette). Recent study by Goette has thrown important light on the heavily damaged figure immediately to the right of Heracles. Goette believes this to have been presented frontally, like Heracles. Unlike all the other figures, the remaining traces show that the body was curved into a reverse S form, accentuated by the way in which the head falls to its right, further making the left shoulder higher than the right. A number of iconographic markers (discussed in Goette and Wilson *forthcoming*) suggest that this may have been Apollo.

The figure to the left of Heracles is certainly not a Muse (as Buck thought, but cf. Merriam at Buck 1892, 118 n. 30). It is probably male (evidence of the outlines of a beard under the chin and on the left cheek confirm the gender), wears a short chiton cinched high above the belly and is bare-legged. Agelidis' proposed identification as Dionysus (2009, 48) has some attractions, but convincing iconographical parallels are hard to find. This figure's position and likely gesture need more careful consideration: the right arm is lifted quite high, the head turned up and towards the right, suggesting that he is engaged in the act of crowning his neighbour, Heracles. It is not immediately obvious why Dionysus would crown Heracles, and Agelidis' identification must be regarded as unproven. It is also a possibility, though of course unprovable, that Dionysus did appear – as the (lost) figure to the viewer's right, probably the last on the relief.

On the more heavily damaged side B there are the remains of ten human figures, facing right (ca. 0.12 m distance between figures). The observation that there are ten human figures rather than nine is owed to Goette, who identified the vestigial remains of a tenth figure on both sides of the break (seen most easily on β). The fact that this figure occupied the space between the two fragments permits some confidence in determining their relative disposition (as indicated on our reproduction, where the two fragments are arranged by Goette to reflect their likely original relative position). The feet of the figures are well preserved and reveal a virtually identical pose, although the first at the left on the right-hand block (β) faces somewhat more frontally. The figures seem to be standing with feet planted apart. The one at the front leads a goat beneath the thick vine that marks the image's border. They are male, considerably smaller than those on side A and thus, evidently, mortals. They wear himatia, quite tightly clasped at their chests (note the gripped fingers of the third and fourth figures from the left on α); and closed shoes.

Agelidis has argued that this was a choregic dedication: on her view, the figures on side B represent the choreuts of a victorious dithyrambic chorus (2009, 48, 78, 194). She bases this on the identical stance of the men and the similarity of their dress to those on the Atarbos base (**V F**) depicted in – as she styles it – a dithyrambic chorus. Her proposed identification of Dionysus on side A is also enlisted in support of this interpretation. If one could have confidence in her argument about the likely symmetry of the figures on side A, we might calculate that there were some four or five more figures before the break on side B. That would produce a group of 14 or 15. In that case, we should suppose that they represented a tragic rather than a dithyrambic chorus, as purely lyric choral performances (described as 'cyclic' in **Vii**, possibly also in **Bii** as 'boys' and 'men's' in **Hii**, never explicitly as 'dithyramb') are not attested in Ikarion and among the demes are found only in Acharnae (**Bii**; cf. **Biii**), Eleusis (**Hii**) and the Piraeus (**Vii**). And while we may doubt an attempt to depict a chorus with an eye to accuracy of its composition, if this chorus did indeed originally number fourteen, a striking comparison may be made with the fourteen *tragoidoi* listed on a monument from Anagyrous (**Ei**; **X** has fifteen). Could this be a tragic chorus, either with its full complement of fifteen choreuts or, if fourteen were depicted, with its fifteenth member perhaps a professional leader, and thus not registered in the lasting memorial? The suggestion of Agelidis (2009, 78, 90; Wulfmeier 2005, 57) that the divine scene with Heracles – and probably Dionysus – on side A formed the subject of the successful dithyramb could be easily transferred to tragedy. Given the doubts raised above about Agelidis' argument from symmetry, it is perhaps more likely that there was just one further figure (or possibly two) at the broken left-hand end of side B, making a total of eleven (or twelve) figures.

Side B is not a typical scene of sacrifice, for there is no altar, unless we are to imagine one beyond the ivy-trunk border. The orientation and disposition of the figures with the animal before them do nonetheless suggest some sort of approach to a deity (also not depicted in the image). This unusual treatment of the goat has led to an interpretation of it as a symbol for the tribe Aigeis, to which Ikarion belonged (Wulfmeier 2005, 57–8). But this, and the further suggestion that the monument celebrates a dithyrambic victory of that tribe (partially endorsed by Agelidis 2009, 78–9), are quite impossible. What tribally organised contest could be celebrated in a deme? The goat might rather perhaps be seen in the light of its cardinal importance to the mythology of Ikarion. Although the story of Icarius and his slaughter in anger of the goat that nibbled at the young vine – a story that serves as an aetiology of drama in Ikarion – is known only from third-century sources (see the discussion of the goat prize in **I Avii**) there is good reason to think that the scholar-poets in question were drawing upon fourth-century Atthidographers, themselves mining (and in some cases fabricating or at least massaging) local traditions. And a case has been made for the existence of an association between Icarius and the goat appearing much earlier in vase iconography (**M Introduction**). The leading historian and publicist of the Lycurgan vision, Phanodemus, is a very likely candidate for the promotion of this myth in Ikarion, and the date of this relief fits such an influence perfectly.

Despite the problems with Agelidis' interpretation, it remains possible that this intriguing object is an unusual instance of the category of votive relief (of rare size and eccentric features) employed as a choregic pinax (parallels in **V F**). It may have as much to do with

Apollo as Dionysus, and possibly reflected the close interaction between the cults of these two deities in Ikarion.

Mxii: Ex-Voto Dedication to Dionysus, ca. 325–300 (by letter forms).

Square marble base with a socket cut in the upper surface (depth 0.038 m) for a votive offering. The socket is closer to the front (0.04 m) than the back (0.125 m).
0.18 × 0.56 × 0.56 m.
Found built into the wall of the Byzantine church separating the narthex from the nave.
Athens EM 13315.
Milchhöfer 1887b, 311; Buck 1892, 105 no. 11; *IG* II 5, 1567b; *IG* II² 4605; *IG* II³ 4, 971.
Text: based on *IG* II² 4605 with autopsy.   Photo: *IG* II³ 4,2 tab. CXVIII.

Κηφίσιος Τιμαρχ[ίδου]
Ἰκαριεὺς
εὐξάμενος ἀνέθηκεν
τῶι Διονύσωι

1 Köhler   Τιμάρχ[ου] Milchhöfer   Τιμαρχ – – Curbera in *IG* II³

Kephisios son of Timarch[ides] of Ikarion dedicated this to Dionysus having made a vow.

This fourth-century ex-voto dedication to Dionysus was found in the same general area as a number of choregic monuments but, given that it lacks any explicit marker of a performance (χορηγήσας, νικήσας, name of didaskalos, etc.), it is just as likely to be an offering made in some other circumstance. A choregic dedication from Thorikos (**Yi**) provides a parallel for an ex-voto dedication by a choregos. The inclusion of the demotic (l. 2) in a deme context is unusual, and is perhaps an indication that non-demesmen also dedicated in the sanctuary. **Miii**, ll. 3–4 suggests that residents of Ikarion who were not demesmen could be called upon to serve as choregoi.

N | Kephale

The deme of Kephale, a member of the coastal trittys of the tribe Akamantis, lay at the northernmost end of the Laurion mining region. Its centre has been placed immediately to the east of the modern village of Keratea (Buchholz 1963; Traill 1986, 133), but we are very poorly served for evidence of the life of this substantial deme (bouleutic quota 9), particularly in terms of public inscriptions, of which not one has been found.

Absent from all accounts of the Rural Dionysia (note however Frederiksen 2002, 83), Kephale merits mention because of an observation made by George Wheler after his journey through Attica in the seventeenth century. When he reached the village of Keratea, he saw ruins that prompted him to write 'This hath been an ancient, and great City … I could discern here, where an *Amphitheater* had been, by the Foundations, and some other remains of it' (1682, 448). Given the likelihood that Wheler was on the territory of ancient Kephale, it is difficult to imagine that what he saw could have been anything other than the remains of a substantial Classical or Hellenistic theatre of that deme. There are moreover some grounds for supposing the existence of an important cult of Dionysus in the deme. The modern place names of Dionysovouni or 'Mountain of Dionysus', and 'Dionysos' itself – an area near and to the north-east of Keratea – may preserve a memory of it (Solders 1931, 41 no. 25). The terraced slopes of Dionysovouni would have served as a fine site for a theatre. And a votive relief (now lost), perhaps to be associated with the ruined Church of Ag. Dionysios (note the name) near Keratea, represented a god or hero, possibly Dionysus, in a temple, approached by a bearded man in an 'adoration' scene (cf. **V F** on Athens NM 1500), a flat round *eschara*-type altar between them (Milchhöfer 1887b, 293 no. 239; others identify the deity as Heracles: Frickenhaus 1911, 121–5; Tagalidou 1993, 243; Despinis 2007, 131). There was also, remarkably, a shrine of Semachos somewhere in the region (*IG* II² 1582, ll. 53–5). This is the father of the eponymous heroines of the deme Semachidai in the far north of Attica, just beyond Ikarion and tied to it by various cultic associations, who with his daughters hosted Dionysus.

Some caution, however, is needed. Chandler (1776, 167) believed that what Wheler named 'Kerateia' was 'probably Thoricus'. The fact that it had taken Wheler three and a half hours to reach Sunium from Keratea might be more grist to the argument that he was further north than Thorikos, in ancient Keratea. But Chandler himself remarks that the track was 'very rocky and bad' and Goette (2014, 105) argues that the theatre seen by Wheler was that of Thorikos, noting that Wheler's term 'Amphitheater' fits quite well with the outline of the curved sides of the koilon of the Thorikos theatre. But on the other hand Hobhouse (1813, 338), who was travelling through the area under very similar conditions fifty years later, took issue with Chandler's view that Wheler had misidentified Thorikos as Kephale (Keratea), believing it a largely arbitrary association of ancient ruins with well-known place names – in this case rendered less plausible because of the existence of 'a port, still called Therico, … about an hour and a half distance to the south-east'.

O | Kollytos

Oi: Aeschines, *Against Timarchos* (1) 157. In 346 Aeschines, facing a trial for misconduct on the embassy sent to make peace with Philip II of Macedon, launched a counter-prosecution against his leading prosecutor, Timarchos, for having 'lived disgracefully' as a younger man and so rendered himself unfit to be a politically active citizen. This trial probably came to court early in 345 (Fisher 2001, 6–8). Text: Dilts.

> πάλιν ἐκ τῶν μειρακίων καὶ τῶν ἐν παισὶν ἔτι καὶ νῦν ὄντων πρῶτον μὲν τὸν ἀδελφιδοῦν τὸν Ἰφικράτους, υἱὸν δὲ Τεισίου τοῦ Ῥαμνουσίου, ὁμώνυμον δὲ τοῦ νυνὶ κρινομένου Τιμάρχου· ὃς εὐπρεπὴς ὢν ἰδεῖν τοσοῦτον ἀπέχει τῶν αἰσχρῶν ὥστε πρώην ἐν τοῖς κατ' ἀγροὺς Διονυσίοις κωμῳδῶν ὄντων ἐν Κολλυτῷ, καὶ Παρμένοντος τοῦ κωμικοῦ ὑποκριτοῦ εἰπόντος τι πρὸς τὸν χορὸν ἀνάπαιστον, ἐν ᾧ ἦν εἶναί τινας πόρνους μεγάλους Τιμαρχώδεις, οὐδεὶς ὑπελάμβανεν εἰς τὸ μειράκιον, ἀλλ' εἰς σὲ πάντες· οὕτω κληρονόμος εἶ τοῦ ἐπιτηδεύματος.

Again, among the youths and those who are even now still boys, there is first the nephew of Iphicrates, the son of Teisias of Rhamnus, the one with the same name as the present defendant, Timarchos. Even though he is good-looking, he is so free from disgrace that the other day at the Rural Dionysia, when comedies were being performed at Kollytos and Parmenon the comic actor was delivering an anapaestic verse to the chorus in which some 'big Timarchean whores' were mentioned, no-one interpreted this as a reference to that youth, but all thought it referred to you. So secure is your inheritance of this practice.

Oii: Demosthenes, *On the Crown* (18) 180. In 336 one Ktesiphon proposed that the People award Demosthenes a gold crown for his services to the city, to be proclaimed in the Theatre of Dionysus. Aeschines attacked the proposal as statutorily illegal. The matter eventually came to trial in the summer of 330. In this passage Demosthenes contrasts his own 'performance' with that of Aeschines in relation to a critical embassy to Thebes in the face of Philip's advance into central Greece. Text: Dilts.

> καίτοι τίνα βούλει σέ, Αἰσχίνη, καὶ τίνα ἐμαυτὸν ἐκείνην τὴν ἡμέραν εἶναι θῶ; βούλει ἐμαυτὸν μέν, ὃν ἂν σὺ λοιδορούμενος καὶ διασύρων καλέσαις, Βάτταλον, σὲ δὲ μηδὲ ἥρω τὸν τυχόντα, ἀλλὰ τούτων τινὰ τῶν ἀπὸ τῆς σκηνῆς, Κρεσφόντην ἢ Κρέοντα ἢ ὃν ἐν Κολλυτῷ ποτε Οἰνόμαον κακῶς ἐπέτριψας;

And which role would you like me to assign you on that great day, Aeschines, and which for myself? Shall I be Battalos – as your abuse, hissing and name-calling would have it; while you are not just any old hero but one of those from the stage – Kresphontes or Creon, or Oenomaus – the one you once wrecked with your bad acting in Kollytos?

Oiii: Demosthenes, *On the Crown* (18) 242. Date: see on **ii** above. Text: Dilts.

> τοῦτο δὲ καὶ φύσει κίναδος τἀνθρώπιόν ἐστιν, οὐδὲν ἐξ ἀρχῆς ὑγιὲς πεποιηκὸς
> οὐδ' ἐλεύθερον, αὐτοτραγικὸς πίθηκος, ἀρουραῖος Οἰνόμαος, παράσημος ῥήτωρ.

But this little fellow is by his very nature a cunning animal, from the start a performer of no sound or noble action but a real ape on the tragic stage, a rustic Oenomaus, a counterfeit orator

Oiv: Anonymous, *Life of Aeschines* 1.7. The author draws here on Demochares, nephew of Demosthenes. On Sannion see **VI J**. Text: Dilts.

> Δημοχάρης δὲ … φησὶν (*FGrH* 75 F6a) Ἰσχάνδρου τοῦ τραγῳδοῦ
> τριταγωνιστὴν γενέσθαι τὸν Αἰσχίνην, καὶ ὑποκρινόμενον Οἰνόμαον διώκοντα
> Πέλοπα αἰσχρῶς πεσεῖν καὶ ἀναστῆναι ὑπὸ Σαννίωνος τοῦ χοροδιδασκάλου
> (ἐντεῦθέν' οὖν ὁ Δημοσθένης Οἰνόμαον αὐτὸν ὀνομάζει, πρὸς εἰδότας τὸ πρᾶγμα
> ἐπισκώπτων), καὶ μετὰ Σωκράτους καὶ Σιμύλου τῶν κακῶν ὑποκριτῶν
> ἀλᾶσθαι κατ' ἀγρούς· εἴη ἂν οὖν ἐντεῦθεν ἀρουραῖος λεγούμενος.

τοῦ τραγῳδοῦ Wagner, teste N   τραγῳδοποιοῦ codd., Dilts

Demochares says that Aeschines became the tritagonist of Ischandros the tragedian and, while acting the role of Oenomaus in pursuit of Pelops he had an embarrassing fall and was helped to his feet by Sannion the chorus trainer (this is the reason Demosthenes names him Oenomaus, mocking him for those in the know), and he wandered through the fields with the dreadful actors Sokrates and Simylos (and that would be why he was thereafter nicknamed 'rustic').

Ov: Demosthenes, *On the Crown* (18) 261–2. Date: see on **ii** above. Text: Dilts.

> ὡς δ' ἀπηλλάγης ποτὲ καὶ τούτου, πάνθ' ἃ τῶν ἄλλων κατηγορεῖς αὐτὸς
> ποιήσας, οὐ κατῄσχυνας μὰ Δί' οὐδὲν τῶν προϋπηργμένων τῷ μετὰ ταῦτα
> βίῳ, [262] ἀλλὰ μισθώσας σαυτὸν τοῖς βαρυστόνοις {ἐπικαλουμένοις} ἐκείνοις
> ὑποκριταῖς Σιμύκκᾳ καὶ Σωκράτει, ἐτριταγωνίστεις, σῦκα καὶ βότρυς καὶ ἐλάας
> συλλέγων ὥσπερ ὀπωρώνης ἐκ τῶν ἀλλοτρίων χωρίων, πλείω λαμβάνων ἀπὸ
> τούτων ἢ τῶν ἀγώνων, οὓς ὑμεῖς περὶ τῆς ψυχῆς ἠγωνίζεσθε· ἦν γὰρ ἄσπονδος
> καὶ ἀκήρυκτος ὑμῖν πρὸς τοὺς θεατὰς πόλεμος, ὑφ' ὧν πολλὰ τραύματ' εἰληφὼς
> εἰκότως τοὺς ἀπείρους τῶν τοιούτων κινδύνων ὡς δειλοὺς σκώπτεις.

And after you were relieved of that post too [of public secretary] – having committed all the offences with which you now accuse others – by Zeus your subsequent conduct brought no shame on your earlier career, [262] when you hired yourself to those famous bellowers, the actors Simykkas and Sokrates; you were the player of the third parts; you collected figs and grapes and olives like a grocer selling stolen fruit, earning more from that than from the contests, in which you competed for your very life. For you waged a war without treaty or truce against the spectators and, battle-scarred from those combats you quite reasonably mock as cowards those of us who have no experience of such dangers.

The Dionysia of Kollytos is of special interest as the only deme Dionysia known to have been held in a deme that lay within the city walls of Athens. Our knowledge of it is based entirely on these few topical references thrown up by the conflict between Aeschines and Demosthenes. Small in terms of citizens (bouleutic quota 3) as also in physical extension, Kollytos will however have been very populous, with demesmen far outnumbered by a combination of Athenians resident in the city, metics and foreign visitors. It was also a centre of wealth, so much so as to generate the saying that 'Not all Athenians live in Kollytos' (Plu. *Mor.* 601b), meaning that not all Athenians were rich. The remains of grand houses on the western and south-western slopes of the Areopagus confirm the truth of the aphorism (Stroud 1998, 89). The deme probably included the Pnyx (or rather 'enclosed' it, as a polis structure), and much of the area between it and the Hill of the Nymphs (for the border with Melite at this point see Lalonde 2006; cf. Traill 1986, 126). And it extended further south and east from there, probably as far as the suburban deme of Diomeia outside the city walls (Hsch. δ 1880 and Phot. δ 636: s.v. Διομεῖς). It may thus have included or bordered on the southern slopes of the Acropolis, and the Sanctuary and Theatre of Dionysus.

Performances of both comedy (**Oi**) and tragedy (**Oii–iii**) are attested. The manner in which Aeschines and Demosthenes refer to them in court suggests that mass citizen audiences will be familiar with them, and that they were no innovation in the 340s. The limited evidence shows both new work (comedy) and classic reperformance (tragedy).

That the *Oenomaus* in which Aeschines performed at Kollytos, evidently in the title role, was the famous play of that name by Sophocles, reperformed some sixty years after its composition (placed before 414: *TrGF* IV, 381) is widely accepted (Wankel 1976 II, 891), and is explicitly stated to be so by an entry in Hesychius that derives from a comment on **Oiii**, though perhaps on no independent evidence (α 7381: ἀρουραῖος Οἰνόμαος· Δημοσθένης Αἰσχίνην οὕτως ἔφη, ἐπεὶ κατὰ τὴν χώραν περινοστῶν ὑπεκρίνετο Σοφοκλέους τὸν Οἰνόμαον, '"rustic Oenomaus": Demosthenes speaks thus of Aeschines, because he used to go round the countryside acting Sophocles' *Oenomaus*'). The possibility that the play was by the otherwise unknown poet Ischandros derives ultimately from a source inimical to Aeschines (**Oiv**) and may reflect that hostility in attempting to airbrush from the historical record Aeschines' association with the hallowed and possibly heroised poet of the Classical past (in a gloss on this passage in Harpocration – 163.14 Dind. – Ischandros is an actor). The role of Creon in Sophocles' *Antigone* had certainly been in Aeschines' repertory (D. 19.246–7 πολλάκις) so both of the two other roles proposed by Demosthenes for Aeschines in **Oii** – Creon and Kresphontes – were probably chosen from the actor's known repertoire, the latter probably from the *Kresphontes* of Euripides (see Carrara 2008, 175–9 for other evidence of its early tradition).

Demosthenes may have singled out the Oenomaus performance at Kollytos because Aeschines did in fact experience an unfortunate theatrical mishap there. But it seems too great a coincidence that these enemy orators should both refer to events at the Dionysia of Kollytos, and Fisher's suggestion (2001, 300) that Demosthenes is engaging in a kind of subtle 'revenge' by selecting this particular performance has much to commend it. As the mastermind of Timarchos' defence, Demosthenes will have suffered acutely from his defeat and been highly sensitised to the arguments that Aeschines used to convict his ally. He may have taken a particular pleasure then in reducing Aeschines' career as an actor to one less than brilliant moment at the very festival that had featured, perhaps with some success, in the earlier attack on Timarchos.

The fact that it was a relatively minor festival was also, evidently, important to Demosthenes' selection. It is impossible to say at what festivals the reperformances of the *Antigone* and *Kresphontes* in which Aeschines took part were staged. Had they also been rural, we might have expected Demosthenes to make more of it. Aeschines had been tritagonist to the great actors Theodoros and Aristodemos for a long period, and both of their troupes had staged the *Antigone* often. But we should not adopt Demosthenes' own caricature of the mediocrity of deme festivals and suppose that these can only have been at major urban events (**Yiv**). Demosthenes does not use the description κατ' ἀγρούς of the festival, as Aeschines had (**Oi**), but he exaggerates to almost absurd degree its 'rural' character, thereby almost single-handedly creating a prejudice of parochialism and second-rate provinciality for the whole sector of theatrical festivals, the effect of which is still felt powerfully today. Although in this passage Demosthenes does not call Aeschines a tritagonist, as he had some years earlier (in D. 19.246–7, of 343), it is implied by the expression 'you hired yourself' that he uses in **Ov** (he had made passing reference to Aeschines' status as tritagonist earlier in this speech, in the curriculum vitae he presents at D. 18.129; **V D**). Yet it is most unlikely that the role of Kresphontes was played by the tritagonist. Some doubt may also attach to those of Creon, and even Oenomaus (Wankel 1976 II, 892).

Demosthenes certainly gives the event, now presumably some twenty or more years in the past, a life of its own. And it went on to have a yet longer life. Issues of family pride no doubt led Demosthenes' nephew Demochares to return to it (**Oiv**), perhaps, as we have seen, further darkening the moment by ascribing the play to a nobody. Demochares also seems to have been responsible for initiating the process by which the metaphorical use of the verb 'to fall' (πεσεῖν) as a colloquial way of saying 'flop' of the actor on stage became literalised, seeing Aeschines require the assistance of a hired trainer to recover (Demosthenes had in fact used a different colloquial term for Aeschines' alleged failure – **Oii**: κακῶς ἐπιτρίβω – used of 'murdering' a theatrical role: cf. Plu. *Mor.* 531b; Lucian *Rh.Pr.* 12). This was at some point further embellished into the story that Aeschines-Oenomaus fell from an overturning chariot on entry (Max. Planud. in Hermog. *Id.* ed. Walz, *Rh. V,* 541.23; see further *TrGF* IV, 381).

When later in the speech Demosthenes returns to Aeschines' acting career (**Ov**), the claim that he got more from 'collecting figs and grapes and olives like a grocer selling stolen fruit' than he earned from the theatrical contests reactivates the nexus between rusticity and mediocrity that he has built for Aeschines' acting career on the basis of the Kollytos Oenomaus. This is certainly how Demochares seems to have interpreted it (**Oiv**). We are presumably to think of the fruit as stolen while on tour in the rural provinces (Yunis 2001, 257) and the image modelled on a stock figure of primitive comic mime (*DTC²* 134–6), or – or in addition – as projectiles gathered by the indigent actor after being thrown by angry audiences (the latter encouraged by what follows in explanation 'For you waged a war without treaty or truce against the spectators'). For the insult of ἀρουραῖος Οἰνόμαος ('rustic Oenomaus') we might compare the ἀρουραία θεά used of Euripides' mother in Ar. *Frogs* 840, and even ἄγροικος Δημοσθένης, apparently turned on Demosthenes himself by Dinarchus (D.H. *Din.* 8).

In **Oi** Aeschines draws on a recent event in the theatre at Kollytos to serve as evidence for the prior condemnation of his opponent in the court of public opinion. We thus find alive and well at this rural festival in the middle of the fourth century newly composed comedy with satirical bite against named, contemporary public figures; comedy moreover performed with a chorus, apparently engaged with an actor in dialogue, and with no sign of any diminution in its importance. Nothing more is known of the play in question, but the words πόρνους μεγάλους Τιμαρχώδεις 'big Timarchean whores' have been thought a direct quotation (forming an anapaestic dimeter: *PCG* adesp. F 73). The actor Parmenon was no second-rate performer. He is known to have won a victory at the Lenaea around the middle of the century (*IG* II² 2325 F, l. 47 M-O) and was remembered long after for his legendary powers of mimesis, with an especially famous pig (Plu. *Mor.* 674b–c; Stefanis no. 2012).

Just where were the performances of the Kollytos Dionysia held? The urban Theatre of Dionysus will have been just a short walk from anywhere in the deme, and it has been suggested that it may have been used for the festival (by e.g. Paga 2010, 374). We know that the city and deme collaborated in some religious matters (*SEG* 44, 42) and some form of short-term rental of the urban venue by the deme is entirely possible. However, Demosthenes' persistent 'rustication' of the Kollytos Dionysia would be a highly risky strategy if the event was routinely staged in the great urban Theatre, perhaps fairly recently magnificently refurbished in stone. And Aeschines, speaking as an ex-actor with none of the motives to besmirch the status of the festival Demosthenes will later demonstrate, uses the characteristic descriptor 'in the fields' τοῖς κατ' ἀγροὺς Διονυσίοις of the event. If it had been held in the urban setting that would make this usage somewhat incongruous, and we might expect it to have fallen off (as seems to have happened in Piraeus: **V Introduction**).

There is no *a priori* reason why Kollytos should not have possessed its own theatre, perhaps of a largely impermanent type, and as Jones (2004, 138) notes, the absence of any visible remains is hardly surprising in this continuously occupied and built-over area. One possible site for such a theatre is in part of the 'narrows (στενωπός) called Kollytos', said by the fourth-century AD rhetorician Himerios to have been named after the deme and to have served as its agora, 'right in the middle of the city' (*Or.* 31, 63–5 = Phot. *Bibl.* 375 Bekker, vol. 6, 121 Henry). The place was still famous if in sad decline in Himerios' day. This 'narrows' has been identified as the major thoroughfare of the deme, for much of its course some 4 m wide, and of great importance for circulation in the western sector of the city as a whole. It is a road that began at the juncture of two streets, known as 'Melite' and 'Areiopagos' streets, and continued into the valley between the Areiopagos and the Pnyx (Köhler 1872, 112; Judeich 1931, 169; Young 1951; Lalonde 2006, 103 and fig. 1, 84; Ficuciello 2008, 102–5). In its southerly course it comes close to the south-west corner of the Acropolis, where it joins a road that leads east to the Sanctuary of Dionysus. If part of this road served as the deme's agora, it could also have served as its theatre. A possible candidate for that space is the open, roughly triangular area formed by the merger of Melite and Areiopagos streets, right at the head of the Kollytos road and directly west of the Areiopagos hill. It is however equally possible that, as Köhler (1872, 112) suggested, the festival was held in the outlying, more southerly parts of Kollytos, which are likely to have been more properly 'rural'.

Wherever the festival was held, the consequences of its central location will have been significant. It doubtless attracted large audiences and high-quality performers, with all the resources of the city close at hand (among which note the likely presence in the adjacent deme of Melite of a specialist training house for *tragoidoi*: **V D**).

An Honorific Decree of a Tribe (? Erechtheis), Mentioning a Dionysia, Probably at Lamptrai, ca. 325–300 (by letter forms).

Fragment of a stele of 'Pentelic' marble, broken at top and right.

0.24 × 0.173 × 0.08 m.

Found in excavations on the south-west part of the Acropolis (Lolling 1889, 86).

Athens EM 7709.

Lolling 1889, 89 no. 6; *IG* II 5, 565d; *IG* II² 1161.

Text: based on *IG* II² 1161, with assistance of a photograph (Kazuhiro Takeuchi).

```
         [- - - - - - - - - - - - - - - - - - - - - - - - - - - - -]
  1      ΝΚ[- - - εἰς δὲ τὴν ἀναγραφὴν τῆς στ]-   stoich.
         ήλης δο[ῦναι - - - - - - - - - τοὺς ἐπιμ]-
         ελητὰς τὸ ἀ[νάλωμα - - - - - - - - - ἀν]-
         ειπεῖν Λαμπ[τρᾶσι - - - - - - - - - - Δι]-
  5      ονυσίοις τὸ[ν στέφανον - - - - - - - - τ]-
         ῆι φυλῆι κα[θάπερ - - - - - - - - - - - - - -]
         ο ἡ φυλὴ ἐπ[ὶ - - - - - - - - - - - - - - - - - -]
         ος καὶ ἀν[- - - - - - - - - - - - - - - - - - - - -]
         αρχωι κ[- - - - - - - - - - - - - - - - - - - -]
                      vacat
```

1 ΝΚ Takeuchi   νκ Lolling   ν κ Kirchner   4 ειπε. ἵνα ἅμ π Lolling   8–9 [δημ]άρχωι Wilson

(unidentified number of lines lost) [… and the *epim*]*eletai* are to gi[ve] the e[xpense for the inscription of the st]ele […] to [an]nounce ⁵ th[e crown at] Lamp[trai …] at [the Di]onysia […] for [t]he tribe ju[st as …] the tribe a[t …] and an[(?)nounce …] for [the (?) -]arch …

There is little doubt that this is the lower part of an honorific decree issued by a tribe: a φυλή 'tribe' is mentioned twice in ll. 6, 7; the duties of the three tribal *epimeletai* were predominantly administrative and financial, and included taking care of honours awarded by the tribe, as apparently here ll. 1–3; the findspot on the Athenian Acropolis is consistent with a place of erection in a tribal sanctuary, probably in this case the Erechtheion. Lines 3–5 are the remains of a proclamation clause, directing the announcement of awards 'at the Dionysia' [Δι]ονυσίοις. Tribes did not hold Dionysia. The festival in question must therefore be either the City Dionysia or a Dionysia of one of the constituent demes of the tribe. The former can be ruled out (however see Goette 2014, 88–9). By the last third of the fourth century, the city had taken steps to curb the announcement by tribes (and demes) of honours they had awarded at it. In 330, Aeschines (**I Av 4g**) refers to a law in force that prevented both demes and tribes from announcing crowns at the tragic competition of the City Dionysia. Moreover the letters Λαμπ[ ] in l. 4 are most cogently restored as Λαμπ[τρᾶσι] 'at Lamptrai' (the reading of the lambda, seen as an alpha by Lolling, is confirmed by photograph and autopsy by Kazuhiro Takeuchi). This must be a reference to the place at which the announcement is to be made, and thus where the Dionysia was to be held.

This is therefore very probably an award by the tribe Erechtheis of honours, to be announced at the Dionysia of Lamptrai, attested here for the first time (thus N. F. Jones 1999, 163–4; *IG* II² 1204 shows that Lower Lamptrai imposed taxes, possibly including liturgies; Takeuchi 2011). The decree may have directed the tribal *epimeletai* to perform the announcement themselves (as in a Hippothontid decree *IE* 63); or perhaps there was a herald in l. 5 (τὸ[ν κήρυκα …]). Lamptrai was a 'divided' deme, with Upper (bouleutic quota 5) and Lower (bouleutic quota 9) Lamptrai lying adjacent to one another to the south-east of the lower part of the Hymettan range (Bultrighini 2015, 91–143 provides an up-to-date discussion of the full corpus of evidence for the deme). Both were members of Erechtheis. It is impossible to identify which Lamptrai is in question here. The size of Lower Lamptrai might incline us to direct our thoughts towards it. The site of the civic centre – including the place of assembly – of Lower Lamptrai has now been identified with some certainty (Goette 1995b; Goette 2001, 198; Bultrighini 2015, 104–7, 111). It is immediately adjacent to the north of a very ancient hilltop sanctuary, around 800 m to the east of the hill Kiapha Thiti, where a Doric capital dating to the Classical period was found that has been thought to belong to a small cult building. Dionysus has been proposed as the recipient of the cult of this sanctuary, as also have Aphrodite and Athena, but none of these proposals are based on any solid evidence (Goette 1995b, 237; Bultrighini 2015, 140–3).

It is highly likely that these two adjacent demes of the same name shared a Dionysia. Given that the combined size of the two Lamptrai would be very substantial, such a joint Dionysia might have been an event of some scale. It was evidently deemed a worthy occasion for the announcement of honours granted by the very much larger unit of the tribe, representing a tenth of the entire citizenry of Athens. This is therefore a striking instance of a tribe making use of the Dionysia of one of its constituent demes to publicise its activities. It is perhaps likely the honorand was himself from Lamptrai. Such a practice is likely to have required special permission from the deme authorities. We may find a trace of such a request in the closing lines of the decree: for the most likely restoration of the first word of the decree's last line is 'to the demarch' [δημ]άρχωι ll. 8–9, and ll. 6–9 could well describe some form of protocol for interaction between tribe and deme.

A parallel for the use by a tribe of a deme Dionysia in this way may be found in a small fragment of an honorific decree of the tribe Kekropis, dated by possible reference to the Archon Thoudemos (353/2) in l. 7 (*IG* II² 1145; Athens EM 7693; Lawton 1995, no. 107). Lines 6–8 may have mandated the proclamation of a crown by the herald at a Dionysia (we suggest [ἀνειπεῖν τ|ὸν κή]ρυκα Δ[ιονυσίοις]). Even if a date in or near 352 is correct, this is very unlikely to refer to the City Dionysia, and will almost certainly be the Dionysia of Phlya (**U**), one of the tribes of Kekropis and the one to which the honorand belonged.

Such an interpretation is consistent with Ober's thesis that deme theatres were probably used by tribes for many of their large-scale activities, such as tribal assemblies, rehearsals for choruses at the City Dionysia and so on (2008, 205–10, although at least two other Erechtheid demes held theatrical Dionysia: Anagyrous **E** and Euonymon **I**, the latter of which certainly possessed its own theatre). Paga (2010) takes Ober's thesis further and argues that there was one theatral space per trittys, used for political as well as cultic purposes. The existence of a theatre in Lamptrai would disrupt the distribution pattern she detects (Paga 2010, 376–7; there are other problems with Paga's theory: see Goette 2014; Wilson 2017b).

Cult and Festival of Dionysus, with Tragic Performances, 4th c.

The deme of Marathon (bouleutic quota 10) possessed a significant sanctuary and cult of Dionysus. They were evidently important to the ancient Tetrapolis of which Marathon was the leading member (Parker 1996, 331–2; Papazarkadas 2011, 303; Lambert 2014). It was here that decrees of the Tetrapolis were displayed. A copy of one such decree (*IG* II² 1243, ca. 190) is to be erected 'at Marath[on, in the sanctuary of Dio]nysus', though as Lambert 2014, 10 notes, the word for the sanctuary in l. 21 is fully restored: [ἐν τῶι ἱερῶι τοῦ Διο]|νύσου (Wilhelm); [ἐν τῶι τεμένει τοῦ Διο]|νύσου (Köhler). ἐν τῶι θεάτρωι 'in the theatre' cannot be ruled out. (Note that a 100-drachma fine imposed on anyone who mismanaged Tetrapolis funds or broke their oath was, on a likely restoration, to go to Dionysus: ll. 8–10; cf. *IG* II³ 4, 224, mid fourth-century dedication to Dionysus.) While the inscriptional evidence dates from the mid fourth century and later, the sanctuary is much older. Eugene Vanderpool (in Traill 1986, 148) associates the remains of a large, archaic polygonal sanctuary wall at Plasi near Marathon with this Dionysion, although the site of the cult of Dionysus in Marathon is far from certain (Goette and Weber 2004, 37–8; Humphreys 2004, 165–6; Ismard 2010, 239, 244; Humphreys 2018, 1151).

Some tantalising evidence has recently emerged to show that Marathon, or the Tetrapolis, celebrated a Dionysia at which tragic performances took place, and may also have possessed its own theatre. An entry in the sacrificial calendar of the Tetrapolis may conceal a reference to a Rural Dionysia. In the month of Posideon offerings were made, in Marathon, τελετῆι σπυΔια : ΔΔΔΔ (*SEG* 50, 168 A2, l. 10, ca. 375–50). This mysterious offering has been explained as 'baskets for *Telete*: 40 drachmas', with σπυ<ρί>δια by haplography or contraction (Solders 1931, 70) and the baskets containing perhaps winter fruits, or those preserved from summer – some kind of dole for the festival? But who or what is *telete*? Parker (2005, 333) thinks of a deity from the Eleusinian context, *Telete*. Humphreys (in Lambert 2000, 59) proposed that 'Τελετῆι might have the connotation "dramatic performance"', though she later modified this view, regarding the word as more fitting for initiates or some other restricted group, and so thought instead of the Haloa (Humphreys 2004, 171, 234). Pirenne Delforge (2016) plausibly argues that the term is unlikely at this date to refer to a deity, a personification *Telete*, and must be a ceremony. Since we find no parallel for the use of *telete* in connection with deme Dionysia, the Haloa may be preferable, with the baskets in question very probably containing pastries in the shape of human genitalia attested for the festival (Sch. Lucian *DMeretr.* 6.1 Rabe; Parker 2005, 199, 330; Pirenne Delforge 2016, 45). The Haloa known for Eleusis was held, like deme Dionysia, in Posideon, and it also had a place of prominence for Dionysus (Parker 2005, 199; note the construction of special seating, probably for an official observing the festival and perhaps others, recorded in *IE* 177, ll. 206–7). It is quite possible that the Haloa was held in other demes also, Erchia included; and that it and the deme Dionysia sometimes became associated with one another (Humphreys 2004, 234; **Av**). While the Haloa thus seems the most likely candidate for this event at Marathon in Posideon, a Dionysia cannot be ruled out, and involvement of Dionysus would in any case be virtually certain at an Erchian Haloa.

But much more informative is an as yet unpublished decree, dated by letter forms to around 350, that honours an Archon of the Marathonian Tetrapolis (who came from the deme Probalinthos) for the performance of his religious duties (*SEG* 48, 129; cf. *SEG* 50, 166). He is to receive prohedria, and the award is to be announced by a herald 'at the tragedies of the Dionysia' Διονυσίων τοῖς τραγωιδοῖς. The only other information available is that the stele was to be erected 'in the Dionysion' ἐν τῶι Διονυσίωι. One would naturally expect this to be the Dionysion at Marathon in which other Tetrapolis documents are known to have been erected (see above); and the Dionysia in question to be that of Marathon, or perhaps more likely, one celebrated jointly by the Tetrapolis itself. The stele was however discovered, intact, in the fortress of Rhamnus – a neighbouring deme to the north which was not a member of the Tetrapolis (**W**).

Two possibilities present themselves. The first is that, although found in an excavated context within the fortress and not far from the deme theatre, the decree is out of place there, and somehow never found its way to its proper destination in the venerable Dionysion of Marathon. Petrakos (1998) suggests that the job was given to a local cutter of Rhamnus – which with its fortress and sanctuary of Nemesis erected many inscriptions – but for some reason was never delivered (he also believes the marble comes from the local quarry of Ag. Marina in Rhamnus). The Dionysion and Dionysia in question are on this view those of Marathon, the latter testified here clearly for the first time, and showing performances of tragedy in the middle of the fourth century at a theatre in Marathon.

The second possibility is that the stele was quite properly in Rhamnus because the Tetrapolis was making use of the theatre and Dionysion there for the purpose of honouring one of its own – and indeed for the celebration of its Dionysia. Some important implications follow. This would present the first instance of the use of one deme's theatre by an outside body (the case made by Lohmann 1993 for Myrrhinous doing so is faulty: **R**), implying that a deme might offer – under lease, or some other contractual arrangement – the use of its facilities to others (Goette 2014; Wilson 2017b). Partial parallels for such 'cultic extra-territoriality' can be cited, for instance the use by the Thorikians of the sanctuary of Poseidon at Sunium (*SEG* 33, 147, ll. 19–20), or of the sanctuary of Zeus Epakrios on Hymettus by the Erchians (*SEG* 21, 541, E ll. 59–64: these and others are cited in Lambert 2000, 69–70). But these are more akin to theoric offerings at important sanctuaries in the worshipping deme's region than to the wholesale temporary takeover of infrastructure, including the offering into the future of prohedria to a non-demesman. Some slight support for this interpretation might come from the existence of cultic ties between Rhamnus and the Tetrapolis (Lambert 2000, 69: the Tetrapolis makes offerings to the hero Aristomachos at *SEG* 50, 168 A2, ll. 19–20, a hero well attested at Rhamnus and buried in Marathon beside the Dionysion: *AB* 1.262.16–17; Lambert 2014, 8–9); and from the fact that three of the four demes of the Tetrapolis – including Marathon – formed, with Rhamnus, the coastal trittys of Aiantis.

Caution is however needed. For it is difficult to see how the Tetrapolis could take it upon itself to erect a permanent document of its own within the sanctuary at Rhamnus and to award prohedria at a theatre that was not its own: surely some further qualification specifying that the award pertained only to festivals of the deme Marathon or of the Tetrapolis would be necessary. Petrakos' view that the decree is out of place and that it therefore testifies to a Dionysia held in a theatre in Marathon may after all be the more likely.

An entry in the sacrificial calendar of the Tetrapolis that related to Elaphebolion 10 shows that the Marathonians sacrificed a goat (probably to Ge) on that day, the first of the City Dionysia (*SEG* 50, 168, A2 ll. 17–18). This may be another case, to set alongside the deme Erchia (**A Introduction**), of a deme marking the city festival for Dionysus locally.

R | Myrrhinous

Ri: Deme Decree Awarding Prohedria at Theatrical Spectacles in Myrrhinous, ca. 330–318 (Loomis: see below).

Stele of 'Hymettan' marble, broken at the top.
0.75 × 0.3 × 0.07 m.
Seen by Fourmont in a ruined church at Merenda and later by Milchhöfer (1887b, 278) built into the door-frame of the church of Ag. Thekla in Markopoulo.
Present whereabouts unknown.
IG II 575; *IG* II² 1182; Vivliodetis 2005, 41–2; Bultrighini 2015, 229–35.
Text: *IG* II² 1182.

```
— — — — — — — ο . . .6. . .          stoich. 21
[. . . . .10. . . . . πρ]οεδρί[αν ἐν]
[ταῖς θέ]αις πάσαις αἷς πο[ι]-
[ο]ῦσι Μυρρινούσιοι· εἶν[αι]
[δ' α]ὐτῶι καὶ τῶν λοιπῶν χρ[η]-
[μ]άτων ἐπιμεληθέν[τ]ι τῆς [ἀ]-
[π]οδόσεως ὑπὲρ τῶν δημοτῶ-
[ν] εὑρέσθα[ι] τι ἀγαθὸν παρὰ
[τ]ῶν δημοτῶν καθότι τιμηθ-
[ή]σεται ἀξίως τῶν εὐεργετ-
[ημ]άτων, ὅπως ἂν καὶ ο[ἱ] ἄλλο-
[ι π]άντες φιλοτι[μ]ῶ[ν]ται εἰ-
[ς] τοὺς δημότας εἰδό[τες] ὅτ-
[ι] χάριτας [ἀ]πολ[ή]ψον[ται πα]-
[ρ]ὰ τῶν δημοτῶν ἀξίας [τῶν ε]-
[ὐ]εργετημ[ά]των. ἀναγρά[ψαι]
δὲ τόδε τὸ ψή[φ]ισμα τὸν δή[μ]-
[α]ρχον ἐν στήληι λιθίνηι [κ]-
[α]ὶ στῆσαι ἐ[ν] τῶι ἱερῶι τ[ῆς]
Ἀρτέμιδος τῆς Κολαινίδο-
ς, εἰς δὲ τ[ὴ]ν ἀναγραφὴν τῆς
στήλης μερίσα[ι] τὸ ἀ[ν]ά[λωμ]-
[α] Φείδιππον κα[ὶ] τὸν ἀντιγ-
[ρα]φέα Μειξ[ί]αν ᵛ ΔΔΔ ᵛ δραχ-
[μ]ὰς ἀπὸ τῆς προ[σ]όδου.
        οἱ δημόται.
```
5

10

15

20

25

[… pr]ohedri[a at] all [the sp]ectacles which the Myrrhinousians hold. [5] And, given the care he took of the remaining money left over from the payment on behalf of the demesmen, may he further have the right to request some benefit from the demesmen so that he be [10] duly honoured for his benefactions, in order that all others will be keen to vie for honour for the demesmen in the knowledge that they will receive favours from [15] the demesmen worthy of their benefactions. The demarch is to inscribe this decree on a stone stele and erect it in the sanctuary of [20] Artemis Kolainis, and Pheidippos and the clerk Meixias are to allocate 30 drachmas as the expense for the inscription of the stele [25] from the income. The demesmen.

Rii: Deme Decree, Probably of Myrrhinous, on the Duties of the Demarch, Mentioning a Dionysia, last quarter of the 4th c. (by letter forms and preponderance of -EI over -HI for morphemic -HI: *GAI* I, 378; Wilson 2011b, 79).

Four joining fragments of a 'Hymettan' marble stele, broken at top and bottom.
0.52 × 0.54 × 0.10 m.
Found near and to the south-west of Markopoulo (Koumanoudes 1874). Traill (1986, 132) assigns it to Hagnous, changing his earlier (1975, 42) ascription to Myrrhinous. Goette (2014, 87) shows that Traill's reliance on the findspots of various grave-markers of Hagnousioi to support an identification of Hagnous at Dardiste has some weaknesses, and suggests that he and others have misread Koumanoudes' indication of the findspot – κατὰ τὴν θέσιν Δαρδίστη – as 'at' rather than 'in the direction of' Dardiste. An earlier section (ll. 27–30) of this decree permits priests to lend sanctuary funds 'on satisfactory security of land or house or tenement house, and they shall place a marker-stone (*horos*) on which they shall inscribe the name of the god to whom the money belongs'. The discovery of a *horos* which precisely fulfils these instructions (Dova 2013), made in the name of 'the community of Myrrhinosioi' (κοι|νῶι Μυρρινοσ||[ί]ων ll. 5–7) and referring to 'the sacred money of Artemis Kolainis' (ll. 7–9), virtually ensures that **Rii** is the enabling decree of the deme Myrrhinous which established this system of cult loans.
Athens EM 7744, 7745 (two small lower fragments).
Koumanoudes 1874; *IG* II 578; *IG* II² 1183; R-O II no. 63; Vivliodetis 2005, E3. A new text based on autopsy is being prepared by Kazuhiro Takeuchi.
Text: *IG* II² 1183, with some improvements as communicated by Takeuchi.   Photo: Vivliodetis 2005, 46.

Only the last five lines of surviving text are presented here.

36   μι· τῆι δὲ ἐνάτει ἐπὶ δέκα τοῦ Ποσιδεῶνο[ς] μ<η>ν[ὸς χρηματίζ]-   stoich. 46
[ε]ιν περ[ὶ Διο]νυσίων, τὰ δὲ ἄλλα πάντα τ[. . . . . . . .16. . . . .]
[. . . . .10. . . . . χρ]ηματίζειν πλὴν τοῦ δ[. . . . . . .17. . . . .]
[. . . .8. . . . τῆι αὐ]τῆι ἡμέραι τὸν δήμα[ρχον . . . . . .13. . . . . .]
40   [. . . . . . .15. . . . . . .] ‾ ὀ[φειλέτ]ω Η : δρα[χμάς . . . . . . .14. . . . . . .]

36 μι Takeuchi   ΛΙ Koumanoudes   μι Köhler   Ποσιδεῶνο[ς] Takeuchi   Ποσιδεῶν[ος]
Koumanoudes   μ<η>ν[ὸς] Takeuchi   ΜΕΝ *lapis*   37 περ[ὶ] Takeuchi   πε[ρὶ]
Koumanoudes   38 [χρ]ηματίζειν Takeuchi   [χρη]ματίζειν Koumanoudes   40
Takeuchi   [. . . . . 16 . . . .] ὀ[φειλέτ]ω Η δρα[χμάς - - - - - -] Köhler

… On the nineteenth day of the mon[th] Posideon [business] concern[ing the Dio]nysia [shall be dealt] with, and all the other things [… d]ealt with except the [… on the sa]me day the dema[rch … ? or] let him o[we] 100 dra[chmas …]

Riii: Boundary Marker (*horos*), Probably of Myrrhinous, Indicating Property Securing a Loan (or Rental Agreement) Made by a Sanctuary of Dionysus, late 4th c. (by letter forms and on the assumption that it post-dates **Rii**).

No recorded physical details.
Seen by Milchhöfer in the house of one Panagiotis J. Orphanos of Markopoulo in 1897 (Wilhelm 1909, 50). The ascription to Myrrhinous is based on the fact that it was seen in Markopoulo and the likelihood that it is another example of a *horos* mandated by ll. 27–30 of **Rii** (see above).
Current whereabouts unknown.
Wilhelm 1909, no. 38; *IG* II² 2767; Finley 1952, no. 163.
Text: *IG* II² 2767.

> ὅρος χωρίου ἀποτίμημα ἐπὶ συνθήκαις
> Διονύσωι ⟨Ρ⟩ΗΗ⟨Ρ⟩.

Boundary marker (*horos*) of land put up as security (*apotimema*) to Dionysus according to the agreement, 750 (drachmas).

The deme of Myrrhinous formed part of the coastal trittys of Pandionis (bouleutic quota 6). Occupying much of the south-east plain of the Mesogaia in the region south of modern Markopoulo, its location has long been known thanks to ancient finds in the region of the church of Ag. Panagia Merenda (Traill 1975, 42; Traill 1986, 129; Vivliodetis 2005, 23–32) and has been given greater precision with the excavations made in the course of the construction of the Olympic Equestrian Centre at Markopoulo, just under 500 m north of Ag. Panagia Merenda. These identified the centre of the ancient deme at the site of the Olympic Equestrian Centre: various roads, shrines, public buildings, farms and cemeteries were found (Kakavogianni 2003; 2009a; Kakavogianni et al. 2009) and the excavators are confident that the foundations of a temple they located here (20 × 11 m) are those of Artemis Kolainis, the deme's principal cult (Kakavogianni 2009a, 59–63; full discussion of the updated corpus of evidence for the deme in Bultrighini 2015, 207–93).

Ri is a decree that confers honours on an individual, apparently for financial services on behalf of the deme (ll. 5–8). It is perhaps somewhat more likely that the honorand was a private citizen applying his financial acumen to deme resources rather than a local official such as a treasurer (*tamias*) but, in the absence of the first part of the decree, this must remain unclear. Bultrighini (2015, 321–2) suggests with some plausibility that he was the Pheidippos (l. 23) who contributed to the cost of the inscription. Pheidippos came from a wealthy family, his father Apemon having served as victorious choregos for the boys' chorus at the Thargelia around 400 (**V F**).

The decree has been dated to the period ca. 330–318 by Loomis on the cogent grounds that the cost of its inscription, at 30 drachmas (ll. 24–5), is high, and that prices for the inscription of public documents rose sharply after ca. 330. (See *SEG* 48, 121. The mid fourth-century date of *IG* II² was based only on letter forms, and Kirchner did not himself see the stone.)

The honorand is to receive 'prohedri[a at] all [the sp]ectacles which the Myrrhinousians hold' (ll. 2–4). Prohedria can certainly be awarded at events other than theatrical performances – as for instance it is to local choregoi at the contest of the Tauropolia for Artemis in Halai Araphenides (*SEG* 34, 103; **Ki**). The stele recording the Myrrhinousian decree is to be erected in the sanctuary of Artemis Kolainis (ll. 20–1). This is no doubt because this was the deme's principal cult, the sanctuary serving as an important centre for the deme's civic business. That it is not to go 'in the theatre' need hardly mean that the deme did not possess one. The spectacles in question ([θέ]αις l. 2 is a safe restoration) may have formed part of the cult of Artemis. But there will have been others: note the force of πάσαις 'all', suggesting a plurality of events. And the phrase seems to mimic an expression frequently used to award prohedria in polis decrees – 'prohedria at all the contests which the city holds' (e.g. *IG* II² 500, of 302/1 προεδρίαν ἐν ἅπασιν το|ῖς ἀγῶσιν οὓς ἂν ἡ πόλις τιθεῖ) – which certainly includes the dramatic contests of the City Dionysia. *Theai* 'spectacles' is in fact a rare term in inscriptions, but it does, despite its rather broad connotations, naturally encourage us to think, first and foremost, of *thea*tre (cf. Thphr. *Char.* 5.7) and on balance it is likely that it encompasses theatrical events, held in a theatre, here. Vivliodetis (2007, 119) notes that the low hills in the deme would provide a good site for a temporary theatre. Bultrighini (2015, 221) airs the possibility that an open space found to the east of the temple uncovered in the recent excavations may have been used for deme gatherings, including festivals and theatrical performances, while Kakavogianni (2009a, 65 n. 90) reports that a number of older residents of Merenda recounted the discovery, at some unspecified point in the past, of a 'theatre seat' (κάθισμα θεάτρου) in the recently excavated sanctuary area of Myrrhinous (near the site tentatively identified by its excavators as a sanctuary of Zeus Phratrios, but note the reservations as to this identification expressed by Bultrighini 2013, 149). It is hard to judge the value of this report, but while it should be noted (with Lauter 1993, 82) that single marble chairs are found in use in a variety of sanctuaries, not just as theatre prohedria, we do find them certainly so used in the Attic theatres of Rhamnus (**W Introduction**; **Wi**), Ikarion (**M Introduction**) and possibly Anagyrous (**E Introduction**). Kakavogianni and Anetakis (2012, 185–8) report the discovery in the same area of what is likely to have been a commercial agora of the deme.

Lohmann (1993, 288–9; cf. Moreno 2007, 72) has argued that the phrasing of this clause implies the existence of spectacles held, perhaps under a temporary leasing arrangement, by groups other than the Myrrhinousians in their theatre – possibly by other demes or private entrepreneurs. But the expression does not necessarily have the limiting sense which Lohmann requires – namely that its specification of spectacles held by the Myrrhinousians requires that spectacles were held by others in the same venue. (As an alternative he suggests that Myrrhinous had no theatre of its own, but occasionally staged spectacles in the theatre of another deme, such as that of Thorikos.)

Rii lacks any internal indication of its deme, but it is now clear that it must derive from Myrrhinous (see above). The decree of which these form the last few surviving lines of text (how many followed is unclear) dealt with various aspects of the duties of the demarch. In what remains, three seemingly distinct subjects are covered: the scrutiny of the demarch (to l. 27); the lending of money by deme sanctuaries (ll. 27–32); and sacrifices and assembly meetings for which the demarch is responsible (ll. 32–40; see the commentary of R-O II; Wilson 2011b on possible connections between these subjects).

Lines 36–40 instruct the demarch to hold an assembly concerning the Dionysia of Myrrhinous. This meeting will have followed the festival, and treated matters arising from it. The nineteenth of Posideon (l. 36) would be too late to do much by way of advance preparation for it (an interpretation urged by Lipsius *IG ad loc.*), and the verb χρηματίζειν is conclusive, for it normally refers to retrospective assessment – 'to treat matters arising' (Wilhelm 1906, 238–9). This is the only certain case of a deme assembly specifically associated with a Dionysia, though it is very probable that Ikarion had one from the fifth century (**Miii**). The nineteenth of Posideon is therefore likely to be the first available day after the festival finished, which places Myrrhinous' Dionysia ca. 17–18 Posideon. The need to hold such a meeting makes it clear that the festival was of some scale, and while it does not prove that it included theatrical performances, it certainly tends strongly in that direction.

The business of such a meeting will have been similar to that of the comparable event held after the Great Dionysia (and the Pandia) in the city (**I Aix 1**): to deal (first) with the management of the festival by the Archon (demarch in the case of Myrrhinous); and with alleged wrongdoing or violations of law committed in respect of the festival. To this list of the activities of the meeting derived from Demosthenes' account of the city event, one should add the function of honouring theatre benefactors (known for the city from the closing decades of the fourth century: cf. **I Av 4**; Lambert 2008). Similarly in the demes, assembly meetings held after Dionysia are a likely point of origin for the surviving honorific decrees for theatre people, especially choregoi.

Humphreys (2004, 162) has argued that the guiding rationale of this section of the decree is not to register the annual sacrifices to be made by the demarch, but rather to list a number of statutory deme assembly meetings. On this cogent interpretation, in these lines the decree not only mandates that the deme meet on 19 Posideon to consider the conduct of the Dionysia, but also that it convene as a regular *ekklesia* to treat deme affairs more broadly. The fragmentary remains of this meeting's 'standing agenda' could be interpreted along these lines: issues arising from the Dionysia are to be treated first: [χρηματίζ|ε]ιν πε[ρὶ Διο]νυσίων '[business] concern[ing the Dio]nysia [shall be dealt] with'. While rather different matters are to be treated after that: τὰ δὲ ἄλλα πάντα τ[.......|........ χρη]ματίζειν 'and all the other things […] dealt with'. (The alternative would be to construe all of ll. 37–40 with reference to the agenda of matters concerning the Dionysia: [χρηματίζ|ε]ιν πε[ρὶ Διο]νυσίων would serve as an opening general rubric, while τὰ δὲ ἄλλα πάντα τ[... would open the agenda for that meeting, and move on – just as our text, infuriatingly, fails completely – to specify in detail a restriction on matters to be treated [... χρη]ματίζειν πλὴν τοῦ δ[........] l. 38.) The very last surviving words suggest that the demarch must do something in connection with this assembly 'on the same day', the nineteenth of Posideon, or suffer a very substantial fine (cf. **Miii**). This may have been an obligation to proceed with any legal actions arising from the meeting (cf. **I Aix 1a**), or perhaps to provide some form of financial accounting for the festival.

The manner in which an assembly to treat the Dionysia has apparently been co-timeta-bled with a general deme meeting suggests that the 'natural' disinclination of demesmen to participate in frequent assembly meetings (D. 57.9, 13; Whitehead 1986a, 92, 357) was addressed in Myrrhinous by attaching an important deme assembly to the diagnostic as-sembly for the festival – and, of course, thereby to the festival itself, with its manifold attractions. The festival will have drawn large numbers of demesmen to town from their farms, while others will have returned to their home deme from residences further afield, in particular in the city, to see the festival and at the same time to renew family ties and deal with business related to their deme properties.

The fact that **Riii** was seen on a property in the region of Markopoulo in the nineteenth century makes it likely to have derived from the deme of Myrrhinous. It marked out a piece of land that was to serve as security (*apotimema* is a term for real security, whether for a lease, a dowry or a loan: Harris 1993) for the god Dionysus, as further specified by the terms of a written agreement or contract. Dionysus of Myrrhinous had thus made a loan of 750 drachmas; or, perhaps, rented out a property for which that was the annual rental. If the lat-ter, the sum will be at the high end of income from land or property rentals in the demes and one may be tempted to think of the local theatre as the property offered for rent. However, another clause in the deme decree from Myrrhinous (**Rii**) – ll. 27–32 – permits the priests of the deme to offer loans, 'on satisfactory security of land or house or tenement house, and they shall place a *horos* on which they shall inscribe the name of the god to whom the mon-ey belongs'. This could well be just such a *horos* as stipulated by the decree, which makes it more likely that the transaction in question was a loan rather than a rental agreement. (Wilson 2011b made the case for **Riii** deriving from Hagnous, but the *horos* published by Dova 2013 virtually guarantees that both it and **Rii** are from Myrrhinous: see above.)

The fact that, in the later decades of the fourth century, the sanctuary of Dionysus in Myrrhinous had sufficient accumulated cash funds to make a sizeable loan shows that the god's affairs were in good health. Suggestions for the rate of interest applied to loans made within a deme by its sanctuaries and other public bodies range from a gentle ca. 2.5 per cent (Blok 2010, 71–2) to ca. 12 per cent (Whitehead 1986a, 159). Applied to this loan, the former would have generated around 18 drachmas, 4½ obols, the latter, 90 drachmas. The higher range is more likely, especially given the existence of instructions like those made to financial officials in Plotheia to offer loans to 'whoever gives the highest interest' (*IG* I³ 258, ll. 18–20). Moreover, other evidence for deme sanctuary credit suggests that it was usual to lend in 'packets' of money of equal value, divided up from a large sum. In one year in the 440s the goddess Nemesis of Rhamnus lent some 185 such 'packets' worth 200 drachmas each; in another year, 45 lots of 300 drachmas; and in a third, 40 of 300 drachmas (*IRhamn.* 182). Dionysus in Myrrhinous may have done something similar (it is notewor-thy that 750 drachmas is one-eighth of a talant), or the land in question may have been one of several properties mortgaged for a larger sum. It is a reasonable surmise that the funds generated by a loan such as this were destined to support the cult in the deme whose major annual enterprise was a theatrical Dionysia.

Two further possibly relevant items are a decree authorising a leasing agreement of the phratry of the Dyaleis, based in Myrrhinous (*IG* II² 1241). This is evidence for the activity of a Dionysian association in the deme, given Hsch. δ 2473: Δύαλος· ὁ Διόνυσος, παρὰ Παίωσιν 'Dyalos: Dionysus, among the Paeonians' (cf. Lambert 1998, 303; Bultrighini 2015, 281–2 for other Dionysian interpretations of the phratry name). The second is an object, found in a cemetery, described in a preliminary report as a round bronze theatre token, marked on one side with a M above an owl, with the head of Athena on the other (*SEG* 53, 227). As it has not yet been properly published, given that the identification of theatre-tokens is a notoriously difficult business, and that the limited description available offers little reason to associate it with the theatre (rather than, say, a dikast's token), judgement must be suspended (Bultrighini 2015, 290–1). Finally, Pausanias (1.31.4) attests the existence of a cult of Dionysus Anthios in the deme, as also at Aixone (**D Introduction**) and Phlya (**U**), but there is no reason to think that this was the cult associated with the Dionysia of **Rii**.

Choregic Victory Monument, late 4th c. (by letter forms).

> Fragment of a small quadrangular base of 'Hymettan' marble. The left-hand side appears to be intact and original. The upper surface is intact and has a circular cavity towards the rear, possibly for a small statue. Its position in the centre of the stone permits an approximate calculation of its original width (ca. 0.40–0.50 m).
> L. 0.24 × W. 0.18 m.
> Found in the vicinity of an ancient farm at Liotrivi, near the village of Koropi in the Mesogaia. Present whereabouts unknown.
> Lionis 2005, 192 no. 2 = *SEG* 57, 181; *IG* II³ 4, 516.
> Text: based on *IG* II³ 4, 516.   Photos: Lionis 2005, fig. 3; *IG* II³ 4,1 tab. LXIX.

> 1   Λυκίσκος .. ^{ca. 6–8} .. [χορη]-
>   γῶν νικήσ[ας ἀνέθηκε].
>   *vacat*
>
> 2   τῶν ? Goette   ΙΩΝΝΙΚΗΣ Lionis   1–2 [χορη]γῶν Makres

> Lykiskos … ? *patronymic*… [dedicated this] after a victor[y as chore]gos.

The possible existence of a Dionysia in the small and rather low-profile deme of Oa in the Mesogaia (a member of the inland trittys of Pandionis, bouleutic quota 4) has been proposed on the basis of this fragmentary inscription, which was found in the vicinity of an ancient farm (Lionis 2005). It is unclear whether it had been moved there for reuse, as was the case with a horos found in the same area that was built into a later wall (Lionis 2005, 192 no. 4). The farm is east of the modern village of Koropi, on territory that almost certainly formed part of Oa. The location of Oa has long been disputed (Dow 1963). Traill (1986, 129) placed it much further to the north in the Mesogaia, beyond Paiania, but a site north of Koropi was one of several already canvassed by Steinhauer (2002, 91, 145). It is now almost certain that the deme is to be identified with the area east and north-east of Koropi. Three funerary inscriptions of the fifth and fourth centuries that record demesmen of Oa (Ὄηθεν) were excavated in a large cemetery at the northern end of the village of Koropi and published in 2009 (Kakavogianni and Galiatsatou 2009; *SEG* 48, 295–7), and another three are kept in the archaeological collection of the school of Koropi. The area controlled by the deme probably extended to the east of Koropi as far as the river Erasinos, between the demes of Paiania and Sphettos. The farm at Liotrivi where this inscription was found is around 1 km to the east of the ancient cemetery.

Makres notes (and the published photograph shows) that the first letter of the second line was a gamma (not an iota, as Lionis thought; a tau might also be a possibility). This makes it likely that the word was χορηγῶν 'as choregos', and thus that the object was a choregic dedication following a victory (the restoration νικήσ[ας] 'after a victor[y]' can be regarded as certain). If this is indeed evidence of a choregia in the deme Oa, it is all the more striking for being late in the fourth century, and thus possibly at a time when the choregia was undergoing radical modification (**Bvii**; **Dii**; **Vii**; **Wii**).

Choregic contests in the demes are almost exclusively associated with Dionysia (one possible exception is a contest in pyrrhic dance supported by choregoi at the Tauropolia for Artemis in Halai Araphenides: *SEG* 34, 103; **Ki**). Given the rarity of evidence for lyric choruses at deme Dionysia, and the fact that they appear only in very large demes like Piraeus (**Vii**) and Acharnae (**Bii–iii**), the likelihood is that the choregia here was for drama. If there was a Dionysia with drama in Oa, we find a very intense concentration of dramatic festivals in this area of the Mesogaia.

T | Paiania

Choregic Dedication for Tragedy of Demosthenes, Son of Demainetos, ca. 350 (by letter forms and prosopography).

Two non-joining marble fragments.
No recorded dimensions.
Found in front of the church of Evangelistria in the village of Kokla ca. 2 km to the east of Liopesi, the site of ancient Paiania (Traill 1975, 43).
Current whereabouts unknown.
Ross 1855, 216; *IG* II 1277 (fr. a) + Le Bas 1847, no. 482bis; *IG* II 1256 (fr. b); Preuner 1924, 108–9; *IG* II² 3097 (a+b); *IG* II³ 4, 503.
Text: based on *IG* II³ 4, 503.

fr. a   *fr. b*

[τ]ραγωιδοῖς χ[ορηγῶ]ν ἐνίκα
[Δη]μοσθένης Δ[ημαινέ]το Παιανιεύς.

1 _ NE Le Bas   ENE Pittakes   2 ΤΟΠΑΙΑΝΙΕΥΣ Le Bas   Δ[ημαινέτ]ο Kirchner

[De]mosthenes son of D[emainet]os of Paiania was victorious as ch[orego]s in [t]ragedy.

Paiania in the Mesogaia, to the east of the northern foothills of Hymettus, was one of the curious 'divided' Attic demes: Lower Paiania was among the very largest of demes for population, with a bouleutic quota of 11 (cf. Osborne 1985, 44); Upper Paiania by contrast among the smallest, bouleutic quota 1. The size alone of Lower Paiania is sufficient to encourage an expectation that this deme may have sustained its own theatre, and its known concentration of wealthy families tends in the same direction (Osborne 1985, 202). At present the only solid evidence is this choregic dedication for a victory in tragedy, probably won at the local Dionysia. It is a safe assumption that the two Paianias would have celebrated such a festival as one (Upper Paiania could hardly have sustained one with dramatic performances on its own).

Nothing can be said about the original form of this monument, since there is no published description of the stones, now lost. The association of the two fragments, proposed originally by Pittakis and argued by Preuner (1924, 108–9) is probably beyond doubt, though it is worth noting that the transcription of fr. b by Pittakis (in a notebook sent to the Berlin Academy) reports the remains of an epsilon where the restoration requires an omega (see apparatus; Le Bas' report also suggests an epsilon rather than an omega).

While the deme Dionysia must be the most likely candidate for this tragic choregia, this is one instance where the possibility that Demosthenes' was a victory won at the City Dionysia and commemorated in the deme is worth canvassing. Milanezi (2004 II, 331) does so, also Goette (2014, 88). The case rests in part on a judgement as to the political prominence of the family of Demainetos, and the observable phenomenon that men who devoted their abilities and resources to their deme tended not to go on to do the same at the urban level. This Demosthenes has been thought likely to be a relative of his famous namesake (*DFA²* 50). Davies however (*APF* 103) is sceptical, on the grounds that the family of Demainetos apparently maintained their local roots in the Mesogaia while that of Demosthenes the orator evidently migrated to the city back in the fifth century. However matters are not quite so clear. For Demainetos and his two sons – Demosthenes (our choregos), and the elder Demeas – each served as cavalry commanders of their tribe (phylarchs), and together they dedicated the fine victory monument known after its sculptor as the Bryaxis base (NM 1733; *IG* II³ 4, 252) for victories won as cavalry commanders in the *anthippasia* or 'mock cavalry charge' contest, probably at the Olympieia (Shear 2001, 341–2) or Panathenaea. (Duplouy 2015, 77 plausibly suggests that there was one victory alone, that of the father, who chose in a dynastic gesture to associate his sons with the victory by inclusion on the monument.) Although they commanded the cavalry in tribal units, phylarchs were elected by the People as a whole, not their tribe (Arist. *Ath.* 61.1, 61.5) and will almost always have been men of considerable wealth. The office, and its agonistic opportunities, gave its holder prominence in the city context. Davies thus somewhat misrepresents its nature when he writes that 'The family seems to have been active in deme and tribal affairs in the middle of the fourth century. There is no very convincing evidence for supposing that it was active on a national level.' The tenure of the phylarchy by all three members of the family, and the victory monument they dedicated, may in fact indicate a certain prominence at the national level, and considerable wealth.

A striking feature of this choregic inscription is the presence of the demotic Παιανιεύς, l. 2. The best parallels for the inclusion of demotics by choregic dedicants in their own demes come from Rhamnus (**Wii**, **Wiii**), where the practice is more readily intelligible given the way the fortress and sanctuary of Nemesis drew numerous visitors from beyond the deme (cf. also **Mxii**). No such reason is obviously present for Paiania (unless its local Eleusinia was a greater attraction than the surviving evidence indicates: *IG* I³ 250). We might instead think of imitation of urban practice (close familiarity with which is demonstrable for these men from their *anthippasia* monument). The use of this habit of personal identification, standard in the city context, might conceivably reflect the fact that the victory was won in the city. And the apparent absence of a stable idiom for commemorating in the city urban tragic victories in a permanent manner (unlike those won in tribal choruses) may be another consideration (Wilson 2000, 236–44). On the other hand, no weight can be put on the fact that we have a singleton choregos where we might have expected synchoregoi, since deme choregiai are found with one, two or three choregoi.

An entry in the Byzantine work known as the *Lexica Segueriana* s.v. 'Paiōnia' may preserve a garbled memory of a theatre in Paiania (if the reference is not to a region in Thrace): '"Paiōnia": a place in which there was a theatre where they held a contest' (Παιωνία.

τόπος ἐν ᾧ θέατρον ἦν, ὅπου ἀγῶνα ἐπετέλουν, *AB* 1.299.14). Corruption of Παιανία to Παιωνία might have been made the easier by the existence of Ionic Παιών alongside Attic Παιάν, and further assisted by the paronomasia common with deme names and attested for Paiania itself by Menander *Dys.* 407–9, though there the play is with the name Pan, not Paian / Paion. And for what it is worth, Harpocration felt the need to distinguish the name of the demesmen of Paiania from those of Paiŏnidai (Harp. s.v. Παιανιεῖς καὶ Παιονίδαι). On the other hand, the *Lexica Segueriana* did know how to use the term δῆμος = 'deme' correctly (e.g. *AB* 1.210.3). Παιώνιος is attested (Hsch. π 115) as an epithet of Dionysus (and an Athena Paionia received a dedication in the sanctuary of Dionysus to the north-west of the Athenian Agora, Paus. 1.2.5). This might have been a sufficient prompt for the *Lexica Segueriana* to postulate the existence of a theatre in a place named Paionia.

U | Phlya

Isaeus, *On Kiron* (8) 15–16. Date of delivery ca. 375, with reference to ca. 400. Text: Roussel.

> οἷα γὰρ εἰκὸς παίδων ὄντων ἐξ ἑαυτοῦ θυγατρός, οὐδεπώποτε θυσίαν ἄνευ
> ἡμῶν οὐδεμίαν ἐποίησεν, ἀλλ᾽ εἴτε μικρὰ εἴτε μεγάλα θύοι, πανταχοῦ παρῆμεν
> ἡμεῖς καὶ συνεθύομεν. καὶ οὐ μόνον εἰς τὰ τοιαῦτα παρεκαλούμεθα, ἀλλὰ
> καὶ εἰς Διονύσια εἰς ἀγρὸν ἦγεν ἀεὶ ἡμᾶς, [16] καὶ μετ᾽ ἐκείνου τε ἐθεωροῦμεν
> καθήμενοι παρ᾽ αὐτὸν καὶ τὰς ἑορτὰς ἤγομεν παρ᾽ ἐκεῖνον πάσας.

For, as you would expect, given that we were the sons of his own daughter, Kiron never offered a sacrifice without our presence; whether he was performing a great or a small sacrifice, we were always there and took part in it with him. And not only were we invited to such rites but he also always took us to his farm for the Dionysia, [16] and we sat beside him as we watched the spectacles, and observed all the festivals in his company.

Lying to the north of the Hymettan range in central Attica, Phlya – the home deme of Euripides – was an inland member of the Kekropis tribe, of above average size (bouleutic quota 7). The existence of a Dionysia in this deme is attested solely by this oration of Isaeus, although Pausanias 1.31.4 notes that Phlya, as well as Myrrhinous (**R**; see also **D Introduction**), had a prominent cult of Dionysus Anthios (see also on **P**). The speaker seeks to establish his claim to be a rightful grandson of Kiron and proper claimant to his (significant) estate, which we know from a later passage (35) was in Phlya. As evidence of their close relationship he describes the various social and religious activities in which Kiron included his grandchildren, among them the Dionysia of his home deme.

    Although it suits his forensic goal to depict it thus, deme Dionysia were generally occasions on which families came together (back) in their home demes (Kiron himself lived in the city). The expression 'he also always took us to his farm for the Dionysia' is a bit like saying 'our grandparents invite us to celebrate Christmas with them every year'. Given that the speaker is recalling distant childhood days and a grandfather's established habit, we may say that Phlya had a Dionysia at the start of the fourth century, if not earlier. The phrase 'and we sat beside him as we watched the spectacles' need not be limited to the 'spectacles' of the Dionysia, but strongly implies that the Dionysia of Phlya included theatrical performances. 'Seating' side-by-side indicates that the viewers were stationary. That suggests that they were in a theatron of some sort.

V | Piraeus

Introduction

The Piraeus was no ordinary deme, and its Dionysia, no ordinary deme festival. Already before the middle of the fifth century the harbour town was a true second urbanised centre, its opportunities for commerce and trade a magnet for foreigners, large numbers of metics and internal Athenian émigrés. With a bouleutic quota of (probably) 8 (Traill 1986, 16–18; it was 10 after 307/6), it was well above average size as a deme. But the nominal 320 / 480 adult male demesmen represented by that quota will have been a tiny minority in a town with a population estimated as equal to that of the city of Athens ca. 432 (Garland 1987, 60).

The Dionysia in the Piraeus has a recorded history stretching over three and a half centuries. Euripides is said to have competed there (**Vi**), confirming the festival's operation by the last quarter of the fifth century, while at the same time ensuring its status as a place where the best poets were keen to perform. A more direct testimony to theatrical life in the Piraeus ca. 410–400 is the (probably) choregic relief representing Dionysus in the company of choreuts that is likely to have come from the god's sanctuary associated with the theatre (**V F** on Athens NM 1500), while contemporary literary evidence reports the use of the theatre in the summer of 411 as a military and political meeting place for the hoplites of the Piraeus during the period of oligarchic rule (Th. 8.93.1, writing of τὸ πρὸς τῆι Μουνιχίαι Διονυσιακὸν θέατρον, with Tozzi 2016, 157–60; cf. X. *HG* 2.4.33) and, also under politically disturbed circumstances, again in 405 when just prior to the regime of the Thirty an Assembly was held there at which the names of those who were allegedly opposed to the peace terms with Sparta were declared (Lys. 13.32 with Tozzi 2016, 161–72).

Although our sources – no doubt more interested in the extraordinary case – thus record meetings held in the Piraeus theatre in the fifth century only by 'irregular' political bodies, it was probably not unusual for the Athenian Assembly itself to meet here in the fifth century from time to time. Construction work on Pnyx II late in the fifth century is a possible factor behind these meetings, and may ultimately be more significant than the (supposed) small size of the Mounichia theatre, thought to be appealing to oligarchs (Frohberger 1880, 129; Tozzi 2016, 168–71). Another possible fifth-century case is a meeting mandated to discuss the Sicilian expedition in 415 (McDonald 1943, 53 on *IG* I² 98, now *IG* I³ 93). This certainly happened in the fourth century, when business to do with the navy seems to have been conducted there, perhaps regularly (D. 19.60, cf. 125, 209 with MacDowell 2000, 233). Ordinary Assembly meetings – normally the last of the prytany – were frequent in the Piraeus theatre from the last quarter of the third and through much of the second century (McDonald 1943, 54; Tozzi 2016, 240–52). An early example may be provided by a polis decree, dated to 302/1, that shows a meeting on 29 Posideon (*Agora* 16, 124, l. 7, restored:

ἐκκλησία ἐμ Πειραιεῖ; Meritt 1936, 415 no. 12 prefers ἐν Διονύσου, presumably a meeting in the city Theatre; Tozzi 2016, 240). It is likely that in the second century the theatre in question was the one newly built at Zea (below). Constructed with a theatron of stone, it was equipped with permanent seating and so was better suited for meetings all year round, unlike the older theatre at Mounichia, the seating for which was evidently wooden and temporary (**Vvi**).

The Piraean theatre may even in some sense have been regarded as a duplicate of the city Theatre in the harbour town, for it is one of a number of physical institutions of the city that had counterparts in this deme. It is listed in a decree of the Augustan era concerning the restoration of sanctuaries, alongside a Bouleuterion and a Strategeion (*IG* II² 1035, ll. 43–4; cf. *SEG* 26, 121). The latter two clearly represent duplicates of city structures rather than structures of the deme as a constitutional entity. The fact that the theatre of the deme was used by the city in this way is consistent with the high degree of involvement of the city in the deme and its theatrical life (below). That the relationship of co-usage of the theatre for public gatherings goes back into the fifth century does not prove that the collaboration over the festival likewise goes back that far, but it certainly tends in that direction and is in any case very likely.

The Theatre and Sanctuary of Dionysus

In 1766 Richard Chandler saw 'traces of a small theatre in the side of the hill of Munychia' (1825, 25; cf. 1774, xxxi: 'Theatri … locum saepe vidi') and its remains were still visible in Leake's day (1841, 387) though annoyingly he recorded nothing of them. As recently as the 1950s Dilke (1950, 22) claimed that part of a retaining wall could still be glimpsed. Its site is thus reliably known. It lay about halfway up the north-west flank of the Mounichia hill. The theatron faced north-west, looking towards Kantharos harbour and the Saronic gulf beyond (Judeich 1931, 451; see map in Curtius and Kaupert 1904, sheet 2; Bressan 2009, 39). Those who had at least seen such remains as could be viewed in the later nineteenth century noted that it lay beyond the Hippodamian market quarter, while being linked to it by a network of streets (Milchhöfer in Curtius and Kaupert 1881, 63, no. 71). This might imply that the theatre was integral to Hippodamus' design of Piraeus town ca. 450 or a little later (some down-dating, even as far as the Periclean period, is now in vogue: Shipley 2005, 352; Gill 2006), or that a pre-existing theatre was accommodated within it. Given the evidence that Hippodamus was particularly concerned with areas and buildings that had specific public functions, we might in any case suppose that the theatre in the Mounichian *nemesis* or 'layout' of his town plan would have received his attention. Good evidence that Mounichia did come within Hippodamus' remit comes in the form of a boundary marker, dated approximately to the middle of the fifth century, which it is agreed reflects the work of the Milesian urban planner (*IG* I³ 1113 [ἄ]χρι τ[ε̃|σ]δε τε̃ς | hοδõ τε̃|ιδε hε Μ|ονιχία|ς ἐστὶ νέ|μησις 'Here, as far as this street, is the layout of Mounichia'; McCredie 1971, 97; Jones 2004, 231).

The theatre was subjected to an emergency 'excavation' in the early 1880s prior to domestic construction on the site. This was so hasty as to exclude even the most basic understanding of its morphology, with the result that virtually nothing can be said with any confidence about this important early Attic theatre. Part of a covered drain around the orchestra was found, and the first row of seats above it, and from the limited indications available about the nature of these finds it appears that the orchestra was rectilinear, as one would have in any case expected in a theatre of this age (Dragatsis 1879; Philios 1881, 57–61; Anti 1947, 136–8; Travlos 1988, 342; Eickstedt 1991, 167–8; Goette and Hammerstädt 2004, illust. 51; Bressan 2009, 40; Tozzi 2016, 71).

A sanctuary of Dionysus (Dionysion) attested by a fifth-century boundary marker was probably close to the theatre (*IG* I³ 1077 ὅρος | Διονυσίο: place of erection not recorded; for other views as to the site of the sanctuary see Garland 1987, 221). Two somewhat similar boundary markers at some point found their way into the garden of the French School at Athens, but it is impossible to say to which Athenian sanctuary of Dionysus they refer (*IG* II³ 4, 1837–8 ὅρος | Διον(υσίο)). The proximity of sanctuary to theatre is suggested by the decree of 324/3 concerning the lease of the theatre (**Vvi**), which permits the lessees 'to use stones and earth from the san[ctuary] of Dionysus' ἐκ τοῦ τεμ[ένους] τοῦ Διονύσου l. 4 in building works related to the theatre. Langdon (2000, 249) believes the phrase refers to quarrying and excavating and suggests that the sanctuary of Dionysus in Piraeus may have contained one of the many quarries of fine limestone known in the area. (Note the likelihood that the theatre of Thorikos was constructed on the site of a pre-existing stone quarry: **Y Introduction**.) It was here that the superbly named hero 'Neat Drinker' – Akratopotes – probably had his home (Πολέμων φησὶν ἐν Μουνυχίαι ἥρωα Ἀκρατοπότην τιμᾶσθαι: Ath. 2.39c. citing Polemon, fr. 40 Preller). To the west of this site there was, at least in a later period (second century), a private, family-based sanctuary of Dionysiastai, founded by a Dionysios son of Agathokles who was himself heroised and worshipped by the association (Jacottet 2003 I, 163–71). Note also the recent discovery of the handle of an Archaic kantharos inscribed as belonging to Dionysus (ΤΟ ΔΙΟΝΥΣ) in a building on the road from Athens to Piraeus, not far from Mounichia (Syropoulos 2013, 63–4; *SEG* 62, 44). The building may have been the meeting place of a Dionysiac thiasos in the area.

Although beyond the chronological limits of this book, it is worth noting that a second, small theatre was built in Piraeus, at Zea, in the first half of the second century, at least in part funded by public subscription (*IG* II² 2334 with Migeotte 1992; Perrin 1997, 202–3; Moretti 2010). Excavated late in the nineteenth century and not over-built, this had a curvilinear orchestra, and appears never to have been modified along Roman lines but maintained its Greek structure well into the Roman period, while continuing to remain in use (Dörpfeld and Reisch 1896, 98; Bressan 2009, 45).

The Festival

Such evidence as we have suggests that the Piraean festival was, like other deme Dionysia, held in Posideon. In the so-called 'dermatikon accounts' recording receipts from the sale of hides of beasts sacrificed at major Athenian festivals, those festivals are listed chronologically. In these accounts the Dionysia in Piraeus falls between the Theseia, which took place on Pyanopsion 8, and the Lenaea, held in Gamelion (**I C**). Only Maimakterion and Posideon intervene. And when, meeting on the last day of the month Maimakterion, the Athenian Assembly arranged for ambassadors from Colophon to be given seats at the

Piraean Dionysia, it is clear that this festival was chosen because the ambassadors would still be in town in the coming days, during the start of the month of Posideon (**V H** on *IG* II² 456; cf. **Vii**). Meetings of the Assembly held in the Piraeus theatre seem not to have taken place outside the winter months until about the second century, when the second Piraean theatre was built at Zea, which may suggest that the wooden theatre remained in place through to Elaphebolion, serving other functions (**Vvi**). If the deme festivals were timetabled in something of a 'cycle' throughout Posideon (**Aiii**), one can well imagine the grand Piraean Dionysia placed early to form a kind of opening to the 'season'.

As in other demes, the festival was known locally simply as 'the Dionysia' (cf. Arist. *Ath.* 54.8, quoted below). When viewed from the city it might be called 'the Dionysia in Piraeus' (*IG* II² 1496, ll. 70, 136, 144 of 334/3) or 'the Piraean Dionysia' (**V H** on *IG* II² 456, of 307/6). By the late second century it was simply the *Peiraia*, Πειραῖα (**I Aiii 1a**, l. 25, of 127/6; **I Aiii 1c**, l. 13, of 118/17; cf. *IG* II² 1028, l. 16; *IG* II² 1029, l. 10). By this time it included a ritual Introduction (*eisagoge*) of the god, like – and probably modelled on – that at the City Dionysia (**I Aiii**). This striking (re)naming of the festival after the place very much implies that this was 'the' festival of the harbour town. The usage will also have something to do with a need to distinguish the Piraean from the City event – a need implied especially by an ephebic inscription of 79/8 (**I Aiv 31d**), listing among the service of the year's ephebes: 'they performed the sacrifices at the Proeresia and the Mysteria and the Peiraia and the Dionysia', where the 'Dionysia' is the City festival. This coheres with other indications that the Piraean festival was in a sense perceived as one in a 'cycle' of Athenian-urban Dionysia (**I Avi 1**).

In fact, the Piraean Dionysia stood, both in constitutional, administrative terms and in its scale and ambition, somewhere between an 'ordinary' deme Dionysia and a major ur-ban festival. Uniquely for a deme, the Athenian People appointed (by lot) the demarch of Piraeus – the man whose job it was to run the Dionysia and nominate its choregoi (Arist. *Ath.* 54.8 κληροῦσι δὲ καὶ εἰς Σαλαμῖνα ἄρχοντα, καὶ εἰς Πει[ραι]έα δήμαρ[χ]ον, οἳ τά τε Διονύσια ποιοῦσιν ἑκατέρωθι καὶ χορηγοὺς καθιστᾶσιν 'And they appoint by lot the Archon for Salamis (**IV Dxii**) and the demarch for Piraeus, who run the Dionysia in each place and nominate their choregoi'). It is not known whether he had to be a demesman of Piraeus. If not, the office was in some sense an Athenian magistracy. The festival was directly controlled by Athenian polis legislation (**I Avi 1**; **Vii**; **Viv**). Although firm evidence for this arrangement can only take it back to the early fourth century, there is no reason to doubt that it pertained also in the fifth. It is moreover clear that the cult of Dionysus in the Piraeus was a polis cult, though administered locally, for its priest was not required to be a demesman of Piraeus. A decree of the Athenian Assembly that honours one such priest of Dionysus, among others, was originally intended to be set up in the Piraeus theatre, but ended up in the city Theatre, suggesting that either site was felt to be an appropriate place to honour the Priest of Dionysus in Piraeus – a consideration that has even led Lambert to speculate that the office of Priest of Dionysus in the city and that in the Piraeus may have been held by the same man (**Viii**).

The city also shouldered significant financial responsibility for the event. Evidence re-lating to the 330s shows that one of the big-ticket items, the mass sacrifice, was funded or at least heavily subsidised by the polis: in 334/3 well over fifty bovines were slaughtered at state expense (**I C**). The strategoi offered sacrifices at the festival in 331/0 – and perhaps regularly – as they did at other major state festivals, including the Lenaea and City Dionysia (**I C**). The polis authorities of the sanctuary at Eleusis apparently made a modest sacrifice at – or at least on the occasion of – the Piraean Dionysia (*IE* 177, l. 168), perhaps signifying a desire to mark an important, quasi-state event rather than an intimate religious link between Dionysus of the Piraeus and the Goddesses. The fact that Lycurgus provided generous state funds for the prizes in the new choral contest he added by law to the festival may imply that the city had long since funded the theatrical contests too (**Vii**). The city also funded, through the monies it disbursed to the Piraean Market-wardens (*agoranomoi*), the cost of maintaining and preparing the roads for the parade (**Viv**).

The deme nonetheless exercised a fair degree of control over the theatre itself. It held the power to grant prohedria (**Vv**; **Vvi**), though this was evidently not an exclusive power over entrance to the theatre, for the city retained a power to grant seating at least, as it did by decree in 307/6 to ambassadors from Colophon (**V H** on *IG* II² 456). And the state also mandated the erection of an honorific decree in the Piraean theatre in the 330s (**Viii**). Most notably, the deme leased the theatre to entrepreneurs for the significant sum of 3,300 drachmas in 324/3. The principal duty of the leaseholders was it seems to construct the seating, which they were then entitled to sell to all those to whom the deme had not granted prohedria (**Vvi**). However, the inscribed decrees relating to this lease were it seems kept in the Athenian Agora rather than the Piraeus – or at least, the copy of them of which fragments survive was probably erected there. This suggests some degree of polis interest in this theatre lease that is not immediately apparent from the surviving text.

The programme of the festival may have aspired to match or at least to mimic that of the City Dionysia. To judge from the fact that in the second century ephebes spent a full four days in the Piraeus while performing their religious duties at the festival, it would appear that it may have lasted that long (**I Aiii 1a**, ll. 24–6, of 127/6: ἔθυσαν δὲ καὶ τοῖς ᵛ ᵛ | [Πει]-ραίοις τῶι Διονύσωι [καὶ] εἰσήγαγον τὸν θεὸν παρακ[αθί]σαντες ἐν τῶι Πειραεῖ ἡμέρα[ς ᵛ | τέτταρ]ας εὐτάκτως). As in the city, there was an important parade (*pompe*) (**I Avi 1**; **Viv**) through the broad streets of Piraeus. Its full course cannot be mapped, but will at least have included the passage between the 'Hippodamian' agora, where the office of the demarch will presumably have been situated, and the theatre. The agora was to the south-west of and quite close to the hill of Mounichia. The appearance in the second century of the ritual Introduction (*eisagoge*) of the god replicates the unusual double processional structure of the city event (**I Aiii**), no doubt deliberately.

Although only tragedy is mentioned for the fifth century (**Vi**), the presence of both comedy and tragedy known for the fourth (**I Avi 1**) is quite likely to have pertained earlier. Circular choruses were added ca. 330 (**Vii**), another elaboration probably designed to mimic the programme of the City Dionysia. As in many other demes, choregoi supported the cost of these performances. The demarch appointed them (Arist. *Ath.* 54.8), and one can only speculate as to just who might have been liable for the duty (the name of no choregos for the festival has been preserved). Sufficiently well-heeled demesmen of Piraeus were no doubt the most likely to be called upon, but given that these will have formed such a tiny minority in the town's huge population, and given too the scale of the event, it seems a fairly safe guess that the choregic net was in this case cast somewhat more widely, at least as far as the large body of resident Athenians who were not members of the deme, many of whom will have settled there for the economic advantages offered by the place. But it is also likely that the numerous metics who lived in the Piraeus were invited or even required to serve as choregoi. Some of these will certainly have had the wealth and liquidity to do so, and the *philotimia* to underpin it. Demosthenes may have had these in mind when he spoke of the 'metic liturgies' at the polis level (**II A**). Lysias and his brother Polemarchos are likely candidates. Almost certainly resident in Piraeus, Lysias declares that he and his brother have 'performed all the choregiai' (**II A**). Again, the context is that of service to the polis, but that certainly need not rule out the Piraeus Dionysia as one occasion for such service.

Vi: Euripides Competes at the Piraeus Dionysia. Aelian, *Miscellany of Stories* 2.13.

Target date: ca. last quarter 5th c. Aelian was a Roman writer active in the second half of the 2nd and early 3rd c. AD. He shared the enthusiasm for the Athenian Classical past of his learned predecessors and contemporaries in the Second Sophistic, demonstrated in his style and interests, but that need not imply a devotion to historical accuracy (N. Wilson 1997, 8–12). The *Miscellany of Stories* was left unfinished at his death. Text: Dilts.

> ὁ δὲ Σωκράτης σπάνιον μὲν ἐπεφοίτα τοῖς θεάτροις, εἴ ποτε δὲ Εὐριπίδης ὁ τῆς τραγῳδίας ποιητὴς ἠγωνίζετο καινοῖς τραγῳδοῖς, τότε γε ἀφικνεῖτο. καὶ Πειραιοῖ δὲ ἀγωνιζομένου τοῦ Εὐριπίδου καὶ ἐκεῖ κατῄει· ἔχαιρε γὰρ τῷ ἀνδρὶ δηλονότι διά τε τὴν σοφίαν αὐτοῦ καὶ τὴν ἐν τοῖς μέτροις ἀρετήν.

> Socrates seldom attended the theatre, but if the tragic poet Euripides was competing with new tragedies, why then he would go. And when Euripides was competing in the Piraeus he even went down there, for he took pleasure in his work, evidently on account of its wisdom and its poetic quality.

This anecdote forms part of a longer section treating Socrates, and in particular his relationship to the theatre – inimical to comedy, as it was inimical to him, but an admirer and intellectual companion of Euripides. It draws on a tradition of friendship between the poet and philosopher that goes back at least as far as Aristophanes' *Frogs* 1491–5 (E. *TrGF* T Fe). To this tradition Aelian (or his source) has introduced another famous topos of Socratic biography – namely that the city-loving philosopher never left Athens except on military campaign, 'not for a festival spectacle (ἐπὶ θεωρίαν), or anywhere else' (Pl. *Cri.* 52b) – but gives it a twist: so great was his admiration for Euripides that when he was producing in the Piraeus, Socrates made a trip 'even there'. The wit, such as it is, depends on knowledge that the theatre in Piraeus was hardly very distant or un-urban.

The logic of the passage implies that Euripides produced new plays in Piraeus, but it would be putting too much weight on Aelian's expression and authority to insist upon the point. Similarly, Aelian's use of the verb ἀγωνίζεσθαι for Euripides' activities is somewhat ambiguous. While it is a natural choice to refer to formal competition, in Aelian's day the verb did not necessarily have this meaning. From Hellenistic times it could be used of performers who 'gave a recital' outside an agonistic context; and often appears to have meant little more than 'perform', as in the case of the musical performers at the festival for Artemis in Eretria, ca. 340. They are certainly formal competitors and described as such. But they are also required to ἀγωνίζεσθαι a parade song for the sacrifice that precedes the contest. The verb seems simply to mean 'to perform' (*IG* XII 9, 189 = R-O II no. 73, ll. 12–14).

Vii: Lycurgus Introduces a Law Establishing a Contest of Circular Choruses in the Piraeus. **[Plutarch]**, *Lives of the Ten Orators: Lycurgus (Moralia)* **842a**. Preserved in the manuscripts of Plutarch's *Moralia*, the *Lives of the Ten Orators* is generally thought not to be a genuine work of Plutarch but may have been composed not long after his era (1st c. AD). It contains material that is demonstrably Classical. The period of Lycurgus' political supremacy (**VI I**) was 336/5–325/4 though he was prominent from at least 338 and until 307/6. Text: Mau.

> ἔτι δέ, ὡς τοῦ Ποσειδεῶνος ἀγῶνα ποιεῖν ἐν Πειραιεῖ κυκλίων χορῶν οὐκ ἔλαττον τριῶν, <καὶ> δίδοσθαι μὲν τοῖς νικῶσιν οὐκ ἔλαττον δέκα μνᾶς, τοῖς δὲ δευτέροις ὀκτώ, ἓξ δὲ τοῖς τρίτοις κριθεῖσιν.

> Ποσειδεῶνος Körte   Ποσειδῶνος codd.

> And further, [he introduced a law] to create a contest in the Piraeus of circular choruses in the month of Pos(e)ideon [or 'choruses for Poseidon'] with no fewer than three choruses, stipulating that not less than ten mnai (1,000 drachmas) be given to the winners, eight (800 drachmas) to the second place-getters and six (600 drachmas) to the third.

This appears in a section of the *Life of Lycurgus* that lists some five laws introduced by the statesman (*Mor.* 841f–42c). There are no indications of chronology, but the action will have derived from the period in which Lycurgus exercised control over the city's finances and public policy, namely 336/5 to 325/4. The addition of a new contest to a festival by Lycurgus comes as no surprise, for he oversaw an extensive refurbishment of the cults of Athens and of their financial base, as well as, more specifically, ensuring the healthy state of the theatre (**VI I**; Csapo and Wilson 2014, 422–3). At a more local level, this may also be seen as part of the systematic attention paid to the Piraeus by Lycurgus, who completed the ship-sheds and armoury there and rebuilt the navy.

The evidence is, however, not without its problems of interpretation. Was this new contest for Poseidon, as the transmitted text claims? Or was it an addition to the Piraeus Dionysia – held in the month Pos(e)ideon – which we know had hitherto hosted only tragedy and comedy, not the circular chorus (**I Avi 1**)? Since it was introduced by the full authority of a law, it at least seems clear that the contest was meant to be a permanent addition rather than a special, one-off event. It would be no surprise to learn that a festival of Poseidon took place in Piraeus, but as it happens none is recorded (for the unexpectedly limited evidence for the cult of Poseidon in Piraeus see Garland 1987, 132; Mikalson 1998, 42 thinks of the cult of Poseidon Pelagios testified in **Viii**, ll. 17–18). More surprising, though not impossible, would be the presentation of circular choruses to him, for these are largely confined to the cults of Dionysus and Apollo in Attica. A candidate for such a choral song has been identified in the pseudo-Arionic and probably 'New Musical' fragment of a hymn for Poseidon preserved by Aelian (*PMG* 939; Ieranò 1997, 273).

There is however a more serious problem. For the normal way to describe a 'contest for X-divinity' is 'ἀγών + dative of X-divinity's name'. Many instances can be adduced (e.g. ἀγῶνα … τῶι Δι\[ὶ τ]ῶι Σωτῆρι καὶ τῶι Ἀπόλλωνι τῶι Πυθίωι *IG* II³ 1, 1005, ll. 7–8), and none for the use of the genitive of the god's name, as here. In a note on the text Körte (1902) made the palmary emendation that, with the addition of a single letter, removed Poseidon and his 'unattested and implausible festival' (Parker 1996, 246) and replaced him with the month of the Rural Dionysia, Pos(e)ideon. The addition of the circular chorus, so familiar from the City Dionysia, to the festival that in some sense sought to rival it and which had hitherto hosted only drama, makes excellent sense.

The new contest is to have at least three competing choruses, and these are to be award-ed substantial cash prizes. These prizes are a particularly noteworthy novelty. Hitherto Athenian choruses appear to have received only symbolic or social prizes – the shared sacrificial ox and the bronze tripod (**I Avii 1**; **V F**). The development may suggest the existence of professional choreuts (**V E**). The 2,400 drachmas budgeted for the first, sec-ond and third-placed choruses were presumably funded under Lycurgus' law by the city. In this very period (334/3) the city was funding large-scale sacrifice at the festival (**V Introduction**). The total for the three prizes is more than twice that provided by the city of Eretria on Euboea for the fourteen place-getters in the musical contests newly added to its major festival of Artemis around 340 (R-O II no. 73). We may at least be confident that any plan authored by Lycurgus will have been economically effective as well as ritually and theatrically satisfying. In keeping with the 'Lycurgan' spirit of the times, the deme charged its own members to attend the Dionysia in the 320s (**Vvi**).

The offering of valuable prizes may imply that the competition was – unlike all other circular choruses in Athens, so far as we know – open to metics and foreigners and not con-fined to demesmen, nor even to Athenian citizens, whether resident in the Piraeus or not. For lucrative prizes frequently aim to draw talent from a wide, supra-polis field. Moreover, although any assessment of how many choreuts were likely to have been in such a chorus can be little more than a guess, it is hard to see how the urban standard of fifty could have applied, and we may wonder whether the deme could have supplied from among its own members (at least) three choruses of sufficient size and quality as not to appear a risible imitation of the city prototype. The population of Piraeus may at certain periods have come close to matching that of the city, but the number of adult male Piraeans will always have been fewer than 500. The fact that the Piraeus Dionysia was something between a deme and a polis festival (**V Introduction**) might also have liberalised its rules of choral participation.

The fact that the law apparently envisaged the possibility that more than three choruses might compete – and consequently that there was not a fixed number of competing chorus-es known in advance – should not make us doubt its authenticity. On the contrary, one may compare the situation envisaged by the decree regulating the Thorikos Dionysia, which seems to countenance a similar uncertainty and that certainly offers a close parallel for a desired minimum of three choruses (or rather choregiai) at that festival (**Yii**). A number of other features suggest the language of a formal Athenian law: the qualifier *kyklios* is attest-ed in official documents at this date (**I D** on *SEG* 25, 177), from which the term 'dithyramb' is absent (**I Avi**). And in a fragmentary law regulating an unknown Athenian festival, dated approximately to the era of Lycurgus, the section on the award of prizes shows similarities with the language reported by pseudo-Plutarch: e.g. [… τοῖς δὲ δευτέροι]ς εἴκοσιν τοῖς [δὲ τρίτοις …] 'twenty (drachmas) [to the second place-gette]rs, […] to the [third …]' (*IG* II³ 1, 449, ll. 23, with Walbank 1982).

Many questions remain unanswered. Did these choruses, like those at city festivals, represent some sort of socio-political groups – perhaps the mysterious 'Thirties' (*Triakades*) into which Piraeans were it seems subdivided for cultic purposes (**Vv**)? The arguments put above in favour of an open policy for the membership of these choruses tell against this. Were choregoi appointed to fund their performance? To this second question we may perhaps suggest a negative response (cf. Davies 1967, 39). For the valuable prizes may have served as the incentive to motivate choral groups to organise themselves independently of any choregic structure.

Viii: Decree of the Athenian Polis Honouring Four Priests of Cults in Piraeus, Including the Priest of Dionysus, and a Board of Ten *Hieropoioi*, ca. 340–330 (by orthography: occasional use of -o for -ou; prosopography: Himeraios, the brother of Demetrius of Phaleron, l. 18, died in 322/1; and likely historical circumstance: Lambert 2003 urges a date soon after the battle of Chaeronea, perhaps 338/7).

Largely intact stele of white marble, broken at top.
1.15 × 0.510 × 0.12 m.
Found near the Theatre of Dionysus in Athens 'πρὸς νότον τῆς σκηνῆς … παρὰ τὴν δενδρόφυτον λεωφόρον' (Koumanoudes 1877b).
Athens EM 7239.
Koumanoudes 1877b, 482–6 no. 3; *IG* II 5, 184b; *IG* II² 410; Lambert 2003; *IG* II³ 1, 416.
Text: based on *IG* II³ 1, 416.   Photo: Lambert 2003, 56, 58.

```
 1      [- - - - - - - - - - - - - - - - - - - - - - - - - - - - - - -]κτο Σκ[αμβωνίδ?]- stoich. 45
        [ης εἶπεν· περὶ ὧν ἀπαγγέλλουσι ὁ ἱερεὺ]ς τοῦ Διο[νύσ]ο[υ . .]
        [. . . . . . . . . . 19 . . . . . . . . καὶ οἱ ? ἱεροποι]οὶ οἱ αἱρε[θ]έντε[ς]
        [ὑπὸ τῆς βουλῆς περὶ τῶν ἱερῶν ὧν ? ἔ]θυον τῶι Διονύσωι καὶ
 5      [τοῖς ἄλλοις θεοῖς οἷς προ]σῆκε θύειν ὑπὲρ τῆς βουλῆς κα-
        [ὶ τοῦ δήμου τοῦ Ἀθηναί]ων· ἀγαθῆι τύχηι· ἐψηφίσθαι τῆι βο-
        [λῆι τοὺς προέδρου]ς οἳ ἂν λάχω[σ]ι προεδρεύειν ἐν τῶι δήμ-
        [ωι εἰς τὴ]ν πρώτην ἐκκλησίαν προσαγαγεῖν τὸν ἱερέα καὶ
        [τ]οὺς ἱεροποιοὺς πρὸς τὸν δῆμον καὶ χρηματίσαι περὶ ὧν
 10     λέγουσιν, γνώμην δὲ ξυμβάλλεσθαι τῆς βουλῆς εἰς τὸν δῆ-
        [μ]ον ὅτι δοκεῖ τῆι βουλῆι, τὰ μὲν ἀγαθὰ δέχεσθαι τὸν δῆμο-
        ν, ἃ ἀπαγγέλλουσι ὁ ἱερεὺς καὶ οἱ ἱεροποιοὶ γεγονέναι ἐ-
        ν τοῖς ἱεροῖς οἷς ἔθυον τῶι Διονύσωι καὶ τοῖς ἄλλοις θε-
        οῖς ἐφ' ὑγιείαι καὶ σωτηρίαι τῆς βουλῆς καὶ τοῦ δήμου τὸ
 15     Ἀθηναίων καὶ παίδων καὶ γυναικῶν καὶ τῶν ἄλλων κτημάτ-
        ων τῶν Ἀθηναίων· ἐπαινέσαι δὲ τὸν ἱερέα τοῦ Διονύσου Με-
        ιξιγένην Χολλείδην καὶ τὸν τοῦ Ποσειδῶνος τοῦ Πελαγί-
```

ου Ἱμεραῖον Φαληρέα καὶ τὸν τοῦ Διὸς τοῦ Σωτῆρος Νικοκ-
λέα Ἁγνούσιον καὶ τὸν τοῦ Ἄμμωνος Παυσιάδην Φαληρέια
20 φιλοτιμίας ἕνεκα τῆς πρὸς τὴν βουλὴν καὶ εὐσεβείας τῆ-
ς πρὸς τοὺς θεοὺς καὶ στεφανῶσαι [ἕκ]αστον αὐτῶν χρυσῶι
στεφάνωι ἀπὸ : ⟙ : δραχμῶν ἐπειδὰν τ[ὰς] εὐ[θ]ύνας δ[ῶ]σ[ι]· ἐπειδὴ δὲ οἱ ἱεροποιοὶ οἱ αἱρεθέντες ὑπὸ τῆς βουλῆς καλῶς
καὶ φιλοτίμως ἐπεμελήθησαν τ[ῆ]ς παρασ[τάσ]εως τῶν ἱερέ-
25 ων καὶ τῶν θυσίων [. . . . . traces 20 . . . .] τῶν ἡρ[ώ]ων καὶ
τἆλλα τὰ περὶ τὴν Ι[. . . . . traces 22 . . . .]ΙΛ[.] ἐπιμε-
μέληνται δικαίως καὶ φι[λ]οτ[ίμ]ως, [ἐπαι]νέ[σ]αι τοὺς ἱεροποιοὺς Εὔνομον Εὐωνυμέα, [Σ]υ[β]α[ρ]ίτην [Γ]αρ[γήττι]ον, Γνωσία-
ν Κυδαθηναιέα, Φιλέαν Παιονίδην, [Χα]ι[ρεφάνην Σφήτ]τιον,
30 Ἀπολλόδωρον Πτελεάσιον, [Α]ὐτο[σθ]ένην [Ξυπεταιόν]α, Ἀμία-
ντον Αὐρίδην, Ἐπικράτην Ἀφιδναῖ[ο]ν, Φιλ[όστρατ]ον Παλλη-
νέα ἀρετῆς ἕνεκα καὶ δικαιοσύνης τῆς εἰς τὴν βουλὴν κα-
ὶ τὸν δῆμον τὸν Ἀθηναίων καὶ ἐπιμελεία[ς] τῆς περὶ τὰ ἱερ-
[ὰ] καὶ στεφανῶσαι ἕκαστον αὐτῶν χρυσῶι στεφάνωι ἀπὸ : ⟙
35 δραχμῶν, ἐ[π]ειδὰν τὰς εὐθύνας δῶσ[ι]. δοῦναι δὲ αὐτοῖς καὶ
[ε]ἰς θυσίαν καὶ ἀνάθημα : [. : δρ]αχμὰς τὸν ταμίαν τοῦ δήμο
[ἐ]κ τῶν κατὰ ψηφίσματα ἀναλισκομένων τῶι δήμωι· ἀναγράψαι δὲ τόδε τὸ ψήφισμα τὸν γραμματέα τῆς βουλῆς ἐν στήλ-
ηι λιθίνηι καὶ [σ]τῆσαι ἐν τῶι θεάτρωι τοῦ Διονύσου [τ. . .]
40 [μ. . .7. . .] εἰ[ς] δὲ τὴν ἀναγραφὴν τῆς στήλης δοῦναι τὸν ταμίαν τοῦ δήμου : ΔΔΔ[.] : δραχμὰς ἐκ τῶν κατὰ ψηφίσματα [ἀ]ν-
αλισκομένων τῶι δήμωι.

(in crowns)

(I)	(II)	(III)
Φιλέαν	Ἀπολλόδωρον	Χαιρεφάνην
Ἀντιγένου[ς]	Εὐκτήμονος	vacat
Παιονίδην	Πτελεάσιον	Σφήττιον

(IV)	(V)	(VI)
Ἐπικράτην	Εὔνομον	Συβαρίτην
Γλαύκων[ος]	vacat	vacat
Ἀφιδναῖον	Εὐωνυμέα	Γαργήττιον

(VII)	(VIII)	(IX)
Αὐτο[σ]θένην	Ἀμίαντον	Φιλόστρατον
Εὐκλ[-]	vacat	vacat
Ξυπεταιόν[α]	Αὐρίδην	Παλληνέα

(X)
Γνωσίαν
Χαιρήμονος
Κυδαθηναιέα

2–3 [κα|ὶ οἱ τῶν ἄλλων θεῶν καὶ οἱ δέκα ἱεροποι]οὶ Wilhelm   25 perhaps [τῶν θεῶν
καὶ] τῶν ἡρ[ώ]ων Lambert   39–40 [τ. . .][[μ. . .7. . .], erased text   [τ[ῶι ἐ|μ [Πειραεῖ]]
Lambert: 'slight traces of Πειραεῖ are perhaps visible'   [τοῦ Ἐλ|ευθερέως] Wilhelm   41
ΔΔΔ[ˇ] or ΔΔΔ[Δ] Lambert

[... son of ...-]ktos of Sk[ambonidai proposed: in connection with the report made by the pries]t of Dio[nysus ... and the hieropoi]oi elec[t]ed [by the Council concerning the sacrifices which] they made to Dionysus and [5] [the other gods to whom] it was [appr]opriate to sacrifice on behalf of the Council an[d Assembly of Athen]s: with good fortune: the Cou[ncil] resolved that [the proedro]i who are allotted to serve in the Assemb[ly] should bring the priest an[d t]he hieropoioi before the Assembly [at its] ne[x]t meeting and deal with their [10] report; that the opinion of the Council as to the appropriate course of action be conveyed to the Asse[m]bly; that the Assembl[y] accept the good outcome which the priest and the hieropoioi report as having transpired at the sacrifices which they made to Diony[s]us and the other gods for the health and safety of the Council and Assembly [15] of Athens, and of the children, women and other possessions of the Athenians. And that we should praise the priest of Dionysus, Meixigenes of Cholleidai, and the priests of Poseidon Pelagios – Himeraios of Phaleron –; of Zeus Soter – Nikokles of Hagnous –; and of Ammon – Pausanides of Phaleron – for their [20] ambition towards the Council and their piety towards the gods; and, when they re[n]d[er] the[ir] acc[o]unts, crown them [ea]ch with a gold crown worth 500 drachmas. And since the hieropoioi elected by the Council oversaw t[h]e prov[isi]on of the sacred offerings [25] and the victims [...] of the heroes, and all the rest for the [...] they oversaw in a just and am[b]it[io]us manner, that we should [pra]is[e] the hieropoioi Eunomos of Euonymon, [S]y[b]a[r]ites of [G]ar[gett]-os, Gnosias of Kydathenaion, Phileas of Paionidai, [Cha]i[rephanes of Sphet]-tos, [30] Apollodoros of Ptelea, [A]uto[sth]enes of [Xypet]e, Amiantos of Auridai, Epikrates of Aphidna, Phil[ostrat]os of Pallene for the virtue and justice they have demonstrated towards the Council and Assembly of Athens and for the car[e] they showed for the sacred ri[tes], and crown them each with a gold crown worth [500] [35] drachmas w[h]en they rende[r] their accounts. And the treasurer of the Assembly should also give them [... dr]achmas from the money budgeted by the Assembly for matters relating to decrees [f]or a sacrifice and a dedica-tion. The secretary of the Council should inscribe this decree on a stone stele and [e]rect it in the theatre of Dionysus [i[n the [40] Piraeus]]. The treasurer of the Assembly should give [thi]rty (or [fo]rty) drachmas from the money [b]udgeted by the Assembly for matters relating to decrees for the inscription of the stele.

(the names below inscribed in crowns)

(I) Phileas son of Antigenes of Paionidai (II) Apollodoros son of Euktemon of Ptelea (III) Chairephanes of Sphettos (IV) Epikrates son of Glaukon of Aphidna (V) Eunomos of Euonymon (VI) Sybarites of Gargettos (VII) Auto[s]-thenes son of Eukl[-] of Xypete (VIII) Amiantos of Auridai (IX) Philostratos of Pallene (X) Gnosias son of Chairemon of Kydathenaion

Meixigenes, from the small deme Cholleidai (ll. 16–17), is the only Classical Athenian priest who served a polis cult of Dionysus whose name has survived. He was the son of a merchant, Mikon, who spent much of his time at sea, and a member of a wealthy family whose fortunes can be traced over several generations ([D.] 58; *APF* 56–8). Meixigenes' was not the major urban cult of Dionysus Eleuthereus (as some have thought: Wilhelm 1943–1947; Humphreys 2004, 111), but rather that of Dionysus in the Piraeus. For the priesthood of Dionysus Eleuthereus we know of no single incumbent. (**I Aiii 4**; however Lambert 2004, 106 notes that the honorand of a fragmentary decree of 326/5, *IG* II³ 1, 365, may have been a priest of Dionysus in Athens, since it was found built into a modern house east of the Theatre of Dionysus; see further below.)

That Meixigenes' priesthood was that of Dionysus in Piraeus is clear from the fact that the other cults whose priests are honoured with him are patently Piraeus-based (but polis) cults – certainly in the case of Zeus Soter (l. 18) and of Ammon (l. 19), very probably for the otherwise unattested Poseidon Pelagios (ll. 17–18); and also from the fact that Meixigenes was on another occasion honoured by the Paraloi, the crew of the sacred ship Paralos (he may have been their treasurer: *APF* 58) – and they were based in Piraeus (*IG* II² 1254). Lambert's demonstration that the original intention was to set up this decree in the Piraean theatre (below) is virtually conclusive on this point.

This document also shows that the cult of Dionysus on the Mounichia hill (**V Introduction**) was in an important sense a polis cult. Meixigenes was not a member of the deme, though he probably resided there and, although the circumstances seem exceptional, he has performed sacrifices on behalf of the Athenian state (ll. 14–16, 20), which now honours him. The priesthood was therefore either a state appointment and, like all those known to have been established in the Periclean phase of 'democratisation' of religious offices, was appointed 'from all Athenians'. Or, if it had been in existence for a long period and remained untouched by this democratising development, it is likely to have been filled by a genos which included men who were not demesmen of Piraeus, and remained so into later times (see Lambert and Blok 2009; Lambert 2010, esp. 170).

The inscription records a recommendation of the Athenian Council that the Assembly should honour a group of four priests and an associated board of ten hieropoioi. The priest of Dionysus is clearly the lead figure in this group, placed above even the priest of the major cult of Zeus Soter. The honours arise from the conduct by these fourteen men of sacrifices and other offerings 'to Dionysus and the other gods for the health and safety of the Council and Assembly of Athens, and of the children, women and other possessions of the Athenians' (ll. 13–16), and more specifically, in response to the report of good news that emerged from the conduct of the sacrifices. These offerings were evidently substantial, the situation that gave rise to them momentous. At least one of these men had a known interest in the theatre. In the same general period, Phileas of Paionidai (l. 29) may be found proposing a polis decree honouring an actor (**I Aix 3d**).

The prominence of the priest of Dionysus within the group is mirrored by the prominence of the god himself as recipient (l. 13). This appeal to Dionysus as a saviour in times of crisis finds many parallels. Lambert has convincingly interpreted the tone of 'defensive anxiety' that can be heard here as echoing from the moment of crisis occasioned by Athens' defeat at Chaeronea in August 338. But he also detects a sense of gratitude and relief in the wake of Philip's decision not to march on Athens: the sacrifices had after all proved positive, implying that the most immediate threat has passed (Lambert 2003, 62; cf. Mikalson 1998, 42–4). Was this joint and major set of offerings made on the occasion of the Piraean Dionysia, some three or four months after the battle in August 338? As that conflict loomed, the Piraeus served briefly as a place of potential refuge for the Athenians. A plausible scenario sees the Council, in the face of the defeat at Chaeronea, having made a special request of the priests of these four major cults in the town that was looked to as a place of sanctuary to sacrifice for the health and safety of the state, turning above all to the priest of Dionysus and his god. The scale of the honours awarded is correspondingly significant – a huge outlay of well over 7,000 drachmas.

A particularly fascinating feature of this inscription concerns the directions for its place of erection, ll. 37–40: 'The secretary of the Council should inscribe this decree on a stone stele and [e]rect it in the theatre of Dionysus […]'. Wilhelm (1943–1947) noticed that the final part of these instructions had been deliberately erased in antiquity. But his proposed restoration of 'in the theatre of Dionysus *Eleuthereus*', τοῦ Ἐλευθερέως cannot stand since it has one letter too many for the space. And Lambert has identified, among other traces, the first letter of l. 40 as a mu, ensuring that the original reading was 'in the theatre of Dionysus *in the Piraeus*' τῶι ἐ|μ Πειραεῖ.

The intention to erect such an honorific decree in the deme theatre is entirely in keeping with the habit of demes to set up such decrees in their local theatres, although this instance differs notably from other cases (but in a manner entirely in keeping with the distinctive administrative arrangements for the Piraeus and its theatre) in that the city is the awarding body, not the deme; and none of the recipients are Peiraieis.

Why and when was the specification 'in the Piraeus' removed? The answer lies in the fact that the stele was found by the Theatre of Dionysus in Athens, indicating that it was eventually erected in the city Theatre. Without the erased words, the instruction is most naturally read as mandating just this: 'and erect it in the Theatre of Dionysus'. One can only guess at what led to this change of plan. But the fact that the original instructions were inscribed suggests that the decision to place it in the city Theatre was an afterthought; or even that it represents a decision to move to the city a stele that had already been set up in the harbour town. We have seen reason to believe that this decree was mandated some months after the battle of Chaeronea – sufficiently long after to show signs of relief, but perhaps not so much time had passed as to remove all fear for the future. The necessity on grounds of security for commemoration in the Piraeus may not yet have disappeared. But as time went on and civic life returned more or less to normal, the city Theatre may have seemed the more appropriate place to commemorate this important and successful intervention with Dionysus. Lambert (2003, 66 n. 42) airs the further possibility that the polis priesthood of Dionysus in Piraeus was held along with that of Dionysus in the Athenian cult (Eleuthereus), comparing the way in which the priest of Zeus Soter may have had joint tenure of the city and the Piraean cult at this time. And he suggests that this may be one factor behind the redirection of the decree to the city, since priests had a degree of control over the disposition of their precincts. Meixigenes would surely have preferred the greater publicity offered by the urban site for this record of his moment of glory, but the grounds for supposing joint tenure of the cults remain slender.

Viv: Polis Decree Giving the Market Wardens of Piraeus Responsibility for the Route of the Parade for Dionysus, 320/19 (by Archon, l. 2).

Damaged stele of 'Hymettan' marble, with pediment.
0.72 × 0.42 × 0.07 m.
Found in Piraeus.
Athens, EM.
Koumanoudes 1877a, 157–8; *IG* II 192c; *Syll.*[1] 337; *IG* II[2] 380.
Text: based on *IG* II[2] 380.

1	ἀναγραφεὺς Ἀρχέδ[ι]κος Ναυκρίτου Λαμπτ[ρεύ]ς.	stoich. 31
	ἐπὶ Νεαίχμου ἄρχοντος ἐπὶ τῆς Ἐρεχθη-	
	ΐδος δευτέρας πρυτανείας εἶ Θηρα[μ]έν-	
	ης Κηφισιεὺς ἐγρα[μμ]άτευε· Βοηδρ[ομ]ιῶ-	
5	νος ἑνδεκ[ά]τει, [μ]ιᾶι καὶ τ[ρ]ιακοστεῖ τῆ-	
	ς πρυτ[α]νείας· τῶν προέ[δρ]ω[ν] ἐπεψήφ[ιζ]ε	
	Διόδοτος Ἰκαριεύ[ς]· ἔδ[οξ]εν [τ]ῶι δήμωι· Δ-	
	ημάδη[ς] Δημέου Παιανιεὺς εἶπεν· ὅπως ἂ-	
	ν ἡ ἀγορὰ ἡ ἐ[μ] Πειραε[ῖ] κ[α]τασ[κε]υασθ[εῖ] κ-	
10	αὶ ὁμαλισθεῖ ὡς κάλλιστα κ[α]ὶ τὰ ἐν τῶι	
	ἀγορανο[μ]ίωι ἐπι[σ]κευασθεῖ ὅσων προσ-	
	δεῖται ἅπαν[τ]α, ἀγαθῆ[ι τ]ύχηι δεδό[χ]θαι	
	τῶι δήμωι τοὺς ἀγορανό[μ]ους τοὺς ἐμ Π[ε]-	
	ιραιεῖ ἐπι[μ]εληθῆν[α]ι ἁπάντων τούτων, τ-	
15	ὸ δὲ ἀνάλωμα εἶναι εἰς ταῦτα [ἐκ] τοῦ ἀργ-	
	υρίου οὗ οἱ ἀγορανόμοι διαχειρίζουσ-	
	ιν· ἐπειδὴ δὲ καὶ ἡ τῶν ἀστυνόμων ἐπιμέ-	
	λεια προστέτακται τοῖς ἀγορ[α]νόμοις,	
	ἐπιμεληθῆναι τοὺς ἀγορανόμους τῶν ὁ-	
20	δῶν τῶν πλατειῶ[ν], ἧι ἡ πομπὴ πορεύεται	
	τῶι Διὶ τῶι Σωτῆ[ρι κα]ὶ τῶι Διονύσωι, ὅπ-	
	ως ἂν ὁμαλισθῶσιν καὶ κατασ[κ]ευασθῶσ-	
	ιν ὡς βέλτιστα, τ[ὰ] δὲ ἀν[αλ]ώματα εἶν[α]ι ε-	
	ἰς ταῦτα ἐ[κ] το[ῦ] ἀργυρ[ίο]υ οὗ ο[ἱ ἀ]γορανό-	
25	μοι διαχειρίζουσιν. ἐπαναγκαζόντων	
	δὲ καὶ τοὺς τὸν [χ]οῦν κατα[βε]βληκότας ε-	
	ἰς τὰς ὁδ[ο]ὺς ταύτας [ἀ]ναι[ρ]εῖν τ[ρ]όπωι ὅ-	
	τωι ἂν ἐπίστων[τα]ι. ἐπε[ιδὰ]ν δ᾽ ἐπισκευα-	
	σθεῖ το[ῦ] ἀγορανομ[ί]ο[υ ἃ ἐνδε]ῖται καὶ τ-	
30	ῆς ἀγο[ρ]ᾶς καὶ τῶν ὁδῶν [δι᾽ ὧν] ἡ πομπὴ τῶι	
	τε Δι[ὶ] τῶι [Σ]ωτῆρι καὶ τῶι [Διον]ύσωι πέμ-	
	πεται, τὰ λο[ι]πὰ χρήμ[ατα κατ]α[βά]λλειν α-	
	ὐτοὺς πρὸς [το]ὺς [ἀθ]λοθ[έτας κατὰ τ]ὸν νό-	
	μον. ὅπως δ᾽ ἂν καὶ εἰς τὸ[ν] λο[ιπὸ]ν χρόνον	
35	ὡς βέλτισ[τα] ἦι [κα]τ[εσκευασμ]έ[ν]α τά τ᾽ ἐν	

τῆι ἀγο[ρ]ᾶι τῆι ἐμ Π[ε]ι[ραεῖ] καὶ τὰ [ἐ]ν ταῖ-
ς ὁδοῖς, μὴ ἐξεῖναι [μηδενὶ μήτε] χοῦν κα-
[ταβά]λλειν μήτε ἄλλ[ο μηδὲν μήτε] κοπρῶ-
[σαι μήτ᾽ ἐ]ν τῆι ἀγορᾶι [μήτ᾽ ἐν τα]ῖ[ς ὁ]δοῖς
40   [ταύταις· ἐὰν δέ τις] τ[ο]ύτων τι π[ο]εῖ, ἐὰμ μ-
[ἐν δοῦλος . . . . . 11 . . . . . λ]αμ[βαν]έτω 𝈖 πλ-
[ηγὰς . . . . 16 . . . . ἐὰν] δ᾽ [ἐλε]ύθερ-
[ος . . . . 20 . . . .] = ΣΛΥΤΩΙΕ[. .]
[- -]ΣΛΣΛ[. . .]
45   [- -]. N[. .]

38–9 [μήτε] κοπρῶ|[σαι μήτ᾽ ἐ]ν τῆι ἀγορᾶι [μήτ᾽ ἐν τα]ῖ[ς ὁ]δοῖς Vatin   [μήδε]
κοπρῶ[σαι μήτ᾽ ἐ]ν τῆι ἀγορᾶι Kolbe   [μήτε] κοπρῶ|[να . . 4 . . ἐ]ν τῆι ἀγορᾶι
Kirchner   40 ταύταις Owens   μηδαμοῦ Köhler   40–1 ἐὰμ μ| [ἐν δοῦλος ἦι
ἢ μέτοικος] Kirchner   41 [δεδέσθω καὶ λ]αμ[βαν]έτω Oikonomides *SEG* 21,
307   43–4 - - - - - - - - αὐτῶι ε . | - - - - - - - - τες αν . . | - - - - - - - - ον . . Dittenberger

The registrar (*anagrapheus*): Archedikos son of Naukritos of the deme
Lampt[rai]. In the Archonship of Neaichmos; in the second prytany, of
Erechtheis, for which Thera[m]enes of Kephisia was the secretary. On the eleventh [5] of Boedromion, the thirty-first day of the prytany. Diodotos of Ikarion
was the proedros who put the motion to the vote. The people decided; Demades
son of Demeas of the deme Paiania proposed: in order that the agora in Piraeus
be made ready [10] and as beautifully level as possible, and in order that all the
needs of the Office of the Market Wardens (*agoranomoi*) might be met, with
good fortune the Athenian people decided that the Market Wardens in Piraeus
should oversee all these matters, and that [15] the expenses for them should come
from the money which the Market Wardens manage. And since the responsibilities of the City Wardens (*astynomoi*) has been additionally laid upon the Market
Wardens, the Market Wardens are to have responsibility for the [20] broad streets,
on which the parade for Zeus the Saviour and Dionysus travels, to see to it that
they are as level and as well prepared as possible, and the expenses for these
matters are to come from the money which the Market Wardens [25] handle. And
further, they are to compel those who deposit refuse on these roads to remove it
by whatever means at their disposal. And when [the ne]eds of the Office of the
Market Wardens (*agoranomoi*) have been provided, and those of [30] the agora,
and of the roads [through which] the parade for Zeus the Saviour and Dionysus
is sent, they are to [trans]fer the remaining fun[ds] to [th]e [ath]loth[etes in accordance with t]he law. In order that in the future the conditions of the agora in
Piraeus and of the roads might be [35] as good as possible, it is to be forbidden [for
anyone] to de[po]sit soil or any[thing else or] to defec[ate either i]n the agora
[or in th]ese [40] [r]oads. And if anyone d[o]es any of th[e]se things, if [he is a
slave or metic], he is to [be b]eaten […] and [if a fr]ee man […]

The date is exactly two years after the Macedonian occupation of the Mounichia hill, and
the end of the democracy that came with it. This is one of the nineteen surviving decrees

proposed by the Athenian politician Demades, at least three of which (this one aside) were concerned in some way with the Dionysia (**VI J**). Demades is best known for his political interventions on the international stage, but here we see him, in the last phase of his career – as the most powerful politician in Athens under the oligarchy imposed by Antipater – with a more local preoccupation. It is however not entirely without an 'international' angle, for the fact that the market and major roads of the Piraeus are in need of special care shows that they had fallen into disrepair, and the urban and religious repair introduced by this decree must have something to do with the Macedonian occupation of Mounichia (Brun 2000, 148; Mikalson 1998, 51).

The proposal involves an administrative reform: the Market Wardens (*agoranomoi*) are given greater powers over the agora in Piraeus, assuming responsibilities that had previously belonged to the City Wardens (*astynomoi*). Special attention is paid to the parade route: 'the broad streets, on which the parade for Zeus the Saviour and Dionysus travels' (ll. 19–20). Mikalson (1998, 52) argues that this shows that the great state-funded cult of Zeus Soter in Piraeus has become enmeshed with that of Dionysus, at least to the extent that they share a parade. Given that the festival for Zeus Soter took place some full six months later than the Dionysia, in Skirophorion, the practicalities of this are hard to imagine, even if a political context for such cultic collegiality could be imagined (based perhaps on the 'salvational' qualities of the two deities in question). It is probably safest to assume that two separate parades are intended in this decree.

And it is further at least implied that the parade met in or passed through the agora of Piraeus. Perhaps the demarch of Piraeus had his office in the agora. The roads in question are to be made smooth and kept in good condition. Other 'preparation' (ll. 22–3) might have included the construction of bleachers for viewers, as is likely in the city. If Owens (1983, 46) is right to restore 'these' ([ταύταις]) roads in l. 40, the remit of the Market Wardens will be not the general sanitation of public streets of Piraeus but only the route of the parade.

The new arrangements mean that, in financial terms, the Market Wardens have some responsibility for the festival's parade in the future. Their office in the busy and lucrative port town was doubtless well-resourced (as is implied by the prospect of a surplus at ll. 28–34).

Vv: Deme Decree of Piraeus Honouring Kallidamas of Cholleidai with Prohedria and a Crown at the Tragic Agon, (?) shortly after 260 (a date after the reunification of the city with Piraeus is implied by ll. 3–4, 9–11, 32–3: this is placed ca. 261 by Garland 1987, 51; ca. 281 by Gauthier 1979, 394–6; letter forms indicate a range ca. 300–250).

Unbroken white marble stele, surmounted by a plain pediment. Beneath the inscription is sculpted an olive crown. Chandler 1825, 26: 'This inscription is not more remarkable for its antiquity, which is very great, than for its fine preservation, being as fair as when first reposited in the temple of Vesta.'
0.6096 × 0.3175 × 0.06985 m.
From the Piraeus: Chandler 1774, xxxi: 'in Piraeo effossum et ab Albano sive colono in casa eius prope templum Thesei servatum.'
British Museum No. 1785,0527.7.

Chandler 1774, 72–3 no. 108; *IG* II 589; *IG* II² 1214.
Text: based on *IG* II² 1214.

```
1        Διόδωρος Πειραιεὺς εἶπεν· ἐπειδὴ Καλλ-    stoich. 32
         ιδάμας Καλλιμέδοντος Χολλείδης ἀνὴρ
         ἀγαθός ἐστιμ περί τε τὸν δῆμον τὸν Ἀθην-
         αίων καὶ τὸν δῆμον τὸμ Πειραιέων καὶ πο-
5        εῖ ἀγαθὸν ὅτι δύναται καὶ τὴν εὔνοιαν ἐ-
         νδέδεικται ἐπὶ τῶγ καιρῶν, δεδόχθαι Πε-
         ιραιεῦσιν ἐπαινέσαι Καλλιδάμαντα κα-
         ὶ στεφανῶσαι θαλλοῦ στεφάνωι ἀρετῆς ἕ-
         νεκα καὶ δικαιοσύνης τῆς εἰς τὸν δῆμον
10       τὸν Ἀθηναίων καὶ τὸν δῆμον τὸν Πειραιῶ-
         ν καὶ ὅταν θύωσι Πειραιεῖς ἐν τοῖς κοιν-
         οῖς ἱεροῖς νέμειν καὶ Καλλιδάμαντι με-
         ρίδα καθάπερ καὶ τοῖς ἄλλοις Πειραιεῦ-
         σιν καὶ συνεστιᾶσθαι Καλλιδάμαντα με-
15       τὰ Πειραιέων ἐν ἅπασι τοῖς ἱεροῖς πλὴν
         εἴ που αὐτοῖς Πειραιεῦσιν νόμιμόν ἐστ-
         ιν εἰσιέναι, ἄλλωι δὲ μή· κατανεῖμαι δὲ α-
         ὑτὸν καὶ εἰς τριακάδα ἣν ἂν αὐτὸς βούλη-
         ται. εἶναι δὲ αὐτῶι καὶ προεδρίαν ἐν τῶι
20       θεάτρωι, ὅταμ ποιῶσι Πειραιεῖς τὰ Διον-
         ύσια, οὗ καὶ αὐτοῖς Πειραιεῦσι κατανέμ-
         εται καὶ εἰσαγέτω αὐτὸν ὁ δήμαρχος εἰς
         τὸ θέατρον καθάπερ τοὺς ἱερεῖς καὶ τοὺ-
         ς ἄλλους οἷς δέδοται ἡ προεδρία παρὰ Πε-
25       ιραιέων· τελεῖν δὲ αὐτὸν τὰ αὐτὰ τέλη ἐν
         τῶι δήμωι ἅπερ ἂγ καὶ Πειραιεῖς καὶ μὴ ἐ-
         γλέγειμ παρ᾽ αὐτοῦ τὸν δήμαρχον τὸ ἐγκτ-
         ητικόν. ἀνειπεῖν δ᾽ ἐν τῶι θεάτρωι τὸν κή-
         ρυκα τραγωιδῶν τῶι ἀγῶνι ὅτι στεφανοῦ-
30       σι Πειραιεῖς Καλλιδάμαντα Καλλιμέδο-
         ντος Χολλείδην ἀρετῆς ἕνεκα καὶ εὐνοί-
         ας τῆς εἰς τὸν δῆμον τὸν Ἀθηναίων καὶ τὸ-
         ν δῆμον τὸμ Πειραιέων, ὅπως ἂν εἰδῶσι πά-
         ντες ὅτι ἐπίστανται Πειραιεῖς χάριτα-
35       ς ἀξίας ἀποδιδόναι τοῖς φιλοτιμουμέν-
         οις εἰς αὐτούς. ᵛ ἀναγράψαι δὲ τόδε τὸ ψή-
         φισμα ἐν στήληι λιθίνηι καὶ στῆσαι ἐν τ-
         ῶι ἱερῶι τῆς Ἑστίας. *vacat*
```

olive crown

Diodoros of Piraeus proposed: since Kallidamas son of Kallimedon of Cholleidai is a good man towards the Athenian demos and that of Piraeus, performing whatever [5] good service he can; and since he has demonstrated his goodwill in these times of crisis, the Piraeans decided to praise Kallidamas and to crown him with a crown of olive leaves for his virtue and honesty towards the [10] Athenian demos and that of Piraeus; and, whenever the Piraeans offer sacrifices in their communal cults, to distribute a portion to Kallidamas also, the same as for the Piraeans, and to permit Kallidamas to share the feast with [15] the Piraeans in all their cults, except in any cases where it is customary for the Piraeans to engage in them alone; but otherwise he is not to be excluded. And it was decided to allocate him to whichever *Triakas* he should choose. And he is to have prohedria in the [20] theatre, whenever the Piraeans hold their Dionysia, where it is allocated for the Piraeans themselves, and the demarch is to conduct him into the theatre as he does for the priests and others to whom prohedria is awarded by the Piraeans. [25] He is to pay the same taxes in the deme as the Piraeans, and the demarch is not to collect the *enktetikon* (property tax) from him. The herald is to make an announcement in the theatre at the contest of tragedies that [30] the Piraeans crown Kallidamas son of Kallimedon of Cholleidai for his virtue and benevolence towards the Athenian demos and that of Piraeus, so that all may know that the Piraeans know how to [35] return gratitude to those who are ambitious on their behalf. This decree is to be inscribed on a stone stele and erected in the sanctuary of Hestia.

This is one of the few public documents from the Attic demes dating from the third century. Although it falls outside the chronological limits of this book, it is included because it is evidence for a certain degree of continuity, or of resurgence, in the life of the Attic theatre in the deme which was most directly affected by the Macedonian occupation. (Macedonian power had been centred precisely on Mounichia hill, home of the Piraean theatre.) Indeed, this is the first sign of life from any major cult in Piraeus after Demetrius the Besieger expelled the garrison.

The decree honours a man of the deme Cholleidai who is clearly a resident of Piraeus. It gives rare information on a range of religious and constitutional practices: providing, for instance, the only known case of a deme charging the *enktetikon*, or property tax levied on non-members (ll. 26–7) – an arrangement that Jones (1999, 65) plausibly sees as aimed at achieving a considerable revenue to the public purse from the many internal émigrés to this deme. It also reveals that there was an inner core of sacrificial feasts from which even one as lavishly honoured as Kallidamas must be excluded (ll. 15–17). And it provides one of only two attested examples of a form of religious and social sub-grouping of deme members (for the other, in Aixone, see Ackermann 2011), in the mysterious *Triakades* or 'Thirties' (l. 18) into whose membership Kallidamas is admitted. If the Dionysia had been affected by the recent 'times of crisis' (l. 6), it was certainly active now that the harbour town and city had been reunited. The award of prohedria in the Piraean theatre – 'whenever the Piraeans hold their Dionysia' (ll. 20–1) – and the public proclamation of a crown at the tragic agon (ll. 28–9), remain valuable honours. As in a number of other demes, the demarch himself is to escort those to whom the Piraeans have awarded prohedria to their place (ll. 22–5), no doubt as an extra honour. This temporal clause – 'whenever the Piraeans hold their Dionysia' – need not imply anything less certain than the traditional, annual periodicity for the festival. And the phrase suggests that, however much the city was involved in the management of the festival, it remained in local perceptions a local event.

The decree specifies a particular area of prohedria where the honorand was to be given a seat: 'where it is allocated for the Piraeans themselves' (ll. 21–2). This implies a map of the Piraean prohedria with sections reserved for different categories. It is presumably in this same area reserved for 'the Piraeans themselves' that the deme's priests, as a category – and evidently *ex officio* – took their place (l. 23). It follows that there was also an area for non-Piraean honorands: Kolophonian ambassadors received it in 307/6 (**V H** on *IG* II² 456). Or perhaps the management and plan of the prohedria was even more complex. We know that the Athenian polis could award it, apparently without consulting the deme (**V H** on *IG* II² 456). Was there a further section especially reserved for these awardees?

As at the City Dionysia and in a number of other demes (**Eiii**; **Hii**; **Hv**; cf. Salamis *IG* II² 1227, ll. 31–3, of 131/0), it is at the agon of tragedies that the crown is to be announced (ll. 28–9). The term agon may here be taken at face value as implying a competitive format for the tragic performances of the festival. Aelian speaks of Euripides 'competing' (**Vi**) there – though the verb can also mean simply 'perform' – and the choral agon introduced by Lycurgus was certainly meant to be a genuine contest (**Vii**).

The decree is to be erected not in the theatre but in the sanctuary of Hestia (ll. 37–8). This was situated in the deme's agora, and its presence there evidently carried the same religious and political symbolism as in the city of Athens, where Hestia resided in the Prytaneion. The Piraeus agora probably had its own local Prytaneion (Garland 1987, 75, 141) which is likely also to have been the site of the demarch's office, and perhaps the starting point of the Dionysian parade (**Viv**). We can only guess at the services that prompted these honours. Nothing in the phraseology suggests that they had anything to do with the Piraean theatre (moreover, the crown depicted under the inscription is of olive, not ivy).

Vvi: Decrees Relating to the Lease of the Theatre of Piraeus, 325/4 (l. 9: Hegesias was Archon in 324/3).

Four fragments of a stele of 'Hymettan' marble (a–d), three (a–c) joining.
a: 0.079 × 0.105 × 0.038 m; b: 0.17 × 0.12 × 0.055 m; c: 0.085 × 0.11 × 0.048 m; d: 0.225 × 0.219–0.229 × 0.044–0.065 m.
a–c come from the central part of the stele. The section they form is broken at the top and bottom, but the left and right sides are preserved. d preserves the bottom of the stele, with preserved left and right sides. The gap between a–c and d can be estimated at ca. 0.10 m (Carusi 2013, 112).
a was found during excavation in 1935 in the wall of a modern house over the East Stoa of the Athenian Agora (Agora grid O 14). Its left side and back are preserved. b was found during excavation in 1952 in the foundation of a modern house NW of the Church of the Holy Apostles (also Agora grid O 14). Its right side and back are preserved. c is of unknown provenance. Its back and left side are preserved. d was acquired by Chandler in 1765 (1776, 23), and taken by him to London. Chandler records only 'Athens' as the findspot (1774, 74). It is a bit precarious to infer anything from the fact that the previous item in Chandler's collection (**Vv**), copied at the house

of an 'Albanian or peasant' near the 'Theseion', is also a deme decree of Piraeus and said to have been 'dug up in Piraeus' (1774, xxxi; cf. Stroud 1974, 291 n. 22). Its back, bottom, left and right sides are preserved.

a: Athens EM 13447; b: Athens EM 7719; c: Athens EM 13446 (a–c plastered together). d: London BM Inscription 12.

d: Chandler 1774, 74 no. 109; *IG* II 573; b+d: Wilhelm 1906, 235–9; *IG* II² 1176; a+b+d: Meritt 1960, 1 no. 1 (= *SEG* 19, 117); **c**: Meritt 1963, 12–13 no. 10 (= *SEG* 21, 521). a+b+c+d: Stroud 1974, 290–8 no. 3 (= *SEG* 33, 143); *Agora* 19 (Walbank 1991), 194–6, L13; *SEG* 57, 130 (Csapo 2007, 90–4); Carusi 2013.

Photos: Stroud 1974, pl. 4 (a–c); *GIBM* 12 (d); Carusi 2013, figs. 1–2 (a–d).

<table>
<tr><td></td><td align="center">*lacuna*</td><td align="right">non-stoich. 29–44</td></tr>
</table>

a   [τὴν] σκηνὴν προ[. . . . .]ασι[- - - ca. 12 - - -]   c
       [ἐ]άν τι βο[ύ]λωντ[αι πε]ρὶ τὴν οἰκοδομίαν,
       ἐξεῖναι δὲ αὐ[τοῖς χ]ρῆσθαι λίθοις καὶ
       γῆι ἐκ τοῦ τεμ[ένους]· τοῦ Διονύσου· ὅταν δ'
5   ἐξίωσιν παρα[διδόναι] ἅπαντα ὀρθὰ καὶ ἑ-
       στηκότα. ἐὰ[ν - ca. 5 - ἀμ]είψωσιν πρὸς τῆι σκη-
       νεῖ, κέρα[μον καὶ ξ]ύλα ἀπίτω λαβὼν πα-
b   ΝΚ[- ca. 5 -]ΛΛἰ · [ὁ δὲ χ]ρόνος ἄρχει τῆς μι-
       σθώσεω[ς] Ἡγησίας ἄρχων· τοὺς δὲ δημό-
10   τας θεωρεῖν ἀργύριο[ν] διδόντας πλὴν ὅ- ᵛ
       σοις οἱ δημόται προ[εδρίαν δ]εδώκασι·
       τούτους δ' ἀπογράψα[ι πρὸς τοὺς π]ρια[μέ]-
       νους τὸ θέατρον· εἶν[αι δὲ καὶ προεδρίαν]
       καὶ τῶι δημάρχωι κα[ὶ τοῖς ἱερεῦσι καὶ τῶι κή]-
15   ρυκι καὶ εἴ τωι ἄλλωι [δεδώκασιν οἱ δημόται]
       [τὴ]ν προεδρίαν· ὅσοι δ[ὲ - - - ca. 17 - - -]
       [- - - ca. 13 - - -]Νἰ[- - - ca. 24 - - -]

        (ca. 10 lines missing)

d   [- - - - - - - - - - - τοὺς πριαμένους τὸ θέ]ατρ[ο]ν πα[ρέ]-
       [χειν τοῖς δημότ]αις ἡδ[ω]λιασμένην τὴν θέαν [κα]-
       [τὰ τ]ὰ πάτρια· ἐὰν δὲ μὴ ποήσωσιν κατὰ τὰς συνθ[ή]-
       κας τὰς περὶ τὸ θέατρον, οἰκοδομῆσαι μὲν Πειρα-
5   έας τὰ δεόμενα, τὰ δ' ἀναλώματα τοῖς πριαμένοις
       εἶναι· ἐπιτιμητὰς δὲ αἱρεῖσθαι Πειραέας ὅταν πα-
       ραδιδῶσι τὸ θέατρον τρεῖς ἄνδρας ἐκ Πειραέων·
       ἀναγράψαι δὲ τὸν δήμαρχον καὶ τοὺς ταμίας ἀντί-
       γραφα τῶν συνθηκῶν εἰς στήλην λιθίνην καὶ στῆσα-
10   ι ἐν τῆι ἀγορᾶι τῶν δημοτῶν· παραγράψαι δὲ καὶ τὸ
       ὄνομα, παρ' ὧι ἂν κείωνται αἱ συνθῆκαι· ὠνηταὶ Ἀρι-
       στοφάνης Σμικύθο : ⲄΗ : Μελησίας Ἀριστοκράτο : ΧΗ

Ἀρεθούσιος Ἀριστόλεω Πήληξ : Γ゙ : Οἰνοφῶν Εὐφι-
λήτου Πειραιεύς : ΧΗ.   *vacat*

15   Καλλιάδης εἶπεν· ἐψηφίσθαι Πειραεῦσι· ἐπειδὴ Θεαῖος
φιλοτιμεῖται πρὸς τοὺς δημότας καὶ νῦν καὶ ἐν τῶι
ἔμπροσθε χρόνωι καὶ πεπόηκεν τριακοσίαις δρα-
χμαῖς πλέον εὑρεῖν τὸ θέατρον, στεφανῶσαι αὐτὸν θαλλῶ στεφάνωι ἀρετῆς ἕνεκα καὶ δικαιο-
20   σύνης τῆς εἰς τοὺς δημότας· στεφανῶσαι δὲ
καὶ τοὺς πριαμένους τὸ θέατρον Ἀριστοφάνην
Πειραέα, Μελησίαν Λαμπτρέα, Οἰνοφῶντα
Πειραέα, Ἀρεθούσιον Πήληκα.   *vacat*
    vacat ca. 0.35

a–c 1 e.g. [εἴ τι περὶ τὴν] σκηνὴν προ[στιθέ]ασι Csapo   5 παρα[διδόναι]
Woodhead   παρα[δοῦναι] or παρα[δόντων] Stroud   6 [ἀλ]είψωσι Meritt   ἐὰ[ν δὲ
παραλ]είψωσιν Stroud   ἐὰ[ν τι ἐξαμ]είψωσιν / ἐὰ[ν δὲ παραμ]είψωσιν Csapo   ἐὰ[ν μὴ]
Slater   7 κέρα[μον καὶ ξ]ύλα Stroud   7–8 e.g. πᾶ[ν καὶ ὅτι ἄλλο] Csapo   13
εἶν[αι δὲ καὶ προεδρίαν] Woodhead   14 κα[ὶ τοῖς ἱερεῦσι] Stroud (cf. **Vv**, ll. 23–5)
κα[ὶ τῶι ταμίαι] Woodhead   κα[ὶ τοῖς ταμίαις] Wilhelm   15 [δεδώκασιν οἱ δημόται]
Walbank and Woodhead   17 ϝ̣ι Wilhelm

[? if they make any additions around the] stage building […] If they want anything [in rel]ation to the construction, they are permitted to [u]se stones and
earth from the san[ctuary] of Dionysus. But when [5] they leave the premises,
they are to re[turn] everything in good repair. I[f they have made alt]erations to
('If they plaster': Stroud) the stage building, let them (lit. 'him') leave taking
a[ll] ti[le and w]ood [? and any other material]. The lease [ta]kes effect when
Hegesias becomes Archon. [10] The demesmen are to pay cash to attend performances, all except those to whom the demesmen have granted proh[edria].
These are to be registere[d with the] theatre [less]ees. The demarch, [? the
priests, and the [15] he]rald [are to have] prohedria as is anyone else to whom [the
demesmen have granted it]. All those who [? come from outside the deme …
    (lacuna of ca. 10 lines)
… the lessees are to] pro[vide the demes]men with the viewing area, fitted with
benches, [according t]o custom. If they do not act according to the terms of the
agreement concerning the theatre, then [5] the people of Piraeus will build what
is required and the cost will fall to the lessees. When they hand over the theatre,
the people of Piraeus will choose three men from Piraeus to act as inspectors.
The demarch and the treasurers will have copies of the agreement inscribed
on a stone stele and placed [10] in the deme's agora. They are also to add the
name of the person with whom the agreement is deposited ('they are also to
add the name [sc. of the lessees] at the place where the terms of the contract
will be deposited [?]': Carusi). Lessees: Aristophanes, son of Smikythos: 600
dr.; Melesias, son of Aristokratos: 1,100 dr.; Arethousios, son of Aristoleos, of
Pelekes: 500 dr.; Oinophon, son of Euphiletos, of Piraeus: 1,100 dr. [15] Kalliades
spoke. It was decreed by the Piraeans: because Theaios shows ambition in

pursuing the interests of the people of Piraeus now, as in times past, and has made the theatre bring in three hundred additional drachmas, they are to crown him with an olive crown for his virtue and [20] justice towards his fellow demesmen, and they are also to crown the lessees of the theatre, Aristophanes of Piraeus, Melesias of Lamptrai, Oinophon of Piraeus, Arethousios of Pelekes.

The inscription records an honorary decree (d, ll. 15–23) for a man named Theaios who had negotiated a lease for the Piraeus theatre (at Mounichia) at a cost 10 per cent higher than the anticipated price. Also honoured are a group of four lessees, evidently for agreeing to pay the extra 10 per cent. Above this honorary decree we have what appears to be part of a decree setting out the general terms of the lease (a–c; d, ll. 1–14). Because the second, honorific, decree is followed by the names of the purchasers, it is likely that both decrees were inscribed on the stone at the same time. We have a close parallel in an inscription of 332/1 from Eleusis (*IE* 85; see on **Hvi**). In that case a decree honours a man for negotiating the purchase of the lease of a sanctuary quarry, and in particular for extracting an additional hundred drachmas over the purchase price, although oddly this hundred drachmas then goes to the cost of a crown for the negotiator himself, suggesting a high degree of self-interest (in the Piraean case no such fee for Theaios is apparent, since the crown he receives is olive). The Eleusinian honorary decree is immediately followed on the same stele by the text of the decree setting out the reasons and terms for leasing the quarry and it is interesting to note that the leasing decree was proposed by the man who also negotiated the purchase and collected the surplus. Unlike the Eleusinian decree, the Piraean decree first gives the text preserving the general terms of the lease, then the honorary decree, possibly out of deference to chronological order.

The decree establishing the lease contains provisions (d, ll. 8–10) for 'copies' of the contract (*synthekai* συνθῆκαι) to be written on stone, and for one copy to be set up in the agora of Piraeus (our inscription may have been set up in the Athenian Agora: see below). The text of the decree inscribed here is not one of these copies (Behrend 1970, 87, 111–12; Carusi 2006, 21; Carusi 2013, 117). This is clear from, among other things, the absence of the name of the trustee with whom the actual written contract was to be deposited, although the leasing decree apparently requires that his name be added to the copies (d, ll. 10–11). Nor does the leasing decree contain the kind of detail one would expect to find in a viable contract: there is no surety, no guarantor, no payment dates, no expiry date, and no breakdown of the obligations of each of the contracting parties. We have no way of knowing whether these details had been established at the time the honorary decree for Theaios was passed (but see below). The present decree may possibly represent an agreement to purchase the lease even before the fine details are negotiated. In any case its principal aim was it seems formally to enable the lease by deme authority, not to record the details of a commercial transaction.

It is interesting that the contract is to be deposited with a trustee who is a private individual (otherwise the text at d, ll. 10–11 would, in conformity with normal practice, refer to the office and not the individual). This is a normal procedure for private contracts. The trustee must be a neutral party mutually agreeable to the contracting parties. Perhaps similar considerations could apply even when one of the contracting parties is the deme itself.

This is the usual interpretation of the important but difficult clause at d, ll. 8–10. However Carusi (2013, 118–20), proceeding on the assumption that the full details of the contract existed in the *synthekai*, suggests that d, ll. 10–11 may be a directive to record the name not of the third-party trustee but of the future lessees themselves, since there is no Attic parallel for a contract involving a public entity, as here, not being deposited in that entity's own archive; and further because even in the case of contracts between private individuals, when a third party trustee is involved, they are always explicitly named (Carusi 2013, 119: 'the reference to a third party yet to be named is completely without parallel'). She further suggests (2013, 120) that the, certainly unusual, expression used for the site of deposition παρ' ὧι ἂν κείωνται αἱ συνθῆκαι d, l. 11 – might refer to a place rather than a person: 'to the place where the συνθῆκαι will be deposited'. This would then be a directive to the demarch and the treasurers not only to set up stone copies of the contract in the deme's agora, but also to record the names of the lessees wherever the archival copies of the contract are to be deposited, probably a reference to the place in the deme's record office where they were to be lodged. Perhaps we might obviate some of these problems by supposing that the referent in παρ' ὧι ἂν κείωνται αἱ συνθῆκαι (d, l. 11) is to the office of a priest or other official with whom the contract was to be lodged.

Though a unique testimony to the economic management of a deme theatre, there is nonetheless reason to suppose (*pace* Slater 2011) that the general arrangement represents a widespread practice at this time in Attica and possibly elsewhere (see **Bvi**; Euboea: *ATD* I, TE 1) and, in particular, in the Athenian Theatre of Dionysus before the completion of the stone theatron towards the middle of the fourth century (**VI H**). The inscription sits within the period during which the influence of Lycurgus and his associates on Athenian politics was at its height (**VI I**; Carusi 2013, 135) and some of its features may reflect the developed techniques of financial management brought to bear on cult characteristic of the age (Csapo and Wilson 2014 with earlier bibliography). The specific interest taken by Lycurgus in the Piraean Dionysia is directly attested (**Vii**) and we may find another echo of it here in the leasing arrangements for the theatre.

The inscription gives an intriguing glimpse of the structure of a corporate venture in the management of a deme theatre. Only two of the four lessees are from Piraeus. From the figures mentioned, the cost structure indicates an original price of 3,000 drachmas for the lease, which was divided into thirds between the lessees, with one third further subdivided into halves (Behrend 1970, 87 n. 176). The extra 10 per cent was evenly divided between the thirds, but not between the sixths. Not surprisingly Aristophanes, the man with the one-sixth interest who pays the extra hundred drachmas, is a Piraean. Arethousios who pays no extra is nonetheless a recipient of a crown (though he is listed last). If this is right, the arithmetic tells against Stroud's suggestion (1974, 298) that there is another lessee involved who for some reason remains unnamed in the surviving portion of the text. We note that demesmen of the Piraeus pay 51.5 per cent of the costs, though it is impossible to know if this represents a 'controlling interest' of any sort. It is also unclear whether the original cost of 3,000 drachmas was arrived at by a process of bidding (auction), known from comparable contexts of leasing (**Yii** for another theatrical example and other parallels).

That theatres were subject to leasing arrangements should come as no surprise. We have many leases of public and sanctuary properties. Indeed Aristotle identifies the leasing of sanctuaries as one of the main tasks of the Archon Basileus (*Ath.* 47.4). Only a partial parallel is offered by the leasing of the Panathenaic stadium for pasturage between Panathenaic festivals (*IG* II² 1035, l. 50) at a much later date (1st c.). Closer in time is evidence for the leasing, for pasturage, of the Hippodrome in Delos and the stadium in Libadia (Csapo 2007, 104). The Piraeus lease, however, is something quite different from an attempt to extract profit from unused land in the interval between festivals. On the contrary, it is primarily concerned to ensure the preparation of installations for the Dionysia itself. 'Such "performance leases" may have been quite common, but this is the only undoubted example to survive' (Walbank 1991, 151). Its singularity has, however led to doubts, by Jameson (1982, 73) and by Walbank himself (1991, 159), that it is a true lease at all: they suggest that the lease is a commercial fiction that conceals a form of liturgy under the guise of a commercial transaction.

The stipulated 'performance' falls far short of the 'repairs and extensions to the theatre' assumed by Walbank (1991, 159) let alone the massive construction projects assumed by Behrend (1970, 87–8). The largely lost early part of the inscription clearly makes provisions for alterations to the stage building (*skene*), but the conditional clauses in a–c, ll. 2 and 6 suggest that this is limited to the upkeep or voluntary improvement of a pre-existing structure (see below). The only construction required of the lessees, at least in the preserved text, is the 'customary' benches for spectators at the Dionysia (d, ll. 1–3). In return the lease stipulates that the lessees are to receive admission charges from all demesmen (and presumably other spectators: it is likely that terms of payment for non-demesmen are mentioned as the text fails at a–c, ll. 16ff.) except those to whom the Piraeans have granted prohedria (see further below). Jameson and Walbank doubt that this would be adequate compensation. They were however probably influenced by Behrend's calculation of the profits from seat sales (1970, 88 n. 178). Behrend estimates, reasonably enough, a theatre of 5,000 capacity and entrance costs (as at Athens: **I C**) of 2 obols a person and 2 days of performance adding up to 3,333 drachmas, which is barely more than the lessees paid. But against this he estimates building costs many times the cost of the lease itself to conclude that ten days of performance are required before the lessees can turn a profit.

We should probably assume at least three days of performance, including a minimum of three lyric choruses, competitions in tragedy and competitions in comedy (**Vi, Vii; I Avi 1**). If we estimate a *per diem* payment of 2 obols by 5,000 visitors over three days, we have an income, from the festival alone, of 5,000 drachmas (a 60 per cent profit on the original cost of the lease). A full four-day Dionysia (implied by the four-day period of official duties of ephebes during the Dionysia at the Piraeus, albeit a good two centuries later: **V Introduction**) gives the lessees 100 per cent profit in the first year.

We do not know the term of the lease. The start date is given but not the end date. This may suggest that the legislation assumes a term of ten years, which Aristotle regarded as standard for leases of sanctuary property in Athens (*Ath.* 47.4). Or it may be that the decree leaves this open to negotiation. With a ten-year term the lessees might expect an income fifteen times greater than the cost of the lease, even if we exclude potential uses of the theatre before or after the annual Dionysia. It is in any case likely (*pace* Stroud 1974, 298) that a longer term is envisioned: the end date seems to be left vague in lines a–c, ll. 4–5 (ὅταν δ' ἐξίωσιν) and the use of continuous aspect verbs might imply a plurality of opportunities to generate income (a–c, l. 10 ἀργύριο[ν] διδόντας) and d, ll. 1–2 (if πα[ρέ|χειν] is correctly restored). Note that the expression in a–c, ll. 4–5 (ὅταν δ' ἐξίωσιν) 'when they leave' is much less abstract than expressions meaning 'when the contract expires' in which ὁ χρόνος ('the time') is the subject of the verb ἐξιέναι. The expression in a–c, ll. 4–5, while it implies expiry of the contract, actually refers to the vacation of the premises by the lessees (cf. Stroud 1974, 297). It may be deliberately vague in order to allow for an open term, a possibility of renewal or an early termination of the agreement. Wilson (2008, 93 n. 32) has suggested that the 10 per cent extra paid by the lessees and diplomatically presented by the inscription as a gift may in fact represent a 10 per cent renewal fee, such as we find attested in leases at Delos (Osborne 1988, 297).

The real value of the lease, of course, depends on the estimate of associated cost. This is much more difficult, but there is nothing to warrant the assumption that large-scale building is involved: as stated above, the conditional clauses in fragments a + b indicate that changes to the stage building (*skene*) are envisioned rather than required. It is true that the expression at a–c, ll. 3–4 which concedes the right to the lessees to employ earth and stones from the sanctuary of Dionysus 'if they want anything [in rel]ation to the construction' could point to other works, especially since parallel expressions (given by Carusi 2013, 126; see also Marginesu 2012) for such concessional granting to contractors of the right to use materials on or near the site appears in other works projects. But this is in itself an entirely insufficient basis from which to deduce that the lessees were here required to refill and consolidate the earthen slope that supported the theatron (Carusi 2013, 116 airs this as a likely possibility), an operation often required in the maintenance of theatres and known, in particular from **IV Eiii**, by the name of χῶσις or ἀνάχωσις τοῦ θεάτρου (Slater 2011, 283–5).

The only construction actually required in the surviving text is the building of benches. The word used for fitting out the theatron with benches, *hedoliazein,* is a rare but well-attested term. Usage indicates wooden seating (Orlandos and Travlos 1986, 92; Csapo 2007, 93; *IG* XI 2, 287 A 81; see also Poll. 2.197 and **VI I** for a contemporary usage in connection with the Theatre of Dionysus). The lexicographers use it for temporary wooden benches 'put-together [seating] in simple fashion from assembled planks in any given location' (*AB* 1.259.32; cf. Suda ε 257: ἐδωλιάσαι καὶ ἰκριῶσαι; *EM* s.v. ἐδωλιάσαι). It is equated to the term *ikriosai,* and so represents a seating arrangement similar to that used in the Athenian Theatre of Dionysus before the building of the stone theatre (**VI I**). Both words imply temporary seating which contractors erected in Athens for festivals, law courts and assemblies, and for which fixed postholes have been found in the Agora and most recently in the Theatre of Dionysus (Csapo 2007, 93, 103–8; Papastamati-von Moock 2014; Csapo 2015, 99–100). We do have epigraphic evidence for the cost of erecting benches of this sort: 28 staters (56 dr.) for assembling the benches (*bathra*) of the Pythian theatre at Delphi in or around 247/6 (*CID* II 139, l. 27); 2 dr. for 200 benches (*bathra*) at Delos in 302 (*IG* XI 2, 145, ll. 37–8 with addenda); and 1½ dr. to hired men who bring in the wood and 51 dr. to the man who assembles them into *ikria* in Delos in 246 (*ID* 290, ll. 240–1; **V H**). These figures may be limited to assembly, and may not include the cost of renting the planks, but they suggest that fitting a theatre with benches for even 5,000 spectators was not a huge expense (for other inscriptions recording costs for bench-work, see Csapo 2007, 104–5). The language used to describe such temporary bench-work implies that the planks were pre-cut for easy assemblage and dismantling, and that they were rented for a period of days or weeks, when needed, at relatively low cost.

As it stands therefore the lease offers a potential for huge profit. Indeed the greed of theatre managers was notorious and proverbial (**V A** on *POxy.* 4502). There is therefore no reason at all to suppose this is a liturgy disguised as a commercial transaction and every reason to think otherwise. Why after all would a liturgy be disguised this way? Official rhetoric invariably runs in the opposite direction if the true nature of a transaction is to be distorted: it disguises potentially lucrative transactions as acts of euergetism, not largesse as commerce. The fact that two of the lessees are not demesmen should also indicate that theatre management in Piraeus was no 'liturgy'. This remains true even when we acknowledge, with Papazarkadas (2004–2009, 104–5; 2011, 153–4) and Carusi (2013, 129) that one lessee, Aristophanes, is also known as a lead contributor, along perhaps with his father, to the dedication of a statue and the repair of a shrine (*IG* II² 2329, ll. 4, 10 ca. 330–320: cult unknown but Papazarkadas airs the possibility of Dionysus), and that the father of a second lessee, Arethousios of Pelekes, may have been another contributor to the same project (an Aristoleos appears at l. 11). Such euergistic commitment to local cult in the deme is far from incompatible with an interest in generating income from leasing its theatre.

Finally, we should note that the honorary decree is mainly directed at the negotiator, possibly the deme's 'leasing agent' (Walbank 1991, 160), Theaios, who convinced the lessees to pay extra, though it would be difficult to understand why his intervention is celebrated in this way, if he merely acts as a facilitator of other people's generosity.

The leasing arrangement indicates that the theatron of the Mounichia theatre was built of wood until at least the late 320s and probably until the time it went out of use: the nineteenth-century excavations recovered no hint of stone seating (though they were extremely limited and poorly documented: **V Introduction**). The reference to 'tile and wood' in a–c, l. 7, almost certainly with reference to the stage building, indicates a wooden skene with a pitched roof. There is no suggestion that the skene was temporary, but the terms of the lease do presuppose a desire to make periodic alterations and possibly regular renovations at the time of the Dionysia (compare the Delian inscriptions which indicate frequent reconstruction of the skene before it was finally built of stone in 274: Hellmann 1992, 373–5). A pitched and tile roof is hard to reconcile with the belief that the skene roof served as a theologeion or platform for divine appearances. Pitched and tiled roofs appear to be normal for surviving skene buildings, though most of the evidence is Hellenistic (Moretti 1992b, 100; Moretti 2014a, 123–33; **IV A Introduction**).

The lacuna (of some 10 lines) between joining fragments a–c and non-joining fragment d must have contained (among other things) provisions for charging visitors from outside the deme for seating in the theatre, though nothing permits us to guess whether it was more, less or the same amount as charged to demesmen. In addition to noting prohedria granted by the deme (above), the lacuna probably also contained provisions for free seating to any to whom the Athenian assembly granted prohedria: the city of Athens took a direct interest in the Dionysia at Piraeus (**V Introduction**) and assumed the right to grant free seats at it, as it did to visiting ambassadors from Kolophon in 307/6 (**V H** on *IG* II² 456). This interest may be reflected in the fact that the fragments of this decree were found in Athens and at least two of them close together in the Agora. One is tempted to conclude that this copy of the decrees was originally set up in the Athenian Agora (Behrend 1970, 87; Woodhead 1997, 139), but given the information relating to the findspot of the previous inscription (no. 108) in Chandler's collection (see above) we must acknowledge the possibility that the Piraean inscriptions were brought to the city from the Piraeus in the eighteenth century.

W | Rhamnus

Introduction

The deme of Rhamnus (tribe Aiantis; bouleutic quota 8) derived its distinctive character in large part from its position at the most northerly edge of Attic territory, far from the city and not well linked by land routes to the rest of Attica, though strategically positioned for the crossing of the Euripos and securing navigation in the Euboean gulf. This isolated frontier community took on a new dimension after the loss of Oropus in the middle of the fifth century. Finding itself very close to the Boeotian frontier, Rhamnus was equipped with its formidable garrison manned by Athenian soldiers (Petrakos 1999 I, 47–184). The military character of the place will have been given a new accent when, after the reforms of 335/4, ephebes spent their cadet year here. The presence of large numbers of temporary residents, many adolescent males among them, created a mixed community. It is clear that these groups contributed actively, and so far as we can tell harmoniously, to the life of the deme – for instance the soldiers issued their own decrees – and they are part of the explanation as to why we find evidence of a vigorous public life continuing well into and beyond the third century, when this has largely disappeared elsewhere in Attica (Oetjen 2014).

The other distinctive feature of the deme is its sanctuary of the goddess Nemesis, lying some 500 m to the south of the acropolis and garrison, and connected to it by the main road of the deme (Petrakos 1999 I, 185–303). This major cult was of much more than local significance (it may even have been under state control: Whitehead 1986a, 160) and was another draw for outsiders to this corner of Attica. A remarkable feature of the sanctuary was its operation as a credit centre. Around the middle of the fifth century it issued cash loans totalling annually between eight and ten talents, offered in packets of two and three hundred drachmas (*IG* I³ 248, ca. 450–440; *IRhamn.* 182). Likely borrowers include choregoi who had their wealth tied up in land and were in need of liquidity.

It is clear, from numerous fragments of black-figure cups with Dionysiac scenes found in the garrison, that Dionysus had a place in this community from as early as ca. 550 (Petrakos 1999 I, 324). A small clay tragic mask said to date from the first half of the fifth century and found in the tower of the gate to the acropolis might indicate a more specifically theatrical interest at this early date (referred to by Petrakos 1999 I, 326 but apparently unpublished). Clear evidence for a local festival of Dionysus with theatrical performances appears in the second half of the fourth century, and – unlike most other demes – persists into the third (and we accordingly include a number of items from this period, even though they fall outside our chronological limit: **Wiv–vii**). As in other demes, this is called simply 'the Dionysia' in an honorific decree of the third century that grants its honorand 'prohedria at the Dionysia', with an announcement to be made 'at the agon of the Dionysia' (**Wv**). Viewed in isolation one would naturally suppose that this refers to a familiar rural Dionysia, held in Posideon. Some cause for hesitation comes in the form of a dedication by the strategos Kallisthenes to Dionysus Lenaios, found in the theatre (**Wiv**). This leads

Petrakos (1999 I, 324; cf. Pouilloux 1954a, 153) to believe that the Dionysia in Rhamnus was a festival of Dionysus Lenaios, which he would accordingly place in Gamelion, the month of the City Lenaea (**II A**). The fact that only comedy is attested for the deme event is adduced in further support. Given the small sample of evidence (two items), the latter argument carries little weight, and it should be noted that tragedy was also performed at the Lenaea in the city, even if comedy seems to have had the more prominent place.

But the epithet leaves no doubt that Dionysus was worshipped under that cult title in Rhamnus. Whether that means the 'Dionysia' was also a 'Lenaea' – and whether we should place it in Gamelion – must remain open questions. The cult of Dionysus Lenaios is nowhere else attested in the demes. The Eleusinian religious authorities made a modest sacrifice at the City Lenaea (*IG* II² 1496, ll. 74–5; *IE* 177, l. 244; **H Introduction**), but that is indicative of a link between the Eleusinian Mysteries (run by the city of Athens, not the deme of Eleusis) and the (City) Lenaea, not evidence for a local Lenaea in Eleusis. It is possible that in Rhamnus the cult was offered to Dionysus Lenaios (in Gamelion) while a rural Dionysia was held in Posideon, as in other demes. Perhaps the choice to dedicate to Dionysus Lenaios was in some way connected to the control of Attica by the Macedonians during the period in question. If there were two cults of Dionysus there is no reason that they should not have had adjacent or even shared cult sites. But this extremely rare evidence of a specific cult epithet of Dionysus in association with a deme theatre provokes an important, larger question: who exactly *was* the Dionysus of the deme Dionysia? (**A Introduction**)

The Theatre (see also Petrakos 1999 I, 87–94, with photographs and plan, images 46–7).

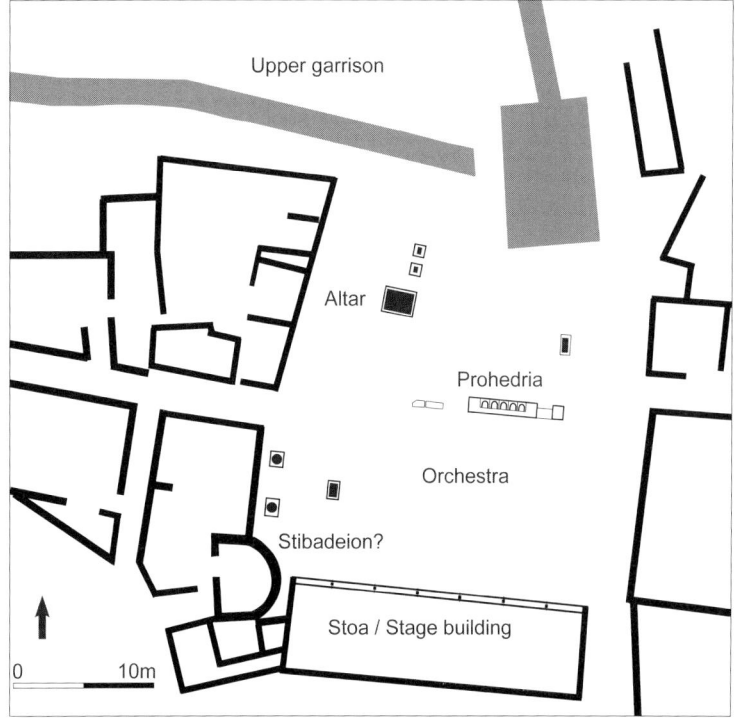

Plan of the Rhamnus theatre site.

The deme's main road enters the outer southern gate of the garrison and, passing a substantial gymnasium, opens to the east onto a space where the slope has been terraced to create an even, rectangular area some 10 × 25 m, directly below the southern gates of the upper garrison. This area formed a simple theatre, recognisable as such by the remains of its prohedria only. These, along with a number of stelai and other bases, delimit the orchestra to the north. There appears to have been no other permanent seating. The gently rising rocky ground behind the prohedria (best seen in Pouilloux 1954a, pl. 35.1), despite the presence of various dedications and altars, constituted the modest koilon. Some may even have watched from the fortress walls.

On the western edge of this theatre space there are two bases which carried columns, one originally with a statue atop; the other, probably a bronze tripod (Petrakos 1999 I, 99), affording another example of a tripod dedication associated with a deme theatre (**Hiv**; **Mviii**). In front of these, at the western edge of the playing area, was an altar, doubtless of Dionysus (1.13 × 1.82 × 0.81 m; Petrakos 1999 I, 94–5 image 51). Parallel to the prohedria a stoa (21.4 × 6.6 m) with wooden superstructure delimited the southern edge of the playing area, and probably also served as the stage building for performances (Petrakos 1999 I, 93–4 image 50). It was however a multi-functional structure, in which decrees could be erected (*IRhamn.* 30, l. 6) and probably hosted market stalls and public meetings at other times. Immediately to the west of this stoa and adjacent to the orchestra (at a level lower than it by ca. 2 m) was a semicircular construction (Stais 1891, 14–15) identified by Pouilloux (1954a, 71–2) as an example of the Dionysiac cult space known as a *stibadeion* (Picard 1944). In the absence of proper archaeological study of this and a series of associated structures, this proposal must remain hypothetical but it is supported not only by the location (ca. 5 m from the altar of Dionysus) and shape of the structure, but also by the fact that it was equipped with a water tank at its centre (that filled to a depth of 4.3 m). It evidently served some significant role in the cult of Dionysus and may have formed a focal point of the god's sanctuary. (Scant remains of a very small temple in the north-west corner of the theatre zone have been tentatively identified as belonging to Dionysus: Pouilloux 1954a, 70; note also the *mensa sacra* found in the fortress, inv. no. 2300, inscribed as 'Sacred to Dionysus' ἱερὰ Διονύσ[ου] and dated by letter-forms to the third century: *IG* II³ 4, 972.)

The theatre itself was a multi-functional space. It evidently also served as an agora (though agora, sanctuary of Dionysus and theatre could all be sufficiently distinguished, at least conceptually, so as to serve as distinct locations for the erection of decrees; cf. e.g. *IRhamn.* 23, l. 18; 43, l. 28). The space was shared by other deities – most prominently the ephebes' god Hermes, the base of whose altar lay near and to the north-west of the prohedria and who had at least one statue in the area. Another, larger altar base to the east probably belonged to Zeus Soter and Athena Soteira (Petrakos 1999 I, 95; Hermes' statue: Petrakos 1999 I, 99; other dedications in the theatre-agora area: Petrakos 1999 I, 97–100).

The set of five (or seven: **Wi**) connected marble prohedric seats was the dedication of a priest of the deme's anonymous Founding Hero, a good example of the way demes often relied on individual benefactors for significant theatrical infrastructure, and also of the interaction between the cults of the deme-hero and of Dionysus (as at Ikarion: **M Introduction**). Indeed the provision and control of prohedria in Rhamnus seems to have been in the gift of the deme's leading men of wealth and status, and to have had a primary function of preserving a record of their achievements. Directly east of the seats, and standing on the same plinth, was a statue dedicated by the priest to Dionysus. The nature of this statue is unclear (**Wi**), but Dionysus himself had at least one statue in the area (Athens NM 2328 is a large fragment of a fourth-century statue, H. 0.91 m; Petrakos 1999 I, 99, 326 image 234) and a fragmentary marble bull (Petrakos 1994, 14 no. 4) found in the vicinity of the orchestra also attests to his presence.

Directly to the west of and in line with the prohedria stood a number of stelai, the presence of which must have interfered with the view of those sitting behind them. These no doubt included honorific decrees of the deme and other local bodies, fragments of many of which survive. *IRhamn.* 1, of 356/5, honouring two chiliarchs, was to be erected 'in the sanctuary of Dionysus' ἐν | [τ]ῶι ἱερῶι τοῦ Διονύσου (ll. 21–2; so too *IRhamn.* 8). And one of the two copies of the major stele honouring Dikaiarkhos son of Apollonios at some length for his military assistance in the region to the Macedonian kings in the 'Demetrian' war of 238/7 (*IRhamn.* 17) was to go 'in the precinct of Dionysus' ἐν τῶι τεμένει τοῦ Διονύσου (l. 40; the other in the sanctuary of Nemesis). The same man was further honoured in **Wvi**, to be erected 'in the theatre'. (The site of *IRhamn.* 55, second half of the third century, is also restored by Petrakos as 'in the theatre', l. 14; cf. *SEG* 22, 129.) It seems unlikely that there was much if any distinction between 'sanctuary' (*hieron*) or 'precinct' (*temenos*) of Dionysus and 'theatre' in Rhamnus. These last examples give a rare glimpse of theatrical culture remaining active in Attica in this period (cf. also **Wvii**).

As it happens no surviving example of a decree honouring choregoi of the sort known from other deme theatres has been found. And the pattern in which honorific decrees are located at various sites around the garrison shows that a position in the theatre is unlikely necessarily to entail a theatrical aspect to the service for which honours are being awarded (see on **Wvi**; cf. Pouilloux 1954a, 129). There is in fact a certain predilection for leaving the place of erection up to the honorand (e.g. *IRhamn.* 22, l. 15; 26, ll. 28–9; 28, ll. 1–2; 38, l. 17; 39, l. 10).

At least three more individual seats were added at a later stage to the prohedria, likewise as dedications by individuals. Two of these carried inscribed honorific crowns. In the case of the first (*IRhamn.* 113, second half of the 4th c.), one crown had been awarded by the Council; in the second (*IRhamn.* 113α) 'the islands' are the awarding body, probably the Cyclades honouring a general stationed locally. It seems that in Rhamnus dedicated chairs of prohedria served as permanent records of individual civic honours. The evidence for the third seat is a little more tenuous but this one appears to have been the gift of a successful choregos in comedy (**Wii**).

Two items of evidence show that Rhamnus had a choregic system in operation (**Wii** and **Wiii**). Both date to the late fourth or even early third century, and both refer only to comedy. Given the small sample of evidence no conclusions should be drawn concerning a preference for this genre on the part of Athenian soldiers and nineteen-year-old males. In both cases the choregos appears to have served as a singleton. (There may in addition be one or two 'lost' choregoi hidden in fragmentary monuments: note the possible tripod dedication mentioned above; a small piece from a bench found near the west gate of the garrison has an inscription, dated by letter forms to the second half of the third century, that was initially restored by Petrakos to reflect a choregia: *SEG* 40, 181 [- - - χορη]γήσα[ς - - -], but he subsequently decided it was more likely to derive from a monument recounting a military career: *IRhamn.* 141 [- - - στρατη]γήσα[ς - - -]; and the 'Xenokrates son of [Phan]okrates of Rhamnus' whose name is inscribed on a large, carefully worked marble base found in the theatre near the prohedria – *IRhamn.* 116, 4th c., cf. *IRhamn.* 117 – may have been a choregos, but the lack of any correspondence between theatrical space and theatrical nature of dedication noted above prompts caution.)

For the possibility that the Rhamnus theatre was used by the deme of Marathon or the Tetrapolis for its Dionysia, see **Q**.

Wi: Dedication of a Row of Five or Seven Seats of Prohedria, second half of 4th c. (by letter forms).

The remains of five or seven connected marble seats of prohedria.
0.63–0.66 × 0.45 m (approx. dimensions of the three surviving seats, II–IV); full width of the base, with extensions for stelai: 13.90 m.
Found *in situ* in the theatre. The inscriptions are placed across the front of the base of each seat.
in situ (Rhamnus inv. nos. 1695, 1696, 1697 Φ).
IG II 3, 1191; *IG* II² 2849; *IRhamn.* 82; *IG* II³ 4, 969.
Text: based on *IRhamn.* 82.   Photos: Pouilloux 1954a, pls. 52.1, 53.1–2, 54.1–2; reconstruction: Petrakos 1999 II, 75.

I	II	III	IV	V
[- - - - -]	ἀνέθηκεν	Διονύσωι	ἱερεὺς ἥρω	Ἀρχηγέτου
[ἐπαινεθεὶς]	καὶ στεφανωθεὶς	ὑπὸ τῆς βουλῆς	καὶ τῶν δημοτῶν	καὶ τῶν στρατιωτῶν

2 [γενόμενος] Eustratiades *SEG* 40, 197

[…], priest of the Founding Hero, dedicated this to Dionysus [after being praised] and crowned by the Council and the demesmen and the soldiers.
(*Or possibly*, '[…], on becoming priest of the Founding Hero, dedicated this to Dionysus after being crowned by the Council and demesmen and the soldiers'.)

The remains *in situ* of a set of marble prohedria are the single clear physical sign of the existence and site of the theatre in Rhamnus. They were dedicated by a priest of the (otherwise anonymous) 'Founding Hero' of the deme to Dionysus, and so to the deme. (For discussion of the possible identity of the priest in question see Whitehead 1986a, 449.) The priest has been crowned by various bodies, presumably over an extended period of time: by the Council – surely that of the city, as no case of a deme equivalent is attested (Whitehead 1986a, 88–9), and explaining why this honour from the highest political organ is listed first; by his fellow demesmen; and by the community of locally stationed Athenian soldiers. The crowns were doubtless represented somewhere on the prohedria (see below). The services that prompted them are unknown. Some are likely to have been in connection with his service as priest, an office he appears still to hold at the time of dedication. The restoration of Eustratiades in l. 2 'on becoming priest' would connect his accession to that office more closely with the dedication (rendering a connection between work done as priest and the honours impossible), but this alternative has not won acceptance.

Had any of these honorific crowns also been accompanied by the award of prohedria (as for instance in **Wv**)? And so was the dedication an elaborate and particularly well-considered counter-gift, a permanent set of prohedric seats for himself and others? While there is no indication that any of the seats was reserved for a particular individual or officer – not even for the priest of Dionysus – one might assume that during his lifetime the seat that carried his name would effectively have been his own. (If there were seven seats rather than five, the one before the first as restored above is likely to have carried the priest's name, while the first as restored above, his patronymic: cf. **Wii**.) The seat inscribed with his name on the reconstruction above, at the far right (left), was the one most centrally placed to the orchestra, as the row of seats as a whole was not centred.

Large parts of three seats survive (II–IV above – a fourth disappeared some time after 1923). They have all lost their backs, but surviving fragments enable an accurate reconstruction of their form (Petrakos 1999 II, 75). The seats were connected and set on a marble base made up of three joined blocks. Petrakos interprets the sockets at either end of the upper surface of the podium as designed to hold poles for a sun-shade. Couvenhes and Moretti (2003, 769) suspect rather that these were designed to fix two more seats at either end, making seven in total. If true, we may have to assume that the inscription as restored above requires further supplementation at the beginning and end.

Petrakos argues that the upper corner of the back of another marble seat (assembled from eight fragments: *IRhamn.* 83) represents the remains of the first prohedric seat (I, the most western: it has no anathyrosis on the side). This has three inscribed crowns of olive, and a fourth, in central position, of ivy. This last and one of the others is inscribed 'the demos'. Below these words there was doubtless once the name of the honorand – on Petrakos' view, that of the priest of the Founding Hero, whose various civic crowns have been assembled in summary on this seat (presumably his own). If those four crowns represent the full complement that were carved on the seat, and if Petrakos is correct in associating it with the monument, some further weight is given to the case of Couvenhes and Moretti. For the fourth crown-awarding body could have appeared on the seventh and last (most easterly) seat proposed by their reconstruction.

The remains of this most easterly seat may be represented by four small joining fragments from a backrest (*IRhamn.* 84), and the few surviving letters of the inscription on its upper surface indicate another likely dedication to the Founding Hero: ([- - - - - - - - - - - - -] ο[- - - - - - - - - - -]ρ[.]ι, possibly [Ἥ]ρ[ω]ι 'to the [He]r[o]', at the end of the line). A striking feature of this seat is that, at some time in the third century, it was inscribed (*IRhamn.* 85, by letter forms) on its back with a graffito, albeit one completed by a skilled hand using an implement suited to the task. A few unintelligible letters aside, this represents three attempts – the last successful – to inscribe the iambic dimeter ἔπος δ' ἐφώνησεν τόδε (*IRhamn.* 85, l. 4) 'He uttered the following word'. The phrase will have been used by various poets at different times (West 1978, 2), including tragic poets (Peek 1977). It clearly featured as part of a well-known school exercise, as it appears as a graffito on the Hill of the Muses at Athens at around the same time (*SEG* 26, 274: ἔπος δ' ἐφώνη[σεν τόδε]); on a Ptolemaic ostrakon from Edfu in Egypt of the second century (*O.Edfu* 326, l. 2 = *SH* 989, where it is followed by a hemiepes that encourages West 1978 to think of an Archilochean epode); and on a wall of the Treasury of the Cyreneans at Delphi in the first century (*FD* II 107, 6, l. 2). It is possible that someone was simply practising their school exercise on the surface of the prohedric seat in Rhamnus, but Petrakos (1997, 77) makes the appealing suggestion that the writer was more targeted: the theatre was also the space of the local assembly (**W Introduction**) and this elevated poetic phrase might have occurred to someone who wished to ridicule a pompous speaker, if only in the restricted space of a graffito.

Directly east of the prohedric seats, and standing on the same plinth, was a statue, presumably also dedicated by the priest of the Founding Hero to Dionysus. All that remains are the feet of a male figure in a himation, and the base is inscribed on its right-hand side with an inscription, the few surviving letters of which indicate a date in the mid fourth century and suggest a dedicatory epigram (*IRhamn.* 112: μνημ[- - - -]‖θεοι[- - - -]‖θνη[- - - -]‖ψ[- - - -]).

Wii: Dedication of a Single Seat of Prohedria by (?) a Choregos, 4ᵗʰ (or 3ʳᵈ) c. (by letter forms).

'part of a chair' (Gandy in 1813); 'base of a large marble chair' (Walpole in 1818).
No recorded dimensions.
Seen by Leake (1835 II, 435) 'in the middle of the enclosure of the fortress'.
Present location unknown.
IG II 1278; *IG* II² 3108; *SEG* 36, 163; *IRhamn.* 115.
Text: based on *SEG* 36, 163.

1   [ὁ δεῖνα]   [τοῦ δεῖνος]   Ῥαμνούσιος
     [ἀνέθηκεν]   [νικήσας]   κωμωιδοῖς

1 [Μεγακλῆς Μεγακλέους] Petrakos *IRhamn.*

[… son of …] of Rhamnus [dedicated this after a victory] in comedy.

On a basis of a full study of the remains of the prohedric seating of the Rhamnusian theatre, much of it assembled only in the 1980s and 1990s, and drawing on unpublished notes of early travellers, Petrakos (1979, 53 no. 75; 79 pl. 40) has proposed a restoration of this monument and its inscription radically different from earlier editions. The stones are now lost, but descriptions made in the nineteenth century clearly indicate that this was part of prohedric seating. And comparison with the way continuous inscriptions are placed across the front of other connected prohedric seats (**Wi**) suggests that the inscription recorded here formed one part of a set of more than one seat. Petrakos' reconstruction makes it three.

We print above Petrakos' initial restoration of 1979 rather than that of his corpus, since the only reason for introducing the name of Megakles is that he is known from **Wiii** as a comic choregos. There were surely many others.

Wiii: Dedication by Megakles son of Megakles of Rhamnus of a Statue, Probably of Themis, after being Crowned for Various Services and having Won a Number of Agonistic Victories, Including as Choregos in Comedy, second half of 4th c. or 300–275 (see below).

A female statue, probably of Themis, on inscribed base: ll. 1–3 inscribed directly under moulding; ll. 4–5 lower on base.
0.296 × 0.904 × 0.786 m.
Found near the corner of the cella of the small temple (probably of Themis) within the sanctuary of Nemesis.
Athens NM 231.
IG II 5, 1233c; *IG* II² 3109; *IRhamn.* 120; *IG* II³ 4, 513.
Text: based on *IG* II³ 4, 513.
Photos: Pouilloux 1954a, pl. 58.3, 59.2–6; Petrakos 1991, 22 fig. 13; *IG* II³ 4,1 tab. LXIX.

```
1      Μεγακλῆς Μεγακλ[έους Ῥαμ]νούσ[ι]ος ἀνέθηκεν Θέμιδι στεφανωθεὶς ὑπὸ τῶν
          δημοτῶν δικαι-
       οσύνης ἕνεκα ἐ[πὶ ἱ]ερείας Καλλιστοῦς καὶ νικήσας παισὶ καὶ ἀνδράσι
          γυμνασιαρχῶν
       καὶ Φειδοστράτης Νεμέσει ἱερείας     κωμωιδοῖς χορηγῶν
                              vacat
                     Χαιρέστρατος Χαιρεδήμου
5                     Ῥαμνούσιος ἐπόησε.
```

Megakles son of Megakl[es of Rham]nus dedicated this to Themis after being crowned by his fellow demesmen for his justice, when Kallisto was priestess (sc. of Themis) and Pheidostrate was priestess of Nemesis; and after a victory with boys and with men as gymnasiarch; and as choregos in comedy.
Chairestratos son of Chairedemos[5] of Rhamnus made this.

The date of this monument is much disputed, the argument resting largely on the rather soft terrain of stylistic grounds for the sculpture; while assumptions about the abolition of the choregia by Demetrius of Phaleron that rest on foundations nearly as insecure have played a part in keeping the date before ca. 310 (**V I**). The letter forms have suggested to most experts a date in the first quarter of the third century. Most recently, Petrakos opts broadly for the second half of the fourth century, apparently identifying the sculptor, Chairestratos son of Chairedemos of Rhamnus, with a Rhamnusian of that name known to have served on the Council in 328/7 (*Agora* 15, 49, l. 49), rather than seeing the latter as a homonymous grandfather. Megakles' choregia is the latest approximately datable choregia in Attica, though it could have been performed some time before this dedication.

This dedication poses many questions of interpretation, most of which may be safely left to one side since tangential to the subject at hand: Is the statue truly of the goddess Themis? What is the relationship between the two priestesshoods, and their role as dating formulae? Do the agonistic victories date from the same time as the civic crown, or are they earlier, or later? Palagia (1994, 118) offers a good summary to that date of the disputed identification of the figure as Themis. She thinks the addition of the agonistic victories is 'an afterthought'. Perhaps we should talk rather of a poorly drafted layout for the inscription.

This is the best evidence for choregia in the Rhamnus theatre, since the comic performance was surely at the local Dionysia (the gymnasiarchies were doubtless local too, probably at the Great Nemesia, with its gymnic agon: *IRhamn.* 7; Petrakos 1999 I, 294–6). The syntax of the inscription is far from clear (some important clarifications by Wilhelm 1940), but we must understand the 'after a victory' νικήσας used of the gymnastic victories in l. 2 also with the present participle 'as choregos' χορηγῶν in l. 3, suggesting that the performance of comedy was also agonistic.

Megakles chose to memorialise his array of achievements with a major dedication to Themis. The only certain record of a choregic victory in Rhamnus thus comes not from the theatre but the great sanctuary of Nemesis, and in fact it is a record that has seemingly been appended to a commemoration primarily of other civic activities. It appears from this that the deme's major sanctuary was the preferred site for the commemoration of a career of achievements, civic and agonistic. The evidence of the theatre's prohedria shows similarly that civic and agonistic commemoration coexisted there (though the former is also more abundantly in evidence in the theatre).

Wiv: Dedication to Dionysus Lenaios by the Strategos Kallisthenes, 253/2–252/1 (on the assumption that *IRhamn.* 136 is to be associated with *IRhamn.* 137).

Small, nearly complete Ionic cornice made up of four fragments: ll. 1–2 (*IRhamn.* 136) inscribed on cornice; fragmentary marble base with six inscribed crowns: ll. 3–7 (*IRhamn.* 137).
Cornice: 0.22 × 1.15 × 0.39 m.
Both found in the region of the theatre during the excavations of 1891 by Stais.
Cornice: *ex* Athens EM 12725 + 13124, now joined with two other fragments and in Rhamnus (1001); fragments of base now lost.
Stais 1891, 16; *IG* II² 2854; *IRhamn.* 136 + *IRhamn.* 137; *IG* II³ 4, 292.
Text: based on *IRhamn.* 136–7.   Photo: Petrakos 1999 II, 110 (*IRhamn.* 136).

1   Καλλι[σθ]ένης Κλεοβούλου Προσπάλτιος στρατηγὸς χ[ε]ιροτονηθεὶς ἐπὶ τὴν
      παραλίαν
      στεφα[νω]θεὶς ὑπὸ τῆς βουλῆς καὶ τοῦ δήμου Διονύ[σωι] Λ[η]να[ί]ωι
      ἀνέθ[η]κεν.

crown	*crown*	*crown*	*crown*	*crown*	*crown*
3 οἱ ἱππεῖς	ἡ βουλή,	ἡ βουλή, ὁ	ἡ βουλή, ὁ	ἡ βουλή, ὁ	οἱ ἱππεῖς
φυλαρχή-	ὁ δῆμος φυ-	δῆμος στρα-	δῆμος στρα-	δῆμος ἱππαρ-	ἱππαρχή-

5 σαντα	λαρχήσαν-	τηγήσαντα	τηγήσαντα	χήσαντα	σαντα
ἐπὶ Φιλο-	τα ἐπὶ Φι-	ἐπὶ Φανο-	ἐπὶ Φει-	ἐπὶ Ἀντι-	ἐπὶ Ἀντι-
[στ]ράτου	λοστράτου	στράτου	[δο]στράτου	μάχου	μάχου

Kalli[sth]enes son of Kleoboulos of Prospalta, after his election as strategos for the coast and crow[n]ing by the Council and Demos, made this dedication to Diony[sus] L[e]na[i]os.

(*in a crown*) The cavalry, after his service as phylarch, in the Archonship of Philo[st]ratos. (*in a crown*) The Council, the Demos, after his service as phylarch, in the Archonship of Philostratos. (*in a crown*) The Council, the Demos, after his service as strategos, in the Archonship of Phanostratos. (*in a crown*) The Council, the Demos, after his service as strategos, in the Archonship of Phei[do]stratos. (*in a crown*) The Council, the Demos, after his service as hipparch, in the Archonship of Antimachos. (*in a crown*) the cavalry, after his service as hipparch, in the Archonship of Antimachos.

The dedicatory inscription (ll. 1–2 above) is on the front of the geison of the cornice. The inscribed crowns were on a separate marble base (the fragments of which seen in the past are now lost). Since its first publication by Stais (1891, 16) these were treated as part of the same dedication, but most recently Petrakos has published the dedication and crowns as separate entries, casting doubt on the certainty of the association, which depends on the testimony of Stais and Reiske. It is however more economical to continue to view them as a single monument (thus also Couvenhes in Couvenhes and Moretti 2003, 783).

If so, this is a dedication to Dionysus Lenaios by the general Kallisthenes for a succession of major military offices held entirely under the Macedonian occupation of Attica, inevitably associating him with the politics of Antigonus and Demetrius. Pouilloux (1954a, 122) sees this as evidence that in this period of reduced independence there were friendly relations between the garrison and deme in Rhamnus. Bulle (1928, 4) interpreted the monument as a small shrine to Dionysus Lenaios, but it seems rather to be the base of a significant dedication (Pouilloux 1954a, 122). On the epithet see **W Introduction**.

Wv: Deme Decree in honour of Kallippos Son of Theodotos Granting Honours at the Dionysia of Rhamnus, mid 3rd c. (by letter forms).

Pedimental stele of 'Pentelic' marble.
1.26 × 0.46 × 0.12 m.
Found in the sanctuary of Nemesis.
Rhamnus 4.
Mastrokostas 1958; *SEG* 22, 120; *IRhamn*. 15.
Text: based on *IRhamn*. 15.   Photo: Petrakos 1999 I, 21.

1   ἔδοξεν Ῥαμνοσίοις, Ἱερόποιος εἶπεν· ἐπαινέσ[αι]
    Ḳάλλιππον Θεοδότου Μελιτέα καὶ στεφανῶσαι

[χρ]υσῶι στεφάνωι ἀνδραγαθίας ἕνεκα καὶ δικαιοσ[ύ]-
[νης τῆ]ς εἰς τὸν δῆμον τὸν Ῥαμνουσίων, ὅτι καλῶς κ-
5 [αὶ δικα]ίως ἐπεμελήθη τῆς φυλακῆς· εἶναι δὲ καὶ προ[ε]-
[δρίαν αὐ]τῶι Διονυσίοις· ἀνειπεῖν δὲ τὸν κήρυκα ᵛ
[Διονυσ]ίων τῶι ἀγῶνι τὸ ψήφισμα· ἀναγράψαι δὲ ᵛ
[ἐν στ]ήληι λιθίνηι καὶ στῆσαι τοὺς ἱεροποιοὺς ἐν τῶι ἱερῶ-
[ι τ]ῆς Νεμέσεως.

The Rhamnusians decided, on the proposal of Hieropoios: t[o] praise Kallippos son of Theodotos of Melite and to crown him with a [g]old crown for his bravery and justic[e] shown towards the deme of Rhamnus, because he supervised the garrison in a fine and ⁵ [jus]t manner. He is to have proh[edria] at the Dionysia. And the herald is to announce the decree at the agon of [the Dionys]-ia. The sacred officials are to inscribe it [on a] stone [st]ele and erect it in the sanctuar[y of] Nemesis.

Kallippos, a member of the intramural deme of Melite, had been the strategos of the coast and thus had special charge of the garrison of Rhamnus. The deme honours him for his service. The award consists of a 'classic' set of theatrical honours: a crown (in this instance of gold), prohedria, announcement at the agon of the Dionysia, and a commemorative stele. The fact that this decree was erected in the sanctuary of Nemesis, rather than the theatre, suggests that, while the theatre remained an attractive site for the award of honours, the sanctuary of Nemesis was the most illustrious place in the deme for their permanent record. Evidently the prohedria of Rhamnus was not quite so fully personalised and individual as to prevent such *ad hoc* awards. The use of the phrase 'at the agon of the Dionysia' without further qualification may suggest that the performance programme of the festival was not very elaborate or differentiated – or perhaps that it was not known in advance.

Wvi: Decree of the Athenian Troops in Rhamnus in Honour of Dikaiarchos, ca. 240 (if dated early in the career of Dikaiarchos: Pouilloux 1954a, 129) or after 235/4 (if dated after the honours recorded in *IRhamn*. 17).

Fragment of a stele of local marble, broken at the top.
0.61 × 0.42 × 0.09 m.
Found by Stais during the excavations of 1890/1891.
Athens EM 4213.
IG II² 1311; *IRhamn*. 19.
Text: based on *IRhamn*. 19.   Photo: Pouilloux 1954a, pl. 49.

1 [- - - - - - - - - - - - - - - καὶ στεφανῶσαι κατὰ τὸν νό]-
μον [ἀρετῆς ἕνεκεν καὶ εὐνοίας, εἰδότες ὅτι χάριτας]
ἀξίας [κομι]οῦντα[ι ὧν ἂν εὐεργετήσω]σ[ιν, ἀγαθῆι] τύχη[ι]·
δεδόχθαι Ἀθηναίων [τ]ο[ῖ]ς στρα[τε]υομέν[ο]ις Ῥ[α]μνοῦν-

5   τι ἐπαινέσαι Δικαίαρχον Ἀ[π]ο[λλ]ωνίου Θριά[σιον]
           καὶ στεφανῶσαι θαλλοῦ στεφάνωι ἀρετῆς ἕνεκα καὶ φι-
           λοτιμίας τῆς εἰς ἑαυτούς· ἀναγράψαι δὲ τόδε τὸ ψήφισ-
           μα ἐν στήλει λιθίνει καὶ στῆσαι ἐν τῶ[ι θ]εάτρωι, εἰς δὲ
           τὴν ἀναγραφὴν εἰσενενκεῖν τοὺς γομ[- - - - - ·]
10   ἑλέσθαι δὲ καὶ τρεῖς ἄνδρας ἐξ ἑαυτῶν οἵτινες συντελοῦ-
           σιν τὰ ἐψηφισμένα. οἵδε εἱρέθησαν, Λέων Ἅγνωνος Ὄαθεν,
           Θεόδωρος Νικωνύμου Φλυεύς, Γλαύκων Σωσικράτου *vacat*
           Χολλείδης.

                      in a crown
                      Ἀθηναίων
15   οἱ στρατευόμενοι
                      Ῥαμνοῦντι
                      Δικαίαρχον.

[… and crown him in accordance with the l]aw [for his virtue and benevolence, in the knowledge that] they will [rec]eive worthy [returns for the good services they perfor]m: [with good] fortune: the Athenian sold[ie]rs stationed at Rh[a]mnus decided [5] to praise Dikaiarchos son of A[p]o[ll]onios of Thria[sia] and to crown him with a crown of olive leaves for his virtue and ambition towards them; and to inscribe this decree on a stone stele and erect it in the [th]eatre, and the […] are to contribute for the inscription […]; [10] and three men are to be elected from among them to see to what has been decreed. The following were elected: Leon son of Hagnon of Oa; Theodoros son of Nikonymos of Phlye; Glaukon son of Sosikrates of Cholleidai. (*in a crown*) The Athenian [15] soldiers stationed at Rhamnus, for Dikaiarchos.

The services recognised here are unlikely to have had a theatrical dimension. Dikaiarchos was a military commander with charge over Rhamnus, here honoured by the Athenian soldiers of the garrison, just as the general Kallippos had been honoured by the deme in **Wv**, and as he himself was honoured also by the deme for his military assistance during the 'Demetrian' war of 238/7 (*IRhamn.* 17). The soldiers give him a crown – of olive rather than gold – and a commemorative stele in the theatre. They do not grant prohedria. It is probably beyond their power, as temporary residents, to do so. Pouilloux (1954a, 73–4) remarks that the dimensions of the socle on the base extension immediately to the east of the five- or seven-seat prohedria (**Wi**) would fit this stele perfectly. It is thus likely to have stood right beside the prohedria.

Wvii: Honorific Deme Decree of Rhamnus, 3rd c. (by letter forms).

Small fragment of a stele of local marble.
0.20 × 0.375 × 0.075 m.
Found in the garrison.
Rhamnus 1388.

IRhamn. 58.
Text: based on *IRhamn.* 58.   Photo: Petrakos 1999 I, 59.

1   [- - - - ca. 16 - - - - καὶ στεφανῶσαι αὐτὸν χρυσῶι]
        [στεφάνωι κατὰ τὸν ν]όμον· εἶναι δὲ αὐ[τῶι καὶ]
        [προεδρίαν ἐν τ]οῖ[ς ἀγ]ῶσιν οἷς Ῥαμνούσιοι τ[ίθησιν· ἀνα]-
        [γράψαι] δὲ τόδε τὸ ψήφισμα ἐν στήλαις δυο[ῖν καὶ]
5   στῆσαι τὴν μὲν ἐν τῶι ἱερῶι τοῦ Διονύσου [τὴν δὲ ἐν τῶι]
        [τῆς Νε]μέσεως ἱερῶι· εἰς δὲ τὴν ἀναγραφὴν [καὶ ποίησιν]
        τῶν [στη]λῶν μερίσαι ὅ τι ἀνάλωμα [γ]ένηται [τοὺς ἐπι]-
        με[λη]τάς.

[… and crown him with a gold crown according to the l]aw; and may h[e have prohedria at t]he [con]tests which the Rhamnusians h[old]; and this decree is to be [inscribed] on two stelai [and] ⁵ erected, one in the sanctuary of Dionysus, [and the other in the] sanctuary [of Ne]mesis; and for the inscription [and construction] of the [ste]lai [the *epi*]me[*le*]*tai* are to allocate whatever expense is incurred.

While the strategos Kallippos had been awarded prohedria at the Dionysia of Rhamnus (**Wv**) earlier in the century, the honorand of this third-century decree is given prohedria at all the contests held by the deme. The Dionysia is no doubt among those intended, indicating that performances were still taking place there regularly in the third century. The second copy of the stele is to be erected in the sanctuary of Nemesis, and the Great Nemesia will also be intended, with its gymnic agon (*IRhamn.* 7, ll. 8–9) and various other events for ephebes, including a torch race (*IRhamn.* 98). Surviving fragments of marble seats (*IRhamn.* 121–2) may be part of the prohedria to be offered in the sanctuary of Nemesis.

X | Sphettos

Introduction

Near the southern foothills of Hymettos in the Mesogaia, Sphettos was a deme of above-average size (bouleutic quota 5; av. ca. 3.6) and wealth (Osborne 1985, 202; Marchiandi 2011, 513–14). The existence of a theatre with prohedric seating which saw dramatic performances in the fourth century, supported by choregoi, is securely attested by two items of evidence (Goette 2014, 89–90, 105; Takeuchi and Wilson 2014): the fragmentary deme decree below; and a probably choregic relief representing a tragic chorus (**V F** on Athens NM 2400). Among the ancient remains found in the area Milchhöfer also noted a number of other 'dionysiaca': a fragmentary torso of a Papposilenos with infant Dionysus and a life-size bull's foot (1887b, 97–8 nos. 99, 101).

Sphettos was strategically situated at the eastern end of the only pass through the Hymettan ranges. One branch of this pass – the 'Sphettian Road' (Σφηττία όδός Philoch. *FGrH* 328 F 108; Plu. *Thes.* 13.2; *IG* I³ 1023; Steinhauer 2009, 58–9; Kakavogianni 2009b, 188–90) – provided a more direct (though non-carriageable) route directly to Athens than the alternatives, reducing the time of travel between the city and the deme by over an hour and a half (Korres and Tomlinson 2002, 43; Takeuchi and Wilson 2014, 43). Another branch of this pass leading west from Sphettos went between the greater northern and the smaller southern peaks of Hymettos and emerged through the Pirnari gorge, thus also providing Sphettos with good access to the coastal demes on the western side of the mountains, among them Aixone, which also held a Dionysia in the fourth century (**D**). The accessibility afforded by these roads will, among many other advantages, have made it possible for performers and spectators to have made their way with relative ease from the city to the eastern side of the Hymettan range and between the demes in the central and southern parts of Attica that held Dionysia at around the same time of year. In fact there appears to have been a marked concentration of theatrical activity in the Mesogaia and Laureion: the case for the existence of a theatre in Kephale is very uncertain, but not out of the question (**N**). Kephale lay immediately to the south of Myrrhinous, which certainly held a Dionysia with theatrical performances (**R**); while Thorikos with its Classical stone theatre and vigorous Dionysia was less than 10 km further south (**Y**) – not to forget Lamptrai immediately to the south of Sphettos (**P**); Aigilia still further south (**C**); and Paiania to the north (**T**) and possibly also Oa (**S**), between Sphettos and Paiania. And on the western side of the range, accessible by the Sphettian way, were Aixone (**D**), Halai Aixonides (**J**), Halimous (**L**) and Euonymon (**I**).

Honorific Deme Decree Mentioning a Theatre, Prohedria and Priest of Dionysus, ca. 350–300 (by letter forms).

Fragment of a greyish-white marble stele, broken on all sides. The original rear side is rough-picked. A zone of 0.04 m beneath the surviving text is uninscribed.

0.2 × 0.07 (top) – 0.09 (line 13) × 0.048 m.

Found in or before 1967 in the village Philiati, west of Koropi, the site of ancient Sphettos (Traill 1975, 48; Takeuchi and Wilson 2014, 41–7 further on the archaeological and topographical context).

Brauron Museum BE 848 (with thanks to Giorgos Papadopoulos and Angelos Matthaiou).

Kalogeropoulou 1986 (= *SEG* 36, 187); Takeuchi and Wilson 2014.

Text: based on Takeuchi and Wilson 2014, with autopsy.   Photos: Kalogeropoulou 1986, 5; Takeuchi and Wilson 2014, 47 fig. 2.

```
      - - - - - - - - - - - - - - - - - - - - - - - - - - - - - -
1     [- - - - - - - - - δρα]χμὰς Ε![- - - - - - - - - - - - - -]      non-stoich.
      [- - - - - - - - - - - - -]αι περιοικο̣[δομῆσαι - - - - - -]
      [- - - - τῆς (?) Δήμ]ητρος τὸ ἱ[ερὸν (?) - - - - -]
      [- - ἐπαινέσαι Ἀπολ]λόδωρον Α[- - - - - - - - -]
5     [- - - - - - - - - - - - - - -]ιει εἰς τὸ ἱε[ρὸν - - - - - - -]
      [- - - - - - - - - - - - - ε]ἰσφέρει ἄμ[α - - - - - - - - - ]
      [- - - - - - - - - - - - - -]ν τὴν ΕΣΤΗ[- - - - - - - - - -]
      [- - - - - - - - - - - - - -]ΙΣ εὐσεβέσ[τατα - - - - - -]
      [- - (?) δεδόχθαι τοῖ]ς δημόταις [(?) δοῦναι - - - -]
10    [- - - - - - - προεδρία]ν ἐν τῶι θεά[τρωι - - - - - - -]
      [- - - - παρὰ τὸν Διο]νύσου ἱερέ[α. (?) ἀναγράψαι]
      [- - - - - τόδε τὸ ψήφ]ισμα τὸν δή[μαρχον - - - - - -]
      [- - - - - - - - - - - - καὶ] στῆσαι ἐν [(?) τῶι θεάτρωι]
      [- - - - - - - - - (?)]      vacat 0.04
```

1 [δρα]χμὰς εἰ[σέφερεν] Kalogeropoulou, who also suggested εἰ[ς τὸν or τὴν]. At the right edge a vertical stroke is clear, but it is broken on the top and to the right. The letter looks like an *iota* (Kalogeropoulou), but it could also be a pi or kappa, e.g. εἰ[σήνεγκε(ν)], ἐπ[έδωκε(ν)], ἐκ.   2 περιοικο̣[δομῆσαι] or possibly περὶ οἰκο̣[δομίαν] Takeuchi and Wilson   [τῶ]ν περιοικο[ύντων] Kalogeropoulou   3 [- - Δήμ]ητρος τὸ ἱ[ερὸν] Kalogeropoulou   [τῆς Μ]ητρὸς is also possible   5 [ὅτι . . . . . ἀφ]ίει Kalogeropoulou (?)   possibly [πο]ιεῖ or [α]ἰεί Takeuchi and Wilson   6 [ε]ἰσφέρει ἄμ[α τὰ] Kalogeropoulou   possibly ἄμ[α καὶ] Takeuchi and Wilson   6–7 (?) [χρήματα] Wilson   7 [ἐς τὴν σκηνὴ]ν τὴν ἑστη[κυῖαν] Takeuchi and Wilson or (less likely) [- -]ν τὴν ἐς τὴ[ν - -]   [ἐς τὴν στήλη]ν τὴν ἑστη[κυῖαν] Kalogeropoulou   9 [δεδόχθαι τοῖ]ς δημόταις Kalogeropoulou   [ἐψηφίσθαι τοῖ]ς δημόταις is also possible   9–10 [δοῦναι (δὲ) αὐτῶι] or [εἶναι (δὲ) αὐτῶι] Takeuchi and Wilson   10 [. . . προεδρία]ν ἐν Stroud, *SEG*, correctly   [. . . προεδρίαν ἐ]ν Kalogeropoulou   11–13 [παρὰ τὸν Διο]νύσου ἱερέ[α. ἀναγράψαι | δὲ τόδε τὸ ψήφ]ισμα τὸν δή[μαρχον ἐν στήληι λιθίνηι κα]ὶ στῆσαι ἐν [τῶι θεάτρωι]. Kalogeropoulou   Possibly e.g. [καθάπερ τῶι τοῦ Διο]νύσου ἱερε[ῖ] Takeuchi and Wilson   13 [τῶι θεάτρωι] Kalogeropoulou   possibly [τῶι θεάτρωι Σφηττοῖ] Takeuchi and Wilson

[? he] con[tributed … dra]chmas […] to build an enclos[ing wall] (*or* in con-nection with build[ing …]) the s[anctuary] of [Dem]eter [… to praise Apol]-

lodoros A[-… ⁵ because …] he [? mak]es for the san[ctuary … and] he [co]ntributes at the same t[ime ?? money for] the erec[ted ? stage building …] most pious[?ly … th]e demesmen [decided ? to give him ¹⁰ prohedri]a in the thea[tre … ? alongside *or* just as for the] pries[t] of [Dio]nysus. The de[march … is to inscribe this de]cree [? on a stone stele an]d erect it in [? the theatre ? at Sphettos].

The reported findspot of this inscription at Philiati, west of Koropi, makes it certain to derive from the deme of Sphettos. It is the tattered remains of an honorific decree for one Apollodoros (*PAA* 142150). If as is likely the alpha following the name in l. 4 ([Ἀπολ]-λόδωρον Α[-]) is the start of his patronymic, this Apollodoros may himself have been the son of an Apollodoros. This is true of his namesake from Sphettos (*PAA* 143240) who was honoured as secretary to Akamantis when presiding over the Council in 222/1 (*IG* II³ 1, 1153, ll. 52–3), and whose father was named Apollodoros (*PAA* 143235). These later Apollodoroi of Sphettos may indeed be relatives of the man honoured here, who is likely to have been a member of the deme.

Lost with the upper part of the stone is the name of the proposer; an initial statement of resolution of the deme (δεδόχθαι τοῖς δημόταις· *vel sim.*: see on l. 9 below, where the motion clause appears to be recapitulated); and much of the grounds for the award of honours. Lines 1–3 are what remain of these grounds, apparently followed by an additional motivation clause (ll. 5–8) that refers to another, ongoing contribution. The great piety mentioned in l. 8 can only be that of the honorand. Lines 9–11 then appear to be a motion formula, after which we have the award clause, granting prohedria in the theatre (ll. 10–11). Lines 12–13 (and possibly part of a lost l. 14) contain the publication formula.

A contribution of money is prominent, made by the honorand to a sanctuary (ll. 1–3). The restoration of the verb εἰσφέρειν (l. 1: εἰ[σέφερεν] Kalogeropoulou '[he] con[tributed]') was deduced by Kalogeropoulou from its clear appearance in l. 6: [ε]ἰσφέρει. While it is entirely plausible that the verb describing the honorand's further meritorious activity at l. 6 repeated the one used for the earlier action, the visible traces of the last preserved letter at the end of l. 1 could also be consistent with a pi or kappa, making ἐπ[έδωκε(ν)] '[he] cont[ributed X dra]chmas' another possibility (cf. *IE* 85, ll. 8–9, of 332/1). Whatever the verb, an aorist is in any case preferable to the imperfect. Or it may be that we are not dealing with the remains of a verb at all. A simple preposition is also possible: εἰ[ς] 'to' or ἐκ 'from'. The matter at hand will nonetheless remain one of money being directed 'to' some end or 'from' some source by Apollodoros.

The remains of ll. 2–3 are most plausibly treated as a reference to construction works related to the sanctuary, for which Apollodoros contributed funds. That the sanctuary was Demeter's is fairly certain. It is however worth recalling that among the remains from Philiati, found near the findspot of the choregic relief, is a late Classical or early Hellenistic relief of two seated goddesses, generally identified as Kybele (Meter) and Demeter, making [τῆς Μ]ητρὸς (l. 3) '[of the M]other' a possibility. Payment for the construction of or repairs to shrines is a matter very familiar in the economy of honour as it appears in deme documents (e.g. *IG* II² 1215, ll. 12–16, Erikeia?; *SEG* 21, 519, ll. 11–14, Acharnae). The most likely restoration in line 2 is part of the compound verb περιοικοδομέω, probably the aorist infinitive περιοικο[δομῆσαι] 'to build around', 'to enclose', 'to build an enclosing wall', making this a reference to the construction (of part or all) of an enclosing wall for the sanctuary. A close and contemporary parallel can be found in the motivation clause of a decree issued by the *genos* Krokonidai, praising members of a commission it had appointed to build a shrine of Hestia (*IG* II² 1229, ll. 4–7). A much less likely alternative is to read περὶ + οἰκο[δομίας/ν: 'in connection with construct[ion]'. While the sense is good, the absence of the article after περί cannot be paralleled (Takeuchi and Wilson 2014, 51–2).

Line 4 contains the proposal to honour, ἐπαινέσαι 'to praise' being a virtually certain restoration before the honorand's name. But rather than moving straight on to the stipulation of awards, the decree then has another clause outlining some further grounds for award, evidently another action in relation to a sanctuary. One promising possibility is the verb [πο]ιεῖ, used with reference to something Apollodoros had made for the sanctuary, or more generally of his 'good deeds' ([εὖ πο]ιεῖ) in respect of it. This is very probably a reference back to the delivery of funds for the sanctuary of Demeter just mentioned. By contrast line 6 has the almost complete verb [ε]ἰσφέρει 'he contributes'. The fact that this verb is in the present tense indicates that the further meritorious action it describes remains ongoing at the time of this award. It is very likely that this further contribution is directed to a different target from the sanctuary of Demeter. The probable restoration ἅμ[α] 'at the same time' points in the same direction. It appears therefore that line 5 refers back in explanation of the proposal to honour to the action already described in the preceding lines, while with line 6 the decree moves on to a further, still current, action, viz. 'to praise Apollodoros because he did good for the sanctuary (sc. of Demeter) and further because he continues at the same time also to …'.

Our only indication of the nature and purpose of Apollodoros' further benefaction consists of the remains of lines 7–8. But it is important also to bear in mind the nature of the honours which Apollodoros received for his generosity, which are of a rather unusual kind. For it is clear that he was awarded only one honour, namely prohedria in the theatre, and perhaps prohedria of a special sort (below on ll. 8–11). It is therefore quite likely that his further contribution related to the theatre in some way, since he was honoured by 'theatrical' means. A reference to theatre infrastructure could be introduced to this sentence in a variety of ways (Takeuchi and Wilson 2014, 55–6 for further discussion), but the most promising approach is to see in the letters ΕΣΤΗ (l. 7) the remains of a perfect participle of ἵστημι. The result is a contribution made towards some 'fixed' or 'standing' (probably architectural) feature of feminine grammatical gender. Kalogeropoulou's suggestion that this feature was a stele ([ἐς τὴν στήλη]ν τὴν ἑστη[κυῖαν]) is not convincing (Takeuchi and Wilson 2014, 56). The reference is very probably to the theatre's skene, for (unlike stele) this is a word to which we should expect the qualifying term ἑστηκυῖα to be applied. Apollodoros will thus have contributed funds [εἰς τὴν σκηνή]ν τὴν ἑστη[κυῖαν] '[for the sken]e that is set [up]'.

Although we are familiar with the use of the word skene alone as a technical term in modern handbooks for a theatrical stage building, it did not have that as its sole, and perhaps not even as a possible, meaning when it appeared without further qualification in texts of the Classical period. Rather, σκηνή referred to a wide variety of impermanent structures – tents, booths, cabins (Ducat 2007; Slater 2011, 282; Malouchou 2015). In Classical texts it is necessary to disambiguate the sense of *skene* and to clarify when a theatrical skene is meant. ἑστηκυῖα would have been used to indicate that the *skene* in question in Sphettos was 'the standing' or 'fixed' skene or, perhaps better – in order to capture a sense of the impermanence or provisionality that still attached to theatrical *skenai* in this period – 'the one that is now set up'.

This is not the same as what in general modern usage is often called a 'permanent' theatrical skene – by which is usually intended a skene built entirely of stone. A 'fixed' or 'standing' skene in a theatre might have been made entirely of wood (and thus be open to deconstruction), or with a stone stylobate into which wooden uprights were inserted (and from which they could potentially be removed). Its main feature is that it is not the sort of entirely temporary structure that could be taken up and moved to another place to serve another function, like a tent. And while epigraphically rare, the perfect participle of ἵστημι is in fact used precisely in connection with the skene of a theatre, the theatre in the deme of Piraeus. It appears in the phrase ἅπαντα ὀρθὰ καὶ ἑστηκότα in the inscription that records the lease of the Piraeus theatre in 324/3, in an immediate context that includes two explicit references to its skene (**Vvi**, l. 1). This is to be left 'all in good order and upright / standing' at the end of the lease. The conferral of honours on a benefactor for contributing funds for a reconstructed or restructured skene would come as no surprise.

The space available for the awards granted Apollodoros is confined to what follows the motion formula (after δημόταις in l. 9) and the start of the publication formula (end l. 11 or l. 12). And the remains of lines 10–11 make it clear that they deal with the award of prohedria, with some reference in elaboration to the priest of Dionysus. In other words, there is no space for additional awards. Apart from the praise he receives by virtue of the award of this decree and its publication, prohedria is the only concrete benefit which Apollodoros is granted for his efforts. As noted, this unusual concentration on prohedria lends considerable weight to the suggestion that the second cause to which Apollodoros contributed was the local cult and theatre of Dionysus.

The involvement of the priest of Dionysus in some connection with the award of prohedria is also entirely unique. Just what the precise nature of this involvement was is unclear (Takeuchi and Wilson 2014, 59–62). The two most likely possibilities are locational or comparative: in the first case, Apollodoros will have been offered a seat of honour '[alongside the] pries[t] of [Dio]nysus' [παρὰ τὸν Διο]νύσου ἱερέ[α]; in the second, he will have been given '[prohedri]a in the thea[tre in the same way as the] priest of [Dio]nysus' [εἶναι δὲ αὐτῶι καὶ προεδρία]ν ἐν τῶι θεά[τρωι καθάπερ τῶι τοῦ Διο]νύσου ἱερε[ῖ]. It is hard to decide which is the more likely alternative. A seat beside the priest would presumably place Apollodoros in the most prestigious seat in the theatre, offering a nice example of the possibilities in the economy of prohedric distinction available even in what was presumably a relatively small theatre. And if, as we have argued, Apollodoros had made – or was in the process of making – some sort of substantial contribution to the skene of the theatre, such a seat would give him an excellent view of the result of his own generosity and thus be an eminently appropriate means of acknowledging the benefaction. On the other hand the (imprecise) parallels are somewhat stronger for the comparative alternative (**Vv**; *IE* 80: **H Introduction**; Takeuchi and Wilson 2014, 61–2). The singular importance of prohedria to the honouring of Apollodoros, on top of the likelihood that he was thereby being thanked for contributing to the infrastructure of the deme theatre, makes it all the more likely that the stele inscribed with his decree was itself erected 'in [the theatre]' ἐν [τῶι θεάτρωι] (l. 13), possibly even 'in the theatre at Sphettos' ἐν [τῶι θεάτρωι Σφηττοῖ] (**Diii**; *SEG* 46, 155, ll. 3–5, Gargettos ca. 350–300).

By the second half of the fourth century, the theatre of Sphettos was thus furnished with prohedric seating (probably made of stone) that was granted to distinguished members and benefactors of the deme, and also – a fact only directly attested for demes here – to its priest of Dionysus. If our interpretation of line 7 as a reference to the fixed skene is valid, this theatre was also equipped with a stage building, which was in the process of being refurbished or extended thanks to the generosity of a private benefactor (**Ii**).

This is the only direct evidence in the entire corpus for a priest of Dionysus in the demes, with the (partial) exception of the priest of Dionysus in Piraeus attested by a polis decree (**Viii**; **A Introduction**). In Semachidai the daughters of the eponymous hero Semachos, who provided hospitality to Dionysus in myth, served as priestesses in his cult (Philoch. *FGrH* 328 F 206), but that cult is not known to have included a theatrical Dionysia (for the possibility that the deme joined with its neighbours Ikarion and Plotheia to share in the Dionysia in Ikarion, within the religious association known as the Epakreis, see **M Introduction**). At Sphettos on the other hand the close connection between the priest of Dionysus and the theatre is guaranteed, for his presence *ex officio* in prohedric seating was evidently the norm.

It is difficult to judge whether the pig clearly being led to sacrifice to Dionysus in **V F** (on Athens NM 2400) reflects a norm of his cult in Sphettos. The sacrifice of a pig to Dionysus is only very rarely attested, but is extremely common practice for Demeter. This might encourage us to ask whether there was some form of interconnection or interaction between the cults of Dionysus and Demeter in Sphettos, something which in itself would not be surprising and for which the decree might be thought to provide some support (**H Introduction**; **Hii**; **Hv**). For it is virtually certain that Apollodoros contributed materially to the cultic infrastructure of Demeter in Sphettos; probable that he did the same for the cult of Dionysus; and certain that he was honoured in the local theatre of Dionysus. This in turn raises the question of the physical location of the two cults, and of the theatre. The fact that Demeter and Dionysus are apparently associated in this decree – at a minimum by virtue of being the object of one man's beneficence – might suggest that the sanctuaries of the two also stood in some physical proximity to one another, or (or perhaps in addition) that they together served as the main cults of the deme. As for the theatre itself, while there is no further evidence to attest to its location and form, possibilities within the target region include a site on the slopes of the hill of Christ (which very possibly served as a kind of acropolis for the deme); or at the open area just north-east of the hill (the possible site of the deme's agora?), where the 'Sphettian Road' passed by.

Y | Thorikos

Introduction

The deme of Thorikos on the south-eastern coast of Attica (bouleutic quota 5) is the site of one of the oldest surviving Greek theatres, the oldest known theatre built almost entirely of stone, and the only theatre of fifth-century date to have survived to any significant degree. The deme was rich in mineral resources, exploited since the Bronze Age and, as the centre of works for the silver mines of the entire Laurion, will have had an industrial character unlike any other. It is a fair guess that the presence of these resources helps explain the existence of a permanent theatre from such an early date. All the major phases of expansion of the Thorikos theatre coincide with a marked acceleration in mining activity in the Laurion (Hackens 1967, 77; Mussche 1998, 62).

Though much, if not most, of this subterranean wealth left the deme and made its way to the polis and to the wealthy industrialists who bought the mining concessions from the polis (and who tended not to be members of the deme: Faraguna 2006), some of it also no doubt remained in the deme, or at least in the pockets of those Thorikians wealthy enough to exploit what lay beneath their own land (Osborne 1985, 116–19) or who were the indirect beneficiaries of these operations at a local level. Moreover a recent salvage excavation in the orchestra of the theatre has confirmed an older hypothesis (Hackens 1967, 83–4) that the orchestra, and presumably the theatron too, were constructed on the site of a pre-existing marble and limestone quarry, taking advantage of the way in which the slope had been conveniently terraced through the activity of mining (Kapetanios *forthcoming*). It is worth noting that, while Athens maintained a monopoly on the right to extract and coin silver in the Laurion, and the demes played no part in the administration of the mining operations, the situation was very different with stone quarrying (Faraguna 2006, 143). The oldest retaining wall was built partly on bedrock and partly on a layer of gravel introduced to even out the gaps in its elevation.

The theatre was constructed between the spurs of the hill known as Velatouri (ca. 150 m high) that served as the deme's acropolis, with a view from the theatron south-west, out across the straits to the island Helena and the sea beyond. A mining works (washeries) and a quarry were nearby. And immediately adjacent, directly to the south of the orchestra, lay a cemetery. Fifth-century domestic dwellings virtually abutted the theatre at at least one point to the west (Mussche 1998, 34–5 fig. 63).

Three relatively clear phases of construction have been identified. The first has been dated from as early as 525–480 – that is, either shortly before or after the introduction of Cleisthenic democracy (Hackens 1967, 80–4; Mussche 1998, 31) – but the most recent study of the relevant stratigraphy suggests a *terminus post quem* of ca. 460 (Kapetanios *forthcoming*). All that remained of this phase when excavated was the western end of the

253

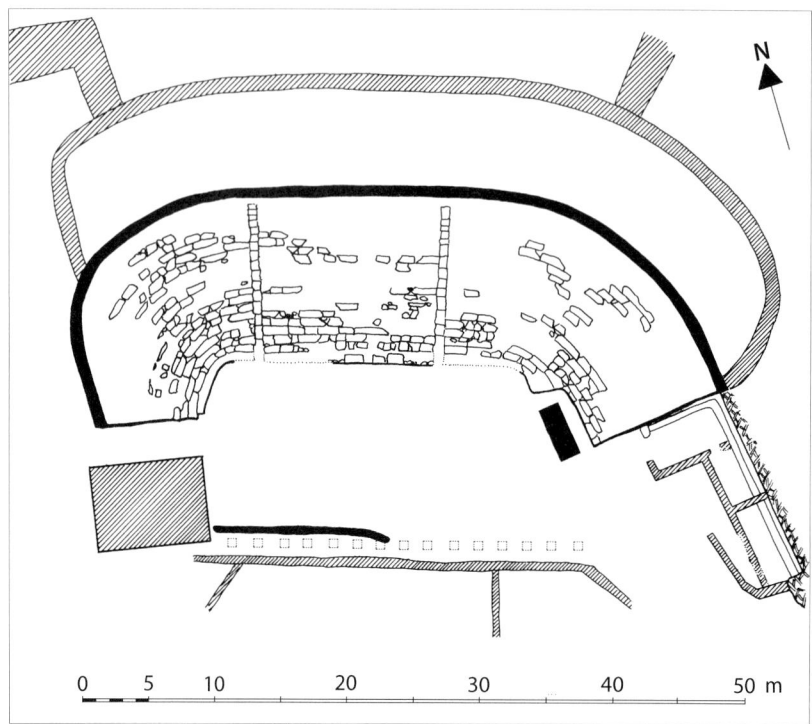

Plan of the theatre at Thorikos.

retaining wall of the orchestra (Mussche 1994, 213). This earliest orchestra constituted a broadening and terracing of a pre-existing east–west road of fifth-century date, mentioned in a mining lease as 'the road to the Dionysion, heading east' ([ἡ ὁδὸ]|ς ἡ εἰς τὸ Διονύσιον φ[έρουσα π]ρὸς ἡλίου ἀνι[όν] *Agora* 19, P 29, ll. 14–15). The part of it that in effect formed the western parodos of the theatre was rather narrow (ca. 2.2–2.5 m wide), and led along-side the temple towards the town, soon passing domestic dwellings, washeries for ore and mine works. Wiles (1997) is probably right to think of the eastern parodos as the one used for significant processional entries.

    In the absence of any other sign of stonework from this date, it is likely that, if in use as a theatre at this time, temporary wooden seating was constructed on the natural slope to the north that was the site of the later stone theatron (Gebhard 1974, 429). But were plays per-formed here from as early as the late sixth century? Some certainly think this possible (Van Looy 1994, 17). Others reject the idea and believe that this structured open space was a site of worship, or a civic meeting place, or both; perhaps a simple agora created in the wake of the fall of the Pisistratids in 511, a sign of early local democratic spirit (Mussche 1998). If the *terminus post quem* of ca. 460 proposed by Kapetanios is confirmed by more thorough study of the pottery in the stratigraphy, this limited evidence for a theatre proper in the late sixth century disappears. More recently Ober (2008, 205–6; see also Paga 2010) has even sought a political explanation for the size of the developed, late fifth-century theatre, which he believes implies a purpose that transcends the limits of the deme and the function of a theatre, and views it rather as a meeting place of the entire Akamantis tribe, whose population size the capacity of the theatre better suits. But economic motives for the capacity of the theatre are as likely to be as relevant as political, and Ober's argument that (2008, 206) 'mine slaves … seem unlikely theatre-goers' is probably misguided (**Aiv**). The claim that this peripheral deme could not have had a stone theatre when there was as yet none in the city centre (Bulle 1928) carries no weight. It is probably safest to assume that such a significant structure as the Thorikos 'theatre' was always meant to be multi-functional and would not have stood empty for most of the year.

It should also be noted that recent excavation and geophysical study of the zone lower in the valley where the fine Doric double stoa stood, dated to the second half of the fifth century, suggests that this was an area with a very substantial collective, civic focus for the deme. The Doric stoa, once thought to be a religious structure, perhaps a temple of Demeter, now seems more likely to have been part of a substantial agora, situated with good access to the ancient harbour (Miles 2015; Kakavogianni and Anetakis 2012, 198–9). If this proves to be true, Thorikos was clearly rich in civic structures and spaces for gathering in the fifth century. It is virtually certain that the agora in the valley had a commercial rather than a political focus, with the theatre better suited to speechmaking, whether dramatic or political. The fact that the site of the theatre appears to have been associated with the worship of Dionysus from an early date encourages belief in its early use for drama, without by any means proving it. Dating from this period (ca. 460–440) is an unpublished inscription thought by Lewis (Matthaiou 2009, 206) to be a deme decree of Thorikos (*SEG* 59, 58). This is reported to contain the conditions of a lease of two *temene*, one of them a Dionysion (the other a Herakleion). It seems that the deme authorities were seeking to make the resources of the god as profitable as possible, perhaps with a view to assisting works on the theatre.

The theatre's second phase is dated (by the stratigraphy of the second retaining wall of the orchestra: Kapetanios *forthcoming*) to ca. 425 and coincides with a period of great expansion in the deme. It has been suggested that the concentration of mining activity in Thorikos town at this time (especially the construction of washeries) was designed to protect the vital economic resources of the silver mines of the Laurion in the face of incursions into Attic territory during the Peloponnesian War (an effect somewhat comparable to the concentration of population within the city walls of Athens itself). During this phase the theatre was furnished with a much larger orchestra, through the construction of a new longer retaining wall to the south of its predecessor. The orchestra was now some 443 m^2 (Mussche 1998, 31), considerably larger than that of the Theatre of Dionysus in Athens. The lower theatron, made of local limestone, dates from the same time (Froning 2002, 41 pl. 39 for a model reconstruction of this phase). This was divided by two vertical stairways whose alignment suggests that they reflect the plan of earlier – wooden – seats (Gebhard 1974, 431–2). The elongated rectilinear shape of the Thorikos orchestra is interpreted by the excavators as deliberate rather than a consequence of constricted spatial circumstances (Mussche 1994, 213; 1998, 3; already thus Bulle 1928, 9–15). And Gebhard's (1974) cogent argument that a rectilinear orchestra is no abnormality but closer to a norm than the circular form (which appears with certainty only late in the fourth century) has not been overturned.

The inscriptions found in the theatre demonstrate that it was home to performances of both comedy and tragedy by around 420 (see below). The desire which they evince to give the activities of the theatre expression in a permanent, monumental form is consistent with the archaeological evidence that this was a period of energetic investment in the theatre. If Hughes (2006) is right to argue that the painter of the 'Perseus Dancer' vase (**V D**), with its (?) comic actor on a raised wooden stage, was attempting to represent the curved corners at the sides of the trapezoidal theatron at Thorikos, this further confirms the presence of comic performances there ca. 420. The findspot of the vase in Anaphlystos is only some 8 km from Thorikos (but on the 'curved corners' see **IV Bi** commentary).

The same general sense of civic pride and vigour is seen in the publication at around this time of the deme's sacrificial calendar (Athens EM 13537; *SEG* 33, 147; Lewis 1985, 108 n. 3 for a date of 440–430; Mattingly 1990, 119 places it ca. 420, precisely the same period as e.g. **Yii**; Matthaiou 2009, 206 apparently concurs). In this handsome and high-quality document, the entry for the month of the deme Dionysia, Posideon, is strikingly different from all of the others. Elsewhere, divine or heroic recipients are usually listed, along with the victim and sometimes the amount to be spent on it. Among other information occasionally added is the location of the sacrifice, the precise day of the month on which it is to take place and various technical details for its conduct. Posideon has nothing other than the festival name 'Dionysia', leaving a large *vacat* of some twelve stoichoi, as the list begins a new line for each month: Ποσιδειῶνος, Διονύσια. *vacat* (*SEG* 33, 147, l. 31). The use of the festival name suggests that it was viewed as a complex event rather than a regular sacrifice to the god and may thus point to theatrical performances by this date. The form of the entry certainly indicates that the Dionysia dominated the deme's religious horizon for the entire month and may suggest that it lasted for more than a single day. While little can be made of the fact that the date for the Dionysia within Posideon is not specified, since on only two or three occasions in the entire calendar is the day of the month explicitly enumerated (Daux 1983, 162–3 has in addition identified two further day-specific formulations in ll. 5–6, 38), one cannot rule out a wish to maintain flexibility in the scheduling of the festival as one reason for this lack of specificity (Henrichs 1990, 262). The fact that no sacrifices are listed suggests that the – doubtless significant – sacrifices necessary for the festival were not accounted for from the regular deme budget. It is true that the Thorikos calendar lists relatively few prices overall and so cannot be treated as an itemised budget of the deme's annual sacrificial expenditure, in the way that those of Erchia and Teithras for instance may. But the absence from this entry of a named sacrifice of any kind for Dionysus, as well as of an associated price, is very striking. Perhaps these too were covered, at least in part, by the deme's wealthy choregoi.

The small Ionic temple of Dionysus at the western parodos; the altar in front of the first row of seats at the eastern end of the koilon; and the chamber on the eastern parodos are all integral to the fifth-century architectural ensemble, suggesting that the theatre and temple formed an integrated sacred space from that time. They are described as a Dionysion by ca. 340 (τὸ Διονύσιον *Agora* 19, P 29, ll. 14–15). The entrance to the temple lay at its eastern end, with three steps that opened directly onto the orchestra. An inscribed stele some 0.26 m high (present location unknown) with the word 'to Dionysus' ΔΙΟΝΥΣΩΙ at its head was seen by the early American excavators and associated with the temple, although accounts of the findspot are ambiguous. (Another places it near the eastern chamber. 'Head of *stele* found in rock chamber' is the caption on the crude drawing at Cushing 1888, pl. 2, fig. 8. The nature of the object is also open to doubt. Cushing 1888, 31 refers to a stele; Miller 1888, 6 to a fragment of an acroterion.) The placement of this temple in relation to the acting space is not unlike the arrangement in Athens, or at Ikarion, though in Athens the temple lay at a lower level rather than, as in Thorikos, at the same level as the acting area.

The altar on the eastern side of the orchestra interrupts the line of the east wing of the theatron and the first row of seats for its length and seems to pre-date the fifth-century development of the theatre, encouraging the excavators to see in it the Archaic *éléos* (Mussche in Van Looy 1994, 24–5; Van Looy 1994; Hackens 1967, 94 pl. 139 for an image). That certainly suggests that the whole space was sacred to Dionysus from a very early period. It is likely that in the age of developed theatre it served as a stage altar for actors; and that the temple and east room could likewise have been integrated into productions as needed (Van Looy 1994, 13, 19).

Directly adjacent to the east wing of the theatron, and facing the eastern parodos, is the so-called 'east room' (or 'rooms' in earlier accounts, before the discovery that the interior dividing wall was of much later construction; Mussche 1998, 118–19; Froning 2002, 41 pl. 39 for model reconstruction). Dating to the second phase of the theatre and built as one large hall of ca. 14 × 7 m, this covered room had bench seats along its northern and eastern sides carved directly into the rock wall, and was perhaps a multi-functional building that could serve as a kind of *lesche* for Dionysus, in association with the temple to the east; a meeting place for the Council; a banquet hall; a gathering place for the chorus and actors; perhaps even a skenotheke, though the bench seats make this last less plausible. Another hall, to the west of the theatre ('P' in Mussche 1998), some 4.75 × 11.50 m, was also probably part of the theatre complex, as it lay exactly on a line with the western parodos. Possibly contemporary with the construction of the fifth-century theatre, this is perhaps a more likely candidate for a skenotheke (Mussche 1998, 32). That it began to be filled with waste deposits at the very end of the fourth century provides a likely date for the abandonment of the theatre.

The – highly unusual – fact that the theatre directly abutted a necropolis (but see **E Introduction**) which pre-dated it and remained in active use while performances were held there has led some to suppose that the cult of the god in Thorikos featured chthonic aspects (Mussche 1998, 32, 40–4 and figs. 74–6). The fact that the Thorikians also took care to sacrifice to the Dionysus worshipped at the Anthesteria may also be relevant (*SEG* 33, 147, ll. 33–4). In Eratosthenes' learned epic poem *Erigone* of the third century, Thorikos was one of the significant stopping points on the religious itinerary of Icarius as he toured Attica initiating his fellow countrymen into the worship of the god. Fr. 23 *CA* (*SSH* p. 49) reads 'until he reached the fair abode of (the hero) Thorikos' εἰσότε δὴ Θορικοῦ καλὸν ἵκανεν ἕδος. This myth may not pre-date the Hellenistic period, and could conceivably represent Ikarian propaganda or scholarly speculation in support of that deme's claim to be the birthplace of drama and the metropolis from which other Attic towns – and for that matter the city itself – learnt of the practice (**M Introduction**). But it is also possible that the subject is Dionysus himself, and that the god's mythic appearance in the home of the hero Thorikos may reflect the long-standing importance of that site in the god's Attic mythology (Hollis 1992, 9).

The third and final phase in the development of the theatre dates to some time shortly before 350. This is the period of 'Eubulan' politics of economic resurgence and theatrical investment in the city, as well as of local industrial growth. The main feature of this development was an increase in the size of the seating capacity by around 50 per cent, or 1,000 places, through the construction from local limestone of a new analemma wall at the rear of the theatron that increased its size by some 550 m², though it remained an earthen slope without stone benches. In this new upper section ten rows (rather than twelve, as on an early plan: Mussche 1998, 33) were added to the twenty-one of the lower theatron. At the same time two entry ramps were constructed to admit spectators from the higher slope of the Velatouri directly into the rear of the theatron.

Preliminary results from a recent salvage excavation carried out in the orchestra tend to confirm the existence of these three major phases of construction, although they suggest that each phase may have been more segmented and gradual too (Kapetanios *forthcoming*). They have also been able to give greater precision (involving down-dating) to their likely *termini post quem* (as noted above).

It is extremely difficult to estimate capacities of Greek theatres that lack individually articulated seats, since the process depends on highly variable estimates of the necessary minimal required space for a single spectator, or on the identification of lateral markers on stones, the results of which are open to surprising disparities. Hackens (1967, 76, 96) claimed average widths on the basis of such markers, which have been identified only in the straight middle section of the lowest rows of seats of the Thorikos theatre, at ca. 0.60 m, while Lohmann (1993, 287) found the markers to be at intervals of ca. 1.0 m. More recently, Palyvou (2001, 56) puts them at ca. 0.70 m. The resultant calculations of the theatre capacity, including the fourth-century upper addition to the theatron, are 3,200 (Palyvou 2001, 56–8) and 3,500 (Lohmann 1993, 201). Palyvou has argued that the design of the seats in the Thorikos theatre was aimed at maximising capacity rather than comfort. In addition to the unusually narrow allocation of individual seat width, the benches are so shallow and so low as to prompt the suggestion that, when used at capacity, the audience may have stood rather than sat. The elaborate and good-quality new construction of this phase (in terms of materials and technique – from the spectators' perspective, the new seating space was more cramped than on the lower tiers) shows that audience demand had outstripped the capacity of the old theatre. This is consistent with a wider pattern of flourishing theatre construction and attendance in the mid fourth century. That maximising capacity was such a concern also suggests that financial motivation may have played a part.

There is no evidence for elaborate prohedria in the Thorikos theatre, certainly not of the throne-like type known from a number of other demes (**I**; **L**; **M**; **W**). However a number of letters engraved on several stones in the second tier of the central section of the lower theatron have been plausibly interpreted as markers of prohedria: Ι, Η, Θ, and ΚΘ (Hackens 1967, 76–7; Gebhard 1974, 431; image: Froning 2002, 40, pl. 36). And the two lowest tiers of seats are slightly deeper than the rest (0.62–0.65 m as opposed to 0.60 m: Palyvou 2001, 56). Several blocks of white marble placed on the foundations of the first tier, and sometimes (e.g. Wiles 1997, 31) referred to as prohedria, are modern (Hackens 1967, 77 n. 1).

The stage building was made of timber. Two large square stone blocks found immediately to the south of the retaining wall (1 × 0.90 m and 0.97 × 0.68 m), each with a central

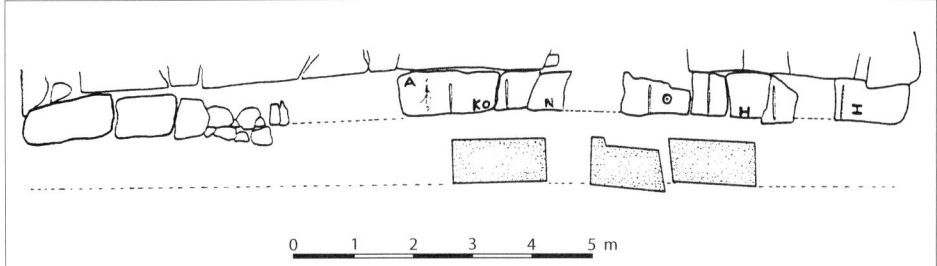

Drawing of prohedria at Thorikos.

square hole for receiving a timber pole (0.13 × 0.13 m), have been associated with the skene and suggest the use of a temporary low- and flat-roofed structure with uprights fixed into these blocks (Mussche 1998, 118 fig. 51 for the blocks; Froning 2002, 38 pl. 37 for a model reconstruction of the wooden skene).

As a deme, Thorikos has not produced a rich crop of inscriptions, and the five relating to the theatre form the largest single group. All were found immediately to the south of the retaining wall of the orchestra. The collapse of that wall after the abandonment of the site to some extent preserved these inscriptions (Bingen 1991, 31). This might suggest that they were originally displayed on the retaining wall itself, overlooking the orchestra. But the fact that, among the many vicissitudes suffered by the theatre, the mayor of Laurion employed a bulldozer to clear the orchestra for a festival in the 1950s limits any confidence that these stones remained undisturbed after the collapse of the wall. An original placement on the retaining wall would however mean that they would probably be obscured on festival days when the stage building was erected at the back of the orchestra, and against (or at least very near) the retaining wall. (Palyvou 2001, 52 has argued that the old retaining wall, some 2 m to the north of and parallel to the later one, remained visible and possibly retained some function after its construction. If she is right in guessing that it was used for the rear wall of the skene, there will have been a gap of some 2 m between the back of the skene and the new retaining wall.) It is perhaps more likely that the theatre inscriptions originally stood at the eastern extremity of the retaining wall, where it meets the eastern parodos; or more generally in the area where the eastern parodos enters the theatre, an ideal spot for display of theatre documents. We may compare the use of the eastern parodos of the Theatre of Dionysus in Athens, and its effective extension into Tripod Street, for epigraphic and other monumental display. Another good parallel is the theatre of Iasus in Caria (**IV E Introduction**). To enter that theatre from the agora, spectators passed along a wall and through a gated parodos covered with inscriptions that bore the names of those who had made the performances possible (Crowther 2007, 301–2).

The working life of a theatre that lasted for more than a century can hardly be conjured from five highly fragmentary inscriptions, but a number of noteworthy features do stand out. The inscriptions are a mix of public and private documents – two dedications by past choregoi; and two decrees and a third document issued under the authority of the Thorikian demos. They span a period from the last third of the fifth to the late fourth century, and show that a choregic system of theatrical financing operated in the deme over that time. Comedy and tragedy were produced, and there is no sign of dithyramb or any other event.

In at least one year it seems that there were two performances of comedy and one of tragedy (**Yiv**).

By the start of the fourth century the deme took steps to keep a permanent record, on stelai erected in the theatre, of those who had funded its drama. The names of poets and plays were apparently not included. At least on occasion, those of the actors were (**Yiv**). There seems to have been a minimum of three choregoi for each festival. In fact, we have a precious fragment of a decree dating to around 420, authored by one Teleas, that regulated the operation of the choregia and apparently required there be a minimum of three choregoi each year (**Yii**). Two later documents show three in action, and apparently covering all the performances of the festival, both comic and tragic. The implication is that in Thorikos a small team of choregoi bankrolled the entire suite of performances at a festival. The decree of Teleas, with its likely direction to 'allot' or 'sell' – or indeed 'lease' – three choregoi to the highest bidders suggests that the tenure of a choregia in Thorikos was assimilated to a sale or lease. The Thorikians were much more familiar than most Athenians with the practices of leasing, for the extensive mineral resources of their territory were managed with an elaborate set of leases, many fragments of which survive from copies kept in the Agora.

In keeping with such corporate, collaborative funding of drama, we find no sign that there was any formal contest at the Thorikos Dionysia. Moreover choregoi seem, uniquely, to have dealt directly with the actors. Theatre in Thorikos was clearly of high quality. There is no reason but urban prejudice to sustain judgements like that of an early excavator of the theatre, who wrote of 'the community's poverty of taste and resources, … now only deepened by an investigation of the theatre and the irregular and mean workmanship of its interior … it seems reasonable to attribute the irregularities in the construction of the theatre to the want of means or want of taste under which the remote rural deme of Thorikos labored' (Cushing 1888, 32). One striking sign of the quality of performance that was made possible by these conditions is the appearance at the Thorikos Dionysia of the greatest tragic actor of his day, Theodoros (**Yiv**).

Yi: Ex-Voto Dedication of a Choregos, ca. 435–410 (by letter forms).

> Marble plaque, left-hand side smooth, top rough-picked; broken on the right-hand side; a large chip lost from lower left-hand corner.
> 0.127 × 0.165 × 0.048 m.
> Found south of the retaining wall of the orchestra in the theatre of Thorikos.
> Lavrion Museum 593.
> Bingen 1990, no. 85 (= *SEG* 40, 179); *IG* I³ 1027bis; Summa 2006, 80–1 (= *SEG* 56, 68).
> Text: based on *IG* I³ 1027bis, with autopsy.   Photo: Bingen 1990, 149 (squeeze).

1	[τ]όνδε Πύ[θων (?) ἀνέθηκε]	1–2 stoich.
	χορηγήσ[ας Διονύσωι]	
	εὐξάμε[νος - - - - - - -]	
	σὺ δ' ἀντι̣[δίδο χάριν ἐ]-	
5	σ̣θλὴν κα[- - - - - - - - - -]	
	[. .]ντος [- - - - - - - - - -]	
	[. . 3–4. .]κ[λ]ῆς ἐ[ποίησε].	

2 Possibly χορηγησα[χορηγησε[Bingen   3 [? τριποδίσκον] Summa   4 σὺ δ'
Ἀντι[…] Bingen   5–6 κα[ὶ τιμὴν διὰ | πα]ντός [μοι κτλ.] Summa   7 ? ἐ[δίδασκε]

Py[thon dedicated t]his [?] after serving as chorego[s for Dionysus], having
made a vo[w …]. You [grant] in return ⁵ [g]ood [favour] an[d …] […-]k[l]es
m[ade this].

This fragment of a marble plaque records an ex-voto dedication made by a choregos. The
restoration of the name of Dionysus as the recipient in l. 2 is very likely, given that the
dedication was sited in the Thorikos theatre. The inscription is metrical, probably to be
restored as hexameters. The last line (7), written in smaller letters (0.007 m in height compared to ca. 0.011 m of the rest), is not part of the poetic epigram and is almost certainly a
craftsman's signature (thus Stroud in *SEG* 40, 179), rather than the name of the didaskalos.
Other examples of such signatures associated with choregic monuments are **V F** on *IG* II³
4, 439 (men's cyclic chorus in the city); **Wiii** (comedy at Rhamnus); cf. also *SEG* 23, 101;
SEG 30, 128; **V F** on *IG* II³ 4, 433.

   This is one of a small number of choregic dedications that employed metrical inscriptions. Others are the comic dedication from Anagyrous (**Eii**); the early monument for a
men's chorus found on the Acropolis (though in this case the dedicant is probably the
poet rather than the choregos: **V C** on *IG* I³ 833 bis); and the epigram transmitted in the
literary tradition that probably preserves an inscription from a monument for a victory of
the Akamantid tribe in the men's cyclic choruses of the Great Dionysia early in the fifth
century (**V F** on *AP* 13.28).

   It is also the only certain example of an ex-voto dedication by a choregos, though Ikarion
may provide another in the possibly choregic dedication to Dionysus made in fulfilment of

a vow by one Kephisios, late in the fourth century (**Mxii**). Py[thon] is discharging an earlier vow to Dionysus and, in keeping with the reciprocal logic of Greek religion, is requesting – in a personal direct address to the god σύ 'you' l. 4 – some benefit in return. '[g]ood [favour]' is a relatively safe guess, though the continuation proposed by Summa 'an[d honour through a]ll [time]' somewhat less so. It has been generally assumed that a formal agonistic victory must lie behind the discharge of this ex-voto vow, but there is no clear evidence that the Thorikian Dionysia had a formally agonistic structure, and this does not provide it. It is safer to suppose that this vow was discharged after and because of a generally 'successful' choregia. The fact that we apparently find here a single choregos acting alone, whereas a form of joint choregia seems to have been the norm at Thorikos, may imply that variation was possible. It may alternatively imply that Py[thon] was particularly keen to mark out his own contribution with this personal dedication from what had in fact been a group effort. On the other hand it is important to recognise just how little of this inscription survives, and, now that Bingen's reading of χορηγησε['was choregos (sing.)' in l. 2 has been dismissed, nothing in the surviving text rules out the possibility that the dedication was in fact made by more than one person.

This plaque will have been attached to the main object of dedication (though no sign of any physical join is evident), made by the craftsman of l. 7. This was perhaps described simply by the demonstrative pronoun 'this' with which the epigram opens; or, more fully, with the addition of a noun: one suggestion that fits both the metre and the dedicatory context is τριποδίσκον 'a small tripod'. Compare the epigram recording the dedication of a small tripod to Athena, *IG* I³ 757; a choregos for tragedy in Ikarion included a tripod on his monument (**Mviii**), as did a comic choregos in Eleusis (**Hiv**), perhaps in imitation of the dedication of prize tripods for dithyramb at the City Dionysia.

Yii: Deme Decree from Thorikos on the Administration of the Choregia, ca. 420 (by orthography and letter forms).

Fragment from the upper left-hand corner of a stele or architectural block of white marble; back broken off; left-hand edge intact and quite smooth; top rough-picked with a shallow (ca. 0.025 m) roughly worked cutting, possibly from secondary usage.
0.137 × 0.205 × 0.063 m.
Found south of the retaining wall of the orchestra in the theatre of Thorikos.
Lavrion Museum TE 83.02.
Bingen 1984, no. 75 (= *SEG* 34, 107); Summa 2006, 77–8 (= *SEG* 56, 199).
Text: based on *SEG* 34, 107, with autopsy.   Photo: Bingen 1984, 176.

[Θ]εοί
Λυσιππίδο δη[μαρχõντος καὶ]   stoich. 23
ἐπιψηφίζοντο[ς, ἔδοξεν Θορι]-
κίοις· Τηλέας ε[ἶπεν· ? μισθõσα]-
5   ι τρẽς χορηγία[ς τοῖς τὸ πλεῖ]-
στον διδõσιν κ[αὶ . . . . 9 . . . .]
ἔλαττον ἢ τρ[ẽς . . . . . 11 . . . . .]

το [. . . . . 21 . . . .]

- -

4 ? [μισθο̃σα]ι, [ἐπιτρέψα]ι, [ἀποδο̃να]ι Whitehead   6 κ[αὶ Wilson   ΔΙΔΟΣΙΝΙ *lapis*   κ[or η[Bingen   6–7 [... εἰ δὲ]‖ ἔλαττον ἢ *vel sim*. Rhodes   6–8 ? κ[αὶ εἰ χορεγοὶ]‖ ἔλαττον ἢ τρ[ε̃ς ἐπαγγείλαιν]το Wilson   7–8 [ἑκάστο ἐνιαυ]‖το̃ Hallof *apud* Summa

[G]ods. Lysippides was de[march and] put the motion to the vote. [The Thori]-kians [decided]; Teleas pro[posed: that we ? sell/leas]e ⁵ three choregia[i to those] who give mo[st] a[nd …] fewer than thr[ee …]

This important document is dated by letter forms and orthography (note esp. the use of ε and ο for the false diphthongs ει and ου) to around 420 (Matthaiou 2009, 206), making it among the earliest of theatre-related inscriptions in Attica. We know from **Yiii** that both tragedy and comedy were being performed at Thorikos by this time.

This is a decree dealing with the choregic system of the Thorikos theatre. As much is clear from the slender remains of the opening clause of the motion, with its reference to 'three choregiai' (l. 5) and '[those] who give mo[st]' (ll. 5–6), showing that it dealt with the number of choregoi and the manner of their appointment. The plan was proposed by one Teleas (l. 4) and put to the vote by the presiding demarch, Lysippides (ll. 1–2) – a circumstance that implies the collaboration of the deme's leading officer in a significant proposal relating to the finance and administration of the local theatre. Neither man is otherwise known. The decree from Ikarion of somewhat earlier date (**Miii**) offers the closest parallel, enacting, like this, a substantive practical programme for that deme's theatre administration. Both begin with the appointment of choregoi.

Given the shape and size of the fragment, it is certain that the decree continued for many more lines. If the restoration of the stoichedon pattern of 23 is correct (and it cannot be incorrect by any great order of magnitude), the width of the stone is just under half its original extension, which we may place at around 0.40 m. It necessarily follows as likely that the stele will have been at least 0.80 m in height. That would allow some 50 lines of script. While we have no way of telling how much of the stele was inscribed, it is certain that much of its surface will have been used and likely that it will have been devoted to this single *psephisma*. It is therefore very likely that the thirty or more lost lines ranged widely over the financial and other organisation of the Dionysia and that the decree represents an important overhaul of the administration of the festival. (Some slight caution is in order, given the characteristics of the surviving stone: while it was most likely a stele, with the loss of the back we cannot know its original thickness and the cavity on the upper surface, if original, would be unusual for a stele. It is possible that the decree was inscribed not on a stele but some other structure, perhaps even a block from or attached to a wall.) Since the Thorikos theatre had been in existence for nearly half a century (**Y Introduction**), and since the choregic dedication **Yi** pre-dates this decree, if only by a decade or so, Teleas' decree probably modified an existing system of theatre administration rather than introducing dramatic performances and choregia altogether (as Summa 2006, 78 suggests).

One highly distinctive feature of Teleas' plan is clear. Even with the loss of the main verb, enough of the text of ll. 4–6 survives to say that it establishes a kind of auction – or indeed, an actual auction. Three choregiai are it seems to be 'leased', 'sold' or 'assigned' to the highest bidders. Although we must restore virtually the entire infinitive verb-form in ll. 4–5, the range of possibilities is very much defined, and narrowed, by the securely restored phrase in the dative that immediately follows (Whitehead 1986b). The best parallels are a number of deme documents that award leases to 'the highest bidder' τῶι τὸ πλεῖστον διδόντι – employing the same expression that appears (in the plural) in ll. 5–6 of this document, τοῖς τὸ πλεῖστον διδῶσιν, translated above as '[those] who give most'. The aim of such leases is often, as here, to secure the financial basis of a local festival or cult (Aixone *IG* II² 2492, l. 36 of 345/4; Eleusis *IE* 85, ll. 23–4 of 332/1). Another good parallel is the polis law that sought to put the festival of the Little Panathenaea on a more solid financial footing in 335/4 by leasing out the Nea, likewise 'to the highest bidder', ll. 9–10 (*IG* II³ 1, 447). A further set of congeners is to be found in the language used for securing or offering the highest rate of interest on sanctuary loans (e.g. from the deme Plotheia *IG* I³ 258, ll. 19–20, of around the same date as this decree: ὅ[στι]ς ἂν πλεῖστον τόκον διδῶι 'whoever may give the most interest'). But in none of these is the business of arranging theatrical performances itself put up for sale (but see on **Miii**, ll. 4–5).

Whatever the precise nature of the process envisaged by Teleas, we evidently have here a model of choregic self-appointment by competitive voluntarism. Voluntarism is built into the expression 'those who give most', for the phrase primarily denotes willingness, not ability, to give. Would-be choregoi in Thorikos are to express their interest at this call for offers, not to await nomination by a civic agent, as in the city, where at the equivalent moment in the timetable of preparations for the Dionysia, it was the task of the Archon to appoint 'the richest men' as dramatic choregoi (**I Bi 2**). We can only guess at how such a system might have worked. Presumably it involved a public process that saw the demarch review potential candidates at a pre-arranged time and place (in the theatre itself? imme-diately following the previous Dionysia?) and negotiate with them to identify the highest sums on offer (Wilson 2007a; *SEG* 57, 126; Wilson 2013; *SEG* 63, 42).

How might such a 'sale' of choregiai have worked in practice? A number of hypotheses present themselves:

1. The cash sums declared at sale by 'the highest bidders' were the actual sums these men went on to spend on their choregiai. The sale represented an undertaking to spend the stated sum in the future.
2. The sale was a transaction separate from the money the choregoi went on to spend on their productions. In other words, what they 'bought' at auction was the right to serve only.
3. The monies received in the sale went directly to the demarch or his agents as a lump sum up-front – the usual practice in leases. The choregia thus consisted merely of this pur-chase, while the actual business of managing the production and deploying the money on the necessary items was separate from the act of funding them. The choregos – more than ever the 'money man' – thus received the glory while the practicalities were left to others.

Whatever the correct interpretation, the emphasis of this scheme lies on voluntarism, not legal compulsion. It presents the undertaking of a choregia as the result of a public contest in generosity. The restoration proposed above in the app. crit. of the next clause (ll. 6–8) – κ[αὶ εἰ χορεγοὶ] | ἔλαττον ἢ τρ[ὲς ἐπαγγείλαιν]το 'a[nd if] fewer than thr[ee choregoi ma]ke [an offer]' – is in accord with this, since the verb ἐπαγγέλλω is used (in the Middle) for the making of voluntary offers (LSJ s.v. 4; *IG* I³ 101, l. 34, of 410/9; *IG* I³ 125, ll. 16–17, of 405/4; Wilson 2013). It seems fairly clear that the decree went on to ensure that a minimum of three choregiai was enabled in this way.

However, even granted the importance of euergetistic motivation to Teleas' plan, the buyer of a lease expects some sort of *quid pro quo* to offset the cost of its purchase. Perhaps for the choregoi of Thorikos that consisted entirely in the honour achieved before his peers in supporting his local theatre. But it is also possible that, as with all other Attic leases, a more concrete, material return was involved. There can be little doubt what that would have been – the same that we know the leaseholders of the Piraeus theatre received for con-structing its wooden seats: namely, the takings from the sale of seats in the theatre (**Vvi**). The Thorikians could afford to do this because, being possessors of a fine stone theatre, they did not need to relinquish this income to the men who built the wooden theatre seating on lease each year and who in return took all of the entrance charges.

Such an arrangement need not be viewed as taking with one hand what had been given with the other. For in the deme context, the holding of a lease regularly had a very signif-icant component of social, euergetistic motivation, built on strong foundations of local social reciprocity. For instance, the successful buyer of the lease on the right to quarry stone in Eleusis cited above made an outright gift of a hundred drachmas to the god on top of his payment for the lease (*IE* 85, ll. 6–9 with Alipheri 2009, 187–8). And the deme went on to honour him 'because he saw to it for his fellow demesmen that the income be maximised' (l. 15). Likewise, the men who bought the lease to construct the seating of the Piraeus theatre were honoured with crowns for paying 10 per cent, or 300 drachmas, beyond the expected price (**Vvi**, fr. d, ll. 15–23). As Michael Jameson has put it, 'On both sides the religious and social aspects may have been at least as important as the strictly financial' (Jameson 1982, 73–4). If this hypothesis is valid, the arrangements devised by the Thorikians to fund their theatre represent a brilliant innovation. They unlocked the necessary liquidity for ensuring high-quality theatre by offering to producers the prospect of an economic return as an additional incentive to the usual social honour.

If the proposed restoration above of ll. 6–8 is even approximately correct, it appears that the Thorikians wished to ensure a minimum of three choregoi for their festival. It is possible that voluntarism here gave way to some form of compulsion. The stipulation of a minimum of three choregiai may lead us to think of the perceived minimal needs of a single agonistic event, namely the desire to avoid a two-horse race. We may compare the provision made by Lycurgus when setting up a new choral contest in the Piraeus that there be χορῶν οὐκ ἔλαττον τριῶν 'no fewer than three choruses' (**Vii**). This consideration would apply if the three choregiai in question were all for the same performance category, or in some other way in direct competition with one another.

But caution is advisable. The dossier of evidence for Thorikos nowhere proves that there was a competitive format for performance (see on **Yiv**). And the lack of any specification of the type of choregia at issue in the (admittedly fragmentary) opening clause of this decree suggests that these choregiai are to cover all of the performance requirements of a single festival. Moreover the evidence of **Yiii** and **Yiv**, from the period immediately subsequent to this decree, and thus likely to be under its authority, indicates that the minimal complement of three choregiai was an annual norm, and designed to supply resources for *both* tragedy and comedy.

Yiii: (?) Honorific Deme Decree of Thorikos Requiring the Making of a Record of Choregoi for Comedy and (Probably) Tragedy, ca. 420 (by letter forms).

Fragment of a stele of local white marble, broken on top, left and bottom. The right edge (rough-picked) is preserved, but only at the rear of the stone (the front surface of the right edge is chipped off).
0.275 × 0.265 × 0.055–0.070 m.
Found on 24 September 1988 in the course of excavation south of the retaining wall of the orchestra in the theatre.
Lavrion Museum 594 (= TE 85.105).
Bingen 1990, no. 83 (= *SEG* 40, 128); *IG* I³ 258 bis; Summa 2006, 78–80 (= *SEG* 56, 200); Takeuchi 2010–2013, 102–5 (= *SEG* 63, 41).
Text: based on Takeuchi 2010–2013, with autopsy.   Photo: Bingen 1990, 144.

```
        [- - - - - - - - - - - - - - - - - - - - - - - -]      stoich. 26
  1     [. . . . . . . . . . .19. . . . . . . . .]ΗΓ[. . .5. . ]
        [. . . . . . . .16. . . . . . . . κ]ωμωι[δ. . . .]
        [. . . . . . . .15. . . . . . .] ἐχορήγ[?ησαν / ουν .]
        [. . . . . .12. . . . . .] χορηγίας Θο[ρικ . ]-
  5     [. . . . . 10. . . . .]ν χρόνον καὶ κωμ[ωιδ]-
        [οῖς καὶ τραγ]ωιδοῖς καὶ ἀναγ[ράψ]-
        [αι τὸς ἀναγρα]φέας ἀναγραφή[ν . .]
```

[. . . . . .12. . . . . .] Ἀμειψίας Μνησ[. .]

[ᵛ ᵛ ᵛ ᵛ οἴδε κεχο]ρηγήκασι· ᵛ ᵛ ᵛ ᵛ

10   [. . . . . . .14. . . . . . .]. ΛΙΔΟ, Μνησ . [. .]

[. . . . . 15. . . . . . .]ος Δωροκλέο̲[ς]

   vacat 0.035

1 ΗΓ Takeuchi .ΗΒ[....] Bingen   3 ἐχορήγ[ησαν] Summa   ἐχορήγ[Lewis   ἐχορηγ[Takeuchi   4 χορηγίας Θο[ρικίοις] Summa   χορηγίας Θο[ρικ?-] Bingen   5 Takeuchi [καὶ τὸ]ν χρόνον Bingen   [κατ' αὐτὸ]ν χρόνον Hallof (in Summa 2006, 79), but cf. Stroud and Papazarkadas *SEG* 56, 200   Also possible: [καθ' ἕκαστο]ν χρόνον   6–7 Bingen   καὶ ΑΝΑΓ[...|......11.....]ΦΕΑΣ ἀναγραφῆς [..] Takeuchi   8 [καθότι εἶπεν] Ἀμειψίας? Bingen   [εἶπεν] Ἀμειψίας Summa   Possibly Μνησ[ίο] 9 Lewis   [οἴδε κεχο]ρηγήκασι: Summa   [. . .5. . οἴδε κεχο]ρηγήκασι· ᵛᵛᵛᵛ Takeuchi   10 –λιδο (or –διδο) Μνησι[..] Bingen   υλίδο Μνησι Lewis   χά[ρ]μο, Μνησᾳ Summa Κ̲ΛΙΔΟ, Μνησ . [. .] Takeuchi   Possibly Μνησ[ίας], cf. Takeuchi 2010–2013, 104

(unknown number of missing lines)

[? for c]omed[y ...] were choreg[oi ...] choregiai [for the] Tho['?rikians ⁵ ... (?) *possibly* at the same *or* each] time both for com[edy and for trag]edy, and [the secret]aries are to insc[ribe] a recor[d ...] Ameipsias son of Mnes[-... (?) proposed. The following men] have served as [cho]regoi: ¹⁰ [*name, son of ...*-] lides; Mnes[-... son of ... ; ...-]os son of Dorokles.

The fragmentary state of this inscription renders most conclusions tentative. It is difficult to guess how many lines are lost from the beginning. The line length of stoich. 26 is how-ever fairly secure, since part of the right-hand edge of the stele is preserved, and we can be relatively confident in the restoration across ll. 5–6 καὶ κωμ[ωιδοῖς κα|ὶ τραγ]ωιδοῖς 'both for com[edy and for trag]edy'.

It is also very likely that the document is, or includes, an honorific decree. Lines 6–7 are cogently restored as instructions to secretaries (only attested here in a deme, but see **Bvi** and **Bvii**) to record the names of choregoi, no doubt for the purpose of acknowledg-ing and honouring their service, although the precise form the instructions take cannot be paralleled in every detail. This may be our very earliest example of an honorific decree (as Takeuchi 2010–2013, 105 notes), at least for an Athenian individual (rather than a city or foreigner). If so it is striking that this class of decree appears first in the realm of theatrical sponsorship, and at the local level. The instructions to secretaries can only have been issued on the authority of a deme assembly. It is unclear whether we should think of the ἀναγραφή[ν] of l. 7, which the secretaries are to inscribe, as the 'record' of choregoi that follows (on which see below); or as the decree itself, meaning in effect that this is the publication clause for the decree (Takeuchi 2010–2013, 105 favours the latter). Both senses are perhaps encompassed in the phrase.

The names and patronymics of three choregoi follow a 'header' in l. 9 '[The following men] have served as [cho]regoi' [ᵛᵛᵛᵛ οἴδε κεχο]ρηγήκασι· ᵛᵛᵛᵛ. Bingen was probably right to conclude that the name of the decree's proposer has been placed after it (though Takeuchi 2010–2013, 104 notes that the inclusion of the patronymic for the proposer is not necessarily to be expected): this is the Ameipsias of l. 8 who, to judge from the remains of his patronymic (Μνησ[- l. 8), may be a relative (the son, or father?) of one of the choregoi listed below (Μνησ.[- l. 10; Takeuchi 2010–2013, 104 for the prosopography; too little of the names of the choregoi remains to see whether they were related to one another). Takeuchi draws attention to the Athenian comic poet Ameipsias who was active in this very period. His patronymic and deme are unknown, but the name is far from common (only seven other attestations in Attica) and so it is possible that we see here the comic poet active in a context of local theatrical administration, leading the cause for public recognition of dramatic choregoi.

It is difficult to go much further, but three main possibilities present themselves:

(i) The decree honours and records the names of the three choregoi in ll. 10–11 at the Dionysia of one (presumably the present or just past) year (or perhaps over a number of years), because they had, extraordinarily, served for both comedy and tragedy.
(ii) The decree honours and records the names of the three choregoi in ll. 10–11 and establishes the maintenance of a record of the names of choregoi for tragedy and comedy thereafter.
(iii) The document is not strictly speaking an honorific decree at all but a deme decree that establishes the project of recording the names of all choregoi.

In favour of (i) is the fact that only one set of names in fact appears (ll. 9–11), below which is an uninscribed space slightly greater than two lines of text in height. If the intention was to record a succession of future choregoi it was not carried out in this space, though it could of course easily have been executed elsewhere. And in fact more than half a century later **Yv** appears to be a public record of choregoi from a number of years. More significant however is the emphasis on some aspect of 'time' (χρόνον l. 5), in close proximity to the phrase 'for both com[edy and trag]edy'. Even though Hallof's restoration of '[at the same] time' [κατ' αὐτὸ]ν χρόνον has its difficulties, some version of it is plausible. One (admittedly inelegant) possibility might be χορηγίας Θο[ρικι|οῖς τὸν αὐτὸ]ν χρόνον καὶ κωμ[ωιδ|οῖς καὶ τραγ]ωιδοῖς, 'choregiai for the Tho[rikians during the sam]e time/period for both com[edy and trag]edy'. The emphasis would thus fall on the – probably unusual – fact that the choregoi of this year funded both dramatic genres at once (perhaps further implying that some sort of oscillation between tragedy and comedy from one year to the next was the norm?). This would no doubt represent a burdensome and costly undertaking that merited special praise. Or perhaps the emphasis lay on the fact that the same three men served as choregoi for a number of years (with the imperfect ἐχορήγ[ουν] l. 3) and 'each time' (see the restoration along these lines suggested below) served 'for both comedy and tragedy'.

On the other hand, the intention to initiate a longer-term record of the names of all choregoi (ii) is to an extent significantly implied by the 'header' of l. 9 '[The following men] have served as [cho]regoi' [ᵛᵛᵛᵛ οἵδε κεχο]ρηγήκασι· ᵛᵛᵛᵛ, suggesting as it does the beginning of a list of some extension. And, as already noted, **Yv** implies that the practice of recording the names of choregoi continued much later. The practice of keeping a public record of the names of choregoi at the City Dionysia was already by this date of long standing, though we do not know of any attempt to monumentalise that record in stone until the one that produced the great inscription known as the *Fasti*, which can be dated between

347/6 and 343/2 (Millis 2014). As Millis (2014, 443) notes, the *Fasti* is functionally akin to honorific decrees. Moreover the phraseology of ll. 6–7, though far from secure in its restoration, tends in this direction. The plural 'secretaries' (l. 7 [ἀναγρα]φέας) would more likely refer to a succession of future secretaries rather than multiple contemporaries in a single deme. This suggests that the decree looked to the longer term, rather than just requiring that the choregoi of a single year or festival be recorded. And while l. 5 is perhaps most cogently interpreted to refer to the special service of one set of choregoi, even this is far from certain. It is possible that the emphasis was not on an outstanding multi-generic act of liturgical service by the same men at all but on specifying that the record was to extend to 'each time', or 'for all future time' or the like, with the specification 'for both comedy and tragedy' serving to ensure somewhat pedantically that records of choregoi for both dramatic forms were to be kept. Rough *exempli gratia* restoration along these lines might be χορηγίας Θο[ρικο|ῖ καθ᾽ ἕκαστο]ν χρόνον καὶ κωμ[ωιδ|οῖς καὶ τραγ]ωιδοῖς, 'choregiai at Tho[rikos each] time, both for com[edy and trag]edy'; or (though they might seem somewhat over-ambitious on the part of the deme authorities) two other possibilities are χορηγίας Θο[ρικί|οις ἐς τὸν ἀε]ὶ χρόνον καὶ κωμ[ωιδ|οῖς καὶ τραγ]ωιδοῖς, 'choregiai for the Tho[rikians for all future] time, both for com[edy and trag]edy' / χορηγίας Θο[ρικο|ῖ εἰς τὸν αἰε]ὶ χρόνον καὶ κωμ[ωιδ|οῖς καὶ τραγ]ωιδοῖς, 'choregiai at Tho[rikos for all future] time, both for com[edy and trag]edy'.

Nothing definitively eliminates the possibility that the purpose of the decree was to establish the project of recording the names of all choregoi and not to honour those of any one year in particular (iii). It probably post-dates the decree of Teleas (**Yii**) – with its apparent insistence that there be a minimum of three choregiai in any year – but not perhaps by very far. The list of three choregoi (ll. 10–11) shows that it is at any rate congruent with it. It might even follow close in the wake of Teleas' efforts to establish the Thorikian choregic system on a firmer footing, and be part of an administrative overhaul of the Dionysia that sought to stimulate continued financial support by establishing a roll-call of benefactors.

We should probably draw no firm conclusions (in terms of perceived priority, or order of performance) from the placement of comedy before tragedy. The sequence 'comedy – tragedy – comedy' in the somewhat later choregic dedication (**Yiv**) is perhaps a better guide for the order of performance, at least in that year, and it is not inconsistent with the evidence of this decree.

If the interpretation (i) which sees this decree responding to an unusual circumstance in which three men elected to fund both comedy and tragedy is not correct, we are free to suppose that it was normal for a choregos in Thorikos to fund just one dramatic genre, as in the city. It is however worth noting that there was no space to mark the generic affiliations ('for tragedy', 'for comedy') against the names of the choregoi listed in ll. 10–11. Even in the case where such generic specificity of choregic service is marked, however (**Yiv**), it would seem that collaboration between a year's choregoi in Thorikos was the norm. The (admittedly highly fragmentary) opening clause of Teleas' decree (**Yii**) also lacks any specification as to the type of the three choregiai to be instantiated.

Yiv: Choregic Dedication in Comedy and Tragedy Listing the Names of Actors, early 4ᵗʰ c. (by letter forms and style of cutting: below); ca. 350–325 (Makres).

Large fragment preserving much of the front of a quadrangular base of white marble, damaged on the lower left-hand corner, bottom and back; right-hand side original. Part of a circular cavity on the upper surface (0.016–0.022 m deep) is preserved, the rest broken off with the back.
0.145 × 0.265 × 0.060 m.
Found on 24 October 1983 in the course of excavation south of the retaining wall of the orchestra in the theatre.
Lavrion Museum 231 (= TE 83.03).
Bingen 1984, no. 76 (= *SEG* 34, 174); Summa 2006, 81–4 (= *SEG* 56, 231); *IG* II³ 4, 512.
Text: based on *IG* II³ 4, 512 with advice, based on autopsy, from K. Takeuchi.
Photos: Bingen 1984, 178; Summa 2006, 81 (squeeze); *IG* II³ 4,1 tab. LXIX.

1	[Δ]ημοχαρίδης ⋮ κωμωιδοῖς,	non-stoich.
	[Σπ]ευσιάδης ⋮ ὑπεκρίνετο·	
	[Δη]μοχάρης ⋮ τραγωιδοῖς,	
	[? Θε]όδωρος ⋮ ὑπεκρίνετο·	
5	[. . 3–4 . .]άδης κωμωιδοῖς,	
	[. . 4–5 . .] ὑπεκρίνετο.	
	vacat	
	[χορηγήσα]ντες ἀνέθεσαν	
	[?τῶι Διονύ]σ[ω]ι	

4 [Θε]όδωρος or [Δι]όδωρος Bingen   5 [Ἀρχι]άδης Jordan-Curbera   [Δημ]άδης Summa   6 ?Λύκων Summa   7 [νικήσα]ντες Makres *IG* app. crit.   8 [- - - - - - -].[.].[- - - - - ?]   possibly [τῶι Διονύ]σ[ω]ι Takeuchi

[D]emocharides for comedy : [Sp]eusiades was the protagonist; [De]mochares for tragedy : [? The]odoros was the protagonist; ⁵ [...-]ades for comedy : [...] was the protagonist. After serv[ing as choregoi] (the above-named) dedicated this (possibly [to Diony]s[us]).

This important document is unique in the corpus of Classical Attic inscriptions for listing the names of actors in close association with those of choregoi. Normally a sharp division is maintained between the spheres of the choregos (and his chorus) and of the actor. It can only be dated approximately, by letter forms and its distinctive rough style of cutting, to the early fourth century (A. Matthaiou pers. comm.). The prosopographic arguments of Whitehead (1986b, 216–17) also suit such a date, for ca. 400 Demochares (l. 3) will have been around thirty-five.

This is almost certainly a dedication by a group of three choregoi. The alternative view of Makres holds that it is a dedication by victorious actors (see app. crit. and *IG* app. crit.), but as there is no doubt that [D]emocharides, [De]mochares and [...-]ades are choregoi, this will surely be their monument. The cavity on the upper surface probably received a small statue or perhaps the base of a column. Kazuhiro Takeuchi has detected traces of two letters in l. 8 that are compatible with '[to Diony]s[us]' [τῶι Διονύ]σ[ω]ι. Three performances are recorded – comedy, tragedy, comedy. The name of the choregos comes first, followed after a punctuation mark by the relevant generic indicator (κωμωιδοῖς, τραγωιδοῖς); then, on a new line, the name of the protagonist (this is certainly the meaning of ὑπεκρίνετο; compare the use of the abbreviation ΥΠΕ to denote the protagonists at city festivals in the Didascalic Lists: Millis and Olson 2012, 61). Because he believed the performances recorded here were victories, Bingen thought they must derive from different years. But there is no compelling reason to think that these performances represent victories, and Bingen withdrew his suggested restoration of [νικήσα]ντες l. 7 'After winning the contest (*the above-named*) dedicated this', which does not fit the available space and arrangement of the text as well as [χορηγήσα]ντες. (Though it should be noted that the absence of an explicit verb of victory does not in itself preclude the event having been agonistic: e.g. **Biii**.) It is much more likely that these men are the three choregoi of a single festival required by the terms of Teleas' decree (**Yii**) and that, in this year at least, the Thorikos Dionysia saw the performance of two comedies and one tragedy.

The three choregoi have elected to join together in erecting a monument commemorating their support of the year's festival. It is thus likely that they also co-operated, if not fully collaborated, in their choregiai. This would not be synchoregia as that term is normally used, for here a plurality of choregoi join to prepare a plurality of performances in different genres, whereas synchoregia is usually understood as a plurality of choregoi preparing a single performance (**A Introduction**). The fact that these three men were probably related further increases the likelihood that they acted in concert throughout. It is suggested by the absence of patronymics (Whitehead 1986a, 218), and the similarity of their names (especially true if [Dem]ades is the comic choregos in l. 5 – Summa 2006, 82 – but see below).

Democharides (l. 1) was almost certainly the Thorikian of that name who appears on a curse tablet in the company of numerous wealthy and politically prominent Athenians (NM inv. 14470, A ll. 13, 17, 26, 128, dated to ca. 345–335: Jordan and Curbera 2008 = *SEG* 58, 265). Since his name was inscribed four times, more than any of the other hundred-odd individuals on the tablet, he was very probably a high-profile public figure from urban politics, and thus looks like an example of an individual prominent in civic life at both urban and deme levels. Demochares (l. 3) can be identified as a member of a prominent family of the deme, known from a substantial funerary monument in the city of Athens (*IG* II² 6218 with Whitehead 1986b, 215–17; Marchiandi 2011, 351–2). The most plausible restoration for the name of the third choregos (l. 5) is Archiades (rather than Demades, not attested in Thorikos). A Thorikian of that name was cursed on the same tablet as Democharides (*SEG* 58, 265, l. 16). If this is he, their co-presence there adds some further weight to the likelihood that he and Democharides were related. Marchiandi (2011, 352) thinks it likely that [Archi]ades the comic choregos was son of [D]emocharides – also, it is worth noting, a comic choregos.

The association of a particular protagonist with each of the three choregoi, who otherwise show every indication of operating as a group, is an intriguing feature of this document. It suggests that each choregos from the trio had a primary responsibility for one of the performances, perhaps for one play. One plausible hypothesis is that the choregoi dealt directly with protagonists, and were not just the providers of the chorus. In fact it seems quite likely that a choregia in Thorikos consisted of payment for a performance of tragedy or comedy, the full provision of which – perhaps even extending to its chorus – was put into the hands of the leading actor in a troupe. That the actors played a significant part in the overall preparation and provision of these productions is suggested by the absence of any reference to didaskaloi. The contractual arrangements may have been conducted by the choregos himself; or they may have been undertaken by the demarch, having secured the promised commitment of funds from choregoi well in advance by the 'sale' of choregiai (**Yii**) distinctive to this deme. If so, this is a precious insight into the sort of administrative and financial arrangements that preceded and led to the appearance of the more formal, organised corporations of actors in the third century.

As for the actors themselves, given the extreme rarity of the name and the common generic affiliation, the comic actor Speusiades (l. 2) is almost certainly the same man as the Speuseades (*sic*) recorded (by an undisputed restoration) as didaskalos for comedy in Acharnae (**Bii**; oscillation between the vowel groups *ea* and *ia* is common in inscriptions: *GAI* I, 145).

Theodoros is a preferable restoration to Diodoros (l. 4), the latter not known as a tragic actor's name. Theodoros was one of the greatest tragic actors of all time (Stefanis no. 1157; **IV Dxvi**). Probably Athenian by birth (rather than, as many actors, by gift of the popular Assembly), he appears to have been a specialist in female parts – among them, frequently, the *Antigone* of Sophocles (D. 19.246) and a Merope that made Alexander weep (**IV Cx 3**). Wealthy enough to make a substantial donation towards the construction of the temple of Delphian Apollo in 361 (*FD* III 5.3 = *Syll.*³ 239B), an appearance of this celebrity at Thorikos is likely to have cost the deme's choregoi dear. Ghiron-Bistagne (1976, 157–8) suggests that the statue dedicated on this monument may have been of Theodoros, but however much greater his fame than the other actors listed upon it, he is unlikely to have been singled out for such attention in a composite dedication like this. Some have hesitated to identify this as the famous Theodoros, on the grounds of date and the inadequate prestige of the Rural Dionysia (Summa 2006, 83). This should rather be treated as further evidence against the entrenched view that deme Dionysia saw only second-rate performances. And given the higher date suggested by Matthaiou for this inscription there is absolutely no concern on chronological grounds: Theodoros' first victory as a tragic actor at the City Dionysia is very close in date to this dedication from Thorikos (ca. 400: *IG* II² 2325B, l. 23 M-O); his first of four at the Lenaea somewhat later (*IG* II² 2325H, l. 26 M-O).

No part of the name of the comic actor associated with the third performance survives (l. 6). It can only have been four to five letters in length, and the single attested candidate is Λύκων (Stefanis no. 1567; identification proposed by Summa 2006, 83). A famous and highly successful *komoidos* from Skarpheia in east Locris, Lykon was regarded as supreme in his art by some (Phld. *Rh.* I.197.9–10). He was twice victor at the Lenaea in the middle of the fourth century (*IG* II² 2325F, l. 48 M-O) and followed Alexander to Tyre in 331, where he is said to have earned himself ten talants from the king from the amusing insertion of a 'begging verse' (στίχον αἰτητικὸν) into a comedy (Plu. *Mor.* 334e). Meineke suggested that he was the object of attack in a comedy named after him (*Lykon*) by Antiphanes: *PCG* F 145.

Yv: Public Record of Choregoi?, second half of 4ᵗʰ c. (by letter forms).

> Left-hand lower corner of a marble stele, left and lower sides partially preserved.
> 0.285 × 0.283 × 0.11 m.
> Found south of the retaining wall of the orchestra in the theatre of Thorikos.

Lavrion Museum inv. 591.
Bingen 1990, no. 84 (= *SEG* 40, 167); Summa 2006, 84–5 (= *SEG* 56, 232).
Text: based on *SEG* 56, 232.   Photos: Bingen 1990, 147; Summa 2006, 84 (squeeze).

```
1      [---]ΛΛ[-]Χ[-]ΔΟΣ[--]      non-stoich.
       Πίνδαρος Πρωτέο·
       ἐπ' Εὐσθένος δημαρ[χõντος]
       Δίφιλος Ἀστυφίλο̣
5      Διότιμος Ἑρμοδ[-....]
              vacat
       Μικίνο δημαρχõντ[ος]
       Πολυκράτης Πολυκρ̣[άτος]
       Πολύστρατος Πολυκ[ράτος (?)]
              vacat
```

1 - - Λ-Χ-ΙΔ-Δ - -Bingen   3 Ἐπευσθένος Bingen

(Unknown number of missing lines. Partial remains of a name)
Pindar son of Proteos. In the demarchy of Eusthenes: Diphilos son of
Astyphilos; [5] Diotimos son of Hermod[-…]. *vacat* In the demarchy of Mikinos:
Polykrates son of Polykr[ates]; Polystratos son of Polyk[rates] *vacat*

This is the lower left-hand corner of a stele whose original dimensions cannot be guessed.
It is however of exactly the same thickness as the stele that carried an earlier decree that
mandated the keeping of an inscribed record of the choregoi of Thorikos (**Yiii**), and the
two were found in the same area. While it is unlikely to be part of that same block, it may
have been a subsequent panel of similar form that continued the deme's public record of
choregoi (erected on the walls of the parodos?) in the fourth century. Summa has persuasively argued that this is indeed part of a list of choregoi, introduced as a kind of dating
formula by the name of each year's demarch whose responsibility it was to organise the
festival and appoint its choregoi (ll. 3, 6). The earlier view (Bingen) that it was a list of victors in a competition of actors rested entirely on the identification of Pindar (l. 2) with the
tragic actor said by Aristotle *Po.* 1461b35 to have demonstrated the same excesses of technique as the tragic actor Kallippides, nicknamed 'the monkey'. This inherently weak case
is further undermined by the absence of any parallel for records of actors being kept by
civic authorities (and **Yiv** is not an exception, since that is a dedication erected by choregoi
with the addition of actors' names). Also the inclusion here of the patronymics is appropriate to choregoi, but not actors. None of the others named are otherwise known as actors.

Much of the record for three, presumably consecutive, years survives. Of the first year
only one full name remains, and a few letters of another. No gap has been left after the
name of the last choregos of this year and before the next year's entry (ll. 2–3), as it was
between the other years, but this is of little consequence. It is clear that the record was updated year by year (the last entry, ll. 6–8 is in somewhat smaller letters) and practice in such
editorial matters between deme secretaries was doubtless variable. One might compare the

way the formula used to register the demarchy varies lightly between the second and the third year (from ἐπί with a genitive l. 3 to a genitive absolute l. 6).

In each of the two years for which a full record has survived, only two choregoi are listed. In an earlier period (**Yiii**) there were three, and three was mandated as a minimum by the decree of Teleas (**Yii**). This might reflect difficulty in securing willing candidates. But it need not. It could equally be an example of fewer but more substantial benefactors, symptomatic of trends in Athenian euergetism from the time of the Lycurgan period that saw for instance substantial civic projects being funded by individuals and that in the theatrical sphere eventually witnessed the replacement of the choregia by the single office of agonothete (**V I**). In the third year two brothers evidently took on the charge. It is possible that those in the previous year were also related.

No attempt has been made to signal any affiliation of these choregoi with particular performance types. This is consistent with other evidence that in Thorikos the year's set of choregoi took on the responsibility of funding the deme's theatrical performances, tragic and comic, as a group.

PART IV

BEYOND ATTICA

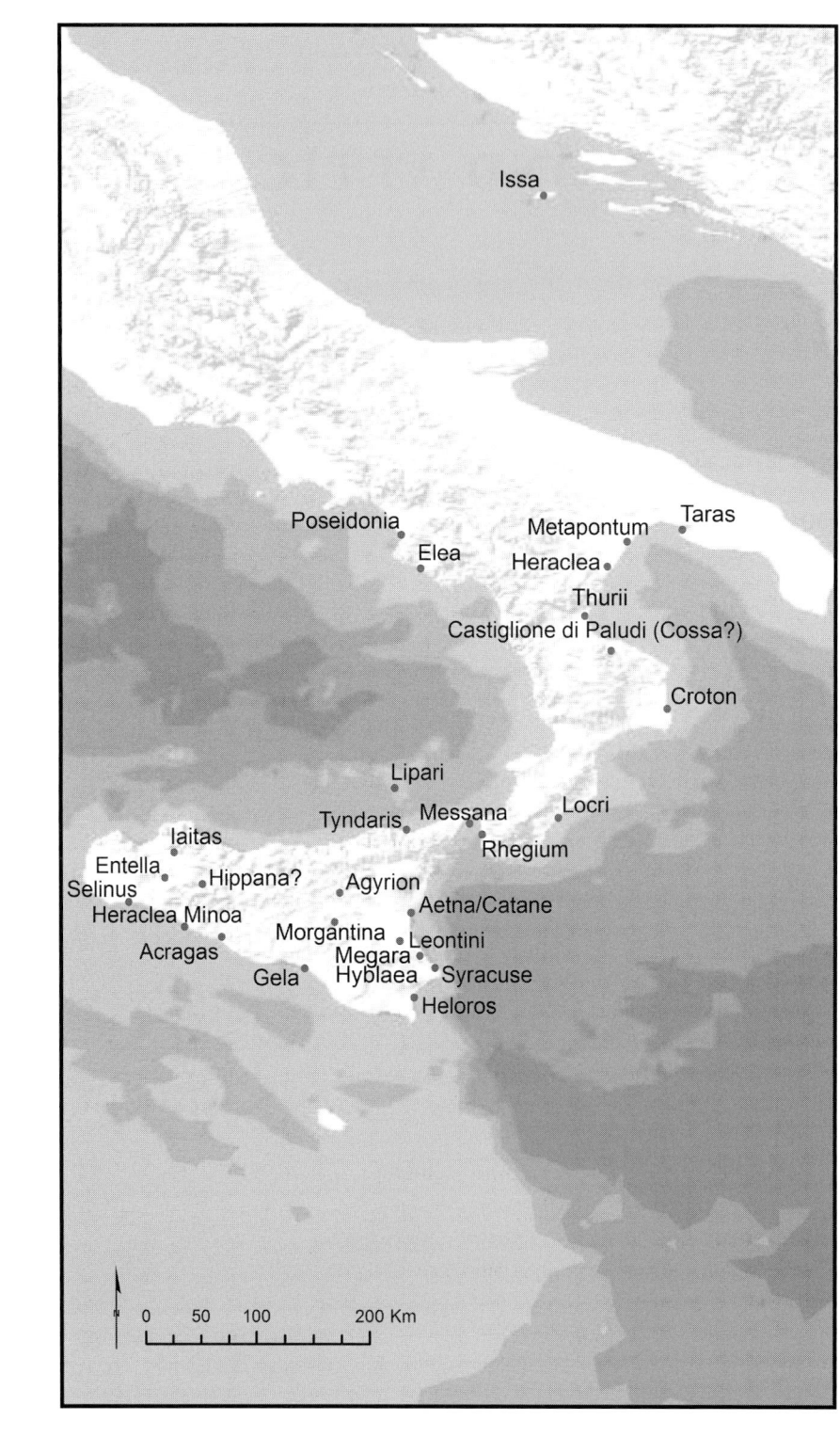

Issa

Poseidonia
Elea

Metapontum   Taras
Heraclea
Thurii
Castiglione di Paludi (Cossa?)

Croton

Lipari
Tyndaris   Messana   Locri
Iaitas   Rhegium
Entella
Selinus   Hippana?   Agyrion
Heraclea Minoa   Aetna/Catane
Acragas   Morgantina   Leontini
                Megara
Gela   Hyblaea   Syracuse
                Heloros

0   50   100   200 Km

A │ West Greece

Introduction

The manner in which Plato refers to the 'present-day Sicilian and Italian custom of entrusting judgment of the winner to a vote of hands by the mob of spectators' (**Axii 4**) shows that, by the middle of the fourth century, this broad region could be treated as a homogeneous unit when it came to at least some aspects of theatrical practice. But while affinities of practice evidently extended across Magna Graecia by the fourth century, the spread of theatre to the West requires careful attention to local specificities.

One important feature of the evidence for theatrical culture here (as elsewhere: **Ciii**) is the presence of so-called 'theatral areas' in close association with cult sites. This is a term used for non-canonical theatres, often a series of linear steps facing an open space, the primary purpose of which is likely to have been to enable worshippers to view more or less performative activities associated with particular cults – processions, rituals involving music, hymns, choral song and sacrifice, extending perhaps to something that might be called 'sacred drama', notably in the context of mystery cults (on the phenomenon see Nielsen 2002, with the important predecessor Anti 1947; Hollinshead 2015, 42–9 on architectural aspects). One such space has recently been identified at Selinus, a stepped viewing area, of sixth-century date, in the urban sanctuary zone, probably designed for watching cult activities for Demeter Thesmophoros in the adjacent Temple R (**Axiv**). Other examples in West Greece include the rectilinear theatre in the Neapolis sanctuary complex at Syracuse (**Ai**) and the phases of the structure at Metapontum that preceded the construction on the same site of a canonical theatre ca. 330 (below).

One cannot exclude in principle the possibility that drama of some kind was performed in such spaces (Marconi 2014, 110), not least since theatres proper, in the West as elsewhere in Greece, are themselves routinely associated directly with sanctuaries (and note the clear evidence for the first performance of Plautus' *Pseudolus* on the steps of the temple of the Magna Mater on the Palatine, the dedication of which it honoured: Cic. *Har. resp.* 24; Goldberg 1998). For our purposes, however, we include such sites only when a case for dramatic performance can be made with some conviction.

Another distinctive feature of theatre culture in this region is the frequent use of theatres as places for political gatherings and action, in a variety of political climates: where the Assembly met, where foreign ambassadors were received and heard; where trials were held. The phenomenon was remarked upon by the first-century AD Roman observer Valerius Maximus, who describes it as 'the Greek fashion' (2.2.5: *ut est consuetudo Graeciae*; Gallo 2003; Marconi 2012, 185–7). In the Greek West a combination of literary evidence and topographical markers – such as the proximity of theatre to agora – tends to support the truth of the claim.

Sicily

In the early years of the fifth century, formal comedy with dramatic plots was more advanced in Sicily than in Athens, or so it appeared to Aristotle when researching the subject (**Bii 1**; **Aiii 2**; **Aiv**). Other innovations at the level of dramaturgy and the use of theatrical space are recorded (**Aiv**) and there is ample evidence for lively interaction between a group of Sicilian comic poets, and between them and visiting theatrical and other poetic luminaries from Greece (**Aii**; **Aiii**; **Aiv**; **Av**). The picture is dominated by Syracuse (**Ai**; **Aiii**; **Avi**; **Aviii**; **VI A**; **VI E**). The Neapolis sanctuary zone was probably the site of a theatre already in Gelon's day (tyrant 485–478). Dionysius I (tyrant 405–367) may have had a large semicircular theatron constructed in the early decades of the fourth century, as much as half a century before the first curvilinear stone theatre was completed in Athens (Papastamati-von Moock 2015; **VI E**). Comedy was performed in Syracuse from ca. 485 under the tyrant Gelon. But the leading exponent of the new form, Epicharmus, appears already to have been producing his work in nearby Megara Hyblaea as early as ca. 510 (**Aiii**). Gelon's brother and successor Hieron (**VI A**) imported the tragedians Phrynichus and Aeschylus from Athens to Syracuse (**VI A** on Aeschylus' *Aitnaiai* and *Persians* for Hieron) and may have transplanted theatre to his new imperial foundation of Aetna after 476 (**Axiii** on the Greek theatre in Catania and the theatrical activities of a later tyrant from that city, Mamerkos).

The particular variety of comedy that flourished under the Deinomenids was not so patently critical of (or indeed engaged with) its political context as (Aristophanic) Old Comedy, and may to some extent have served to bolster some of the tyrants' imperial ambitions (**Aiii**). Although the Deinomenids energetically sponsored a variety of choral genres, above all epinikion (**VI A**), there is no positive evidence to place these in a theatrical setting (but see **Axiii**), or for other theatrical genres in Syracuse prior to the emergence of the form known as *hilarotragoedia* (ἱλαροτραγῳδία), also called *phlyakographia* (φλυακογραφία 'farce-writing') and comi-tragedy (κωμικὰ τραγικά) associated with Rhinthon (ca. 323–285) of Taras and Syracuse (**Axxi**; on *phlyakes* see now Favi 2017d). Predecessor forms to such farce, of an improvisatory (and probably non-versified) nature, are often supposed to be among the elements that flowed into the genesis of western comedy (Willi 2015, 133).

The half-century or so (ca. 466–406/5) that followed the fall of the Deinomenids and preceded the rise of Dionysius I is a particularly obscure period of Sicilian theatre history. This is especially unfortunate, not least since in Syracuse some or all of this period is marked by a democratic form of constitution, and would thus afford an interesting comparison with the relationship between theatre and democracy in Athens at the same time (**Ai**). So far as we can tell, the theatre continued to serve as the place of political assembly. That is the clear implication of the evidence of Chariton (**Ai**), and there is none to suggest any attempt to disentangle political and theatrical actions by providing them with separate spaces. This is the period during which the Athenians sent Euripides as an official ambassador to the Syracusans, to plead for peace and friendship (**Axi**) – presumably making his case in the theatre. The attested shift in the way the process of judging in the Syracusan theatre operated, from a panel of five judges to 'a vote of hands by the mob of spectators', must have taken place between ca. 470 and ca. 360 (**Axii**). We might suppose this democratic period a likely moment for this change, noting at the same time that it was evidently a change that one or both of the Dionysii subsequently found it expedient to maintain. An epochal phase of construction in the Syracusan theatre also took place in this period, probably towards the end of the fifth century (**Aviii**).

During the last quarter of the fifth century Sophron, writer of mimes, also flourished in Syracuse. In this earliest observable phase of the long history of mime, this took the form of a short dramatic sketch in prose that dealt with comic scenes from everyday life (Hordern 2004, 4; *PCG* T 1). Sophron's mimes had affinities with Epicharmean comedy but with a greater emphasis on bawdy, low-register sexual and scatological humour and personal abuse. They were written in Doric, which has been seen as a deliberate assertion of local identity in the face of the increasing dominance of Athenocentric theatre culture (Hordern 2004, 1); but a decision to write in Attic-Ionic would have been much more surprising. Despite being in prose, Philodemus felt drawn to refute a claim that Sophron wrote 'poems / verses', and some later authors refer to him as a poet (*PCG* T 17, 19). However the issue may be little more than an accidental by-product of Aristotle's description of Sophron's mimes as 'mimetic', like Platonic dialogues, despite not being in verse (*On Poets* fr. 44a Janko), a description that is very far from implying that he thought of them as a properly poetic genre (Janko 2011, 511) and no basis for thinking they were regarded as a theatrical form. This need not rule out the possibility that Sophron's mimes may have been performed in the Syracusan theatre, of which one surviving fragment reflects precious knowledge (**Aviii**; Hordern 2004, 8 argues for sympotic performance). Whether the tradition is reliable that makes Xenarchos, also a writer of mimes, the son of Sophron (*PCG* T 2), it clearly reflects sound chronology, since Xenarchos is reported as having mocked the people of Rhegium in a mime at the behest of Dionysius I, who led a protracted siege of the city and finally took it in 386 (*PCG* T 2; **VI E**). The account provides evidence for yet another genre put to the services of a Syracusan tyrant.

In addition to Dionysius I himself (**VI E**), Syracuse produced two tragic poets of note in the fourth century: the Achaeus (*TrGF* 79) who had ten tragedies known to the Suda (α 4682) and who, like Dionysius, seems to have achieved success (once) at the Athenian Lenaea (*IG* II² 2325G, l. 35 M-O, around 356); and the productive Sosiphanes (*TrGF* 92), credited by Suda (σ 863) with a remarkable 73 dramas and seven victories. The fact that the Suda describes him as active 'in the latter days of Philip, though some say it was under Alexander the Macedonian' might reflect some memory of his having been professionally associated with one or both of this pair. Syracuse was also the home of a major poet of (New) comedy in the later fourth century, Philemon, the slightly older contemporary of Menander (active ca. 330-ca. 270: for his Syracusan origins: *PCG* T 1, 2, 11). Philemon's career was evidently international in scope. He was granted Athenian citizenship (*PCG* T 2), no doubt in some connection with his theatrical activity and successes there (**V I** on *IG* II³ 4, 518). He also produced plays on Delos (**Dvi**) and probably in Alexandria too (**Gi**). The eccentric tradition reported by Strabo (14.5.8; *PCG* T 3) that made him a native of Soli in Cilicia may reflect time spent producing comedy there. Athens asserted its claim on the poet in the second century AD with a statue on the Acropolis that gave his patronymic and Attic demotic, studiously avoiding the ethnic (*PCG* T 12). The fact that a bust in Piso's Villa at Tivoli recorded him emphatically as Syracusan (*PCG* T 11) probably reflects a reassertion of his western origins, not least since he had, like Menander, long since become a model for Roman dramatists.

We are also confident that the more broadly based civic polity in Gela that followed the fall of the Deinomenids hosted Aeschylus in that city in the last years of his life (**Aix**), perhaps introducing tragedy to an already flourishing tradition of choral performance (**Avii**). It is possible too that Selinus had a theatre (in addition to the 'theatral area' already mentioned) in the fifth century (**Axiv**). For activity elsewhere, we are heavily dependent on the archaeological remains of theatres, often the sole direct testimony to the theatrical culture of a city. In the absence of associated literary material (which when present tends to be late), choregic dedications, theatre-related decoration, or inscriptions (fewer in Sicily where the epigraphic habit was less vigorous and the available stone less good), the performance of drama in these theatres can only be assumed from the more general evidence for Sicilian love of drama, especially Euripidean tragedy (**Axi**), although the presence of major centres of production and use of theatre-related ceramic iconography in a region sometimes further bolsters the case. In general, iconographic evidence tends to be of a more generic value rather than tied to specific performances or sites, although cases such as **Axviii**, **Axix**, which demonstrate clear markers of theatricality and an intention to depict climactic scenes of known dramas, suggest a rather closer knowledge of specific performances (note too the unusual case of Lipari). Nor does the evidence of iconography always necessarily repeat a narrative of influence radiating from Athens alone: recently Green (2014a) has highlighted the extent to which a tradition of Corinthian comedy made itself felt in comic terracottas of the middle and later fourth century that were exported to or made in Western Greece.

Given that by ca. 450 tragedy was performed in both Syracuse and Gela, it is very likely that an appetite for drama was fired in other centres and that they too began to invest in dramatic festivals and theatre. The large and powerful city of Acragas further to the west of Gela on the south coast, itself founded (in part or whole) by Gela around 580, is a case in point. The Emmenid tyrants of Acragas, like the Deinomenids of Syracuse, were keen patrons of poetry early in the fifth century and recognised the power of epinikia and enkomia in particular to project their image (e.g. Morrison 2007; Budelmann 2012; Clear 2013). Midas the star piper, for whom Pindar composed *Pythian* 12 for his victory at the Pythia of 490, was an Acragantine, and it has been plausibly suggested that it was Theron who commissioned the ode on Midas' behalf, as part of a campaign of self-representation prior to his accession to the tyranny in 488 (Gentili et al. 1995, 307; Pavlou 2012, 83–7). In addition to his victory at Delphi in 490, Midas had another at the next Pythia (486), and another of unknown date at the Athenian Panathenaea (Sch. inscr. Pi. *P.* 12), so he was clearly a musician of the very highest attainments on the Panhellenic scene.

We have (as yet) no compelling reason to believe that the Emmenids were early adopters of the new musical forms of drama, as the Deinomenids certainly were, but there is spectacular new evidence emerging for theatrical culture in the city, which may ultimately throw further light on the question. Acragas expelled the tyrant Thrasydaeus around 472, leading to what most regard as a form of democracy rather like that experienced in Gela at the same time (Robinson 2011, 92–5). As at Syracuse, comedy may have pre-dated tragedy, as the comic poet Deinolochos, a younger contemporary and rival of Epicharmus, was almost certainly an Acragantine (**Av**). Though apparently Athenian, the family dynasty of tragic poets and performers best known for homonymous grandfather and grandson Carcinus (*TrGF* 21 and 70) evidently had significant connections with both Syracuse under Dionysius II and Acragas (**Ax**). There is even some evidence (admittedly open to divergent interpretation) that, around the middle of the fifth century, Aeschylus' son Euaion may have been active in Acragas (**Aix**). Another likely Acragantine tragic poet is the homonymous grandson of the philosopher Empedocles (*TrGF* 50) who lived early in the fourth century.

Until very recently, the evidence for a theatre in Acragas was modest: a passage in Frontinus of uncertain reliability and a passing comment by the sixteenth-century 'father of Sicilian history', the Dominican friar and antiquarian Tommaso Fazello. Frontinus refers to a speech given by Alcibiades to the citizens of Acragas assembled in the theatre (**Axiii 2**). 'Acragas' is widely supposed to be an error for 'Catane', and the occasion thought to be the one mentioned by Thucydides as taking place in Catane in 415 (6.51.1), but it remains a possibility that Frontinus was reporting a different event in Acragas in the same context of the Sicilian expedition, and is thus evidence for a theatre in the city (also used as a place of political assembly) by ca. 420. As for Fazello, he remarked that in 1558 one could still just make out the theatre from its submerged foundations, not far from the church of S. Nicola (1560, 129: 'Quod hodie ex obrutis fundamentis, quae a templo S. Nicolai non procul absunt, vix etiam cognoscitur').

Sporadic attempts had been made since at least the early nineteenth century to find this theatre, but Fazello's observation has received striking confirmation, for in September 2016 it was announced in the press that a large semicircular stone structure had been identified directly south-east of the S. Nicola church, the site of the present Museum and Archaeological Park of Agrigento. Early excavation reports indicate that the upper part of an extremely large curvilinear theatron has been found, with an original diameter of ca. 100 m. The theatre will have faced south, in the direction of the sea, not far below the so-called Temple of Concordia and in close proximity to the city's agora to the north (an ancient access route has already been identified). A preliminary report confidently dates the structure to the late third century. This apparently rests on stratigraphic evidence from the foundation trench of the analemma wall, of which only the lowest, foundation, course remains. Fragments of theatrical masks made of terracotta have been found and mention also made of architectural remains compatible with an orchestra and stage building of 'Hellenistic-Roman' date. The site is within the zone of the upper agora of Hellenistic Acragas. Excavation began in October 2016, by a team from the Politecnico in Bari (Luigi Maria Caliò and Monica Livadiotti) and the Archaeological Park of Agrigento (Maria Serena Rizzo, Valentina Caminneci, Maria Concetta Parello). Livadiotti et al. 2017, 41–76 publish some preliminary findings.

The question of whether the structure known as the ekklesiasterion, immediately northwest of the S. Nicola church, served as a theatre as well as a place of political assembly (De Miro 2006, 2012; Marconi 2012, 187, 189) is now likely to be settled in the negative, although it remains a possibility that it was used for drama prior to the construction of the large theatre in the third century. Dated to ca. 350–300 (though some suspect an earlier date: Hansen and Fischer-Hansen 1994, 57), the so-called ekklesiasterion, in the form of a three-quarter circle made up of some twenty steps, was largely carved directly into the rock, and held up to 3,000 people. Its shape, its immediate proximity to a bouleuterion, and the fact that it apparently lacks any stage building, lie behind the categorisation as an ekklesiasterion.

The Timoleontic era has long occupied an important place in the history of Sicilian theatre. According to the dominant account, with the arrival of the Corinthian general in 344, tyrants were expelled from the shores of Sicily, its population replenished, the economy boomed, democracy flourished – and, as a key feature of a wider growth in urbanism and monumental architecture, theatres sprang up all over the island as expressions of the new sense of civic freedom and autonomy that came with democracy (Marconi 2012, 182). A lot rests on a passage of Diodorus, who explicitly links the construction of 'the finest theatre of those in Sicily after that of Syracuse' in his hometown of Agyrion in central Sicily with this era of prosperity (**Axv**). While in many ways an attractive interpretation, this orthodoxy runs the risk of reintroducing a subtle Athenocentrism, in its implicit and largely unargued assumption that theatre is essentially expressive of and natural to democracy. The interpretation is subject to a number of other qualifications. The extent of the economic boom and associated public building is being questioned on archaeological grounds (De Angelis 2016, 129–32, 218–19; Portale 2015, esp. 699 on the 'interpretative cliché' of the 'Timoleontic revival'). And many stone theatres that were once thought to fit within this context are now being down-dated, often far beyond the Timoleontic period, as part of a more general corrective to the tendency to date monumental architecture in Sicily high in the Hellenistic period (Campagna 2006; Campagna 2011; De Vincenzo 2013, 161–78). These theatres will instead be the product of another period of economic and social renewal for much of Sicily under Roman control, at the end of the second and start of the first century.

Two that do still seem to sit properly in the Timoleontic period are Heraclea Minoa and the theatre at Monte dei Cavalli, probably ancient Hippana (Plb. 1.24). Both of these are in the area of Punic control; and both seem to have been built following their liberation from Carthaginian domination. This has led to the view that their construction was a way of reasserting the cities' Hellenicity as well as political liberty (De Vincenzo 2013, 164). But even here, care is needed, for it is striking that, at least in the case of Heraclea, the theatre survived the return of Punic control. And the cult associated with the theatre suggests an unproblematic syncretism of Punic and Greek religion. Heraclea Minoa was a sixth-century colony of Selinus (Hdt 5.46.2; **Axiv**) that some time before 500 was taken by the Lacedaemonians who had survived the failed expedition of Dorieus to take the city. It fell into Carthaginian hands by a treaty of 383 between Carthage and Dionysius I (D.S. 15.17.5), reverting again by treaty in 339 to the Greek area when it was refounded by Timoleon (D.S. 16.82.3). It is to this Timoleontic period that the stone theatre has been dated by its excavator (De Miro 2014, 63–72 is the definitive publication), although it should be noted that even in this instance some would place the theatre around the middle or towards the end of the third century (La Torre 2006, 90, 93). By 314 the city was once again in Carthaginian control, but there is no sign that the theatre was abandoned at that time.

Some regard this theatre as the first in Sicily known to have adopted the 'Athenian/ Attic' model of horseshoe-shaped theatron combined with a circular orchestra. No traces of a stage building were found, which was therefore probably made of wood (De Miro 2014, 64–5, 72). A stage building with some wooden parts was introduced only in a second stage of construction that took place in the third or second century. The theatron shows an interesting combination of seating types (De Miro 2014, 68). At the front each of the nine kerkides had prohedric benches with straight backs and armrests at each end. Above this there were ten rows of stone steps; then a section of almost equal size to the ten stone rows, of 'unmade' seating, thought by its excavator to be left to 'private' organisation. At the very top of the theatron, carved into the rock, there was a walkway and small wall. On a terrace above the theatre there was a sanctuary that very probably stood in some relation to the theatre and was in use from the fourth to the second century. De Miro (2014, 77) believes the deity was a chthonic female figure, possibly Demeter or Aphrodite in the Punic–Hellenistic syncretism (or the Aphaia attested by graffiti on vases).

The recently excavated theatre at Monte dei Cavalli (Hippana), dramatically situated just outside the city walls on a steep hillside over a thousand metres above sea level (capacity ca. 3,000), has secure stratigraphic dating for its construction in the second half of the fourth century. Offerings thus datable were found under the pavement of the orchestra that can be associated with the initial dedication of the theatre, and it seems clear that it was built as part of a new city plan (ca. 350–325) in the era of Timoleon. Its falling into disuse is also securely dated, since in 258 the city as a whole was abandoned with the Roman conquest (Vassallo 2012; Vassallo and Zirone 2012). As a result it constitutes a rare example of an early Hellenistic Sicilian theatre not subject to later alterations.

Among the theatres whose traditional dating in the Timoleontic period is open to increased scrutiny, that of Iaitas in the north-west of the island is especially important, since it was excavated according to modern scientific principles and because the dating of a number of comparable theatres – notably Soluntum, Segesta and Tyndaris – hangs together with it (La Torre 2004, 130–1; La Torre 2006). Iaitas is also a striking case of an Elymian city in Phoenician territory, though one that seems to have been receptive to Greek influence from as early as the seventh century. (Another Elymian centre, also heavily influenced by Greek culture from an early date, which may have had a theatre is Entella in the central west of the island, but the evidence consists only of a number of inscriptions of third- or possibly late fourth-century date that mention prohedria and agones, which need not imply drama: Todisco 2002, 173; Tosi 2003, 601; Marconi 2012, 195; de Cesare 1992 and Taplin 2007, 263 for a theatrical vase-fragment found at Entella.) The theatre rests in part directly on the rocky slope at the top of Mt. Iato, and is situated near the ancient agora (to the north-west), facing south. It had some thirty-five rows of seating, with an estimated capacity of around 4,400 (Isler 2003, 276).

Its excavator, Hans Peter Isler, dates its first phase to the last quarter of the fourth century (Isler 1981; Isler 2000a; Isler 2003), but his arguments have come under some stringent criticism (Campagna 2006; De Vincenzo 2013, 173–4). Affinities with the theatre of Segesta, which is now dated stratigraphically to the second half or end of the second century, are an important part of the picture (D'Andria 1997 for the new dating; critique: A. De Bernardi 2000, M. De Bernardi 2000, maintaining the possible existence of a fourth-century phase; Green 2008, 68). And Isler's tentative reconstruction and dating of the dedicatory inscription of his proposed first, fourth-century, phase of the Iaitas theatre cannot stand (Isler 2000b, 724–5; *SEG* 36, 835; *SEG* 50, 1002). Palaeographical criteria place the fragments of this inscription that certainly come from the theatre in the second century

(Dimartino *forthcoming*). If there was a phase prior to the second century, this inscription must refer to a later act of construction or restoration.

A further weighty argument for down-dating the Iaitas theatre and others of a similar style is the simple observation that they depend heavily in their general morphology, the design of their stage building and their architectural decoration on the theatre of Syracuse in the phase demonstrably associated with the latter part of the reign of Hieron II, 238–215 (**Ai**). Perhaps the single most characteristic architectural form is the use of supporting caryatids or telamons (Di Stefano 1996). These appear not only in Hieron II's theatre in Syracuse but are a stylistic marker of much of his monumental architecture, featuring in his vast altar to Zeus south of the theatre and also on the great wooden three-masted ship *Syrakosia* commissioned as a symbol of his power and the technical advances his city fostered. It is very unlikely that a relatively insignificant centre such as Iaitas would have innovated in the use of this motif in its theatre as much as a century before Syracuse and much more plausible that its use spread from Syracuse to other Sicilian centres, placing those which show it some time after 215. The question of whether the Iaitas theatre is a re-markable innovator or one of many epigonic variants on the Syracusan prototype of Hieron II should be settled with its full publication by Isler. One suggestive indicator that a late fourth-century date should not yet be ruled out is the discovery of original roof tiles from the stage building with terracotta antefixes attached in the form of theatrical masks of New Comedy (identified by Green 2008, 69 as *MNC³* 1ST 67a and 1ST 68a; Isler 2003, 280). These carry the name of their maker, Portax, whose workshop has been located.

Other theatres whose dating has been drawn down include Tyndaris, placed by Bernabò Brea (1964–1965) towards the end of the fourth century, but without any systematic ar-chaeological study and recently revised down to the late second (La Torre 2004), although without the full study required for a definitive answer (Spigo 2006, 101). As with Iaitas, affinities with the theatre of Segesta are an important part of the picture. The same is true of the small theatre of the Syracusan foundation of Heloros (capacity ca. 1,250, probably associated with the sanctuary of Demeter within the city walls to the north-east). Until recently this was placed broadly in the fourth/third centuries (Todisco 2002, 171–2; Tosi 2003, 602–3; Merlino and La Mattina 2008, 128). A date after the new construction by Hieron II of the theatre at Syracuse is inherently more likely in the case of a city such as Heloros that remained very firmly in the cultural orbit of its vastly greater metropolis (Campagna 2006, 19).

The same argument applies for the better-preserved theatre of another Syracusan foun-dation, Akrai, where a date some time from ca. 230–150 now seems most likely (Merlino and La Mattina 2008; Viola 2008). And it applies to the theatre of Morgantina, where the archaeological evidence indicates a date soon after 250, which would fit within the context of the monumentalisation of the city's agora undertaken under the stimulus of Hieron II (Bell 1988, 338; 2012, 114; Campagna 2006, 20; Sposito 2011; Stone 2014, 10, 85; De Miro 2016, who draws attention to a likely connection between the theatre and the important chthonic sanctuary immediately to its east). The conclusion is also supported by Dimartino's redating of the dedicatory inscription of the theatre on palaeographical grounds (Dimartino *forthcoming*). This dedication was carved along the tenth row of seats and indicates that the theatre was consecrated to Dionysus (Sjöqvist 1962, 138; Dubois

1989, 228) and, apparently, was the gift of a private individual (the long rectilinear stairs that bounded the agora immediately to the north of the chthonic sanctuary appear to be part of the same programme of monumental building and probably served as an ekklesterion).

A consensus holds that the first phase of the spectacular theatre of Tauromenium (Taormina) dates to the third century (Sear 2006, 193), although the view of Polacco (1982, 438–40) that the existing remains imply a prior structure remains unanswered in the absence of a definitive study (Tauromenium was founded as a Greek polis early in the fourth century: *IACP* 231). Dimartino (2009) has analysed the epigraphic evidence from the Taormina theatre, showing it to be of second-century date and possibly relating to the theatre's foundation (or perhaps a restoration at that time).

If further research confirms this down-dating of several Sicilian stone theatres, it does not necessarily follow that these places had no theatre before that date. Many could have had theatres with wooden structures, and the fact that no remains of permanent theatres have yet been found in larger and more culturally prominent cities, such as Gela, Camarina, Leontini and Megara Hyblaea, does not mean that these places had no theatre, permanent or otherwise. In the case of Gela other considerations make it very likely that drama was performed in the city from the fifth century (above). There is a variety of evidence for theatre culture in Megara Hyblaea, and some have argued for the existence of a theatre in the city's Archaic agora (**Aiii**). As for Leontini, a single passage of Plutarch recounts an assembly held in a theatre in the city in 355 (**Axvi**). Messana is a similar case. Plutarch places the capture of the tyrant Hippo in that city's theatre in 338, implying it had one sufficiently robust for the task by that date. In addition some evidence for a theatre of Roman date in the city has recently emerged (**Axvii**). As for the Syracusan foundation of Camarina, Di Stefano (2013) has published important evidence of theatrical terracottas from the city (miniature masks and statuettes, the latter relating to Middle and New Comedy and satyr play) ranging in date from around the second quarter of the fifth to the third century, found in a combination of funerary, public and domestic contexts. Several were discovered in a furnace (Pisani 2008); others in a context that suggests they had been dedicated to Demeter and Persephone (or their local equivalents); others near the agora, leading Di Stefano (2013, 176) to wonder whether there may have been a building for theatrical performances nearby. Some of these objects show affinities with the materials from Lipari.

The evidence from Lipari is a case apart, although as Green (2008, 22) notes, it is difficult to believe that the theatrical interests of the Aeolian island were an isolated phenomenon, and he points to the way in which material from Cefalù on the Sicilian north coast, and that from Adrano and Biancavilla further south on the plains below Etna, 'indicates a participation in the same cultural values' (and one can add the material recently published from Camarina, just mentioned). Lipari was – from the fifth century until its destruction by the Romans in 252 – a centre of intensive production of theatre-related objects: terracotta statuettes of actors, miniature masks and vases with theatre-related iconography. The city has left the single largest corpus of such materials (over 1,500 items) relating to tragedy, comedy and satyr play (Bernabò Brea and Cavalier 1965; Bernabò Brea 1973; 1981; 1994; 2001; Bernabò Brea and Cavalier 2002; Schwarzmaier 2011; Madella 2015; Ollà et al. 2018). The vast majority of these were found during excavation in a large undisturbed necropolis, showing that the Lipariotes had a predilection for taking such items to their graves. Sometimes a single mask (tragic, satyric or comic) was placed on top of a tomb; sometimes groups of statuettes (comic or satyric). Many other masks (tragic, satyric or comic) were found separately in votive trenches within the necropolis.

Although no theatre has yet been found, it is clear that this habit was based on a powerful attachment to theatre rather than a general attachment to the Dionysiac or to a particular form of Dionysiac eschatology. Much of the iconography is too specifically theatrical for a narrow interpretation of these as 'Dionysiac'. Thus for instance some eight terracottas have been found in votive pits in the necropolis that represent a portrait of the comic poet Menander, almost contemporary in date with the marble statue which they copy, erected in Athens ca. 290. Another series of terracotta figurines and heads is thought to represent Euripides (Bernabò Brea and Cavalier 2000). No theatre-related material dated to the fifth century has been found in the necropolis. The oldest seems to be a series of tragic, satyric and Old-Comic masks of the first decades of the fourth century (Bernabò Brea 2001, 16). The only fifth-century finds are some comic terracottas found in the 'great bothros' or votive well for Aeolus on the acropolis. There can be little doubt that these materials emerge from a context in which the cult of Dionysus was prominent and if, as seems probable, drama was performed on Lipari, it is likely that it was in some association with a cult of Dionysus. The recent finds from Adranon (**Axiii**), in domestic urban habitations, of comic terracottas akin to some from Lipari implies that they were intended as much for the living as the dead, and so likely serve as evidence for theatre as a social and economic institution rather than for the involvement of theatrical motifs in Dionysiac eschatology. The connection with Dionysus is not true of a number of Sicilian sites where we have an idea of the cultic associations of theatres. In Syracuse, Heloros, Heraclea Minoa, and Iaitas, the theatre seems to have been associated with a cult of Demeter (though in the cases of Heraclea Minoa and Iaitas the deity has sometimes been identified as Aphrodite).

Dionysius I (**VI E**) founded a number of cities during his rule, designed to secure wider territorial control: Tyndaris in 396 (D.S. 14.78.5); Andranon ca. 400. The former was named after the cult of the Tyndaridai (the Messenian Dioscuri). Both show signs of a vigorous theatre culture, the former at least quite possibly including a theatre as part of its original design (above). It is therefore noteworthy that one of the other very probable Dionysian foundations, Issa (Vis) in the Adriatic, has a Roman theatre on the city's harbour peninsula that has been thought to overlie a Greek predecessor (Gabričević 1981a). An oinochoe from the nearby cemetery has recently been published which has a red-figured comic scene (late 4th c., possibly of local manufacture: Ugarković 2016, 90), as has a terracotta theatrical mask, from a child's grave (Ugarković 2016).

An object made of ivory and thought by Gabričević (1981b) to be a 'theatre ticket' is reported as having been found in connection with this theatre (Gabričević 1981b, 152–4, with image 2; *IGR* I, 555). This is inscribed (in Greek) with the (abbreviated) name of one of the Tyndaridai, Polydeuces, and also has the number 15 in both Roman and Greek numerals (XV | Πολυδεύκ(ης) | ιε′). Gabričević thinks it may reflect the division of the theatron of Issa into sectors named after gods and heroes, after the model of the theatre of Hieron II in the mother-city of Syracuse. The identification of theatre tickets or tokens is a formidably difficult task, and the use of a valuable material such as ivory seems an unlikely choice for their manufacture. But if a connection with the theatre is sound, the presence of the name of Polydeuces hints at an intriguing association between the cult that held such prominence under Dionysius I (Rossignoli 2004; Musti 2005) and the theatre, an institution that played a prominent role in his cultural politics. No date is given for the object but it evidently comes from a period of Roman control and would thus also be evidence for the persistence of the cult of the Tyndaridai in Issa.

Like Leucas (**Cvii**; **C Introduction**), Issa was also an extremely important staging point on an ancient maritime route, in this case between the southern and the northern Adriatic Sea (one of the reasons behind its establishment by Dionysius). We do not know of any centres in northern Italy with theatre culture at this time that might help to explain the opportunistic construction of a theatre in Issa to take advantage of the regular passage of theatrical talent, although Leigh (1998, 87–90) assembles evidence that demonstrates considerable interest in and close familiarity with traditions of the upper Adriatic on the part of Aeschylus, Sophocles and Euripides – interests that sat alongside the more pragmatic Athenian need for trade in grain with the area (R-O II no. 100). Adria (between the Po and Adige rivers), a city perhaps founded by Aegina in the sixth century but certainly in receipt of Syracusan settlers under Dionysius I (*IACP* 327), had a Roman theatre (destroyed for its materials) dated to the second century AD, the design of which has been thought (controversially) to reflect a Hellenistic model (Tosi 2003, 505). But whether or not there was a local appetite for drama in northern Adriatic sites such as Adria, the favourable position of the city of Issa for maritime travel may have been one factor in encouraging or assisting its development of theatre, which could have been driven directly by its theatre-loving founder.

South Italy

Evidence for theatre culture begins rather later on the Italian peninsula. The powerful Greek city of Taras on the northern coast of the great gulf of Taranto had a Dionysia by the 360s, the attractions of which raised Plato's ire (**Axxi 1**), but, despite a strong literary tradition that the city was devoted to theatre, there is no certain evidence for theatre there (or at any other site) until some time before the 320s. Outside of the evidence of the vases, there is no strong case for the performance of tragedy or comedy in the fifth century (the evidence for theatre in Croton in the fifth century provided by Iamb. *VP* 126 is unreliable), but the less concrete evidence of theatre-related vase imagery plays a considerably larger role here than in Sicily. From around the 420s, Taras was the main centre for the production of Apulian vasepainting, and is overwhelmingly dominant among those places which have revealed theatre-related vases, making the softer evidence of vase iconography in this case that much more persuasive (**Axxii**; **Axxiii**; **Axxiv**; **Axxv**; **V E**).

The cities of Metapontum, Heraclea and Thurii, further to the west on the gulf of Taras, are often invoked in discussion of theatre in the Greek West – Thurii above all because, as a largely Athenian foundation of mid fifth-century date (444/3), directed by none other than Pericles, it is plausibly thought to have served as an important bridgehead for the spread of Athenian theatre and culture to South Italy, notably the craft of red-figured vasepainting (Taplin 1993). There is however no direct evidence for the performance of drama in Thurii. Closest is the comedy *Thurio-Persians* by Metagenes (last decades of the fifth century), with its chorus of Persified citizens of Thurii and lavish praise of the city, well suited to production in the city itself, as Revermann (2006, 71–2) notes, commenting in particular on the fact that Athenaeus' (6.270a) description of the work as ἀδίδακτον 'unproduced' must mean that it could not be found in the Athenian *Didaskaliai*. The fact that Thurii was the birth place of a number of successful theatre professionals is also suggestive – notably the comic poet Alexis, who won at the Athenian Dionysia in 348/7 (*IG* II² 2318, l. 1471 M-O, perhaps early in his career: Arnott 1996, 10) and at the Lenaea by the 340s (*IG* II² 2325E, l. 45 M-O; *IG* II² 2322, l. 2); as well as the tragic actor Archias, who had a Lenaea victory around 330 (*IG* II² 2325H, l. 43 M-O; Stefanis no. 439). Alexis is credited with a large production of some 245 comedies (Suda α 1138 = *PCG* T 1), which some have interpreted as evidence for performance in Magna Graecia, in addition to the Athenian festivals (Blume 1978, 9–10) though Arnott (1996, 15) is sceptical. Clement knew of a tragic poet by the name of Patrokles from Thurii (*Protr.* 2.30.4) who wrote a tragedy that concerned the Dioscuri, the prominence of whose cult in Magna Graecia might suggest that it was aimed at a local audience. (The Athenian tragedian of the same name mentioned only by Sch. Ar. *Wealth* 83 is probably a phantom: Sommerstein 2001, 140; Millis and Olson 2012, 206; *TrGF* 57–8.)

Only a small part of the ancient city has been excavated, but its rectilinear street plan is clearly revealed, very probably the work of Hippodamus of Miletus, one of its colonists, or at least under his influence. This consists of a grid of broad avenues (*plateiai*) forming large blocks (ca. 300 × 300 m), subdivided into smaller (domestic) units by narrow cross-streets. One of the broad avenues was named Dionysias (others are Heraclea, Olympias and Aphrodisia: D.S. 12.10.7), and it is very likely that a major sanctuary of the god stood alongside or at the end of it (Mertens 2006, 362–7; the theatre built over the excavated grid plan of Thurii is part of the later Roman city of Copia, dates in its first phase to the second century AD and does not seem to relate to a pre-existing Greek structure: Tosi 2003, 233; Marino 2010, esp. 134–8).

The evidence is stronger for Metapontum, which certainly had a theatre (unusual for being built up artificially, though necessarily, on a flat site) in the area of the agora, close to sanctuaries of Zeus Agoraios (a stele inscribed 'agora of Zeus' was found near the theatre: *SEG* 29, 955, ca. 600–550) and of Dionysus. Around 330 a conventional theatre with stage building (capacity of ca. 6,500) was built (Mertens and De Siena 1982; Tosi 2003, 243–5; Magnolo 1995, on marks on blocks in the central sector of the theatre that may have to do with a restoration project of the second half of the fourth century: *SEG* 45, 1449). The construction of this new-style theatre appears to have followed the partial destruction by fire of an older building (which the evidence of carbonised wood suggests may have employed wooden *ikria*), directly on top of which the new theatre stood. Two phases of this earlier structure have been identified, the first (I) ca. 550, the second (II) early fifth century, when some stone seats were added (previously it seems that only embanked earth was used).

This earlier two-phase building is generally referred to as an ekklesiasterion because it is thought to have been solely or primarily a place for political gathering rather than performance. It consists of two semicircular theatra that meet at a large rectangular orchestra, approached by two wide access ways (capacity ca. 7,500–8,000). It is however clear that this cannot have been only, and perhaps not even primarily, a political structure. Its seating capacity – excessive for the needs of the citizenry alone – suggests other than purely political usages (Mertens and De Siena 1982; Hansen and Fischer-Hansen 1994, 65–7); and marks (*grammai*) made in chalk in the orchestra of phase II are best explained as guiding the placement of choruses (Todisco 2002, 155; Mertens 2006, 336–7; Moretti 2014a, 118). It appears that early in the fourth century part of the building was destroyed and abandoned for a period, and there is some indication that wooden benches may have been used in the interim before the new theatre was built. The political organisation of the city is not clear: a tyranny is likely in the Archaic period and a subsequent oligarchy has been inferred from little more than the story that Pythagoras took refuge and died there, but there is some evidence for democratic inclination at the end of the fifth century, when Metapontum supported Athens against Syracuse (Th. 7.33; 7.57.11).

The city produced one of the most famous actors of the fourth century, Aristodemos, victor at the Athenian Lenaea around 370 (*IG* II² 2325H, l. 23 M-O) and possibly earlier (ca. 390) at the Dionysia (*IG* II² 2325B, l. 26 M-O) and who, after being granted Athenian citizenship, served on several critical occasions as an ambassador to Philip (**VI F**). Metapontum was also an extremely important centre of vase production with theatrical motifs around the turn of the fifth and fourth centuries (Taplin 2007, 15). A small number of the most significant theatre-related items once thought to be Tarantine are now considered by some more likely to derive from Metapontum (notably **Axxii** and **Axxiv**; note also Green 2014b on the importance of this figurative tradition in Metapontum in the years before and around 400).

Heraclea in Lucania, jointly founded in 432 by Taras and Thurii and on the coast approximately between them, was another important centre of production. Many vases, dating from ca. 400, found in funeral contexts have mythological subjects thought to reflect theatrical performances, and perhaps locally performed tragedy (Taplin 1993, 16–17; Taplin 2007, 17, 129–30, 187–88; Taplin 2012). Euripides' *Captive Melanippe* (ca. 424–413) sutures figures originally at home in Thessalian myth into a South Italian context that ends with a prophecy of the foundation of Heraclea, and may well have been composed with production there or at nearby Metapontum in mind (Collard et al. 1995, 245; Nafissi 1997; Allan 2001, 85–6, who also suggests performance of Euripides' *Herakleidai* in the city, citing two vases from the area with depictions of the story; Taplin 2007, 193–6 for discussion of an Apulian volute krater of ca. 320s that seems to depict one of the two *Melanippe* plays by Euripides, as he would argue *Melanippe the Wise*; see now Stewart 2017, 144–58, who also plausibly argues that Euripides in his *Aeolus* deliberately merged the two previously separate figures of Aeolus, the son of Hellen, founder of the mainland Greek Aeolic race, and Aeolus, the master of the winds located in the Aeolian islands off the north-east coast of Sicily, the composite becoming the father of the founding kings of Italy and Sicily).

Further south on the Ionian coast, theatres have been found in the old rival cities of Locri and Rhegium. The construction of the former is usually placed in the period after the fall of Dionysius II in 344, when the pro-Syracusan élite was replaced by a more democratic constitution that appears to have ushered in a period of considerable economic and cultural fertility (Barra Bagnasco 2005). (Prior to this and from its earliest days in the seventh century Locri seems to have had a narrow, hereditary, oligarchy.) Local vasepainting and terracotta production show close links with Sicily (Elia 2014). The Locri theatre, which was close to a sanctuary zone in the upper part of the city and connected by a road to an area of domestic dwellings, has a horseshoe-shaped theatron, made of local sandstone, with a capacity estimated at over 4,500. It probably dates to the later fourth century, when it apparently had a wooden stage building, with which a number of silen antefixes have been associated (Parra 1998, 307–8; Todisco 2002, 145–9; Tosi 2003, 239–41). Decoration of this sort – on top of the fact that a number of terracotta votive offerings of theatrical subject matter were found in wells or drains in the area of the stage building (including a terracotta statuette of an actor dressed as a frog, 4th c., and a miniature terracotta mask of a comic actor, 3rd c.: Parra 1998, 308 pl. 61, 309 pl. 60) – strongly suggests that this was a theatre where drama was performed. The full spectrum of votive deposits found in the area implies a range of divine recipients, including Dionysus, Artemis, Athena, Persephone and a local hero. An as yet unproven suggestion is that the theatre may have been associated with the significant sanctuary of Olympian Zeus (Costabile 1992), which has left an important archive of public documents inscribed on bronze tablets (mid 4th to 3rd c.), some relating to the finance of public works (Parra 1998, 310–12; Costabile 1992).

The small Rhegium theatre discovered under the modern city of Reggio di Calabria (Todisco 2002, 160–3; Tosi 2003, 248–9) might possibly date from the same general period, for the city was refounded by Dionysius II (having been sacked by Dionysius I in 387) and gained its independence in 351, at which point it may already have had a democratic form of government (Robinson 2011, 114) after a long period of largely tyrannical and narrowly oligarchic-aristocratic rule. It certainly pre-dates the Roman conquest of 270. The modest size of the structure (capacity ca. 1,500–1,600) has encouraged the view that it may have been an ekklesiasterion rather than a theatre (Martorano 1985), but the discovery of three terracotta capitals for columns implies the existence of a stage building, with wooden columns. The presence in the city by the second century of a local Association of Artists of Dionysus (*ATD* I, 317–19) shows that it had an active theatre culture by that date (note also Cic. *Arch.* 5) and may incline us to suppose that the building in question had long since been used as a theatre (the inscription was found in reuse in the mediaeval city wall near the theatre).

Two cities on the Tyrrhenian coast, Elea (Hyele) and Poseidonia, are strong candidates for theatrical performance by the fourth century, and it also remains a real possibility that there was a Greek predecessor to the Roman theatre in Neapolis (Tosi 2003, 149). Elea, founded ca. 540 by Phocaeans (**Ev**) from the failed venture of Alalie in Corsica, may in fact have had a theatre much earlier. A number of studies of the theatre on the south-east side of the acropolis in 1979 and again in the 1990s and in 2001–2002 have clarified the existence of three phases. The second, Hellenistic, phase has been dated with little controversy to ca. 300 (Steskal 2002, 278; Krinzinger 2003, 25). A long portico to the west of the theatre has also been attributed to this building phase (Gassner 2016, 94). Part of its prohedria survives (Krinzinger and Gassner 1997, 235 with fig. 2). The surviving seats in the theatron date from the third, Roman, phase, which is placed in the third century AD (Krinzinger and Gassner 1997).

The most difficult to date and interpret is the evidence of the first phase. That evidence consists of the remains of part of an analemma wall, situated at the north-east corner of the higher of the two terrace walls that run along the south-east side of the acropolis, at the level supporting the theatron. This analemma wall is of high-quality polygonal construction and was found in a good state of preservation, covered in a fine white plaster that sought to imitate the effect of marble (Krinzinger and Gassner, 1997, 242–3, with fig. 7). From it to the east there led another curved stone wall (Krinzinger and Gassner, 1997, 242–3, with fig. 6). The full reconstructed shape of this theatron in its eastern part must remain hypothetical, given that the rest of it was destroyed by the construction of the Hellenistic theatre above it (Krinzinger 2003, 25). But although preserved only for ca. 2.0 m of its course, the curved wall that might have delimited the orchestra of the theatron allows us to calculate that the original diameter of the orchestra would have been ca. 14.0 m. The structure has been dated as early as ca. 470–460 (Bencivenga Trillmich 1994, 92–4), but its most recent excavators put it in the first half of the fourth century, mainly from the evidence of the backfill (Krinzinger and Gassner 1997, 243). Analysis of the limited remains at the level under the outer side of the wall (Steskal 2002, 280) permits only the determination of a *terminus post quem* in the second half of the fifth century.

The function of this earlier theatron cannot be determined. Bencivenga Trillmich (1994) considers it most likely a bouleuterion, while acknowledging that a multi-functional usage for such a structure is likely, and assuming that it could also readily have served for theatrical performances. Krinzinger and Gassner (1997, 243) note that its position dictates that it must have been designed for important public and cultic activity. The fact that a standard, new-style Greek theatre was built directly above it ca. 300 is suggestive, and moreover, it has also long been noted that if a wish to construct a theatre for dramatic performances had been the primary motive, other areas would have offered more suitable options, such as the southern slopes of the acropolis at the level of the first terrace (Bencivenga Trillmich 1994, 94 citing Lenormant). Nearby there were found numerous post holes and other cuttings in the rocky outcrops to the side, which Krinzinger (2006, 171, pl. II.3) interprets as indications of an area designed for festivals, richly ornamented with votive gifts and honorific monuments placed along the sacred way.

Founded by Sybaris ca. 600, the city of Poseidonia (Paestum) has a circular building to the east of its agora, in use from ca. 450 to the Roman conquest, which is sometimes identified as a theatre. Its small capacity (ca. 1,100–1,400) has rightly been seen as suggesting a (primarily) political function though some argue it might also have been used for performances (Todisco 2002, 159–60; Tosi 2003, 246). Of generic rather than specific value is the intense concentration of possibly theatre-related vases produced from ca. 360 in a local tradition derived from the Sicilian. The painter As(s)teas who signed around a dozen surviving pieces has been thought to reflect comedy and tragedy, especially Euripidean tragedy (Taplin 2007, 19), but it is disputed as to whether the thirty-odd vases with 'theatrical' subject matter (some by another signing artist, Python) show intimate familiarity with performance or simply copy motifs from the Sicilian repertoire (Hughes 2003; Green 2008, 214–15; Bacilieri 2001, 55–65 makes a case that the relevant Paestan iconography depicts a distinctive type of stage building that must have been specific to the city). The most cogent single example (**Axxvii**) indicates a direct dependence on a performance tradition of the *Demes* of Eupolis, a comedy composed more than half a century earlier, and is certainly good evidence for the developing comic canon in the fourth century. The fact that Poseidonia fell under the control of Lucanians soon after 400 would mean that any Greek drama being performed in the city would have appealed to them. Aristoxenus (fr. 28) may refer to a time before 400 when the Poseidonians had a properly Greek theatrical culture, after which it was 'barbarised' (Meriani 2003).

The question of whether and to what extent non-Greek ('barbarian') peoples in the West adopted Greek drama has only been posed very recently (Robinson 2004; 2014; Carpenter 2014). One of the key types of evidence for theatre culture in this part of the Italian peninsula – Apulian red-figured vases with possibly theatrical scenes, including comic scenes with specifically theatrical markers such as stage buildings and actors (**Axxiii**; **Axxiv**; **Axxv**; **Axxvi**; **V E**) – derives in large part, when their contexts of discovery are known, from graves in non-Greek Italic communities, notably in Peucetia, and most spectacularly at Ruvo di Puglia (probably ancient Rubi), some 90 km north-west of Taras. Simple prejudice has prevented the drawing of the plausible conclusion that those who took such care to have these images in their graves were themselves interested in and closely acquainted with the practices alluded to upon them. The fact that Peucetia was directly accessible from Greece by an ancient maritime route up the Adriatic (Kirigin et al. 2009) would also support the thesis that the Greek trade in ceramics with the peoples of Peucetia may have been direct, rather than through the intermediary of Taras. Robinson (2004) has convincingly shown that various indigenous Italian communities in Apulia enjoyed comic performances (note also the suggestive evidence of **Axxvi**). Carpenter (2014) makes a similar case for tragedy.

One indigenous centre – Bruttian (in modern Calabria) rather than Apulian – has even left a theatre 'of Greek type' (Sear 2006, 145). Castiglione di Paludi, probably ancient Cossa, was a fortified garrison town in a zone disputed between Bruttians and Greeks, but archaeological finds increasingly make it clear that the place was substantially urbanised, adopting architectural and iconographic forms from the Greeks (there is in addition evidence of bilingualism: Fronda 2010, 152–3). The excavation conducted on the theatre has not been properly published, but a number of fragmentary Ionic capitals (dated to the fourth century) and a clay antefix in the form of a woman's head have been treated as evidence of a stage building (Brienza et al. 2011, 274 air the possibility that rectilinear cuttings in the rock into which the theatron was cut may reflect an earlier phase for the structure). Given the theatre's small size and the absence of definitive evidence for a stage building, some think of it as an ekklesiasterion (Brienza et al. 2011, 272). The theatre is situated in the central public zone of the site, not far from the agora and other public structures; a building thought to have some cultic function was identified close to the theatre (Brienza et al. 2011, 272–3; Todisco 2002, 139–41; Tosi 2003, 234–5). In general Bruttian culture in the late fourth and third centuries shows the same sort of pattern as appears in Apulia: 'the emergence of a Hellenised political elite whose status was bound up with wealth and military success' (Fronda 2010, 154). It would be rash to conclude that Greek tragedy or comedy were performed in this theatre by the fourth century; but rash also to exclude the possibility.

Ai: The Theatre in Syracuse

1. **Diodorus of Sicily, *Library of History* 13.94.1**. Written ca. 50–30, and referring to Dionysius' arrival from Gela and seizure of power in Syracuse in 406. Text: Vogel.

> θέας δ' οὔσης ἐν ταῖς Συρακούσαις, τὴν ὥραν τῆς ἀπαλλαγῆς τῶν ἐκ τοῦ
> θεάτρου παρῆν εἰς τὴν   πόλιν. συνδραμόντων δὲ τῶν ὄχλων ἐπ' αὐτὸν
> καὶ πυνθανομένων περὶ τῶν Καρχηδονίων, ἀγνοεῖν αὐτοὺς ἔφη, διότι τῶν
> ἔξωθεν πολεμιωτέρους ἔχουσι τοὺς ἔνδον τῶν κοινῶν προεστῶτας, οἷς οἱ μὲν
> πολῖται πιστεύοντες ἑορτάζουσιν, αὐτοὶ δὲ διαφοροῦντες τὰ δημόσια τοὺς
> στρατιώτας ἀμίσθους πεποιήκασι

κατὰ τὴν ὥραν Rhodoman   ὑπὸ or περὶ τὴν ὥραν Reiske

A show was on at Syracuse, and (Dionysius) arrived at the time when people were leaving the theatre for the city. As the hurrying crowds converged on him and asked about the Carthaginians, they were unaware, he said, that they had greater enemies among those within the city in charge of public affairs than among those outside the city: the citizens put their trust in these men while they were holding their festival, but they meanwhile were plundering the public funds and had made the soldiers go without pay

2. **Plutarch, *Life of Dion* 38.2–4**. Written ca. 115 AD. Target date: mid summer 356 (38.1). It is generally agreed (Muccioli 1990, 170) that Plutarch depends heavily on the *History* of Timonides of Leucas, who was himself a key participant in events, including the planning of Dion's return from exile to Syracuse in 357 narrated in the broader context of this passage. In the struggle between Dion and his old admiral Herakleides for control of Syracuse while Dionysius II was in Italy, the people meet in assembly (ἐκκλησιάζουσι 38.1) to appoint new commanders. Text: Ziegler.

> ἐπεὶ δὲ φυλάξαντες εὐδίαν σταθερὰν οἱ δημαγωγοὶ συνετέλουν τὰς
> ἀρχαιρεσίας, βοῦς ἁμαξεὺς οὐκ ἀήθης οὐδ' ἄπειρος ὄχλων, ἄλλως δέ πως τότε
> πρὸς τὸν ἐλαύνοντα θυμωθεὶς καὶ φυγὼν ἀπὸ[3] τοῦ ζυγοῦ, δρόμῳ πρὸς τὸ
> θέατρον ὥρμησε, καὶ τὸν μὲν δῆμον εὐθὺς ἀνέστησε καὶ διεσκέδασεν, οὐδενὶ
> κόσμῳ φεύγοντα, τῆς δ' ἄλλης πόλεως[4] ἐπέδραμε σκιρτῶν καὶ ταράττων
> ὅσον ὕστερον οἱ πολέμιοι κατέσχον. οὐ μὴν ἀλλὰ ταῦτα χαίρειν ἐάσαντες οἱ
> Συρακόσιοι πέντε καὶ εἴκοσι στρατηγοὺς ἐχειροτόνησαν, ὧν εἷς ἦν Ἡρακλείδης·

And when after looking out for settled fair weather, the popular leaders started to hold the elections for office, a draught-ox, not at all unfamiliar or inexperienced with crowds, but for some reason or other at this moment angry at his driver, fled from[3] the yoke and made a rush for the theatre. It immediately made the people get up and scattered them in disorderly flight, and then it ran, leaping up and throwing eveything into turmoil, over as much of the rest of the city [4] as the enemy later occupied. But the Syracusans paid no attention to this and elected twenty-five generals, one of whom was Herakleides.

3. Plutarch, *Life of Timoleon* **34.5–7**. Written ca. 115 AD. Target date: 338. The *Timoleon* is widely held to draw heavily on Timaeus of Tauromenium (late 4th – early 3rd c.), though Westlake (1938) argued for the primacy of a Peripatetic biography, itself based on Timaeus, with additional direct consultation of Timaeus. At 34.1–3 Timoleon pursues Mamerkos, tyrant of Catane, to his place of refuge with Hippo, tyrant of Messana, and beseiges the city with both men in it. The Messanians capture Hippo and execute him in their theatre (**Axvii**), bringing their children from their schools to watch the edifying spectacle of the tyrant's punishment. Mamerkos surrenders and faces a similar fate in the theatre of Syracuse. Text: Ziegler.

> ὁ δὲ Μάμερκος ἑαυτὸν Τιμολέοντι παρέδωκεν ἐπὶ τῷ δίκην ὑποσχεῖν ἐν Συρακοσίοις μὴ κατηγοροῦντος Τιμολέοντος. [6] ἀχθεὶς δ᾽ εἰς τὰς Συρακούσας καὶ παρελθὼν εἰς τὸν δῆμον, ἐπεχείρει μέν τινα συγκείμενον ἐκ παλαιοῦ λόγον ὑπ᾽ αὐτοῦ διεξιέναι, θορύβοις δὲ περιπίπτων καὶ τὴν ἐκκλησίαν ὁρῶν ἀπαραίτητον, ἔθει ῥίψας τὸ ἱμάτιον διὰ μέσου τοῦ θεάτρου, καὶ πρός τι τῶν βάθρων δρόμῳ [7] φερόμενος, συνέρρηξε τὴν κεφαλὴν ὡς ἀποθανούμενος. οὐ μὴν ἔτυχέ γε ταύτης τῆς τελευτῆς, ἀλλ᾽ ἔτι ζῶν ἀπαχθεὶς ἥνπερ οἱ λῃσταὶ δίκην ἔδωκε.

As for Mamerkos, he gave himself up to Timoleon on condition that he should undergo trial at Syracuse, and that Timoleon should not prosecute him. [6] So he was brought to Syracuse, and when he came before the people, tried to rehearse a speech he had composed a long time before; but being received with noisy uproar, and seeing that the assembly was inexorable, he flung away his cloak, ran right across the theatre, and [7] dashed his head against one of the bench seats, in an attempt to kill himself. However, he was not so fortunate as to die in this way, but was taken away, still living, and crucified like a robber.

4. Plutarch, *Life of Timoleon* **38.5–7**. Written ca. 115 AD. The events date to near the end of Timoleon's life, so ca. 336. Cornelius Nepos, *Timol.* (20) 4.2 offers a briefer version of the same material. Text: Ziegler.

> καλὴν δὲ καὶ τὸ περὶ τὰς ἐκκλησίας γινόμενον ὄψιν εἰς τιμὴν αὐτοῦ παρεῖχε· τὰ γὰρ ἄλλα δι᾽ αὐτῶν κρίνοντες, ἐπὶ τὰς μείζονας διασκέψεις ἐκεῖνον ἐκάλουν. [6] ὁ δὲ κομιζόμενος δι᾽ ἀγορᾶς ἐπὶ ζεύγους πρὸς τὸ θέατρον ἐπορεύετο, καὶ τῆς ἀπήνης <ἐφ᾽> ἧσπερ ἐτύγχανε καθήμενος εἰσαγομένης, ὁ μὲν δῆμος ἠσπάζετο μιᾷ φωνῇ προσαγορεύων αὐτόν, ὁ δ᾽ ἀντασπασάμενος, καὶ χρόνον τινὰ δοὺς ταῖς εὐφημίαις καὶ τοῖς ἐπαίνοις, [7] εἶτα διακούσας τὸ ζητούμενον ἀπεφαίνετο γνώμην. ἐπιχειροτονηθείσης δὲ ταύτης, οἱ μὲν ὑπηρέται πάλιν ἀπῆγον διὰ

τοῦ θεάτρου τὸ ζεῦγος, οἱ δὲ πολῖται βοῇ καὶ κρότῳ προπέμψαντες ἐκεῖνον, ἤδη τὰ λοιπὰ τῶν δημοσίων καθ᾿ αὑτοὺς ἐχρημάτιζον.

Moreover, the proceedings in their assemblies afforded a noble spectacle in his (Timoleon's) honour, since, while they decided other matters by themselves, for the more important deliberations they summoned him. [6] Then he would proceed to the theatre carried through the market place on a mule-car; and when the vehicle in which he sat was brought in, the people would greet him with one voice and call him by name, and he, after returning their greetings and allowing some time for their felicitations and praises, [7] would then listen carefully to the matter under debate and pronounce his opinion. And when this opinion had been adopted, his retainers would conduct his car back again through the theatre, and the citizens, after sending him on his way with shouts of applause, would proceed at once to transact the rest of the public business by themselves.

5. **Diomedes,** *Art of Grammar* (*Gramm. Lat.* 1, pp. 486–7). The *Art of Grammar*, in three books, was written in the second half of the 4th c. AD or somewhat later (Kaster 1988, 270–1). This passage comes from a discussion of the Sicilian origins of the bucolic genre. Favi (2017b) convincingly demonstrates that the Hieron in question in this passage must be Hieron II (in power 275–ca. 216) and not Hieron I (in power 478–died 467/6). Hieron I did not conquer Syracuse (note *expugnaret*) but took over rule after the death of his brother Gelon I, whereas Hieron II did impose himself on Syracuse militarily (Plb. 1.8.3–5). This also accords with a passage of pseudo-Probus ([Prob.] *Comm. in Verg. Buc. et Georg.* p. 324, 23 – p. 325, 3 Hagen) that treats the same subject, and which is not dependent on Diomedes but very probably derives from a common source (Reitzenstein 1893, 194). According to this, *ante Gelonem tyrannidem Syracusis lue pecora interibant* 'Before the tyranny of Gelon the animals were dying because of a plague'; the people's response was to dedicate a temple to Artemis, *quam Lyaeam vocaverunt propter quod malis essent absoluti* 'whom they called Lyaea because they had been freed from ills'. This is chronologically compatible with Diomedes' text only if the Gelon in question is Gelon II. Text: Keil.

> *antequam Hiero rex Syracusas expugnaret, morbo Sicilia laborabat. variis et adsiduis caerimoniis Dianam placantes finem malis invenerunt eamque Lyaeam cognominaverunt, quasi solutricem malorum. inde res in consuetudinem tracta est, ut greges rusticorum theatrum ingrederentur et de victoria canerent.*

Before king Hieron conquered Syracuse, Sicily was afflicted with the plague. They discovered a way to end their ills by appeasing Diana with a variety of non-stop rituals, and they gave her the epithet 'Lyaea', as the looser of their evils. Thereafter it became an established practice for the bands of country-folk to enter the theatre and sing of the victory.

It is highly likely that the Phormis from Arcadia who served Gelon militarily in the 480s is to be identified with the Phormos who served him culturally, as tutor to his children, and also as a major comic poet in the orbit of his court (**Aiv**), in a tradition characteristic of the Sicilian tyrants (**VI A**; **VI E**). The ultimate source for the dramaturgical innovations ascribed to the comic poet Phormos is unrecoverable, but Lycophron of Chalkis (Lowe 2013) is an attractive candidate, given his likely responsibility for cataloguing (and commenting upon) the comedies in the library of Alexandria. The very oddity of the notice concerning his introduction of 'a stage building (skene) of purple skins' (**Aiv 1**) speaks in favour of its credentials, and the various attempts to correct the text so as to mean 'purple <costumes instead of> skins' (Phormos *PCG* T 1 app. crit.) should be avoided. The echo it establishes with the tradition, reported unfavourably as quintessentially vulgar behaviour by Aristotle (**Bi 5**), of the use of purple (costumes or scenery? Sifakis 1971; Wilson 2000, 94) in comic performances at Megara, is suggestive. Some have thought that Aristotle had Sicilian Megara Hyblaea in mind, a city in which Epicharmus very probably produced his work and which Gelon destroyed in 483 (**Aiii**). At a minimum the use of a stage building for Syracusan comedy ca. 485 is implied. Perhaps the most likely sense to draw from this report is that the 'walls' of this stage building were made of soft fabric (rather than wood or stone) and that Phormos' innovation related to the introduction of (presumably tanned) sturdy skins dyed purple (or maybe the reference is merely to a backdrop in front of the stage building: *DTC*² 231; Polacco and Anti 1981, 33, 166; **Bi** for the use of leather hangings on parodoi and elsewhere on the stage).

Aviii is solid evidence for the completion of a phase of major works, perhaps around 410. That will be the theatre in which **1** locates the arrival of Dionysius I from Gela on his way to take power in Syracuse in 406. An author with access to such abundant local sources as Diodorus is unlikely to have been loose or inventive on this point, which also accords with the rich evidence for a tradition in Syracuse (and more broadly in Sicily), stretching over hundreds of years, of using theatres as a site for political communication and action, in a variety of political climates – to listen to autocrats as readily as to execute them (**2–4**; Just. *Epit.* 22.2.8–12). **2–4** identify the theatre as the site where the Syracusans routinely held their assemblies in the second half of the fourth century, as does the novel *Chaereas and Callirhoe* by Chariton, composed ca. 25 BC–50 AD and largely set in fifth-century Syracuse (e.g. 1.1.12; 3.4.7; 8.7.1; similarly in Plutarch's account of Dion in Leontini, where ekklesia and theatre are identified: **Axvi**; Gallo 2003). It is likely that the theatre(s) served as a, and perhaps the primary, place of civic assembly in Syracuse long before the era of Timoleon.

The presumed site of the Syracusan agora in southern Achradina remains unclear (Zirone 2005, 165–6) and in any case the widely held assumption that a city's agora served as its assembly place rests on little firm evidence (Hansen and Fischer-Hansen 1994, esp. 45–6). Robinson (2011, 88) rightly notes that one of the theatres of Syracuse is the most likely location for assemblies during the period of more democratic politics from 466 to 406. Whether

Syracuse should be called a democracy as early as the 460s (Robinson 2011, 67–88), or only in the last decade or so of the century, is a matter of live debate (Rutter 2000; Hornblower 2008, 53; de Angelis 2016, 206–10). Those who tend to the latter view recognise the existence of a mixture of oligarchic-aristocratic and democratic elements in the earlier part of the period. The growth of the navy in the 430s and the likely 'trickle-down' benefits of imperial expansion seem to have alleviated class tensions and indicate that the voice of the lower orders was making itself heard. It was, somewhat ironically, the defeat of democratic Athens in 412 that led to the introduction of properly democratic reforms in Syracuse.

Dionysius' devotion to drama, both personally and as an integral part of his broad cultural politics, is well established (**VI E**). From **1** he emerges as a canny exploiter of theatrical space for political ends, stage-managing the delicate politics of his arrival in the city over which he intends to establish himself as tyrant through the space afforded for mass communication, the theatre. Though it is represented as mere chance, Dionysius will surely have foreseen this opportunity of the presence of the populace gathered at a festival in the theatre on his march towards the city. Trojani (in Polacco and Anti 1981, 42) makes the observation that he in all likelihood approached Syracuse from Gela by travelling down the Anapos valley, and so will have reached the city in the region of Neapolis, implying that a theatre on the Temenites hill is meant.

The theatre appears as a political space at another key moment in Syracusan history in **2**. This event sounds more like a reality conveniently turned into a significant historical symbol than a literary artifice manufactured to serve as symbol for political and historical reality. We may therefore be justified in focusing on the detail: the fact that the ox could not readily escape the theatre suggests a somewhat confined space, like a theatre with a solid, built-up theatron and constricted entrances (Trojani in Polacco and Anti 1981, 42). Similarly in **3**, where the tyrant's attempt to commit suicide on one of the *bathra* in 343 could only be convincing if these were already made of stone.

5 can no longer (as has been the case hitherto: Trojani in Polacco and Anti 1981, 41–3) be treated as the earliest literary evidence for the Syracusan theatre (Favi 2017b) but it does accord with the abundant evidence for the enormous resources devoted to the theatre by Hieron II (below) and throws further light on the particular importance attached to the bucolic genre by Hieron II and Gelon II (note the sixteenth *Idyll* of Theocritus, dedicated to Hieron II, and the tradition that Theocritus composed an epigram for Epicharmus which was inscribed in the Syracusan theatre: **Aiii 6**).

The Archaeological Remains

More than a century of archaeological study shows little sign of producing a consensus on the most basic issues concerning the cultic context, the form and the dating of the earliest phases of the Syracusan theatre(s). (For reports and amateur study prior to Orsi's excavations see Zirone 2005, 172–3.) On the northern edge of the district called Neapolis, outside the Gelonian walls and around 1 km to the north-west of the city's centre, the Temenites hill is the location of the Syracusan theatre. Neapolis had probably already become a suburb of the city by the fifth century, in the wake of Gelon's deliberate mass expansion of the population in the 480s. It has recently become clear that the theatre was situated close and parallel to a significant ancient road, of fifth-century date or even earlier, that passed east to west from Acradina to Neapolis and its sanctuaries, part of a network connecting the urban centre of Syracuse to its necropolis (Voza 2001, 208; 2007, 74). What follows is a selective survey of some of the more salient features of the long debate over the history of the Greek phases of the Syracusan theatre. (On the so-called gymnasium with small theatre and Italic temple west of the agora, dated to the first–second century AD, see Sear 2006, 192.)

The Rectilinear Theatre

There are remains of two distinct but adjacent theatrical structures on the Temenites hill. On the south-west slope is the set of some seventeen rows of rock-carved seats, around 27.5 m in length and divided by two staircases, of late sixth- or fifth-century date (no stratigraphic study was ever undertaken to narrow the range). This lies some 24 m to the south-west of a small quadrangular sanctuary (excavated by Stucchi), at the south-western corner of the retaining wall of the later, great theatre. This sanctuary revealed a number of altars, the earliest dating to the late seventh century, as well as various votive stelai and stone receptacles for cult purposes (Stucchi 1952; Neutsch 1954, 604; Stucchi 1954; Polacco 1990, 144–9; no full publication emerged and the original excavation notebooks are lost: Polacco 1990, 135–6). The rectilinear theatre – sometimes called instead a 'theatral area', largely because of its non-canonical shape and uncertain association with dramatic performances – was probably directly associated with this Archaic sanctuary for cult purposes (Polacco 1990, 153 is confident to that effect). For Gentili (1952) this was the place where Epicharmus, Phormos and their peers put on their comedies. The deity of the sanctuary is uncertain: Apollo Temenites and the pair Demeter and Kore have both been argued (below). The use of the site as a theatre for dramatic performance prior to the construction of the great theatre remains hypothetical, but their proximity is itself highly suggestive. Further bibliography in Marconi 2012, 203–4.

The Great (Curvilinear) Theatre

The great theatre of Syracuse was carved directly into an accommodating corner of the limestone hillside of the Temenites (for a reconstructed image of the morphology of the hillside prior to human intervention that indicates its natural suitability to accommodate a curvilinear theatron, see Voza 2007, 77 fig. 12). The excavations of Orsi in 1907 and 1916 laid the basis for the first systematic study, the monograph by Rizzo (1923), who identified three phases of construction – Classical, Hellenistic (under Hieron II) and Roman. To the Classical phase he attributed (1923, 62), as an example of 'Charonian stairs' (Green et al. 2015, 328–31), the long underground passageway carved directly into the rock beneath the orchestra, leading to its centre from a point behind the stage building. This however looks like an example of a phenomenon common in the archaeology of the Syracusan theatre, where the desire to identify the stage of Aeschylus – in this case the means by which the ghost of Darius appeared in the *Persians* – has unduly influenced interpretation of the material remains (Bernabò Brea 1967, 127–8 attributes the 'Charonian stairs' to his third phase, of the 2nd/1st c. below). Rizzo's second, Hellenistic, phase is virtually the single fixed point of agreement in the study of this theatre, for its date is securely established by inscriptions (below).

Somewhat more systematic excavation began in the 1940s and 1950s. Those conducted by Anti and the architect Gismondi (1946–7) found a trapezoidal channel under the Roman floor of the orchestra, leading to the claim to have discovered the 'theatre of Epicharmus' (Siracusa I: Anti 1947, 86, 88–92), an Archaic theatre with rectilinear theatron. This had parodoi that led away from the orchestra alongside and at right angles to the stage building. A series of cavities in the area of the stage were thought to have supported a basic rectangular stage building (Anti 1947, 83–106; Polacco and Anti 1981). Anti's next phase – the 'theatre of Damokopos' (Siracusa II: Anti 1947, 87, 92–106) – also has a rectilinear theatron, extending to around the height of the nineteenth row of seating in the later semicircular theatron. Key to the interpretation of this phase was the idea that its stage building employed the most southerly of the long trenches still visible in the stone. Anti tentatively dated the first semicircular theatron (Siracusa III) to the fourth century, as the likely work of Dionysius II. His Siracusa IV is the phase of major renovations under Hieron II, which included the extension of the theatron to its present height; while Siracusa V (a–c) represents a series of later phases in the Roman period up to the fifth century AD.

There followed in 1967 an important study by Bernabò Brea that profited from further excavation by Adamesteanu, Gentili and Stucchi in the 1950s, and which delivered a bracing riposte to Anti. Bernabò Brea described Anti's thoughts on the stage building as 'fantastical and illogical' (1967, 98) and found that the trapezoidal channel, the key to Anti's early phases, was demonstrably later than the two semicircular ones, dating from the Roman Imperial era. Bernabò Brea argued that in fact none of the visible remains of the Syracusan stage and theatron can be older than Hieron II, since the works for his theatre levelled to the ground anything that might have stood there beforehand. Thus for Bernabò Brea the existence prior to the Hieronian II period of a more ancient theatre on the site remained purely hypothetical. Bernabò Brea (1967, 97–8) was also critical of those (notably Rizzo, Pace and Anti) who placed what he saw as too much weight on the literary evidence, and he reserved praise for Bulle's more cautious approach to the physical remains, endorsing his view (Bulle 1928, 152) that those remains suggest that the surviving theatron could not be the product of successive adaptations and augmentations but was conceived as a single entity, which could be no earlier than Hieron II. Bernabò Brea's own first phase for the surviving theatre is therefore the third-century Hieronian theatre (1967, 119, fig. 36). Only with a second phase, in the third to second century, did he find evidence (in agreement with Drerup 1901) for a stylobate to receive columns for a modest wooden stage building (1967, 121 fig. 40; 123 fig. 44).

Bernabò Brea's view on the absence of any evidence for a theatre earlier than the third century is approaching what passes for an orthodoxy among archaeologists (with the endorsement of e.g. Mertens 1984; 2004, 32; Marconi 2012, 179–80). The hyper-sceptical approach to the literary evidence that this entails may however have gone too far, for even if the value of **1** and **5** is open to dispute, **2–4** and **Aviii** are together strong support for the existence of a Classical phase to the theatre on the Temenites hill. It is however the most recent excavations, undertaken in the 1970s and 1980s by Voza but still only published in a frustratingly preliminary fashion, that will challenge the view that all material evidence of the Classical Syracusan theatre has disappeared. These excavations promise to throw remarkable new light on the early phases of the theatre and its related sanctuary (Voza 2001, 2007, 2008, 2014; note the cautions expressed by e.g. Portale 2015, 702 concerning Voza's findings, given the lack of evidence as yet furnished).

In the first place, Voza has shown that the theatre was integrally linked to the city's early Classical network of roads (above). But the most significant discoveries come from the large terrace immediately to the north of and directly associated with the theatre, at the top of the Temenites hill. Here, the picture emerging is of a vast monumental sanctuary complex centred on the theatre: this was dominated in the first instance by an L-shaped stoa at the top and to the west of the theatron, incorporating at its centre the so-called Nymphaeum with its waters channelled by an aqueduct that Rizzo (1923, 116) dated to the Deinomenids; and then, at a higher level – reached by a rock-carved stair – by a second monumental U-shaped stoa with sides ca. 100 m long that embraced the entire sanctuary area (Voza 2001, 208–9). These two large stoas were built in the Hellenistic period, almost certainly as part of the major transformation carried out under Hieron II. The whole area was more clearly defined by the construction of the U-shaped stoa, open at the south side facing the theatre, and forming a unity with it (Voza 2001, fig. 2). At the south-eastern corner of this were built two temples which it seems collapsed into the adjacent quarry below during the Middle Ages, and which Voza identifies – on the basis of numerous architectural remains found in the 1980s (2007, 75) – with the temples of Libera and Ceres (viz. Demeter and Persephone) mentioned by Cicero (*Verr.* 2.4.52, 53: *ad summam theatrum maximum, praeterea duo templa sunt egregia, Cereris unum, alterum Liberae, signumque Apollinis, qui Temenites vocatur, pulcherrimum et maximum*; a different view is taken on the location of these temples by Polacco et al. 1989, who would place them further to the west, on a triangular rocky terrace near the western side of the U-shaped stoa).

At the very centre of the great stoa, and aligned precisely with the central axis of the theatre, were found the remains of an Archaic Greek temple (28.5 × 14.25 m; Voza 1993–1994, 1289–90, pl. 182; Voza 2008, fig. 4), with an altar and access stair directly to the south, towards the theatre, and evidence that there had been a sacred grove on its eastern side (cf. Th. 6.99). At a later date (the construction indicates the fifth century but no further detail has been given) this temple was completely dismantled and in the rear part of its cella were installed two subterranean monumental tombs, robbed in antiquity, that had once had a mausoleum above them (Voza 2007, 78 with fig. 15, noting the evidence of mouldings and plasterwork on a number of limestone blocks). Voza has made the bold suggestion that the tombs were those of Gelon (I) and Demarate, known from Diodorus Siculus (14.63.3) to have been destroyed by the Carthaginians under Himilco in the siege of Syracuse in 397, but there are difficulties in making the site where Diodorus himself places the tombs of Gelon and Demarate (11.38: 200 stades or ca. 40 km from the city centre) compatible with the theatre (Collin Bouffier 2011, 103). If, however, Voza's theory is correct (and one might wonder what other couple of the age could have merited burial in such a spot), it shows in spectacular fashion just how central to Gelon's political identity and legacy the theatre had already been. Voza does not make the point in support of his theory, but the burial of Gelon in the theatre would make perfect sense, in that his actions in Syracuse had effectively made of him a city founder (Luraghi 1994, 297–8). As such, we should expect burial at the centre of the city; and hero cult at the site (D.S. 11.38 refers to heroic cult honours for Gelon; Malkin 1987, 96, 237–8).

Voza is confident that the temple and its associated terrace sanctuary belonged to Apollo Temenites (below). The unusual orientation of this temple (north–south) suggests a desire to co-ordinate its position with that of the theatre, for the axis of the temple and its altar aligns precisely with that passing through the centre of the theatre itself (Voza 2008, fig. 5), indicating that the two were conceived as an entity. The implication would follow that the cult with which the theatre was primarily associated was that of Apollo (**Gi**), and that there was a theatre of some sort already below the hill in the late Archaic period (Voza 2007, 78 with fig. 13). Wilson (1988, 112) suggests that the temple may have been rebuilt when Hieron monumentalised the terrace, but Voza seems to have found no indication to that effect, since he proposes (2014, 35–6) that in the centre of what must have been the largest stoa in Sicily was placed the 'very beautiful and very large' statue of Apollo Temenites seen by Cicero.

Clearly defined early phases for the theatre do not emerge from Voza's preliminary publications, but he appears confident of the existence of a theatron on the site of the great theatre already in the late sixth century, remodelled and expanded in the fifth. Voza (2008) suggests that in its earliest phase the upper and middle parts of the theatron employed the natural rocky slope, to some extent worked smooth, for seating. He (2007, 79; 2008) ascribes a significant phase of the theatre to Dionysius I's plan of grand public building mentioned by Diodorus: 'He also constructed large gymnasia along the Anapos river, and likewise temples of the gods and whatever else tended towards the growth and glory of the city' (D.S. 15.13.5). One would have liked an explicit reference to the theatre in this passage, especially given that it stands as something of an appendix to a more extended account of Dionysius I's efforts in building up Syracuse's military security (Mertens 2004, 31–2). Perhaps the best archaeological evidence for the intervention of Dionysius I will emerge with proper publication of an area in front of the U-shaped stoa that faces the theatre, at around the very centre of the top of the theatron. Here Voza identified remains of the foundations of part of a retaining wall of the theatre (Voza 2001, fig. 2 feature 2), which he ascribes to Dionysius I. (He suggests that in a phase prior to its construction, the retaining wall came up to only around half the height of the present theatron.) This 'Dionysian' retaining wall is said to be curved, like its later incarnations, and to have continued around the entire perimeter of the theatron, turning inward to form a recess at its south-western corner, respecting the presence of the Archaic sanctuary at this point (the one discovered in the 1950s and excavated by Stucchi: Voza 2007, 79 with figs. 16–17).

If it proves to be true that Dionysius I had constructed a semicircular theatron, this will present the earliest instance of a monumental curvilinear theatron anywhere. Papastamativon Moock (2015, 60, 73–4) has argued for the existence of an unrealised curvilinear plan for the Theatre of Dionysus in Athens that was begun in the Periclean era (on the basis of a stratigraphic date of ca. 430–425 for the inner, conglomerate element of the western retaining wall of the Theatre of Dionysus, which has a curved northern extension; cf. Moretti 2014a, 117). The Peloponnesian War and subsequent fiscal problems delayed its advance and it was only finally achieved a century later, under Lycurgus in the 330s (**VI I**).

On the other hand Dionysius I's close association with the theatre in Syracuse, and its importance to his public image, are not in doubt. There is even reason to suppose that in his day and with his support the sanctuary of the Muses associated with the theatre, also almost certainly located on the upper terrace, served as some sort of base for the theatrical professions in Syracuse, as also for the dedication of the literary relics of Euripides (**VI E**). The walls of this area (as in much of the theatre zone) are full of niches designed to receive pinakes and larger cavities for small rock-cut buildings, well-suited to dedications associated with theatrical performances. It would be neat (perhaps too neat) to be able to associate the 'theatre of Damokopos' with the late fifth-century theatre sponsored by Dionysius I, but the evidence for the former points to a somewhat earlier period in the century (**Aviii**; Wilson 2017a).

The Hieronian II Phase

The extent to which Hieron II developed the theatre and the associated upper terrace is beyond doubt, and – to whatever extent the stringent position of Bernabò Brea may come to require qualification – this phase provides a fixed chronological anchor for the archaeology of the site. A series of inscriptions in large letters on the front and centre of the blocks that form the wall of the nine seating sections (I–IX) in the larger of the two passageways (diazoma) in the theatron provide the most secure means of dating the surviving stone theatre (*CIG* IV, 5369; *IG* XIV 3; *SGDI* no. 3232; *Syll.*[3] 429; Dimartino 2006, 704–5; Dimartino 2011, 91, 106; Dimartino *forthcoming*). On the first four blocks (counting from the left) are inscribed (all in the genitive) the names of members of the Syracusan royal dynasty: '[of King Gelon]' (I : no longer legible, but see *SEG* 42, 820.1), 'of Queen Nereis' (II: wife of Gelon), 'of Queen Philistis' (III : wife of Hieron), 'of [K]in[g Hier]on' (IV). The fifth, central block is inscribed 'of Olympian Zeus'; while of the remaining four blocks only on VII can any inscription be read: 'of [Her]acles [*K*]*rate*[*ro*]*phron*' (VI, VIII and IX are all damaged and severly worn: Campagna 2004, 175–83).

These inscriptions can be dated to the second half of the third century on palaeographical and historical grounds. They indicate a date after Gelon II had joined Hieron II as regent and married Nereis in 238, and before Gelon's death ca. 216. Dimartino (*forthcoming*) is perhaps right to conclude that the central position of Zeus implies that the major works conducted by Hieron II and his son on the theatre were in some sense dedicated to the Olympian. The way in which the inscriptions set living members of the royal family of Syracuse and its divinities side-by-side, and on something of an equal footing, is highly suggestive (Campagna 2004, 177). It is also possible that these inscriptions served some practical function in identifying sections of seating (thus already Rizzo 1923, 50; Guarducci 1967–1978 II, 571–4; cf. Campagna 2004, 176).

It is clear Hieron II drew great propagandistic value for his dynasty from this project (Campagna 2004, 171–83), which put him in the company of Hellenistic rulers devoted to the grand development of their capital's monumental architecture. Among its various stylistic innovations is the first use of satyrs and maenads as telamons in the decoration of the stage building (Rizzo 1923, 97–105; Lehmler 2005, 128–30), a motif favoured by Hieron II in a variety of contexts, including the gigantic 'altar near the theatre' which he built as part of the same programme (D.S. 16.83.2, ca. 200 m long, still extant; Zirone 2005, 171). This was very probably also dedicated to Zeus (Lehmler 2005, 142) and was possibly designed to serve, along with the theatre, for meetings of the *koinon* of Sicilian Greeks (Karlsson 1996). (The fact that Diodorus specifies the altar but not the theatre as among the public works erected by Hieron II suggests that the theatre itself already existed.) Hieron II does not appear to have instituted a personal ruler cult, but he certainly promoted a close association between his own royal power and the cult of Olympian Zeus, the traditional source of legitimacy for monarchic authority. And he used the theatre and its adjacent shrines to accomplish this, as also to communicate with his citizens in a space that had long since served a political function (**1–4**).

The Cults of the Theatre

The primary cult with which the theatre of Syracuse was associated (on the assumption that there is likely to have been a single one) remains quite unclear. The main contenders are Apollo 'Temenites' and Demeter and Kore. In favour of Apollo are Voza's confidence (as yet not properly documented) that the Archaic temple on the upper terrace, aligned with the axis of the theatre, belonged to him; and more general indications that the area may have been the location of his cult: Thucydides uses 'Temenites' of the site (6.75, 100) and mentions a sacred grove (6.99), without specifying Apollo; Cicero (above) speaks of 'a statue of Apollo, who is called Temenites, that is very beautiful and very large' on the heights of Neapolis. Apollo's preeminence as Syracuse's founder deity might also be cited, with the Temenites cult on the outskirts of the old city possibly serving in a 'bipolar' capacity with the temple on Ortygia. Apollo Temenites has also been seen as a possible owner of the Archaic quadrangular sanctuary on the southern side of the hill (above): this was Stucchi's view, and Doepner (2002, 107–9) has since associated the stelai found there with an aniconic cult of the god.

On the other hand, the case for Demeter and Kore gains weight from the general predominance of the pair in the religious life of the western Greeks, and above all in the cultic politics of the Deinomenid tyrants, patrons of and protected by Demeter and Kore (Hdt. 7.153; Sch. Pi. *P.* 2.27b; White 1964; Luraghi 1994, 120–3; De Angelis 2006; Kowalzig 2008, esp. 144–5). Pindar (*O.* 6.94–6) describes how, in a Syracusan context, Hieron 'attends on red-footed Damater, and the festival of her daughter with her white horses' (φοινικόπεζαν ἀμφέπει Δάματρα, λευκίππου τε θυγατρὸς ἑορτάν), phraseology that could readily include his organisation of theatrical performances in the goddess' honour. Moreover the passage of Cicero (above) is better evidence for temples for the pair on the top of the hill than for Apollo (the latter has a *signum*, the pair *duo templa … egregia*), and Voza is certainly ready to locate these two temples on the stoa, doubtless built in the Hieronian II period (see above for the alternative location – still on the heights of the hill – proposed for these temples by Polacco et al. 1989).

Polacco (1990, 144–9) has made a case, in part on the basis of some very fragmentary inscriptions and ritual remains, that the quadrangular Archaic sanctuary below was dedicated to Demeter and Kore (Reichert-Südbeck 2000, 243–7: one of the inscriptions is more likely to refer to Artemis). His further view (1990, 139, 157) that the hill carried the name Temenites because it was in its entirety a temenos, and that Apollo's epithet Temenites is a secondary derivation, may carry some weight. If it did in some sense mean 'Apollo of the temenos', it implies that Apollo was a secondary presence in the temenos, to which Demeter and Kore were primary (cf. Reichert-Südbeck 2000, 206–7, 243–7). If theirs was the primary cult on the site from the late seventh century, it is entirely likely that the rectilinear theatre served as the first location for performances in the goddess' cult (comparison with the viewing areas / theatres at Eleusis has long been made), with the great theatre being a later expansion as the needs of the cult grew, and with eventual interaction with and involvement of other cults (compare the situation in Cyrene, with an urban theatre in the sanctuary of Apollo and an extraurban theatre in that of Demeter and Kore: **Gi**).

For there is no doubt that the site was (eventually) home to multiple deities: Polacco's (1990, esp. 157) list includes Apollo, Demeter and Kore, Artemis, Dionysus, the Muses and the Nymphs (we should add Olympian Zeus: above). Dionysus is far from prominent, but we may note the development of explicitly Dionysiac motifs in the Hieronian II phase and the possibility that the temple of Dionysus and his son Aristaeus mentioned by Cicero without indication of location or age (*Verr.* 2.4.57) might have been in some physical and cultic association with Demeter and Kore (Reichert-Südbeck 2000, 247). Preliminary publication of recent archaeological discoveries slightly to the east of the theatre point to the likelihood of a sanctuary of Dionysus, probably dating to the era of Agathocles (ruled 316–288; Ciurcina 2014). It is possible that an association between the Syracusan theatre and Dionysus should be traced back to a deliberate policy of Dionysius I (Wilson 2017a; **VI E**).

Aii: Aristoxenos of Selinus and Early Sicilian Iamboi

1. **Hephaestion,** *Handbook on Metres* **8.3 (p. 25, 12 Consbruch)**. Hephaestion of Alexandria (2nd c. AD) wrote an influential metrical treatise in 48 books, of which only an epitome, the *Handbook*, largely undertaken by Hephaestion himself, survives. His practice is to introduce and discuss metrical structures and illustrate them with quotations from ancient authors (Dickey 2007, 104–5). In a chapter on anapaests Hephaestion explains that while the anapaestic tetrameter catalectic is called the Aristophaneion, it was in fact used by poets earlier than Aristophanes – Cratinus, Epicharmus (**Aiii**) and Aristoxenos of Selinus. Suspicion that the quoted line of Aristoxenos is a fake (Wilamowitz 1875, 334; Holford-Strevens 2009) seems unfounded. While Hephaestion or his source may not have had direct access to the poetry of Aristoxenos, some is likely to have been preserved in the work on Epicharmus in ten books by Apollodorus of Athens (2nd c.), who may also be the source of the information as to Aristoxenos' homeland. Sch. Ar. *Wealth* 487a, III 4b, 129–30 Chantry cites this passage. Text: Consbruch, with modifications.

> Ἀριστόξενος δὲ ὁ Σελινούντιος Ἐπιχάρμου πρεσβύτερος ἐγένετο ποιητής, οὗ καὶ αὐτὸς Ἐπίχαρμος (*PCG* F 77) μνημονεύει ἐν Λόγῳ καὶ Λογίνᾳ

> τοὶ τοὺς ἰάμβους καὶ τὸν † ἄριστον τρόπον,
> ὃν πρᾶτος εἰσαγήσαθ᾽ Ὡριστόξενος

καὶ τούτου τοίνυν τοῦ Ἀριστοξένου μνημονεύεταί τινα τούτῳ τῷ μέτρῳ γεγραμμένα (*PCG* F 1)

τίς ἀλαζονίαν πλείσταν παρέχει τῶν ἀνθρώπων; τοὶ μάντεις·

οὐ τοὺς ἰάμβους Willi   οἱ codd. (Willi notes this should be τοὶ)   καὶ τὸν ἄριστον ADI   καττὸν ἀρχαῖον Porson   ὦ (or οἴ) τοὺς ἰάμβους καττὸν ἀχάριστον τρόπον Ahrens   καὶ τὸν ἀμπαιστὸν τρόπον Vaillant   κὰτ τὸν Ἀνανίου τρόπον Rotstein   κὰτ τὸν ἄδιστον Willi

Aristoxenos of Selinus was a poet older than Epicharmus. Epicharmus himself even mentions him in his *His and Her Argument* (*PCG* F 77): 'those who the iambs and † the finest style (or 'in the ancient / old-fashioned style': Porson; 'Ah, the *iamboi* in that ugly style': Ahrens; 'in the anapaestic manner': Vaillant; 'in the manner of Ananios': Rotstein), which Aristoxenos was the first to introduce'. Now of this Aristoxenos too some things are remembered, written in this metre (*PCG* F 1): 'Which sort of men are the biggest of charlatans? Seers!'

2. **Athenaeus**, *Sophists at Dinner* **5.181c**. Written ca. 200, with probable general reference to the Classical past. The passage forms part of a rambling discussion by the jurist and musician Masurius on sympotic customs, which opens out to a discourse on song and dance in the context of symposia and beyond. It is possible, given the Sicilian origin of the *iambistai*, that the whole passage goes back to Timaeus of Tauromenium, who wrote a now lost *History of Sicily* in 38 books, from ca. 315 to ca. 265. Text: Olson.

οἱ δὲ λεγόμενοι Λακωνισταί, φησὶν ὁ Τίμαιος (*FGrH* 566 F 140) ἐν τετραγώνοις χοροῖς ἦδον. καθόλου δὲ διάφορος ἦν ἡ μουσικὴ παρὰ τοῖς Ἕλλησι, τῶν μὲν Ἀθηναίων τοὺς Διονυσιακοὺς χοροὺς καὶ τοὺς κυκλίους προτιμώντων, Συρακοσίων δὲ τοὺς ἰαμβιστάς, ἄλλων δ' ἄλλο τι.

The so-called Lakonistai, as Timaeus (*FGrH* 566 F 140) says, sang in rectangular choruses. Music was generally varied among the Greeks, with the Athenians preferring Dionysiac and cyclic choruses, the Syracusans *iambistai*, other peoples other things.

Hephaestion (**1**), with access to a wealth of earlier literature and scholarship, was in no doubt that Aristoxenos of Selinus was earlier than Epicharmus. How much earlier is very difficult to say: while Hephaestion evidently had more information about Aristoxenos than F 77 of Epicharmus, he may not have had a lot more and, whatever its correct original text (below), the fragment is naturally interpretable as implying that Aristoxenos was a predecessor of Epicharmus. The chronographic tradition (*PCG* T 2) offers a floruit date in the 29th Olympiad (664/0), more precisely in 664/3 in the case of Eusebius (Hicron. p. 94b, 15 Helm), who registers for that year 'Archilochus and Simonides and Aristoxenos the musician were famous'. Evidently this tradition located Aristoxenos in the earliest generation of iambists, alongside Semonides of Amorgos and Archilochus (perhaps an error for Hipponax: Ornaghi 2010). This however would be before the likely foundation of Selinus ca. 650 (D.S. 13.59.4), which Thucydides (6.4.2) puts even later, in 628/7 (**Axiv**). Further doubt on the value of the chronographic tradition derives from its confusion of the Selinuntine Aristoxenos with the famous fourth-century musical theorist Aristoxenus of Taras (note Eusebius' *Aristoxenus musicus*). West left open the possibility of a seventh-century date ('s. vii vel vi'), while Kassel and Austin put Aristoxenos in the sixth century. It is possible that Aristoxenos was an older contemporary of Epicharmus.

However much earlier the activity of Aristoxenos, *PCG* F 77 of Epicharmus is remarkable for the way it presents the contribution made by an earlier poet to a tradition to which Epicharmus very probably saw himself as belonging. The drama from which it comes, the *His and Her Argument*, is generally supposed (from its title alone) to have featured an agon between the allegorical figures of a male and female *logos*, possibly a model for the debate between the Just and Unjust Arguments of Aristophanes' *Clouds* (Willi 2015, 123 points to the slender basis for this view). The work has thus been thought to have interacted with an intellectual environment in which the early Sicilian masters and instructors of rhetoric, notably Gorgias of Leontini, were making their presence felt (Demand 1971; Conti Bizzarro 1999, 27). Yet it is clear from *PCG* F 76, a dialogue between two characters, one of whom has been invited by Zeus to a feast of Pelops, that *His and Her Argument* was set in a mythological milieu. The mythological frame is absent from *PCG* F 77, which looks very much like a parabasis *avant la lettre* (Oliverio 1946, 67). Its reference to an earlier poet suits the self-positioning strategies familiar from later Aristophanic parabases and it is probably safe to assume that the speaking voice is to be thought of as the poet Epicharmus himself.

The first line is unmetrical and corrupt at a critical point (ἄριστον), but it is safe to say that Epicharmus credits Aristoxenos with an innovation in the performance of iamboi, and that that innovation possibly relates specifically to music – the last word in the line τρόπον 'style' is less likely to have suffered corruption, whereas the καί 'and' which makes 'the iambs' and the 'style' two separate objects is somewhat more likely to have been (the identification of Aristoxenos as an iambographer hangs largely, but not entirely, on the emendation of καί into κάτ: Lennartz 2010, 131–6). It is probable that τρόπος is used here in its sense (LSJ s.v. IV) of (general) musical style. The correct reading and hence the nature of Aristoxenos' style as described by Epicharmus are irrecoverable. The transmitted 'best' (ἄριστον *ariston*) may have been introduced in error from the adjacent name of *Aristo*xenos, albeit in the form Ὠριστόξενος (*Oristoxenos*). This is more likely than the alternative: that 'best' may in fact be correct and Epicharmus was aiming at a (rather jejune) word play between musical style and its innovator's name. Qualities proposed by emendation for Aristoxenos' iambic style are 'ancient / old-fashioned' (Porson), 'ugly' (Ahrens), 'anapaestic' (Vaillant), 'Ananian' (Rotstein) or 'sweet' (Willi).

Ahrens' more extensive correction – 'Ah, the *iamboi* in that ugly style' – makes the reference to Aristoxenos polemical, almost certainly out of keeping with the inherently eulogistic tendency of protoheuristic remarks. Rotstein (2009, 218–19) is rightly doubtful of Vaillant's (1927) 'and the anapaestic style' (or, in Rotstein's own improvement, 'in the anapaestic style' καττὸν ἀμπαιστὸν τρόπον), given the improbability that the word 'anapaestic' would fall out from a learned discussion precisely of anapaests. Rotstein herself

(2009, 219–20) proposes 'in the manner of Ananios', suggesting that Epicharmus was referring to the introduction by Aristoxenos of iambics in the manner of the Ionian poet Ananios, a poet to whom Epicharmus himself refers elsewhere, using the phrase κὰτ τὸν Ἀνάνιον 'like Ananios' (*PCG* F 51). If Rotstein is correct, Epicharmus would be making a very explicit claim that the Sicilian (and Dorian) poet Aristoxenos had introduced the iambic style of an exponent from the Ionian world. Irrespective of the merits of Rotstein's suggestion (which does risk seeming a little contrived), *PCG* F 51 is important evidence of Epicharmus' familiarity – and of a presumed familiarity among his audience – with Ionian iambic poetry (Carey 2016). Willi's suggestion 'not iambic lines of the very sweet type which Aristoxenos was the first to introduce' (2015, 123–4) has merit, despite its further correction of the line by the introduction of the negative at its beginning, for it would have the speaking voice both respect and observe a distance from the iambs of Aristoxenos.

Porson's emendation has found considerable favour (West 1974, 34; *IEG*). If it is correct, Epicharmus will have referred to Aristoxenos' introduction of 'iambs in the ancient/old-fashioned style', in an implied contrast to a contemporary style, a contrast familiar from Attic Old Comedy's depiction of changes in music and poetry, notably in Eupolis *PCG* F 326, ll. 1–2 ἄγε δή, πότερα βούλεσθε τὴν <νῦν> διάθεσιν | ᾠδῆς ἀκούειν ἢ τὸν ἀρχαῖον τρόπον; 'Well now, do you want to hear the modern arrangement of song or the old style?' (Telò 2007, 637–8; Olson 2014, 11–14). In Epicharmus an evaluation of Aristoxenos as ἀρχαῖον could be positive or negative, depending on whether he was stressing a continuity of tradition or seeking to identify a breach in musical style. Again, given the protoheuristic context, the former is more likely. It is quite plausible that Epicharmus should here be signalling an affinity or inheritance, for we know that he composed at least two works, *Choral Dancers* (Χορεύοντες or Χορευταί) and *Epinik(i)os*, entirely in anapaestic tetrameters catalectic (**Aiii**). The first line of *PCG* F 77 refers to a group τοί 'those who …', but the syntax as quoted is incomplete and a verb is missing that described the activity of this group. They were presumably said to be adherents to the style introduced by Aristoxenos, and Epicharmus probably included himself among them. 'Ancient' would also suit a high date for Aristoxenos, but is, needless to say, of little value as evidence for dating him. In Attic Old Comedy 'ancient' used in such contexts can refer to poets as little as two generations or more than two centuries earlier, as in Eupolis' *Helots* of the 430s, where a speaker describes it as ἀρχαῖον to sing works of Alcman, Stesichorus and Simonides (*PCG* F 148). If Epicharmus was using the phrase in a comparable manner, Aristoxenos might be placed anywhere between the early seventh century and 540.

What were the performative and generic contexts into which Aristoxenos introduced his *iamboi*? εἰσαγήσαθ' 'he introduced' may hint at a theatrical context, although this verb is more generally used of introducing a new custom or practice (e.g. Hdt. 2.49) while εἰσάγω (LSJ s.v. II) is reserved for the more specific idea of 'bring on stage'. Debate has centred on whether the Selinuntine should be categorised as a comic poet (Kassel and Austin) or an iambographer (West). The imposition of such a neat distinction may be inappropriate in the context of Archaic West Greek performance culture. The negative sentiments against seers expressed by the speaker of the single surviving line of Aristoxenos himself (*PCG* F 1) would be equally at home in comic and iambic poetry as we know them, and are found among the fragments of Epicharmus himself (*PCG* F 9). The chronographic tradition seems to have treated Aristoxenos as an early iambist (above), but the fact that Hephaestion introduces Aristoxenos in the company of Epicharmus, Cratinus and Aristophanes as the earliest poet to use a metrical structure characteristic of Classical comedy suggests that for the traditions upon which he drew, Aristoxenos made a contribution to early comedy. Epicharmus' own words (*PCG* F 77) are readily interpretable in the same vein. From the acutely limited evidence Rotstein concludes (2009, 221) that Aristoxenos 'wrote plays similar to those of Epicharmus'. West (1974, 35, following Wilamowitz 1907, 52–3) argued that Epicharmus (or someone not much prior to him) added dialogue, more often in tetrameters than trimeters, to the type of anapaestic address employed by Aristoxenos, under the direct influence of Attic tragedy.

There is no good reason to suppose that Aristoxenos did not put on his performances in his home city of Selinus, but the earliest evidence for a possible theatre in that city is some time in the fifth century (**Axiv**). It is equally likely that he was drawn by the cultural magnet of Syracuse. He was clearly a very early contributor to the tradition of iambic performance that **2** shows to have continued to be of enormous importance in Syracuse well into the Classical period, where it was as culturally central as the Dionysian performances of tragedy, comedy and dithyramb were for the Athenians. The nature of the performances by these *iambistai* (a *hapax*) in Syracuse is unclear. The context in Athenaeus might suggest the involvement of choral dance, a possibility upon which West's theory (1974, 35) of the existence of a Dorian form of choral iambos largely rests. At a minimum, we can say that Aristoxenos' contribution to an iambic tradition appears to have been acknowledged by Epicharmus, who in turn probably saw himself as participating in that evolving tradition. For his part Aristotle acknowledged the advances that Sicilian poets made upon it, with huge consequences for Attic comedy (**Aiii 2**).

Aiii: Epicharmus

1. **Plato, *Theaetetus* 152e.** Written ca. 369; dramatic date of the main dialogue 399. Socrates marshals support for the theory that 'nothing ever *is*, but is always *coming into being*' (ἔστι μὲν γὰρ οὐδέποτ᾽ οὐδέν, ἀεὶ δὲ γίγνεται). In citing Homer (as often, cf. Pl. *Rep.* 598d) as the exemplary poet of tragedy, Socrates intends all serious poetry (epic and tragic); while Epicharmus stands for all comic poetry. The manner in which Plato refers in passing to Epicharmus' position on this issue suggests he could assume his (admittedly narrow) audience was familiar with the play in question (Kerkhof 2001, 173). Plato (*Grg.* 505e of ca. 380 = *PCG* F 161) and Xenophon (*Mem.* 2.1.20 of ca. 370 = *PCG* F 236, 271) offer the earliest examples of direct quotation of single or part-lines of Epicharmus. Text: Burnet.

> καὶ περὶ τούτου πάντες ἑξῆς οἱ σοφοὶ πλὴν Παρμενίδου συμφερέσθων,
> Πρωταγόρας τε καὶ Ἡράκλειτος καὶ Ἐμπεδοκλῆς, καὶ τῶν ποιητῶν οἱ ἄκροι τῆς
> ποιήσεως ἑκατέρας, κωμῳδίας μὲν Ἐπίχαρμος, τραγῳδίας δὲ Ὅμηρος, ὃς εἰπών
>
> Ὠκεανόν τε θεῶν γένεσιν καὶ μητέρα Τηθύν
>
> πάντα εἴρηκεν ἔκγονα ῥοῆς τε καὶ κινήσεως· ἢ οὐ δοκεῖ τοῦτο λέγειν;

And on this topic all the wise men, except Parmenides, may be gathered together in a line – Protagoras, Heraclitus, Empedocles, and the chief poets in each kind of poetry, Epicharmus in comedy and Homer in tragedy, who, in saying 'Ocean the origin of the gods, and Tethys their mother' (Hom. *Il.* 14.201, 302) has said that all things are the offspring of flow and motion. Or don't you think he means that?

2. Aristotle, *Poetics* **1449a36–b8.** Written ca. 335–330. In the context of an abbreviated and somewhat disjointed discussion of the origins and evolution of tragedy and comedy (1448a19–1449b20), Aristotle reports the claims of Dorians to have invented both (**Bii 1**). As for comedy, the matter is disputed between 'the Megarians here' (in mainland Greece) and 'those from Sicily'. The syntax makes it virtually certain that the Megarians of Megara Hyblaea are meant, with 'those from Sicily' οἱ ἐκ Σικελίας picking up and balancing 'the Megarians here' οἱ Μεγαρεῖς οἵ τε ἐνταῦθα rather than the earlier 'the Dorians' οἱ Δωριεῖς. The claim of the Sicilians is advanced on the basis of the fact that 'the poet Epicharmus, who was much earlier than Chionides or Magnes, came from there' οἱ (sc. Μεγαρεῖς) ἐκ Σικελίας, ἐκεῖθεν γὰρ ἦν Ἐπίχαρμος ὁ ποιητὴς πολλῷ πρότερος ὢν Χιωνίδου καὶ Μάγνητος (on the issues of dating this raises see below). After going on to explain that, unlike tragedy, comedy's origins and early innovators are unknown, Aristotle notes in this passage that the important shift from iambic lampoon to the construction of acted dialogue and coherent plots began in Sicily. Crates of Athens was active in the mid fifth century, his first victory at the City Dionysia probably in 450: *IG* II^2 2325C, l. 16 M-O.

The phrase Ἐπίχαρμος καὶ Φόρμις 'Epicharmus and Phormis' is present in the major manuscript tradition of the *Poetics* (though apparently not in the Arabic translation: Gutas 2012, 334–6), but was excluded by Susemihl and some subsequent editors as ungrammatical. This is far too drastic a response and the text can be defended or explained in a number of ways. Bonanno (1972, 23) offers the most effective defence in her suggestion (which we follow) that with 'Epicharmus and Phormis' we should understand the verb ἀπέδωκεν from the previous clause (i.e. ἀπέδωκαν), viz.: 'Epicharmus and Phormis (sc. introduced) the composition of plots. This originally came from Sicily …'. If this is thought too abrupt, the phrase could also be an (authentic) disjointed note: Else 1957, 197; Janko (2011, 365) compares the awkward phrase 'three and scene-painting Sophocles' earlier in the same section (*Poet.* 1449a18–19). Alternatively it might be an interpolation (Taran and Gutas 2012, 245), possibly deriving from Aristotle's own *On Poets* (Janko 2011, 366). Among proposed emendations, Gallavotti's has the benefit of minimalism – 'The composition of plots, <like> Epicharmus and Phormis, originally came from Sicily' – if not the elegance of Janko's more extensive repair: 'The composition of plots originally came from Sicily. <For> Epicharmus and Phormis <came from there>'. The relationship between this passage and Themistius *Or.* 27.337b (**Bv 2**: κωμῳδία τὸ παλαιὸν ἤρξατο μὲν ἐκ Σικελίας – ἐκεῖθεν γὰρ ἤστην Ἐπίχαρμός τε καὶ Φόρμος 'comedy long ago had its beginning in Sicily – because Epicharmus and Phormos were from that place') cannot be determined. Janko (2011, 366, 492) argues that Themistius is based on Aristotle's *On Poets* but see Heath (2013, 5). Text: Tarán, with adjustments.

αἱ μὲν οὖν τῆς τραγῳδίας μεταβάσεις καὶ δι᾽ ὧν ἐγένοντο οὐ λελήθασιν, ἡ δὲ κωμῳδία διὰ τὸ μὴ [1449b] σπουδάζεσθαι ἐξ ἀρχῆς ἔλαθεν· καὶ γὰρ χορὸν κωμῳδῶν ὀψέ ποτε ὁ ἄρχων ἔδωκεν, ἀλλ᾽ ἐθελονταὶ ἦσαν. ἤδη δὲ σχήματά τινα αὐτῆς ἐχούσης οἱ λεγόμενοι αὐτῆς ποιηταὶ μνημονεύονται. τίς δὲ πρόσωπα ἀπέδωκεν ἢ προλόγους ἢ πλήθη ὑποκριτῶν καὶ ὅσα τοιαῦτα, ἠγνόηται. τὸ δὲ μύθους ποιεῖν Ἐπίχαρμος καὶ Φόρμις. τὸ μὲν ἐξ ἀρχῆς ἐκ Σικελίας ἦλθε, τῶν δὲ Ἀθήνησιν Κράτης πρῶτος ἦρξεν ἀφέμενος τῆς ἰαμβικῆς ἰδέας καθόλου ποιεῖν λόγους καὶ μύθους.

τὸ δὲ μύθους ποιεῖν Ἐπίχαρμος καὶ Φόρμις ABY   [Ἐπίχαρμος καὶ Φόρμις] Susemihl <ὡς> Ἐπίχαρμος καὶ Φόρμις Gallavotti   τὸ δὲ μύθους ποιεῖν τὸ μὲν ἐξ ἀρχῆς ἐκ Σικελίας ἦλθε. <ἦσαν γὰρ ἐκεῖθεν> Ἐπίχαρμος καὶ Φόρμις Janko *exempli gratia*

So tragedy's stages of development and those who brought them about have not been forgotten, but comedy was forgotten, on account of the fact that it was not taken seriously from the beginning. It was only at a rather late date that the Archon granted a comic chorus: they used to be volunteers. It is from a time when comedy already had some formal features that named poets of it are remembered. Who introduced masks, prologues, the numbers of actors and everything else like that, is lost to knowledge. Epicharmus and Phormis (sc. introduced) the composition of plots. This originally came from Sicily, but of those at Athens Crates was the first to relinquish the iambic form and to construct spoken dialogue and plots with a general scope.

3. **Suda s.v. Ἐπίχαρμος ('Epicharmus', ε 2766)**. Compiled ca. 1000 AD. Like many of the Suda's entries on Greek authors, this one may derive in part from Hesychius' (5th or 6th c. AD) catalogue of writers and their works from earliest times (the *Onomatologos*), now lost, which in turn drew on earlier scholarship. The proposition about Krastos is probably dependent on **5** and ultimately on Syracusan Philistus, active under Dionysius I (Franco 2010, 198–9). The identity of the Lykon whose authority is cited for the (lower) number of productions by Epicharmus is unknown. He is most probably the scholarch of the Peripatos of that name (268–244; D.L. 5.65–74). The idea that he might be the early 3rd c. poet and scholar Lycophron of Chalkis (Lowe 2013) has some appeal, given his likely responsibility for cataloguing (and commenting upon) the comedies in the library of Alexandria (Kaibel 1907, 35). Reference to 'the Persian Wars' as a chronological marker is traditionally assumed to refer to the battles of 480, which gives a dating for Epicharmus' production of comedies in Syracuse in either 486/5 or 485/4. Euetes may be a tragic poet, victorious at the Athenian Dionysia in 484/3 or soon after (*IG* II² 2325A, l. 12 M-O), but there is some evidence for a comic poet of the name, of uncertain date: *PCG* V, 276. Euxenides and Mylos are both comic poets, the former possibly to be (very heavily) restored to the list of comic poets successful at the Athenian Dionysia in the 480s (*IG* II² 2325C, l. 6 M-O with Foucart 1906, 596). For Phormos see **Aiv**. Text: Adler with adjustments, substantially as in *PCG*.

Ἐπίχαρμος, Τιτύρου ἢ Χειμάρου καὶ Σηκίδος, Συρακούσιος ἢ ἐκ πόλεως
Κραστοῦ τῶν Σικανῶν· ὃς εὗρε τὴν κωμῳδίαν ἐν Συρακούσαις ἅμα Φόρμῳ.
ἐδίδαξε δὲ δράματα νβ′, ὡς δὲ Λύκων φησὶ λε′. τινὲς δὲ αὐτὸν Κῷον ἀνέγραψαν,
τῶν μετὰ Κάδμου εἰς Σικελίαν μετοικησάντων, ἄλλοι Σάμιον, ἄλλοι Μεγαρέα
τῶν ἐν Σικελίᾳ. ἦν δὲ πρὸ τῶν Περσικῶν ἔτη ἕξ, διδάσκων ἐν Συρακούσαις·
ἐν δὲ Ἀθήναις Εὐέτης καὶ Εὐξενίδης καὶ Μύλος ἐπεδείκνυντο. οὗτος εὑρετὴς
καὶ τῶν μακρῶν στοιχείων η καὶ ω. καὶ Ἐπιχάρμειος λόγος, τοῦ Ἐπιχάρμου.

Χειμάρου Α   Χιμάρου Bernhardy   σικίδος codd.   Σηκίδος Bernhardy   Μεγαρέα
Kaibel   Μεγάρων codd.   ἦν δὲ τῶν πρὸ τῶν Α   οὗτος εὑρετὴς καὶ τῶν μακρῶν
στοιχείων η καὶ ω. IVM marginal note

'Epicharmus': son of Tityros or Cheimaros and Sekis (or, maintaining the
manuscripts' reading, 'Sikis'); Syracusan or from the Sican city Krastos. He
was the inventor of comedy in Syracuse, along with Phormos. He produced
52 dramas, or 35 according to Lykon. Some recorded him as a Coan, one of
those who migrated to Sicily with Kadmos; others as a Samian; others as a
Sicilian from Megara. He was producing plays in Syracuse, six years before
the Persian Wars; in Athens (sc. at this time) Euetes and Euxenides and Mylos
were putting on their works. He was also the inventor of the long vowels eta
and omega. Also (sc. attested in the phrase) 'Epicharmian argument', (meaning
that) of Epicharmus.

4. **Parian Marble 55 (*IG* XII 5, 444, ll. 71–2; *FGrH* 239 A 55)**. Date of inscription: 264/3
or soon after. Target date: 472/1 (by Archon). The sentence on Epicharmus is one of
several 'postscripts' in the inscription that follow the Archon date and that are thought
to have been added at a later stage of the chronicle's composition (Jacoby *FGrH* 239
Commentary, 668).

ἀφ᾽ οὗ Ἱέρων Συρακουσσῶν ἐτυράννευσεν, ἔτη ΗΗΓΙΙΙ, ἄρχοντος Ἀθήνησι
Χ[άρ]ητος· ἦν δὲ καὶ Ἐπίχαρμος ὁ ποιητὴς κατὰ τοῦτον.

From the time Hieron became tyrant of Syracuse, 208 years, when Ch[ar]es
was Archon in Athens (472/1). The poet Epicharmus also lived at this time.

5. **Neanthes of Kyzikos, *On Famous Men*, *FGrH* 84 F 13 (= St.Byz. κ 209)**. Neanthes was
an historian active ca. 300. His *On Famous Men* is a work of biography innovative for its
use of eyewitness sources and remarkable for its attention to local details of topography
and place name (Schorn 2007). A famous courtesan named Laïs was captured in Sicily
during the Peloponnesian War and brought to Corinth (Plu. *Nic.* 15.4; Ypsilanti 2006,
198–201 on the chronology of courtesans named Laïs). The claim that Epicharmus came
from Krastos also appears to go back to Neanthes (and in turn probably to Philistus:
introduction to **3** above), whose interest in highly specific local traditions and the Greek
West is attested elsewhere (Schorn 2007, 144). Neanthes had his critics in antiquity for
reliability (*FGrH* 84 T 4; Ath. 13.602f), but see below. Text: Billerbeck.

Κραστός· πόλις Σικελίας τῶν Σικανῶν. Φίλιστος Σικελικῶν ιγ΄. ἐκ ταύτης ἦν
Ἐπίχαρμος ὁ κωμικὸς καὶ Λαῒς ἡ ἑταίρα, ὡς Νεάνθης ἐν τῷ Περὶ ἐνδόξων ἀνδρῶν.
ἔχει δὲ ἡ πόλις εὐπρεπεστάτας γυναῖκας, ὡς Φιλήμων. Ἀπίων δὲ ὅτι μόνος
Πολέμων ἔφη τὴν Λαῒδα Κορινθίαν. ὁ πολίτης Κραστῖνος καὶ Κραστίνη τὸ θηλυκόν.

Krastos, a city in Sicily of the Sikans. Philistus (*FGrH* 556 F 44) in the 13th
book of *Sikelika*. Epicharmus the comic poet was from here, and Laïs the courtesan, according to Neanthes in his *On Famous Men*. The city had very beautiful women, according to Philemon (*PCG* 182). According to Apion (*FGrH* 616
F 30), only Polemon (fr. 44 Preller) said that Laïs was Corinthian. The citizen
(was called) Krastinos and Krastine in the feminine.

6. Theocritus, *Epigram* **18 (*AP* 9.600).** Early 3rd c. Theocritus of Syracuse spent time on
Cos before emigrating to Alexandria and the court of Ptolemy Philadelphus (ruled ca.
282–246). He was known best for developing the bucolic genre, but also undertook
radical innovations in epic. This is one of 24 epigrams ascribed to him, and there is
little reason (as there is with some others) to doubt its authenticity. Wilamowitz (1905,
87) thought it to have been inscribed on a statue of Epicharmus in the Syracusan theatre newly developed by Hieron II (endorsed by Gow 1952 II, 542); but the view now
prevails that the memorial is a fiction and the epigram is as much to do with Theocritus'
own rivalrous relation to his poetic predecessor as a public tribute to him (Bing 1988;
Rossi 2001, 291–2). In particular, the statement (l. 3) that the statue has been erected 'in bronze, not flesh and blood (or 'instead of the real thing')' χάλκεόν νιν ἀντ᾽
ἀλαθινοῦ has the air of literary artifice unsuited to a monumental setting, by which 'the
poet compels us to acknowledge the distance between life and art' (Bing 1988, 122).
Furthermore, the lack of reference to any characterising detail in the statue that 'stands
for the real thing' suggests a statue that entirely fails to achieve the contemporary artistic
ideal of verisimilitude. On the metre see Handley 2003, 143–4. Text: Gow (also Dover,
Kassel and Austin), with modifications.

1   ἅ τε φωνὰ Δώριος χὠνὴρ ὁ τὰν κωμῳδίαν
            εὑρὼν Ἐπίχαρμος.
       ὦ Βάκχε, χάλκεόν νιν ἀντ᾽ ἀλαθινοῦ
            τὶν ὧδ᾽ ἀνέθηκαν
5   τοὶ Συρακούσσαις ἐνίδρυνται, πελωρίστᾳ πόλει,
            οἷ᾽ ἄνδρα πολίταν.
       σοφῶν ἔοικε ῥημάτων μεμναμένους
            τελεῖν ἐπίχειρα·
       πολλὰ γὰρ ποττὰν ζόαν τοῖς πᾶσιν εἶπε χρήσιμα.
10   μεγάλα χάρις αὐτῷ.

7 σωρὸν γὰρ εἶχε Κ, Gallavotti   6–8 οἷ᾽ ἀνδρὶ πολίται | (σωρὸν γὰρ εἶχε ῥημάτων)
μεμναμένοι | τελεῖν ἐπίχειρα· see Handley 2003   9 παισὶν KCD   πᾶσιν *AP*

Dorian is the speech and Dorian too is the man – Epicharmus the inventor of
comedy. For you, Bacchus, those who dwell in [5] Syracuse, a giant of a city,

have set him here in bronze, not flesh and blood, as the man was a fellow citizen. It is fitting that those who remember his wise words should recompense him (or with Handley's text '… remembering to pay their dues to him – for he had a heap of sayings – as a fellow-citizen'); for many are his sayings for the whole community useful for life. [10] Great gratitude to him.

7. **Diogenes Laertius,** *Lives of the Eminent Philosophers* **8.78**. Written 3rd c. AD. Diogenes treats Epicharmus as a (Pythagorean) philosopher, placing him between the notable Pythagoreans Empedocles and Archytas and ascribing to his father a name – 'Helothales' – known otherwise only as the title of a pseudo-Pythagorean work (D.L. 8.7). The physical, ethical and medical works mentioned at the end are widely deemed pseudepicharmic (Kerkhof 2001, 59–115). The quoted epigram (= *AP* 7.125; *FGE* 35B; *PCG* T 9), said to come from an inscribed statue of the poet in Syracuse, is like **6** probably a literary fiction and 'cannot be dated without a margin of error of almost half a millenium' (Page *FGE* 340). The same is true of a third (in this case, funerary) epigram preserved at *AP* 7.82 = *PCG* T 19. Text: Dorandi.

> Ἐπίχαρμος Ἡλοθαλοῦς Κῷος. καὶ οὗτος ἤκουσε Πυθαγόρου. τριμηνιαῖος δ᾽ ὑπάρχων ἀπηνέχθη τῆς Σικελίας εἰς Μέγαρα, ἐντεῦθεν δ᾽ εἰς Συρακούσας, ὥς φησι καὶ αὐτὸς ἐν τοῖς συγγράμμασιν. καὶ αὐτῷ ἐπὶ τοῦ ἀνδριάντος ἐπιγέγραπται τόδε·
>
> > εἴ τι παραλλάσσει φαέθων μέγας ἄλιος ἄστρων
> > καὶ πόντος ποταμῶν μείζον᾽ ἔχει δύναμιν,
> > φαμὶ τοσοῦτον ἐγὼ σοφίᾳ προέχειν Ἐπίχαρμον,
> > ὃν πατρὶς ἐστεφάνωσ᾽ ἅδε Συρακοσίων.
>
> οὗτος ὑπομνήματα καταλέλοιπεν ἐν οἷς φυσιολογεῖ, γνωμολογεῖ, ἰατρολογεῖ· καὶ παραστιχίδα γε ἐν τοῖς πλείστοις τῶν ὑπομνημάτων πεποίηκεν, οἷς διασαφεῖ ὅτι ἑαυτοῦ ἐστι τὰ συντάγματα. βιοὺς δ᾽ ἔτη ἐνενήκοντα κατέστρεψεν.

έαυτοῦ Diels   αὐτοῦ codd.   συγγράμματα PF   συντάγματα B

Epicharmus of Cos, son of Helothales, was another pupil of Pythagoras. When three months old he was sent to Megara in Sicily and thence to Syracuse, as he tells us in his own writings. On his statue this epigram is written: 'If the great sun outshines the other stars, and the sea has power mightier than the rivers, just so, I say, does Epicharmus stand out in wisdom, whom Syracuse his fatherland crowned here.' He has left memoirs containing his physical, ethical and medical doctrines, and he has made marginal notes in most of the memoirs, which clearly show that they were written by him. He died at the age of ninety.

8. **Anonymous,** *On Comedy* 9 (***Prolegomena de Comoedia* III)**. The author of this essay on the history and form of comedy, which is included in a number of Aristophanic manuscripts, is unknown. It was probably composed in the Byzantine period but drew, at

least indirectly, on a variety of older sources, including Aristotle. The author subscribes to a strict periodisation of comedy and this passage consists of the discussion of 'Old Comedy' and the first named author of it, Epicharmus. The restoration of the name of Epicharmus is secure (Ornaghi 2016, 132) as he is the only poet in the list who lacks such a rubric to the summative discussion that follows. γέγονε 'he was' will refer to a floruit, not birth (Rohde 1878). Text: based on Koster.

> οἱ μὲν οὖν τῆς ἀρχαίας κωμῳδίας ποιηταὶ οὐχ ὑποθέσεως ἀληθοῦς, ἀλλὰ παιδιᾶς εὐτραπέλου γενόμενοι ζηλωταὶ τοὺς ἀγῶνας ἐποίουν· καὶ φέρεται αὐτῶν πάντα τὰ δράματα τξε′ σὺν τοῖς ψευδεπιγράφοις. τούτων δέ εἰσιν ἀξιολογώτατοι Ἐπίχαρμος, Μάγνης, Κρατῖνος, Κράτης, Φερεκράτης, Φρύνιχος, Εὔπολις, Ἀριστοφάνης.
> <Ἐπίχαρμος>. οὗτος πρῶτος τὴν κωμῳδίαν διερριμμένην ἀνεκτήσατο πολλὰ προσφιλοτεχνήσας. χρόνοις δὲ γέγονε κατὰ τὴν ογ′ Ὀλυμπιάδα, τῇ δὲ ποιήσει γνωμικὸς καὶ εὑρετικὸς καὶ φιλότεχνος. σῴζεται δὲ αὐτοῦ δράματα μ′, ἐξ ὧν ἀντιλέγονται δ′.

> <Ἐπίχαρμος> Dindorf   <Ἐπίχαρμος Συρακόσιος> Kaibel   Possibly <Ἐπίχαρμος Μεγαρεύς> PCG

The poets of Old Comedy, becoming keen on witty amusement rather than true plots, began to hold competitions. In all 365 of their dramas are transmitted, including those falsely attributed. The most noteworthy of them are Epicharmus, Magnes, Cratinus, Crates, Pherecrates, Phrynichus, Eupolis, Aristophanes. <Epicharmus>. He was the first to recover the scattered material of comedy and made many artistic additions. In date he was in the 73rd Olympiad (488–485); his poetry was full of maxims, inventive and artistic. 40 of his dramas are preserved, of which 4 are disputed.

9. Plutarch, *How to Tell a Flatterer from a Friend* (*Moralia*) 68a (= *PCG* T 14). Written ca. 100 AD. Addressed to C. Julius Antiochus Philopappus, grandson of the last king of Commagene, Antiochus IV, as a warning to men of power of the dangers from skilled flatterers. Text: Babbitt.

> Ἐπίχαρμος δ᾽ οὐκ ὀρθῶς, τοῦ Ἱέρωνος ἀνελόντος ἐνίους τῶν συνήθων καὶ μεθ᾽ ἡμέρας ὀλίγας καλέσαντος ἐπὶ δεῖπνον αὐτόν, ᾽ἀλλὰ πρῴην,᾽ ἔφη, ᾽θύων τοὺς φίλους οὐκ ἐκάλεσας.᾽

But Epicharmus was not right in his reply to Hieron, who had made away with some of his intimate friends and then a few days later invited him to dinner, when he said: 'But the other day, you held a sacrifice without invitation of friends!'

10. Plutarch, *Sayings of Kings and Commanders* (*Moralia*) 175c (= *PCG* T 15). Written ca. 110 AD. In the wake of Beck (2002), the dedicatory epistle to the Emperor Trajan (ruled 98–117) is widely regarded as genuine. Pelling (2002, 65–90) persuasively argues that this work, a collection of pithy sayings by famous rulers and military commanders, ordered approximately chronologically, was written later than the *Lives*, collected from them and from other notes made in their production, probably by Plutarch himself, to provide 'some leisure-reading for a busy man who would not have time to read through the longer work'. This passage is from a short section of sayings of Hieron (and his wife), largely concerned with issues of speaking freely before the tyrant. The preceding anecdote reports an exchange between Hieron and Xenophanes of Colophon. Text: Nachstädt.

> Ἐπίχαρμον δὲ τὸν κωμῳδοποιόν, ὅτι τῆς γυναικὸς αὐτοῦ παρούσης εἶπέ τι τῶν ἀπορρήτων, ἐζημίωσε.

ἀπορρήτων Σ   ἀπρεπῶν *alii*, Bernardakis

And he fined Epicharmus the comic poet for saying something forbidden in the presence of his wife.

11. **Iamblichus, *On the Pythagorean Way of Life* 166, 266 (= *PCG* T 12)**. Written ca. 300 AD. Iamblichus was a leading Neoplatonic philosopher from Chalcis in Syria who studied with Porphyry and went on to found his own school. His *On the Pythagorean Way of Life* is the first book of a compendium of Pythagorean philosophy that draws extensively on earlier writers, including Pythagoras himself, Plato, Aristotle, Aristoxenus and Apollonius of Tyana. 'On the whole, *VP* [*On the Pythagorean Way of Life*] is not a biography of Pythagoras, but a systematic presentation of the way of life and doctrines which he taught to his followers and other human beings' (Dillon and Hershbell 1991, 1). The latter section (266), thought by many (Baron 2013, 164; Horky 2013, 127–32) to derive from Timaeus, gives an account of the followers of Pythagoreanism and puts Epicharmus among the so-called 'exoteric' Pythagoreans who were more active in public life, as opposed to the 'esoteric' Pythagoreans who were devoted to rigorous ritual and ethical practices that included secrecy and a long period of silence. Text: Dillon and Hershbell.

> [166] ... ἀπὸ δὴ τούτων τῶν ἐπιτηδευμάτων συνέβη τὴν Ἰταλίαν πᾶσαν φιλοσόφων ἀνδρῶν ἐμπλησθῆναι καί, πρότερον ἀγνοουμένης αὐτῆς, ὕστερον διὰ Πυθαγόραν Μεγάλην Ἑλλάδα κληθῆναι, καὶ πλείστους παρ᾽ αὐτοῖς ἄνδρας φιλοσόφους καὶ ποιητὰς καὶ νομοθέτας γενέσθαι. τάς τε γὰρ τέχνας τὰς ῥητορικὰς καὶ τοὺς λόγους τοὺς ἐπιδεικτικοὺς καὶ τοὺς νόμους τοὺς γεγραμμένους παρ᾽ ἐκείνων εἰς τὴν Ἑλλάδα συνέβη κομισθῆναι, καὶ περὶ τῶν φυσικῶν ὅσοι τινὰ μνείαν πεποίηνται, πρῶτον Ἐμπεδοκλέα καὶ Παρμενίδην τὸν Ἐλεάτην προφερόμενοι τυγχάνουσιν, οἵ τε γνωμολογῆσαί τι τῶν κατὰ τὸν βίον βουλόμενοι τὰς Ἐπιχάρμου διανοίας προφέρονται, καὶ σχεδὸν πάντες αὐτὰς οἱ φιλόσοφοι κατέχουσι. ... [266] ... τῶν δ᾽ ἔξωθεν ἀκροατῶν γενέσθαι καὶ Ἐπίχαρμον, ἀλλ᾽ οὐκ ἐκ τοῦ συστήματος τῶν ἀνδρῶν·

ἀφικόμενον δὲ εἰς Συρακούσας διὰ τὴν Ἱέρωνος τυραννίδα τοῦ μὲν φανερῶς φιλοσοφεῖν ἀποσχέσθαι, εἰς μέτρον δ' ἐντεῖναι τὰς διανοίας τῶν ἀνδρῶν, μετὰ παιδιᾶς κρύφα ἐκφέροντα τὰ Πυθαγόρου δόγματα.

[166] ... As a consequence of these pursuits (the reference is to the many fields of Pythagorean study generally), then, all Italy was filled with philosophers and while it was formerly unknown, later, because of Pythagoras, it was called Great Greece, and very many men there became philosophers, poets and law-givers. For rhetorical treatises, display speeches and laws written by them were brought into Greece, and all those who have mentioned the physicists cite as authorities first Empedocles and Parmenides of Elea, while those who wish to propound maxims about the conduct of life cite as authority the wise sayings of Epicharmus. ... [266] ... And Epicharmus (is said to have) become one of the disciples outside the school, and not from the inner circle of men. When he arrived in Syracuse, he abstained from philosophising openly because of the tyranny of Hieron, but put the thoughts of these men in metre and under the guise of foolery published the secret teachings of Pythagoras.

12. Hesychius, _Lexicon_ s.v. ὀροὐα ('sausage', o 1290). Date: 5th or 6th c. AD. Hesychius' entry glosses a rare word for a (perhaps boiled) sausage: note Hsch. o 1342: ὀρύα· χορδὴ ἐφθή '"_orya_": boiled sausage'. Ath. 3.94f reports that 'Epicharmus mentions sausages, which he calls _oryai_ (ὀρύας), even naming one of his dramas _Orya_ (Ὀρύαν)'. Ὀρύα _Orya_ will be the correct spelling for Epicharmus. The word has been restored to the corrupt _PCG_ F 81 of the _Megarian Woman_. Causabon's conjecture – σύστημα πολιτικόν 'political system' – is bland and weak. Meineke's σύστρεμμα πολιτικόν has the advantage of attested application in an explicitly political context, referring to a 'mob of internal insurgents' (Phot. σ 844 Theodoridis συστρέμματα· στασιαστῶν πλῆθος), but neither improves upon the transmitted text. Text: Kassel and Austin.

> ὀροὐα· χορδή. καὶ σύντριμμα πολιτικόν, εἰς ὃ Ἐπιχάρμου δρᾶμα.
>
> σύστημα Casaubon   σύστρεμμα Meineke

'_oroua_': sausage; and a political smash-up, on which Epicharmus (sc. wrote) a drama.

13. Polemon of Ilium, _In Response to Timaeus_, fr. 45 Preller (Ath. 15.698c = _PCG_ T 20). Polemon lived ca. 220–160. He was an important author of periegetic literature, with works on the Athenian Acropolis, the mythological traditions of several Greek regions, painters, marvels and various antiquarian subjects. Athenaeus quotes from a work (in at least 12 books!) that responds to the western Greek historian Timaeus. Baron (2013, 133) argues for the translation of the title as _In Response to_ rather than _Against Timaeus_, because in at least one identifiable case Polemon is in agreement with Timaeus. Text: Kaibel.

> Πολέμων δ' ἐν τῷ δωδεκάτῳ τῶν πρὸς Τίμαιον περὶ τῶν τὰς παρῳδίας γεγραφότων ἱστορῶν τάδε γράφει· 'καὶ τὸν Βοιωτὸν δὲ καὶ τὸν Εὔβοιον τοὺς

τὰς παρῳδίας γράψαντας λογίους ἂν φήσαιμι διὰ τὸ παίζειν ἀμφιδεξίως καὶ
τῶν προγενεστέρων ποιητῶν ὑπερέχειν ἐπιγεγονότας ... κέχρηται δὲ καὶ
Ἐπίχαρμος ὁ Συρακόσιος ἔν τισι τῶν δραμάτων ἐπ᾿ ὀλίγον καὶ Κρατῖνος ὁ
τῆς ἀρχαίας κωμῳδίας ποιητὴς ...᾿

Polemon, in the twelfth book of his *In Response to Timaeus*, speaking of those
who have written parodies, writes thus: 'I would refer to both Boiotos and
Euboios, who wrote parodies, as learned men, since they make witty remarks
that can be understood in several ways and are better than the poets of earlier
generations, despite coming later ... And Epicharmus of Syracuse also uses
parody, to a limited degree, in some of his plays; as does Cratinus, a poet of
the Old Comedy ...'

14. **Suda s.v. Διονύσιος ('Dionysius', δ 1179)**. Compiled ca. 1000 AD. Dionysius the
Younger succeeded to the tyranny of Syracuse in 367 after the death of his father, the
elder Dionysius (**VI E**), and was definitively ejected from it by Timoleon in 344 after
a rule marked by severe factional strife. His brother-in-law Dion brought Plato to his
court in 367 to cultivate an interest in philosophy and in an attempt to realise the ideal
state; the philosopher returned in 361. The *Letters* will be those of Dionysius himself
rather than Epicharmus. Text: Adler.

Διονύσιος, υἱὸς τοῦ Σικελίας τυράννου καὶ αὐτὸς τύραννος καὶ φιλόσοφος.
Ἐπιστολὰς καὶ Περὶ τῶν ποιημάτων Ἐπιχάρμου.

'Dionysius': son of the tyrant of Sicily and himself tyrant and philosopher.
[Wrote] *Letters* and *On the Poems of Epicharmus*.

Date and Life

With a wealth of evidence before him, Aristotle (**Bii 1**) reports that Epicharmus was 'much
earlier' than the Athenian comic poets Chionides and Magnes. The Suda (χ 318) records a
production by Chionides in 487/6, and the irregular expression used in the entry – ὃν καὶ
λέγουσι πρωταγωνιστὴν γενέσθαι τῆς ἀρχαίας κωμῳδίας 'whom they go as far as to call
the protagonist of Old Comedy' (tr. Whitehead) – looks like the garbled descendant of a
didascalic notice that Chionides was the first recorded winner (viz. πρῶτον ἀγωνιστήν) in
the comic contest at the Athenian Dionysia, in 486 (Olson 2007, 16; fully restored to that
year in *IG* II² 2325, l. 41). As for Magnes, the Suda (μ 20) describes him as a (considerably) younger contemporary of Epicharmus (ἐπιβάλλει δ᾿ Ἐπιχάρμῳ νέος πρεσβύτῃ 'and
he overlapped in his youth with the aged Epicharmus'), which is consistent with Athenian
archival evidence that records him as victor at the Dionysia in 472 (*IG* II² 2318, l. 3 M-O),
not necessarily for the first time. This would lead us to suppose that Epicharmus was already active by around 510–500, perhaps even earlier (born ca. 540), but that conclusion
has been thought to conflict with other evidence. Epicharmus' own Suda entry (**3**) has him
'producing in Syracuse' in 486/5 or 485/4 and **8** gives a floruit of 488–484 – precisely the

period in which Chionides appears to have won the first Athenian comic contest. **4** synchro-
nises Epicharmus with the accession to power in Syracuse of Hieron I – namely 472/1 –
and a variety of other evidence confirms that the poet was active under the Deinomenid in
the 470s, including reference in his own works to Hieron's military intervention in southern Italy on behalf of the Locrians in 477/6 (below) and clear signs of interaction with
Aeschylus, presumably in the wake of the latter's productions in Sicily in the 470s, though
conceivably also in response to his later residence at Gela from 458 (**Aix**; other sources that
situate Epicharmus chronologically in relation to Hieron's tyranny: **9**; **10**; **11**; *PCG* T 8).

Aristotle is unlikely to be in error; nor is the text of the *Poetics* (though some, e.g. Janko
2011, 364, follow a suggestion advanced and then withdrawn by Butcher that the text of
1448a33 should read <οὐ> πολλῷ πρότερος ὢν Χιωνίδου καὶ Μάγνητος '<not> much earlier than Chionides and Magnes'). 'Much earlier' may involve an element of exaggeration,
but if exaggeration is present, it will belong to the Megarian Sicilian tradition Aristotle is
reporting rather than to Aristotle himself. However, the impression of somewhat incongru-
ent dates is likely to be due in large part to the fact that recorded knowledge of Epicharmus'
activity became more secure after he moved to Syracuse, and within the context of the
Deinomenid tyrants, with their capable channels of self-publicity. Conversely, his home
city of Megara Hyblaea entered a period of non-existence in 483 from which it did not
fully emerge until the 330s (below). Kerkhof (2001, 58–9) also suggests that Aristotle was
thinking of the beginnings rather than the peaks of the respective poets' careers. The fact
that **3** and **8** situate Epicharmus in Syracuse a couple of years either side of 486 indicates
that he was already active under Gelon (tyrant from 485). He continued to be so under
Hieron I (tyrant from 478 – died 467/6) and he may well have still been producing after the
fall of the Deinomenids in 466, a period generally seen as introducing a democratic form
of constitution (Robinson 2011, 67–88; some would place this development only in the last
decade or so of the century, identifying a mixture of oligarchic-aristocratic and democratic
elements in the earlier part of the period: Rutter 2000; de Angelis 2016, 206–10). The claim
of **7** that he lived to be at least 90 (supported by Aelian *VH* 2.34, *PCG* T 16; [Lucian] *Macr.*
25) suggests he could have lived until ca. 445.

The evidence with which to sketch the life and career of Epicharmus is slim (*DTC*²
230–9; Berk 1964, 3–10; testimonia in *PCG* I; Millino 2000, 114–27). The substantial
tradition that grew up around him from at least as early as the late fifth century shows
every sign of being the product of a variety of motives removed from a purely documentary interest in the early history of the theatre, notably his appropriation (at an uncertain
date) by Pythagoreanism. The earliest source certainly to claim that Epicharmus 'shared
the Pythagorean way of life' (τῆς Πυθαγορικῆς διατριβῆς μετεσχηκώς) is Plutarch (*Num.*
8.17), although it has been argued that the fuller assertions of **11** go back to the Sicilian
historian Timaeus (ca. 350–260). **11**'s patriotic claims for the philosophical and wider cultural riches of 'Great Greece' suggest as much. The idea that Epicharmus used comedy
as a cover for disseminating the secret teachings of Pythagoras (**11**) is extremely implausible and if, as is possible, 'Pythagorean' material did feature in his works, it must have
served the needs of its dramatic and comic context (below). It is at any rate very likely that
Timaeus and another western Greek intellectual, Aristoxenus of Taras, played a lead role
in the depiction of Epicharmus as a Pythagorean (on the processes of the formation of the

Pythagorean Epicharmus and the related pseudepicharmea: Cassio 1985; Álvarez Salas 2007a; Willi 2015; Favi 2017c; further on the early reception of Epicharmus below).

Of the parental names given by **3**, 'Sekis' for his mother – 'Slave girl' – is evidently derived from a scene of Epicharmean comedy (**Aiv 2**) in which a 'Basket' was quizzed as to its parentage and the answer was 'Slave girl' (Σακίς). The target in that play appears to have been Epicharmus' contemporary, the comic poet Phormis/os, and the ascription of the insult to the mother of Epicharmus may be the result of later confusion in the biographical traditions of the two contemporary poets. It might however be worth considering maintaining the manuscript reading of Σικίδος 'Sikis' (Σηκίδος is an emendation by Bernhardy) and associating it with the tradition of a Sicanian origin for the poet (**3, 5**), as Sikis may be (or at least be meant to suggest) a Sicanian name, or at least a hyper-Sicilian name (compare the personal name Σίκων 'Sikon', sometimes thought to be a hypocoristic of Σικελός and Σικανός: Poccetti 2012, 53).

At first sight the paternal names of Ch(e)imaros and Tityros seem no more promising. A χίμαρος (*chimaros*) is a billy goat, making Epicharmus 'Son of Billy goat', while some ancient scholars report Tityros as the Sicilian term for silens, satyrs or male goats (Sch. Theoc. 3.2a, c). Both thus smack of an attempt to endow early Sicilian comedy with a Dionysian and bucolic pedigree that it very probably did not have (Oliverio 1946, 4), an operation for which a plausible historical context can be found in the time of Hieron II, when explicitly and exuberantly Dionysiac motifs appear in Hieron II's great renovation of the Syracuse theatre and for which we find Theocritus providing the literary cover (see on **6** below; **Ai**), although we cannot rule out the possibility that the 'Dionysian' tyrant Dionysius II (**VI E**) initiated the process in his own work on Epicharmus (below). Before consigning the Suda's sources on this topic to 'futility' and 'evident invention' (*DTC*[2] 237), however, it is noteworthy that both names are genuine anthroponyms: Chimaros appears in the first half of the fifth century as a personal name in Selinus, a colony of Megara Hyblaea (*IGDS* 34; *SEG* 16, 572); another is likely from the Syracusan colony of Akrai in the late sixth century (*IG* XIV, 227; *IGDS* 107; some nine others are recorded elsewehere in Greece). This onomastic spread is highly suggestive. Tityros is also attested, though rather less well (five cases in *LGPN*, none in Sicily).

The tradition shows clear evidence of debate and contestation over the place of Epicharmus' birth. The evidence that associates him with Syracuse is all compatible with his having adopted that city as a place of residence during his long career. Even the epigram of Syracusan Theocritus (**6**) stresses his status as a citizen of that city (ἄνδρα πολίταν 'a fellow citizen', l. 6) with an emphasis that suggests an awareness that he was accorded citizenship rather than being born into it. **3**, after offering 'Syracusan' as one possibility, goes on to speak of Epicharmus inventing comedy and producing his work 'in Syracuse', as though distinguishing place of work from the place of origin (note also **11**'s claim that he came to Syracuse during the tyranny of Hieron). **3** leaves the evidence of divergent traditions apparent, whereas **7** stitches three places together in a somewhat novelistic attempt to reconcile them. While it can hardly be disproved, it is difficult to imagine how Diogenes might have gained knowledge of the infant Epicharmus' migration from Cos to Megara Hyblaea. The detail about travelling in the company of the abdicating tyrant of Cos, Kadmos, seems designed to affect an historical veracity the claim did not possess, and may be a fiction spun from nothing more than Herodotus' account of Kadmos' westward move, to Zancle (6.23; 7.163–4; Lorenz 1864, 47). Given the island's associations with medical science, Coan origins are likely to be the product of manipulation by those who created and promoted the circulation of medical texts under the name of Epicharmus. Similarly, the Pythagoreanising tradition will lie behind the assertion of origins in the homeland of Pythagoras, (Ionian!) Samos (**3**; *DTC*² 236). At some point the Coan tradition mobilised an etymological argument that tied the name of the genre (κωμῳδία *komoidia*) to that of the island where Epicharmus, as an exile, supposedly put on the first comedy (Κῶς, Cos: Diom. *Gramm. Lat.* I 489, 8 Keil). Perhaps this was an attempt somehow to leverage (or contest?) the value of the argument made by fellow Dorians of the Peloponnese for the origin of comedy from activity in the 'villages' (*komai*; **Bii**; Ornaghi 2016, 167–8).

The claim for Sicanian Krastos (**3, 5**) is particularly interesting (Willi 2008, 120 inclines to it). It is one of the few for which a named and relatively early ancient authority is adduced, the late fourth-century Neanthes of Cyzicus, whose reputation is on the rise (Schorn 2007; Baron in *BNJ* s.v. 'Neanthes') and who had a demonstrated interest both in highly localised traditions and the Greek west. Krastos is perhaps to be identified with a small isolated inland settlement on the heights above Castronovo in western Sicily, though no completely secure identification has been made and the Castronovo site has as yet revealed no evidence of Sicanian culture (assimilation to Greek culture accelerated in all known Sicanian sites in the fifth century: Corsaro 1987; Falco in *BNP* s.v. 'Sicani'). Others have proposed Terravecchia di Cuti in central Sicily, the site of a large and significant Sicanian settlement that from the end of the seventh century entered the sphere of influence of Gela and Himera and, later, of Acragas. If a fabrication, we might think of a biographising interpretation by a later scholar of some reference to Krastos in an Epicharmean comedy; or possibly of a resurgent expression of indigeneous ethnic identity (in the wake of Ducetius?) that sought to claim the island's most prominent Greek poet as its own.

There can however be little doubt that Megara Hyblaea was the early home of Epicharmus. **Bii** shows that, for Aristotle, Epicharmus was not simply from Sicily, but from Megara Hyblaea. In fact it shows that Aristotle knew him to have produced his work there: 'the claim would have been pointless unless he had actually written there' (*DTC*² 230). The quality of this evidence marginalises the rest. Poli Palladini (2013, 44) tentatively suggests that a funerary stele from the Galera Bagliazzo necropolis of Selinus inscribed 'I belong to Epicharmos son of Mnasandridas' Ἐπιχάρμο εἰμὶ τõ Μ|νασανδρίδα and dated ca. 475–450 (by letter forms: Manni Piraino 1967, 196; *IGDS* 76; Raccuia 1995) might actually mark the very grave of the poet. While this is unlikely (the dating tells somewhat against it, and the name is not as rare as once thought, with *LGPN* recording a total of 34 from a wide range of sites), the tomb does place the name Epicharmus, early in the fifth century, among the families of a major city founded by Megara Hyblaea (**Axiv**), further reinforcing the likelihood that that was the birthplace or at least the early home of the poet (recall too the evidence above for the name Chimaros – said to be that of Epicharmus' father by **3** – in Selinus in the first half of the fifth century). The title Μεγαρίς *Woman of Megara* and its nugatory fragments (*PCG* F 79–81) do not enable us to decide whether it was set in Megara Hyblaea or treated the figure of the 'Megarian courtesan' well-known from later comedy, or something else altogether (Oliverio 1946, 67).

It is thus highly likely Epicharmus began his career in Megara before moving to Syracuse, 22 km to the south. The move will have been before 483, the year in which Gelon destroyed the city and incorporated its wealthy citizens (the *pacheis*) into the citizenry of Syracuse (Hdt. 7.156.2; the family of Epicharmus may have been among them: Raccuia 1995, 162); and it was evidently before around 486 (above). At the start of the fifth century, social upheaval in Syracuse saw slaves and free citizens join forces against the dominant aristocratic landowners (*gamoroi*) to produce a short-lived democracy (Arist. *Pol.* 1302b27–32). We do not know enough about the nature of Epicharmean comedy to say whether this would be a likely context in which it flourished. The Megara in which Epicharmus had launched his new type of drama was it seems a fairly narrow land-owning aristocracy.

Megara Hyblaea

Megara Hyblaea was virtually non-existent for the entire Classical period, destroyed in 483 and largely deserted until around 338, when archaeology shows it was refounded, on a somewhat smaller scale, under Timoleon (Talbert 1975, 149; *IACP* 214–15; limited archaeological evidence suggests some sort of vestigial, partial reoccupation in the 460s: Tréziny 2012, 121). There are however a few modest signs of theatre culture before the city was destroyed and at the time of its renewal. The first is a striking and unique mask made of terracotta, of slightly larger than human dimensions (ca. 0.23 m frontal height), which was found in pieces in a well in the agora (now in the Museo Regionale Paolo Orsi). Bernabò Brea (in Vallet 1973, 168 with pl. 56) dates it to the late sixth or very early fifth century, on the basis of the find context (the well otherwise contained fragments of late Archaic amphoras), while the city's destruction provides a firm *terminus ante*. Of fine craftsmanship, the mask has large openings for eyes, nostrils and mouth, and a highly expressive face that relates to no obvious character type. Bernabò Brea regarded it as a true theatrical mask rather than an object of dedication (although its material seems hardly ideal for performance). He also noted from the presence of a hole on the upper edge the likelihood that it was designed to have a wig attached to the top (Vallet 1973, 168; Frontisi-Ducroux 1995, 5).

The findspot – around 25 m from a long Archaic portico that bordered the agora to the north – has been thought significant. This portico (ca. 22 m long) had an opening at its rear (8.15 m wide), made of three wooden columns (Gras et al. 2004, 432–5 with fig. 415) to give access to the street behind it. The site will have served a variety of public gatherings, and it has been suggested that one of these might also have been as a kind of 'proto-theatre' (Villard 2013, 174). The access point at the rear of the portico could have functioned well as a point of entrance and exit out of range of viewers watching from the agora, with the road behind serving as a place to change costumes – in other words, the ensemble looks very much like a proto-stage-building. Another hypothesis has been aired for the possible location of a theatre in Megara Hyblaea. The city occupied two coastal plateaux, divided by the natural depression known as the Arenella. In the centre of this depression a wall of considerable scale, extending for some 62 m, was discovered in 1962, broken at its centre by a monumental door. Excavations undertaken in the 1990s remain unpublished (Gras et al. 2004, 288–92) but Tréziny (2012, 119) deduces from what is known of the structure that it was a large public place of assembly, and possibly used as a theatre (against this enticing possibility one should note however that from its technique of construction and stratigraphy a date of late 8th–early 7th c. has been proposed: Vallet 1993, 464–5).

A recently published modest corpus of Attic and early Sicilian red-figured ceramic demonstrates an appetite for theatre-related iconography and an interest in the early products of Sicilian iconography with comic subjects in Megara Hyblaea in the fourth century (Enríquez de Salamanca Alcón 2015). The most suggestive item is a set of fragments of a large calyx krater which shows a wooden stage with hanging curtains below it and two sets of access stairs. Enríquez de Salamanca Alcón ascribes this to the Group of the Louvre K 240, placing it ca. 400–390 but J. R. Green (pers. comm.) would place it in the Lentini-Manfria Group, and thus ca. 350–325 (Green 2012a, 319). It is therefore likely to be evidence for an interest in comic drama at the very time of the reemergence of the city in the later fourth century, an interest further demonstrated by a considerable number of terracotta figurines representing comic actors (said to range from Old to New) and comic masks, one of which has close affinities with the Lipari material, if it is not in fact from Lipari (Enríquez de Salamanca Alcón 2015, 80–1).

Though modest in scope, these artefacts suggest that the new city of Megara looked to its comic theatre culture as it emerged from long oblivion. It is moreover to precisely this period that we should assign the mobilisation by the Sicilian Megarians of their claim to being the creators of comedy, for there is no other period in which they could have done so. Aristotle was reporting the claim in the 330s, the decade of the city's refoundation. The issue was not only live in Aristotle's day; it is evidently a product of it. It might be an outside possibility that the Megarians of the mainland, at a period earlier than the 330s, and when Megara Hyblaea still lay in ruins, bolstered their claim by pointing to the ancient tradition of Epicharmus in their (abandoned) colony, the issue becoming a matter of dispute once Megara Hyblaea had been repopulated.

The General Nature of Epicharmean Comedy

The combined evidence of **3** and **8** suggests that scholarly opinion in the early Hellenistic period leant towards setting the authentic output of Epicharmus at around 35–40 plays. There are grounds for thinking that at least that many dramas, and probably more, were still being read in later antiquity. Part of a 'catalogue of some provincial library or a reading list' surviving on papyrus of the second century AD (*POxy.* 2659 = *PCG* T 3; Rea 1968, 70; Otranto 2000, 29–38) records comic poets and their plays in alphabetical order, from Ameipsias to Epicharmus. The remains of the entry for Epicharmus covers the letters alpha to eta, with 19 titles, including three apparent doublets. (The doublets have been explained in various ways: scribal error in one case, where there is also disruption to the alphabetical order, Ἁρπαγα[ί] | Βούσειρ[ις] | Ἁρπαγαί [ ] *PCG* T 3, ll. 7–9; multiple copies of the work kept in the library; reworked versions of the same play; different works with the same title.) A conservative extrapolation of the likely full complement of titles on the original list would put it somewhere in the range of 50–60. This significant rate of survival into later antiquity may be in part due to a tradition of reperformance (Hartwig 2014, 223), for which there is the limited evidence of plays that were reworked: from Athenaeus 3.110b we learn that the *Muses* was a reworking of the *Marriage of Heba*; the multiple titles *Pyrrha and Promatheus*, *Deukalion* or *Leukarion* may likewise reflect reworking.

Some 300 fragments survive, many of them nugatory, a full fifth deemed pseudepigraphic by Kassel and Austin. An assessment of the nature of his work is extremely difficult (nor is this the place to attempt it). Epicharmus' dramas evidently covered a striking variety of themes and tones (Willi 2015, 128 describes them as 'fundamentally heterogeneous'). A distinction between mythological and non-mythological works as a means of categorisation may go back to Apollodorus of Athens (2nd c.), the first critic known to have engaged in editorial activity on Epicharmus. As much is implied by a fragmentary catalogue of Epicharmus' works in iambic trimeters generally ascribed to Apollodorus (*POxy.* 2426 = *PCG* T 35, 2nd c. AD). Apollodorus produced an edition in ten books (*PCG* T 34, cf. *PCG* T 35; Kerkhof 2001, 63–5). His *On Epicharmus* is generally believed to be a separate work (*FGrH* 244 F 213). The non-mythological plays seem to have drawn from scenes of daily life in a vernacular register, and specialised in the careful drawing of character types. Among the mythological plays material from (Homeric and Cyclic) epic features prominently, and the figures of Odysseus and Heracles stand out as favourites (e.g. *Heracles with Pholos*, *Heracles in Search of the Belt*, *Marriage of Heba*, *Bousiris*, *Odysseus the Deserter*, *Odysseus Shipwrecked*, *Sirens*), though titles such as *Antanor*, *Bacchae*, *Dionysuses*, *Cyclops*, *Medea*, *Philoctetas*, *Pyrrha and Promatheus* speak to a breadth of range. Some promising work has been done to identify the possible impact of Epicharmus' treatment of myth on the imagery of western Greek vasepainting (Reinhardt 1996), but in the absence of specific signifiers of theatricality as such in these images, the argument remains highly hypothetical. Works such as *Festival*, *Months*, *Sausage*, *Islands*, *Epinik(i)os*, *Thearoi* and *Choral Dancers* are thought to be examples of non-mythological plays closer to daily life (though largely on the basis of their titles alone). The *Old Woman*, *The Rustic* and the *Megarian Woman* are likely instances of non-mythological works centred on character types. Some of these show types that appear to anticipate Middle and New Comedy, such as the parasite in *Wealth* or *Hope* (*PCG* F 32–34; Arnott 1968) and (probably) the hetaera in the *Megarian Woman*.

Aristotle's observation that plot comedy came from Sicily need not entail that all Sicilian and Epicharmean comedy was plot based (Willi 2015, 128). The *Marriage of Heba* (reworked as *Muses*) is a case in point. The fragments suggest a detailed and leisurely catalogue of a divine banquet, seemingly delivered as a monologue. The nearest parallels lie in the cook monologues of Middle Comedy (Nesselrath 1990, 297–308) and the cookbooks that we first hear of from late fifth-century Sicily, notably Mithaikos of Syracuse, active ca. 400. The tradition of gastronomic Sicilian poetry continues with, among others, the hexameter *Life of Luxury* of Archestratos of Gela, mid fourth century. The presumably dithyrambic *Dinner* of Philoxenos (*PMG* 836), probably the poet from Cythera, may derive from his sojourn at the court of Dionysius I (Sutton 1989, 70–75; Le Ven 2014, 115–18).

It has been argued that an Epicharmean play will have been short, only around 300–500 verses long. This assumes that each of the ten volumes of Apollodorus' edition will have contained some four dramas, given that he is reported to have written around 40 in all; and, since a single play of Aristophanes (of ca. 1,500 lines) appears to have filled a single volume, it follows that an Epicharmean work was around a quarter of that length (Millino

2000, 127). These assumptions are however open to question and are further challenged by the fact that the mutilated papyrus containing *Pyrrha and Promatheus* (*PCG* F 113) shows remains of over 500 lines, with no sign that that was close to the totality of the work.

There are numerous instances of dialogue between two characters. Whether a third actor was used cannot be conclusively determined, though some plays certainly had (at least) three characters (*DTC*² 264; Kerkhof 2001, 138); the use of the phrase 'This [is said by] the other actor' [τ]οῦθ' ὁ ἕτερος τῶν ὑποκριτῶν by the scholar commenting on *Odysseus the Deserter* – *PCG* F 98, l. 52 – does not necessarily imply that there were only two actors in that work, let alone in others.

Whether Epicharmean comedy had a chorus is insoluble on current evidence (*DTC*² 278–9; Kerkhof 2001, 151–5; Willi 2015, 134–6). The fragments offer no unambiguous trace of lyric metre. When of sufficient length to judge, they appear to be from spoken dialogue, or monologue. The dominant metres are trochaic tetrameters and iambic trimeters. Some plays had mixed metres (e.g. *Odysseus the Deserter* with trochaic tetrameters and anapaestic dimeters), but once again the evidence is limited and ambiguous (Kerkhof 2001, 152; Willi 2015, 135). **Aii 2** indicates the considerable cultural prominence of a tradition of iambic performance in Syracuse, a tradition to which the earlier poet Aristoxenos of Selinus evidently made a significant contribution, as acknowledged it would seem by Epicharmus himself (**Aii 1**). Riu (2011) has made the interesting but speculative case that Epicharmus' heavy use of trochaic tetrameter is compatible with a chorus, at least one that may have only danced, or spoken in recitative, possibly in dialogue and with musical accompaniment. Riu draws on the fact that Aristotle (*Po.* 1449a21–23, cf. 11460a1; *Rh.* 1404a26–33) saw a close relation between the trochaic tetrameter and the chorus in the context of early drama, describing an early development in tragic metre from the use of trochaic tetrameters to iambics, the former being used because the poetry of early tragedy was 'satyric' and involved more dancing (διὰ τὸ σατυρικὴν καὶ ὀρχηστικωτέραν εἶναι τὴν ποίησιν *Po.* 1449a21–23). We are told that *Choral Dancers* (Χορεύοντες or Χορευταί) and *Epinik(i)os* were composed entirely in anapaestic tetrameters, a metre associated with choral movement (recitative and 'marching', if not song and dance: *PCG* F 100, 108), which has led some to suppose these two works were performed entirely by a chorus (**Axii** on the possibly 'parabatic' quality of these works).

The title *Choral Dancers* Χορεύοντες or Χορευταί is not in itself proof of a chorus (Willi 2015, 135), but it is highly suggestive and at an absolute minimum presupposes a work that engaged with choral culture. (The same is demonstrably true of Sophron's prose mimes, with their somewhat comic references to someone who entered a chorus and farted, and a choragos suffering an attack of the itches: *PCG* F 136, 147.) This remains so notwithstanding the fact that in Epicharmus' dialect χορός could also be used as a word for 'school-room' (*PCG* F 13, 103). More specifically, Pollux reports that in his comedy the *Seizures* (F 13) Epicharmus used the word χορηγεῖον *choregeion* rather than διδασκαλεῖον *didaskaleion* (in fact Epicharmus will have used the form χοραγείων *chorageion*); while his *Odysseus the Deserter* (*PCG* F 103) is referred to without quotation for the more general phenomenon: 'they also called the *didaskaleion choros* (*choregeion* Kaibel), whenever (they also called) the didaskalos choregos and used χορηγεῖν for διδάσκειν, above all the Dorians, like Epicharmus in the *Odysseus the Deserter*' (ἐκάλουν δὲ τὸ διδασκαλεῖον καὶ χορόν, ὁπότε καὶ τὸν διδάσκαλον χορηγὸν καὶ τὸ διδάσκειν χορηγεῖν, καὶ μάλιστα οἱ Δωριεῖς, ὡς Ἐπίχαρμος ἐν Ὀδυσσεῖ αὐτομόλῳ). In *PCG* F 108 χορεύει means 'dances', used of Semele. Whatever the correct interpretation of this fragment, a choral dance is clearly implied (Rotstein 2009, 234–7).

The argument that other plural titles might refer to a chorus, as in the Attic context, has been criticised (Kerkhof 2001, 152–4) but some remain obstinately evocative: *Choral Dancers* Χορεύοντες or Χορευταί, *Bacchae* Βάκχαι, *Komasts* Κωμασταί, *Muses* Μοῦσαι, *Persians* Πέρσαι, *Sirens* Σειρῆνες; to which one might add *Atalantas* Ἀταλάνται (**Aiv 1**) and probably *Dionysuses* Διόνυσοι and *Diktyes* Δίκτυες, noting Lowe's suggestion (2007, 22–3) that in the case of some plural personal names, this could be 'a curious form of pluralized celebrity name that in the mid-century Athenian comedy of Cratinus refers to a chorus of followers of the named hero: *Archilochoi* ("The Archilochus Boys"), *Odysseis* ("The Odysseus Boys")' – thus e.g. 'Followers of Atalanta'. A (somewhat less compelling) alternative would be to think of plays that deal with the mistaken identity of the individual in question (Willi 2015, 135). Willi draws attention to the presence of first-person plural references in a number of fragments of trochaic tetrameters, notably *PCG* F 40, l. 11 from the *Marriage of Heba* ('we … the gods') and *PCG* F 84 'we call' (καλέομες) from the *Muses* (said to be a reworking of the *Marriage of Heba*). His overall conclusion is that 'the picture emerges of a chorus who speaks or recites in the iambic mode, but – crucially – does not sing'.

The absence of a formal chorus in Epicharmean comedy would hardly require the genre as a whole to ignore the existence of such a universal Greek phenomenon as choruses. Significant choral poetry in a variety of genres was performed in Syracuse in Epicharmus' day (**VI A**) and the Greek West had a tradition of choral performance stretching back at least as far as the seventh century.

Epicharmus' comedy appears to have been of a decidedly more gnomic bent than its Attic counterpart. The characteristic remains visible in what survives: 'One hand washes the other: give something, and take something' (*PCG* F 211); 'the gods sell us all good things for hard work' (*PCG* F 271). This lent his drama to the excerpting of maxims (*gnomai*) from at least the fourth century and probably earlier. These came to be circulated separately from the works in their complete form, and their popularity generated the fabrication of others under his name (Kerkhof 2001, 79–108; Battezzato 2008; De Cremoux 2011; the presumed pseudepicharmic maxims are presented as *PCG* F 244–73). Philochorus in the third century (*FGrH* 328 F 79) and Apollodorus of Athens in the second (*FGrH* 244 F 226) named the person responsible one Axiopistos from Locri or Sicyon ('Mr. Trustworthy': the name undermines itself; Ath. 14.648d). The generation and contestation of pseudepicharmea began even earlier. Already in the fourth century Aristoxenus of Taras identified the fifth-century piper Chrysogonos, doubtless the man associated with the triumphal return of Alcibiades to Athens in 408 (Duris *FGrH* 76 F 70; Stefanis no. 2637) rather than his fourth-century homonym, as the true author of a *Politeia* ascribed to Epicharmus.

The further question as to the extent and manner in which Epicharmus engaged with developments in contemporary philosophy, mathematics and (possibly) rhetoric remains open to debate. As noted, the claim that he used comedy as a cover for the dissemination of Pythagorean doctrine is implausible. A more nuanced view is that Epicharmus sympathetically staged philosophical arguments that Pythagoreans might have employed (Horky 2013, 125–67), although some of the claims for the philosophical earnestness of Epicharmus seem a little forced: for instance that *PCG* F 147, in which one speaker objects to the use of the term τρίπους – 'literally 'tripod', but in common usage just 'table' – for a table with four feet, 'suggests that Epicharmus' jokes about numbers and naming represent some of the earliest evidence of philosophical speculation concerning what would later become thematised by Plato and brought forth by Aristotle as problems of identity, parts of wholes, alteration, and predication' (Horky 2013, 136).

At the other extreme his approach has been characterised as that of an anti-sophist *avant la lettre*, attacking the ideas and practices of philosophers, but on the basis of a familiarity and facility with their methods, with the aim of controlling and restricting intellectual elites as Aristophanes was to do half a century later (Álvarez Salas 2016). The truth probably lies somewhere in-between. Epicharmus clearly drew on contemporary philosophical and other intellectual trends, but is unlikely to have done so primarily as their zealous exponent and advocate. His aims will have been comic, but that encompasses more than the zero-sum approach to intellectual authority of Attic Old Comic poets. It is also likely that he dramatised certain views without explicitly indicating their intellectual paternity, so enabling later writers to ascribe them to him (Rodríguez-Noriega Guillén 2012, 87). Xenophanes of Colophon (and Elea) – philosopher, rhapsode and Homeric critic – looks like a special case. He was one of the cultural luminaries at Hieron's court and it seems likely that he came more explicitly under fire from Epicharmus (*PCG* F 143; Álvarez Salas 2007b; Rodríguez-Noriega Guillén 2012, 95; Morgan 2015, 106–7).

The most important evidence for Epicharmus' use of philosophical argument is that pertaining to a play (of unknown title) in which the (ultimately Heraclitean, though arguably more immediately Pythagorean) fluxist ontological idea of constant change was rhetorically and comically exploited in the form of the so-called 'growing argument', the αὐξόμενος λόγος (*PCG* F 136), with the invention of which Plutarch (*Mor.* 559b) credits him (Kerkhof 2001, 68–70, 171–3; Willi 2008, 170–5; Willi 2012, 58–63; Rodríguez-Noriega Guillén 2012, 89–93; Battezzato 2008 makes it virtually certain that *PCG* F 276, often considered to be pseudepicharmic, is also an authentic fragment from the play in question). It is relatively clear that this argument received more than a passing reference in the drama. From the reported fragments, it appears that the following events were enacted or at least reported: a man is invited to a dinner; refuses to pay his contribution as a guest; subsequently argues that he is no longer the same man who had accepted the invitation; is beaten by his host who, when indicted for the assault, argues that he is no longer the same man as the one who did the striking. The comparison with Strepsiades of Aristophanes' *Clouds* has long been made (Süss 1905, 35–6).

Our knowledge of Epicharmus' use of this material derives from an ancient commentary to **1** (*PCG* F 136), which stands for us at the head of a long tradition that depicted Epicharmus as a sage, a poet of philosophical disposition. For the Platonic Socrates, only two poets – Homer for 'tragedy' (serious poetry) and Epicharmus for comedy – merited the status of wise man (*sophos*) capable of holding and expressing serious philosophical ideas in their works. Plato's choice of Epicharmus may evince the possibility that he found Western Greek comedy more sympathetic than Attic, with its amply demonstrated anti-(Socratic) intellectualism and demotic vulgarity. But it also suggests that Epicharmus did engage with subjects and methods of contemporary philosophical and rhetorical debate. Whether he personally held those views is another matter. The easy habits of ancient biographical criticism will have enabled any view expressed by a speaker in an Epicharmean comedy to be attributed to its author. Theocritus (**6**) notably combines the topos of generic inventor (below) with that of Epicharmus' wisdom, and the nature of that wisdom is not that of an attachment to more or less abstruse philosophical doctrine but an essentially practical, gnomic wisdom useful for civic life.

As to developments in rhetoric, the title Λόγος καὶ Λογίνα *His and Her Argument* is suggestive, and it has been conjectured that it featured an agon between these two allegorical figures in a manner anticipatory of the agon of Aristophanes' *Clouds* (Demand 1971). But in truth its three short fragments offer no insight into the nature of the work (though they do make it clear that it included reference to a poetic predecessor, **Aii**). Aristotle cites Epicharmus as a practitioner of the rhetorical trope of accumulation (τὸ ἐποικοδομεῖν *Rh.* 1365a16–19) and for the use of false antithesis (*Rh.* 1410b4–6), but the poets are a standard quarry for Aristotle's search for examples of tropes and these hardly flattering references scarcely make Epicharmus a pioneer in rhetoric or a model to emulate.

Significance

Aristotle admitted that the earliest history of comedy lay beyond the reach of even his research, but he was able to credit to Sicily the first major development in comedy that could be identified (**2**). Epicharmus and Phormis (**Aiv**) are the first nameable poets of comedy (οἱ λεγόμενοι αὐτῆς ποιηταί) that could be remembered, from an era when the genre 'already had some formal features' (ἤδη δὲ σχήματά τινα αὐτῆς ἐχούσης). Willi (2015, 140–1) makes a major advance in our understanding of Aristotle's account of the Sicilian contribution by drawing attention to the distinction (hitherto glossed over or ignored) that Aristotle makes between λόγοι and μῦθοι in the last phrase in this sentence: 'Epicharmus and Phormis (sc. introduced) the composition of plots. This originally came from Sicily, but of those at Athens Crates was the first to relinquish the iambic form and to construct spoken dialogue and plots (ποιεῖν λόγους καὶ μύθους) with a general scope.' As Willi argues, λόγοι must here refer to the introduction of spoken word in enacted dialogue, while μῦθοι will mean 'plots'. It follows that Attic comedy prior to this development – and prior to Crates – had neither mimetic dialogue nor developed plots (both demonstrably present in Epicharmean comedy). The Sicilian contribution is thus very substantial indeed. Epicharmus' real influence on later Attic comedy should not be sought at the microscopic level, in specific allusions to works or passages. It had made itself felt at the macroscopic level more than a generation before the first Attic comic poets composed works that had plots which could be compared to their Sicilian predecessors (Willi 2015, 138–9). Willi's challenge to Athenocentric orthodoxy goes even further, proposing (2015, 142) that it was his experience of Epicharmean dramatic-dialogic comedy during his visit to Sicily in (or soon after: **VI A**) 476 that inspired Aeschylus to introduce the second actor to Attic tragedy. This bracing argument will no doubt stimulate further debate. (The drama he produced on that visit, the *Aitnaiai*, itself almost certainly had two actors: *TrGF* F 6.)

What name Epicharmus and his contemporaries gave to his works is not known. It was probably not 'comedies' (κωμῳδίαι), a term that – whatever its later contestation – was probably developed in Athens after the model of τραγῳδία (Wilamowitz 1907, 54). Plato (**1**) and (implicitly) Aristotle (**2**) spoke of them as 'comedy', as did Theocritus (**6**). It is difficult to judge what if any significance should be attached to the use of the broader term 'poems' in the title of the work by Dionysius II (**14**). Epicharmus' status as the 'inventor of comedy' (along with Phormos) reappears in **3**: 'he was the inventor of comedy in Syracuse, along with Phormos'; and, unsurprisingly, it features prominently in Syracusan Theocritus (**6**), who also emphasises the linguistic and Dorian ethnicity of Epicharmus himself and his poetry – 'Dorian is the speech and Dorian too is the man – Epicharmus the inventor of comedy' (ll. 1–2). **8** expresses the point somewhat differently – 'he was the first to recover the scattered material of comedy and made many artistic additions' – but this may be largely an elaboration of Aristotelian discussion. *DTC*² 276 observes that 'recovered' is probably misleading in that it implies an earlier organised form of comedy that Epicharmus reconstituted, 'but he did unite various elements into a structure which was sufficiently coherent to be regarded as the beginning of artistic comedy'. Bosher (2014, 83–4) takes the phrase to mean that he to some extent drew together local comic traditions. For Aristotle and others Epicharmus and Phormis merited equal credit for the beginnings of literary comedy. If we are correct to interpret **Aiv 2** as an attack on Phormis in the *Skiron* of Epicharmus, there may well have been more competitive friction between the pair than this discreet account implies. And if as we argue the slur related to Phormis' position within the household of Gelon, this is important evidence for a degree of possible 'free speech' in Epicharmean comedy in at least indirect connection with the Syracusan autocrat himself.

The Politics of Epicharmean Comedy

Recent scholarship has persuasively argued that the poetic production of Pindar, Bacchylides, Simonides and Aeschylus under the Deinomenids was powerfully aligned with the ideology of the regime and directly supported some of its specific imperial ambitions (**VI A**). The picture as regards Epicharmus and his peers active in Syracuse is much less clear, largely for want of sufficient evidence. The simple fact that comedy flourished under Gelon and Hieron proves that they tolerated it and is probably enough to show they actively supported it (Bosher 2014, 96). Cantarella (1970, 179–83) assumed tyrannical patronage and explained the apparent absence of political polemic by reference to it. Perhaps most telling is the report of **Aiv 1** that Epicharmus' contemporary Phormis/os had the closest possible affinities to the ruling family, being 'a member of the household of the Sicilian tyrant Gelon and tutor to his children', and the possibility that Epicharmus cast the latter's status as a slur against him in his *Skiron* (**Aiv 2**). The report that Hieron fined Epicharmus for saying something inappropriate when his wife was present (**10**) implies a tension of some sort, but is of very uncertain lineage and likely to be in part or whole the product of later anti-tyrannical literature (Rodríguez-Noriega Guillén 1994, 664–5). Wilamowitz took it as proof that a comic poet should not be found at a prince's table in company with the likes of Pindar (1922, 229). It is much more likely that Hieron, like Gelon before him, welcomed all poets and publicists who could aid him in communicating with his mixed populace and with the wider world in and beyond his Sicilian and South Italian empire: 'gentle mockery, especially when directed at poets rather than the monarch, could help parade Hieron's security and generosity' (Morgan 2015, 108). Another anecdote (**9**), even if a 'late figment' (Jebb 1905, 11; Bonanno 2010, 97 is more accepting of its veracity), suggests that Hieron did indeed cultivate an intimacy with Epicharmus but one that was underpinned by a very clear knowledge of the steep imbalance of power upon which their relationship rested.

Evidence from the surviving fragments is limited but suggestive. It is certain that *Islands* referred to regional politics and very likely that this constituted more than a passing allusion, for two separate testimonies indicate reference to the activities of Anaxilas, tyrant of Rhegium and Messana on the straits, the latter refounded as such from Zancle by Anaxilas in ca. 490. A seemingly well-informed scholiast to Pindar (Sch. Pi. *P*. 1.99a = *PCG* F 96) reports that in his *Islands* Epicharmus gave an account of how 'Anaxilaos wished utterly to destroy the Locrians and was prevented by Hieron' (Ἀναξίλαος Λοκροὺς ἠθέλησεν ἄρδην ἀπολέσαι καὶ ἐκωλύθη πρὸς Ἱέρωνος). The date will be 477, when Anaxilas exploited the unsettled moment of Hieron's accession to power to renew his expansionist policies in South Italy by moving against Locri and was rebuffed, it seems by diplomacy and threat rather than the direct use of military force, by Hieron (Pi. *P*. 2.18–20; Sch. Pi. *P*. 2.27c, 38; Bonanno 2010, 75–84; De Sensi Sestito 2014, 18–27). The scholiast's report certainly implies that Hieron was depicted in the image of a timely saviour of the city (with its famously grateful maidens) from the aggressive ambitions of the potentate – an image consistent with that presented in Pindar's laudatory *Pythian* 2 (Currie 2005, 258–95).

The second reference to Anaxilas in the *Islands* is deduced from putting together two items: the first is an indirect report of Aristotle that the tyrant introduced hares to the island of Sicily at the same time as he won the mule-car race at Olympia, and subsequently had both the hare and the mule car depicted on the coinage of Rhegium (Arist. fr. 568 Rose, *apud* Poll. 5.75: καὶ μὴν Ἀναξίλας ὁ Ῥηγῖνος οὔσης, ὡς Ἀριστοτέλης φησίν, τῆς Σικελίας τέως ἀγόνου λαγῶν, ὁ δ' εἰσαγαγών τε καὶ θρέψας, ὁμοῦ δὲ καὶ Ὀλύμπια νικήσας ἀπήνῃ, τῷ νομίσματι τῶν Ῥηγίνων ἐνετύπωσεν ἀπήνην καὶ λαγών. 'And – as Aristotle says – at a time when Sicily still had no population of hares, Anaxilas of Rhegium introduced and reared them and, on the occasion of his victory in the mule car at Olympia, he had struck an image of the mule car and the hare on the coinage of the Rhegians'); the second is the statement of Zenobius (Ath. 1.80) that Epicharmus used the proverb 'Carpathian, the hare' ὁ Καρπάθιος τὸν λαγών in his *Islands* (*PCG* F 93). This proverb (attested as early as Archilochus, fr. 248 West) illustrated the way people can launch themselves, wittingly or not, into actions that lead to their own ruin. It told of the introduction of the hare by the Carpathians to their island, its rapid multiplication and subsequent destruction of their crops.

In Pollux's report, Aristotle stated that Anaxilas introduced the actual animal to Sicily, but it is clear that Pollux or his source has here adopted an erroneous interpretation of Epicharmus, and that the reference in the *Islands* was to the use of the symbol of the hare on a special issue of tetradrachms by Anaxilas in the 480s, in both Rhegium and Messana (Luraghi 1994, 219). These bore a running hare on the reverse, with a mule car on the obverse. The latter referred to the victory of Anaxilas at Olympia in either 484 (Luraghi 1994, 219–22) or 480, for which Simonides composed on epinikion (Rawles 2012, 22–5) and from which the tyrant sought to derive maximum publicity. What the hare symbolised in this imagery of Anaxilas is not entirely clear – possibly a reference to Pan and his cities' Arcadian roots (Zunino 1997, 206–7); to fertility (Arist. *HA* 5.542b; *GA* 4.774ab); or simply to the speed that led to his victory in the mule-car race. Millino (2001, 125–36) argues for an association with Artemis – goddess of hunting who had a prominent cult in both cities on the straits – and her likely role in their foundation.

There can be little doubt that Epicharmus applied the proverb of the destructive hare as a way to undermine Anaxilas' propagandistic employment of the animal to proclaim his Olympic victory and more generally his imperial self-assertion. There is however debate as to whether the imagery of the coinage represents the innovative forging of an iconography of victory by Anaxilas in the mid 480s, when his regime was at its height (assuming the higher date of 484 for the mule-car victory: Luraghi 1994, 218–22; Millino 2001, 114–25, arguing further that the imagery of the mule car evokes the foundation of the new city of Messana; Morgan 2015, 71–2) or rather demonstrated subordination to Syracusan supremacy by adapting and echoing the existing quadriga and Victory motif already exploited by the Deinomenids on their coins for the less prestigious mule-car event (Nicholson 2016, 181–2).

The case for the higher date and Anaxilas as the iconographic innovator is stronger, but given the reference to the fate of Locri in the comedy, there can be no doubt that the *Islands* itself dates to some time (soon?) after 477. By that time, in the wake of Himera and the definitive exclusion of Carthaginian aid in favour of Anaxilas, Hieron had taken the tyrant's daughter as wife in a dynastic marriage that signified the supremacy of Syracuse. Given that Anaxilas issued his new coins in Messana as well as Rhegium, he could readily have been said by Epicharmus to have introduced 'hares' to another island, that of Sicily itself, with destructive consequences for himself. The unanticipated disaster for Anaxilas was doubtless the battle of Himera and its consequences. Millino (2001, 140) makes the further attractive suggestion that the 'hares' had been used as pay for Carthaginian mercenaries at Himera. It is thus extremely likely that Epicharmus applied the proverb to Anaxilas in a manner that undermined a central image of the tyrant's system of self-presentation to the wider world, suggesting again that the politics of the comedy aligned with the interests of Hieron.

More speculative cases have been made for other works. Rodríguez-Noriega Guillén (1996, 19) suggests that the title of the drama *Seizures* might refer to looting that took place in some Sicilian cities during a period of disturbance in the reign of Hieron. One surviving fragment of the play (*PCG* F 9) is the evocative 'Sicily has suffered' (ἁ δὲ Σικελία πέποσχε). Sofia (2003) situates the *Bousiris* in the context of Sicilian relations with Egypt. Piva (2011) proposes that the *Marriage of Heba* (revised as *Muses*) was political satire against Hieron and his court, with specific parody of Pindar's symbolic equation of Hieron with Castor in *Pythian* 2. On the other hand, Millino (2000, 130–50) offers an alluring hypothesis that the *Heracles in Search of the Belt* affirmed Deinomenid ideology by evoking Gelon's victory against the Carthaginians at Himera through a comic battle, localised in the region of Etna, between Heracles and the Pygmies. The clinching point is the fact that the Phoenicians had distinctive Pygmy-like effigies on the prows of their warships (Hdt. 3.37.2). Epicharmus' comic *Persians* is often, and plausibly, assumed to have interacted with Aeschylus' *Persians*, known to have been performed in Syracuse by tyrannical fiat between 472 and 467 (**VI A**). There is however no direct evidence with which to gauge the politics of the play. Some kind of parody of the tragic original is widely assumed (Kerkhof 2001, 136; Morgan 2015, 107), but who was the principal target – Aeschylus? Hieron? the defeated Carthaginians and Etruscans thought to stand by analogy behind the vanquished Persians? – and, along with them, the Deinomenids' imperial rival, Anaxilas of Rhegium and Messana, who with Terillus of Himera had sided with the Carthaginians defeated at Himera?

Finally, we have the tantalising notice (**12**) that Epicharmus' *Sausage* (Ὀρύα) was a σύντριμμα πολιτικόν, a 'political fracture' or 'smash-up': 'metaphorically of a political "hash"' (*DTC*[2] 271). This opens up the possibility that the drama may have been an inspiration for the figure of the sausage seller in Aristophanes' *Knights* (Oliverio 1946, 71). Millino (2000, 120–1) conjectures that the politics in question were more likely to have been primarily external rather than internal, and that Anaxilas was once again the target. Millino sees in the image a reference to the tyrant's attempt to make a new city from a mix of ingredients (peoples), like a sausage, in his conquest of Zancle and (re)foundation of Messana. Negative views expressed in the work against Anaxilas might in turn explain how the biography of Epicharmus became associated with Anaxilas' predecessor in Zancle, Kadmos (**3**).

Relation to Other Poets and Cultural Figures

Epicharmus made explicit reference in *His and Her Argument* to an earlier Sicilian poet of iambs, Aristoxenos of Selinus, to whom he may have looked to some extent as a precursor (**Aii**). In his *Marriage of Heba* he referred to the Ionian poet Ananios (*PCG* F 51), demonstrating that his poetic horizons – and those of his audience – were far from parochial. He also parodied the cultural luminaries gathered at Hieron's court. In addition to Aeschylus (**Aix**), Pindar (Rodríguez-Noriega Guillén 2012, 83; Morgan 2015, 107–8) and Xenophanes, it has been suggested that the comic poet went further, possibly even mocking 'the culture of celebration in the city in the 470s and early 460s' (Morgan 2015, 106) that was itself central to Deinomenid self-representation. The case is intriguing but rests on inherently weak foundations, namely the suggestion that Epicharmus' *Epinik(i)os* 'can profitably be understood as playing on the fever of epinician production that characterized Hieron's reign' (Morgan 2015, 107).

Epicharmus' relationship to Homeric epic forms part of the same debate and intersects with the question of the politics of Epicharmean comedy. His drama presupposes an audience entirely familiar with epic, with which it engages extensively and subtly. There had been a tradition of competitive rhapsodic performance of epic in Syracuse from at least the latter decades of the sixth century, doubtless organised by the ruling *gamoroi* who preceded the Deinomenid takeover. The Chian rhapsode Kynaithos was reported (Sch. Pi. *N.* 2.1c) to have been the first to recite Homer at Syracuse in the sixty-ninth Olympiad (504–501). As West (1975, 166) notes, the only way such an event would have been recorded with its date would be because it was a victory in a formal contest, making it likely that this was not in fact the first performance of Homer in Syracuse but the first victory in an established contest. West (1999b, 368) plausibly posits as a stimulus for the decision on the part of the Syracusans to keep a record of the victors in this contest the recent undertaking on the part of the Athenians to record the victors in tragedy and men's and boys' choruses at the Dionysia. A sixth-century inscription from Gela may record the erection of a statue of the poet in that city, indicating significant activity there also, although an alternative reading (τὸ [σᾶ]μα *IGDS* 129 rather than τὸ [ἄγαλ]μα *IGASMG* II² 5) makes this a funerary monument, and the identification of this Kynaithos with the Chian rhapsode, while highly plausible (the name is recorded only in the Geloan inscription and for the Chian), cannot be regarded as certain (Burkert 1979, 55).

Epicharmus' (limited) use of parody was noted by Polemon in the second century (**13**). Willi (2012; 2015, 128–30) has argued that Epicharmean comedy adopts an iconoclastic approach to the cultural canon as exemplified above all by epic, and that this gives his comedy a fundamentally democratic character. Willi substantially bases his case on the one drama for which some significant fragments survive, the *Odysseus the Deserter*, suggesting that in it Epicharmus attacks the epic ethos head-on in the interests of a more egalitarian ideology, producing an Odysseus who deserts the heroic station he was given in *Iliad* 10. Qualifications are required. Some are provided by Morgan (2015, 108) and Favi (2017a), who note that Epicharmus was developing tendencies in the representation of Odysseus' heroism that were already part of the epic tradition.

Early Reception

The tyrant of Syracuse Dionysius the Younger is reported as having written a work *On the Poems of Epicharmus* (**14**). This is unlikely to have been a piece of scholarly philology or in any sense an 'edition' of his oeuvre. More probably Dionysius enlisted the figure of Epicharmus as an icon of the cultural (and perhaps philosophical) power of his city, at the same time forging a link between his own regime and that of the Deinomenids under whom Epicharmus had flourished. It is also possible that Dionysius' work played some part in developing the claim for the Dorian, Sicilian origins of comedy. The cultural capital of Sicilian Epicharmus seems also to have been mobilised by the Dionysian propaganda machine against Dion and Plato. Given the history of his relations with the Athenian philosopher, we might detect the hand of the tyrant in the project that asserted Plato's plagiarism of Epicharmus for both his central doctrines and key characteristics of his style. That claim is ascribed to a contemporary of Dionysius, the Sicilian historian Alkimos, in a work of four books entitled *To* (or *Against*) *Amyntas* (πρὸς Ἀμύνταν; *FGrH* 560; D.L. 3.9–17; *PCG* [F] 275–9; the fragments of Epicharmus cited from Alkimos and excluded from the genuine works by *PCG* are coming to be viewed as more probably authentic: Favi 2017c). Jacoby argued that Alkimos was a member of the tyrant's court, and that the work was designed to besmirch Dion as much as Plato at the time when they were at odds with Dionysius (Cassio 1985, 45). The Amyntas in question may be the son of Perdiccas III of Macedon, Amyntas IV, who was eliminated by his cousin Alexander the Great in 336 (Jacoby). But if we are to take the title as indicating an explicit polemic *Against Amyntas* – or possibly *In Reply to Amyntas*, assuming the existence of a work by Amyntas that was the focus of Alkimos' attack – he is doubtless the pupil of Plato of that name from Pontic Heraclea (Gaiser 1973,

63–4). There is even more reason to suppose that Alkimos was involved in promoting Sicilian claims in the origins of comic drama (Willi 2015, 110). One of the few things we know about his work is that in it Alkimos asserted that the inventor of the literary form of *Paignia* or light verse was a Sicilian from Messana (*FGrH* 560 F 1).

Epicharmus was very probably also a useful figure for a later ruler of Syracuse, Hieron II (in power 275–ca. 216). Hieron II drew great propagandistic value for his dynasty from the monumental transformation he effected on the Syracusan theatre (**Ai**), which put him in the company of Hellenistic rulers devoted to the grand development of their capital's monumental architecture, notably those of Asia Minor and Egypt, above all Alexandria. Even though **6** is unlikely to have been inscribed on a statue of Epicharmus in Hieron's transformed Syracusan theatre (above), Theocritus will have been careful to ensure that it conformed to the cultural and political aspirations of his Syracusan patron, and the likelihood that there was in fact a statue of Epicharmus in Hieron's theatre is high (this despite the paucity of evidence for an iconographical tradition of the poet: a seated Epicharmus appears in a third-century AD mosaic in Trier which has, in a series of octagons, images of the nine Muses, each accompanied by a mortal practitioner of a relevant art: the surviving octagons feature Homer, Hyagnis, Epicharmus, Thamyris, Cadmus, and Aratus: Daniel 1996). Rossi (2001, 292–3) found in the epigram's claim for the Dorian origin of comedy a concern of literary scholars, not civic authorities and hence a reason to suspect its status as a real inscription, but the scholarly claim might well have been aligned with Hieronian propaganda. It would be no surprise if Hieron II did in fact harness the cultural prestige of Theocritus to bolster the specific claim of his city to have given birth to the founder of comedy – of a kind characterised by a broad gnomic wisdom and civic utility.

Aiv: Phormis or Phormos

1. **Suda s.v. Φόρμος ('Phormos', φ 609)**. Written ca. 1000 AD. Like many of the Suda's entries on Greek authors, this one probably derives from Hesychius' (5th or 6th c. AD) catalogue of writers and their works from earliest times (the *Onomatologos*), now lost, which in turn has roots in Hellenistic scholarship. The entry shows that the sources on which the lexicographer drew were incomplete (as one might expect for such an early author), since the list of titles did not include one known to Athenaeus (14.652a), the *Atalanta(i)*. The title of this play is in the plural in Athenaeus, singular in the Suda entry. Epicharmus wrote a work on the same subject (below) for which the plural *Atalantai* is most likely (see *PCG*). *Atalantai* is probably correct for Phormos. The plural may refer to the 'followers of Atalanta', and may or may not imply a chorus (**Aiii**). (It is intriguing that the Athenian comic poet Callias, fl. ca. 445, appears to have written an *Atalantai* in which the Sicilian tyrant Dionysius I was ridiculed: *PCG* F *3.) The list itself appears to have suffered some form of corruption since it does not add up to seven, but six. The problem is aggravated by Kaibel's plausible suggestion that *The Sack of Troy* and *The Horse* are alternatives (Stesichorus composed a work which almost certainly had the same two alternative titles: Davies and Finglass 2014, 395–461). West (1982) suggests that *Kepheus*, *Kephalaia* and *Perseus* may represent three different

plays. For Κεφάλαια (*Kephalaia*) West (1982) suspected Κεφαλλῆνες (*Kephallenians*). It is however worth noting that κεφάλαια is used by Antiphanes (*PCG* F 111, l. 5; Pl. *Laws* 811a) and later critics (e.g. Hypoth. A. *Pr.*, S. *Ant.*) in the sense of 'plot' or 'summaries' and might have already been used by Phormis/os with a (meta)theatrical meaning (cf. Deinolochos' *Komoidotragoidia* **Av**). The transmitted figure of seven plays can stand if, with Kaibel, we treat *The Sack of Troy* and *The Horse* as alternatives and, with West, *Kepheus*, *Kephalaia* and *Perseus* as three different plays; or if *The Sack of Troy* and *The Horse* are treated as separate works and *Kepheus*, *Kephalaia* and *Perseus* represent two works, two of the three titles presumably serving as alternatives. In both cases *Atalanta*(*i*) is an eighth play, as implied by the use of ἕτερος 'another'. Some (including Welcker and Kaibel) have thought that the *Halcyons* should rather be *Alkyoneus*, the name of the giant fought by Heracles, which is confirmed as the title of an Epicharmean drama (Rodríguez-Noriega Guillén 1996, 15).

Φόρμος, Συρακούσιος, κωμικός, σύγχρονος Ἐπιχάρμῳ, οἰκεῖος δὲ Γέλωνι τῷ τυράννῳ Σικελίας καὶ τροφεὺς τῶν παίδων αὐτοῦ. ἔγραψε δράματα ζ′, ἅ ἐστι ταῦτα· Ἄδμητος, Ἀλκίνους, Ἀλκυόνες, Ἰλίου πόρθησις <ἢ> Ἵππος, Κηφεὺς † ἢ Κεφάλαια † ἢ Περσεύς. ἐχρήσατο δὲ πρῶτος ἐνδύματι ποδήρει καὶ σκηνῇ δερμάτων φοινικῶν. μέμνηται δὲ καὶ ἑτέρου δράματος Ἀθήναιος ἐν τοῖς Δειπνοσοφισταῖς, Ἀταλάντης.

<ἢ> Ἵππος Kaibel   Ἵππος codd.

'Phormos': Syracusan, comedian, contemporary of Epicharmus, a member of the household of the Sicilian tyrant Gelon and tutor to his children. He wrote 7 dramas, which are as follows: *Admetus*, *Alkinous*, *Halcyons*, *The Sack of Troy* <or> *The Horse*, *Kepheus* † or *Kephalaia* † or *Perseus*. He was the first to use a garment that reached to the feet and a stage building (skene) of purple skins. Athenaeus in the *Sophists at Dinner* (14.652a) also mentions another play, the *Atalanta*.

2. **Epicharmus, *Skiron*, *PCG* F 123**. Date: early 5th c. A scholion (V) to Aristophanes' *Peace* 185 comments on the exchange between Hermes and Trygaeus in which the former asks the name, place of origin and father of the latter, who responds to each enquiry 'Arch Scum' (μιαρώτατος). The scholiast goes on to report that this 'takes its starting-point from the *Skiron* of Epicharmus, where he makes the basket (τὸν φορμόν) reply when asked "Who is your mother?" (τίς ἐστι μήτηρ;) that it is "Servant Girl" (σηκίς) and to "Who is your father?" (τίς ἐστι πατήρ;) he says "Servant Girl" (σηκίς) and likewise to "Who is your brother?" (τίς ἀδελφός;), "Servant Girl" (σηκίς).' From this Kaibel, following Ahrens, reconstituted the original lines of Epicharmus and introduced the Doric form Σακίς. The identity of the questioner is unknown. With Kassel and Austin we deduce from the scholion that the second speaker was Φορμός (Phormos / 'Basket'). As to whether this Φορμός was represented on stage literally as a speaking 'basket' or

as a person named Phormos, see below. The situational similarity with the passage of Aristophanes' *Peace* that provoked the scholar's reference is attenuated: Aristophanes is parodying the Attic process of dokimasia, Epicharmus echoing the Homeric practice of enquiring after a stranger's lineage and, in particular, alluding to the exchange between Andromache and Hector in *Iliad* 6 (below). Nonetheless something led the ancient critic to declare the Epicharmean scene the 'starting-point' (ἀφορμή) of the Aristophanic, and 'starting-point' explicitly opens the possibility of heading in a different direction. The scholiast goes on to observe differences between the two exchanges: 'But he (sc. Phormos) seems to answer the questions in a consistent manner, since there is a certain relation between baskets and servant girls. But in this case (i.e. the passage of *Peace*) he (Trygaeus) does not respond any further in terms of their relation' (ἀλλ᾽ ἐκεῖνος μὲν ἔδοξε πρὸς τὸ ἐρωτώμενον τὸ ἑξῆς ἀποκρίνεσθαι· ἔστι γάρ τις τοῖς φορμοῖς συγγένεια πρὸς τὰς σηκίδας. ἐνταῦθα δὲ οὐκέτι κατὰ τὸ συγγενὲς οὗτος ἀπεκρίθη). It may be that the tripartite questioning was a sufficient parallel to attract the scholar's notice: thus Kerkhof (2001, 145), who stresses the quality of the scholarship behind the scholion. Text: Kassel and Austin.

> (A) τίς ἐστι μάτηρ; (Φο.) Σακίς. (A) ἀλλὰ τίς πατήρ;
> (Φο.) Σακίς. (A) τίς ἀδελφεὸς δέ; (Φο.) Σακίς. (A) - ˘ -
>
> (A) Who is your mother? (Phormos) Slave Girl. (A) Your father?
> (Phormos) Slave Girl. (A) And your brother? (Phormos) Slave Girl. (A) - ˘ -

3. **Pausanias, *Guide to Greece* 5.27.1–2, 7**. Composition date: ca. 150 AD. Date of Phormis' dedications between ca. 485 and 478/7, probably closer to the former, given the greater likelihood that Phormis was awarded Syracusan citizenship (evidently recent at the time of his dedication) in connection with the refoundation of the city rather than for his efforts at the battle of Himera (Luraghi 1994, 295–6). Pausanias is describing the dedications in the sanctuary of Zeus at Olympia that line the Sacred Way leading to the temple of Zeus. Those of Phormis are close to the precinct of Pelops (the Pelopion). A rectangular base (ca. 8.0 × 1.7 × 0.40 m) between the Pelopion and the west wall of the Altis has been identified as that of Phormis' dedications (Eckstein 1969, 43–7; Zizza 2006, 252–4; Ma 2013, 197–8). Pausanias leaves it unclear whether Phormis' dedication bears any relation to an equestrian victory, but does emphasise that it consists of two horses, each with a charioteer (ἡνίοχος) beside. Some translate this as 'jockey', doubtless because of the lack of reference to a chariot, but perhaps Phormis' dedication alluded to Gelon's chariot victory at Olympia of 488, for which he dedicated a life-size bronze chariot group (Paus. 6.9.4; *IvO* 143). It is impossible to tell whether the statues representing Phormis in battle are a separate dedication or part of the group of horses and charioteers (Zizza 2006, 251–2). Ma (2013, 197–8) suggests the military statues must have formed a 'limpet' structure on the semicircular base immediately to the west of the main rectangular one and notes its status as an unusually early, private portrait dedication. It is worth stressing that the 'vulgate' tradition, mentioned but rejected by Pausanias (5.27.2), held that all the statues were dedicated by Phormis, without reference

to Lykortas. Zizza (2006, 253–4) may be right to suggest that Pausanias' motive, driven by his dislike of tyrants in general and Gelon in particular, was to diminish the scale and prestige of Phormis' dedication, which is also consistent with the cursory and somewhat disparaging manner in which he discusses his dedications as a whole. In his lengthy discussion of Delphi in Book 10, Pausanias makes no reference to the dedications made there by Phormis. Ἀρκάς 'Arcadian' (5.27.2) is a regional ethnic, Μαινάλιος 'Mainalian' a second ethnic for a subgroup of Arcadians possibly organised as a tribal state (Nielsen 1999). Lykortas (5.27.7), 'a good Arkadian name' (Hornblower 2004, 186), was very probably another Arcadian who had gone to join the Syracusan enterprise under Gelon (below). Ma (2013, 197) notes that Pausanias' comment that the military statues were 'clearly' dedicated out of friendship suggests a deduction 'rather than the paraphrase of an explicitly declared motive in the inscription', although telling somewhat against this is the use of the optative ἀναθείη as if in indirect quotation of the inscription; and the fact that friendship is frequently expressed as a motivation for the dedication of a funerary memorial (e.g. *IG* I³ 1329). It is possible that Lykortas set up the military statues for Phormis/os after his death. Text: Rocha-Pereira.

> ἐν δὲ αὐτοῖς καὶ τὰ ἀνατεθέντα ἐστὶν ὑπὸ τοῦ Μαιναλίου Φόρμιδος, ὃς ἐκ Μαινάλου διαβὰς ἐς Σικελίαν παρὰ Γέλωνα τὸν Δεινομένους καὶ ἐκείνῳ τε αὐτῷ καὶ Ἱέρωνι ὕστερον ἀδελφῷ τοῦ Γέλωνος ἐς τὰς στρατείας ἀποδεικνύμενος λαμπρὰ ἔργα ἐς τοσοῦτο προῆλθεν εὐδαιμονίας, ὡς ἀναθεῖναι μὲν ταῦτα ἐς Ὀλυμπίαν, ἀναθεῖναι δὲ καὶ τῷ Ἀπόλλωνι ἄλλα {δὲ} ἐς Δελφούς. 27.2 τὰ δὲ ἐς Ὀλυμπίαν δύο τέ εἰσιν ἵπποι καὶ ἡνίοχοι δύο, ἑκατέρῳ τῶν ἵππων παρεστὼς ἀνὴρ ἡνίοχος· ὁ μὲν δὴ πρότερος τῶν ἵππων καὶ ὁ ἀνὴρ Διονυσίου τοῦ Ἀργείου, τὰ δεύτερα δὲ ἔργα ἐστὶν Αἰγινήτου Σίμωνος. τῷ προτέρῳ δὲ τῶν ἵππων ἐπίγραμμα ἔπεστιν ἐπὶ τῇ πλευρᾷ, τὰ πρῶτα οὐ σὺν μέτρῳ· λέγει γὰρ δὴ οὕτω·

> > Φόρμις ἀνέθηκεν
> > Ἀρκὰς Μαινάλιος, νῦν δὲ Συρακόσιος.

> … 27.7 ἔστι δὲ ἐν τοῖς ἀναθήμασι τούτοις καὶ αὐτὸς ὁ Φόρμις ἀνδρὶ ἀνθεστηκὼς πολεμίῳ, καὶ ἐφεξῆς ἑτέρῳ καὶ τρίτῳ γε αὖθις μάχεται. γέγραπται δὲ ἐπὶ τούτοις τὸν στρατιώτην μὲν τὸν μαχόμενον Φόρμιν εἶναι τὸν Μαινάλιον, τὸν δὲ ἀναθέντα Συρακόσιον Λυκόρταν· δῆλα δὲ ὡς οὗτος ὁ Λυκόρτας κατὰ φιλίαν ἀναθείη τοῦ Φόρμιδος. τὰ δὲ ἀναθήματα τοῦ Λυκόρτα καλεῖται Φόρμιδος καὶ ταῦτα ὑπὸ Ἑλλήνων.

Among them there are also those dedicated by Mainalian Phormis, who crossed from Mainalos to Sicily to join the court of Gelon the son of Deinomenes. After a spectacular display of military achievements both for him and, later, for his brother Hieron, he reached such a level of prosperity that he made these dedications at Olympia and others also for Apollo at Delphi. [27.2] Those at Olympia consist of two horses and two charioteers, with a charioteer standing by each of the horses. The first of the horses and its man are the work of Dionysius of Argos, the second set of works are by Simon of

Aegina. On the first of the horses there is an inscription on the flank, its first part not in verse. This is how it goes: 'Phormis dedicated [this], an Arcadian from Mainalos, but now a Syracusan' … [27.7] Among these dedications there is also a statue of Phormis himself making a stand against an enemy, and he also fights against another and then yet a third opponent. It is inscribed on these that the soldier fighting is Phormis of Mainalos, while the dedicator is the Syracusan Lykortas. Clearly this Lykortas dedicated them out of friendship for Phormis. These dedications of Lykortas are also called by the Greeks dedications of Phormis.

Known to us by a single, one-word fragment and a handful of (disputed) testimonia, Phormis/os was nonetheless a very significant figure in early comedy – in form, dramaturgy and use of theatrical space. Aristotle pairs him (seemingly on equal footing) with Epicharmus as the originator of plot construction in comedy, 'which came first from Sicily' (**Aiii 2**). (Given this, it is striking that the best way to make sense of the transmitted title (**1**) *Kephalaia* is to interpret it in the sense, attested later, of 'plot' or 'main points': perhaps something like *The Main Points of the Story*.) Aristotle's words imply synchronicity, about which **1** is explicit. The association with Gelon (**1**, see also **3**) places his active career, like Epicharmus', high in the fifth century. If Phormis/os the poet and soldier (**3**) are the same, we might suppose that his career as a dramatist in Syracuse (and tutor to the tyrant's children) began after his military successes, some time in the late 480s.

It is difficult to judge the value of the claim that Phormis/os was the first to use a garment that reached to the feet (**1**). It might not rest on much more than a scholarly desire for symmetry with the history of costume in tragedy, which, among various innovations, ascribed (mostly) to Aeschylus a trailing robe (*Life of Aeschylus* 14; cf. Ath. 1.21d). Even so, it shows that Phormis/os had a sufficient prominence in later scholarship to attract attention or identification as the innovator in question. The term used (ἔνδυμα ποδήρες) is not especially technical but evokes the ξυστίς *xystis* said to be worn by tragic heroes (along with charioteers, wealthy women and, according to some sources, also comic actors, possibly female). A number of sources use the same phrase to explain the ξυστίς (Tim. *Lex.* s.v. Ξυστίδες; Phot. ξ 71–2; Hsch. ξ 195–6; *Lex. Seg. Gloss. Rhet.* s.v. Ξύστις). For discussion of Phormis/os' supposed introduction of a stage building (skene) of purple skins see **Ai**.

The uncertainty over the orthography of the name cannot be resolved. Aristotle calls the poet Phormis (**Aiii 2**: the passage has been thought an interpolation, we think without sufficient cause). The Suda (**1**; **Aiii 3**) and Athenaeus (14.652a) have Phormos. Themistius (**Bv 2**, possibly deriving from Aristotle) also has Phormos, but it is worth noting that this is a correction by Themistius' first editor, Denis Pétau (Dionysius Petavius, seventeenth century AD), of the manuscripts' μόρφος and ἄμορφος (Janko 2011, 426). The authority of Aristotle urges acceptance of Phormis, as does the name's extreme rarity, attested only for the comic poet and the individual in **3**. Phormos is far from common (eight attestations), but it was held by a number of prominent Athenians, which might have inclined later scholars mistakenly to adopt the more familiar form (but see on **2**). This uncertainty is tied to another: whether the Phormis of **3**, an Arcadian soldier in the entourage of Gelon and Hieron and immigrant to Syracuse, is to be identified with the poet.

We believe that the poet and mercenary are very probably one and the same person. It is possible that the name of the poet was properly Phormis and that Epicharmus himself (**2**) is responsible for the introduction of the near-homonym Phormos into the tradition by virtue of a pun. The source of the confusion would be contemporary with the poet himself. (Both φορμός and the related diminutive φορμίς are common nouns for a wicker basket generally used for domestic or light agricultural work.) It is even possible that Epicharmus used and punned on the name Phormis in **2**, and that this was later wrongly 'normalised' to the more common name (Φόρμος, Phormos) and noun (φορμός, *phormos*): the fragment of Epicharmus is not only preserved indirectly, but is reconstructed from a scholiastic paraphrase. In his comedy *Skiron*, Epicharmus had a speaker inquire of a basket – φορμός (*phormos*) or possibly φορμίς (*phormis*) – the identity of its mother, father and brother. The answer comes each time 'slave girl' (Σακίς, 'Sakis'). The slave girl is – to an object destined always to be by her side or in her hands – a basket's entire family. Since Schneidewin (1837a, 55), scholars have detected a reference to Epicharmus' contemporary.

The poet was clearly working in the same innovative sphere as Epicharmus. The existence of an agonistic relationship between the early comic poets of the Sicilian tradition is implied by the evidence of **Axii** that there were formal contests in the Syracusan theatre, and by the reference to an antagonistic professional relationship between Epicharmus and Deinolochos (**Av 2**). We know that Epicharmus mocked Aeschylus in his works, at least for stylistic matters (**Aix 3**). It is possible that he engaged in a form of explicitly rivalrous discourse against practitioners in his own genre that bears comparison to the later embedded rivalry of the Athenian comic poets. The isolated letters φορμον found in a second-century AD fragmentary papyrus commentary on Epicharmus' *Odysseus the Deserter* may well refer to the comic poet. This scholar provides frequent references to passages in authors with which Epicharmus is engaging, including Homer, Sophron and the tragedians (*PCG* F 98, cf. F 97). It is thus entirely likely that in this instance he was identifying engagement by Epicharmus with the work of Phormos (*PCG* F 98, l. 16).

The comic exchange in **2** establishes a nicely bathetic allusion to Andromache's words to Hector at *Iliad* 6.429–30: Ἕκτορ ἀτὰρ σύ μοί ἐσσι πατὴρ καὶ πότνια μήτηρ | ἠδὲ κασίγνητος, σὺ δέ μοι θαλερὸς παρακοίτης· 'Why, Hector, you are my father and my queenly mother – and my brother; you are my sturdy husband'. The fact that the means by which Epicharmus mocks his rival draws on a resource of their shared medium is also suggestive – namely, rechannelling a famous moment of epic intensity to comic effect in a mythological burlesque (Favi 2017a). That there was some abusive or parodic intent in the exchange that went beyond the humour of a basket outlining its own servile origins seems clear. Lesi (1975–1977, 86) notes that starting the enquiry with the mother's name, rather than the father's, is itself a slight in terms of the norms of social address. Berk (1964, 124) was the first to suggest that the scene involved a besmirching of the comic poet's origins as servile: Epicharmus puts his rival 'the Basket' on stage (disguised as a basket?), and makes him declare his own servile origins. (Petrides 2003, 76 accepts the possibility of introducing a contemporary individual within a mythological spoof in this way, but opts for an entirely different interpretation that draws on the dramaturgy of much later Roman adultery mime scenes in which an adulterer hides in a basket.)

The absence of extended fragments of Epicharmian (not to mention Phormian and Deinolochian) comedy, and the skewing of quotation of Epicharmus in antiquity in favour of the gnomic, leaves us unable to give parallels for such an *ad hominem* attack on a contemporary, but western comedy is unlikely to have been entirely free of such 'iambic' elements. In addition to his mockery of Aeschylus, it is clear that Epicharmus directly parodied, or at least openly criticised, the philosopher-poet Xenophanes of Colophon (the authority is Arist. *Met.* 1010a, with the commentary of Alexander of Aphrodisas: *PCG* F 143), who spent time in Catane, Zancle and Elea and probably also in Syracuse (D-K 21 A8; Álvarez Salas 2007b).

The (rare) word σηκίς *sekis* means a domestic slave born within the household (Ar. *Wasps* 768 with Biles and Olson 2015, 323). It was also a proper name given to such slaves, taken from the social role (Pherecr. *PCG* F 10.1, is a literary example, and a scholion to Ar. *Wasps* 768a makes the generalisation that the noun was so used: below), so that both characters will have had names that elevated a common noun for a lowly thing to a proper name. A female figure inscribed with the name Σακίς, in the Doric form, appears on a Corinthian pyxis dating to ca. 590–570 (Amyx 1988 II, 33.4; Wachter 2001, 60 thinks it more likely a noun 'slave' than a name): presumably a servant in a heroic context (other names include Agamemnon, Dorimachos, Alka, Thersandros). More remarkable is the evidence for Σάκις as a man's name in a very pertinent place and time (Arena 1994, 13 supposes a female, but this is virtually impossible): a Sakis is attested as a citizen of Camarina, dated to around or just before the middle of the fifth century (Cordano 1992, no. 41; *SEG* 42, 846, 4). This name may be local and of Sicel origin, a homonym to the Greek noun / name Sakis, but without the core semantic sense of 'slave'. The citizens of Camarina were among those made to join in the refoundation of Syracuse by Gelon in 485. It is difficult to gauge what, if any, relevance this may have to **2**. Perhaps knowledge of the male name Sakis enabled, by bilingual pun, a 'real' name for mother, father and brother of 'Basket' that could be male as well as female – for there can be little doubt that the scene nonetheless depends on the name having or at least implying the sense of 'slave girl'. The fact that Sakis was a 'real' (if rare) name, for both men and (slave) women, is further grounds for thinking that Phormis/os as used in the scene drew on knowledge of its role as a 'real' name.

According to one tradition, Sekis was also the name of Epicharmus' mother (**Aiii 3**, albeit by emendation). It has been plausibly suggested that this passage of Epicharmus' *Skiron* lies at the origin of this tradition (Kaibel 1899, 114), though none have proposed a route by which such an ascription might have developed. If the scene did operate at a metapoetical level, with a comic literalisation of the poet Phormis/os' name deployed as a strategy of attack, a confused memory of which poet's mother was alleged to be 'Sakis' in the drama may have generated such a tradition.

The Phormis from Mainalos in Arcadia of **3** was undoubtedly one of the 10,000 foreign mercenaries given citizenship by Gelon in return for military aid in the refoundation of Syracuse (D.S. 11.72.3), and one of a small group of these new Syracusans that have been identified as hailing from the Peloponnese (Luraghi 1994, 295). Other Arcadians in this group include Hagesias of Stymphalos, member of the prophetic genos of Iamids, described by Pindar as a *synoikister* of Syracuse (*O*. 6.5–9); and Praxiteles of Mantinea, subsequently of Camarina, then Syracuse – as evidenced by his dedication at Olympia, which demonstrates a similar epigraphic biography to that of Phormis in **3** (*IvO* 266; *CEG* I, 380;

SEG 36, 391: Πραξιτέλες ἀνέθεκε Συρακόσιος τόδ' ἄγαλμα | καὶ Καμαριναῖος· πρόσθαρ ἐ Μαντινέαι | Κρίνιος huιὸς ἔναιεν ἐν Ἀρκαδίαι πολυμέλο‹ι› | hεσλὸς ἐόν, καί ϝοι μνᾶμα τόδ' ἐστ' ἀρετᾶς 'Praxiteles of Syracuse – and Camarina – dedicated this object of delight. Son of Krinis, formerly he dwelt in Mantinea, in flock-rich Arcadia, a man of worth; this is a memorial of his excellence'; Luraghi 1994, 291–6). The Lykortas involved in the dedication of Phormis' statue group at Olympia was very probably another (above).

Eckstein (1969, 116) firmly rejects the identification ('sicher nicht identisch'); Janko (2011, 493) endorses it with equal energy ('Phormis must be the same person as the comic poet Phormis/Phormos; otherwise entries regarding two people, *both* with *both* forms of the name, have been conflated in Suda φ 609': Janko presumably hypothesises two separate entries in an earlier version of the lexicon); most are understandably non-committal (e.g. Körte 1941). To our knowledge the case in favour has never been made in any detail. Onomastics urge it: the only occurrences from all antiquity of the name Phormis are those for the poet and the mercenary. Moreover both of these are associated, very closely, with Gelon: the poet was 'a member of the household of the Sicilian tyrant Gelon and tutor to his children' (**1**), the mercenary emigrated 'to Sicily to join the court of Gelon the son of Deinomenes' and served 'both for him and, later, for his brother Hieron' (**3**). While Pausanias makes no mention of a later career as a poet, this was not evident in the Olympian dedications he had before him, which may have been all he had to go on. It is possible that one detail the significance of which he failed to notice does hint at that career. Pausanias thought the first part of the inscription – Φόρμις ἀνέθηκεν – was not in verse, but the situation may be more complex: Gallavotti (1978, 26) proposed that it could be treated as the (lyric) colon known as a 'reizianum' (or acephalic pherecratean), essentially a variation on the dactylic dimeter: x | — ◡ ◡ — | x. This has been thought an over-complex interpretation (Casevitz et al. 1999, 261), but if Phormis were also an accomplished (or an aspiring) poet, that objection falls away. (The presence of ephelkystic *nu* in ἀνέθηκεν could be another sign of a poetic composition.) Other explanations of the highly unusual form of the inscription fail to satisfy: that Pausanias could not see the first part of the inscription, so that the line he thought not in verse was in fact incomplete (Eckstein 1969, 116); or that a line in prose is followed by a single pentameter (Preger 1891, 45 no. 55).

Another suggestive thread between the 'comic' and the 'military' Phormis/os is the drama that attracted the attention of Athenaeus, the *Atalantai* (**1**). There can be no doubt that that work will have followed the dominant tradition that located the heroine Atalanta in Arcadia. Atalanta shunned marriage and devoted herself to hunting in the wilds of the Mainalian mountains, participating in the Calydonian boar-hunt, the funeral games of Pelias, and sometimes joining the Argonauts (Fowler 2013, 110). Atalanta was not simply from Arcadia, but from the very homeland of Phormis, Mainalos. In a tradition represented for us by Hellanicus (*EGM* F 162) her father Mainalos, son of Arkas, was the eponym of the place (even when her father is given the name Ias(i)os, the location around Mainalos persists, e.g. Call. *Dian.* 224; A.R. 1.769–70). His auto-description in his dedication at Olympia as 'an Arcadian from Mainalos ...' makes it clear that Phormis was proud of his Arcadian origins, and indeed of his regional attachment to Mainalos, just as it also shows that he was keen to advertise his new status as a Syracusan: '... but now a Syracusan'. It is entirely likely that he should have drawn on a central figure of the Panhellenic mythology of his region when in his adopted city. A poetic work created for another prominent figure among the Deinomenids' Arcadian emigré supporters shows just such a phenomenon. In *Olympian* 6, Pindar forges a powerful link between Arcadian Stymphalos, the homeland of its honorand Hagesias, and Syracuse, of which he is described as a *synoikister* (*O*. 6. 8–9, 77–100; Stamatopoulou 2014). The epinician komos is explicitly said to travel 'from one home to another' οἴκοθεν οἴκαδ' l. 98, between Stymphalos and Syracuse. Aeschylus composed an *Atalante*; Epicharmus an *Atalantai* (above). This (very near) homonomy of titles might be taken as further evidence for creative interaction between these poets, and is suggestive too of the impact the 'Arcadian' theme had in and beyond Syracuse. Another Arcadian theme in the oeuvre of Phormis/os might hide in the title *Kepheus* (**1**). If this is a separate work from the *Perseus* (above), this Kepheus is most likely to have been not the father of Andromeda of that name, but the Arcadian king and Argonaut who took part in Heracles' expedition against Hippocoon (Fowler 2013, 109–10).

Some further support for the identification of the Arcadian Phormis of **3** with the comic poet results from the (plausible) hypothesis that **2** is an attack on the social status of the poet Phormis/os. Gelon's Syracuse was an amalgam of migrants, forced and willing, and it would be interesting to know what ideological distinctions were made between the different groups with which Gelon increased the population. Were the citizens of Camarina, the wealthy aristocrats of Megara Hyblaea (among which may have been Epicharmus' family) and Euboea, not to mention the local Syracusan elite and demos, thought of as in some sense superior to the thousands of mercenaries brought in from Arcadia and elsewhere? The attack on Phormis/os in **2** could be not (simply) an attack on a poetic rival but evidence of an operative ideological distinction that asserted an inferior status for those in Syracuse who had come from elsewhere as 'economic migrants'.

The choice of the term σα/ηκίς for Phormis/os' parentage (or broader family, since a brother is included), is striking. The distinctive character of a σηκίς is that he or she is a slave *born within the oikos*: thus Hsch. σ 480: σηκίς· οἰκογενὴς δοῦλος, ἢ δούλη. οἷον ἐκ τοῦ σηκοῦ; Sch. Ar. *Wasps* 768a: σηκὶς· ἡ κατ' οἶκον διάκονος, ἡ θεράπαινα. This takes on significance when set against the striking biographical detail recorded by **1**, to the effect that the poet was 'a member of the household of the Sicilian tyrant Gelon and tutor to his children', οἰκεῖος δὲ Γέλωνι τῷ τυράννῳ Σικελίας καὶ τροφεὺς τῶν παίδων αὐτοῦ. Here οἰκεῖος evidently means 'belonging to one's house or family' (LSJ s.v. A.III). Other meanings, such as 'friendly' and 'related' can be ruled out. The point is that Phormos was given a station within the tyrant's household, honorific no doubt but nonetheless not a matter of friendship or equality based on relation by blood or marriage. The relevant concept of household in the case of the tyrant is somewhat like the enlarged, Homeric household that could include subordinate free men, as well as family and slaves (Luraghi 1994, 225).

There is an excellent parallel for the status held by Phormos in that of Mikythos, who was regent of Rhegium and Messene after the death of the tyrant Anaxilas in 476 and very probably another westward migrant from Arcadia (Luraghi 1994, 224–5). Mikythos also made a dedication, of enormous scale, at Olympia, that included a personified Agon alongside Dionysus, Orpheus and Zeus and statues of the poets Homer and Hesiod (Eckstein 1969, 33–42). The Homer statue is the earliest securely attested portrait of the poet, contemporary with the original of an Imperial copy dated to ca. 460 (Zanker 1995, 20). Mikythos was a member of Anaxilas' household (οἰκέτης) and the guardian of his sons (Hdt. 7.170.4; Paus. 5.26.2; D.S. 11.48.2, 11.66.1–2; Just. 4.2.4–5; *SEG* 28, 431). It has been suggested that in describing Phormos as it does, **1** was confusing Phormos for Mikythos (Eckstein 1969, 116), but no explanation for why or how such a confusion might have arisen has been given and it is entirely plausible that a man with the skills of a poet (and warrior) would have been well suited to the task of educating a tyrant's offspring. Epicharmus appears to have depicted this special status of Phormos and his family as that of chattels of Gelon's household. If he was in fact tutor to the tyrant's children, the dynamic of the attack may not simply be the assertion of servile birth but the disparagement of his position as a low-status and utilitarian one – useful, like a basket.

Av: Deinolochos

1. **Suda s.v. Δεινόλοχος ('Deinolochos', δ 338)**. Compiled ca. 1000 AD. Like many of the Suda's entries on Greek authors, this one derives from Hesychius' (5th or 6th c. AD) catalogue of writers and their works from earliest times (the *Onomatologos*), now lost, with roots in earlier scholarship. Text: Adler.

> Δεινόλοχος, Συρακούσιος, ἢ Ἀκραγαντῖνος, κωμικός. ἦν ἐπὶ τῆς ογ΄ Ὀλυμπιάδος, υἱὸς Ἐπιχάρμου, ὡς δέ τινες, μαθητής. ἐδίδαξε δράματα ιδ΄ Δωρίδι διαλέκτῳ.

> 'Deinolochos': Syracusan or Acragantine, a comic poet. He was in the 73rd Olympiad (488–485), son of Epicharmus; according to some, his pupil. He produced 14 dramas in Doric dialect.

2. **Aelian, *On the Characteristics of Animals* 6.51**. Written late 2nd or early 3rd c. AD. Aelian was a Roman writer from Praeneste who became famous for his mastery of Attic Greek and shared the enthusiasm for the Classical past of his learned predecessors and contemporaries in the Second Sophistic. While generally reticent about his sources, it is clear that he was a master of research and synthesis. Here he gives an aetiology of the name of the snake called the Dipsas ('Thirst-maker') that situates it in the mythology of Prometheus. Zeus offered a drug that would ward off mortality to anyone who denounced the thief of fire. The ass tasked with carrying the drug exchanges it for a drink at a spring, guarded by the snake. The snake receives the gift of renewed life, the ass the drink. On the identity of Aristias, possibly the tragedian from Phlious known for his satyr plays active in the 460s (**Bvi**), see Davies 1987, 72; Aristias *TrGF* 9 F 8. Text: Scholfield.

> τί οὖν; ἐγὼ τοῦ μύθου ποιητής; ἀλλ᾽ οὐκ ἂν εἴποιμι, ἐπεὶ καὶ πρὸ ἐμοῦ Σοφοκλῆς ὁ τῆς τραγῳδίας ποιητὴς καὶ Δεινόλοχος ὁ ἀνταγωνιστὴς Ἐπιχάρμου καὶ Ἴβυκος ὁ Ῥηγῖνος καὶ Ἀριστίας καὶ Ἀπολλοφάνης ποιηταὶ κωμῳδίας ᾄδουσιν αὐτόν.

> Ἀριστοφάνης καὶ Ἀπολλοφάνης Schneidewin

What then? Am I the poet of the story? I will deny it, for before me it is celebrated also by Sophocles the poet of tragedy (*TrGF* F 362); Deinolochos, the
rival of Epicharmus (*PCG* F 8); Ibycus of Rhegium (*PMG* 342; Van Dijk 1997,
159–60); and the comic poets Aristias and Apollophanes (*PCG* F 9).

The ascription of paternity and status as teacher to a major predecessor in the same field (**1**)
are standard reflexes of the ancient biographical tradition and, in the case of Epicharmus
and Deinolochos, both are doubtless false. They will reflect an awareness that Deinolochos
was younger than Epicharmus, perhaps by as much as a generation. But the date given for
his activity (a floruit rather than birthdate will be intended by 'he was …' ἦν) – 488–485 –
is the same as the floruit of Epicharmus in **Aiii 8**, which in turn is consistent with **Aiii 3**,
that has Epicharmus producing in Syracuse in 486/5 or 485/4. A likely conclusion is that
Deinolochos was a considerably younger contemporary of Epicharmus. This would fit with
the tradition preserved by **2** of agonistic rivalry between the two. The most likely explanation for the uncertainty expressed over Deinolochos' place of birth is that he was from
Acragas (**A Introduction**) but spent much of his career based in the city that was, already
by the start of Gelon's tyranny (485), developing a new and highly sophisticated tradition
of comic theatre.

It is unlikely that the notice Deinolochos 'produced' (ἐδίδαξε) 14 dramas (**1**) rests on
any didascalic information comparable to that available for Classical Athens, and more
probably simply reflects the number of attributed works known to an anterior source (the
Suda uses the same verb for Epicharmus: **Aiii 3**). A dozen or more of Deinolochos' works
were still being read in Aelian's day. Part of a 'catalogue of some provincial library or a
reading list' that survives on two small papyrus fragments of the second century AD (*POxy*.
2659 = *PCG* T 3; Rea 1968, 70; Otranto 2000, 29–38) records comic poets and their plays
in alphabetical order, from Ameipsias to Epicharmus. The entry for Deinolochos has the
broken names of at least ten works, six of which were not known before the publication
of the papyrus in 1968: *The Doctor*, *Kirka* or ? *O*[*dysseus*], *Meleag*[*er*], *Oineus*, *Oreste*[*s*],
Pholos. A seventh, *Leu*[*ka*]*r*[*ion*] (as restored by Rea), was also new. Rea thought this last
the erroneous ascription of an Epicharmean work recorded by a variety of names, *Pyrrha
and Promatheus*, *Deukalion* or *Leukarion* (a variant form for the name Deukalion; see below). Kassel and Austin detected traces of a tenth name at the join between the two small
fragments (app. crit. *PCG* T 3, l. 9), possibly *Od*[*y*]*sse*[*us*], also hitherto unknown for
Deinolochos (though note the possible alternative title for *Kirka* above). Among the five
further plays already known from other sources – *Althaea*, *Amazons*, *Komoidotragoidia*,
Medea and *Telephus* – the last two also appear on the papyrus list. The preponderance of
mythological subject matter is clear.

Aelian's description (**2**) of Deinolochos as 'the rival of Epicharmus' may have been designed to introduce an obscure author by reference to a more famous contemporary working in the same genre. But Aelian chooses his words carefully, and 'rival' (ἀνταγωνιστής)
implies a context involving structured contest (**Axii**) or a more general but nonetheless historically and culturally embedded relationship of competitive interaction. Clear evidence
of one or both may have been available to Aelian in the surviving works of the two authors.

Schneidewin (1833, 197) suggested that Deinolochos' *Medea* might have been a suitable
home for the story of Dipsas, assuming it included Medea's rejuvenation of Aeson, but the

Leukarion is a much more likely candidate. For Leukarion was the son of Prometheus, who with his wife Pyrrha survived a flood sent by Zeus, and Aelian makes it clear that the story of Dipsas was associated with the mythology of Prometheus. Prometheus and his theft of fire also featured in Epicharmus' treatment of the subject in his *Leukarion* (or *Deukalion*, or *Pyrrha and Promatheus*; *PCG* F 113, ll. 241–53). In addition to the *Leukarion*, Deinolochos and Epicharmus are reported to share the title *Medea*; while Deinolochos wrote a *Pholos*, Epicharmus a *Heracles with Pholos*.

Epicharmus wrote (at least) two plays entitled *Odysseus* (such that they were given distinguishing epithets, the *Deserter* and *Shipwrecked*) and Deinolochos very probably wrote one, or possibly two plays about Odysseus (above). Similarly, an *Atalanta(i)* is ascribed to both Epicharmus and Phormis/os (**Aiv**). And some (including Welcker and Kaibel) have thought that the *Halcyons* reported by the Suda for Phormis/os should rather be named *Alkyoneus* after the giant fought by Heracles, which is confirmed as the title of an Epicharmean drama (Rodríguez-Noriega Guillén 1996, 15). An intriguing feature of the Epicharmean work is that it made Diomos the father of Alkyoneus and (according to Athenaeus or his source) the former was also the founder of Syracusan bucolic poetry (*PCG* F 4).

This phenomenon of common titles has been interpreted as evidence for uncertainty of ascription by later critics of plays from the early western tradition (Lobel 1959), but it may be preferable to view it within a framework of agonistic rivalry between this group of comic poets interacting within the vibrant context of the Syracusan theatre. The evidence of titles common between Epicharmus and Aeschylus, notably *Persians*, tends to support this line of reasoning (**Aix**). Aelian's description of Deinolochos as 'the rival of Epicharmus' (**2**), precisely in the context of a theme that had also been treated by the elder dramatist, may thus take on greater significance. Moreover, the fact that the tradition concerning the Epicharmean play offers a number of variant titles may in part be due to the existence of one or more reworkings in or after the poet's lifetime (**Aiii**), hinting at a popularity of the story that would be in keeping with its having also been taken up by Deinolochos. In other words, it is possible that Aelian's description might be based on some knowledge that Deinolochos had engaged in rivalry with Epicharmus precisely by composing a work that responded to Epicharmus' treatment of the *Leukarion* story. An alternative but related interpretation of the phenomenon would be that the Deinolochean titles were in fact reworkings of the Epicharmean dramas, or represent some other type of collaboration between the two poets. This would sit well with the tradition of **1** that makes Deinolochos the son or pupil of Epicharmus, though accords rather less well with the emphasis on rivalry between them in **2**.

The title *Komoidotragoidia* further suggests that Deinolochos was working in a context in which, as later at Athens, comedy existed in a parodic or symbiotic relationship with tragedy. Some unnecessary doubt over the ascription has been expressed (Kerkhof 2001, 116). The title is reported by the Antiatticist in his entry on πέπαυνται (π 34 Valente) – 'The same (sc. author); in the *Komoidotragoidia*'. It has been suggested that, between the immediately prior entry in the Antiatticist (π 33 Valente), which reports that the word πιττάκιον was used by Deinolochos in his *Telephus*, and the entry reporting the use of πέπαυνται in the *Komoidotragoidia*, another may have fallen out that recorded a usage by one of the comic poets Anaxandrides or Alcaeus, for whom the title *Komoidotragoidia* is also reported (Valente 2015, 230). But with *DTC*[2] 290 we find no reason Deinolochos could not have written such a work that travestied tragedy, a novelty he would have seen staged at Syracuse. Epicharmus parodied Aeschylean tragedy (**Aix 3**; **Aiii**) and the comment of an ancient critic on Epicharmus' *Odysseus the Deserter* hints at a broader range of tragic targets: passages of that comedy were said to have been directed 'at the tragedians' (*PCG* F 97, commentary on ll. 1–10, l. 2: πρὸ(ς) τοὺς τραγικοὺς λέγετ(αι); *PCG* F 98, l. 48).

Avi: Phrynichus in Sicily. Anonymous, *On Comedy* 32 (*Prolegomena De Comoedia* III = *TrGF* 3 T 6). The (unknown) author of this treatise on comedy of late composition, preserved with the manuscripts of Aristophanes, demonstrates quite good knowledge of the life, times and number of works of the comic poets. Phrynichus the Athenian tragic poet was a leading member of the first generation of tragedians, active from around the last decade of the sixth century (Suda φ 762 = *TrGF* 3 T 1 calls him a student of Thespis and mentions a victory in the 67th Olympiad: 511–508), while **VI B** attests a victory in 476 with Themistocles as choregos, possibly including his *Phoenician Women*. Another Phrynichus, an Athenian comic poet, was active in the last thirty years of the fifth century. Text: Koster.

> Φρύνιχος †† <Πολυ>φράδμονος ἔθανεν ἐν Σικελίαι.

> Phrynichus […] son of <Poly>phradmon died in Sicily.

The author proceeds by listing in chronological order the names of famous comic poets and giving brief accounts of their careers. The entry on Phrynichus, which comes after that of Pherecrates and before that of Eupolis – and thus chronologically suits the comic poet – has suffered disturbance. Phrynichus the tragic poet is otherwise reported to have been the son of Polyphradmon (Suda φ 762), while the scholion to Aristophanes' *Frogs* 13 gives Eunomides as the name of the comic Phrynichus' father. It is therefore clear that the tragic poet is being referred to here (the error – Phradmon for Polyphradmon – is probably a result of textual corruption). The author made mention of the tragic poet in his entry on his comic namesake, no doubt in order to distinguish the two, and we know that ancient scholars devoted considerable energy to distinguishing between at least four Athenian Phrynichi (Sch.RVEΘM Barb Ar. *Frogs* 13; Sch.RV Ar. *Birds* 750), but at some point the material relating to the comic poet was removed, leaving only this tattered entry (the detection of the lacuna after the name 'Phrynichus' and the restoration 'son of <Poly>phradmon' go back to Dindorf). Because of the disturbance to the text there is some question as to which of the two Phrynichi is reported as having died in Sicily: some think that text might also have been lost after the patronymic, which would separate the son of <Poly>phradmon from the verb (see Koster). But the most economical solution is that this tradition reported that the death of the tragic Phrynichus took place in Sicily (Guardì 1980, 35–7; Bosher 2012, 102; Stewart 2017, 223–5. Harvey 2000, 114–15 and Stama 2014, 28 argue that the comic poet is meant). The fact that in the first half of the fourth century members of the court of Dionysius II are, on the authority of Timaeus (*FGrH* 566 F 32), said to have sung works by Phrynichus after dinner (the tragic poet is clearly meant), along with those of Stesichorus and Pindar, is suggestive of an enduring acquaintance with his works in Syracuse that may derive in part from a sojourn there during the poet's life.

It is possible that Gelon (tyrant of Syracuse 485–478) was responsible for bringing Phrynichus to Sicily – with notable consequences for the extent to which we regard Hieron as the great cultural innovator who saw the value of the new dramatic form for his purposes. The suggestions that Phrynichus was somewhat older than Aeschylus point to such a possibility, and it now seems possible that Gelon had already developed the great theatre in Syracuse. It may however be more likely that Phrynichus was among the many poets and intellectuals brought to the court of Gelon's brother and successor, in the period from 478 to the death of the tyrant in 467 (**VI A**). It has been remarked that his *Phoenician Women*, almost certainly successful at the Athenian Dionysia in this same period (476: **VI B**), would have held a similar appeal to Hieron as we know Aeschylus' *Persians* did, for it treated the defeat of Xerxes at Salamis in 480, an event which Hieron's publicists were busy assimilating to his own victory in 474 over the Etruscans at Cumae. Some have thus supposed that Hieron saw in Phrynichus another poet whose work might glorify his achievements (Guardì 1980, 35–6) and the hypothesis of a reperformance of *Phoenician Women* at Syracuse (Guardì 1980, 37; Morgan 2012, 49) is attractive. (The possibility that Phrynichus' work could have been reperformed in the fifth century is already attested by Herodotus: **V H** on Hdt. 6.21.2.) In a significant sense the two tragedies form a kind of pair, not only because they stand out as treating the recent historical conflicts with Persia, but because we know on the excellent authority of Glaucus of Rhegium (*TrGF* 3 T 5) that Aeschylus paid direct homage to his older colleague's work in the opening lines of the *Persians*, which allude explicitly to those of the *Phoenician Women* (*TrGF* 3 F 8).

Phrynichus will have been in advanced age in the 470s. It is eminently possible that he did die in Sicily (Molyneux 1992, 235–6), and that Hieron in fact offered his poets a permanent final residence in fine conditions, as Archelaus was to do later. Two other of Hieron's poets suffered (or enjoyed) the same fate – Aeschylus, though in Gela and after the fall of the tyranny (**Aix**) and Simonides, apparently in Acragas (Call. fr. 64.3–4 Pfeiffer; Suda σ 441). It may be that the topos of poets' deaths in Sicily might have an independent life of its own, possibly one born out of Deinomenid (and Emmenid) propaganda (Kowalzig 2008, 141 n. 40; Barbantani 2010).

Avii: A Lead Tablet from (?) Gela with a Curse against Choragoi in a Local Competition, ca. 470–450 (see below).

An opisthographic lead tablet, originally folded; complete at top, bottom and right-hand side. Inscribed in West Greek. Side A, in the later 'blue' alphabet, records a financial transaction that took place in the presence of a proxenos of Leontini, for which Apellis was guarantor. Side B (below) is in the older 'red' alphabet.

0.062 × 0.171 m.

From a grave in south-east Sicily (according to the dealer from whom it was purchased).

Rare Book Room, Library of the University of North Carolina at Chapel Hill.

Miller 1973, 65–108; Jordan 1985, no. 91; *IGDS* no. 134b; *IGASMG* II² 45; Jordan 2007 = *SEG* 57, 905B.

Text: based on *SEG* 57, 905B.   Drawing: Dubois 1989, 155.

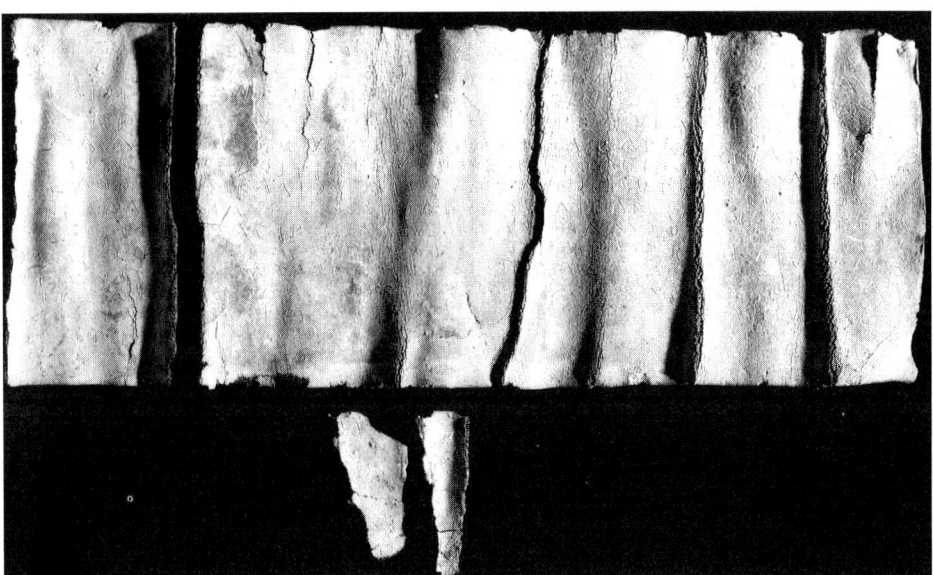

1 Ἐὐχά. Ἀπέλλις ἐπὶ φιλότατι τᾶι ΕὐνίϘο <—> μεδέν΄ [Ε]ὐνίϘο σπευ-
δ[αι]ότερον ἔμεν μεδὲ φιντίονα, ἀλλ' ἐπαινε̄<ν> καὶ ἑΦόντα κἀέΦ-
οντα καὶ φιλετᾱν. ἐπὶ φιλότατι τᾱι ΕὐνίΦο ἀπογαράφο τό-
ς χοραγὸς πάντας ἐπ' ἀτελεία<ι> κὲπέον καὶ ἔργον καὶ τ-

5 ὸς παῖδ{ι}ας ἀπὸ τένον καὶ τὸς πατέρας κἀπρακτίαι κὲν ἀγõ-
νι κὲχθὸς ἀγόνον οἵτινες μὲ παρ' ἐμ' ἀπολείποιεν. Καλεδίαν
[ἀπογ]αράφο ἀπ' Ἀπέλλιος καὶ τὸς{ς} τενε̄ι πάντας ἐπὶ μεσοτερ-
[ο. ^{ca. 3} . .] ἐντάδα. Σοσίαν ἀπογράφο ἀπὸ τõ καπελείο Ἀλκιαδᾶν ἐπὶ τᾱ-
[ι Μελ?]ανθίο φιλότατι. Πυρία<μ>, Μύσσκελον, Δαμόφαντον καὶ τὸν

10 [χοραγ]ὸν ἀπογράφο ἀπὸ τõμ παιδõν καὶ τõμ πατέρον καὶ τὸς ἄλλ-
[ος πά]ντας οἵτινες ἐντάδε ἀφικνοίατο, μεδέν' Εὐνίκο σπευδαιό-
[τερο]ν γενέσθαι μέτ' ἄνδρεσι μέτε γυναικέσσι. ὸς οὗτος <ὸ> βόλιμος, τὸς ΤΕ-
[. . ^{ca. 5} . .]ΟΔΙΑΙΤΙΜΑΝ ἐρύσαιντο. Εὐνίκοι ἀὲ νικᾶν παντε̄. ἐμ βολύμοι ἐπ-
[ὶ φιλ]ότατι τᾱι Εὐνίκο γάρφο.

1 Εὐχά Miller, Dubois, Arena   Τύχα Jordan   1–2 σπευδότερον Miller   2
Φίντονα Miller, Dubois   3 Φιλέταν Miller, Dubois   6 οἵτινές με Dubois   8
καπελείο· Ἀλκιάδαν Miller, Dubois   10 [χοραγ]ὸν Jordan 2007, 349   12 τοσοῦτος
Miller   τοσούτος Dubois   12–13 βόλιμος, τος τε‖[....]ọ Διοτίμαν Miller   βόλιμος
τὸς τε‖[νε̄ι, β]ολίμο τιμάν Dubois   12–13 perhaps ὸς οὗτος <ὸ> βόλιμος, τὸς τέ‖[νον ?
ἐπ]ọ<ι>δ{ι}αι τιμάν ἐρύσαιντο. Εὐνίκοι ἀὲ νικᾶν παντε̄.   13 ἐμ βολύμοι: εμοαψψσον
Miller   ΡΜΟΑΥ... Dubois

Prayer (or 'Fortune'): Apellis, for love of Eunikos <sc. prays> that no-one
be taken more seriously or be more popular than [E]unikos, but <all> should
praise and admire (him) both willingly and unwillingly (or perhaps 'that no-
one be more enthusiastic or more affectionate than [E]unikos, but (he) should
praise and be affectionate to (me) both willingly and unwillingly'). For love of

Eunikos I mark down all the choragoi so that they be ineffectual both in word and in deed, along with [5] their sons and fathers, and so that they fail both in the contest and outside the contests – whoever does not leave him (sc. Eunikos) with me (or perhaps 'whoever in my entourage should let me down' or 'whoever does not desert and come over to my side'). Kaledias I mark [down] (?) to separate him from Apellis, along with all those (??) in betw[een] there and here (or perhaps 'all those there against the arbiters here' or, less likely, 'all those there for more mediocre places here'). Sosias I mark down, from the shop of the Alkiadai, for his love of [Mel]anthios. Pyria<s>, Mysskelos, Damophantos and the[ir [10] (?) chorag]os I mark down, along with their sons and fathers, and [a]ll the other[s] who arrive here. May none be taken [mor]e seriously than Eunikos either among men or women. As this lead (sc. does), so may [the sp]ells against tho[se men] draw away their honour. For Eunikos may there be victory always, completely (Reading τέ|[νον ἐπ]οδ{ι}αὶ τιμὰν ἐρύσαιντο. Εὐνίκοι ἀὲ νικᾶν παντε̃.) I write on the lead for [l]ove of Eunikos.

This curse is inscribed on a lead tablet that had done service as a receipt in a financial transaction for which Apellis served as guarantor (on Side A see Jordan 2007, 336–42 with earlier bibliography). The record of that transaction is inscribed in the 'blue' alphabet, which began to replace the older 'red' alphabet in south-east Sicily around 470. The inscription on Side A can therefore be dated to around 470, or slightly later. Even though it is written in the older 'red' alphabet, the curse on Side B is certainly later than Side A, given that after the curse was inscribed the tablet will have been buried in the earth; and because the curse occupied a slightly smaller extent of lead than the text of Side A: evidently the left-hand edge had broken off in the interim. We can date the curse some time before 450, perhaps ca. 470–450 (cf. Jordan 2007, 336). Secure information about its provenance is unavailable, but the best indications – dialect, letter forms and onomastics – suggest Gela as most likely.

Much is obscure about this intriguing document, among the very earliest surviving curse tablets. It is one of a very small group of curses against public performers (the others are Attic: **V D**; **V F**). It provides a rare glimpse into the mechanics of a choral contest in Greek Sicily before the middle of the fifth century. The key aim of Apellis, the author of the curse, was to affect the outcome of choragic contest on behalf of his friend Eunikos, a competitor. A relationship of φιλότας 'friendship' or 'love' unites Apellis to Eunikos. Apellis declares himself to act 'for love of Eunikos' (ll. 1, 3, 14). This may imply erotic attachment as opposed to simple friendship, but we do not follow Jordan (2007, 346; cf. Dubois 1989, 156) in his interpretation of ll. 2–3 as an attempt by Apellis to secure Eunikos' love by magical means (see his alternative translation above).

One reason for preferring 'Prayer' Ἐὺχά to 'Fortune' Τύχα as the first word (below for another) is the absence of a main verb in ll. 1–3, since 'Prayer' could provide the verbal idea needed for what follows – a wish that Eunikos be successful, attractive and praised by all. Eunikos is not a rare name but may suggest that its holder came from a class that had aspirations for the agonistic future of its offspring. It is also the name of one of the choreuts on the Pronomos Vase (no. 1 in Taplin and Wyles 2010, fig. 0.0; Wilson 2007c, 372–4). The pragmatic core of the prayer follows in ll. 3–4: ἐπὶ φιλότατι τᾶι Εὐνίϙο ἀπογαράφο τὸ|ς χοραγὸς πάντας ἐπ' ἀτελεία<ι> κέπέον καὶ ἔργον 'For love of Eunikos I mark down all the choragoi so that they be ineffectual both in word and in deed'. Rival choragoi are cursed. This first statement is generic and inclusive. More specific named targets follow. The use of the verb ἀπογράφο in curses is not paralleled directly but is not difficult to explain, drawing on legal meanings of 'denounce', 'accuse' (LSJ s.v. III.1). The preposition ἀπό appears sometimes to be used in this inscription in close association with this verb (with a sense of 'mark down as *or* to keep separate from' e.g. l. 7), but it is difficult and probably unhelpful to try to make every instance conform to the same usage (thus in l. 8 we translate it as signifying place of origin, in ll. 5 and 10 with the meaning of 'along with').

The extension of the prayer to encompass the sons and fathers of the rival choragoi (l. 5) may simply reflect the expansive root and branch rhetoric of curse; but it might in this instance imply that the performance in question was a family business that drew on multiple generations (cf. the organisation of the theatrical professions along family lines: Sutton 1987). The issue arises again with the addition of the 'sons and fathers' to a list of those targeted later in the document (ll. 9–10). The consignment of rival choragoi to failure 'both in the contest and outside the contests' (ll. 5–6) shows that what lies behind this curse is a specific competitive event (the initial singular ἀγῶνι probably shows that one special occasion is in mind, while the following plural in 'and outside the contests' generalises without detracting from the primary focus).

At this date the term choragos will certainly mean that the event involved a contest of choruses. Eunikos was himself possibly a choragos competing against the (other) choragoi cursed by his friend and supporter, Apellis. But it is perhaps more likely that Eunikos was a performer within a choral contest organised by 'liturgical' choragoi, his own being Apellis. Much turns on how we take the relative clause that redescribes the cursed choragoi, l. 6: οἵτινες μὲ παρ' ἐμ' ἀπολείποιεν. Our preferred translation – 'whoever does not leave him (sc. Eunikos) with me' – is most readily compatible with a situation in which Eunikos was a star performer working with Apellis, who fears he might be taken from him by others.

Other interpretations cannot be ruled out, though they all bring more substantial difficulties: thus for instance Jordan (2007, 347) airs the possibility of locating Kaledias (l. 6) not in the following sentence but treating him as the object of the verb in this one: 'those who would not leave Kaledias in my hands'. But what role Kaledias (thus abruptly introduced) might have served in Apellis' team and how it might have related to that of Eunikos remains unclear. Two further interpretations that have been offered both have the disadvantage of requiring a more or less rough breach of syntax: 'whoever in my entourage should let me down' (Dubois 1989, 157) and 'whoever does not desert and come over to my side' (Eidinow 2007, 159). Both these descriptions cannot easily be referred back to the competing choragoi (as strict grammar requires) and look rather like an extension of the curse against entirely new targets.

Apellis has left virtually no other clues as to the context for which he made his curse. The choral contest will certainly form part of a festival and cult. If Gela is the right locale, among that city's major cults are those of Athena Lindia; the founder-hero Antiphamos; Apollo; Gelas; and, above all, Demeter and Kore (Wilson 2007c, 354). A dramatic as opposed to purely choral context remains a (perhaps more remote) possibility. The Deinomenid tyrants, notably Hieron, engaged in energetic patronage of festivals, poets and – in all likelihood – the theatre (**VI A**). Aeschylus is said to have spent his last days in Gela (ca. 458–456) and the date of the tablet is early enough to refer to a contest in tragedy in which Aeschylus himself might have competed. Alternatively the cult offered to the heroised tragic poet in Gela might have seen the competitive reperformance of his dramas by actors from across the Greek world (**Aix**; note the strong emphasis on contestants arriving from outside; Wilson 2007c, 356–8).

One illuminating detail is the addition to the list of names of those targeted at ll. 9–11: 'and [a]ll the other[s] who arrive here' καὶ τὸς ἄλλ|[ος πά]ντας οἵτινες ἐντάδε ἀφικνοίατο. Of these it is wished that 'none be taken [mor]e seriously than Eunikos either among men or women'. This shows that Eunikos was facing competitors (in the plural) coming from outside his own town or region where the festival was held. The event was therefore of some scale and at least regional importance. The fact that women are listed alongside men as those whose support for Eunikos is sought quietly reveals that the audience for the contest in question included women in it. We interpret the preceding list of names as members of a rival choral group, regarding as very likely Jordan's suggested restoration of [χοραγ]-ὸν at the start of l. 10. This is perhaps most likely a local group, or at least part of one, as too the other named individuals. The outsiders are it seems referred to as an anonymous group.

The extremely difficult phrase at ll. 7–8 looks somewhat similar in shape and perhaps content: καὶ τὸς{ς} τενἔι πάντας ἐπὶ μεσοτέρ|[ο . ca. 3 . .] ἐντάδα. The sentence of which it forms the end is most plausibly construed as targeting one Kaledias as a rival or enemy of the curser himself, Apellis: 'Kaledias I mark [down] to (?) separate him from Apellis'. Kaledias may be the individual whom Apellis sees as his greatest potential threat in the agon and that is why he is the first to be named after the generic 'all the choragoi' of ll. 3–4. He is thus probably a rival choragos. No fully satisfactory analysis of the final phrase has been proposed, but an interpretation that treats it as akin to the later curse against rivals from outside has much to be said for it, though quite how the desired meaning is to be extracted from the surviving Greek is not clear: 'along with all those (??) in betw[een] there and here'. The particularising deictic τενἔι 'there' l. 7 implies an important centre from which rival performers are anticipated (and perhaps, feared): Syracuse is a possibility. A less satisfactory alternative is to treat the word μεσοτερ- as a comparative form of μέσος used after ἐπὶ in the sense of 'middling', 'mediocre' to describe the placements to be achieved by the rivals from 'there': 'and (sc. I also mark down) (??) all those there for more mediocre places μεσοτέρ|[ους] here'.

A third and promising solution is adumbrated by Arena, who draws attention to a term preserved in a gloss of Hesychius (μ 959): μεσσωτήρ· ὁ μεσιτεύων κατὰ τὸν ἀγῶνα. 'messoter: one who acts as an arbiter in the contest'. One might then suppose a restoration thus: καὶ τὸς{ς} τενἔι πάντας ἐπὶ μεσ<σ>οτέρ|[?ασι] ἐντάδα 'and (sc. I also mark down) (??) all those there against / after the arbiters here'. Arena (2002, 44) writes: 'In altre parole qui sono contemplate tutti i generi di imbroglio che possono venire effetuati nelle gare, compreso quello di "comperare" l'arbitro'. The notion that this extremely rare word for a 'mediator' or 'arbiter' in a contest might be present here is attractive, but Arena gives no sense of how he thinks the term might work within the sentence. Could the aim be to control unscrupulous contestants from 'there' who, when they come 'here' for the event, are 'against' or 'at' the judges? (A dative might be most likely in such a construction, thus ἐπὶ μεσ<σ>οτέρ|[?ασι] above; but we might have expected the correct form of the plural to be μεσ<σ>οτράσι and, rather than supposing another error – ἐπὶ μεσ<σ>οτ{ε}ρ|[άσι] – an accusative is perhaps also feasible: ἐπὶ μεσ<σ>οτέρ|[ας].) An additional problem for this line of interpretation is the absence of the article.

At ll. 8–9 Apellis marks down Sosias, 'from the shop of the Alkiadai, for his love of [Mel]anthios'. Sosias is probably another competing choragos and Melanthios his own star performer, the counterpart to Apellis' Eunikos. The intriguing 'shop' or 'bar' of the Alkiadai may indicate the source of Sosias' finances, or (or also) a form of localised, collegial choral organisation. Alternatively, this may simply be a way of identifying which Sosias is meant, since we know of at least one other in Gela. It may be local custom to identify people by their house or place of employment (and it is perhaps relevant that no patronymics are used in this tablet). Sosias was himself doubtless an 'Alkiad': a Sosias and an Alkias appear together on a funerary monument dating to ca. 500 from the necropolis of Gela (*IGDS* 131 with Wilson 2007c, 369–72).

The curse concludes with what looks like a trope of sympathetic magic (Jordan 2007, 349): '*as* this lead (has certain qualities), *so* may X have that quality, *vel sim.*' l. 12: ὅς οὗτος <ὁ> βόλιμος, τὸς .... Jordan's improved readings permit a number of speculative suggestions for this sentence (we withdraw from the even greater speculation of Wilson 2007c, 375–7). The correlative function of the clauses in this sentence evidently extended to both the adverbs ὅς 'as' and τὸς 'so'; and also to their related demonstratives: οὗτος 'this' should thus be paired with a 'that', part of τῆνος. Given that a plural verb follows (ἐρύσαιντο) the grammatically equivalent τῆνος is ruled out. But the remaining text (TE[. . ᶜᵃ·⁵ . . .] ΟΔΙΑΙΤΙΜΑΝ) could certainly conceal a plural subject, accompanied by a genitive of τῆνος. The five letters before the verb ἐρύσαιντο are most easily articulated as the accusative τιμὰν, leaving the likely ending of a nominative noun form before it: ὅς οὗτος <ὁ> βόλιμος, τὸς τέ‖[νον . . ᶜᵃ·² .]οδιαι τιμὰν ἐρύσαιντο. If we may suppose a slip in the placement of an iota (compare l. 5 παῖδ{ι}ας), it is possible to complete the word that precedes τιμὰν with part of the contextually pertinent noun ἐπωιδά 'spell': ὅς οὗτος <ὁ> βόλιμος, τὸς τέ‖[νον ? ἐπ]ọ<ι>δ{ι}ạὶ τιμὰν ἐρύσαιντο. 'As this lead (sc. does), so may [the sp]ells against tho[se men] draw away (LSJ s.v. ἐρύω A.1) their honour (sc. of the rival choragoi and their supporters and performers listed)'. On this reading Apellis aims to achieve his goal both by the efficacy of his lead tablet and by spells intoned over it (most probably by himself while burying it), securing by this oral performance the full magical power of the written curse (Wilson and Favi 2017).

If 'spells' ἐπῳδαί did in fact feature here at the end of the curse, Εὐχά 'Prayer' becomes the more likely candidate for its first word, since it would define the nature of the *defixio* as a whole, and there are parallels for the close association between prayers and contextual spells (e.g. Pi. *P.* 4.217; Pl. *Laws* 909b4). The following phrase Εὐνίκοι ἀὲ νικᾶν παντῆ 'For Eunikos may there be victory always, completely' is thus a free-standing wish for victory for Eunikos, always and completely, with a play – perhaps with magical force – on the name of his friend 'Good winner' (Wilson 2007c, 373). The word translated as 'completely' (παντῆ) might in this context mean 'by all the votes' (**Axii**).

Opinion varies as to whether the agonistic choragia to which this tablet testifies was liturgical in the sense familiar from Athens – namely a primarily financial and organisational duty (Eidinow 2007, 162 inclines towards this); or rather a performative service of choral leadership (thus e.g. Dubois 1989). We may adduce the evidence of Pollux (9.41–2).

When describing parts of the Greek city, he notes that 'they [the subject is the Greeks in general] call the training room (*didaskaleion*) the chorus, whenever they also call the trainer (*didaskalos*) a choregos and "to train", "to be a choregos" – especially the Dorians, as Epicharmus shows in his *Odysseus the Deserter* (*PCG* F 103), while in his *Seizures* (*PCG* F 13) he names the training room (*didaskaleion*) the *choregeion*.' ἐκάλουν δὲ τὸ διδασκαλεῖον καὶ χορόν, ὁπότε καὶ τὸν διδάσκαλον χορηγὸν καὶ τὸ διδάσκειν χορηγεῖν, καὶ μάλιστα οἱ Δωριεῖς, ὡς Ἐπίχαρμος ἐν Ὀδυσσεῖ αὐτομόλῳ, ἐν δ' Ἁρπαγαῖς χορηγεῖον τὸ διδασκαλεῖον ὠνόμασεν. Pollux is making the point that Dorian Greeks in particular used the word *choregos* where others used *didaskalos* and the verb χορηγεῖν where others used διδάσκειν. Given the thoroughly Dorian character of Gela, this gives us some reason to incline to the view that the choragoi of this tablet are more likely to serve as trainers/poets/choreographers than as financier liturgists (cf. Wilson 2007c, 359–64).

Nonetheless, we cannot rule out a liturgical meaning: it should be noted that Pollux qualifies his remark with the word 'especially', which indicates that Dorian practice was not necessarily uniform (Wilson 2007c, 364). And the tablet may date from a period after the fall of the tyrants in Gela, which would be a fertile time for liturgical service to take root, with the new broadening of elite participation in public life. In sum, while there can be little ground for confidence, it is perhaps most probable that Apellis was himself a competing liturgical choragos (we know from the financial transaction on Side A that he was a man of substance), while Eunikos was a key performer in his team. Also somewhat in favour of this interpretation is what looks like the same two-tier relationship of 'backer'-choragos and performer in the pair Sosias and Melanthios ll. 8–9. If on the other hand the alternative interpretation of the evidence of Pollux above is correct, the two tiers could be that of poet-director on the one hand (perhaps Apellis himself) and Eunikos, on the other, his performer and (?) love object.

Aviii: The Architekton of the Theatre in Syracuse. Sophron, *PCG* F 123 (Eust. *Comm. Hom. Od.* 3.68, 1.113 Stallbaum). Sophron was a Syracusan composer of mime, short dramatic sketches in prose (**A Introduction**). An approximate contemporary of Euripides, he was probably most active in the last quarter of the 5th c. (Hordern 2004, 2–4). Eudaimon is a grammarian from Egypt of uncertain date. His knowledge of Sophron may derive ultimately from the major work on him by Apollodorus of Athens in the 2nd c. (Hordern 2004, 30–1). Eudaimon is quoted by Eustathius for providing examples of the unusual masculine nouns in -α, like the epic ἱππότα, the word in the *Odyssey* passage under comment. Text: based on Kassel and Austin.

> καὶ Συρακούσιον τὸ ὁ Μύριλλα, οὗ μεμνῆσθαι λέγει τὸν Σώφρονα, ἱστορῶν καὶ ὅτι τοῦ Συρακουσίου τούτου ⟨τὸ⟩ κύριον Δημόκοπος ἦν ἀρχιτέκτων. ἐπεὶ δὲ τελεσιουργήσας τὸ θέατρον μύρον τοῖς ἑαυτοῦ πολίταις διένειμε, Μύριλλα ἐπεκλήθη.

> ⟨τὸ⟩ Kaibel

And (Eudaimon of Pelousion compares) a Syracusan example – the name Myrilla, which he says Sophron mentions, reporting that this Syracusan's real name was Demokopos, an architekton. And he was called Myrilla because, after he finished work on the theatre, he distributed perfume (μύρον *myron*) to his fellow citizens.

This passage is our only evidence for a named individual associated with the practical con-struction of a Classical theatre, with the possible exception of Poykleitos II, said to have been the architekton who built the theatre of Epidaurus in the late fourth century (**Bviii 2**; although some follow Roux 1961 I, 185–7 in his argument that Pausanias' identification is in error, leaving the name of the architekton of the Epidauros theatre unknown). It purports to give the name of the architekton of the Syracusan theatre – a Syracusan himself named 'Demokopos' (probably better in its Doric form 'Damokopos'), nicknamed 'Myrilla'. Even while there are doubts about the historicity of these name(s) (below), there can be no doubt that this theatre architekton featured prominently in one of Sophron's mimes at some time in the last quarter of the fifth century (thus Fabricius 1903).

It is unclear how much of the information about Damokopos/Myrilla is being ascribed directly to the authority of Sophron. The grammatical subject of the participle 'report-ing' (ἱστορῶν) is Eudaimon of Pelousion, but the substance of the report will belong to Sophron. It is in any case unlikely that Eudaimon will have had a source independent of Sophron (whose work was probably in any case mediated by way of Apollodorus and his later tradition) for the information that follows, and his philological interests make a pro-pensity to fantasy improbable. This implies that the whole account goes back to Sophron in some form. Whether his mimes were performed in a theatre (as implied by Solin. 5.13 = Sophron *PCG* T 12: *hic* (Sicilia) *primum inventa comoedia: hic et cavillatio mimica in scaena stetit*) or not (Hordern 2004, 8), Sophron will have had an intimate acquaintance with the Syracusan theatre of his day, and it is no surprise that he included jocular comment on its architekton in one of his mimes.

Just what sort of activity is implied by the description of Damokopos as an architekton who worked on the Syracusan theatre? It is possible that the word ἀρχιτέκτων may here mean something close to the modern 'architect', as in the Pausanias passage mentioned above, where it is used of Polykleitos, praised for his skills in 'harmony and beauty' and described as 'the one who made this theatre and the circular building'. But in Sophron's day the usage of the term was somewhat different. In Classical contexts the word generally refers as much to a master builder, engineer or chief of works as an artistic designer (Hdt. 3.60, 4.87); or to a commissioner of public works whose skills are as much managerial and financial as artistic (Coulton 1977, 15–29). This is notably the case in Athens, where the architekton who appears ca. 350 was an elected official, and to that extent involved in the political sphere, and was responsible for the arrangement of all the contracts for civic building, including (but not only) in the Theatre of Dionysus (**I Bvi**). It is entirely likely the word is used here in some such sense, for if Damokopos was an architekton of this sort – not (just) an architectural designer and maker but involved in the political sphere (implied by his election to the office) and in the realm of high-value public contracts – this would more readily explain the fact that he was open to comic attack; and moreover that he had the power to give the people assembled in the theatre a gift upon its completion. Both as-pects are attested for the forerunner of the architekton in Athens, the *theatropoles*, who for instance had the power to grant free admission, and was evidently exposed to Aristophanic ridicule as a figure in the public eye (**V A**). The appearance of the Syracusan architekton would pre-date that of his Athenian homonym by at least half a century.

The (unusual) verb used of Damokopos' actions in relation to the theatre (τελεσιουργήσας) suggests more than just 'finish' but rather 'bring (a major project) to a final state of completion'. It is thus precious evidence for what must have been an epochal event in the history of the Syracusan theatre. Such an occasion would be a fitting moment for a gift of the sort described at the inauguration. It is difficult to determine the period in question, since it is hard to gauge how topical the reference to Damokopos in Sophron's mime might have been. If we can accept the possibility that the nickname Myrilla might have been genuinely applied, that it required explanation to a (presumably Syracusan) audience might suggest he was a figure from the past (Hordern 2004, 188), but it is more likely that the nickname was invented by Sophron himself and applied to a contemporary. Nor does the explanation of the nickname in itself necessarily undermine confidence. It is not out of line with the attested practice of benefactors making distributions of wine, food or other gifts to theatre audiences on momentous occasions (Wilson 2000, 275). But some doubts persist, not least the difficulty of explaining why the name might have been given such a recondite, pseudo-epic form. This has led some instead to suppose a reference in Sophron to the architekton's association with a prostitute named Myrilla (Stephanus vol. V, p. 1282 s.v. Μύριλλα); but that leaves unexplained what might have led Eudaimon or his sources to categorise a name that ostensibly looked like a regular feminine form as masculine.

While Eudaimon (Sophron) says that Demokopos was the architekton's 'real' name, this is unlikely to be true. 'Demokopos' is not otherwise attested as a personal name (this instance is accepted as genuine by *LGPN* IIIA s.v. 'Damokopos'), but it does appear as a noun in the sense of 'demagogue' (e.g. in Pollux' list of terms of political abuse: 4.37). Phrynichus the Atticist reports (*PS* p. 99, l. 14) that the verb πολιτοκοπεῖν (used at Sannyr. *PCG* F 7 and Diph. *PCG* F 132) is a later word than δημοκοπεῖν, implying that the latter was in use by the fifth century. He also says that the two are synonyms, meaning to apply pressure with smooth talk and to persuade the demos against its judgement. If Damokopos was in fact the architekton's real name it would certainly have lent itself in the world of mime to the etymology of the nickname Myrilla, for making an expensive and luxurious gift to an entire theatre audience might well be construed as the action of a demagogue, and the etymology would activate the sense latent in the name Damokopos. But it is much more likely that both names are fabrications by Sophron, suggesting that the construction of the Syracusan theatre was implicated in charges of demagoguery. Pöhlmann (2015, 153–4) has recently suggested that Damokopos was applied as an insulting nickname in the sense of 'demagogue', but his further claim that Myrilla was the architekton's real name cannot stand. While he notes that Myrilla is attested as a real name twice (Delos, 1st c.: *ID* 2619 b II, 21; Acarnania, 2nd/3rd c.: *IG* IX 1² (2) 530), in both cases it is the name of a woman, a problem Pöhlmann leaves unresolved.

Plutarch (*Mor.* 802d) draws an illuminating distinction between *demagogos* and *demokopos*: the former attempts to persuade the people by means of words alone; the latter uses bribery – free distributions of food and drink, and festival spectacles. What has probably happened is that the person in question's name was sufficiently close to Damokopos – something like Damokrates, Damoxenos or Damophilos – to permit Sophron, in good comic tradition, to morph it into an insulting variant to make his point. This elected official – 'Mr Bludgeoner of the People' – exploited his elected office to buy the people's favour with bread and circuses – or rather, perfume and performances.

Voza (2007, 79) is inclined to place Damokopos under Dionysius I. Polacco and Anti (1981, 177–8), followed most recently by Pöhlmann (2015), thought that 'il teatro di Damocopo' was the one in which Aeschylus directed his works. They are all, surely, wrong: the latter decades of the fifth century is the period when the political and cultural climate of Syracuse produced demagogues and talk of them (Robinson 2011, 67–89), and more particularly a date soon after 412, the year of the reforms of Diokles – a man described as 'the most powerful of the demagogues' (D.S. 13.34.6) – that enhanced the democratic character of the constitution. So 'Mr Bludgeoner of the People', *aka* 'Give them Perfume', was an official responsible for the completion of a major phase of the Syracusan theatre late in the fifth century, not long after the Athenians had been seen off from the shores of Syracuse. We might even speculate that the defeat of the Athenians had triggered an enthusiastic burst of investment in theatrical infrastructure, to add cultural insult to massive military injury.

Aix: Aeschylus at Gela (458–456) and Elsewhere in Sicily

1. ***Parian Marble* 59 (*IG* XII 5, 444, ll. 74–5; *FGrH* 239 A 59 = *TrGF* T 3).** Date of inscription: 264/3 or soon after. Target date: 456/5 (by Athenian Archon date). The author of the Parian Marble, who has a powerful interest in literary and cultural history, may draw ultimately on the Hellenistic and earlier sources mentioned under **2**. Text: Radt.

   > ἀφ' οὗ Αἰσχύλος ὁ ποιητὴς, βιώσας ἔτη ⊓ΔΓΙΙΙΙ, ἐτελεύτησεν ἐγ [Γέ|λ]αι τῆς Σικελίας, ἔτη ΗⓅΔΔΔΔΙΙΙ, ἄρχοντος Ἀθήνησι Καλλέου τοῦ προτέρου.

   > From the time Aeschlyus the poet, 69 years old, died at [Gel]a in Sicily, 193 years; when Kalleas the elder was Archon at Athens (456/5).

2. ***Life of Aeschylus* 10–11 (= *TrGF* T 1, ll. 35–47; cf. T 162).** The *Life*, a composition probably of the Imperial period (Kimmel-Clauzet 2013, 149, 414) found in the oldest manuscripts of Aeschylus' works, includes much that is fiction spun from the plays of Aeschylus himself and the comedies in which he appeared, notably Aristophanes' *Frogs* (Lefkowitz 1981, 71–3). But it also draws on authors who had access to sources outside this tradition. These include: Ion of Chios (mid fifth century), who had met Aeschylus and mentioned him in his *Visits* (*FGrH* 392 F 7, 22; *TrGF* III, TQ); possibly the late fifth-century Glaucus of Rhegium in South Italy, the first-attested scholar who worked on Aeschylus (on the assumption that the Glaukos mentioned in Arg. A. *Pers.* = *TrGF* T 86 as the author of *The Myths of Aeschylus* is the Rhegine); the fourth-century Peripatetics Heraclides of Pontus, who wrote a work *On the Three Tragedians*; Chamaeleon of Pontus, who wrote a work *On Aeschylus* (frr. 42–44, cf. 61–64C Martano); and Dicaearchus of Messana (explicitly at *Life* 15), who had an interest in dramatic productions (frr. 99–104 F-S) and whose Sicilian origins are noteworthy.

The other ancient authors who cite the epigram in whole or part (notably Plutarch, Athenaeus and Pausanias: *FGE* 131–2) do so with variations that are little more than scribal, increasing the likelihood that the tradition is anchored in reality. Text: Radt.

κατὶ σφόδρα τῶι τε τυράννωι Ἱέρωνι καὶ τοῖς Γελώιοις τιμηθεὶς ἐπιζήσας τρίτον ἔτος γηραιὸς ἐτελεύτα τοῦτον τὸν τρόπον. ἀετὸς γὰρ χελώνην ἁρπάσας, ὡς ἐγκρατὴς γενέσθαι τῆς ἄγρας οὐκ ἴσχυεν, ἀφίησι κατὰ πετρῶν αὐτὴν συνθλάσων τὸ δέρμα, ἡ δὲ ἐνεχθεῖσα κατὰ τοῦ ποιητοῦ φονεύει αὐτόν. χρηστηριασθεὶς δὲ ἦν, ʻοὐράνιόν σε βέλος κατακτενεῖ.ʼ [11] ἀποθανόντα δὲ Γελῶιοι πολυτελῶς ἐν τοῖς δημοσίοις μνήμασι θάψαντες ἐτίμησαν μεγαλοπρεπῶς, ἐπιγράψαντες οὕτω·

> Αἰσχύλον Εὐφορίωνος Ἀθηναῖον τόδε κεύθει
> μνῆμα καταφθίμενον πυροφόροιο Γέλας·
> ἀλκὴν δʼ εὐδόκιμον Μαραθώνιον ἄλσος ἂν εἴποι
> καὶ βαθυχαιτήεις Μῆδος ἐπιστάμενος.

εἰς τὸ μνῆμα δὲ φοιτῶντες ὅσοις ἐν τραγωιδίαις ἦν ὁ βίος ἐνήγιζόν τε καὶ τὰ δράματα ὑπεκρίνοντο.

11 Γέλας Plu. *Mor.* 604f reporting ll. 1–2   σέλας BXc   πέλας others

He was accorded great honour by both the tyrant Hieron and the Geloans, and continued to live there for two more years and died an old man in the following way. An eagle snatched up a tortoise, but it did not have the strength to stay in charge of its prey, so let it fall over rocks with the intention of crushing its shell but, carried over the poet's head, it killed him. He had received a prophecy: 'A missile from the heavens will slay you'. [11] When he died the Geloans honoured him magnificently with costly burial in their public memorials, which they inscribed as follows: 'This memorial covers Aeschylus, son of Euphorion, the Athenian, who perished in wheat-bearing Gela. Of his famous prowess the plain of Marathon could tell, and the thick-haired Mede – who knows it all too well.' Those who made their livelihood in tragedy made regular trips to his memorial, where they made offerings and staged (his) dramas.

3. **Scholion (M) to Aeschylus, *Eumenides* 626 (= Epich. *PCG* F 221).** Text: Kassel and Austin.

τιμαλφούμενον· συνεχὲς τὸ ὄνομα παρ' Αἰσχύλωι· διὸ σκώπτει αὐτὸν Ἐπίχαρμος.

'Honoured': the word occurs frequently in Aeschylus. Epicharmus mocks him for it.

4. **Scholion to Aristophanes, *Peace* 73b.** The lemma goes on to quote passages from Sophocles' *Daedalus* (*TrGF* F 162) and Plato the comedian's *Festivals* (*PCG* F 36). Text: Holwerda.

αἰτναῖον κάνθαρον· μεγάλοι λέγονται εἶναι κατὰ τὴν Αἴτνην κάνθαροι. μαρτυροῦσι δὲ οἱ ἐπιχώριοι. Ἐπίχαρμος ἐν Ἡρακλεῖ τῷ ἐπὶ τὸν ζωστῆρα (F 65)

> <ὁ> Πυγμαρίων λοχαγὸς ἐκ τῶν κανθάρων
> τῶν μειζόνων, οὕς φαντι τὴν Αἴτναν ἔχειν.

τρόπον δέ τινα καὶ Αἰσχύλος ἐπιχώριος· λέγει δὲ ἐν Σισύφῳ πετροκυλιστῇ (F 233)

> Αἰτναῖός ἐστι κάνθαρος βίᾳ πονῶν.

'Aetnaean dung beetle': the dung beetles on mount Aetna are said to be big. The locals bear witness to this. Epicharmus in *Heracles after the Belt* (F 65): '<The> captain of the Pygmies is one of the larger dung beetles which, they say, inhabit mount Aetna.' Aeschylus too is a local, after a fashion. And he says in *Sisyphus the Stone-roller* (F 233): 'He is an Aetnaean dung beetle, toiling forcefully.'

5. Athenaeus, *Sophists at Dinner* 9.402b–c. Athenaeus wrote ca. 200 AD. The use of the word *aschedoros* by Aeschylus is also reported by Eustathius in his commentary on *Od.* 19.439, where it is noted as 'Italiote', viz. of Greeks in the Italian peninsula. Text: Olson.

> οὐκ ἀγνοῶ δ' ὅτι οἱ περὶ τὴν Σικελίαν κατοικοῦντες ἀσχέδωρον καλοῦσι τὸν σύαγρον. Αἰσχύλος γοῦν ἐν Φορκίσι παρεικάζων τὸν Περσέα τῷ ἀγρίῳ τούτῳ συί φησιν (*TrGF* F 261)
>
> > ἔδυ δ' ἐς ἄντρον ἀσχέδωρος ὥς.
>
> ... ὅτι δὲ Αἰσχύλος διατρίψας ἐν Σικελίᾳ πολλαῖς κέχρηται φωναῖς Σικελικαῖς οὐδὲν θαυμαστόν.

I am well aware that those who live in Sicily refer to the wild boar as an *aschedoros*. For instance Aeschylus, comparing Perseus to this wild boar in *The Phorkides*, says (*TrGF* F 261) 'he plunged into the cave like a wild boar' … That Aeschylus, who spent time in Sicily, uses many Sicilian phrases is no surprise.

6. Macrobius, *Saturnalia* 5.19.17. Macrobius wrote the *Saturnalia* around the middle of the 5th c. AD. It is a fictitious learned discussion of Roman culture and antiquarian lore held during the festival of Saturn after which it is named. The information in this passage is thought to derive from Macrobius' learned contemporary Serenus Sammonicus (Fraenkel 1954, 61–2; Champlin 1981, 193) and beyond that, from an Alexandrian source, perhaps Didymus. An ultimate source might be the late fifth-century Glaucus of Rhegium in South Italy (see on **2**). Text: Kaster.

> *nam primum ut Symaethus fluvius, cuius in his versibus meminit, in Sicilia est, ita et di Palici in Sicilia coluntur; quos primus omnium Aeschylus tragicus, vir utique Siculus, in litteras dedit, interpretationem quoque nominis eorum, quam Graeci* ἐτυμολογίαν *vocant, expressit versibus suis.*

First of all, just as the river Symaethus mentioned in these verses [Verg. *Aen.* 9.581–5] is in Sicily, so too the gods Palici are worshipped in Sicily: they were first given a literary treatment by the tragedian Aeschylus (**VI A**) – a man thoroughly Sicilian – and moreover in his verses he also provides an explanation of their name, what the Greeks call an 'etymology'.

Aeschylus in Gela

2 somewhat elliptically compresses Aeschylus' association with Hieron I of Syracuse in the 470s (**VI A**) with a period spent at Gela on the south coast of Sicily at the end of his life, from 458 – doubtless after the Athenian production of the *Oresteia* in the spring – to 456/5. The latter is given by **1** as the year of his death 'at [Gel]a in Sicily' (the restoration is certain), and is corroborated by other evidence (*TrGF* T B). A similar confusion appears in Plutarch (*Cim.* 8.9; **I Av**) where defeat by Sophocles at the Athenian Dionysia of 468 is said to have precipitated Aeschylus' departure to Sicily soon after 'where he died and was buried near Gela' ὅπου καὶ τελευτήσας περὶ Γέλαν τέθαπται. Despite the uncertainty as to the context of the trip to Gela, and despite the colourful story of the manner of his death there by falling tortoise (on the roots of which in fable and myth see Kimmel-Clauzet 2013, 73–80 and Poli Palladini 2013, 267–84, who intriguingly notes a characteristic Geloan usage of tortoise-shaped vessels as ossuaries and in cult contexts), there is no reason to doubt the fact of Aeschylus' sojourn and death in the city. Indeed if it were a fiction, it is difficult to imagine its motivation and harder still to see how such a fabrication might have been sustained and propagated. There is no evidence that any other city, Athens included, made a claim to be the site of the poet's death and burial (Val. Max. 9.12 ext. 2 puts it in 'a city in Sicily').

The motivations for Aeschylus' departure, aged 66, from Athens at the height of his fame have been matter for speculation since antiquity (see now Smith 2018, 13–15). The *Life* advances a number of more or less impossible, implausible and contradictory motivations for his departure(s) from Athens, to which Suda (αι 357) adds the no less implausible exile following collapse of the *ikria*. Herington (1967) refocused attention away from the fanciful push factors of the ancient embroiderers to the pull of the intellectual, cultural and political ferment of Sicily and of Gela in particular. Among the ancient motives proffered, Herington (1967, 77) rightly pointed to the outrider given for Aeschylus and a number of other voluntary exiles by Plutarch's *On Exile* (*Mor.* 604e–605b) as the most plausible, namely the hunt for greater glory and honours (δόξαν οὗτοι καὶ τιμὰς ἐθήρευον 'these men went in quest of fame and honours') – a suggestion taken further by Poli Palladini (2013, 87), who thinks that the prospect of great honours in life and even of posthumous cult was 'the major drive'.

The Geloans had a tradition of competitive choral performance before they invited Aeschylus to stay among them (below), and the invitation certainly reflects a powerful appetite for tragedy. If Aeschylus introduced tragic drama to the city, his presence is likely to have been a magnet and stimulus for further practitioners. A decision on the part of the civic authorities in Gela to invite and honour a poet who had ties to the fallen Deinomenid regime (**VI A**) cannot have been neutral, and may reflect an attempt to reclaim the genre of tragedy and this practitioner of it for political ends (half a century later Dionysius I seems to have attempted to wrest the Aeschylean legacy back for Syracuse: **VI E**).

By 458 Gela was experiencing a period of renewal and prosperity after the fall of the tyrants, and after an even longer period under the shadow of Syracuse. Along with other Greek cities of Sicily, it had liberated itself from tyrannical rule and restored those citizens who had been ejected under the tyrants (Arist. *Pol.* 1312b9–16; D.S. 11.76.4–6). Among this returning elite some will have been keen to renew the cultural glory of their city (Poli Palladini 2013, 85). It also joined in the 'common resolution' to drive out foreign constitutions and reapportion land back to all citizens. In 461 it refounded Camarina (destroyed by its own founder, Syracuse, in 552). It is noteworthy in this context that the physical layout of the new Camarina and its civic subdivisions into phratries drew heavily on musical symbolism (Cordano 1994). The picture overall has been described as one of 'vigorous democratization' (Robinson 2011, 100). The exact nature of the constitution at this date is unknown, and while unlikely to be democratic on precisely the Athenian model, it was certainly closer to it than it ever had been (D.S. 11.53.5, 11.68.5; Robinson 2011, 100–2). De Angelis (2016, 212) would qualify the more 'democratic' interpretation and characterises the period thus: 'on balance, the picture suggests the creation of new social and economic elements, but on top of an old elite that continued to remain firmly in place'. Despite the darkness of the historical and material record, it is highly likely that Gela had a strong commercial partnership with Athens in this period, not least given the high prevalence of imported Attic ceramic (Panvini and Giudice 2003).

The evidence of all other international invitations to poets, tragic and other, shows that this will have been driven by some broadly political purpose. What distinguishes this case from others is that it came from the Geloans as a civic entity (**2** τοῖς Γελῴοις): a demos rather than a dynast was Aeschylus' host. The Geloans buried Aeschylus at considerable public expense, perhaps in part of their necropolis dedicated to war dead and other civic benefactors (with ἐν τοῖς δημοσίοις μνήμασι θάψαντες, cf. e.g. D. 18.208: ἐν τοῖς δημοσίοις μνήμασιν; Kimmel-Clauzet 2013, 148–50; Poli Palladini 2013, 290–6, with speculation on its location). Kimmel-Clauzet (2013, 149) draws attention to the corroborating implication of the epitaph of a famous Geloan doctor named Pausanias (*AP* 7.508) that it was the city's established practice in the later fifth century to accord public burials to its benefactors. Aeschylus was doubtless given these lavish honours because of his prominence in the life of the city, a prominence predicated upon his status as a major Panhellenic poet in their midst and to some extent as a cultural figurehead of the most energetic Greek democratic city, one that had both seen off its own tyrants and taken a lead role in repelling the tyranny of Persia.

Several ancient authors believed the epitaph in **2** was composed by Aeschylus himself, or under his direction (Ath. 14.627c–d; Plu. *Mor.* 604d–f; Paus. 1.14.5; *TrGF* T 162 with Kimmel-Clauzet 2013, 169–70 on the variance in these citations). Wilamowitz thought it fifth century in date and by an Athenian, but not Aeschylus. His claim (1914, 11) that an epitaph placed on a monument in Gela would not, as here, name the city where the deceased was buried was answered by Pohlenz (1954 II, 17), who compared an epitaph on a public burial monument in the Ceramicus (*IG* I³ 1154) in which 'the Athenians' are said to bury the proxenos Pythagoras of Salymbria. The practice reflects the fact that a city was burying a non-native resident and was additionally attractive in this particular context in the way it drew attention to the city in which Aeschylus had produced the great majority of his work and that was the metropolis of tragedy itself (Bosher 2013, 95). Page (*FGE* 131–2) declared the epitaph a Hellenistic fabrication, but its authenticity has been stoutly defended by Sommerstein (1996b), who shows that the linguistic features claimed to be Hellenistic are in fact well attested in the Classical period and in particular that the unusual use of ἄλσος (l. 3) in the sense of 'level expanse' rather than 'sacred grove' is confined to Aeschylus and his contemporaries, making it highly probable that it was written by him or a contemporary (or someone with an astonishingly nuanced appreciation of Aeschylean usage). Aeschylus himself or a member of his family (possibly his son Euaion? – below) are perhaps the most likely candidates, but a possible implication of **2** is that the epigram was composed, rather than simply being inscribed, by 'the Geloans'. One of the single most telling indications of its status as an authentic epigram (whether or not by Aeschylus) is its striking omission of any reference to Aeschylus' poetic art, scarcely imaginable if it had been composed much later than the date of the poet's actual death. Scodel (2003, 132) nicely adds that the omission involves a deliberate and impressive reticence.

The silence of this monument on Aeschylus' art and the attention it focuses on his military prowess against the Mede are entirely intelligible in context. If it was composed by Aeschylus himself, it is consistent with the family's reputation for their martial contribution in the Persian Wars. Herodotus (6.114) writes that Aeschylus' brother Cynegirus lost an arm and died while attempting to seize a Persian ship by the stern at Marathon; and Ion (*FGrH* 392 F 7) reported that Aeschylus also fought at the battle of Salamis. The epigram is also consistent with a very recent development in Athenian public iconography, for the poet was depicted, perhaps even named, along with his brother in the famous painting of the battle in the Stoa Poikile of ca. 460 (Paus. 1.21.2; De Angelis 1996).

Perhaps on balance the most likely scenario is that the epigram was composed by Aeschylus in close collaboration with the Geloan authorities. In that case, the remarkable emphasis on his contribution in the fight at Marathon may reflect a considered reinterpretation of the poet whose *Persians* had been reperformed as a centrepiece of Deinomenid propaganda in the 470s, propaganda that had urged an image of Hieron as a champion of Greek freedom against the barbarians in the west to mirror that of the Greeks fighting at Marathon and Salamis. In a democratic city that had more recently ejected the tyranny of Hieron himself and his family, the poet who had bolstered their regime with his drama of Salamis was better memorialised as a combatant in the earlier battle, rather than as the creator of representations open to reuse and even misapplication. Another benefit of stressing Aeschylus' participation at Marathon was that it made of him a warrior-poet. As such he had the twin attributes of the only other poet prior to Aeschylus who it can be said with some confidence was a recipient of hero cult, Archilochus. The emphasis on Aeschylus' martial prowess may in fact have been a necessary consequence of the decision to accord him heroic honours. In later ages poets could receive cult without this emphasis. The fact that it is present for Aeschylus is another indication of the Geloan cult's historicity.

The language of the final sentence makes it clear that heroic cult, based at the resting place of the mortal, is indeed meant. The verb ἐναγίζω makes this virtually certain, for it is used of offerings made to the dead by non-family members, particularly in heroic cult (Ekroth 2002, 74–128). Taken at face value, it might appear that it was not the city of Gela as such that offered the cult, but the international acting community – 'those who made their livelihood in tragedy'. But while the civic funeral honours and the subsequent cult appear to be distinguished to some extent, it is virtually certain that they were conceived together. At the very least such cult honours could only have been offered with the approval of the city. The Western Greek world was the epicentre of heroisation of the recently dead, notably athletes but also city founders, not least Aeschylus' powerful old associate Hieron of Syracuse (and Gela).

It is probable that one intention on the part of the Geloans in granting Aeschylus lavish burial and heroic honours was to make of his tomb and their city a centre for the (re)performance of Aeschylean tragedy, the religious claim on the poet underpinned by an economic aim: to make Gela a new player in the regional and international contest of tragic theatre (an ambition cut short by history, with its sack in 405 by Carthage). This is the most likely interpretation of the phrase τὰ δράματα ὑπεκρίνοντο 'they staged *his* dramas' (Clay 2004, 127; Wilson 2007c, 357). **2** suggests but need not require that these performances took place at the tomb. They are akin to the musical or athletic contests associated with festivals that honour heroised or divinised mortals and are more likely to have formed part of a formal 'Aeschylia' than to have been spontaneous recitations by visiting pilgrims (Kimmel-Clauzet 2013, 242).

Despite the enthusiastic efforts of local antiquarians, no theatre site has ever been securely identified in Gela, but this is hardly surprising given the lack of any systematic study of the ancient city (and the destruction of 405) and the likelihood that a theatre of ca. 450 will have been of largely impermanent construction (Todisco 2002, 175, 222 and Poli Palladini 2013, 88–9 on the efforts of nineteenth-century antiquarians; *IACP* 194 is more optimistic: 'The stay of Aeschylos at Gela surely implies that the city had a theatre in C5m.'). In 406, immediately prior to his coup in Syracuse, Dionysius I resolved a stasis initiated by the wealthiest citizens in Gela. He did so 'at an assembly' (D.S. 13.93.2), and was in return honoured by decree as the liberator of the demos. Although Diodorus does not identify the space of that assembly as the theatre of Gela, it is more than likely that at Gela, as at Syracuse and elsewhere in Sicily, the same space served both functions.

It is possible, as Poli Palladini (2013, 308) suggests, that the Athenian decree enabling (re)performance of Aeschylean dramas (**I Avi**) should be seen as evidence of an assertion of proprietorial feelings and a response on the part of Athens to the Geloan cult of their poet (so far as we know Athens never granted any of its poets hero cult). This entirely new and exceptional honour effectively treated Aeschylus as though he were still alive, and to that extent could be viewed as an act of one-upmanship on the Geloan heroic honours. The *Life* (12) refers to the decree immediately following the reference to the honours in Gela. Whether or not the juxtaposition is significant, Geloan cult and Athenian decree are both concerned with the immediate afterlife of Aeschylus, and with the ongoing (re)-performance of his works in the distant locales of the poet's two homes, Athens and Sicily.

In **Avii** we glimpse the kind of infrastructure that was available in Gela to support performances in the lifetime of Aeschylus himself or soon after his death. We find a choral contest, or possibly contests, of some scale and complexity, with (probably liturgical) choragoi operating in an intensely competitive environment. It is even possible that such infrastructure was used to support theatrical contests in the city during Aeschylus' lifetime, or that it was applied to the cult offered to the heroised tragic poet by visiting actors. In this connection it is worth noting the strong emphasis on contestants arriving from outside (**Avii** on ll. 9–11; Wilson 2007c, 356–8).

The evidence of vase iconography points to Gela as a Sicilian centre with a special attachment to theatre, with some hints of a specifically Aeschylean emphasis. It is one of the first Greek cities in Sicily to import Archaic Corinthian aryballoi and alabastra (ca. 600) with 'padded dancers' (Todisco 2002, 47) and the city's interest in dramatic subjects on ceramic is well represented in the record (Catucci 2003, 7, 28). The preponderance in Western Greece generally of themes from tragic myth plausibly associated with Aeschylean drama over those similarly associated with Sophocles or Euripides on imported Attic and local western ceramic has been noted (Kossatz-Deissmann 1978; Taplin 2007, 48–87; Poli Palladini 2013, 302–8; Nervegna 2014, 172–6).

Somewhat sharper focus is given by the fact that three of some ten vases that evidently refer to Euaion – the name of one of the two sons of Aeschylus who followed him into the tragic profession – have findspots in Sicily, one of them certainly, the other reportedly, in Gela itself (Krumeich 2002; Poli Palladini 2013, 89–92). Euaion is attested as a son of Aeschylus only by Suda α 357 and the evidence of these vases (Euaion *TrGF* 13), but the name is not common (some seventeen attested in all Greece by *LGPN*, eight of which from Attica) and there are no good grounds to doubt these vases as evidence of his existence. The vases carry the acclamatory inscription ΕΥΑΙΟΝ ΚΑΛΟΣ, in six cases with the addition of ΑΙΣΧΥΛΟ, 'Euaion (son of Aeschylus) is beautiful!' (Shapiro 1987, 108–9), placed in close proximity to a figure more or less explicitly involved in a mythical scene that may relate in some way to a tragedy. Some examples are more readily linked to a tragic drama, whether identifiable or not, than others; for instance a relatively strong case is Argiope, mother of the eponymous hero of Sophocles' *Thamyris*, on a red-figured hydria from Vulci (*ARV*² 1020 no. 92). These inscriptions evidently serve to label a particular figure in the scene, suggesting that Euaion had acted in that role in some production and was lauded for it on a vase. In some cases the figure so labelled is strikingly generic and far from being emphatically theatrical.

This is true of the evidence from Gela. The example with a secure provenance was found in the necropolis on Capo Soprano (Siracusa Mus. Arch. Reg. 21146). It is a white-ground lekythos of Attic manufacture, dated to around 460–430 (Griffo 1987, 103) or 440–430 (Catucci 2003, 50), on which a woman wearing a long chiton and mantle moves to the left, her head turned backwards, a phiale in her left hand, an oinochoe in her right. The inscription ΕΥΑΙΟΝ ΚΑΛΟΣ is immediately to her right, below a suspended piece of fabric. There are no markers of theatricality, and it would be stretching plausibility – though perhaps not to breaking point – to suggest that the image refers to Euaion in some female role. More likely perhaps, though still highly speculative, is that the lekythos itself was used in connection with the offerings made to Euaion's father in Gela. The second vase that was (reportedly) found in Gela is another white-ground lekythos of ca. 460–450 and is especially striking for its addition of the patronymic ΑΙΣΧΥΛΟ 'son of Aeschylus' on a third line, written in stoichedon style next to a youth dressed in a chlamys and petasos who moves to the right, holding a drawn sword (Getty Museum Malibu CA83.AE.41, formerly in Palermo and said to be from Gela).

At a minimum these two vases indicate a fascination for the celebrity actor-poet in Gela ca. 450 (**Gi 1** is a late fifth-century *kalos* inscription from a theatre in Cyrene that may refer to an actor). It would come as no surprise if Aeschylus' younger son played a significant role in the theatrical pilgrimage cult of his father in the city, perhaps living in the city for an extended period. Involvement in this cult may have been an important part of the family's wider control of the poet's legacy. Euaion's rather older brother Euphorion competed in Athens, winning in 431 against Sophocles and Euripides (Arg. E. *Med.* = *TrGF* I DID C 12), and is said to have won four victories with works of his father left unproduced at his death (Suda ε 3800 = *TrGF* 12 T 1). Unlike his elder brother, Euaion has left no trace of a professional life in Athens.

A variety of evidence (**A Introduction**) suggests that, by around the middle of the fifth century, the powerful city of Acragas further to the west on the south coast of Sicily, and itself founded (in part or whole) by Gela, had its own theatrical culture. This could provide some context for another, well-known 'Euaion vase' found in that city. A white-ground calyx krater, dated ca. 450–440 (Agrigento Mus. Arch. Reg. AG 7, Phiale Painter), features two figures only, both with their mythic names inscribed: Perseus, wearing winged cap and boots, has his left foot set upon a rock, his chin supported by his left hand, as he gazes at the figure of Andromeda, who is tied to three posts. To the right and just above the head of Perseus is the further inscription ΕΥΑΙΩΝ | ΚΑΛΟΣ | ΑΙΣΧΥΛΟ. This image is widely seen as drawing inspiration from a tragedy, usually identified as Sophocles' *Andromeda* (Webster 1967, 147; Poli Palladini 2013, 89–90). It may also be evidence for the activity of Aeschylus' son in Acragas.

Aeschylus the Sicilian

3 shows that Epicharmus was intimately acquainted with Aeschylean language and parodied it in his own works. But it also implies a Sicilian public sufficiently familiar with Aeschylus to make such fine-grained allusion effective. The word τιμαλφέω is not used in the *Persians* and so Epicharmus' and his audience's acquaintance cannot derive from the performance of that play in Sicily (whether it appeared in the *Aitnaiai* we simply cannot say). It is however used five times in the *Oresteia*, a concentration which might suggest that Aeschylus produced the trilogy in Sicily after 458. Epicharmus is said to have lived a long time, perhaps dying as late as ca. 440 (**Aiii**; Kerkhof 2001, 59). Both Syracuse and Gela are plausible sites for such a reperformance at this date. On the other hand, συνεχές 'frequently' leaves open the possibility that Aeschylus used the word in non-extant works and that some of these were well known to Sicilian audiences. The fact that Epicharmus composed plays with the same or very similar titles to those of Aeschylus – among them, notably, a *Persians* (others include *Promatheus, Bacchae, Philoctetas, Thearoi*) – has been taken as further evidence of parody on his part (Kerkhof 2001, 136; Willi 2008, 166–7) but it is worth noting that Epicharmus' career was very well advanced by the time Aeschylus came to Hieron's court. Smith (2018, 38–9) suggests other examples of influence between the two poets, noting that in each case it is impossible to determine which text came first and thus who might be imitating or mocking whom.

The suggestion that Aeschylus' own works were influenced by his time spent in Sicily has been challenged (Griffith 1978, 106–9), but readers in antiquity with far greater access to his plays and to information about them believed in Aeschylus' Sicilianisms, not to mention his 'Sicilianness'. **4–6** reflect a strong and persistent tradition that Aeschylus could in some sense be called 'Sicilian'. **4** qualified the claim that he was a native Sicilian by adding τρόπον δέ τινα 'after a fashion'. **6** draws ultimately on sources with learned knowledge of Aeschylus' *Aitnaiai*, a play we know received scholarly treatment that survived at least into the second century AD (**VI A**). The expression it uses of Aeschylus – *vir utique Siculus* 'a man thoroughly Sicilian' – has been thought to press the claim too far, leading Herington (1967, 79) to deduce textual corruption and suggest that the correct reading may be *vir quasi Siculus* 'just like a Sicilian man'. But the adverb can be used in cases where the existence of evidence or circumstances indicating the contrary exists (*OLD* s.v. 3), which is precisely the situation here.

Sicilianisms – of language (**5**) and subject (**4**, **6**) – might suggest anticipated performance in Sicily. And the claim of **5** that such linguistic usage was frequent suggests that the influence derived from an extended sojourn other than that of the last two years of his life (Herington 1967, 80). Poli Palladini (2013, 93–161, 211–66) makes an energetic and at times highly ingenious case for the intended Sicilian and specifically Geloan performance of several works, most convincingly perhaps for the *Daughters of the Sun* (2013, 113–61, 141–2). This tragedy's attested interest in the geography of the far west and the importance of its myth to Rhodian identity make it a suitable work for production in Gela (a foundation of Rhodians and Cretans) after the fall of the tyrants, when Rhodian interests in the west may have revived, and Gela may have found it expedient to look back to its older associations. Poli Palladini (2013, 264–6) also advances some arguments in favour of a performance of *Sisyphus the Stone-roller* (**4**) at Gela as part of a tetralogy about Odysseus, noting the appearance in it of a word – ἄμβωνες 'ridgeways' (F 231) – said by ancient grammarians to have been specifically Rhodian. Marconi (2005) elegantly develops an idea of Snell that the surviving passage of Aeschylus' satyr play *The Sacred Delegation* (*Theoroi*), in which the satyr chorus marvel at likenesses of themselves which they intend to attach to the temple of Poseidon, may (in addition to being an allusion to the dedication of dramatic masks after performance: **V F**) refer to the (almost exclusively) Sicilian practice of attaching silen antefixes to temples. If the Epicharmean comedy Θεαροί (*Thearoi*) was a parodic response to Aeschylus, it follows as likely that the satyr play was performed in the West (Smith 2018, 39–40 on possible forms of interaction between these works).

A fourth-century AD mosaic image found in a Roman villa near Helorus (roughly halfway between Syracuse and Gela) appears to depict the key scene in Aeschylus' *Phrygians* or *The Ransom of Hector* – and one that distinguishes it from its epic precursor (*TrGF* F 365) – the literal weighing of Hector's corpse on a set of scales against gold (Pelagatti and Voza 1976, 573; Poli Palladini 2013, 305–8). This might possibly reflect a tradition of iconographic copying of images that derive from a much older iconography, closer to the time of Aeschylus, or even some tradition of local performance.

Ax: Carcinus and Sicily

1. Suda s.v. Καρκίνος ('Carcinus', κ 394). Compiled ca. 1000 AD. The end of the passage quoted appears to be a corrupted citation of Athenaeus (see app. crit.). The lemma continues with quotations and glosses about the word καρκίνος 'crab' in various literal and metaphorical senses, none of which appears to have anything to do with a poet of the name. Text: Adler.

> Καρκίνος, Ἀκραγαντῖνος, τραγικός. καὶ Καρκίνος, Θεοδέκτου ἢ Ξενοκλέους, Ἀθηναῖος, τραγικός. δράματα ἐδίδαξεν ρξ΄, ἐνίκησε δὲ α΄. ἤκμαζε κατὰ τὴν ρ΄ ὀλυμπιάδα, πρὸ τῆς Φιλίππου βασιλείας τοῦ Μακεδόνος. τῶν δραμάτων αὐτοῦ ἐστιν Ἀχιλλεύς, Σεμέλη, † ἢ ἀρχή †, ὡς Ἀθήναιός φησιν ἐν Δειπνοσοφισταῖς.

> α΄ <ι>α΄ Köhler, from *IG* II² 2325A M-O, l. 43   † ἢ ἀρχή †, ὡς Ἀθήναιός φησιν ἐν Δειπνοσοφισταῖς   Καρκίνος δ' ὁ τραγικὸς ἐν Σεμέλη, ἧς ἀρχή 'Ὦ νύκτες,' φησίν (F 2) Ath. 13.559f

> 'Carcinus': from Acragas, a tragedian. And Carcinus, son of Theodectes or Xenocles, Athenian, a tragedian. He produced 160 plays and had 1 victory (or, reading Köhler's emendation, '11 victories'). He was in his prime during the 100th Olympiad (380/79 – 377/6), before the kingship of Philip of Macedon. Among his plays are *Achilles*, *Semele* † or beginning †, as Athenaeus says in *Sophists at Dinner*.

2. Diogenes Laertius, *Lives of the Philosophers* 2.63. Writing in the 3rd c. AD, Diogenes is here discussing the philosopher and follower of Socrates, Aeschines of the Attic deme Sphettos. Very little is known about Polykritos of Mende, but Jacoby (*FGrH* 559) placed his career ca. 370–340, making him a contemporary of Carcinus (II). In addition to the *On Dionysius* he is credited with a *Sikelika* (*History of Sicily*). The reference to Dion's return – which took place in 357/6 – indicates that the Dionysius in question is Dionysius II of Syracuse. The correction by Meineke (1839, 507) of κωμῳδοποιόν 'comic poet' to τραγῳδοποιόν 'tragic poet' is widely accepted (Olson 2001), but note Rothwell 1994. Text: Dorandi.

> φησὶ δὲ Πολύκριτος ὁ Μενδαῖος ἐν τῷ πρώτῳ τῶν Περὶ Διονύσιον ἄχρι τῆς ἐκπτώσεως συμβιῶναι αὐτὸν τῷ τυράννῳ καὶ ἕως τῆς Δίωνος εἰς Συρακούσας καθόδου, λέγων εἶναι σὺν αὐτῷ καὶ Καρκίνον τὸν τραγῳδιοποιόν.

> τραγῳδιοποιόν Meineke, Dorandi   κωμῳδοποιόν PF

> Polykritos of Mende, in the first book of his *On Dionysius* (*FGrH* 559 F 1), says that he [sc. Aeschines] lived with the tyrant until his [sc. Dionysius'] expulsion, and until the return of Dion to Syracuse, and that with him also was Carcinus the tragic poet.

3. Diodorus of Sicily, *Library of History* **5.5.1**. Composed ca. 50–30. Diodorus'
Bibliotheke or *Library* was a universal history from mythical times to 60. As a Sicilian
(from Agyrion: **Axv**) his treatment of Sicilian matters is extensive and draws heavily
on well-informed sources, notably Timaeus (ca. 350–260). Book 5 treats the history of
islands and begins with the mythic and cultic traditions of Sicily. Although he is not explicitly mentioned by name, Jacoby was confident that all of 5.1–23 was from Timaeus
(*FGrH* 566 F 164). The account of the abduction of Kore referred to is the tradition that
places her abduction in Sicily and makes the Sicilians the first recipients of the gift of
grain. Text: Fischer and Vogel.

> περὶ δὲ τῆς κατὰ τὴν Κόρην ἁρπαγῆς, ὅτι γέγονεν ὡς προειρήκαμεν, πολλοὶ
> τῶν ἀρχαίων συγγραφέων καὶ ποιητῶν μεμαρτυρήκασι. Καρκίνος μὲν γὰρ ὁ
> τῶν τραγῳδιῶν ποιητής, πλεονάκις ἐν ταῖς Συρακούσαις παρεπιδεδημηκὼς
> καὶ τὴν τῶν ἐγχωρίων τεθεαμένος σπουδὴν περὶ τὰς θυσίας καὶ πανηγύρεις
> τῆς τε Δήμητρος καὶ Κόρης, κατεχώρισεν ἐν τοῖς ποιήμασι τούσδε τοὺς
> στίχους (*TrGF* 70 F 5)·

>> λέγουσι Δήμητρός ποτ' ἄρρητον κόρην
>> Πλούτωνα κρυφίοις ἁρπάσαι βουλεύμασιν,
>> δῦναί τε γαίας εἰς μελαμφαεῖς μυχούς·
>> πόθῳ δὲ μητέρ' ἠφανισμένης κόρης
>> μαστῆρ' ἐπελθεῖν πᾶσαν ἐν κύκλῳ χθόνα.
>> καὶ γῆν μὲν Αἰτναίοισι Σικελίαν πάγοις
>> πυρὸς γέμουσαν ῥεύμασιν δυσεμβόλοις
>> πᾶσαν στενάξαι, πένθεσιν δὲ παρθένου
>> σίτων ἄμοιρον διοτρεφὲς φθίνειν γένος.
>> ὅθεν θεὰς τιμῶσιν εἰς τὰ νῦν ἔτι.

Concerning the abduction of Kore, many of the old historians and poets report
that it took place as I have described. Carcinus the poet of tragedies, for example, who had resided in Syracuse several times and observed the eagerness
which the inhabitants displayed in their sacrifices and festivals for Demeter
and Kore, recorded these lines in his poems (*TrGF* 70 F 5): 'They say once
Demeter's daughter, whom none may name, Pluto stole by secret schemes,
and she went into the earth's depths whose light is darkness. Longing for the
girl who disappeared her mother went in search to every land in turn. And the
Sicilian land by Aetna's crags was filled with fiery streams unapproachable
and groaned throughout its length, and in grief over the maiden the people,
nurtured by Zeus, were perishing with no share of grain. And so they honour
the goddesses even now.'

The family, whose earliest attested member is Xenotimos, father of the tragic poet Carcinus
(*TrGF* 21), is one of the most striking instances of a dynasty involved, over a number of
generations, in the business of tragic theatre (Sutton 1987; Stewart 2016; *APF* 283–5; **V
C**). Of the career and output of Carcinus I himself very little is known (even the victory at
the Dionysia in 446 supposed from *IG* II² 2318, l. 297 M-O is open to doubt, with Rothwell

1994, 241–2 suggesting Κα[λλίστρατος ἐδίδασκε] instead of Κα[ρκίνος ἐδίδασκε]). We know more of the sons who followed their father into the theatre under his direct tutelage. They appear to have received training in various aspects of the craft and perhaps began their careers on stage in the role of proficient and innovative tragic dancers, perhaps working principally as choreuts (maybe *koryphaioi*-cum-*chorodidaskaloi*) in dramas produced by their father (and the fact that they could do so is, incidentally, revealing of one manner in which members of a tragic chorus might be supplied to a choregos: **V E**). As much is clear from comedy of the latter years of the 420s: in Aristophanes' *Wasps*, Lenaea 422 (ll. 1498–1537: MacDowell 1971, 330 thinks the performance at the end of the play is to be viewed not as ridicule but a bravura display by the Carcinus family, in person, of their expertise in modern tragic dance; cf. Biles and Olson 2015, 506–14); *Peace*, Dionysia 421 (ll. 781–95) and Pherecrates' *Wild Men*, Lenaea 420 (*PCG* F 15).

The number and names of Carcinus' sons were matters of ancient dispute, but it is fairly clear that there were three rather than four (the fourth seems to be the product of a misunderstanding of Pherecrates *Wild Men PCG* F 15; Stewart 2016, 12–14) and that their names were: Xenocles, who went on to become a tragic poet like his father (Xenocles I, *TrGF* 33), probably already composing or at least contributing to tragedies himself by the late 420s (Stewart 2016, 11–15 on Ar. *Wasps* 1511); Xenotimos, doubtless the eldest, given that this was the name of Carcinus I's own father (*IG* I³ 874); and Xenarchos (on the other names proffered by ancient sources see *APF* 285). The fact that Xenotimos was engaged as a diplomatic courier of a letter to Athens from the Spartocid king of the Cimmerian Bosporus, Satyros I, suggests that he may have gone on to have a career as an actor about which we otherwise remain uninformed (**Fiii**).

Xenocles I in turn fathered Carcinus II, the tragedian mentioned in the second sentence of **1**, who was one of the most prominent and prolific tragic poets of the fourth century, mentioned on several occasions by Aristotle on matters of plot construction, rhetoric and (in one instance) faulty stagecraft (Webster 1954, 300–1). That Xenocles is the correct one of the two patronymics proffered by **1** is secured by the evidence of Lysias (fr. 235 Carey) and scholia (Sch.[VAld] Ar. *Wasps* 1502; Sch.[VGAld] Ar. *Wasps* 1509; Sch.[RVG] Ar. *Wasps* 1510; Sch.[RV] Ar. *Peace* 778; Sch.[RV] Ar. *Peace* 791; Sch.[RV] Ar. *Peace* 793; Sch.[RV] Ar. *Peace* 794–5). How Theodectes – presumably the Lycian tragic poet from Phaselis who was active in the mid fourth century, and in the service of the Hecatomnid dynasty of Caria (**Eviii–ix**) – became identified in later scholarship as the father of Carcinus II can only be guessed at. It is possible that the theatrical activity of the family extended into a fourth generation (Meineke 1839, 515–16). The scholion to Aristophanes' *Frogs* reports that there were two *tragoidoi* by the name of Xenocles, and the second has plausibly been thought to be a grandson of the first, a poet or actor in the third century, son of Carcinus II (Xenocles II, *TrGF* 268).

The younger Carcinus (II) was active as a tragic poet early in the fourth century (*TrGF* 70 and 235; fl. 380–377: **1**), the first of his eleven victories won at the Dionysia not long before 373 (*IG* II² 2325A M-O, l. 43; probably also victorious at the Lenaea in the mid 370s: *SEG* 26, 203 col. 1, l. 12). He was however clearly at work some time before this, since Lysias, who retired from public life around 380, quoted him (fr. 235 Carey), providing us incidentally with the only known case of a fifth-century orator citing tragic poetry (but note Hermocrates' possible quotation of Euripides at the conference of Gela in 424: Timaeus

FGrH 566 F 21; **Axi**). Carcinus II had more than a passing association with Sicily. **2**, which derives from sources contemporary with the poet, indicates that he was, along with Aeschines the Socratic (and Plato: *Seventh Letter*), a member of the circle of intellectuals and celebrities gathered around the younger Dionysius of Syracuse, in a tradition that goes back not only to his father (**VI E**) but to the Deinomenids in an earlier generation (**VI A**). The care with which **2** specifies that the poet did not remain in Syracuse during the period of Dionysius II's exile (356–346) is evidence of the extent to which he was identified with the tyrant's regime.

   3 speaks of multiple periods of residence as a foreigner (this is the import of the compound παρεπιδημεῖν) in Syracuse. We may assume that a certain proportion of his enormous output of 160 dramas (**1**), larger than that reported for any other tragedian, was tailored for production in that city. His *Medea*, new fragments of which were published in 2004 (Bélis 2004; West 2007; Martinelli 2010), is one possibility, given the play's setting in the metropolis of Syracuse, Corinth. The case is much stronger with the work from which the fragment quoted in **3** derives. This contains the earliest known telling of the version of the Demeter and Kore myth that places the abduction of and search for Kore in Sicily. Carcinus' tragedy evidently also provided an aetiology for the origin of grain and its diffusion to mankind from Sicily, rather than Eleusis. In presenting this mythic innovation, doubtless as though it were hoary tradition – note the introductory λέγουσι 'they say' – in a tragedy composed for Dionysius II, Carcinus will have been serving the tyrant's imperial ambitions by promulgating the primacy of the Sicilian–Syracusan, in a direct challenge to the Athenian–Eleusinian, tradition. Epicharmus *PCG* F 99 from *Odysseus the Deserter* is evidence of a local, probably Syracusan, Eleusinia at which worshippers sacrificed pigs over a century earlier, but whether this festival already had the characteristics ascribed to it by Carcinus is not known. (Hsch. ε 2026 testifies to the existence of an Eleusinia in Sicily, but in honour of Artemis rather than Demeter and Kore.) This was moreover a time when Dionysius II was turning away from the friendly relations that his father had cultivated with Athens and when Athens needed to go seeking grain from Sicily (D. 32; 56.9; note also somewhat later, after Chaeronea, *IG* II³ 1, 432 of 337–325, honours for Sopatros of Acragas for bringing grain to Athens: **I Ai 2b**, and *IG* II³ 1, 339 of (?) 333/2, praise for men of Pontic Heraclea for selling Sicilian wheat and barley at fixed prices in Athens; De Angelis 2016, 305).

   The traditions that flowed into the Suda (**1**) distinguished an Acragantine tragic poet named Carcinus from an Athenian Carcinus. The possibility that it was the elder Carcinus (I) who hailed from Acragas (*TrGF* I, p. 128) deserves more serious consideration. Strong evidence makes of him an Athenian from Thorikos who served in high public roles reserved for citizens (below), but as he will have been born some three decades or more before Pericles' citizenship law, it is entirely possible that his mother came from Acragas. The meaning of the common noun καρκίνος as 'crab' was irresistible for comic purposes, and that, in combination with the perceived orchestic and physical peculiarities of Carcinus I and his sons, made crab jokes an inevitability (esp. Ar. *Wasps* 1500–10). But the crab was also an identifying symbol of the city of Acragas, still prominent on its coins in the latter decades of the fifth century, as it had been earlier in the century. The comic jokes do not depend on an Acragantine association of the 'Crab' Carcinus, though they would have gained added force if the family had a relationship with the city. On the other hand, the mockery itself cannot have been enough to generate the tradition that ties a Carcinus to Acragas (**1**), especially in light of the other evidence (**2–3**) for time spent by the younger Carcinus in Sicily. (It is also striking that one of the dozen or so attested Karkinoi from all periods and regions was the father of the Sicilian tyrant Agathocles, who came from Rhegium to live in Himera in exile in 317: D.S. 19.2.)

Given that Acragas was sacked by Carthage in 406 and not resettled until the era of Timoleon ca. 340 (Plu. *Tim.* 35.2), it is much more likely that Carcinus II inherited his Acragantine citizenship from a time when the city was closer to Athens, as it was for at least some of the tumultuous period of its history from the end of the tyranny in 472 to 406. Unions with non-Athenian women made by members of the élite often served to strengthen a family's important economic links outside Attica. The Carcinus family had strong maritime associations, and the appellation of Carcinus I as 'Lord of the sea' ὁ ποντομέδων ἄναξ (Ar. *Wasps* 1531), of his children as 'sons of the seaman' τέκνα τοῦ θαλασσίοιο (Ar. *Wasps* 1518–19) and of Xenocles in particular as 'the son of the seaman Carcinus' (Pl.Com. *PCG* F 143 ὁ Καρκίνου παῖς τοῦ θαλαττίου) seem to go beyond the 'crab' pun. Carcinus I was involved in naval operations around the Peloponnese when general in 432/1 (Th. 2.23.2; D.S. 12.42.7; *IG* I³ 365, ll. 31, 36, 38) and served as trierarch around the middle of the century (*IG* I³ 874). Perhaps the family was also involved in maritime trade (in grain?) between Athens and Greek Sicily, and their work in the world of theatre equally found opportunities in the West, as in Athens? (Involvement in the grain trade might also lie behind Xenotimos' presence in the Bosporus early in the fourth century: above.) The recent discovery of a large theatre in Acragas adds to other evidence which suggests that the city had its own theatrical culture by the fourth century (**A Introduction**).

Axi: Euripides and Sicily

1. Aristotle, *Rhetoric* 1384b11–16. Written ca. 330. Target date: probably 427–415 (Baiter and Sauppe 1850, 216; Stevens 1956, 91; with Cagnazzi 1993 making a case for 427), but 411 is a possibility (Jameson 1971, 544 n. 12). In a chapter on shame (ch. 2.6), Aristotle lists the kind of people before whom we tend to feel shame. Text: Kassel.

> καὶ ἐν οἷς μηδὲν ἀποτετυχήκασιν· ὥσπερ γὰρ θαυμαζόμενοι διάκεινται· διὸ
> καὶ τοὺς πρῶτον δεηθέντας τι αἰσχύνονται ὡς οὐδέν πω ἠδοξηκότες ἐν αὐτοῖς.
> τοιοῦτοι δ᾽ οἱ ἄρτι βουλόμενοι φίλοι εἶναι – τὰ γὰρ βέλτιστα τεθέανται· διὸ
> εὖ ἔχει ἡ τοῦ Εὐριπίδου ἀπόκρισις πρὸς τοὺς Συρακοσίους – καὶ τῶν πάλαι
> γνωρίμων οἱ μηδὲν συνειδότες.

> And we feel shame in front of others before whom we have never yet shown our inadequacies, since they are disposed to think well of us. For that reason we feel ashamed to refuse those who ask a favour of us for the first time because they have seen only our best side. Such, for example, is the case with men who have recently conceived a desire to become our friends, because they have seen our best side only – hence the beauty of Euripides' reply to the Syracusans – and also with old acquaintances who are unaware of our failings.

2. Anonymous commentary on Aristotle, *Rhetoric* 1384b (*CAG* XXI 2, p. 106–7). See **1** for target date. Text: Rabe.

Εὐριπίδης πρὸς τοὺς Συρρακουσίους πρέσβυς ἀποσταλεὶς καὶ περὶ εἰρήνης καὶ φιλίας δεόμενος, ὡς ἐκεῖνοι ἀνένευον, εἶπεν ʽἔδει, ἄνδρες Συρρακούσιοι, εἰ καὶ διὰ μηδὲν ἄλλο, ἀλλά γε διὰ τὸ ἄρτι ὑμῶν δέεσθαι [107] αἰσχύνεσθαι ἡμᾶς ὡς θαυμάζοντας'. τὸ δὲ ὅλον τοιοῦτόν ἐστι· φησὶν ὁ Εὐριπίδης πρὸς τοὺς Συρρακουσίους ὡς ʽοὐ δεῖ ἀποπεμφθῆναι παρ' ὑμῶν, διότι ἅπαξ ὑμῶν ἐδεήθημεν ὡς ὑμᾶς θαυμάζοντες'.

Euripides was sent on an embassy to Syracuse and made a plea for peace and for friendship. As they were about to reject his plea, he said 'Men of Syracuse, you should feel shame before us, if for no other reason than because we only now (for the first time) made this request, [107] thinking well of you'. In short, Euripides tells the Syracusans that 'we should not be rejected by you because, thinking well of you, we have only once made a request'.

3. Timaeus of Tauromenium, *Sicilian History*, FGrH 566 F 22, ll. 34–44. Written from ca. 315 to ca. 265. Polybius (12.26) paraphrases a speech purportedly delivered by the Syracusan politician and general, Hermocrates, at a conference at Gela in 424. The conference was attended by Sicilian leaders for the purpose of discussing the threat posed by Athens to Sicilian independence. The speech cites Homer and Euripides on war and peace. Thucydides 4.59–64 also reports the speech, but in his version there is no mention of Euripides. Euripides' *Cresphontes* (*TrGF* F 453) is datable between 428 and 421 (see commentary). Text: Jacoby.

ὁμογνωμονεῖν δὲ τῷ ποιητῇ καὶ τὸν Εὐριπίδην ἐν οἷς φησιν

Εἰρήνα βαθύπλουτε,
καλλίστα μακάρων θεῶν,
ζῆλός μοι σέθεν, ὡς χρονίζεις.
δέδοικα δὲ μὴ πρὶν ὑπερβάλλῃ με γῆρας,
πρὶν σὰν χαρίεσσαν προσιδεῖν ὥραν
καὶ καλλιχόρους ἀοιδὰς
φιλοστεφάνους τε κώμους.

ἔτι δὲ πρὸς τούτοις ὁμοιότατον εἶναί φησι τὸν μὲν πόλεμον τῇ νόσῳ, τὴν δ' εἰρήνην τῇ ὑγιείᾳ· τὴν μὲν γὰρ καὶ τοὺς κάμνοντας ἀναλαμβάνειν, ἐν ᾧ δὲ καὶ τοὺς ὑγιαίνοντας ἀπόλλυσθαι. καὶ κατὰ μὲν τὴν εἰρήνην τοὺς πρεσβυτέρους ὑπὸ τῶν νέων θάπτεσθαι κατὰ φύσιν, ἐν δὲ τῷ πολέμῳ τἀναντία. τὸ δὲ μέγιστον, ἐν μὲν τῷ πολέμῳ μηδ' ἄχρι τῶν τειχῶν εἶναι τὴν ἀσφάλειαν, κατὰ δὲ τὴν εἰρήνην μέχρι τῶν τῆς χώρας ὅρων· καὶ τούτοις ἕτερα παραπλήσια.

And he (Timaeus) claims that Euripides shares the poet's (Homer's) views where he says: 'Supremely wealthy Peace, most beautiful of the blessed goddesses, I yearn for you as you delay. I fear that old age will overwhelm me before I lay eyes upon your graceful beauty, and the songs accompanied by beautiful choruses and the garland-loving revels.' Furthermore he says that war is most like a disease, peace like health: in the latter even the sick are revived, but in the former even the healthy perish. And in peace the old are buried by the young as is natural, in war the opposite. And above all in war one is not safe even as far as the city wall, but in peace one is safe as far as the country's borders. And so on like this.

4. **Satyrus,** *Life of Euripides*, **F 6 fr. 39 col. xix (Schorn)**. The text is based on a papyrus, *POxy*. 1176 of 150–200 AD. Satyrus of Kallatis was probably active 240–170 (Schorn 2004, 6–10). The target date is from 413, date of the defeat of the Athenians by Syracuse. Satyrus' *Life of Euripides* is a biography written in dialogue form in which the main speaker (who delivers the lines below) presents himself as a somewhat overweening authority in a largely monologic discussion between three (or possibly only two) characters. This is important because it shows that Satyrus does not necessarily vouch for the information he gives: note especially the 'they say at any rate' that introduces the anecdotes. The *Life of Euripides* is part of a larger compilation of *Lives*, book 6 of which included Aeschylus and Sophocles as well as Euripides, probably in a continuous text. Euripides is credited with an epigram for the victims of the Battle of Syracuse (*TrGF* T 92). Text: Schorn.

> οὐ κακῶς εἴρη|κας· τὰ μὲν | γὰρ τῶν Ἀθή|νηισιν [οὐ]δὲ | λέγειν ἄξιον, | οἵ γε
> ποιητὴν | τηλικοῦτον | Μακεδόνων | καὶ Σικελιω|[10]τῶν ὕστερον | ἤισθοντο.
> λέ|γεται γοῦν, ὅτε | Νικίας ἐστρά|τευσεν ἐπὶ Σι|κελίαν καὶ πολ|λοὶ τῶν
> Ἀθη|ναίων ἐγένοντ' | αἰχμάλωτοι, | συχνοὺς αὐτῶν |[20] ἀνασωθῆναι | διὰ τῶν
> Εὐρι|πίδου ποιημά|των, ὅσοι κατ|έχοντες τῶν | στίχων τινὰς | διδάξειαν |τοὺς
> υἱεῖς τῶν | εἰληφότων | ὑποχειρίους |[30] αὐτούς· οὕ|τως ἡ Σικελ[ί]α | ἅπ[ασ]α
> τὸν Εὐ[ριπίδη]ν ἀπε[θαύμαζ]εν. καὶ | [.....]παρτε |[......]..[...

You put it well. The attitude of the Athenians is [no]t worth mentioning. They [10] recognised the greatness of the poet after the Macedonians and the Sicilians. They say at any rate that, when Nicias led the armada against Sicily and many Athenians became prisoners, Euripides' poems [20] saved a large number of them – namely those who retained some of his verses and taught them to the sons of those who took [30] them prisoners. So greatly did a[ll] Sicil[y] ad[mir]e Eu[ripide]s and …

5. **Plutarch,** *Life of Nicias* **29**. Written ca. 114 AD and describing events after the Battle of Syracuse in September 413. Text: Ziegler.

τῶν δ' Ἀθηναίων οἱ μὲν πλεῖστοι διεφθάρησαν ἐν ταῖς λατομίαις ὑπὸ νόσου καὶ διαίτης πονηρᾶς, εἰς ἡμέραν ἑκάστην κοτύλας δύο κριθῶν λαμβάνοντες καὶ μίαν ὕδατος, οὐκ ὀλίγοι δ' ἐπράθησαν διακλαπέντες ἢ καὶ [2] διαλαθόντες ὡς οἰκέται. καὶ τούτους ὡς οἰκέτας ἐπώλουν στίζοντες ἵππον εἰς τὸ μέτωπον· ἀλλ' † ἦσαν οἱ καὶ τοῦτο πρὸς τῷ δουλεύειν ὑπομένοντες. ἐβοήθει δὲ τούτοις ἥ τ' αἰδὼς καὶ τὸ κόσμιον· ἢ γὰρ ἠλευθεροῦντο ταχέως, ἢ τιμώμενοι παρέμενον τοῖς κεκτημένοις. ἔνιοι δὲ καὶ δι' [3] Εὐριπίδην ἐσώθησαν. μάλιστα γὰρ ὡς ἔοικε τῶν ἐκτὸς Ἑλλήνων ἐπόθησαν αὐτοῦ τὴν μοῦσαν οἱ περὶ Σικελίαν, καὶ μικρὰ τῶν ἀφικνουμένων ἑκάστοτε δείγματα καὶ γεύματα κομιζόντων ἐκμανθάνοντες ἀγαπητῶς μετεδίδοσαν [4] ἀλλήλοις. τότε γοῦν φασι τῶν σωθέντων οἴκαδε συχνοὺς ἀσπάζεσθαί τε τὸν Εὐριπίδην φιλοφρόνως, καὶ διηγεῖσθαι τοὺς μὲν ὅτι δουλεύοντες ἀφείθησαν, ἐκδιδάξαντες ὅσα τῶν ἐκείνου ποιημάτων ἐμέμνηντο, τοὺς δ' ὅτι πλανώμενοι μετὰ τὴν μάχην τροφῆς καὶ ὕδατος μετελάμβανον [5] τῶν μελῶν ᾄσαντες. οὐ δεῖ δὴ θαυμάζειν ὅτι τοὺς Καυνίους φασι πλοίου προσφερομένου τοῖς λιμέσιν ὑπὸ λῃστρίδων διωκομένου μὴ δέχεσθαι τὸ πρῶτον, ἀλλ' ἀπείργειν, εἶτα μέντοι διαπυνθανομένους εἰ γιγνώσκουσιν ᾄσματα [6] τῶν Εὐριπίδου, φησάντων δ' ἐκείνων, οὕτω παρεῖναι καὶ συγκαταγαγεῖν τὸ πλοῖον.

Of the Athenians most perished in the stone quarries from disease and malnutrition as they received a pint (2 *kotylai*) of barley and a half pint (1 *kotyle*) of water per day. Not a few were sold because they were taken to be slaves either through concealment (by the Syracusans who captured them) or [2] inattention. These they branded on the forehead with the image of a horse and sold as slaves – (there is some problem with the text here) indeed there were some who even suffered this indignity in addition to slavery. Modesty and good behaviour saved them: either they soon regained their freedom or they stayed with their masters enjoying privileged conditions. Some were even saved by [3] Euripides. Beyond all other overseas Greeks the Sicilians, it seems, were infatuated with his music and poetry. Whenever new arrivals brought little bits and pieces they eagerly learned them by heart and passed them on [4] to one another. At any rate they say that at that time many who had found themselves safely home warmly greeted Euripides and told their story: some that they were freed from slavery after they had taught all they remembered of his poems; others that after the battle they received food and water in their wanderings in exchange for [5] singing some of his songs. Little wonder then that they say they (the Sicilians) refused to allow Caunians to enter their harbours when chased by pirates, but at first repelled them, until they asked if they knew any of the songs [6] of Euripides, and when they said yes, they let them pass and beach their ship on these terms.

There is no good reason to doubt **1–2**'s claim that Euripides was a member of an embassy to Syracuse. By this date Greek cities seem to have made good use of their culture heroes in international diplomacy: e.g. Gorgias (Pl. *Hp.Ma.* 282b; D.S. 12.53; Paus. 6.17; cf. Th. 3.86), Prodicus (Pl. *Hp.Ma.* 282c–d), Hippias (Pl. *Hp.Ma.* 281a; Philostr. *VS* 1.11.5), even possibly Thrasymachus (White 1995). And though the earliest attestations favour men associated with sophistry and rhetoric (as was indeed Euripides), more literary figures are common from the fourth century onwards (Chaniotis 1988b). Euripides may have been an inspired early example of this practice. Knowledge of poetry and myth, as C. P. Jones 1999 makes very clear, was vital to ancient diplomacy (cf. Patterson 2010), but the choice of Euripides must imply some anticipation that his fame would lend authority and good will to the Sicilian embassy.

Modern scholarship has however received the information sceptically largely because this kind of public service seems out of tune with the reclusive and misanthropic behaviour attributed to the poet in the biographical tradition, itself allegedly responsible for Athens' putative reluctance to recognise Euripides' genius (a premise of **4** and **5**). Modern scholars, largely out of reliance on this biographical fiction (see Stevens 1956), have long disregarded the excellent testimony of Aristotle (**VI Di 2**), by supposing that Euripides' name is either reported by **1** and **2** in error for another, or, if the text is correctly transmitted, assumed to be the poet in error for another Euripides. Ruhnken argued that 'Euripides' is an error for 'Hyperides', the well-known fourth century politician (1768, 71; 1823, 346; followed by Webster 1967, 27–8); Jameson (reluctantly) suggests an error for Epikerdes (1971, 545 n. 12). Against the emendation to Hyperides, Sauppe (Baiter and Sauppe 1850, 216) pointed out that nothing was known of an embassy by Hyperides either. As for Epikerdes, he appears to have ransomed some Athenian prisoners in 413 (D. 20.41; *IG* I³ 125), but was not an Athenian, let alone an Athenian ambassador, and there is nothing to connect him with the kind of official representation implied in **1** and explicit in **2**.

Though happy to dismiss Hyperides, Sauppe ended his discussion by asking if the passage might refer to a late fifth-century Euripides of Melite (Th. 2.70.79 = *APF* no. 5951). Wilamowitz (1899, 617–18) favoured a 'Eurip(p)ides/Heurip(p)ides', early fourth-century Athenian politician = *APF* no. 5949 (see **V F** on *IG* II² 1138). Jameson, however, points out that 'to the Syracusans' would sit awkwardly after 406 in a context that must presuppose an embassy to Dionysius and not the Syracusan democracy (1971, 544 n. 23). The same objection would have to be levelled against Wilamowitz's candidate. But the possibilities are rich for those who are disinclined to accept the obvious: *LGPN* lists twelve Athenians of the fifth and fourth centuries with the name Euripides. Cope (1877, 83) and Grimaldi (1988, 119–20) accept the reference to the tragedian, mainly on the grounds that there is no reason to doubt it. But there are also positive reasons for accepting this conclusion. There is little chance that Aristotle would refer to anyone but the poet with the name 'Euripides' *tout court*, and, with Jameson, 'we should note that "the reply of Euripides" was evidently so familiar as a paradoxical argument that Aristotle did not need to quote it in order to make his point' (1971, 544). What other Euripides would be so well remembered as to need so little prompting either with respect to his name or his utterances? None of the proposed substitutes for Euripides is remembered for his *apothegmata* (unpublished famous sayings): those of Euripides the poet were collected and repeated by Aristotle himself.

1 and **2** indirectly attest the popularity of Euripides in Syracuse in the third or second last decade of the fifth century, as it is very likely that Euripides was chosen for the embassy because of the esteem in which he was held in Sicily. This would seem to confirm **4–5**'s claim that the Sicilians (along with the Macedonians) were the first among the Greeks to recognise Euripides' genius (though we might freely doubt the story that the Athenians were slow to do so).

From the fact that Plutarch's version (**5**) of the tales about the liberation of Athenian prisoners by the songs of Euripides is fuller and more detailed than that of Satyrus (**4**), it is clear that Plutarch is not drawing upon Satyrus, but upon another author who probably also served as Satyrus' source. Arrighetti guesses that Plutarch's and Satyrus' source is Philochorus (1964 on fr. 39 col. x, ll. 1–22; Schorn 2004, 58, 380). Philochorus appears indeed to be the first to tell a tale that we find again in Satyrus' *Life of Euripides* fr. 39 col. ix that the tragedies of Euripides were written in a cave on Salamis (**Dxii**; Gell. 15.20.5; Frey 1919–1920, 17–18; Schorn 2004, 278). Philochorus' (ca. 340–260) sources remain obscure and it is as hard to believe, on such doubtful authority, that 'many' Athenians were saved by Euripides' songs as it is hard to believe in Euripides' troglodytic writing habits. The anecdotes seem however to be predicated upon the belief that 'beyond all other overseas Greeks the Sicilians were infatuated with his music and poetry' not vice versa.

Doubtful as the tale of salvation by Euripides (**4–5**) may be, there is no reason to doubt the anecdote's premises. Sicily's admiration for Euripides seems well attested, quite apart from any inferences we can draw from **1** and **2**. Euripidean subjects appear on Sicilian red-figured vases very soon after the first use of the technique, and although the number of tragedy-related vasepaintings is not many, Euripidean subjects predominate. Of the twenty 'tragic' Sicilian red-figured vases listed in *CFST*, 493–8, thirteen are certainly or possibly ascribed to Euripidean drama (**Axviii**). Sicilian importations of Attic vases with Euripidean subjects begin as early as ca. 440, according to the same authors (Catucci 2003). Moreover, Dionysius I's adulation and imitation of Euripides is indicated both by anecdote and fragments (**VI E**).

We cannot be certain that written texts of Euripides' dramas were wholly unavailable in Sicily in this period, although anything that we could recognise as a 'book industry' was certainly in its infancy in the late fifth century. We should note however that the emphasis in the anecdote of **4** and **5** is upon the songs and music of Euripides. It is unlikely, though not impossible, that texts with musical notation existed as early as 413: West conjectures the origin of the system of notation for vocal music in 'the late fifth or the fourth century' (1992, 263) and Hagel 'the first invention of a melodic notation perhaps not long after 500' (2009, 443). But if notation were available, it could hardly have affected the popular transmission of the music (even in a much later period ancient musical notation was only intelligible to professionals; for the issues, see Prauscello 2006, 7–121, esp. 40 51). The primary vehicle for the popular transmission of Euripidean song is likely to have been, in the first instance, the many Athenian citizens who served in his choruses at the city and rural festivals, and in the second instance, the popular performance of these songs in schools and at symposia (Csapo 2010, 170–1).

It would be an excellent confirmation of Euripides' celebrity in Sicily if we could rely on Timaeus' claim that Hermocrates cited Euripides (next to Homer) in a speech made to delegates from all over Sicily (**3**), and indeed a speech designed to unite the Sicilians in an alliance against Athens, a fact that might recommend the view that Euripides was regarded as less of an Athenian, than a Panhellenic poet. It is unfortunately unlikely that Timaeus had access to actual records in composing the speech and in any case Polybius cites it precisely as the 'clearest proof' that Timaeus' speeches are 'wilful', 'ignorant', 'pedantic' and 'scholastic' misstatements, and not the 'real speeches made' (Plb. 12.25i–k). Polybius specifically lists the quotation of the passage of Euripides among a catalogue of clichés worthy of a schoolboy. Thucydides' version of Hermocrates' speech cites no poetry and interestingly begins by dismissing as pointless precisely the kind of arguments with which Timaeus has filled this speech, since 'all are agreed that peace is better than war' (4.62.2). The dating of Euripides' *Cresphontes* does nothing to confirm or exclude the possibility of Hermocrates' citation. On metrical criteria it is probably later than 428 and certainly no later than 421, when it was parodied by Aristophanes (Collard et al. 1995, 125). There is a good chance that it was a recent play at the time of the Geloan conference, but this cannot be taken as in any way confirming the possibility of a citation: Baron suggests that Timaeus, who was fond of creating synchronisms, may have put the speech in Hermocrates' mouth for this very reason (Baron 2013, 110). The most we can hope to salvage from **3** is that a writer born in Tauromenium three generations after these events had no difficulty presenting recent quotations from Euripides as viable rhetorical currency in Sicily in 424, and on a par with Homer for poetic authority. But this alone is perhaps not inconsiderable.

Axii: Theatrical Judging in South Italy and Sicily

1. **Epicharmus, *PCG* F 237**. Epicharmus is closely associated with the production in Syracuse of the earliest known comedy, from the 480s or earlier (**Aiii**). This fragment, from an unknown drama, is preserved in **2**. Text: Kassel and Austin.

> ἐν πέντε κριτᾶν γούνασι κεῖται.
>
> κριτᾶν Ahrens   κριτῶν codd.

> It rests on the knees of the five judges.

2. **Zenobius, *Proverbs* 3.64**. Zenobius was a 2nd c. AD sophist who taught rhetoric in Rome. In addition to making a Greek translation of Sallust's *Histories* he produced a compilation of proverbs from pre-existing collections, notably those of Didymus and Lucillus of Tarrha (Suda ζ 73), which survives in abridged form. Suda ε 1425 is a redacted version of the same entry: παρ' ὅσον τὸ παλαιὸν ε' κριταὶ ἔκρινον τοὺς κωμικούς, ὡς φησιν Ἐπίχαρμος 'inasmuch as, long ago, 5 judges used to judge the comedies, as Epicharmus says'. A number of other sources gloss the proverb in very similar language, without mentioning Epicharmus: [Plu.] *Prov.* 1.76: τὸ παλαιὸν πέντε κριταὶ ἔκρινον τοὺς κωμικούς 'long ago, five judges used to judge the comedies'; Phot. ε 1006: τοσοῦτοι γὰρ τοὺς κωμῳδοὺς ἔκρινον 'for that many used to judge the comedies'. Text: Schneidewin and von Leutsch.

> ἐν πέντε κριτῶν γούνασι κεῖται· παροιμιῶδες, οἷον, ἐν ἀλλοτρίᾳ ἐξουσίᾳ εἰσίν.
> εἴρηται δὲ ἡ παροιμία, παρόσον πέντε κριταὶ τοὺς κωμικοὺς ἔκρινον, ὡς φησιν

Ἐπίχαρμος. σύγκειται οὖν παρὰ τὸ Ὁμηρικόν, θεῶν ἐν γούνασι κεῖται. ἐπειδὴ
οἱ κριταὶ ἐν τοῖς γόνασιν εἶχον, ἃ νῦν εἰς γραμματεῖα γράφεται.

Crusius (1891–1893, 282) posited a lacuna after εἶχον, possibly ψήφους

'It rests on the knees of the five judges': a proverbial way of saying 'They are
under the control of others'. The proverb came into use insofar as five judges
used to judge the comic poets, as Epicharmus says. So it is composed on analogy with the Homeric phrase 'It rests on the knees of the gods', since the judges
kept on their knees what is now written on tablets.

3. Hesychius, *Lexicon* **s.v. πέντε κριταί ('five judges', π 1408).** Compiled in the 5th or 6th c.
AD, drawing on material many centuries older. Text: Hansen.

πέντε κριταί· τοσοῦτοι τοὺς κωμικοὺς ἔκρινον, οὐ μόνον Ἀθήνησιν, ἀλλὰ καὶ
ἐν Σικελίᾳ

'Five judges': that many used to judge the comic poets, not only in Athens, but
also in Sicily.

4. Plato, *Laws* **659b–c.** Written probably in the 350s. The discussion, led here by the
Athenian, concerns the importance of assigning judgement in matters of poetry and per-
formance to the best educated, with no consideration of the views of the mass audience.
Text: Burnet.

οὐ γὰρ μαθητὴς ἀλλὰ διδάσκαλος, ὥς γε τὸ δίκαιον, θεατῶν μᾶλλον ὁ κριτὴς
καθίζει, καὶ ἐναντιωσόμενος τοῖς τὴν ἡδονὴν μὴ προσηκόντως μηδὲ ὀρθῶς
ἀποδιδοῦσι θεαταῖς. ἐξῆν γὰρ δὴ τῷ παλαιῷ τε καὶ Ἑλληνικῷ νόμῳ, <οὐ>
καθάπερ ὁ Σικελικός τε καὶ Ἰταλικὸς νόμος νῦν, τῷ πλήθει τῶν θεατῶν
ἐπιτρέπων καὶ τὸν νικῶντα διακρίνων χειροτονίαις, διέφθαρκε μὲν τοὺς
ποιητὰς αὐτούς ᶜ – πρὸς γὰρ τὴν τῶν κριτῶν ἡδονὴν ποιοῦσιν οὖσαν φαύλην,
ὥστε αὐτοὶ αὐτοὺς οἱ θεαταὶ παιδεύουσιν – διέφθαρκεν δ' αὐτοῦ τοῦ θεάτρου
τὰς ἡδονάς· δέον γὰρ αὐτοὺς ἀεὶ βελτίω τῶν αὑτῶν ἠθῶν ἀκούοντας βελτίω
τὴν ἡδονὴν ἴσχειν, νῦν αὐτοῖς δρῶσιν πᾶν τοὐναντίον συμβαίνει.

[ἐξῆν γὰρ δὴ τῷ παλαιῷ τε καὶ Ἑλληνικῷ νόμῳ] England   <οὐ> Winckelmann 1839

For, under a just arrangement, the judge takes his seat not as the student but the
teacher of the spectators, and ready to oppose those who offer them pleasure
in a way that is inappropriate or wrong. This was in fact possible under the old
Hellenic custom, not as with the present-day Sicilian and Italian custom of entrusting judgement of the winner to a vote of hands by the mob of spectators, which
has corrupted the poets themselves, ᶜ for they compose with a view to the pleasure – which is base – of their judges, so that the spectators themselves are their
educators – and it has also corrupted the pleasures of the theatre. For while they
should be improving their standard of pleasure by always listening to characters
better than their own, what they are doing now has the opposite effect on them.

The expression 'it rests on the knees of the five judges' (**1**) is recorded as a proverb relating to the judging of comedy in a variety of sources, but only in **2** and Suda ε 1425 is it referred to Epicharmus. One might have even doubted whether **2** preserved the *ipsissima verba* of Epicharmus, for the gloss could be taken to imply merely that Epicharmus made reference in some way to the rule of five judges for comedy, but as Hermann (1839, 94) saw, the fact that the phrase is in anapaestic metre points to a comic author. Crusius (1891–1893, 284) thought the *Epinikios* or the *Choral Dancers* of Epicharmus likely contenders, since both works are reported by Hephaestion (*Ench.* 8.2) to have been composed entirely in anapaestic tetrameters. Nothing more is known of these plays, though the metatheatrical potential of their titles is certainly suggestive. Precisely what kind of dramas they were is unknown, perhaps pieces sung and danced entirely by a chorus, possibly with a 'parabatic' quality akin to that familiar from Aristophanic comedy in which the poet spoke in his own voice (Riu 2011; **Aiii**). In that case **1** would be the dramatised voice of Epicharmus speaking of the power of the judges in the theatre and of his work's fortunes at their hands in the competition. There can be little doubt (Willi 2008, 160 expresses some) that this points to the existence of a formal contest of comedy in early fifth-century Syracuse, for which a tradition of agonistic rivalry between Deinolochos and Epicharmus offers further support (**Av 2**). The existence of choral contests in south-east Sicily is even more securely established by the evidence of the curse tablet (**Avii**) probably from Gela, of around 470–450.

It is possible that the panel of judges was greater than five and that Syracuse employed a system akin to the one found in use in Athens several decades later, according to which the result depended on the vote of five judges, but there were more in total (**I Avii**). The absence of the article – 'five judges' rather than '*the* five judges' – might urge us in this direction, as might the direct claim of **3** that the phrase 'five judges' had currency in both places (with Athens as the primary point of reference). But **3** looks like a later effort to make the two great centres of fifth-century comic performance conform (**2** makes no such reference to Athens), an effort informed by a generalised Athenocentrism. Such Athenocentrism lies behind some influential modern interpretations, such as that of Pickard-Cambridge (*DTC*[2] 284–5), who thinks that both the custom and the proverb may have been imported to Sicily from Athens (Trojani in Polacco and Anti 1981, 38, also takes it to imply a system of organisation modelled on the more famous Athenian exemplar). But given the intimate connection between the procedure for judging in the Athenian theatre and the structures and values of the democracy, this seems an inherently implausible practice for the Deinomenids to copy, and much more likely that five was the full complement of judges in Syracuse (whether this can be generalised to 'Sicily' as in **3** is unclear, but note below on **4**).

We should not hope to extract any authentic information from the probably corrupt final clause of **2**, 'since the judges kept on their knees what is now written on tablets', which looks like nothing more than a deduction on the part of Zenobius or a source that over-literalises the metaphor (there is no need to explain the reference to 'knees' at all). The fact that the phrase is calqued on a Homeric formula – ταῦτα θεῶν ἐν γούνασι κεῖται 'that rests on the knees of the gods' (e.g. *Il.* 17.514, 20.435; *Od.* 1.267, 1.400, 16.129) – is consistent with Epicharmus' practice of engagement with epic tradition. For all its undercutting hyperbole in the comic context (Willi 2012, 71–2), the comparison of theatrical judges to omnipotent Olympians underscores a perception of their power. The restriction of that power to a small group of five doubtless reflects the situation under the Deinomenids, and a certain desire to control what was accorded validation in the theatre, for all the tyrants' populist tendencies. The fact that the great majority of early theatrical production in Sicily was the result of tyrannical patronage has been very plausibly proffered as one reason why our sources for formal, institutional arrangements for Sicilian theatre are so few (Privitera 1980, 411). Such patronage tends to remain closely identified with the figure of the tyrant and not to develop more persistent institutional structures.

Plato writes with intimate knowledge of the region for, despite the doubts over the authenticity of the *Seventh Letter*, it is virtually certain that he had been in South Italy and in Sicily with the two Dionysii in the 380s, in 366 and in 361 (Nails 2002, 247–9). **4** shows that, by that time, competition was the norm in Sicilian and Italian theatres, and that the practice was to judge performances by a show of hands of the whole theatre audience – a practice that, in the view of Plato, had catastrophic ethical and political consequences. The 'old Hellenic custom' to which he opposes it, that saw the theatrical judge 'not as the student but the teacher of the spectators', sounds like little more than a conservative fantasy. The casual manner in which Plato refers to the 'present-day Sicilian and Italian custom' also shows that, by the middle of the fourth century, this broad region could be treated as a homogeneous unit when it came to the practice of theatrical judging.

Axiii: Catane – Aetna

1. Thucydides, *History of the Peloponnesian War* 6.51.1. Thucydides was writing soon after the events in question, dated to the summer of 415. Text: Jones and Powell.

> καὶ ἐκκλησίας γενομένης τὴν μὲν στρατιὰν οὐκ ἐδέχοντο οἱ Καταναῖοι, τοὺς δὲ στρατηγοὺς ἐσελθόντας ἐκέλευον, εἴ τι βούλονται, εἰπεῖν. καὶ λέγοντος τοῦ Ἀλκιβιάδου, καὶ τῶν ἐν τῇ πόλει πρὸς τὴν ἐκκλησίαν τετραμμένων, οἱ στρατιῶται πυλίδα τινὰ ἐνῳκοδομημένην κακῶς ἔλαθον διελόντες, καὶ ἐσελθόντες ἠγόραζον ἐς τὴν πόλιν.

> An assembly was called, and while the Catanians would not receive the army they told the generals to enter and say whatever they wished. While Alcibiades was speaking and the people of the city paid attention to the proceedings of the assembly, the soldiers secretly pulled down a postern gate which had been poorly built, and entering the city gathered in the agora.

2. Frontinus, *Stratagems* 3.2.6. Frontinus was an experienced military commander who served as governor of Britain 73/4–77 AD, proconsul of Asia in 86 AD and superintendent of aqueducts in 97 AD. The 'Stratagems' (*Strategemata*), one of several treatises on technical subjects, aims to advise contemporary military commanders with practical examples from the past. The surviving work appears to be an appendix to a lost comprehensive treatment of the art of war (Frontin. *Str.* 1 *Pref.* 1; Wheeler 1988, 19). Frontinus gathered his material both from Greek and Roman historians and from pre-existing collections of *exempla* (*Str.* 1 *Pref.* 2–3). The events referred to date to 415 (below). Text: Gundermann.

Alcibiades, dux Atheniensium, cum civitatem Agrigentinorum egregie munitam obsideret, petito ab eis concilio diu tamquam de rebus ad commune pertinentibus disseruit in theatro, ubi ex more Graecorum locus consultationi praebebatur: dumque consilii specie tenet multitudinem, Athenienses, quos ad id praeparaverat, incustoditam urbem ceperunt.

Alcibiades, the Athenian commander, while besieging the well-fortified city of the Agrigentines, sought a meeting of the citizens, and, as though discussing matters of common concern, addressed them at length in the theatre, where according to the custom of the Greeks it was usual to afford a place for consultation. And while he held the crowd on the pretence of deliberation, the Athenians, whom he had prepared for this move, took the city, thus left unguarded.

3. **Monogram of the letters K A T in ligature on the theatre**. Date: probably 4th c. (see below).

The inscriptions appear on the internal faces of the blocks of white stone (probably from a Leontinian coastal quarry: Privitera 2009, 43) that make up an imposing wall of isodomic construction in the area of the western parodos. Sometimes the monogram is right-way up; others upside-down or on its side. It is evidently an abbreviation for Κατ[άνη/α] 'Catane/a' or Κατ[αναίων] 'property of the Catanians'.
ca. 0.30 (max.) × ca. 0.35 m (max.).
Fiorelli 1884, 433–4; Libertini 1929, 15–16; Tortorici 2008, 110–15; Branciforti 2010, 194.
Photos: Branciforti 2010, 194 fig. 93 (photo and sketch); Tortorici 2008, 112 fig. 24, 114 fig. 25 (sketch).

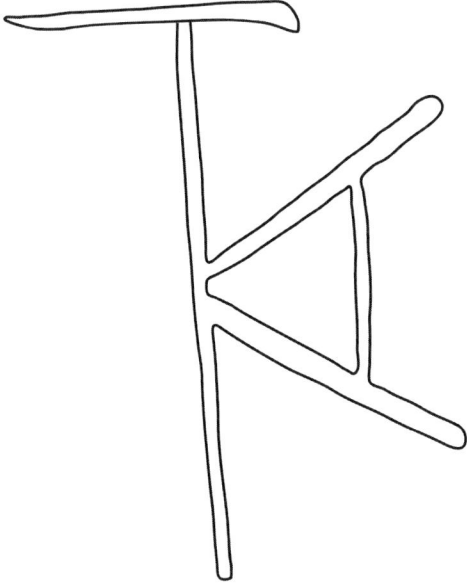

The event in question in **2** may be the one recorded by **1** as taking place in the summer of 415, but in the eastern Sicilian city of Catane rather than Acragas (**A Introduction**).

Polyaenus (1.40.4) and Diodorus (13.4.4) follow Thucydides' account. Unless we suppose that Alcibiades adopted the same ruse on an otherwise unattested occasion in Acragas, it follows that Frontinus or his source is in error (Dederich 1855, xi 'error ipsius auctoris, ut videtur. Ad Catinam res pertinent'). However only Frontinus speaks of the event taking place in the theatre: in Polyaenus and Diodorus the occasion is described as an assembly without topographical marker. While it is entirely likely that the theatre in Catane served as the place where the city's assembly met, it is perhaps less likely that Frontinus, whose account is already suspect because of the presumed error, would have had access to a source for the event that had greater detail than Thucydides (Privitera 2009, 41). The much-read *Histories* of Timaeus (early 3rd c.) or the (in modern times lost) Thirteenth Book of Diodorus (1st c.) are however two realistic possibilities.

While this literary evidence for the existence of a theatre in Catane by 415 is therefore open to doubt, it is now abundantly clear that the Greek city had a theatre that long predates the relatively well-preserved first-century AD Roman one built above it (on which see Branciforti 2010, 196–209). Indeed, some (recently Fischer-Hansen, Nielsen and Ampolo in *IACP* 185) assume on the basis of the fact that Aeschylus composed and performed his *Aitnaiai* in honour of the newly founded city (**VI A**) that the construction of a theatre in the city may be attributable to Hieron himself, who founded Aetna on the site of Catane in 476 and who is highly likely to have commissioned poetic performance for its foundation, and at festivals in the city thereafter, notably the Aitnaia in honour of Zeus Aitnaios. The Pindaric scholia attest an agon for the latter at which 'Hieron's supporters sang the epinikia composed for the crown games' (ἐν τῷ ἀγῶνι καὶ ἐν τῇ πανηγύρει τοῦ Αἰτναίου Διὸς ᾖδον οἱ περὶ τὸν Ἱέρωνα τοὺς ἐπὶ τοῖς στεφανίταις ἀγῶσι πεποιημένους ἐπινίκους: Sch. Pi. *N.* 1.7b; cf. Sch. Pi. *O.* 6.162a, c; *N.* 1.7a).

A grid system of streets partially revealed within the Archaic city walls is attributed to Hieron, as too is the catastrophic destruction wrought on domestic buildings in the first quarter of the fifth century, doubtless those of the Catanians expelled to make way for his new Dorian population (Privitera 2009, 38, 41). Given that Hieron evidently intended the new city to serve as a monument to himself after his death and elevation to heroic status, the notion that he would have equipped it with a theatre is far from implausible, and indeed to be expected if, as is possible, his elder brother Gelon had closely associated himself with the construction of a theatre in Syracuse (**Ai**). It is also clear that Hieron energetically pro-moted the cult of Demeter and Kore, that sign and vehicle of Deinomenid religious author-ity, at a sanctuary very near the eventual theatre – probably, as is becoming increasingly clear, in the sanctuary of the theatre itself (below). A number of excavations starting in the 1990s and still in progress, conducted by the Archaeological Superintendency of Syracuse and the Archaeological Section of the Superintendency of Catania, in collaboration with the Institute of Archaeology of the University of Catania and under the direction of Maria Grazia Branciforti, has brought to light evidence for the Greek theatre that supplements other features seen by earlier investigators (Branciforti 2010, 183–5, 191–2 for a history of the earlier studies; Buda 2015 on the project to restore the monument).

The theatre rested on the slopes of the city's acropolis (the hill of Montevergine), fac-ing the south and overlooking the plain of Catania. New evidence for its Greek phase (or

phases) comes from excavation in the areas of the stage building; the central theatron; a
zone to the north of and outside the theatre; and a number of sites on the eastern side of the

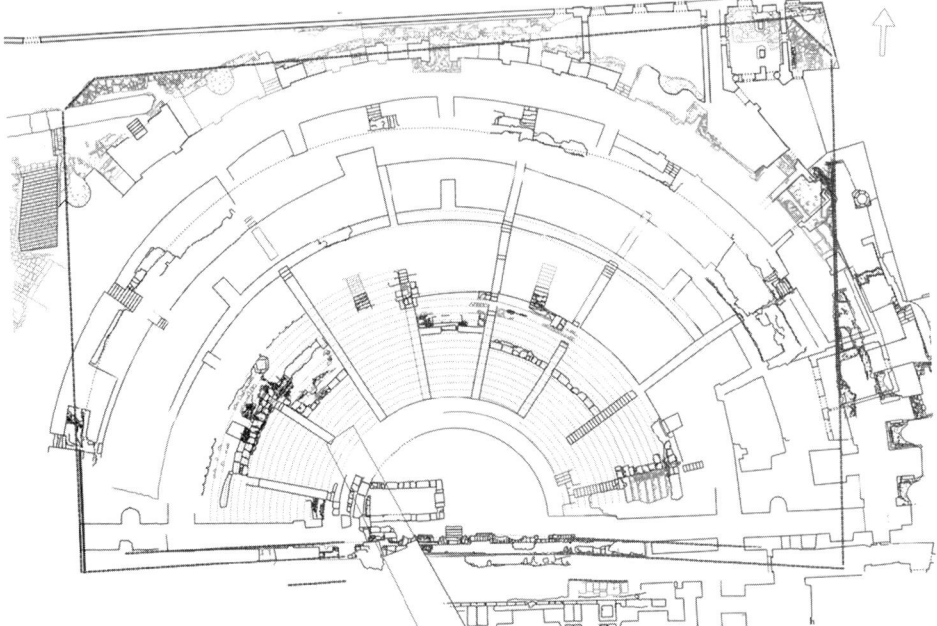

Plan of the theatre in Catane. See also Colour Plate 8 where the Greek structures are marked in red.

monument, including the eastern parodos, the continuation of which seems to have been a
major entranceway to the theatre, providing access to and from the lower part of the city.

One of the most important discoveries is a length of some 5.20 m of the eastern end of
the foundations for the stage building itself, made up of six blocks of limestone (Branciforti
2010, 195 with figs. 94–5; Taormina 2015, 321–2 with fig. 82). Its original width is hard
to gauge because the rear has been cut off by the foundations of the Roman stage building,
but one block of ca. 1.50 m may reflect the original dimension. Fragments of two Doric columns possibly associated with the stage building were found nearby, and part of a retaining
wall for the eastern parodos of the Greek theatre (in the same limestone) was also recently
identified (Taormina 2015, 322). Branciforti (2010, 196) deduces that the orchestra will
have been roughly horseshoe in shape.

As for the theatron, it is possible that some of its lower parts preserve a level of Greek
seating directly under a Roman overlay (Branciforti 2010, 196; Taormina 2015, 309–11),
positioned directly on the natural slope (thus also Libertini 1929, 15). The most recent
work in this area, still in progress, suggests that the curvature of the seating was slightly
different from the later Roman phases, but the difficulty of securing undisturbed Greek
levels and the various later reconstructions of the seating render analysis enormously
difficult. The most recent excavations, in the zone immediately to the north of the theatre where good stratigraphy is preserved, have revealed a number of structures from the

Greek period. One of these is a polygonal wall of Archaic (7th–early 6th c.) date, of which more than 12 m is preserved, plus a further 4.5 m at an obtuse angle to the south-west (Taormina 2015, 287–91). The presence here of votive objects of the same kind as found in the very rich deposit discovered under the nearby Piazza San Francesco d'Assisi suggests that this structure was part of the major Archaic temenos devoted to a female goddess (perhaps, prior to the 5th c., Hera) and where, since the early fifth century, Demeter and Kore had been worshipped (Pautasso 2010; Branciforti 2010, 209–10, 240; Taormina 2015, 290). Indeed there is no doubt that the change in dedicatory practice in evidence in the first quarter of the fifth century towards a more 'thesmophoric' cult of the Twain was the direct result of the refoundation of Catane as Aetna in 476 by Hieron (Rizza 2008). The new discoveries reveal important evidence for the cult structures and show beyond doubt that the theatre was constructed in direct association with them. This Archaic wall runs parallel to the line of the stage building, and Taormina (2015, 291 with fig. 13) has made the cogent suggestion that it may have been joined to the two stone retaining walls (discussed immediately below) when they were constructed, to form a large, roughly trapezoidal theatron.

In the late nineteenth and early twentieth century a substantial stretch (ca. 24 m) of an imposing rectilinear wall (E–W) of large quadrangular blocks of limestone (ca. 1.50 × 0.72 × 0.50 m: Anti 1947, 125) in isodomic construction, marked with the monogrammatic inscription in **3**, had been seen in the area of the western parodos (and serving as the foundation of its later phases), leading Anti (1947, 125–8) to deduce the existence of a trapezoidal theatre of unusual form in Catane by the fifth century (its most unusual feature is that the retaining walls do not converge towards the theatron, but towards the orchestra – 'uno schema trapezoidale inverso': Anti 1947, 127). This wall was rediscovered in recent excavations, to a length of some 11 m (Branciforti 2010, 191 with fig. 88). Anti had also seen a retaining wall of the same construction (N–S; ca. 24 m seen, at points to a height of around 10 m: Anti 1947, 126) that met this wall at a gently obtuse angle (Anti 1947, 125–6; Branciforti 2010, 192, fig. 89), evidently forming the south-east corner of the theatron at its western parodos. The blocks were only finished on the outside and rough on the inside, further indicating to Anti that this was an analemma wall. Anti also saw evidence for a further set of small buttress walls (ca. 1.50 m) set at right angles, internal to the corner where these two large walls meet.

These details have not yet been fully confirmed by recent research, in part because the area is often inundated by water. Most importantly, however, excavation at the eastern side of the theatre has revealed decisive evidence for the corresponding eastern retaining wall: a section of similar rectilinear wall with three courses made of large limestone blocks in isodomic construction, exactly as in the western wall (Branciforti 2010, 194 with fig. 91; Taormina 2015, 333–41). These two retaining walls stand some 32.40 m apart (Branciforti 2010, 196), suggesting a theatron of some amplitude, and one that will certainly be of a non-canonical shape (Taormina 2015, 291 fig. 13 has the clearest hypothetical plan). Branciforti (2010, 189) notes that the dimension of the structure leaves no doubt it was a theatre rather than an ekklesiasterion, odeion or telesterion. The suggestion that the structure seen by Anti formed part of the city's defensive walls (Tortorici 2008, 113–14; 2010) now appears to be definitively excluded by the discovery of the corresponding eastern wall.

The dating of these retaining walls will hold a key to the, or an, early phase of the Greek theatre in Catane. Future stratigraphic study of their foundation trenches will, it is hoped, provide conclusive evidence. But at the moment we must depend largely on general morphological and physical considerations relating to the construction of the walls and, perhaps more promisingly, on the evidence of **3**. On the former grounds Privitera (2009, 43) finds a close analogy in the design of the western retaining wall seen by Anti with that employed in the theatre of Morgantina, leading him to situate the Catane theatre in the flurry of theatre construction that took place in a number of Sicilian cities between the conclusion of the second Punic War (241) and the end of the second century. He would place it more specifically in the third century (Privitera 2009, 44), when the city once more enjoyed a certain prosperity as a *civitas decumana* under Rome.

However the epigraphic evidence (**3**), though far from easy to interpret, points rather towards a fourth-century date. Since Fiorelli (1884, reporting the opinion of A. Salinas) the inscriptions on the blocks have been interpreted as marks made as they were quarried to indicate that their destination was Catane (on mason's marks: Richter 1885; Saflund 1937; Rizza 2000, 46–50 for the evidence from defensive walls at nearby Leontini, where however some 35 different signs that include most of the letters of the alphabet appear, their function entirely unclear). The inscriptions are intriguing evidence in their own right, for it is likely that they symbolised not merely a delivery destination for the blocks of stone, but the fact that they were public property of the city of Catane: thus Anti (1947), interpreting them as both quarry marks and as sure evidence that this structure was a major public building.

Comparison with the corpus of Sicilian inscriptions can set a broad date range for the letter forms: the alpha with horizontal crossbar is attested from the second quarter of the fifth to the second half of the third century (before the first date the stroke extends diagonally downwards; after the latter it is usually broken). That produces a very broad range of ca. 460 (the city only became 'Catane' once more in 461) to ca. 200, but it can be narrowed. The very same ligature appears inside a laurel garland on the reverse of a rare bronze coin of the city, of which the obverse has an owl (*CNS* 2C; Hoover 2012, no. 631), a parallel already noted by Fiorelli (Salinas). The dating of this issue is difficult (Mirone 1918, 53) and has been put in the period between 404 and 338 (Hoover 2012, 174), more particularly under the tyranny of Mamerkos, ca. 344–337 (Hoover 2012, 161); or after 212 (Mirone 1918, 54 no. 114; Minì 1979, 129 no. 11). The latter proposal would however appear to be excluded on the palaeographical grounds already noted (the alpha also has an unbroken horizontal crossbar on the coin). The fact that the same unusual ligature abbreviation for the city name appears on both blocks and coins suggests that it may have been in use as an identifying symbol for the city during a particular period. The evidence of the coins points to a time after Catane was taken by Dionysius I in 403/2, who in reprisal for the city's support of Athens during the war with Syracuse sold its population into slavery and repopulated it with Campanian mercenaries. Then, following the naval victory of the Carthaginians over Syracuse off the coast of Catane in 396, there followed more troubled years for the city under Carthaginian influence and a series of tyrants, the last of whom was Mamerkos (ca. 344–337).

The period of Mamerkos' tyranny is a promising context for the construction of these retaining walls and hence of the theatre itself, or certainly of a significant monumental phase. For Mamerkos was evidently a tyrant who knew the value of theatre and who followed the lead set by earlier Sicilian tyrants in its use. In what was doubtless conscious emulation of Dionysius I, he combined the roles of tyrant and tragic poet (*TrGF* 87). No fragment of his tragedies survives, and the single surviving instance of his poetry is what Plutarch calls an 'insolent elegiac couplet' inscribed on the shields Mamerkos had taken in a victory over Timoleon's mercenaries (Plu. *Tim.* 31).

> καὶ γὰρ ὁ Μάμερκος, ἐπὶ τῷ ποιήματα γράφειν καὶ τραγῳδίας μέγα φρονῶν, ἐκόμπαζε νικήσας τοὺς μισθοφόρους, καὶ τὰς ἀσπίδας ἀναθεὶς τοῖς θεοῖς ἐλεγεῖον ὑβριστικὸν ἐπέγραψε·
>
> τάσδ' ὀστρειογραφεῖς καὶ χρυσελεφαντηλέκτρους ἀσπίδας ἀσπιδίοις εἵλομεν εὐτελέσιν.

> For Mamerkos, who valued himself highly as a writer of poems and tragedies, boasted of his victory over the mercenaries, and in dedicating their shields to the gods inscribed the following insolent couplet: 'These bucklers, purple-painted, decked with ivory, gold, and amber we captured with our simple little shields.'

We are very poorly informed about Mamerkos and his career as tyrant of Catane, and we first hear of him near the end of his story, when, under attack from Timoleon, he fled to Messana, which was under his friend, the tyrant Hippo. Hippo was executed by the Messanians in their theatre (**Axvii**) 'as at a most beautiful spectacle' (ὡς ἐπὶ θέαμα κάλλιστον), while Mamerkos himself was put on trial soon after in the theatre of Syracuse, when he is reported to have 'tried to rehearse a speech composed by him a long time before; but being received with noise and clamour, and seeing that the assembly was inexorable, he flung away his cloak, ran right across the theatre, and dashed his head against one of the stone benches, in an attempt to kill himself. However, he was not so fortunate as to die in this way, but was taken away, still living, and crucified like a robber' (Plu. *Tim.* 34.6–7; **Ai 3**). One of the most striking things we know about Mamerkos is that he was not ethnically Greek, but an Italiote (Nep. *Tim.* 2.4) – probably a Campanian (Poccetti 1989, 119) or Lucanian; perhaps an Etruscan (Sordi 1992, 113–15). His attachment to Greek culture, and to theatre as the key institution of Greek culture, was however clearly an important part of his entrepreneurial toolkit. He had attained competence in the highest realms of Greek cultural expertise, and did so for political ends. He may have given his son the élite Greek name of Alkippos, although the latest epigraphical view holds that the name should be read as Kipos, elsewhere known as Etruscan / Oscan, including in Entella (*SEG* 42, 291; Poccetti 1989, 120).

The practice attested by the passage of Plutarch above for Mamerkos of inscribing poetry on dedicated weapons from a defeated enemy is eminently Greek. In these verses we see the Italiote *capitano di ventura* occupying the cultural high ground of his defeated enemy, the Corinthian general Timoleon. He uses the medium skilfully, in a tradition of calculated rebranding that aligns him with Hieron before him, who used poetry to brand his rule as a legitimate monarchy (**VI A**). Thus he categorises his opponents as *misthophoroi*, mercenaries. For all we can tell, Mamerkos himself started his career in Sicily as a gun for hire, and here he is clearly rescripting himself as an established ruler. The fact that the shields of his men were 'simple', 'cheap' even (εὐτελής), while those of the enemy were made of purple, ivory, gold and amber, works against the claim that Mamerkos and his men were driven by motives of material gain. In fact, the couplet sets up a sharp opposition between the luxury of the defeated opponent and the frugality of the victor, and aligns Mamerkos with an adherence to Dorian and specifically Spartan customs. This may well deliberately hark back to the image factory of Hieron, who recreated Catane as Aetna in an idealised Dorian mould. It is clear at any rate that Mamerkos was an immensely skilled manipulator of the ideological possibilities of Greek poetry, and seems very likely to have invested in theatre and drama in the city over which he ruled for less than a decade.

We must await further evidence (of which the prospects are quite good) for more secure dating of the Greek phase or phases, but at the moment it looks on balance most likely that the unusual ('reverse') trapezoidal theatre of Catane with stone walls dates to the second half of the fourth century, perhaps the product of the leadership of the tyrant Mamerkos. But a much earlier phase cannot be ruled out: the existence of an important sanctuary on the site since the Archaic period and the fact it lay within the Archaic city walls are consistent with the possibility that already in the 470s Hieron had a theatre built on the slopes of the acropolis of the new city designed to make him immortal. The water that periodically floods the theatre comes from a subterranean aquifer that popular tradition has long, and perhaps correctly, identified with the river Amenas (Chiavetta 2015, 29), the river that features prominently in Pindar's *Pythian* 1 for Hieron. By etymologising the name of this river for the 'eternal remaining' of the new city in the Dorian tradition (αἰεὶ μένειν l. 64, αἰεὶ δὲ . . . Ἀμένα παρ' ὕδωρ l. 68) the poet rhetorically granted the new foundation the permanence and Hellenicity its founder so desired (Dougherty 1993, 94–5). If, as seems very likely, the Amenas was indeed in the vicinity of the Greek theatre and its adjacent sanctuary in antiquity, it would have made an ideal site for the performance not only of Aeschylus' foundation tragedy but of Pindar's foundation epinikion.

The popularity of theatre in the wider area in the fourth century is also attested by a number of terracotta figurines and masks relating to Middle Comedy found, significantly, in a settlement rather than a funerary context at the site of the small city of Adranon on the southern slopes of Etna, less than 30 km to the north-west of Catane (Lamagna 2000; Falco 1997; from the same area fragments of red-figured vases with comic scenes of the later fourth century: Barresi 2002). The city was founded by Dionysius I around 400 (D.S. 14.37.5).

Axiv: Selinus

1. *Diegesis* on the *Iambs* of Callimachus 9, ll. 12–24 (= Call. fr. 201 Pfeiffer of *Iamb* 11).
Callimachus wrote his *Iambs* probably around the middle of the 3rd c. (soon after 268: Cameron 1995). The *Diegesis* is a prose summary of the *Iambs* known from a 1st–2nd c. AD papyrus that draws on earlier and more scholarly works (Harder 2012 I, 70). Text: Pfeiffer.

ἀλλ' οὐ τὸν Ὑψᾶν, ὃς τὸ σᾶμά μευ (Call. fr. 201 Pf.) διημαρτημένως λέγεται παροιμία 'ἁρπαγὰ τὰ Κοννάρου'· 'Κοννίδα' γὰρ χρὴ λέγειν. [15] ἐντεῦθεν γὰρ παρῆλθεν· Κοννίδας μέτοικος ἐν Σελινοῦντι πλουτήσας ἐκ πορνοβοσκίας παρὰ μὲν τὸν ἄλλον χρόνον .εν ἐφήμιζεν, ὡς τὴν οὐσίαν τῇ τε Ἀφροδίτῃ καὶ τοῖς φίλοις [20] διανεμεῖν. τελευτήσαντος δὲ αὐτοῦ ἡ διαθήκη εὑρέθη περιέχουσα 'ἁρπαγὰ τὰ Κοννίδα'· ὅθεν ὁ δῆμος ἐξελθὼν τοῦ θεάτρου ἥρπασεν τὰ Κοννίδα. Σελινοῦς δὲ πόλις Σικελίας.

18 χρόνον .εν A letter or ligature cannot be read before εν. Possibly αἰὲν from the text of Callimachus, so Pfeiffer (but Kerkhecker 1999, 213 says this does not fit the traces)   ἐνεφήμιζεν Gallavotti   οὐσίαν Norsa-Vitelli   αισιαν Π   αἰσίαν Kerkhecker

'No, by Hypsas, which (passes by) [or you who (pass by)] my tomb …' (Call. fr. 201 Pf.). The proverb 'The possessions of Konnaros are up for grabs' is wrongly quoted. One should say 'Konnidas'.[15] This is how it came into use: Konnidas was a metic in Selinus who became rich from running a brothel. During his lifetime he used to promise that he would [20] divide his property between Aphrodite and loved ones (or perhaps, reading αἰσίαν, 'that he would distribute their due share to Aphrodite and loved ones'), but when he died his will was found to include the statement 'The possessions of Konnidas are up for grabs'. And so the populace left the theatre and seized the possessions of Konnidas. Selinus is a city in Sicily.

2. **Timaeus, *Sicilian History?*, FGrH 566 F 148 (= Zen. *Proverbs* 1.31)**. Timaeus of Tauromenium in eastern Sicily (ca. 350–260) is the most important historian of Western Greece. He wrote his *Sicilian History* – going up to the death of Agathocles in 289/8 – in exile in Athens some time after ca. 315. The reference to Callimachus' *Iambs* in Zenobius' introduction will be **1**. Text: Leutsch and Schneidewin.

ἁρπαγὰ τὰ Κιννάρου· ταύτης μὲν μέμνηται Καλλίμαχος ἐν Ἰάμβοις· Τίμαιος δὲ ἔφη, ὅτι Κίνναρος ἐγένετο πορνοβοσκὸς Σελινούσιος· πλουσιώτατος οὖν ἐκ τῆς ἐργασίας γενόμενος, ζῶν μὲν ἐπηγγέλλετο τὴν οὐσίαν ἱερὰν τῇ Ἀφροδίτῃ καταλεῖψαι, τελευτῶν δὲ τὰ ὄντα προύθηκεν εἰς ἁρπαγήν.

'The possessions of Kinnaros are up for grabs'. Callimachus has mentioned this in his *Iambs*. But Timaeus says that Kinnaros was a Selinuntine brothel keeper. Becoming very rich from the business, while alive he made it known that he left his property as sacred to Aphrodite, but in dying he gave his possessions up to seizure.

Selinus was the most westerly Greek colony in Sicily, founded ca. 650 (D.S. 13.59.4, but see Hornblower 2008, 288–9 on the divergent Thucydidean date, 6.4.2, of ca. 628/7) by Megara Hyblaea (**Aiii**), itself founded by Megara in mainland Greece – on the confines of Elymian and Phoenician territories. Around the middle of the sixth century, Selinus in turn founded Heraclea Minoa (for its theatre see **A Introduction**), though by the early fifth it was under the control of Acragas.

According to a commentary on the Eleventh *Iamb* of Callimachus (**1**) that draws on Timaeus (**2**), Selinus had a theatre in the time of one Konnidas, an immigrant and wealthy brothel keeper in the city. Callimachus dramatises Konnidas in the *Iamb*, who featured in a proverb ἁρπαγὰ τὰ Κοννάρου, 'snatching the things of Konnaros'. Whether it was Callimachus or the *Diegesis* that corrected the tradition which maintained that the correct name was Konnaros is not entirely clear (Kerkhecker 1999, 214). Konnidas speaks after death from his tomb near the city of Selinus (the river Hypsas passed some 3 km to the east of the city). He was said to have been a metic who enriched himself in Selinus as a brothel keeper. Timaeus (**2**), doubtless a source for **1**, included the story of how on his death, against his formerly declared intentions, he left his accumulated wealth to open seizure rather than dedicating it to Aphrodite (**1** adds καὶ τοῖς φίλοις, probably with the primary sense of 'and her loved ones' rather than 'and his friends', with reference to those who had frequented Konnidas' brothel).

Robertson (2010, 60–2) argues that the whole story is the garbled residue of an aetiology for the important Selinuntine festival of the Kotyttia, in which ritual snatching of cakes and nuts featured (Jameson et al. 1993, 23–5 on the ἁρπαγὰ Κοτυττίοις). He notes that the name given to the brothel keeper by what might be called the vulgate tradition – Konnaros – is the word for the jujube tree (κόνναρος), and suggests that the fruit of this tree may itself have been snatched at this festival, or made into something like a cake to be snatched. The theory is attractive, but requires us to assume that the meaning of the snatching ritual was already lost to Timaeus, and not recovered by the indefatigable scholar of aetiology Callimachus, who has substituted for the strange name Konnaros ('Jujube') the more intelligible Konnidas (Robertson 2010, 62).

Another possibility is that the story of Konnaros'/Konnidas' promised gift to Aphrodite alludes to a form of sacred prostitution (D'Alessio 1996, 633; Iannucci 2010) – the 'possessions of Konnaros' being his portfolio of prostitutes, to be dedicated on death to the goddess who oversaw their sphere of activity. Iannucci (2010) locates **1** and **2** within the cult of Aphrodite in Selinus, proposing that Temple E was hers. This stood on the eastern hill of Selinus alongside the older Temple F (ca. 520), which with its unusual, high intercolumnial wall that closed off access to the rear of the temple looks likely to have been designed for mystery cult. Iannucci suggests that Selinus replicated the cult structure of its metropolis, mainland Megara, where a temple of Aphrodite Epistrophia stood on the acropolis beside one of Dionysus Nyktelinos (Paus. 1.40.6). A problem with this cogent idea is that Temple E is generally agreed to belong to Hera, on the basis of a dedication found inside it (*IGDS* 56).

The detail that the brothel keeper's last will was read out in the theatre of Selinus may have featured in Callimachus, but is likely also to go back to Timaeus. Even if the story is a fabrication by Timaeus or his source, the fabrication assumes the existence of a theatre at the time of the story, and it would serve the interests of a fabricator to include realistic detail. It may have been introduced because the Selinuntine theatre was known to be a place for the transaction of public business, operating in the familiar capacity of an assembly space, and the reading of a will of concern to the whole community fell into the category of action appropriate to such a space. If Robertson's interpretation is valid, another possibility is that the theatre was a site of the festival Kotyttia and reference to it has somehow persisted in the story explaining the proverb. And if Iannucci is right to bring the story into the orbit of Aphrodite – and perhaps Dionysus with her – the presence of a theatre may likewise reflect its role in associated cult activity.

The time at which the story is supposed to have taken place is difficult to pinpoint. Timaeus' *History* treated the Carthaginian sack of Selinus in 409 (*FGrH* 566 F 103), which might have offered a context for the story. The reference will certainly be to a time prior to the fourth century, since the account is located by Timaeus in the unspecified and seemingly somewhat distant past, and the fourth century itself is an unlikely time for the construction of a theatre, given that Selinus was sacked by Carthage in 409 and resettled only later in the fourth century by a mixed population of Greek and Punic refugees, under Punic control. While a theatre in Punic territory is not entirely implausible, a fifth-century date for the story and the theatre is much more likely.

No archaeological evidence for a theatre has been produced, but Hulot and Fougères (1910, 152 with plate 2) hypothesised a possible site near the eastern entrance to the city, which connects the city via a sacred way to the temples (including E and F) on the eastern hill. They refer to a circular recess seen in the slope of the plateau and explain the absence of visible remains due to its being a fifth-century theatre made without use of shaped stone. A circular pattern would tend to imply a structure of fourth-century (or later) date, and might perhaps reflect the remodelling of a later phase.

Selinus produced the important poet of (probably) iambs, Aristoxenos, said to be older than Epicharmus (**Aii**). The nature of his work is very unclear, but was quite possibly performed in a theatrical or at least festival context. The city was also the home of an important innovator in music and poetry of the later fifth century, Telestes, best known for his dithyrambs, but quite possibly a practitioner in a variety of genres, including comedy. He probably left his city definitively after the Carthaginian sack of 409 (Berlinzani 2008), but the (limited) evidence in any case suggests the peripatetic career expected of an important international poet (Stewart 2017, 81). He won a victory in Athens in 402/1 (*Marm. Par.* 65). The one surviving fragment of the *Life of Telestes* written by Aristoxenus of Taras informs us that he also visited Italy (fr. 117 Wehrli), and the report that Aristratos of Sicyon (mid 4th c.) had a statue of the poet erected in Sicyon (Plin. *HN* 35.36.109) implies a visit there. Another major poet who may have had connections to Selinus is Epicharmus. A funerary stele from Selinus dating to the second quarter of the fifth century reads 'I belong to Epicharmos son of Mnasandridas' (*IGDS* 76). The rarity of the name Epicharmos in Sicily makes some connection with the comic poet likely. It seems improbable that the Selinuntine tomb is that of the poet himself (suggested by Poli Palladini 2013, 44), but the tradition that makes Megara Hyblaea – metropolis of Selinus – the native city of Epicharmus, does point to a family association with the city (**Aiii**).

A large rectangular structure has recently been identified in the central urban sanctuary zone of Selinus (Marconi 2014; Marconi and Scahill 2015). This has been described as a 'theatral area', rather than a theatre, largely because of its non-canonical shape, relatively small size (it could accommodate some 500 people) and its close association with the sanctuary complex (on such 'ritual theatres' or 'theatral spaces' more widely see Nielsen 2002). It dates to around the end of the sixth century and apparently served as a viewing area for ritual performances and processions, notably for a cult of Demeter Thesmophoros in the adjacent Temple R. Marconi (2014) reports on the discovery of aulos fragments dedicated in this area, possibly associated with the performances that took place there. It is difficult to judge whether this could be the theatre referred to in **1**. It is far from the site on the eastern hill where the circular depression was viewed, and may be thought unsuitable for the sort of public meeting involved in the story of the brothel keeper's will.

Axv: Agyrion. Diodorus of Sicily, *Library of History* 16.83.3. Diodorus' *Bibliotheke* or *Library* was a universal history from mythical times to 60, written ca. 50–30. The period of prosperity to which Diodorus refers is under the leadership of Timoleon in Syracuse (345–336), who established peaceful conditions and repopulated the island. Agyrion is the native city of Diodorus himself. A Sicel centre, it was made a colony of Syracuse under Timoleon ca. 339 and undertook a programme of major civic works. Text: Fischer.

> ἐν δὲ ταῖς ἐλάττοσι πόλεσιν, ἐν αἷς ἡ τῶν Ἀγυριναίων καταριθμεῖται, μετασχοῦσα τῆς τότε κληρουχίας διὰ τὴν προειρημένην ἐκ τῶν καρπῶν εὐπορίαν, θέατρον μὲν κατεσκεύασε μετὰ τὸ τῶν Συρακοσίων κάλλιστον τῶν κατὰ Σικελίαν, θεῶν τε ναοὺς καὶ βουλευτήριον καὶ ἀγοράν, ἔτι δὲ πύργων ἀξιολόγους κατασκευὰς καὶ <κατὰ> τάφους πυραμίδων πολλῶν καὶ μεγάλων διαφόρων ταῖς φιλοτεχνίαις.

> Among the lesser cities is to be reckoned Agyrion, although when it had its share of the influx of cleruchs due to the agricultural prosperity I have already mentioned, it built the finest theatre of those throughout Sicily after that of Syracuse, as well as temples of the gods, a council chamber, and an agora. There were also noteworthy constructions of towers, as well as pyramidal monuments of architectural distinction over tombs, many and great.

In his account of the period of great revival and prosperity experienced by Sicily under the Corinthian general Timoleon, who arrived in 344, expelled Dionysius II from Syracuse and repopulated the island, Diodorus reports the effect on his own hometown, the relatively minor city of Agyrion in central Sicily. Like others, it marked its new surge in prosperity and civic autonomy by a programme of urban development and associated monumental architecture, including the construction of a theatre (Gallo 2003; Marconi 2012, 182). Diodorus puts the theatre first in his list of the new structures undertaken in this project, granting it alone elaboration in the detail that it was 'the finest theatre of those throughout Sicily after that of Syracuse'. Local pride doubtless plays a significant part in this assessment (Tosi 2003, 593), and it is perhaps noteworthy that Diodorus stresses beauty rather than size in his bold comparison to the Syracusan theatre. But equally, Diodorus' local origins ensure that he knew what he was talking about. The comparison also implies without exactly specifying that there were many theatres in Sicily at the time of its construction (rather than at the time of writing in the first century, when they were certainly very numerous). The construction of a number of other stone theatres has been associated with the Timoleontic period (Gallo 2003, 539), although a recent reassessment of the evidence is tending to push many of those proposed to a much later date, the end of the second and start of the first century (**A Introduction**).

Agyrion had been a Sicel centre, though already heavily influenced by Greek culture in the Archaic period. Under Timoleon the tyranny of Apolloniades was brought to an end and the city was refounded, and made either a colony or a subordinate ally of Syracuse. It is hard to judge whether it was effectively a fully Greek city at the time of the construction of its theatre, but an appetite for theatre in places with mixed or largely non-Greek ethnic and cultural traditions is a striking feature of the Sicilian and South Italian picture (**A Introduction**).

The site of the theatre in Agyrion has been plausibly hypothesised on the basis of an unpublished history of the town written by G. P. Sinopoli between 1929 and 1933 that is kept in the Biblioteca Comunale of Agira (Sinopoli 1929–1933). Sinopoli drew on a document dating to 1225, that was destroyed by fire in 1904, which spoke of a Church of S. Erasmus *juxta proscenio* and of a church of SS. Trinità (S. Agostino) 'in chirchia', which it has been suggested might derive from the word κερκίδες (Patanè 1992, 78): until 1876 the Discesa Roselli that passed by S. Agostino from S. Pietro was made up of high, wide, old steps carved into rock. The site of these churches forms a natural basin on the hillside with an open space facing west. Various other topographical indications and notices of random archaeological finds, such as the remains of seats in the lower part of the ex-Augustinian convent and a large mask with open mouth found carved into the wall of a building attached to S. Pietro, have been adduced in support (Favaloro 1922). Sinopoli also had oral reports from those associated with the Augustinian convent that materials for its construction, as for that of the bell-tower of S. Pietro in 1838, had been found on the site itself.

Axvi: Leontini. Plutarch, *Life of Dion* 42.8–43.3. Written ca. 115 AD. Target date: 356. Plutarch draws on a range of sources close in time to the events, including Dion's older contemporary and opponent Philistus (**VI E**), Timonides of Leucas (cited by Plu. *Dio* 22.5 as a supporter of Dion), letters that circulated under Plato's name in the fourth century, and Timaeus of Tauromenium (late 4th–early 3rd c.), although he has been criticised for the way he handled the evidence of contradictory accounts (Sanders 2008, 193–6). Dion of Syracuse, brother-in-law and son-in-law of Dionysius I, friend and student of Plato and defender of his philosophy since Plato's early involvement with Dionysius I, was banished in 366 because of his attempts to transform the despotic rule of Dionysius II according to Platonic political ideals. In 357 he returned from exile with a modest military force that gathered considerable support from various Greek cities including, eventually, the citizens of Syracuse itself. Dion was elected to lead Syracuse but his proposed reforms lacked broad appeal and he withdrew to Leontini (356) after civil conflict broke out with the more democratically inclined Heracleides. A delegation approaches Dion in Leontini to ask him to return and help eject Dionysius II from Syracuse. Text: Ziegler.

> εὐθὺς οὖν ἡγεῖτο πρὸς τὴν ἐκκλησίαν αὐτοῖς, καὶ συνδραμόντων προθύμως, οἱ
> περὶ τὸν Ἀρχωνίδην καὶ τὸν Ἑλλάνικον εἰσελθόντες ἐξήγγειλάν τε βραχέως τὸ
> μέγεθος τῶν κακῶν καὶ παρεκάλουν τοὺς ξένους ἐπαμῦναι τοῖς Συρακοσίοις, τὸ
> μνησικακεῖν ἀφέντας, ὡς μείζονα δίκην δεδωκότων αὐτῶν, ἢ λαβεῖν ἂν οἱ κακῶς
> πεπονθότες ἠξίωσαν. 43.1 παυσαμένων δὲ τούτων, σιγὴ μὲν εἶχε πολλὴ τὸ θέατρον·
> ἀναστάντος δὲ τοῦ Δίωνος καὶ λέγειν ἀρξαμένου πολλὰ τῶν δακρύων ἐκπίπτοντα
> 43.2 τὴν φωνὴν ἐπέσχεν· οἱ δὲ ξένοι παρεκάλουν θαρρεῖν καὶ συνήχθοντο. μικρὸν

οὖν ἀναλαβὼν ἐκ τοῦ πάθους ἑαυτὸν ὁ Δίων, Ἄνδρες, ἔφη, Πελοποννήσιοι καὶ σύμμαχοι, βουλευσομένους ὑμᾶς ἐνταῦθα περὶ ὑμῶν αὐτῶν ⁴³·³ συνήγαγον.

At once, then, Dion led them to the assembly, the people eagerly gathered there, Archonides and Hellanikos with their entourages came forward, reported briefly on the scale of the disaster, and called upon the mercenaries to put away their feelings of resentment and come to the defence of the Syracusans, since those who had wronged them had suffered a heavier punishment than those who had been wronged would have thought it right to exact. ⁴³·¹ When they had stopped speaking, there was a profound silence in the theatre. Then Dion rose and began to speak, but copious tears ⁴³·² checked his utterance. But his mercenaries sympathised with him and encouraged him to take heart. Accordingly, after he had recovered a little from his emotion, he said: 'Men of the Peloponnese and allies, I have brought you together here to deliberate upon your own course of action. '

The territory of Leontini, an early colony founded in the last quarter of the eighth century by Chalcidians from Sicilian Naxos, included much of the rich plain of Catania. Some 40 km north-west of Syracuse, the city was subjected to a series of drastic population transplantations in the fifth and fourth centuries (*IACP* 209). Politically it was dominated by tyrants in the early period, though its later arrangements are unclear. Leontini's mistreatment by Syracuse was the pretext for the Athenian Sicilian expeditions of 427 and 415, and Robinson (2011, 103–5) has plausibly argued that a period of democracy is likely at least in the last quarter of the century, when the rhetorician Gorgias of Leontini was at the height of his powers and said by Plato to have long experience addressing the masses in assemblies, courts and council meetings (Pl. *Grg.* 452e, 454b: ἐν τοῖς δικαστηρίοις καὶ ἐν τοῖς ἄλλοις ὄχλοις, 456b), and may date from as early as the overthrow of the tyrants in the 460s.

The public meeting which Dion convenes in Leontini to hear the overtures from those seeking to eject Dionysius II from Syracuse is described as an 'assembly' (ἐκκλησία), with reference both to its place and its function and then, immediately after, the location of the meeting is named as the theatre (τὸ θέατρον) of Leontini. The use of the city's theatre as its place of political assembly is likely to reflect the reality of the fourth century, attested elsewhere for western Greek cities (**A Introduction**; **Ai**; **Axvii**). Enthusiastic locals have made tentative identifications of the site of the theatre on the hillside of S. Mauro to the south of the modern city, but no good evidence has been forthcoming.

Axvii: Messana. Plutarch, *Life of Timoleon* 34.3–5. Written ca. 115 AD. Target date: ca. 337. The *Timoleon* is widely held to draw heavily on Timaeus of Tauromenium (late 4ᵗʰ – early 3ʳᵈ c.), though Westlake (1938) argued for the primacy of a Peripatetic biography, itself based on Timaeus, with additional direct consultation of Timaeus. In his campaign to expel tyrants from the Greek cities of Sicily, the Corinthian general Timoleon pursues Mamerkos, tyrant of Catane (**Axiii**), to his place of refuge with Hippo, tyrant of Messana, and besieges the city with both men in it. After the capture of Hippo recounted below, Mamerkos surrenders and faces a similar fate in the theatre of Syracuse (**Ai 3**). Text: Ziegler.

Μάμερκος δὲ δυσθυμῶν ταῖς ἐλπίσιν, ἔπλει μὲν εἰς Ἰταλίαν, ὡς Λευκανοὺς ἐπάξων
Τιμολέοντι καὶ Συρακοσίοις· ἐπεὶ δ' ἀποστρέψαντες οἱ σὺν αὐτῷ τὰς τριήρεις καὶ
πλεύσαντες εἰς Σικελίαν τῷ Τιμολέοντι τὴν Κατάνην παρέδωκαν, ἀναγκασθεὶς
καὶ αὐτὸς εἰς Μεσσήνην κατέφυγε πρὸς Ἵππωνα [4] τὸν τυραννοῦντα τῆς
πόλεως. ἐπελθόντος δὲ τοῦ Τιμολέοντος αὐτοῖς καὶ πολιορκοῦντος ἔκ τε γῆς καὶ
θαλάττης, ὁ μὲν Ἵππων ἀποδιδράσκων ἐπὶ νεώς ἥλω, καὶ παραλαβόντες αὐτὸν
οἱ Μεσσήνιοι, καὶ τοὺς παῖδας ἐκ τῶν διδασκαλείων ὡς ἐπὶ θέαμα κάλλιστον
τὴν τοῦ τυράννου τιμωρίαν [5] ἀγαγόντες εἰς θέατρον, ᾐκίσαντο καὶ διέφθειραν·

With his hopes disappointed, Mamerkos sailed to Italy with the thought of
bringing Lucanians against Timoleon and Syracuse. But when his followers
turned back the triremes, sailed to Sicily and handed over Catane to Timoleon,
Mamerkos himself was also compelled to seek refuge in Messene with [4] the
tyrant of the city, Hippo. Timoleon attacked them and besieged the city by land
and sea, and Hippo was captured as he was trying to run away by ship. The
Messenians took him into the theatre, bringing the children from their schools,
as though to a most beautiful spectacle, to witness the [5] tyrant's punishment,
and tortured and put him to death.

The city of Zancle, on the Sicilian side of the straits between the toe of Italy and the eastern
corner of Sicily, was founded in the eighth century by Chalcidians from Kyme in Italy,
later joined by other Chalcidians and Euboeans; although another tradition holds that it
was founded by Sicilian Naxos (*IACP* 234). The city's name was changed from Zancle to
Messana around 488, after Hippocrates tyrant of Gela betrayed the Zanclaians to a group of
Samian aristocrats fleeing Samos after the Ionian revolt, who were in turn promptly driven
out by the tyrant Anaxilas of Rhegium (**Aiii**). Anaxilas refounded the city as Messana. A
tradition of participation by Messanians in choral performance at a festival in Rhegium is
attested for the fifth century by Pausanias (5.25.2–5), and has been plausibly related to the
city's refounding by Anaxilas (Cordano 1980).

After the fall of the sons of Anaxilas in the 460s the city was chosen as the place where
the mercenaries of the ejected tyrannies (of Syracuse, Gela, Himera, Acragas, Rhegium as
well as Messana) were settled (D.S. 11.76.5–6). It was under the control of Syracuse early
in the fourth century, destroyed by the Carthaginians in 396 and repopulated by Dionysius
in 395. Its constitutional arrangements thereafter are unclear until we learn that the tyrant
Hippo was in power some time prior to 337.

Although this account of the manner in which the Messanians employed their theatre is
decidedly lurid, this need not undermine its basic factuality. That the theatre served, even
under a tyranny, as a multi-functional political space is consistent with attested Sicilian
practice elsewhere (**Ai**). Thus while the action described has something of the character of
an impromptu uprising against tyrannical power, it also suggests a reflex to employ their
theatre as a place of juridical activity on the part of the Messanians. Whatever the historicity of the further detail that children were brought into the theatre from their schoolrooms
to witness Hippo's punishment, the fact that Plutarch ironically ascribes the motive 'as to
a most beautiful spectacle' (ὡς ἐπὶ θέαμα κάλλιστον) points both to the primary function
of the city's theatre as an institution of spectacle, and the extent to which politics and theatre interacted in the Western Greek context in particular (**A Introduction**). Only limited

excavation of the Greek city has been attempted and many of its remains lie some 4–5 m below the present surface level, but in recent years evidence for a theatre of Roman date has emerged under the palazzo Comunale of Messina, and there are as yet unsubstantiated suggestions that, like so many others, this sat above a Greek predecessor (Bacci and Spigo 1991; Tosi 2003, 609). A nearby necropolis has revealed evidence of red-figured ceramic of the mid fourth century, some of it produced locally or in Syracuse, with subjects drawn from the world of theatre and Dionysiac myth, that show affinities to the material from Lipari (Spigo 1992–1993; 2003, 108–9). A notable example is the calyx krater of ca. 330 excavated in a cemetery and attributed to the Manfria painter, which has a comic scene depicted on a stage and is thought by Handley (1997, 194–6) and Green (2010, 82–6 with fig. 6) to owe its inspiration to Diphilus' *Kleroumenoi* (Milazzo Antiquarium 11039).

Axviii: The Antiope Krater, 390–380 (by painting style).

> Sicilian red-figured calyx krater, Dirce Painter (name vase).
> H. 0.52 m.
> Found at Palazzolo Acreide in or shortly before December 1875 and acquired by the Berlin Museum in 1876.
> Berlin F 3296; *LCS* 203 no. 27; *LCS* Suppl. 3.99; *RVSIS* pl. 61; *LIMC* Antiope I.6, Dirke 5, Lykos 1.1; *CFST* S 5; Taplin 2007, 188–9. See also Colour Plate 9.

Sicilian red-figured vasepainting begins about 400. Its similarities with Apulian and Lucanian production are strong enough that one can speak of red-figure technique 'spreading' from Southern Italy to Sicily, but Sicilian production reveals a 'substantial autonomy'

(Sisto 2003, 121) in its choice of shape, its choice of subjects, and in its treatment of its subjects. These features are evident in vasepainting with theatre-related subjects, which appear by preference on (usually large) calyx kraters (five times more often than in Apulian), are generally more original in their choice of subject, and, in some cases, go a good deal farther than any other West Greek fabric in emphasising a connection with tragic theatre. The most unambiguously tragic of West Greek vasepaintings are produced in Sicily in about 330 (**Axix**), but tragic subjects, tragic motifs, and a dramatic style (Sicilian has, for example, many more frontal and three-quarter faces), are remarkably strong already in the first generation of Sicilian vasepainters. This vase is a particularly good example of a vasepainting that depicts not tragedy, but myth, while nonetheless depicting a myth so as to evoke a very specific canonical tragic narrative of that myth.

Euripides produced a tragedy named *Antiope* probably sometime between 411–408 (E. *TrGF Antiope* T ii; Collard 2004, 269). More fragments of this play survive than for any other lost tragedy, enough to show that Euripides' version of the myth completely dominated later accounts. Among the mythographers who recount the entire tale, Hyginus (*Fab.* 8) is probably the most faithful to Euripides:

> Antiope was the daughter of Nycteus who was king in Boeotia. Jupiter attracted by her outstanding beauty made her pregnant. When her father threatened her because he wished to punish her for her disgrace, Antiope fled. By chance Epopeus of Sicyon was staying in the place she came to. He took the woman home and married her. Nycteus bore this ill and as he died he made his brother Lycus, to whom he left his kingdom, swear that Antiope would not go unpunished. After Nycteus' death Lycus came to Sicyon, killed Epopeus and dragged Antiope to Cithaeron in chains. She gave birth to twins and abandoned them. But a cowherd raised them and called them Zethus and Amphion. Antiope was given over to Dirce, Nycteus' wife, for torture. But when she got the chance Antiope fled. She came to her sons. Zethus supposing her to be a runaway slave would not take her in. Dirce was brought to the same place in her celebration of Bacchic rites for Dionysus. There she discovered Antiope and as she was dragging her off to her death the cowherd who had raised the young men informed them that she was their mother. They quickly followed, snatched their mother away and killed Dirce by tying her to a bull by her hair. Though they wanted to kill Lycus, Mercury forbade them and at the same time ordered Lycus to cede his kingdom to Amphion.

The Dirce Painter clearly depicts two scenes from this myth on three different planes. Above a tree on the left one sees the prostrate body of a dead or dying woman. Her head hangs limply to the side and her eyes are closed. She has evidently been dragged by the rampant bull above her and whose hind legs are still planted on her stomach. Traces in added white of ropes tying the woman to the horns of the bull were at least once visible on the pot (Dilthey 1878, 43 n. 3; they are not visible on any photographs). Since Dirce is the only woman in myth to die this way, there can be no doubt about her identity.

Immediately to the right of the bull and on a somewhat higher plane we see the upper body of Hermes (traces of his kerykeion in added white were visible to Dilthey 1878, 43 n. 3). He looks down upon a group of figures on the rightmost and lowest plane. Under an arch, overhung in the middle by a panther skin, we see four figures on a rocky platform. Two beardless youths stand naked but for elaborate boots and the wind-blown cloak of the youth to the right who holds a sword. They subdue an older (bearded) man and are clearly threatening his life. The older man wears elaborately decorated costume with sleeves of the sort normally associated with orientals and tragic actors. He holds up his arm in a gesture that may suggest an appeal for aid or mercy. To the right a woman runs out making the hand to mouth gesture that shows anxiety and alarm (cf. Jocasta in **Axix**). Each of the three males under the arch looks to one of the other three: the leftmost youth to Dirce, the kneeling man to Hermes, and the rightmost youth to the running woman beside him.

The story of Antiope was not much told in antiquity and we have insufficient traces of any pre-Euripidean version to be sure that the particular form of Dirce's death, being dragged by a bull, was original with the tragic poet. For the configuration of Dirce and the bull we can be sure that the painter's imagination is uninformed by the visual impact of a tragic performance. In Euripides' play this episode was described by a messenger. One small detail may, however, register the impact of the messenger's verbal description. There is a branch caught in Dirce's hair that Joyce takes to be the bedraggled traces of the garland worn by Dirce while performing bacchic rites (2001, 225). This is no wreath but evidently intended to show a fragment of a bush (like that just below Dirce) that got caught in her hair as she was dragged. The stem of the branch is too thick for a garland and there is nothing garland-like about the three branches of leaves that issue from it. It is, moreover, not depicted as ivy, the plant that one would expect a bacchant to wear: it has not the distinctive heart shape of ivy in Greek iconography (such as we see in the decoration under the rim of the krater). A fragment of the messenger speech of Euripides' play included a description (*TrGF* F 221) of the way the bull circled about dragging 'woman, rock, oak along with it as it ranged about continually' (Collard's translation, though I suspect that γυναῖκα πέτραν δρῦν μεταλλάσσων ἀεί implies something like 'continually scrambling together woman, rock, oak'; Taplin 1998, 34 translates 'dragging at everything, rock, woman, oak, juggling with them all'). This detail may have been inspired by this line, but there is certainly no studious imitation. The leaves are not oak either.

By contrast the visual impact of a production of the play is very strongly marked in the tableau to the right of the vasepainting. As often with dramas set in rustic environs, a cave formed the backdrop to the performance of Euripides' play (Collard 2004, 268–9). Indeed *Antiope*'s cave had an unusual thematic and symbolic importance. The cave mouth, represented by the skene door, was also identified by the fragments as the cult site of Dionysus at Eleutherae (*TrGF* F 179, 203), the home of the cowherd and his adoptive sons Amphion and Zethus (*TrGF* F 223.58, 61–2, 70, 76, 83), and it was presumably also the cave in which Antiope was said to have given birth to the twins. As elsewhere in West Greek vasepainting, the Dirce Painter's 'rocky arch' represents the mouth of a cave. The panther skin hanging from the arch is probably a clue to Dionysus' presence within.

Certainly original with Euripides is the action we see inside the cave. A papyrus discovered in Egypt in 1890 preserves the text of the play's climactic final moments (text based on E. *TrGF Antiope* F 223.57–99).

	(ΒΟΥ.)	.[ ]σας ἥδομαι κακὸν ..α[
	(ΛΥ.)	οὐκ ἀσφαλὲς τόδ' εἶπας, ἄνθρωπε, στέγ[ος;
	(ΒΟΥ.)	δρᾶν δεῖ τι· κείνους δ' οἶδ' ἐγὼ τεθνηκό[τας.
60	(ΛΥ.)	καλῶς ἄρ', εἴπερ οἶσθα, ταξώμεσθα νῦν.
	(ΒΟΥ.)	τάξιν] τίν' ἄλλην ἢ δόμων στείχει[ν] ἔσω
		ca. 14 letters] καὶ πρὶν οἰκοῦμεν[
	(ΛΥ.)	] τοὺς ξένους ἐῶν μ.[..].[
	(ΒΟΥ.)	] δορυφόρους ἔξω πέτ[ρας.
65		]νταινακ[.]σιν π.[
		ca. 12 letters ἡμ]εῖς καὶ σὺ θήσομεν καλῶς.
	(ΛΥ.)	πλ]ῆθός εἰσιν οἱ ξένοι;
	(ΒΟΥ.)	]δ' οὐκ ἔχουσιν ἐν χεροῖν.
	(ΛΥ.)	φ]ρουρεῖτε περίβολον πέτρας
70		]ντες, κἄν τι[ς ἐ]κπίπτηι δόμων,
		· ἐγὼ] δὲ παῖδα Νυκτέως ἐμῆι
		]σαι χειρί, καὶ τάχ' εἴσεται
		ca. 14 letters]ντας ὡς μάτην λόγων
		συ]μμάχους ἀνωφελεῖς.
75	(ΧΟ.)	]ος, ἢν θεὸς θέληι,
		] τήνδ' ἀνὰ στέγην τάχα.
		]ριων σθένος βρόχοισι κατα-
		] βροτῶν δ' αὖ τέχναις
79a		.].[ ]όν;
79b	(ΛΥ.)	ἰώ μοί μοι.
80	(ΧΟ.)	ἔ]α ἔα ·[
		καὶ δὴ [πρὸς ἔργω]ι τῶν νεανιῶν χέρες.
	(ΛΥ.)	ὦ πρόσπ[ολοι ....]ντες οὐκ ἀρήξετε;
	(ΧΟ.)	ἀλαλάζετα[ι στ]έγα· βοᾶι θανάσιμον μέλος.
	(ΛΥ.)	ὦ] γαῖα Κάδ[μου κ]αὶ πόλ[ισ]μ' Ἀσωπικόν.
85	(ΧΟ.)	κλύεις; ὁρᾶι<ς>; πα[ρα]καλεῖ πόλιν
		φοβερὸς αἵματος·
		Δίκα τοι Δίκα χρόνιος, ἀλλ' ὅμως
		ἐπιπεσοῦσ' ἔλαθεν ἔλαβεν, ὅταν ἴ[δ]ηι
		τιν' ἀσεβῆ βροτῶν.
	(ΛΥ.)	οἴμοι· θανοῦμαι πρὸς δυοῖν ἀσύμμαχος.
	(ΑΜ.)	τὴν δ' ἐν νεκροῖσιν οὐ στένεις δάμαρτα σήν;
90	(ΛΥ.)	ἦ γὰρ τέθνηκεν; καινὸν αὖ λέγεις κακόν.
	(ΑΜ.)	ὁλκοῖς γε ταυρείοισι διαφορουμένη.
	(ΛΥ.)	πρὸς τοῦ; πρὸς ὑμῶν; τοῦτο γὰρ θέλω μαθεῖν.
	(ΑΜ.)	ἐκμανθάνοις ἂν ὡς ὄλωλ' ἡμῶν ὕπο.
	(ΛΥ.)	ἀλ]λ' ἦ τινῳ[ν] πεφύκαθ' ὧν οὐκ οἶδ' ἐγώ;
95	(ΑΜ.)	τί τοῦτ' ἐρευν[ᾶ]ις; ἐν νεκροῖς π[ε]ύσει θανών.

(ΕΡΜΗΣ)   παῦσαι κελ]εύω [φόν]ιον ἐξορμ[ωμ]ένους
　　　　　　 ὁρμήν, ἄνα]ξ Ἀμφῖον· ἐντολὰς δὲ σοὶ
　　　　　　 Ἑρμῆς ὁ Μ]αίας τ[　　　].εͺνͺος
　　　　　　 .....] Διὸς κήρυγ[μ᾽ ἀφικόμη]ν φέρωͺνͺ·

Cowherd: I am glad [I got you well away from] danger. **Lycus**: Did you not say sir that the hu[t] would be safe? **Cowherd**: Something must be done. But I know that they are dea[d]. [60] **Lycus**: If you are certain, let's make the proper arrangements. **Cowherd**: What [course] is there but t[o] go inside this dwelling? […] it has long been my home […] **Lycus**: [I would be crazy to] allow the strangers [to catch] me. **Cowherd**: [But you must leave your] bodyguard outside the cave. [65] [… inside] you and I will set things right. **Lycus**: [How] many are the strangers? **Cowherd**: […] but they don't carry any [weapons] in their hands. **Lycus** (to his bodyguards): […] guard the area around this cave [70] [looking in all directions?] and if anyone runs out of this dwelling [seize them. I want to kill] the daughter of Nykteus with my own hand. She will soon learn how vainly she boasted [about her divine lovers when she sees what] useless allies they are. [75] **Chorus**: God willing, [may his cries ring out] throughout this hut soon [… god will easily] tie down the strength [of the blessed tyrants] with his snares, but with the plots of men […] **Lycus**: Ay, me, me! [80] **Chorus**: Listen, listen. The youths' hands are indeed [at work!] **Lycus**: Attendants (i.e. the bodyguards), won't you come [runn]ing to save me? **Chorus**: The [h]ut resounds with cries, he shouts forth the tune of death! **Lycus**: O Land of Cad[mus!] Ci[t]y of Asopos! [85] **Chorus**: Do you hear? Do you see? Afraid for his own blood he calls the city to his aid. Retribution, aye, retribution is slow to come but nonetheless, whenever it sees an impious mortal it swoops down and seizes him unawares. **Lycus**: Alas! I will die at the hands of two men without an ally. **Amphion**: Aren't you going to grieve for your dead wife? [90] **Lycus**: Is she dead? This is a new disaster you speak of! **Amphion**: Yes, torn apart by being dragged by a bull. **Lycus**: Who is responsible? You? I want to know! **Amphion**: I would like it to be very clear to you that she died at our hands. **Lycus**: I wouldn't be acquainted with your parents would I? [95] **Amphion**: Why do you ask? Once dead you can inquire among the ghosts. **Hermes**: [I com]-mand [you to stop this murderous] assault! […] Lord Amphion. Hermes the son of Maia […] you these orders […] bringing the proclamation of Zeus. (There follow about fifty lines of a very typical *deus ex machina* solution in which Hermes commands Lycus to hand his kingdom over to Amphion and Zethus.)

The Dirce Painter unequivocally shows the moment of Hermes' arrival to interrupt the killing of Lycus when ambushed within the cave by Amphion and Zethus. The running woman, we must suppose, is Antiope who has also taken refuge within the cave, though it is very unlikely that she appeared as a mute in the final scene of Euripides' tragedy. The influence of tragedy is not, however, confined to the narrative. Two aspects of the vasepainting's use of space imitate the visual effects of the tragic theatre. The first is Hermes' appearance on a higher plane above the cave, strangely emphasized by his truncated form, which recalls the use of the mechane for which Euripides was notorious (**V B**). The second is the placement of the heroes and their victim at the very mouth of the cave – note that each of the twins has one foot shown to be in front of the cave mouth. But the ambush takes place, at least notionally, inside the cave. There are, moreover, good reasons why Amphion and Zethus cannot bring Lycus out to kill him: Lycus' bodyguards are stationed, as the papyrus shows, at the entrance.

In the tragic theatre notionally interior scenes were made visible by the use of the ekkyklema (**V B**), a device that rolled an interior tableau through the skene door to make it visible, though without compromising its notional interiority (and despite the fact that it is often used in combination with the mechane). Ekkyklema scenes are often prepared (or cued) by the chorus (or others) saying 'look!' or, as in *Antiope*, 'do you see?' In this painting the high rocky platform upon which the twins stand and Lycus kneels adds another 'stagey' feature to the composition. There is no need to insist that both mechane and ekkyklema were used in the original production of *Antiope*, although most experts suppose this to be the case. Collard's flat and unargued denial of the possibility is very eccentric and seems to be based on a misguided attempt to vindicate for Euripides a minimalist Aristotelian aesthetic (see Collard 2004, 269, 318) that is quite out of keeping with the testimony of Aristotle himself. The vase does, however, strongly suggest the use of theatre machinery in a Sicilian production within a couple of decades of its performance in Athens.

Taplin (2007, 37–41) has a helpful 'index of signals' used by West Greek vasepainters to give a tragic colouring to their compositions. Each of the eight types of signals is frequently used in isolation and need not indicate any significant relationship between a scene and a tragedy. They do however appear in high density in vasepaintings that otherwise show a demonstrable connection with a tragedy, and this is the case here. Signals that West Greek painters use to evoke a 'tragic' atmosphere include details of costume (particularly sleeved and ornate costume, especially cross-banded decoration such as we find on Lycus here), ornate high boots (or kothornoi), such as those worn by Amphion and Zethus and which later became a conventional symbol of the tragic stage, rocky arches, and supplications (including figures like Lycus who are 'down on their knees pleading with another'). To these I would include women who turn or run in horror from a central scene of violence. This is the function of the woman at the right, whether or not we decide to label her Antiope. Running women are perhaps meant to be included in Taplin's signal number 5, 'Anonymous witness figures', but in this case anonymity is misleading, and in any case running women seem to us to be a particularly strong index of a desire to show that a scene has a strong charge of contagious tragic pathos.

Axix: The Oedipus Krater, ca. 330 (by painting style), although the assumptions behind this Timoleontic dating have been challenged and a date closer to the 350s cannot be ruled out.

Several joining fragments of a red-figured Sicilian calyx krater, Gibil Gabib Group, probably Capodarso Painter.
H. 0.24 m; diam. 0.30 m.
Excavated in Syracuse in 1969 in an area south of the city hospital, tomb 34.
Syracuse, Museo Archeologico Regionale 'Paolo Orsi' 66557.
LCS Suppl. 3.276/98a; *RVSIS* fig. 429, pl. 236; *LIMC* Oidipous 83, Antigone 1, Iokaste 5, Ismene I.1; *CFST* S14; Taplin 2007, 90–2 no. 22.

Architectural details in Greek vasepainting signify that the scene takes place in an unusual location whose identity is important for an understanding of the visual narrative. Here the columns are emphasized by added white. They are all somewhat different from one another, possibly drawing attention to the artificiality of the environment. That on the left descends to the very edge of a platform, even overhangs it somewhat, and thereby emphasises the confined and narrow nature of the platform. The three-dimensionality of the ground is marked by lines showing the depth of the floor boards, and, lest anyone fail to get the point, the front edge of the floor joists is clearly outlined underneath. The platform ends abruptly at the back and sides. The details signify that the action takes place on a wooden stage in front of columns that represent the palace. This fragment is one of two West Greek vases that show the performance of a tragedy on stage. Both are Sicilian. Both produced around 330. Both are probably by the Capodarso Painter (**Axx**). Stages otherwise appear only on vasepaintings related to comedy.

Atop the stage stand six figures: from left to right are an old man, a young girl, a younger man, a girl, a woman, and on the far right, not visible in the reproduction, a second woman who runs away from the scene. Details of stage costume are clearest in the character of the old man. His arms clearly show the sleeves of the actor's tights, coloured black, emerging from underneath his cloak (sleeves are not part of ordinary Greek clothing). Ornate sleeves can also be seen on the younger man's right arm. A mask is suggested by the vacant look on the old man's face, emphasised by the rare frontal view, though this may also serve to signal his extreme old age as do the pupils of his eyes that are rendered with vertical strokes. He wears the cloak and boots characteristic of a figure, most commonly identified as the *paidagogos*, that Green (1999) and Taplin (2007, 40–1) regard as an iconographic index in West Greek vasepainting of tragic action. The *paidagogos* or old nurse frequently serves as a messenger in tragedy and New Comedy. A mask is also suggested by the stiffness, angularity and the larger-than-life size of the younger man's head.

Most of all, however, it is the configuration of the scene that suggests a stage action. J. R. Green points out to us that one of the more generally 'histrionic' aspects of Sicilian vasepainting is its preference for three-quarter or frontal faces (as opposed to a more decided tendency in the other fabrics to show figures in profile). This can of course be found on vases that have nothing particularly dramatic about them, but it is especially frequent in vasepaintings that do (cf. for example four of the six figures of **Axviii**). On the Oedipus krater the connection to contemporary acting style seems very direct. The old man to the left stares straight out towards the viewer, but makes a conventional 'speaking gesture' toward the younger man and woman at centre stage. In non-dramatic scenes people look as well as gesture towards those to whom they speak. But this odd bi-directionality is a common feature of the comic messenger known from the highly realistic theatre art of the Hellenistic period (Csapo 1993a). The New Comic messenger delivers his narrative 'upfront', looking towards the audience, but gestures with his left hand towards the characters he notionally addresses. The younger man, at centre stage, strokes his beard in thoughtful puzzlement at the old man's words; the woman to the right holds her left hand to the side of her cheek in an expression of shock (their stance and gestures are also paralleled by Hellenistic representations of dramatic messenger scenes, see Csapo 1993a, 52 n. 69).

The Capodarso Painter very probably intends to show a performance of the climactic messenger scene of Sophocles' *Oedipus the King*, where an old shepherd from Corinth brings news of the death of Oedipus' presumed parents. Upon questioning, he reveals that they were not Oedipus' natural parents: the infant Oedipus was given to the old man by a slave of Laius and taken to the childless Corinthian couple. Jocasta's gesture captures the moment of her recognition soon after the old man releases the vital information at line 1042.

Even in the most realistic depictions of tragic performance, however, there are illusionistic details. Tragic vases never achieve the degree of realism that comic vases show from the start. The mouths of the actors are not quite as open as we expect from a tragic mask. Moreover, the stage realism is compromised, paradoxically, by some of the standard forms of theatrical 'rhetoric' one finds on the mythological vases (**Axviii**). Oedipus' daughters Antigone and Ismene are added for pathos, even though they are not part of this scene in Sophocles' play, though they do appear later. The anonymous woman just behind Jocasta turns away with a gesture of alarm, like many other female onlookers who typically register emotional reactions on the margins of South Italian mythological scenes. Yet in this scene it is only Jocasta and the audience who have the requisite knowledge to feel alarm. The anonymous running woman simply serves as the concrete and conventional symbol of tragic horror. The artist's desire to show the production is compromised by a desire to tell the story. He possibly felt the daughters necessary to show that this recognition scene was that of Oedipus (in Sophocles' play Oedipus' children/siblings do not appear until much later, but they are symbolically important to the present moment that marks the first recognition of the confusion of the natural order of generations that Oedipus' crime represents).

Axx: Theatre Realistic Scene Showing a Tragic Performance, 330s (by painting style), although the assumptions behind this Timoleontic dating have been challenged and a date closer to the 350s cannot be ruled out.

Sicilian red-figured calyx krater attributed to the Capodarso Painter, recomposed from a number of fragments, with some missing pieces, surface badly damaged. The beard of the figure on the right is described by Trendall as white, which may imply that he saw some traces of added paint. The reverse shows a satyr with a torch, a panther chariot drawn by a silen and followed by Pan. H. 0.46 m, diam. 0.37 m.

Found during excavations conducted by Dinu Adamesteanu of the necropolis at Gibil Gabib on Monte Capodarso about 5 km south of Caltanissetta in central Sicily.

Museo Archeologico, Caltanissetta inv. 1301bis.

LCS 601 no. 98, pl. 235.2–3; Trendall and Webster 1971, 114–15 no. III.6.1; Green 1999, 60 no. 51; Taplin 2007, 261–2 no. 105. See also Colour Plate 10.

The scene is unique. No non-comic vasepainting from ancient Greece shows this degree of theatre realism, though **Axix**, attributed to the same painter, comes very close. The stage, supported by a central Ionic column and posts on each side, occupies the bottom third of the painted scene. The viewer is meant to see this as a stage performance. With the probable exception of **Axix**, this can be said of no other scene on West Greek pottery that can be related to tragedy. Despite various (sometimes quite striking) tragic 'effects', West Greek tragedy-related vasepaintings seem meant to be viewed primarily as mythological scenes.

Tragic costume is evident from the dotted and black-bordered actor's sleeves on the female character second from the right. The leftmost figure, whose costume is otherwise identical, also shows the black border of the actor's sleeve on her right arm. The state of preservation makes it difficult to discern if sleeves are marked on the kneeling female figure or the male figure on the far right. Yet, the otherwise unprecedented degree of performance realism falls short of that of West Greek comic vases: the figures here have naturalistic faces, although the treatment is in some ways unusual. Two of the figures have a three-quarters frontal view (**Axix**), and the unusual care given to the figures' hair, sometimes rendering strand-by-strand, makes them stand out as elaborate and artificial. The male figure has a particularly large head and eyes. His age, boots, cloak and pilos mark him out as a paidagogos type, who frequently adopts the role of messenger (Green 1999; Taplin 2007, 262). He makes a 'speaking gesture' with his right hand and the women respond to his words with gestures of grief and horror. The scene has structural similarities to the same painter's **Axix**: both are messenger scenes, both show four main figures on a stage, the messenger and three other adults, the rightmost of which, like the leftmost in this image, turning away from the messenger in grief and/or horror.

The kneeling woman offers an unparalleled display of tragic emotion, falling to her knees and spreading her arms in both directions. She is the visual centre of the scene and her kneeling posture and the stretching out of her left hand, with open palm, might seem a gesture of despair, but it is combined with a gaze and raised arm towards the woman on the left, who turns her back, and might be interpreted as an appeal that is being rejected. Whatever the specific meaning of these gestures, there can be no reasonable doubt that they display overwhelming and 'tragic' emotions. This seems to be a hallmark of the Capodarso Painter. One could compare the pathos of **Axix**, and particularly the interpolated children and the woman who turns away from the scene. The shorter hair and less ornate clothing of the kneeling woman might at first suggest a difference in caste, but as J. R. Green suggests to us they probably show that she is a respectable matron in contrast to the younger maidens, who both have longer hair and more ornate costumes. It is possible, given the lack of any obvious interaction between the two groups of characters, that we have two moments in a tragedy (Taplin 2007, 262; cf. the interpolation of children in **Axix**), and even possible that the woman on the left and the woman on the right are meant to be the same character.

Is the scene a generic representation of the climax of a tragedy? Taplin argues that it is 'scene-specific', meaning that the painter had a specific tragedy in mind while painting the scene, though the suggestion that this is a scene from Euripides' *Hypsipyle* (Trendall and Webster 1971, 114) does not correspond with the remains of that play (Taplin 2007, 262). There is one detail that might help identify the play. The woman facing the messenger holds up her hands, it is said 'as if in horror' (Trendall and Webster 1971, 114), but her fingers on both hands are bent with index fingers raised and folded in the middle like a person holding to eye level a necklace or a string, the ends of which are secured in her palms but draped over her index fingers. Perhaps some such object was drawn in added paint that has since disappeared (we thank J. R. Green for this observation). Aristotle in the *Poetics* 1454b24–5 mentions necklaces as typical recognition tokens, but names no specific examples. The necklace is a recognition token in Euripides' *Ion* 1431 (in a scene very different from this), and doubtless other tragedies, as the device is commonplace in New Comedy (Men. *Epit.* 303 A; *Pk.* 815 A; and probably *Plokion*; cf. *PCG* adesp. F 1084 and Satyrus, *TrGF* V.1 T 137, where 'recognitions through necklaces' are listed among the Euripidean innovations received by New Comedy).

The inhabitants of Monte Capodarso were indigenous Sicilians. They are usually in this region labelled 'Sican', but neither archaeological nor linguistic evidence permits a clear ethnographic or cultural difference between Sican and Sicel (Poccetti 2012). The settlement had strong commercial ties with Gela in the Archaic period, and Greek and particularly Attic pottery were imported and the shapes imitated locally from the middle of the sixth century, specifically, it is said, for use as grave goods (Panvini 2005). Here, as elsewhere in Sicily, all traces of the indigenous language disappear by the end of the fifth century (Poccetti 2012, 72). The homogenisation of the indigenous with Greek culture, attested by Diodorus (5.6.6), was probably well advanced in the Gibil Gabib area by the time this vase was purchased (Poccetti 2012, 59–60).

Axxi: Taras

1. **Plato, *Laws* 637a–b**. Written probably in the 350s. Plato visited Taras at least once, probably in 388/7, when he spent time with the Pythagorean philosopher, mathematician and politician Archytas (Huffman 2005, 32–43). Megillos the Spartan is lauding his city's restraint when it comes to indulgence in pleasures. Text: Burnet.

> Σπάρτη κάλλιστ' ἀνθρώπων δοκεῖ μοι κεῖσθαι τὰ περὶ τὰς ἡδονάς· οὗ γὰρ μάλιστ' ἄνθρωποι καὶ μεγίσταις προσπίπτουσιν ἡδοναῖς καὶ ὕβρεσι καὶ ἀνοίᾳ πάσῃ, τοῦτ' ἐξέβαλεν ὁ νόμος ἡμῶν ἐκ τῆς χώρας συμπάσης, καὶ οὔτ' ἂν ἐπ' ἀγρῶν ἴδοις, οὔτ' ἐν ἄστεσιν ὅσων Σπαρτιάταις μέλει, συμπόσια οὐδ' ὁπόσα τούτοις συνεπόμενα πάσας ἡδονὰς κινεῖ κατὰ δύναμιν, οὐδ' ἔστιν ὅστις ἂν ἀπαντῶν κωμάζοντί τινι [637b] μετὰ μέθης οὐκ ἂν τὴν μεγίστην δίκην εὐθὺς ἐπιθείη, καὶ οὐδ' ἂν Διονύσια πρόφασιν ἔχοντ' αὐτὸν λύσαιτο, ὥσπερ ἐν ἁμάξαις εἶδόν ποτε παρ' ὑμῖν ἐγώ, καὶ ἐν Τάραντι δὲ παρὰ τοῖς ἡμετέροις ἀποίκοις πᾶσαν ἐθεασάμην τὴν πόλιν περὶ τὰ Διονύσια μεθύουσαν· παρ' ἡμῖν δ' οὐκ ἔστ' οὐδὲν τοιοῦτον.

The arrangements as regards pleasures at Sparta seem to me the best in the world. For our law banished entirely from the land that practice which gives the greatest opportunity for people to fall into the greatest pleasures and violent excesses and foolishness of every description. Neither in the country nor in the cities controlled by Spartiates would you see symposia and everything that goes with them that powerfully stimulates all kinds of pleasure. There is not a man who would not punish at once and most severely any drunken reveller he happened to come across; [637b] nor would he get away with it even if he had a Dionysia as an excuse, like I once saw 'on the wagons' among your people; and among our colonists at Taras, too, I witnessed the whole city drunk at the Dionysia. But with us no such thing is possible.

2. Aristoxenus, *Sympotic Miscellany*, fr. 124 Wehrli (= Ath. 14.632a). Aristoxenus composed the *Sympotic Miscellany* ca. 335–320 (Meriani 2003). Himself from Taras, he was a prolific writer of philosophical works and the most famous musical theorist of antiquity. Text: Wehrli.

> διόπερ Ἀριστόξενος ἐν τοῖς Συμμίκτοις συμποτικοῖς· ὅμοιον, φησί, ποιοῦμεν
> Ποσειδωνιάταις τοῖς ἐν τῷ Τυρρηνικῷ κόλπῳ κατοικοῦσιν. οἷς συνέβη τὰ μὲν
> ἐξ ἀρχῆς Ἕλλησιν οὖσιν ἐκβεβαρβαρῶσθαι Τυρρηνοῖς [ἢ Ῥωμαίοις] γεγονόσι,
> καὶ τήν τε φωνὴν μεταβεβληκέναι τά τε λοιπὰ τῶν ἐπιτηδευμάτων, ἄγειν
> δὲ μίαν τινὰ αὐτοὺς τῶν ἑορτῶν τῶν Ἑλληνικῶν ἔτι καὶ νῦν, ἐν ᾗ συνιόντες
> ἀναμιμνήσκονται τῶν ἀρχαίων ἐκείνων ὀνομάτων τε καὶ νομίμων, καὶ
> ἀπολοφυράμενοι πρὸς ἀλλήλους καὶ ἀποδακρύσαντες ἀπέρχονται. οὕτω δὴ
> οὖν, φησί, καὶ ἡμεῖς, ἐπειδὴ καὶ τὰ θέατρα ἐκβεβαρβάρωται καὶ εἰς μεγάλην
> διαφθορὰν προελήλυθεν ἡ πάνδημος αὕτη μουσική, καθ᾽ αὑτοὺς γενόμενοι
> ὀλίγοι ἀναμιμνησκόμεθα οἵα ἦν ἡ μουσική.

[ἢ Ῥωμαίοις] Wilamowitz

That is why Aristoxenus says in his *Sympotic Miscellany*: 'We act like the Poseidonians who live on the Tyrrhenian gulf. What happened to them is that they were originally Greeks but have been completely barbarised and become Tyrrhenian [or Romans]. They have changed their language along with all their other practices and still today they hold just one of their Greek festivals, at which they come together and recall their ancient words and customs: after they bewail them deeply to one another and weep much they depart. And we actually do the same', he says, 'since our theatres have also been completely barbarised and that popular music has reached a level of great corruption, so we few by ourselves recall what music was like.'

3. Hesychius, *Lexicon* s.v. δρόμος ('dromos', δ 2402). Hesychius (of Alexandria) compiled his lexicon of obscure words in the 5th or 6th (Latte) c. AD, drawing on material many centuries older. Text: Latte.

> δρόμος· ἡ ὀρχήστρα τοῦ Διονυσιακοῦ θεάτρου παρὰ Ταραντίνοις.

'dromos': the orchestra of the Dionysiac theatre among the Tarantines.

4. Dionysius of Halicarnassus, *Roman Antiquities* 19.5.1–4, 19.8.1–3. Dionysius was a Greek critic and historian who taught rhetoric at Rome. He published the first part of the *Roman Antiquities* around 7 BC (D.H. 1.7). Target date: 282. Rome sent ambassadors to Taras led by Lucius Postumius Megellus to recover Romans captured by Taras following Roman entry into the bay of Taras in violation of a treaty. The Tarantines then (19.8) sought to enlist the aid of King Pyrrhus of Epirus against the prospect of reprisals from Rome. Text: Jacoby.

ὅτι Ποστόμιος πρέσβυς ἐστάλη πρὸς Ταραντίνους· καὶ τινα αὐτοῦ διεξιόντος
λόγον οὐχ ὅπως προσεῖχον αὐτῷ τὴν διάνοιαν ἢ λογισμοὺς ἐλάμβανον
οἱ Ταραντῖνοι σωφρόνων ἀνθρώπων καὶ περὶ πόλεως κινδυνευούσης
βουλευομένων, ἀλλ᾽ εἴ τι μὴ κατὰ τὸν ἀκριβέστατον τῆς Ἑλληνικῆς
διαλέκτου χαρακτῆρα ὑπ᾽ αὐτοῦ λέγοιτο παρατηροῦντες ἐγέλων, καὶ πρὸς
τὰς ἀνατάσεις ἐτραχύνοντο καὶ βαρβάρους ἀπεκάλουν καὶ τελευτῶντες
ἐξέβαλλον ἐκ τοῦ θεάτρου. 5.2 ἀπιόντων δ᾽ αὐτῶν εἷς τῶν ἐφεστηκότων ἐν
τῇ παρόδῳ Ταραντίνων, Φιλωνίδης ὄνομα, σπερμολόγος ἄνθρωπος, ὃς ἀπὸ
τῆς οἰνοφλυγίας, ᾗ παρὰ πάντα τὸν βίον ἐκέχρητο, προσηγορεύετο Κοτύλη,
μεστὸς ὢν ἔτι τῆς χθιζῆς μέθης, ὡς ἐγγὺς ἦσαν οἱ πρέσβεις, ἀνασυράμενος
τὴν περιβολὴν καὶ σχηματίσας ἑαυτὸν ὡς αἴσχιστον ὀφθῆναι, τὴν οὐδὲ
λέγεσθαι πρέπουσαν ἀκαθαρσίαν κατὰ τῆς ἱερᾶς ἐσθῆτος τοῦ πρεσβευτοῦ
κατεσκέδασε. 5.3 γέλωτος δὲ καταρραγέντος ἐξ ὅλου τοῦ θεάτρου καὶ
συγκροτούντων τὰς χεῖρας τῶν ἀγερωχοτάτων ἐμβλέψας εἰς τὸν Φιλωνίδην ὁ
Ποστόμιος εἶπεν· δεξόμεθα τὸν οἰωνόν, ὦ σπερμολόγε ἄνθρωπε, ὅτι καὶ τὰ μὴ
αἰτούμενα δίδοτε ἡμῖν. ἔπειτα εἰς τὸν ὄχλον ἐπιστραφεὶς καὶ τὴν ὑβρισμένην
ἐσθῆτα δεικνύς, ὡς ἔμαθεν ἔτι πλείονα γινόμενον ἐξ ἁπάντων <τὸν> γέλωτα
καὶ φωνὰς ἤκουσεν ἐνίων ἐπιχαιρόντων 5.4 καὶ τὴν ὕβριν ἐπαινούντων·
γελᾶτε, ἔφησεν, ἕως ἔξεστιν ὑμῖν, ἄνδρες Ταραντῖνοι, γελᾶτε· πολὺν γὰρ τὸν
μετὰ ταῦτα χρόνον κλαύσετε. ἐκπικρανθέντων δέ τινων πρὸς τὴν ἀπειλήν·
καὶ ἵνα γε μᾶλλον, ἔφησεν, ἀγανακτήσητε, καὶ τοῦθ᾽ ὑμῖν λέγομεν, ὅτι πολλῷ
τὴν ἐσθῆτα ταύτην αἵματι ἐκπλυνεῖτε.

8.1 τῶν Ταραντίνων βουλομένων ἐκ τῆς Ἠπείρου Πύρρον μετακαλεῖν ἐπὶ
τὸν κατὰ Ῥωμαίων πόλεμον καὶ τοὺς κωλύοντας ἐξελαυνόντων Μέτων τις
καὶ αὐτὸς Ταραντῖνος, ἵνα τύχοι προσοχῆς καὶ διδάξειεν αὐτούς, ὅσα μετὰ
τῆς βασιλικῆς ἐξουσίας εἰς πόλιν ἐλευθέραν καὶ τρυφῶσαν εἰσελεύσεται,
συγκαθημένου τοῦ πλήθους παρῆν εἰς τὸ θέατρον ἐστεφανωμένος ὥσπερ
ἐκ συμποσίου, παιδίσκην περιειληφὼς αὐλητρίδα κωμαστικὰ μέλη
προσαυλοῦσαν. 8.2 διαλυθείσης δὲ τῆς ἁπάντων σπουδῆς εἰς γέλωτα, καὶ
τῶν μὲν ᾄδειν αὐτὸν κελευόντων, τῶν δὲ ὀρχεῖσθαι περιβλέψας κύκλῳ καὶ τῇ
χειρὶ διασημήνας ἡσυχίαν αὐτῷ παρασχεῖν, ἐπειδὴ κατέστειλε τὸν θόρυβον·
Ἄνδρες, ἔφη, πολῖται, τούτων, ὧν ἐμὲ ποιοῦντα ὁρᾶτε νῦν, οὐδὲν ὑμῖν ἐξέσται
ποιεῖν, ἐὰν βασιλέα 8.3 καὶ φρουρὰν εἰς τὴν πόλιν εἰσελθεῖν ἐάσητε. ὡς δὲ
κινουμένους καὶ προσέχοντας εἶδε πολλοὺς καὶ κελεύοντας λέγειν, σῴζων ἔτι
τὸ προσποίημα τῆς κραιπάλης τὰ συμβησόμενα αὐτοῖς ἠριθμεῖτο κακά· ἔτι
δὲ αὐτοῦ λέγοντος οἱ τῶν κακῶν αἴτιοι συλλαβόντες αὐτὸν κατὰ κεφαλῆς
ἐξωθοῦσιν ἐκ τοῦ θεάτρου.

Postumius was sent as ambassador to the Tarantines. As he was making a
speech to them, the Tarantines, far from paying attention to him or thinking
seriously, as sensible people do who are taking counsel for a city which is in
peril, watched rather to see if he would make any slip in the finer points of the
Greek language, and then laughed, became exasperated at his effortfulness,

which they called barbarous, and finally were about to drive him out of the theatre. [5.2] As they were departing, one of the Tarantines standing in the parodos whose name was Philonides, a frivolous fellow who because of the drunken state in which he passed his entire life was nicknamed the Tankard, being still full of yesterday's drink, when the ambassadors drew near, pulled up his garment, and assuming a posture most shameful to behold, sprayed the sacred robe of the ambassador with the filth that is indecent even to be uttered. [5.3] When laughter burst out from the whole theatre and the most arrogant clapped their hands, Postumius, looking at Philonides, said: 'We shall accept the omen, you frivolous fellow, in the sense that you Tarantines give us what we do not ask for.' Then he turned to the crowd and showed his defiled robe; but when he found that the laughter of everybody became even greater and heard the cries of some who were exulting over [5.4] and praising the outrage, he said 'Laugh while you may, Tarantines, laugh! For long will be the time that you will weep hereafter.' When some became embittered at this threat, he added 'And that you may become yet more angry, we say this also to you, that you will wash out this robe with much blood.'

[8.1] When the Tarantines wished to summon Pyrrhus from Epirus to aid in the war against the Romans and were banishing those who opposed this course, a certain Meton, himself a Tarantine, in order to gain their attention and show them all the evils that would come from introducing royal power into a free and luxury-loving city, came into the theatre, at a time when the multitude was seated there, wearing a garland, as if returning from a symposium, and embracing a young piper girl who was playing komastic tunes. [8.2] When the seriousness of all gave way to laughter and some of them bade him to sing, others to dance, Meton looked round him on every side and waved his hand for silence; then, when he had quieted the disturbance, he said: 'Citizens, of these things which you see me doing now you will not be able to do a single one if [8.3] you permit a king and a garrison to enter the city.' When he saw that many were moved and paying attention and urging him to go on, he proceeded, while still preserving the pretence of drunkenness, to enumerate all the evils that would befall them. But while he was still speaking, those responsible for these evils seized him and threw him head first out of the theatre.

5. Annaeus Florus, *Two Books of the Epitome of All the Wars of Seven Hundred Years from Livy* 1.13.3–4. Florus was a Roman historian who lived in the time of Trajan and Hadrian, writing a brief history of Rome from its foundation to the year 25, drawing on Livy, Sallust and Caesar among others. Target date: 282, referring to events immediately prior to those in **4**. Text: Malcovati[2].

> *inminet portui ad prospectum maris positum maius theatrum, quod quidem causa miserae civitati fuit omnium calamitatum. ludos forte celebrabat, cum adremigantes litori Romanas classes vident, atque hostem rati emicant, sine discrimine insultant.*

Above the harbour there lies a rather large theatre, so placed as to command a view of the sea, and this was the cause of all the misfortunes that befell the unhappy city. They happened to be celebrating a festival when they saw the Roman fleet rowing towards the shore, and thinking that they were enemies, they rushed out and began to hurl indiscriminate insults at them.

6. Cassius Dio, *Roman History* 9.39.5–10. Cassius Dio was a Roman senator of Greek origins who wrote his *Roman History* in the years 211–233 AD. Target date: 282. Text: Boissevain.

ὅτι Λούκιος ἀπεστάλη παρὰ Ῥωμαίων ἐς Τάραντα. οἱ δὲ Ταραντῖνοι Διονύσια ἄγοντες, καὶ ἐν τῷ θεάτρῳ διακορεῖς οἴνου τὸ δείλης καθήμενοι, πλεῖν ἐπὶ σφᾶς αὐτὸν ὑπετόπησαν, καὶ παραχρῆμα δι᾽ ὀργῆς, καί τι καὶ τῆς μέθης αὐτοὺς ἀναπειθούσης, ἀντανήχθησαν, καὶ προσπεσόντες αὐτῷ μήτε χεῖρας ἀνταιρομένῳ μήθ᾽ ὅλως πολέμιόν τι ὑποτοπουμένῳ κατέδυσαν κἀκεῖνον καὶ ἄλλους πολλούς. ⁶ πυθόμενοι δὲ ταῦθ᾽ οἱ Ῥωμαῖοι χαλεπῶς μέν, ὥσπερ οὖν εἰκός, ἔφερον, οὐ μὴν καὶ στρατεῦσαι ἐπ᾽ αὐτοὺς εὐθὺς ἠθέλησαν. πρέσβεις μέντοι, τοῦ μὴ κατασεσιωπηκέναι δόξαι κἀκτούτου θρασυτέρους αὐτοὺς ποιῆσαι, ἔστειλαν. καὶ αὐτοὺς οἱ Ταραντῖνοι οὐχ ὅπως καλῶς ἐδέξαντο, ἢ τρόπον γέ τινα ἐπιτήδειον ἀποκρινάμενοι ἀπέπεμψαν, ἀλλ᾽ εὐθύς, πρὶν καὶ λόγον σφίσι δοῦναι γέλωτα τά τε ἄλλα καὶ τὴν στολὴν αὐτῶν ἐποιοῦντο. ⁷ ἦν δὲ ἡ ἀστική, ᾗ κατ᾽ ἀγορὰν χρώμεθα· ταύτην γὰρ ἐκεῖνοι, εἴτ᾽ οὖν σεμνότητος ἕνεκα εἴτε καὶ διὰ δέος, ἵν᾽ ἔκ γε τούτου αἰδεσθῶσιν αὐτούς, ἐσταλμένοι ἦσαν. κατὰ συστάσεις τε οὖν κωμάζοντες ἐτώθαζον (καὶ γὰρ καὶ τότε ἑορτὴν ἦγον, ὑφ᾽ ἧς καίτοι μηδένα χρόνον σωφρονοῦντες ἔτι καὶ μᾶλλον ὕβριζον), καὶ τέλος προστάς τις τῷ Ποστουμίῳ καὶ κύψας ἑαυτὸν ἐξέβαλε καὶ τὴν ἐσθῆτα αὐτοῦ ἐκηλίδωσε. ⁸ θορύβου δὲ ἐπὶ τούτῳ παρὰ πάντων τῶν ἄλλων γενομένου, καὶ τὸν μὲν ἐπαινούντων ὥσπερ τι θαυμαστὸν εἰργασμένον, ἐς δὲ δὴ τοὺς Ῥωμαίους πολλὰ καὶ ἀσελγῆ ἀνάπαιστα ἐν ῥυθμῷ τοῦ τε κρότου καὶ τῆς βαδίσεως ᾀδόντων, ὁ Ποστούμιος Γελᾶτε ἔφη, Γελᾶτε, ἕως ἔξεστιν ὑμῖν· κλαυσεῖσθε γὰρ ἐπὶ μακρότατον, ὅταν τὴν ἐσθῆτα ταύτην τῷ αἵματι ὑμῶν ἀποπλύνητε. ⁹ ἀκούσαντες τοῦτ᾽ ἐκεῖνοι τῶν μὲν σκωμμάτων ἐπέσχον, ἐς δὲ τὴν παραίτησιν τοῦ ὑβρίσματος οὐδὲν ἔπραξαν, ἀλλ᾽ ὅτι καὶ σῶς αὐτοὺς ἀφῆκαν, ἐν εὐεργεσίας μέρει ἐτίθεντο. ¹⁰ ὅτι Μέτων ὡς οὐκ ἔπεισε Ταραντίνους τὸ μὴ Ῥωμαίοις ἐκπολεμωθῆναι, ἔκ τε τῆς ἐκκλησίας ὑπεξῆλθε καὶ στεφάνους ἀνεδήσατο, συγκωμαστάς τέ τινας καὶ αὐλητρίδα λαβὼν ὑπέστρεψεν. ᾄδοντος δὲ αὐτοῦ καὶ κορδακίζοντος ἐξέστησαν τῶν προκειμένων καὶ ἐπεβόων καὶ ἐπεκρότουν, οἷα ἐν τῷ τοιούτῳ φιλεῖ γίγνεσθαι. καὶ ὃς σιγάσας αὐτοὺς Νῦν μὲν καὶ μεθύειν ἔφη καὶ κωμάζειν ἔξεστιν ἡμῖν· ἂν δ᾽ ὅσα βουλεύεσθε ἐπιτελέσητε, δουλεύσομεν.

Lucius was despatched by the Romans to Taras. Now the Tarantines were celebrating the Dionysia, and sitting gorged with wine in the theatre one afternoon, they suspected that he was sailing against them. Immediately, in a fit of anger and in part under the influence of intoxication, they set sail in turn; and thus, without any show of force on his part or the slightest suspicion of any hostile act, they attacked

and sank both him and many others. [6] When the Romans heard of this, they naturally were angry, but did not choose to take the field against them at once. However,
they despatched envoys, in order not to appear to have passed over the affair in
silence and so render them more arrogant. But, far from receiving them decently
or even sending them back with an answer in any way suitable, the Tarantines
at once, before even granting them an audience, made fun of their clothes and
general appearance. [7] It was the urban attire, which we use in the Forum; and this
the envoys had put on, either for the sake of dignity or else out of fear, thinking
that for this reason at least they would respect them. So revellers in small groups
jeered at them – they were again celebrating a festival, which, though they were
at no time temperate in their behaviour, rendered them still more arrogant – and
finally a man planted himself in the way of Postumius, and stooping over, relieved
his bowels and soiled the envoy's clothing. [8] At this an uproar arose from all the
rest, who praised the fellow as if he had performed some remarkable deed, and
they sang many licentious verses against the Romans, accompanied by clapping
and capering steps. But Postumius said: 'Laugh, laugh while you may! For long
will be the period of your weeping, when you shall wash this garment clean with
your blood.' [9] Hearing this, they ceased their jests, but made no move toward
seeking pardon for their outrageous behaviour; indeed, they regarded themselves
as having performed a generous act by letting them withdraw unharmed. [10] Meton,
failing to persuade the Tarantines not to engage in war with the Romans, withdrew
unobserved from the assembly, tied garlands on his head, and returned along with
some fellow revellers and a piper girl. At the sight of him singing and dancing
the cordax, they gave up the business in hand to accompany his movements with
shouts and hand clapping, as people are apt to do under such circumstances. But
he, after reducing them to silence, said: 'Now we may both be drunk and revel, but
if you accomplish what you plan to do, we shall be slaves.'

7. **Polybius, *Histories* 8.30.7**. Written ca. 150–140. Target date: 212. Philemenos was a
member of a faction of aristocrats in Taras, then under the control of Rome, that admitted Hannibal to the city in an attempt to revolt from Roman control. Livy (25.10.4) refers to the same event (*Errorem et tuba audita ex theatro faciebat*) though in his account
because the trumpet was sounded by an inexperienced Greek its signal was not clearly
understood. Text: Büttner-Wobst.

> κατὰ δὲ τὸν καιρὸν τοῦτον οἱ περὶ τὸν Φιλήμενον, ἡτοιμασμένοι σάλπιγγας
> Ῥωμαϊκὰς καί τινας τῶν αὐταῖς χρῆσθαι δυναμένων διὰ τὴν συνήθειαν,
> στάντες ἐπὶ τὸ θέατρον ἐσήμαινον.

> Meanwhile those with Philemenos had provided themselves with Roman trum-
> pets, and some men who were able to blow them, from being used to doing so.
> They stood in the theatre and sounded a call.

The large, prosperous and powerful Greek city of Taras on the northern coast of the great gulf
of Taranto was founded late in the eighth century by Sparta, but introduced a form of democracy after the Persian Wars that, in the fourth century at least, combined democratic use of the

lot with oligarchic election (Arist. *Pol.* 1303a5, 1320b11–14). For much of the fourth century the city was effectively the hegemonic Greek state in Magna Graecia (μεγίστη τῶν ἐν Ἰταλίᾳ Τάρας 'Taras mightiest city in Italy': [Scymn.] 330), its great wealth and cultural energy drawing many towards it from other centres in Western Greece, and beyond. Literary testimony to the city's theatre and Dionysia is plentiful (**1–7**), but much of it is coloured, and perhaps substantially shaped, by a topos of Tarantine luxury and a ridiculously high frequency of publicly funded festivals that seems to derive from anti-democratic circles (Clearch. fr. 48 Wehrli; Theopomp. *FGrH* 115 F 233; Str. 6.3.4; see also Walbank 1967, 101 on the likely origins in Tarantine aristocratic circles of the theory of Tarantine decline found in Polybius). Roman historiography adopted and energetically developed this topos in propaganda that sought to exculpate Rome from the accusation of having provoked the Tarantine War, whereas in fact the Roman action in entering the gulf of Taranto was clearly a violation of a treaty that had existed since the later fourth century and posed a direct threat to Tarantine security and trade (Lomas 1993, 50). The whole edifice has a foundation in **1**, which assimilates the Dionysiac excesses of (democratic) Athens and Taras, in sharp opposition to the abstemious ways of Sparta.

The theatre features at two critical junctures of Tarantine history: the prelude to conflict with Rome in 282 (**4–6**; Zonaras 8.2. 370A adds that once in the city Pyrrhus 'closed the theatre' to prevent any gathering to foment a revolt; Orosius 4.1 confirms that the Roman fleet was met at sea some distance from the Tarantine harbour); and during the factional introduction of the Carthaginians into the city in 213–212 to support a revolt from Roman control (**7**). In the first case it is difficult to decide whether the theatre is given a prominent role as the site both from which the Roman fleet was first seen and for subsequent audiences with ambassadors simply because it permits such a grotesque and graphic depiction of Tarantine decadence in the face of the restrained and dignified Romans. It is however very likely that the theatre in Taras was used for meetings of a political nature. Such multi-functionality is especially well-attested for Magna Graecia (**A Introduction; Ai**) and this is the event which prompts Valerius Maximus (who also reports the story, in abbreviated form: 2.2.5), to note that such usage was 'the custom of Greece' *ut est consuetudo Graeciae*. The familiar fact of this multi-functionality, in Taras as elsewhere, probably enabled the effective rhetorical development of the picture (Lippolis et al. 1995, 185–6).

1 indicates a Dionysia by around 360. Dionysus is otherwise attested as a god of considerable importance in Taras, although we know little of the concrete realities of his cult (Lippolis et al. 1995, 180–8). A set of inscribed drinking cups dedicated to him in the second half of the fourth century was found in the area of Via Anfiteatro (*IG* XIV 668a with Lippolis et al. 1995, 91–2, 181–2, 187), and there are indications of a mystery cult particular to the city (Firm. 26.1; Arnob. 5.21). The Dionysiac toponym Satyrion is possibly to be identified with the city's very acropolis (Lippolis et al. 1995, 291–2; but cf. Lo Porto 1964).

2 puts theatre in the city some time well before the 320s. The speaker of this passage was probably its author, Aristoxenus of Taras himself, but if not there can be no doubt that he was mouthing views of the conservative musical theorist. The work evidently pictured a group of like-minded such conservatives in conversation at a literary symposium, discussing the qualities of 'old' and 'new' music, perhaps with performative displays of each (Meriani 2003). Aristoxenus compares the way this small circle gets together to remember music before the 'barbarisation' of their theatres with the practice of the citizens of the Greek city of Poseidonia (**A Introduction**). They underwent a process also described as 'barbarisation' – their language is the focus of attention, rather than their music, although 'and all their other practices' casts a wide net – and subsequently only on one occasion, at one of their Greek festivals, did the Poseidonians still assemble to 'recall their ancient words and customs'. This reveals much about the cultural conservatism of Aristoxenus and his circle, and the way in which, more than a century after their appearance, the musical changes referred to – what modern scholarship has dubbed 'the New Music' – still had the power to cause anguish. It also gives us a fairly direct reference to the already long-established existence of theatre in Taras by ca. 320 – although, given the somewhat undefined nature of the group for whom the speaker speaks, the 'our' of 'our theatres' may have a wider reference to theatres of Greek cities more generally. (The passage does not offer any evidence for theatre in Poseidonia, in the present or the imagined past of the speaker. The alleged degeneration of Poseidonian culture lamented in this work must be dated to the high fourth century, and can have nothing to do with the establishment of a Latin colony in the city in 273, with which archaeologists have tried to co-ordinate it. It has been cogently argued that the Greek festival referred to may in reality have been the cult of the founder-hero of the city: Meriani 2003.)

No remains of a theatre have been securely identified and proposed sites are conjectural. The sources suggest that there may have been two – one near the agora (the context of **7**, which is the oldest source after **2**, implies this); and one above the port (**5**) – but Todisco (2002, 165) may be right to argue that the one which Florus places near the port during the Greek period is a later Roman theatre misidentified. If Florus' *maius* means 'the greater theatre' as opposed to a 'rather large' one, he or his source was distinguishing this from a second theatre in the city. But since the Tarantine harbour lies in the direction of the interior, north of the city and separated by it from the great gulf of Taranto, a theatre that overlooked the harbour would place its spectators with their backs to the open sea. This does not inspire confidence in the detail, which may have been fabricated in a maladroit attempt to make the story work, affording the Tarantines an easy view of the Roman fleet from theatre at the cost of reality. On the other hand there is nothing inherently implausible about such a site, and it has been endorsed by some (e.g. Lippolis: Lippolis et al. 1995, 186).

The remains of a large Roman amphitheatre were found not far from and facing the gulf of Taranto (in the area of present-day Via Anfiteatro) at the western end of the city, and some maintain that this had been built above a Greek theatre (Tosi 2003, 220–3; Sear 2006, 144; Todisco 2015 assembles and discusses the relevant brief accounts of the nineteenth-century archaeological study and is inclined to the view that the amphitheatre could have been built over a Greek theatre, but on a different orientation). The inscribed drinking cups dedicated to Dionysus in the fourth century were found in the area of the amphitheatre (above). The Roman amphitheatre could also be the 'rather large' theatre that Florus or his source has misidentified as Greek, though it is not above the port but looking out to the open gulf. A complicating factor is that the treaty which the Romans are thought to have violated prohibited them from sailing into the gulf of Taranto itself (east of cape Lacinium), rather than specifically the harbour of Taras (App. *Samn.* 7.1). A theatre on the site of the amphitheatre would have afforded a view of ships entering the gulf. The suggestion that a Greek theatre was rebuilt in Roman times may receive some further support from the fact that the sole attestation in Latin of the word *prohedria* comes from Taras, in a first-century AD dedication to Jupiter by one M. Cocceius Pudens, for having received *honorem prohedriae* (*ILS* 6462; Lippolis et al. 1995, 201–22).

Polybius refers to a 'building called the *Mouseion*' near the agora (Plb. 8.25.11, 27.1) where heavy drinking had been taking place. This may derive from the Spartan origins of the city, for the cult of the Muses was prominent in Sparta, with a sanctuary on the acropolis next to that of Athena Chalkioikos, and the kings sacrificed to them before battle (Plu. *Lyc.* 21.7). The influence of Pythagorean culture, in which the cult of the Muses was connected to political harmony, has also been detected (Lippolis et al. 1995, 205–6; Wuilleumier 1939, 485). It is possible that this shrine to the Muses, whatever its structure, is to be identified with the *auleterion* that Hesychius records as 'a place at Taras' (Hsch. α 8294: αὐλητήριον· τόπος παρὰ Ταραντίνοις). It may have been close to the theatre (**Ai**). The name *auleterion* certainly suggests that pipe music featured prominently in the city (cf. **4**).

Only with **6** do we have the explicit connection of Dionysia to theatre, but it can be safely deduced both for the target date (282) and doubtless much earlier. **3** indicates that the (or a) theatre in Taras was dedicated to Dionysus, or rather, that it was 'Dionysiac'. No significant distinction is probably intended by this form of expression, but note the view, based largely on the so-called Carneia vase that was probably made in or near Taras, that the festival of the Carneia for Apollo in Taras was heavily influenced by Dionysiac performance (Casadio 1994, 265–75; Krausskopf 2012, 86–7). No source explicitly places the performance of drama at the Tarantine Dionysia. Little can be drawn from **4**'s (8.1) account that a piper was playing 'komastic tunes' to a full theatre while in **6** (39.5) the only detail given of the Tarantines at their Dionysia is that they were sitting in the theatre gorged with wine in the afternoon. The description of the unspecified festival later in the passage (**6**, 39.6–8) strongly suggests some kind of Dionysiac revelry, perhaps held in the streets, of the sort mentioned in **1**.

3 also reports that the orchestra of the theatre was called a *dromos*. The point seems to be that the term used for the orchestra was unusual, not necessarily that the form of the orchestra itself was especially unusual, although this has not unreasonably been deduced. Todisco (2002, 165) calls to mind the wide corridors of the so-called ekklesiasterion of Metapontum (**A Introduction**) and suggests formal and functional parallels between these two buildings in the area. The fact that it was the orchestra – rather than the parodoi (note **4**, 5.2) – which was called the *dromos* in Taras suggests that there may have been less spatial distinction between the two elements, as at Metapontum. It has been suggested that the term reflects an original use of the site as a place for horse racing (Wuilleumier 1939, 249), but if the name alludes to a previous or primary function, (perhaps ritual) foot races of some sort are more likely (Lippolis et al. 1995, 187). Another possibility is that the name reflects the refunctioning of a pre-existing broad public walkway (**III Y Introduction**).

The most substantial body of evidence for theatrical culture in Taras is iconographic (Taplin 1993, 12–14; Taplin 2007). Taras was the main centre for the production of Apulian vasepainting, and dominates among those places which have revealed theatre-related vases (**Axxiii**; **Axxv**; **V E**). Of Todisco's list of tragedy-related vases, 243 are 'Apulian', probably all produced in Taras, and 56 'Lucanian', which probably means between Metapontum and Thurii (2006, 246–50). These begin from ca. 420s and by ca. 400 these vasepainters are 'thoroughly conversant with the details of mask, costume and stage, and are not likely to have come by this knowledge through any means other than frequent contact with living theater' (Csapo 2010, 98). Many Tarantines took to their graves choes painted with comic scenes or masks (Robinson 2004, 198), though as Green (2008, 20) notes, most vases decorated with comic material are symposium vessels, while the same is not true for tragedy.

But when their contexts of discovery are known, Apulian red-figured vases with certainly or possibly theatrical scenes derive in large part from graves in non-Greek Italic communities of the hinterland, notably in Peucetia, and most spectacularly at Ruvo di Puglia (probably ancient Rubi), some 90 km north-west of Taras. The graves of the native elite of Ruvo also show them to be great importers of Attic ware with theatrical motifs, including the Pronomos Vase (**V E**). As Carpenter (2014) notes, it is largely simple prejudice that has prevented the drawing of the plausible conclusion that those who took such care to have images of tragedy in their graves were themselves interested in and closely acquainted with the practices alluded to upon them. And Robinson (2004) has convincingly shown that various indigenous Italian communities in Apulia probably had direct knowledge of comic performances. Carpenter makes a similar case for tragedy. A further argument that theatre-related iconography in this region was designed for the market of its indigenous 'warrior aristocracy', seeking to distinguish themselves socially by this adoption of Hellenic culture, is the prominence of a motif that rarely appears in purely Greek contexts – namely the image of a youth in a funerary naiskos with a theatrical mask suspended above him, suggesting an attachment to theatre (see **V E**).

Some regard the fragment of a bell krater from Taras depicting a tragic actor (Würzburg Martin-von-Wagner Museum H 4600) as 'alone sufficient evidence to prove that tragedies were performed at Tarentum around the mid-fourth century' (Vahtikari 2014, 204). Green (2012b) has recently shown that a locally made funerary relief of ca. 400 shows a young man costumed as a tragic choreut, which is rather stronger evidence for local performance of tragedy (with choruses): **V E**.

Taras produced various theatrical poets and performers, including a parodist of dithyramb in the fourth century called Straton (Stefanis no. 2316). And Tarantine performers show a particularly high degree of mobility across the eastern Mediterranean (Nocita 2012, esp. 215). Taras was also the home of a key figure in the development of Roman drama, Livius Andronicus, said to have been a Greek from Taras who produced a comedy and a tragedy at the Ludi Romani of 240. The city was also very probably the home of Rhinthon (ca. 367–283), remembered (Suda ρ 171) as the inventor of a new dramatic form known as *hilarotragoedia* (ἱλαροτραγῳδία), also called *phlyakographia* (φλυακογραφία 'farce writing') and comi-tragedy (κωμικὰ τραγικά). This involved burlesque of tragic subjects and may owe much to traditions from indigenous Italian centres, the Western Greek comic tradition (note, already in the fifth century, the comic title *Komoidotragoidia* of Deinolochos: **Av**) as well as the, by this date, wider international theatrical tradition. The surviving titles suggest that Euripidean tragedy was a favourite target. Rhinthon may have made Syracuse his adopted home. The poetess Nossis of Locri refers to him as Syracusan in an epitaph (*AP* 7.414 = *PCG* T 2; Gigante 1971a; on Rhinthon see now Favi 2017d, 54–263).

Axxii: 'New York Goose Play', ca. 400 (by painting style).

> Apulian (or Lucanian?) calyx krater, probably Dolon Painter (Denoyelle and Silvestrelli 2013) and not Tarporley Painter as Trendall thought (the two painters had a history of collaboration and worked at a time when painters moved freely between Taras and Metapontum). The inscription was probably made before firing.

H. 0.306 m, diam. 0.318 m.

In the Alessandro Pizzati collection before it was purchased by the Metropolitan. Museum records report a findspot 'Near Taranto, or between Naples and Capua', but Montanaro (2007, 905, 910) makes the case that the vase came from tomb 324 at Ruvo, which also contained vases datable to the second quarter of the fourth century.

New York, Metropolitan Museum of Art 24.97.104; *PhV²* 84; *RVAp* 46.3/7; *PCG* adesp. F 57. See also Colour Plate 11.

(right to left) ΕΓΩ ΠΑΡͰΕΞΩ

(left to right) ΤΡΑΓΟΙΔΟΣ

ΝΟΡΑΡΕΤΤΕΒΛΟ

(right to left) ΚΑΤΕΔΗΣΑΝΩΤΩΧΕΙΡΕ

3 possibly ΝΟΡΑΡΕΤΤΕΡΛΟ, but this is excluded by the Circassian reading (below)

I hand (him) over.

Tragedian

Norarettblo (if Circassian = 'Indeed he is the one who stole it/them from them over there in their yard (or barn)'. See below).

He tied up my hands.

The vasepainting has recently been reassigned to the Dolon Painter, whose mature work was produced in Metapontum (Denoyelle and Silvestrelli 2013). Previously Trendall's attribution to the Tarporley Painter and Taras was universally accepted. Both painters, however, show signs of close collaboration about the time this vase was painted, consistent with the notion that the Dolon Painter was an apprentice at the same workshop, though it is not clear whether the workshop was in Taras or in Metapontum (Denoyelle and Silvestrelli

2013, 66–8). The alphabet of the inscription has little in common with either the (by now moribund) epichoric alphabets of either Taras or Metapontum, and conforms easily to standard Ionic, with the exception only of the heta. Jeffery (1990, 29) notes that this is the first appearance of this form of heta ('tack heta'), but it appears on several Apulian vases, especially those of the Darius Painter, and on fourth-century coins from Heraclea in Lucania (Carpenter 2016, and for other 'theatre-related' appearances, Csapo 2010, 49 n. 54). We are probably dealing therefore with a local alphabetic form, probably developed in Taras. But the other alphabetic features indicate a strong Ionian influence (one might guess from Thurii). Whatever the origin of the painter (or inscriber), he appears to have absorbed broader regional influences.

The calyx krater shows three masked and costumed actors performing. A fourth figure to the far left wears no costume or mask and stands at a higher level to show he does not share the same space. The masked actors have open mouths and the inscriptions are arranged so that the first letter of each phrase is juxtaposed to the mouth. This is the conventional method, at least in Attic iconography, of showing that the words are intended to be taken as speech emanating from the mouth of the character. By contrast the simple juxtaposition of 'tragedian' to the figure upper-left, well away from the mouth, acts as a label to indicate that the figure is a tragedian (the Greek word can indicate a tragic poet, actor or choreut). Although the dialect of Taras is Doric (and that of Metapontum Achaean), the phrases are written in the Attic dialect.

The characters are poised as if interacting, but there is no way of determining the order of speech, whether left to right or top to bottom, and it may be a matter of indifference. Beazley (1952) attempted to join the phrases together into a line and a half of comic iambic trimeter: κατέδησ' ἄνω τὼ χεῖρε – νωραρεττεβλω / ἐγὼ παρέξω. This defies any systematic directionality, whether left to right, right to left, or top to bottom, that can be extracted from the position of the texts. Moreover it arbitrarily lengthens two syllables in the speech of the figure on the lower left by turning omicrons into omegas, and will not work at all if the word is 'noraretterlo'. It is true that in labelling the tragoidos our painter has written an omicron rather than an omega, but the error is particularly unlikely in the transcription of metrical verse in which three omegas otherwise correctly appear. It is perhaps noteworthy however that each individual phrase could fit easily into an iambic trimeter line.

The three actors wear standard Old Comic masks and costumes. The actor on the stage to the right is an old woman (Mask U). She says 'I hand him over to you', which appears to be a legalistic formula of the sort one uses when offering a slave up for torture by a civic authority (the only condition under which evidence from slaves was admissible under Athenian law). The old man (Mask E) in the centre of the orchestra on tiptoes with his hands raised says 'he has tied up my hands'. Slaves were often suspended before a beating. The young man behind him (Mask B?) and holding a stick is presumably going to do the work. He appears to be clean-shaven to show that he is young. He says 'noraretteblo' which means nothing in Greek. In Athens Scythians were used as police, and his barbarism might indicate that he is supposed to be a Scythian. A recent study indicates that the language is Circassian (one of many 'Scythian' languages) and means 'He stole it/them from them over there in their yard (or barn)' (Mayor et al. 2014, 468; sceptical, Chiarini 2018, 197–203). The decipherment helps eliminate the alternative reading 'noraretterlo' as meaningless, but does not help determine whether the first syllable of noraretteblo is long or short as Circassian may (like the conservative Bzyb dialect of Abkhaz) have an 'emotomorpheme' that lengthens the first syllable and 'conveys a sense that the speaker is surprised, perhaps even incredulous, or expects the hearer to agree' (Colarusso pers. comm.).

Beazley (followed by Taplin 1993 and Schmidt 1998) interprets the dialogue differently. In response to Trendall's concern about the apparent contradiction between the central character's complaint that he was tied up and the absence of visible ropes in the painting, Beazley suggested that the Greek verb καταδεῖν here meant 'to cast a spell', a meaning that it can take in addition to its normal meaning which is simply 'tie'. The adverb ἄνω is, however, a problem for Beazley's interpretation: 'tie up' is far more likely than 'hex up', for which we know no parallels. The decipherment of 'noraretteblo', if correct, is clearly against the spell-binding interpretation.

This is one of the earliest examples of close to a hundred scenes of comic performance in West Greek art. Yet there are several unique features in the painting that are never matched by later painters, though all attempt to capture the specificity of theatrical performance. It is the only vasepainting to transcribe dramatic dialogue. It is the only vasepainting that attempts to capture an interaction between actors on stage and actors in the orchestra. Indeed it is the only attempt to render the full topography of the theatre, including the skene doors, the stage, the orchestra, and possibly the theatron in the figure of a naked youth watching on the left. He seems to float as if rising in the theatron and the puzzling label, *tragoidos*, does not suffice to make him part of the play. Whoever he is, he functions here as a spectator, not a performer.

Most remarkable of all, however, is the stark theatrical realism of the vase. Costumes and masks are rendered without any compromise. The detail of the buckle that joins the buttocks to the belly of the old man's body suit is never otherwise reproduced in ancient theatre art. Like the Tarporley Painter, the Dolon Painter is interested in the contrast between theatrical (and artistic) illusion and reality. Here he has chosen a subject that vividly presents the performance reality that creates the dramatic illusion. The old man in the centre of the orchestra tells us that he has been strung up for a beating, but (as Trendall noted) there is no sign of ropes or of anything to tie him to. Here both the humour and the art of the actor's performance depend precisely upon the viewers' (and audience's) awareness that the actor is posturing and dancing about like a man suspended without actually being so.

The originality of this scene is breathtaking. There is, however, Attic precedent, especially in the Perseus Dancer Vase (**V D**), for the majority of its most striking features: the detailing of mask and costume, the representation of the stage, the attempt to capture the full sweep of the theatre, including both the orchestra and the suggestion of an audience. The main difference is that the Dolon Painter does it much better, much more consistently and with a level of specificity and detail that is unprecedented. The Dolon Painter has attempted to capture on the surface of a pot what only theatre can give. We are left with the impression of seeing not just a scene but as it were a film clip of an ancient comedy: the characters speak, interact and even move (Marshall 2001, observes how the rising script emerging from the Old Man's mouth rises up – reading from left to right – as if leaving a trail as he is hoisted in the air; even the floating mask probably points to another character who appears earlier or later in the narrative).

The scene relates to an unknown comedy with a complex plot (despite Todisco 2012's arbitrary attempt to connect it to Aristophanes' *Thesmophoriazusae*), but one for which we have (uniquely for comedy) the representation of another scene in **Axxiv**.

Axxiii: Berlin *Frogs*, ca. 375–350 (by painting style).

Apulian red-figured bell krater. Green thinks it 'quite likely by the Iris Painter'.
H. 0.35 m.
Purchased by the Berlin Museum from the Neapolitan art dealer, Raff. Barone in summer, 1847.
Once Berlin St. Mus. F 3046. The vase is reported lost or destroyed during World War II. *PhV²* 22.
Panofka 1849; Taplin 1993, 45–7; Csapo 2010, 58–61, fig. 2.4.

Only one photograph and one drawing of the vase are known. The drawing is from the original publication by Panofka in 1849 and is inaccurate in several details. The photograph
shows the vase had suffered much surface damage. It may also be misleading in places,
since it has very probably been 'touched up' either before or since its acquisition.

From left to right one sees a Doric pilaster or column representing a building, apparently
a porch, since the figure immediately to the right rises up to enter (despite the high variabil-
ity of the groundline in this painting). The figure appears stage naked (with body tights and
somation). There are apparently remnants of an original phallos, but the rest of the phallos
was either eradicated or not restored: it appears that the two lines marking its projection
over the body tights were assimilated to wrinkles, but the phallos in the line drawing,
which was not meant to be seen by the general public, is more explicit, if impossibly small.
The figure has a thick beard and bushy hair and a face close enough to Mask J, the Heracles
mask. J. R. Green draws our attention to the white aura around Heracles' head, which may
be the remnant of the head of the lionskin. He holds a club in his right hand, evidently to

beat the door. His left hand holds an animal skin by one leg. On the line drawing this is interpreted as a bow, but that is doubtful, given the appearance of the skin's other legs. Under the animal skin that falls awkwardly from the actor's back is an altar. J. R. Green points out to us that the white circles strung across the top of the scene do sometimes appear in Apulian sanctuary scenes. Behind the altar is a donkey ridden by another actor (the stripes on the legs are characteristic of Greek donkeys that are derived from a Nubian strain that interbred with zebras: Griffith 2006, 194 n. 31). The lines of the actor's tights at the wrist and ankle are distinct. Over his shoulder is an exaggeratedly large bundle. It could only be attached to a stick although the lines of the stick are barely visible behind the figure's chin.

At the beginning of Aristophanes' *Frogs*, Dionysus, disguised as Heracles with a lionskin and club, makes his way to Heracles' home to ask directions to the Underworld. There is nothing in the text of the play to suggest that Heracles lives in a shrine, but the idea that a god lives in his temple is natural enough. Dionysus' slave sits on a donkey, but absurdly also carries a large pack suspended on a pole that presses against his shoulder. Dionysus then proceeds to bang violently on Heracles' door with his club. Despite the condition of the vase when photographed, the details that correspond to this scenario are clear enough: a comic actor dressed as Heracles in a lionskin bangs at a door with a club, while a slave carrying a heavy pack sits on a donkey behind him. The general configuration of the scene conforms in every detail. Doubt attaches only to the details of the costume worn by the figure who bangs at the door with his club. His costume appears to be that of Heracles rather than that of Dionysus disguised as Heracles: the text of *Frogs* makes it certain that Dionysus is supposed to be wearing boots and a diaphanous gown beneath his lionskin. Indeed, the figure's face appears to be that of Heracles rather than Dionysus.

The problem appears insuperable if one expects perfect conformity between an image of a theatre scene and the production details indicated by a text. It is considerably less severe, if we accept that West Greek painters might omit and even alter details to enhance the beauty, clarity or recognisability of their paintings. The painter of this scene may well have baulked at the confusion likely to result from an attempt to render an actor disguised as Dionysus disguised as Heracles, and for the sake of clarity has chosen only to render the beginning and end points of this chain of impersonation. It is, after all, difficult iconographically to signal a 'Heracles' if you add boots, an effeminate gown, and someone else's face.

How much weight can we give to the minor costume details when we throw them in the balance beside the general outline of the scene? Hoffmann (2002, 175) explicitly accepts the premise that other determined sceptics would rather not voice: that this precise scenario could have appeared in any number of ancient comedies. Even supposing that scenes juxtaposing a Heracles-like figure clubbing a door and a slave carrying a large pack on his shoulders while seated on a donkey became all the rage in Classical Greece, there are good reasons why *Frogs* might particularly be represented by this scene. Not only is it the opening scene of the play, but the dialogue draws particular attention to the details. The violence of Dionysus' knocking generates one of the most brilliant 'gatekeeper' scenes in Greek comedy (there are many); Dionysus' Heracles-costume is the object of a good deal of ridicule by Heracles himself; and finally the detail of the slave carrying a pack while sitting on a donkey is important because the slave complains about the pole pressing into his shoulder, which elicits an elaborate joke as Dionysus tries to prove that it is the donkey and not the slave who is doing the work. The details we see in this image generate the humour of the opening fifty lines of *Frogs*. But are we seriously to entertain Hoffmann's hypothesis that there were many lost Heracles-banging-at-the-door-with-his-club-accompanied-by-the-pack-bearing-donkey-riding-slave comedies? The jokes do not really bear repeating. It is hard to imagine Aristophanes winning first prize with such an opener and at such length if the joke was as stale as the hyper-sceptics suggest.

For methodological reasons it is necessary to point out that our painter is not a consummate artist, but was, to his credit, at least aware of his limitations and wisely did not attempt to render the triple disguise required by the performance. The manner in which the lionskin floats behind the Heracles figure with no connection to his body and the manner in which the pack carried by the slave floats above the slave in relative independence of his stick or his back all inspire little faith in the artist's skill. But although a poor picture may obscure the importance of his image, it cannot compromise it. One should, however, acknowledge the possibility that such desired minor costume details as a diaphanous gown on a figure that was so apparently Heracles were misrecognised and omitted when the vase was restored in the nineteenth century. We will never know unless the missing vase resurfaces.

Axxiv: 'Boston Goose Play', ca. 370 (by painting style).

Apulian red-figured bell krater, McDaniel Painter.
0.286 × 0.231 m (below handles).
From Pisticci.
Boston, Museum of Fine Art 69.695; *RVAp* 100.4/251.
Vermeule 1970, figs. 103–4; Taplin 1993, 32, 112 no. 11.3; Padgett et al. 1993, 68–70, no. 13 and pl. V (colour). See also Colour Plate 12.

Positioned on top of a stage supported by columns, we see on the far left a herm (in the Attic style) covered with a himation on top of which sits an aryballos. The herm probably marks the space as a gymnasion or wrestling ground and the aryballos holds oil used to lubricate the bodies of wrestlers before a match. To its right stands an actor with the comic costume of a young man (Mask B?) and holding a stick (not a walking stick, but a switch that might be used for punishment). The man on the right is an actor in the costume of a comic old man. He holds an aryballos in his right hand and pours oil into the palm of his left. On the far right of the stage is a yoked double-basket, with a goat in each panier. In front of it stands a goose.

The bell krater offers an important index that Apulian vasepainters derived their knowledge of comedy from performance, not texts. The McDaniel Painter produced the vase as much as thirty years after the Dolon Painter's krater (**Axxii**) but both vasepaintings clearly evoke a different moment from the same comedy. The same two male characters reappear with very nearly the exact same costume and masks. The young man still carries his stick. The reappearance of the same masks and the stick do not of course suffice to show that we are dealing with the same play as the Dolon Painter's calyx krater. It is rather the baskets at the lower right of each vase that establish this beyond reasonable doubt. Each vase shows two goats in baskets and on each vase a goose stands or lies beside them. (On the Dolon Painter's vase there is damage to the face of the rightmost goat, but its ears, and the back of its head are clearly visible on the vase, though this detail is generally ignored in the literature.) Moreover, both baskets appear to be yoked double-baskets: the Dolon Painter's baskets are seen in profile, but he is careful to outline the profile of the second basket. Since this is anything but a standard prop in Greek comedy, it can leave no serious doubt that we are dealing with a different scene from the same comedy. This is the only certain instance in Greek art in which a single comedy is represented by two different scenes in the artistic tradition. If we can judge by the life cycle of the goose, the McDaniel Painter's scene precedes that of the Dolon Painter in the play since the goose is still alive.

It seems unlikely that the McDaniel Painter simply imagined an earlier scene to an image he found on a pot in the storeroom. In all likelihood the McDaniel Painter had never seen the Dolon Painter's vase: its condition suggests that it had been sold and sealed in a tomb soon after its production. The retention of the precise details of the appearance of costumes and props over thirty years (if Trendall's dating is correct) surely tells against any theory that our painters are working from texts: the texts of plays rarely provide descriptions of what is visually obvious in a production, and could not provide the details of masks, props and costume that both vasepaintings share. But the very minor differences between the two paintings are no less revealing. If both painters were copying two closely related images, as for example from a single illustrated manuscript, one might have expected absolute consistency. But here the baskets, though close, are not identical in their shape or weave; the thug has the same mask but different hair length and a ribbon on the McDaniel Painter's vase; the old man's hair has changed colour; and the stages are very different. The images sooner testify to the continuance and conservatism of a local performance tradition.

Axxv: Scene from Aristophanes' *Thesmophoriazusae*, ca. 370 (by painting style).

Apulian bell krater, attributed by Trendall to the Schiller Painter.
0.193 × 0.205 m (at mouth).
No known provenance: acquired in Rome in 1977.
Martin-von-Wagner Museum, University of Würzburg, H 5697.
Kossatz-Deissmann 1980; *RVAp* 65.4/4a; *RVSIS* 109; *CVA* Würzburg 4, 4.1–4; Taplin 1993, 36–40; Csapo 2010, 53–8, fig. 2.3; Green 2014a, 347–9, figs. 13–19.

This tiny bell krater shows two comic actors atop a raised ground line. The actor on the right, whose body tights are clearly visible, kneels astride an altar. His right hand holds a sword, his left a wineskin. The wineskin is fitted with little closed shoes tied at the arch in the Persian style (**V E**). From the left an actor in female costume rushes in carrying an over-sized skyphos. Above and between them hangs a mirror in profile. The mirror's reflective surface faces the figure on the altar.

It is not entirely clear whether the actor on the altar is playing a male or female role. On other vases and on figurines of this date the standard comic costume for mature male characters includes a beard and a very short tunic (although they can also wear a *himation* over the tunic). The standard comic male tunic is designed not to cover but to reveal the phallos. The character atop the altar has no beard and a knee-length tunic. He is in fact sexually indeterminate, and, on the evidence, deliberately so: though beardless, there are a dozen clearly marked splotches about his mouth rendering what appears to be razor stubble; and while his garment is too long to be male it is definitely too short to be female, but it is nevertheless girded above the waist like female dress. Other feminine features of the costume are the headband and the rather fluffy hairdo, both of which are paralleled by female characters on other Apulian vases (e.g. ΧΑΡΙΣ on Milan AO.9.284, Taplin 1993, no. 12.5 'Milan Cake-eaters', *PhV*² 45).

The actor's stance on the altar is well known to iconographers as the *position agenouillée* (Moret 1975, 101). It characterises mythological scenes showing heroic suppliants fleeing to take sanctuary at altars, and sometimes – normally in the case of Telephus, often in the case of Orestes at Delphi – with swords drawn. The stance probably originates with scenes of Telephus taking the baby Orestes as hostage. It is in any case most closely associated with the climactic scene of Euripides' *Telephus* (see Cropp 1995; Preiser 2000). Euripides' *Telephus* begins with the arrival of Telephus, the King of Mysia, in Argos disguised as a beggar. He has come to infiltrate the war council of the Greeks that takes place in the palace of Agamemnon. He explains in the prologue how the first Greek expedition to Troy went off course and landed in Mysia and how he was forced to repulse them when they began laying waste to the country. In the course of the fighting Telephus was wounded in the leg by Achilles' spear and when the wound began to fester, Telephus sought help from the oracle of Apollo. The oracle responded that 'the wounder would heal'. Thinking that this meant Achilles, Telephus entered Argos in disguise in order to await the safest opportunity to confront Achilles. During the war council, however, news came that the enemy had infiltrated the council and suspicion falls on Telephus. In desperation Telephus jumps upon an altar to seek asylum but also grabs Agamemnon's infant son as a hostage and threatens him with a sword. A truce follows and a deal is struck whereby Telephus will guide the Greek expedition to Troy in exchange for being healed (as it turns out by the rust from Achilles' spear).

The Würzburg krater has numerous correspondences with Aristophanes' parody of the climax of the *Telephus* in *Thesmophoriazusae*. In Aristophanes' play Euripides' 'in-law' is shaved, and then disguised with an effeminate headband, fancy shoes, and a dress in order to infiltrate the Thesmophoria (an exclusively women's festival characterised by fasting and abstinence) where the women of Athens plan revenge against Euripides for his misogyny. News comes that a man has infiltrated the rites and suspicion falls upon the in-law who is discovered to be male when they lift his tunic. The in-law then grabs what appears to be the baby of one of the women and jumps upon an altar threatening it with a sword. As several women run in search of kindling to burn the in-law off the altar and away from his sanctuary, the following dialogue takes place (lines 730–55 Wilson):

730	KH.	ὕφαπτε καὶ κάταιθε· σὺ δὲ τὸ Κρητικὸν
		ἀπόδυθι ταχέως· τοῦ θανάτου δ᾽, ὦ παιδίον,
		μόνην γυναικῶν αἰτιῶ τὴν μητέρα.
		τουτὶ τί ἐστιν; ἀσκὸς ἐγένεθ᾽ ἡ κόρη
		οἴνου πλέως, καὶ ταῦτα Περσικὰς ἔχων.
735		ὦ θερμόταται γυναῖκες, ὦ ποτίσταται
		κἀκ παντὸς ὑμεῖς μηχανώμεναι πιεῖν,
		ὦ μέγα καπήλοις ἀγαθόν, ἡμῖν δ᾽ αὖ κακόν,
		κακὸν δὲ καὶ τοῖς σκευαρίοις καὶ τῇ κρόκῃ.
	MI.	παράβαλλε πολλὰς κληματίδας, ὦ Μανία.
740	KH.	παράβαλλε δῆτα. σὺ δ᾽ ἀπόκριναί μοι τοδί,
		τουτὶ τεκεῖν φῄς; MI. ⟨καὶ⟩ δέκα μῆνάς ⟨γ᾽⟩ αὔτ᾽ ἐγὼ
		ἤνεγκον. KH. ἤνεγκας σύ; MI. νὴ τὴν Ἄρτεμιν.
	KH.	τρικότυλον ἢ πῶς; εἰπέ μοι. MI. τί μ᾽ ἠργάσω;
		ἀπέδυσας, ὦναίσχυντέ, μου τὸ παιδίον
745		τυννοῦτον ὄν. KH. τυννοῦτο; μικρὸν νὴ Δία.
		πόσ᾽ ἔτη δὲ γέγονε; τρεῖς Χοᾶς ἢ τέτταρας;
	MI.	σχεδὸν τοσοῦτον χὦσον ἐκ Διονυσίων.
		ἀλλ᾽ ἀπόδος αὐτό. KH. μὰ τὸν Ἀπόλλω τουτονί.

	MI.	ἐμπρήσομεν τοίνυν σε. ΚΗ. πάνυ γ᾽· ἐμπίμπρατε.
750		αὕτη δ᾽ ἀποσφαγήσεται μάλ᾽ αὐτίκα.
	MI.	μὴ δῆθ᾽, ἱκετεύω σ᾽· ἀλλ᾽ ἔμ᾽ ὅ τι χρῄζεις ποίει
		ὑπέρ γε τούτου. ΚΗ. φιλότεκνός τις εἶ φύσει.
		ἀλλ᾽ οὐδὲν ἧττον ἥδ᾽ ἀποσφαγήσεται.
	MI.	οἴμοι, τέκνον. δὸς τὸ σφαγεῖον, Μανία,
755		ἵν᾽ οὖν τό γ᾽ αἷμα τοῦ τέκνου τοὐμοῦ λάβω.

In-law: (*to the women*) Go ahead, kindle! Burn! (*to the baby*) But you, off with this wrap right now! For your death, child, you have only your mother to blame. Hey, what's this? The girl has turned into a skin full of wine and wearing Persian booties at that! [735] O most flagrant women! O most bibulous of creatures, stopping at nothing to contrive an opportunity for a drink! Great boon for the bartender; great bane for mankind! Bane too for dishes and the loom! **Mika**: (*to her servant*) Mania, throw lots of brushwood beside the altar! [740] **In-law**: Go ahead throw it down alongside. But you! Answer me this question! Do you claim to be the mother? **Mika**: To be sure I bore her for ten months! **In-law**: YOU bore her? **Mika**: Yes, by Artemis! **In-law**: At three pints an obol, or what? **Mika**: What have you done? You've stripped my child naked, [745] tiny as she is, you pervert! **In-law**: Tiny! I'll say she's tiny! How old is she? Three or four Wine Pitchers? (The reference is to the annual drinking contests on the second day of the Anthesteria.) **Mika**: About that, plus however many months since the Dionysia. But give her back! **In-law**: No, by this Apollo here! **Woman**: We'll set you on fire, then! **In-law**: Go ahead! Burn! [750] But this baby's going to get her throat cut, this instant! **Woman**: No! I beg you! Do whatever you like to me, but spare her! **In-law**: I see you have a very maternal nature. But her throat will be cut nonetheless! **Woman**: Oh my child! (*to her servant*) Mania, give me the sacrificial basin [755] so that I can at least save the blood of my baby.

The details on the vase correspond accurately to the implied action: the *Telephus* parody on the altar, the wineskin with little Persoid baby-booties, the woman rushing towards the threatened wineskin with a vessel to catch the 'blood', the headband of the figure on the altar, the longish tunic which hides the actor's phallos, the beardless face and razor splotches. Even the mirror has a place in the shaving scene before this episode. It is clear that we have something very close to what we might legitimately call a representation of the climactic moment in the performance of Aristophanes' *Thesmophoriazusae*.

There are, however, also discrepancies. Austin and Olson list several details that show that the artist is not giving us a perfectly accurate representation of every detail that from the text we know a stage production must have included (2004, lxxvi–lxxvii). Our scene, for example, does not show the brushwood that the text suggests was already by this point in the dialogue piled around the altar. An omission of this sort does not cast doubt upon the connection between this painting and a scene from Aristophanes' play. It does, however, demonstrate that vasepainters are generally less interested in accurately documenting every detail of a performance than in producing an attractive, clear and recognisable

image. One must first take into account the fact that artists and actors have different resources at their disposal. On stage there could be no doubt that the in-law is on an altar: the
audience sees him take refuge on the altar and then the brushwood is piled up around it.
The viewer of the vase painting, however, does not share the knowledge that an audience
would gain from the sequence of action seen in a performance. The painter needs to show
that the in-law is on an altar and it would be counterproductive to obscure or hide the altar
by surrounding it with brushwood. Indeed, as Austin and Olson remark, the recognition of
this scene as the climax of *Thesmophoriazusae* depends on the iconic clarity with which
the configuration of the altar and suppliant conform to the visual patterning of Euripides'
play. This would only be frustrated by the addition of incidental performance details we
can infer from the text, such as the presence of brushwood, a servant, a statue of Apollo and
the very un-beggar-like (and hence un-Telephean) effeminate shoes we know were worn
by the in-law. In other words, many (on the whole minor) discrepancies between the painter's image and the actors' performance may arise, paradoxically, out of the painter's very
desire to provoke recognition of the specific performance from whose details he deviates.

The details that are in the text, but not in the painting, are much less revealing than the
details that are in the painting, but not in the text. On this vase, there are two types of added
detail that we find interesting. The first is detail that recalls or foreshadows moments elsewhere in the narrative. Though it is true that West Greek vases in general aim to capture
a single important moment within a narrative, deviations from the temporal unity of the
image may actually aid in the recognition of the scene. There is, for example, no reference
to a mirror at this point in the play. The mirror does however appear in an earlier scene (Ar.
Th. 234–5) in which the in-law is shaved and dressed in female disguise. Here the mirror
appears to allude to the dressing scene for the sake of imparting essential background to the
visual narrative, because it is important that we recognise that the person of ambiguous gender is only 'dressed up' as a woman. The mirror, in other words, is added as a clue to the interpretation of a scene to which it does not strictly belong. (There is no need to suppose that
the mirror was left hanging on the stage at the end of the dressing scene and continued to be
visible in this one.) The razor splotches on the in-law's face are also there by the painter's
art and not by the mask maker's: a mask in production might well have had such splotches,
but they would not be easily visible to even the closest members of the audience. These too,
by alluding to the shaving scene, appear to serve as clues to facilitate recognition.

But there are also some details that are not in the text at all, not even hinted at, though
they make perfect sense once we see them. The bibulous woman in the *Thesmophoriazusae*
asks for a sphageion which is a large basin employed in sacrificial ritual to catch the blood
of a sacrificial victim. Instead, we see the old woman rushing forward with a giant drinking
cup or skyphos (for oversized props, see Revermann 2006, 244–6). The substitution is perfectly consistent with a text that systematically confuses the language of sacrifice and the
language of wine tippling, but nothing in the text would have justified our extension of this
pattern of incongruity to the shape of the vessel used to collect the 'blood' of the wineskin.
The detail surely reproduces the stage action of the play in production – it is unlikely that
a vasepainter invented the detail in the expectation that his customer would remember that
the text called for a sphageion.

Another detail that enriches our knowledge of the stage action beyond anything we
might have guessed from the text is the fact, evident from the mask, that Mika is an old

woman well past the age of childbirth. In light of this detail the in-law's incredulous 'YOU bore her?' has an extra dimension of comic meaning. It is also noteworthy that it is particularly old women who are caricatured as winos in Greek comedy.

Both the absence of details in the text and the presence of details not in the text indicate that the artist is not in fact illustrating a text. Details imported from earlier moments of the play show that he is concerned to enhance the recognisability of an action that would simply be 'given' in the case of a book illustration. Other details, however, that cannot be inferred from the text cannot plausibly derive from any source other than a stage production.

Axxvi: Telephus Parody in *Acharnians*, late 4th c. (by style).

> Apulian relief guttus.
>
> H. 0.08 m.
>
> Provenance unknown. E. Robinson has pointed out to us that no gutti have been found in either the 300+ tombs at Pantanello or apparently in the thousands excavated in the urban necropoleis of Metapontum. But they were certainly produced in Metapontum, as the finds from the Ceramicus show; and they are commonish in Italic tombs in Apulia and Basilicata. So our comic gutti, surely all from tombs, were probably produced in Metapontum with an Italic clientele in mind.
>
> Naples MN Santangelo 368. *CVA* (2) pls. 23, 1 and 27, 1; *LIMC* Telephos 83. Two other copies of the relief, apparently from the same mould, are in the Tampa Museum, Zewadski Collection (illustrated by Green 1994, 66, fig. 3.8 and Csapo 2010, 64–5, fig. 2.6), and in a Private Collection in Westfalia, Germany (illustrated by Nieswandt 1984).

The gutti show a single comic actor (the stomach padding and the phallos are immediately visible and there is a strong suggestion of breast padding). One can make out the wrinkling of the body tights that represent 'stage skin'. He appears to wear a felt cap (*pilos*) and the line of his baldric is visible across his chest. The actor kneels upon an altar (certainly indicated by the raised ends of the top surface).

The actor's kneeling position and the aggressive manner in which he holds the sword make the scene an easily recognisable comic parody of Euripides' *Telephus* (**Axxv**). The *pilos* or felt cap, often worn by Telephus in the vasepaintings, is specifically attested for the performance tradition of Euripides' play (by Sch.REΓ Ar. *Ach.* 439: τὸ πιλίδιον· πρὸς τοὺς νῦν ὑποκριτάς, ὅτι χωρὶς πίλου εἰσάγουσι τὸν Τήλεφον 'the little felt hat: contrary to modern actors, because they bring Telephus on without his felt hat'). The *pilos* has associations with Odysseus, travellers, the ill, and beggars in Greek art and literature (see Preiser 2000, 181 n. 266; Kannicht on *TrGF* V.2, 683, iv a, l. 439; Pipili 2000). It is in any case borrowed from 'Euripides' and worn by Dikaiopolis, the hero of Aristophanes' *Acharnians*, when he parodies Euripides' *Telephus* by jumping onto an altar when assaulted by the chorus of farmers from Acharnae, and threatening with a sword a charcoal bucket (*larkos*), which he calls one of their demesmen (Acharnae was the centre of charcoal production in Attica).

The concave object with a raised rim which the actor holds in his left hand is the comic substitute for the baby that served as a hostage in Euripides' play (it is analogous to the wineskin in *Thesmophoriazusae*, **Axxv**). Some scholars claim that the oval object is a shield, not a bucket, evidently without the benefit of a careful inspection of the gutti. It is oval and concave, far too small for a shield, and not held like any shield known to military science: the actor's fingers are clearly wrapped around the rim. Strauss (*LIMC* Telephos 83) and Small (2003, 67) identify the object as a wineskin (a claim no experienced iconographer could possibly endorse). The object corresponds to the shape and dimensions of a vessel illustrated on Attic pottery that is used to store coal and tentatively identified by Sparkes (1975, 134 and fig. 17d) as a *larkos*.

Comic subjects on gutti are rare, but late fourth-century relief gutti with comic subjects are known. Green's current (unpublished) catalogue lists three scene types in addition to the *Acharnians* Telephus parody, and all display a close similarity in style: seven gutti are impressed with the image of a comic slave sitting on a stool; four with a comic Heracles; and one with a frontal mask of an old man. Green draws attention to the fine detailing that only survives in traces in some of the better examples (note the wrinkles on the tights, visible on the *Acharnians* guttus, and the trace of a decorative element, perhaps a blood splash on the altar). It is unlikely to have been composed originally for oil bottles of this sort and Green thinks of metalware archetypes. The Old Comic costume with padding and phallos, long out of date by the time the gutti were moulded, indicates a much earlier date for the composition of the archetypes.

Axxvii: Phrynis and Pyronides, ca. 350 (by painting style).

Paestan red-figured bell krater by Asteas.
H. 0.305 m.
Excavated from a fourth-century necropolis at Pontecagnano sometime 1953–1958.
Salerno, Museo Provinciale Pc 1812; *PAdd* no. A7; *PhV*² 58; *RVP* 2/19, pl. 20.
Sestieri 1960, 156–9, pls. 40–2; Trendall and Webster 1971, iv 31; Gigante 1971a, pl. 6; Taplin 1993, 16.16; Revermann 2006, 330–4, pl. 14; Piqueux 2006; Csapo 2010, 61–4, fig. 2.5. See also Colour Plate 14.

ΦΡΥΝΙΣ	ΠΥΡΩΝΙΔΗΣ
Phrynis	Pyronides

Asteas (sometimes signed Assteas) is a Sicilian painter who emigrated to Poseidonia (Paestum: **A Introduction**) some time before the middle of the fourth century. The name is Greek (*LGPN* has 14 entries including our artist). Asteas is responsible for a large number of vases with theatrical subjects. This is among his earliest works.

The vasepainting shows two figures in masks and comic costume. The character on the left has the mask of a younger man (possibly Z) with a laurel crown. He holds a concert kithara in his left hand and a plectrum in his right. The kithara is hung with ribbons showing that he is a contest winner. An older man wears mask M and the costume of a respectable citizen (his phallos is covered and he carries, or rather presses against his chest, a walking stick). With his right hand the older man grabs the younger's left arm. The younger man evidently resists being dragged by digging in his heels and leaning hard in the opposite direction. On the ground below the younger man's plectrum is a Maltese dog. Maltese dogs are associated with musicians, women and children, and the attribute may suggest effeminacy (J. R. Green pers. comm.; Cinaglia 2012). The sash in the upper right of the image probably suggests a sanctuary setting.

Both characters are labelled. The musician is the famous singer and composer 'Phrynis'. This Phrynis can be none other than the dithyrambic poet and kitharode from Mytilene, active throughout Greece in the second half of the fifth century (sources and chronology in Telò 2007, 28–33). His appearance on a Paestan vasepainting by Asteas more than half a century after his death is no surprise: he was canonised as one of the founders of the controversial 'New Music', which by 350 was the norm. The New Music was condemned by conservative critics as effeminate (hence probably the Maltese dog). Phrynis' musical innovations are the object of jokes in several Old Comedies: a personified 'Music' names him in a list of composer/poets who have violated her in Pherecrates' *Cheiron* (*PCG* F 155); his innovations are ridiculed in Aristophanes' *Clouds* (966–72); and the Suda (φ 761) says he was 'often' named by the comic poets. An afterlife on the comic stage as well as notoriety in West Greece is indicated by a recently published Apulian bell krater, probably a little later than this one, that shows a comic mask of a man with the laurel crown of a victor juxtaposed to a kithara and inscribed 'Phrynis' (Vandlik 2002). A comedy is possibly the source of Ister's information that Phrynis' father was a cook for the tyrant Hieron.

The ribbons and sash (which suggest a musical victory in a festival setting) might indicate that Phrynis has just been performing. The elderly gentleman appears to lead the resisting Phrynis away. He is named 'Pyronides'. Few now believe that the name is a comic distortion pointing to the Athenian general 'Myronides' (see Plepelits 1970, 116–32; Heath 1990, 154–5; Storey 2003, 117–19). The connection with an Old Comedy depends mainly upon this label. 'Pyronides' is the name of the main character of Eupolis' *Demes* (Storey 2003, 116–17), a partially extant comedy produced sometime between 417 and 410 (for the date see Telò and Porciani 2002; Storey 2003, 112–14). *Demes* is largely concerned with restoring the virtues of the simple and virtuous old order to a troubled and degenerate Athens. The hero brings up from the underworld the great statesmen of the past and together they rid Athens of various personifications of its ills: at least we still have the text of a scene in which a sycophant is arrested and further fragments to suggest that other undesirables suffered a similar fate (Storey 2003, 165–74). Pyronides possibly drags Phrynis away for punishment for offences against traditional music (Storey 2003, 170 thinks of an intruder scene after the model of Cinesias in Aristophanes' *Birds*).

Piqueux has recently expressed the view that 'onomastics do not allow one to connect this image with a known play' (2006, 3) and others suppose the name was common. It is worth setting out the evidence in some detail. 'Pyronides' is an extremely rare name. As a fictional name it is attested three times: on Asteas' vase, in Eupolis' *Demes*, and in Lucian's totally fictitious *True Histories* (1.20.13). As a historical anthroponym it appears only once in all the historical and epigraphical texts of antiquity: in Athens and in the late fifth century, at the time of the production of Eupolis' play (Lys. frr. 26, 29 Carey). There is no need to suppose that Eupolis means to spoof this Pyronides, though it is certainly a possibility: this Pyronides was a wealthy and well-connected citizen and may have been well-enough known to serve Eupolis as a model for his comic hero. The name is not only extremely rare but somewhat improbable.

Eupolis and Lucian exploit Pyronides as a speaking name, as if it came from the root *pyr*, meaning 'fire' and suggesting ardour in the case of Eupolis' hero, and, in Lucian, suggesting a more literally combustible gentleman (Lucian's Pyronides appears in a list of humorous speaking-names given to leaders of the people of the Sun and Moon where Pyronides is, of course, one of the Sunnies). As a real name it derives not directly from *pyr* but from *pyrrh*, a root meaning ruddy or red-headed, from which several other names are derived, most notably 'Pyrrhus' (Chantraine 1968–1980 III, 959). We do, in fact, have one and only one (not very securely attested) Pyrrh[on]ides from early fifth-century Athens (*Agora* 21, D 37) and one and only one (possibly fictional) Doric variation, Pyrrhonidas, dubiously reported to be the father of the lyric poet Pratinas (Suda π 2230, **Bvi 1**). Pyrrh- names do sometimes appear as Pyr- names, but as Chantraine notes the phenomenon is 'tardif'. For example, the five volumes of the *LGPN* attest 196 different people named 'Pyrrhus' from Greek antiquity, but only 14 named 'Pyrus'. Moreover at least 5 of these 14 are treated by the experts as simple spelling mistakes (they appear in semi-literate graffiti) and the remaining 9 all date to the first three centuries AD, with a single possible exception from third-century BC Crete (see further Csapo 2010, 80–1 n. 95).

The Athenian Pyronides attested by the Vienna papyrus of Lysias therefore had a name that was not only extremely rare, but spelled in a form that, so far as we know, was unique except for its comic exploitation. Pyronides is no John Smith. The odds are overwhelming that if an ancient purchaser, even in Paestum, recognised these characters, he recognised them as the famous kitharode named Phrynis and the famous citizen named Pyronides who appeared in Eupolis' play, even if the latter were based on the one attested Athenian citizen of that name. Gould and Lewis were correct therefore in taking the presence of the name as an almost certain link with Eupolis' play, and all studies of the *Demes* written since the Würzburg *Thesmophoriazusae* krater (**Axxv**) came to light are right to regard Asteas' dependence upon the play as a virtual certainty (Gould and Lewis in *DFA*[2] 219; Storey 2003, 169–70; Revermann 2006, 318; Telò 2007, 28–36). In this case onomastics do help – they are indispensable to the recognition of the scene, which is doubtless why the painter thought it important to add the names.

This is the only identifiable scene on West Greek pottery by a comic author other than Aristophanes. However an Attic polychrome oinochoe of ca. 410 (Agora P 23985; *MMC*[3] AV 14) almost certainly shows a scene from Eupolis' *Taxiarchoi*. In this case, the survival of the image from Old Comedy until the mid fourth century, whether or not it is based on a performance, is good evidence for the beginning of the process of canonisation that made Cratinus, Aristophanes and Eupolis the big three of Old Comedy.

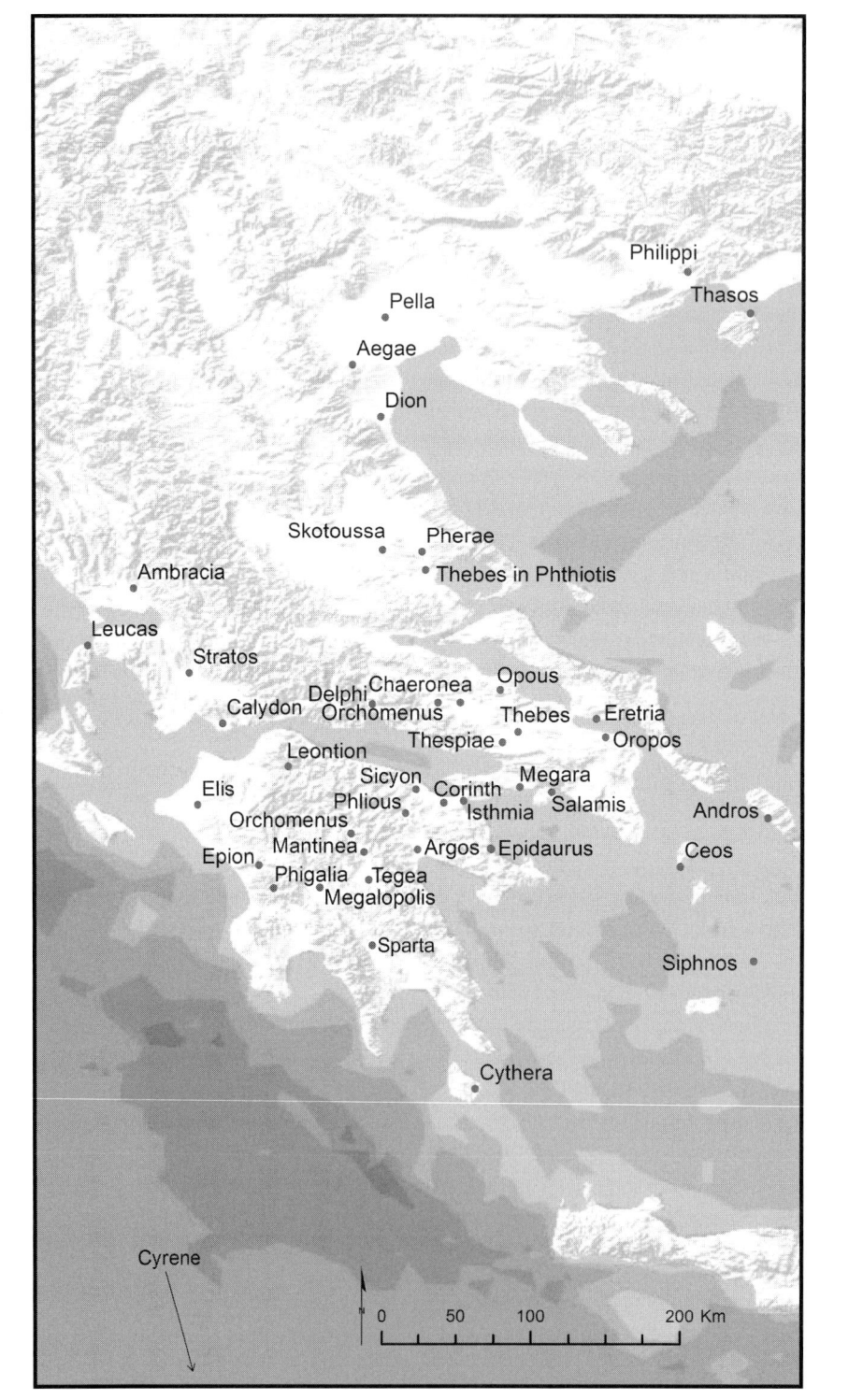

Philippi

Thasos

Pella

Aegae

Dion

Skotoussa

Pherae

Thebes in Phthiotis

Ambracia

Leucas

Stratos

Chaeronea

Opous

Delphi

Calydon

Orchomenus

Thebes

Eretria

Thespiae

Oropos

Leontion

Sicyon

Megara

Elis

Corinth

Phlious

Isthmia

Salamis

Andros

Orchomenus

Ceos

Epion

Mantinea

Argos

Epidaurus

Phigalia

Tegea

Megalopolis

Sparta

Siphnos

Cythera

Cyrene

0   50   100   200 Km

B | Megarid, Isthmus and Peloponnese

Introduction

Several cities in the Megarid, Isthmus and Peloponnese are remarkable for the early date of their development of theatre culture, and for the independence of their theatrical traditions, despite proximity to Athens. The varietal and chronological patterns make it easiest to divide this region into three main subgroups: the Megarid, Isthmus and north-eastern Peloponnese; Laconia; and Arcadia.

The Megarid, Isthmus and North-eastern Peloponnese (**Bi–Bviii**)

Very early and, in some cases, distinctive traditions allowed many cities of this region to challenge Athens' claim to the invention of drama: Megara claimed to have invented comedy (**Bii**); the Sicyonians claimed the invention of tragedy and also possibly comedy (**Bv 1–5**); and the Phliasians claimed satyr play (**Bvi**). All these cities were careful to place their inventors in the seventh or sixth centuries well before the documented history of the Attic theatre.

Megara has the oldest recoverable theatre tradition after Attica and Sicily. Comic performance is attested from at least the middle of the fifth century (**Bi 1**). By Aristotle's day (**Bii 1**) the city claimed to have invented comedy in the time of its democracy (probably 6th c.). Aristotle adds that both the Megarians in Sicily and those of the mainland claimed to have invented comedy. This probably indicates that performances originated in a period of frequent cultural exchanges between the mother city (mainland Megara) and the colony, Sicilian Megara. The cultural exchange would necessarily predate the expulsion from their city of the Sicilian Megarians by Gelon in 483 (**Aiii**). If this is right, then Megarian comedy is at least as old as the recorded performances in the Athenian theatre (ca. 480: Millis and Olson 2012, 156–7) and probably as old or older than those of Syracuse (**Ai**).

Our sources for Megarian comedy (**Bi**) show that it was very like Attic in form: choral, produced in competition at a Dionysian festival in theatres structurally similar to the Athenian, sponsored by choregoi, performed by masked actors and sharing many stock characters and stock jokes. Our Athenian sources attest only differences in taste and assume a general identity in style.

The Athenian writers who refer to Megarian comedy, even in the mid fifth century, rely upon their audience's and readers' familiarity with the genre. They indicate, moreover, that it had a powerful influence upon Attic comedy and that it even contributed to the standard repertoire of masks used in the fourth century (**Bi**; **Biii**). In the fifth century Megarian comedy produced international stars (**Bi 9**; **Biii**), and in the fourth century international stars performed in Megara's theatre (**Bi 4**). Though Aristotle in the second half of the fourth century still singles out Megarian productions for gaudiness and poor taste (**Bi 5**), Megarian comedy seems never to have been very far from the mainstream of the genre and doubtless merged with it in the fourth century.

Surprisingly there is no evidence in Megara for any other theatrical genre or even for a permanent stone theatre. As Megara was firmly oligarchic for most of the fifth and fourth centuries (Legon *IACP* 464), the city was probably shy of the more aggressively democratic theatrical culture that spread from neighbouring Attica. The one passage that *might* suggest some imitation of the political comedy developed from the 440s onwards in Athens implies an imitation of the mockery of *Athenian* tragedians and politicians (**Bi 3**). Megara evidently embraced its comedy as part of a native tradition. It shows therefore a very different pattern from the Aegean cities (**D**), where theatre's democratic culture seems to have been a major factor in its reception. Oddly, Megara's claim to the invention of comedy, which cannot be much later than the mid fourth century, draws precisely upon an assumption of an essential connection between democracy and comedy (**Bii 1**).

Sicyon made a much bolder claim (**Bv**). By ca. 400 the Sicyonians erected a monument in their marketplace celebrating the city's cultural achievements. In it one Epigenes of Sicyon was listed, probably along with several others, as a tragic poet of the first half of the sixth century (**Bv 2–3**). Herodotus' mention of Cleisthenes transferring 'tragic choruses' to Dionysus in the early sixth century is probably best understood in the context of this claim (**Bv 1**). Aristotle's statement that 'some of the Peloponnesians' claimed the invention of tragedy (**Bii 1**) doubtless includes Sicyon. Only one source from the first century AD mentions Sicyon in connection with the invention of comedy and this tradition is probably late (**Bv 5**), and possibly draws upon the assumption that tragedy and comedy stemmed from a common ancestor (cf. **Bii**; **I Avii 2**). A large number of theatre people had Sicyonian connections in the fifth and fourth century, but this circumstantial evidence does not permit much confidence that Sicyon actually had tragic performances at the time it made its claim to the invention of the genre. It is not until the late fourth century that Sicyon certainly had a theatre and probably also drama (when Demetrius the Besieger rebuilt the city in 303). Sicyon, like Megara, was an oligarchic state for most of the fifth and fourth centuries (Legon *IACP* 470; Robinson 2011, 50–3), and it would be of interest to know how this may have tempered the reception of theatre.

Phlious' claim to have invented satyr play may be no earlier than the beginning of the third century, when it seems to have appealed to the pro-Dorian and pro-Peloponnesian propaganda of the Attalids (**Bvi 7–9**). The Phliasians Pratinas and Aristias were said to have first introduced satyr play to Athens. The evidence for these two figures does suggest a tradition of satyr choruses in Phlious dating back to the sixth century and the antiquity of the choruses doubtless gave some substance to the claim. Evidence uncovered by the excavation of the theatre in Phlious suggests a wooden precursor no later than the fourth century and quite possibly of the fifth. Despite the normal connection of satyr choruses with Dionysus, Pausanias seems to connect the theatre with Asclepius (2.13.5). Non-Dionysian drama is a significant anomaly that we find elsewhere in the region.

The first theatres of Isthmia and Corinth are probably both constructions of the second half of the fifth century (Gebhard 2015, 107; **Biv**). The theatre in Isthmia is located in a sanctuary of Poseidon (Gebhard 1973). The earliest theatre competition attested in Corinth is part of a festival of Artemis, while the closest identifiable sanctuary to the theatre is that of Apollo (**Biv 1**). And yet both Corinth and Isthmia are significant for the history of dithyramb and Dionysian cult (for Corinth: Hdt. 1.23; Pi. *O.* 13.18–19; Kowalzig 2013, 31–4, 48–9; for Isthmia: Seelinger 1998; Reichert-Südbeck 2000, 171–8, cf. 131–3; Csapo 2003, esp. 85–6; Kowalzig 2013, 52; Ieranò 2013, 370). The Isthmian theatre seems to have been physically unsuited to the needs of drama (Gebhard 2015) and only used for the purpose in 66 AD when Nero, according to Philostratus (or pseudo-Lucian), won the contests for kitharodes and heralds and then demanded the creation of a tragic competition (Philostr. 641.14–16: 'though the established custom at Isthmia was that there were no competitions in comedy or tragedy, Nero thought he could beat the other tragic performers', Ἰσθμοῖ γὰρ νόμου κειμένου μήτε κωμῳδίαν ἀγωνίζεσθαι μήτε τραγῳδίαν ἐδόκει Νέρωνι τραγῳδοὺς νικᾶν). The earliest record of performance in the Isthmian theatre, which dates to 300–250, probably attests musical performances: a kitharodic performance or a kitharodic dithyramb (*IG* II² 3779, l. 15; *ATD* I, 130–1; Gebhard 2015, 114).

In Corinth too only musical performances are directly attested, though there is indirect evidence in the form both of fourth-century tragic actors sojourning in Corinth and comic vasepaintings and terracotta figurines produced in Corinth from about 375 (Green 2014a, 344–62). These indicate a regional style (of comic performance, apparently, and not just its artistic representation). Most striking is a figurine that appears to be extracted from a scene of Aristophanes' *Thesmophoriazusae* (Green 2014a, 347–9, fig. 13.18a–b). The earliest securely datable testimony for the Corinthian theatre (**Biv 1–2**) belongs to a period of civil war that initiated the short democracy in Corinth (and union with Argos) that lasted from 392 to 386 (Robinson 2011, 22). Otherwise 'for most of the classical period Corinth appears to have been reliably oligarchic in government' (Robinson 2011, 21; cf. Legon *IACP* 467). Corinth, like Sicyon and Megara, is thus one of the relatively rare examples of an oligarchic state that had a theatre, but here as in Megara, the evidence points partly to a regional tradition of comedy, and, as in Isthmia, to a possible preference for musical rather than dramatic performances. The evidence for regional comedy surviving well into the fourth century suggests a reluctance to embrace the now international, mainly Athenian-influenced, model of theatre culture. We do not hear of a Dionysia in Corinth until the mid second century.

Evidence for mainstream theatre culture is unavailable even in the case of the region's democratic states, Argos and probably Epidaurus. The traces of a rectilinear stone theatron, with a seating capacity of about 2,500, are visible underneath and beside a Roman period Odeon at Argos (Ginouvès 1972; Moretti 1993, 30–2). There is no trace of a skene building. The construction dates back to ca. 450 making it the earliest known stone theatre in the Peloponnese. At the date of its construction Argos had established a democratic constitution and had taken control of the Argive Plain (Robinson 2011, 9). Argos' democracy and its rivalry with Sparta made it a natural ally of Athens and a foe of Athens' oligarchic enemies for much of the fifth century (Piérart *IACP* 603). Given these circumstances, it would not be surprising to find evidence for the early development of a theatre culture, but we have none apart from the theatre itself. Argos' desire to consolidate its political and cultural hegemony over the newly incorporated cities of the Argive plain seems to have made the sanctuary of Hera at Prosymna, two hours' walk north-east of Argos, the focus of its festival culture (Hall 1995; Kowalzig 2007, 161–80). From the 460s until the late third century Argos sponsored the festival of the Hekatombaia at the Heraion (Amandry 1980; Hall 1995, 611–12). The festival was mainly athletic but included at least one musical competition, in kitharody, before the mid third century (*IG* II² 3779, l. 14). These competitions, however, had no connection with the theatre at Argos and we have no evidence for its use: it is generally supposed that the rectilinear theatre served chiefly or exclusively for civic assemblies or popular courts (Piérart *IACP* 605).

A new and very large theatre, with an audience capacity of 20,000, and a skene with proskenion, was built in the first quarter of the third century (Moretti 1993, 7–17). It was presumably built to accommodate the musical events associated with the transfer of the Nemean Games to Argos. Argos took control of the Nemean Games in 271 and permanently moved its musical events to its own theatre (Miller 2004, 108; Kyle 2015, 140, 143). Nemea itself had no theatre and probably had no musical events except perhaps during an earlier period of Argive control in 410–330 and then again after 271. But it is only from the second Argive period that we have clear evidence of musical competitions, beginning in 207 when Plutarch tells us that Philopoemen entered the theatre during a kitharodic competition (*Phil.* 11; Miller 2001, 8 n. 13). From the end of the third century the large theatre at Argos also seems to have absorbed the musical content of the Hekatombaia. The festival apparently outgrew the capacities of the Heraion at Prosymna and was reorganised as the 'Heraia' and held at Argos (Amandry 1980, 248–50; 1983). It is here in the early second century that tragedy is first attested (*Syll.*³ 1080). Probably also connected to the Heraia is a list of performers at Argos from the early first century which includes comic actors, tragic chorodidaskaloi and actors, a kitharode and 'singers' (Vollgraff 1919, 252–8 = *SEG* 33, 290).

We have no direct evidence for the use of the large theatre between its construction (300–275) and 207, but it seems very likely that the Argive theatre housed musical competitions for the Nemean Games very soon after its construction, and these may have included drama. The Isthmian–Nemean Artists' Association, which included actors, was probably formed during the time the Nemean Games were held in the Argive theatre, and the Association presumably had its headquarters at Argos (*ATD* I, 131–2). The large theatre in Argos was evidently designed for drama, as indicated not only by the skene building, an underground 'Charonian' passage from the skene to the orchestra, but also by a circle with tangential lines marked by limestone blocks sunken into the orchestra, which Moretti believed was designed to orient circular and dramatic choruses (Moretti 1993, 14, 39).

Despite the historical importance of Dionysus to Argos and the Argolid (Casadio 1994; Piérart 1996) and despite the city's distinguished musical traditions, including Dionysian music (Franklin 2013, 222–6), we have no evidence of music or drama being performed for him at Argos. The large theatre may have been consecrated to Zeus, as were the Nemean Games, but in Argos specifically to Zeus Eubouleus or to Demeter (Moretti 1993, 16).

In the fifth century Epidaurus was most often allied with Sparta against Athens and more particularly against Argos. Though the city appears to have had a democratic constitution, this seems not to have affected its external relations in the fifth or for most of the fourth century. After the Battle of Chaeronea (338) Epidaurus may have come under Argive control (Piérart *IACP* 607). Its small theatre probably predates this event. The conversion of the theatron into stone begins ca. 350 and continues into the second century (**Bvii 1**). The city of Epidaurus has one of the earliest surviving semicircular (horseshoe-shaped) theatres in Greece, and its design and production were probably undertaken in conjunction with the much larger theatre at the Asclepieion that was under Epidaurus' control (**Bviii**). The inscriptions suggest religious rather than political use of the theatre (dedications to Dionysus and Apollo by religious officials), and the existence of a skene suggests musical performances as at the Asclepieion. The somewhat later, but much more magnificent, theatre in the Asclepieion almost certainly formed part of the healing cult of the sanctuary (see on **Bviii**), with a likely emphasis on music, including choral performances, but drama is not specifically attested at Epidaurus, sanctuary or city, until the second century when both tragedy and comedy appear at the Asclepieia and Apollonia.

In sum, the north-east Peloponnese, including the Isthmus and the Megarid, is distinctive:

- For the large number of cities for which theatres or some degree of theatre culture is attested in the fifth century (Megara, Sicyon, Phlious, Corinth, Isthmia, Argos).
- For the number of cities that, with the backing of local tradition, laid claim to the creation of a dramatic genre by the Hellenistic period (Megara, Sicyon, Phlious) and with this group we could perhaps associate Corinth's claim to the invention of dithyramb (asserted as early as Pi. *O.* 13.13–19 and Hdt. 1.23), the ancestor of the theatrical men's and boys' (circular) choruses. This region seems to rival rather than imitate Athenian theatre culture.
- For the complete absence of direct evidence for the production of any normative form of drama in the Classical period, despite widespread pretensions to the creation of drama. It seems nonetheless likely that Megarian comedy merged with the mainstream and that Corinth had some drama.
- For a very large number of theatres or theatre festivals associated with gods other than Dionysus: Isthmus (Poseidon), Corinth (Artemis), Argos (Hera, Zeus or possibly Demeter), Phlious (Asclepius), Epidaurus Sanctuary (Asclepius and Apollo). This too testifies to the independence of their traditions.

Laconia (**Bix–Bx**)

Many of these characteristics are also found in Sparta, which seems to play a large role in the theatre history of the Peloponnese (see further below). Sparta's theatre is attested as early as 490–486 (**Bix 1**) and so is among the very oldest theatres in Greece. If the arguments that connect this theatre with the so-called Round Building in the Spartan Agora are correct, it is also the earliest known semicircular design, making the Peloponnese truly the origin of the form assumed by theatres everywhere in later antiquity (cf. Moretti 2014a, 133).

Drama, so far as we know, was not produced in Sparta's theatres until the first or second century AD (tragedy). We hear only of competitions in kitharody and in choral dance, where the kitharodes were international competitors and the choral dance was local, divided into age, tribal and phratry divisions, and sponsored by local choregoi. The choregic system in Sparta goes back at least to the Archaic period (Arist. *Pol.* 1241a33–7 = **V F** on Thrasippos' pinax) and probably well into the sixth century. Sparta may have served as a model for the introduction of tribal, choregically funded men's and boys' choruses at the Athenian Dionysia, ca. 508.

Ancient writers at least from the time of Sosibius (a Laconian historian of the 3rd–2nd c.) attempted to connect Sparta with the Dorian invention of tragedy (**Bix 4**) and especially comedy (**Bx 3**; cf. **5–12**). But the connections with tragedy are remote, fanciful and forced, while the connections with comedy amount to nothing more than cultic dances and crude entertainments at the Spartan syssitia. There is in fact no record of anything an ancient observer might have called comedy (κωμῳδία) ever being performed in Sparta. This is a surprising and surely significant fact, given all the attention paid to any activity that could vaguely remind later antiquity of some aspect of comedy. Indeed some of our testimonia rely for their intelligibility upon the assumption that tragedy or comedy was never performed in Classical Sparta (esp. **Bx 4**). Recent suggestions that Sparta produced forms of Dionysian music like dithyrambs remain speculative and, from the evidence used in the scholarship, it would seem, if it did exist, to be of a cultic rather than theatrical character like the men's and boys' choruses at Athens. Our sources show Spartan theatres being used for festivals of Apollo (**Bix 1, 3, 4, 6, 8**) and Athena Alea (**Bix 2**). The cultic dances and entertainments Hellenistic and later scholars likened to comedy or mime seem to have been performed mainly for Artemis.

Even in antiquity Classical Sparta often served as the paradigm case for an oligarchic constitution. It frequently does so today. In fact even in antiquity its classification was regarded as an idiosyncratic mix. But Sparta notoriously supported oligarchies elsewhere, and Sparta's political sympathies fitted the pattern for oligarchic states in the Peloponnese, the Aegean, and elsewhere of a general avoidance of theatre, or, in the few oligarchic states that had theatres, of an avoidance of drama or even the men's and boys' choral competitions that characterised Athenian theatre.

Arcadia (**Bxi–Bxv**)

Politics, internal and external, seem to play a large role in the history of theatre in Arcadia. Mantinea was a democratic state from at least 421 (Th. 5.29.1, cf. 5.54). Its theatre must date from about this time, but we cannot be sure that it was used for anything other than political purposes (**Bxi**). Sparta imposed an oligarchy in 385, but after the Battle of Leuctra in 371 Mantinea, like other Arcadian cities, threw off the Spartan yoke. Mantinea restored its democracy and became a founding member of the Arcadian League taking a leading role in the creation of the confederate city of Megalopolis in 371/0. Both creations, the League and its new capital, Megalopolis, were apparently designed to protect Arcadia from any future Spartan resurgence (D.S. 15.72.4; Paus. 8.27). The cities of the League seem all to have adopted a democratic constitution (Robinson 2011, 34–44; Nielsen *IACP* 521).

Megalopolis' theatre was probably part of the original design of the new city (Goette 1995a, 34–5; **Bxii**), even if the precise date of its completion in stone is disputed. The theatres in Tegea (**Bxiii**) and Orchomenus (**Bxiv**) were probably also built in the mid fourth century. Megalopolis had public funding through an agonothete and, as the name implies, competitions (**Bxii 1**). The same official appears in Tegea and Orchomenus and the same practice of dedicating prohedric benches in the theatre at the end of the official's term in office. This suggests a common theatre culture stretching back to the earliest days of the Arcadian League.

The competitions almost certainly included men's and boys' choruses in all theatres of the League cities (**Bxii 2**). The theatres and theatre festivals were in all cases theatres or festivals for Dionysus (**Bxii 2**; **Bxiii**; **Bxiv**; **Bxv**). Even remote Phigaleia (**Bxv**), which is assumed to be a member of the League, had a theatre and a Dionysia immediately after throwing off the Spartan yoke and becoming democratic: indeed the residual oligarchic faction chose the theatre and the Dionysia – doubtless a symbolic as well as convenient location – for a last brutal attack on the new democracy before the oligarchs withdrew to the safety of Sparta (**Bxv 1**).

The sudden appearance of theatres, public funding, competitions in men's and boys' choruses and Dionysia in the newly democratised and Laconophobic Arcadia looks like an attempt to embrace the kind of democratic theatre culture developed by Athens. We are specifically told by Polybius that the New Musicians Timotheus and Philoxenus dominated the League's theatres. Timotheus and Philoxenus seem inspired choices not only because they were the darlings of the Athenian theatre in the fourth century but, at least in the case of Timotheus, because he was famously loathed by the Spartan oligarchs who had so long oppressed Arcadia. Indeed Polybius, himself an Arcadian, claims that Timotheus and Philoxenus became the staple not only of theatrical entertainment but of public education (**Bxii 2**). The Megalopolitan theatre, still reputed to be the largest in Greece in Pausanias' day (7.32.1), seems an extravagant emblem of new cultural aspirations. Unfortunately we have no evidence that drama was part of this new democratic theatre culture, though the attestation of a skenotheke in Megalopolis strongly suggests drama at least from the middle of the third century (*SEG* 55, 539; *SEG* 47, 386; cf. *IG* V 2, 469), and possibly from the fourth century (Moretti 2014a, 113).

Elsewhere in Arcadia, a theatre has recently been uncovered in Stymphalus. Stymphalus was rebuilt between 375 and 360 (archaeological dating) and one is tempted to connect the rebuilding of the city with the general Arcadian resurgence after the defeat of Sparta at Leuctra. The city was an early member of the Arcadian League (X. *HG* 7.3.1). The earliest theatre, which has a stage building, is difficult to date. It was associated with early Hellenistic pottery and likely to be fourth century (Williams et al. 2002, 160–7; Williams 2005, 403–4), but further study may well permit an earlier mid-century date for the first phases of use in conformity with the general pattern we find across Arcadia (H. Williams pers. comm.).

Other Parts of the Peloponnese

Worthy of mention are a few theatres that lie on the periphery of the Peloponnese and possibly only at or beyond the lower end of our chronological time frame. All are in need of further exploration and unsupported by documentary evidence that might merit a more substantial inclusion in this volume.

Still more remote than Phigaleia is a large theatre some 50 km by road to the south at Messene. This is thought to have been built at the beginning of the third century (Themelis 2010, 19–20; Themelis and Sidiropoulos 2015). It was presumably here that the acting troupes performed that the Spartan king Cleomenes encountered coming from Messene through Megalopolitan territory in ca. 226/5 (Plu. *Cleom.* 12.1–4). Another

20 km to the south-east brings one to Thouria where preliminary exploration under Xeni Arapogianni of the recently discovered stone theatre suggests a third-century date (Petrakos 2017).

To the north and east there are theatres at Leontion on the border of Achaea, and of Elis and Ep(e)ion/Aipion in Triphylia, all thought, on archaeological grounds, to go back to fourth- or third-century foundations. In the case of Elis, a fragment of a locally made red-figured ceramic attests local knowledge of comedy in the late fifth century (Green 2014a, 333–4, fig. 13.1). The theatre at Aigeira seems no earlier than the early third century (Gauss et al. 2015).

Bi: Megarian Comedy

1. **Ecphantides, *PCG* F 3**. Ecphantides was active from ca. 455 to ca. 430. Cited in **6** below. The corruption at the end of the first verse is evident from the metre as well as the impossible verb form. The first two words of the apparent citation do not fit into an iambic trimeter. They may not be verse at all but comment from the anonymous commentator on Aristotle. The same may be true of the second line of the apparent citation. There have been many attempts to restore the fragment: in addition to the minimal apparatus here, see Conti Bizzarro 1994, 155–6; Bagordo 2014, 89–93. Text: after Kassel and Austin.

> ἀλλὰ καὶ Ἐκφαντίδης παλαιότατος ποιητὴς τῶν ἀρχαίων φησὶ·
>
> > Μεγαρικῆς κωμῳδίας † ἆσμα δίειμαι †
> > αἰσχυνόμενος τὸ δρᾶμα Μεγαρικὸν ποιεῖν.
>
> φησὶ <περὶ Μεγαρικῆς κωμῳδίας> Kaibel   ἆσμα codd.   ? <παραπέτ>ασμα cf. **6** and commentary below   δίειμαι codd.   δίειμι Meineke   μεθίεμαι Bywater

> But even Ecphantides a very old poet of Old Comedy says (Kaibel would read 'about Megarian comedy'): 'I will go through (reading δίειμι) a song (? or curtain?) ?of Megarian comedy though I (or 'he', i.e. Ecphantides) feel(s) ashamed to compose Megarian drama'.

2. **Eupolis, *Prospaltians, PCG* F 261**. Produced: 429 or 428? (Storey 2003, 231). The fragment is quoted by Anon. Arist. *EN* below (**6**). The second line is quoted by Sch.[V] and Sch.[LH] (Triclinius) to Ar. *Wasps* 57b and said to be from *Prospaltians.* The title implies a chorus representing members of the Attic deme of Prospalta (south-east of Athens in the Mesogaia). 'Heracles!' in line 1 is probably an oath, not a vocative address to a character in the play as Schiassi 1955 thought (Storey 2003, 238). Text: after Kassel and Austin.

> (Α.) τὸ δεῖν᾽, ἀκούεις; (Β.) Ἡράκλεις, τοῦτ᾽ ἔστι σοι
> τὸ σκῶμμ᾽ ἀσελγὲς καὶ Μεγαρικὸν καὶ σφόδρα
> ψυχρόν. † γελᾷς ὁρᾷς τὰ παιδία

1 τὸ δεινῆς cod.   τὸ δεῖν᾽ (or ὁ δεῖν᾽) Meineke   οὐ δεῖν᾽ ἀκούειν; Herwerden   3 σέλας cod.   γελᾶς Anon. ed. Ald.   γελᾷ γάρ, ὡς Cobet   ψυχρὸν γελᾷς· <γελῶσ᾽,> ὁρᾷς, τὰ παιδία Bergk   ψυχρόν· γέλως <τόδ᾽ ὡς> ὁρᾷς τοῖς παιδίοις Luebke

A. Well then … do you hear? **B.** Heracles! The joke is filthy, Megarian and really flat, you see it is the boys who are laughing (reading γελῶνθ᾽ ὁρᾷς).

3. Aristophanes, *Wasps* 54–63. Produced: Lenaea 422. Note the use of ἀνασελγαινόμενος ('violated') for Euripides, from the same root as ἀσελγές ('filthy') in **2**, as if part of a stock vocabulary for Old Comic descriptions of Megarian comedy. The slave 'Xanthias' speaks in the prologue. Text: Wilson.

φέρε νυν, κατείπω τοῖς θεαταῖς τὸν λόγον,
55   ὀλίγ᾽ ἄτθ᾽ ὑπειπὼν πρῶτον αὐτοῖσιν ταδί,
μηδὲν παρ᾽ ἡμῶν προσδοκᾶν λίαν μέγα,
μηδ᾽ αὖ γέλωτα Μεγαρόθεν κεκλεμμένον.
ἡμῖν γὰρ οὐκ ἔστ᾽ οὔτε κάρυ᾽ ἐκ φορμίδος
δούλω διαρριπτοῦντε τοῖς θεωμένοις,
60   οὔθ᾽ Ἡρακλῆς τὸ δεῖπνον ἐξαπατώμενος,
οὐδ᾽ αὖθις ἀνασελγαινόμενος Εὐριπίδης·
οὐδ᾽ εἰ Κλέων γ᾽ ἔλαμψε τῆς τύχης χάριν,
αὖθις τὸν αὐτὸν ἄνδρα μυττωτεύσομεν.

Well then, let me reveal the plot to the audience, [55] just first prefacing these few words for them. Don't expect anything too magnificent from us, nor, again, a joke stolen from Megara. Because there will be no pair of slaves throwing about nuts to the audience from a large basket, [60] nor a Heracles who has been cheated of his dinner, nor a Euripides being violated, nor, if Cleon has been brilliant thanks to his good luck will we once again make hash of the man.

4. Callisthenes, *Apophthegmata*, *FGrH* 124 F 5 (= Ath. 8.350f). Callisthenes died in 327. The famous wit and kitharode Stratonicus was active in the first half of the 4th c. (Stefanis no. 2310). Nothing else is known of Phaon (Stefanis no. 2465). The fragment deals with Stratonicus' clever repartees to celebrities and especially famous musicians. We can infer from the way Phaon is introduced that he was also famous and the anecdotes imply that he is a piper, probably of the very prolific Theban school (hence the pun on Cadmus and Harmonia). The pun on Cadmus has not to our knowledge been explained: possibly it refers to the expression 'Cadmean victory' which entails the destruction of the victor. Text: Kaibel.

τὸν Φάωνα δὲ ἔφη αὐλεῖν οὐχ ἁρμονίαν, ἀλλὰ τὸν Κάδμον. προσποιουμένου δὲ εἶναι Φάωνος αὐλητικοῦ καὶ ἔχειν φάσκοντος Μεγαροῖ χορόν, ληρεῖς, ἔφη· ἐκεῖ μὲν γὰρ οὐκ ἔχεις, ἀλλ᾽ ἔχει.

He (Stratonicus) said that Phaon did not pipe a scale (*harmonia*, puns on Harmonia, wife of Cadmus), but a Cadmus. When Phaon pretended to have great skill as an aulete and said he had a chorus at Megara, he (Stratonicus) said 'Nonsense! You do not possess anything there, but are possessed.'

5. **Aristotle,** *Nicomachean Ethics* **4.2, 1123a19–27**. Written ca. 330. In this chapter Aristotle examines the virtue of magnificence (*megaloprepeia*), which is a great expenditure on a fittingly grand and honourable object (for which dedications and choregiai are given as prime examples). Like all virtues there are vices corresponding to an excess or deficiency of the same disposition, in this case crass vulgarity and mean-spiritedness respectively. Vulgarity is excessive spending on a trivial object or ostentation in inappropriate circumstances. Text: Bywater.

> ὁ δ᾽ ὑπερβάλλων καὶ βάναυσος τῷ [20] παρὰ τὸ δέον ἀναλίσκειν ὑπερβάλλει, ὥσπερ εἴρηται. ἐν γὰρ τοῖς μικροῖς τῶν δαπανημάτων πολλὰ ἀναλίσκει καὶ λαμπρύνεται παρὰ μέλος, οἷον ἐρανιστὰς γαμικῶς ἑστιῶν, καὶ κωμῳδοῖς χορηγῶν ἐν τῇ παρόδῳ πορφύραν εἰσφέρων, ὥσπερ οἱ Μεγαροῖ. καὶ πάντα τὰ τοιαῦτα ποιήσει οὐ τοῦ [25] καλοῦ ἕνεκα, ἀλλὰ τὸν πλοῦτον ἐπιδεικνύμενος, καὶ διὰ ταῦτα οἰόμενος θαυμάζεσθαι, καὶ οὗ μὲν δεῖ πολλὰ ἀναλῶσαι, ὀλίγα δαπανῶν, οὗ δ᾽ ὀλίγα, πολλά.

The man who is excessive and vulgar [20] spends beyond what is appropriate, as we said. He lavishes his money on small objects and is ostentatious beyond measure, like someone who brings a wedding feast to a potluck dinner, or when a choregos brings purple cloth in the parodos, as do those in Megara. And he will do such things not for any [25] noble end but in order to show off his wealth, and anticipates that he will be admired because of these things, but spends little on the things that deserve large expenditure, while spending a lot on the things that deserve little.

6. **Anonymous commentator on Aristotle,** *Nicomachean Ethics* **1123a23 (*CAG* XX, p. 186)**. The same source seems to be used by the scholia to Ar. *Wasps* 57a–58b (Ornaghi 2016, 110). A much shorter version of this appears in the scholia to Arist. *EN* 1123a22.3. Moraux argues that the commentator's source is a literary-historical work by the Aristotelian philosopher and polymath Adrastos of Aphrodisias, a scholar active probably in the mid 2nd c. AD, who was steeped in the writings of Aristotle and Theophrastus (1984, 323–9; Kerkhof 2001, 19). Indeed the words ἐπεὶ καὶ ἀντιποιοῦνται αὐτῆς seem to echo Aristotle's own διὸ καὶ ἀντιποιοῦνται τῆς τε τραγῳδίας (**Bii 1**; cf. Ornaghi 2016, 112–13). The comic fragment of Myrtilus (*PCG* F 1) was lost in transmission: he was a contemporary of Aristophanes who, according to the Victor List, won the Lenaean contest of ca. 427. The commentary is meant to explain the reference to the choregia in **5**. Text: Heylbut.

σύνηθες ἐν κωμῳδίᾳ παραπετάσματα δέρρεις ποιεῖν οὐ πορφυρίδας. Μυρτίλος ἐν Τιτανόπασι τὸ *** (quotation of **2** omitted) διασύρονται γὰρ οἱ Μεγαρεῖς ἐν κωμῳδίᾳ, ἐπεὶ καὶ ἀντιποιοῦνται αὐτῆς ὡς παρ᾽ αὐτοῖς πρῶτον εὑρεθείσης, εἴ γε καὶ Σουσαρίων ὁ κατάρξας κωμῳδίας Μεγαρεύς. ὡς φορτικοὶ τοίνυν καὶ ψυχροὶ διαβάλλονται, καὶ πορφυρίδι χρώμενοι ἐν τῇ παρόδῳ. καὶ γοῦν Ἀριστοφάνης ἐπισκώπτων αὐτοὺς λέγει που ᾽μηδ᾽ αὖ γέλωτα Μεγαρόθεν κεκλημένον᾽. (The commentator continues with the quotation of Ecphantides in **1**.) δείκνυται γὰρ ἐκ πάντων τούτων ὅτι Μεγαρεῖς τῆς κωμῳδίας εὑρεταί.

In comedy it was customary to make hangings of leather and not purple cloth. Myrtilus in the *Titanopanes* (the quotation from Myrtilus has been lost, instead the text continues with the fragment of Eupolis in **2**, above). The Megarians are mocked in comedy, especially because they are rival claimants to it, on the grounds that comedy was first invented by them, if indeed Susarion the originator of comedy is Megarian. They are moreover discredited as vulgar and insipid, and as using purple cloth in the parodos. Aristophanes, at any rate, mocks them, saying somewhere 'nor, again, a joke stolen from Megara' (**3**, l. 57). (The commentator continues with the quotation of Ecphantides in **1**.) It is demonstrated by all this that the Megarians were the inventors of comedy.

7. Proverbia Bodleiana 285. Shorter versions of this entry appear in the collection of Pseudo-Diogenianus *CPG* 3.88 = Apostolius 5.29.2 and in Suda γ 115. The 'proverb' seems to come ultimately from **3**, l. 57. Text: Gaisford.

γέλως Μεγαρικός· ἐπὶ τῶν ἀώρως θρυπτομένων. ἤκμασε γὰρ ἐπὶ χρόνον ἡ Μεγαρικὴ κωμῳδία, ἣν Ἀθηναῖοι καταμωκώμενοι ἐγέλων.

'Megarian joke': used of those who are prematurely withered, because Megarian comedy blossomed for a time, a comedy which the Athenians laughed at scornfully.

8. Hesychius, *Lexicon* s.v. γέλως Μεγαρικός ('Megarian joke', γ 317). Compiled in the 5th or 6th c. AD. The 'proverb' seems to come ultimately from **3**, l. 57. Text: Latte.

γέλως Μεγαρικός· ὁ σκωπτικός.

'Megarian joke': one that mocks.

9. *Etymologicum Genuinum* AB s.v. Τολύνιον ('Tolynion' = *EM* p. 761, 46). Compiled 9th c. AD. Meineke (1839, 38) conjectured 'Telleneion' for 'Tolynion' in order to make a connection with a piper and poet known from other sources (cf. Körte 1937; Stefanis no. 2384). Text: Gaisford.

Τολύνιον· τὸ καλούμενον Κρατίνειον μέτρον πολυσύνθετον. καλεῖται γὰρ ἀπὸ τοῦ Μεγαρέως Τολύνου· ἔστι δὲ προγενέστερος Κρατίνου.

'Tolynion': the so-called Cratinean metre that is a compound of many elements. It is named after the Megarian Tolynos. He was born before Cratinus.

Since late antiquity discussion of Megarian comedy has been dominated by the Megarian claim that they invented drama (**6**; **Bii**). Modern scholarship has been even less successful in separating information about Classical Megarian theatre from questions of the prehistory of Greek comedy. Information about comedy contemporary with our fifth- and fourth-century sources is often misappropriated to discussions of the prehistory of drama. Quite unlike the humorous performances at Sparta (**Bx**), our ancient sources speak unambiguously of Megarian 'comedy' (possibly **1**; certainly **5** etc.; **Bii 1**), but scholarship persistently speaks of Megarian 'Possenspiel', 'Stegreifspiel' or 'farce' and openly challenges the notion that Megarian comedy really deserves to be classed as comedy (e.g. Körte 1921, 1222; Ornaghi 2016, 247 would take the reference to 'drama' in **1** to indicate farce rather than comedy). While our ancient sources speak of bad taste, modern scholarship speaks of primitive ritual. The whole question of Megarian drama is bedevilled by the evolutionary and anthropological framework into which nineteenth-century German scholarship inserted it as if a missing link in the evolution of comedy from religious mummery to literary artefact (history in Kerkhof 2001, 1–12). Scholars pointed to the South Italian 'phlyax vases' as proof of the survival of primordial forms of Doric 'folk drama' into and beyond the Classical period. But these 'phlyax' vases are now known to depict Attic drama. Might the posited species gap between Megarian and Athenian comedy also be the residue of false assumptions and outdated research agendas?

It is true that our Attic sources characterise Megarian comedy as vulgar (**2**, **3**, **5**, **6**), frigid (**2**, **6**), unimaginative (**3**), and inclined to personal abuse (**3**, **8**). But our main sources are Megara's rivals, the Athenian comic poets. Aristophanes adopts the same posture towards his Attic rivals and they to him. If we are obliged to take with a grain of salt ancient comic poets' statements about their rivals, we should apply the same caution to their statements about a rival theatre. The examples of the kinds of jokes 'stolen from Megara' offered by **3** have abundant parallels in Attic comedy and even in Aristophanes' own work (supposing the γάρ in **3**, l. 58 is meant to introduce a list exemplifying the claim). Slaves throwing nuts to the audience appear to be a regular feature of Old Comedy, and is almost certainly practised by Aristophanes himself at *Peace* 962–7 and elsewhere (**V H**). The bulimic Heracles is a well-known stereotype in Attic comedy (Ar. *Peace* 741 with Sch. *ad loc.*; *Frogs* 52–65; *Birds* 1574–1693; Ephippus *PCG* F 3 with Konstantakos 2011; Alexis *PCG* F 88 and 140; Sch. Ar. *Wasps* 60; Galinski 1972, 81–100; Casolari 2003, 249–95; Konstantakos 2015), and it is with reference to Attic comedy that Aristophanes boasts 'I first drove off the stage with contempt those kneading and starving Heracleses' (*Peace* 741–2). Most surprising, however, is **3**'s apparent ascription to 'Megarian comedy' of such standard Attic and Aristophanic traits as abuse of Euripides and Cleon. Most scholars feel that Aristophanes is no longer describing Megarian comedy here, but now thinking in general about comedy that is 'too magnificent' (**3**, l. 56; Pickard-Cambridge 1927, 277 n. 1; Kerkhof 2001, 20–1; Konstantakos 2012, 126), arguing that the change of conjunctions from οὔτε to οὐδ' αὖθις must show a change of topic in his list from typically Megarian to typically Attic (though as we have seen even the first pair of examples are typically Attic).

Such paradoxes led Wilamowitz at one point in his career to doubt that 'Megarian comedy' had any reference to a distinct local performance tradition, but rather interpreted 'Megarian' to be nothing more than Athenian slander for 'vulgar' Attic comedy (1875; cf. Breitholz 1960, 62–71). But this theory is inconsistent with the language of our sources, which is not figurative: **3**'s 'joke stolen from Megara' is explicitly and concretely geographical. In a small way, nonetheless, the young Wilamowitz and Breitholz are right: Aristophanes' target is not Megarian comedy directly but his Athenian rivals who, he claims, copy Megarian comedy. It would be more accurate to say that our sources attest not the crudeness of Megarian comedy so much as its similarity to Attic, however much our Attic comic poets might affect to despise it. In any case the syntax of **3** is not helpful for those who might argue that Megarian comedy shared only vulgar and buffoonish humour with Attic comedy. Even at its lowest level Megarian humour was popular in the Attic theatre. Konstantakos (2012) persuasively argues that one of the funniest scenes in Aristophanes, the Megarian merchant in *Acharnians*, makes extensive use of the themes and techniques of Megarian comedy.

Given the similarities, it was an easy thing for an Attic comic poet to accuse his rivals of emulating Megara. The fault outlined by Aristotle in **5** is similarly directed at the non-Megarian choregos who 'brings purple cloth into the parodos', in imitation of what he implies to be the regular practice of the Megarian theatre. The evidence suggests that **6**'s explanation of the 'purple' is correct (against the interpretation of Sifakis 1971). In the Attic theatre it was customary during performances to put leather hangings on the gates at either parodos of the theatre in order to screen the gathering of the chorus or actors before their entry into the view of the audience (Kerkhof 2001, 18). These leather screens were surely mentioned in the lost fragment of Myrtilus (**6**) and they are mentioned probably in reference to the Athenian theatre by the comic Plato (*PCG* F 267) and in a fragment of a probably Old Comic author (*PCG* adesp. *307) preserved by Hesychius (δ 689). Hesychius glosses the word 'pegged up with screen' (δερριδόγομφοι) with 'gates with leather screens' (πύλαι δέρρεις ἔχουσαι, παραπετάσματα). Screens of this sort seem also to have been used around the skene (cf. Zonaras α 345.5: αὐλαῖαι· αἱ δέρρεις τῆς σκηνῆς 'curtains: the screens of the skene', if this means 'the stage building' and not 'the tent' – δέρρεις is also regularly used of the door flaps of tents). Froning (2014, 310) makes a good case that the 'screens' discussed by these authors are shown on the 'Perseus Dancer Vase' in **V D**. The use of purple hangings around the stage building is attested for Syracuse in the early fifth century (**Aiv 1**), so the extravagance was not confined to Megara (cf. Pickard-Cambridge 1927, 414), and indeed Aristotle's words can be taken to imply that some Athenian choregoi undertook the expense.

Scholars rightly argue that **5** *need* not imply the existence of a choregic system in Megara (Wilson 2000, 285; Konstantakos 2012, 125), though it is far more natural to take 'someone … when choregos, brings purple cloth into the parodos as do those in Megara' as meaning 'the choregoi in Megara', than to take it simply as an equivalent of 'the Megarians' (a reading that would make οἱ Μεγαροῖ strictly equivalent to οἱ Μεγαρεῖς). Aristotle's example has in any case more force if the comparison is to individual Megarians pretending to magnificence, since he is concerned in the *Ethics* with the manner in which individuals spend their wealth, not nations. The ascription to Megara of such comic routines as actors throwing food to the audience is a strong point in favour of a choregic competition, since at Athens at least it is a rather transparent device by which choregoi curried audience favour (**V H**). We know from **4** in any case, that Megara had choral performances (though here no genre is named) to which pipers of international stature were assigned and, on a strict reading of the text, one per chorus, suggesting a competitive environment. **9** gives evidence of a Megarian poet who used the lyric metre that came to be associated with Cratinus in later antiquity. Those who believe in Tolynos' existence usually suppose he is a comic poet, but this is not stated and cannot securely be inferred from the later history of the metre. While the evidence for the choral content of Megarian comedy may not be conclusive, Körte's confident denial of a chorus in Megarian comedy is completely unwarranted (1937).

In sum, though Attic sources 'discredit' (**6**'s διαβάλλονται could be translated as 'slander') Megarian comedy as lumpish and tasteless, they at the same time suggest a picture of Megarian comedy which seems very much like the comedy we know in Attica and does not at all justify the attempt by modern scholars to place it in an entirely different genre from Attic comedy by using words like 'farce' or 'Possenspiel'. The interpretation of the sources is admittedly difficult, but an unprejudiced reader could conclude from the material we have just examined that Megara had famous composers and actors, that its comedy had subjects and themes that were familiar from Attic comedy (and indeed emulated by it), that its comedy was performed by actors wearing masks (**Biii**) and playing roles familiar from Attic comedy (and in some cases directly borrowed by Attic comedy), that it was sponsored by choregoi, performed in competition, had songs performed to the music of famous international pipers (**4**), was performed in theatres with a topography comparable to that of the Theatre of Dionysus and decorated in ways that once again provoked the emulation of Attic choregoi.

Apart from Maison (**Biii**), there are no comic actors or poets known from fifth- or fourth-century Megara. There are however two Megarians active in the Athenian theatre in the training of men's and boys' lyric choruses: Antiphilos, a didaskalos for boys' choruses, who was victorious at the Athenian Thargelia in 354/3 (*SEG* 26, 220; Stefanis no. 223); and the aulete, Telephanes, who was victorious in Salamis and was probably the Telephanes who did double duty as chorodidaskalos for Demosthenes when he served as choregos for a men's lyric chorus (**Dxii 2**; D. 21.14–18 in **V G**; Stefanis no. 2408).

It is not until the third century that we find Megarians internationally active in dramatic genres: there are three tragoidoi (Stefanis nos. 450, 584, 1162), a komoidos (Stefanis no. 2393), a didaskalos of comedy (Stefanis no. 1656) and a comic choreut (Stefanis no. 764). In addition third-century Megara had other successful theatre performers: a choreut for men's choruses (Stefanis no. 815), an aulete (Stefanis no. 44) and a kitharode (Stefanis no. 790).

No physical trace of a theatre has been found in Megara (Rune Frederiksen has very kindly confirmed for me that his doubts about the reported theatre setting in 2002, 116 no. 145 were correct). No theatre is mentioned either by Pausanias, though it is unclear what inference if any could be derived from his silence. A theatre and a Dionysia are attested by inscriptions of the early second to first century (*IG* VII 19; *IG* VII 20; *IG* VII 21, l. 24; *IG* VII 190, l. 19). There was a cult of Dionysus in Megara from Archaic times (Ornaghi 2016, 432–44), and a cult of Melampus in Aegosthena (Paus. 1.44.5), the mythic missionary of

Dionysus who is said by Herodotus (2.49) to have introduced phallic rites for Dionysus to Greece.

Bii: Megarian Susarion?

1. Aristotle, *Poetics* 1448a28–b1. Written ca. 335–330. The Megarian democracy is usually dated to the 6th c. (Robinson 1997, 114–17; Wallace 2007, 57; Ornaghi 2016, 344–51; on the question of how 'democratic' the supposed democracy was see Forsdyke 2005, 48–59; the category betrays the perspective of the mature or late Classical period: Ornaghi 2016, 291–2). For the translation 'wronged out of the city', see commentary below. Text: after Tarán.

> ὅθεν καὶ δράματα καλεῖσθαί τινες αὐτά φασιν, ὅτι μιμοῦνται δρῶντας. διὸ καὶ [a30] ἀντιποιοῦνται τῆς τε τραγῳδίας καὶ τῆς κωμῳδίας οἱ Δωριεῖς - τῆς μὲν γὰρ κωμῳδίας οἱ Μεγαρεῖς οἵ τε ἐνταῦθα ὡς ἐπὶ τῆς παρ᾽ αὐτοῖς δημοκρατίας γενομένης καὶ οἱ ἐκ Σικελίας, ἐκεῖθεν γὰρ ἦν Ἐπίχαρμος ὁ ποιητὴς πολλῷ πρότερος ὢν Χιωνίδου καὶ Μάγνητος· καὶ τῆς τραγῳδίας ἔνιοι [a35] τῶν ἐν Πελοποννήσῳ - ποιούμενοι τὰ ὀνόματα σημεῖον· αὐτοὶ μὲν γὰρ κώμας τὰς περιοικίδας καλεῖν φασιν, Ἀθηναίους δὲ δήμους, ὡς κωμῳδοὺς οὐκ ἀπὸ τοῦ κωμάζειν λεχθέντας ἀλλὰ τῇ κατὰ κώμας πλάνῃ ἀτιμαζομένους ἐκ τοῦ ἄστεως· [b1] καὶ τὸ ποιεῖν αὐτοὶ μὲν δρᾶν, Ἀθηναίους δὲ πράττειν προσαγορεύειν.

That is why some say they are also called dramas (*dramata*), because they imitate men in action (*drontas*). And for this reason [a30] the Dorians are rival claimants both to tragedy and to comedy – in the case of comedy the Megarians here, on the grounds that it came into being at the time of their democracy, and those from Sicily because the poet Epicharmus, who was much earlier than Chionides or Magnes (Athenian comic poets), came from there. In addition some [a35] of the Peloponnesians claim tragedy – they use the names as evidence. They say they call their outlying settlements 'villages' (*komai*), whereas the Athenians call them 'demes' (*demoi*), supposing that comedians (*komoidoi*) are not named from carousing (*komazein* = 'perform a *komos*'), but from the wandering about the villages of men who have been slighted (the word can also mean 'disenfranchised', but see commentary) from the city. [b1] Also for 'doing' they say *dran* (same root as *drama*), while the Athenians say *prattein*.

2. John Tzetzes, *Prooemium* I, Koster XIa I 78–88 (= Susarion *PCG* F 1). Written 12th c. AD. The same information in different wording is given in Tzetzes, *On the Distinctions between Poets* (Koster XXIa). Diomedes (Koster XXIV) and Stobaeus (4.22c.69) also cite the iambic verses purporting to be by Susarion, but without the second line that identifies him as Megarian. All four lines are however given by John the Deacon (Koster XIX) and by **4**. Tzetzes is drawing on a common source (Ornaghi 2016, 183–225), though with some significant difference in detail. Stobaeus alone adds a fifth line to the 'fragment': 'marrying is an evil and so is not marrying' which some editors believe to be excerpted from another poet (it would be an easy thing for a poet's name to fall out of Stobaeus' text: Kerkhof 2001, 40–4). Text: Koster.

> τῆς οὖν κωμῳδίας τῆς καλουμένης πρώτης πρῶτος καὶ εὑρετὴς γέγονεν ὁ
> Μεγαρεὺς Σουσαρίων ὁ Τριποδίσκιος, υἱὸς ὢν Φιλίνινιου, ὃς φαύλῃ γυναικὶ
> συνοικῶν ἀπολιπούσῃ αὐτὸν Διονυσίων ἠγμένων εἰσελθὼν εἰς τὸ θέατρον
> τὰ τέσσαρα ἰαμβεῖα ταυτὶ ἀνεφθέγξατο, ἃ μόνα τῶν ἐκείνου συγγραμμάτων
> ἐφεύρηινιται τῶν ἄλλων ἁπάντων ἠφανισμένων·

>> ἀκούετε λεῴ· Σουσαρίων λέγει τάδε,
>> υἱὸς Φιλίνινιου, Μεγάρόθεν Τριποδίσκιος·
>> κακὸν γυναῖκες, ἀλλ᾿ ὅμως, ὦ δημόται,
>> οὐκ ἔστιν εὑρεῖν οἰκίαν ἄνευ κακοῦ.

> οὕτως ἡ πρώτη κωμῳδία τὸ σκῶμμα εἶχεν ἀπαρακάλυπτον· ἐξήρκεσε δὲ τὸ
> ἀπαρακαλύπτως οὑτωσὶ κωμῳδεῖν μέχρις Εὐπόλιδος.

So of the so-called first comedy the founder and first practitioner was the Megarian Susarion of Tripodiskos, the son of Philinnos, who cohabited with a worthless woman and when she left him, as it was the time when the Dionysia was being celebrated, he entered the theatre and uttered these four iambic verses. These alone have been found. All his other compositions have disappeared. 'Oyez, people. Susarion says this, the son of Philinnos, from Megara, of Tripodiskos: Women are an evil thing, but nonetheless, demesmen, it is not possible to find a home without evil.' And so the first comedy had undisguised mockery. Mocking (*komoidein*) remained undisguised in this way until Eupolis.

3. Anonymous Crameri I, *On Comedy* (Koster XIb 3–26). There are several versions of this tale (closest in detail and expression are: Anon. *On Comedy* Koster IV; *EM* 764.13–24 Koster XVI; **4**). Text: Koster.

> τὸ παλαιὸν ἐν ταῖς κώμαις ἀδικούμενοί τινες ὑπὸ τῶν ἐν Ἀθήνησι πολιτῶν
> καὶ θέλοντες ἐλέγχειν αὐτοὺς κατῄεσαν [5] ἐν τῇ πόλει καὶ νυκτὸς καθευδόντων
> πάντων παριόντες παρὰ τὰς ἀγυιὰς ἔλεγον ἀνωνύμως τὰς βλαβάς, ἃς
> ἔπασχον ὑπ᾿ αὐτῶν, τοιαῦτα λέγοντες· ʼἐνταῦθα μένει τις τάδε καὶ τάδε
> ποιῶν τισι τῶν γεωργῶν καὶ οὐ μετρίας βλαβὰς ἐπιφέρων αὐτοῖςʼ, ὥστε τοὺς
> γειτνιῶντας ἀκούοντας ἡμέρας γινομένης πρὸς ἀλλήλους λέγειν, ἃ νύκτωρ
> παρὰ τῶν [10] γεωργῶν ἤκουσαν. ἐπονείδιστον δὲ ἦν τοῦτο τῷ ἀδικοῦντι,
> ὥστε καὶ πολλοῖς τῶν ἀδικούντων τὸ τοιοῦτο διορθώσεως γέγονεν αἴτιον
> αἰσχυνομένοις τὴν ὕβριν· ὅθεν τοῖς τῆς πόλεως ἔδοξεν ἐπ᾿ ἀγαθῷ γεγονέναι
> τὸ ἐγχείρημα τῶν ἀγροίκων καὶ ἀναζητήσαντες αὐτοὺς ἠνάγκασαν καὶ
> ἐπὶ θεάτρου τοῦτο ποιεῖν. οἱ δὲ δειλιῶντες τοῦτο ποιεῖν ἐμφανῶς τρύγα
> περιχρίοντες τὰς ἑαυτῶν ὄψεις [15] οὕτως εἰσῄεσαν· ὅθεν κἀκ τούτου μᾶλλον

τῶν ἀδικούντων ἐλεγχομένων ἐπὶ θεάτρου συστολὴ τῶν ἀδικιῶν ἐγίνετο. ἐπεὶ δὲ ἡ πόλις ἐκ τούτου μεγάλης ἀπήλαυσεν ὠφελείας, ποιητὰς ἔταξαν ἐπὶ τούτῳ κωμῳδεῖν, οὓς ἂν βούλωνται ἀκωλύτως. πρῶτον οὖν Σουσαρίων τις τῆς ἐμμέτρου κωμῳδίας γέγονεν ἀρχηγός· οὗ τὰ μὲν ποιήματα λήθῃ κατενεμήθη, δύο δὲ ἢ τρεῖς ἴαμβοι [20] ἐπὶ μνήμῃ φέρονται τούτου· εἰσὶ δὲ οὗτοι·

> ἀκούετε λέξιν· Σουσαρίων λέγει τάδε·
> κακὸν γυναῖκες, ἀλλ' ὅμως, ὦ δημόται,
> οὐκ ἔστιν οἰκεῖν οἰκίαν ἄνευ κακοῦ.

ἀρχὴν οὖν λαβόντος τοῦ πράγματος πολλοὶ γεγόνασι κωμικοὶ ἐλέγχοντες τοὺς [25] κακῶς βιοῦντας καὶ ἀδικίαις χαίροντας, καὶ ἐντεῦθεν ὠφέλουν κοινῇ τὴν πολιτείαν τῶν Ἀθηναίων.

5 ἐν τῇ πόλει Reg. R.   εἰς τὴν πόλιν MCVP

Long ago in the villages (*komai*) some men who were wronged by the citizens in Athens and wishing to expose them went down [5] in the city and when at night all were sleeping they presented themselves in the streets and began without mentioning names to describe the harms which they suffered at their hands, saying this: 'Here lives someone who is doing this and that to some of the farmers and inflicting no small harm upon them.' As a result the listening neighbours when day came discussed with one another the things they heard from the farmers during the night. [10] This became a cause of reproach to the wrongdoer, with the result that this kind of action became the cause of atonement by many of the wrongdoers when they felt shame for their arrogant behaviour. As a result the people of the city decided that the enterprise of the country people had brought a benefit and they sought them out and forced them to do this in the theatre. The latter, afraid to do this openly, covered their faces with wine lees (*tryges*), [15] and entered the theatre in this way. And so, as a result, as more and more of the wrongdoers were exposed in the theatre, there was a cessation of injustices. As the city had enjoyed a great benefit from this, they thereafter ordered poets to compose mockeries (or 'comedies') against whomever they wished with impunity. So a certain Susarion first became the founder of versified comedy. His poems have by chance been consigned to oblivion, but two or three iambic verses [20] of his are transmitted in memory. They are: 'Oyez the saying! So speaks Susarion: Women are an evil thing, but nonetheless, demesmen, it is not possible to have a home without evil.' Once the thing had a start many comic composers arose to expose those [25] who led wicked lives and delighted in wrongdoing. And from that time they conferred a public benefit on the constitution of Athens.

4. Commentary on Dionysius of Thrace's *Ars Grammatica*, Koster XVIIIb 1–29 (= *Grammatici Graeci* I 3, p. 18.15–19.15; Susarion *PCG* T 12). The tale in *EM* 764 (Koster XVI) is much briefer but nearly identical in language. In addition to an etymology of comedy from *komai* ('villages'), this narrative makes allowance for the derivation of 'comedy' from *koma* ('sleep') that we find in several other sources by insisting that the farmers went to the city 'around bedtime', cf. **3** 'at night'. The odd fact that the commentator mentions 'two or three verses' of Susarion that survive but then cites four suggests to Cantarella (1949, 29) that the second, identifying Susarion as from Megara, was added by a later interpolator, but note that John the Deacon (Koster XIX), who seems to use a common source, has all four lines (Ornaghi 2016, 183–216). The second line is notably absent in **3**. Text: Koster.

ἐφευρέθη δὲ ἡ κωμῳδία, ὥς φασιν, ἔκ τινος τοιαύτης αἰτίας. βλαπτόμενοί τινες γεωργοὶ παρὰ τῶν πολιτῶν τῶν ἐν Ἀθήναις καὶ θέλοντες ἐλέγχειν αὐτούς, κατήεσαν ἐν τῇ πόλει, καὶ περὶ [5] τὸν καιρὸν τοῦ καθεύδειν περιιόντες τὰς ἀγυιάς, ἔνθα ἔμενον οἱ βλάπτοντες αὐτούς, ἔλεγον ἀνωνύμως τὰς βλάβας, ἅς ἔπασχον ὑπ' αὐτῶν· ἵνα δὲ σαφέστερον εἴπωμεν, τοιαῦτά τινα ἐβόων· 'ἐνταῦθα μένει τις τάδε καὶ τάδε τισὶ ποιῶν τῶν [10] γεωργῶν καὶ οὐ μετρίας βλάβας ἐπιφέρων αὐτοῖς', ὥστε τοὺς γειτνιῶντας ἀκούοντας ἡμέρας γινομένης πρὸς ἀλλήλους λέγειν, ἅτινα νύκτωρ παρὰ τῶν γεωργῶν ἤκουσαν — ἐπονείδιστον δὲ ἦν τῷ ἀδικοῦντι — τὸν δὲ ἐμφανιζόμενον τοῖς τῆς πόλεως αἰδεῖσθαι καὶ παύεσθαι τῆς τοιαύτης ἀδικίας. τούτοις πολλάκις παρακολουθήσαντες ἄλλοι πολλοὺς τῶν ἀδικούντων ἀνέστειλαν· ὅθεν τοῖς τῆς πόλεως ἔδοξεν ἐπ' ἀγαθῷ γεγονέναι τὸ ἐγχείρημα τὸ τῶν κωμικῶν, καὶ ἀναζητήσαντες αὐτοὺς ἠνάγκασαν καὶ ἐπὶ θεάτρου τοῦτο ποιεῖν. οἱ δὲ αἰδούμενοι, [15] μᾶλλον δὲ φοβούμενοι, τρυγίᾳ περιχρίοντες αὐτῶν τὰς ὄψεις οὕτως εἰσῄεσαν. καὶ ἔτι μᾶλλον κατηγορουμένων καὶ ἐλεγχομένων τῶν ἀδικούντων ἐπὶ θεάτρου ἀνοχὴ τῶν ἀδικιῶν ἐγένετο τῆς αἰδοῦς ἔτι συνοικούσης τοῖς ἀνδράσιν. ἔδοξεν οὖν τοῖς τῆς πόλεως τὸ ἐγχείρημα καλὸν ὑπάρχειν καὶ λογίους ἄνδρας αὐτὸ μετιέναι. πρῶτος οὖν Σουσαρίων τις τῆς ἐμμέτρου κωμῳδίας ἀρχηγὸς ἐγένετο, [20] οὗ τὰ μὲν δράματα λήθη κατέλαβε, δύο δὲ ἢ τρεῖς ἴαμβοι τοῦ πρώτου δράματος αὐτοῦ ἐπὶ μνήμῃ φέρονται. εἰσὶ δὲ οὗτοι·

ἀκούετε, λεώς· Σουσαρίων λέγει τάδε,
υἱὸς Φιλίνου, Μεγαρόθεν, Τριποδίσκιος·
κακὸν γυναῖκες, ἀλλ' ὅμως, ὦ δημόται,
οὐκ ἔστιν οἰκεῖν οἰκίαν ἄνευ κακοῦ. [25]

ἀρχὴν οὖν δεξαμένου τοῦ πράγματος πολλοὶ γεγόνασι κωμῳδοί διακωμῳδοῦντες καὶ ἐλέγχοντες τοὺς κακῶς βιοῦντας καὶ τοὺς ταῖς ἀδικίαις χαίροντας, ἀναστέλλοντες τὰς ἀκαίρους καὶ ἀδίκους αὐτῶν πράξεις, καὶ ὠφέλουν κοινῇ τὴν πολιτείαν τῶν Ἀθηναίων.

Comedy was invented, they say, from a cause of this sort. Some farmers who had been harmed by citizens in Athens and wishing to expose them went down in the city and around [5] bedtime went about the streets where those who harmed them lived, and they began without mentioning names to describe the harms which they suffered at their hands. To be more precise they started shouting

this sort of thing: 'Here lives someone who is doing this and that to some of the
[10] farmers and inflicting no small harm upon them.' As a result the neighbours
hearing these things when day came discussed with one another the things
they heard from the farmers during the night. This became a cause of reproach
to the wrongdoer. The men informed against felt shame before the men of the
city and stopped their wrongdoing. On many occasions others followed the
example of these farmers and did away with many of the wrongdoers. As a
result the people of the city resolved that the enterprise of the comedians had
brought a benefit and they sought them out and forced them to do this in the
theatre. The latter feeling shame, [15] or rather fear, covered their faces with wine
lees (*trygia*), and entered the theatre in this way. And as more and more wrongdoers were charged and exposed in the theatre, there was a halt to wrongdoing,
since shame still cohabited with men. So the people of the city decided that
the enterprise was good, and that literary men should pursue it. So a certain
Susarion first became the founder of versified comedy. [20] Oblivion has fallen
upon his dramas, but two or three lines of iambic verse from his first drama
are transmitted in memory. They are: 'Oyez, people. So speaks Susarion, the
son of Philinnos, from Megara, of Tripodiskos: Women are an evil thing, but
nonetheless, demesmen, it is not possible to have a home without evil.' [25] Once
the thing got a start many comic composers arose to scoff at and expose those
who led wicked lives and delighted in wrongdoing and they did away with
their inconvenient and unjust actions, and conferred a public benefit on the
constitution of Athens.

Our earliest sources give or imply an Attic origin for Susarion. The very earliest surviving
mention of Susarion (264), the Parian Marble (**I Avii 3a**), mentions Ikarion in connection
with Susarion's invention of comedy. Clement of Alexandria, the second extant source to
mention Susarion (*Strom.* 1.16.79.1), towards the end of the second century AD, is explicit
that he was Ikarian (for a discussion of Clement's sources, see Ornaghi 2016, 67–97). The
Anonymous *On Comedy* speaks of 'Sannyrion and his associates' inventing comedy in
Attica, and it is very likely that 'Sannyrion' is an error for Susarion (Ornaghi 2016, 136–8).

The earliest datable testimony of Susarion's Megarian origin is **2** (John Tzetzes, twelfth
century AD). But Tzetzes clearly did not himself invent Susarion's Megarian origins: he
cites an iambic poem purporting to be by Susarion and this poem explicitly declares him to
be from Megara. The poem, though echoed by Q. Caecilius Metellus Macedonicus in 131
(Erler and Ungern-Sternberg 1987, 254–5), is not actually cited until the time of Diomedes
(4th c. AD) and Stobaeus (late 5th c. AD), but without the second line that identifies Susarion
as Megarian (see introduction to **2**). This might encourage one to think that the Megarian
Susarion is a Byzantine invention. Yet **Bi 6**, drawing upon a much earlier source (2nd c.
AD), knows of the theory of Susarion's Megarian origins and also knows that it was con-
tested. It is hard to imagine what motive any Imperial or Byzantine scholar might have
had for contesting the Attic origins of Susarion and comedy, and most scholars have been
willing to speculate that it goes back much earlier. We think there is compelling evidence
for a fourth-century source.

Since the dawn of modern scholarship the verse ascribed to Susarion (**2**) has been regarded as a forgery (e.g. Bentley 1699, 199–211; Wilamowitz 1875, 338; Pickard-Cambridge 1927, 282; Olson 2007, 329). Many even suppose that Susarion himself is a fiction (Pickard-Cambridge 1927, 283; Dover in *OCD*[3] 1458; Rusten 2006). But Susarion's historicity is defended by West (1974, 183). He regards Susarion as a sixth/fifth-century iambic poet, chosen by the Megarians to serve as a first comedian 'because, while he was no more a comedian than Semonides, he was a Megarian'. West makes the reasonable point that 'if Susarion had been an invented person, he would surely have been credited with verses more suited to the purpose he was to fulfil. As it is, the fragment manifestly belongs to the genre iambus' (1974, 184). This of course leaves open the possibility that a forger wished to create proof of an inventor of iambus, or an Urform from which both iambus and comedy developed (see below). We should note that one source (*PCG* T 11) does in fact make Susarion the inventor of iambus, rather than comedy.

If Susarion was an historical figure, the evidence does not favour a Megarian origin. The same is true even if we regard Susarion as a historical fiction. He seems, despite West, to have been of Attic origin or invention and only later claimed by some to be Megarian. A chief reason for doubting his Megarian origins is the language of the verses ascribed to Susarion. The language is standard Attic (not Ionic) and he invokes his audience as 'demesmen'. The Megarian claim, first reported by Aristotle (**1**), that they use the word κῶμαι for the extra-urban communities (and not δῆμοι) is confirmed by inscriptions (*IG* VII 1, l. 17). These Atticising and un-Megarian features cannot be explained as a simple reflex of adopting the Ionic dialect appropriate to the iambic genre. They do seem to indicate that, whether authentic or forged, the verses presuppose an Attic audience addressed in Attic fashion. This may even extend to Susarion's self-identification with patronymic and demotic (albeit from Tripodiskos), in formal Attic style, and the information that he is 'from Megara', which would hardly be necessary if the verse was designed for delivery in Megara. We cannot exclude the possibility that Susarion is a Megarian addressing an Attic audience (a possibility favoured by Meineke 1839, 18), but if so, then it undermines the purpose for which it is normally cited: namely to demonstrate either an Attic or a Megarian origin for comedy. A further point in favour of regarding the second of the four verses ('the son of Philinnos, from Megara, of Tripodiskos') as an interpolation is the fact that our texts **3** and **4** refer to the survival of only 'two or three iambic verses' (**2** 'corrects' this to 'these four iambic verses'). This may imply that the archetype of this tale really did have only two or three verses and the line was copied as it appeared despite the addition of a fourth verse.

The oddness of the name 'Susarion' has played a larger role than it merits in this debate. Körte inferred that because the name was not Attic it was probably Megarian (1931, 974). But this, of course, does not follow. Others have regarded the oddity of the name as proof of its fictionality. But this does not necessarily follow either: Kerkhof urges that unique names are less likely to appear in forgeries, since they lack credibility (2001, 48). Rusten takes the name as a sign of its mythical fictionality and wonders if it is not some compound formed from the name 'Arion' (2006, 43). The name is however not unique, though it is exceedingly rare. It appears as an ordinary anthroponym on a Hellenistic relief from Nicaea in Bithynia (*IK Iznik* 1588), while names beginning with 'Σουσ-' (an Aeolic form corresponding to Attic/Ionic 'Σωσ-') are quite common (*LGPN* has 80 names beginning with Σουσ-, apart from Susarion), though interestingly none of these comes from Megara where

Σω- names are normal. The shift from 'ω' to 'ου' takes place in Aeolic from at least the fifth century and possibly earlier (Bechtel 1921, 136, 143; Buck 1955, 27, 29; Morpurgo Davies 1965, 245). The name itself reveals nothing.

Since Bentley (1699, 204), many have placed evidentiary weight upon the silence of Aristotle regarding Susarion. Some take this as proof that Susarion was invented sometime in the half century between Aristotle's lifetime and the inscribing of the Parian Marble (**I Avii 3a**). Kerkhof, however, takes Aristotle's silence to indicate that Susarion was indeed Megarian, as Aristotle should otherwise have mentioned Susarion, rather than Chionides and Magnes, if he really were Attic (2001, 50). But Aristotle's silence is not a very solid foundation for argument: it is just as likely that Aristotle knew of Susarion but either did not believe him to be historical or did not believe him to be a comic poet. Even the premise of the argument, that Aristotle never named him, may also be wrong. A seventh-century AD commentator on Dionysius the Thracian's *Ars Grammatica* (*Grammatici Graeci* I 3, p. 306.9 = Sus. *PCG* T 12) actually reports that 'Aristotle says that Susarion began it' (ἄρξασθαι δὲ αὐτῆς Ἀριστοτέλης Σουσαρίωνά φησι). In the immediate context 'it' seems to refer to tragedy, which is one reason why the editor Hilgard treated the line as an ignorant interpolation; but Gudeman (1929) argued that the hasty transcription by the commentator, Stephanos, of an earlier commentator (Choiroboskos?) skipped over a reference to the origin of comedy, but included the sentence with the now-orphaned shifter 'it' appearing now to refer to tragedy when it had originally referred to comedy. Gudeman, moreover, argued on the basis of parallel material in other commentators on Dionysius the Thracian that the ultimate source was Aristotle's dialogue *On Poets*, which included discussion of the originators of various aspects of tragedy (Them. *Or.* 26, 316d Hardouin) and presumably included similar contents relating to comedy.

Else 1957, 112 also independently argued that Susarion was mentioned in Aristotle's *On Poets*. He was struck by the way Aristotle's language in **1** was echoed by the commentator on Aristotle's *Ethics* (cf. Webster in *DTC*² 187). The commentator on the *Ethics* writes (**Bi 6**): 'the Megarians are mocked in comedy, especially because **they are rival claimants to it, on the grounds that** comedy was first invented by them, if indeed Susarion the originator of comedy is Megarian' (διασύρονται γὰρ οἱ Μεγαρεῖς ἐν κωμῳδίᾳ, ἐπεὶ **καὶ ἀντιποιοῦνται αὐτῆς ὡς παρ' αὐτοῖς** πρῶτον εὑρεθείσης, εἴ γε καὶ Σουσαρίων ὁ κατάρξας κωμῳδίας Μεγαρεύς; the boldfaced words reproduce and abbreviate the language of **1**). It is clear that the commentator on the *Ethics* thought Susarion relevant to **1**, even though he is not mentioned by name in the text. 'There are', wrote Else (1957, 112–13), 'three possibilities':

1. The commentator is echoing the *Poetics*. But the *Poetics* does not mention Susarion; the commentator would have to have supplied his name (and the connection between it and the question raised in the *Poetics*) on his own initiative, which is perhaps not very likely.
2. The *Poetics* passage echoes the commentator. This is possible if the passage is an interpolation, but not very likely; although the omission of Susarion this way is more plausible than the addition the other way.
3. Both passages derive from the same source, which mentioned Susarion, but the *Poetics* passage had dropped him. Notice that if the author of the *Poetics* passage is Aristotle this

hypothesis gives a solid fourth-century source for Susarion; and that source might even be, say, Aristotle's own dialogue *On Poets*.

But whether or not Aristotle mentioned Susarion in the *Poetics* or in *On Poets*, his function is implicit in Aristotle's language in **1**. Aristotle cites the Megarian argument from the etymology of comedy, not being from *komos*, but from *komai* 'villages'. **1**'s expression adds a significant detail: comedy is named 'from the wandering about the villages of men who have been wronged from the city' (τῇ κατὰ κώμας πλάνη ἀτιμαζομένους ἐκ τοῦ ἄστεως). The word ἀτιμαζομένους is sometimes translated as 'men banned from the city' (e.g. Storey 2011 II, 5). Although this is a possible meaning of the word, it is secondary to 'slight', 'dishonour' or 'wrong' and a very indirect way of saying 'banish' (for which φεύγοντες would be normal, or if the reference is to people who have legally been deprived of their citizen rights, then ἀτιμούμενοι). Others understand the word in the sense of slighted but take 'from the city' (ἐκ τοῦ ἄστεως) in close combination with wandering (πλάνη): thus Bywater translates 'comedians got the name not from their comoe or revels, but from their strolling from hamlet to hamlet, lack of appreciation keeping them out of the city' (1909, 9). But to take 'from the city' in this way is not only redundant with 'wandering in the villages', it does not respect the actual word order. The expression ἀτιμαζομένους ἐκ τοῦ ἄστεως should mean 'those who were dishonoured from the part of the city' i.e. by men in the city. Moreover, the verb ἀτιμάζω, when used of persons, does not normally mean to 'not value' (as if equivalent to ὀλιγωρεῖν), but to diminish actively someone's honour by not treating them as law or convention requires. The detail shows that there is a narrative of injustice and retribution behind the etymology which involve a tension between the countryside and the city. It is also clear from Aristotle's words in **1** that the Megarian theory must be one in which comedy appears as an exercise of 'free speech', the distinctive feature of democracy, since the early democracy in Megara is cited by them as proof of the correctness of their claim to have first invented comedy (**1**). The use of free speech is somehow connected to retribution by the country people against the city people. Precisely these elements lie behind the 'political' theory of the evolution of comedy that we find in several late sources, and most clearly articulated in **3** and **4**.

Aristotle's words (**1**) show that, by the time they were written, some theatre historian had already formulated the germ of the theory that comes down to us from various sources (Anon. *On Comedy* Koster IV; Anon. Crameri I Koster XIb; *EM* 764.13–24 Koster XVI; Sch. D.T. Koster XVIII). It presupposes, like the pro-Megarian theory, a derivation of comedy from *kome* ('village') combined with a political interpretation that theorised the necessity of a democratic environment for comedy to take root. The protagonists in the theoretical history presented by **3** and **4** are 'some country people' who have been wronged by some city people (**3** ἀδικούμενοί τινες ὑπὸ τῶν ... πολιτῶν, **4** βλαπτόμενοί τινες γεωργοὶ παρὰ τῶν πολιτῶν). The other main elements implied in Aristotle's report (**1**) are there: the tension between city and countryside; the righting of wrongs; the adaption to democratic ends by the democracy of the public denunciations. (For other possible connections with the history of the Megarian democracy, see Ornaghi 2016, 335–400.)

There are some discrepancies between the story in **3–4** and the pro-Megarian tale implied by Aristotle. The most obvious is that the 'city' named in both **3** and **4** is explicitly

Athens. Another is that the 'wandering' expressed in Aristotle (**1**) is quite different from the simple visits to the city mentioned in **3–4**, since Aristotle speaks of it as 'wandering about the villages', in conformity with the view that comedy was first created in rural Attica. In this respect **I Avii 3d** is closer to the version assumed by Aristotle. In **I Avii 3d** the Attic farmers wander about the countryside. This suits the Attic version of the story where trage-dy and comedy both arose in the demes, and specifically Ikarion, before they were adopted by the city. Note that **1** also indicates that the Megarians claimed to have invented tragedy, in addition to comedy. The mention of 'trygedy' in **I Avii 3d** and of wine lees in **3–4** implies that our tale is meant to embrace the origins of tragedy as well as comedy, since 'trygedy' functions in the fuller histories as an Urform from which they both branch out (cf. **I Avii 2-3**). Our late sources therefore contain elements of both a pro-Attic and a pro-Megarian version of the origin of comedy, but in basic outline the plot of the narrative is the same.

It seems to us that the most economical way of explaining the various stages of this narrative is as follows. Fourth-century Attic theorists had developed a theory of wandering and singing rustics based on the assumption that drama originated in Ikarion and associated it with the figures of Icarius, Thespis and Susarion, who, whatever their historical reality, became the protagonists of a heavily mythologised history of drama (cf. **I Aiv 21**; **I Avii 2**): Icarius invented the Urform of 'trygedy' and the Ikarian demesmen Thespis and Susarion created from trygedy tragedy and comedy respectively. **1** shows that a pro-Megarian criti-cism of this tale had been made before Aristotle's day.

Wilamowitz (1906, 619) guessed that Dieuchidas, author of a Megarian history in five books, with a particular interest in early literary history, was responsible for Megara's pretensions to the invention of comedy. He is probably fourth century (cf. *FD* III 5, 58; *FD* III 5, 60A with Davison 1959, 221), but arguably later (Davison 1959; Piccirilli 1975, 14–15). Other named possibilities are Praxion (Jacoby *FGrH* vol. 3b, p. 396), probably the father of Dieuchidas and also an historian, as well as Hereas, author of a polemically an-ti-Athenian Megarian history of ca. 300 (Gudeman 1934, 111; Piccirilli 1974, 1295, 1298). Ornaghi (2016, 299–334) details the chauvinistic, pro-Dorian and anti-Athenian nature of these historians, and in particular their tendency to take Attic accounts and pervert them to pro-Megarian ends.

This Megarian history seems to have rejected the Ikarian origins of drama by urging the derivation of comedy from *kome* 'village', and pointing out that Ikarion was not a 'village' but a 'deme'. The pro-Megarians did not however propose a different narrative so much as modify the Attic tale, presumably locating the event in the villages around Megara at the time of their democracy. The Megarian version necessarily involved a rejection of Icarius and probably Thespis, but was content to claim that Susarion was a Megarian. The Megarian version presumably introduced or heightened the element of class tension between country folk and city folk in order to add credibility to their claim that comedy could only arise in democracy and in this way urge their claim to priority as their democra-cy was much earlier than the Athenian. In the pro-Megarian version known to Aristotle, it appears that, as in the older Attic version, the disaffected country people wandered around the villages before embarking on a performance in the city: a significant incubation in the villages is required by the etymological argument, and was a standing feature of the Attic myths relating to Icarius and Thespis (cf. **I Avii 2**; **I Avii 3**; **I Aiv 21**).

The importance of the villages would have remained something of an embarrassment, however, for pro-Megarian narratives, as Attica has a very large extra-urban territory, while Megara has very little. At some point, possibly after **1** was written, someone produced a fragment of Susarion. It is written as iambus because the established narrative framework of Susarion's first performance was a denunciation of wrongdoers performed, it would seem, by isolated wronged individuals and not by choral groups. It is also 'anonymous' as the tale requires, since it speaks of the evil of women in general and does not focus on Susarion's wife. That the forgery of early documents relating to the origins of drama was a common enough practice in the later fourth century is suggested by Aristoxenus' denunciation of Heraclides of Pontus for forging plays of Thespis (D.L. 5.92; Aristox. fr. 114 Wehrli). It seems highly likely, given the evidence examined above, that the second line of the poem of 'Susarion' that we find in **2** and **4** is an interpolation in a fragment that was probably invented to prove an Attic origin. In this interpolation 'Tripodiskos', a village (*koma*) in the territory of Megara, is of obvious importance in a narrative in which the few existing Megarian villages needed to be worked rather hard to permit the relevance of the etymology of 'comedy' from 'village'.

All of this tells us much more about the importance of theatre to the economies and prestige of Athens and Megara in the fourth century than about the remote origins of drama. Clearly Megarian comedy had a long enough tradition reaching well back into the fifth century (**Bi**) to permit a challenge to Athenian priority. This was bolstered no doubt by claims of some share in the creation of Sicilian comedy through Epicharmus of Megara Hyblaea (**Aiii**). **1**'s reference to 'some of the Peloponnesians' claiming tragedy seems to exclude Megarian pretensions to that genre. The claim to Susarion and a tradition of denouncing people while wearing wine lees does, however, tap into the Attic theory of the common dramatic Urform of trygedy, and it is perhaps significant that Aristotle mentions only a Megarian etymology for 'drama', in addition to that for comedy, leaving tragedy very much in the background.

Biii: Megarian Maison

1. Athenaeus, *Sophists at Dinner* 14.659a (= Chrysipp. *SVF* 3, App. II, p. 200 von Arnim). Athenaeus wrote ca. 200 AD; Chrysippus in the mid to late 3rd c. BC. Eustathius *Od.* 14.78, p. 1751.53, draws directly upon Athenaeus. Text: von Arnim.

> ἐκάλουν οἱ παλαιοὶ τὸν μὲν πολιτικὸν μάγειρον μαίσωνα, τὸν δ' ἐκτόπιον τέττιγα. Χρύσιππος δ' ὁ φιλόσοφος τὸν Μαίσωνα ἀπὸ τοῦ μασᾶσθαι οἴεται κεκλῆσθαι, οἷον τὸν ἀμαθῆ καὶ πρὸς γαστέρα νενευκότα, ἀγνοῶν ὅτι Μαίσων γέγονε κωμῳδίας ὑποκριτὴς Μεγαρεὺς τὸ γένος (Athenaeus continues directly with **3**).

> The ancients called the local (or 'citizen') cook Maison and the foreign cook Cicada. Chrysippus the philosopher thinks 'Maison' is derived from 'chewing' (*masasthai*), as if of an ignorant and gluttonous man. He is ignorant of the fact that Maison was an actor of comedy, Megarian by nationality.

2. Hesychius, *Lexicon* s.v. μαίσων ('maison', μ 96). Compiled in the 5th or 6th c. AD. It evidently derives from Chrysippus. Text: Latte.

> μαίσων· μάγειρον. ἄλλοι βορόν· ἀπὸ τοῦ μασᾶσθαι.
>
> μαγειρίον βόρον cod.   μασσᾶσθαι cod.

> 'maison': a 'cook'; according to others 'food'; from 'chewing' (*masasthai*).

3. Athenaeus, *Sophists at Dinner* 14.659a–b (= Ar.Byz. *On Masks* fr. 363 Slater). Written ca. 200 AD. This follows from **1**, above. Aristophanes of Byzantium was the head of the Library at Alexandria in the late 3rd and early 2nd c. It is unclear if the last sentence is also taken from Aristophanes. Text: Slater.

> ὃς καὶ τὸ προσωπεῖον εὗρε τὸ ἀπ᾽ αὐτοῦ καλούμενον Μαίσωνα, ὡς Ἀριστοφάνης [659b] φησὶν ὁ Βυζάντιος ἐν τῷ Περὶ προσώπων, εὑρεῖν αὐτὸν φάσκων καὶ τὸ τοῦ θεράποντος πρόσωπον καὶ τὸ τοῦ μαγείρου. καὶ εἰκότως καὶ τὰ τούτοις πρέποντα σκώμματα καλεῖται μαισωνικά ...

> and he (Maison) invented the mask called 'Maison' after him, as Aristophanes [659b] says in his *On Masks*, claiming that he invented both the mask of the slave and the mask of the cook. And, appropriately, the jokes suited to these characters are called 'Maisonic'.

4. Pollux, *Onomasticon* 4.148–50 (possibly citing Aristophanes of Byzantium, *On Masks*). Pollux's lexicon was compiled ca. 180 AD. It has been doubted that Pollux draws upon Aristophanes of Byzantium (*MNC*[3] vol. 1, p. 6 dismisses it as a 'sanguine guess'). In favour of this guess is the fact that a mask type, the Maison, discussed by Pollux was listed by Aristophanes' *On Masks* and clearly discussed in more detail than survives in Pollux (**3**, **7**). *DFA*[2] 178 is wrong, however, to say that **3** 'seems to conflict with the account of Pollux'; Pollux simply gives less information: he does not identify the mask as typically a cook and seems only to name the 'slave mask' (see below). It should in any case be borne in mind that the surviving text of Pollux's *Onomasticon* is an abridgement of the original, which itself belonged to a selective tradition. In general Pollux is known to have drawn extensively on the works of Aristophanes of Byzantium (Dickey 2007, 93, 96). *MNC*[3] vol. 1, p. 6 n. 20, through the study of artefacts, posits an Early Hellenistic–early Middle Hellenistic source for Pollux's list of masks, which should be precisely the time of Aristophanes, and since Aristophanes is the only person known to have written on masks at this time, most scholars regard Aristophanes as Pollux's probable source (Nesselrath 1990, 183 and n. 99). Text: Bethe.

> τὰ δὲ δούλων πρόσωπα κωμικὰ πάππος, ἡγεμὼν θεράπων, κάτω τριχίας, θεράπων οὖλος, θεράπων Μαίσων, [149] θεράπων Τέττιξ, ἡγεμὼν ἐπίσειστος ... [150] ὁ δὲ Μαίσων θεράπων φαλακρὸς πυρρός ἐστιν. ὁ δὲ θεράπων Τέττιξ φαλακρὸς μέλας, δύο ἢ τρία βοστρύχια μέλανα ἐπικείμενος, καὶ ὅμοια ἐν τῷ γενείῳ, διάστροφος τὴν ὄψιν.

The comic masks of slaves are: Pappos, Leading Slave, the Hairy-Lower-Down, the Curly Slave, the Slave Maison, [149] the Slave Cicada, the Leading Slave with hair overhanging his face … [150] The Slave Maison is red-haired and bald on top. The Slave Cicada is dark and bald, with two or three black braids on his head, and similar (i.e. black, braided?) in his beard, and cross-eyed.

5. Hesychius, *Lexicon* s.v. τέττιξ ('cicada', τ 671). Hesychius' lexicon was probably compiled in the 5th or 6th c. AD. The entry evidently preserves information ultimately derived from Aristophanes of Byzantium. Text: Hansen and Cunningham.

> τέττιξ· ἔξω τοῦ συνήθους ζώου παρὰ Ἀττικοῖς οἱ τῶν μαγείρων ὑπηρέται ξένοι, οἱ δὲ ἐντόπιοι μαίσωνες.
>
> μαίσονες cod.   μαίσωνες Schmidt

'cicada': aside from the ordinary creature the foreign underlings of cooks are called this by Attic speakers, the local ones are called 'maisones'.

6. Hesychius, *Lexicon* s.v. μούσωνες ('mousones', μ 1759). Lexicon compiled 5th or 6th c. AD. This entry evidently preserves information ultimately derived from Aristophanes of Byzantium. The word 'mousones' may just be a corruption of 'mai-sones' (see **2, 5**), but it may also be a comic condensation of Muses (Μοῦσαι) and Maisons (Μαίσωνες). The word for 'chiefs' (κορυφαῖοι) is normally a choral term in Attic and seems unusual for cooks. Conceivably the entry originated as a gloss on a word found in comedy. Text: Latte.

> μούσωνες· οἱ κορυφαῖοι τῶν μαγείρων. καὶ οἱ τεχνῖται.
>
> τεχνῆται cod.   τεχνῖται Schmidt

'mousones': the chiefs among cooks; and the actors.

7. Festus, *On the Meaning of Words* s.v. Maeson (p. 118 Lindsay). Sextus Pompeius Festus, in the later 2nd c. AD, epitomised the twenty-volume encyclopaedic diction-ary of Marcus Verrius Flaccus (55 BC–20 AD). The entry preserves information from Aristophanes of Byzantium. Text: Lindsay.

> *Maeson: persona comica appelatur, aut coci, aut nautae, aut eius generis. dici ab inventore eius Maesone comoedo, ut ait Aristophanes grammaticus.*

'Maeson': a name given to a comic mask, either of a cook, or a sailor, or some-one of that sort. It is named after Maeson, the comedian, who invented it, as Aristophanes the Grammarian (i.e. of Byzantium) says.

8. Philodemus, *On Rhetoric* Book 4 (?) (*PHerc.* 1007 cols. 6a–8a). Philodemus was an Epicurean philosopher whose floruit was mid 1ˢᵗ c. The papyrus (*PHerc.* 1007 = N in the apparatus criticus) was discovered at the time of the excavation of the Villa of the Papyri in Herculaneum in 1752. An apograph of the papyrus, made soon after its first unrolling in 1799, was brought to England by John Hayter and given to Oxford University in 1810 (this is O in the apparatus; early history in Scott 1885, 1–15). The passage comes from a discussion of good diction or verbal style (*lexis*). Text: re-edited from Sudhaus and a high resolution image of the apograph from 'The Imaging Papyri Project' site of Oxford University, Faculty of Classics.

καί⁷ᵃτοι διαφέρουσιν οὐ[δὲν οἱ] καὶ
μετὰ τὴν ἰσχὺν τ[ῶ]ν δια-
τριβῶν ἀνιστόρητοι γεγο-
νότες ἁπάσης τῶν πρὸ τοῦ
5 παρελθεῖν αὐτὰ[ς] καὶ κατισ-
χῦσαι διαλεχθέντω[ν], ἀλλ' οὐ-
θὲν ἧττον ὁ[ρ]ῶνται φανε-
ρῶς οἱ μὲν οὐχ ἧττον ἁγνεύ-
[ο]ῠτες ἐν λέξει τῶν ἄκρως
10 διατριβικῶν, οἱ δὲ μᾶλλον,
ἀναρίθμητοι δὲ τῆς οὕτω
προχείρου καχεξίας. ὀ-
κνῶ [γὰ]ρ εἰπεῖν, ὅτι τὸν τρόπον τοῦτον, ὃν διὰ τῶν
15 παραδειγμάτων οὗτος
ὑπέδειξεν, ὁ σκαπανεὺς
καὶ Μα[ί]σων μόνος λαλεῖ,
δοκῶ δὲ μηδ' ἀγυμνάσ-
των μόνον ἐν λόγοις ταύ-
20 τας εἶναι τὰς καχεξίας
ἀλλὰ καὶ τὸν κοινὸν λεγό-
μενον νοῦν οὐ προσφερο-
μένων, ὥστε κινδυνεύ-
ειν ἡμᾶς κατὰ τὸν λόγον
25 καὶ τοῦτο περιποιεῖσθαι
παρὰ τῆς ἰσχύος τῶν ῥη-
⁸ᵃτορικῶν διατριβῶν.

7a 17 μαθων N   μασων O   Μαίσων Usener

And ⁷ᵃ yet people who remained ignorant of all (rhetoric) after its establishment as a discipline are no better than those who lived before the discipline came along and established itself, but some are no less distinguished for purity of style than the greatest pundits of the rhetorical schools, and others are even more so, though there are countless many with this degree of common bad style. I hesitate to say that only a furrow-digger or Ma[i]son speaks in the manner which this man (a critic whose name is lost to us) reveals through his examples. I think this poor speech is not only characteristic of those who are uneducated but also of those who are not applying what we call 'common intelligence', and consequently we run the risk of doing this even despite the rigour of [8a] rhetorical study.

9. **Philodemus, *On Frank Criticism* (*PHerc.* 1471 col. XIIb)**. Date: mid 1st c. The treatise is mainly about how to apply and receive criticism and mainly interested in student–teacher relationships and the reactions of different personalities to different manners of criticism. Many editors suppose that the sentence mentioning Maison is a quotation of some sort, but we agree with Gigante (1971b) that the text makes better sense if Philodemus takes Maison as an example in his own voice (as in **8**). Text: Konstan et al. (but without the quotation marks).

> ποή[σ]ει δ᾽ αὐτοῖς φα-
> γερόν, ὅτι [σ]υνπεριφερό-
> μενος αὐτ[οὐ]ς φέρει. ἄ-
> λυπος γὰρ ὁ Μαίσων φρε-
> 5 [ν]ούμενος καὶ ἀπάγει τοῦ
> χωρίου. τῶν δ᾽ ὑπ᾽ αὐτοῦ
> κατασκευασομένων οὐ
> πάνυ μὲν ἀνέξεται παρ-
> ρησίας, οὔτ᾽ αὐτὸς ἡδέως
> 10 [κ]αταναρκ[ώ]μενος π[ρὸς] ἐ-
> κείνους τ[ετ]ράφθαι [πρ]ο-
> [αιρήσεται]

2–3 [σ]υνπεριφερόμενος Konstan   [ν]υν περιφερόμενος Olivieri   11–12 [πρ]ο-[αιρήσεται] Philippson   [όμ]ο[νοήσει] Olivieri

He (the wise man?) will make it clear to them that he will be [i]ndulgent and bear with the[m]. For Maison when being instructed takes no offence and gives ground. But he will not easily put up with the frank criticism of those who are to be instructed by him, nor will he happily become passive towards them and choose (or 'agree') to be redirected.

10. **Zenobius, *Proverbs* 2.11**. Zenobius, the sophist, was active in the early 2nd c. AD. According to the Suda (ζ 73) he collected proverbs from Didymus (ca. 63 BC–10 AD) and Lucillus of Tarrha (1st c. AD). This formed the core of a collection, added to by several later scholars, that has come down under his name. Maison's use of 'Achaean' here is also reported, without mention of Maison, by Suda (α 2637; cf. **11**). But the Suda

has 'avenge' rather than 'tie up', and says the proverb is aimed at those who 'commit outrage against their benefactors'. Text: von Leutsch-Schneidewin.

ἀντ᾽ εὐεργεσίης Ἀγαμέμνονα δῆσαν Ἀχαιοί· αὕτη κατὰ τῶν ἀχαρίστων λέγεται. φασὶ δὲ αὐτὴν ὑπὸ Μαίσωνος τοῦ Μεγαρέως πεποιῆσθαι.

Μέσωνος codd.   Μαίσωνος Schneidewin   πεποίηται δὲ ὑπὸ Μέσωνος τοῦ Μεγαρέως Β

'In exchange for his good deeds the Achaeans tied up Agamemnon': this (proverb) is used against the ungrateful. They say it was composed by Maison the Megarian.

11. **Harpocration, *Lexicon of the Ten Orators* s.v. Ἑρμαῖ ('Herms', 134–5 D.) (= Menekles or Kallikrates, *On Athens*, FGrH 370 F 2)**. Harpocration's lexicon was compiled in the 1st or 2nd c. AD; the guide book *On Athens* must have been written before the city's destruction by Sulla in 86 (Hanslik 1931, 796). The Menekles cited as author is sometimes identified with Menekles of Barca who wrote in the 2nd c. (e.g. Wycherley 1957, 6), though the identification is based on nothing but homonymy. We are in no better position than Harpocration to decide whether Menekles is the author and Kallikrates the source of the citation or vice versa. The fragments of the work are praised by Hanslik for 'gute und genaue Sachkenntnis' (1931, 796). If the testimony is correct, the words 'in archaic letters' must refer to the pre-Euclidean alphabet and so dates the herm before 403 (Schneidewin 1837b, 854). For 'the Herms', see on Onesippos' herm in **II A**. Text: Dindorf.

Ἑρμαῖ. … Μενεκλῆς ἢ Καλλικράτης ἐν τῷ περὶ Ἀθηνῶν γράφει ταυτί 'ἀπὸ γὰρ τῆς Ποικίλης καὶ τῆς τοῦ βασιλέως στοᾶς εἰσὶν οἱ Ἑρμαῖ καλούμενοι· διὰ γὰρ τὸ πολλοὺς κεῖσθαι καὶ ὑπὸ ἰδιωτῶν καὶ ἀρχόντων ταύτην τὴν προσηγορίαν εἰληφέναι συμβέβηκεν. ἐφ᾽ ἑνὸς δὲ τῶν ἑρμῶν ἐπιγέγραπται γράμμασιν ἀρχαίοις· ἀντ᾽ εὐεργεσίης Ἀγαμέμνονα δῆσαν Ἀχαιοί.' …

'Herms': … Menekles or Kallikrates in the book *On Athens* writes the following: 'Because (moving on) from the Painted (Stoa) and from the Royal Stoa are the so-called Herms. It happened to get this name from the fact that many (herms) were dedicated both by private individuals and by Archons. On one of the herms is inscribed in archaic letters 'in exchange for his good deeds the Achaeans tied up Agamemnon'.

12. **Polemon, *In Response to Timaeus* fr. 46 Preller (= Ath. 14.659c)**. Polemon wrote in the early 2nd c. His 12-volume work is a polemic against, or response to (**Aiii 13**), Timaeus of Tauromenium who wrote a now lost *History of Sicily* in 38 books, from ca. 315 to ca. 265. Polemon may be reacting to a claim by Timaeus that Maison was from mainland Megara (Preller 1838, 85). In claiming that Maison is from Sicilian Megara,

Polemon may be suggesting that he was born before the destruction of Megara Hyblaea in 483. Possibly he is trying to connect Maison with the generation of Epicharmus. Text: Kaibel.

τὸν δὲ Μαίσωνα Πολέμων ἐν τοῖς πρὸς Τίμαιον ἐκ τῶν ἐν Σικελίᾳ φησὶν εἶναι Μεγάρων καὶ οὐκ ἐκ τῶν Νισαίων.

Μάσωνα A   μεγαρέων A   νησαίων A

Polemon in his work *In Response to Timaeus* says that Maison was from the Megara in Sicily and not from Megara Nisaea (mainland Megara).

13. Pseudo-Diogenianus, *On Proverbs* 1.9–12. A preface to a 2nd-c. AD collection of proverbs. Text: Schneidewin.

ἔστι δὲ ἡ παροιμία τρόπος καὶ τῆς καλουμένης ἀλληγορίας· παράκειται δὲ αὐτῇ λόγος αἶνος Αἰσώπειος, Καρικὸς αἶνος, Συβαριτικὸς λόγος, Κύπριος, Λιβυκὸς αἶνος, Μαισωνικὴ παροιμία.

A proverb is a mode also of what is called allegory. Closely connected to it are: Aesopic fable, Carian fable, Sybaritic tale, Cyprian tale, Libyan fable, the Maisonic proverb.

Our earliest sources, Aristophanes of Byzantium (**1, 3, 7**) and Polemon (**12**), speak of Maison as a historical person: either an actor (**1**, cf. **6**) or a poet (**7**'s *comoedus* can mean both; cf. **10**) or, like many fifth/fourth-century comic artists, both an actor and a poet. This is important to keep in mind as it contradicts the prevailing modern view, originated by Zielinski (1887, 63–6) and Körte (1928), that Maison was not the name of a real person but of a stock character of Doric comedy, comparable to Maccus or Bucco in Atellan farce (still taken as a 'hard fact' by Henderson 1991, 225). The belief that Maison is a stock character depends partly upon the belief that Maison was not a Greek name (now disproven: Cabanes 1976, 563 no. 40), and also upon acceptance of Chrysippus' alleged derivation of Maison from chewing (**1, 2**), just as Bucco means 'big cheeks', but it has been shown that Chrysippus' etymology is incorrect (Frisk 1960, 162; Chantraine 1968–1980 III, 659). It also depends heavily upon the outmoded assumption that Megarian 'farce' was a primitive folk genre, receding into the mists of time, pre-literate and without nameable authors and actors: this is also disprovable (see on **Bi**).

The fact that two theatre masks (see below), and also genres of jokes (**3**) and proverbs (**13**), bear the name Maison shows that we are also dealing with stock typologies. But there is no reason to suppose that we are dealing with exclusively stock typologies. Another pair of comic masks in Pollux's list (and probably originating from Aristophanes of Byzantium's list), the 'Hermonios', is almost certainly named after the famous comic actor, Hermon, who was active in the last quarter of the fifth century (Stefanis no. 910). The Lykomedes who gave his name to the comic mask called 'Lykomedeios' is unknown.

Athenaeus reports that Aristophanes of Byzantium (**3**) indicates that Maison invented the mask of a slave and another mask used for free characters (**7** is less clear whether one mask or two bear Maison's name). That there were two masks named Maison seems to receive some confirmation from Pollux (**4**) who is careful to specify 'Slave Maison' (θεράπων Μαίσων), in the same way as he specifies 'Leading Slave' and 'Curly Slave', distinguishing them from masks for free men which are also called 'Leading' and 'Curly'. The description of the Maison as πολιτικόν in **1** also should imply that he is a citizen and free: the word could hardly be used of a 'slave' in the sociologically neutral sense of 'local' (we would expect a word like **5**'s ἐντόπιοι).

Both **1** and **3** state that the free Maison is the cook and cooks in comedy are normally free men (though of low citizen status). Chrysippus' (or Athenaeus') words (**1**) indicate that the stock character associated with Maison and/or his mask was one who is uneducated and preoccupied with eating: both of these suit a cook. Philodemus' descriptions confirm that the stock character created by Maison was notorious for low speech patterns (**8**) and the kind of touchy sensitivity to social rank that would suit a low echelon of free man (**9**), but **9** also suggests that he is a professional man who gives instruction to others beneath him and this certainly suits the imperious nature of comic cooks who are often accompanied by assistants of various sorts (cf. **6**). Aristophanes indicates that the mask of the free man was not limited to cooks, but used of other low characters like sailors 'or someone of that sort' (**7**).

Through the surviving comic artefacts Green is able to trace the mask type back to the first quarter of the fourth century (2003, 120–4). Both slave and free characters appear in the mask: slaves appear from the early fourth century, but it is not clearly used of freemen until soon after 350 when it regularly begins to appear on characters who can be identified as cooks. The earlier date is certainly suggestive for dating the career of Maison, but we need not suppose that he is also responsible for the evolution of the mask type after the middle of the century. The artefacts show an increasing tendency after the mid fourth century to distinguish the costumes of slaves and free men by giving free men a more naturalistic physiognomy and retaining much of the grotesque features of earlier comedy for slaves. Free characters of low status, including professional characters (cooks, pimps, parasites, etc.), developed features midway between these polarities (Csapo 2002, 143–4). We would from ca. 350 expect a traditional mask, if it were used both for slaves and free men, to develop free and servile variations, though slight ones in this case, given the free Maison's low sociological status.

Maison's theatrical career must, therefore, have made its impact on Attic comedy by the first quarter of the fourth century. A still earlier date is suggested by **10** and **11**, because **10** preserves a proverbial saying attributed to Maison, while **11** reports the inscription of this same proverb upon an Attic herm in 'archaic letters', which must mean the old Attic alphabet in use before 403. Maison's authorship of the proverb can however be doubted, not because the writing down of a 'Doric farce' beggars belief (Crusius 1893, 275), but because, as **13** shows, a whole genre of proverbs came to be classified as 'Maisonic', and it was too easy for a later writer to mistake a description of type for an assertion of authorship. The proverb probably entered the lexica through the description of Menekles/Kallikrates (**11**) and not from any memory of a performance by Maison. But some proverbs came to be known, possibly for their acerbic character, as Maisonic (**13**), and it is an easy guess that Zenobius or his copyist misinterpreted a proverb marked 'Maisonic' as an indication of authorship, not type. Nothing about Maison therefore need be derived from the date, Attic dialect, or metre of the inscription.

1, **10** and **12** all assert that Maison was a Megarian, though Polemon (**12**) claimed he came from Megara Hyblaea (mainland Megara's Sicilian colony) 'and not from Megara Nisaea (mainland Megara)'. Whether the last clause comes from Polemon or Athenaeus who quotes him, the phrase makes it clear that others believed Maison to be a mainland Megarian. If we could be sure that Polemon here was arguing against Timaeus, we would be able to date the tradition of his mainland Megarian origin back to an early third-century source who (like Polemon) knew Sicily well. Whatever the origins of Maison, it is clear that he left a measurable impact upon the mainstream of Greek comedy, and this fact alone should have modified the scholarly orthodoxy of Megarian comedy's regionalism and primitivism (**Bi**). It is perhaps an even more remarkable testimony to the internationalism of Maison's art that a mask so closely associated with a Megarian should come to be the mask of an Athenian *citizen* cook (as opposed to the dark-skinned and exotically tonsured Tettix, which is the foreign cook). Both adoption of Maison's mask and the lingering memory of his verbal and performance style strongly suggests that Maison's professional circuit extended well beyond Megara and included successful performances in Athens of a comedy not very different from 'Athenian comedy'.

Biv: Corinth

1. Xenophon, *Hellenica* **4.4.2–3**. Work completed in 350s; the passage refers to spring 392. Xenophon describes the massacre, on the final day of a festival for Artemis Euklea, of the large pro-Spartan faction in Corinth by democrats and supporters of the Greek confederacy against Sparta. This episode initiates the only period of democratic rule we know of in otherwise solidly oligarchic Corinth (X. *HG* 4.4.1–8; Robinson 2011, 21–5). Text: Marchant.

> καὶ πρῶτον μὲν τὸ πάντων ἀνοσιώτατον ἐβουλεύσαντο· οἱ μὲν γὰρ ἄλλοι, κἂν νόμῳ τις καταγνωσθῇ, οὐκ ἀποκτιννύουσιν ἐν ἑορτῇ· ἐκεῖνοι δ' Εὐκλείων τὴν τελευταίαν προείλοντο, ὅτι πλείους ἂν ᾤοντο λαβεῖν ἐν τῇ ἀγορᾷ, ὥστε
> ⁴·⁴·³ ἀποκτεῖναι. ὡς δ' ἐσημάνθη οἷς εἴρητο οὓς ἔδει ἀποκτεῖναι, σπασάμενοι τὰ ξίφη ἔπαιον τὸν μέν τινα συνεστηκότα ἐν κύκλῳ, τὸν δὲ καθήμενον, τὸν δέ τινα ἐν θεάτρῳ, ἔστι δ' ὃν καὶ κριτὴν καθήμενον.

> The first part of their plan was the most irreligious of all. Other men, even when someone is condemned by the law, refrain from killing during a festival. But these men chose the last day of the Eukleia, because they thought they would find and kill in the marketplace the greatest number of their enemies. [4.4.3] When a signal was given, those who were assigned a list of victims drew their swords and began striking them down, some standing in the midst of a circle of friends, some sitting in the theatre, and even some who were sitting as judges.

2. Diodorus of Sicily, *Library of History* **14.86.1**. Written ca. 50–30; the passage refers to spring 392, as above. Text: Vogel-Fischer.

ἐν δὲ τῇ Κορίνθῳ τινὲς τῶν ἐπιθυμούντων δημοκρατίας συστραφέντες ἀγώνων ὄντων ἐν τῷ θεάτρῳ φόνον ἐποίησαν καὶ στάσεως ἐπλήρωσαν τὴν πόλιν.

In Corinth some of the democratic faction banded together while contests were being held in the theatre and perpetrated a massacre that filled the city with strife.

3. Inscribed Foundation Block for a Theatre Seat. After mid 5th c. (by letter forms).

Reused poros block with 'characteristic rebate' (Stillwell 1952, 110), all sides preserved, anathyrosis on left end.
0.62 × 0.42 × 0.105 m.
Found during excavation of Kerkis II of Roman theatre, June 1948.
Corinth Excavations inv. no. 2441.
Stillwell 1952, 110 no. 49; *Corinth* 8.3, 4 no. 11.
Text: *Corinth* 8.3 no. 11.   Photo: *Corinth* 8.3, pl. 2.

ΓΑΡΕΙ⅃

[Με]γαρεῖς

[Me]garians

4. Inscribed Foundation Block for a Theatre Seat. Near end 5th c. (by letter forms).

Reused 'complete' poros seat block, with notches 0.36 m apart 'to mark the seating spaces available to individual spectators' with 'rudely cut letters'; but the depth of the strokes shows that the cutting of the letters involved not a little physical effort, so that the words can scarcely be the 'scratchings of some excited spectator' (*Corinth* 8.3, 5 no. 16). The inscription is nonetheless far more casual than the other inscriptions, even if it did take a prolonged physical effort.
0.295 × 1.47 × 0.36 m.
Found in row 32, west of Stair IX of the cavea of the Roman theatre in March 1929 (Stillwell 1952, 31; *Corinth* 8.3, 5).
Corinth Excavations inv. no. 2440.
Shear 1929, 518; Stillwell 1952, 30–1, fig. 23; *SEG* 13, 230; *Corinth* 8.3, 5 no. 16.
Text: *Corinth* 8.3 no. 16.   Photo: *Corinth* 8.3, pl. 2.

ΝΙΚΑ̣ ΝΙΚΑ

Victory! Victory! *or* He wins! He wins!

5. Inscribed Foundation Block for a Theatre Seat. Early 4th c. ? (by letter forms).

Inscribed reused poros block, parts of all sides preserved; anathyrosis at right end; 0.09 m rebate at top back.
0.28 × 0.75 × 0.41 m.

Found in foundations of lower west cavea (Kerkis XI) of Roman theatre in May 1948.
Still in theatre foundation; Corinth Excavations inv. no. 2438.
Stillwell 1952, 110 no. 46, fig. 86; *Corinth* 8.3, 5–6 no. 17.
Text: based on *Corinth* 8.3 no. 17.   Photo: *Corinth* 8.3, pl. 2.

[- - ἐ]κγόν[ων - - -]

[- - of the d]escendan[ts - - -]

6. Inscribed Foundation Block for a Theatre Seat. Early 4th c. ? (by letter forms).

Inscribed fragment of reused poros block, broken at right, all other sides partially preserved,
anathyrosis at left end, rebate of 0.095 m at top back.
0.295 × 0.65 × 0.37 (top) – 0.415 (bottom) m.
Found in foundations of the lower west cavea (Kerkis XI) of Roman theatre in May 1948.
Still in theatre foundation; Corinth Excavations inv. no. 2439.
Stillwell 1952, 110 no. 47; *Corinth* 8.3, 6 no. 18.
Text: *Corinth* 8.3 no. 18.   Photo: *Corinth* 8.3, pl. 2.

[- - - -]EΛE[- - - -]

7. Inscribed Foundation Blocks for Theatre Seats. Early 4th c. ? (by letter forms).

Two reused inscribed poros blocks. From the letter size, style and position Kent deduced that they
formed a continuous text (*Corinth* 8.3, 6). The first (inv. 2435) has anathyrosis on left side. 0.27
× 0.70 × 0.37 m. The second (inv. 2437) has rebate of 0.09 m at top back.
0.295 × 1.16 × 0.37 (top) – 0.42 (bottom) m.
Found in foundations of lower west cavea (Kerkis XI) of Roman theatre in May 1948, and in
foundations of south wall of west parodos of Roman theatre in April, 1929, respectively.
Still in theatre. Corinth Excavations inv. nos. 2435, 2437.
Shear 1929, 521–2; Stillwell 1952, 110 nos. 44–5, fig. 86; *SEG* 13, 230; Jeffery 1990, 132 no. 39,
pl. 21; *Corinth* 8.3, 6 no. 19.
Text: *Corinth* 8.3 no. 19. Photos: Shear 1929, 521 fig. 5; Stillwell 1952, 56 fig. 49b; *Corinth* 8.3, pl. 2.

[- - - -]OYKA![- - - -]IKOPFAN[- - - -]

[…] of the ?? and? […] and? of maidens (*or* maiden)

8. Inscribed foundation block for a theatre seat. Early 4th c. ? (by letter forms).

Reused poros seat block, all sides partly preserved.
0.30 × 1.42 × 0.395 m.
Found in the lowest course of the east end of the north wall of the parodos of the Roman theatre in May 1948.
Still in theatre. Corinth Excavations inv. no. 2447.
Stillwell 1952, 109–10 no. 43; *Corinth* 8.3, 6 no. 20.
Text: *Corinth* 8.3 no. 20.   Photo: Stillwell 1952, 56 fig. 49a.

[- - - -]ΙΣΤΙΑΙΩΤΟΝ[- - - -]

[- - - -]?of ?Histiaios ?the [- - - -]

1 and **2** prove the existence of a theatre in Corinth by the earliest years of the fourth century. **1** refers to a κριτής, which normally signifies a judge of a musical or dramatic contest (the word is only 'rarely' used of a judge at a legal trial: LSJ). In any case, **2** explicitly refers to contests (cf. **4**). Despite Kolb (1981, 82) and others (Kenzler 1999, 213; Dubbini 2010, 172) there is no reason to suppose that the theatre mentioned by Xenophon was in a different location from the excavated theatre: the centre of ancient Corinth has been extensively explored and no other plausible site exists (Stillwell 1952, 5 n. 3, 131). The theatre, moreover, is close enough to the area now called the 'agora' to explain **1**'s general (and not necessarily punctilious) localisation of the action 'in the marketplace'.

Excavations in the theatre in Corinth reveal at least one Classical phase before the theatron was enlarged, built in stone, and an outer perimeter wall was built at the back of the theatron (Williams and Zervos 1989, 25–8). The theatron associated with the Classical phase extended to the 45th row of seating in the Roman theatre. The second phase of the theatre is dated to sometime after the beginning of the last quarter of the fourth century by the material recovered from the fill of the theatron above the 45th row of seats. Scahill (2015) dates the second phase from ca. 300 and associates it with the activities of Demetrius the Besieger in Corinth after he took the city in 303 (cf. **Bv 8**; **VI L**). The skene may have been built in stone at this time and fitted with a proskenion (Scahill 2015, 198–9). The theatre was rebuilt again in Roman times: Williams counts several phases, dating probably from the earthquake of 22/3 AD until the theatre went out of use sometime after 400 AD (2013, 489).

The excavators identify as 'first phase' a wooden theatron of the Classical period of 45 rows: beyond the last row the excavators posit 'unstructured seating' (Williams 2013, 488; Williams and Zervos 1989, 26) meaning that the fixed seating gave onto the hillside without any wall or barricade, suggesting a free space for spectators to stand, such as that posited by Roselli for members of the Athenian public who did not pay for seats (see on **V H**). Excavations in 2011 uncovered the west analemma of the early theatre showing that the parodos here extended ca. 41.2–41.3 m from the orchestra towards the north-west (Williams 2013, 489).

The excavators variously date the 'first phase' theatre to the late fifth or early fourth century. Stillwell dated the earliest Corinthian theatre to ca. 415 (1952, 131). Sturgeon dates 'late fifth to early fourth' (2004, 4). Williams and Zervos (1989, 26–7) date to the early fourth century. Stillwell's dating is based primarily upon the stratigraphy below what he took to be the earliest stone theatre ('Phase 1'). According to Stillwell 'from the soundings made between and below the rows of seats and their foundations … none of the pottery found contained any sherds later than the fifth century' (Stillwell 1952, 131). Stillwell referred to Shear 1928, 482–3, as his authority, but Shear says something quite different: the sounding was in the area 'where no remains of seats or of foundations for seats were found' and the fifth-century stratum began 'at a point about two metres below the present level of the ground' (Shear 1928, 482; cf. Shear 1929, 518). There is, in other words, no direct connection between the stone theatron that Stillwell thought to be the earliest Greek phase and the fifth-century stratum. That this is so is confirmed by more general considerations. When Stillwell wrote it was believed that a round stone theatre already existed or was being built in Athens in the later decades of the fifth century (Stillwell 1952, 131). On present knowledge, stone construction of any sort is rare in the fifth century, and circular theatra rare and uncertain before the building of the Lycurgan theatron ca. 340 (Papastamati-von Moock 2014; Moretti 2014a; **Bix**).

Such general considerations support Williams and Zervos' belief that the Corinthian theatre was built of wood until ca. 320. Gebhard very plausibly argued, partly on evidence for the shape of the Isthmian theatron, and partly on irregularities in the shape of the late fourth-century theatron, that Corinth in the fifth century had a rectilinear theatron (Gebhard 1973, 16–17). Anti and Polacco (1969, 103–26) believed they found traces of an early (presumed) rectilinear theatre in a series of wedge-shaped cuttings just behind the front wall of the Hellenistic skene (cf. Bressan 2009, 158 and 422 'Korinthos I, Plan 1').

In support of his fifth-century date for the stone theatre Stillwell also appealed to a series of rudimentary limestone seat blocks that were reused in the later theatre (**3–8**). The seats could be ascribed to the early Hellenistic construction, but the inscriptions include, amongst standard forms, epichoric letters that are not or very rarely found in the fourth century. The rho in **3** 'appears in the late archaic period' (Jeffery 1990, 116). The digamma on **7** is said by Jeffery to be 'apparently still in use at Corinth in the last years of the 5th or even the start of the 4th c.' (1990, 115; cf. Stroud 2013, 7 with further bibliography in n. 11). The inscribed seats do not easily fit current interpretations of the history of the theatre in Corinth. Gebhard (1973, 17 n. 19) and even Stillwell (1952, 131) cast doubt upon Kent's dating of the letter forms, but neither is prepared to think that they could be as late as the early Hellenistic theatre. Kolb argued that the inscriptions were unsuited to a theatre and surmised that the blocks must have been brought into the Hellenistic theatre, already inscribed, from elsewhere (1981, 82 n. 18). The inscriptions are, however, not obviously *unsuited*, and, on the contrary, are at least in some cases eminently suited to a theatre environment: **4** reads like an early form of acclamation (*Corinth* 8.3, 5 remarks that 'there can be little doubt that the words refer in some way to theatrical contests'); **3** conceivably reserves seats for Megarian theoroi or ambassadors; the genitive forms on **7** and **8** conform to the type of the labels found in the early prohedria of the Theatre of Dionysus at Athens (Moretti 1999–2000, 382–5). Note that Shear (1929, 522) suggests that 'the maidens' in **7** may have been 'the famous hierodoules of the temple of Aphrodite who are called by this name in Pindar's hymn to Xenophon, the Corinthian' (fr. 122.19). The label on **5** can only be supplemented by some form of the word 'descendant'. Prohedria (**V H**) granted to the descendants of honorands is attested in Athens from 393 (*IG* II² 20, ll. 9–10), and many other cities, including probably Corinth (see the supplement to *Corinth* 8.1 no. 5, ll. 2–3, undated, possibly Hellenistic). On the most obvious interpretation, **8** perhaps reserves prohedria for 'the descendants of Histiaios'. In addition to the fifth-century theatre in Athens, prohedric inscriptions are known from the fourth-century theatres of Rhamnus and Euonymon (**III Wi**; **III Wii**; **III I**), though in these instances they are donors' inscriptions.

If these are stone foundation blocks for the prohedria, like the inscribed blocks from the fifth-century Athenian theatre, then it is worth noting that they are, like their Athenian counterparts, rectangular and appear to have anathyrosis on their preserved ends. Originally they probably, like their Athenian counterparts, formed a straight line on three sides of the Archaic orchestra. If this interpretation is correct then the blocks confirm both the fifth-century date of the theatron, as well as the general conformity of its shape to the rectilinear or trapezoidal patterns found in other theatres of this date. With the exception of **3**, the height of these blocks (**4–8**) ranges from 0.28 to 0.30 m. Most of the Athenian blocks are 0.24 m in height, although the highest, like **3**, is a little over 0.6 m (Moretti 1999–2000, 383). Up to a third of the height of the lower blocks was buried in the ground (see Moretti 1999–2000, 388 fig. 3). Cushions or possibly wooden chairs were placed upon the blocks. Apart from one or two steps of prohedria the rest of the theatron was of wood. The rebate of 0.09 m (**3**, **5–7**; not reported on **4** or **8**, possibly not visible as these blocks are still built into the theatre) was presumably to provide extra foot room for the row behind.

The only direct evidence for performance in the Corinthian theatre relates to musical contests, for which Corinth was particularly famous (Stratonicus ap. Ath. 8.350b–c). Plutarch (*Arat.* 17.4) and Polyaenus (4.6.1) both mention a performance in the theatre by the famous kitharode Amoibeus (Stefanis no. 159) in 245/4. Other musical performances in the theatre are probably to be inferred from the sojourn of the still more famous early fourth-century kitharode Stratonicus (Ath. 8.349d–e) and Stratonicus' slightly later contemporary, the piper Ismenias (Lucian *Ind.* 5).

For dramatic competitions the evidence is indirect but not altogether negligible. Various hints of dramatic performance in Corinth come from closer to the middle of the fourth century. Vases with scenes from comedy and figurines of comic actors are produced in Corinth from the second quarter of the fourth century (*MMC*³ CV 2–4, CT 2–4; and esp. Green 2014a; earlier material, *MMC*³ CV 1 and CT 1, is 'comic' in a broad sense, but not related to drama). The three vases that certainly relate to comic drama (*MMC*³ CV 2–4) are bell kraters that come from the upper Lechaion valley, 'an area devoted to various important cults and related festivals', and may have been used at festival banquets (McPhee 2004, 11). Green finds that the earliest figurines reveal regional characteristics that are in some ways closer to the art of Sicily and West Greece than to Athens (Green 2014a) and it is worth recalling that Corinth's colony, Syracuse, had drama from the beginning of the fifth century. More significant, perhaps, is the presence in Corinth from the early to mid fourth century of the tragic actors Hipparkhos ([D.] 59.26–8) and Andronikos (reported by the Corinthian, or Sicyonian, Machon, 349–86 Gow), and the poet Xenokleides, assumed to be tragic from his association with the Hipparkhos just mentioned (Stefanis nos. 179, 1278, 1901). Sometime around 338 we also find the famous tragic actor Thettalos in Corinth (Plu. *Alex.* 10.2–3), possibly, as Stefanis notes, for performance (no. 1200).

The theatre at Corinth cannot be directly associated with any sanctuary: an Archaic temple, probably of Apollo, is some 250 m to the south-east. Moreover the testimony of **1–2** that connected competitions with Artemis Euklea has encouraged speculation that the theatre and theatrical, even dramatic, performance had a particular connection to Artemis (Kolb 1981, 82–3). The archaic dancers known as 'komasts' (often described as 'pre-comic' or 'pre-dramatic' performers) are especially linked with Corinth (Smith 2010), and it has been argued that komasts are also closely connected with Artemis in Corinth (Jucker 1963; Seeberg 1965, 109; Amyx 1988 II, 652–7; Seeberg 1995) as well as in other Peloponnesian states (Pipili 1987, 71–5; Scullion 2002b, 114–16). This may be true, but Peloponnesian komasts also nonetheless had a strong connection with Dionysus (Csapo and Miller 2007, 20–1). In any case, Corinth was, from at least the early fifth century, famous for its Dionysian choral performances: it was said to have invented the dith-yramb, which has possible links with komast dancing (Csapo and Miller 2007, 18), and in Pindar, at least, the Corinthian dithyramb is unequivocally labelled an entertainment for Dionysus (Hdt. 1.23; Pi. *O.* 13.18–19; note however that the performance of dithy-ramb does not presuppose a theatre, *pace* Bressan 2009, 158 – dithyrambs were probably processional in the early 6th c.). Direct evidence for a Dionysia in Corinth comes only in the mid second century in a fragmentary inscription that is most plausibly supplemented to include a reference to dramatic competitions as well (*Corinth* 8.1 no. 4, l. 13).

Bv: Sicyon

1. Herodotus, *Histories* 5.67.5. Written 440–420, referring to ca. 600–570. Cleisthenes, the tyrant of Sicyon, took measures to weaken Argive influence upon Sicyon and Dorian power within Sicyon. In the context from which this passage is taken Herodotus argues that Cleisthenes of Sicyon's division of the Sicyonians into tribes was the model for the tribal divisions of his grandson, the Athenian Cleisthenes. It has been suggested that Herodotus' sources also mentioned the tragic choruses in the context of cultural transfer from Sicyon to Athens (Pohlenz 1927, 300). Text: Wilson.

> τά τε δὴ ἄλλα οἱ Σικυώνιοι ἐτίμων τὸν Ἄδρηστον καὶ δὴ πρὸς τὰ πάθεα αὐτοῦ τραγικοῖσι χοροῖσι ἐγέραιρον, τὸν μὲν Διόνυσον οὐ τιμῶντες, τὸν δὲ Ἄδρηστον. Κλεισθένης δὲ χοροὺς μὲν τῷ Διονύσῳ ἀπέδωκε, τὴν δὲ ἄλλην θυσίην Μελανίππῳ.

> The Sicyonians honoured Adrastus in all ways but they particularly paid hon-our to his sufferings with tragic choruses, as they did not worship Dionysus, but Adrastus. Cleisthenes gave the choruses to Dionysus and the other sacri-fices to Melanippus.

2. Themistius, *One Should Regard Men not Places* (*Or.* 27) 337b (Harduin). Written mid 4th c. AD. Text: after Schenkl, Downey, Norman.

> ἀλλ᾿ οὐδὲν ἴσως κωλύει τὰ παρ᾿ ἑτέροις ἀρχὴν λαβόντα πλείονος σπουδῆς παρ᾿ ἄλλοις τυγχάνειν, ἐπεὶ καὶ κωμῳδία τὸ παλαιὸν ἤρξατο μὲν ἐκ Σικελίας – ἐκεῖθεν γὰρ ἤστην Ἐπίχαρμός τε καὶ Φόρμος – κάλλιον δὲ Ἀθήναζε συνηυξήθη. καὶ τραγῳδίας εὑρεταὶ μὲν Σικυώνιοι, τελεσιουργοὶ δὲ Ἀττικοὶ ποιηταί.

> But perhaps nothing prevents a thing originated by some from getting more serious attention from others, since even comedy long ago had its beginning in Sicily – because Epicharmus and Phormos were from that place – but coming to Athens it grew better. And the inventers of tragedy were Sicyonian poets, but the perfecters were Athenian.

3. Suda s.v. Θέσπις ('Thespis', θ 282). Compiled ca. 1000 AD possibly from a 4th c. source, Heraclides of Pontus: West suggests that Heraclides found the names on an inscription in Sicyon, the *Anagraphe*, cited elsewhere by Heraclides, listing 'poets and musicians' and reaching far back into mythical times ([Plu.] *Mor.* 1131f–32a; West 1989, 252). Another possible intermediary is the 4th-century local historian Menaechmus of Sicyon who probably used the *Anagraphe* in a work *On Experts in the Arts*, Περὶ τεχνιτῶν (Pfister 1913, 535–6; Jacoby on *FGrH* 131; Chaniotis 1988a, 90). The inscription is thought to go back to ca. 400 (*FGrH* 550 F 1; Griffin 1982, 159–60; Chaniotis 1988a, 89–91; Möller 2001, 258–9; Christesen 2007, 517–18; Franklin 2012, Excursus). Text: Adler.

> Ἰκαρίου, πόλεως Ἀττικῆς, τραγικὸς ις΄ ἀπὸ τοῦ πρώτου γενομένου τραγῳδιοποιοῦ Ἐπιγένους τοῦ Σικυωνίου τιθέμενος, ὡς δέ τινες δεύτερος μετὰ Ἐπιγένην· ἄλλοι δὲ αὐτὸν πρῶτον τραγικὸν γενέσθαι φασί.

> Of Ikarion, a city of Attica, he is ranked as the 16th tragedian after Epigenes of Sicyon, the first tragic poet. But some say he was second after Epigenes. Others say he was the first tragedian.

4. Suda s.v. οὐδὲν πρὸς τὸν Διόνυσον ('Nothing to do with Dionysus', o 806). Compiled ca. 1000 AD. Photius o 618 (Theodoridis) is virtually identical. We cite only the first of the many explanations for the proverb in the entry in Suda. Text: Adler.

> Ἐπιγένους τοῦ Σικυωνίου τραγῳδίαν εἰς τὸν Διόνυσον ποιήσαντος, ἐπεφώνησάν τινες τοῦτο· ὅθεν ἡ παροιμία.

> When Epigenes of Sicyon wrote a tragedy for Dionysus, some of them shouted this (i.e. 'nothing to do with Dionysus!'), whence the proverb.

5. Epigram of Honestus, *Palatine Anthology* 11.32, celebrating the Sicyonian origin of comedy. Composed: 1st c. AD. Although originally generally thought to refer to satyr play, Cohn (2016) shows convincingly that the language evokes comedy. The most popular etymologies of comedy are alluded to in the explicit reference to a komos in l. 2 and the implicit reference to farmers bringing their reproaches to the town-dwellers in l. 4 (see **Bii**). Cohn (2016, 17) argues that the *Anagraphe* (see on **3**) is the most likely source for the theory of the Sicyonian origin of comedy. Text: Gow and Page.

> Μούσης νουθεσίην φιλοπαίγμονος εὕρετο Βάκχος,
>   ὦ Σικυών, ἐν σοὶ κῶμον ἄγων Χαρίτων·
> δὴ γὰρ ἔλεγχον ἔχει γλυκερώτατον ἔν τε γέλωτι
>   κέντρον· χὠ μεθύων ἀστὸν ἐσωφρόνισεν.

> Bacchus invented the chastisement of the playful Muse,
>   leading a komos of Graces in you, O Sicyon,
> For truly it has the sweetest reproach and in laughter
>   a sting; and the drunken man chastens the townsman.

6. Menander, *Synaristosai* fr. 12 (Arnott). First produced ca. 320–292. The scholiast to Aristophanes' *Acharnians* 292 says only that the fragment is from Menander. It is widely assigned to the *Synaristosai* and thought that the *Synaristosai* is set in Sicyon. For details, see on **7** below. Text: Arnott.

> τραγῳδὸς ἦν ἀγών, Διονύσια.

> It was the tragic contest, the Dionysia.

7. Plautus, *Cistellaria* 156–63. Produced ca. 209–207 (Woytek 2004, 293; Stockert 2012, 40–1). The *Cistellaria* is based on Menander's *Synaristosai*. As far as we can tell from overlapping fragments, the plot closely follows the Greek play. The play is set in Sicyon (cf. 130, 190) and, since we know of no motive Plautus may have had to change the location, it is widely supposed that *Synaristosai* was also set in Sicyon, that **6** is the Greek original for the first lines of **7**, and that **6** therefore also refers to Sicyon (see below). The prologue, delivered by the god Auxilium (Help), gives the background to the plot. Text: Stockert.

> *fuere Sicyoni iam diu Dionysia.*
> *mercator venit huc ad ludos Lemnius,*
> *isque hic compressit virginem, adulescentulus,*
> *<vi>, vinulentus, multa nocte, in via.*
> 160   *is ubi malam rem scit se meruisse, ilico*
> *pedibus perfugium peperit, in Lemnum aufugit,*
> *ubi habitabat tum. illa, quam compresserat,*
> *decumo post mense exacto hic peperit filiam.*

> It was already the time of the Dionysia at Sicyon. A Lemnian merchant came here to the competitions; he, a young man, here raped a maiden violently, being

drunk on the street late at night, [160] and when he realised that he deserved harsh punishment he took to his heels in flight back to Lemnos where he lived at that time. And the maiden whom he raped gave birth here to a daughter after ten months passed.

8. Diodorus of Sicily, *Library of History* **20.102.2–3**. Composed ca. 50–30, referring to 303. Demetrius the Besieger ousted a Ptolemaic garrison by breaking through the city's defences at night. He refounded the city on more defensible ground (Griffin 1982, 23–4; Lolos and Gourley 2011), named it Demetrias, and instituted a founder cult for himself. Text: Vogel-Fischer.

> ὁ δὲ Δημήτριος τοὺς Σικυωνίους εἰς τὴν ἀκρόπολιν μετοικίσας τὸ μὲν τῷ λιμένι συνάπτον μέρος τῆς πόλεως κατέσκαψεν, <ἀν>οχύρου παντελῶς ὄντος τοῦ τόπου, τῷ δὲ πολιτικῷ πλήθει συνεπιλαβόμενος τῆς οἰκοδομίας καὶ τὴν ἐλευθερίαν ἀποκαταστήσας τιμῶν ἰσοθέων ἔτυχε παρὰ τοῖς εὖ παθοῦσι· Δημητριάδα μὲν γὰρ τὴν πόλιν ὠνόμασαν, θυσίας δὲ καὶ πανηγύρεις, ἔτι δ' ἀγῶνας ἐψηφίσαντο συντελεῖν αὐτῷ κατ' ἐνιαυτὸν καὶ τὰς ἄλλας ἀπονέμειν τιμὰς ὡς κτίστῃ.

> Demetrius relocated Sicyon to the acropolis and destroyed the part of the city that joined the harbour, as the area was completely without defences. By aiding the political majority through his participation in the building and his restoration of liberty he received divine honours from the grateful citizens. They called the city Demetrias, and they voted to celebrate sacrifices and festivals, even competitions annually for him and to give him the other honours due the founder of a city.

Herodotus' choice (**1**) of the term 'tragic choruses' rather than simply 'tragedy' looks like a deliberate attempt to distinguish a choral precursor from actual tragedy even while assimilating the two. Herodotus probably draws upon a Sicyonian tradition. This tradition is carved in stone by ca. 400 when Sicyon erected a monument commemorating its great poets and musicians (introduction to **3**). The Sicyonians of the late fifth century were, it seems, sanguine enough to name fourteen other 'tragedians' before Thespis. One need allow little more than two years between 'tragedians' to bring the beginning of the series into the time of the Sicyonian Cleisthenes (using Suda's ca. 536 for Thespis: see **I Avii 2a**). Knowledge of the Sicyonian tradition survived until late antiquity when Epigenes (not mentioned by Herodotus) was remembered as 'the inventor of tragedy' (**2–4**). Aristotle must in part be thinking of Sicyon in *Poetics* 1448a30 when he writes that 'some of the Peloponnesians claim tragedy' (**Bii 1**). If Sicyon is part of the Dorian claim to the invention of tragedy, then the irony of **1**'s emphasis upon the act of the creation of tragedy being an anti-Dorian measure becomes rather poignant.

　　5 is all that remains of the Sicyonian claim to have invented comedy. If Sicyon was a contender for the invention of comedy, it was not recognised by Aristotle, who mentions only the Megarian and Sicilian claims as well as the 'Peloponnesian' claim to tragedy, yet the etymologising arguments reported by Aristotle (**Bii 1**) both appear in **5**.

None of this, of course, necessarily implies more than the existence of choral performances for Dionysus in or near the sanctuary of Dionysus in Sicyon, though it would be
surprising if the claims to the invention of tragedy and possibly comedy, represented by
2–5, stemmed from a time when neither genre was actually performed in the city.

   The later theatre was built adjacent to the ancient sanctuary (for the possible remains,
see Bressan 2009, 228; Lolos 2011, 379). Pausanias (2.7.5) traces the foundation of the
sanctuary back before the return of the Heraclidae. The temple housed a chryselephantine
statue of Dionysus and a marble sculpture of bacchae thought by Furtwängler to be by
Scopas (1895, 396–7), both of which seem in any case to be works of the fifth or fourth
century (Casadio 1999, 98). Of greater chronological significance is a cult statue said by
Pausanias to be kept out of the public eye (ἐν ἀπορρήτῳ) and which Casadio shows to be
of a very archaic type with connections to Phigaleia, Megara, Corinth and Argos (1999,
101–43). On Pausanias' testimony the latter was processed in a nocturnal torch-lit procession annually (2.7.5). From the third-century antiquarian Sosibius we learn that the
Sicyonian Dionysus was also honoured with the more usual phallic processions (**Bx 3b**).

   The surviving theatre of Sicyon is one of the largest of the Peloponnese with an estimated seating capacity of 9,000–10,000 (Hayward and Lolos 2015, 174). There is no firm
evidence for dating the extant theatre, beyond the *terminus ante* provided by Plutarch's
mention of the theatre in reference to the events of 251 (*Arat.* 8.6; the theatre is only mentioned again in Plb. 29.25.2 in reference to 168). A fourth-century date is urged, however,
by **6**, thought to be a fragment of Menander's *Synaristosai*, the Greek model for Plautus'
Cistellaria (**7**). *Cistellaria* is set in Sicyon, and it is generally supposed that this was also
true of Menander's *Synaristosai* (e.g. Süss 1938, 103–5; Ludwig 1970, 47; Webster 1974,
188 n. 106; Arnott 2000, 330–1, 358–61). If this is correct, then **6** gives evidence for tragedy at the Sicyonian Dionysia, ca. 310 (for even if the play was written in the last year of
Menander's life, it refers back, we might expect with some historical realism, to events that
passed at least sixteen years earlier). But Kuiper (1936, 177–80, 190–1) and more recently
Brown (2005) have argued that the Menandrian original was set in Athens. In support of a
Sicyonian setting, Ludwig (1970, 47) pointed out that an important element of Plautus' plot
relied on a detail that implied precise knowledge of Sicyonian topography. The heroine in
Cistellaria, the child born of the rape in **7**, was exposed in the hippodrome (549), one of the
two most imposing buildings of Sicyon, along with the theatre just south-east of it (Lolos
and Gourley 2011, 140). The 'stadium', just west of and below the theatre, was one of the
most prominent landmarks in Sicyon, and remains clearly visible. Horse and chariot races
are attested for Sicyon ca. 474 (Pi. *N.* 9.9), and are generally thought, on the testimony of
the scholia to Pindar (Sch. Pi. *N.* 9.20, 9.25, 10.49, 10.76; cf. Hdt. 5.67), to begin with the
foundation of the Sicyonian Pythia in the time of Cleisthenes (early 6th c.). The surviving
stadium has never been excavated. It is usually supposed to be Early Hellenistic, but coins
found in the stadium may suggest use as early as 330 (Miller 2001, 235). It is impossible
to say whether the surviving stadium was built on top of an earlier stadium or whether the
stadium served for horse-racing and might therefore have been known locally as a hippodrome (cf. Skalet 1928, 16). Brown's suggestion that the mention of the hippodrome better
suits Athenian topography is incorrect, however (2005, 67). Athens had no hippodrome as
such and ancient references by Athenian authors to a hippodrome must refer to that of New

Phaleron (Kyle 1993, 96–7). Some scholars have guessed that the *Synaristosai* was written for a performance in Sicyon (Legrand 1917, 52; Ludwig 1970).

The majority of archaeologists and historians regard the most likely date for the beginning of the construction of the extant theatre as the refounding of the city in 303 by Demetrius reported in **8** (e.g. Fiechter 1931, 32; Griffin 1982, 10; Hayward and Lolos 2015, 161–2): the orthogonal plan of the new city certainly conforms to the style of new foundations by the Successors of Alexander (Haverfield 1913, 38–49; Lolos and Gourley 2011, 94–5). Fossum however long ago (1905) noted that the theatre (as also the stadium) was completely out of alignment with the streets of the planned city and therefore argued for an earlier date for the theatre (cf. Lolos 2013, esp. 475–6 figs. 7–8). This he placed in the early to mid fourth century, largely because of similarities to the theatre of the Asclepieion in Epidaurus which he took to be a later construction. Hayward and Lolos argue that the theatre's non-alignment to the grid plan of the post-Demetrian city was a deliberate choice based on the local topography and calculated to minimise the need to import stone as most of the koilon could be cut from bedrock (2015, 162, 166–9). Fossum also drew attention to irregularities in the foundations, interpreting certain features to be traces of an earlier theatre, though these remain doubtful (1905, esp. 274–5). Even Bressan, who assigns a late fourth-century date to the Sicyonian theatre, acknowledges similarities with the theatre of the Asclepieion of Epidaurus (2009, 227–8). The latter however may be as early as the 330s (**Bviii**) and Fossum (1905, 273; cf. Skalet 1928, 14) supposed that, because the theatre at Sicyon is more crudely styled in sections than Epidaurus, it was the earlier construction. It seems likely that contests for Dionysus were among those transferred to Demetrius at Sicyon, as at Athens (**VI L**). Diodorus tells us that after renaming the city Demetrias the people of Sicyon 'voted to celebrate sacrifices and festivals, even competitions annually for him' (**8**).

We hear of competitions for kitharodes in Sicyon by the mid fourth century (Ath. 8.351f). An early importance of drama at Sicyon is suggested by the large number of poets and performers that came from the city. In addition to the doubtless mythical Epigenes (**3, 4**), Sicyon was home to the fifth-century tragic poets Amymon (P. Wilson 1997, 177–8) and Neophron (*TrGF* 15). The latter wrote 120 plays, if we can trust the Suda (*v* 218), and his *Medea* (of which three fragments survive) was imitated by Euripides in his *Medea* (431) according to Dicaearchus (fr. 63 W = 62 Mirhady), Aristotle (fr. 635 Rose: possibly written by Theophrastus) and Diogenes Laertius (2.134, drawing on Antigonus of Carystus: Wilamowitz 1880, 487). Wilamowitz, however, compared this information about Neophron with the information about Epigenes (**3–4**), declaring the tradition that Neophron came from Sicyon (and that Euripides copied him): 'fraud, nothing but malicious, tendentious, Peloponnesian fraud' (1880, 487). The belief that Neophron's priority over Euripides is in the service of advancing Dorian pretensions to the origin of tragedy is revived by Sommerstein (in Mossman 2011, 25–6), but much recent scholarship has been less dismissive of the claim that Neophron produced a *Medea* earlier than Euripides, whether or not the extant fragments belong to that play (Michelini 1989; Mastronarde 2002, 57–64).

Sicyon was also possibly the place of origin of the fourth-century comedian Sophilus (Suda σ 881 also mentions Thebes), whose comedies certainly include Athenian settings

(Ath. 3.123d, 6.228b). Most impressive and significant among specifically theatrical personnel is the number of fifth- and fourth-century Sicyonian trainers and pipers for men's and boys' theatrical lyric competitions, most of whom are known from their activities in Attica. These include Ariphron the lyric poet and possibly chorodidaskalos (**III Biii**; cf. Ath. 15.702a) and the chorus-trainers/didaskaloi Bacchiadas (Stefanis no. 510), who competed at the Mouseia in Thespiae (**Cv 3**), and Epikouros, who trained the boys' chorus of Pandionis and Akamantis for the Athenian Thargelia of 344/3 (*IG* II³ 4, 494). Fourth-century Sicyon exported several pipers known from monuments commemorating victories of boys' or men's choruses at Athens: Kleanthes (Thargelia 362/1 and 360/59: Stefanis no. 1416), Alkathous (Thargelia 359/8; cf. **Dvii 6**; Stefanis no. 130), Satyros (Thargelia 344/3: Stefanis no. 2237), Pantaleon (Dionysia 320/19: Stefanis no. 1997), and two pipers whose names have been lost (Dionysia mid 4th c.: Stefanis no. 2772; Dionysia 344/3: Stefanis no. 2943). Another Sicyonian piper Kleagoras was successful in Delos in the late fourth century (Stefanis no. 1411). D'Alessio has suggested that the dithyramb *Achilles* of the Sicyonian poetess, Praxilla, was composed for performance in her hometown (2013, 125).

It is perhaps relevant that the grave of the great Athenian Old Comic poet Eupolis was to be found in Sicyon (Paus. 2.7.3). If Pausanias is right, we are clearly to infer that Eupolis died in Sicyon (and that the Eupolis on the Athenian casualty list *IG* I³ 1190, l. 52, is not the poet). Sidwell argues that Eupolis went to Sicyon in exile (2009, 38–41). If so, the specific choice of Sicyon by a comic poet, still in his prime, possibly had something to do with its theatre. It is, in any case, tempting to infer from the various and disparate evidence just reviewed that a Dionysia with a full slate of competitions existed at Sicyon from the early fourth century, and possibly from some time in the fifth. The Dionysia, presumably renamed Demetrieia (cf. 'Dionysia and Demetrieia' at Athens), probably provided the main part of those competitions which **7** indicates were later held in Demetrius' honour, qua founder (as elsewhere, see Brenk 1998, 169 n. 38).

Bvi: Phlious

1. **Suda, *Lexicon* s.v. Πρατίνας ('Pratinas', π 2230)**. Date: 10th c. AD, but drawing on much earlier compilations. The 70th Olympiad referred to is 499/6. The omitted portion of the text relating to the collapse of the Athenian *ikria* can be found in **9** on Ikria in **V H**. Text: Adler.

> Πρατίνας· Πυρρωνίδου ἢ Ἐγκωμίου, Φλιάσιος, ποιητὴς τραγῳδίας· ἀντηγωνίζετο δὲ Αἰσχύλῳ τε καὶ Χοιρίλῳ ἐπὶ τῆς ο′ Ὀλυμπιάδος, καὶ πρῶτος ἔγραψε Σατύρους … καὶ δράματα μὲν ἐπεδείξατο ν′, ὧν Σατυρικὰ λβ′· ἐνίκησε δὲ ἅπαξ.

> 'Pratinas': son of Pyrronides or of Enkomios, of Phlious, a poet of tragedy. He used to compete against Aeschylus and Choerilus in the 70th Olympiad, and he first wrote satyr plays … and he put on 50 dramas, of which 32 are satyric. He won once.

2. Pseudo-Acronian Scholia to Horace's *Art of Poetry* 216 (Keller). Probably 7th c. AD, referring to the early 5th c. BC. The commentary is directed at lines 220–2 of Horace's *Art of Poetry*: 'and the man who first competed for a goat with tragic song / soon also undressed rustic satyrs and / while still in earnest made trial of rough humour'. Something has evidently dropped out of the text before this passage. Text: Keller with Casaubon's emendation.

> [lacuna] … *ponebant tragoediis satyrica dramata, in quibus salva maiestate gravitatis iocos exercebant secundum Pratinae institutionem. is enim primus Athenis, Dionisia dum essent, satyricam fabulam induxit.*

> *Cratini* codd., Keller   *Pratinae* Casaubon, Fabricius   *satyricam* v c   *satiricam* Γ *f* V

> [missing text] … to tragedies they added satyric dramas, in which without compromising the grandeur of solemnity they employed humour after the manner of Pratinas (the manuscripts say 'Cratinus'). For he first, during the Dionysia, introduced a satyr drama.

3. Hypothesis to Aeschylus' *Laios* (*POxy.* 2256, fr. 2; A. *TrGF* T 58b). The papyrus was written ca. 200 AD, most of the information is probably drawn from a 4th-c. source, most likely Aristotle's *Didaskaliai*, and ultimately goes back to 5th-c. archival records (cf. **4**, and commentary below). It refers to the Dionysia of 467. The papyrus roll contains hypotheses to the plays of Aeschylus. Text: after Radt and archive photograph; see also *CLGP* I 1.1, 34–51.

> [Λαίος]
> [Αἰσχύλο]υ
> [ἐπὶ ἄρχοντος Θεαγ]ενίδου Ὀλ[υ]μπιάδος [οη′ ἔτει] α[′]
> [ἐνίκα Αἰσχύλ]ος Λαίωι, Οἰδ[ί]ποδι, Ἕπτᾳ ἐπὶ Θήβα{ι}ς,
> [Σφιγγὶ σατ^υ·] δεύτερος Ἀριστίας ταῖς τοῦ πα-
> [τρὸς Πρατίνο]υ τραγωιδ[ί]αις· τρί[τ]ος [Πο]λυ-
> [φράσμων] Λυκουργε[ίαι] τ[ετρ]αλογίαι·

> [*Laius*]
> [of Aeschylu]s
> [in the Archonship of Theag]enides [year] 1, [78th] Ol[y]mpiad
> [Aeschyl]us [was victorious], with *Laios, Oed[i]pus, Seven Against Thebes*,
> [*Sphinx* satyr.]; second Aristias with the traged[i]es of his fa-
> [ther Pratinu]s; thi[r]d [Po]ly-
> [phrasmon with the] *Lycurg[an]* t[etr]alogy.

4. Hypothesis to Aeschylus, *Seven Against Thebes* (*TrGF* I, DID C 4b). The hypothesis comes down to us attached to the manuscripts of Aeschylus. It clearly draws upon the same source as **3**, whose information is in some respects superior, but in others inferior. The name of the Archon of 468/7 is Theagenides (Develin 1989, 70), not Theogenes, but the names of the tragedies of Aristias are missing in **3** (one title is probably missing in **4** as well), and consequently **3**'s claim that the tragedies were written by Aristias' father, Pratinas, looks like an abbreviated and confused version of **4**'s much more specific claim that only the satyr play was composed by Pratinas (see further below). Polyphrasmon is also the son of a 'first-generation' poet, Phrynichus. Text: Snell.

ἐδιδάχθη ἐπὶ Θεαγένους Ὀλυμπιάδι οη΄. ἐνίκα Λαΐῳ, Οἰδίποδι, Ἑπτὰ ἐπὶ Θήβας, Σφιγγὶ σατυρικῇ. β̄ Ἀριστίας Πέρσεῖ, Ταντάλῳ, <...>, Παλαισταῖς σατύροις τοῖς Πρατίνου <τοῦ> πατρός. γ̄ Πολυφράσμων Λυκουργείᾳ τετραλογίᾳ.

<Ἀνταίῳ> Garrod

It was produced in the Archonship of Theagenes in the 78th Olympiad. He was victorious with *Laius*, *Oedipus*, *Seven Against Thebes*, *Sphinx* satyric. 2nd Aristias with *Perseus*, *Tantalus*, ... *Wrestlers* the satyr play of his father Pratinas. 3rd Polyphrasmon with the *Lycurgan Tetralogy*.

5. Aristias Named in the Tragic Victor Lists (*IG* II² 2325 A, col. 1, ll. 11–17 M–O). From an agonothetic monument of ca. 279. This fragment comes from the beginning of a list of tragic poets in order of their first victory at the Dionysia. After their names is written the total number of Dionysian victories achieved by the poet. There is room for about eight names before Aeschylus. Aristias' victory must have been in 465 or later (cf. **3–4**). The fragment breaks off after line 17. Text: Millis-Olson.

11	[Αἰ]σχύλ[ος - - -]	(484)
	[Εὐ]έτης Ι	
	[Πο]λυφράσμ[ων - - -]	(492–471)
	[Νόθ]ιππος Ι	(late 470s?)
15	[Σοφο]κλῆς ΔΠΙΙΙ[-]	(468)
	[Μέσα]τος ΙΙ	
	[Ἀριστ]ίας [- - -]	

11	[Ae]schyl[us ...]	(484)
	[Eu]etes 1	
	[Po]lyphrasm[on ...]	(492–471)
	[Noth]ippus 1	(late 470s?)
15	[Sopho]cles 18[+]	(468)
	[Mesa]tos 2	
	[Arist]ias [...]	

6. *Life of Sophocles* (*TrGF* T 1, ll. 78–9). The anonymous *Life*, a late composition, draws extensively on earlier sources, including Peripatetic authors such as Satyrus, Aristoxenus and Hieronymus of Rhodes (all cited by name) and shows direct or indirect access to the works of Aristotle and Sophocles' contemporary, Ion of Chios. Text: Radt.

συνηγωνίσατο δὲ καὶ Αἰσχύλῳ καὶ Εὐριπίδῃ καὶ Χοιρίλῳ καὶ Ἀριστίᾳ καὶ
ἄλλοις πολλοῖς καὶ Ἰοφῶντι τῷ υἱῷ.

He competed with Aeschylus, Euripides, Choerilus, Aristias and many others
including Iophon his son.

7. A Dedicatory Epigram from a Statue Base from Pergamon. Date: 241–197 (letter
forms; internal reference to Attalos I of Pergamon), and probably 230–220 (prosopographical considerations relating to Dionysodoros, an admiral of Attalos, and Thoinias,
the sculptor: Müller 1989, 508–21). There appears to be some connection between this
monument and **9**, but it may be that both are inspired by an earlier monument or poem.

Marble statue base with epigram, work of Thoinias, an artist of the Lysippan school. The front
face is broken on the right side (the inscription is intact except the end of the last line); the corners,
sides and part of the back face are missing; anathyrosis on underside. Two dowel holes in upper
surface, both dug out apparently for removal of lead. The position of the dowel holes for the satyr
suggests that the satyr is dancing (Nicolucci 2003, 337). This certainly suits his name, Skirton,
which means 'Leaper' (cf. Skirtos in **9**).
0.285 × 0.69 × 0.5 m.
Found in excavations, reused in a first-century foundation wall on the Via Sacra of the Asklepieion
of Pergamon (sector 32A) on 23 October 1966. Other fragments of dedications were removed
from nearby structures suggesting that they have not moved far from their original position.
Pergamon inv. 66 III; *SEG* 39, 1334.
Müller 1989; Lebek 1990; Kerkhecker 1991; Nicolucci 2003.
Text: Kannicht.

> παῖς ὁ Δεινοκράτους με σοί, Θυώνης
> κοῦρε, καὶ βασιλῆι τὸν φίλοινον
> Ἀττάλωι Διονυσόδωρος εἶσεν
> Σκίρτων οὐΞικυῶνος· ἁ δὲ τέχνα
> 5   Θοινίου, τὸ δὲ λῆμμα Πρατίνειον·
> μέλοι δ᾽ ἀμφοτέροισιν ὁ ἀναθείς [με].

The son of Deinokrates, Dionysodoros from Sicyon, set me, wine-loving
Skirton, up for you, son of Thyone, and for King Attalus. The craftsmanship ⁵
belongs to Thoinios; the conception is Pratinian. May both (dedicatees) look
after the man who dedicated [me].

8. Funerary Epigram for Sophocles by Dioscorides (*AP* **7.37; Diosc. fr. 22 Gow-Page;
S. *TrGF* T 179)**. Written: ca. 250–200. Dioscorides of Alexandria composed some forty
of the epigrams in the Greek (a.k.a. Palatine) Anthology. The speaker is the statue of a
satyr on the tomb of the tragedian Sophocles. Text: Radt-Snell.

> 1   ʽτύμβος ὅδ᾽ ἔστ᾽, ὤνθρωπε, Σοφοκλέος, ὃν παρὰ Μουσῶν
>   ἱρὴν παρθεσίην ἱερὸς ὢν ἔλαχον·

ὅς με τὸν ἐκ Φλιοῦντος, ἔτι τρίβολον πατέοντα,
    πρίνινον ἐς χρύσεον σχῆμα μεθηρμόσατο
5 καὶ λεπτὴν ἐνέδυσεν ἀλουργίδα. τοῦ δὲ θανόντος
    εὔθετον ὀρχηστὴν τῇδ᾽ ἀνέπαυσα πόδα᾽.
'ὄλβιος, ὡς ἀγαθὴν ἔλαχες στάσιν· ἡ δ᾽ ἐνὶ χερσὶ
    κούριμος ἐκ ποίης ἥδε διδασκαλίης;᾽
'εἴτε σοὶ Ἀντιγόνην εἰπεῖν φίλον, οὐκ ἂν ἁμάρτοις,
10   εἴτε καὶ Ἠλέκτραν· ἀμφότεραι γὰρ ἄκρον᾽.

'This, sir, is Sophocles' tomb which from the Muses I acquired as a sacred trust
being (his) holy (servant). He took me, a native of Phlious, still treading the
tribulum (a kind of threshing sledge), made me over from holm oak into golden
form [5] and dressed me in a purple cloak. The moment he died I brought my ag-
ile dancing foot to rest here'. 'How lucky you are to have gotten so good a post;
but the (mask of a) girl in your hands with the cropped hair, what production
is she from?' 'If it please you to say *Antigone*, you would not be wrong, [10] or
even *Electra*: both are supreme'.

9. Funerary Epigram for Sositheus by Dioscorides (*AP* 7.707 = Diosc. fr. 23 Gow-Page; *TrGF* 99 T 2). Written: ca. 250–200. The second last line is hopelessly corrupted. Text: after Snell.

1 κἠγὼ Σωσιθέου κομέω νέκυν, ὅσσον ἐν ἄστει
    ἄλλος ἀπ᾽ αὐθαίμων ἡμετέρων Σοφοκλῆν,
Σκίρτος ὁ πυρρογένειος. ἐκισσοφόρησε γὰρ ὡνὴρ
    ἄξια Φλιασίων, ναὶ μὰ χορούς, σατύρων
5 κἠμὲ τὸν ἐν καινοῖς τεθραμμένον ἤθεσιν ἤδη
    ἤγαγεν εἰς μνήμην πατρίδ᾽ ἀναρχαΐσας,
καὶ πάλιν εἰσώρμησα τὸν ἄρσενα Δωρίδι Μούσῃ
    ῥυθμόν, πρός τ᾽ αὐδὴν ἑλκόμενος μεγάλην
† ἑπτὰ δέ μοι ἐρσων οὐχερὶ † καινοτομηθεὶς
10   τῇ φιλοκινδύνῳ φροντίδι Σωσιθέου.

3 Σκιρτός cod.   Σκίρτος Reiske   6 πατρίδος ἀρχαίας Emperius   9 εὐαδέ μοι
θύρσων κτύπος Jacobs   εὐαδέ μοι θύρσων τύπος Hermann   ἔσπετό μοι or ἔπλετ᾽/
ἔπτατ᾽ ἐμοί Stadtmüller   ταρσῶν τύπος Cipolla   ἐν χερί/οὔρεσι Jacobs   οὐν χερί
Hecker   εὖ χερί van Herwerden   εὐχερί Desrousseaux   αὖ χερί Beckby

And I look after the remains of Sositheus, just as in the city another of our
tribe looks after Sophocles, I, red-bearded Skirtos. For the man wore ivy wor-
thily of Phliasian satyrs – yes by choruses! – [5] and he restored me, who had
already been bred in new fashions, to homeland tradition making me old once
more, and once again I thrust that manly rhythm into the Dorian Muse and
being drawn towards great utterance the beat of thyrsoi in hand pleased me
who was invented (reading Jacobs' emendation) [10] by the adventurous fancy
of Sositheus.

10. The Early Life of Timon: Diogenes Laertius, *Lives of the Philosophers* **9.109**. Written: 3rd c. AD. The date of Timon's birth is usually set at about 325 (Clayman 2009, 15). Diogenes cites the authority of Apollonides of Nicaea *On the Silloi* 1, a 1st-c. AD work dedicated to the emperor Tiberius. Apollonides probably found the details of Timon's early career in Timon's own writings (Clayman 2009, 7) and in any case his original occupation as a choreut is confirmed by the 1st-c. Peripatetic writer Aristocles of Messene (ap. Eus. *PE* 14.18.15 = Decleva Caizi 52 = Chiesara F 4.14). Diogenes calls Apollonides 'one of ours' possibly because he belongs to the same philosophical school (sceptic) or because Diogenes is also from Nicaea. 'Silloi' are philosophical satires written in hexameters, said to have been invented by Timon. Stilpo (ca. 360–280) was head of a philosophical school and teacher of Zeno of Citium, the founder of stoicism. Text: Dorandi.

Ἀπολλωνίδης ὁ Νικαεὺς ὁ παρ᾽ ἡμῶν ἐν τῷ πρώτῳ τῶν Εἰς τοὺς Σίλλους ὑπομνήματι, ἃ προσφωνεῖ Τιβερίῳ Καίσαρι, φησὶ τὸν Τίμωνα εἶναι πατρὸς μὲν Τιμάρχου, Φλιάσιον δὲ τὸ γένος· νέον δὲ καταλειφθέντα χορεύειν, ἔπειτα καταγνόντα ἀποδημῆσαι εἰς Μέγαρα πρὸς Στίλπωνα …

κατληφθέντα Β   ἐπιδημῆσαι Β

Apollonides of Nicaea, one of ours, in the first book of his commentary *On the Silloi*, which he dedicates to Tiberius Caesar, says that Timon's father was Timarchos and his birthplace Phlious. When he (Timon) was young he was orphaned and made a living as a choreut, then he grew tired of it and left his home for Megara to stay with Stilpo …

Speculation about theatrical activity in Classical Phlious revolves around the activities of two Phliasian dramatists, Pratinas and his son Aristias (**1–6**). According to **1**, Pratinas competed in the tragic competitions in Athens at the very beginning of the fifth century. Doubt has been thrown upon the accuracy of the dating (Scullion 2002a, 81–2). Other details, like the names for Pratinas' father, suggest mythicisation. 'Enkomios' implies a man who participates in *komoi* (drunken or jubilant processions) and Pyrronides, 'Redhead', suggests the normal colouring of satyrs: both are names that prognosticate an inventor of satyr drama (Shaw 2014, 55).

The information we have about Aristias (**3–6**) is more secure. It looks solidly based on Athenian archives, especially as regards competitors, dates and possibly the names of plays (Sickinger 1999, 45). The same confidence cannot be extended to the mention of Pratinas' authorship of a play or plays performed by Aristias in **3–4**. Contest officials might conceivably have taken an interest in Pratinas' authorship of the plays if Aristias merely functioned as a stand-in for his father. It is in fact often assumed that Aristias produced his father's plays posthumously (*DTC*² 19; Ostwald 1992, 324; Millis and Olson 2012, 160; Shaw 2014, 43). But there is no reason to suppose this was the case. The didascalic notices of the posthumous productions of Euripides' *Bacchae* (Arist. *Didascaliae* fr. 627 Rose) and Sophocles' *Oedipus at Colonus* (Hyp. S. *OC*) name both author and didaskalos, but in those cases the didascalic notices specifically mention the recent deaths of the older poets. Moreover, **3**, the source of the claim that Aristias produced tragedies written by his father, looks like an abbreviation and confusion of **4**, where we are clearly told that only the satyr play was written by Pratinas. The information in **3–4** relating to Pratinas' authorship appears therefore less likely to have been of use to festival officials than of interest to fourth-century or Hellenistic literary scholars. The later addition is comparable to the didascalic material in the hypothesis to Aristophanes' *Wealth* which indicates that the play was the last Aristophanes produced in his own name and that 'wishing to introduce his son Araros he produced his last two plays through him' (facts that could not be recorded in festival records). There are no grounds therefore to suspect the death of Pratinas by 467, nor to impugn Aristias' authorship of the tragedies performed in 467.

The most we can say is that **1**'s date of 499/6 is within the archival period (West 1989, 251; Csapo 2015, 81) and if **1**'s information that he won a victory at the Dionysia is correct, and if it is true that he was the father of Aristias, and if we can therefore assume that he was active in Athens before Aristias, then **5** shows that it must have been before Aeschylus' victory, which is dated to 484 by the Parian Marble and which cannot be far wrong (Scullion 2002a, 82). **1**'s date for Pratinas must, therefore, be within ten years of Pratinas' production. Moreover, both the precision of the date in **1**, limited as it is to a single Olympiad, and the fact that only two competitors are named for Pratinas suggest that all the didascalic information relates to a single event: if so Pratinas' single victory was achieved within a ten year radius of 499/6 and it was won against Aeschylus and Choerilus, and no other archival information about any other competitions entered by Pratinas survived.

The most serious doubt adheres to the claim (**1, 2**) that Pratinas introduced satyr plays to the Athenian Dionysia. Possibly the archives once retained the name of a satyr play by Pratinas and it was the earliest known to Hellenistic scholars and therefore came to be treated as 'the first' (see below). More likely the early date was fancifully connected with a satyr drama that was the main product of Pratinas to survive into the Hellenistic period. In any case the information that he introduced satyr performances is hard to reconcile with what we know: satyrs appear in Athenian iconography from as early as 580 and satyr choruses can be associated with the Dionysian Parade from its inception (**I Aiv 23**; **I Aiv 26**). The claim that Pratinas first produced satyr plays is unlikely to have entered the ancient scholarly repertoire through Aristotle's *Didaskaliai* since Aristotle derived tragedy from satyr drama, whereas Pratinas' invention of it would see satyr performances coming after the invention of tragedy and from a Doric source.

Pohlenz long ago (1927) identified the information about Pratinas as a cornerstone of an Alexandrian, un-Aristotelian and pro-Dorian theory of the origin of satyr play (cf. Napolitano 1979). Webster, however, argued that **1** was not irreconcilable with Aristotle on the grounds that **1**'s 'first wrote satyr plays' simply 'means that satyr-plays of the fifth-century type with the chorus in the normal fifth-century satyr costume were first recorded for Pratinas' (*DTC*² 96). This may well be what happened but it is surely not what 'first wrote' meant, and is in any case irreconcilable with **2**'s testimony that explicitly says 'first introduced'. The evidence of **7–9** is against any attempt to soften the incompatibility of the theory of Pratinas' invention of satyr play by supposing he first made a traditional Attic form of entertainment 'literary' or 'refined': not only do **7–9** stress that Phlious is the original home of dancing satyrs, but they stress the primordial vigour of Pratinas' performances.

Despite speculation about late fourth-century sources in Aristoxenus and Heraclides of Pontus (Pohlenz 1927, 312–13), we cannot trace any direct mention of Pratinas earlier than the third to second century, but in that era, though our literary remains are sparse, he is an established culture hero, mentioned or alluded to no less than six times:

- three times as a founder of satyr play (**7–9**);
- once for his excellence in directing choral dance (Aristokles probably in *On Choruses*, in Ath. 1.22a = *TrGF* 1 T 11, though even there some manuscripts confuse 'Pratinas' for 'Cratinus' as in **2**);
- once for the contents of his poetry (Diogenes of Babylon is the likely source of *TrGF* 4 F 9: see Woodward 2010, 66–8);
- and finally in a third-century papyrus with at least nine epigrams that appear to relate to the contents of plays (*TrGF* V.2, 1105 *Add.* 10).

The epigrams **7–9**, between them, presuppose a history of satyr drama, from rude and rustic (esp. **8**, l. 3) beginnings in Phlious, reaching a state of perfection in Athens under Sophocles (**8**, **9**) and then losing its vigour through innovation (**9**, l. 5), until the time of Sositheus, who archaised and reinvigorated the genre (Fantuzzi 2007, 118–21, who notes also Dioscorides' claim, *AP* 7.708, that Machon's restoration of Old Comedy's pungency put Alexandria on a par with Athens). Sositheus, whose nationality is variously given as Syracuse, Athens or Alexandria Troas (the latter's obscurity recommends it), was an important member of the Pleiad in Egyptian Alexandria. Alexandria in the early to mid third century had adopted 'an overtly anti-Peripatetic impetus in both the literary poetics and … scholarly practice' (Lowe 2013, 347), despite the contribution of the exiled Demetrius of Phaleron in establishing the cultural and intellectual life of Ptolemy's court, and indeed perhaps because of it – as he fell precipitously from Ptolemy's favour (**VI K**). If it was not here that the Dorian origins of satyr play (and by implication tragedy: cf. **Bv 1–4**) were first asserted, **8** and **9** show that the theory was here happily received as an important component of its self-proclaimed cultural renaissance. The third-century Alexandrian scholar Istros, notably, claimed that even Sophocles, the supposed perfecter of satyr play, was born in Phlious (*FGrH* 334 F 34) and this may explain the preeminent importance of Sophocles in this tradition (**8**, **9**).

That the theory appealed to Doric pride and to the cultural ambitions of the new capitals of the Diadochi is obvious from **7**, the epigram on a statue base found in Pergamon. The satyr who notionally speaks the verses speaks in Doric dialect, though this is unusual for epigrams and foreign to Aeolic Pergamon. Unusual for the genre too is the use of the metre named after the Doric Phalaikos. Doric is evidently designed to present the satyr as Peloponnesian if not specifically Phliasian. The dedicator and the sculptor, Thoinias, are from Sicyon, less than 20 km distant from Phlious along the banks of the river Asopos (and Sicyon was the reputed home of Epigenes, the inventor of tragedy: **Bv 1–4**). Together with the references to Thyone, a specifically Peloponnesian name for Semele, and to Pratinas as the originator of the 'concept' of a dancing satyr, the dedication is a manifestation of local pride (Kerkhecker 1991, 31–2), and one that may have a specific appeal to Attalid interests, both because of the royal Dionysus cult (Müller 1989, 542–53; Nicolucci 2003, 329–36) and the claimed origin of the Attalids from Tegean Telephus.

If Pratinas was reinvented as the inventor of satyr play in the third century it was certainly not *ex nihilo*. Recent scholars have made a good case that one extended fragment of Pratinas that survives belongs to a satyr performance (D'Alessio 2007; Cipolla 2009, 65–74; Shaw 2014), and though the fragment has been assigned to a different Pratinas, scholarly consensus now strongly favours the Phliasian (Griffith 2013, 273; Shaw 2014, 44–55). This fragment may have been preserved because it illustrates the satyrs' assertion of their primitive, robust and spontaneous affinity to dance against musical refinements and innovation, in short because it supports a view of Pratinas and the origins of satyr play that appealed to Alexandria and other Hellenistic rivals of Athens' claims to cultural supremacy. More particularly, the last line of the fragment ἄκου᾽ ἄκουε τὰν ἐμὰν Δώριον χορείαν 'listen, listen to my Dorian dance/song' (*TrGF* 4 F 3, l. 17), appears to assert the essential and original Dorianness of satyr dance, and may indeed constitute the main justification for the Alexandrian assertion that Pratinas, the poet of Dorian Phlious, first introduced Peloponnesian satyr performances to Athens. Many scholars (Pohlenz 1927, 319–20; Fantuzzi 2007, 115; Cipolla 2009, 55–6) persuasively argue a direct allusion to this line in **9**'s lines 7–8 καὶ πάλιν εἰσώρμησα τὸν ἄρσενα Δωρίδι Μούσῃ ῥυθμόν, 'and once again I thrust that manly rhythm into the Dorian Muse'. An anonymous epigram (*AP* 7.82) possibly comes from the same cultural milieu and oddly reinforces the Dorian claim to satyrs through Epicharmus: 'I (the tomb) hold Sicilian Epicharmus, a man armed by the Dorian Muse for Bacchus and satyrs.'

For our immediate purposes it is important to know the nature of Pratinas' and Aristias' connection with Phlious. It is often assumed that migration and permanent displacement to Athens was a condition of their theatrical careers. But Athenaeus twice speaks in a manner that indicates he thought of Pratinas either as performing in Phlious, or performing in a primarily Phliasian context: in **I Bi 13d** Pratinas is said to complain that pipers no longer 'piped to the choruses, in accordance with local custom (καθάπερ ἦν πάτριον), but choruses sang to the pipers'. The expression would be an odd one spoken by a foreigner in Athens. Elsewhere in Athenaeus (9.392f) the speaker comments upon Pratinas' expression 'sweet-voiced quail' (*TrGF* F 1) and wonders if quails sound differently in Phlious. Both these passages indicate that Athenaeus and perhaps his sources imagined Pratinas to be performing in Phlious, not Athens. Moreover, it has long been noticed that the proportion of satyr plays in Pratinas' output (64%), as reported by **1**, sits awkwardly in an Athenian context where one satyr play to three tragedies was the norm. If the figures are correct (and, as Shaw 2014, 44 points out, manufactured data would likely be far less anomalous), then Pratinas could not have been working and performing in Athens alone (*DTC*² 65). This would also explain why of eighty-two dramas only four (?) were successful at Athens at a time when there were very few tragedians to be had (witness the reported twenty-eight victories of Aeschylus and Choerilus' thirteen). Neither Pratinas nor, it seems, Aristias (**3**, **4**) confined themselves to the Athenian norm of writing connected tetralogies. Pratinas, at least, seems to have written and performed single satyr plays and possibly gave one to his son to complement the three tragedies with which he performed in 467.

There is at least a possibility that Pratinas and Aristias performed in Phlious and in other locations besides Athens. Certainly Phlious claimed Aristias for its own: a memorial to, or tomb of, 'Aristias, son of Pratinas' was seen in the marketplace of Phlious by Pausanias (2.13.6; oddly enough he reports none to Pratinas himself, an oddity so unexpected that many misread the text to include both: e.g. Snell at *TrGF* 7 T 4). Unfortunately the earliest theatre at Phlious allows for no more precise dating than the fourth century or earlier. The first phase of the theatre, certainly of wood (Moretti 2014a, 112), was built upon a surface that was covered over with another upon which the stone skene was built and which contained no pottery later than the fourth century (Biers 1975, 62; Bressan 2009, 220). The later orchestra had an oval or rectangular shape (Biers 1971, 443), which presumably indicates that it respected the original layout of the theatre that conformed to fifth- and early fourth-century norms. Moreover, near the theatre, reused in a Byzantine grave monument, was found an unfluted Ionic column with a rectangular cutting at the top, apparently to hold a statue, and interpreted by Biers as a choregic monument of fifth-century date (1973, 110–11). In Pausanias' day (2.13.5) the theatre may have been connected to a sanctuary of Asclepius or Demeter: Pausanias' language is very imprecise. Dionysus was nonetheless an important deity in Phlious (Casadio 1994, 24–5; Fearn 2003, 365–6). The city derived its name from a son of Dionysus (Meyer 1941, 288).

The testimony of **10** has been ignored by previous discussions of theatre in Phlious, but it confirms use of the theatre at Phlious by the later fourth century. Timon, who was orphaned as a child in Phlious, survived by taking up a career as a choreut. This is one of our earliest clear pieces of evidence for a choreutic profession. **10** does not mention the theatre but it is hard to imagine where else a choreut in Phlious could practise his trade. Timon later became a writer of, among other things, tragedies, satyr plays, and comedies, the first poet we know of to write in all genres (*TrGF* 112), a versatility to which his early activity as a choreut probably contributed. Phlious was home to other famous theatricians in the fourth century: the aulete Asopodoros (Stefanis no. 468); the tragic actor Hegemon (Stefanis no. 1051); as well as the magician Kratisthenes (Stefanis no. 1496).

Bvii: Epidaurus, City

1. Dedicatory inscription of the Damiourgoi on theatre seats (kerkis B, row 7). Date: second half 4th c. (letter forms).

Inscribed across four adjoining limestone seats of the second wedge and seventh row of the theatre of the city of Epidaurus.
A: 1.4 × 0.38 × 0.37 m; B: 1.31 × 0.29 × 0.39 m; C: 1.07 × 0.3 × 0.4 m; D: 1.49 × 0.31 × 0.41 m. This section of the theatre was excavated in 1997.
in situ.
Petrounakos 2015, 114–15, fig. 16.
Text: Petrounakos.

δαμιουργο[ὶ] Διονύσῳ
Σωκράτης Τιμόκριτος Δαμοχάρης Λυσίξιππος
Εὔκλιππος Τέλων Τιμοσθέ[ν]ης Ἀριστοκράτης

The Demiourgo[i] (dedicate these seats) to Dionysus.
Sokrates, Timokritos, Damochares, Lysixippos,
Euklippos, Telon, Timosthe[n]es, Aristokrates.

2. Plautus, *Curculio* **644/5–50**. Written ca. 193. The Greek model has been dated by the reference to the siege of Sicyon (*Curc.* 393–94) to some time soon after 303 (Wilamowitz 1886, 37 n. 8), but this may be Plautus' own allusion to Flamininus' campaign against Nabis of Sparta (Naudet 1845 II, 2). Lefèvre speculates that Plautus is himself responsible for the Epidaurian setting of the play (1991, 90). This passage explains how the leading female character of the play, Planesium, while a young child, became separated from her family and came into the possession of a pimp. She describes events that took place some 10–15 years before the action of the play. This is part of the recognition scene in which she is proven to be a freeborn citizen of Epidaurus and can therefore legally marry the leading young man, Phaedromus. Text: Lindsay.

644/5	*ea me spectatum tulerat per Dionysia.*
	postquam illo ventum est, iam, ut me collocaverat,
	exoritur ventus turbo, spectacla ibi ruont,
	ego pertimesco: [tum] ibi me nescioquis arripit
	timidam atque pavidam, nec vivam nec mortuam.
650	*nec quo me pacto apstulerit possum dicere.*

She (the nurse, Archestrata) had taken me to view (the proceedings) at the time of the Dionysia. After we arrived there, as soon as she had found me a place, a whirlwind suddenly descended, then the stands of seating collapsed, I was terrified: then someone grabbed me livid and frightened, neither dead nor alive, [650] and I can't say how he took me from that place.

The theatre in the city of Epidaurus was discovered only in 1970 and was excavated sporadically from 1972 until 1995 and again from 2000 to 2010 (Lambrinoudakis and Kazolias 2006). The discovery was unexpected as Pausanias makes no mention of the monument (2.29.1), though he does mention several shrines and temples in the city of Epidaurus, among them a temple of Dionysus. It was a small theatre with a capacity of some 2,000 (Benos 2009, 2). Until Petrounakos 2015 only very brief reports of the theatre and its inscriptions (*SEG* 26, 452) were published.

The earliest datable phase of the theatre is the gradual installation of a stone prohedria and theatron which took place in stages from the mid fourth to the beginning of the second century (Petrounakos 2015, 72–5). The limestone seats are all inscribed with dedicatory inscriptions of which **1** is one of the fullest of the one hundred published texts. All the seats in the theatron (including the prohedria) appear to be dedicated, usually by groups of two, four, six or eight magistrates, either *damiourgoi* or *phrouroi*, and in one case (E15), the *phrouros* Bykos (see below) adds that he also served as an *agoranomos*. The even numbers of the officials are convincingly related to the tribal structure of Epidaurus, which had two of the traditional Doric tribes (Hylleis and Dymanes), and two non-Doric tribes

(Azantioi and Hysminates; see Petrounakos 2015, 34–9). The *damiourgoi*, of whom eight were in office at the time of our inscriptions, may have the general political function of Archons, though at Epidaurus they are only attested in relation to festival activities where they seem to represent the polis and share their authority with agonothetes and hellanodikai (Petrounakos 2015, 44–6). The *phrouroi* are argued by Petrounakos to be officials related to a sort of ephebate (see further below).

The magistrates of each class generally seem to have made, during or at the end of their term in office, a collective dedication within a kerkis of a row of benches or prohedric seats in stone. In this way the theatron was slowly filled with rows of stone benches over a period of a century and a half. Sometimes the officials dedicate more than one row of seats within the kerkis; in one case the same pair of *phrouroi*, Bykos and Kalliphon, dedicated ten rows in the fifth kerkis, presumably on a single occasion, while Bykos also appears as one of the *damiourgoi* dedicating a row of seats in the second kerkis (Petrounakos 2015, 111, 166–74). Clearly, even if the dedications were prescribed by law or custom, public zeal or ambition played a role in motivating the largesse.

Even so, the inscriptions are all fairly minimalistic. The names of the dedicators are without patronymic, tribe name, or the names of the thirty-nine regional units used in formal identifications (Piérart *IACP* 607). At times the dedicators are entirely nameless and the dedication is simply marked 'the *damiourgoi*' or 'the *phrouroi*'. First names (and even no names) evidently sufficed. But the rest of the inscription is equally minimal. A verb of dedication is rarely expressed. Most of the inscriptions do not even name the god to whom the seats are dedicated (and to whom presumably the theatre belongs): Dionysus is certainly or probably named as dedicatee some thirty-five times in the published corpus. Surprisingly 'Lykeios' (Apollo) is named as dedicatee, with no further text, three times (Petrounakos 2015, 94, 262, 268, 275–6, nos. 220, 245, 283). A late third-century dedication to Apollo was also found just above the theatre (Petrounakos 2015, 54). Petrounakos supposes these were dedications by the *phrouroi*, who elsewhere show a strong connection with Apollo Lykeios, and particularly with the gymnasium, dedicated to Lykeios, beside the theatre (2015, 48–58).

There is no indication whether the remainder of the theatron was covered with *ikria* or remained a bare hillside. It is not unlikely that the theatre was in use before stone architecture was introduced. The mid fourth-century date makes the theatron one of the earliest theatres in Greece to adopt a horseshoe-shaped theatron, and may even have been somewhat earlier in design than the theatre in the nearby Sanctuary of Asclepius (**Bviii**). The first phase probably also included a skene building (some of its poros blocks were reused in the subsequent phases of the theatre), parodoi, analemma walls and a drainage canal (Lambrinoudakis and Kazolias 2006, 61; Petrounakos 2015, 75–6). There is no evidence for the shape of the orchestra in this phase, as it was obliterated in the two phases that followed (1st–2nd c. AD; late antique–Early Byzantine).

Epidaurus provides a close parallel for the gradual conversion over many decades of a wooden to a stone theatron, such as is indicated by the Delian inscriptions (see on **Dvi**; Petrounakos 2015, 74) and was probably also the case in Athens (Papastamati-von Moock 2014, esp. 20–3). **2** might be a witness to the use of *ikria* and the incompleteness of the process of conversion by ca. 320, but it is much more likely that the *spectacla* which collapsed were those set up along the route of the Dionysian procession (as in *Cistellaria* 89–90;

Bv 5–6). It is, rather, evidence of a Dionysia with an important procession in Epidaurus, certainly by the early second century, but more likely in the late fourth (assuming this plot detail was transferred from the Greek model). The Epidaurian Dionysia is not again attested until ca. 74 (*IG* IV² 1, 66, ll. 38–42, 67–9).

There is no evidence for drama at the Dionysia at Epidaurus. Epidaurus seems to have been a democracy in the fourth century, when the decrees are passed by the Council and the People (Piérart *IACP* 607), but an oligarchic tradition lay somewhere in its past, probably in the Archaic period: Plutarch, probably drawing upon Aristotle, says 180 individuals constituted the full citizen caste (*Mor.* 291e). The constitution may also have been affected by Epidaurus' possible dependency on democratic Argos after Chaeronea (338; Piérart *IACP* 607). The fact that the theatre seats are dedicated by *damiourgoi* and *phrouroi* whose primary responsibilities are, so far as we can tell, religious, and that the seats are dedicated to Dionysus, does suggest that the theatre was conceived primarily as a performance space, not a political assembly. The presence of a skene building in the first phase of the theatre suggests dramatic or at least musical performances.

Bviii: Epidaurus, Asclepius Sanctuary

1. Building Accounts Probably Related to the Theatre, 330–320 (letter forms, contents, prosopography: see below).

Lower sections of a limestone stele with remains of tenons. Front, back and right edge inscribed.
Front (**a**) and back (**c**) badly damaged; right side (**b**) well preserved except at top.
Possibly 0.45 × 0.43 × 0.16 m (there are obvious errors in Peek's record of the dimensions).
No record of date or location of discovery. Left neglected in the museum store rooms at Epidaurus until studied by Peek in the ?1960s.
Presumably still Epidaurus museum inv. 012.
Burford 1966, 296 no. XIV; Peek 1972, no. 19; *SEG* 25, 394.
Text: Based on Peek with minor modification.

a. Front
(three illegible lines)   stoich.

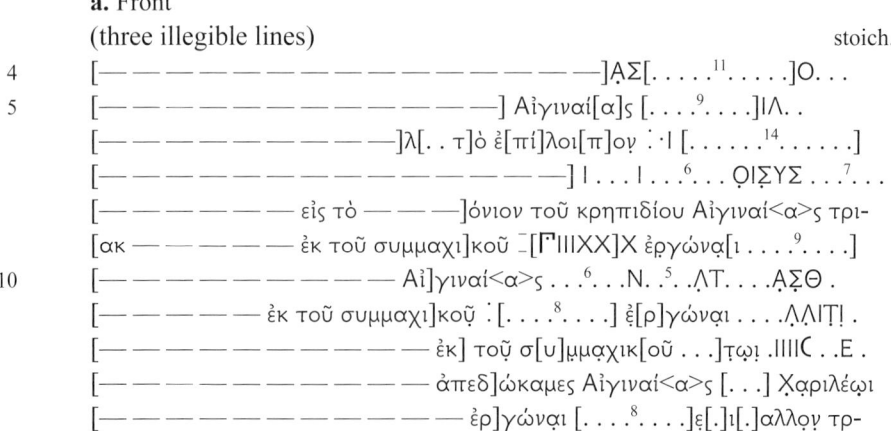

15 [— — — — — — — — — — — — — — — —]ω[. . .⁷. . .] ὀβο[λ]ο[ὺ]ς Λα[μ]προνί-
[κωι — — — — — — — — — — — — — — —]νωτροι ἀπεδώκαμε[ς] τὰ ἐπὶ λ[.]
[— — — — — — — — — — — — — — — — —]ρ[. . .] τούτων Ι.
[— — — — — — — — — — — — — — — —]Λ. .ΙΣΣΟΝΙ. . . .ΣΕ . ΟΝΗ .
[— — — — — — — — — — — — — — — ἀπ]εδώκαμες [δρ]αχμὰς [. .]
20 [— — — — — — — — — — — — — — —] Δαϊμένει ἐδώκαμες ᵛ
[— — — — — — — — — — — — — — ἐρ]γώνα]ι Νί[κ]ωνι Αἰγιναίας
[— — — — — — — — — — — — — —]σιν[ίκ]ωι ἀπεδώκα-
[μες — — — — — — — — — — — — —]ια ἑπτά, τρ[ε]ῖς χαλκ-
[έους — — — — — — — — — — — — τ]οῦ κρηπιδίο<υ> Αἰγι-
25 [ναίας — — — — — — — — — ἐκ τοῦ συμ]μαχικοῦ ⁼ – ΓΙΙΙΧ[Χ]Χ
[— — — — — — — — — — — — — —] εροι ἐπὶ [τ]ὰ [. . .]
[— — — — — — — — — — — — — ἑλ]ομένωι τὰ [. . . .]
[— — — — — — — — — — — — — — —]τίων δαπ[άν]α ᵛ᙮
vacat

(three illegible lines) [… ⁵ …] Aeginet<a>n (drachmas) [… t]he r[e]main[d]er
[…] for the […-]*onion* of the row of seats thirty (or less likely 'three hundred')
Aeginet<a>n (drachmas) [… ??from the alliance f]und 2[5 drachmas, 3 obols,
3] chalkeoi for the contracto[r … ¹⁰ … Ae]ginet<a>n (drachmas) [from the
alliance fu]nd […] c[on]tractor [… from] the al[l]ian[ce fund …] 4 drachmas
and 6 chalkeoi […] we [pa]id […] Aeginet<a>n (drachmas) to Charileon […]
to the [con]tractor […¹⁵ …] obo[l]s to La[m]proni[kos …] we pai[d] the things
at […] of these 1 obol […] we pai[d dr]achmas [… ²⁰ …] we gave to Daimenes
[… to the contracto]r Ni[k]on Aeginetan (drachmas) […] to [?]sini[k]os we
pai[d … X] and seven, thre[e] chalk[eoi …] of [t]he row of seats ²⁵ Aegi[netan
(drachmas) … from the all]iance fund 35 drachmas, 3 obols, 3 chalkeoi […]
for [t]he […] to the one who [to]ok up the contract for the […] of the […]
exp[en]ses.

b. Right Side
. ΡΕ[— — — — — — — —]   stoich. 16–18
[—]ΟΤ[— — — — — — —]
!. . . .Ι[— — — — — — —]
του ἔργο[υ . ᵛ . . .⁸⁻⁹. . .]
5 [.]ων σκαν[ᾶ]ς [. . .⁶. . .]
νων ἐν π[.]ΙΕ[. . .]ΣΥΛ[.]
ων τῶν ἐν τᾶι [σκανᾶι]
[τρί]ταν δόσιν στύ[λο]-
υς [τ]ρι[ά]κο<ν>τα δύο, ἑλο[μ]-
10 έν<ωι> τὰν στῦλον ἑκά[σ]-
[τ]αν [δ]ραχμᾶν τριάκο-

ντα ὀκτώ· καὶ τῶν πα-
ρασταμάτων δυωδε-
καποδίαν ἑκατὸν ἐγ-
15   νέα, ἑλομέν‹ω›ι τὰν δυ-
[ω]δεκαποδίαν δραχμ-
[ᾶ]ν δύο· ὑφαιρεθέντο[ς]
[τ]οῦ ἐπιδεκάτου πα[ντ]-
ὸς γίνονται δραχμ[αὶ]
20   ḤΗΗΗΓ⌐_– ΙΙΤΧ ᵛ καὶ Αἰσ[χυ]-
[λ]ίδαι Σθενείδαι τοῖ[ς]
[ἐ]γγύοις Καλλία τοῖς
[δε]κάτας κονιάσιος
. . *vacat*

[…] of the work […] ⁵ of the sken[e …] for a [th]ird instalment for the
[th]ir‹t›y-two columns on the [skene] to the man who too[k] ¹⁰ up the contract thirty-eight drachmas for each column. And for the one hundred and
nine twelve-foot lengths of door jambs (and/or window frames, or possibly
'pilasters'?), ¹⁵ to the man who took the contra‹c›t two drachm[a]s for each
tw[e]lve-foot length. Withholdin[g] the ten-percent from each item the total
comes to ²⁰ 480 drachmas 2 obols and 4 chalkeoi. And to Ais[chyl]idas,
Sthenidas, th[e g]uarantors of Kallias, for whom [te]n percent for plastering ...

c. Back

(*four illegible lines*)   non stoich. ca. 70–75

5   . . . . . .¹². . . . . .Γ⌐: ΟΙ[— — — — — — — — — — — — — — — — —]
. . . . . .¹³. . . . . .ΠΛ. . .⁷. . .ΙΛΛ.Ο[— — — — — — — — — — — — —]
. . . . .¹⁰. . . . . παρὰ Σθεν[είδα] ἐ[ρ]γώναι [— — — — — — — — — — —]
[. . .⁶. . .]ει .ΙΙΙΧ [Π]ερικ[λ]εῖ Λ[ακ]ρ[άτ]ει το[ῖς ἐγγύοις — — — — — — —]
[. . . .⁸. . . .]ένει ΙΙΙΙΙ λ[ό]γ[ος] δ[α]πάνας πά[σας — — — — — — — —]
vacat
10   [ἐπισ]τάταις τοῦ θ‹ε›άτρου Δυμάνων [—, Ἀζαντίων —, Ὑλλέων —, Ὑσμ]-
[ινατᾶ]ν Κλειδίκωι, γροφεῖ Πανκράτ[ει — — — — — — — — — — — δ]-
[ραχμὰ]ς Γ⌐ΙΙ . . . Χ Καλλ[ιτέ]λε[ι] Νέστ[ορι τοῖς ἐγγύοις — — — — — —]
[. .⁵. .] λόγος [λά]μματος [Η]ΗΗΙΙℂ ᵛ [— — — — — — — — — — — — —]
[.]α τῶν θώκων ἐ[ρ]γασίας Πε[ρ]ίλ[αι — — — — — έλομένωι τὰν τετρα]-
15   ποδίαν δραχ[μᾶ]ν δέκα δύο καὶ τ[ὸ ἐπιδέκατον — — — — — — δρα]-
χμᾶν δύο δέ[κα κα]ὶ τὸ ἐπιδέκ[ατον — — — — — — — — — — ὀ]-
κτὼ ποδῶν [καὶ ἡ]μιπόδιον [— — — — — — — — — καὶ τὸ ἐ]-
πιδέκατ[ο]ν δραχμαὶ Γ⌐_: [— — — — — — — — — έλομένωι τὰν]
τετραπο[δ]ίαν ἑξήκοντα [— — — — — — — — — — — — — — —]
20   κα[.]αν ἁπάντων δέκα τά[λαντα — — — — — — καὶ τὸ ἐπιδέκα]-
τον Η_–Ι . . ἐγγύωι Θεμ[ι— — — — — — — — — — — — — — —]

δραχμὰς Ⲫ— ⋮ ·ΙΙΙΙΤΧ ᵛ Γ[— — — — — — — — — — — — — — — παρὰ]
Παρμενίωνος δραχμᾶ[ν — — — — — — — — — — — — — — λόγος]
λάμματος Ἀρισ[τ]ομή[δ— — — — — — — — — — — — καὶ τὸ ἐπι]-
δέ[κατον].ΙΙ.Τ δαπά[ναι — — — — — — — — — — — — — —]
vacat

14 [.]άτων θώκων Peek   19–20 δα|πα[ν]ᾶν ἁπάντων Burford

[…] 8 drachmas […] from Sthen[eidas] for the co[n]tractor […] 3 obols 1
chalkeos to [P]erik[l]es, L[ak]r[at]es, th[e guarantors …-]enes 4 obols. An
a[c]c[ount] of a[ll] e[xp]enditure [… (*empty line*)] [10] To the [over]seers of the
th<e>atre: [to …] of the Dymanes [to … of the Azantioi, to … of the Hylleis,
to] Kleidikos of the [Hysmiata]i, to the secretary Pankrat[es …] 7 (or up to 9)
[drachma]s and 1 (or up to 9) chalkeoi; to Kall[ite]le[s], Nest[or the guarantors
…] account of the [re]ceipt 400 drachmas, 2 obols, 6 chalkeoi. […] of the
wo[r]king of the thrones to Pe[r]il[as …] who took the contract at [15] twelve
drach[ma]s per four feet and the ten p[ercent …] twe[lve] drachmas and the
ten percent [… e]ight [and a h]alf feet [… and the] ten percent 72 drachmas […
who took the contract at] sixty (drachmas) per four feet […] [20] of all ten ta[lants]
(or reading with Burford '(the sum) of all expenditures is ten ta[lants]') [… and
the ten percent] 130 drachmas, one (or more) obols to the guarantor Them[i-…]
65 drachmas, 4 obols and 4 chalkeoi. […] from Parmenion […] drachmas […
the account] of the receipt of Aris[t]ome[d-… and the ten] [25] per[cent …] 2
obols and 3 chalkeoi expen[ditures …]

2. Pausanias, *Guide to Greece* 2.27.5. Composition date: ca. 150 AD. The 'round building'
is the Tholos that Pausanias described earlier. Text: Spiro with emendation.

Ἐπιδαυρίοις δέ ἐστι θέατρον ἐν τῷ ἱερῷ μάλιστα ἐμοὶ δοκεῖν θέας ἄξιον· τὰ
μὲν γὰρ Ῥωμαίων πολυτελείᾳ ὑπερῆρε τῶν πανταχοῦ τῷ κόσμῳ, μεγέθει
δὲ Ἀρκάδων τὸ ἐν Μεγάλῃ πόλει· ἁρμονίας δὲ ἢ κάλλους ἕνεκα ἀρχιτέκτων
ποῖος ἐς ἅμιλλαν Πολυκλείτῳ γένοιτ' ἂν ἀξιόχρεως; Πολύκλειτος γὰρ καὶ
θέατρον τοῦτο καὶ οἴκημα τὸ περιφερὲς ὁ ποιήσας ἦν.

πολυτελείᾳ ὑπερῆρε Csapo   πολὺ δή τι [καὶ] ὑπερῆρ<κ>ε Bekker, Spiro, Musti   πολὺ
δή τι καὶ ὑπερῆρε β

The Epidaurians have a theatre in the sanctuary that I think especially worth
seeing. The theatres of the Romans surpass all the world in opulence, but in
size the theatre of the Arcadians at Megalopolis. What architect could be a serious rival to Polykleitos for harmony and beauty? Polykleitos was the creator
of this theatre and the round building (the 'Tholos').

The theatre of the Asclepieion of Epidaurus is the best known and most photographed
theatre in Greece. It is one of the earliest and largest curvilinear stone theatres in Greece.

The seating capacity, estimated at 12,300 (von Gerkan and Müller-Wiener 1961, 80) and 13,000–14,000 (Tomlinson 1983, 90), has recently been calculated at no more than 12,196 to 13,551 by Kampourakis, depending on whether 0.5 m or 0.45 m seating space is given per person (in Gogos 2011, 76: note error in final addition). Controversy surrounds the precise date of the monument and in particular its relationship to the 'Lycurgan' theatre in Athens, which is commonly assumed to be the model and precursor of all curvilinear stone theatres in Greece.

The Sanctuary of Asclepius in the territory of Epidaurus began a major building programme, probably 375–370. The programme upgraded the rural sanctuary to one of the chief Panhellenic centres of the healing god, Asclepius. The building began with a new temple of Asclepius, which was completed within five years, but construction continued in various parts of the sanctuary for another century or more. Because Epidaurus, through a board of *hieromnamones*, made individual contracts with hundreds of suppliers and craftsmen from throughout Greece, the city kept a detailed account of the moneys paid to the contractors. Non-Epidaurians would not be subject to legal proceedings in Epidaurus and so, to protect the city against default, each foreign contractor had to name an Epidaurian guarantor. The guarantors are also mentioned in the accounts. As further security, large contracts at Epidaurus were normally paid in instalments. And finally, as in other sanctuaries with major building programmes like Delphi and Lebadeia, one-tenth of each instalment was reserved until completion, as a deposit against possible fines incurred by the contractor (Burford 1969, 97). As a result of these complex arrangements, Epidaurus has left one of the largest archives of building accounts from antiquity.

At Epidaurus it was customary to assign separate stones to the accounts relating to each individual building. Despite the poor preservation of the stone, the collocation of terms relating to theatre architecture make it virtually certain that **1** preserves sections of the accounts relating to the construction of the theatre (cf. **1c**, l. 14). Not diagnostic in itself, the word *skene* (**1b**, ll. 5, 7) can mean, in addition to its technical theatrical meaning, any kind of tent, shed or temporary building. But the association of the term with the construction of thirty-two columns removes all doubt that the theatrical term is meant. The *skene* is also associated with *parastamata*. Burford (1966, 300) interprets *parastamata* as 'window frames' but in addition to 'window frames' and 'door jambs', the word can be generally applied to pillars or pilasters (see Hellmann 1992, 322–4; cf. on the parastadion of Eubulus' skene in **VI H**). There is no doubt that we are dealing with monumental architecture. Also multivalent is the term *krepidion* (**1a**, ll. 8, 24). It can refer to a socle or foundation, to a containment wall by a river or quay, as well as to a row of seating in the theatron (Hellmann 1992, 242). The word *thokos* (**1c**, l. 14) is a little more restricted: it is well attested in the form *thakos* in Delian inscriptions relating to the construction of the theatre. There it refers to marble benchwork, but the term can also refer to benches outside of a theatre (Hellmann 1992, 149–50). It is therefore uncertain that the individual terms on the stele refer to construction of the theatre, but the collocation of terms with possible theatrical reference and especially the highly elaborate *skene* make the conclusion more than likely. *Thokos* is thought to refer to the seats with backs that formed the first row (prohedria) of seats bordering the orchestra, but in the Asclepieion theatre the term could also refer to the seating in the rows below and above the diazoma (Burford 1966, 299). In Athens and Attica (Euonymon, Rhamnus, Halimous and Ikarion) individual or double thrones border the orchestra; but in the Peloponnese longer benches with backs designed for three or more occupants stretch between staircases (Megalopolis, Sicyon, and Epidaurus city as well as Asclepieion; see Moretti 2014a, 123).

The text on the front and back (**1a**; **1c**) is badly abraded, lacunose and the readings often suspect. In particular, the source of the payments 'from the alliance fund' ἐκ τοῦ συμμαχικοῦ (**1a**, ll. 9, 11, 25) is doubted by Grandjean (1995, 2: 'restitutions pour le moins audacieuses, que l'état de mutilation du texte dissuadait de suivre'). Burford even argues an error in the inscribing of **1b**, l. 20 (1966, 300). She finds that the sums do not work out: the total cost of the columns and pillars is 1,432 drachmas which with 10 per cent retained should equal 1,291 + drachmas. But Burford seems to be overlooking the fact that the money laid out for the columns is a third instalment of unknown amount. As 10 per cent is withheld on the third instalment of the work on the *skene* (**1b**, ll. 17–18), it is clear that at least four instalments were envisaged. For the recorded figures to work out the instalment must have been roughly a quarter of the total for pillars (i.e. 304 drachmas), but we do not actually know what other items appeared before the legible text. In all Burford (1969, 81–5) estimates the cost of a century of work on the sanctuary at 290 talants, of which 10 talants were spent building the theatre (1969, 83). But the latter figure is itself extracted from **c**, l. 20, reading the 'ten ta[lants]' as the grand total of expenditures (see apparatus). She notes however that Peek's restoration is not 'completely assured, but δεκατά would not make sense here either' (1966, 300).

Attempts to date the theatre generally range from about 340 to 300. Von Gerkan and Müller-Wiener (1961, 79) most influentially dated the theatre to the very end of the fourth century or the beginning of the third; Roux (1961, 417) dated it to the early third century. These scholars did not know our inscription. Subsequent to Burford and Peek's publication of **1** scholars have generally been disposed to accept an earlier date for the theatre, somewhere between 330 and 310 (Tomlinson 1983, 87; Moretti 1997, 16; Froning 2002, 53–8; Bressan 2009, 96). Gogos 2011, 63–70, however, retains the late dating of the theatre to ca. 300, but is influenced by incorrect assumptions about dramaturgical practice.

No precise date can be given to **1**, but a number of factors seem to indicate a date around 330. Polykleitos is said by **2** to have designed both the theatre and the Tholos at Epidaurus. If true, one would expect work to have begun on both buildings around the same time or in close succession. According to Burford (1969, 63–4) the building accounts indicate that work on the Tholos began about 365–360, soon after the Temple of Asclepius was built, but continued for twenty-seven years, thus to about 338–333. As corroboration of the common origin of these buildings it is notable that the Tholos and theatre in fact share uncommon decorative elements (Goette 1995a, 33) and they may even have served a common function since Schultz and Wickkiser identify the Tholos as a music room (2010; Schultz et al. 2017). Three bits of internal evidence to **1** allow a closer dating:

1. Sometime towards the end of the series of inscriptions relating to the Tholos, there is a change in the composition of the Building Commission, when projects were directed by Overseers (*Epistatai*), one from each of the Epidaurian tribes, and a secretary (Burford 1969, 133–4). This is the composition of the Building Commission we find in our inscription (**1c**, ll. 10–11). This should date the inscription to or close to the 330s.
2. One of the overseers, with the rare name Kleidikos, is also secretary to the building commission in *IG* IV² 1, 106, l. C 41 and as *katalogos* in *IG* IV² 1, 103, l. 144, which relate to construction that probably took place within the years 365–320 (the Tholos and the temple of Artemis: Burford 1969, 70–3, 208). There is also a Kleidikos who served as a guarantor in *IG* IV² 1, 102, l. 30 (ca. 370; cf. Peek 1969a, no. 52 A, l. 36, ca. 370–365). If any or all of these are the same Kleidikos, then a date ca. 340–330 is perfectly reasonable.
3. The lettering style of **1** is said to be close to *IG* IV² 1, 106 (Burford 1966, 297; Tomlinson 1983, 87), the temple of Artemis, where Kleidikos is also secretary to the building commission (see above). Tomlinson dates the temple of Artemis to around 330 (1983, 75). There is no reason to think that Kleidikos served as secretary before serving as overseer, as Tomlinson seems to do (1983, 87). But it is a plausible scenario and in any case a close chronological relationship between these activities and the inscriptions that record them is likely and this consideration too points to a date ca. 330.

The inscription only indicates a date at which there was building activity in the theatre. It does not settle the question of when construction began or when it was completed, unless of course we take the grand total of ten talants on **1c** as its total cost (as did Burford, above). **1**, however, does indicate a fairly advanced stage of construction on the theatron, with activity both in the main body and on the edges. At the same time the erection of columns and jambs for the skene suggest that construction is well beyond its initial phases. Construction in the theatre has been put as early as ca. 350, Goette's date for the gates of the parodos (1995a, 33; though contrast von Hesberg 1994, 126). Active work at this time on the theatre of the Asclepieion at least harmonises well with the evidence for the construction of the theatre in the city of Epidaurus, which is dated by inscriptions from 350 (**Bvii**). It is likely that the Epidaurians were encouraged to take advantage of the presence of the architects, skilled craftsmen and materials to build their own theatre in conjunction with that of the sanctuary (cf. Petrounakos 2015, 31). As it stands, the city theatre is possibly the earliest horseshoe-shaped stone theatron in Greece, if its completion does indeed antedate the sanctuary theatre.

Most scholars have assumed that the theatre at the Asclepieion must be later than the 'Lycurgan Theatre' in Athens. Athens, on this theory, was at the forefront of theatre design and alone responsible for the radical innovation of curvilinear stone-theatron construction (so von Gerkan and Müller-Wiener 1961, 79; Tomlinson 1983, 87). But the dating of the 'Lycurgan Theatre' is not as straightforward as it once seemed. The recently confirmed bonding of the Theatre of Dionysus' east retaining wall and the retaining wall north of the Odeion show that the plan for the 'Lycurgan' theatron was envisioned already in the fifth century, begun about 350 and essentially complete around 340 (Papastamati-von Moock

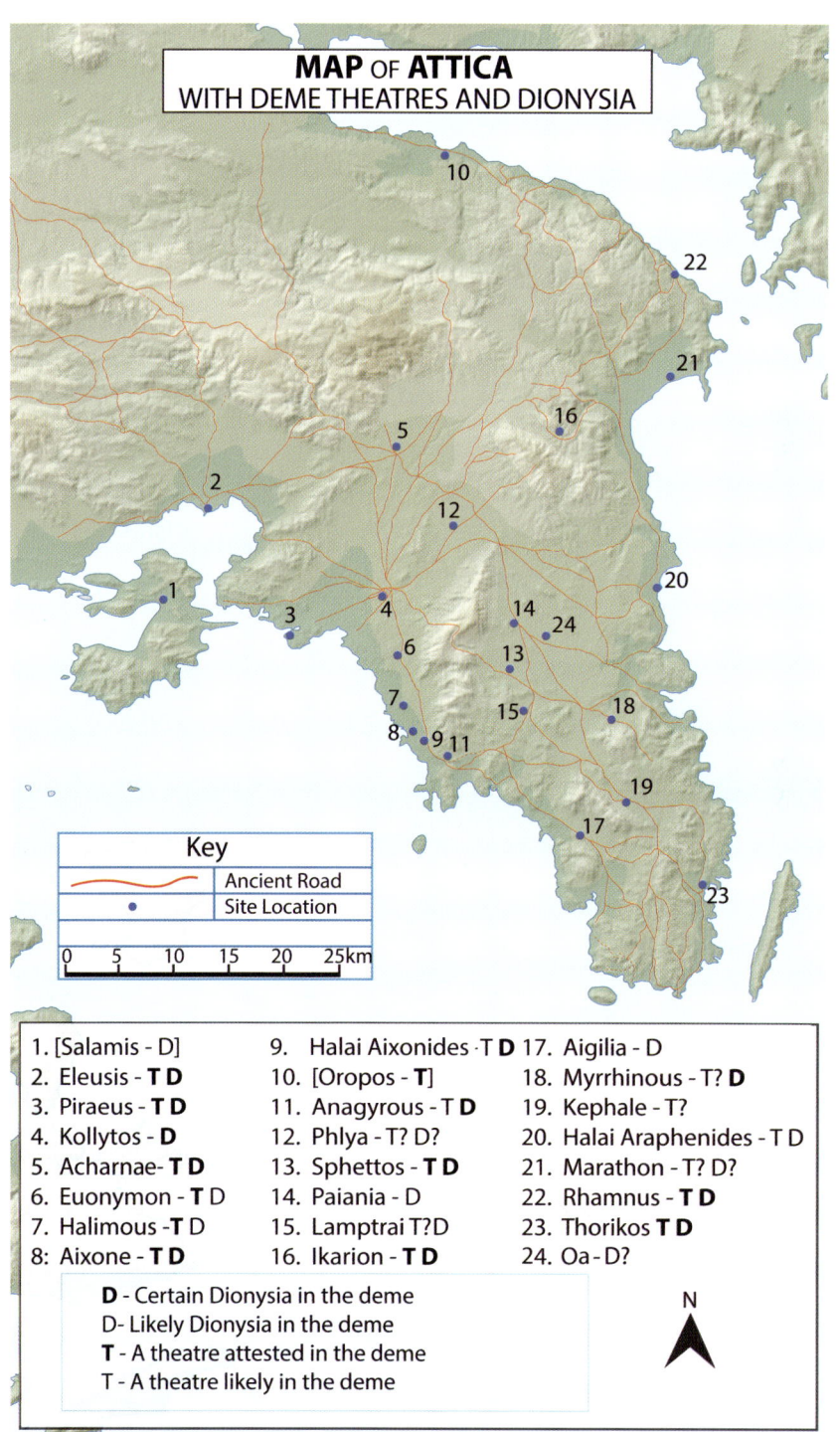

MAP OF ATTICA
WITH DEME THEATRES AND DIONYSIA

Key

⁓	Ancient Road
•	Site Location

0   5   10   15   20   25km

1. [Salamis - D]
2. Eleusis - **T D**
3. Piraeus - **T D**
4. Kollytos - **D**
5. Acharnae- **T D**
6. Euonymon - **T** D
7. Halimous -**T** D
8: Aixone - **T D**
9. Halai Aixonides ·**T D**
10. [Oropos - **T**]
11. Anagyrous - **T D**
12. Phlya - T? D?
13. Sphettos - **T D**
14. Paiania - D
15. Lamptrai T?D
16. Ikarion - **T D**
17. Aigilia - D
18. Myrrhinous - T? **D**
19. Kephale - T?
20. Halai Araphenides - T D
21. Marathon - T? D?
22. Rhamnus - **T D**
23. Thorikos **T D**
24. Oa - D?

D - Certain Dionysia in the deme
D- Likely Dionysia in the deme
T - A theatre attested in the deme
T - A theatre likely in the deme

N

Plate 1

Plate 2

Philippi

Thasos

Pella

Aegae

Dion

Skotoussa   Pherae

Ambracia   Thebes in Phthiotis

Leucas

Stratos

Opous

Delphi Chaeronea
Calydon Orchomenus   Thebes   Eretria
        Thespiae   Oropos

Leontion

Sicyon   Megara
Elis   Phlious   Corinth   Salamis   Andros
Orchomenus   Isthmia

Epion   Mantinea   Argos   Epidaurus   Ceos
    Phigalia   Tegea
    Megalopolis

Sparta   Siphnos

Cythera

Cyrene

0   50   100   200 Km

Plate 3

Plate 4

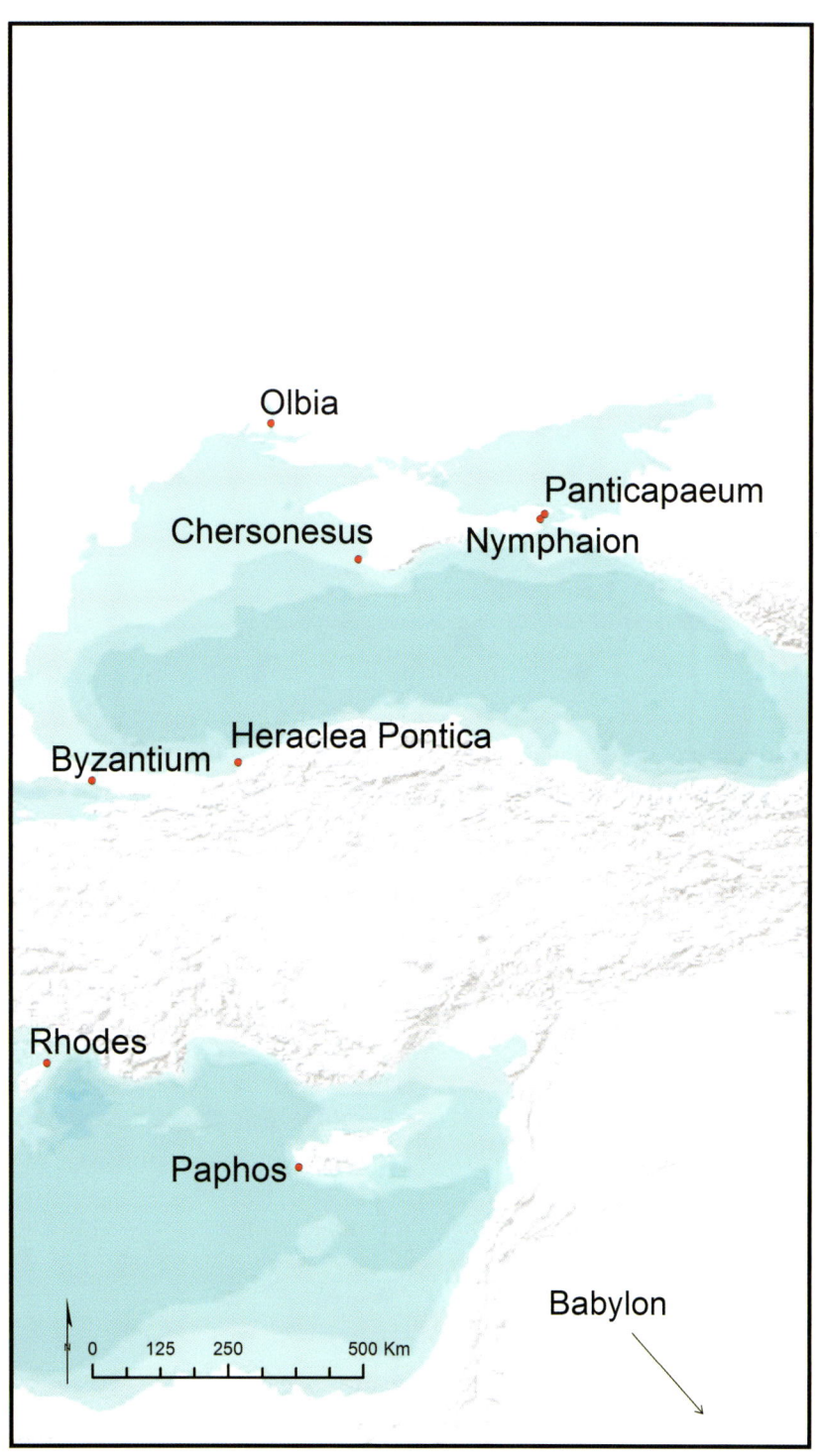

Olbia

Panticapaeum

Chersonesus   Nymphaion

Heraclea Pontica

Byzantium

Rhodes

Paphos

Babylon

0   125   250   500 Km

Plate 5

Plate 6

Plate 7

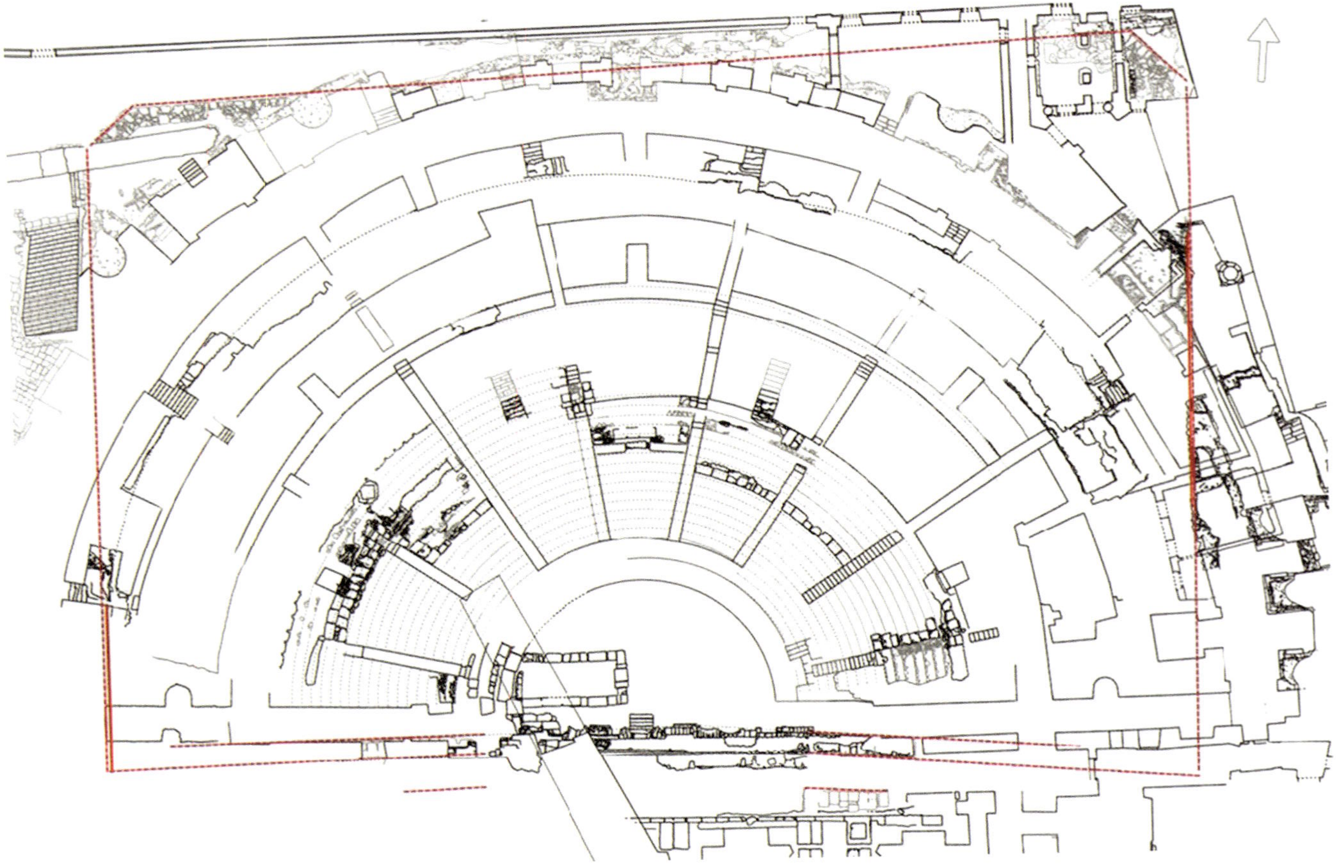

Plate 8

Plate 9

Plate 10

Plate 11

Plate 12

Plate 13

Plate 14

Plate 15

Plate 16

2014, 21–2, 33–4; Papastamati-von Moock 2015, 62–4; cf. Csapo and Wilson 2014, 395–6). Von Gerkan and Müller-Wiener also argue that the theatre at the Asclepieion is later than the Lycurgan theatre precisely because the Asclepieion has a proskenion, and the Lycurgan theatre none, concluding that proskenia were invented between the completion of the Lycurgan theatre and the designing of the theatre of the Asclepieion (1961, 79). But this assumes for proskenia a utility and importance, once they came into use, which made them indispensable to all theatres. Moretti (1997) has, on the contrary, shown that they were purely aesthetic additions. Developments at Athens do not therefore provide any kind of control over the beginning of the construction of the Epidaurian theatre. Nothing excludes the possibility that Polykleitos first designed the proskenion and Epidaurus first acquired one (Moretti 1997, 16; 2014a, 134). It is, in any case, easily possible that work began on the Asclepieion theatre as early as the 350s and that it was completed by the 330s or 320s. Indeed, given the therapeutic function of the circle, which we discuss in the next paragraph, it would not be unreasonable to think that the circular design of the Epidaurian theatre was conceived without reference to developments in Athens and before construction on the Lycurgan theatre began.

Von Gerkan and Müller-Wiener argued that the theatron of the Asclepieion was built in two phases, with a first phase that extended the seating only to the diazoma, and a second that doubled the seating capacity by building the epitheatron beyond the diazoma (1961, 80–1). But Käppel 1989 and Svenshon 2012 have shown that the theatre's geometric proportions indicate that the entire theatron was part of the original design. The theatre is built upon the Pythagorean pentagram which the Pythagoreans identified as 'Health' and used as a symbol for health (Käppel 1989, 104–5). More specifically the theatre is based upon the pentagram within a circle, and the Pythagoreans regarded the circle as the most perfect geometrical form and as a symbol of eternal life (Huffman 2005, 526–7). Archytas himself regarded geometry and music as kindred sciences (fr. 1 Huffman), and as music and dance therapy were apparently practised by the Pythagoreans (Iamb. *VP* 110–11; Porph. *VP* 32–3; Schultz and Wickkiser 2010; Schultz et al. 2017, 109–11, 122), and music therapy was practised at Epidaurus (Edelstein and Edelstein 1945 II, 199–208), we should entertain the possibility that the round theatre was designed with an eye to enhancing music's therapeutic value.

It is argued that the presence of a skene building at Epidaurus 'is a clear indication that the Theatre was intended for the performance of plays' (Tomlinson 1983, 88). This is possible, but far from certain. More purely musical performances may have better served the sanctuary's evident therapeutic programme. Athletic games are known at Epidaurus from Pindar (*N.* 3.148, 5.97; *I.* 8.147–50), who recalls victories that took place ca. 520 (Sève 1993, 305). But poetic competitions also existed well before the building of the theatre. A rhapsodic competition at the Asclepieion is attested in Plato's *Ion* 530a (probably written ca. 395). Drama is not explicitly attested until well after the construction of the theatre. Inscriptions listing fines for cheating athletes and defaulting performers (*IG* IV² 1, 99, ll. 24–6 with supplements by Peek 1969a, no. 44; *IG* IV² 1, 100) attest both tragedy and comedy at the festival of the Asclepieia and Apollonia (2nd or possibly 3rd c.: see Sève 1993, 310). The same inscriptions mention a defaulting aulete. Epidaurus' erection in the sanctuary of a statue for the celebrated Athenian comic poet Diomedes also points to comic competitions in the second century (*IG* IV² 1, 626; *PCG* V, 31).

The most that can be said is that some features of the proskenion and the orchestra seem suited to, if not designed for, drama or choral performance generally. The proskenion seems to have been designed to enable performance at orchestra level, and the pillars of the proskenion were designed to receive pinakes as a backdrop to performance at orchestra level, including panels with door openings, and the communication with the skene was through three doors suggesting an easy adaptability to the needs of comedy. Moreover, Moretti (2001, 169) interprets the paving slabs that define the orchestra circle as guidelines for choral dance, such as attested by Hesychius (s.v. γραμμαί) and Eustathius (*Il.* 2, 790). Another small slab seems to have marked the centre of the orchestra circle (von Gerkan and Müller-Wiener 1961, 8). We can guess that purely musical performances might more appropriately take place on the proskenion roof against the backdrop of the second storey of the skene. Though drama may not seem as obviously germane to the sanctuary's therapeutic purposes, we may note that a connection between drama and Asclepius is paralleled elsewhere, most conspicuously in the juxtaposition of Asclepius' sanctuary to the Theatre of Dionysus, and the contiguity between the Festival of Asclepius and the Dionysia (see **I Ai 4**; for a general study of Asclepius and drama, see Mitchell-Boyask 2008).

Bix: Spartan Theatres

1. **Herodotus, *Histories* 6.67**. Written ca. 440–420. Demaratus' kingship ended between 491 and mid summer 490. The festival of the Gymnopaidiai, the setting for Herodotus' narrative, took place between that time and before 486 (Richer 2012, 385). Demaratus was the Eurypontid Spartan king, but deposed through a conspiracy led by the other Spartan king, the Agiad Cleomenes, who, according to Herodotus, bribed the Pythia in Delphi to give a negative response to the question of the legitimacy of Demaratus' birth, and hence impugned the legitimacy of his succession. Text: Wilson.

> κατὰ μὲν δὴ Δημαρήτου τὴν κατάπαυσιν τῆς βασιληίης οὕτω ἐγένετο, ἔφυγε δὲ Δημάρητος ἐκ Σπάρτης ἐς Μήδους ἐκ τοιοῦδε ὀνείδεος· μετὰ τῆς βασιληίης τὴν κατάπαυσιν ὁ Δημάρητος ἦρχε αἱρεθεὶς ἀρχήν. ἦσαν μὲν ⁶⁷·² δὴ Γυμνοπαιδίαι. θεωμένου δὲ τοῦ Δημαρήτου ὁ Λευτυχίδης, γεγονὼς ἤδη βασιλεὺς αὐτὸς ἀντ᾽ ἐκείνου, πέμψας τὸν θεράποντα ἐπὶ γέλωτί τε καὶ λάσθῃ εἰρώτα τὸν Δημάρητον ὁκοῖόν τι εἴη τὸ ἄρχειν μετὰ τὸ βασιλεύειν. ⁶⁷·³ ὁ δὲ ἀλγήσας τῷ ἐπειρωτήματι εἶπε φὰς αὐτὸς μὲν ἀμφοτέρων ἤδη πεπειρῆσθαι, ἐκεῖνον δὲ οὔ· τὴν μέντοι ἐπειρώτησιν ταύτην ἄρξειν Λακεδαιμονίοισι ἢ μυρίης κακότητος ἢ μυρίης εὐδαιμονίης. ταῦτα δὲ εἴπας καὶ κατακαλυψάμενος ἤιε ἐκ τοῦ θεήτρου ἐς τὰ ἑωυτοῦ οἰκία, αὐτίκα δὲ παρασκευασάμενος ἔθυε βοῦν τῷ Διί, θύσας δὲ τὴν μητέρα ἐκάλεσε.

So this is how Demaratus' kingship came to an end. But Demaratus left Sparta and lived in exile among the Medes (Persians) because of the following kind of insult. After the end of his reign Demaratus was elected to a magistracy. It was the time [67.2] of the Gymnopaidiai. Demaratus was in the audience. Leotychides, who had become king in his stead, sent a slave to mock and insult him. He asked Demaratus what it was like to be a magistrate after being a king.[67.3] Demaratus took offence at the question but said that he admitted that he had experience of both offices, which Leotychides had not, but that this question would be the cause either of great trouble or great happiness for Sparta. After saying this he covered his head with his cloak (a conventional sign of shame) and left the theatre for his house where he immediately prepared and sacrificed an ox to Zeus and then summoned his mother.

2. Hexameter dedication on a theatre seat from Sparta. Date: probably 400–375 (letter forms, and dialect features: Kourinou-Pikoula 1992–1998, 264–5; Kourinou 2000, 160–3).

A marble throne inscribed on a smooth band at top of inner concave surface of backrest.
Preserved dimensions: 0.425 × 0.52 × 0.04–0.07 (top)–0.10–0.105 (bottom) m.
Reused as building material.
Found during salvage excavations in 1988 from the Georgakopoulos property, south of the present Eurotas bridge, north-east of Sparta.
Sparta Museum inv. ΜΣ 7730.
Kourinou-Pikoula 1992–1998 (*SEG* 46, 400); Cassio 2000 (*SEG* 50, 394); Lanérès 2012a (*SEG* 62, 212).
Text: Lanérès.   Photos: Kourinou-Pikoula 1992–1998, pl. 42; Kourinou 2000, pl. 33.

> μνᾶμα γεροντείας Ηιππανσίδας | τοῦτ᾽ ἀνέσηκε
> τᾶι Ηαλέαι καὶ σᾶ|τρον, ηαμ᾽ ἐνκάλη ηώστ᾽ ἀπὸ τούτω |
> σᾶσθαι, τὼς δὲ νέως τοῖς περγυ|τέροις ηυποχάδδην.

τᾶι Ηαλέαι καὶ σᾶ|τρον· Kourinou, Cassio   ηα μὲν καλῆ Kourinou   ηα μέν κα λῆ
Cassio

Hippansidas dedicated this (seat) (or reading with Kourinou and Cassio 'and theatron') as a memorial of his entry into the Gerousia | to Halea (Athena Alea), at the same time he invites the public (or 'gives an invitation') to spectate from it, | on condition that the young yield the seat to their elders.

3. Xenophon, *Hellenica* 6.4.16. A work completed in the 350s and referring to events after the Battle of Leuctra in 371 (cf. **6** below). Text: Marchant.

> γενομένων δὲ τούτων, ὁ μὲν εἰς τὴν Λακεδαίμονα ἀγγελῶν τὸ πάθος
> ἀφικνεῖται Γυμνοπαιδιῶν τε οὔσης τῆς τελευταίας καὶ τοῦ ἀνδρικοῦ χοροῦ
> ἔνδον ὄντος· οἱ δὲ ἔφοροι ἐπεὶ ἤκουσαν τὸ πάθος, ἐλυποῦντο μέν, ὥσπερ,
> οἶμαι, ἀνάγκη· τὸν μέντοι χορὸν οὐκ ἐξήγαγον, ἀλλὰ διαγωνίσασθαι εἴων.
> καὶ τὰ μὲν ὀνόματα πρὸς τοὺς οἰκείους ἑκάστου τῶν τεθνεώτων ἀπέδοσαν·

Once these events took place (i.e. the Battle of Leuctra), the man who brought news of the disaster to Lacedaemon arrived on the last day of the Gymnopaidiai and the men's chorus was within. The ephors, when they learned of the disaster, were upset, as was, I suppose, inevitable. They did not, however, ask the chorus to leave, but allowed them to continue competing, and they had the names of the dead delivered to each of their families.

4. Aristoxenus, fr. 108 Wehrli (= Ath. 14.631c). Written ca. 335–320. Aristoxenus is known to have written a work *On Tragic Dance* (frr. 104–6), which may have been part of a more general work on choral dance (Wehrli 1967, 80–1). It looks very much as if Aristoxenus, in the broader context from which this fragment was extracted, was writing in support of Peloponnesian claims to the invention of tragedy. He may have divided lyric poetry into three fundamental genres, pyrrhiche, gymnopaidike and hyporchematike, and seems to have likened the gymnopaidike to the (typical) tragic dance called emmeleia (frr. 103–4, 106 Wehrli; Wehrli 1967, 80–2), thus giving a derivation of a stereotypical tragic form, via pyrrhiche, from gymnopaidike. For the location of this development, Aristoxenus is probably thinking primarily of Sparta, and not e.g. his native Taras (a colony of Sparta) for which there is almost no evidence of pyrrhiche (Ceccarelli 1998, 146–7; **Axxi**). Winkler's suggestion (1990, 55) that the passage could refer to Athens is very unlikely: the category gymnopaidike (cf. below) clearly relates to a theoretical category of dance that evolved into and became characteristic of performance at the Spartan festival of the Gymnopaidiai. Moreover, Ceccarelli (1998, 223) notes that the majority of fragments of Aristoxenus transmitted by Athenaeus and relating to the pyrrhiche refer to Laconia. Aristoxenus indeed claims (probably in the same work) that Sparta invented the pyrrhiche (fr. 103 Wehrli). The most convincing way to take this fragment, therefore, is as a comment on the historical evolution of the genre pyrrhiche. It is, however, also possible to read this fragment as a description of three stages in a festival programme (as does Richer 2012, 386); or indeed as three stages in an 'athletic-cultural *cursus*' (Winkler 1990, 56). For the different interpretive possibilities, see Ceccarelli 1998, 223–4. The term gymnopaidike is probably a coinage of Aristoxenus: it appears only here and in Aristoxenus fr. 103 Wehrli, the passage of Athenaeus that cites Aristoxenus, and in Philodemus, *On Music* IV, where gymnopaidike is similarly part of a tripartite categorisation of dance genres (col. 40, ll. 7–8 Delattre; Philodemus is citing Diogenes of Babylon: Woodward 2010, 61–2, and 173–89 for Aristoxenus' influence on Diogenes, esp. as regards Spartan music). Text: Wehrli.

Ἀριστόξενος δέ φησιν ὡς οἱ παλαιοὶ γυμναζόμενοι πρῶτον ἐν τῇ γυμνοπαιδικῇ εἰς τὴν πυρρίχην ἐχώρουν πρὸ τοῦ εἰσιέναι εἰς τὸ θέατρον.

Aristoxenus says that the ancients, who took exercise first in the gymnopaidike, then advanced to the pyrrhiche before entering the theatre.

5. Polykrates, *Spartan History (Lakonika)*, *FGrH* 588 F 1 (= Ath. 4.139c–f). Athenaeus quotes Didymus (died ca. 10 AD) quoting Polykrates. Nothing is known of Polykrates unless he is the same author as the Polykrates of Athens who in the early 4th c. wrote on Sparta, and, according to Josephus, did so in a slanderous fashion (*Ap.* 1.120; *FGrH* 597 F 1). The lack of any such tone here has been advanced as an argument against the identification. Text: close to Jacoby.

Πολυκράτης ἐν τοῖς Λακωνικοῖς ἱστορεῖ, ὅτι τὴν μὲν τῶν Ὑακινθίων θυσίαν οἱ Λάκωνες ἐπὶ τρεῖς ἡμέρας συντελοῦσι, καὶ <τῇ μὲν πρώτῃ> διὰ τὸ πένθος τὸ γενόμενον περὶ τὸν Ὑάκινθον οὔτε στεφανοῦνται ἐπὶ τοῖς δείπνοις οὔτε ἄρτον εἰσφέρουσιν, <οὔτε> ἄλλα πέμματα καὶ τὰ τούτοις ἀκόλουθα διδόασι, καὶ τὸν εἰς τὸν θεὸν παιᾶνα οὐκ ᾄδουσιν, οὐδ᾽ ἄλλο τι [5] τοιοῦτον εἰσάγουσιν οὐδέν, καθάπερ ἐν ταῖς ἄλλαις θυσίαις ποιοῦσιν, ἀλλὰ μετ᾽ εὐταξίας πολλῆς δειπνήσαντες ἀπέρχονται. τῇ δὲ μέσῃ τῶν τριῶν ἡμερῶν γίνεται θέα ποικίλη καὶ πανήγυρις ἀξιόλογος καὶ μεγάλη· παῖδές τε γὰρ κιθαρίζουσιν ἐν χιτῶσιν ἀνεζωσμένοι, καὶ πρὸς αὐλὸν ᾄδοντες πάσας ἅμα τῷ [10] πλήκτρῳ τὰς χορδὰς ἐπιτρέχοντες ἐν ῥυθμῷ μὲν ἀναπαίστῳ, μετ᾽ ὀξέος δὲ τόνου, τὸν θεὸν ᾄδουσιν· ἄλλοι δ᾽ ἐφ᾽ ἵππων κεκοσμημένοι τὸ θέατρον διεξέρχονται· χοροί τε νεανίσκων παμπληθεῖς εἰσέρχονται, καὶ τῶν ἐπιχωρίων τινὰ ποιημάτων ᾄδουσιν, ὀρχησταί τε ἐν τούτοις ἀναμεμιγμένοι τὴν κίνησιν [15] ἀρχαϊκὴν ὑπὸ τὸν αὐλὸν καὶ τὴν ᾠδὴν ποιοῦνται. τῶν δὲ παρθένων αἱ μὲν ἐπὶ κανάθρων [καμαρωτῶν ξυλίνων ἁρμάτων] φέρονται πολυτελῶς κατεσκευασμένων, αἱ δ᾽ ἐφ᾽ † ἁμίλλαις ἁρμάτων ἐζευγμένων πομπεύουσιν. ἅπασα δ᾽ ἐν κινήσει καὶ χαρᾷ τῆς θεωρίας ἡ πόλις καθέστηκεν, ἱερεῖά τε παμπληθῆ [20] θύουσι τὴν ἡμέραν ταύτην, καὶ δειπνίζουσιν οἱ πολῖται πάντας τοὺς γνωρίμους καὶ τοὺς δούλους τοὺς ἰδίους· οὐδεὶς δ᾽ ἀπολείπει τὴν θυσίαν, ἀλλὰ κενοῦσθαι συμβαίνει τὴν πόλιν πρὸς τὴν θέαν.

1 <τῇ μὲν πρώτῃ> Jacoby   <τὴν μὲν πρώτην τοῦ Ὑακίνθου ἰδίαν νομίζουσι καὶ> Bölte   4 <οὔτε> ἄλλα Schweighäuser, Jacoby, et al.   ἀλλὰ A   16 [καμαρωτῶν ξυλίνων ἁρμάτων] Dobree, Wilamowitz   17–18 'intellegerem ἐφ᾽ ἁρμάτων ἡμιόνοις ἐζευγμένων, sed latet fortasse glossema' Kaibel   22–3 πρὸς τὴν θέαν A   πρὸς τὴν θοίνην Bölte, Jacoby

Polykrates in his *Spartan History* recounts that the Spartans celebrate the festival of the Hyakinthia for three days, and <on the first> (or with Bölte 'they think the first day to be a special day of Hyacinth and') because of the misfortune that befell Hyacinth they neither wear garlands nor do they bring bread to their meals, <nor do> they give cakes and such like, nor sing a paean to the god, nor do they introduce anything else [5] of the sort they do at all other sacrifices, but in orderly fashion they eat their meal and leave. On the second of the three days there is a varied spectacle and a well-attended and noteworthy assembly. Boys play the kithara in girded-up chitons and, singing in high-pitched voices to the music of pipes while [10] striking all the strings with a plectrum in an anapaestic rhythm, they praise the god. Others in elegant dress move through the theatre on horseback. Large choruses of youths enter and sing some compositions of local poets, and dancers mixed among them [15] perform ancient movements to the music of the pipes and the song. As for the maidens, some ride in lavishly decorated *kanathra* (wicker carriages) [covered wooden chariots (this is thought to be a later gloss)], others move in procession † in a competition of yoked chariots (the text appears to be corrupt here; Kaibel suggests 'move in procession on chariots yoked to mules'). The whole city is caught up in the movement and joy of the spectacle, and they sacrifice an enormous number of victims [20] during this day, and the citizens give a feast to all of their acquaintances and to their own slaves. No one is left out of the feast. As a result the whole city is emptied because everyone has gone to the spectacle (or with Bölte and Jacoby 'to the feast').

6. Plutarch, *Life of Agesilaus* 29. Written ca. 100 AD and referring to 371. Cf. **3**, which lacks the explicit mention of the theatre (but see commentary below). Text: departing from Ziegler (see apparatus).

> ἔτυχε μὲν γὰρ ἡ πόλις ἑορτὴν ἄγουσα καὶ ξένων οὖσα μεστή - Γυμνοπαιδίαι γὰρ ἦσαν - <καὶ> ἀγωνιζομένων χορῶν ἐν τῷ θεάτρῳ· παρῆσαν δ' ἀπὸ Λεύκτρων οἱ τὴν συμφορὰν ἀπαγγέλλοντες. οἱ δὲ ἔφοροι, καίπερ εὐθὺς ὄντος καταφανοῦς ὅτι διέφθαρται τὰ πράγματα καὶ τὴν ἀρχὴν ἀπολωλέκασιν, οὔτε χορὸν ἐξελθεῖν εἴασαν οὔτε τὸ σχῆμα τῆς ἑορτῆς μεταβαλεῖν τὴν πόλιν, ἀλλὰ κατ' οἰκίαν τῶν τεθνεώτων τοῖς προσήκουσι τὰ ὀνόματα πέμψαντες, αὐτοὶ τὰ περὶ τὴν θέαν καὶ τὸν ἀγῶνα τῶν χορῶν ἔπραττον.

μεστή (γυμνοπαιδίαι γὰρ ἦσαν) ἀγωνιζομένων Ziegler   μεστή· γυμνοπαιδίαι γὰρ ἦσαν, ἀγωνιζομένων Flacelière and Chambry   μεστή <καὶ> (γυμνοπαιδίαι γὰρ ἦσαν) ἀγωνιζομένων Reiske

The city (Sparta) was celebrating a festival and full of foreigners – it was the Gymnopaidiai – <and> of competing choruses in the theatre (or with Ziegler's text apparently 'full of foreign choruses competing in the theatre', or with Flacelière and Chambry 'full of foreigners, because it was the Gymnopaidiai, with choruses competing in the theatre'), when the men arrived with the news from Leuctra. The ephors, although it was clear that Sparta was ruined and had lost its hegemony, would not permit any chorus to go out, nor any change to the festival programme, but sent the names of the dead to the houses of their relatives, while they themselves attended to the business of the spectacle and the contest of the choruses.

7. Lucian, *Anacharsis* 38. Probably written sometime between 157 AD and 170 AD. Anacharsis was a semi-mythical half-Greek Scythian king thought to have lived in Greece in the early 6th c. For the ball games in the theatre, see Kennell 1995, 38–40. For the ritual combat in the field surrounded by water see: Paus. 3.14.8–10; Richer 2012, 457–545 and, for the location, Sanders 2009. While Lucian's descriptions in this dialogue are certainly anachronistic, it should be noted that Spartan ball games are attested as early as the 4th c. (Kennell 1995, 131). Text: Macleod.

ἐπεὶ δὲ φής, ὦ Ἀνάχαρσι, καὶ τὴν ἄλλην Ἑλλάδα ἐπελεύσεσθαι, μέμνησο ἤν
ποτε καὶ εἰς Λακεδαίμονα ἔλθῃς, μὴ καταγελάσαι μηδὲ ἐκείνων μηδὲ οἴεσθαι
μάτην πονεῖν αὐτούς, ὁπόταν ἢ σφαίρας πέρι ἐν τῷ θεάτρῳ συμπεσόντες
παίωσιν ἀλλήλους ἢ εἰς χωρίον εἰσελθόντες ὕδατι περιγεγραμμένον, εἰς
φάλαγγα διαστάντες, τὰ πολεμίων ἀλλήλους ἐργάζωνται γυμνοὶ καὶ αὐτοί,
ἄχρις ἂν ἐκβάλωσι τοῦ περιγράμματος τὸ ἕτερον σύνταγμα οἱ ἕτεροι, τοὺς
κατὰ Λυκοῦργον οἱ καθ' Ἡρακλέα ἢ ἔμπαλιν, συνωθοῦντες εἰς τὸ ὕδωρ· τὸ
γὰρ ἀπὸ τούτου εἰρήνη λοιπὸν καὶ οὐδεὶς ἂν ἔτι παίσειε.

Since, Anacharsis, you say you intended to visit the rest of Greece (beyond
Athens), recall if you ever also went to Sparta, not to laugh at them, nor to suppose that they struggle in vain, when, in a ball game, they fall upon one another
in the theatre and bash each other, or when they go into a field surrounded by
water, and place themselves in ranks and do to each other what their enemies
do, naked as they are, until one group pushes the other beyond the boundary,
whether the Heracles team pushes the Lycurgus team into the water or vice
versa, an event that brings peace and no one would strike another thereafter.

8. Pausanias, *Guide to Greece* 3.11.9. Composition date: ca. 150 AD. Pausanias is describing the agora of Sparta of his day. Text: After Spiro.

Σπαρτιάταις δὲ ἐπὶ τῆς ἀγορᾶς Πυθαέως τέ ἐστιν [καὶ] Ἀπόλλωνος καὶ
Ἀρτέμιδος καὶ Λητοῦς ἀγάλματα. ῾χορὸς᾽ δὲ οὗτος ὁ τόπος καλεῖται πᾶς, ὅτι
ἐν ταῖς Γυμνοπαιδίαις – ἑορτὴ δὲ εἴ τις ἄλλη καὶ αἱ Γυμνοπαιδίαι διὰ σπουδῆς
Λακεδαιμονίοις εἰσίν – ἐν ταύταις οὖν οἱ ἔφηβοι χοροὺς ἱστᾶσι τῷ Ἀπόλλωνι.

In the agora the Spartans have images of Apollo Pythaeus, of Artemis, and
of Leto. All this space is called the *choros* (= 'Chorus', or 'Dancing Place'),
because in the Gymnopaidiai – the Spartans take this, if they take any festival,
seriously – the ephebes organise choruses for Apollo.

The dedication on the marble throne from the sanctuary of Athena Alea (**2**) provides a
unique usage in Classical Sparta of the word σᾶτρον, a Laconian dialect word corresponding to Attic 'theatron'. Unfortunately the uncertainty of the text leaves it unclear whether
the word refers to a viewing place for spectators (as suggested by earlier interpretations
of the text), a single seat (namely the marble throne itself) or spectators. If the first, the
'viewing place' is probably little more than a landscaped hillside, since the emphasis of the
dedication is on the marble throne ('this marble throne and the theatron'). If the second
(construing 'Hippansidas dedicated this as a memorial and a viewing place'), it is a unique
usage, since *theatron* never means a single seat (for which Attic–Ionic use θέα/θέη or a
word from some other root). Lanérès is probably right therefore to interpret σᾶτρον as a
reference to the spectators, a common meaning of 'theatron' in Attic (2012a, 723). Even
in Attic–Ionic, however, this meaning is metonymic. The formation of the word θέατρον,
derived from the root of the verb θεάομαι 'to view' and the instrumental suffix -τρον
(sometimes also feminine -τρα) designates 'meistens ein Werkzeug oder ein Mittel zur

Erreichung gewisser Zwecke' (Kühner and Blass 1892, 271–2, sec. 27) including the place where one performs an action, in this case 'the place where one views', 'lieu où se trouvent les spectateurs' (Chantraine 1968–1980 II, 425; cf. λουτρόν 'the place where one washes', and indeed ὀρχήστρα 'the place where one dances'). Therefore, even if σᾶτρον were used of the audience in this instance, this meaning still attests a broader usage of the term in Laconian to refer to a place from which to view a spectacle. Moreover, **2** is written on a marble throne, expressly for the function of viewing spectacles, and the dedication of this throne in the Sanctuary of Alea is clear evidence for the existence of a permanent 'viewing place' in the sanctuary: **2** makes explicit reference to reuse by future 'spectators', to say nothing of the use of a permanent material like marble for the throne itself. The Sanctuary of Athena Alea can, partly with the help of **2**, be located in the north-eastern sector of the city (Kourinou-Pikoula 1992–1998, 266–76; Kourinou 2000, 163–7). Unfortunately, nothing is known of festivals or spectacles related to the sanctuary.

The existence of another or other theatres in Classical Sparta is indeed highly likely. At least two of the sources (Herodotus, Plutarch and perhaps Aristoxenus) mention a theatre in Sparta in the context of the festival of the Gymnopaidiai (**1**, **4**, **6**). Plutarch draws upon Xenophon (**3**) in this account, who makes no explicit mention of a theatre, yet the existence of some kind of building or at least a spatially circumscribed precinct seems implicit in **3**'s language (ἔνδον 'within'; οὐκ ἐξήγαγον 'they did not ask the chorus to go out'; cf. Richer 2012, 386) and Plutarch's inference that the performance mentioned by Xenophon took place in a theatre is probably correct.

The testimony of Pausanias (**8**), though much later, indicates part of the Spartan agora was used for the choruses of the Gymnopaidiai and was for that reason called the *Choros* ('Dancing Place'). **8** might seem to imply, on the analogy of the *Orchestra* in the Athenian Agora (**I Aiv 6**), that the 'theatre' was an open space converted into a 'viewing space', a *theatron*, for each Gymnopaidiai. This is, however, not a necessary conclusion. Martin (1951, 234–5; cf. Kolb 1981, 79–80; Ducat 2006, 266–8; Dubbini 2010, 166–7), and more fully Kourinou (2000, 114–27), have argued that the *Choros* mentioned by Pausanias should be identified with the so-called Round Building on the western edge of the Spartan agora. Recent study argues that the building was indeed 'semi-circular rather than circular, and … not so much a building as the encasement of a natural rock outcrop with blocks of conglomerate stone from a nearby quarry, arranged as a three-stepped base, surmounted by orthostats, with an impressive diameter of 43.3 metres' (Waywell 1999, 11). The half circle could then represent the analemma wall of the theatron mentioned by our Classical sources (**1**, **3**, **4**, **6**, **8**).

The date of the surviving building is unfortunately unknown. Waywell and Wilkes think the building may possibly be of 'late classical, hellenistic, or even later date' (1994, 418). This is revised in Waywell 1999, 11 to 'it could go back in date to the Archaic or Classical Greek periods'. As we write this, rumours circulate that recent work on the Round Building has uncovered evidence of an early date, possibly late seventh or early sixth century. In any case, the *Choros* would appear to be the earliest semicircular theatre building known from the ancient world, if it was semicircular. But the semicircularity and the identification of the Round Building with the *Choros* continue to be disputed. Greco has more recently (2011, 56–66) defended the identification of the building as circular and as the *Skias*, mentioned by Pausanias 3.12.10, built by Theodorus of Samos in the mid sixth century. This building served originally, Greco argues, for musical performances (2011, 60): it is notably the building where in Pausanias' day the famous 'kithara of Timotheus' was displayed with its cut strings (3.12.10). If the news of a late seventh- or early sixth-century foundation is correct, it could modify the one criticism raised by Salapata against Kourinou's identification of the Round Building with the *Choros*, namely that 'K's conclusion that the agora existed already in the first half of the seventh century (pp. 127, 132) because of the celebration of the Gymnopaidiai since 669 BC seems bold' (2001).

Polykrates (**5**) mentions a theatre in connection with another major Spartan festival, the Hyakinthia. The festival appears to have been divided between Sparta and Amyklai, some 6 km south of the Spartan acropolis (on the festival, generally, see Richer 2012, 343–82). No trace of a theatre has been found at Amyklai. Richer proposes that the first day and a half of the activities described by **5** took place in Sparta, including those related to the theatre, and the remainder in Amyklai (Richer 2012, 358–9: 'It is possible, in fact, to conclude that the theatre Polykrates mentioned was the theatre of Sparta itself and not a theatre of Amyklai, otherwise unknown'). Possibly the processions described in **5** relate to the removal from Sparta to Amyklai. This might explain how Polykrates is able to say in one sentence that 'the whole city is caught up in the movement and joy of the spectacle' and in the next that 'the whole city is emptied'. If this is the case we might suppose, though without any reason but a consideration for economy, that the same theatre used for the Gymnopaidiai was used also for the Hyakinthia (conceivably, as stated above, the *Choros* mentioned in **8**).

Lucian (**7**), despite the Early Archaic setting of his tale, probably has the extant Roman theatre on the south-west slope of the acropolis in mind. This very large theatre (only slightly smaller than the sanctuary theatre at Epidaurus: Waywell 1999, 17) was known since the late eighteenth century and has been investigated several times, beginning in 1906 (Dickins 1905–1906). Its construction is no earlier than the Late Hellenistic period and probably built around 30–20 in the time of C. Julius Eurykles (Waywell 2002, 247). There are no traces of an earlier theatre on this site. The theatre was renewed in the time of Vespasian and may have continued to be used as a performance space until the Visigothic incursion of 396 AD.

Our sources name only lyric (non-dramatic) choral performances in Sparta's theatre(s). These choral performances were by the Classical period competitive (**3, 6**). The evidence we have suggests that these competitions were limited to local choruses (cf. **5**): probably representing age, tribal and phratry divisions (Pettersson 1992, 87–90; Wilson 2000, 299–300; Richer 2012, 389–404, 425–7; but see also Parker 1989, 144). Choral competition appears to have been exclusively civic, like the lyric competitions of the Athenian Dionysia. The Carneia, Gymnopaidiai, and Hyakinthia (see also **I Av 3**) made Sparta famous throughout Greece both for music and musical festivals (see recently Massaro 2018). This fame was probably due more to the international competitions in kitharody than to the local choruses. Consistent with the notion that the choral competitions were composed of Spartan citizens and were competitive is the notice by Aristotle that Sparta had a choregic system and that the choregoi themselves served as pipers (Arist *Pol.* 1241a33–7; **V F** on Thrasippos' pinax). Since Archaic times, and in the case of the Carneia from the early seventh century, the kitharodic contests were open to, and apparently dominated by, international competitors (see Franklin 2012 on the historical tradition).

These major international musical festivals in Classical Sparta are festivals of Apollo. There were other less well attested and possibly more locally attended festivals. We have some evidence of a musical competition for Eleusinian Demeter (Hsch. ε 2026; Prauscello 2009, 172–88), and also of choral competitions or performances for Artemis (Calame 1997, 142–74), though these appear to be of a more local and cultic character. A case has been made for Dionysian content in the Hyakinthia (Richer 2012, 366–76), but the Spartan Dionysus remains elusive. There is even some evidence for dithyrambic performances in Classical Sparta (D'Alessio 2013, 123–32; Battezzato 2013, 99–110), possibly in a competitive format (D'Alessio 2013, 130), though here too the performances appear to have been cultic rather than theatrical (Battezzato 2013, 108).

It is only as late as 105/6 AD that we have evidence for drama, a tragedy, being performed in a Spartan theatre (*IG* V 1, 662; cf. *SEG* 11, 838, l. 6, probably of 143–8 AD), though we can probably, on this evidence, assume that the tragic competition dates to the foundation of the festival at which this tragic competition took place, the Ourania, in 97 or 98 AD (Cartledge and Spawforth 2002, 185–6). At the end of the second century AD, we even have evidence of pantomime in Sparta (*IK Ephesos* 2070 + 2071, l. 10; Slater 1995). There is, however, no evidence for canonical comedy being performed in Sparta, despite the indigenous Spartan 'comic' tradition (**Bx**). At best we know of a comic actor, Nikon, of Spartan origin, who won a prize at the Soteria festival around 270 (Stefanis no. 1881; cf. *SEG* 13, 248 for a supposed group of Spartan actors in first-century Argos).

Bx: Spartan 'Comedy'

1. **Plato,** *Laws* **816d–17a**. Written probably in the 350s. At *Laws* 637a–b the Spartan Megillos explained that Sparta rejected sympotic and festival jesting and frivolity. This passage appears in a general discussion of dance. The 'Athenian' speaks about rules governing the representation of ludicrous behaviour in the ideal state. Text: Burnet.

> τὰ μὲν οὖν τῶν καλῶν σωμάτων καὶ γενναίων ψυχῶν εἰς τὰς χορείας, οἵας εἴρηται δεῖν αὐτὰς εἶναι, διαπεπέρανται, [816d5] τὰ δὲ τῶν αἰσχρῶν σωμάτων καὶ διανοημάτων καὶ τῶν ἐπὶ τὰ τοῦ γέλωτος κωμῳδήματα τετραμμένων, κατὰ λέξιν τε καὶ ᾠδὴν καὶ κατὰ ὄρχησιν καὶ κατὰ τὰ τούτων πάντων μιμήματα κεκωμῳδημένα, ἀνάγκη μὲν θεάσασθαι καὶ γνωρίζειν· ἄνευ γὰρ γελοίων τὰ σπουδαῖα καὶ πάντων τῶν [816e1] ἐναντίων τὰ ἐναντία μαθεῖν μὲν οὐ δυνατόν, εἰ μέλλει τις φρόνιμος ἔσεσθαι, ποιεῖν δὲ οὐκ αὖ δυνατὸν ἀμφότερα, εἴ τις αὖ μέλλει καὶ σμικρὸν ἀρετῆς μεθέξειν, ἀλλὰ αὐτῶν ἕνεκα τούτων καὶ μανθάνειν αὐτὰ δεῖ, τοῦ μή ποτε δι' [816e5] ἄγνοιαν δρᾶν ἢ λέγειν ὅσα γελοῖα, μηδὲν δέον, δούλοις δὲ τὰ τοιαῦτα καὶ ξένοις ἐμμίσθοις προστάττειν μιμεῖσθαι, σπουδὴν δὲ περὶ αὐτὰ εἶναι μηδέποτε μηδ' ἡντινοῦν, μηδέ τινα μανθάνοντα αὐτὰ γίγνεσθαι φανερὸν τῶν ἐλευθέρων, μήτε γυναῖκα μήτε ἄνδρα, καινὸν δὲ ἀεί τι περὶ αὐτὰ φαίνεσθαι τῶν μιμημάτων. [816e10] ὅσα μὲν οὖν περὶ γέλωτά ἐστιν παίγνια, ἃ δὴ [817a1] κωμῳδίαν πάντες λέγομεν, οὕτως τῷ νόμῳ καὶ λόγῳ κείσθω.

So, we have covered the subject of how we said beautiful bodies and noble souls should be disposed to choral dance. [816d5] But we must still examine and get acquainted with the topic of ugly bodies and dispositions and the people who practise comedic activities for the sake of laughter, in respect of vocabulary, song, dance, and the comic imitations of all these things. We need to do this because without the ridiculous [816e1] it is impossible to recognise the serious, or indeed any category without its opposite, if one is to be a sensible person. One cannot however practise both, if one is to have even the smallest share of excellence, but one has to learn these things precisely so as never [816e5] to do or say anything ridiculous out of ignorance when one should not. We should rather order slaves and hired foreigners to mimic such behaviour. Yet no one is to develop any interest for these things, and no free man or woman is to be seen learning such things. Moreover something new should always appear in the imitations. [816e10] So, as far as concerns amusements related to laughter, which [817a1] we all call comedy, let the law and the argument be laid down in this way.

2. **Plutarch**, *Life of Lycurgus* **28.4–5**. Written: ca. 115 AD and referring to Classical times. The passage belongs to a discussion of the abuse to which the Spartans regularly subjected the helots. Just after this passage Plutarch expresses the opinion that these practices were too wicked and barbarous to be the work of Lycurgus and go back no earlier than 465. At latest the practices existed by 370–362 as indicated by the reference to the Theban invasion. Plutarch's 'they also say' (5.1) indicates that he is following an earlier source or sources throughout this passage. There is no reason to think that it is Sosibius, although he did show an interest in Spartan sympotic entertainments (Plu. *Lyc.* 25.2 = *FGrH* 595 F 19). Cf. Plu. *Demetr.* 1.5 where the forced drinking is said to take place 'during festivals'; *Mor.* 239a, 455e. Text: minor punctuation variation on Perrin.

καὶ τᾶλλα δὲ τραχέως προσεφέροντο καὶ σκληρῶς αὐτοῖς, ὥστε καὶ πίνειν ἀναγκάζοντες πολὺν ἄκρατον εἰς τὰ συσσίτια παρεισῆγον, ἐπιδεικνύμενοι τὸ μεθύειν οἷόν ἐστι τοῖς νέοις, καὶ ᾠδὰς ἐκέλευον ᾄδειν καὶ χορείας χορεύειν ἀγεννεῖς καὶ καταγελάστους, ἀπέχεσθαι δὲ τῶν ἐλευθέρων. [5.1] διὸ καί φασιν ὕστερον ἐν τῇ Θηβαίων εἰς τὴν Λακωνικὴν στρατείᾳ τοὺς ἁλισκομένους εἵλωτας κελευομένους ᾄδειν τὰ Τερπάνδρου καὶ Ἀλκμᾶνος καὶ Σπένδοντος τοῦ Λάκωνος παραιτεῖσθαι, φάσκοντας οὐκ ἐθέλειν τοὺς δεσποσύνους. ὥστε τοὺς λέγοντας, ἐν Λακεδαίμονι καὶ τὸν ἐλεύθερον μάλιστα ἐλεύθερον εἶναι καὶ τὸν δοῦλον μάλιστα δοῦλον, οὐ φαύλως τεθεωρηκέναι τὴν διαφοράν.

And they inflicted many other harsh and difficult torments upon them (the helots). They even brought them into their *syssitia* (common dining halls) and kept forcing them to drink large quantities of unmixed wine in order to show the young what drunkenness was like. And they forced them to sing and dance demeaning and ridiculous songs and dances, while ordering them to refrain from singing or dancing those practised by free men. [5.1] Consequently they also say that later during the Theban invasion of Laconia captured helots refused, when asked, to sing the songs of Terpander, Alcman or Spendon the Spartan, saying that the masters would not like it. Those therefore who say that in Lacedaemon the free man is especially free and the slave especially slavish have acquired a pretty accurate concept of the difference.

3. Sosibius, *On the Mummers in Laconia.*

a. Suda s.v. Σωσίβιος ('Sosibius', σ 859) (= *FGrH* 595 **T 1**; *PCG* I, **T 3**). Written ca. 1000 AD. Sosibius, of unknown date, probably somewhere between 250 and 150 (commentary to *FGrH* 595, p. 636; Boring 1979, 56), is identified as a Laconian by two other sources. He is to be distinguished from the 'problem-solver' (Boring 1979, 55–6) who was active at the court of Ptolemy Philadelphus in Alexandria (hence the square brackets in the first sentence below). The Laconian Sosibius appears to be a reasonably careful and judicious local historian: Jacoby calls him the Spartan Philochorus (commentary to *FGrH* 595, p. 636). Sosibius was one of the first Greek scholars to collect and preserve dialect words (Pfeiffer 1968, 202; Montana 2015, 72 n. 34). Most of the fragments of Sosibius come from a work entitled *On Sacrifices in Lacedaemon*, though this may be part of a larger work on customs (Laqueur 1927, 1146). The work 'On Representations' named by Suda is not necessarily a separate work (it is cited only here). Text: revised from Jacoby and Adler.

> Σωσίβιος, Λάκων, γραμματικὸς [τῶν ἐπιλυτικῶν καλουμένων]. Περὶ τῶν μιμηλῶν <τῶν?> ἐν Λακωνικῇ ἱστορουμένων παλαιῶν. ἐν τούτοις δ' ἱστορεῖ καὶ τοῦτο, ὅτι εἶδός τι κωμῳδίας ἐστὶ καλούμενον δικηλιστῶν καὶ μιμηλῶν, καὶ ἄλλα.

[τῶν ἐπιλυτικῶν καλουμένων] del. Jacoby, cf. Ath. 11.493c–e   ἐν τούτοις δ' ἱστορεῖ καὶ τοῦτο, ὅτι εἶδός τι κωμῳδίας ἐστὶ καλούμενον δικηλιστῶν καὶ μιμηλῶν. Περὶ τῶν μιμηλῶν ἐν Λακωνικῇ ἱστορουμένων παλαιῶν. καὶ ἄλλα. Suda codd.   Jacoby transposed Περὶ etc. before ἐν τούτοις   Περὶ τῶν ἐν Λακωνικῇ ἱστορουμένων παλαιῶν μιμηλῶν. Bernhardy   Περὶ τῶν μιμηλῶν ἐν Λακωνικῇ ἱστορουμένων παλαιῶν παλαιῶν· (ἐν τούτοις δ' ἱστορεῖ καὶ τοῦτο, ὅτι εἶδός τι κωμῳδίας ἐστὶ καλούμενον δικηλιστῶν καὶ μιμηλῶν)· καὶ ἄλλα. Jacoby

Sosibius, the Laconian, a literary scholar [of those called 'problem-solvers']. *On the Mummers of the Ancients Researched in Laconia* (or with Bernhardy *On the Researched Ancient Mummers in Laconia*). In it he reports both that there is a form of comedy called 'of the *dikelistai* (pageant players)' and 'of the *mimeloi* (mummers)', and other things (Jacoby's punctuation and Suda's mss. order implies 'And [he wrote] other writings'; but the text could imply 'and other things [are said in the work mentioned]').

b. Athenaeus, *Sophists at Dinner* 14.621d. Athenaeus wrote ca. 200 AD. The irrelevant quotation from Alexis (*PCG* F 146) is 'certainly added' by Athenaeus (Olson 2007, 5), not Sosibius' contribution. Olson also argues that the style of the final sentence equating *d(e)ikelistai* with *phallophoroi, autokabdaloi* etc. is also 'most likely Athenaeus' composition' (2007, 5). The reference to 'an old type of comic play' and the use of past tenses with respect to Sparta (contrast the use of the present 'call' in the last sentence listing the supposed equivalents) suggests that this entertainment was already a folk-memory in Sosibius' day (cf. Sonnino 2014, 130–1 n. 12). Text: Kaibel.

παρὰ δὲ Λακεδαιμονίοις κωμικῆς παιδιᾶς ἦν τις τρόπος παλαιός, ὥς φησι
Σωσίβιος, οὐκ ἄγαν σπουδαῖος, ἅτε δὴ κἀν τούτοις τὸ λιτὸν τῆς Σπάρτης
μεταδιωκούσης. ἐμιμεῖτο γάρ τις ἐν εὐτελεῖ τῇ λέξει κλέπτοντάς τινας
ὀπώραν, ἢ ξενικὸν ἰατρὸν τοιαυτὶ λέγοντα, ὡς Ἄλεξις ἐν Μανδραγοριζομένῃ
διὰ τούτων παρίστησιν·

> ἐὰν ἐπιχώριος
> ἰατρὸς εἴπῃ, τρυβλίον τούτῳ δότε
> πτισάνης ἕωθεν, καταφρονοῦμεν εὐθέως·
> ἂν δὲ πτισάναν καὶ τρυβλίον, θαυμάζομεν.
> καὶ πάλιν ἐὰν μὲν τευτλίον, παρείδομεν·
> ἐὰν δὲ σεῦτλον, ἀσμένως ἠκούσαμεν·
> ὡς οὐ τὸ σεῦτλον ταυτὸν ὂν τῷ τευτλίῳ.

ἐκαλοῦντο δ᾽ οἱ μετιόντες τὴν τοιαύτην παιδιὰν παρὰ τοῖς Λάκωσι δικηλισταί,
ὡς ἄν τις σκευοποιοὺς εἴπῃ καὶ μιμητάς. τοῦ δὲ εἴδους τῶν δικηλιστῶν πολλαὶ
κατὰ τόπους εἰσὶ προσηγορίαι. Σικυώνιοι μὲν γὰρ φαλλοφόρους αὐτοὺς
καλοῦσιν, ἄλλοι δ᾽ αὐτοκαβδάλους· οἱ δὲ φλύακας, ὡς Ἰταλοί· σοφιστὰς δὲ οἱ
πολλοί· Θηβαῖοι δέ, τὰ πολλὰ ἰδίως ὀνομάζειν εἰωθότες, ἐθελοντάς.

Among the Lacedaemonians there existed a very old type of comic entertainment, as Sosibius says. It was not taken very seriously as even in this Sparta
pursued austerity. Someone imitated in plain speech men stealing fruit, or a
foreign doctor speaking in like manner as Alexis in *The Woman who Drank
Mandrake* presents with these words: 'If a local doctor says "give this man a
bowl of porridge first thing every morning" we despise him straightaway. If he
says "parridge" (the same word with a Doric accent) and bowl, we hold him
in awe. And again if "beet" we give him no heed, but if "bate" (the same word
with a Doric accent), we listen eagerly as if the "bate" was not the same thing as
the "beet".' They called those who pursued such jests among the Spartans *dikelistai*, as one would say 'impersonator' (literally 'maskmaker') and 'imitator'.
Many are the regional appellations of the genre *dikelistai*. The Sicyonians call
them *phallophoroi* (literally 'phallos-bearers'); others call them *autokabdaloi*.
Some call them *phlyakes*, as do the Italian Greeks; the many (the majority?) call
them *sophistai* (literally 'sophists'). The Thebans, who customarily name things
in their own idiosyncratic fashion, (call them) *ethelontai* (literally 'volunteers').

4. **Plutarch**, *Life of Agesilaus* 21.4. Written: ca. 115 AD. Anecdotes about the tragic actor
Kallippides (Stefanis no. 1348) seem mainly to be set in the period ca. 420–400. One of
his five victories at the Lenaea was in 418 (*IG* II² 2319, ll. 82–3 [= col. II, ll. 16–17 M-O];
IG II² 2325, l. 252 [= H, l. 7 M-O]). He was famous for his innovation (Csapo 2010, 117–
39), as Spartans were for their cultural conservatism, so the pairing of Kallippides and
Agesilaus in this anecdote is likely to have other than historical reasons. The same anecdote reappears, in slightly fuller form, in *Apophthegmata Laconica* 212e–f, a work largely
excerpted from and attributed to Plutarch. Cf. also Apostol. *Cent.* 13.66. Text: Perrin.

καί ποτε Καλλιππίδης ὁ τῶν τραγῳδιῶν ὑποκριτής, ὄνομα καὶ δόξαν ἔχων ἐν τοῖς Ἕλλησι καὶ σπουδαζόμενος ὑπὸ πάντων, πρῶτον μὲν ἀπήντησεν αὐτῷ καὶ προσεῖπεν, ἔπειτα σοβαρῶς εἰς τοὺς συμπεριπατοῦντας ἐμβαλὼν ἑαυτὸν ἐπεδείκνυτο νομίζων ἐκεῖνον ἄρξειν τινὸς φιλοφροσύνης, τέλος δὲ εἶπεν· ʻοὐκ ἐπιγινώσκεις με, ὦ βασιλεῦ;ʼ κἀκεῖνος ἀποβλέψας πρὸς αὐτὸν εἶπεν· ʻἀλλὰ οὐ σύγε ἐσσὶ Καλλιππίδας ὁ δεικηλίκτας;ʼ οὕτω δὲ Λακεδαιμόνιοι τοὺς μίμους καλοῦσι.

Once Kallippides the tragic actor, whose name and fame was known to all Greeks and who was celebrated by all, first encountered and greeted him (Agesilaus), and then with energetic display inserted himself into his entourage expecting to inspire some friendly recognition. Finally he said 'King, do you not know who I am?' Agesilaus cast a glance at him and said 'Aren't you Kallippides the pageant player (*deikeliktas*, Spartan dialect for *deikelistes*)?' This is what the Spartans call mimes.

5. **Hesychius, *Lexicon* s.v. δεικηλισταί (ʻdeikelistaiʼ, δ 453)**. Compiled in the 5th or 6th c. AD. Weber (1887, 42–64) and Latte (1913, 9) argue that Hesychius draws upon Sosibius for his glosses related to Laconian cult (i.e. possibly here but more especially for **6, 8–12**). This is very likely. Hesychius directly names Sosibius as his source for three different glosses (Hsch. η 310 Latte; π 2011 Hansen; σ 165 Hansen = *FGrH* 595 F 16–18; cf. also Hansen ad Hsch. π 2410 and *FGrH* 595 F 9; for this gloss, cf. *EM* 260, 42; Sch. A.R. 1.745–6a). Text: Latte.

> δεικηλισταί· μιμηταὶ παρὰ Λάκωσι.
>
> δεικελισται cod. *EM*, Valesius

'*deikelistai*': imitators in Laconian.

6. **Hesychius, *Lexicon* s.v. δίκηλον (ʻdikelonʼ, δ 1821)**. Compiled in the 5th or 6th c. AD. Cf. Hsch. δ 1820, 1823; Tim. *Lex.* Ruhnken[3] p. 51; Sch. A.R. 4.1672. Text: Latte.

> δίκηλον· φάσμα. ὄψις. εἴδωλον. μίμημα. ὅθεν καὶ ὁ μιμολόγος παρὰ Λάκωσι δικηλίκτας
>
> δικην λικτας cod.   δικηλίτας Musurus

'*dikelon*': apparition; vision; image; imitation; whence *dikeliktas* a mime actor in Laconian.

7. **Pollux, *Onomasticon* 4.104–5**. Written ca. 180 AD. This information may be derived from Sosibius (**3**; cf. Paus. 3.25 with Wilamowitz 1898, 515–16). Cape Malea is not strictly speaking Spartan territory, but inhabited by Spartan-dominated perioikoi. Text: after Bethe.

ἦν δέ τινα καὶ Λακωνικὰ ὀρχήματα, διὰ Μαλέας· σειληνοὶ δ᾽ ἦσαν, καὶ
ὑπ᾽ αὐτοῖς σάτυροι ὑπότρομα ὀρχούμενοι. καὶ ἴθυμβοι ἐπὶ Διονύσῳ,
καὶ καρυάτιδες ἐπ᾽ Ἀρτέμιδι. καὶ βαρυλλικά, τὸ μὲν εὕρημα Βαρυλλίχου,
προσωρχοῦντο δὲ γυναῖκες Ἀρτέμιδι καὶ Ἀπόλλωνι. οἱ δ᾽ ὑπογύπωνες
γερόντων ὑπὸ βακτηρίαις τὴν μίμησιν εἶχον· οἱ δὲ γύπωνες ξυλίνων κώλων
ἐπιβαίνοντες ὠρχοῦντο, διαφανῆ ταραντινίδια ἀμπεχόμενοι. καὶ μὴν
Ἐσχάρινθον ὄρχημα ἐπώνυμον ἦν τοῦ εὑρόντος αὐλητοῦ, [4.105] τυρβασίαν δ᾽
ἐκάλουν τὸ ὄρχημα τὸ διθυραμβικόν, μιμητικὴν δὲ δι᾽ ἧς ἐμιμοῦντο τοὺς ἐπὶ
τῇ κλοπῇ τῶν ἑώλων κρεῶν ἁλισκομένους. λομβρότερον δ᾽ ἦν ὃ ὠρχοῦντο
γυμνοὶ σὺν αἰσχρολογίᾳ.

βαρυλλικά A C   βαρβυλλικά Π   Βαρυλλίχου Bethe   βαρυλλύχου A   βαραλλίκου
C   βαρβυλλίκου Π

There were also some Laconian dances throughout Malea. There were silens and
satyrs subject to them dancing a panic dance. And *ithymboi* for Dionysus, and *kar-
yatides* for Artemis. And *baryllika* (or *barbyllika*) are the invention of Baryllichos
(or 'Baryllychos' or 'Barallikos' or 'Barbyllikos'), and women danced it in worship
of Artemis and Apollo. The *hypogypones* made imitation of old men accompanied
by walking sticks. The *gypones* danced mounted on wooden limbs (presumably
'stilts'), covered by diaphanous Tarentine wraps. And indeed (they danced) the
Escharinthos dance named after the piper who invented it. [4.105] They called a dithyrambic dance *tyrbasia* (the name implies 'tumultuous' or 'confused') and (they
called a dance) the imitative (dance) with which they imitated men caught in the
act of stealing maggoty meat. The *lombroteron* (the name implies 'phallic': see
Hsch. s.v. λόμβαι) they danced naked with obscene language.

8. Hesychius, *Lexicon* s.v. βρυδαλίχα ('brydalicha', β 1243). Compiled in the 5th or 6th c.
AD (see on **3a**, **5**). Text: Latte.

βρυδαλίχα· πρόσωπον γυναικεῖον. παρὰ τὸ γελοῖον καὶ αἰσχρὸν †ὄρρ(ος)
τίθεται †ὀρίνθω τὴν ὀρχίστραν καὶ γυναικ(εῖα) ἱμάτια ἐνδέδυται. ὅθεν καὶ
τὰς †μαχρὰς <βρυδαλίχας> καλοῦσι Λάκωνες.

ὁ Ῥίνθων Meursius, Stephanus   τὴν ὀρχήστριαν Küster   μαχλάδας Musurus

'*brydalicha*': a female mask. Beside the ridiculous and disgraceful †rum(p)
is placed (hopelessly corrupt word or words; Meursius and Stephanus emend
to 'Rhinthon [calls it] the orchistra') the dancing place and women's clothing
is put on. Whence the Laconians also call wanton women (reading Musurus'
emendation μαχλάδας) <*brydalichai*>.

9. Hesychius, *Lexicon* s.v. βρυλλιχισταί ('bryllichistai', β 1245). See on **5**. Possibly
related to this gloss are β 1309 '*byllichai*: some choruses of dancers amongst the

Lacedaemonians' (βυλλίχαι· χοροί τινες ὀρχηστῶν, παρὰ Λάκωσι) and β 1246 '*bryllon*: getting tipsy' (βρύλλων· ὑποπίνων) and Ar. *Knights* 1126. Text Latte.

> βρυλλιχισταί· οἱ αἰσχρὰ προσωπεῖα περιτιθέμενοι γυναικεῖα καὶ ὕμνους ᾄδοντες.

> βρυλλοχισται cod., Schmidt

> '*bryllichistai*': the men putting on ugly female masks and singing hymns.

10. Hesychius, *Lexicon* s.v. κυριττοί ('kyrittoi', κ 4684). See on **5**. Cf. Hsch. s.v. κυλίνθιον (κ 4501), κύνθιον (κ 4585), and κύριθρα (κ 4678), all of which give the meaning 'wooden mask' (προσωπεῖον ξύλινον). The name *kyrittoi* suggests rams butting horns. Nilsson imagines a phallic fertility rite (1906, 184). Artemis Korythalia was worshipped in Sparta. Athenaeus is our main source for this (4.139a–b): 'they (the Spartans) celebrate *kopides* (a kind of picnic festival) in the city at the festival called the Nursing Festival (*Tithenidia*) which they celebrate on behalf of their children. The nurses take the male children on this occasion into the countryside to the Artemis called Korythalia, whose sanctuary is near (the stream) Tiassos in the district towards Kleta'. The epiklesis *Korythalia* for Artemis seems to be connected with the *korythale*, a laurel wreath (Nilsson 1906, 182–3). Although Hesychius names only Italy, it is assumed that the Italian rites spread from Doric colonies including Spartan Taras, and that therefore this information relates also to Sparta (Nilsson 1906, 184). This would be all the more probable if the gloss is from Sosibius. Text: Latte.

> κυριττοί· οἱ ἔχοντες τὰ ξύλινα πρόσωπα κατὰ Ἰταλίαν, καὶ ἑορτάζοντες τῇ Κορυθαλίᾳ γελοιασταί.

> '*kyrittoi*': those wearing the wooden masks throughout Italy, and clowns celebrating the festival for Korythalia.

11. Hesychius, *Lexicon* s.v. κορυθαλίστριαι ('korythalistriai', κ 3689). See on **5**. Text: Latte.

> κορυθαλίστριαι· αἱ χορεύουσαι τῇ Κορυθαλίᾳ θεᾷ.

> '*korythalistriai*': the women who dance for the goddess Korythalia.

12. Hesychius, Lexicon s.v. καλαβίς ('kalabis', κ 378), καλαβῶται ('kalabotai', κ 379), καλαοίδια ('kalaoidia', κ 409), καλλιβάντες ('kallibantes', κ 471). See on **5**. These glosses are often treated as from the same root and mutually explicative (Latte 1913, 23–6). Nilsson (1906, 185; cf. Ahrens 1839–1843 II, 48 n. 20; Weber 1887, 44) explains the presence of β in καλαβίς/καλαβῶται and its absence in καλαοίδια as the result of a differential treatment of an original digamma. The expression 'he walks *kallabides*' (καλλαβίδας δὲ βαίνει) is used in a caricature by Eupolis in *Kolakes* (*PCG* F 176), a play performed in 421 (*Hyp.* 3 Ar. *Peace*): *kallabides* is the plural of *kalabis:* see **13**. Dereatis was worshipped on Taygetos (Paus. 3.20.7). Text: Latte.

> καλαβίς· τὸ περισπᾶν τὰ ἰσχία.
>
> καλαβῶται· ἐν τῷ τῆς Δερεατίδος ἱερῷ Ἀρτέμιδος αἰδόμενοι ὕμνοι.
>
> καλαοίδια· ἀγὼν ἐπιτελούμενος Ἀρτέμιδι παρὰ Λάκωσιν.
>
> καλλιβάντες· ὅμοια σμιλίοις καὶ ψαλίσιν, ἐν αἷς τὰς ὀφρῦς κοσμοῦσιν αἱ γυναῖκες. [ἄνθη.] [ἢ γένος ὀρχήσεως ἀσχημόνως τῶν ἰσχίων κρατουμένων].

'*kalabis*': drawing the thighs about.

'*kalabotai*': hymns sung in the sanctuary of Artemis Dereatis.

'*kalaoidia*': a contest held for Artemis among the Laconians.

'*kallibantes*': like the blades and scissors with which women trim their eyebrows. [flowers.] [or a type of dance in which the thighs are held indecorously].

13. Photius, *Lexicon* **s.v. καλλαβίδες ('kallabides', κ 104).** Date: 9th c. AD. Photius and Athenaeus (14.629f) probably draw upon the 1st-c. BC grammarian Tryphon and ultimately Eupolis (cited in **12**), hence also the gemination of lambda, required by the metre in Eupolis (Latte 1913, 26). Text: Theodoridis.

> καλλαβίδες· τὸ διαβαίνειν ἀσχημόνως καὶ διέλκειν τὰ ἰσχία ταῖς χερσίν.

'*kallabides*': walking in an indecorous manner and tugging at the thighs with one's hands.

The genre labels attached to local performance traditions in Sparta have had a large impact on the writing of theatre history. Many commentators urge that some or all of the performance genres attested in **1–13** be understood as a form of drama, or at least put in some significant relationship with a dramatic genre or genres. Modern scholarship is particularly generous in its range of labels, including, to name just a few, 'ritual drama', 'mummery', 'antecedent of drama', 'pre-drama', 'Dorian farce', 'Dorian comedy', 'drama', 'mime', and 'comedy'. The problem in the variety is exacerbated by the vagueness of many of the terms, and most especially by the ambiguity of the label 'comedy', which even within a single discussion can appear to refer to the theatre-historical genre, or to comedy in the broad sense of any performance that generates laughter. Since the question of the applicability of genre labels is principally a question of historical reception, it is important to scrutinise just how our sources use them. Our ancient sources, for example, are universal in applying the label 'comedy' to the dramatic performances attested in Megara, and this is a fact of some importance, as it calls into question the modern impulse to classify them as something more primitive (**Bi**). Interestingly, a close look at our sources on Spartan performances reveals a very different and in some ways opposite pattern. Some reveal the same vagueness and ambiguity in their labelling as the moderns. This offers precedence, but not justification to the modern habits. Plato (**1**) and Sosibius (**3** and, indirectly, possibly the source behind **5–12**) especially seem to want to force the genre classifications of 'comedy' or 'mime' upon Spartan entertainment for purposes of their own, while others, like Plutarch (**4**) and Athenaeus (**3b**), seem content to draw facile equations between the Spartan entertainments and comedy or mime, either to explain a joke through anachronistic comparisons, or to license a display of superficial but broad historical and literary learning.

There is no specific reference to Sparta in **1** but it is generally and probably correctly supposed that Plato had Spartan practice (**2**) in mind when he spoke of ordering 'slaves and hired foreigners to mimic such [ridiculous] behaviour' (David 1989, 10; Murray 2013, 297). It would be a mistake however to suppose that **1** can serve as testimony for performance of 'comedy' in any strict sense. While it is true that Plato at the end of **1** sums up his argument with a general reference to 'amusements related to laughter, which we all call comedy', it is striking that **1**'s earlier descriptions of these laughter-producing activities deliberately play upon the *komoid-* root, but avoid using the actual term *komoidia*. Plato speaks rather in vaguer terms of *koimoidemata* or *kekomoidemena*, and even *paignia*, terms that are rhetorically designed to encompass just about any activity that might generate laughter. Plato evidently does this to permit his general discussion to embrace a good deal more than his contemporaries would classify as *komoidia* (Morrow 1960, 371–2). As Prauscello observes (2013, 323): 'the "comic", like the "tragic", is for Plato a universal concept, a modality of perceiving and being that is not limited to the dramatic world'. The final equation to 'comedy' of 'all amusements related to laughter' is a rhetorical inflation at least partly for the purpose of sustaining the contrast between Spartan custom and one of the most cherished institutions of Plato's contemporary Athenian culture. It may seem paradoxical, but Plato's roundabout insinuation that the drunken dancing that went on in Sparta should be regarded as 'comedy' serves as proof that he felt his contemporaries would not easily accept the categorisation. In any case **2** indicates that the Spartan performances took place in the *syssitia* (hence are what we might call sympotic entertainments) and not in theatres, and that they consisted of nothing more than performances of obscene or funny dances and songs by slaves poisoned with alcohol.

The word *komoidia* also appears in **3a**, though it is unclear whether it is the vocabulary of Sosibius or of Athenaeus and the Suda. But one must be cautious here too of the same promiscuous use of the term that we find in **1**. **3a** speaks of a 'kind of comedy' and **3b** of 'a comic entertainment', but the actual genres are called, by Sosibius, 'of the *deikelistai*' and 'of the *mimeloi*'. Deikelistai (a.k.a. *dikelistai* / *deikeliktai* / *dikeliktai*) are defined in **5** as *mimetai* (μιμηταί, 'imitators'). The root of the word *mimetai* is the same as the proper term for 'mime artists' but mime artists are never in antiquity referred to by this word (contrary to Reich 1903, 232: 'was soviel wie Mime bedeutet'). If Sosibius had no qualms he would have used the term μῖμοι. His choice of word indicates that these performances are not 'mime' even if they are in some way comparable to mime.

Etymologically, a *deikelistes* should mean someone who performs a *deikelon,* a rare word that **6** defines broadly as 'apparition, vision, image, imitation'. The root is the same as the verb δείκνυμι which means 'show'. Normally *deikelon* is used in Greek of an icon or simulacrum, something that 'manifests' a deity, and Herodotus uses the word (2.171) of a religious pageant performed in Egypt to commemorate the sufferings of Osiris (on which see Leprohon 2007, 265–6). As Sonnino (2014, 132) states, 'Δείκηλα is the cor-rect term for a religious spectacle … and not light entertainment'. Referring to **4**, LSJ simply equates *deikelistes* with dramatic actors (s.v. δεικηλίκτας '= ὑποκριτής'). But the success of Agesilaus' put-down of Kallippides (**4**) depends on the proper meaning of the word *dikeliktas* (Laconian dialect for *deikelistes*) being in some way comparable while at the same time very different from 'actor', and decidedly more primitive and common.

The essentially cultic nature of the *deikelistai* might also emerge from the nature of its congeners in the crude equation Sosibius (or Athenaeus?) draws at the end of **3b**: *phallo-phoroi* (phallos bearers) are choral entertainers in Dionysian processions (**I Aiv 7**); *auto-kabdaloi* are also Dionysian processional choruses as indicated by Semos (*FGrH* 396 F 24); the term *phlyax* (pl. *phlyakes*), described by Hesychius (φ 649 Hansen, Cunningham) as 'drunken, drunkard, clown' (μέθυσος, μεθυστής, γελοιαστής), is by Pollux juxtaposed to words relating to ritual abuse, though Pollux incidentally doubts that it is a proper word (9.149). The *sophistai* and *ethelontes* are probably also ritual performers, if one is to take **3b**'s claims about 'the many' and about the Thebans seriously. (The last words on the list are not paralleled anywhere and it is hard in this void to believe that 'most Greeks' had clowns they called 'sophists'!) The main problem with these equations is that **3b** and **4–6** suggest that *deikelistai* were actor-impersonators who performed in skits, while *phallo-phoroi* and *autokabdaloi* are processional choruses (and so probably also are the other con-geners). They cannot have had much in common except to the eyes of someone who was determined to equate anything funny with comedy. This very promiscuous sense of 'com-edy' obviously favoured Dorian claims that they had invented comedy and it is probably in part regional patriotism that drives these clumsy and misleading equations. The modern historian is advised to read the ancient testimony, to some extent at least, against the grain.

Deikelistai and *mimeloi* might for their part be classed as somehow antecedent to comedy, but they certainly are not a recognisable species of the genre. With actual comedy they need have nothing in common beyond laughter, ritual obscenity and abuse and, as would appear from **3b**, rudimentary impersonations or scenarios, but without any evidence of dialogue or anything one might comfortably call a plot. Though scholars frequently compare the two, **3b**'s description of a *deikelon* as an imitation 'in plain speech' of 'men stealing fruit' is rather undermined than corroborated by **7**'s imitation of 'men caught in the act of stealing maggoty meat', as the latter is a dance, and if accompanied would surely have been accompanied by song, not 'plain speech'. It is unclear how and if these food-stealing performances were related to actual food-stealing rituals practised in everyday life by ephebes and by groups at the festival of Artemis Ortheia (X. *Lac.* 2.9; Parker 1989, 148 n. 33; for the spelling Ortheia rather than Orthia see also Davison 1968, 169–72). That impersonations or dances should have any narrative element is of course interesting and important, but falls short of justifying or corroborating Sosibius' attempt to characterise the activities as forms of comedy or mime.

Ritual choral dance performances are exclusively the topic of **7**, **10–13**, and probably also **8–9**: **8** mentions costumes in the plural and seems to reference 'a dancing place'; **9** mentions the singing of hymns. The wearing of female masks, mentioned in **8** and **9**, gained considerable interest in 1906 when a trove of fragments of some six hundred clay masks, dating from ca. 600 to ca. 450, were uncovered in the excavation of the Spartan sanctuary of Artemis Ortheia. Some of the masks are life-sized and this has encouraged the inference that they were used directly, whether worn or held, or the more likely inference that they imitate wooden or linen originals that were worn in some kind of performance. The excavators sorted the masks into seven types (Dickins 1929, 165), though a large class is miscellaneous 'Caricatures' and another category equally miscellaneous 'Portraits'. The most common type was a heavily wrinkled face taken to be the mask of 'Old Women' (though some have beards). There are in addition 'Youths', 'Warriors', 'Satyrs' and 'Gorgons'. Though the masks were dumped and buried together, there is no evidence that all types were used together, and indeed the excavators note that mask types come and go at different periods (Dickins 1929, 166–9). Carter, by contrast, would reduce the categories 'to four or even two': the 'Old Woman' and Youths/Warriors (distinguished by the presence or absence of a beard), and possibly Satyrs and Gorgons, though these may just be a variation of the 'Old Woman' type (1987, 356–7).

Carter's very rich discussion persuasively argues that the mask of the 'Old Woman' and the Youths/Warriors derive from Near Eastern prototypes of Humbaba and Gilgamesh and she proposes that some ritual drama of Phoenician origin was performed at the Ortheia sanctuary. Other finds from the Ortheia sanctuary suggest music and dance formed part of her worship: auloi of bone, plectra for stringed instruments and lead figurines of musicians (Carter 1987, 380), as well as vases and figurines depicting komast dancers (Pipili 1987, 71–5; Smith 1998). There are also mythical and literary attestations of dance performance for Ortheia: Helen is said to have been abducted by Theseus and Perithous while dancing at the sanctuary of Artemis Ortheia (Plu. *Thes.* 31) and some poems of Alcman are sometimes supposed to have been performed for Ortheia (but see Calame 1997, 169).

In general, Artemis, or goddesses later identified as Artemis, seems to have had patronage of most phallic, obscene or otherwise ritually transgressive activity in Sparta (in addition to **7–13**, see *DTC*[2] 162–9; Parker 1989, 151, 168 n. 45; Calame 1997, 142–74), despite the presence of a cult of Dionysus there (Stibbe 1991; Stibbe 1992; Calame 1997, 173; Constantinidou 1998). It is not easy to reconcile this information with **1–2**'s claim that no Spartan citizen performed unseemly dances (cf. Halliwell 2008, 46–50). Indeed if we accept the information derived from our native informant, Sosibius, we would have to conclude that either such rites were entirely discontinued ca. 450, when the Ortheia mask-series stops, or that Plutarch (**2**), if not also Plato (**1**), is overlooking a great deal in his eagerness to embroider the myth of Spartan austerity. Given the importance the role 'Sparta' plays in the Greek imagination, from about 430 onwards, as the mythical opposite of Athens, this latter option is not unlikely.

The initial collection and comparison of our sources for Laconian ritual and dance took place at a time when Mannhardtian theories of Vegetation Magic were at the height of their popularity in Germany and 'Cambridge Ritualism' reigned in Britain. The agenda for both of these closely related trends was to map the evolution of culture from primitive ritual beginnings. Cambridge Ritualism especially focused on a supposed moment of transition from ritual to drama as a kind of big bang that historically and symbolically separated civilisation from savagery (Csapo 2005, 145–61). The framework and even the conclusions to be drawn from our material were in an important sense already 'given' before the enterprise began. Körte, for example, used the evidence of **2–13** to develop a broad concept of 'Doric comedy' which served as an intermediary between ritual and Attic comedy (1893, 92). Reich used the material, somewhat incompatibly, to construct an early history of mime (1903, 231–3). More significantly however both anthropological trends were deeply rooted in a promiscuous nineteenth-century comparativism that characteristically tarred quite disparate phenomena with a very large same brush. Both the aims and the methods of nineteenth-century anthropology, as we will see, still dominate the question of Spartan drama.

The discovery of the masks of Ortheia in 1906 secured Sparta a prominent role in the question of the origin of drama. In the first publications Bosanquet freely accessed the full gamut of evidence found in **3–13** as a framework for interpreting the masks (1905–1906, 338–43). Schnabel (1910) extended this framework by adding the testimony of performances not specifically Laconian such as the *kordax* (connected with Elis) and the *mothon* (the name of a sailor's dance and not derived from the Spartan word for 'house slave': Chantraine 1968–1980 III, 708), and compared these with scenes on komast vases (particularly the Corinthian Dümmler krater), and even went so far as to enlist the evidence of the mimetic fertility magic of 'Naturvölker' of indigenous North America and Indonesia in support of his conclusion that all the rituals, including those that used the Ortheian masks, were so many ritual impersonations of fertility demons. Most exciting however was the parallel attestation of a food-robbing ritual (**7**) with a food-robbing 'drama' (**3b**), capturing the moment of the great evolutionary fission when drama emerged from ritual: 'Man wird zugeben, daß dies sehr an den Käseraub und die Züchtigung der Räuber im Kult der Ὀρθία erinnert: nur daß, was dort sakral war, hier profan geworden ist, was dort *Kulthandlung war, dramatisches Spiel*' (Schnabel 1910, 46–51, his italics). Cornford was briefer but no less free in mixing categories of evidence, when he concluded that the masks belonged to a *deikelon* that spread from Sparta to the Doric Peloponnese and West as the original matrix of mime/vulgar comedy/phlyax drama (1914, 180).

The intellectual climate in which these testimonia were first collected and compared had an enduring effect upon the form and style of almost all subsequent discussion. Körte's concept of 'Doric comedy' (1893; 1921, 1221–5) remains the preferred framework for interpreting our Spartan performances (see the discussion in Kerkhof 2001, 1–12), despite a detailed dismissal of the concept as pure hypothesis by Breitholz (1960). David cites **1–13** in support of the proposition that Sparta, despite 'the absence of a developed form of drama', had drama and 'a sort of comedy' (1989, 7). Relying on **2**'s distinction between the seriousness appropriate to citizens and the ridiculous behaviour appropriate to helots, he thought that this 'comedy' was performed entirely by helot *deikeliktai* at festivals and 'in the Spartan theatre' (1989, 8–17). Others followed Reich (and indeed Sosibius) in identifying some or all of these performances as mime (see the list of works cited in Sonnino 2014, 131–2 n. 15). Nobili adds the origin of iambus to the mix (2016, 42). The importance of Sparta to the evolution of the dramatic genres continues, therefore, to be much overstated. Nielsen positively identifies Ortheia as the place where drama began in Greece (2002, 88). Rosenberg supposes that the masked performances at Ortheia 'stand at the beginning of the shift from a purely ritual drama to a drama in which a broad range of masks was marshalled' (2015, 259). Di Clemente thinks Sparta 'probabile patria delle più antiche *performances* farseche che si svilupperanno nel mondo dorico' (2008, 183).

There are serious obstacles to vague equations modern scholars urge between the various types of performances reported in **1–13**. Minimal as they are, the descriptions indicate genres quite incompatible with one another in terms of performance venues, personnel, and mimetic modes. **10–12** speak of performances at sanctuaries of Artemis, but different sanctuaries and Artemises from Ortheia. For their part, **1** and **2** are performed at *syssitia* and presumably have nothing to do with Artemis. The *baryllika* reported in **7** are expressly performed in Malea, not in Sparta. *Bryllichistai* are evidently men wearing female masks (**9**), while *baryllika* are explicitly danced by women who presumably do not need female masks and in any case are not reported to have them (**7**). Though they both perform for Artemis Korythalia the genders of the participles in **10** and **11** show that the mask-wearing clowns called *kyrittoi*, men, are different from the female choruses of *korythalistriai*. The dancers of **1** and **2** are drunken helots. The *baryllika* are presumably performed by Malean *perioikoi*. The choruses for Artemis in **7** appear to be Laconian women of citizen class. The *deikeliktai* are apparently thought by Sosibius to include Spartan males of citizen class (**3b**'s 'even in this Sparta pursued austerity'). The rites described in **10–11** combine Spartan citizens (the boys) with slaves or helots (the nurses: see Parker 1989, 145 n. 13), if they relate to Sparta at all. The rites described in **7–13**, and probably **1–2**, are choral songs and dances, but the *deikelistai* are evidently speaking actors who perform skits (**3b**, **4–6**).

The danger of lumping all ritual activity together as *baryllika*, or whatever, is no less than that of lumping all rituals that involve obscenity, humour, impersonations or masks together as 'comedy' – or even to conflate them, as is frequently done, under the hazy classification of 'the roots of comedy' *vel sim*. This is not to imply that rituals that employ masks, mockery, obscenity, phalloi, or cross-dressing rituals are not relevant to understanding the background against which comedy came into being. It is a caution against mistaking that background for an actual early history of the genre as Doric historians did in attempting to stake a claim to comedy's or drama's invention. The kind of transgressive rituals we find in Laconia have parallels throughout Greece, and we have no reason to think Sparta was exceptional either in the range or quality of such ritual practices and entertainments. Ridgeway in an early criticism of Cornford wisely noted that: 'It is … futile to inquire in what particular community lampooning first began, or where the farce first started into life, even though we may happen to know that at Sparta … there were some such rude performances … we might as well attempt to prove that the practice of laughing and the appreciation of the grotesque started in some one particular tribe, race or town, and that from thence it spread to other less gifted communities' (1915, 402).

What is special about Sparta in this context may be no more than the fact that the rites are better recorded than most, probably because certain ritual forms lasted longer in Laconia, due either to Spartan conservatism or to the fact that these activities were not eclipsed by the sophistication generated by exposure to real drama. Still more important in this regard perhaps was Hellenistic and Roman scholarship's nostalgic and sometimes fanciful resuscitation (and in some cases 'construction') of an idiosyncratic heritage for the once glorious city.

Bxi: Mantinea. Terracotta tesserae, extending from late 5th–3rd c. (letter forms: Fougères 1898, 531; Svoronos 1900, 198–9).

Terracotta tesserae or tokens of five different shapes and hues, normally with pre-firing inscriptions of personal names in the nominative, often followed by patronymic in the genitive, on one side and single letters of the alphabet, written larger, on the other side (with all letters, including digamma, represented). The entire alphabet is distributed across each of the five different shapes.

Excavated by the French School at Athens in 1887–1888. Some 200 found in the theatre of Mantinea or in the Stoa of Epigone (about 100 m east of the theatre). Of these nos. 1–19 are assigned by Svoronos (1900, 206–18) to 425–385, no. 20 to 371–340, and nos. 22–107 to the 3rd c. (ca. 226).

Athens, NM inventory numbers unreported.

Fougères 1898, 531–4; Svoronos 1900; *IG* V 2, 323.

Photos and drawings: Fougères 1898, 356 fig. 50, 361 fig. 51; Svoronos 1900, pls. 9–10; *IG* V 2, 323. The two examples below are from Svoronos 1900, pl. 10.

ΓΟΡΓΙΑΔΑΣ	ΘΕΟΧΑΡΗΣ
ΓΟΡΓΥΘΩ	ΑΓΗΣΙΔΑ
	ΜΩ
Gorgiadas	Theochares
son of Gorgythas	son of Agesidamas
H	Z

Mantinea had the oldest democracy we know of in Arcadia, going back at least a half-century before the creation of the Arcadian League in 371, and possibly much earlier (Robinson 2011, 35–6). Thucydides claims that Mantinea's democratic constitution facilitated its alliance with Argos and Athens in 421 and 418 (Th. 5.29, 5.54). Sparta imposed an oligarchy and dispersed the city into its villages in 385 (X. *HG* 5.2.6–7), but the democracy and the city were restored after Sparta's defeat in the Battle of Leuctra in 371 (X. *HG* 6.5.3–5). Just how democratic Mantineian democracy actually was has been a matter of contention among modern scholars (cf. Amit 1973, 143–7; Robinson 2011, 34–40). Aristotle (*Pol.* 1318b23–5) speaks of democracies where the majority are satisfied if they retain the power to deliberate 'even if the people do not participate (i.e. stand as candidates?) in election to office, but some are selected section by section (? or 'in turns': see Robinson 2011, 38) from the entire populace (ἀλλά τινες αἱρετοὶ κατὰ μέρος ἐκ πάντων) as in Mantinea'.

Identification tokens of this kind have been found in a number of ancient cities, most, if not all, of them democracies (Robinson 2011, 37), and in most cases connected to the democratic selection of offices by lottery: in Athens such tokens were used to select jurors (Kroll 1972); analogous functions are supposed for the tokens from Argos (Robinson 2011, 14), Rhodes (Fraser 1972b, 119–24; Bingen 1982), and Camarina (Cordano 1992; Robinson 2011, 96–100). Tokens are attested by a decree of Iasus (R-O II 508–13 no. 99). Similar tokens were found at Styra in Euboea but there the form of the constitution is unknown. At Mantinea the tokens seem to be closely connected to the representative democracy described by Aristotle above.

The citizens of Mantinea were divided into five *demoi* or *komai*, but apparently also five tribes (*IG* V 2, 1; *IG* V 2, 271; Pritchett 1969, 50–2; Jones 1987, 132–3). This probably explains why the tokens are divided into five shapes. The letters of the alphabet (with the addition of digamma) are twenty-five, suggesting that each division was divided into five groups (5 × 5), and this seems to be confirmed by the fact that each letter is represented. The scheme seems designed to group citizens from the different tribes and demes together in a single space, not to separate them (Jones 1987, 150 n. 4). The aim is to ensure that the votes of the representatives of the twenty-five sections 'be cast for the interests of the polis and not for those of the demes' (Amit 1973, 143). Amit envisions a scheme by which the entire citizen body, distributed by their tokens into 'sections' that were each tribally and demotically mixed, voted to elect their ruling magistrates (1973, 144–5). Robinson imagines that at a special meeting in the theatre the tokens for each section were taken and the appropriate number randomly selected to serve as representative electors (2011, 38). The letters and shapes seem to have been generally fixed for each individual, since four of the tokens repeat the same name, and these have the same shape, and only one has a different letter from the homonymous token (Fougères 1898, 532).

Excavations of the theatre at Mantinea revealed a division of the theatron into seven kerkides (Fougères 1890, 249). Fougères and Svoronos interpreted the letters on the tokens each to relate to a different segment of the theatron. Reserving front and central sections for officials, the scheme suggested by Svoronos is as follows:

Δ	H	Λ	M	Π	Y	Ω
Γ	Z	K		O	T	Ψ
B	F	I	proh-	Ξ	Σ	X
A	E	Θ	edria	N	P	Φ
pro	*hed*	*ria*		*pro*	*hed*	*ria*

Theatre Seating Plan after Svoronos 1900, 224.

That the token letters correspond to a sector of the theatron receives a striking corroboration from the fact that different parts of the theatron in Mantinea were marked by inscribed letters (Fougères 1890, 249; Svoronos 1900, 225), including one recorded ΜΕ Θ which Svoronos takes to be an abbreviation for ΜΕ(ΡΟΣ) Θ, i.e. Section Θ (1900, 225). A further confirmation may be taken from the fact that one token, instead of a letter, has the word τάξις (= 'section') written on it, where the actual letter was presumably added or to be added in paint now lost (Fougères 1898, 533).

If this is correct then the theatre must be at least as old as the earliest tokens, i.e. late fifth century or beginning of fourth, since the tokens we have were mainly found in the theatre and in any case presuppose the theatre. This evidence has unfairly been neglected in dating the theatre. The theatre is universally dated from its architectural remains to the fourth century and usually to the mid fourth century (virtually all commentators from Bulle 1928, 248 to Bressan 2009, 180). Possibly the earliest tokens are the only remains of the theatre that pre-dated the construction of the extant stone theatron.

The skene building may be of very late date (Bulle 1928, 248; Arias 1934, 97; Bressan 2009, 181, 183–4), so does not help in determining this question. Ridgway discusses evidence for a possible fourth-century choregic sculpture in the theatre of Mantinea (1997, 206–9). The estimated capacity of the theatre is about 4,000 (Frederiksen in Forsén 2000, 51 n. 49), more than ample space to accommodate the citizen population of Mantinea which according to Lysias (34.7) was under 3,000 (Hodkinson and Hodkinson 1981, 271–9), but not so much larger as to suggest that the theatre was designed for non-political purposes (cf. Hansen and Fischer-Hansen 1994, 51–3). In the apparent absence of a skene, the use of the Mantinean theatre for musical or dramatic performances in the Classical period remains in doubt. Indeed we know of only one Mantinean involved in a theatrical profession and that is not until the Hellenistic period: a didaskalos of tragedy in the first half of the third century (Stefanis no. 2033).

On the other hand Polybius' comments on the efflorescence of theatrical music in Arcadia are very likely to extend to Mantinea (see **Bxii 2**). Mantinea was a founding member of the Arcadian League and even though the League split as early as 363, when Mantinea served as an alternative capital (*IACP* 519), it may have shared in the evident expansion of theatre and festival culture attested in the other major cities of the region (**Bxii–Bxv**).

Bxii: Megalopolis

1. **Dedicatory inscriptions on prohedric benches**. Date: 4th c. (letter forms; possibly prosopography – see commentary).

A dedication inscribed on three of the nine marble prohedric benches, one at the bottom of each kerkis, in the Megalopolitan theatre. The benches have arms at each end, a slightly curved back and hollowed seats, four seats to the central benches and five to each of the outer benches. For the type cf. Sicyon, Epidaurus city, Epidaurus Asklepieion, and partly Delos (Moretti 2014a, 123). Some of the Megalopolitan theatre benches bear the names of the different Arcadian tribes with inscriptions that date from the 2nd and possibly from the 3rd c., with names reassigned and recut some centuries later (Gardiner et al. 1892, 74–5). **a** is written over the back of three slabs in a not very straight line and with letters of varying size a quarter of the distance from the top of the back of the easternmost prohedric bench (the bench is 6.6 m long and the first inscribed line extends 3.82 m); **b** is from the central bench; **c** is from the first and third slabs of the western bench, with a blank slab interrupting the letters of the second word.

Found during excavations by the British School at Athens in the spring of 1890.

In situ.

Richards in Gardiner et al. 1892, 122–3; *IG* V 2, 450.

Text: Richards.

Photo: Gardiner et al. 1892, 123 (transcription), fig. 2 (benches; inscription not visible).

> **a.** Ἀντίοχος ἀγωνοθετήσας ἀνέθηκε τὸς θρό|νος πάντας καὶ τὸν ὀχετόν.
>
> **b.** Ἀντίοχος ἀγωνοθετήσας ἀ|νέθηκε.
>
> **c.** Ἀντίοχος ἀγωνοθετ||ήσας ἀνέθηκε.
>
> **a.** Antiochos after serving as agonothete dedicated all the thro|nes and the drain.
>
> **b.** Antiochos after serving as agonothete de|dicated (this bench).
>
> **c.** Antiochos after serving as agonothet| |e dedicated (this bench).

2. Polybius, *Histories* 4.20.8–21.1. Written ca. 150–140 with reference to 'traditions' that defined the Arcadians down to 220 (the reference to Philoxenus and Timotheus suggests that the customs here described are those of the mid 4th c. onwards). In a long excursus Polybius tries to explain how the people of Kinaitha degenerated into treachery and savagery, whereas all other Arcadians are famous for their piety and humanity. The Kinaithans alone of all Arcadian cities neglected music. Text: Foucault.

> ταῦτα γὰρ πᾶσίν ἐστι γνώριμα καὶ συνήθη, διότι σχεδὸν παρὰ μόνοις Ἀρκάσι πρῶτον μὲν οἱ παῖδες ἐκ νηπίων ᾄδειν ἐθίζονται κατὰ νόμους τοὺς ὕμνους καὶ παιᾶνας, οἷς ἕκαστοι κατὰ τὰ πάτρια [20.9] τοὺς ἐπιχωρίους ἥρωας καὶ θεοὺς ὑμνοῦσι· μετὰ δὲ ταῦτα τοὺς Φιλοξένου καὶ Τιμοθέου νόμους μανθάνοντες πολλῇ φιλοτιμίᾳ χορεύουσι κατ᾽ ἐνιαυτὸν τοῖς Διονυσιακοῖς αὐληταῖς ἐν τοῖς θεάτροις, οἱ μὲν παῖδες τοὺς παιδικοὺς ἀγῶνας, οἱ δὲ νεανίσκοι τοὺς [20.10] τῶν ἀνδρῶν λεγομένους. ὁμοίως γε μὴν καὶ παρ᾽ ὅλον τὸν βίον τὰς ἀγωγὰς τὰς ἐν ταῖς συνουσίαις οὐχ οὕτως ποιοῦνται διὰ τῶν ἐπεισάκτων ἀκροαμάτων ὡς δι᾽ αὑτῶν, ἀνὰ μέρος ᾄδειν ἀλλήλοις προστάττοντες. [20.11] καὶ τῶν μὲν ἄλλων μαθημάτων ἀρνηθῆναί τι μὴ γινώσκειν οὐδὲν αἰσχρὸν ἡγοῦνται, τήν γε μὴν ᾠδὴν οὔτ᾽ ἀρνηθῆναι δύνανται διὰ τὸ κατ᾽ ἀνάγκην πάντας μανθάνειν, οὔθ᾽ ὁμολογοῦντες ἀποτρίβεσθαι διὰ τὸ τῶν αἰσχρῶν παρ᾽ αὐτοῖς [20.12] νομίζεσθαι τοῦτο. καὶ μὴν ἐμβατήρια μετ᾽ αὐλοῦ καὶ τάξεως ἀσκοῦντες, ἔτι δ᾽ ὀρχήσεις ἐκπονοῦντες μετὰ κοινῆς ἐπιστροφῆς καὶ δαπάνης κατ᾽ ἐνιαυτὸν ἐν τοῖς θεάτροις ἐπιδείκνυνται τοῖς αὑτῶν πολίταις [21.1] οἱ νέοι.

It is a fact known and familiar to all that in Arcadia, almost uniquely, children are first of all by law (or possibly 'in measure': Walbank 1957, 467) from earliest childhood trained to sing the hymns and paeans by which each locality traditionally [20.9] celebrates its heroes and gods. After that they learn the *nomoi* of Philoxenus and Timotheus and dance competitively each year to the music of professional (literally 'Dionysiac' referring probably to members of the Artists of Dionysus) pipers in the theatres, the boys at the boys' contests, and the youths at those [20.10] called 'men's competitions'. In the same way for the whole of their lives they observe the customary entertainments at social gatherings not through hired musicians, but by their own music, asking each to sing to the others in turn. [20.11] And they think it no disgrace to admit ignorance in other fields of study, but they can admit no ignorance of any song since they are forced to learn them, nor can they refuse to sing a song, while admitting that they know it, as such an act is [20.12] considered shameful. Indeed the youths at public initiative and expense practise marching in good order to the music of the pipes and also train hard in dance and then display (the dances) for their fellow citizens in the theatres [21.1] each year.

After the Spartan hegemony over the Peloponnese was broken at Leuctra in 371, the cities of Arcadia formed a league, probably mainly motivated by a desire to offer a common front against the likelihood of a Spartan resurgence. The League's constitution was almost certainly democratic (Robinson 2011, 41–4). Megalopolis was founded in 371/0 through the synoecism of some forty Arcadian cities to serve as the Arcadian League's capital (Hornblower 1990). The city was planned and laid out in a previously uninhabited plain. The plan was ambitious: Pausanias regarded the theatre as 'the biggest in Greece' (when complete it seated an estimated 20,000) and the Council House (Thersilion) was 'built for the Ten Thousand (i.e. representatives of the) Arcadians' (8.32.1). The latter was built immediately to the north of the theatre and together they form a functional and architectural unity. As Goette points out, this plan must have existed in some form from the beginning: 'after 362 BC and the death of Epaminondas in the Battle of Mantineia, the end of Theban hegemony and the division of the Arcadian League, such a magnificent building concept is no longer imaginable' (1995a, 35).

The date of the completion of the Thersilion is usually thought to be the 360s or 350s (Roy 2000, 315). The dating of the surviving stone theatre is much disputed. **1** has played a primary role in the argumentation. Gardiner et al. 1892 (Richards) give **1** a date of 370–350 based on letter forms (for nu and sigma) and orthography (o for ou). They also argued the identification of the donor with the Antiochos who was a pancratiast and representative of the Arcadian league in an embassy to Persia in 367 (X. *HG* 7.1.33–8; Gardiner et al. 1892, 123–4; Goette 1995a, 35). Assuming Antiochos was of a mature age when he served as ambassador, the dedication would not be much later than 350. In favour of this identification it could be pointed out that no other fourth-century Antiochos is known from Arcadia, and only two others from the whole of the Peloponnese: the name is reasonably uncommon at this time (*LGPN* IIIb 45–6 nos. 17, 48).

Both the epigraphic and the prosopographic datings are disputed, however. The epigraphic date is challenged by Dörpfeld and Reisch 1896, 141, though without argument, and by Hiller in *IG* V, who adds that the form of the alpha looks later. These authors nonetheless all agree on dating **1** within the fourth century. The identification of Antiochos with the pancratiast is disputed by Lauter and Lauter-Bufe (2004, 148–9). Their study of the chronology of the theatre, the most authoritative to date, is based on stonework construction techniques and styles (e.g. use of swallow-tail clamps rather than T-clamps – already a concern in Dörpfeld and Reisch 1896, 140; wall construction; shapes of column capitals and roof tiles). Lauter and Lauter-Bufe propose a date in the last quarter or end of the fourth century. A later fourth-century date may be supported by the findings of a small trench laid in the epitheatron in 1997 which yielded no material earlier than the late fourth century but also showed construction techniques similar to those used in the lower theatre, suggesting that both parts of the theatron were built at the same time (Zabbou 1997, 203). On the other hand, the recent uncovering and examination of the analemma of the eastern parodos revealed a construction technique typical of the second quarter of the fourth century (Karapanagiotou 2001, 334–5).

A date around 330–320 for the stone theatre is just possible, without compromising the likelihood that Antiochos is the known athlete: he would have been a very old man at the time of his dedication. It is, however, also likely that the building of the theatron in stone took many decades and that the earliest part of the theatre to be converted was the prohedria, thanks in part to Antiochos' dedication. There need be no conflict with the impression of a substantially later completion of the stone construction.

Re-used blocks of an earlier skene in the skene of the
Late Classical or Early Hellenistic theatre at Megalopolis

The surviving stone skene, illustrated above, incorporates at least four large blocks with cuttings designed to hold wooden beams (marked 1–4), and from their position it is clear that they belonged to an earlier construction which was freed for reuse by the building of the stone skene (H. R. Goette pers. comm.). The most likely interpretation is that these blocks belonged to an earlier skene constructed of wood. So if the date of the stone theatre, ca. 330–320, is correct, we should posit the existence of a wooden skene some time before ca. 330, and for reasons given by Goette above the wooden theatre would most probably belong to the original plan for Megalopolis, and have a likely construction date in the 360s. Bressan supports this conclusion in positing four phases of construction: the first in the mid fourth century; the second in the later fourth to early third; the third in the second century and the fourth in imperial times (2009, 187–95).

Antiochos' dedication (**1**) is to Dionysus. A second-century agonothetic dedication, also found in the theatre, was explicitly dedicated 'to Dionysus and the city' (*IG* V 2, 453). Parallels in other Arcadian cities (see below) make it an easy inference that the theatre was dedicated to Dionysus from the beginning. The theatre, the largest in Greece according to Pausanias (2.27.5), continued to be used without interruption until at least the second century AD.

In introducing **2** Polybius speaks of an 'Arcadian constitution' (4.20.7), language that would seem to look primarily to the years following the foundation of the League. The conclusion gets some confirmation from **2**'s reference to the requirement that youths learn the *nomoi* of Timotheus (ca. 450–ca. 360) and Philoxenus (ca. 435–ca. 380), the most famous lyric poets of the fourth century. Interestingly enough, both poets were associated with democratic music, and Timotheus at least was also associated with anti-Spartan sentiment (Prauscello 2009, esp. 169–70). **2** speaks of competitive performances to 'Dionysian pipes', though not explicitly at 'Dionysia' (see on **1**), by choruses of boys and choruses called 'men's' which must be a reference to the same form of lyric competition (a.k.a. 'circular chorus' or 'dithyramb') known at Athens and broadly across the Aegean. **2** also declares that these Dionysian choruses are publicly sponsored, and our evidence from Megalopolis (**1**), Tegea (**Bxiii**), and Orchomenus (**Bxiv**) shows a common culture of sponsorship through officials called 'agonothetes' well before Athens abandoned the choregic system to adopt this practice. Arcadian theatre culture also seems to have shared the agonothetic practice of dedicating prohedric seating on the conclusion of one's term of office (**1**; **Bxiii**; **Bxiv**), though we find prohedric seat dedication elsewhere in the fourth century. Moretti (2010, 162) lists also Oropus (**Ci**), Euonymon (**III I**), Rhamnus (**III Wi**; **III Wii**) and Priene (**Evii**): one could add also Sparta (**Bix 2**) and Epidaurus City (**Bvii 1**).

Unfortunately **2** makes no mention of drama, nor does any other ancient source for Classical Arcadia. It is possibly significant that the tragic actor Ischandros (Stefanis no. 1303) was chosen by the pro-Athenian faction in Arcadia to represent their interests to the Athenian Assembly in 348 (D. 19.303). Several third-century boy choreuts of Megalopolitan origin do some credit to **2**'s claims of a strong choral tradition (Stefanis nos. 851, 2855, 2873, 2896), but it is not until the second century that we hear of a tragic actor who was a citizen of Megalopolis (Stefanis no. 1886).

Bxiii: Tegea. Dedicatory inscription on the face of a prohedric bench in the theatre, second half or last third 4th c. (by letter forms and prosopography).

Stoichedon dedicatory inscription on the front face of a rectilinear marble bench in the prohedria of the earliest theatre, formed of seats H. 0.45 m × W. 0.45 m.

Excavated by the French School at Athens in autumn 1912. About 5 m of the bench were exposed. *In situ.*
Vallois 1926, 166; *SEG* 11, 1070.   Drawing: Vallois 1926, 166.

      Κύμβαλος   stoich.
      ἀνέθηκε
      Διονύσῳ
      ἀγωνοθετήσας

Kymbalos dedicated (this bench) to Dionysus after serving as agonothete.

A Kymbalos, son of Ariston, appears on a list of names from Tegea (*IG* V 2, 38, l. 52). The list, of unknown function, is dated by letter forms to the fourth or third century. Vallois was almost certainly right to suppose the son of Ariston to be either the dedicator of the theatre prohedria or the grandson of the dedicator (1926, 167). The name Kymbalos is, so far as we know, not only rare, but unique to this single individual or family.

The first phase of the extant theatre is dated to the second half of the fourth century and more probably 330–300 (Bressan 2009, 245–6). The dating is largely based on the dating of the dedicatory inscription. But the theatre itself has several very early features, including a rectilinear plan for the theatron (Vallois 1926, 168; Arias 1934, 97; Gebhard 1974, 436–8; Bressan 2009, 245, 459). The theatron above the row of prohedric seating where the inscription was found was either formed of the bare hillside (Vallois 1926, 167) or of wooden *ikria* (Bulle 1928, 260). For this first phase we are probably to imagine a wooden skene, though it unfortunately left no trace (Bulle 1928, 260). We can conclude from Kymbalos' dedication to Dionysus as agonothete and its placement in the theatre that the Tegean theatre served as the venue for some kind of musical competition, and presumably in the context of a Dionysia.

Sometime later, though probably still within the fourth century, a drain and another more elaborate prohedric bench with back and arm rests were placed about 2 m in front of Kymbalos' prohedria. This was also rectilinear. Also found, and presumably belonging to this same later phase, were two single prohedric thrones, now in the Tegea Museum (Bulle 1928, 259; Micheli 1987, 69). The thrones are stylistically dated by Micheli to the late fourth century (1987, 79). The theatre was not rebuilt with a circular theatron until ca. 174, by Antiochus Epiphanes (Livy 41.20.6). In the imperial period a stone skene with a deep proskenion was built.

Tegea produced a tragic poet, Aristarchus (*TrGF* 14), said to be contemporary with Euripides (Suda α 3893) and whose drama may have been performed in Rhodes ca. 380 (see Snell's supplement to **Dxi 2**, l. 4). In the fourth-century Tegea produced some distinguished auletes who performed for boys' choruses in Athens (Stefanis nos. 1359, 2949), but it is not until the second quarter of the third century that we hear of comic actors (Stefanis nos. 1261, 2136), auletes for comedy (no. 2544) or choreuts from Tegea (nos. 1308, 2136), and just a little later (190–170) that we hear of a tragic actor of Tegean origin (*Syll.*[3] 1080).

In the aftermath of the defeat of Sparta at Leuctra, several cities in the Peloponnese that were previously under Spartan hegemony adopted democratic constitutions. This seems to have happened in Tegea following a civil war in 370 which resulted in the exile of 800

(X. *HG* 6.5.6–9; *IACP* 532; Robinson 2011, 41). The Tegean democracy was one of the founding members of the Arcadian League and its capital Megalopolis (Paus. 8.27.2). The League was partly formed to unify the Arcadian cities against the prospect of a Spartan resurgence, and probably also governed by a democratic constitution (**Bxii**). All the available evidence suggests that it was within the framework of this democracy that Tegea established its theatre and its Dionysia. The fact that the theatres of several cities in Arcadia are attested at this time (**Bxii**; **Bxv**; **Bxiv**; cf. **Bxi**), that they have Dionysia (**Bxv 1**; **Bxiv**; probably **Bxii**), and that, like Tegea, at least two of the other Dionysia are publicly funded and managed by an agonothete (**Bxii**; **Bxiv**) – all suggest that a kind of common theatre culture existed within the Arcadian confederacy.

Bxiv: Orchomenus. Agonothetic dedication to Dionysus of prohedric theatre bench,
4ᵗʰ–3ʳᵈ c. (by letter forms and the general morphology of the theatre which suggests a similar date range).

Dedicatory inscription on back of continuous prohedric limestone bench with back and arm-rests in theatre of Orchomenus. Two ornamented marble thrones with high backs (1.05 m) and traces of inscription (Arias 1934, 83: 'Δ.... Ο.... A forse resti di un nome') were also found in the orchestra and are of a form that is common in the 4ᵗʰ–3ʳᵈ c. (Bulle 1928, 248).
Found during excavations by the French School in the autumn of 1913 (Blum and Plassart 1914, 80).
In situ (cf. Steinhauer 1973–1974, 301 pl. 193).
Text: Blum and Plassart 1914, 80; *SEG* 11, 1104.   Photos: Burmeister 2006, 38; Theatrum website (http://www.theatrum.de/275.html) has excellent photos of the prohedria by K. Böhne).

>] Ἐπιγένεος ἀγωνοθετήσας Διονύσωι

>] Son of Epigenes (dedicated this) to Dionysus after serving as agonothete.

Orchomenus' theatre is small (Bulle 1928, 249: 'das kleinste aller griechischen'). The cavea of the extant theatre is dated to the fourth century by Isler (*TGR* II, 268) and, with some hesitation, by Moretti (2014a, 109); but to the third century by Arias (1934, 83) and others. The use of an agonothete and the dedication of theatre seats upon expiration of office is a pattern in Arcadia that can certainly be dated elsewhere to the fourth century, and may well have its origin in the common culture of the Arcadian League (**Bxii**; **Bxiii**).

Bxv: Phigaleia

1. **Diodorus of Sicily, *Library of History* 15.40.1–2**. Written 50–30, referring to 374 or 371–370 (Roy 1973). Diodorus' source is probably the *Histories* of Ephorus, who lived at the time of these events (Lauffer 1959, 346; Roy 1973, 137–5). Diodorus himself dates the events to 374 but his account confuses details relating to two different peace treaties: the renewal of the King's Peace in 375 and the peace that followed the Battle of Leuctra in July 371. According to Diodorus civil disturbances took place in several

Peloponnesian cities following the renewal of the King's Peace which included a requirement that all cities be free and independent of foreign garrisons (D.S. 15.38.2). As
a consequence Phigaleia was apparently freed from Spartan hegemony. Phigaleia, best
known for its rural temple to Apollo at Bassae, is located in the south-west corner of
Arcadia, but it is cut off from Arcadia by high mountains and its cultural and political ties
were with Messenia. The 'g' in the name of the town became obsolete over the course
of the fourth century and the second 'i' is variable (Meyer 1938, 2065–7). Text: Vogel.

μετὰ γὰρ τὴν συγχωρηθεῖσαν τοῖς δήμοις αὐτονομίαν αἱ πόλεις ἐνέπιπτον
εἰς ταραχὰς μεγάλας καὶ στάσεις, μάλιστα δὲ αἱ κατὰ τὴν Πελοπόννησον.
ὀλιγαρχικοῖς γὰρ πολιτεύμασι κεχρημέναι, καὶ ταῖς τῆς δημοκρατίας
ἐξουσίαις ἀπειραγάθως χρώμεναι, πολλοὺς τῶν ἀγαθῶν ἀνδρῶν ἐφυγάδευον
καὶ κρίσεις ἐπιβάλλουσαι συκοφαντώδεις κατεδίκαζον. διόπερ εἰς στάσεις
ἐμπίπτουσαι φυγὰς καὶ δημεύσεις οὐσιῶν ἐποιοῦντο, μάλιστα δὲ πρὸς τοὺς
ἐπὶ τῆς Λακεδαιμονίων ἡγεμονίας προεστηκότας τῶν πατρίδων. ² ἐν γὰρ
τοῖς τότε χρόνοις ἐπιτακτικῶς ἐκείνων τοῖς πολίταις προσενηνεγμένων,
ὕστερον ὁ δημοτικὸς ὄχλος ἀπολαβὼν τὴν ἐλευθερίαν ἐμνησικάκει. πρῶτον
δὲ τῶν Φιαλέων οἱ φυγάδες συστραφέντες κατελάβοντο τὴν καλουμένην
Ἡραίαν, χωρίον ὀχυρόν. ἐκ ταύτης δ' ὁρμηθέντες παρεισέπεσον εἰς τὴν
Φιάλειαν, καὶ Διονυσίων κατὰ τύχην ὄντων ἐπιπεσόντες ἀπροσδοκήτως τοῖς
ἐν τῷ θεάτρῳ καθημένοις, καὶ πολλοὺς ἀποσφάξαντες, οὐκ ὀλίγους δὲ καὶ
συναπονοήσασθαι πείσαντες, ἀνεχώρησαν εἰς τὴν Σπάρτην.

After autonomy had been conceded to the various peoples, the cities experienced great upheavals and civil unrest, especially those in the Peloponnese. For
they used to have oligarchic constitutions and as they were unused to the liber-
ties of democracy they abused them by attempting to exile and condemn with
trumped-up lawsuits many of the good citizens (i.e. oligarchs). As a result they
fell headlong into civil war and banishments and confiscations of property, especially as directed against those who at the time of the Spartan hegemony held
power. ² At that time they (the pro-Spartan oligarchs) dealt with their fellow citizens in an authoritarian fashion and once the democratic mob recovered its liberty it nursed bitter memories of the wrongs it had suffered. First the Phigaleian
citizens that had been exiled (i.e. the oligarchs) gathered together and seized
the stronghold called Heraia. They set out from there and swooped down upon
Phigaleia and assailed the citizens without warning as they sat in the theatre,
since it happened to be the time of the Dionysia, and they slaughtered many
and persuaded not a few to share in their madness, and then retreated to Sparta.

**2. Harmodios of Lepreon, *On the Customs of the Phigaleians*, FGrH 319 F 1 (= Ath.
4.148f–149b)**. Harmodios is probably a Hellenistic author, possibly 3rd c. (Jacoby 1912).
He describes how Phigaleians organised their town banquets. It is clear from the 'even
now' in the last sentence of the passage that he is writing about what he supposed to
be ancient customs. The fragment is a few sentences longer than what is quoted below:
its length encouraged Zecchini to speculate that our source Athenaeus had a full text

of Harmodios before him, though mediation through Didymus (1st c.) is also a named possibility (1989, 147–8). Text: close to Jacoby.

ὁ κατασταθεὶς ⁵ παρὰ Φιγαλεῦσι σίταρχος ἔφερε τῆς ἡμέρας οἴνου τρεῖς χόας καὶ ἀλφίτων μέδιμνον καὶ τυροῦ πεντάμνουν, καὶ τἄλλα τὰ πρὸς τὴν ἄρτυσιν τῶν ἱερείων ἁρμόττοντα· ἡ δὲ πόλις παρεῖχεν ἑκατέρῳ τῶν χορῶν τρία πρόβατα καὶ μάγειρον ὑδριαφόρον τε καὶ τραπέζας καὶ βάθρα πρὸς τὴν καθέδραν καὶ τὴν τοιαύτην ¹⁰ ἅπασαν παρασκευήν, πλὴν τῶν περὶ τὸν μάγειρον σκευῶν ὁ χορηγός. τὸ δὲ δεῖπνον ἦν τοιοῦτο· τυρὸς καὶ φυστὴ μᾶζα νόμου χάριν ἐπὶ χαλκῶν κανῶν τῶν παρά τισι καλουμένων μαζονόμων, ἀπὸ τῆς χρείας εἰληφότων τὴν ἐπωνυμίαν· ὁμοῦ δὲ τῇ μάζῃ καὶ τῷ τυρῷ σπλάγχνον καὶ ἅλες προσφαγεῖν. ¹⁵ καθαγισάντων δὲ ταῦτα ἐν κεραμέᾳ κοτταβίδι πιεῖν ἑκάστῳ μικρόν, καὶ ὁ προσφέρων ἀνεῖπεν 'εὖ δείπνειας'. εἶτα δ' εἰς τὸ κοινὸν ζωμὸς καὶ περίκομμα, πρόσχερα δ' ἑκάστῳ δύο κρέα. ἐνόμιζον δ' ἐν ἅπασι τοῖς δείπνοις, μάλιστα δὲ τοῖς λεγομένοις μαζῶσι — τοῦτο γὰρ ἔτι καὶ νῦν ἡ Διονυσιακὴ ²⁰ σύνοδος ἔχει τοὔνομα — τοῖς ἐσθίουσι τῶν νέων ἀνδρικώτερον ζωμόν τ' ἐγχεῖν πλείω καὶ μάζας καὶ ἄρτους παραβάλλειν ...'

10 τὴν δὲ K   πλὴν περὶ A   πλὴν τῶν περὶ Kaibel   τὸν μάγειρον codd.   τὸ μαγειρεῖον Kaibel   14 προφαγεῖν A   16 ἀνεῖπεν 'εὖ δείπνειας' Müller   ἂν εἶπεν ευδειπνιαις A, Jacoby   ἂν εἶπεν 'εὐδειπνίας' Dobree, Kaibel   cf. ἀνεῖπεν ευδειπνειας Ath. 11.479c   17 πρόσχερα codd.   πρόχειρα Schneider   πρὸς χεῖρα Kaibel

The man who is appointed ⁵ as superintendent of food contributes three *choes* of wine and a *medimnos* of barley and five *minai* of cheese and everything else that is appropriate accompaniment to sacrificial meat. The city provided three sheep, a cook and a water-carrier for each of the choruses, and tables, and benches for seating, and all such ¹⁰ furnishings, with the exception of the equipment for the cook that the choregos provided. The meal was of this sort: cheese and puffed barley-cake was served by custom in baskets of bronze that were called by some *mazonoma*, a name they acquired from their use (etymology from *maza* = barley-cake and *nomos* = distribution); together with the barley-cake and cheese they ate tripe and salt, ¹⁵ and, when these had been offered to the gods, they gave everyone a little wine to drink in a ceramic cottabus bowl and the man who brought the wine said 'May you dine well!' Then they set broth and mince on the table and placed two pieces of meat in addition for (if that is what πρόσχερα means; or reading Schneider's emendation 'within reach of') each diner. And it was a custom in all their dinners, and especially those called *mazones*, for even now the Dionysian ²⁰ club (or 'gathering' or 'guild') has that name, to ladle out more broth and place extra barley loaves beside young men who ate with a manlier appetite …

Dionysus was the chief god of Phigaleia (Meyer 1938, 2083–4; Jost 1985, 84–5, 425–38) and was worshipped under at least two different cult titles. Lycophron, *Alexandra* 212 (δαίμων Ἐνόρχης Φιγαλεὺς Φαυστήριος) and the scholia to this verse attest that the epiklesis of the Dionysus at Phigaleia was 'Enorches', 'With Testicles'. The obvious implication of the name, i.e. that Dionysus was worshipped in Phigaleia in phallic form, is confirmed by the aetiology given by the scholia which mention Dionysus fulfilling a promise to have sex with the deceased Prosymnos by strapping on an artificial phallos of figwood and leather (Csapo 1997, 259, 275–6). Pausanias 8.39.6 reports the cult epiklesis of the main temple of Dionysus in Phigaleia as 'Akratophoros' meaning 'unmixed' (of wine), a name Dionysus shares with a kind of wine pitcher. 'Akratos' is the name given to a Dionysian demon in Attica (Paus. 1.2.5) and 'Akratopotes' is the name of a hero worshipped near the temple of Dionysus in Piraeus (**III V Introduction**). But Pausanias' description of the icon as bright red with the lower part hidden by ivy suggests that Akratophoros is also a phallic icon, and raises the possibility that both epikleseis may belong to the same Dionysus (with the eponymous testicles hidden from view: the scholia describe the rites of Enorches as mysteries).

The Dionysia at Phigaleia (attested in **1**) therefore presumably included a phallic procession, but the massacre of the Phigaleian demos seems to presuppose an entertainment exclusively or mainly localised in the theatre. **2**, albeit indirectly, attests a plurality of choruses as well as the existence of at least one choregos in Phigaleia. We may infer that one of the Phigaleian banquets at which choruses and choregos played such a prominent role included feasts connected to the Dionysia, especially given that a special sub-variety of the banquets described was given a name (*mazones*) that was appropriated by the local Dionysian association. We find the same word in a late inscription from Tegea, on the other side of Arcadia, in a funerary epigram where a 19-year-old man is said to have been 'distinguished among all the *mazones* for his character, [lost word], and beauty' (*IG* V 2, 178). It seems safe to assume, from **2**'s information about choruses and their implied connection with Dionysus, that the entertainment which brought the Phigaleians together in the theatre in the unlucky circumstance described by **1** was a choral entertainment of some sort. The Dionysian association, referred to by **2** as a *synodos*, may be an actors' guild, since this is the formal nomenclature used of other known Hellenistic actors' unions. If this is the case, we should assume that the Phigaleian Dionysia, even if simple in 374, soon came to offer more than mere choral competitions. *Synodos* could imply a local branch of a larger, more broadly based union such as the Isthmian and Nemean Artists of Dionysus (cf. *ATD* I, 101 n. 327; Aneziri 2011, 219–20).

An inscription found near the presumed site of the temple of Dionysus (Jost 1985, 436) and dated by letter forms to the second or first century confirms the existence of a Dionysia at Phigaleia, but it indicates that by that date, at least, it was not an annual event (*IG* V 2, 422: ἂν | [δ]ὲ κωμάζει ἁ πόλις τὰ Διονύσια ἐν | τῶι ἐνιαυτῶι ἐν ὧι δεῖ τὰ Ἀνδρίνει|α γίνεσθαι, γινέσθω παρὰ τρία, 'If the city celebrates the Dionysia in the year in which the Andrineia take place, let it take place by a three-year interval'). The decree seems to be concerned to make sure that the Andrineia, probably a festival held in memory of a private donor, not be held in the same year as the Dionysia. From the fourth line we can infer that the Andrineia was to be held normally every three years. This would seem to indicate that the Dionysia of Phigaleia was penteteric, i.e. held every four years. The schedule would thus conflict every twelfth year, but the inscription remedies this potential clash by making the interval every two years ('by a three year interval' in inclusive reckoning) in cases where the Andrineia would otherwise conflict. The use of the verb *komazei* for 'celebrate' the Dionysia, a word that normally implies processional activity (see on **I Aiv 23a**), supports our hypothesis that a chief entertainment of the Dionysia at Phigaleia was a phallic parade.

2's mention of a plurality of choruses but only one choregos (unless it is just a careless expression) would seem to imply a situation somewhat like the one we have inferred for some of the Attic Rural Dionysia such as Thorikos (**III Y**), where it seems that a small team of three choregoi might have bankrolled the entire suite of performances, including both tragedy and comedy, at a single festival (a system which in some ways resembles the agonothetic system adopted by the other Arcadian cities: see **Bxii 1**; **Bxiii**; **Bxiv**).

Phigaleia produced a piper for a men's chorus, Anakos, at the Valley of the Muses (**Cv 3**), probably in the fourth century (Stefanis no. 172), but no other theatrical performers until the first century (Stefanis nos. 576, 2833, 2843, 2951).

It is assumed that Phigaleia was a member of the Arcadian League, though it is not specifically attested (*IACP* 528). If so, it seems more than coincidental that its theatre is first attested at the same time and under the same circumstances as most of the other early Arcadian theatres in Megalopolis (**Bxii**), Tegea (**Bxiii**), and Orchomenus (**Bxiv**) and that its main theatre festival should be a Dionysia, something that cannot be taken for granted in the Peloponnese, but is a pattern shared by the Arcadian cities.

C | Central Greece (Mainland, Ionian Islands, Macedon and Thrace)

Introduction

Central Greece seems to display the full spectrum of the modes of reception of theatre that we find in other parts of Greece. Most distinctive are: the conservative, largely oligarchic and usually Athenophobic Boeotia, in which theatre culture suddenly seems to flourish (as in Arcadia, **Bxi–xv**) after the Theban democratic revolution of 379 and during the Theban hegemony that lasted until 338; the spread of theatre up along the coast of the Corinthian Gulf and the Ionian Sea, apparently following the trade routes to Italy and Sicily; and the rapid spread of theatre through the monarchic, non-Greek realm of Macedonia.

Boeotia (**Ci–Cv**)

Throughout antiquity Boeotia, the home of the Heliconian Muses, was famous for its musical life. The region had at least a dozen theatres in antiquity. Of these only three (Oropus, Chaeronea, Orchomenus) offer architectural evidence of use before 300. The oldest remains are the stone foundations of a rectilinear wooden theatron and an early skene, underneath the Hellenistic theatre of Oropus (**Ci**). These are datable to around 420.

The second oldest physical remnant of a theatre in Boeotia may be a rock-cut section of the theatre at Chaeronea, dated to the late fifth or beginning of the fourth century (Anti and Polacco 1969, 18–44; Kyriazi 2013, 76). The surviving theatron, built some time probably in the fourth century, is curvilinear, but there are traces of earlier rectilinear rows of benches. An agonothetic dedication of a proskenion to Dionysus survives (*IG* VII 3409) but no case has been presented for its date (*LGPN* V3b, 34553 assigns a 2nd c. date; Moretti 2010, 168 suggests 'fin de l'époque hellénistique ou début de l'Empire'). This theatron was very small, in the earliest phase seating only about 500, and it may have served as an Assembly building (Frederiksen 2002, 67). Chaeronea appears to have been oligarchic (*IACP* 439), which may explain the small size of the building and the complete lack of any evidence for performance in the theatre: some suggest that it functioned only as a council house, a function for which it might seem too large.

The archaeological remains of the theatre of Orchomenus (**Civ**) indicate a fourth-century date. It was apparently part of the plan of the city refounded by Philip II of Macedon and it was in any case in operation by ca. 300. From that time we have a series of epigraphically datable choregic monuments. A similar date is tentatively assigned to the remains of the theatre at Plataea which has only recently been located by electrical ground-resistance and magnetic survey (Konecny et al. 1999; Konecny et al. 2013, 144–6). This city too was rebuilt under Philip and the theatre is guessed to belong to the original plan of the reconstruction (Paus. 4.27.10; 9.1.8; Konecny et al. 2012, 134–5; Konecny et al. 2013, 34, 38). If so, it was probably at least partially rebuilt in later antiquity: the survey detected a possible stage building but its size suggested a Roman-style *scaenae frons* (Konecny et al. 2013, 145).

Though the surviving theatres at the Cabirion, the Valley of the Muses, Thebes and Tanagra are of later construction, various bits of evidence indicate that they replace earlier structures dating back to the fourth or fifth century. The theatre at the Cabirion (**Ciii**) was not built until ca. 200–125, about the same time as the theatre constructed in the Cabirion in Samothrace. But the Cabirion theatre was built on a natural slope (which scholars call the 'Cavea') that probably served as a theatral area from the middle of the fifth century and which was artificially extended ca. 370–330. This theatral area is of greater interest to theatre history than most cultic viewing places because of the comic entertainments that many think are attested by several Cabiric vasepaintings ca. 410–325.

Another modified natural semicircular depression was used as a theatron in the Valley of the Muses near Thespiae (**Cv**). Attached to it are the foundations of a proskenion that can be dated by the letter forms of the mason's marks to the early second century. Inscriptions and literary sources, however, make it clear that competitions were held in the theatre from as early as the 370s. In the same way literary texts indicate that the third-century theatre at Thebes (**Cii**) also had a precursor by the 370s.

So little is left of the theatre at Tanagra that its construction cannot be dated (Germani 2015b, 352). It is thought by many to go back to the fourth century (Charami 2013, 49), but the theatre was only certainly in use in the first century for the musical competitions of the Sarapieia, well attested by inscriptions, some of which were found near the theatre. The festival was probably only founded in the first century. It included old and new tragedy, old and new comedy, and satyr play (Manieri 2009, 261–79). We would have no reason to suspect an earlier use of the theatre were it not for the local interest and knowledge of comedy attested by Boeotian terracotta comic figurines, for which Thebes and Tanagra became the two major centres of production. Recent studies have begun to establish criteria, largely through analysis of the clay, to distinguish Theban from Tanagran production (e.g. Charami and Jeammet 2015). Nothing yet permits one to attribute the earliest of the Boeotian series of figurines of comic actors, which begins about 400, to one city or the other (Green 2014a, 338–44). Tanagran production dominates after 335, with the destruction of Thebes, though Theban production also seems to continue (Jeammet 2010, 9).

We have very little information about the remaining Boeotian theatres. The urban theatre of Thespiae (see on **Cv**) and the theatre of Coronea have only recently been located by surface survey in 2006 (Slapšak 2007, 17–20; Bintliff et al. 2012, 6, 14 fig. 7, 22–3). Dramatic performances are not epigraphically attested for Coronea before the second century (Schachter and Slater 2007). Two Boeotian theatres, at the Ptoion and at Akraiphiai, are only epigraphically attested and both later than the period of our inquiry. The theatre at the Ptoion is known epigraphically from the late second or early first century (*IG* VII 2712, 4148, 4149). It was the site of the contests of the festival of the Ptoia (from ca. 230 BC to 3rd c. AD) for poetry, instrumental music, kitharody, as well as choruses (χοραῦλαι, κύκλιοι αὐληταί). The festival, so far as we know, never included dramatic competitions (Manieri 2009, 73–5). Since the sanctuary of Apollo Ptoios has no trace of a theatre, Manieri thinks the theatre referred to by the inscriptions was a temporary wooden theatre erected for each festival in the sanctuary (2009, 70). Germani argues that the performances took place in the urban theatre of Akraiphiai (also epigraphically attested but unlocated: Germani 2015b,

357). At Akraiphiai the musical and athletic games of the Soteria (probably founded in the mid 2nd c.) by 80 had musical contests and included tragedy, comedy and satyr play (Manieri 2009, 78–9, 130–2). At Leuctra and Lebadeia theatre seats have been found re-used in Byzantine buildings (Germani 2015b, 356). Lebadeia was the site of the Basileia, a festival created to celebrate, in the name of all Boeotians, the victory of the Thebans over the Spartans at Leuctra (Schachter 1994, 111–12). There is no evidence that the festival contained a musical competition until about the middle of the third century when an Athenian statue base for the kitharode Nikokles records among many others a victory at the 'Basileia' without further qualification (though the 'Basileia in Macedon' and 'Basileia in Alexandria' are candidates: *IG* II² 3779; Manieri 2009, 150–1 Leb. 6). Somewhat later we have a heavily restored victor list from Lebadeia that is restored to mention [προσόδιον], [ἐπῶν ποιητ]ής and [ῥαψῳδ]ός (*SEG* 3, 368).

The density of theatres in largely oligarchic Boeotia may seem to go against the grain of the observation made elsewhere, that oligarchic states are generally reluctant to embrace theatre culture. It was Athens, however, that built the theatre at Oropus (**Ci**), and it is noteworthy that the earliest mentions of theatre and theatrical performances in Thebes (**Cii**) come from the time of its democracy, 379–335. This Theban democracy extended its military and cultural influence through the restoration of the Boeotian Confederacy, under Theban hegemony, and the theatre at Chaeronea may date only from this time. Certainly the theatre at Lebadeia (see above) was built for the celebration of the Theban (and Boeotian Confederacy's) victory at Leuctra in 371. The theatre in the Valley of the Muses, though it may have been conceived under Spartan domination (**Cv 4**), was initially nurtured in this era. The theatres in Orchomenus and Plataea were, for their part, planned and built in conjunction with the refoundation of these cities by the Macedonian monarchs Philip and Alexander. It is likely therefore that none of Boeotia's fifth- and fourth-century theatres was constructed on the initiative of a local oligarchic government.

Even so, Boeotia seems not to have unreservedly embraced the Athenian and increasingly Panhellenic model of theatre culture in the same way we find democratic regimes doing throughout the Aegean. A likely exception is Oropus, whose theatre, as we noted above, was built by Athens (**Ci**) when it founded the sanctuary of Amphiaraus in the city's territory, ca. 420. This was a time when Oropus, though in Boeotia and disputed by Thebes, had been incorporated into Attica for nearly a century, but was at risk of slipping from Athenian control, as it did in the latter part of the Peloponnesian War. Oropus seems nonetheless to have preferred Athenian to Theban domination and ca. 374 voluntarily joined Attica once again (Isoc. 14.20, 37). Athens' hold on Oropus was still not permanent and the city changed hands again before Philip restored it to Athens after 338. At that time Athens again took the initiative in refurbishing the sanctuary and creating a quadrennial Panhellenic athletic and musical festival for the sanctuary, the Amphiareia. Athens' concern to build up the sanctuary, both in the fifth and fourth centuries, reveals an avid policy of political and cultural integration of this pocket of Boeotian territory into Attica. Though performances of tragedy, comedy and satyr play are only attested from the first century, honorary decrees for tragic and comic actors make it virtually certain for the third and, on the analogy of the Attic deme Dionysia (**III**), to which the Oropan festival seems to have been in part assimilated, drama is highly likely from the time of the theatre's initial construction.

Significant Attic cultural influence is likely, but undocumentable, in the case of the Plataean theatre. Democratic Plataea clung to Athens as a bulwark against oligarchic Thebes for most of the fifth century until its capture by Thebes in 428/7. At that time the Plataean demos removed to Athens where it was given citizen rights. Plataea was restored, this time with Spartan aid, after 386, but was then destroyed by Thebes in 373. The Plataean refugees again settled in Athens, with special privileges, until Plataea was rebuilt by Philip and Alexander sometime in the aftermath either of the destruction of Theban hegemony or of Thebes itself in 338 and 335 respectively. With the refoundation of Thebes by Cassander in 316, however, Plataea once again came under Theban domination (Konecny et al. 2013, 27–36). The Plataeans, from their time in Athens, were intimately familiar with Athenian theatre culture. Yet the only hint that they transplanted it to their own city is the theatre with stage building mentioned above. Just north of the theatre is a sanctuary, identified as that of Dionysus, but this is based on the assumption that a sanctuary connected with the theatre must be that of Dionysus (Konecny et al. 2008, 63–5; Konecny et al. 2012, 121–2; Konecny et al. 2013, 146–8).

The model of Athenian theatre culture seems otherwise remote in Boeotia. We have no evidence of tragedy until late in the third century. Evidence for comedy is, by contrast, very early, but it is comedy of epichoric varieties distinct from what we find in Athens or elsewhere. Though we doubt that the grotesque Cabiric vasepaintings are evidence of a cultic comedy at the Cabirion (**Ciii**), another distinctive form of comedy is attested by Boeotian terracotta figurines of comic actors. The figurines, though distinct, are much closer in costume to the Attic and Panhellenic norm than the images on the Cabiric vases. These figurines begin early in the fourth century, not necessarily earlier than 379, probably in Thebes, but possibly Tanagra (see above). If they are an experiment in adapting local traditions to the theatre stage, their distinctiveness does not survive long. Sometime after the middle of the century the costumes and style of presentation seem to merge with the Panhellenic norms.

There are no other traces of drama in Boeotian theatres in the fifth and fourth centuries. Boeotian theatres seem to have been dominated by more strictly musical performances. Were it not for the comic figurines just mentioned we would have evidence only for men's choruses in the newly democratised Thebes (and choregically sponsored by the new political leaders, **Cii**). But other Boeotian territories also uniquely attest lyric choruses: in the Valley of the Muses men's choruses are more securely attested than boys' (**Cv 3**); and even the relatively abundant monuments from Orchomenus attest only men's lyric choruses until late in the third or in the second century (**Civ**). These performances, moreover, seem to have deviated from the Athenian and later Panhellenic norm in including soloists who are named on the monuments.

It appears therefore that oligarchic Boeotia generally avoided theatre, possibly adopting it only after the democratic revolution in Thebes or, in the case of Plataea and Orchomenus, only after the cities were refounded by Philip. But even so, those cities that had theatre avoided drama or admitted only a regional form of comedy, and made use of choral genres that may also have had regional characteristics (see on **Civ**). Indeed many of the festivals in the fourth and third centuries had more of a Panboeotian than Panhellenic character. There is little evidence that, apart from the likely instances of Oropus and Plataea, Boeotia was attracted to an Athenian model of theatre culture, saving perhaps only the choregia (**Cii**; **Civ**). This may help explain why, with the likely exception of Thebes (**Cii**) and possibly Plataea (above), Boeotian theatrical festivals were not Dionysia and not dedicated to Dionysus, though in some cases they were dedicated to deities closely associated with Dionysus. At Orchomenus, the choregic dedications are expressly 'to Dionysus' and the theatre was probably in his sanctuary, but the musical festival was probably for his 'daughters', the Graces (**Civ**); at the Cabirion the performances, if there were any, were for deities whose connection with Dionysus is vague and disputed (**Ciii**); at Thespiae the festival was for the Muses (**Cv**); at Oropus the festival was for Asclepius (**Ci**). Other musical festivals that later included theatrical performances were to Zeus (Lebadeia's Basileia, Akraiphiai's Soteria), Serapis (Tanagra), and Apollo (Ptoia).

Southern Mainland (Phocis, Aetolia, Acarnania, Leucas), Ambracian Gulf, Epirus (**Cvi–vii**)

Delphi (**Cvi**) is unusually rich in literary and epigraphic sources of information for the performance of musical genres beginning long before the construction of the surviving theatre in the mid second century. Temporary theatres are directly attested only from the last quarter of the fourth century (**Cvi 2–3**), yet some kind of theatral area was required by the Pythian Games, the first regular Panhellenic musical competitions in Greece, which date back to the sixth century. We have no evidence of competitions for drama until the Soteria festival was established, probably in the 270s, but Delphi did host performances of the important theatrical genre of circular choruses in the Classical period. A distinction must be made between the dithyrambs that were performed annually for Dionysus in Delphi at least from the first half of the fifth century (**Cvi 4–5**) and the circular choruses introduced in the 330s. The dithyrambs were cultic, processional, non-competitive and presumably performed on the Sacred Way and at the temple. 'Circular choruses' were introduced to the programme of the Pythia in the 330s, apparently under strong Athenian influence. These were performed as part of a regular competition and were probably held in a theatrical space built for the occasion (**Cvi 6**). The introduction of the competition was part of a broader campaign to develop the importance of Dionysus in the sanctuary. We do not know the performance format of a non-competitive boys' chorus in a Pythaid celebrated by Athens in Delphi probably in the mid fourth century (**Cvi 7**).

Moving westward from Delphi along the north coast of the Gulf of Corinth, Aetolia has three ancient theatres (Calydon, Makyneia, Pleuron). Beyond the gulf, moving into the Ionian Sea and then northward up the Adriatic Coast there are three theatre sites in Acarnania (Stratos, Oeniadae and Amphilochian Argos), one in Leucas, a further two on the Ambracian Gulf, both in Arta, thirteen in Epirus and a theatre at Corcyra (we do not include Nicopolis, a foundation by Octavian). Of these twenty-three ancient theatres only one certainly dates back to the fourth century, though four or five are probably of fourth-century date.

The medium-sized theatre at Calydon (seating capacity estimated at 5,000) was constructed by the mid fourth century. The recent Dano-Greek excavations uncovered stratigraphy and pottery that indicated use of the theatron 'throughout most of the fourth century BC' and a fourth-century date is confirmed for the skene building as well by the style of some of its architectural remains (Vikatou et al. 2014, 230, 225; Frederiksen 2015, 89–92). An early date is further supported by the rectilinear Π-shape of the theatre. The lower nine rows of stone benches in the centre of the theatron meet the benches of the lateral wings at

90° angles, but beyond that there survive some fifteen rows that join the benches of the lateral wings with increasingly rounded corners. This difference may reflect a second phase of expansion, 'but it is also possible that the change in design has a merely practical explanation due to function or construction' (Vikatou et al. 2014, 224). The style of construction is most like the theatre at Euonymon (**III I**) where the orchestra, as defined by the prohedria, is Π-shaped, but the rows meet with increasingly rounded corners in the upper sections. It is not, on present information, possible to say if the construction dates back to the years when Calydon was a member of the Achaean Federation in the early fourth century (certainly by 389), when the city was thought to be oligarchic in constitution, or to the years after 366 when Epaminondas had conquered the cities of the Federation and briefly changed their constitutions to democratic (*IACP* 384, 474, 478).

Fourth-century dates have also been suggested for the theatres of Oeniadae and Stratos. The mid fourth-century date assigned to the theatre at Oeniadae (Gogos 2004; Kolonas et al. 2009, 43) is based on fairly general historical grounds and is doubted by Isler 2011 and Moretti 2014b, 211–12. It was in any case renewed if not first built in the second half of the third century (*IG* IX 1² 2, 420). At Stratos recent excavations have distinguished three phases of the small to medium-sized theatre (seating over 6,000) of which the first, including both theatron and skene, is placed towards the end of the fourth century (Schwandner 2006, 536–7; Kolonas et al. 2009, 48). Probably third century is the small theatre at Makyneia (estimated capacity of 700). Its unusual shape seems due rather to unambitious than early construction. It is curvilinear in the central part of the theatron and completely rectilinear on the north side (the south side of the theatre is lost, but a wall, if contemporary, suggests that the theatron did not include a south wing: Stiros et al. 2005; Kolonas et al. 2009, 16–17). There are only traces of the foundations of a skene. Some have dated the nearby fortifications to the fourth or third century and, if correct, the same range is likely for the theatre (Stiros et al. 2005, 300). Certainly of third-century date, or later, is the theatre at Pleuron: it is thought to have been built immediately after the foundation of the city in 235/4 (Kolonas et al. 2009, 31). The location of the theatre at Amphilochian Argos is known but it remains unexcavated (Kolonas et al. 2009, 55).

The city of Leucas (**Cvii**) was a crucial point on the shipping route between the northern route that linked Greece and the Adriatic and the western route that linked Greece to the Ionian Sea and hence to Italy and Sicily. Because westerly winds made treacherous the west coast of the peninsula, the inhabitants of Leucas, soon after the city's foundation in the seventh century, dug a canal through the very narrow neck on the north-east side of the peninsula turning Leucas into an island. Sometime, probably in the third century, the Leucadians again connected themselves to the Acarnanian mainland by building a bridge across the Sound of Leucas, a little to the south of the canal (Fiedler and Hermanns 2011). In this way Leucas controlled shipping between Greece and the north and west, and this fact may be significant for understanding the history of theatre on the island and in the wider region. Of particular importance is Leucas' control of the two main routes from Greece to Southern Italy and Sicily: the route from Leucas to Cape Lakinion (near Croton in Bruttium) was a longer alternative to the usual crossing from Corcyra to Cape Iapygia (Morton 2001, 171–2), but even those ships that crossed from Corcyra were likely to pass through the Leucas canal.

Although Leucas' theatre was partly excavated, the excavation was left unpublished. Demosthenes has, however, provided an important testimony of the chance presence in Leucas of the famous actor Kleandros in the very early fourth century (**Cvii**). We do not know if he was performing in Leucas, or simply passing through on his way to or from Italy, by one or the other of these main sea routes. Further excavation of the theatre might show if Leucas in the early fourth century took advantage of the regular passage of theatrical talent to create a theatre festival of its own, but an opportunistic scenario of this sort seems necessary to explain the early development of theatre on the island and its early efflorescence generally in the otherwise remote regions of Aetolia, Acarnania and Epirus. Cities like Makynia, Calydon, Pleuron, and Oeniadae border the main sea link westward through the Corinthian Gulf to the Adriatic, and, as we will see, there are heavy concentrations of early theatre sites on the extremely remote cities of Epirus en route to and in the hinterland of Corcyra. It is noteworthy that Oeniadae was a sea port in the fifth century (Freitag 1994) and that Leucas, Oeniadae and Calydon are all prominently listed as stops on the shipping route between Italy and Corinth described by the *Periplus* of Pseudo-Scylax (34–5; Freitag 1994, 230). Some Athenian influence in the spread of theatre is possible, but less likely to have been a major factor. Oeniadae was of special interest to Athens because of its strategic position guarding the Gulf of Corinth and it appears to have served as an Athenian naval base for some part of the fourth century (certainly in 389: X. *HG* 4.6.14).

The coastal cities north of Leucas have remains of relatively early theatres. Arta has a large theatre and a more recently discovered small theatre, both dated to the late fourth or early third century and both apparently connected to sanctuaries of Apollo (Hammond 1967, 142, 147, 584, 664; Andreou 1976, 199, 201; Karatzeni 1982, 263; Andreou 1983; Merkouri 2012, 151–3). The small theatre covered traces of what might have been an older and larger theatre (Andreou 1976, 199, 201) and it is noteworthy that Epicrates, a poet of Middle Comedy, is of Ambracian origin: he was an author of at least six plays, and appears to have been active from ca. 380–350 (Ath. 10.422f; Nesselrath 2016). We do not hear of theatre performers from Ambracia before the third century (Stefanis nos. 581, 875, 1085, 1838, 1906, 2560), assuming that the fourth-century tragic actor Hippasos mentioned by Alciphron (3.12) is fictitious (Stefanis no. 1280).

Serious archaeological investigation of the large theatre at Cassope on the Thesprotian coast only began in 2011 (Riginos 2012, 143). Baçe dates it to the first quarter of the fourth century stressing formal parallels with Corinth, Isthmia, Argos, Oropus, Apollonia, Cyrene and Hephaistia on Lemnos, especially the U-shaped theatron and the skene with side ramps (2002–2003, 374). But curvilinear theatres, let alone theatres of this 'Peloponnesian type' with side ramps leading to the skene, are not known until well into the second half of the fourth century (Moretti 2014a, 133). Riginos sees close parallels with Dodona and posits a more plausible third-century date (2012, 140).

Corcyra's theatre has not been found but it is epigraphically attested (*IG* IX 1² 4, 798). The document, known only from a transcript published by De Montfaucon, an eighteenth-century Benedictine monk, has been variously dated on historical and orthographic grounds: between 272 and 229 by Guarducci (1967–1978 III, 251); to the second century by Dittenberger and Hallof; and to the end of the third century or the very beginning of the second by Le Guen (2004, 97). The decree establishes a fund for hiring performers, notably three comic and three tragic actors, for a biennial Dionysia. This does not however look like a first foundation. Migeotte argues that the insufficient funds made by the donors, and the anxiety about interruptions caused by a state of war, suggest that the donation was designed to restore to the festival 'un éclat qu'elle avait perdu' (2010, 64). Location and perhaps political development (Corcyra was a democracy until at least 361: Robinson 2011, 122–8) favoured an early development of theatre in this region, but evidence before the third century is entirely lacking.

Third-century starts are also likely for the theatres in neighbouring Thesprotis of Gitana and Dodona. The theatre of Gitana (Goumani) has only recently been excavated: after surface clearing and some preliminary investigation in 1996–1997 (Touchais 1998, 801), excavation began in 2006 and continues to the present day (Preka-Alexandri 2012, 111). Baçe, who examined the visible surface remains before excavation, assigned the theatron a fifth-century date on the belief that the seating within each wedge was rectilinear, giving the theatron a polygonal form (2002–2003, 367–9). The seven rock-cut wedges of the theatron are in fact curvilinear (Preka-Alexandri 2012, 111 fig. 2). The excavator thinks the stone theatre is the first in this location and assigns a third-century date on the basis of architectural parallels, letter forms of the manumission inscriptions on the seats, and coins found in the theatre (Preka-Alexandri 2012, 115). The first construction at the magnificent theatre at Dodona is also dated no earlier than 297–272 (Antoniou 2015, 180; Pliakou and Smyris 2012). The theatres of Elea (= Chrisavgi-Veliani) and Amotopos have not been excavated (Sear 2006, 410).

Bouthrotum, immediately across the strait from Corcyra, may also have had a fourth-century start. Ugolini (1931–1932), followed by Baçe (2002–2003, 394), dates the theatre to the fourth century, but the most complete publication of the evidence dates it to the beginning of the third century (Gilkes 2003, esp. Sear 2003, 181–2). Unfortunately the manumission inscriptions in the theatre do not (*pace* Baçe) support an earlier date (Cabanes 1974). Sear (2003) however suspects that there may have been an earlier phase. Nothing can be said of the now scarcely visible theatre at Onchesmos, the port city just to the north of Bouthrotum and very little of the port of Orikon's theatre, whose rock-cut seats are dated to the second century (Sear 2006, 414). The poor remains of the two theatres in the hinterland of Onchesmos, at Phonike and Antigoneia, are undatable.

A shorter and more northerly route across the Adriatic went from Apollonia to Hydruntum (Otranto): so close that Pyrrhus is said to have wanted to bridge the strait (Plin. *HN* 3.101). The crossing from Apollonia became more important as the power of Rome grew and especially after the Via Appia was extended to Brundisium in 264. It is in the second half of the third century that the theatre at Apollonia, one of the largest in the Mediterranean, was built in the sanctuary of the city's patron god, Apollo (Fiedler 2014, 260; Fiedler et al. 2011; von Hesberg and Eck 2008; Franz and Hinz 2015). Excavation in the orchestra did uncover the traces of a curvilinear wooden construction of the same orientation and size as the stone theatron, allowing for speculation that the third-century theatre replaced a possibly much earlier one (Fiedler 2014, 261, fig. 14). A third-century development of the theatre industry in the area is supported by the evidence for the theatres of Bylis and Nikaia in the hinterland of Apollonia. The theatre at Byllis is dated by Baçe to 'the second half or sooner the end of the fourth century', claiming that the plan of the stoa and theatre indicate that they were built at the same time as the city wall (2002–2003, 385). Soueref dates the theatre more plausibly to the middle of the third century (2012, 17) and this agrees with the probable dates of the theatre inscriptions (Ceka 1987, 73–5 nos. 1–3, 117). According to Baçe, the letter forms and formulae used in manumission inscriptions on the analemma walls of the smaller theatre at ?Nikaia (= Klos; *SEG* 38, 559–68f) indicate a fourth-century date, while architectural features (drains, irregular form of the orchestra, single narrow parodos) indicate a date before the middle of the fourth century (2002–2003, 391 and n. 73). Ceka dates the inscriptions to the second century (1987, 85–91 nos. 23–40, 117) and the theatre to the late third (1987, 116). The latter date is supported by Soueref on the basis of its integration with the agora and broader urban setting (2012, 17). No theatre performers of Epirote origin are known before the third century (Stefanis nos. 1846, 1883).

Central Mainland (Opous, Magnesia, Thessaly) (**Cviii–Cxi**)

The evidence for theatre in the eastern mainland between Boeotia and Macedon is mainly literary for the fifth and fourth centuries. The earliest attests a performance by Kallippides in 406/5 in Opous, but relies on an obviously fictional anecdote (**Cviii**). There are no remains of ancient theatres in Locris (what was once reported to be an unexcavated theatre in Naryx in Epiknemidian Locris is merely a concavity produced by the collapse of a hillside: González et al. 2013, 29; Pascual 2013, 179).

More believable is the textual tradition that Euripides received honours in Magnesia and from there departed to Macedon (**Cix 1**). The information seems to echo the language of a local decree and, if historically accurate, is likely to relate to Euripides' main occupation as a tragedian: though he seems occasionally to have done ambassadorial duty (**Axi 1–2**), this too was doubtless ultimately based on his fame as a tragedian. The relatively early development of theatre in Thessaly is attested by questionable anecdotes connected to the behaviour of Jason of Pherae (**Cx**), and by a marginally more reliable account of the fall of Skotoussa (**Cxi**). The sources are only weakly corroborated by reported remains of theatres in both locations: the actual theatre of Pherae (**Cx**), though it has been located, remains unexcavated; while that at Skotoussa (**Cxi**), though reported as 'clearly visible' by early twentieth-century travellers, is now no longer so.

Of the other theatres in Thessaly, a fourth-century phase has only been suggested for the small theatre (seating about 3,000) of Thebes in Phthiotis, though the visible remains are third century. The supposition of a wooden predecessor for the Hellenistic theatre is based on the large amount of pottery and coins of the fourth century found during the excavation of the theatre (Adrimi-Sismani 2011, 53, 63–5). The two theatres at Larissa can be dated to the beginning of the third and the first century respectively (Tziafalias 2011, 23, 27). A second-century theatre with competitions and a prohedria is attested for Phalanna (*IG* IX 2, 1230, ll. 25–20). In Magnesia, the medium-sized theatre at Demetrias was probably built at the time the city was founded by Demetrius the Besieger in 293 (Intzesiloglou 2011). It, along with his refoundations of Corinth (**Biv**) and Sicyon (**Bv**), attest the importance Demetrius attributed to theatre (**VI L**).

Macedon and Thrace (**Cxii–Cxiv**)

The documentation for the reception of theatre in Macedon from the late fifth century onwards is particularly rich. This volume collects only the documents related to the Festival of Zeus and the Muses and theatrical remains relevant to that festival (**Cxii**). Volume 3 (**VI**)

collects the evidence relevant to the patronage of poets and actors and other theatrical competitions organised by Archelaus (**VI D**), Philip (**VI F**), Alexander (**VI G**) and Demetrius
the Besieger (**VI L**).

Macedonia and Thrace are rich in wood and poor in marble. The earliest theatres, consequently, were of wood and have left only scant traces (Velenis 2012). It is to ancient historical and literary texts that we must turn to reconstruct the initial importation of theatre into
Macedon by Archelaus in the last decade of the fifth century. Archelaus usurped the throne
in 413 and until his assassination in 399 he pursued a policy of Hellenisation in which
theatre played a pivotal role. From about 410 he invited many of the most preeminent
culture heroes of the Greek world to take up residence at the court. These included such
celebrities as the lyric poets Melanippides and Timotheus, the epic poet Choerilus, the phy-
sicians Hippocrates and Thessalus, his son, the architect Callimachus, the painter Zeuxis,
as well as the tragedians Euripides and Agathon and possibly the comic poet Plato (**VI D**).
Archelaus seems also to have encouraged more local talent: the earliest Macedonian poet,
Arribaeus, and Krateuas of Thessaly are said by Suda (ε 3695; cf. Headlam's emendation
to Hermesian. 7.68) to have been poets, jealous of Euripides, which some take to imply
that they wrote tragedy.

It seems likely that Archelaus' guests resided primarily in the older capital, Aegae
(Vergina), though Archelaus is credited with the construction of a new palace in Pella, a
city he probably redesigned to serve as his new capital. The presence at Archelaus' court
of the architect Callimachus presumably had something to do with the designing of the
new capital and Zeuxis is specifically said to have been commissioned to paint Archelaus'
'house' (**VI Div 11**). But that the palace at Pella was still under construction during much
of this time is strongly suggested by the discovery of the tomb of Callimachus at Aegae,
which should indicate that Aegae was the architect's main residence during the construction
of the new palace at Pella (**VI Div 9**). Both locations would have suited Archelaus' guests.

The palace at Pella had many guest rooms, but there is no trace of a theatre at Pella
and no literary attestation of Pella's theatre until ca. 335 when Alexander is said to have
been dissuaded from building a proskenion of bronze (Plu. *Mor.* 1096b). Nonetheless, the
discovery at Pella of a very large number of terracotta tragic, satyric and comic figurines,
both imported and locally made, dating from as early as 400–375, suggests that the theatre
Alexander wished to renovate formed part of Archelaus' plan for his new capital (Chasapi-
Christodoulou 1991–1992 counts 16 tragic and satyric and 18 Old and Middle Comic figurines from Pella; cf. Adam-Veleni 2012, 21; Giannou 2016, 52). The palace at Aegae
(**Cxii**), on the other hand, appears to have had a theatre built onto it in Archelaus' day.
There are archaeological traces of an early fourth-century phase, and an inscription, found
in the area of the theatre, has been taken to indicate a late fifth-century phase. Aegae would
of course have been an ideal location for the production of Euripides' *Archelaus*, a play that
ancient sources tell us was written to please Archelaus (**VI Di 14**; Diom. 3.9.3) and that
dealt with the foundation of Aegae and the dynasty whose legitimate issue was Archelaus
himself. It is, however, not till the day that Philip was assassinated in 336 (D.S. 16.92) that
we can be sure a tragic performance was envisioned for Aegae's theatre.

The theatre festival founded by Archelaus for Olympian Zeus and the Muses is certainly
to be located at Dion (**Cxii**). The festival probably included drama from its foundation, but

comedy is only specifically attested in 348 (**Cxii 7**; cf. Hartwig 2014, 220 n. 98). Dion also had a Dionysia with theatrical performances by the last quarter of the fourth century (**Cxii 5**). Archaeological exploration of Dion's theatre reveals a pre-Hellenistic phase which some think goes back to the fifth century (**Cxii**). All told, it seems likely that drama was performed at Aegae and Dion from the time of Archelaus and then at Pella from late in his reign or soon afterwards. No other sites in old Macedonia are relevant to our investigation: Beroia's theatre and musical contests are only epigraphically attested from the early second century (*EKM* 1 Beroia 140; *SEG* 17, 315; Giannou 2016, 76), while the theatre at Mieza appears to be of very late Hellenistic date (Sear 2006, 418; Allamani-Souri et al. 2012).

Philip and Alexander shared Archelaus' enthusiasm for all genres of theatre and integrated it into their lives and campaigns in a way that anticipated (and indeed served as a model for) the use of theatre in Hellenistic ruler cult (**VI F–G**). In the present volume we are mainly interested in their role in the spread of theatre to other cities through Greece, Asia Minor and beyond. Philip seems to have been responsible for building the palace and theatre at Aegae whose remains were excavated in the last two decades of the twentieth century: the buildings interact structurally and must both have formed part of the original plan (Velenis 2012, 35–44). Philip was also responsible for introducing theatre in other locations. In 356 Philip conquered and refounded the city of Crenides in a slightly different location and named it, after himself, Philippi. We are told that he built the city's walls (App. *BC* 4.105) but he evidently planned the monumental buildings of the town as well, since the east side of the theatron bonds with the walls (Koukouli-Chrysanthaki and Karadedos 2012, 193–5). This could be compared with Philip's introduction of theatre into the refounded cities of Boeotian Orchomenus (**Civ**) and Plataea, mentioned above. Some (e.g. Manieri 2015) think him primarily responsible for the first competitions of cyclic choruses at Delphi (**Cvi**). Alexander's role in spreading theatre is far more important, though all lasting effects appear to have had more to do with the political realities of the Hellenistic world he created than to his rapid passage through Asia Minor and the Near East. This topic will be explored in the Introduction to theatre in Asia Minor (**E**).

Theatre culture may have existed in a number of cities on the north coast of the Aegean before they were incorporated into the Macedonian empire. The theatre at Amphipolis has been located but not systematically excavated (Peristeri 2012). As an Athenian colony (from 427/6) theatrical activity seems likely from the fifth century, but we have no evidence except for a few comic figurines (Chasapi-Christodoulou 1991–1992, 275) before Aemilius Paulus held victory games in Amphipolis after the Battle of Pydna in 168 (Liv. 45.32.8–33.5). Olynthus too is a likely candidate for theatre based on the very large number of figurines of tragic and comic actors and on the fact that several important fourth-century theatricians were natives of Olynthus: the tragic poet Euphantus (*TrGF* 118), the famous comic actor Satyros (Stefanis no. 2235) and the kitharode, Aristonikos (Stefanis no. 367). Chasapi-Christodoulou (1991–1992, 271–2) records 1 tragic and 35 comic figurines from Olynthus, some of which are Attic imports and some local imitations, all from the first half of the fourth century (Olynthus was destroyed in the summer of 348). Robinson (1930, 6, figs. 43, 45) identified a naturally hollowed hillside as a possible site for a theatre, but excavation yielded no remains. This should not be too discouraging, given the region and the early date, as the theatre was probably entirely of wood which could leave few traces. Abdera (**Cxiii**) and Maroneia (**Cxiv**) may have acquired their theatre culture under Athenian influence, if not under Philip when he took the cities in 354–353.

Ci: Oropus, Sanctuary of Amphiaraus

The territory of Oropus (Oropia), between Attica and Boeotia, fell successively for much of its history in the Classical period under the power of these two. It became an Athenian possession either after the Athenians gained the upper hand over Boeotia around 506, or some decades later, following the destruction of Eretria in the Persian Wars. Prior to this time it appears to have been under the strong influence of Eretria, directly opposite over the Euripos on the island of Euboea. Oropus remained under Athens for most of the fifth century, but was never incorporated into the Cleisthenic system of demes. Its famous shrine of the healer hero Amphiaraus was founded in the last quarter of the fifth century, following the decline of the Amphiareion of Thebes. The new foundation was doubtless presented as a transference of the Theban cult and the shrine thereafter became the identifying polis cult of Oropus (Petrakos 1995, 12; Str. 9.2.10).

The fourth century presents a rather more complicated picture. After a short period of independence from 411 to 402, Oropus briefly fell under the power of Thebes, then became a member of the Boeotian Confederacy. It presumably gained independence when the Confederacy was dissolved in 386, but chose to join Athens again some time around 374. By 366 it had been captured by the tyrants of Eretria, and the ensuing threat of conflict with Athens ended up seeing Oropus under Theban control, though retaining some form of political independence. The Oropia was transferred to Athens perhaps by Philip in 338, or by Alexander in 335 after the destruction of Thebes, when its territory was divided between the Athenian tribes (Papazarkadas 2011, 102–6). Athens held it until 322, when Oropus became independent once more, but only until it was seized by the Antigonid general Ptolemaios, under whose influence it rejoined the Boeotian Confederacy, until Antigonus' son Demetrius the Besieger withdrew it from the Confederacy and (briefly) restored it to Athens (Petrakos 1995, 5–11; Parker 1996, 146–9; Hansen in *IACP* 448–9 no. 214 'Oropos'; Knoepfler 2001a, 371–80).

The sanctuary of Amphiaraus, just over 2 km east of the city of Oropus, has a relatively well-preserved Hellenistic theatre, situated immediately behind the large Doric stoa, to the north-east of the temple and baths, and clearly integral to the overall design of the sanctuary (Fiechter 1930; Petrakos 1968, 84–94; Travlos 1988, 302 and fig. 380; Goette 1995c; Bressan 2009, 69–75). This is dated to the late third or early second century, largely on the basis of two dedicatory inscriptions, one of which attests to the construction and dedication by an agonothete of the proskenion and its pinakes around that time (*IOrop.* 430); while the other is evidence for a substantial rebuilding of the skene in the middle of the second century (*IOrop.* 435). This was long thought to be the oldest theatre at the site, but a few scholars, notably Dörpfeld and Reisch (1896, 103), had already concluded that there had been a Classical phase to the Oropus theatre, although without detailed argument. Goette (1995c) provided this, arguing convincingly that the first theatre was constructed out of wood around 420. This is the time when the sanctuary complex was being established under Athenian control. It was also a time when Oropus was essential to Athenian strategic needs, notably for the secure access it gave to the major Athenian holdings on Euboea (Moreno 2007, 115–18).

Two significant features indicate the existence of this earlier phase. The first is four courses of parallel, basically rectilinear blocks of poros on the east side of the theatron, best seen in the photographs of Anti and Polacco (1969, 54–74), who report a study of them made in 1955 that first revealed their importance. Fiechter (1930) noted them on his plan but made no reference to them in his text. These were evidently seating and/or standing terraces for spectators from an earlier structure, incorporated into the later semi-circular theatron. Anti and Polacco (1969, 71–4) effectively dispense with the notion of Leonardos and Dörpfeld that they merely served to secure the ground as part of the works for the Hellenistic theatre. Goette (1995c, 254) argues on this basis that the earlier theatre had a rectilinear seating system with an orientation that differs by about 45 degrees from the later one.

The second point concerns the skene. Goette interprets a number of stone blocks found immediately to the south of the poros wall at the stage building as evidence of an earlier phase of the skene. These were designed to receive wooden uprights, and are therefore very probably to be associated with a front wall made of wood of an early stage building. The back of this simple stage would have consisted of breccia foundations in front of a retaining wall, with earth fill. This is also consistent with the evidence of Fiechter's section drawing through the stage building (Fiechter 1930, Taf. 2).

The first concrete evidence for performances of drama in the Oropus theatre appears only in the first century, when satyr play, tragedy and comedy are all attested (*IOrop.* 523–6, 528, 531), as well as epic, in the context of the Amphiareia and Rhomaia (on the appended festival in honour of Rome, see Buraselis 2012, 255–6). But there is no doubt that drama dates back at least to the third-century phase of the theatre and probably also back to its rectilinear late fifth-century precursor. In the third century the Oropians award substantial honours to a number of theatre people: the comic actor Polyaratos from Cyrene (Stefanis no. 2090; **Gi**) – along with his descendants – is granted proxeny, status as benefactor and various other valuable honours 'because of his ongoing good-will and usefulness to the city' (*IOrop.* 25, ll. 3–5); Kleonikos the *tragoidos* from Rhodes is similarly honoured, notably in this case because he offered his services to the city both in a public capacity and in private (*IOrop.* 179, ll. 2–4: ἐπειδὴ Κλεόνικος ὁ τραγωιδὸς | εὔνους ὢν διατελεῖ τῆι τε πόλει κοινῆι καὶ ἰδίαι τοῖς δεομέ|νοις τῶν πολιτῶν παρέχεται χρείας ἐμ παντὶ καιρῶι, with Manieri 2009, 229); the prompt for the honours to Demokrates son of Philokles of Athens is his 'good-will and usefulness to the city' as a poet who 'elected to compose poetic enco-mia for the god' (*IOrop.* 63, ll. 3–4: καὶ τὸν θεὸν προαιρεῖται ἐνκωμιάζειν | διὰ ποιημάτων; cf. *IOrop.* 211).

We thus have an instance of drama performed for a god other than Dionysus, though still within a festival context. There may have been a cult of Dionysus in the region, at a place called Aulon that lay within the Oropia, but there is no evidence for a Dionysia: a cult table dedicated to Dionysus Auloneus was discovered near Oropus in reuse in the wall of a chapel at Kako-Salesi (*IG* II² 4745, 1ˢᵗ c. AD; Solders 1931, 42 no. 32; Gill 1991, 45–7 no. 15). This may have been an offering set up in the Amphiareion, which would bring Dionysus into the orbit of the sanctuary. Intriguingly, the only other evidence for this cult comes from a prohedric seat inscription in the Theatre of Dionysus in Athens, where the priest of Dionysus Auloneus had a seat in Imperial times (*IG* II³ 4, 1886).

A theatre is thus virtually certain and drama in it likely under the period of Athenian control of Oropus in the later fifth century. They will have served as a marker of Athenian culture on a site that played such an important role in external relations with neighbouring Boeotia, the previous owners of the cult; but also as a familiar appurtenance for those Athenians who lived in the area, far from the city of Athens. Whether performed in the context of the Amphiareia at the earlier date (as much later), or at an unattested local Dionysia, the performance of drama at Oropus may have formed part of the same 'circuit' as the Attic deme Dionysia (the place in the calendar of the Amphiareia is unknown). The Amphiareia is best attested in the (late) Classical period from a victor list of the 'Great', quadrennial, version (*IOrop.* 520 with Manieri 2009, 225–8), probably that of 329 or perhaps 325, perhaps under a new refurbishment by the luminaries of the Lycurgan establishment, notably Phanodemus (*IOrop.* 298 of 329/8; cf. *IOrop.* 297; *IG* II³ 1, 449, ll. 21–6; Scafuro 2009). Drama does not appear in this document, and the contests are athletic, equestrian and (on a somewhat more restricted basis) musical, plus an event in 'sophistry' (*IOrop.* 520, l. 8). Manieri (2009, 214) intriguingly suggests that this last – no doubt a contest in oratory of some kind – may have been a sort of homage to the illustrious contemporary orators such as Demades and Lycurgus. Petrakos thinks of speeches in praise of Amphiaraus, of which *IOrop.* 301 may partially preserve an example. The events are open to contestants from all over Greece. The festival – with equestrian contests in some form – is attested as early as ca. 400 (*IOrop.* 335).

We have evidence for a second theatron at the Amphiareion from the Classical period. In a set of inscribed instructions to the contractor in a contract for works of ca. 335–322 designed to improve the plumbing in the men's baths (*IOrop.* 292, ll. 28–33), the contractor is instructed to 'make use of stones from the theatre which is opposite the altar' (λί<θ>οις δὲ χρήσεται τοῖς ἐκ τοῦ θεάτρου τοῦ κατὰ τ|ὸ[μ] βωμόν). This 'theatre opposite the altar' will refer to a 'theatral structure' (θεατροειδὲς κτίσμα Petrakos 1968, 98) the remains of which have been found directly in front of the altar of Amphiaraus (Petrakos 1968, 98–9 with plan 19 and image 17). Only three bow-shaped tiers of poros seating around 20 m long survive. As the contract indicates, it already went out of use in the fourth century, since its materials were given over for reuse in other structures. This theatron was doubtless designed for observation of sacred activities at the altar and the small temple behind it. Given the absence of virtually anything that might serve as an acting space, it is extremely unlikely ever to have hosted drama. (Dörpfeld 1922, 26–8 thought that it went out of use when the large theatre was built, implying a continuity of purpose, but Petrakos 1968, 99 rightly emphasises the very different purposes of each structure.) It is however possible, perhaps likely, that the use of the specification in the contract 'the theatre opposite the altar' was in part intended to distinguish this theatron from the other one that already existed.

From at least the early third century, and continuing into the second, the city of Oropus held a choral contest, possibly dithyramboid, for the nymph Halia, daughter of Ocean, sister of the Telchines and lover of Poseidon (according to D.S. 5.55–6; for the dithyramb's associations with Poseidon see Csapo 2003; Kowalzig 2013, 52; and note that at Argos Haliai was the name of maenads in Dionysus' train: Paus. 2.22.1). This was supported by choregoi, and the prize was a tripod, subsequently dedicated by the winner (*IOrop*. 511–19; Manieri 2009, 217–18, 253–8; Agelidis 2009, 19–20, 32–3, 107–8, 122–3, 238–44). The form of these choregic dedications bears notable similarities with those from the Eretrian theatre (**Dvii**), and Knoepfler (2010a, 234) intriguingly suggests that the Oropians, newly liberated from Athenian control, may have turned to the city with which they had ancient ancestral links for the model. Although the shrine of Halia has not been securely located, there is no doubt that it was somewhere near the city of Oropus, close to the sea (Petrakos 1997, 401–3; Agelidis 2009, 122–3). Manieri (2009, 217) thinks the choral contest will have been held at the nymph's sanctuary near the city, but Agelidis (2009, 123) proposes the use of the theatre in the Amphiareion, given its availability and the unlikelihood that there will have been two suitable performance spaces in the rather sparsely populated area around Oropus.

Cii: City of Thebes. Plutarch, *Precepts of Statecraft* (*Moralia*) 799e–f. Written (perhaps soon) after 96 AD and relating to the first of possibly two trials of Epaminondas in the spring and summer of 369 (for the confusion of the different trials see Cary 1924; Cuff 1954; Beister 1970, 75–80; Stylianou 1998, 468–9). Epaminondas, Pelopidas and the other boiotarchs were put on trial for having extended their command while they took the war with Sparta to the Peloponnese. Advising that anyone going into politics must understand the character of their fellow citizens, Plutarch illustrates with examples what public actions different nations are willing to tolerate. The episode of the captured letters of Philip mentioned by Plutarch is also referred to in the second letter of Philip that has come down with the Demosthenic corpus (D. 12.2). Text: Fowler.

> οἶμαι δ᾽ ἂν ἔγωγε μηδὲ Θηβαίους ἀποσχέσθαι γραμμάτων πολεμίων κυρίους γενομένους, ὡς Ἀθηναῖοι Φιλίππου γραμματοφόρους λαβόντες ἐπιστολὴν ἐπιγεγραμμένην Ὀλυμπιάδι κομίζοντας οὐκ ἔλυσαν οὐδ᾽ ἀπεκάλυψαν ἀπόρρητον ἀνδρὸς ἀποδήμου πρὸς γυναῖκα φιλοφροσύνην· οὐδέ γ᾽ αὖ πάλιν Ἀθηναίους, Ἐπαμεινώνδου πρὸς τὴν κατηγορίαν ἀπολογεῖσθαι μὴ [799f] θέλοντος ἀλλ᾽ ἀναστάντος ἐκ τοῦ θεάτρου καὶ διὰ τῆς ἐκκλησίας εἰς τὸ γυμνάσιον ἀπιόντος, εὐκόλως ἐνεγκεῖν τὴν ὑπεροψίαν καὶ τὸ φρόνημα τοῦ ἀνδρός·

> I think, if they got hold of them, the Thebans would not be able to keep their hands from the letters of the enemy, as did the Athenians after they seized the letter bearers of Philip who were carrying a letter addressed to Olympias. They neither unsealed nor opened the private greetings of a travelling man to his wife. Nor, conversely, would the Athenians have borne easily the contempt and arrogance of Epaminondas, when he [799f] refused to defend himself on the charge, but stood up and left the theatre, going through the assembly into the gymnasium.

This passage provides the only textual evidence for a 'theatre' in fourth-century Thebes, albeit in this instance, functioning as an Assembly and a Court. It is difficult to assess the reliability of Plutarch's testimony.

Plutarch was himself a Boeotian (from Chaeronea) and took a particular interest in the history of the region. The first five pairings of his *Parallel Lives* seem to have been chosen for their Boeotian connection (Stadter 2014, 123): a *Life of Epaminondas*, paired with Scipio, was the first biography in Plutarch's original work (Peper 1912; Irigoin 1986; Georgiadou 1997, 6–8). Despite his regional interests, Plutarch is not uncritical, especially as regards the Thebans and their poor treatment of Epaminondas, whom he greatly admired (Georgiadou 1997, 8–9). Plutarch had a variety of sources for this period of Theban history, but probably relied mainly on Ephorus and Callisthenes of Olynthus, both contemporaries of Epaminondas, and both admirers of the Theban statesman and general (Georgiadou 1997, 15–29). All this might seem to encourage belief in the accuracy of Plutarch's account. But comparison with other mentions of the same trial in Plutarch (*Pel.* 25; *Mor.* 194a–c, 540d–e, 817f) shows that in this passage Plutarch 'has put a different coloring on Epameinondas' conduct in that he now describes it as contemptuous rather than patient' (Buckler 1978, 38). Indeed, none of the other treatments implies that he left the proceedings before being acquitted. It may be that Plutarch has dramatised this version, but could the dramatisation have extended to his characterising the venue as a 'theatre'? Plutarch in *Pelopidas* 25 refers to the location as a *dikasterion* (cf. App. *Syr.* 218; Ael. *VH* 13.42), but this may be because it was functioning as such.

Despite Thebes' close associations with Dionysus (Schachter 1981, 185–92), we know very little about the Dionysia in Thebes. A festival of Dionysus may have been celebrated in Thebes from at least the early fifth century and have served as the venue for Pindar's second dithyramb, which is said to have been 'for the Thebans' (Lavecchia 2000, 121–2). Moreover this dithyramb appears to be referred to as 'circular' (D'Angour 1997, 344) and so may allude to the term 'circular chorus', though that term is not attested for the lyric choruses that performed in the Athenian theatre until 415. We have, however, no direct attestation of a Dionysia in Thebes until the first half of the third century.

In Pindar's day when Thebes was securely oligarchic, Theban choruses appear to have been sponsored and also physically led by wealthy aristocratic families (Wilson 2000, 280–1; 2011a, 23–5). No form of the verb χοραγείω, the proper Boeotian term for the formal sponsorship of a chorus (as in the choregia at Athens), is attested earlier than the inscribed monuments at Orchomenus (**Civ**). Plutarch, however, informs us that Pelopidas and his associates lent money to Epaminondas so he could serve as choregos for a men's chorus (Plu. *Arist.* 1.4; discussed in **V F**). Not only does this passage imply the existence of a formal liturgy that could be filled by any man who had the means, but it also suggests the importation of the theatrical genre properly known as 'men's chorus', for which we have no earlier attestation in Thebes. The connection with Pelopidas and his followers points to the decade after the coup of 379 that brought the democrats into power in Thebes (**Cv 4**) and before 369, the date of Epaminondas' trial. Otherwise we hear only a century later of Pythokles who won a crown 'for Dionys[us K]admeios' (**Cv 5**). Pythokles seems to have had many talents but the most clearly attested connect him with theatrical choruses (see on **Cv 4**). The trieteric Theban festival for Dionysus Kadmeios included tragedy and comedy at least by the 220s. This is clear from a series of decrees in which the Delphic Amphictyony grants *asylia* (safe passage) to performers (including tragic and comic) attending the festival (*CID* IV 70–2; *ATD* I, 134–9 no. 20; Rigsby 1996, 68–75; Aneziri 2003, 358–60). The festival was probably renamed Agrionia when the games were reorganised before 170 (Robert 1990, 778; *ATD* TE 45) and then later became the Dionysia-Herakleia (Robert 1990, 765–80).

A theatre may have been found in the north-east part of Thebes, near the Proetid Gate (recently relocated by Osanna 2008), where Pausanias puts it (Paus. 9.16.6; Germani 2012; Germani 2015b). Sporadic excavations over the last fifty years have uncovered what appear to be analemma walls and part of a skene (Germani 2012, 988) or proskenion (Oikonomou 2013, 51–3), drainage channels and a fragment of a prohedric marble seat (Germani 2012, 988). The excavation of other stone seats was reported by neighbours (Symeonoglou 1985, 139). Most of the pottery associated with the walls and 'skene' or 'proskenion' was from Roman times and is associated with the skene that was rebuilt by Sulla (Plu. *Sull.* 19; and the inscription recorded by Aravantinos 1998). Germani dates the skene to the third century (2015b, 355). While earlier reports mentioned only Roman pottery, these conclusions are put in doubt by a recent cleaning of the analemma walls (2008) which yielded classical sherds (Germani 2012, 990). Germani dates the remains stylistically, on the analogy of the theatre at Eretria, to the third century (2012, 990–1). Conceivably it is the same location as the theatre mentioned in which Epaminondas sponsored a men's chorus and was tried – but that theatre was presumably destroyed when Alexander levelled Thebes in 335.

Thebes produced an extraordinary number of often very famous pipers. We know of at least twenty from the fifth and fourth centuries (Stefanis nos. 196, 390, 1295, 1387, 1475, 1564, 1633, 1932, 1936, 1938, 1957, 2131, 2149, 2388, 2417, 2594, 2598, 2613, 2619, 2926), as well as kitharists/kitharodes (Stefanis nos. 345, 1198, 1572), singers (no. 1465) and a didaskalos, Polyzelus, who trained the winning boys' chorus at the Thargelia in 363/2 (no. 2097). By contrast, it is not until the second and first centuries that we hear of Theban poets or performers in any dramatic genre.

Several comic figurines of Boeotian manufacture have been found in and around Thebes from the second quarter to the end of the fourth century. It is not known which if any are of Theban or Tanagran manufacture, so it is unclear what relevance they may have to possible performances in the city of Thebes itself. They reveal a distinctive form of comedy, though one that is gradually assimilated to the Panhellenic norm as the century advances (Green 2014a, 338–44).

Ciii: 'Comic' Vase from Cabirion, late 5th to second quarter of 4th c., and more narrowly to 410–400 (style: Braun and Haevernick 1981, 8).

> Boeotian black-figured 'Cabiric' skyphos attributed to Mystes Painter ('Mystenmaler': Bruns; a.k.a. 'Thetis Painter': Ure).
> H: 0.154 m.
> The scene of Odysseus and Circe is generally known as Side A. The other side has a scene of Odysseus (inscribed) fleeing over the sea on a pair of amphorae and blown by Borias (inscribed). Said to be from Thebes. Acquired by the Ashmolean Museum from the collection of the Belgian Alphonse van Branteghem (Tsingarida 2002; 2014) which was auctioned in Paris, 15–18 June 1892 (Froehner 1892, no. 210).
> Oxford, Ashmolean Museum G 249 (V 262).
> Walters 1892–1893, 79, 81 fig. 2; Gardiner 1893, 18–19 no. 263, pl. 26; Wolters and Bruns 1940, 109 M16; *MMC*[3] BV 1; Walsh 2009, 315 no. 93.
> Photos: Vickers 1999, 52 no. 46; Walsh 2009, 200 pl. 77a–b.

The sanctuary of the Cabirion is located about 6 km south-west of Thebes. It was the site of a mystery religion for a father and son, Kabiros and Pais, known collectively as the Cabiri, and for a goddess known as 'the Mother' (Schachter 2016b, 339). Active worship of the Cabiri is attested from ca. 600 until the second century AD or later. The earliest evidence comes in the form of some 400 lead or bronze figurines of bulls, 37 of which bear inscriptions. Among them the dedication 'KA' offers a fairly clear indication that the Cabiri were worshipped in the sanctuary from the late seventh or early sixth century (Schachter 2016b, 329).

The name 'Kabiros', as it appears in the Boeotian inscriptions, has long been thought related to Phoenician Kabir 'Lord' (Schachter 1986, 96 n. 4), but Beekes more recently argued that the name is of Anatolian origin (2004). Ancient and modern authors compare the cults of Samothrace and Lemnos (Bedigan 2008, 38–44), though it is not entirely clear how useful comparison with these cults can be for understanding the origins and nature of the Boeotian cult. The identification of the Lemnian and Samothracian cults as Cabiric depends upon the more or less syncretistic impulses of our Greek sources (Bremmer 2014, 32–8, 54; Schachter 2016b, 315).

Though within Theban territory for most of its existence the Cabirion was probably independent and only came under Theban administration in the late fourth century (Schachter 2016b, 316). It appears that the mysteries, like those of Eleusis or Samothrace, were open to all, regardless of ethnicity, gender or social status, but the use of the sanctuary was limited in practice to inhabitants of Boeotia (Schachter 2016b, 316–17).

No ancient literary or epigraphic source connects the sanctuary with theatrical performances. The connection is made by modern scholarship for two reasons:

1. The Cabirion had a theatral area.
2. Several modern scholars have taken the images of vasepaintings associated with the Cabirion as depictions of a form of comedy that was performed there, whether a strictly cultic performance related to the mysteries, or something more akin to contemporary comedy performed elsewhere in Greece.

Both reasons are highly problematic.

The extant 'theatre-like' structure, which seats ca. 1,400 spectators, was built in the Cabirion in the second half of the first century AD (Sear 2006, 408). Of its irregularly shaped theatron there survive six rows of seats divided into eleven kerkides. There was never a stage building. The Roman theatre is therefore half a millennium later than the vasepaintings. It appears, however, that the natural hillside upon which the theatre was built had a long use as a theatral area prior to the construction of the Roman theatre. The hillside was extended and shaped several times: in the fourth century; in the second quarter of the third century; and in the second half of the first century (Schachter 2016b, 320–4). It is therefore possible and even likely that the bare hillside served as a viewing area in relation to sanctuary activities from at least the fourth century. Ceramic finds suggest that the hillside was at the hub of cultic activities from at least 380 to 334 (Bedigan 2008, 194–5).

Far more important than the existence of a theatral area are a small but very suggestive group of images found on Cabiric wares. Significant ceramic remains of drinking vessels, both local and imported, are found at the Cabirion from the sixth century onwards. The remains show a sharp increase in ceramics relating to feasting at the beginning of the fifth century, especially drinking vessels, like skyphoi, bowls and kantharoi, while large quantities of cooking vessels appear then for the first time (Bedigan 2008, 178–81). Cabiric Ware begins to be produced around 450 (a couple of later sixth-century precursors are dubbed 'Proto-Cabiric': Bedigan 2008, 166–7, 171), and it continues until the early third century, with most of the figured vases produced ca. 400–330 (Braun and Haevernick 1981). There are very good reasons for supposing that the vessels were used for ritual feasts that took place in the sanctuary. The range of uses to which the Cabiric wares could be put is indeed limited by the fact that they did not leave the environs of the sanctuary: they were produced by potters and painters at the Cabirion and evidently for the Cabirion (Sparkes 1967, 125; Heimberg 1982) and most were dedicated in the sanctuary, presumably directly after use (Wolters and Bruns 1940, 43–80; Heimberg 1982, 4; Schachter 1986, 67). The fragments of Cabiric ware that have been excavated are predominantly associated with buildings that appear to be designed for feasting (Cooper and Morris 1990, 66), although a few were found in tombs in Thebes, Thespiae and possibly Tanagra, and at the end of the fourth century as far away as Ceos and Aegina (Bedigan 2008, 178, 204).

The earliest painters of Cabiric ware's figural scenes, like the Argos Painter (dated '445/440–400/395' by Avronidaki), have a naturalistic if sometimes naive, or clumsy appearance (Avronidaki 2007; Bedigan 2008, 186–7). The images are of a highly original and idiosyncratic style, so the focus on sanctuary activities is generally free of the conventionality that is typical of other Boeotian wares: as Sparkes puts it, with the Cabiric vases 'Boeotian painting abandons its slavish imitation of Attic and pours out examples of a style of painting both individual and unmistakable' (1967, 125). It is not until after 410–400 that we find the grotesque or comic scenes that are the most distinctive products of Cabiric production. The early representative of the grotesque style and its application to mythological subjects is the Mystes Painter (Sparkes 1967, 126; Bedigan 2008, 189–90, 210–18 Appendix 5.9; a.k.a Mystai Painter after 'Mystenmaler', the original coinage by Bruns, or the Thetis Painter as named by Ure). He is dated ca. 410–370 (Braun and Haevernick 1981, 7–9). The Mystes Painter illustrated our scene of Odysseus and Circe. The style finds its mature development in the Kabir Painter (Bedigan 2008, 191, 219–26), who is thought to be 'contemporary with the latter half of the Mystes Painter' (Bedigan 2008, 191). Between them these painters are responsible for all the attributed vasepaintings that are believed to represent comic theatre (Bedigan 2006, 13–18; and see below).

For the most part Cabiric ware's figured decoration offers images that can easily be associated with activities at the sanctuary. The majority are sympotic scenes (Bedigan 2008, 130). Most others show what are clearly or plausibly classifiable as scenes of cultic activities: processing, sacrificing, feasting, or dancing (Schachter 1986, 100–3; Bedigan 2008, 130, 244–65). That the subject matter may reflect activities that take place in the Cabirion is further suggested by the number of figures who wear knotted fillets or crowns of foliage on their heads as these are thought to reflect the dress of initiates in the sanctuary. But in some cases the mirroring of cultic activities seems remote: several scene types refer to athletics or hunting, which could not have taken place in the sanctuary (Bedigan 2008, 265–71). The grotesque vasepaintings, as mentioned above, are predominantly mythological, but also extend to scenes of cult, athletics, hunting or everyday life. So the question of the connection between the imagery of Cabiric vases and the cultic activities of the Cabirion is far from straightforward.

The belief that the grotesque vasepaintings reproduce the visual impressions of dramatic performances that took place in the sanctuary goes back to the time of the first excavation in the sanctuary. Otto Kern, on the analogy of presumed parallels in the Orphic mysteries, thought the Cabiric vases showed dramatic performances that formed part of the Cabiric initiations: 'Auf den local boiotischen Vasen erscheint also ein Theil der mystischen δρώμενα, die auch für die thebanischen Mysterien von Pausanias ausdrücklich bezeugt sind, im Bilde' (1890, 8). It was under the combined influence of Kern and Jane Harrison's primitivistic ritual interpretations of Greek iconography, that Walters, in the first discussion of our Odysseus and Circe vase (1892–1893, 87) together with another similar scene in the British Museum, supposed that the Cabiric rites included dramatic parodies of myth. Neither Kern nor Walters addressed the awkward question how vasepainters could so freely publish the mystery *dromena* that Pausanias felt constrained to guard under silence (9.25.5; cf. Schachter 1986, 93 n. 2). Alfred Körte (1894, 348–9), on the other hand, offered a more secular interpretation, identifying our image and its congeners as examples of Boeotian 'Volksposse' (cf. 1893, 71). He first drew attention to the large bellies, buttocks and phallos that he thought parallel to the 'phlyakes' of South Italy (considered at the time also to be a regional farce).

For a long time the ritual and the dramatic interpretations sat comfortably together. Bieber (1920, 153) for example expresses in the strongest terms a belief that the vases reproduced a precise visual record of Cabiric mystery rites ('wir dürfen nicht daran zweifeln, daß uns die Vasen, aus denen die Festteilnehmer bei den heiligen Trinkgelagen tranken, einen Teil der mystischen δρώμενα des Kabirenkultus vollständig naturgetreu zeigen'), but also, with no apparent change of heart, the view that these mysteries were also a traditional Volksposse (1961, 49 'the Kabeirion vases attest the continuation of the old farce of the archaic period'). Séchan also walked the border between ritual and drama, echoing Aristotle's words that the earliest comedy, lost in the mist of time, was put on by volunteers 'burlesques qu'improvisaient des acteurs volontaires (ἐθελονταί)' (1926, 51; cf. **Aiii 2; Bx 3b**).

Since 1960 strong doubts have arisen about one or both of these interpretations and this has also awakened doubt about their compatibility. In 1960 Breitholz's *Die dorische Farce* cast serious doubt on the value of all the supposed evidence for folk theatre in Greece, including the Cabiric vases, which he claimed had no connection with theatre (1960, 198–201). Webster in his review of Breitholtz agreed that the Cabiric vases had no connection with a folk comedy (1961, 456). He had, he states, been moving to the same conclusion independently (1961, 452; *DTC*² 138). But he did not agree with Breitholtz's conclusion that that they had no connection with theatre: rather they had no specific connection with regional traditions or Cabiric theology. Webster thought the images related to contemporary comedy in the Attic tradition (1961, 456), in much the same way that he thought the West Greek comic ('phlyax') vases related to Middle Comedy (Webster 1948). For this reason, the first edition of his *Monuments Illustrating Old and Middle Comedy* (1960) included eight Cabiric vases (first among them our Circe and Odysseus) with attributions to standard comic mask types, and these were expanded to ten entries in the subsequent edition (*MMC*² p. 81, BV 9–10; cf. *MMC*³ p. 4 and BV1–10). Braun and Haevernick (1981, 10–11) added several more vases with mask attributions from Webster's mask typology (all on paintings by the Mystes Painter). They also compared the subject matter with known titles of Middle Comedies, but without abandoning the notion that the presumed productions were 'populäre Stegreifstücke' or 'farcenhaften Possen': a local farce with strong connections to contemporary Athenian comedy was performed separately from the sanctuary's mystic *dromena* (Braun and Haevernick 1981, 26–9). Bedigan 2006 enlarges to twenty-nine the number of Cabiric vases that show figures wearing standard Middle Comic masks (cf. Bedigan 2006; 2008, 272–7).

While one branch of scholarship has come to regard the Cabiric grotesques as something very close to contemporary drama, another branch has moved away from drama to more purely ritual interpretations. The detailed study by Daumas (1998) relates virtually all the vases to the mystery initiations performed at the Cabirion. Strongly in her favour, as she points out (1998, 25), is the fact that the Cabirion's theatral area could not easily have been used for anything like a traditional dramatic performance at the time the vases were produced. As Schachter puts it (2016b, 333):

> There was, after all, a stream running across the valley at the bottom of the slope, and there were buildings on the opposite bank. The theatral area of the Archaic and Classical periods may have been used only for the needs of initiation, as was the case of the Hellenistic and Roman periods, when a large podium filled the orchestra.

Indeed, in Schachter's view, the podium, built in the third century just when this area begins to take the form of a proper theatre, 'effectively rules out any possibility that the

Hellenistic and Roman caveas could have been used for theatrical purposes' (1986, 82). As there is no telesterion, however, initiations must have taken place in the open air of the sanctuary, and it could be supposed that, even though traditional comedy could not be performed in the sanctuary, something much more intimate like initiation rites might have centred on the theatral area.

Mitchell goes still further from dramatic towards ritual interpretation (2009, 248–79). He denies that the grotesque figures wore masks or costumes at all (except in the case of the man dancing with a bull's head on Wolters and Bruns 1940, pl. 32.2–3). On the contrary, the images show grotesque bodies and faces, not costumes and masks (Mitchell 2009, 254–7). They are related neither to drama nor to mystic *dromena,* but are rather visual parodies of myth, cultic and other activities. They do not record the contents but rather translate the carnival spirit of the Cabiric festival (which Mitchell takes to be a form of local Dionysia). On this interpretation they may resemble the iconography of choes, a drinking vessel used at the Anthesteria, with which they are sometimes compared (Burkert 1985, 282; Mitchell 2009, 276–7): the images on the choes relate to themes connected to the Anthesteria, above all childhood and the Dionysia, but developed freely and independently of any particular rituals or activities engaged in at the festival (Hamilton 1992).

More evidence is needed before one can safely take a stand on the question whether the vases are simply grotesques or testimonials to actual performances, whether of ritual or comedy. We remain unconvinced, however, that the iconography supports the theory that comedy, in any form, was produced at the Cabirion, and convinced, rather, that, if it was, it had little or no relationship to the contemporary Middle Comedy performed in Athens and elsewhere in Greece. The features of the grotesque figures are 'comic' only in the broad non-theatrical sense. They are generally described as negroid or dwarfish, or both together: the scholarly literature sometimes describes them as pygmies. These are features that can be found elsewhere in grotesque vasepainting entirely unrelated to theatre (Mitchell 2009, 105–9, 235–46). The large bellies, buttocks, breasts and phalloi, and distorted faces are similarly not unique to comic costume (Walsh 2009, 245–58). Even the attempts to identify Middle Comic masks in the Cabiric scenes require far too much good will: Mitchell for one finds all the faces fairly regular, unvaried and consistent (Mitchell 2009, 254–7) and far from resembling Middle Comic masks or even reproducing the variety presupposed by Webster's mask typology. We share his scepticism, especially as Dick Green (pers. comm.) tells us he has 'little confidence in the mask attributions in *MMC*³ BV1–10' and would leave them out if he were to do a new edition.

The vasepainting we illustrate has always been at the centre of the small core of vases upon which the performance theory rested. It is one of seven Cabiric vases that show the confrontation of Odysseus and Circe (Walsh 2009, 316–17 nos. 96–103; Mitchell 2009, 272–4; Bedigan 2008, 191, 273). They allude to the first encounter between Odysseus and Circe, as known from the tenth book of the *Odyssey*. After their arrival on Circe's isle, a party of Odysseus' men were sent out to investigate the territory. They came to Circe's hut and were received with apparent hospitality. Circe mixed them drinks, but once they had imbibed, she was able, with a touch of her wand, to turn them into pigs. One of Odysseus' comrades escaped and reported to Odysseus. Odysseus set forth in anger but was met by Hermes who gave him an antidote to the potion and was told that as soon as he had drunk the potion Circe would offer him he must draw his sword and threaten her until she swore not to harm him and to restore his men to their former selves.

It is this canonical myth that appears on our vase and it is rendered in a canonical style except for the grotesquery of the figures and the frontal face of Odysseus that is probably intended to display a state of panic. Circe is depicted with a mixing bowl which she stirs with her magic wand, both of which are the identifying attributes of Circe in depictions of this scene (or scenes of the initial transformation of Odysseus' comrades) in Greek iconography from Attica to Sicily since the mid sixth century (Buitron-Oliver and Cohen 1995, 36–8). The treatment of Odysseus is similarly conventional in its iconographic attributes: the pilos (traveller's hat) upon his head, and the sword in his right hand is directly drawn from the long-established iconography of this scene (Buitron-Oliver and Cohen 1995, 53 n. 48). What is unique to the Cabiric vases is the presence of the loom (normally the attribute of Penelope), a touch which adds perhaps to Circe's seductiveness as an alternative wife (Buitron-Oliver and Cohen 1995, 53 n. 44; Brilliant 1995, 171). But it is a symbol and unlikely as a stage prop.

The other mythic Cabiric vases also represent scenes familiar from myth and epic and scenes for the most part favoured by iconographic tradition. None evokes a fictional narrative known mainly from drama and certainly none offers anything like the narrative perplexity of the New York Goose Play (**Axxii**), which could be fully understood only by persons familiar with the specific lost comedy after which it was drawn. When words appear on the Cabiric scenes, they are the kind of name labels we find on mythological vases: not lines as in a drama, and not the names of fictional characters. Thus on the reverse of our vase we find the same grotesque Odysseus (labelled Olyseus) being blown by Borias (sic) paddling with a trident over the Ocean on a pair of amphorae (one for each foot). This is not a likely scene from the stage, but made for viewers who know the tale of Odysseus' wanderings from myth and epic. Despite its humorous deformation, it clearly alludes to the story of the windstorm created by Poseidon in the fifth book of the *Odyssey*, with a blow of his trident (291), to ruin Odysseus' raft with which he left Calypso's island, a storm that would have drowned him, were it not for the intervention of the quasi-Nereid Leucothea, who persuades Odysseus to abandon his raft just before it shattered apart and who then wrapped the hero in her veil and brought him to shore.

In short only the grotesquery of the characters in these scenes departs from the canonical myth, unlike our West Greek or Attic comic scenes which, when based on myth, retain the characters but typically pervert the actions and events if they do not depart from the myth altogether. Even the grotesquery of the characters has little in common with comic iconography. It is true that their distorted faces, big bellies and phalloi resemble the costumes of the comic actors known from vasepaintings and figurines, but the Cabiric vases are otherwise quite unlike the vasepaintings that we know to depict comedy. There are none of those performance-realistic details that allow us to be sure we are seeing a scene of comedy. In contrast to such vasepaintings as the New York Goose Play (**Axxii**) there is nothing that confirms the impression of costume or masks: we see no buckles to secure the parts of the somation, no wrinkles on the arms and legs to confirm the existence of actor's tights, no floating or, as elsewhere, removed masks, and nothing that resembles a stage. Perhaps most troubling for the performance hypothesis, the Cabiric grotesques bear little resemblance to the costume or mask types found on those Boeotian comic terracottas that appear to depict the regional comic style which remained in full vigour at least during the most productive period of Cabiric grotesques (Green 2014a).

Mitchell's interpretation that they are grotesques that relate to themes suggested by, and in the spirit of, the Cabiric festival seems the likeliest on present evidence. The grotesques that relate to cult or drinking are easy enough to comprehend in this light, but so are many of the mythic scenes. The Circe vases have not only to do with mind-altering drugs in a cult which evidently relied heavily on the intoxicating effects of wine, but also Circe's character as a transformatrix and initiatrix (cf. Daumas 1998, 149–86; Cruccas 2007). Similarly other favoured mythological scenes, like the Nereids transporting the arms for Achilles (Louvre CA 4502; Berlin 3265), have mystic and eschatological symbolism which is borrowed from a broader mystic repertoire and not specifically Cabiric (see Csapo 2017, 127–35; *contra* Robertson in Sparkes 1967, 125 n. 71).

The hypothesis that the grotesque Cabiric vases relate to comedy is sometimes said to be confirmed by the claim that 'theatrical masks' were found at the sanctuary (Schmaltz 1974, 132–5; Demand 1982, 67). This unfortunately makes a lot of a little, and only tangentially related evidence. The masks are miniature terracotta representations of 'theatrical masks', which Schmaltz took to be dedications in the sanctuary, even though the only firm context recorded for any of them was a burial (1974, 133). He lists ten items as 'Theatermasken' (1974, 181–2 nos. 352–61) of which only three are accepted by Webster and Green as representations of comic masks: all miniature. All three are standard New Comic types, probably all third-century or later (*MNC*[3] 1AT 51b, 1BT 14–15), and thus all much later than the vasepaintings, and they relate to an entirely different and later form of comedy. Their scarcity on the site, compared with all the other figurine types, does not encourage one to allow Schmaltz's inference that they relate to comic performances at the Cabirion, quite the opposite. Of the terracotta figurines that Schmaltz calls 'Grotesken und Schauspieler' (1974, 177–80 nos. 312–45), there is no reason to regard them as actors and they are of a different type from the comic figurines studied in Green 2014a.

A word should also be said about the claim that the cult of the Theban Cabiri is 'Dionysiac'. The impression is based largely on the evidence of communal feasting and drinking on the site and on the imagery of artefacts associated with the sanctuary, and particularly the Cabiric vases. Just how Dionysiac is a matter largely of how one interprets the evidence. For Schachter the association 'with Dionysus and his circle, or with Hermes and Pan' exists 'only in a casual, unsystematic way' (2016b, 315). For Bedigan the Theban cult is 'Dionysiac in nature, both in terms of iconography and activity' (2008, 43, 289–92; Blakely 2006, 16–17; the process of syncretism is studied by Cruccas 2014). In Schachter's view the assimilation to Dionysus is largely the result of the vasepainters themselves who in the later fifth century were confronted with a need to decorate vases intended for use in the sanctuary and for gods who had no iconographic tradition of their own. Given the fertility function of the Cabiri and their nature as patrons of a mystery cult, the assimilation to the well-established Dionysian iconography of local drinking vessels was an obvious solution (2016b, 327). On one of the earliest pieces (Athens NM 10426), probably produced around the same time as the Pronomos Vase (**V E**) or the Piraeus Relief (**V F**), Kabiros (labelled) appears in precisely the same monoposiast position that typifies Dionysus in Attic iconography at that time, reclining on a couch, with Pais (labelled) at his feet fetching wine from a krater.

Civ: Orchomenus in Boeotia

1. Choregic tripod dedication of Pedakleis. Late 4th c. (letter forms, linguistic features, prosopography and deviation from later formulaic pattern). Amandry and Spyropoulos (1974, 177) find the lettering typical of the end of the 4th and beginning of the 3rd c. ('trait fin, avec *apices* à peine marqués'). More significant is the Kaphisiadas, son of Pedakleis, who is a polemarch in the Archonship of Philokomos, 286 or 285 (*IG* VII 3175; for the date: Knoepfler 2014, 70–1, 86) and is likely to be the son of the Pedakleis mentioned here. The use of the dual (l. 3) is rare in the Boeotian dialect after the time of Alexander (cf. **2** and the language of Amandry and Spyropoulos 1974, nos. 3–4, and contrast nos. 5–20). In addition the patronymic adjective in l. 2 is a feature rarely found after the middle of the 3rd c. Because of these features Amandry and Spyropoulos consider this the earliest of a series of twenty-five choregic monuments (see below) and its earliness seems confirmed by a number of deviations from the other monuments both in language and in form which suggest that the established patterns we see in the other dedications had not yet had time to develop. Only one or possibly two other choregic dedications from Orchomenus (Amandry and Spyropoulos 1974, nos. 3 and perhaps 4) fail to include a verb indicating the victory, a verb of dedication, and the names of the Archon, piper and singer. Noteworthy, also is the dative in ωι in Διωνύσωι, a rare instance, and unique among these dedications, of the *koine* form in place of the dialect form in οι as in **2** (see Knoepfler in Amandry and Spyropoulos 1974, 242–3).

A rectangular limestone base with mouldings above and below the front inscribed surface and extending three-fifths of the length of the sides: the rest of the sides remained unfinished. On the top there are cuttings to receive the three feet of the tripod (unusually with one foot in front and two in back), plus a large and deep central rectangular cutting for a support pillar (also unique for this series).
0.307 × 0.85 m.
Found in the theatre of Orchomenus during the excavations of 1973 (cf. Amandry and Spyropoulos 1974, 173 fig. 1).
Amandry and Spyropoulos 1974, 175–7 no. 1; Manieri 2009, 187–8 ORC 3. Photos: Amandry and Spyropoulos 1974, 174 figs. 2–3; drawings: Amandry and Spyropoulos 1974, 176 fig. 4 and 211 fig. 33.

> Πεδακλεῖς Καφισιάδαο
> Διωνύσιος Δαματρίχιος
> ἄνδρεσσι χοραγείσαντε
> Διωνύσωι.

> Pedakleis, son of Kaphisiadas, Dionysios, son of Damatrichos, after serving as choregoi for the men, to Dionysus.

2. Choregic tripod dedication of Eucharidas. 300–285 (letter forms, prosopography and linguistic forms). 'Malgré la relative grandeur des lettres rondes et la forme de l'oméga en arche de pont, l'écriture paraît, dans l'ensemble, plus récente que celle de la base 1' (= **1** above; Amandry and Spyropoulos 1974, 179). Eucharidas, son of Damatrichos (l. 1), was a polemarch at the same time as Kaphisiadas, son of Pedakleis (see on **1**). For the use of the dual (ll. 2–3) and the patronymic adjective, see on **1** above. Amandry and Spyropoulos 1974, 178 n. 6 (cf. Stefanis no. 2714) suggest that the piper may be the Damasias who was honoured at Eleusis in the mid 4ᵗʰ c. (**III Hii**), though this might imply a somewhat earlier date. 'Damasias' is by far the most likely supplement for l. 4, though Timasias and Thaumasias (not attested in Boeotia) are possible. The inscription does not perfectly adhere to the normal formula (see on **1**), as the name of the singer is omitted.

Triangular limestone base with an upper moulding on front and sides. The top surface has holes for the tripod legs, two of which still contain metal, and a round central hole for the support column.
0.19 × 0.91 m.
Found in or near the theatre of Orchomenus and placed in the Treasury of Minyas sometime before 1970 (Fossey 1991, 65).
Amandry and Spyropoulos 1974, 177–80 no. 2; Manieri 2009, 187–8 ORC. 4. Photos: Amandry and Spyropoulos 1974, 178 fig. 5; profile drawing: Amandry and Spyropoulos 1974, 176 fig. 34.

> [Εὐ]χαρίδας Δαματρίχιος,
> [. . .]ειρος Ἀρξιλαΐδαο ἄνδρεσσι χοραγείσαντε
> [νικά]σαντε Διωνύσοι ἀνεθέταν,
> [. . . . .]ιος (or [. . . . .]νος) ἄρχοντος, ᵛ [. . .]μασίας αὔλι *vacat*

> [Eu]charidas, son of Damatrichos, [...-]eiros, son of Arxilaidas, after serving as choregoi for the men, having [won], dedicated to Dionysus, when [...-]ios (or [...-]nos) was Archon, [...-]masias was piper.

3. Agonothetic dedication of doors. Dated by letter forms to the late 4ᵗʰ c. (Roesch 1980, 9) or 250–200 by Knoepfler 1992, 490–1 no. 162, who puts this fragment together with another fragment of an epistyle block, *IG* VII 3209, to read '[A]pollodoros, son of Nikon, having served as agonothete, dedicated to Dionysus the doors and the panels that go together with the doors', [Ἀ]|πολλόδωρος Νίκωνος τὰ πρόθυρα κὴ τὼς πινάκας τὼς | [σὺν] προθύροις ἀγωνοθετείσας Διωνύσοι ἀνέθεικε|[ν] (= *SEG* 42, 418). But the recently rediscovered epistyle block of *IG* VII 3209 shows that the two blocks have different dimensions and do not belong together (Germani 2015a, 791, fig. 4). Schachter takes the *prothyra* to be an 'entry-way' into the theatre (1981, 180; Moretti 2010, 170 'des portes des *parodos*', cf. Moretti 2010, 162). Hesychius connects the word with 'propylaea' (π 3645 Hansen) as used of the gateway to the Theatre of Dionysus at Athens even in the fifth century (Andoc. 1.38), but 'propylaeon' seems to be reserved for gateways that are more monumental in style than what one might term a *prothyron* (Hellmann 1992, 349).

Fragment of a Doric epistyle of bluish limestone.
0.33 × 1.76 × 0.5 m.

Found in 1957 on the road beside the theatre (Lauffer 1980, 173).

Presently kept in the garden of the Church of the Dormition of the Virgin at Skripou (modern Orchomenus).

Lauffer 1980, 173 no. 12 (= *SEG* 30, 445); Roesch 1980, 9 no. E.80.17; Knoepfler 1992, 490 no. 162 (= *SEG* 42, 418; Manieri 2009, 186–7 ORC. 2); Germani 2015a, 791. Photo: Lauffer 1980, pl. 5; drawing: Germani 2015a, fig. 4.

> [… e.g. σὺν τοῖς] προθύροις ἀγωνοθετείσας Διωνύσοι ἀνέθεικε.

> [*X*] after serving as agonothete dedicated to Dionysus [… e.g. with] the gateways.

1 and **2** are the first of a series of fragments of twenty-five choregic monuments, all but one tripod bases (Amandry and Spyropoulos 1974; Manieri 2009, 186–98). Originally they were probably placed in the theatre of Orchomenus, or along the road leading into the parodos of the theatre (Papalexandrou 2008, 276), although no more than nine of them (certainly including **1**) were actually found in the theatre in the unpublished excavations of 1972–1973 (Fossey 1991, 65). Several others had been reused, along with fragments of the theatre buildings, in 873/4 AD in the building of the Church of the Dormition of the Virgin, immediately north-east of the theatre. In date the choregic monuments range from the late fourth century to at least the end of the third century. The surviving inscriptions (Amandry and Spyropoulos 1974, nos. 1–20) commemorate a choral competition for Dionysus of men accompanied by pipes (**2**, l. 4 and Amandry and Spyropoulos 1974, nos. 2–3, 5–20), with each chorus sponsored by a joint choregia of two Orchomenian citizens.

The choruses would be indistinguishable from the men's Dionysian lyric chorus known from Athens and very many other sites, except for one unique feature: the fullest inscriptions (Amandry and Spyropoulos 1974, nos. 5–20) also all list a singer (ἀΐδοντος) after the name of the piper (restored on Amandry and Spyropoulos 1974, nos. 10 and 18). Wilson (2000, 297) suggests the 'singer' is a lead singer and also had some part in training the chorus, so might be the equivalent of a chorus leader (like the κορυφαῖος or ἡγεμὼν χοροῦ we find mentioned elsewhere). But possibly the presence of a 'singer' indicates that a solo part was mixed with the choral song and so implies a different form of performance to that attested in Athens and elsewhere. This practice may conceivably be attested at Delphi in 259/8 or 255/4 where the catalogue of performers at the Soteria mentions Menalkes son of Speuson in the chorus of men and later lists a Boiskos (probably the same who appears in the Orchomenian series) as having accompanied him on the pipes (Nachtergael 1977, Actes 8, ll. 35, 82; Amandry and Spyropoulos 1974, 191). But we also know that Menalkes performed as a kitharode at the same festival outside the competition and it is likely that Boiskos accompanied him at that time (Nachtergael 1977, 326). In Athens the Dionysian lyric choruses are thought sometimes to have included solo song (Zimmermann 1993, 127–8), but the soloist never achieved official recognition nor, it seems, did the solo song achieve any level of regularity. Possibly we are dealing with a specifically Boeotian form, perhaps more like a cultic dithyramb, where the soloist derived from the *exarchos* of the processional form (cf. on **Gi**).

The earliest four inscriptions of this series and the associated monuments show considerable diversity, whereas the later inscriptions and monuments are relatively uniform and formulaic (see on **1** and **2** above; Manieri 2009, 178). One might infer from this that these

monuments were erected before a uniform pattern had imposed itself on the artists responsible for the monuments and possibly therefore in the earliest years of choregic competition. On this evidence we could infer a late fourth-century date for the beginning of men's
choral competitions at Orchomenus. This is consistent with the evidence for the dating of
the earliest phase of the extant theatre.

The theatre at Orchomenus was discovered during excavations in 1972–1973 with additional sondages in 1997–1998, and again in 2012 in anticipation of a restoration project
under the auspices of Diazoma. Although the surviving theatre was refurbished in the second or first century, the most recent studies identify an earlier phase that can be no earlier
than the time of the Battle of Chaeronea in 338 and forms part of the reconstruction of
the city after successive destructions by Thebes in 364 and 345. In 364 Thebes destroyed
Orchomenus and killed the men, enslaved the women and children (D.S. 15.79.3–6; D.
16.4, 16.25, 20.109), and gave the city to settlers loyal to Thebes (Hansen *IACP* 447). But
in 354 the Phocian general Onomarchus seized Orchomenus, and some of the original
Orchomenians seem to have returned while the city was under Phocian occupation (D.S.
16.33.4, 16.58.1; D. 16.25. 19.148; Aeschin. 2.141; Sch. D. 6.21 Dilts = § 13); however the
city was again taken and enslaved by Thebes in 345 (D. 19.112, 141, 325). It was Philip II
of Macedon after his victory at Chaeronea in 338 or after the destruction of Thebes in 335,
who rebuilt Orchomenus on a new plan and returned the city to the Orchomenians (Paus.
4.27.10, 9.37.8; Kyriazi et al. 2013, 85–6; Germani 2015a).

The theatre is located within the acropolis walls of Philip's city, but in an area that was a
remote cemetery in the earlier city. This suggests that it was planned as part of the political
and religious centre of the new city (Germani 2014, 32; 2015a, 790). Moreover, the theatre
reuses parts of the older city wall, probably that built in 364 and subsequently destroyed
by the Thebans in 345. But the *terminus ante* for the completion of the theatre ultimately
depends upon the dating of the choregic monuments (**1–2**) that were evidently placed in
the theatre, and especially the inscribed epistyle (**3**) which was assuredly part of its (not
necessarily initial) construction. Amandry's dating of **1** and **2** has not been challenged, but
the dating of **3** ranges from the fourth (Roesch 1980, 17 E8) to the second half of the third
century (Knoepfler 1992, 491 no. 161). However Knoepfler's dating is based on a feature
of an inscription (the use of a genitive for the patronymic on *IG* VII 3209) which he is
probably wrong to join with **3** (Germani 2015a, 791).

Associated with the building of the fourth-century theatre are vestiges of a skene (Germani
2015a, 792–3). In 2012 the excavations and cleaning operations around the orchestra and
foundations of this older skene uncovered two bronze Chalcidian coins of 480–445 which
may suggest an older cultic usage of the site (Kyriazi et al. 2013, 86). The operations in
2012 also resulted in the identification of the foundations, stylobate and floors of a building
to the south of the theatre as a temple built some time earlier than the theatre (Kyriazi et al.
2013, 88–9). This temple presumably belongs to Dionysus as the dedications (**1–3**) clearly
show that the theatre belonged to the god. The cult of Dionysus in Orchomenus dates back
at least to the mid fifth century since we are told that the sanctuary once housed a statue
of Dionysus by Myron (Paus. 9.30.1). The mythic tradition suggests a much older reception of Dionysus, as the Minyadai are granddaughters of the eponymous Orchomenos, for
which our earliest direct source is the probably fifth-century poetess Corinna (Ant.Lib.

10; Gantz 1993, 736–7; and for the dating controversy for Corinna: Larson 2007, 19–20; Guerrera 2013, 76–7 n. 205).

It is unclear for what festival the men's choruses performed. There are three known possibilities: the Agrionia, the Charitesia and the Homoloia (Manieri 2009, 175–83). An Agrionia is attested for Dionysus at Orchomenus by Plutarch (*Mor.* 299c–300a; cf. 717a), and scholars once connected the then-known tripod monument inscriptions (Amandry and Spyropoulos 1974, nos. 5–6) to this festival (Preuss 1879, 33; Reisch 1885, 109; Brinck 1886, 185–6). But little is known of this festival (Burkert 1983, 168–79; Dowden 1989, 82–9; Johnston 1999, 66–72; Manieri 2009, 176–7), and Dionysus is the main link between the festival and the competitions attested by the choregic monuments (**1**, **2**).

The Homoloia is perhaps the best candidate for the festival related to the victories recorded in **1**, **2** and the later tripod bases. The Homoloia had in the early first century, among several musical contests, contests in tragedy, comedy, and both men's and boys' choruses (*IG* VII 3196–7). The inscription of one of the tripod bases from Orchomenus, dating from the third century, differs radically from the formula used by the others. One difference is that the dedication appears in the first line, which is restored by Lauffer (1976, 47–8 no. 58) as [— — — Διὶ Ὁμολ]ωῖυ ἀνέθεικα (= *SEG* 26, 585), and less restrictively by Robert and Robert (1974, 229 no. 283) as [— — — Ὁμολ]ωῖυ ἀνέθεικαν, though other restorations are possible (Amandry and Spyropoulos 1974, 221, 228 n. 57). The problem is that, although a Zeus Homoloios, an Athena Homolois and a Demeter Homoloia, as well as a hero Homolois are all attested for Thebes, there is no evidence for a Dionysus Homoloios anywhere (Schachter 1994, 121). However a month name Homoloios is known at Thebes and throughout Boeotia, central and north-western Greece, and it is possible the games were named, not after the divinity for whom they were held, but for the month in which they were held (Schachter 1981, 143; Schachter 1994, 121).

Also possible is the festival of the Charitesia, named after the Graces (Χάριτες) and obviously dedicated to them. But in Orchomenus the Graces were conceived to be the daughters of Dionysus and Aphrodite (Serv. 1.720; Jameson 2014, 70; though Pi. *O.* 14.14–15 addresses the Orchomenian Graces as daughters of Zeus). This suggests a close cultic connection. Moreover the abrupt juxtaposition in Pausanias' language may imply some proximity between the temple of the Graces and the sanctuary of Dionysus: 'at Orchomenus there is also a sanctuary (or a theatre?) of Dionysus, and the oldest sanctuary is for the Graces' (9.38.1: Ὀρχομενίοις δὲ πεποίηται καὶ <ἱερὸν / θέατρον> Διονύσου, τὸ δὲ ἀρχαιότατον Χαρίτων ἐστὶν ἱερόν – for the supplement, see Schachter 1981, 144 n. 2). The actual location of the sanctuary of the Graces is unknown but generally believed to be adjacent to and north-east of the theatre, near or underneath the Byzantine Church of the Dormition of the Virgin (Frazer 1898, 186; Kyriazi et al. 2013, 82; Guerrera 2013, 44–5).

Pausanias' testimony to the antiquity of the cult of the Graces at Orchomenus is confirmed by sources from Hesiod onwards who claim that the cult goes back to Eteocles (Hes. fr. 71c M-W; Theoc. 16.104 with Sch.; Strab. 9.2.40; Paus. 9.35.1; Sch. Pi. *O.* 14.1). Pindar attests the cult as early as the beginning of the fifth century, and, moreover, associates the Orchomenian Graces with both song and choral dance (Pi. *O.* 14.3–4, 'Graces, much sung Queens of Orchomenus' without whom, ll. 7–9, 'not even the gods arrange choruses and feasts'; and Pi. *P.* 12.26 where Orchomenus is described as the 'city of beautiful dances of the Graces', καλλίχορον … πόλιν Χαρίτων). The description implies that the Graces were worshipped with choral rituals already before 490, the date of the ode's composition, and that the choral music was accompanied by pipes since Pindar specifically associates Orchomenus and the cult of the Graces at Orchomenus with the reed beds, ideal for pipe music, that grew abundantly at the confluence of the Melas and Cephissus on the shores of lake Copais, where Orchomenus was founded (Pi. *P.* 12.26; cf. Thphr. *HP* 4.11.8; Plu. *Sull.* 20.3–5).

Given the close relationship between the Orchomenian Graces, Dionysian music, and indeed Dionysus, is it possible that Dionysus presided at the festival of his daughters to the extent that dedications made in the theatre from competitions at the Charitesia were put in the name of the god of the sanctuary in which the festival competitions took place and the dedication was made (cf. te Riele 1976, 288–9; Barbantani 2000, 165–6; *contra* Manieri 2009, 177)? In any case, the Charitesia of the early first century took place in the theatre (Amandry and Spyropoulos 1974, 224; Schachter 1981, 144). Problematic, however, is the lack of evidence for the men's and boys' lyric choruses, such as existed at this time at the Homoloia (see above), although the Charitesia did include tragedy, comedy, and satyr play (*IG* VII 3195–7).

On the evidence, it seems likely, despite the importance of Dionysus and despite the city's probably ancient history of cultic choruses, that Orchomenus had no theatre before the city was rebuilt by Philip and came under Macedonian domination. Even then the use of the theatre may have been limited to performances of men's lyric choruses, possibly in an idiosyncratic and archaising style, until some time in the third or second century when, like other cities in the Boeotian Confederacy, Orchomenus developed festivals in a Panhellenic style (cf. Barbantani 2000). Orchomenus is a good example of cities that in the Classical period had an oligarchic constitution (Th. 4.76.3; D.S. 15.79.3; Hansen *IACP* 447) and were slow to embrace the popular theatre culture so eagerly adopted by both democracies and autocracies elsewhere.

Cv: Thespiae

1. **Hesiod, *Works and Days* 654–9.** Composed: 8th or 7th c. In *Theogony* 22–34 Hesiod declares that the Muses taught him song and breathed into him a divine voice while he was pasturing lambs under mount Helicon. While giving him his new vocation, the Muses caution him always to begin and end his song with the Muses. This he does in the *Theogony*. The first lines of *Works and Days* are an invocation to the Pierian Muses (of disputed authenticity in antiquity: Paus. 9.31.4; Sch. Hes. *Op.* Proleg.), but the poem does not end with any reference to the goddesses (the poem as we have it continues for another 169 lines after its last mention of the Muses below). The dedication is also mentioned in the *Contest between Homer and Hesiod* 212–14 in a form that may echo the actual dedicatory inscription (Caruso 2016, 224). Text: Most.

> ἔνθα δ' ἐγὼν ἐπ' ἄεθλα δαΐφρονος Ἀμφιδάμαντος
> 655   Χαλκίδα τ' εἰς ἐπέρησα· τὰ δὲ προπεφραδμένα πολλὰ
> ἄεθλ' ἔθεσαν παῖδες μεγαλήτορος· ἔνθά μέ φημι

ὕμνῳ νικήσαντα φέρειν τρίποδ᾽ ὠτώεντα.
τὸν μὲν ἐγὼ Μούσῃς Ἑλικωνιάδεσσ᾽ ἀνέθηκα,
ἔνθά με τὸ πρῶτον λιγυρῆς ἐπέβησαν ἀοιδῆς.

There (Aulis) I crossed to Chalcis for the games of warlike Amphidamas. The sons of the great-hearted man offered these many prizes that were announced in advance. There I claim that I was victorious in song and won a large-handled tripod. I dedicated it to the Heliconian Muses where first they set me upon clear-sounding song.

2. Description of the Sanctuary at the Valley of the Muses: Pausanias, *Guide to Greece* **9.30.1–9.31.3**. Date: ca. 150 AD. Pausanias describes a forest of votives and statues in the Valley of the Muses, and more importantly, for our purposes, he names the artists, which allows some conclusions to be made about the chronology of an important stage of development of the sanctuary. We know of two sculptors by the name of Cephisodotus: one probably the father, and the other the son, of Praxiteles. The former is given a floruit of 372–369 (Plin. *HN* 34.50). His presumed grandson, active 344–293, was the sculptor of the Menander in the Theatre of Dionysus. Lysippus' active career is given by Andrew Stewart as ca. 370–315 (*OCD³*). Assuming, as we must, that the statues of the Muses were a planned group, it is the participation of Strongylion that decides the question in favour of the elder Cephisodotus. Strongylion was born ca. 440–435 and active in the early 4th c. (Corso 2004, 55–75). Strongylion probably took charge of Myron's workshop in the last years of the 5th c. and Corso thinks that Olympiosthenes and the elder Cephisodotus 'must have grown up in his studio in the early 4. c.' (2004, 75). The workshop had links with Athenian oligarchs and with Sparta (Corso 2004, 48, 55; also 9, 52, 85, 115, 126–7, 135). The abundant statues and dedications described by Pausanias came to be emulated by other Mouseia: 'La presenza in uno stesso luogo di molteplici oggetti d'arte fa intendere come possa esser nato proprio presso il santuario dell'Elicona il primo *Museum* nel senso moderno del termine' (Manieri 2009, 315; cf. Fossey 1988, 134–65). We omit a page from the middle of Pausanias' text, mainly a digression on the myth of Orpheus. Text: Spiro.

ταῖς Μούσαις δὲ ἀγάλματα <τὰ> μὲν πρῶτά ἐστι Κηφισοδότου τέχνη πάσαις, προελθόντι δὲ οὐ πολὺ τρεῖς μέν εἰσιν αὖθις Κηφισοδότου, Στρογγυλίωνος δὲ ἕτερα τοσαῦτα, ἀνδρὸς βοῦς καὶ ἵππους ἄριστα εἰργασμένου· τὰς δὲ ὑπολοίπους τρεῖς ἐποίησεν Ὀλυμπιοσθένης. καὶ Ἀπόλλων χαλκοῦς ἐστιν ἐν Ἑλικῶνι καὶ Ἑρμῆς μαχόμενοι περὶ τῆς λύρας, καὶ Διόνυσος ὁ μὲν Λυσίππου, τὸ δὲ ἄγαλμα ἀνέθηκε Σύλλας τοῦ Διονύσου τὸ ὀρθόν, ἔργον τῶν Μύρωνος θέας μάλιστα ἄξιον μετά γε τὸν Ἀθήνησιν Ἐρεχθέα· ἀνέθηκε δὲ οὐκ οἴκοθεν, Ὀρχομενίους δὲ ἀφελόμενος τοὺς Μινύας. τοῦτό ἐστι τὸ ὑπὸ Ἑλλήνων λεγόμενον θυμιάμασιν ἀλλοτρίοις τὸ θεῖον σέβεσθαι. 30.2 ποιητὰς δὲ ἢ καὶ ἄλλως ἐπιφανεῖς ἐπὶ μουσικῇ, τοσῶνδε εἰκόνας ἀνέθεσαν· Θάμυριν μὲν αὐτόν τε ἤδη τυφλὸν καὶ λύρας κατεαγυίας ἐφαπτόμενον, Ἀρίων δὲ ὁ Μηθυμναῖος ἐστιν ἐπὶ δελφῖνος. ὁ δὲ Σακάδα τοῦ Ἀργείου τὸν ἀνδριάντα πλάσας, οὐ συνεὶς Πινδάρου τὸ ἐς αὐτὸν προοίμιον, ἐποίησεν οὐδὲν ἐς τὸ μῆκος τοῦ σώματος εἶναι τῶν αὐλῶν μείζονα τὸν αὐλητήν. ³⁰·³ κάθηται δὲ καὶ Ἡσίοδος κιθάραν ἐπὶ τοῖς γόνασιν ἔχων, οὐδέν τι οἰκεῖον Ἡσιόδῳ φόρημα· ... ³¹·³ ἐν δὲ τῷ Ἑλικῶνι καὶ ἄλλοι τρίποδες κεῖνται καὶ ἀρχαιότατος, ὃν ἐν Χαλκίδι λαβεῖν τῇ ἐπ᾽ Εὐρίπῳ λέγουσιν Ἡσίοδον νικήσαντα ᾠδῇ. περιοικοῦσι δὲ καὶ ἄνδρες τὸ ἄλσος, καὶ ἑορτήν τε ἐνταῦθα οἱ Θεσπιεῖς καὶ ἀγῶνα ἄγουσι Μουσεῖα· ἄγουσι δὲ καὶ τῷ Ἔρωτι, ἆθλα οὐ μουσικῆς μόνον ἀλλὰ καὶ ἀθληταῖς τιθέντες.

The first statues of all the Muses are the art of Cephisodotus. As one moves forward a little one sees three which are again by Cephisodotus, but another group of the same number is by Strongylion, a man who was unrivalled in sculpting bulls and horses, and the remaining three are by Olympiosthenes. There is also at Helicon a bronze Apollo and Hermes fighting over the lyre, and a Dionysus by Lysippus. Sulla dedicated the standing statue of Dionysus, the most noteworthy work of Myron after the Erechtheus at Athens. He did not dedicate it from his own property but took it from the Minyans of Orchomenus. This the Greeks call worshipping the god with other people's incense. ³⁰·² They also set up the following statues of poets or people who are otherwise famous musicians: Thamyris is already blind and holding a broken lyre; Arion of Methymna is on a dolphin; the maker of the statue of Sacadas of Argos, not understanding Pindar's prooemium about him, made no part of the piper's body bigger than the pipes; ³⁰·³ Hesiod too sits holding a kithara on his knees, which is no appropriate posture for Hesiod. ... ³¹·³ Tripods are dedicated on Helicon, and most particularly the oldest, which is that which they say Hesiod won in Chalcis on the Euripos when victorious in song. Men live around the grove and the people of Thespiae hold a festival there and the contest of the Muses. They also have contests for Eros with prizes not only for music but also for athletes.

3. **Amphion of Thespiae, *On the Sanctuary of the Muses at Helicon, FGrH* 387 F 1 (=
Ath. 14.629a)**. It is not known when Amphion wrote: this kind of site guide is characteristic of both the Hellenistic period and the Second Sophistic (Bowie 1974, 185). A Nikokrates also wrote an *On the Contest at Helikon* (Sch. Hom. *Il.* 13.21; *FGrH* 376 F 2) and is dated by Jacoby to ca. 200. The epigram of Bacchiadas is usually dated to the 4th c. (Schachter 1986, 158 n. 2). Podlecki (1981, 99–100) argued for a date in the 5th (but see Lewis 1984, 180). The piper Anakos of Phigaleia is otherwise unknown (Stefanis no. 172). 'I am Bacchiadas' indicates that the object of dedication is a statue of Bacchiadas (cf. Hardie 1997, 26 n. 46, 27). Both the fact that the dedication is a statue celebrating the victory of an individual and the fact that Bacchiadas says he was didaskalos (and not choregos) put considerable doubt upon the view that this dedication is 'choregic' (Schachter 1986, 163; see further on commentary below). Text: Jacoby.

Ἀμφίων δ᾽ ὁ Θεσπιεὺς ἐν δευτέρῳ Περὶ τοῦ ἐν Ἑλικῶνι Μουσείου ἄγεσθαί φησιν ἐν Ἑλικῶνι παίδων ὀρχήσεις μετὰ σπουδῆς, παρατιθέμενος ἀρχαῖον ἐπίγραμμα τόδε·

ἀμφότερ᾽, ὠρχεύμην τε καὶ ἐν Μώσαις ἐδίδασκον
ἄνδρας· ὁ δ᾽ αὐλητὰς ἦν Ἄνακος Φιαλεύς.
εἰμὶ δὲ Βακχι<ά>δα<ς> Σικυώνιος· ἦ ῥα θεοῖσι
ταῖς Σικυῶνι καλὸν τοῦτ᾽ ἀπέκειτο γέρας.

<ἀνδρῶν καὶ> παίδων Kaibel   ἄνδρας codd.   παῖδας Reisch   Βακχιάδας
Meineke   δ᾽ Βακχιδα A

Amphion of Thespiae in his second book *On the Sanctuary of the Muses at Helicon* says that the performances of dances of boys were taken seriously at Helicon and he adduces as evidence this ancient epigram: 'I did both: I danced and I was didaskalos in the sanctuary of the Muses for (a chorus of) men (or reading Reisch's emendation 'boys'); the piper was Anakos of Phigaleia, I am Bacchiadas of Sicyon. This lovely prize is laid in store for the goddesses in Sicyon.'

4. Heracles demands a competition for the Muses: Plutarch, *On the Sign of Socrates* (*Moralia*) 578e–9a. Probably written 96–117 AD. The dialogue is set on the eve of the democratic coup in late 379. In 382 a pro-Spartan faction with Spartan aid overthrew the oligarchic government of Thebes and replaced it with a still narrower oligarchy. Three years later the leaders of the pro-Spartan government were assassinated, the Spartan garrison expelled, and a democracy was created under the leadership of Pelopidas and Epaminondas which would eventually lead to the destruction of Sparta's hegemony in Greece at Leuctra in 371 (Hansen *IACP* 455; Robinson 2011, 56; Cawkwell 2010 argues that a narrow oligarchy was only replaced by a broader one). The story of the gathering of the democratic conspirators at the house of Simmias in Thebes is narrated as a dialogue by Caphisias, Epaminondas' brother. Plutarch's account, which so far as we can tell is in outline historically accurate, probably draws upon Callisthenes' *Hellenica* (*FGrH* 124; Cawkwell 2010, 102). Historical accuracy is less easily attached to Pheidolaos of Haliartus' digression, just before our extract below, which tells of a Spartan excavation and opening of the tomb of Alcmene in Haliartus in order to remove her remains to Sparta (*Mor.* 577e; Parker 2010a). While opening the tomb a bronze tablet with an inscription in unknown script was found. King Agesilaus of Sparta, thinking the characters looked Egyptian, sent the tablet to Egypt to be deciphered. Pheidolaos returns to the narrative where the passage below begins. The deciphered text's command by Heracles to institute a competition for the Muses is rightly taken by Schachter (1986, 157) and others to be an aetiology for the festival of the Mouseia. The aetiology appears to be a Boeotian creation, conveniently attached to a tale that made plausible an intervention by the Boeotian Heracles (Parker 2010a, 135; cf. Manieri 2009, 139). Even if the story of the tablet is a fiction, it is nonetheless of real interest that an aetiology for the Mouseia should be embedded in a tale in which the Spartan King's authority and intervention are required for the delivery of Heracles' command. Text: Russell.

᾽νυνὶ δ᾽ ὑπὲρ ὧν ἀρτίως ἠπορῦμεν, ὦ Σιμμία, γραμμάτων, εἴ τι γιγνώσκεις πλεῖον ⁵⁷⁸ᶠ ἐξάγγειλον ἡμῖν· λέγονται γὰρ οἱ κατ᾽ Αἴγυπτον ἱερεῖς τὰ

γράμματα συμβαλεῖν τοῦ πίνακος, ὃν παρ' ἡμῶν ἔλαβεν Ἀγησίλαος τὸν
Ἀλκμήνης τάφον ἀνασκευασάμενος'. καὶ ὁ Σιμμίας εὐθὺς ἀναμνησθεὶς
'οὐκ οἶδ'' ἔφη 'τὸν πίνακα τοῦτον, ὦ Φειδόλαε, γράμματα δὲ πολλὰ παρ'
Ἀγησιλάου κομίζων Ἀγητορίδας ὁ Σπαρτιάτης ἧκεν εἰς Μέμφιν ὡς Χόνουφιν
τὸν προφήτην, ... τότε συμφιλοσοφοῦντες διετρίβομεν ἐγὼ καὶ Πλάτων
καὶ Ἑλλοπίων ὁ Πεπαρήθιος. ἧκε δὲ πέμψαντος βασιλέως καὶ κελεύσαντος
τὸν Χόνουφιν, εἴ τι συμβάλλοι τῶν γεγραμμένων, ἑρμηνεύσαντα ταχέως
ἀποστεῖλαι πρὸς ἑαυτόν· <ὁ > δὲ τρεῖς ἡμέρας ἀναλεξάμενος βιβλίων τῶν
παλαιῶν παντοδαποὺς [579a] χαρακτῆρας ἀντέγραψε τῷ βασιλεῖ καὶ πρὸς
ἡμᾶς ἔφρασεν, ὡς Μούσαις ἀγῶνα συντελεῖσθαι κελεύει τὰ γράμματα, τοὺς
δὲ τύπους εἶναι τῆς ἐπὶ Πρωτεῖ βασιλεύοντι γραμματικῆς, <ἣν> Ἡρακλέα τὸν
Ἀμφιτρύωνος ἐκμαθεῖν, ὑφηγεῖσθαι μέντοι καὶ παραινεῖν τοῖς Ἕλλησι διὰ τῶν
γραμμάτων τὸν θεὸν ἄγειν σχολὴν καὶ εἰρήνην διὰ Φιλοσοφίας, ἀγωνιζομένους
ἀεὶ Μούσαις, καὶ λόγῳ διακρινομένους περὶ τῶν δικαίων τὰ ὅπλα καταθέντας.

'But for now, Simmias, please tell us if you know any more about the matter of
the writing we were just puzzling over. [578f] They say that the priests made out
the letters of the plaque which Agesilaus took from us when he took apart the
grave of Alcmene.' Simmias immediately recollected and said 'I know nothing
about this plaque, Pheidolaos, but Agestoridas the Spartan came to Memphis
to the house of the high priest Chonouphis carrying a long text … (there is a
lacuna of about 10 letters here) … At that time Plato, Ellopion of Peparethos
and I were staying there studying philosophy. He came on a mission from the
King and asked Chonouphis, if he could interpret the writing, to quickly send a
translation back to him. Chonouphis spent three days researching letter forms
of all sorts from old books [579a] and wrote back to the King and explained to us
that the letters commanded the creation of a competition for the Muses. The
letter forms belonged to writing of the time when Proteus was king. This is
the writing that Heracles the son of Amphitruo learned, and indeed the god
(Heracles) was instructing and advising the Greeks through this text to create
peace and leisure through Philosophy by laying down their arms, becoming
constant competitors for the Muses, and resolving their disputes on matters of
justice through words.'

5. **Verse epigram inscribed on base of a statue of Pythokles,** ca. 265–255 (prosopography). The brothers are known from a series of lists of contestants in the Amphictyonic
Soteria of Delphi, ca. 270/69–258/7 (Nachtergael 1977, 317–23, 406–12, 416–19, Actes
2bis–5, 8; *ATD* I, 166–70, TE 24A–C; Aneziri 2003, 276–7, 338–41, Ga 1–5) as well as
an honorary decree from Delphi (Nachtergael 1977, Actes 15; *SGDI* 2602). Pythokles
also served as priest of the Artists (probably of the Isthmian–Nemean Association). In the
competition lists he is identified as a choreut and as director of a men's lyric chorus (for
the meaning of ἄνδρας ἡγεμών, see Slater 1997, who notes that this is a role frequently
assumed by a musician). Here he is said to be victorious 'in circular choruses' and as
an '[aulo]de' and '[rhapso]de' (ll. 9–10). The inscription lists victories at the Isthmus (**B**

Introduction), at Delphi (**Cvi**), at the festival of Olympian Zeus in Pieria (Robert and Robert 1978, 423; **Cxii**), at the Mouseia in Thespiae, and at the Kadmeia in Thebes (**Cii**).

That the inscribed block is a statue base seems to be an inference from the text.

The text is only known from a copy made by the Abbé Michel Fourmont, not the most reliable of witnesses (Sandys 1908, 99; Macgregor Morris 2009, 389–90; Schnapp 2011, 301). Fourmont's transcription is reproduced in *CIG* 1212. Robert and Robert rightly observe 'le texte est trop mutilé pour être jamais restitué (copie de Fourmont)' (1978, 423). Exceptionally here, the square brackets indicate not only supplements but departures from Fourmont's transcription.

Found at Hermione in 1729.

Now lost or destroyed.

CIG 1212; Kaibel 1878, no. 926; *IG* IV 682; Nachtergael 1977, 429–30 no. 15 bis (= *SEG* 27, 115); Manieri 2009, 354–5 Thes. 7.

Text: close to Nachtergael.

[Παν]τακλῆς μ' ἀνέθηκεν· ἀδελφεός εἰμι δ' ἐκείν[ου]
  [Πυθο]κλέης πλείστων ἀντιτυχὼν ἀέθλων·
[–⏓– ν]ῖκ[αι] τ[ρε]ῖς καὶ δέκα, τὰς [Νεμέῃ τε]
  [καὶ π]αρὰ [Π]ειρήνην Κασταλίαν τ' ἔλ[α]βον,
5 [τὰς ἄλλας Ζεὺ]ς οἶδε[ν] Ὀλύμπ[ι]ος, ὡς ἐτύμας [τοι]
  [εἰπεῖν ἐξ ἱ]ε[ρ]οῦ [φθ]εγγόμενος στόματος·
[–⏓–⏓ φ]ῦλ' οὐ[κ ἄ]ν τις ἀ[ρ]ι[θ]μήσειεν,
  [οὓς ἀν' Ἀχαιίδα] γῆ[ν ἠ]γαγόμ[η]ν στεφάνους.
[ἀλλ' ὁπόσ' αὐλωι]δός τε καὶ ἐγκυκλίοισι χοροῖσιν,
10 [ὅσσα τε ῥαψωι]δός, ταῦτα καταγράφεται·
[ἡνίκα Βοιωτῶν] με [π]αν[ήγυ]ρ[ις] ἐστεφάν[ω]σεν,
  [–⏓–⏓ –] πρῶτ' ἀ[π]ε[ν]εγ[κά]μεν[ον],
[χώ] στέφανος Μούσαις Ἑλι[κω]νίσι καὶ Διονύσ[ωι]
  [Κ]αδμείωι, τρίτατ' ἦν κῦδος ἐμοῖς γενέταις.
15 [κ]αὶ [β]ασιλεῖς δώροισί [μ'] ἐτίμησαν τὸν ἀοιδόν
  [υ]ἱὸν Ἀριστάρχου, θεοῖς φίλον, Ἑρμιονῆ.

3 [Ἑλλαδικαὶ ν]ῖκ[αι] Wilamowitz   7 [ἄσπετα δ' ἄλλων φ]ῦλ' Wilamowitz
9 ΕΓΚΥΚΛΙΟΙΣΟΙΧΟΡΟΙΣΙ Fourmont   10 \ΛΟΣ Fourmont   [κωμ]ῳδός(?) Boeckh,
Kaibel, Fraenkel   [ῥαψωι]δός Nachtergael   11 Γ.Ο.ΙΜΕΤ.ΑΝ...Ρ.ΔΕΣΤΕΦΑΝΟΣΕΝ
Fourmont   13 ΣΤΕΦΑΝΟΣΜΟΥΣΑΙΣΕΛΙΙ..ΝΙΣΙΚΑΙΔΙΟΝΥΣΟΥ Fourmont

[Pan]takles dedicated me. I am tha[t] man's brother [Pytho]kles who won a great many prizes: t[hi]rteen are the (reading Wilamowitz's supplement '[Grecian]') [v]ictor[ies] which I w[o]n [at Nemea and] by [P]eirene and Kastala. ⁵ Olymp[i]an [Zeu]s is abl[e] to [at]test the truth of [the others when he gi]ves utterance [from his h]o[l]y mouth. No one [co]uld e[n]u[m]erate the (reading Wilamowitz's supplement '[vast quantity of other]') crowns which I [g]ather[e]d [across the Achaean] lan[d]. [But how many] both [as aulo]de and in circular choruses, ¹⁰ [and how many as rhapso]de (or reading Boeckh's supplement, '[as com]ic actor' or '[as com]ic poet') is all listed. [When] the [g]ath[eri]n[g of the Boeotians] crown[e]d me (lacuna of 5–7 syllables) first [I w]on, [and the] crown for the Heli[con]ian Muses and [K]admeian Dionys[us] was a third source of pride for my parents. [15] [E]ven [k]ings honoured the singer with gifts, me, the [s]on of Aristarchos, native of Hermione, dear to the gods.

Two sites are relevant to the theatre history of Thespiae: the city of Thespiae itself and the Valley of the Muses below Mount Helicon, 6 km to the west of Thespiae. About theatre in the city of Thespiae, there is little to be said beyond the fact that a theatre building mentioned by Pausanias (9.27.5) has been located recently by resistivity surveys (Slapšak 2007, 17–20; Bintliff et al. 2012, 22–3). The cult of the Muses in the Valley of the Muses is at least as old as Hesiod (**1**), and probably older (Caruso 2016, 114–15). Archaic pottery fragments were found not far from the altar of the Muses, but no architecture before the third century (Ridder 1922, 287–90; Roux 1954, 43).

To judge from the remains, a far more active cult centre in the Archaic period was the nearby summit of Helicon, close to a spring that has been identified as Hippokrene, and just a little more than a kilometre west of and above the theatre (see below). These Archaic remains include a rectangular building of Lesbian polygonal masonry, the head of a kouros, a boundary stone inscribed '[bo]undary of the sanctuary', and fragments of sixth-century pottery including one inscribed 'sacred to Ze[us]' (Caruso 2016, 107–8, 117–18). In the *Theogony*, Hesiod speaks of the Muses performing choral dance 'on the very tip of Helicon' (7), 'around the violet spring and the altar of the mighty son of Cronus' (3–5, cf. 6). Though the polygonal building may not be the altar of Zeus, the inscriptions seem to confirm Hesiod's claim that the summit was sacred to him (Caruso 2016, 118). The most significant of the finds on the summit of Helicon is an inscribed dedication on a fragment of a bronze bowl, apparently inscribed 'I a[m sacred] to Helikon[ios]', in lettering dated by Jeffery to 'c. 625–600' (1990, 91, 94 no. 6, pl. 8). Helikonios is presumably an epithet of Zeus (Schachter 1994, 101, 151) or conceivably Poseidon (Schachter 1986, 206–7). This has led to speculation that the bowl belongs to the tripod dedicated by Hesiod (on which, see Caruso 2016, 117), but by Hesiod's own testimony the Muses descended from the mountain to teach Hesiod song as he herded his flocks 'under Helicon' (*Th.* 9–10, 23) and it was there, in the valley below Helicon, that the Muses first addressed him and there that Hesiod dedicated his tripod (**1**).

It is in the Valley of the Muses that Pausanias (**2**) claims to have seen the tripod Hesiod dedicated (**1**, ll. 658–9) and he states that it was the 'oldest' in the sanctuary. Hesiod's fame probably added to the Archaic sanctuary's renown (cf. Caruso 2016, 125–6). Hesiod's hometown of Ascra was probably just another 2 km to the south-west of the Valley of the Muses (Schachter 1986, 150). When Thespiae took control of Ascra is a matter of dispute (Edwards 2004, 30–79). The Valley of the Muses was certainly under Thespian control from at least the fourth century (Schachter 1986, 153, 157).

The Valley of the Muses may have remained an independent rural sanctuary until the early fourth century. The literary evidence (**2–4**) indicates a significant refurbishment of the sanctuary in the first quarter of the fourth century. Myron's workshop in Athens, now probably headed by Strongylion, received a commission to produce two sets of statues of the Muses for dedication in the sanctuary (see on **2**). The statues by Lysippus, a group of Apollo and Hermes, and a Dionysus, followed within a few decades (**2**). As Schachter observes (1986, 157): 'It can thus be argued that there was in existence by that time an official cult, with an administrative organisation which had the resources to commission a set of statues from at least one of the major sculptors of the period. It is no longer a simple, rustic cult, but one over which the polis of Thespiae must by now have been exercising control.' Confirmation that outside interests were upgrading the sanctuary comes from **4**, which gives evidence of Sparta taking some interest in 'the creation of a competition for the Muses' in Boeotia, during its brief period of control over the region (Schachter 1986, 157; Manieri 2009, 347–9). Although Thebes threw off the Spartan yoke in 379, Thespiae remained under Spartan control from the time of the Spartan incursion into Boeotia in 382 until 374. Sparta's specific interest was doubtless connected with the strategic importance of the stretch of land between Haliartus (cf. **4**) and Thespiae, with the sanctuary midway between them, in controlling the invasion route over Helicon from southern Greece into the Boeotian plain (cf. Edwards 2004, 169–70). It may seem strange that a Spartan-dominated and narrowly oligarchic Thespiae (Hansen *IACP* 457) would commission statues from Athenian workshops, but as Corso (2004) points out, Myron's workshop had a long history of co-operation both with Sparta and with Athenian and foreign oligarchs (see on **2**).

Even if the competitions for the Muses date to the time of the Spartan occupation, they continued after Thespiae was forced by Thebes in 372 to join the Second Boeotian Confederacy. In the period between the battles of Leuctra and Chaeronea, Epaminondas instituted or revived a number of festivals to celebrate, in the name of all Boeotians, the Theban victory over Sparta: the Basileia at Lebadeia, the Ptoia at Akraiphiai and the Panboiotia at Itonion. The Boeotian Confederacy assumed the management of the Mouseia as well as the Basileia, Ptoia and even the Theban Agrionia (Manieri 2009, 140–1). It is indeed possible to interpret **4** as an aetiology for the Mouseia at least partially shaped in this era, since the value of the advice of Chonouphis to the seemingly invincible Spartans to lay down their arms and seek peace lies in its implied prognostication of the irremediable defeat they would suffer at Theban hands (Manieri 2009, 139). Diodorus (15.53) reports an oracle of Trophonius at Lebadea commanding the Boeotians to institute a festival and competition for Zeus (the Basileia) should they be victorious at Leuctra. This doubtless stems from the same context.

We have abundant evidence for the performance of music in the Valley of the Muses from the last third of the third century, probably no later than 230–225 (Schachter 2016a, 344, 357). Inscriptions give evidence of a reorganisation of the festival in three stages (Schachter 2016a, 371): (1) the creation of musical competitions including competitions for pipers, auldes (cf. *IThesp.* 204), kithara, kitharodes (cf. Hesiod's statue in **2**), and epic poetry (cf. *IThesp.* 206); (2) probably in the 210s, the elevation of the five above-named contests to the status of crown competitions (stephanitic; *IThesp.* 156A, ll. 17–21); (3) in ca. 204, the transformation of the competitions into quadrennial (penteteric) festival events, and their expansion, with funding from Ptolemy IV, to include tragedy, satyr play and comedy (Manieri 2009, 333–8; Schachter 2016a, 350–1). It is probable that drama had no part in any earlier Mouseia as *IThesp.* 152–4 specifically records a request by Thespiae, backed by the Boeotian Confederacy to Ptolemy IV and Arsinoe III to permit competitions in tragedy and comedy (cf. Schachter 2016a, 359 no. 1; Manieri 2009, Thes. 15).

We have only **3** and **5** to help fill in the history of the musical competitions that were held at the Mouseia between ca. 380 and ca. 230, a period in which it is assumed that the festival and its competitions were held annually (Manieri 2009, 318). Amphion of Thespiae (**3**) speaks of boys' (circular?) choruses, but Athenaeus has him cite in evidence an inscribed statue base from the sanctuary that speaks rather of men's choruses. **3**, therefore, seems certain evidence of men's and somewhat more problematic evidence of boys' ('dithyrambic' or 'circular'?) choruses. On the usual dating, the epigram quoted by **3** belongs to the fourth century, so probably gives evidence for the musical programme in the first 150 years of the Mouseia, though perhaps not the entire period, as there is nothing to exclude the possibility that the epigram on **3** belongs to the first three quarters of the third century. It is almost certainly no later. Contrary to Lewis 1984, 180, there is no evidence of circular choruses after the reform of the Mouseia, ca. 225, when our epigraphic evidence for competitions is relatively abundant, until only the third century AD (*IG* VII 1776 = Manieri 2009, Thes. 49, l. 21).

More precisely datable (ca. 265–ca. 255), but still less helpful for determining the kind of competitions held in the fourth century, is **5**. Pythokles merely states that he won a 'crown for the Heli[con]ian Muses'. We can only guess at the full range of Pythokles' talents. Apart from 'circular choruses' (**5**, l. 9), two other roles are named in his prize-winning itinerary, but the labels are largely lost. **5**, ll. 9–10 names two different roles that survive only in the form '[- -]δός', with the last three letters probably preceded by two long syllables: [τρᾰγωι]δός is therefore not an option, but aulode, rhapsode or comic actor/choreut ([αὐλωι]δός, [ῥαψωι]δός and [κωμωι]δός) all are options. On other inscriptions Pythokles is listed as a choreut and a leader of a men's chorus (see on **5**). But none of these supplements necessarily throws light on the nature of the victory at the Mouseia and it is probably safest, given **3**, to assume that Pythokles' victory there was with one of the many circular choruses mentioned in **5**, l. 9.

5 is therefore very far from corroborating the existence of dramatic competitions of any kind at the Mouseia before ca. 204 (despite Feyel 1942, 115; Manieri 2009, 318). **3** is even further from supporting any such conclusion, despite Schachter (1986, 163), who wrongly assumed that **3** was a choregic monument, and further that this somehow implicated drama. The tripods attested by Pausanias (**2** at 9.31.3) need not be choregic dedications or even victory dedications relating to the Mouseia, though the latter is not unlikely. Personal dedications by individuals and collective dedications by cities and leagues were common in prominent sanctuaries in Boeotia (Papalexandrou 2008). Apart from Hesiod's (**1**), the only tripod dedication to the Muses at Thespiae for which we have specific information is an early third-century tripod dedication by the Boeotian Confederacy (*IG* VII 1795; Papalexandrou 2008, 270; Mackil 2014, 60–1).

The archaeological remains are also of little help in determining the fourth- to third-century festival programme. The excavations in 1888–1890 by Jamot recovered no buildings that could be dated earlier than the third century (1895). Indeed the Valley seems to have been left deliberately underdeveloped and the natural beauty of the setting deliberately preserved (Manieri 2009, 314; Caruso 2016, 115). In the third century there was a monumental altar in the midst of a large open space bordered by stoas to the west and north (Roux 1954, 25–36; Manieri 2009, 313; Caruso 2016, 108–10). Three hundred metres south-west of the west stoa was a theatron in the form of a natural semicircular depression, enhanced by terracing, but which never had stone benchwork, and was, even in late antiquity, either built of wood or left uncovered for audiences to sit directly on the hillside

(Roux 1954, 36–8). Only the prohedria may have had stone seats (Ridder 1922, 221 no. 5). The theatre was equipped with a stage building of which only the proskenion survives. The letter forms of its mason's marks indicate a date in the early decades of the second century, suggesting that the theatre was built for the dramatic performances added to the Mouseia in and after ca. 204 (Roux 1954, 38; Schachter 2016a, 358 n. 42). Yet nothing prevents us from supposing that the use of the hillside as a theatron was older.

The city of Thespiae became the site of a festival of Eros, the Erotideia, founded in the second century (Manieri 2009, 342–3). It included a kitharodic contest by the mid first century AD (**2**; Plu. *Mor.* 749c) and choral performances are attested in the second (*SEG* 36, 476; Manieri 2009, 432–3 Thes. 57). The music contests were held in the theatre(s?: Plu. *Mor.* 749c). There is no evidence for drama.

Cvi: Delphi

1. Plutarch, *Convivial Questions* (*Moralia*) 674d–e. Probably written after 99 and before 116 AD (Jones 1966, 72–3). The individual discussions in this work have fictional settings of varying date. This discussion contains a reference to the agonothesia of L. Cassius Petraeus (*Mor.* 674f), which can be dated to 99 or 103 AD (*Syll.*³ 825A–C). Plutarch had a keen interest in the affairs of Delphi for most of his life (Stadter 2014, 70–81), and became priest of Pythian Apollo at Delphi from ca. 90 to ca. 120 AD (Jones 1966, 73). Other sources claim the existence of a contest of kitharodes 'singing a paean to the god' even before the foundation by the Pyleo-Delphic Amphictyony of the Pythian Games, ca. 582 (see under **2**). The Amphictyony added to the kitharodes, according to Strabo 9.3.10, athletic games, solo pipes and solo kithara, or, according to Pausanias 10.7.4, *aulodia* and solo pipe-playing (though at 10.7.5 he claims that *aulodia* was withdrawn by the second Pythia). Text: Hubert.

> ἐν Πυθίοις ἐγίνοντο λόγοι περὶ τῶν ἐπιθέτων ἀγωνισμάτων, ὡς ἀναιρετέα. παραδεξάμενοι γὰρ ἐπὶ τρισὶ τοῖς καθεστῶσιν ἐξ ἀρχῆς, αὐλητῇ Πυθικῷ καὶ κιθαριστῇ καὶ κιθαρῳδῷ, τὸν τραγῳδόν, ὥσπερ πύλης ἀνοιχθείσης οὐκ ἀντέσχον ἀθρόοις συνεπιτιθεμένοις καὶ συνεισιοῦσι παντοδαποῖς ἀκροάμασιν· ὑφ᾽ ὧν ποικιλίαν μὲν ἔσχεν οὐκ ἀηδῆ καὶ πανηγυρισμὸν ὁ ἀγών, τὸ δ᾽ αὐστηρὸν καὶ μουσικὸν ⁶⁷⁴ᵉ οὐ διεφύλαξεν, ἀλλὰ καὶ πράγματα τοῖς κρίνουσιν παρέσχεν καὶ πολλὰς ὡς εἰκὸς ἡττωμένων πολλῶν ἀπεχθείας.

At the Pythian Games there was discussion about whether the added competitions should be removed from the programme. When they accepted the tragedian in addition to the three competitors that had been there since the foundation, namely the Pythian piper, the kitharist and the kitharode, it was as if the floodgates had opened and they were no longer able to resist the massed onslaught of musical entertainments of every variety that kept thronging in. As a result the competition had a not displeasing variety and festive appeal, but it lost its austere and musical quality ⁶⁷⁴ᵉ and also created difficulties for the judges and presumably a lot of animosity from defeated contestants.

2. **Accounts of the Pyleo-Delphic Amphictyony**, 326/5? (Bommelaer 2002, 127). The dating is very uncertain. In col. 1, l. 21, there is possibly a reference to the 'Ho[plo]-th[ek]e', which other inscriptions show to be under construction in the sanctuary from 334 until 320 (*CID* II 79A, l. 33 [supplement]; 83, l. 11; 84 col. B, l. 9; 87, l. 3 [supplement]; 109 A, l. 17; 110, l. 35). The name Damoteles of Olynthus appears as a recipient in col. 1, l. 12, which suggests a date not too late in the 4th c. (Olynthus was destroyed in 348; cf. Bourguet 1900, 484). The layout of the accounts in two columns is a style also found in an account dated to 325/4 (*CID* II 100). The 'Pyleo-Delphic Amphictyony' is a modern name for the group of states surrounding Delphi ('amphictyony') that since the First Sacred War in the early sixth century regulated the organisation and finance of the sanctuary of Delphi. The Amphictyony was also responsible for the sanctuary of Demeter at Thermopylae (hence 'Pyleo-Delphic'). Only column 2 line 19 is given below. The line represents a construction expense.

Two fragments of a badly worn limestone plaque, possibly complete at top, bottom missing, left side preserved.
0.85 × 1.04 × 0.215 (originally more than 0.23) m.
The plaque contains two columns of accounts inscribed by two different hands. It is now completely illegible and *CID* II 101 depends on Bourget's text in *FD* III 5, 75.
Found in 1896 in the paving of the opisthodomos in the north-east corner of the Temple of Apollo at Delphi. The plaque served as a pedestal for a statue before it was used as a paving block.
Delphi inv. 4894.
FD III 5, 75; *CID* II 101.
Text: *CID* II 101 with corrected accent.

col. 2, l. 19 σκην[ὴ σταδ]ίου πυθικοῦ Σ[— — — — — —].ΤΕΡ..   stoich. 38–9

            sken[e of the] Pythian [Stad]ium

3. **Accounts of the Pyleo-Delphic Amphictyony relating to works in preparation for the Pythia**, 251/0 or 247/6 (Archon date). The accounts are organised sector by sector: work in the gymnasium ends at l. 23, then follows work in the Pythian stadium up to l. 35, after which the inscription proceeds to work on the hippodrome. We give only lines 25–30 which seem to include preparations for musical and scenic events.

Limestone stele broken into seven fragments, bottom missing, moulding broken at top.
0.725 × 0.52 × 0.12 m.
Found during excavation on 10 June 1896; the fragments were built into the paving of the Sacred Way north-east of the Temple of Apollo at Delphi.
Delphi inv. 3862.
Homolle 1899, 564–9; Pouilloux 1977; *CID* II 139, ll. 25–30; Hellmann 1999, 70–2 no. 20; *CID* IV 57; Jacquemin et al. 2012, 210–13 no. 116.
Text: Jacquemin et al.   Photo: Pouilloux 1977, 104 fig. 1.

25   τ[οῦ ὠ]ιδείου τὰν ποί[η]σιν Νίκων : ΔΔΔΔΣΣΣΣΗΙΙΙ : ἐ[ν τὸ π]υθικὸν
          στάδιο[ν]
      γᾶς λευκᾶς με<u>δίμνους</u> : ΓΗ: Ξενων, τὸν μέδιμνον : ΙϹΧ[Χ : γί]νεται τὸ πᾶν : Γ
      ΔΔΔΣΣΣΙΙΙΙ : τὰν βάθρωσιν [τοῦ] θεά[τρου τοῦ πυ]θικοῦ Μελισσ[ίων] :
          ΔΔΓΣΣΣ : τὰν
      φράξιν τοῦ πυθικοῦ σταδίου Εὐθύδαμο[ς] : Δ : <u>τοῦ προσκανίου τὰν πᾶξιν ἐν
          τ[ῶι]
      πυθικῶι σταδίωι Νίκων : ΓΣ : τὰν βάθρωσιν ἐν τ<u>ῶι</u> πυθικῶι σταδίωι Νίκων,
          πόδας [:.:],
30   στατήρων : Γ :

Nikon for the cons[tr]uction of t[he m]usic hall: 44 staters 1 drachma, 3 obols.
Xenon for 600 medimnoi of white earth i[n the P]ythian Stadiu[m]: at 1 2/3
obols per medimnon, the total [co]mes to 83 staters, 4 obols. Meliss[ion] for
the benchwork of [the Py]thian the[atre]: 28 staters. Euthydamo[s] for the
fencing of the Pythian stadium: 10 staters. Nikon for setting up the proskenion
in t[he] Pythian stadium: 6 staters. Nikon for the benchwork in the Pythian
stadium [at ??] per foot: 5 staters.

4. Plutarch, *On the E in Delphi* (*Moralia*) 389b–c. Written probably not long after 95
AD (Jones 1966, 72). Plutarch here recognises a homology between the proportions
of the Great Year (the periodic creation and destruction of the world) and the Delphic
year: as the former is divided between a stable orderly period and a chaotic destructive
phase, so the latter is divided, in the same proportion of three parts to one, between an
Apollonian and a Dionysian phase. For Plutarch's intellectual background here, see
Rutherford 2013b, 416–18. Text: Bernadakis.

ἐπεὶ δ᾽ οὐκ ἴσος ὁ τῶν περιόδων ἐν ταῖς [389c] μεταβολαῖς χρόνος, ἀλλὰ μείζων
ὁ τῆς ἑτέρας ἣν ᾿κόρον᾽ καλοῦσιν, ὁ δὲ τῆς ᾿χρησμοσύνης᾽ ἐλάττων, τὸ κατὰ
λόγον τηροῦντες ἐνταῦθα τὸν μὲν ἄλλον ἐνιαυτὸν παιᾶνι χρῶνται περὶ
τὰς θυσίας, ἀρχομένου δὲ χειμῶνος ἐπεγείραντες τὸν διθύραμβον τὸν δὲ
παιᾶνα καταπαύσαντες, τρεῖς μῆνας ἀντ᾽ ἐκείνου τοῦτον κατακαλοῦνται τὸν
θεόν· ὅπερ τρία πρὸς ἕν, τοῦτο τὴν διακόσμησιν οἰόμενοι χρόνῳ πρὸς τὴν
ἐκπύρωσιν εἶναι.᾽

Because the time of the cycles in these [389c] transformations is not equal, but
the one they call 'Fullness' is greater, the one they call 'Lack' is lesser, they
preserve the proportion here and perform paeans at their sacrifices for the rest
of the year, but at the beginning of winter they put to rest the paean and rouse
the dithyramb and for three months they invoke the god with this instead. For
just the same ratio, three to one, they ascribe to the time difference between the
period of order and the time of conflagration.

5. Bacchylides, fr. 16, *Dithyramb* 2, lines 1–16. Bacchylides lived ca. 510–ca. 431. The
datable remains are to the first half of the 5ᵗʰ c. Both the title and the contents of this

poem (of which only the first 16 of 35 lines are given here) indicate that Bacchylides wrote for a performance at Delphi. For the Hellenistic origin and variable reliability of the titles of the individual poems (here given in square brackets), see Rutherford 2001, 150–2. Text: After Maehler with minor variation.

[ΗΡΑΚΛΗΣ (or ΔΗΙΑΝΕΙΡΑ ?)
ΕΙΣ ΔΕΛΦΟΥΣ]

[. . .]ιου . ι̣ο̣ . . . ἐπεὶ
[ὁλκ]άδ᾽ ἔπεμψεν ἐμοὶ χρυσέαν
[Πιερ]ίαθεν ἐ̣[ὔθ]ρο̣ν̣ος [Ο]ὐρανία,
[πολυφ]άτων γέμουσαν ὕμνων
5   [. . . . .]ν̣ε̣ι̣τ̣ις ἐπ᾽ ἀνθεμόεντι Ἕβρῳ
[. . . . . ἀ]γάλλεται ἢ δολιχαύχενι κύ[κνῳ]
[. . . . .]δεϊα[[ν]] φρένα τερπόμενος
[. . . . . .]δ᾽ ἵκῃ παιηόνων
ἄνθεα πεδοιχνεῖν,
10   Πύθι᾽ Ἄπολλον,
τόσα χοροὶ Δελφῶν
σὸν κελάδησαν παρ᾽ ἀγακλέα ναόν.

πρίν γε κλέομεν λιπεῖν
Οἰχαλίαν πυρὶ δαπτομέναν
15   Ἀμφιτρυωνιάδαν θρασυμηδέα φῶ-
θ᾽, ἵκετο δ᾽ ἀμφικύμον᾽ ἀκτάν·

5]Ν or]Α̣ι Maehler   εὔχομ]αι Schmidt   ἢ καλό]ν Handley   εἴ τις Milne   6 θηρσίν Jebb   δάφναι Blass   μούσαι Schmidt   μολπᾶι ? Maehler   ἀγάλλεαι Barrett   7 Α³ (an ancient correction to Papyrus A) deletes Ν and writes Ι over it

[*Heracles* (or *Deianeira* ?) for Delphi]

[…] now that [well-th]roned [O]urania has sent me a golden [sh]ip from Pieiria filled with [famo]us hymns ⁵ […] by the flowery Hebrus [r]ejoices (or 'you rejoice' [Barrett]) in the ('beasts' [Jebb], 'laurel' [Blass], 'song' [Schmidt], or the long-necked sw[an]) […] delighting in spirit you come for a share of the flowers of paeans, ¹⁰ Pythian Apollo, all those that the choruses of Delphians sing beside your illustrious temple. But until then we will glorify the departure from Oichalia when it was consumed by fire ¹⁵ of the son of Amphitryon, a brave man. He came to the wave-beaten shore …

6. **Inscribed stele recording Philodamus' Paean for Dionysus and an honorific decree of Delphi**. Date: Archonship of Etymondas, probably 339/8 (Bousquet 1988b, 58) or 340/39 (Vatin 1964, 448–52; Marchetti 1977; Manieri 2015, 27). Internal evidence indicates that the poem was commissioned for performance at the Theoxenia, a sacrifice at Delphi to all the gods held annually in early spring (ll. 110–12: Apollo commands that

'we present this hymn for the holy race of the gods in the annual reception of the gods', δε[ῐξ]αι [δ'] ἐγ ξενίοις ἐτείοις θεῶν ἱερῷ γένει συναίμῳ τόνδ' ὕμνον: see further Käppel 1992, 209–11). Pindar's *Paean* 6 was also performed at this festival (l. 61 'in the reception of the gods', ἐν θεῶν ξενίᾳ; cf. Sch. Pi. *Pae.* 6.62), as were a prosodion, paean, and hymn by Kleochares of Athens in ca. 227 (*FD* III 2, 78). Philodamus may be the poet of a men's chorus at Athens ca. 350: *IG* II³ 4, 450; Stefanis no. 2945. The decree at the end of this inscription is probably just a little earlier than a similar inscription of hymns and an honorary decree of the poet Aristonous (*FD* III 2, 190–2; Vamvouri Ruffy 2004, 211–15). The honours given Philodamus and his brothers by Delphi are those normally given to victorious athletes at the Pythia. Of earlier poets only Pindar is reported to have received such honours from Delphi (Rutherford 2001, 180; for later poets *Syll.*³ 447–52). Only the last two of twelve stanzas and the subscript honorary decree are given here.

Twenty-five fragments of a stele inscribed with two 50-line columns of verse organised into 12 stanzas.
Largest fragment: 0.875 × 0.87 m.
Fifteen fragments found during excavations at Delphi some time between 1892 and 1895 with another ten fragments found before 1897 'in the pavement of the sacred way by the altar of Chians, and lay with text downwards' (Poulsen 1920, 18 n. 3).
Weil 1895; Weil 1897; *CA*, 165–71; Vollgraff 1927; Sokolowski 1936; *SEG* 32, 552; Käppel 1992, 375–80; Furley and Bremer 2001 II, 52–84.
Text: close to Furley and Bremer.

<blockquote>

Πυθιάσιν δὲ πενθετή-
ροις [π]ροπό[λοῖς] ἔταξε Βάκχου θυσίαν χορῶν τε πο[λ]-
[λῶν] κυκλίαν ἅμιλλαν
135   - Εὐοῖ ὦ ἰὸ Βακχ' ὦ ἰὲ Π[αιάν]-
τεύχειν, ἁλιοφεγγέσιν
δ' ἀ[ντ]ο[λαῖς] ἴσον ἁβρὸν ἄγαλμα Βάκχου
ἐν [ζεύγει] χρυσέων λεόν-
των στῆσαι, ζαθέῳ τε τ[εῦ]-
140   ξαι θεῷ πρέπον ἄντρον.
Ἰὲ Παιά[ν, ἴθι σω]τήρ,
εὔφρων τάνδε πόλ[ιν φ]ύλασσ'
εὐα[ίωνι] σὺν ὄλβῳ.

ἀλλὰ δέχεσθε Βακχ[ιά]ς̣-
145   [τα]ν Δι[ό]νυσ[ον, ἐν δ' ἀγυι]-
αῖς ἅμα σὺγ [χορ]οῖσι κ[ι]-
[κλήσκετε] κισσ[οχ]αίταις
- Ε[ὐο]ῖ ὦ ἰὸ Βακχ' ὦ ἰὲ [Παιὰν]-
πᾶσαν ['Ελ]λάδ' ἀν' ὀ[λβί]αμ
150   παν. . . .ετε. .πολ. .υ. . .στα. .νας. .ρεπι.
λω. . . . . .ν. . .ιο.ε. . .κυκλι[

</blockquote>

[χαῖρ' ἄ]να[ξ] ὑγιείας.
Ἰὲ Παι[άν, ἴθι σωτήρ·]
155   [εὔφρων] τάνδε πόλιν φύλασσ'
[εὐαίωνι σὺν ὄλβῳ.]

θ[ε]ο[ί]·
Δελφοὶ ἔδωκαν Φιλοδάμ[ωι Αἰν]ησιδάμου Σκαρφεῖ καὶ τοῖς ἀδελφοῖς
    Ἐπιγένε[ι]
[..]ντίδαι αὐτοῖς καὶ ἐκ[γόνοις] προξενίαν, προμαντείαν, προεδρίαν,
    προδικ[ίαν],
[ἀτέ]λειαν, ἐπι[τιμ]ὰν, καθ[άπερ Δε]λφοῖς· ἄρχοντος Ἐτυμώνδα, βουλευόντων
[Πλ]εισίστωνος Καλλικρ[άτεος — — —].
vacant versus duo
[ἐπεὶ Φιλόδαμος καὶ τοὶ ἀδέλφο]ι τομ παιᾶνα τὸν ἐς τὸν Διόνυσον
[ἐποιήσαν ......¹².... κατὰ τὰ]ν μαντείαν τοῦ Θεοῦ ἐπαγγείλα<ν>τ[ος]
[. . . . . .³⁹. . . . . .αι, τυχἀγαθᾶι

132 [π]ροπό[λοῖς] Sokolowski   [-ι] τροπαῖ[ς] Weil   [ἄρ'] ὁ παῖ[ς] Vollgraff   137
ἀ[ντ]ο[λαῖς] Vollgraff   ἀ[ρχ]ο[ύσαις] Weil   150 γᾶν [χωρε]ῖτ' ἐ[πὶ] πολ[υθ]ύ[του]ς
τ' Ἀ[θά]νας Vollgraff   παν[νυχίζ]ετε Sokolowski   παν[νυχίζ]ετ' ἐ[πὶ] πολ[υθ]ύ[του]ς τ'
Ἀ[θά]νας Croissant

He (Apollo) gave instructions to his [s]erva[nts] to produce at the Pythia of every four years a sacrifice for Bacchus and a circular contest of m[any] choruses [135] – Euoi o io Bacchus o ie P[aean] – and to set up a statue of Bacchus, resplendent like the sun-kissed [d]a[wn], upon a [yoke] of golden lions (i.e. chariot drawn by lions) and to [fas]hion [140] a fitting cave for the radiant god. Ie Paea[n, come Sa]viour! Benevolently [g]uard this cit[y] with ha[ppy] prosperity.

But receive the Bacch[ia]s[t] [145] Di[o]nys[us, and in the stre]ets [summon] him together with ivy-coi[ff]ed [chor]uses. – E[uo]i o io Bacchus o ie [Paean] – throughout all b[less]ed [Gr]eece [150] (reading Croissant's supplements 'celebrate all[-night procession] and t[o] A[the]ns gen[er]o[us in sacrifi]ce') [...] circul[ar. Hail L]ord of health. Ie Pae[an, come Saviour!] [155] [Benevolently] guard this city [with happy prosperity].

G[o]d[s]! The Delphians gave to Philodam[us], son of [Ain]esidamos, of Skarpheia, and to his brothers, Epigene[s] and […]ntidas, both to them and to their off[spring]: proxeny, *promanteia* (the right of priority consultation of the oracle), prohedria, *prodik[ia]* (preferential access to the courts), *ateleia* (freedom from taxation), *epitime* (the enjoyment of citizen rights), just [like the De]lphians (possess): in the Archonship of Eymondas, the councillors being [Pl]eisiton, son of Kallikr[ates …].

(two empty lines)

[Since Philodamus and his brother]s [composed] the paean for Dionysus [… according to th]e oracle, when the God comma<n>d[ed …] with good fortune.

7. Pinax dedication to Apollo by four boy Pythaistai. Date: ca. 370–350 (letter forms, style, orthography, but mainly the prosopographical argument based on a possible identification of Timokritos). A Timokritos, son of Timokrates, was a prytanis and so at least thirty in 341/0 (*Agora* 15, 38, l. 26; Boethius 1918, 27). This may be the homonymous boy Pythaist named in this dedication. If so, Timokritos may be from Ikarion. The syntrierarch of ca. 350 Timokrates of Ikarion has been identified as his father, while another Eupatrid Pythaist of 107/6 Timokrates Timokr[- - - -] may be a descendant (*APF* no. 13768). Some argue therefore that the Pythais in question was that of the Marathonian Tetrapolis (see commentary). Timokrates however is a very common Athenian name (136 entries in *LGPN* II) and Timokritos is not rare.

Relief pinax dedication said to be of Pentelic marble.
0.445 × 0.375 × 0.04–0.06 m.
The relief shows from left to right a seated goddess, doubtless Leto, a standing Artemis and Apollo, who are approached by four boys wearing garlands and wrapped in himatia and accompanied by a single adult male who raises his right arm to greet Apollo.
It is not known how the relief ended up in Rome. It appears in the publication of the collection of Baron Giovanni Barracco (Barracco et al. 1892, 41). Said to have been 'found in Greece': Köhler suspected it came from the Pythion in Ikarion (**III M Introduction**).
Museo Barracco 129.
IG II 5, 1190c; *IG* II² 2816; Boethius 1918, Test. 12; Rutherford 2013a, C5; *IG* II³ 4, 632.
Photos: Barracco et al. 1892, pl. 50; *Enciclopedia dell'arte antica* IV, fig. 590; Lawton 2007, fig. 2.9; *IG* II³ 4, 1 tab. LXXXV.

> Πυθαισταὶ ἀνέθεσαν τῶι Ἀπόλλωνι.
>
> | | | | |
> |---|---|---|---|
> | Πείθων | Τιμόκριτος | Ἀμεινοκλῆς | Ἁγνόδημος |
> | Σωσιγένος | Τιμοκράτος | Ἀμεινίππο | Ἁγνοθέο. |

> The Pythaistai dedicated this to Apollo.
>
> | | | | |
> |---|---|---|---|
> | Peithon | Timokritos | Ameinokles | Hagnodemos |
> | son of Sosigenes | son of Timokrates | son of Ameinippos | son of Hagnotheos |

8. Decree of Pyleo-Delphic Amphictyony honouring Aristotle and Callisthenes for composing the *Register of Pythian Victors*. Date: probably ca. 336 or 335, and at latest by 327 (first record of costs related to inscription of the list: see below). The decree mentions 'treasurers' (l. 11), an office that was instituted in 337/6 (Bousquet *CID* II, pp. 146–9; R-O II 394). This *terminus post* is reinforced by Miller's observation that the inscription on a statue base of Agias, erected sometime between 336 and 332, shows a correction that seems prompted by the publication of the *Register of Pythian Victors* (1978, 140–1). It has been argued that since the decree envisages the crowning of Aristotle and Callisthenes it must be earlier than Callisthenes' departure for Asia with Alexander in 335, but the inference is open to doubt. Since the work is described as collaborative, however, it does imply that the work was at least well underway by that date. Robertson argues for a composition date between 345 and 340 (1978, 58–9). The *Register of Pythian Victors* is thought to have included the history of the Games, established the chronology of the Pythiads, and also listed all the victors in the athletic and musical contests (Arist. frr. 615–17 Rose; Christesen 2007, 179–202, 374–81). The glory and status this conferred on the Pythian festival was enough to license these honours, though political considerations may have played a part. In addition to the Athenian connections mentioned below in the commentary, it should be noted that the decree belongs to a period when Philip (or, after 336, Alexander) dominated the Amphictyonic Council (in 346 at the end of the Third Sacred War the two seats on the Council that had belonged to the Phocideans were transferred to delegates appointed by the Macedonian king: see generally Manieri 2015). After Alexander's death Delphi rescinded the honours for Aristotle and it may be at that time that the decree was broken and this fragment thrown into the well where it was found (Ael. *VH* 14.1; R-O II 395). The inscribing of the *Register of Pythian Victors* at Delphi certainly took place though we have no trace of the monument beyond the accounts for its production. In an account for 327/6 (*FD* III 5, 58), the stonecutter Deinomachos is paid two mnai for inscribing the *Register of Pythian Victors* (ll. 42–3: Δεινομάχω[ι], τῶμ Πυθιονικῶν ἀναγραφῆς, κελευσάντων | [τ]ῶν ἱερομνημόνων, μνᾶς δύο). We know of possibly three other disbursements for inscribing this work in 330 (*FD* III 5, 58B, ll. 6–7 and supplement to 60A, l. 9), and possibly in 324 (*FD* III 5, 61, ll. 36–7). We follow *Syll.*³ and R-O II in assigning the decree to the Delphic Amphictyony (not the city of Delphi: Homolle 1898 et al.), since payment for inscribing the *Pythian Victors* is made by the treasurers of the Amphictyony (l. 11).

Fragment of a marble stele, broken on all but the left side.
0.25 × 0.26 × 0.08 m.
Found on 30 June 1895, in a well south-east of the precinct ('near the Pappaioannou house') at Delphi.
Delphi Museum inv. 2829.
Homolle 1898; *FD* III 1, 400; *Syll.*³ 275; Callisthenes *FGrH* 124 T 23; Bousquet 1988a; R-O II 392–5 no. 80; Jacquemin et al. 2012, 115–16 no. 49.
Text: R-O II.   Photos: *FD* III 1, p. 237 fig. 39; Miller 1978, pl. 2; Mulliez 2013, 153 fig. 4.

```
        [- - - - ¹¹ - - - - ἐπεὶ]     stoich. 15
        [Ἀριστοτέλης Νικο]-
        [μάχου Σταγιρίτης]
        [καὶ Καλλισθένης Δ]-
        [αμοτίμου Ὀλύνθιο]-
   1    [ς συ]νέ[ταξαν πίνακ]-
        [α] τῶν α[...]. [... νεν]-
        ικηκό[τ]ων τὰ [Πύθια]
        καὶ τῶν ἐξ ἀρχ[ῆς τὸ]-
   5    ν ἀγῶνα κατασκ[ευα]-
        σάντων, ἐπαινέ[σαι]
        Ἀριστοτέλην κα[ὶ Κ]-
        αλ[λι]σθένην καὶ [στ]-
        εφανῶσαι· ἀνα[θεῖν]-
```

10   αι δὲ τὸν πίν[ακα το]-
     ὑς ταμία[ς ἐν τῶι ἱε]-
     ρῶι με[ταγεγραμμέ]-
     νο[ν εἰς στήλας — — —]

2 ἀ[πὸ Γυλίδα] Homolle   ἀ[π' αἰῶνος] Preuner, Bousquet   ἀ[μφότερα] Witkowski

[… since Aristotle, son of Nikomachos, of Stagira and Callisthenes, son of Damotimos, of Olynthus [1] put to]ge[ther a table] of those [vic]torious at the [Pythia] ('f[rom ?the Archonship of Gylis]' Homolle; or 'f[rom eternity]' Preuner, Bousquet) and of those who from the beginning org[ani]sed [5] the contest, to prai[se] Aristotle an[d C]al[li]sthenes and to [cr]own them. [10] [T]he treasur[ers in the sa]nctuary are to set [up] the tab[le] tr[anscribe]d [onto stelai …]

Chronological Summary

ca. 600	First Sacred War
582/1	creation of quadrennial Pythian Games
356–346	Third Sacred War
346–323	Macedonian domination of Amphictyony
ca. 300–ca. 275	construction of stadium NW of Sanctuary
279	winter, Celtic invasion of Delphi
279/8?	creation of Soteria
ca. 260–191	Aetolian domination of Delphi
191	Romans 'liberate' Delphi from Aetolians (who sided with Antiochus III in Syrian War)
ca. 170–ca. 140	construction of stone theatre
168–5th c. AD	Roman domination of Delphi (after Third Macedonian War)

The Pythia held every fourth year in Delphi was the second oldest and most prestigious Panhellenic competition in Greece after the Olympic Games. Founded ca. 582 (Mosshammer 1982), it was the first Panhellenic festival to include regular musical competitions. The first competitions were for *kitharoidia* (solo song accompanied by the kithara), unaccompanied piping, and either unaccompanied kithara or *aulodia* (song accompanied by pipes: see on **1**). The early history of kitharodic competitions is especially well attested but for the most part invented at a late date for the glorification of the festival (Power 2010, 371–8).

Plutarch (**1**) states that tragedy was the first of the later additions to the musical contests of the Pythia. The presence of tragedy and comedy in the official programme of the Pythia can only be confirmed from the time of Nero (Philostr. *VA* 5.9 [195], 6.10 [238]) until at least as late as 193–196 AD (Philostr. *VS* 2.27.2 [616]; cf. Plu. *Mor.* 410a-14c; *FD* III 4, 86; Philostr. *VS* 2.1 [553–4]; Bourguet 1905, 89; Vollgraff 1919, 258–60 no. 26). It may be that **1** complains of a relatively recent phenomenon. Earlier we hear only of occasional performances 'dedicated to Apollo' by various musicians (Sifakis 1967, 95–8). Possibly to be connected to the Pythia was a performance at Delphi dedicated to

Apollo in 165 by a tragic actor, Nikon of Megalopolis (*FD* III 1, 48; Sifakis 1967, 97; Stefanis no. 1886).

We know of no dramatic competitions held at Delphi before the creation of the Soteria. The festival of the Soteria was instituted to thank Apollo for saving Delphi from a raid by Celts in 279. The precise date of the foundation of the festival is unknown, but was probably soon after the victory and no later than 266 (Bommelaer 2002, 123) or 254 (Jacquemin et al. 2012, 135). At first the festival was probably biennial (Knoepfler 1995). Some ten lists of competitors survive. They indicate regular competitions in tragedy, comedy and dithyramb (Nachtergael 1977, 404–25 Actes 2–11, and 475–83 Actes 58–68; Aneziri 2003, 403–12 Ga1–7). The list for 253/2 or 248/7 (Knoepfler 1995, 158), for example, names as competitors, in order: 2 rhapsodes, 1 kitharist, 3 kitharodes, 2 pipers, 2 *didaskaloi auleton* (i.e. 2 directors for choruses accompanied by the pipers), 16 choreuts for boys' choruses, 15 choreuts for men's choruses, 3 tragic actors, 1 piper, 4 didaskaloi, 1 piper, 1 didaskalos, 3 comic actors, 1 piper, 7 didaskaloi, 7 comic choreuts, 1 costumer (Nachtergael 1977, 422–4 Acte 10; Aneziri 2003, 410–12 Ga7; Jacquemin et al. 2012, 140–5). These numbers vary somewhat from festival to festival, as do the categories: other Soteria include poets of prosodia as a musical competition (Sifakis 1967, 73–4).

In 247/6 or 246/5 when the Aetolians dominated the sanctuary the Soteria was refashioned as a quadrennial 'Aetolian Soteria' and expanded with the addition of athletic competitions (Nachtergael 1977, 328–73; Manieri 2016). The musical programme was then only slightly reduced but still usually included boys' and men's choruses and tragedy and comedy (Sifakis 1967, 83; Nachtergael 1977, 475–83 nos. 58–68). Whereas the lists for the earlier Amphictyonic festival, probably a money-prize festival (ἀγὼν χρηματίτης), give names of all 'competitors' (οἴδε ἠγωνίσαντο τὸν ἀγῶνα τῶν Σωτηρίων), but without marking the winners, the inscriptions from the era of the Aetolian Soteria, which described itself as a (more prestigious) crown contest (ἀγὼν στεφανίτης: *FD* III 3, 215, l. 15) list only the names of victorious competitors (Nachtergael 1977, 475–83 Actes 58–68; and cf. *Syll.*³ 1080, an early second-century inscription commemorating a tragic actor who won a crown at the Soteria with the *Heracles* of Euripides and the *Antaios* of Archestratos).

We have an Amphictyonic decree of 278 or 277, thus probably soon after the foundation of the Soteria, that grants the Athenian association of the Artists of Dionysus certain guarantees 'so that the gods can receive the honours and sacrifices to which the Artists are assigned' (*FD* III 2, 68, ll. 61–94; *CID* IV 12; *ATD* TE 2; Aneziri 2003, A5A; Jacquemin et al. 2012, no. 68). The Amphictyony gave the performers a number of guarantees aimed at reducing the risk that travelling artists be apprehended, unfairly taxed or abused in foreign states. Negotiating this decree for the Athenian Artists of Dionysus were Astydamas the tragic poet (possibly a scion of the theatrical clan descended from Euphorion – the father of Aeschylus – like the famous Astydamas: Sutton 1987, 12–14) and Neoptolemos the tragic actor (Stefanis no. 1796, probably not the famous Neoptolemos: Stefanis no. 1797). Another decree, probably somewhat earlier than 280, awards privileges to the Commonwealth (κοινόν) of the Artists in Isthmus and Nemea (*ATD* TE 17; Aneziri 2003, B1; Jacquemin et al. 2012, no. 69). These decrees seem to be aimed at assuring the success of the new festival and the presence of actors and musicians upon which that success depended. Although some (e.g. Jacquemin et al. 2012, 139) deny a connection between the foundation of the Soteria and Delphi's negotiations with the actors' associations, especially the Athenian, on the grounds that the Soteria exclusively used artists from the Isthmian–Nemean association, this supposed exclusivity is unprovable, unlikely and generally contrary to Panhellenic festival practice (Aneziri 2007, esp. 77).

Despite regular dramatic performances from ca. 275 onwards no permanent theatre building existed in Delphi until the small extant stone theatre (seating about 4,200–4,600: Kolonia 2013b, 137) was built in the north-west corner of the sanctuary in the mid second century. Anomalies in the construction both of the theatron (Bommelaer 2008; 2010, 66–7) and orchestra (Bommelaer 1996) indicate that a phase of work was interrupted, possibly by an earthquake, in the late 160s, and a second phase begun on a slightly different plan in 158. *FD* III 3, 239 (cf. 237; Jacquemin et al. 2012, 287–307) enables us to date the second phase with precision: Eumenes II of Pergamon in 159/8 (Mulliez 1998 for Archestratos' Archonship) sent specialised slaves and equipment for the recommencement of construction. The theatre was doubtless in use by 140 when the first of many inscriptions was cut upon the pillar bases and the walls of its parodoi (Bommelaer 1996, 292). There is no architectural trace of an earlier theatre in this location nor any other in the sanctuary (Bommelaer 2002, 121–2).

The Amphictyony's plans possibly anticipated the Aetolian expansion of the Soteria to include athletic games. The Pythian stadium above and north-west of the sanctuary is thought to have been built ca. 275: the dating is based on broad stratigraphic and historical considerations but include most notably the Amphictyonic coin of 280/79 in the foundation layer of the first track, though the dating is in part supported by a general assumption of synchrony with the foundation of the Soteria (Aupert 1979, 45–51, 145; Perrier 2013, 159), despite the fact that the original Amphictyonic Soteria did not include athletic games. It was probably here that the musical and theatrical competitions were held before the construction of the theatre (Bommelaer 2002; Kolonia 2013, 129a; Moretti 2014b, 208).

The accounts of the Amphictyony for the preparation of the Pythia of 251/0 or 247/6 (**3**) show costs for the construction of a temporary music hall, a *theatron*, and a proskenion inside the Pythian stadium. *Theatron* can of course mean any seating area, but in this inscription we have separate costs for the benchwork in the *theatron* and in the stadium, indicating that *theatron* means 'theatre' or at least the auditorium for a theatre. A music hall is of course necessary for the Pythian kitharodic, kithara and pipe competitions, but the presence of a temporary proskenion (which should also imply a temporary skene) and a theatre inside the Pythian stadium is more surprising given the apparent absence of drama from the Pythia. Hellmann (1999, 72) suggests that the theatre was built 'pour les déclamations'. It is not impossible that these preparations were made for occasional dedicated dramatic performance (such as mentioned above). The localisation of musical performances in the stadium may explain why the piper Satyros (Stefanis no. 2240), ca. 200 (Bommelaer 2002, 125), is said to have performed additional pieces in the stadium (*FD* III 3, 128). The important point is that even well into the Hellenistic period a major sanctuary known to have had dramatic performances could function with only temporary theatres. These must have been built and dismantled quite quickly in order to avoid interfering with the races that were held in the stadium. Even before the surviving Pythian stadium was built, **2** gives evidence of a temporary skene built into an earlier stadium. The earlier stadium has not been found, but was probably located somewhere on the Plain of Kirrha (Aupert 1979, 149–52 nos. 1–11).

Our knowledge of the performance and theatrical culture of Delphi is complicated by very incomplete information about a variety of occasions for choral performance at the sanctuary. Plutarch (**4**) indicates that 'they' perform paeans to Apollo at sacrifices for nine months of the year and dithyrambs to Dionysus during the winter months. We hear of paeans being composed for Apollo at Delphi from the seventh century (Rutherford 2001, 24–9). By the fifth century regular performances took place not only at the Pythia, but also at the festivals of the Theoxenia (**6**), and the Septerion. The Theoxenia, an annual feast for all the gods, was held in the Delphic month of Theoxenios (roughly March–April) and attracted choral offerings from throughout Greece (Rutherford 2001, 310–11). Pindar's *Paean* 6 appears to have been composed for the Theoxenia – since it relates the festival's aetiology – perhaps in the 470s (Kurke 2005, 117), and for performance by an Aeginetan chorus, possibly in combination with a Delphic chorus (Rutherford 2013a, 244–5; Kurke 2005). The Septerion may have been an octennial summer festival (Alc. 307c V). Snell (1938, 439) and Rutherford (2001, 201–3) connect Pindar's *Paean* 10a with the Septerion.

There may also have been a winter festival, the Theophania(?) (Hdt. 1.51.2; Mommsen 1878, 280–97; Rutherford 2001, 28 n. 21), held in anticipation of Apollo's return from the Hyperboreans, that may have served as a setting for odes simultaneously honouring Dionysus and Apollo. **5** seems to indicate that such a custom goes back at least to the first half of the fifth century. Classified as a 'dithyramb' by Hellenistic scholars, it begins with a figure of *praeteritio*, evoking a paean that might have been sung for Apollo, but that the appropriate season for paeans has not yet arrived. The crossover date is assumed to be Apollo's birthday, celebrated in Delphi on the 7th of the month Bysios in mid-late winter (Zimmermann 1992, 70). **5** is probably correctly identified as a dithyramb, but its style and particularly non-Dionysian contents may owe something to contemporary theatrical men's and boys' lyric choruses (Fearn 2007, 171–2, 226). It is not easy to say if all dithyrambs performed in the winter festival of Delphi were fully comparable to the lyric choruses performed in Athens and at other theatrical competitions throughout Greece. Certainly the Dionysian performances of the Thyiades, if they date back this far, were purely cultic, as they were female and processional (Budelmann and Power 2015, 273–5). We have no reason to think that the Classical choral performances at Delphi before ca. 340 (see on **6** below) were competitive and Plutarch's language, connecting them closely with festival sacrifices, suggests that these paeans and dithyrambs were cultic performances (χρῶνται περὶ τὰς θυσίας) and probably mainly processional, though they may have included circular dance around an altar (as do the theoric paeans: Rutherford 2001, 63–8).

6 preserves the text of a choral performance for Dionysus at the Delphic Theoxenia. It is an unusual combination of Apollonian form with both Apollonian and Dionysian content: it is a paean (identified as such in the subscript), but performed for Dionysus, and contains a creative mixture of paeanic and dithyrambic characteristics (Käppel 1992, 218–84; Rutherford 1995; Strauss-Clay 1996; Rutherford 2001, 131–6; Furley and Bremer 2001 II, 52–84; Calame 2009). The decree appended to **6** tells us that the paean was composed as a special commission from Apollo himself, evidently for an important event. This event is doubtless that announced in lines 131–6, the expansion of the Pythia with a sacrifice to Dionysus and 'a circular contest of m[any] choruses'. The word ἅμιλλα (**6**,

l. 134, 'competition'), though poetic and frequently metaphorical, always seems to imply rivalry and normally indicates competition. That it does not simply refer to choral zeal is suggested by the epithet 'circular', repeated at l. 146. Though the usage is not strict, 'circular chorus' is a word normally used to distinguish a theatrical lyric choral performance from a cultic dithyramb, or from other cultic and processional genres like paeans (see above all Fearn 2007, 163–218; D'Alessio 2013; Ceccarelli 2013b). **6** therefore has justly been taken as an announcement of something new at the Pythia (Käppel 1992, 254; Furley and Bremer 2001 II, 82–3), namely a contest for men's and/or boys' lyric (circular) choruses of the sort familiar from Athens, Delos (**Dvi**), and several other cities by this date. As an announcement of the new competition **6** anticipates the style of 'circular', or more properly men's and boys', choruses, which by this date were a theatrical genre that drew freely upon the conventions of cultic choruses. Elsewhere in the poem Philodamus deliberately attempts to draw an equation between the cultic dance at Delphi (at l. 1 Dionysus is called 'Dithyrambus', ll. 58–62 Muses move 'in a circle' around Dionysus while Apollo 'leads off', ll. 124–5 goddesses circle around ?Dionysus) and the circular choruses that are announced in **6**. This assimilation may appeal to religious conservatism, even in announcing the theatrical innovation, by calling attention to the fact that the new competition is anchored in cultic, and specifically Delphic tradition.

Croissant's definitive reconstruction (2003) of the pediment sculptures on the fourth-century temple of Apollo indicates a more than casual correspondence with Philodamus' *Paean* (though earlier scholars had guessed this, mainly on the basis of the somewhat misleading description of the pediments in Pausanias 10.19.4). The Temple of Apollo was destroyed in an earthquake and landslide in 373 (cf. on actors' incomes in **V D**). Philodamus' *Paean to Dionysus* ll. 118–27, the stanza just before our excerpt in **6**, makes specific reference to the rebuilding of the temple: 'Blessed and happy will be the generation of mortals who will build for Lord Apollo a spotless and ever-new temple … all in gold with sculptures of gold'. Work on the pediment sculptures probably started around 345–340 and they were completed in 327. Croissant has reconstructed the pediments from several previously unidentified fragments of the new temple's pediments only discovered in the museum storerooms in 1971. Unusually, both the east and west pediments show, not a mythological narrative, but a divine epiphany: on the east Apollo seated frontally with Artemis and Leto at his sides and at least eight Muses; on the west a frontal Dionysus in a mitra but otherwise dressed as a kitharode surrounded by eight gracefully poised, if notionally ecstatic, Thyiads and panthers in each corner. The pediments present Apollo and Dionysus as gods of music. They draw a surprising equation between Apollo and Dionysus, particularly given Dionysus' appearance as sole deity front and centre of the west pediment. Though Dionysus' incursion into Apollo's realm is somewhat softened by Dionysus' truly Apollonian posture and dress as a kitharode, the promotion of Dionysus as an equal of the god of the temple and sanctuary is remarkable, as is the celebration of Dionysus in an Apollonian hymnic genre in **6** (Croissant 2003, 163–71).

Croissant's explanation of the bold and, at this level, unprecedented incorporation of Dionysus within Apollo's cult centre has important implications for the history of the spread of theatrical culture. He points out that though the sculptures were not yet finished, the plans must have been known at the time of Philodamus' performance. Indeed Philodamus in his poem refers to the subject of the two pediments, Apollo as Mousagetes (58–62), and Dionysus as leader of the Thyiades (20–3). Behind the sudden emergence of Dionysus as god of the circular chorus Croissant sees the political influence of Athens upon the early phases of the rehabilitation of the sanctuary (2003, 171–82). Athens took a leading role in raising money for the reconstruction of the temple (*Syll.*³ 159, l. 10; Croissant 2003, 175). More significantly, Athenian workshops were put in charge of the production of the new temple's pedimental sculptures (Paus. 10.19.4; Croissant 2003, 145–6, 176). While Philodamus has no obvious Athenian affiliation, Attica is surprisingly present in Dionysus' itinerary in his poem, with a stop at Eleusis (ll. 34–5), and, if Vollgraff's supplement to **6**, l. 150 is correct, a terminus in Athens (Croissant 2003, 177–8). Athens' preponderant influence may also be seen in the addition of a competition in 'circular choruses', for not only were theatrical men's and boys' choruses an Athenian invention and institution, but Athens also, unusually at this time, used these choral competitions to celebrate both Dionysus and Apollo (Wilson 2007b). The addition of competitions in 'circular choruses' to the Pythia, announced by **6**, reveals the same conception of a more integrally Dionysian Delphi, and therefore one more susceptible to Athenian cultural influence.

Several events show a concerted attempt to enhance the prestige of Delphi as a musical and cultural centre during the 330s. To **6**'s announcement of a new competition for circular choruses at the Pythia and the building of a shrine to Dionysus (not yet found but assured by the presence of votives: Jacquemin 1999, 29; Jacquemin 2007, 110; Moretti and Fincker 2008, 147), **8** offers evidence of an attempt to enhance the prestige of the festival by creating an inscription recording the winners of its competitions stretching back to its earliest foundation. **6** and **8** can be compared with evidence of contemporary efforts by Eubulus (**VI H**) and Lycurgus (**VI I**) to enhance Athens' theatre culture not only through the creation of new competitions and festival infrastructure, but also through historical research confirming the antiquity of its festivals and the publication in monumental form of records and victor lists dating back to the origin of competitions at the Athenian Dionysia.

Quite independently of any Delphic festival, Greek cities sent delegations to Delphi to offer sacrifice and choral hymns for the god (Rutherford 2013a, 241). Divine embassies (*theoriai*) of this sort may lie behind Herodotus' mention of a chorus of a hundred Chian youths being sent to Delphi some time before 494 (6.27), and Simonides' paean for an Andrian delegation to Delphi (*PMG* 519 fr. 35b). The Athenian Pythaids are a conspicuous, and doubtless the most elaborate, example. The Pythaids were irregular events triggered by the observation in Athens of certain divine signs and normally celebrated at a time, in early summer, when no major Delphic festival occurred (Sifakis 1967, 86; Parker 2005, 83–5). The practice is best known from lists of participants to Pythaids from 128/7 to 98/7 that were inscribed on the Treasury of the Athenians at Delphi. These numbered from 300 to 500 delegates who took hecatombs and first fruits to Pythian Apollo (Boethius 1918). Three of these Pythaids included musical and dramatic performers (*FD* III 2, 47–9). In 138, for example, the procession included two pipers, seven kithara players, one aulode, two kitharodes, eight comic actors, three tragic actors, three tragic and one comic choreographers (*chorodidaskaloi*; *FD* III 2, 47).

We have no other evidence for drama at earlier Pythaids, but a variety of choral performances were probably normal. **7** seems to indicate performances by boys' choruses at a

Pythais in the mid fourth century. In this case the connections between the boys' families and Ikarion suggest that these performances may have formed part of an independent deme-sponsored Pythais by the Marathonian Tetrapolis (of which Ikarion was a member) and which is attested by Philochorus (*FGrH* 328 F 75; Hatzfield 1907, 139). **7** may however commemorate a local contribution to the Pythais of the city of Athens (Humphreys 2004, 147 n. 43). Rutherford (1990, 172–6) tentatively assigns a fragment of a Simonidean paean (*PMG* 519 fr. 35 [i]) to an Athenian Pythais and in any case Aeschylus' *Eumenides* seems to indicate the practice by 458 (A. *Eu.* 9–14 with Sch.; Parker 2005, 86). The evidence for the second- and first-century Athenian Pythaids suggests actual competitions, especially the plurality of comic and tragic actors. Conceivably Athens may have transplanted the competitive format of its musical culture even in the Pythaids of the Classical period. From as early as 426/5 Athenian delegations to Delos included tribal choruses for competitions on the island (**Dvi 1–6**). It is possible that Athenian Pythaids had introduced occasional 'circular' choral competitions to Delphi even before they became part of the Pythia in the 330s.

Indeed **6**, **7** and **8** all seem to attest an increased Athenian interest in Delphi during the Eubulan and Lycurgan periods (355–324). There are many direct parallels in Athens for the sudden increase in construction relating to sanctuaries, temples and shrines, in the introduction of new festivals or expansion of old festivals with new competitions, and in the enhancement of the status of festivals through a politics of commemoration, and in particular the creation of victor lists (the *Fasti*, normally dated to the 330s) that advertised the antiquity of established festivals and stimulated competitive engagement (**VI H–I**; Csapo and Wilson 2014). It is tempting to see the trademarks of Eubulo-Lycurgan religious politics in the Athenian engagement in the rebuilding of Apollo's temple, the building of a new shrine for Dionysus, the addition of a regular choral competition to the Pythia (**6**) and the publication of victor lists for the Pythia (**8**).

Athens officially asserted a special connection with Delphi in this period. Apollo Patroos, the ancestor of the Athenians through Ion, was equated with Delphic Apollo and Lycurgus gilded his altar in the Athenian Agora (D. 18.141; [Plu.] *Mor.* 843f; Humphreys 2004, 119 n. 31). Aristotle was almost certainly back in Athens at the time the *Register of Pythian Victors* was published and we know from fr. 615 Rose that the work gave Solon a decisive role in the leadership of the First Sacred War that led to the foundation of the Pythia. Indeed, the Lycurgan circle made their presence felt in Delphi at this time. Pythaids mark either end of the Eubulo-Lycurgan era. A Pythais is attested for 355 at the beginning of this period (Is. *Apoll.* 27) and, on the generally accepted chronology, the choreuts of **7** might have belonged to this, but **7** is arguably also as late as a Pythais of 326/5 near the end of that period (Humphreys 2004, 96). An inscription listing the leaders of the Pythais of 326/5 reads like a roll call of the Lycurgan establishment, including Lycurgus, Phanodemus, Demades, Nikeratos, Kephisophon, Neoptolemos of Melite, and Glauketes of Oion (*Syll.*³ 296; Humphreys 2004, 95–7; cf. **VI H–I**). The Delphians honoured Demades, Glauketes, and another Lycurgan associate, Epiteles, with among other things a proxeny, while Epiteles served as naopoios in Delphi for much of the 320s (*FD* III 4, 383; *Syll.*³ 297; *FD* III 1, 408; Humphreys 2004, 95–7, 118 n. 26). This increase in the Athenian cultural and material presence in Delphi itself was a reassertion of Athens' privileged connection with the sanctuary and perhaps also a response to the increasing power of Macedon on the Amphictyonic Council.

In this specific introduction of theatre culture into Delphi, however, there is no need to think that Athens' interests were contrary to Philip's. Aristotle and Callisthenes' work on the history of the Pythian Games (**8**) established the story that the first musical competitions at Delphi were created to celebrate the First Sacred War, ca. 590, when a coalition of Sicyon, Athens and Thessaly liberated Apollo's sanctuary after it had been seized by the people of Crisa (Robertson 1978; Manieri 2015, 38–9). This established a historical precedent and an interpretive paradigm for the refoundation of the Pythia through the creation of new competitions when Philip in the Third Sacred War liberated Delphi after the seizure of the sanctuary by the people of Phocis. One of the earliest advocates of the parallelism between the First and Third Sacred Wars was Eubulus' associate Aeschines (D. 18.149; Robertson 1978, 51–4).

Cvii: Leucas. Demosthenes, *Against Euboulides* **(57) 18–19**. Delivered ca. 345 but referring to events that must have taken place in the late 5th or early 4th c. The Decelean War referred to was 413–404. The speech is not certainly by Demosthenes. The speaker, Euxitheos son of Thoukritos, whose Athenian citizenship has been impugned, responds to the putative evidence adduced by his opponent that his father Thoukritos spoke with a foreign accent. Text: Dilts.

> διαβεβλήκασι γάρ μου τὸν πατέρα, ὡς ἐξένιζεν· καὶ ὅτι μὲν ἁλοὺς ὑπὸ τῶν πολεμίων ὑπὸ τὸν Δεκελεικὸν πόλεμον καὶ πραθεὶς εἰς Λευκάδα, Κλεάνδρῳ περιτυχὼν τῷ ὑποκριτῇ πρὸς τοὺς οἰκείους ἐσώθη δεῦρο πολλοστῷ χρόνῳ, παραλελοίπασιν, ὥσπερ δὲ δέον ἡμᾶς δι' ἐκείνας τὰς ἀτυχίας ἀπολέσθαι, τὸ ξενίζειν αὐτοῦ κατηγορήκασιν. ¹⁹ ἐγὼ δ' ἐξ αὐτῶν τούτων μάλιστα {ἂν} οἶμαι ὑμῖν ἐμαυτὸν Ἀθηναῖον ὄντ' ἐπιδείξειν. καὶ πρῶτον μὲν ὡς ἑάλω καὶ ἐσώθη, μάρτυρας ὑμῖν παρέξομαι, ἔπειθ' ὅτι ἀφικόμενος τῆς οὐσίας παρὰ τῶν θείων τὸ μέρος μετέλαβεν, εἶθ' ὅτι οὔτ' ἐν τοῖς δημόταις οὔτ' ἐν τοῖς φράτερσιν οὔτ' ἄλλοθι οὐδαμοῦ τὸν ξενίζοντα οὐδεὶς πώποτ' ᾐτιάσατο ὡς εἴη ξένος. καί μοι λαβὲ τὰς μαρτυρίας.

> They have denounced my father as speaking with a foreign accent, but they omitted to say that he had been caught by the enemy during the Decelean War and sold (as a slave) to Leucas, where he chanced upon Kleandros the actor and was brought home safe after so many years to his family. Confident of securing my ruin through this misfortune they have charged him (my father) with speaking in a foreign accent, ¹⁹ but I think that by this very thing I can most securely prove to you that I am an Athenian. I will first provide witnesses that he was caught and rescued, and then that he returned and shared part of the family estate with my uncles, and then that not a single member of the deme, the phratry, or any other body ever charged this supposed foreign speaker with being a foreigner. (To the court clerk) Take the depositions of my witnesses!

Athenian courtroom speeches may not be the best place to look for undisguised truth, but if the speaker in this passage is making up a fiction it is certainly in his interest to fill it with details that will strike the jury as plausible. Either way we have good evidence for actors travelling through the Ionian islands at the end of the fifth or in the early fourth century. The language of the text 'chanced upon' (περιτυχών) may, however, suggest that Thoukritos was lucky to come across an Athenian, even an actor, in Leucas, but this may have had more to do with his personal circumstances than the rarity of Athenian actors in the region. Remains of a theatre were partially excavated in 1901 by Krüge and Dörpfeld on the south slope of the western acropolis of Leucas, but never published (Pliakou 1997 publishes material from Krüge's notebooks). Dörpfeld later noted that is was 'sicher der vorrömischen Zeit' (Dörpfeld et al. 1927, 267) and recent surveys suggest it may be pre-Hellenistic (Frederiksen 2002, 116 no. 132; *TGR* II, 253). Leucas is a likely transit stop between South Italy and mainland Greece (see **C Introduction**). Kleandros' role was probably to take news to Thoukritos' relatives in Athens, and possibly to arrange purchase of his freedom when again in Leucas.

Leucas had a democratic constitution in the fifth and fourth century (*IACP* 365), but was part of the Peloponnesian League in the fifth century (Th. 2.9.3; D.S. 12.42.4; Paus. 10.9.10), which would explain how Euxitheos ended up there; but Leucas was allied with Athens from 394 (D.S. 14.82.3; X. *HG* 4.6–7), and so probably by the time Kleandros visited the island. Leucas once again supported Sparta in 373 (X. *HG* 6.2.3). It is not clear if Leucas joined the Second Athenian Confederacy (*IG* II² 104; *IACP* 365), but it was allied with Athens against Philip in 342–340 (D. 18.237).

Kleandros is almost certainly the tragic actor named in the Athenian *Fasti* (*IG* II² 2318, l. 1008 M-O) as a victor at the Dionysia in 387 and competing in Rhodes about the same time (**Dxi 1**; Stefanis no. 1413). He may be related to the Kleandros who was said to be Aeschylus' actor (Stefanis no. 1412; see on poets' actors in **V D**).

Cviii: Opous. *Life of Sophocles* **55–8 (= Ister, *FGrH* 334 F 37; Neanthes *FGrH* 84 F 18; *TrGF* T A 1, 14).** The date of the composition of the *Life of Sophocles* is unknown, though this section draws directly on two 3ʳᵈ-c. authors. Ister compiled a work on Attic history in the second half of the 3ʳᵈ c.; Neanthes wrote biographies of famous men and other historical works in the 3ʳᵈ c. Sophocles died in 406/5. For the use of the term ἐργασία for a 'dramatic performance' or 'production' in Hellenistic and later scholarship, see **I Ai 6c** l. 108 and *PMich* 36 col. 1, l. 5. Text: Radt.

> τελευτῆσαι δὲ αὐτὸν Ἴστρος καὶ Νεάνθης φασὶ τοῦτον τὸν τρόπον·
> Καλλιππίδην ὑποκριτὴν ἀπὸ ἐργασίας ἐξ Ὀποῦντος ἥκοντα περὶ τοὺς Χόας
> πέμψαι αὐτῷ σταφυλήν, τὸν δὲ Σοφοκλέα λαβόντα ῥᾶγα εἰς τὸ στόμα ἔτι
> ὀμφακίζουσαν ὑπὸ τοῦ ἄγαν γήρως ἀποπνιγέντα τελευτῆσαι.

Ister and Neanthes say that he (Sophocles) died in the following manner. Kallippides the actor was coming from Opous from a performance about the

> time of the Choes and sent him a bunch of grapes. Sophocles took a grape into his
> mouth that was still green and because of his extreme old age he died by choking.

This account was known also to Lucian (*Macr.* 24). It is one of three accounts of Sophocles'
death, all cited by the *Life of Sophocles.* The others are even more incredible: Satyrus (fr.
5 Schorn) reported that he died from the strain of reading (out loud) a long and under-
punctuated speech from his own *Antigone*; unnamed others claimed that he died of joy
upon hearing himself declared winner in the tragic competition at an unnamed festival (cf.
VI Eiv 1; Plu. *Mor.* 785b). All the anecdotes seek some 'meaningful' connection between
his death and his dramatic preoccupation: in this case it is a gift of the fruit of his patron
god (Anacreon is said by Val. Max. 9.8 to have died the same way), during the god's festival, from a close associate, who was the most renowned tragic actor of his day (Stefanis
no. 1348).

The Festival of the Choes takes place on the second day of the Anthesteria and as the
Anthesteria is a mid-winter festival, it has long been noticed that the existence of fresh grapes
of any sort, let alone unripe grapes, is an impossibility (Ritter 1845, 50), and this might seem
to rob the anecdote of any historical value at least as regards the circumstances of Sophocles'
death. Schorn, however, makes a case for the accuracy of the background details ('ungewöhn-
lich ausgeprägte Lokalkolorit'). This includes not only knowledge of Kallippides, but also
knowledge of a custom of bringing gifts to one's teachers at the Feast of the Choes (Ath.
10.451d; Plu. *Ant.* 70.2) and even an alleged custom, to which Schorn believes the story
alludes, of hanging the slightly dessicated grapes of the previous harvest outside during
the festival (Schorn 2007, 139; cf. Deubner 1932, 132). It is however not unlikely that the
mythic structure assumes dessicated grapes, sharing Sophocles' extreme old age, and a mi-
raculously youthful grape, like Sophocles' still vigorous genius. Opous evidently took pride
in its grapes, raisins and wine (and still does – the Atalanti Valley wines are reckoned among
the best in Greece). Clusters of grapes are in fact a symbol of Opous, appearing on coinage
of the city from the fifth century (Nielsen 2000, 100). Schorn believes that the knowledge of
Athenian custom is so accurate that the story could only have been composed in the fourth
century. If so, this might increase somewhat the possibility that the background assumption
of tragic performance in late fifth-century Opous has some basis in fact.

No theatre has been found in Opous or in Locris (see **C Introduction**). Locris was,
however, the birthplace of a surprising number of didaskaloi for lyric choruses in fourth-
century Athens: we know of six in all, of which three were from Opous and two from
Skarpheia (*IG* II² 2325, l. 195; *IG* II³ 4, 450, 463, 464, 489, 493; Summa 2010, 112). Opous
also produced the fifth-century piper Bakchylides, known well enough in Athens to have
been parodied in Plato's comedy, the *Sophists* (*PCG* F 149 = Sch. Ar. *Clouds* 331a; Stefanis
no. 514), and the probably fourth-century singer Mnasitheos mentioned by Aristotle (*Po.*
1462a7) who may be identical with the tragic actor, Mnesitheos, active in mid fourth-century Athens (Stefanis nos. 1715, 1723; *IG* II² 2419, l. 10; **Dxi 2**, l. 2). It is not until the
third century that we hear of an Opountian *tragoidos* and not until the first that we hear of
a comic actor from the city. We hear of the Dionysia in Opous again only in Roman times
(*IG* IX 1² 1930), though 'Dia' and 'Aianteia' with musical competitions were also held in
the city from at least the second or first century (Summa 2010, 116, 124).

Cix: Magnesia and Thessaly

1. Anonymous, *Family and Life of Euripides* **6 (*TrGF* T 1, IA)**. The event is dated by Euripides' subsequent removal to Macedonia, and therefore probably some time before 410 (see **VI Di**). Text: Kannicht.

> μετέστη δὲ ἐν Μαγνησίᾳ καὶ προξενίᾳ ἐτιμήθη καὶ ἀτελείᾳ. ἐκεῖθεν δὲ εἰς Μακεδονίαν παρὰ Ἀρχέλαον …

> He relocated to Magnesia and was honoured with an ambassadorship (*proxenia*) and tax-free status. From there he went to Macedonia and spent time at the court of Archelaus.

2. Scholiast[MNOA] **to Euripides,** *Andromache* **445 (II 284.20–1 Schwartz = Call. fr. 451 Pfeiffer = E. *TrGF* T 64)**. The most likely date for the *Andromache* is about 424–422 (Cropp and Fick 1985, 5). The Demokrates here mentioned is often thought to be connected to a Demokrates of Sicyon mentioned in a late 3rd-c. papyrus (*PTeb.* 695 = *TrGF* CAT A 6.5 = *TrGF* 124 T 1), author of (at least twenty) tragedies. The same tragic [Demok]rates is one possible supplement to a fragment of the Lenaean Tragic Victors List, *IG* II^2 2325G, l. 24 M-O, probably from the 370s (cf. Snell on *TrGF* 68). Text: after Kannicht.

> ‘ὦ πᾶσιν ἀνθρώποισιν (ἔχθιστοι βροτῶν Σπάρτης ἔνοικοι’)· ταῦτα ἐπὶ τῷ Ἀνδρομάχης προσχήματί φησιν Εὐριπίδης λοιδορούμενος τοῖς Σπαρτιάταις διὰ τὸν ἐνεστῶτα πόλεμον. καὶ γὰρ δὴ καὶ παρεσπονδήκεσαν πρὸς Ἀθηναίους, καθάπερ οἱ περὶ τὸν Φιλόχορον (*FGrH* 328 F 124) ἀναγράφουσιν. εἰλικρινῶς δὲ τοὺς τοῦ δράματος χρόνους οὐκ ἔστι λαβεῖν· οὐ δεδίδακται γὰρ Ἀθήνησιν. ὁ δὲ Καλλίμαχος ἐπιγραφῆναί φησι τῇ τραγῳδίᾳ Δημοκράτην.

> δεδίδακται Cobett   δέδεικται MNO

> ‘O to all men (most hateful inhabitants of Sparta’): Euripides says these things in the guise of Andromache to revile the Spartans because of the war going on at that time. In fact they had violated a truce with the Athenians, as Philochorus (*FGrH* 328 F 124) records. It is not possible to date the drama exactly because it was not produced in Athens. Callimachus says that ‘Demokrates’ was written on the tragedy.

The information in **1** seems oddly intrusive in the biography of Euripides, connects with no known anecdote or tale, and offers a combination of honours well known from decrees, including Thessalian decrees (albeit from the third century onwards), and so ‘looks like one of the few possibly authentic scraps of information among the fictional constructions’ (Easterling 1994, 76). The information says nothing of performances, but it is an easy inference that Euripides was honoured as a celebrated tragedian, which implies at least knowledge and appreciation of his dramas. Scholarship has traditionally doubted that Thessaly had sufficient cultural sophistication to appreciate Euripidean drama. But the Thessalians patronised poetry and sophists, long before Euripides: Simonides (Molyneux

1992, 117–46), Gorgias (Isoc. 15.155–6; Pl. *Men.* 70a–b; Philostr. *Ep.* 73.2) and possibly Anacreon (fr. 107–8 Diehl); and Isocrates resided in Thessaly in the fifth century (Quint. *Inst.* 3.1.13; cf. Lesky 1972, 655 and Scholl 1994, 250). The same prejudice might exist *a fortiori* against Macedonia, yet the evidence is overwhelming that Euripides did spend his last days there (**VI Di**).

It is not until some forty years after the presumed date of Euripides' sojourn in Thessaly that we have literary evidence there of theatres (**Cx–xi**) and tragic performances – of Euripides, as it happens (**Cx**). Clear archaeological evidence for the first phase of surviving Thessalian theatres is much later (see **C Introduction**). Larissa is also said, among other places, to be the birthplace of the comic poet Antiphanes, who was professionally active from about 385 (*Prolegomena de com.* III, p. 10 Koster).

Whether or not we accept Cobett's emendation, **2** must mean that the *Didaskaliai* did not list an *Andromache* under Euripides' name. If it is true that no *Andromache* appeared in the *Didaskaliai*, then **2**'s inference that the play was not produced at the Athenian Dionysia or Lenaea is surely right (*pace* Harder 1985, 126 n. 4; cf. Allan 2000, 150 n. 5). **2**'s addition of the information from Callimachus can be interpreted in two ways, depending on whether the information that the *Andromache* was ascribed to Demokrates is connected or not connected with the didascalic information given earlier. In the latter case we should understand that the play was not in the *Didaskaliai* and also that some source (a papyrus, or possibly Callimachus himself in his *Pinakes*) ascribed the play to Demokrates. If it is connected and Callimachus' mention of Demokrates is designed to explain the absence of Euripides from Aristotle's *Didaskaliai*, then we should probably conclude that Callimachus (or some later source using Callimachus) explained the apparent absence of an *Andromache* by Euripides in the *Didaskaliai* by claiming that Euripides' play does indeed appear but was listed under the name Demokrates. In this case we have to assume that Demokrates served as didaskalos for the production in Athens (see on didaskaloi in **V J**). In fact the word attributed by **2** to Callimachus, ἐπιγράφεσθαι, is the common term for the displacement of a poet's name by that of the producer (didaskalos) in the didascalic lists (Butrica 2001, 191–5; Kannicht on E. *TrGF* T 64). But if Callimachus had concluded that *Andromache* was produced in Athens and therefore did appear in the *Didaskaliai*, only under the name Demokrates, not Euripides, then why is **2** ignorant of the necessary conclusion, namely that the play was performed in Athens, was in the didascalic lists, and must have been attached to a specific date?

Despite this problem, **2**'s claim that the drama 'was not produced in Athens' has stimulated much speculation about the place of *Andromache*'s original production. Nauck's suggestion (1903, xvii n. 21) that the play was first produced in Argos depends entirely upon Bergk's arbitrary emendation of the name 'Demokrates' to 'Timokrates' (Hinrichs 1883, 491–6; cf. Page 1936, 223–8). Equally arbitrary is Lesky's argument that the play was first produced in Sicyon (**Bv**), the hometown of Demokrates (1972, 338 n. 90). The play is set in Thessaly, at the Thetideion in Phthia (E. *Andr.* 16–20), and contains mention of local cults (43–4, 115, 1263–9). Taplin (1999, 45) and Allan (2000, 149–60) have given good arguments for its suitability to a Thessalian performance venue. Though the *Andromache* must have been produced a good fifteen years before the events mentioned in **1**, **1** is certainly consistent with the notion that the relationship between Thessaly and Euripides had a history established by earlier visits and productions. But as the Molossian royal family is the direct beneficiary of the genealogy given by the goddess Thetis from the machine at *Andromache* 1243–52 (Dakaris 1964, 68–101), many have speculated that the first performance of *Andromache* might have taken place in Epirus, i.e. Molossia (Schmid 1912, 362; Robertson 1923; Hall 1989, 181; Butrica 2001; Stewart 2017, 139–44). Though the literary record suggests that theatre was a fixture of Thessalian life by the fourth century (**Cx–xi**), current archaeological evidence favours neither Thessaly nor Epirus as a venue for a fifth-century production (see **C Introduction**).

Cx: Pherae, Thessaly

1. Plutarch, *Life of Pelopidas* **29.9–11**. Composition date: ca. 115 AD, referring to a period within the tyranny of Alexander of Pherae (369–358). Plutarch inserts the episode into a series of reflections on Alexander's savagery that he places in the mind of Epaminondas in early 367 (Stylianou 1998, 451), when he led the Theban army into Thessaly and secured the release of Pelopidas, whom Alexander had imprisoned at Pherae. Text: Ziegler.

> τραγῳδὸν δέ ποτε θεώμενος Εὐριπίδου Τρῳάδας ὑποκρινόμενον, ᾤχετ᾽ ἀπιὼν ἐκ τοῦ θεάτρου, καὶ πέμψας πρὸς αὐτὸν ἐκέλευε θαρρεῖν καὶ μηδὲν ἀγωνίζεσθαι διὰ τοῦτο χεῖρον. οὐ γὰρ ἐκείνου καταφρονῶν ἀπελθεῖν, ἀλλ᾽ αἰσχυνόμενος τοὺς πολίτας, εἰ μηδένα πώποτε τῶν ὑπ᾽ αὐτοῦ φονευομένων ἠλεηκώς, ἐπὶ τοῖς Ἑκάβης καὶ Ἀνδρομάχης κακοῖς ὀφθήσεται δακρύων.

On one occasion when he (Alexander of Pherae) watched a tragic actor performing the *Trojan Women* of Euripides he suddenly left the theatre. He sent a messenger to the actor asking him to take heart and not compromise his virtuosity because of this (Alexander's departure). He did not depart out of contempt for him, but because he was ashamed to allow his citizens to see him weeping at the hardships of Hecuba and Andromache when he never took pity on any of his own murder victims.

2. Plutarch, *On the Fortune and Virtue of Alexander the Great* **(*Moralia*) 334a–b**. Composition date: ca. 100 AD, referring to the same event as **1**. Text: Nachstädt.

> Ἀλέξανδρος δ᾽ ὁ Φεραίων τύραννος (ἔδει δὲ τοῦτο μόνον αὐτὸν καλεῖσθαι καὶ μὴ καταισχύνειν τὴν ἐπωνυμίαν) θεώμενος τραγῳδὸν ἐμπαθέστερον ὑφ᾽ ἡδονῆς διετέθη πρὸς τὸν οἶκτον. ἀναπηδήσας οὖν ἐκ τοῦ θεάτρου θᾶττον ἢ βάδην ἀπῄει, δεινὸν εἶναι λέγων, εἰ τοσούτους ἀποσφάττων πολίτας ὀφθήσεται τοῖς Ἑκάβης καὶ Πολυξένης πάθεσιν ἐπιδακρύων. οὗτος μὲν οὖν μικροῦ καὶ δίκην ἐπράξατο τὸν τραγῳδόν, ὅτι τὴν ψυχὴν αὐτοῦ καθάπερ σίδηρον ἐμάλαξεν.

Alexander the tyrant of Pherae – one has to call him simply this to avoid disgracing his namesake – while watching a tragic actor, was so taken by the performance that he was moved to tears. He jumped up and left the theatre at more than a walking pace, saying that it would be a terrible thing if while butchering so many citizens, he were seen crying for the calamities of Hecuba and Polyxena. Furthermore the same man nearly took revenge upon the tragic actor for having softened his heart of iron.

3. Aelian, *A Miscellany of Stories* 14.40. Composition date: late 2nd or early 3rd c. AD, referring to the same event as **1–2**. Merope is the chief character in Euripides' *Cresphontes*. Theodoros is without doubt the famous actor (Stefanis no. 1157), even if Aelian calls him a 'poet' (the word may be an interpolation). Text: Wilson.

> Ἀλέξανδρος ὁ Φεραίων τύραννος ἐν τοῖς μάλιστα ἔδοξεν ὠμότατος εἶναι. Θεοδώρου δὲ τοῦ τῆς τραγῳδίας ποιητοῦ ὑποκρινομένου τὴν Μερόπην σφόδρα ἐμπαθῶς, ὁ δὲ ἐς δάκρυα ἐξέπεσεν εἶτα ἐξανέστη τοῦ θεάτρου. ἀπολογούμενος δὲ ἔλεγε τῷ Θεοδώρῳ ὡς οὐ καταφρονήσας οὐδὲ ἀτιμάσας αὐτὸν ᾤχετο, ἀλλ᾽ αἰδούμενος εἰ τὰ μὲν ὑποκριτοῦ πάθη οἷός τε ἦν ἐλεεῖν, τὰ δὲ τῶν ἑαυτοῦ πολιτῶν οὐχί.

ποιητοῦ cod.   ὑποκριτοῦ Nauck

Alexander the tyrant of Pherae was classed among the most brutal men of all time. When Theodoros the poet of tragedy was acting the part of Merope with real feeling, Alexander burst into tears and left the theatre. By way of apology he told Theodoros that he left not because he had no regard for him and disliked his acting, but out of shame for the fact that he was able to feel pity for the suffering of an actor but not for his own citizens.

Nothing could be more implausible than the historicity of this gushing self-incrimination by a notorious tyrant. After his death (murdered in his bed at the hands of his wife and her brothers), Alexander not only became the type of the faithless and hardened 'tragic tyrant' untouched by any human feeling but also, somewhat contradictorily, 'was refashioned into an exemplum of the loneliness of power, hopelessly in love with [his wife] Thebe yet unable to trust her' (Boehm 2015, esp. 223, 234). This would account for the reputation of hidden sentimentality that underlies the choice of Alexander for this tale about how art can tame brutes that real life cannot sway. The details of his death may also incidentally explain the choice of *Cresphontes* in **3**, for in that play the climactic scene brought Merope very close to murdering her own unrecognised son as he lay in bed. Alexander himself became a figure of the tragic stage in a play by the later fourth- or third-century Athenian tragedian Moschion which probably dealt with his murder and the abuse of his corpse (*TrGF* 97 F 3, 7; a more remote possibility is that Moschion's tragedy dealt with Jason's assassination). This tragedy may have served as a source for Plutarch in his account of the tyrant's death (Plu. *Pel.* 35.7; cf. Boehm 2015, 226).

Not only is the play identified differently by Plutarch and Aelian, Plutarch tells a very different tale about Alexander's subsequent treatment of the actor. The fact that Aelian is more specific about the identity of the actor and agrees with **1** on the treatment of the actor could indicate that Aelian is closer to the source. If Aelian did misidentify the actor

Theodoros as a poet, then he is clearly taking Theodoros' name from his source, but mistaking his profession. Theodoros was indeed active at the time of this anecdote, though the fact does little to encourage belief in its historicity: he was the most famous tragedian of Alexander of Pherae's day and so an obvious choice for a fictional anecdote. What is perhaps valuable is the ease with which Plutarch and his source (possibly the fourth-century historian Theopompus or Ephorus) assume the existence of a theatre and a tragic performance of Euripidean drama in Pherae (cf. the theatre attested in the same year at Skotoussa, **Cxi**, where the source is almost certainly Ephorus). There is indeed evidence that Alexander fostered the cult of Dionysus (Theopomp. *FGrH* 115 F 352). The ancient theatre of Pherae is probably located on the north-east slopes of the Kastraki hill just outside modern Velestino, but has not yet been excavated (Doulgeri-Intzesiloglou 2011, 68–9).

Cxi: Skotoussa, Thessaly

1. **Pausanias, *Guide to Greece* 6.5.2–3**. Composition date: ca. 150 AD, referring to 371/0 (contrast **2**) and drawing ultimately on Ephorus (cf. **2**). Pausanias, describing the dedications at Olympia, refers to a statue by Lysippus of Poulydamas, a native of Skotoussa. Text: Spiro.

> Σκοτοῦσσα δὲ ἡ τοῦ Πουλυδάμαντας πατρὶς οὐκ ᾠκεῖτο ἔτι ἐφ᾽ ἡμῶν·
> Ἀλέξανδρος γὰρ τὴν πόλιν ὁ Φεραίων τυραννήσας κατέλαβεν ἐν σπονδαῖς, καὶ
> Σκοτουσσαίων τούς τε ἐς τὸ θέατρον συνειλεγμένους – ἔτυχε γάρ σφισι καὶ
> ἐκκλησία τηνικαῦτα οὖσα – τούτους τε ἅπαντας κατηκόντισε, πελτασταῖς
> ἐν κύκλῳ περισχὼν καὶ τοξόταις, καὶ τὸ ἄλλο ὅσον ἐν ἡλικίᾳ κατεφόνευσε,
> γυναῖκας δὲ ἀπέδοτο καὶ παῖδας, μισθὸν εἶναι τὰ χρήματα τοῖς ξένοις. αὕτη
> Σκοτουσσαίοις ἡ συμφορὰ Φρασικλείδου μὲν Ἀθήνησιν ἐγένετο ἄρχοντος,
> δευτέρᾳ δὲ ὀλυμπιάδι ἐπὶ ταῖς ἑκατόν, ἣν Δάμων Θούριος ἐνίκα τὸ δεύτερον,
> ταύτης ἔτει δευτέρῳ τῆς ὀλυμπιάδος.

> Skotoussa, Poulydamas' home city, is no longer inhabited in our times, because Alexander, the tyrant of Pherae, took the city during a truce. He surrounded with peltasts and slingers and then shot down those of the citizens of Skotoussa who were in the theatre – there happened to be an assembly meeting at the time. Of the others, he murdered the young men and gave the women and children as payment to his mercenaries. This calamity befell the Skotoussans when Phrasikleides was Archon in Athens, in the second year of the hundred and second Olympiad, which Damon of Thurii won for the second time (371/0).

2. **Diodorus of Sicily, *Library of History* 15.75.1**. Written ca. 50–30; the passage refers to 367/6, and draws upon the *Histories* of Ephorus, probably Book 24 (Stylianou 1998, 95). Ephorus was contemporary with these events. Text: Vogel-Fischer.

> ἐπ᾽ ἄρχοντος δ᾽ Ἀθήνησι Πολυζήλου κατὰ μὲν τὴν Ῥώμην ἀναρχία διά
> τινας πολιτικὰς στάσεις ἐγένετο, κατὰ δὲ τὴν Ἑλλάδα Ἀλέξανδρος ὁ Φερῶν

τύραννος ἐν τῇ Θετταλίᾳ περί τινων ἐγκαλέσας τῇ πόλει τῶν Σκοτουσσαίων, ἐκάλεσεν αὐτοὺς εἰς ἐκκλησίαν καὶ περιστήσας τοὺς μισθοφόρους ἅπαντας ἀπέσφαξε, τὰ δὲ σώματα τῶν τετελευτηκότων ῥίψας εἰς τὴν πρὸ τῶν τειχῶν τάφρον τὴν πόλιν διήρπασεν.

When Polyzelos was Archon in Athens (367/6) there was anarchy in Rome because of some civil disturbances; in Greece Alexander the tyrant of Pherae in Thessaly brought a charge on some matter against the city of Skotoussa. He invited the Skotoussans to an assembly, surrounded them with mercenaries, and slaughtered them all. After throwing the bodies of the dead into a ditch in front of the city wall, he plundered the city.

3. Plutarch, *Life of Pelopidas* 29.7. Written ca. 115 AD, referring to the same event as **1–2**, and probably derives his information from the same source. Plutarch lists celebrated examples of the savagery of Alexander of Pherae. Text: Ziegler.

Μελιβοίᾳ δὲ καὶ Σκοτούσσῃ, πόλεσιν ἐνσπόνδοις καὶ φίλαις, ἐκκλησιαζούσαις περιστήσας ἅμα τοὺς δορυφόρους, ἡβηδὸν ἀπέσφαξε.

He (Alexander of Pherae) surrounded with his bodyguards the people of Meliboia and Skotoussa while they were in assembly, though they were allies and protected by a truce, and slaughtered them all from the youth upwards.

Although our sources mention the theatre at Skotoussa on the occasion of an assembly (*ekklesia*), the building is explicitly named a *theatron* (**1**), not an *ekklesiasterion* or *bouleuterion*, and we may safely assume that, in Pausanias' mind at least, the building was a theatre (cf. Frederiksen 2002, 75). It is particularly interesting in this regard that both Kromayer (1907, 64 n. 1) and Stählin (1924, 109 fig. 6, 110), who visited Skotoussa, respectively, in 1900 and either 1904 or 1912, saw the theatre in a natural hollow in the south-west of the city. From the accounts it appears that the German travellers may have had no evidence beyond the contour of the land. On the other hand the theatre is said to have been 'clearly visible' (Kromayer 1907, 64 n. 1: 'das Halbrund … des Theaters am Südabhange … noch deutlich zu sehen'). Stählin also noticed the immediate proximity of the city walls behind the theatre which agreed with **2**'s account that Alexander of Pherae callously tossed the corpses of the Skotoussans slaughtered in the theatre into the ditch before the city walls (1924, 110). No theatre was mentioned by Leake when he visited the site on New Year's Eve 1809 (1835 IV, 455–65), nor by Giannopoulos when he visited in 1902.

Although **1**'s date is surprisingly precise, **2**'s dating of 367/6 agrees with what we know of the career of Alexander of Pherae, who did not become *tagos* until 369/8 (see Stylianou 1998, 480 *ad loc.*). But if we accept Diodorus' and Plutarch's order of events, the massacre at Skotoussa must have happened before Epaminondas led the Theban expedition to free Pelopidas (Stylianou 1998, 480), which is dated 'early in 367' (Stylianou 1998, 451). Early 367 is however too early to be consistent with **2**, given that the Archon year begins only after the middle of our calendar year. The precise dating of the Skotoussa massacre is therefore problematic and its inclusion in the narratives of Diodorus and Plutarch (and ultimately Ephorus?) before the expedition of Epaminondas may owe more to its evocative exemplification of Alexander's treachery than to strict chronology. Despite Pausanias' expression, the town did not remain depopulated down to his day (Plb. 18.20.2–6; Liv. 33.6.8, 36.9.12–13; Plu. *Pomp.* 68.3; Missalidou-Despotidou 1993), but the city's coinage abruptly ceases around 367 and does not recover until the next century. The theatre probably continued to be used until late antiquity.

Cxii: Macedon: Festival of Olympian Zeus and the Muses

1. **Diodorus of Sicily,** *Library of History* **17.16.3–5**. Written ca. 50–30 and referring to 335. Alexander, after the fall of Thebes and before his departure for Asia, holds a festival of Zeus and the Muses. Text: Vogel and Fischer.

> διδάξας οὖν αὐτοὺς περὶ τοῦ συμφέροντος καὶ παρορμήσας διὰ τῶν λόγων πρὸς τοὺς ἀγῶνας, θυσίας μεγαλοπρεπεῖς τοῖς θεοῖς συνετέλεσεν ἐν Δίῳ τῆς Μακεδονίας καὶ σκηνικοὺς ἀγῶνας Διὶ καὶ Μούσαις, οὓς Ἀρχέλαος ὁ προβασιλεύσας ⁴ πρῶτος κατέδειξε. τὴν δὲ πανήγυριν ἐφ᾽ ἡμέρας ἐννέα συνετέλεσεν, ἑκάστῃ τῶν Μουσῶν ἐπώνυμον ἡμέραν ἀναδείξας. σκηνὴν δὲ κατασκευασάμενος ἑκατοντάκλινον τούς τε φίλους καὶ τοὺς ἡγεμόνας, ἔτι ⁵ δὲ τοὺς ἀπὸ τῶν πόλεων πρέσβεις παρέλαβεν ἐπὶ τὴν εὐωχίαν. λαμπραῖς δὲ παρασκευαῖς χρησάμενος καὶ πολλοὺς μὲν ἑστιάσας, πάσῃ δὲ τῇ δυνάμει διαδοὺς ἱερεῖα καὶ τἄλλα τὰ πρὸς τὴν εὐωχίαν ἀνήκοντα προσανέλαβε τὸ στρατόπεδον.

> So he instructed them on the best course of action, and by appeals aroused their enthusiasm for the contests. He performed magnificent sacrifices to the gods in Dion of Macedonia and theatre contests (*skenikoi agones*) for Zeus and the Muses, which Archelaus who was king before him ⁴ first introduced. He performed the festival for nine days, dedicating and naming a day for each of the Muses. He had built a tent that held a hundred banqueting couches and invited to the festivities his friends, the commanders and even ⁵ the envoys from the cities. After entertaining many with lavish offerings he distributed to the army sacrificial meat along with everything else conducive to festivity and uplifted his men's spirits.

2. **Arrian,** *The Anabasis of Alexander* **1.11.1–2**. Written ca. 145–160 AD and referring to the same events as **1**. 'Some say' indicates that Arrian's main source (Ptolemy or Aristobulus?) does not mention the contest for the Muses. Text: Roos and Wirth.

> ταῦτα δὲ διαπραξάμενος ἐπανῆλθεν εἰς Μακεδονίαν· καὶ τῷ τε Διὶ τῷ Ὀλυμπίῳ τὴν θυσίαν τὴν ἀπ᾽ Ἀρχελάου ἔτι καθεστῶσαν ἔθυσε καὶ τὸν ἀγῶνα ἐν Αἰγαῖς διέθηκε τὰ Ὀλύμπια· οἱ δὲ καὶ ταῖς Μούσαις λέγουσιν ὅτι ἀγῶνα ἐποίησε.

> After transacting this business he (Alexander) returned to Macedonia. He both sacrificed the sacrifice to Zeus Olympios which had already been established

by Archelaus, and he arranged the games, the Olympics, in Aegae. Some say that he also held a contest for the Muses.

3. Dio Chrysostom, *On Kingship* (*Oration* 2) 2–3. Delivered ca. 104 AD. Chrysostom reports an anecdote about a conversation between Alexander and his father Philip. The conversation is surely fictitious, but that does not necessarily taint the information Dio gives about the festival he employs as a historical setting. Text: Arnim.

> τότε δ᾽ οὖν ἀπὸ στρατείας ἥκοντες ἐν Δίῳ τῆς Πιερίας ἔθυον ταῖς Μούσαις, καὶ τὸν ἀγῶνα τῶν Ὀλυμπίων ἐτίθεσαν, ὅν φασιν ἀρχαῖον εἶναι παρ᾽ αὐτοῖς.

> So then arriving in Dion after their campaign they (Philip and Alexander) began sacrifices to the Muses and held the contest of the Olympics, which they say is ancient among them (i.e. the Macedonians).

4. Stephanus of Byzantium, *Ethnica* 232.3–5. Written 5th c. AD. Text: Meineke.

> Δῖον, πόλις Εὐβοίας περὶ τὸ Κήναιον. Ὅμηρος ῾Κήρινθόν τ᾽ ἔφαλον Δίου τ᾽ αἰπὺ πτολίεθρον᾽ (*Il.* 2.538). ἔστι καὶ Μακεδονίας, ἔνθα τὸν Ὀλυμπικὸν ἀγῶνα ἐτέλουν.

> Dion, a city of Euboea near Kenaion. Homer 'and Kerinthos by the sea, and the lofty citadel of Dion' (*Il.* 2.538). There is also a Dion of Macedonia, where they used to hold the Olympic contest.

5. Decree of Dion granting prohedria. Date: 325–300 (letter forms).

White marble stele broken at top.
0.47 × 0.385 × 0.095 m.
Discovered at Dion near Roman Odeon.
Dion Museum (formerly Thessaloniki 6670).
SEG 27, 279b; Hatzopoulos 1996, no. 57.

```
             . . . [προ]-            stoich. 18
     εδρίαν ἐν τοῖς γυ[μνικ]-
     οῖς ἀγῶσι καὶ ἐν τοῖς Δ[ι]-
     ονυσίοις καὶ τὸ ψήφισ-
  5  μα τοῦτο ἀναγράψαντας
     εἰστήλην λιθίνην ἀνα-
     θεῖναι πρὸ τοῦ ναοῦ, τή-
     ν δὲ εἰκόνα στῆσαι ἐν τ-
     ῶι τεμένει τοῦ Διὸς τοῦ
 10  Ὀλυμπίου, . . .
```

… [pro]hedria in the gy[mnic] competitions and in the D[i]onysia and that they
[5] write up this decree on a stone stele and erect it in front of the temple and
place the statue in the sanctuary of Zeus [10] Olympios …

6. *Curriculum Vitae* of an Athlete. Date: late 3rd–early 2nd c. (letter forms: Alexander 1970,
132–3).

Marble slab, broken on all sides, projection at middle of bottom, Latin funerary inscription on
back.
$0.35 \times 0.62 \times 0.05$–$0.09$ m.
Dug before or in 1936 in Portes (Poteidaia or Kassandreia) out of the yard of Mr Hadzikoudelios,
along with a marble banquet relief, said to be 'of second century BC' (Robinson 1938, 64).
Once in Nea-Potidea collection. Lost during WWII (Alexander 1970, 133 n. 22).
Robinson 1938, 64–5; Moretti 1953, 141 no. 54; *SEG* 14, 478a; Robert and Robert 1978, no. 232.
Photo: Robinson 1938, pl. XII, fig. 16.

[— — — — — — — — — —]
Ὀλύμπια τὰ ἐν Δίωι ἄνδρα[ς]
ὁπλίτην, Νέμεα ἄνδρας στάδι[ον],
Βασίλεια στάδιον, δίαυλο[ν],
ὁπλίτην τεῖ αὐτεῖ.

Olympics in Dion men's heavy-armoured contest; Nemean Games men's sta-
di[um] race; Royal Games stadium race, double cours[e]; heavy-armoured
contest, (all) on the same day.

7. Demosthenes, *On the False Embassy* (19) 192–5. Speech delivered 343, referring to
an event of 348. The use of the word *technitai* for performers is interesting but does not
imply the existence of actors' unions (*Technitai*). Satyros was one of the most famous
and successful comic actors of the day (Stefanis no. 2235). Text: Butcher.

ἐπειδὴ γὰρ εἷλεν Ὄλυνθον Φίλιππος, Ὀλύμπι᾽ ἐποίει, εἰς δὲ τὴν θυσίαν ταύτην
καὶ τὴν πανήγυριν πάντας τοὺς τεχνίτας συνήγαγεν. [193] ἑστιῶν δ᾽ αὐτοὺς καὶ
στεφανῶν τοὺς νενικηκότας ἤρετο Σάτυρον τουτονὶ τὸν κωμικὸν ὑποκριτήν,
τί δὴ μόνος οὐδὲν ἐπαγγέλλεται; ἢ τιν᾽ ἐν αὐτῷ μικροψυχίαν ἢ πρὸς αὐτὸν
ἀηδίαν ἐνεορακώς; εἰπεῖν δή φασι τὸν Σάτυρον ὅτι, ὧν μὲν οἱ ἄλλοι δέονται,
οὐδενὸς ὧν ἐν χρείᾳ τυγχάνει, ἃ δ᾽ ἂν αὐτὸς ἐπαγγείλαιθ᾽ ἡδέως, ῥᾷστα μέν
ἐστιν Φιλίππῳ δοῦναι [194] καὶ χαρίσασθαι πάντων, δέδοικε δὲ μὴ διαμάρτῃ.
κελεύσαντος δ᾽ ἐκείνου λέγειν καί τι καὶ νεανιευσαμένου τοιοῦτον, ὡς οὐδὲν
ὅ τι οὐ ποιήσει, εἰπεῖν φασιν αὐτὸν ὅτι ἦν αὐτῷ Ἀπολλοφάνης ὁ Πυδναῖος
ξένος καὶ φίλος, ἐπειδὴ δὲ δολοφονηθεὶς ἐτελεύτησεν ἐκεῖνος, φοβηθέντες οἱ
συγγενεῖς αὐτοῦ ὑπεξέθεντο τὰς θυγατέρας παιδί᾽ ὄντ᾽ εἰς Ὄλυνθον. ᾽αὗται
τοίνυν τῆς πόλεως ἁλούσης αἰχμάλωτοι γεγόνασι [195] καὶ εἰσὶν παρὰ σοί,
ἡλικίαν ἔχουσαι γάμου. ταύτας, αἰτῶ σε καὶ δέομαι, δός μοι. βούλομαι δέ
σ᾽ ἀκοῦσαι καὶ μαθεῖν οἵαν μοι δώσεις δωρειάν, ἂν ἄρα δῷς· ἀφ᾽ ἧς ἐγὼ

κερδανῶ μὲν οὐδέν, ἂν λάβω, προῖκα δὲ προσθεὶς ἐκδώσω, καὶ οὐ περιόψομαι
παθούσας οὐδὲν ἀνάξιον οὔθ᾽ ἡμῶν οὔτε τοῦ πατρός.᾽ ὡς δ᾽ ἀκοῦσαι τοὺς
παρόντας ἐν τῷ συμποσίῳ, τοσοῦτον κρότον καὶ θόρυβον καὶ ἔπαινον παρὰ
πάντων γενέσθαι ὥστε τὸν Φίλιππον παθεῖν τι καὶ δοῦναι.

When Philip took Olynthus he held Olympics. He gathered all the performing
artists (*technitai*) to this sacrifice and festival. [193] While he was feasting them
and giving crowns to the winners he asked Satyros the famous comic actor
why he alone had no request to make of him. Was it because he detected some
stinginess or ungraciousness in him? They say that Satyros replied that he had
no need of the kind of thing others requested, but though Philip could easily
grant all that he wanted to ask, [194] he was afraid he would not obtain it. When
Philip asked him to speak and blustered something to the effect that there was
nothing he would not do, they say he (Satyros) explained that Apollophanes
of Pydna had been a friend of his, and, when he was murdered, his relatives in
fear sent his daughters who were children at the time away to Olynthus. 'Now
these girls became captives when the city was taken [195] and they are under your
control and of marriageable age. I ask and beg you, give them to me! I want
you to hear and learn what kind of gift you will be giving me, if indeed you do
give. I do not want any profit from it, if I get my wish, but I will provide them
with a dowry and find husbands for them and I will not permit them to suffer
anything unworthy of myself or of their father.' When those present at the party
heard this, they all gave such loud applause and approval that even Philip was
somewhat moved and gave him his wish.

8. Scholion to Demosthenes, *On the False Embassy* (19) 192 (§ 383). Text: Dilts.

Ὀλύμπια ἐποίει. ἐκ τῆς πανηγύρεως τὸ πάθος τῶν ἀκουόντων ἔτι μᾶλλον
ηὔξησεν. αἱ γὰρ εὐπραγίαι τῶν πολεμίων λυποῦσι τοὺς ἡττωμένους. ὁ
μὲν οὖν πανήγυριν ἤγαγεν ἐπὶ νίκῃ καὶ συμφορᾷ τῶν Ἑλλήνων, ἡ δὲ πόλις
πληγεῖσα τοῖς συμβεβηκόσιν ἔστενε τὰς συμφοράς. τὰ Ὀλύμπια δὲ πρῶτος
Ἀρχέλαος ἐν Δίῳ τῆς Μακεδονίας κατέδειξεν. ἤγετο δ᾽ ἐπ᾽ ἐννέα, ὥς φασιν,
ἡμέρας ἰσαρίθμους ταῖς Μούσαις. συνέζευξε δὲ τὰ κατὰ τὴν Ὄλυνθον, ἵνα δοκῇ
πανηγυρίζειν ἐπὶ τῇ ἁλώσει τῶν Ἑλλήνων καὶ συνεορτάζειν καὶ ὁ Αἰσχίνης,
οἷον ᾽ἐγὼ μὲν ἐθρήνουν, Φίλιππος δὲ ἐτέλει μετὰ Αἰσχίνου πανήγυριν᾽.

'he held Olympics': with this festival he (Demosthenes) increases the emotional effect on the listeners, because the celebrations of the enemy give grief
to the vanquished. The one (Philip) holds a festival on the occasion of victory over the Greeks and a Greek calamity, while the city (Athens) struck by
events mourns the calamities. Archelaus first established the Olympics in Dion
of Macedonia. They say he held them for nine days, a number equal to the
number of the Muses. He (Demosthenes) tried to link them with the events at
Olynthus so that Aeschines would also appear to be celebrating and sharing in

the festivities at the capture of Greeks, as if to say 'I was lamenting, but Philip along with Aeschines was celebrating a festival'.

9. Scholion to Thucydides, *History of the Peloponnesian War* **1.126.5**. Thucydides mentions 'the Olympic games in the Peloponnese' as the time of Cylon's attempted coup (640?) in Athens. The Athenian Olympieia is a minor festival of which we hear little, and nothing before the fourth century (Parker 2005, 477). The Macedonian games are perhaps mentioned first as the more illustrious. Text: Hude.

> τὰ ἐν Πελοποννήσῳ· τοῦτο προσέθηκεν, ἐπειδὴ ἔστιν Ὀλύμπια καὶ ἐν Μακεδονίᾳ καὶ ἐν Ἀθήναις.

'(The Olympic games) in the Peloponnese': he adds this because there are Olympic games both in Macedonia and in Athens.

10. Philostratus, *Life of Apollonius of Tyana* **1.35.44–9**. Written 217–238 AD. Apollonius' argument is that a virtuous man will not allow himself to indulge indiscipline in any place or circumstances. Philostratus' location of the Olympics at Olynthus shows that his knowledge derives from a misreading of **7**. Text. Kayser.

> εἰ δὲ θύοι Φίλιππος Ὀλύμπια πόλεις ᾑρηκὼς ἢ ὁ τούτου παῖς Ἀλέξανδρος ἐπὶ ταῖς ἑαυτοῦ νίκαις ἀγῶνα ἄγοι, χεῖρον ἤδη παρασκευάζειν τὸ σῶμα καὶ μὴ φιλονίκως ἔχειν, ἐπειδὴ ἐν Ὀλύνθῳ ἀγωνιεῖται ἢ Μακεδονίᾳ ἢ Αἰγύπτῳ, ἀλλὰ μὴ ἐν Ἕλλησι καὶ σταδίοις τοῖς ἐκεῖ;

If Philip were to perform Olympics when (or 'because') he captured cities, or Alexander, his son, were to hold a contest on the occasion of his own victories, would you tell the man to relax the training of his body and slacken his resolve, because the contest is to be held in Olynthus or in Macedonia or in Egypt, and not in Greece or on Greek race courses?

Our two principal sources (**1**, **2**) for the festival of Olympian Zeus and the Muses contradict one another: **1** places it in Dion, **2** in Aegae. This has given rise to considerable controversy in modern scholarship. Possibly both are right and **2** means to indicate that Alexander transplanted or replicated the festival of Dion in Aegae (Ziehen 1939, 46). Indeed we have anecdotal evidence from Plutarch (*Mor.* 1096b) that suggests Alexander had a proskenion built for the theatre at Pella, probably sometime before his departure for Asia in 334 (Moretti 2014a, 110). If this is connected in any way to preparations for the festival of Zeus and the Muses, then we might just possibly have to suppose an expansion of the festival by Alexander to several locations in Macedonia, with simultaneous or successive dramatic performances.

The location of the festival of Olympian Zeus and the Muses should not be confused with the question of the location of the first performance of Euripides' *Archelaus*. If it was a possible location at all, Aegae would certainly have been a more suitable location for the

Archelaus, given the themes of the play, which include the city's foundation (Sourvinou-Inwood 2003, 41–5). Modern excavations discovered a theatre in Vergina/Aegae in 1982. But the theatre dates to the second half of the fourth century (and was presumably the theatre in which Philip II was assassinated in 336: see **VI F**). The excavators note earlier phases of the theatre datable to the early fourth century (Drougou 1997, 305; 2012, 51) and an inscription found in the area of the theatre may possibly indicate use of the theatral space in the late fifth century (Saatsoglou-Paliadeli 2002, 482–3; *SEG* 53, 587). Future research may therefore indicate a use of the area (or some other) for theatrical purposes in the late fifth century; at present however nothing more than **2**'s testimony and the themes of Euripides' play argue for fifth-century performances at Aegae.

The evidence, textual, geographical and archaeological, is overwhelmingly in favour of Dion. **2**'s claims are isolated. Five sources name Dion as the site of the festival of Zeus and the Muses (**1**, **3**, **4**, **6**, **8**), including an inscription (**6**), albeit of Hellenistic date. Dion is geographically the most obvious choice for a festival of Olympian Zeus and the Muses: it lies at the foot of and is almost equidistant between the peaks of Olympus and Pieria, the sacred mountains of Zeus Olympios and the Pierian Muses respectively. Vergina (Aegae) on the other hand is located at the north end of Pieria and far from Olympus. The very name of Dion indicates its importance as a sanctuary of Zeus. It contained a large sanctuary of Zeus Olympios (Pandermalis 1997, 29–30; cf. **5**, l. 10), as well as a sanctuary of Zeus Hypsistos discovered in 2003 (Dowden 2006, 58–9; *SEG* 53, 596–600). In this connection it is important to note the prominence of Dionysus at Dion, the existence of a Dionysia (**5**), and evidence of an active cult of the Muses, albeit from a second-century inscription (Pandermalis 2002, 101–3; Giannou 2016, 33–5).

At Dion, as at Vergina, a theatre has been found, but as at Vergina, it is much later in date ('Hellenistic'). There are however some indications of an earlier phase. The theatre is thought to have been built at the same time as the nearby stadium, which yielded coins of 'almost all' the Macedonian kings beginning with Alexander I (498–454; Pandermalis 1997, 80; Adam-Veleni 2010, 75–6; Karadedos 2012a, 71). The weakness of this evidence is of course not only the fact that we appear to have only one coin of fifth-century date but also the fact that we cannot tell how long such coins remained in circulation. More importantly the excavators have found a row of seats, of different construction, and slightly different orientation, underneath the middle of the Hellenistic theatron, which must belong to an earlier phase of the theatre, as do some remains of a limestone prohedria reused as building material in the Hellenistic phase (Karadedos 1986, 335, 339–40; 2005, 38; 2012b, 74). It is difficult to believe that this feature, however, goes back to the fifth century: if it did, then the theatre at Dion is the first round (i.e. horseshoe-shaped) theatre known from antiquity. Moretti is however willing to entertain the possibility, largely on the evidence of the theatre at Aegae, that 'curved seating was known in Macedonia at a time when the Athenian theatre was still under construction' (2014a, 135). A theatre in fifth-century Dion is nonetheless likely, given our literary evidence, and in any case guaranteed for late fourth-century Dion by the granting of prohedria at the Dionysia in **5**.

Dion is also favoured by the fact that both a theatre and a stadium were necessary for the combination of athletic and musical competitions that made up the festival of Zeus and the Muses. Our sources are unclear on whether the festival established by Archelaus had only theatrical contests (**1**), or both athletic and theatrical contests, but athletic games were certainly part of the festival by the late fourth century (**5?, 6, 10**). Finally, the description of Alexander's tent in **1** suits the sanctuary setting of Dion much better than Aegae, where Alexander had a palace (right beside the theatre) in which to receive his guests. Even on current evidence, therefore, one can conclude with reasonable confidence that Archelaus established his festival at Dion, not Aegae. Though many recognise that Arrian (**2**) is wrong to locate the Macedonian Olympics in Aegae, few have been content to regard it as a simple error, but construct complex, often fanciful and generally unpersuasive hypotheses to show how he went astray. These are of no interest to us and are discussed in Mari 1998, 139–42.

The periodicity of the festival is harder to determine. Many of our sources speak of the festival as if it were an 'occasional' festival mounted in celebration of victories by Philip and Alexander (this is the impression in **1–3** and more or less explicit in **7** and **10**). **8** however argues that Demosthenes rhetorically creates the impression of a causal link in order to discredit Aeschines and raise the indignation of his Athenian audience. It is also likely from the reference to Olynthus in **10** that Philostratus' testimony also depends on Demosthenes. Mari (1998, 144–6) argues persuasively that even **1** is tainted by Demosthenes' rhetoric in **7**, since Diodorus' earlier description of Philip's Olympics in 348 (there simply called *epinikia*) follows Demosthenes closely in detail, even if mediated through Diyllus or some other source (16.53–55). The upshot is that all the sources for the 'occasional' epinician character of Philip and Alexander's celebration of the festival may have been caught on the lime of Demosthenes' anti-Macedonian and anti-Aeschinean rhetoric.

In short, the festivals presided over by Philip and Alexander, though celebrated at some time after the fall of Olynthus (autumn 348) and after the fall of Thebes (autumn 335) respectively, may not have been celebrated because of these victories. The first month of the Macedonian year is called 'Dios', after Zeus, and corresponded roughly with October and the normal end of the campaigning season (Mari 1998, 151–2). It is possible therefore that the festival of Zeus was a New Year's festival. If the festivals were regular and took place reasonably soon after the campaigns to which **1–2** and **7** ascribe them, then the festival of Zeus and the Muses cannot be penteteric like the major Panhellenic athletic festivals to which it is compared, or even trieteric, but must be annual. It is possible however that Philip's celebration of the festival took place much later than Demosthenes implies and in the following year, 347. For her part, Mari (1998, 150–2) prefers to suppose that the festival was penteteric but that Alexander arbitrarily held the Olympics in a year in which they would not normally occur (and also in a place, Aegae, where they were not normally held), so, on this hypothesis, a certain arbitrary and occasional quality adheres to the festival notwithstanding.

The dedication of a day of contests to each of the Muses may imply a wide range of contests, though we have no specific evidence of the specialisation of the nine Muses before Plato's *Phaedrus* (Murray 2004, 374–5). This is certainly consistent with the wide range of genres represented by Archelaus' visitors (**VI D**), including tragedy, comedy, lyric, epic, history, philosophy, medicine and the plastic arts. Demosthenes' anecdote (**7**) confirms comedy, through the person of Satyros, and a variety of performing artists through the reference to *technitai*. The singer, aulode and rhapsode, Pythokles, appears to have won victories at the Macedonian Olympics in the third century (**Cv 5**; Mari 1998, 158–9). Athletic contests may have continued at least until the third century AD (Moretti 1953, no. 84, 212–217 AD). Two centuries later they are spoken of in the past tense by **4**.

Cxiii: Abdera

1. **Lucian,** *How to Write History* **1**. Probably written soon after 164–165 AD (the essay mentions events in Lucius Verus' Parthian war up to that date). The target date is the beginning of the reign of Lysimachus (King of Thrace 306–281). The essay is addressed to a friend named Philo. The passage cites Euripides' *Andromeda TrGF* F 136. Text: Kilburn.

> Ἀβδηρίταις φασὶ Λυσιμάχου ἤδη βασιλεύοντος ἐμπεσεῖν τι νόσημα, ὦ καλὲ
> Φίλων, τοιοῦτο· πυρέττειν μὲν γὰρ τὰ πρῶτα πανδημεὶ ἅπαντας ἀπὸ τῆς
> πρώτης εὐθὺς ἐρρωμένως καὶ λιπαρεῖ τῷ [1.5] πυρετῷ, περὶ δὲ τὴν ἑβδόμην τοῖς
> μὲν αἷμα πολὺ ἐκ ῥινῶν ῥυέν, τοῖς δ' ἱδρὼς ἐπιγενόμενος, πολὺς καὶ οὗτος,
> ἔλυσεν τὸν πυρετόν. ἐς γελοῖον δέ τι πάθος περιίστα τὰς γνώμας αὐτῶν·
> ἅπαντες γὰρ ἐς τραγῳδίαν παρεκίνουν καὶ ἰαμβεῖα ἐφθέγγοντο [1.10] καὶ μέγα
> ἐβόων· μάλιστα δὲ τὴν Εὐριπίδου Ἀνδρομέδαν ἐμονῴδουν καὶ τὴν τοῦ Περσέως
> ῥῆσιν ἐν μέλει διεξήεσαν, καὶ μεστὴ ἦν ἡ πόλις ὠχρῶν ἁπάντων καὶ λεπτῶν
> τῶν ἑβδομαίων ἐκείνων τραγῳδῶν, [1.15] 'σὺ δ' ὦ θεῶν τύραννε κἀνθρώπων
> Ἔρως', καὶ τὰ ἄλλα μεγάλῃ τῇ φωνῇ ἀναβοώντων καὶ τοῦτο ἐπὶ πολύ, ἄχρι
> δὴ χειμὼν καὶ κρύος δὲ μέγα γενόμενον ἔπαυσε ληροῦντας αὐτούς. αἰτίαν δέ
> μοι δοκεῖ τοῦ τοιούτου παρασχεῖν Ἀρχέλαος ὁ [1.20] τραγῳδός, εὐδοκιμῶν τότε,
> μεσοῦντος θέρους ἐν πολλῷ τῷ φλογμῷ τραγῳδήσας αὐτοῖς τὴν Ἀνδρομέδαν,
> ὡς πυρέξαι τε ἀπὸ τοῦ θεάτρου τοὺς πολλοὺς καὶ ἀναστάντας ὕστερον ἐς τὴν
> τραγῳδίαν παρολισθαίνειν, ἐπὶ πολὺ ἐμφιλοχωρούσης [1.25] τῆς Ἀνδρομέδας
> τῇ μνήμῃ αὐτῶν καὶ τοῦ Περσέως ἔτι σὺν τῇ Μεδούσῃ τὴν ἑκάστου γνώμην
> περιπετομένου.

1.12 ἐν μέλει Ε Γ Kassel 1973, 106–7   ἐν μέρει other codd. Homeyer

They say that when Lysimachus had just become King, a sickness afflicted the people of Abdera, my dear Philo, which was of this sort. Initially from the first day the whole city came down with a powerful and persistent [1.5] fever. Around the seventh day it was dispelled, for some by profuse bleeding from the nostrils, for others by a sweat just as profuse, but it reduced their minds to a ridiculous state. Everyone became obsessed with tragedy and they would utter iambic lines [1.10] shouting them out loud. Most of all they would sing monodies from the *Andromeda* of Euripides or melodically (or 'in turn') go through the speech of Perseus. The whole city was filled with these thin, pale, seventh-day tragedians, shouting out [1.15] 'Eros, you tyrant over men and gods!' and the rest in a loud voice, and it went on for a long time until winter and a cold snap put a stop to their raving. I think the cause of this affliction was the [1.20] then famous tragic actor, Archelaos, who performed the *Andromeda* for them in the scorching heat of mid summer with the result that most of them became feverish from the moment they left the theatre and when they later rose from their sickbeds they relapsed into tragedy [1.25] while Andromeda still haunted their memory and Perseus still holding Medusa hovered about everyone's mind.

2. Machon, *Sayings* fr. 11.119–33 Gow (= Ath. 8.349b). Machon's *Sayings* (Χρεῖαι) were written in Alexandria in the 3rd c. Stratonicus should be dated from the very late 5th c. to perhaps some time beyond the middle of the 4th c. Cf. on **Cxiv** and **Fiii 4**. Text: Gow.

	Στρατόνικος εἰς Ἄβδηρ᾽ ἀποδημήσας ποτὲ
120	ἐπὶ τὸν ἀγῶνα τὸν τιθέμενον αὐτόθι,
	ὁρῶν ἕκαστον τῶν πολιτῶν κατ᾽ ἰδίαν
	κεκτημένον κήρυκα κηρύττοντά τε
	ἕκαστον αὐτῶν, ὅτε θέλοι, νουμηνίαν
	σχεδόν τε τοὺς κήρυκας ἐν τῷ χωρίῳ
125	ὄντας πολὺ πλείους κατὰ λόγον τῶν δημοτῶν,
	ἐπ᾽ ἄκρων ἐβάδιζε τῶν ὀνύχων ἐν τῇ πόλει
	σχέδην, δεδορκὼς ἀτενὲς εἰς τὴν γῆν κάτω.
	πυνθανομένου δὲ τῶν ξένων αὐτοῦ τινος
	τὸ πάθος τὸ γεγονὸς ἐξαπίνης περὶ τοὺς πόδας,
130	τοῦτ᾽ εἶπε· ᾽τοῖς ὅλοις μὲν ἔρρωμαι, ξένε,
	καὶ τῶν κολάκων πολὺ μᾶλλον ἐπὶ δεῖπνον τρέχω·
	ἀγωνιῶ δὲ καὶ δέδοικα παντελῶς,
	μή ποτ᾽ ἐπιβὰς κήρυκι τὸν πόδ᾽ ἀναπαρῶ.᾽

Stratonicus once on a trip to Abdera [120] for the competition held there, seeing that each of the citizens privately retained a herald and each proclaimed the beginning of the month whenever he wished – there being, one could say, far too many heralds [125] in proportion to the citizens in the place – began walking on tiptoes in the city quickly with his eyes intent on the ground below. When one of the foreigners (i.e. the Abderites) asked what had just happened to his feet, [130] he said: 'I am completely fine, stranger, and I can outrun a parasite to dinner, but I am anxious and very much afraid of stepping on a conch shell/ herald (κῆρυξ can mean both) and injuring my foot.'

Abdera, a refoundation of Teos in 544, was the largest city on the northern Aegean coast. Its prosperity was based on the conduct of trade between Thrace and the Aegean and the export of grain and mineral resources. It was the third largest contributor to the Delian League, paying an annual contribution of 15 talants from at least 454/3, reduced to 10 talants in 432/1, and then rising in 425 to an enormous 75 talants together with Dikaia. Abdera joined the north Aegean revolt against Athenian hegemony, probably after 411, but was brought back in 407. In 376/5 Athenian forces under Chabrias repelled a Thracian attack on Abdera and established an Athenian garrison. In consequence Abdera remained a member of the Second Athenian Confederacy until occupied by Philip by 346/5 when Athens gave asylum to Abderite refugees. Abdera's constitution 'was presumably democratic' (Loukopoulou in *IACP* 873–4, quotation 874; cf. much more confidently, at least for the fifth century, Robinson 2011, 140–5, 249).

1 is clearly a fiction and poor evidence for theatre or performance in Abdera, though it is frequently cited as such. Though the specificity of didascalic details in **1** encourages hope that the anecdote contains a core of historical content, none can be independently verified. The actor Archelaos is unknown apart from this tale (Stefanis no. 432; the tragic actor Archelaos who appears in Delphi in 263, *FD* III 1, 478, l. 17, is probably too late to be the same man). Other details can be explained by the author's literary and narrative intentions. **1** seems to parody Hippocratic literature and the choice of Abdera as a setting may be grounded in nothing more real than the city's reputation for an unhealthy climate (Loukopoulou in *IACP* 872), located as it was on the marshlands at the mouth of the river Nestos, which gave it a prominent place in the Hippocratic corpus (particularly in *Epid.* 3.3.17, 6.8.30, 7.1.97, but also in the *Ep.* 10–12, 17 and other works; see *IThrAeg* T 114–23). The extant corpus offers Abderan parallels for many of **1**'s symptoms (Tschiedel 1986, 184–7). Even the choice of Euripides' *Andromeda* could be determined by the hero's love sickness, every bit as sudden and intense, to judge from Aristophanic parody, as the tragic mania that supposedly afflicted Abdera (*Frogs* 53–4; *Th.* 1008–135, esp. 1116–18, thought by some to be a quotation from the play, where 'Euripides' refers to Eros as a 'sickness', νόσημα). The most that can be said is that Lucian or his source (see below) had accurate knowledge of Euripides' play. The lines cited from Euripides' *Andromeda* are also cited with minor variations by Ath. 13.561b and Stob. 4.20b, and we have independent verification that in the play Perseus makes a flying entrance carrying the head of Medusa (*TrGF* F 124).

Scholars also frequently adduce Abdera's reputation for the stupidity of its inhabitants in explanation of the choice of setting (e.g. Tschiedel 1986 and Klimek-Winter 1993, 102–3), but this is of no obvious relevance, since the anecdote turns on sickness and madness, not stupidity. It is, moreover, not known when Abdera's reputation for stupidity arose: whether by the fourth century as argued by Tschiedel (1986), or not before the first century BC as argued by Klimek-Winter (1993, 102–3), and so, despite Klimek-Winter, offers no purchase for dating the origin of the anecdote.

There is some evidence for a narrative of a plague erupting in the theatre of Abdera earlier than Lucian. Essentially the same story, but set in a 'semi-barbarian' city and in the time of Nero, appears in Eunapius' *Histories* (later fourth century AD; *Hist.* fr. 54), though the setting, both time and place, reveals a general confusion with a completely independent anecdote that we know from Philostratus' *Life of Apollonius* (5.9, written ca. 220 AD; Klimek-Winter 1993, 104–5). Eunapius' version, if anything, seems to indicate that both he and Lucian are ultimately drawing material from an earlier source, though we doubt that this source was (as Möllendorff 2001, 132 argues) 'closer to Eunapius'. How much earlier than Lucian this source might have been is impossible to say. For the purposes of theatre history, **1** at best proves only that some time before 164 AD an unknown author thought not implausible a production of tragedy in Abdera at the end of the fourth century.

2 is only a little more trustworthy in ascribing a musical competition to Abdera some time in the first half of the fourth century (for the date of Stratonicus' death, see **Fiii**). Machon does not say Stratonicus was in Abdera for a *musical* competition, but this is an obvious inference from the fact that the famous kitharode is said to be present 'for the competition held there' (ἐπὶ τὸν ἀγῶνα τὸν τιθέμενον αὐτόθι). As kitharodic competitions are normally held in theatres, this at best improves on **1** by indicating that Machon writing in the third century thought it plausible that Abdera would have had a theatre with a programme of musical competitions by the first half of the fourth century. The evidence would be much stronger if we could prove at this point that Machon was drawing on Callisthenes of Olynthus, who was a contemporary of Stratonicus (see **Cxiv**).

Problematic as these sources are, archaeological and other evidence make it possible and even likely that Abdera had a theatre by the fourth century. The theatre was discovered in 1965 just within the line of the Archaic and Classical fortification wall to the south-west of the city (the Hellenistic city circuit lies to the south: see *Philogelos* 110; Loukopoulou et al. 2005, 177). Though partially excavated the remains offer no evidence for its chronology. Both the theatre and an annual Dionysia that included a (single?) competition are in any case guaranteed for the second century, probably early in the century, by honorary inscriptions (*IThrAeg* E7, ll. 21–4: 'to invite him during his lifetime each year to take a front row seat and to crown him with a golden crown in the theatre at the contest of each Dionysia', καλεῖσθαι δὲ αὐτὸν ἕως ἂν ζῇ καὶ εἰς προε|δρίαν κατ᾽ ἐνιαυτόν, καὶ στεφανοῦσθαι ἐν | τῶι θεάτρωι ἐς ἀεὶ Διονυσίων τῶι ἀγῶνι χρυ|σῶι στεφάνωι; and with almost identical language: E8, ll. 20–2; E9, ll. 19–21). But 'even if [the theatre's] architectural remains date to the 2ⁿᵈ c. BC, its design seems older' (Loukopoulou et al. 2005, 179). Lazaridis was of the opinion that 'it is probable the city also had a theatre in the fifth century' (1971, 38; cf. Lazaridis 1966, 359–61; Dimadis 1974; Triandaphyllos 1984, 32–3).

Of some importance to the dating of Abdera's reception of theatre is the discovery of a production centre for figurines (including moulds), with tragic and comic figurines among them, not far to the south-west of the theatre (Lazaridis 1952), and dating perhaps as early as ca. 350 (Graham 1972; Chasapi-Christodoulou 1991–1992, 321–2). The comic figurines date from the very beginning of the Abderite production (*MMC*³ XT12, XT14; *MNC*³ 2BA1, 2BT1, 2BT3, 2BT7; Lazaridis 1960). In addition comic terracotta figurines of Athenian type were used as grave goods as early as the second quarter of the fourth century (*MMC*³ AT46d, 58d; *MNC*³ 1AT6a). Chasapi-Christodoulou (1991–1992, 276) lists 5 tragic and satyric figurines, 4 Old and Middle Comic and 11 New Comic from Abdera.

From the very little we know about the city, Abdera appears to have had a rich musical tradition from Archaic times. The lyric poet Anacreon is said to have taken part in the Teian refoundation of the city, ca. 544 (Asheri et al. 2007, 189 on Hdt. 1.168). Pindar wrote a paean (*Pae.* 2) for an Abderite chorus probably for performance in Delphi and Delos (Power 2011, 105–6; Hubbard 2011, 361). A transfer from Athens of theatre culture from as early as the fifth century is not unlikely, given that Abdera, like its mother city Teos, was probably a democracy from as early as ca. 490, worshipped Dionysus as its chief deity (Sherk 1991, 225; Chryssanthaki-Nagle 2007, 96), and was an ally of Athens for most of the Classical period (Loukopoulou in *IACP* 872–5; Robinson 2011, 140–5).

Cxiv: Maroneia. Callisthenes, *Apophthegmata*, *FGrH* **124 F 5 (= Ath. 8.351e–f)**.
Written in the third quarter of the 4ᵗʰ c. (Callisthenes died in 327) and referring to an
event that supposedly took place in the very late 5ᵗʰ or first half of the 4ᵗʰ c. when the famous wit and kitharode Stratonicus was active (Stefanis no. 2310). Athenaeus refers to
Callisthenes' work as *Reminiscences of Stratonicus* but the anecdotes about Stratonicus
are thought to be from a larger work, *Apophthegmata* (*Witty Sayings*), generally agreed
to be a genuine work of Callisthenes of Olynthus (Kroll 1919, 1685; Jacoby *FGrH* IID
416; Pearson 1960, 26–7; Prandi 1985, 143 n. 1). It recorded the witticisms of several
famous contemporaries (cf. Poll. 9.93). Text: close to Kaibel.

> ἐν Μαρωνείαι δὲ συμπίνων τισὶν ἐχειν ἔφη γνῶναι κατὰ τίνα τόπον ἐστὶ
> τῆς πόλεως, ἐὰν κατακαλύψαντες ἄγωσιν· εἶθ' ὡς ἦγον καὶ ἠρώτων, 'κατὰ
> τὸ καπηλεῖον' ἔφη, ὅτι καπηλεῖα <πάντα> ἐδόκει εἶναι ἡ Μαρώνεια ... ἐν
> Μαρωνείαι δ' ἔφη οὐ γίνεσθαι ἔαρ, ἀλλ' ἀλέαν.

ἔχειν C   ἐθέλειν Kaibel, Jacoby   <πάντα> Jacoby

In Maroneia he (Stratonicus), drinking with some fellows, said if they were to
blindfold him and take him anywhere he would be able to recognise where in
the city he was. Then when they took him and asked, he said 'in a pub', because Maroneia seemed to him to be all pubs … in Maroneia he said there was
no 'summer' (ἔαρ = spring) but 'simmer' (ἀλέα = heat).

Callisthenes is the best evidence we have for some form of theatre culture in Maroneia
in the late fifth or first half of the fourth century. In the short surviving fragment of his
work (Ath. 8.350d–52c) he locates the kitharode Stratonicus twice in Maroneia and it is
reasonable to conclude that Stratonicus is there for a kitharodic performance (kitharodic performances are normally a theatrical event). The only other evidence is the theatre
building itself. The remains of Maroneia's theatre (10 of originally 20 rows of seating
and a prohedria) were excavated from 1981 to 1994 and again from 2003 to 2007 while
restoration works were in progress. The earliest phase is dated stratigraphically to the
late fourth or early third century, most specifically by coins found in the construction
layers of the cavea and by coins and Thasian stamped amphora handles in the area outside
the cavea and south-east of the stage building (Karadima et al. 2015, 263–4). An earlier
theatre may have existed elsewhere. Nothing of the pre-Hellenistic city of Maroneia has
yet been found and it has been suggested that the entire city was relocated in the early
Hellenistic period.

Dionysus was probably the poliadic deity, judging from the prominence of his image on
the coinage, the use of his sanctuary as the place of publication of official documents (*SEG*
35, 823, ll. 43–4 [ca. 167]), and the connections of the city's eponymous hero, Maron, with
Dionysus. The theatre is built into a natural slope and located 200 m east of a sanctuary of
Dionysus.

Though the evidence scarcely permits any confident conclusions, Maroneia fits well the
profile of Aegean sites that received theatre in the fifth or fourth century under the direct
influence of Athens. It was a site of some strategic and commercial importance, located

on the sea routes of the northern Aegean and guarding the passes into Thrace through the Rhodope mountains and hence a member of both the first and second Athenian leagues, remaining loyal even after the Social War of 357–355 (Loukopoulou in *IACP* 879). Nothing is known of Maroneia's constitution. Philip attacked the city in 353 (D. 23.183; Polyaen. 4.2.22) but probably did not take it until 338 (Hammond and Griffith 1979, 379).

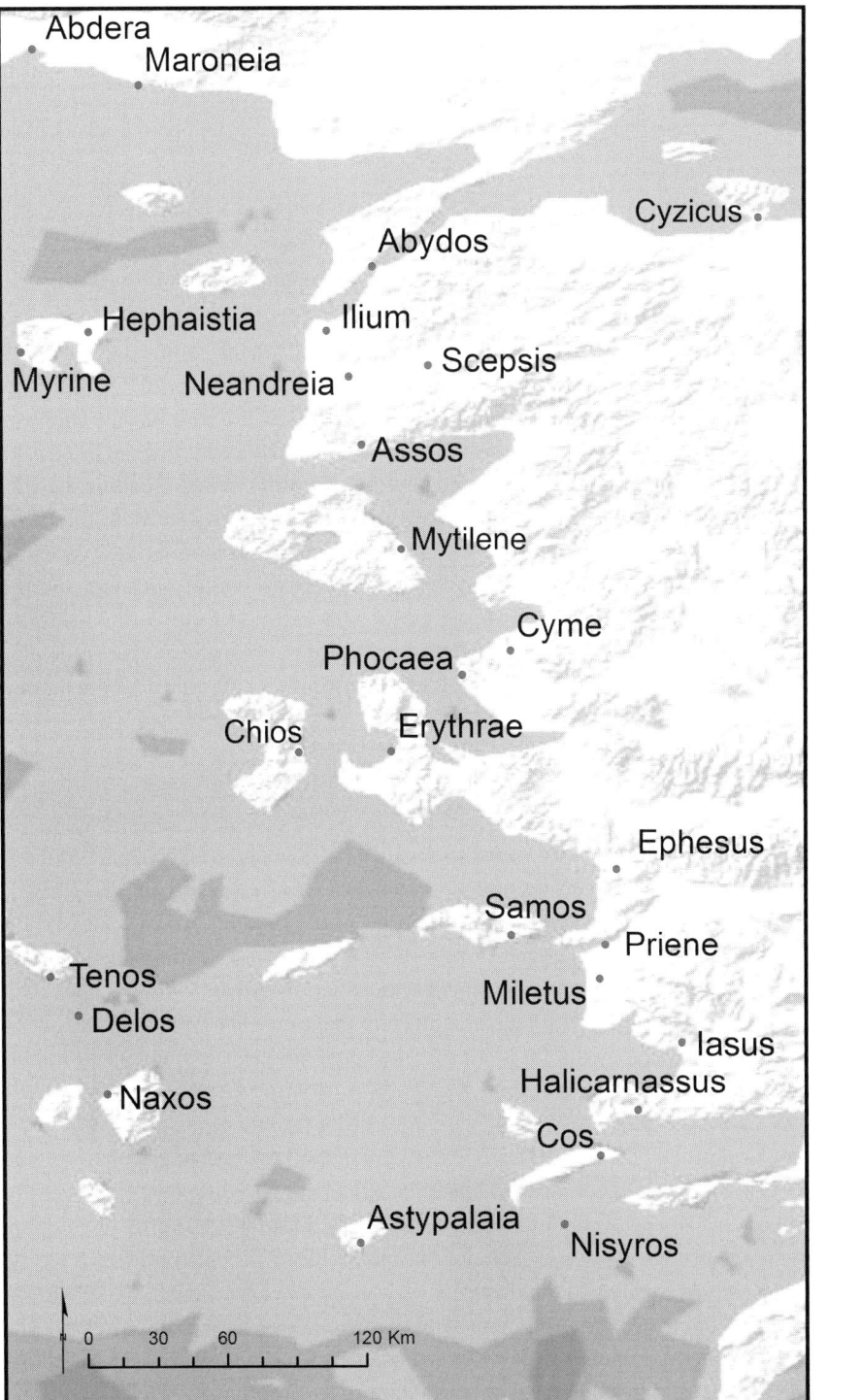

Abdera

Maroneia

Cyzicus

Abydos

Hephaistia

Ilium

Myrine

Neandreia

Scepsis

Assos

Mytilene

Cyme

Phocaea

Chios

Erythrae

Ephesus

Samos

Priene

Tenos

Miletus

Delos

Iasus

Naxos

Halicarnassus

Cos

Astypalaia

Nisyros

0 30 60 120 Km

D | Aegean Islands

Introduction

Athens' role in the dissemination of theatre culture is most easily perceptible in the Aegean. Some sites give evidence of a transplantation of theatre culture through Athenian colonisation while others suggest a reception of theatre at the time of Athens' political and cultural hegemony in this region. Predictably both processes led to the development of a theatre culture with a distinctively Athenian stamp. Aegean theatrical festivals are all Dionysia (Tenos is probably no exception, **Dxv**) until the end of the fourth century when drama begins to spread to other festivals; frequently we have evidence of choregic funding, tribally organised choruses, and competitions in choral lyric (men's or boys' or both), comedy and tragedy. In most cases we find the proclamation of public honours 'at the contest of the tragedies', as the honorary decrees that authorise them are one of our main sources of evidence in this region. In some cases we find details of other festival rituals known from Athens, such as elaborate choral and phallic processions, competitions for actors, the awarding of tripods to lyric choruses, or in one case the awarding in the theatre of panoplies to war orphans once they have come of age.

Cleruchies and Colonies

'The cleruchies of the fourth century were little replicas of Athens, with their own councils and assemblies … and it is scarcely surprising to find such a basic amenity of Attic life as a tragic festival of Dionysos soon attested' (Parker 1994, 343). Salamis (**Dxii**) is an obvious example. Though barely 2 km separate from the Attic mainland, Salamis was never incorporated into the Attic deme system. The island was settled by Athenians in the late sixth century and was probably technically a cleruchy from that time. The Athenians appointed an Archon for Salamis, as they did for other overseas possessions. His single most important duty was to 'run the Dionysia' (Arist. *Ath.* 54.8). A choregic system, as well as tragic and boys' (probably also men's) choruses were in place by the end of the fifth century.

Athens took control of Lemnos (**Dviii**) ca. 500, expelled the native population, who were non-Greek, and planted colonists to make the island entirely their own (Hdt. 6.140). Lemnos' importance for Athens stems from its strategic location on the main shipping route between Athens and the Black Sea and its proximity to Athenian mining interests in Thrace. The earliest remains of the theatre at Hephaistia have been dated to the earliest years of the Athenian occupation (but should probably be redated to the late 5th c.). The theatre was superimposed upon a native Lemnian sanctuary to a mother goddess, whom the Athenian settlers elsewhere on the island worshiped as a form of Cybele/Demeter and associated with Dionysus, a connection sympathetic to the incorporation of the Lemnian Dionysus within Attic and Eleusian cult that we find in Euripides' *Hypsipyle*, which traces the charter of the Athenian Euneidae, priests of Dionysus Melpomenos, back to Dionysus on Lemnos. We have no evidence at Hephaistia for a Dionysia or tragedy until the early third century (**Dviii 2**), but a Dionysia and a competition for tragedy did exist by 348 at Myrina on the west side of the island (**Dviii 1**). A choregic system is also attested at Myrina. Our main information at both locations comes thanks to the imitation of the Athenian custom of announcing public honours at the contest of the tragedies at the Dionysia.

Samos (**Dxiii**) received an Athenian cleruchy in the 440s after the Samian revolt, but the earliest evidence for theatre comes only with the second Athenian cleruchy, 365–322, when, as in Lemnos, the local population was expelled. A series of honorific decrees, beginning ca. 350 (**Dxiii 1**) and extending well beyond the expulsion of the Athenian cleruchs in 322, gives evidence of a Dionysia and a tragic competition. By ca. 306 (**Dxiii 2**) an agonothete is in charge of the competitions at the festival, together with tragic performance at a new festival in honour of Antigonus and Demetrius. By this time there are a plurality of competitions held in the theatre and the famous tragic actor Polos is granted prohedria at all of them. Inscriptions of the mid third century indicate a programme of competitions, funded by choregoi, that include men's and boys' lyric choruses, tragedy and comedy. The tomb of a Bitto, daughter of Glaukos, sat[yrographos] from Samos (*CEG* II, 685), dated to the end of the fourth century, offers some slight (and not unproblematic) evidence for the inclusion of satyr play in the fourth century, although this genre is not otherwise attested on the island until the second century. The choregia and other genres may have come later but at least the Dionysia, the theatre and tragic competitions all originated in the period of Athenian domination.

The evidence is more circumstantial on islands where there was no wholesale displacement of native populations. Andros (**Di**) received a small group of Athenian cleruchs about 450 and was occupied by an Athenian governor and garrison in the mid fourth century, during the Second Athenian Confederacy. An inscription shows that it had a contest for tragedy at its Dionysia by a date around the end of the fourth century, there is material evidence for a theatre about the same time, and suggestive evidence for the existence of comedy on the island from the middle of the fourth.

The remarkable similarities in theatre culture between Eretria (**Dvii**) and Athens may possibly be ascribed to Athenian hegemony rather than Athenian occupation. Eretria celebrated a lavish Dionysia with tribally organised and choregically funded men's and boys' choruses, probably from as early as ca. 500, and these were commemorated, as at Athens, by choregic tripod monuments that lined the main road entering the theatre (**Dvii 1**, **3–8**). Even the relationship of the Eretrian theatre to the sanctuary and temple of Dionysus is analogous to Athens. Moreover, the structure of tribal funding, through paired tribes, resembles that practised at the Athenian Thargelia and the comic competitions of the Athenian Dionysia in the fourth century. The Eretrian Dionysia probably always began with an elaborate parade though we have no specific mention before the late fourth century (**Dvii 9**). Drama is not attested until the Euboean Festival Decree of ca. 290 (*ATD* TE 1) when three tragic choruses and an unknown number of comic choruses competed. Moreover, the decree shows that the same festival structure was shared with the other Euboean cities of Chalcis, Oreos and (with minor modification) Carystus. The genres perhaps had an earlier history on the island; at any rate the early fifth-century tragic poet Achaeus was Eretrian, the early fifth-century tragic actor Mynniskos was from Chalcis, and Menander's statue was placed in the parodos of the theatre at Eretria, already probably within the comic poet's lifetime.

Although we know of only one possible Athenian cleruchy in Eretria, and this only after a revolt from League membership in 446, it is likely that Athenian colonisation had some impact on theatre culture in Euboea generally, even if we cannot establish a direct link in Eretria. The three other cities named in the Euboean Festival Decree (Chalcis, Oreos and Carystus) all had significant cleruchies imposed upon them by Athens at an early date. Chalcis had a large cleruchy imposed by Athens in 506 after the Chalcidian oligarchic elite were expelled, the cleruchs settled on their lands and a democracy established. After Histiaea revolted from the Delian League in 446, Pericles expelled some of the Histiaeans and established the democratic city of Oreos with an influx of 2,000 Athenian colonists (*IACP* no. 372). Thucydides singles out this colony, along with the Athenian colonies of Lemnos, Imbros and Aegina, as one which 'had the same institutions' as Athens (7.57.2: νομίμοις ἔτι χρώμενοι). Archaeological and literary evidence indicates that Carystus, a site controlling the grain route at the southern tip of Euboea, received an Athenian cleruchy after ca. 452 (Keller and Wallace 1988; Figueira 1991, 176–7; Moreno 2007, 96 n. 91).

More questionable is the degree of direct Athenian influence one can ascribe to the theatre culture of Lesbos (**Dix 1**). It is true that we hear of a choregic system at Mytilene shortly after the imposition of a cleruchy following the island's revolt against Athens in 427 (though the choregia may well antedate the cleruchy). The choregia was probably directed towards competitions at the Dionysia, though the festival is only attested sometime before 324/3 (**Dix 2**, cf. **3**: the Dionysia is organised by an agonothete implying competitions). In the late fifth century Mytilene may have produced a poet, Alcaeus, who is one of the earliest non-Athenian comic poets known. Mytilene's theatre is usually thought to be a Late Classical or Early Hellenistic construction, but the theatre, like the choregia, may only have supported purely musical competitions. There is no evidence for drama at Mytilene until Late Imperial times. Important Dionysia were also celebrated at Antissa (**Dix 4**), Eresus and Methymna. The evidence from Antissa is fourth-century, possibly even fifth, but speaks only of the expense and variety of activities at the Dionysia. For Eresus tragic competitions are attested only after the early third century, and for Methymna a 'scenic competition' is not attested until the early second.

Possibly to be included here is Naxos (**Dx**), which received an influx of Athenian settlers in the time of Pisistratus (Hdt. 1.64), and later after revolting from the Delian League was forced to receive 500 Athenian cleruchs in 453–448. Naxian relations with Athens were uneven, but Naxos was an original member of the Delian League, and may have joined the Second Athenian Confederacy in the 370s (Reger *IACP* 761). Naxos became a democracy after the overthrow and expulsion of an oligarchic class ca. 500 (Robinson 1997, 117–18), though we do not know how long it lasted, and no doubt the ups and downs of the relationship with Athens had some connection with the island's own internal factional struggle (Cartledge 2016, 153–4). Local choral performances in honour of Dionysus may be attested by a fifth-century inscription (**Dx**), but are in any case likely given Naxos' connection with the invention of the dithyramb (see commentary to **Dx**). By the late fourth or early third century an inscription indicates competitions in the Naxian theatre. Soon afterwards in 280 we catch our first glimpse of the Naxian 'Great Dionysia' (implying a

Lesser Dionysia) which includes a competition for tragedy preceded by the proclamation of honours. On this evidence it remains uncertain just when Naxos obtained its theatre culture and how great a role, if any, Athens played in the process.

Hegemony

The Delian League (477–404) included nearly all the cities of the Aegean Islands, as did the Second Athenian Confederacy (378–355). To reinforce the initially purely military interests that formed the league, Athens attempted to bind her allies with political and cultural ties. Two of these had particularly important consequences for theatre history in this region. One was a general, if inconsistent, support for the democratic factions of the allied cities (Robinson 2011, 137–40, 188–200). This reinforced Athens' imperial influence not only through the creation of common political values, but also through the fear of political instability and oligarchic reprisals that might follow a withdrawal of Athenian support. The other was a more direct incorporation of Athenian allies within Athens' own festival culture and particularly its City Dionysia.

It was to the Dionysia that the allied cities were required to bring their tribute, probably beginning immediately at the time of the transference of the treasury from Delos to Athens in 453 (**I Ai 3**). Carter's observation (2004) that tragedy tends to present Athens as a benevolent imperial power certainly underscores the ideological significance of the reunion. Particularly revealing for the care Athens took to involve subjects directly in its festival is an Athenian decree of 372 (**I Aiv 9**) which required the city of Paros to 'bring a cow and a phallos to the Dionysia *since they are in fact colonists of the people of Athens*'. This requirement for cow and phallos is said to be 'traditional' and we know that colonists were to bring a phallos from a decree of 445 founding the colony of Brea (**I Aiv 8**). But the only basis for the assertion that Paros was a colony of Athens depended on Athens' own mythic claim to be the mother city of all the Ionians (cf. Hdt. 8.46–8; Th. 7.57.4; Sch. D.P. 525). This example strongly suggests that all the Ionian cities were subject to the same pressure. The phallos and cow would of course require a chorus or choruses to accompany them, so that the delegations from subject states must have been reasonably large, quite independently of officials who went to discuss political or military matters with Athens and other allies. Familiarity with the Athenian Dionysia can be assumed throughout the empire from early times.

The Dionysia was of course set at a convenient time, when the seas opened and the military campaigning season began (**I Ai 1**). But doubtless the Dionysia was an added inducement to the timely presence of the ambassadors from allied cities as well as an opportunity for Athens both to include within its public proclamations honours extended towards cities and individuals within the empire and to assert its power through the magnificence and excellence of its festival. It is not surprising then that many of the Aegean cities created or reshaped their Dionysian festivals after the prestigious Athenian model. That some form of conscious modelling was the norm across the Aegean emerges from the fact that the theatrical festivals created in the fifth and fourth centuries across the Aegean were all initially Dionysia (probably also **Dxv**); that the Aegean cities were all certainly or probably democracies at least at the critical moments when our evidence indicates their reception of theatre; and that so far as we can tell all follow to the best of their financial means the patterns of the Athenian festival sponsorship and structure, many quite closely.

Paradoxically, one of the best examples of Athenian hegemonic influence comes from Rhodes (**Dxi**), a city in the most distant corner of the Aegean and one that, as a thoroughly Dorian city, could never have been categorised as one of Athens' family of Ionian 'colonies'. Most of our information about the vibrant theatre of Rhodes comes from an unlikely source, the so-called 'Roman *Fasti*'. These *Fasti* are a first-century AD didascalic list based on a Hellenistic Alexandrian source. The fragments relating to Rhodes (**Dxi 1–8**) were all found built into the floor paving of St. Paul's Basilica in Rome but are almost certainly part of the same series as the Comic Poets' List (**I Avi**), whose many fragments were found in that part of the Campus Martius in Rome where the theatres of Pompey, Balbus and Marcellus were located. These inscriptions are thought to have once decorated the walls of a large building, possibly the headquarters of the Roman *Artifices Scaenici*. Two honorific decrees for poets or actors in the same lettering style were found in the same area as parts of the Roman *Fasti*, between the Via Arenula and the Theatre of Marcellus, as was a third which mentions the actors' union (*IGUR* I 231–4).

This source proves that, by the 380s, Rhodes had something resembling the Athenian Dionysia in scale. The inscriptions list under the name of each actor, in the chronological order of their first appearance, the prizes they won and plays with which they competed, for the Athenian Dionysia, the Athenian Lenaea and the Rhodian Dionysia: possibly in that order. Because of uncertainty regarding the length of the lines it is hard to know or even guess what parts belong to which competition, but Rhodes is explicitly mentioned in three places. We can see from the fragments that there were at least two entries in the Rhodian tragic competition, but we know that the city, founded by synoecism in 408/7, had three tribes each named after one of the founding cities, Kamiros, Ialysos and Lindos. In two places the assignment of the actor to the tribe is mentioned, showing the existence of public funding by tribes (as in Athens for lyric choruses and, in the 4th c., for comedy). This funding model is amply attested by later Rhodian inscriptions. But it also seems good evidence that there were three entries for tragedy. Indeed, no other source records more than a single prize for fifth- or fourth-century actors either in Athens or anywhere else, so it may be that Rhodes, because of its tribal funding model, ranked all three of the actors. This would partly explain the interest of our list in Rhodes as the city's records may have offered detailed information about early actors not available elsewhere. But it also suggests that all the information on this list relating to second and third actors' prizes relates to Rhodes. Even as it is, more information relates to Rhodes on this sampling than we would expect and that is probably because for actors at least the Rhodian records were much fuller.

The Rhodian competitions drew upon major international competitors: we can recognise the names of actors and playwrights who also performed in Athens, namely Mnesitheos, Thrasyboulos, Eupolemos and Kleandros, and competing with plays that appear to be by Sophocles the Elder and Sophocles the Younger. Other inscriptions of the fourth century show that the tribally organised choregic system sponsored boys' choruses on the Athenian model, and still later inscriptions show the same system supporting men's choruses and comedy. The fragments of the Roman *Fasti* give no evidence of comedy in early fourth-century Rhodes, but we can possibly infer the existence of comic competitions from the fact that Anaxandrides and Antiphanes, two of the most productive comic poets of the first half of the fourth century, were Rhodians.

In other words it looks likely that, from the creation of the democracy in Rhodes, after its revolt against Sparta in 395, the city had a full Dionysia with everything that Athens had, including competitions of men's and boys' lyric choruses, tragic trilogies, or possibly tetralogies including a satyr play, comedy, a competition for actors, a system of choregic funding, a practice of setting up choregic monuments, and accurate archives recording competitors and winners. To all this we can add an item of distinctly democratic theatre culture. Diodorus (20.84.3) tells us that in 305 when under threat from Demetrius the Besieger the Rhodians passed a decree liberating slaves, giving public burial for the war dead and granting a panoply to the sons of the war dead in the theatre at the Dionysia when they had come of age. These provisions are all known from Athens, but the last is of special interest to us because it directly copies a pre-performance ritual of the Athenian theatre from much earlier in the century. The Rhodian theatre culture appears to be following the Athenian model to the letter and arguably does so to reinforce its democratic government with distinctly democratic festival structures and theatre rituals.

Also within the Dorian Dodecanese, we have indirect evidence that Cos (**Div**) had a theatre within a couple of decades of its synoecism in 366, under a democratic constitution, at a time when Cos may have been a member of the Second Athenian Confederacy (Cargill 1981, 38; but cf. Hornblower 1982b, 237). Inscriptions show that Cos had by the third century a full Dionysian programme with a parade and competitions in lyric choruses (cyclic pyrrhiche), tragedy and comedy, most, if not all, funded by choregoi and with tribally organised choruses. As in Athens and Rhodes, actors received prizes separate from the production, and public honours were announced, from at least the end of the fourth century, before the choral agon. There is some evidence that the Dionysia itself was created at the time of synoecism, and the analogy of Rhodes suggests that most of the festival structure and contents could go back to that time.

Two other Dodecanesian islands, Astypalaea and Nisyros, probably had Dionysia and tragic competitions by the end of the fourth century and in any case by ca. 290 (see **Ev 1**). Nisyros' Dionysia had more than one day of circular choruses (as had probably long been the case in Athens) by 300–275 (Schwyzer 1923, no. 271; Peek 1969b, 27 no. 63; Ceccarelli 2010, 129 n. 93). We know more of Astypalaea's Dionysia, held in the month of Iobacchios, but only from inscriptions ranging from the third to first centuries (*IG* XII 3, 169 = *Syll.*³ 946; *IG* XII 3, 170; *IG* XII, 3 190; *IG* XII Suppl. 150; Peek 1969b, 38–9 no. 87). The Dionysia had an elaborate parade, a lyric choral competition for boys and a tragic contest (at which public honours were proclaimed).

Thasos (**Dxvi**) was an original member of the Delian League, a member of the Second Athenian Confederacy, and a democracy for most of the time that it remained in the Athenian orbit. It lay close to Athenian interests in Thrace and conflict between Athens and the island over markets and mines led to a short-lived rebellion in 465–463 (Th. 1.100) and another withdrawal from Athenian hegemony with the restoration of oligarchy on the island in 411–407. Both the theatre and a sanctuary of Dionysus are mentioned as landmarks of the city by Hippocrates, who lived on Thasos in 420–410, or possibly as early as the 460s (**Dxvi 2**; *Epid.* 1.21). The first possible mention of competitions at a Dionysia on Thasos comes from what may be an Athenian decree related to Athens' restoration of democracy in the island in 407 (**Dxvi 1**), though it is possible that the Dionysia mentioned in the decree is the Athenian. The earliest physical remains of the surviving Thasian theatre suggest that it was in place around the mid fourth century, by which time a commemorative monument (**Dxvi 3**) gives clear evidence for the performance of tragedy (cf. **Dxvi 4–5**), comedy and 'dithyramb' (possibly the same as the 'cyclical choruses' in **Dxvi 6**), and also a genre called the *nykterinos*, probably music for a nocturnal procession for Dionysus. Regular competitions in drama and lyric choruses are only indicated by present evidence from the end of the fourth century (**Dxvi 4–6**).

Siphnos (**Dxiv**) was (probably) an original member of the Delian League and an early member of the Second Athenian Confederacy. It proved a loyal and consistently democratic ally except during the brief period of Spartan hegemony that followed the Peloponnesian War. It is from soon after the destruction of the Spartan navy at the Battle of Cnidus and the restoration of democracy in Siphnos in 394 that we have our earliest evidence for a choregia on the island (**Dxiv 1**). A Siphnian, eager to claim descent from one of Siphnos' leading families, but also concerned perhaps to stress the family's democratic credentials, speaks of the magnificent choregiai performed by his ancestors. If we take the speaker at his word, a choregic system seems to have been in place in Siphnos from ca. 440. Though the choregiai are probably to be connected to the island's Dionysia, it is only from inscriptions of the third century that we have direct evidence of tragic competitions and the announcement of honorific crowns in the theatre (**Dxiv 2**; *IG* XII 5, 482).

Little is known of the constitution of Ceos (**Dii**), which was also a member, probably from the beginning, of the Delian League as well as the Second Athenian Confederacy. For most of the Classical period the main cities of the island formed a confederation. It is probably significant that from some time in the fifth century 'the decree formula for all the cities (individually and collectively) is a democratic one and copies the form of Athenian decrees' (Robinson 2011, 214). Stratigraphy dates the circular stone theatre at Karthaia on Ceos (**Dii**) to the mid fourth century and so it appears, remarkably, to have been completed even before the Athenian 'Lycurgan' theatre. Although we have to wait until the early third century for inscriptions attesting a Dionysia with a contest of tragedy (and proclamations of crowns and other honours), it seems likely that this theatre was the site of such activities from its inception. A choregic system is attested for the late fourth century, though only in relation to the sending of theoric choruses to Delos (**Dii 2**), but this practice goes back at least to the early fifth century (**Dii 1**) and is likely to have followed the Athenian model.

Tenos (**Dxv**) was another loyal member of both the Delian League and the Second Athenian Confederacy and a democracy, except perhaps in the time of Athens' own oligarchic revolution in 411. Although the earliest evidence (end of the 4th c.) for the theatre and a competition are at the Posideia, third-century inscriptions indicate that tragic competitions are associated with a Dionysia and, though the two festivals seem to have merged for a while, they also seem to have had an independent tradition. The cult of Dionysus was in any case well rooted in the island's history.

Chios (**Diii**) was one of the few members of the Delian League that provided ships and paid no tribute, but the alliance was not an easy one and in 412 Chios went over to the Peloponnesian side. It was a founding member of the Second Athenian Confederacy but later formed part of an anti-Athenian alliance backed by the Hecatomnids of Caria in 357 and then fell under Hecatomnid domination by 346. As a non-tributary ally of the Delian League, Athens seems not to have interfered much with internal politics in Chios, which throughout its fifth- and fourth-century history seems to have swung from moderate to extreme oligarchy until the island came under Alexander's control (334–330), when he appears to have imposed a form of democracy. It is only from the time of this democracy that we have evidence of a theatre culture in Chios. And yet Chios had a distinguished tradition in dithyramb and choral lyric: including the dithyrambic poets Licymnius and Demokritos, and Ion (*TrGF* 19) who wrote not only dithyrambs but tragedies. Nonetheless, we only have direct evidence in Chios for a Dionysia with a lively procession in the first half of the fourth century (**Diii 1**), evidence, moreover, that implies considerable anxiety that this minimal component of the Dionysia might lead to revolution. Even after the creation of the democracy, Chios' Dionysia may only have included a competition for boys' choruses.

The case of Delos (**Dvi**) is exceptional. In most ways Delos provides a prime example of Athens' role in the transmission of theatre through the Aegean. The island was entirely dominated by Athens from the early fifth century to 404 and again from 394 to 314. We have very good documentation of the international competitions in men's and boys' lyric choruses established by the Athenians in 426/5, apparently after the model of their Dionysian/Thargelian choral competitions, and continued until the late fourth century (**Dvi 1, 3–6**). But the unusual wealth of evidence we have for the island makes it fairly certain that, despite Athens' domination, there was neither a theatre nor dramatic performance until Delos became independent from Athens in 314. At that time, however, the independent Delians created a Dionysia that mimicked the timing, order and organisation of the Athenian Dionysia, including an elaborate phallic procession (**Dvi 8–10**), followed by a choral competition, a comic competition, and a tragic competition, with tribally based citizen choruses all sponsored by choregoi. The evidence seems to suggest that Athens had no interest in developing a Dionysian festival outside of Athens that might have a claim to pan-Ionian status and rival the pre-eminence of Athens' own 'Imperial festival' (Rhodes 2010, 94; **I Ai 3**).

Surprisingly almost all of the larger Aegean islands provide some evidence of theatre culture before 300. The most notable exception is Paros, which apart from its participation in the Parade of the Athenian Dionysia (**I Aiv 9**) and despite the strong tradition in iambic poetry and Dionysian music attested by Archilochus, offers no evidence of theatre until the late third or second century (*IMagn.* 50 + p. 295, ll. 39–42; *IG* XII 5, 129, ll. 33–8; Sear 2006, 403).

Many mainland coastal cities, dealt with more fully in other sections, also probably follow the general pattern we perceive in the Aegean islands of having adopted or developed their theatre culture while under Athenian hegemony and/or under the direct influence of Athens' democratic culture: these are the Aegean coastal cities of Abdera (**Cxiii**), Maroneia (**Cxiv**) and Oropus (**Ci**), the Hellespontine cities of Abydos (**Ei**) and Byzantium (**Fi**), and the coastal cities of Asia Minor: Erythrae (**Evi**), Cyme (**Eiv**), Phocaea (**Ev**), and Priene (**Evii**).

Di: Andros. Decree honouring Antidotos, late 4th or early 3rd c. (by letter forms).

> Block of white (presumably imported) marble, edge preserved on three sides, broken horizontally on top, surface much damaged in places.
> 0.385 × 0.325 (above) – 0.345 (below) × 0.085 m.

Found built into the wall of a house belonging to G. Stylianos in Palaiopolis.
Archaeological Museum of Andros, inv. no. 82 (Televantou 1996, 94).
Weil 1876, 239–40; Dragatsis 1881a, 794; Pernice 1893, 14–15 no. 15; *IG* XII 5, 714 + Suppl. p.
119; Sauciuc 1911; Reger 1994; Sosin 2002.
Text: *IG* XII 5, 714 + Suppl. p. 119 with modifications from Reger 1994 (= *SEG* 44, 699) and
Sosin 2002, 142–4 (= *SEG* 52, 799).   Drawing: Sauciuc 1911, 3. Photo: Reger 1994, pl. 76.

1   [. 3–4 . τ]ὸν̱ μέδ̱[ιμνον τοῦ σίτου ὁρῶν πωλούμενον πλέο]-
      [νος] δ̱ρα̱χ̱μῶν πέντε [ἐν τῆι ἀγορᾶι, εἰσάγων ἐπώλη]-
      [σε τ]οῦ σίτου τοῦ ξενικοῦ εἴκοσιν̱ ἁ̱[μάξαις [πέντε δρα]-
      [χμ]ῶν τοῦ μεδίμνου, ὅπως ἂν ο̱ὖν εἰδῶσιν πάν̱[τες]
5   [ὅτι ἐ]πίσταται ὁ δῆμος χάριτας ἀξίας ἀποδιδ[όναι]
      [τοῖς] εὐεργέταις, ἐπα̱ινέσαι μὲν Ἀντίδοτ[ον . .]
      [. .4–5. .ο]υ̱ς καὶ στεφανῶσαι χρυσῶι στεφάνωι ^{vacat}
      [ἀπὸ χι]λ̱ίων δραχμῶν ἀρετῆς ἕνεκεν καὶ εὐν[οί]-
      [ας τ]ῆς εἰς τὸν δῆμον τὸν Ἀνδρίων· τ̱ὸν δὲ κήρ[υ]-
10   [κα τῆς β]ο̱υλῆς ἀναγγεῖλαι τόνδε τὸν στέφανο[ν]
      [Διο]νυσίοις τραγωιδῶν τῶι ἀγῶνι· εἶναι δ᾽ Ἀντιδό- ^{vacat}
      [τ]ωι καὶ ἄλλο ἀγαθὸν εὑρέσθαι παρὰ τοῦ δήμου, ὅ-
      [τ]ου ἂν δοκεῖ ἄξιος εἶναι· ἐπαινέσαι δὲ καὶ τοὺ[ς]
      [στ]ρατιώτας, ὅσοι τὰς χρείας παρέσχοντο τῶι δή̱-
15   [μωι] καὶ συνήργησαν εἰς τὸ σῖτον εὐμαρέστερο[ν]
      [εἶναι] ἐν τεῖ πόλει· τὸν δὲ γραμματέα τῶν πρυτάν[ε]-
      [ων ἀν]αγράψαι τόδε τὸ ψήφισμα ἐν {εἰς} στήλην λιθίν-
      [ην] καὶ στῆσαι ἐν τῆι ἀγορᾶι πρόσθε τοῦ βουλε[υ]-
      [τηρί]ου· τὸ δὲ ἀνάλωμα τὸ γενόμενον εἰς τὴν ^{vacat}
20   [ἀναγ]ραφὴν δοῦναι τοὺς ταμίας ἀπὸ τῶν προσό-
      [δων] τῶν τῆς πόλεως. ^{vacat}

     1–3 suppl. exempli gratia Sosin   τ]ὸν μέδ[ιμνον ἐπέδωκε τῶι δήμωι τῶι Ἀνδρί|ων]
     δραχμῶν πέντε [καὶ ἤγαγε τῶι δήμωι τῶι Ἀνδρίων | τ]οῦ σίτου τοῦ ξενικοῦ εἴκοσιν
     Hiller   3–4 τ]οῦ σίτου τοῦ ξενικοῦ εἴκοσιν̱ δ[ύ]ο̱ [δρ]α|[χμ]ῶν τοῦ μεδίμνου Reger

[… seeing that] a med[imnos of grain was being sold for more] than five drachmas [in the marketplace, he imported and sold] twenty w[agon-load]s of foreign grain at [five drach]mas the medimnos. So that al[l] may know [5] [that]
the People gives appropriate thanks [to its] benefactors, (X proposed) to praise
Antidot[os …] and to crown him with a gold crown [of a value] of one thousand drachmas for his excellence and ben[evolence] to the People of Andros,
and that the her[ald [10] of the C]ouncil announce the crow[n] at the [Dio]nysia at
the contest of the tragedies, and that Antido[t]os receive whatever other honour
from the People that he seems worthy of, and to praise also all th[e so]ldiers
who provided service to the Peo[ple] [15] and helped make the grain more afforda-
bl[e] in the city. The secretary of the Prytan[eis is to i]nscribe this decree on a
sto[ne] stele and place it in the marketplace in front of the Council [House]. The
treasurers are to pay the expense for the [20] [ins]cription from the city's inco[me].

Pernice thought the inscription fourth century (1893, 15: 'gehört wohl noch dem vierten Jahrhundert an'); Hiller judged it fourth, or first half of the third century; Sauciuc thought the letter forms 'gut der zweiten Hälfte des IV. Jahrh. angehören können' (1911, 15); Reger thinks the letter forms belong to the second or third quarter of the third century. Most attempts at contextualising the document, paying close attention to 'foreign grain' in l. 3 and 'soldiers' in l. 14, have assumed that Antidotos is a foreign garrison commander honoured for making grain available to the Andriots in time of need and that the decree therefore belongs to a period of foreign occupation. Hiller (*IG* XII 5, 713, p. 203) assumed an Antigonid occupation on Diodorus' evidence that Ptolemy liberated Andros and expelled a garrison in 308 (20.37.1: Πτολεμαῖος μὲν ἐκ τῆς Μύνδου πλεύσας ἁδρῷ στόλῳ διὰ νήσων ἐν παράπλῳ τὴν Ἄνδρον ἠλευθέρωσε καὶ τὴν φρουρὰν ἐξήγαγε). Sauciuc (1911, 16–18) argued that the decree honoured the commander of the Athenian occupation of Andros during the Second Athenian Confederacy known from *IG* II² 123 and Aeschin. 1.107. This allows for a date range of probably 363/2–318/17 (Reger 1994, 315). Reger associates the decree with 'a foreign garrison, perhaps of Ptolemaic origin after the liberation of Athens or of Macedonian origin after the Chremonidean war', thus after 287 or after 262 (1994, 318).

Daniela Summa and Klaus Hallof very kindly examined the letter forms on the squeeze of *IG* XII 5, 714 in the Berlin-Brandenburg Akademie der Wissenschaften. In their opinion the optimal date for the letter forms is the end of the fourth century or the beginning of the third (the alphas and omicrons are most indicative) and so do not particularly favour either Sauciuc or Reger. Moreover Sosin (2002) has argued quite convincingly that Antidotos is most likely a grain dealer (cf. **I Ai 2**), and not a garrison commander or foreign governor. There is indeed no reason to think that the soldiers who help transport the foreign grain are themselves foreign. There is no reason therefore to contextualise the inscription within a period of foreign occupation of Andros. Moreover, Sosin casts doubt upon some of the historical and orthographic arguments adduced by Reger to show a third-century date and offers syntactic and formulaic considerations that might indicate that a fourth-century date is after all preferable (2002, 133–4 n. 15, 141 n. 57, 143 n. 63).

Apart from this inscription the only certain direct evidence we have for tragedy from Andros is *IG* XII, Suppl. 258 (2nd c.), another crown proclaimed at the tragedies of the Dionysia. An unspecified choregia is mentioned in *IG* XII, Suppl. 250 (also 2nd c.).

The theatre has not been excavated at Andros. Sauciuc already suggested that the ancient theatre was located in a hollow called by the locals 'Lakoma' just north-east of the summit of Tourlos hill in Palaiopolis (Sauciuc 1914, 21; cf. Televantou 2002, 22). Palaiokrassa-Kopitsa (1996, 218; 2007, 37, 260) favours a location to the south-west on the lower slopes of Tourlos (E 11 on her plan), where fragments of a marble Doric column were found and other marble fragments are still visible, including a marble statue-base lying on the path at the level and to the north-east of the presumed orchestra (autopsy Oct. 2013). The latter suggestion receives some confirmation from an analysis of remote sensing satellite imagery in October 2013 by Adele Sobotkova. A multi-spectral analysis showed an anomaly yielding a reasonably clear outline of a theatron, stretching from about 200–300 m from the sea at the outlet of the main watercourse, and facing north-west. The city wall runs to the south and to the east of the theatre (Palaiokrassa-Kopitsa 1996, pl. 2: Δ 12 – Ζ 11; cf. Tiverios 1993, 211). Two marble seats, probably taken from the prohedria, were found by Sauciuc built into a shed 'near the property of D. Lukrezis' (1914, 23). Sauciuc evidently removed the seats from the building as he was able to provide dimensions (0.34 × 0.485 × 0.195 m), a complete profile showing the depth of the objects (1914, 23 fig. 25) and details of the T-clamps on their upper surface. One of the seats is visible in a photograph taken before the wall was dismantled (Televantou 2002, 35 fig. 23) and it remains in private possession (the whereabouts of the other is unknown). The seats are of a form that is typical from the beginning of the Hellenistic period and can be found, for example, in the theatre at Delos in the first half of the third century. A third possible theatre seat is illustrated by Palaiokrassa-Kopitsa (1996, 219–20 AM 4, fig. 139).

Zaphiropoulou (1977, 308) published what she believed to be a fourth theatre seat (cf. Televantou 2002, 94) inscribed with the name Πυθώνυμος Νικοκράτους (= SEG 46, 1162), but the large rectangular block (Arch. Mus. Andros inv. 185) is a statue base for a late first-century public benefactor well known from several other inscriptions (Palaiokrassa-Kopitsa 2009).

Drama was probably associated with Dionysus on Andros from an early date. The cult of Dionysus dominated the religious life of the island. The mythical founder of the island was Andros or Andreas, a grandson of Apollo on his father's side and a great-grandson of Dionysus on his mother's side (D.S. 5.79; Ov. *Met.* 13.647–9; Paus. 10.13.4l; Serv. *Aen.* 3.80.12–13; St.Byz. s.v. Ἄνδρος). Dionysian theonyms are very prominent in the Andrian onomastikon (Sauciuc 1914, 113). The coinage of the island regularly portrays an ivy-crowned head of Dionysus from the beginning of the fourth century onwards; among the motifs found on the obverse is, perhaps significantly, a tripod (Sauciuc 1914, 112–13; Televantou 2002, 47–8). Tripods are also found on fragments of a triglyph and metope frieze, made of local marble, that Sauciuc found near the theatre in the house of K. Lukrezis and that he judged to be fourth-century work from an altar of Dionysus (1914, 23–4, figs. 27a–b). The winter festival for Dionysus (Theodaisia) was the most famous festival on the island in antiquity (Plin. *HN* 2.231; Paus. 6.26.2; Philostr. *Im.* 1.25).

Further evidence for drama in Andros is merely circumstantial, but not perhaps negligible. One of the more conspicuous patterns for the dissemination of drama is through Athenian colonies and cleruchies (**D Introduction**). Andros received 250 cleruchs probably in 450 (Plu. *Per.* 11.5; Meyer 1939, 672; Meritt et al. 1950, 287, 298; Meiggs 1963, 6–10) and in the mid fourth century during the Second Athenian Confederacy, the island was occupied by an Athenian garrison with an Athenian governor (Reger 1994, 314–15). The city was probably a democracy for most of the fifth and fourth centuries (Reger *IACP* 736). The comic poet Amphis, active from the middle of the fourth century, certainly came from Andros. In 331 he received a golden crown and was made a proxenos for the Athenians (indicating that he was not a citizen, and possibly not a resident, of Athens: **I Aix 3**).

Dii: Ceos (Karthaia and Ioulis)

1. Athenaeus, *Sophists at Dinner* 10.456e–457a (= Chamael. fr. 37 Martano). Simonides lived ca. 556–468. Athenaeus wrote in the 2nd c. AD. He draws here, as in the preceding passage (10.456c–d), on Chamaeleon of Pontus, a 4th-c. Peripatetic philosopher and critic, who wrote an *On Simonides*. Chamaeleon's practice in writing about famous authors was long seen as nothing more than a form of biographical interpretation of their poetry (Leo 1901), but recently he has been adjudged a somewhat more sophisticated writer of lives, 'a serious scholar who also applied methods of historical research when writing biography' (Schorn 2012, 431). Text: Olson.

πεποίηκε δὲ καὶ ἕτερον ἐπίγραμμα ὁ Σιμωνίδης, ὃ παρέχει τοῖς ἀπείροις τῆς ἱστορίας ἀπορίαν (fr. 70 Diehl)·

φῆμι τὸν οὐκ ἐθέλοντα φέρειν τέττιγος ἄεθλον
τῷ Πανοπηιάδῃ δώσειν μέγα δεῖπνον Ἐπειῷ.

λέγεται δὲ ἐν τῇ Καρθαίᾳ διατρίβοντα αὐτὸν διδάσκειν τοὺς χορούς. εἶναι δὲ τὸ χορηγεῖον ἄνω πρὸς Ἀπόλλωνος ἱερῷ μακρὰν τῆς θαλάσσης. ὑδρεύεσθαι οὖν καὶ τοὺς ἄλλους καὶ τοὺς περὶ τὸν Σιμωνίδην κάτωθεν, ἔνθα ἦν ἡ κρήνη. ἀνακομίζοντος δ' αὐτοῖς τὸ ὕδωρ ὄνου, ὃν ἐκάλουν Ἐπειὸν διὰ τὸ μυθολογεῖσθαι τοῦτο δρᾶν ἐκεῖνον καὶ ἀναγεγράφθαι ἐν τῷ τοῦ Ἀπόλλωνος ἱερῷ τὸν Τρωικὸν μῦθον, ἐν ᾧ ὁ Ἐπειὸς ὑδροφορεῖ τοῖς Ἀτρείδαις, ὡς καὶ Στησίχορός φησιν (fr. 100 Finglass)

ᾤκτειρε γὰρ αὐτὸν ὕδωρ αἰεὶ φορέοντα Διὸς
κούρα βασιλεῦσιν.

ὑπαρχόντων οὖν τούτων ταχθῆναί φασι τῷ μὴ παραγινομένῳ τῶν χορευτῶν εἰς τὴν ὡρισμένην ὥραν παρέχειν τῷ ὄνῳ χοίνικα κριθῶν. τοῦτ' οὖν κἂν τῷ ποιήματι λέγεσθαι, καὶ εἶναι τὸν μὲν οὐ φέροντα τὸ τοῦ τέττιγος ἄεθλον τὸν οὐκ ἐθέλοντα ᾄδειν, Πανοπηιάδην δὲ τὸν ὄνον, μέγα δὲ δεῖπνον τὴν χοίνικα τῶν κριθῶν.

Simonides also composed another epigram, which causes perplexity to those who are ignorant of history (fr. 70 Diehl): 'I declare that he who does not want to endure the cicada's task (or 'is not willing to win the prize of the cicada') will give a great meal to Epeius the son of Panopeus.' The story goes that he was spending time in Karthaia training choruses; and that the choral training space (*choregeion*) was on high ground near the temple of Apollo, a long way from the sea. So Simonides and those with him, along with everyone else, used to draw their water from down below, where there was a spring. An ass carried the water up for them. They used to call it Epeius because, according to a tradition, the famous Epeius used to do this, and there was a depiction in the temple of Apollo of the Trojan story, in which Epeius is drawing water for the Atreidai, as Stesichorus also relates (fr. 100 Finglass) 'For the daughter of Zeus pitied him, forever carrying water for the kings.' And as this was the case, they say that any choreut who was not present at the appointed time had the duty of giving the ass a choinix of barley; and that this is also expressed in the same poem: and that what is meant by he who does not want to endure the cicada's task (or 'is not willing to win the prize of the cicada') is one who is not willing to sing; and that by the son of Panopeus is meant the ass, and the great meal is the choinix of barley.

2. Dedications of crowns by choregoi in the temple of Apollo at Karthaia, late 4th or early 3rd c. (by letter forms). This is one of a set of inscriptions from the temple with lists that record various important financial matters. Others record money borrowed by the city from the temple and leases of land with tithes going to a number of sacred funds (Osborne 1988, 318–22; Migeotte 2014, 216–17). Crowns are also recorded as having been received from Archons, generals, ambassadors and market-managers (the last appearing in another inscription of similar type, *IG* XII 5, 1075, ll. 19–23).

Two fragments of a tall stele of white marble, with cymation above, broken to right and at the middle, inscribed on both faces and one short side.
Found in the ruins of the temple of Apollo on the acropolis of Karthaia.
Current location unknown.
IG XII 5, 544 (see for earlier editions).
Text: *IG* XII 5, 544 A2 (we excerpt lines 35–63 from the longer lists).   Drawing (upper fragment): Brønsted 1826, Tab. XXIV.

35	ἐπὶ ἄρχοντος
	Ἀλεξιτέλους
	Ἀριστοπείθης
	Ἐρασικλείους
	χορηγήσας παι-
40	σὶν εἰς Δῆλον
	στεφανωθεὶς
	ὑπὸ τοῦ δήμου
	χρυσῶι στεφά-
	νωι ἀνέθηκεν
45	τὸν στέφανον
	τῶι Ἀπόλλωνι
	δραχμὰς ἑκα-
	τόν.
	παρὰ χορηγοῦ
50	τῶν ἀνδρῶν
	Ἀρετᾶνος τὸν
	στέφανον ἐλά-
	βομεν : H.
	παρὰ χορηγοῦ
55	τῶν παίδων
	Δεξιθέου τὸ[ν]
	στέφανον ἐ[λά]-
	βομεν : H.
	παρὰ χορηγοῦ
60	τῶν παίδων
	[Ἀ]γλωκλείδου
	τὸν στέφανον
	ἐλάβομεν : H.

In the Archonship of Alexiteles, after serving as choregos for the [40] boys on Delos and being crowned by the People with a gold crown, Aristopeithes son of Erasikles dedicated the crown to Apollo, one hundred drachmas. From the choregos [50] of the men Aretan we received the crown: 100 (dr.). From the choregos of the boys Dexitheos we re[ce]ived the crown: 100 (dr.). From the choregos [60] of the boys [A]glokleides we received the crown: 100 (dr.).

Ceos was close to Athens, politically as well as physically, for much of the Classical period. Herodotus describes the Ceans as 'Ionians by race, from Athens' (Hdt. 8.46.2) in line with a tradition maintaining that Ceos was founded by Ionians from Athens (Th. 7.57.4; Sch. D.P. 525). The tradition may be in part or whole a product of Athenian imperial propaganda. The presence of the exploits of Theseus in the iconography of the temple of Athena in Karthaia in the fifth century (*SEG* 25, 948; Mendoni dates the material to the mid fourth century: *SEG* 40, 714) plays an (inconclusive) part in this debate (Mendoni 1990, 287–92), but it has been plausibly argued that Athenian imperial interests had a significant effect on the way in which Ceans represented themselves in choral song on Delos in the fifth century (Fearn 2013).

The four cities of the island – Karthaia, Ioulis, Koressos and Poieessa – may have had some limited form of federated structure already in the fifth century, but it was far from comprehensive since cities continued to mint coins separately (Lewis 1962; Cooper 2008). Constantakopoulou (2005, 8) argues that the existence of a hestiaterion of the Ceans on Delos reflects an effort to represent themselves collectively as citizens of the island (Fearn 2011, 218 expresses some doubts) and the likely sending of theoric choruses by 'Ceans' – rather than 'Karthaians', 'Ioulians' and the like – in the fifth century points in the same direction (below). In the fourth century the three major cities (excluding Poieessa) certainly had a form of federated union (Brun 1989; Reger and Risser 1991), with Ioulis as the political capital. In this period Ceans appear to have held citizenship as a collective body, and to have been divided into *phylai*, *trittyes* and *chôroi* (χῶροι: Jones 1987, 203–4), probably on the model of Eretria (**Dvii**). Whether these divisions played any role in festival performance is not known. In the first half of the fourth century the island had an intensive set of economic, political and cultural connections with a surprisingly wide variety of places in Greece, including Athens and Sparta, but also a strong concentration in the Propontic region, as is clear in particular from a detailed proxeny catalogue (Mack 2015, 182–8, 320–2).

Ceos was forced to dissolve the union and live as separate cities after a defection from the Second Athenian Confederacy in 364 was suppressed. In the 280s or early 270s (under Ptolemy I or II) a Ptolemaic naval garrison was established at Koressos, renamed Arsinoe. Ioulis probably served as the base of operations (Cherry et al. 1991). How long this direct Ptolemaic involvement on the island persisted is not clear (it may have ended with the end of the Chremonidean War in 261), but it is striking that Ioulis appears to acquire a theatre in the third century (below).

Ceos produced two of the greatest melic poets of all time, Simonides and his nephew Bacchylides (both from Ioulis), and had a flourishing tradition of high-quality choral composition and local performance from at least the late Archaic period. In the fifth century a Cean chorus, perhaps from Karthaia (Rutherford 2001, 283), sings: 'Truly, I too, who dwell on a rock, am renowned for achievements among Hellenes in games, and also known for providing poetry in abundance' (Pi. *Pae.* D4, ll. 21–4 Rutherford). The Ceans were highly active participants in the Panionic festivals of nearby Delos, where they had their own hestiaterion near the temple of Artemis (Hdt. 4.35.4; cf. Th. 7.57.4), and where Apollo frequently had his 'heart warmed by choruses of Ceans' (B. 17.130–2). Like his nephew, Simonides also composed theoric choruses for performance by Cean choruses on Delos (note the collection of dithyrambs by Simonides that Strabo tells us went under the name *Deliaka* and included a title *Memnon, PMG* 539: Ieranò 1997, 279–83; Poltera 2008, 587 raises doubts). The language suggests that in their theoric choruses abroad – of which Bacchylides 17, probably for performance for Apollo on Delos, is an example (Kowalzig 2007, 88–94; Wilson 2007b, 177–9; Fearn 2013) – Ceans of the fifth century presented themselves as a single collective, rather than as (e.g.) citizens of Karthaia or Ioulis. There is also evidence of fierce choral traditions of local performance already in the fifth century (Rutherford 2000; Fearn 2011).

Although it was never the most powerful city on the island, Karthaia on its south-east side appears to have had a particularly strong tradition of choral song (Rutherford 2001, 283–4). From **2** we know that choral performances took place in some close association with the temple of Apollo in Karthaia in the fourth century. The existence of a designated train-ing-ground for choruses in Karthaia is thus entirely likely (see on choral training in **V E**), but the explanation offered in **1** for the riddling epigram of Simonides which refers to such a *choregeion* has won little acceptance. Reitzenstein (1893, 117) is scathing in his judgement, regarding it as a foolish attempt on the part of later scholars to interpret an old poem that made no sense. Huxley (1978, 233–4) declares 'we should not assume that the enigmatic pair of hexameters had originally anything to do with Simonides or with Karthaia'. While Lefkowitz (1991, 196) holds that '[t]he association of cicada with singers and dancers (e.g. Archil. fr. 223W; Call. fr. 1.29–36 Pf.; *Anacreont.* 34.15W) would have encouraged the fanciful aetiology'. But the very evidence Lefkowitz cites for the association tends to un-dermine her dismissive statement, and her own 'simpler explanation' of the riddle – 'anyone who doesn't work will pay a penalty' – does scant justice to any of its details.

Chamaeleon will certainly have drawn on older sources and quite possibly on local Cean knowledge. The topographical information in the gloss is corroborated by the evidence of the site itself, with the temple of Apollo on the heights of the acropolis and significant natu-ral springs at its foot (below). Although its interpretation has been influenced by **1** itself, an-other fragmentary inscription on a stone from the left anta of the temple of Apollo has been restored in such a way as to refer to sacrifices made 'in front of the *ch[oregeion]*' (*IG* XII 5, 530 + *IG* Suppl. p. 113, l. 5 [… ὅσ]αι πρὸ τοῦ χ[ορηγείου γίνονται …]; a fourth-cen-tury date is possible). If correctly restored, this shows that the *choregeion* of Karthaia was a well-known site and, while not proving the truth of Chamaeleon's report that it existed already in Simonides' day, the inscription certainly tends to support such a suggestion.

Chamaeleon's explanation thus seems to contain a core of reliable information about the circumstances under which choruses trained at Karthaia. This may depend on knowl-edge of activity that took place in Chamaeleon's own day (when we know choral activity was vigorous: **2**), but it is reasonable to suppose that the guardians of the local traditions of choral training in the late fourth century preserved a memory of their most illustrious chorodidaskalos. It thus at least remains a possibility that the epigram did indeed serve as a didactic maxim in Simonides' *choregeion*, or at the very least that in attempting to bring the epigram into an (inauthentic) association with Simonides' choral training, Chamaeleon has drawn on material concerning the poet's career with a good prospect of being authentic, and likely to derive from local sources (Schorn 2012, 427). The emphasis on the need for water in choral training rings true; as does the use of the cicada as an emblem of musical excellence. The same holds for the jocular 'poetic' ruse to encourage participation, with its pun on 'winning a prize' and 'enduring a task' (φέρειν … ἄεθλον).

If Chamaeleon's research can be trusted in all its details, it further appears that the temple of Apollo depicted some scene from the Trojan myth in which Epeius was 'drawing water for the Atreidai', whether literally or in the sense of performing some act of subservience to the kings. The hero will thus have been of special local relevance. In Homer Epeius was the winner of a mule in the boxing match at Patroclus' funeral games (*Il.* 23.664–75) and the builder of the Trojan Horse (*Od.* 8.495; 11.523), both of which will have served to bring him discursively into the realm of equids and made his name ready for application to a water-drawing ass in the service of a poetic training ground. But it is now clear that the lowly water-carrier Epeius was given a place of remarkable prominence at the start of Stesichorus' *Sack of Troy* (Finglass 2013), where he was described as 'a man learned in measurements and wisdom by the will of the revered goddess [Athena]' (fr. 100.11–12 Finglass). The significant role of Epeius in a major work of a famous choral predecessor may have played a part in Simonides' deployment of this figure in his own choral practice. (For a positive view of Chamaeleon's explanatory method, whether or not the poems are genuine, see Giordano 1990, 172–3; Martano 2012, 257–9.)

2 is an excerpt from a set of inscriptions set up in the temple of Apollo that list crowns received from various public figures, including choregoi. The entries for choregoi follow a standardised form: 'from the choregos for (*category*) men/boys + *name of choregos* (rarely with patronymic: e.g. *IG* XII 5, 1075, ll. 5–6) we received the crown: 100 (sc. dr.)'. Elsewhere in these lists, which were inscribed at different dates, the specification of performance type does not regularly appear. The use of the first person 'we received' is striking, reflecting the 'voice' of the temple authorities. The fact that in every case the crown is worth 100 dr. suggests that these crowns may have been akin to an 'honorific tax' on those who had served as choregos (**I D**), with the inscribed record of the 'gift' serving as a permanent commemoration of the service. That generals, market-managers, ambassadors and others all likewise handed over 100 dr. crowns makes this interpretation more likely than the alternative – namely that the choregos (perhaps only the winner in a competition?) is recorded as dedicating a crown which he had earlier been awarded by the city for his service (Wilson 2010a, 48).

2 is unusual among the (fragmentary) lists for the presence of an Archon date (ll. 35–6). This probably implies that what follows took place in a single civic year. The three choregoi in ll. 49–63 – one for men, two for boys – are thus likely to have served at a local festival or festivals, probably in honour of Apollo. The first entry in the year of Alexiteles is of a different sort altogether. It records the support of a boys' chorus to Delos (on such theoric choral performance at Delos see **Dvi**; Rutherford 2004; Kowalzig 2007, 56–128). In this case it is clear that the choregos Aristopeithes had been crowned by the People for his service and that he went on to dedicate that crown – also worth 100 dr. – to Apollo. It is very likely that a choregic system existed on Ceos long before the late fourth century, the date of **2**.

The theatre of Karthaia lies at the base of the south-west slope of the acropolis, at the mouth of a stream, some 80 m from the sea. Its earliest archaeologically identified phase belongs to the middle of the fourth century, but given the tradition of choral performance associated with the temple of Apollo on the acropolis from the fifth century, it is possible that there was a precursor to the stone theatre for such performances. The theatre was seen and studied by the Danish scholar Peter Oluf Brønsted in 1811–1812, who marked it on his map at Brønsted 1826, 15 (fig. 6). Major work was undertaken on the theatre in 2011–2015, and is still in progress, continuing efforts begun in 1987–1991 (Simantoni-Bournia et al. 2015, with earlier bibliography). A first phase of this theatre has been dated by stratigraphy (ceramic finds in the backfill beneath the seats) to the middle of the fourth century (between 350 and 340). Thus far two phases of the stage building have been identified – the first late-Classical, contemporary with the construction of the rest of the theatre; the second an extension in the early Hellenistic period. The stage building has a base with sockets for seven columns and will have had a single door. In the late Roman period the theatre was rendered unusable by its incorporation into a bathing complex that took advantage of the local supply of water. It may have fallen out of use some time before this, since it shows no signs of modification later than the early Hellenistic period.

The theatre was not large, with a capacity of around 880 spectators on fifteen rows of seats (Simantoni-Bournia et al. 2015, 8; plans: 17, fig. 7; 13, fig. 13; Panagou 2010–2012) and constructed from materials with an eye to economy (Simantoni-Bournia et al. 2015, 10–11). The adult male citizen population of Karthaia in the fourth century has been esti-mated at around 260 (Ruschenbusch 1982), so the theatre was more than adequate to the immediate needs of the local community and doubtless accommodated many non-citizens and visitors. Mendoni (1985–1986, 170) deduces from the extensive wear to the upper sur-face of many rows that the theatre was well used over a long period. Made of local stone, the theatron was divided into four sections by three access-stairs. The retaining wall at its north-western side has an irregular pattern that breaks the expected curve of the theatron, evidently in order to respect the presence of a pre-existing structure of some importance, in the same way as accommodation was made for the Odeion in the construction of the stone Theatre of Dionysus in Athens. The orchestra was circular (Simantoni-Bournia et al. 2015, 8 for more detail). The good supply of spring water in the area (which made it suitable for the later Roman bath complex) was doubtless already managed by civic authorities in the Classical period (Mendoni 1985–1986, 171). It fits precisely with the account in **1** of the springs 'down below' – as viewed from the heights of the acropolis and the temple of Apollo – from which Simonides and his choreuts drew water during their training.

It is extremely likely that drama was performed at a Dionysia held in this theatre from its inception. At present our earliest direct evidence for a Dionysia at Karthaia with a tragic contest (at which honorific crowns were announced) is a decree recently published (Mendoni 2009 = *SEG* 59, 930) which honours the Archon of the previous year – one Theokles, probably to be identified with the homonymous general and choregos known from lists in the sanctuary of Apollo (*IG* XII 5, 544 A1, ll. 5–7; A2, ll. 11–15: another part of **2**). This appears to date from the first quarter of the third century (Mendoni 2009, 72). The festival, and tragedy, continue to be attested throughout the third century and into the second (*IG* XII 5, 529/1064; 531; 535; 536; 538; 1061 dated by Mendoni 1989, 291–2 to 267/6–262/1 and to 264 by Frederiksen 2002, 84; 1070; 1072; *SEG* 14, 543; *SEG* 48, 1130: ca. 194–192). A decree of ca. 200 mentions the further award of invitation to prohedria (*SEG* 14, 544, ll. 23–4: [ἀ]νακηρῦξαι τὸν στέφανον Διονυσίοις τῶι ἀγῶν[ι | τῶν] τραγωιδῶν, καλέσαι δὲ αὐτὸν καὶ εἰς προεδρίαν) which indicates the existence of honorific seating in the Karthaia theatre at this date. The recent archaeological study has concluded that there was no prohedria in stone (Simantoni-Bournia et al. 2015, 9), so this was presumably some form of probably wooden seating placed in front of the first row of stone seats.

Ceos has revealed suggestive evidence for some of the earliest manifestations of the cult of Dionysus anywhere in Greece. An Attic black-figured skyphos of the late sixth century was found in the temple at Ayia Irini, on the north-west coast of Ceos. The sanctuary had been in use from the Middle Bronze Age (15th c.). The cup is inscribed on its base as a votive offering to Dionysus, made by one Anthippos of Ioulis (*SEG* 25, 960; Caskey 1964, 332–5; Gorogianni 2011, 645; a second, less legible, inscription around the edge of the base, contemporary with the first and thought by Mendoni 1990, 300 to be directly related to it but by another hand, may refer to victory in some sort of drinking contest). Caskey (1971, 39; 1980, 200; 2009) is confident that Dionysus was worshipped at this sanctuary from the eighth century and argues for the possibility of Bronze Age worship at Ayia Irini on the basis of various dedications, including the numerous terracotta statuettes of dancing women. The fact that the sixth-century dedication was made by a man from Ioulis adds some weight to the somewhat oblique evidence of Athenaeus 10.456c–d (Simon. fr. 69 Diehl; Chamael. *On Simonides* fr. 37 Martano) that Dionysus was worshipped with ox-sacrifice and dithyrambs in Ioulis in Simonides' day. In the Hellenistic period both Ioulis and Karathaia issued coins with the head of the god or other symbols relating to him, such as grapes (Mantzourani 1991, 157, 159; Reger and Risser 1991, 307; see also *SEG* 40, 711).

Ioulis, a city with a population of perhaps ca. 3,500 in the middle of the fourth century (Reger *IACP* 748) – much larger than Karthaia (above) – had its own theatre in the third century. That is the date of a decree honouring a Timophanes son of Philinos who as Archon of the city has '[fulfilled the obligations in respect of the g]ods in a fine and p[i]ous manner s[o that he has also ded]icated a skene and proskenio[n in the theatre to gratify all the] citizens, and has further donated mo[ney … an]d oversaw the *onopl*(?) […] and has als[o ove]rseen [th]e citizen[s …]' (*SEG* 39, 869, ll. 6–12: [καὶ νῦν]‖ ἄρχων τῆς πόλεως γενόμε[νος συντετέλεκεν τὰ περὶ τοὺς | θ]εοὺς καλῶς καὶ ε[ὐ]σεβῶς ὥ[στε καὶ ἐν τῶι θεάτρωι ἀνέ|θ]-ηκεν σκηνὴν καὶ προσκήνιο[ν χαριζόμενος πᾶσι τοῖς] | πολίταις, ἐπέδωκεν δὲ καὶ ἀρ[γύριον - - - - - - - | κα]ὶ ἐπεμελήθη τοῦ . ΩΝΟΠΛ (?) - - - - - - ‖[ἐπιμ]εμέληται δὲ κα[ὶ τῶ]ν πολιτῶ[ν - - - - - -]; Mendoni 1989, 293–5). It is possible to interpret this as the dedication of a new stage building and proskenion to a theatre which had been in existence for some time, perhaps with a wooden rather than stone stage building. Or it may be that the dedication added these structures to a theatre that was in the course of being built. At any rate, it is possible that Ioulis had had a theatre for some time before the passing of this decree. The city held a Dionysia with tragic contest by the second century (*IG* XII 5, 599; 604).

Diii: Chios

1. **Aeneas Tacticus, *Siege Tactics* 17.5**, before 356 (all datable stories in this treatise on military stratagems are earlier, with a particular concentration of anecdotes relating to the 360s: Hug 1877, 4–8; Vela Tejada and Martín García 1991, 10, 16–17). The story at 11.3, in a section on the need to exercise vigilance against factional treachery (11.1), also describes in some detail and with apparent accuracy the port installations at Chios: 'Eneas parece conocer de cerca los asuntos de Quíos' (Vela Tejada and Martín García 1991, 73). This section of the *Siege Tactics* deals with the dangers of large festival gatherings in cities that are in discord and where the citizens are suspicious of one another. Text: Dain.

> Χῖοι δὲ ἄγοντες τὰ Διονύσια καὶ πέμποντες πομπὰς λαμπρὰς πρὸς τοῦ Διονύσου τὸν βωμόν, προκαταλαμβάνουσι τὰς εἰς τὴν ἀγορὰν φερούσας ὁδοὺς φυλακαῖς καὶ δυνάμεσι πολλαῖς, κώλυμα γοῦν οὐ μικρὸν τοῖς βουλομένοις νεωτερίζειν.

> When the Chians celebrate the Dionysia and perform magnificent parades to the altar of Dionysus they occupy in advance the roads opening onto the marketplace (agora) with guards and copious troops. This at any rate is no insignificant obstacle to those who want a revolution.

2. **Chian decree honouring judges from Andros and Naxos**, ca. 320 (by letter forms: Heisserer 1980, 79–117, esp. 115). The 'Alexander drachmas' mentioned in l. 13 (cf. **3**, ll. 1, 6) are a coinage issued soon after Alexander's death in 323 (Heisserer 1980, 116; Belinger 1963, 86).

Grey limestone stele, inscribed on face (A) and left side (B). Chips on upper right margin of face. From line 9 the stone has been cut in a semicircle and then in a straight line as far as line 31. 1.02 × 0.45 × 0.27 m.
The stone was used to frame a loophole in the Byzantine and Genoese fortress of Chios. It was dismantled and taken to the former museum of Chios from the Kastro at some time before 1938. Chios Archaeological Museum inv. 652 (Malouchou and Matthaiou 2006, 194 no. 5).
Hunt 1940–1945, 46 (= *SEG* 12, 390); Condoléon 1949, 9–13 no. 2; Dunst 1960, 38–9; McCabe and Brownson 1986, no. 12.
Text: Based with minor variations on McCabe and Brownson.   Photos: Heisserer 1980, 114 pl. 11, 117 pl. 12.

> A   ἔδοξεν τῶι δήμωι·   non-stoich.
>   ἐπειδὴ οἱ δικασταὶ οἵ τε Νάξιοι κα[ὶ οἱ]
>   Ἄνδριοι ἐπελθόντες ἐπὶ τὸν δῆμ[ον]
>   ἠξίουν ἀποστέλλεσθαι διὰ τὸ χρόν[ον]
> 5   πολὺν αὐτοῖς εἶναι τῆς ἀποδημίας, δεδ[ό]-

χθαι τῶι δήμωι· ἐπαινέσαι μὲν τὰς π[ό]-
λεις ἀμφοτέρας ὅτι φιλοτίμως καὶ οἰ-
[κ]είως ἀπέστειλαν ἡμῖν τὰ δικαστή-
ρια, ἐπαινέσαι δὲ καὶ τοὺς δικαστάς, ὅτι
10   [κ]αλῶς καὶ δικαίως ἐδίκαζον τὰς [δίκας]
[κ]αὶ στεφανῶσαι ἑκάτερον τ[ῶν δικαστη]-
[ρ]ίων χρυσῶι στεφάνωι ἀπὸ [δραχμῶν ἑκατὸν]
[ἀ]λεξανδρείων· δεδόσθαι δ[ὲ προξενίαν]
[κα]ὶ αὐτοῖς καὶ ἐγγόνοις κα[ὶ προεδρίαν ἐν τοῖς]
15   [ἀγ]ῶσιν καὶ ε̣ἴσπλουν καὶ ἔκ[πλουν καὶ πολέμου]
[κ]αὶ εἰρήνης ἀσυλεὶ καὶ ἀσ[πονδεὶ καὶ δίκας]
[π]ροδίκους καὶ ἀτέλει[αν, ὧν ἂν εἰσάγωσιν ἢ]
ἐξάγωσιν ἐπὶ κτήσε[ι· καὶ αὐτοὺς Χίους]
εἶναι ἐὰμ βο̣ύλ̣ω̣ν̣τ̣[αι· ὅπως δὲ καὶ φανερὸς]
20   ἦι ὁ δῆμος, ὅτι ἐπ̣ί̣[σταται χάριτας ἀποδι]-
δόναι τοῖς δικαίο̣ι̣ς [τῶν ἀνδρῶν, ἀνει]-
πεῖν τ̣ὸ̣ν̣ κ̣ή̣ρ̣υ̣κ̣α̣ Διον̣[υσίοις τόδε τὸ κήρυ]-
[γ]μα· ὁ δῆμος ὁ Χίων [στεφανοῖ τοὺς δι]-
[κ]αστὰς τοὺς ἐγ Νάξ[ου καὶ ἐξ Ἄνδρου δικαι]-
25   οσύνης ἕνεκα τῆς εἰς [ἑαυτὸν χρυσῶι]
[σ]τεφάνωι ἀφ᾽ ἑκατὸν [δραχμῶν· τιμᾶι δὲ]
[πρ]οξενίαι κ̣α̣ὶ πο[λιτείαι αὐτοὺς καὶ ἐγ]-
γόνους· ἐπιμεληθῆναι δ[ὲ τοῦ κηρύγμα]-
τος Μεγαρέα τὸν ἀγωνο[θέτην καὶ τοὺς]
30   πρυτάνεις τοὺς ἐνεστῶτας, [οἳ καὶ ἀναγραψάν]-
των εἰς τὴν στήλην τὴν προξ[ενικὴν τήν]
τε πόλιν ἑκατέρων καὶ τὰ ὀνόμ[ατα πατρό]-
[θ]εν· δοῦναι δὲ τοὺς ταμίας ἑκατ[έρωι τῶν]
[δι]καστηρίων τὸ εἰς τὸν στέφανο[ν ἀργύριον·]
35   [δ]οῦναι δὲ καὶ εἰς κομιδὴν ἑκ[άστωι τῶν]
[δι]καστῶν δραχμὰς πεντήκον[τα τοὺς]
ἐξεταστὰς μετὰ τῶν πολεμάρ[χων· ἐπι]-
[μεληθ]ῆναι δὲ ὅπως ἐπὶ τριήρους κ[ομισθῶ]-
[σιν οἱ δικ]ασταί· ὅπως δὲ καὶ ἀείμνη[στος ἡ]
40   [τῶν ἀν]δρῶν δικαιότης ἦι καὶ οἱ λ[οιποὶ ὁ]-
[μοίως π]ράττωσι πρὸς τὸν δῆμον, [τοὺς πρυ]-
[τάνει]ς ἀναγράψαντας εἰς στήλ[ην λιθί]-
[νην τό]δε τὸ ψήφισμα καὶ τὰ ὀνόματα [τῶν δικα]-
[στῶν π]ατρόθεν καὶ ἐξ ἧς πόλεως [ἑκάτερον]
45   [τῶν δικ]αστηρίων ἐστίν, στῆσαι εἰς τὸ ἱερ[ὸν . .⁴. .]
[. .⁴. . τὸ δ᾽] ἀνάλωμα τὸ εἰς τὴν στήλη[ν]
[. .⁴. . δ]οῦναι τοὺς ταμίας.

B　　ἐγ Νάξο[υ]

　　Ἐπιγενίδης Ἡγησιμάχου

50　　Σωσίλος Ἱππολύτου

　　Ξενόφαντος Ἀρχέλεω

　　Εὐχάρης Εὐστράτου

　　Σώπολις Σωσίου

　　ἐξ Ἄνδρου

55　　Πυθόδωρος Πυθίππου

　　Μυρτίας Ἰδνάδου

　　Κλεόδωρος Κλεονίκο[υ]

　　Θεαγένης Ἀρχαγορίδο[υ]

　　Θεότιμος Ῥίκωνος

14–15 δη[μοσίοις | ἀγ]ῶσιν Hunt　　κα[ὶ προεδρίαν ἐν τοῖς |ἀγ]ῶσιν Condoléon　　18
ἐξάγωσιν· ἐπικτήσε[ις δὲ γῆς καὶ οἰκίας] Hunt　　ἐξάγωσιν ἐπὶ κτήσε[ι· καὶ γῆς (?)
ἔγκτησιν (?)] Condoléon　　22–3 τὸγ κήρυκα νομ[ίμως τόδε τὸ ψήφισ]μα Hunt　　τὸγ
κήρυκα Διον[υσίοις τόδε τὸ κήρυ|γ]μα Condoléon

The People decreed. Since the Naxian an[d the] Andrian judges who came to
the ci[ty] decided to leave because of the great length of tim[e] [5] they had been
away from home, the people have de[c]ided: to give praise to both c[i]ties
for the alacrity and ca[r]e with which they sent us their judges and to give
praise to the judges [10] for the [f]ine and just manner with which they delivered
their [judgements a]nd to crown both o[f the groups of jud]ges with a gold
crown worth [one hundred A]lexander [drachmas] and to grant [proxeny bo]th
to them and to their children and [prohedria in the [15] con]tests and the right to
sail into and out [of our harbour both in time of war a]nd in time of peace with
inviolability and without fo[rmal treaty and to grant them the right to have
their cases heard in ad]vance of others and to be free of taxat[ion for whatever
goods they import or] export for their own us[e. Furthermore, they are to become Chian citizens,] if they wis[h. That it be made manifest that] [20] the People
un[derstand how to show gratitude] to just [men], the herald is to [an]nounce
[this proclamat]ion at the Dion[ysia]: The People of Chios [crown the judg]es
from Nax[os and from Andros] [25] on account of the justice they have shown [it
with a gold c]rown worth one hundred [drachmas and it honours with pr]oxeny
and ci[tizenship both them and their ch]ildren. Megareus the agono[thete and
the] [30] Prytaneis in power at the time are to look after [the proclamat]ion, [and
the same officials are to have inscrib]ed on the prox[enic] stele the city of each
of the groups of judges and their nam[es with patronymic.] The treasurers are
to give to ea[ch group of ju]dges [the expenditure] for the crow[n] [35] and the
auditors along with the Polem[archs] are to give to each [of the ju]dges fif[-
ty] drachmas for their passage [and they are to see] to it that [the ju]dges be
c[onveyed] on a trireme; [40] and so that [the] justice [of the m]en be forever re-
mem[bered] and so that f[uture benefactors] behave [in the same way] towards
the People, [the Prytanei]s after inscribing on a [stone] stel[e] this decree and

the names [of the judges] with patronymic and to which city [each group [45] of ju]dges belongs, are to erect it in the san[ctuary …] the treasurers are to [p]ay [the] cost of the stele.

From Naxos: Epigenides, son of Hegesimachos; [50] Sosilos, son of Hippolytos; Xenophantos, son of Archelaus; Eochares, son of Eostratos; Sopolis, son of Sosias. From Andros: [55] Pythodoros, son of Pythippos; Myrtias, son of Idnades; Kleodoros, son of Kleonikos; Theagenes, son of Archagorides; Theotimos, son of Rikon.

3. **Chian decree honouring Nikomedes, son of Aristandros, of Cos,** 315–305 (by letter forms and prosopography). Nikomedes was a henchman of Antigonus I. This decree is part of a collection of at least 26 decrees honouring Nikomedes, from Athens, from cities of western Asia Minor and from the adjoining islands, that were collected and inscribed on two opisthographic stelae and probably erected in the vicinity of a family monument in Nikomedes' hometown of Cos (**3** is the tenth such decree on the face of the stele). 'We know of at least one or two distant descendants of Nikomedes holding important offices at Kos, which means that the status of the family remained intact for a long time' (Paschidis 2008, 363). The letter forms of these stelae belong after the end of the 4th c., but the decrees recorded on the stelae date to some time between 315 and 305 (Sherwin-White 1978, 86–7 n. 30; Paschidis 2008, esp. 87–8, 365). The decree is massively restored on the basis of the other decrees on the stelae and other Chian decrees (cf. **2** and **4**). Kleandros, son of Themistius, restored in the last line is known from *IG* XI 4, 597, l. 7. On Nikomedes, see Paschidis 2008, 361–5.

Fragment of an opisthographic marble stele.
0.50 × 0.35 × 0.10 (bottom) m.
Part of a larger monument recording honours given to Nikomedes by various states. For the reconstruction see *IG* XII 4, 129.
Reworked to serve as a threshold block.
Found in Cos by R. Herzog.
Once (?) Cos Castle Museum inv. 619.
Dunst 1959 (= *SEG* 18, 333); Segre 1993, ED 71d; *IG* XII 4, 129 (decree no. X).
Text: *IG* XII 4, 129 (decree no. X = ll. 67–78).   Photo: Segre 1993, pl. 24.

non-stoich.

[— — — — — — — — — — — κα]ὶ στεφάνω[σαι χρυσῶι στεφάνωι ἀπὸ
      δραχμῶν Ἀλεξαν]-
[δρείων πεντήκοντα καὶ στῆσαι αὐτοῦ εἰκόνα χ]αλκῆν ἐν τῆ[ι ἀγορῆι·
      δεδόσθαι δὲ καὶ αὐτῶι προεδρίην ἐμ]
[πᾶσι τοῖς ἀγῶσιν οἷς ἂν ἡ πόλις ποιῆι ἀρετῆς ἕ]νεκεν καὶ εὐνο[ίης ἣν ἔχων
      διατελεῖ εἰς τὸν δῆμον· ὅπως δὲ]
[φανερὸς ἦι ὁ δῆμος ὅτι ἐπίσταται ἀποδιδόναι] χάριτας ἀξίας τῶ[ν
      εὐεργετημάτων, ἀνειπεῖν τὸν ἱεροκήρυ]-
5   [κα Διονυσίοις ἐν τῶι θεήτρωι τόδε τὸ] κή[ρυ]γμα ʽὁ δῆμος ὁ Χίων σ[τεφανοῖ
      Νικομήδη Ἀριστάνδρου χρυσῶι]
[στεφάνωι ἀπὸ δραχμῶν Ἀλεξανδ]ρείω[ν π]εντήκοντα, στήσει δὲ [αὐτοῦ καὶ
      εἰκόνα χαλκῆν ἐν τῆι ἀγορᾶι· δί]-

[δωσι καὶ προεδρίην ἐ]μ πᾶσι τοῖς ἀγῶσιν οἷς ἂν ἡ πόλις π[οιῆι, ἀρετῆς καὶ
        εὐνοίης ἕνεκεν᾽. ἐπι]-
[μεληθῆναι τοῦ ποιεῖσθαι τὴ]ν ἀναγγελίην τὸν ἀγωνοθέτην· ἐλέ[σθαι δὲ καὶ
        ἄνδρα ὅστις ἐπιμελεῖται τῆς]
[κατασκευῆς τῆς εἰκόνος· τοὺς] δὲ πρέσβεις οὓς ἂν πρώτους ὁ δ[ῆμος
        πέμψηι πρὸς Ἀντίγονον τοῦτο τὸ ψή]-
10   [φισμα Νικομήδει — — — — — —] ἀποδοῦναι καὶ ἐπαινέσαι καὶ
        στεφα[νῶσαι αὐτὸν παρὰ τοῦ δήμου — — — — —]
[τὸ δὲ ἀργύριον τὸ εἰς τὸν σ]τέφανον δοῦναι τοῖς πρέ[σ]βεσι τὸν [— — —
        — — — — — — —]
[— ἡιρέθη εἰς κατασκευὴν] τῆς εἰκόνος Κλέανδρ[ος Θε]μιστί[ου].

[… an]d to crow[n him with a gold crown worth fifty golden Alexander drachmas and to place a b]ronze [statue of him] in th[e marketplace; and to give
him also prohedria in all the contests which the city puts on] on account o[f
his excellence] and his good wi[ll that he always shows towards the People.
And so that all may know that the People understand how to repay] gratitude
worthy of th[e benefits they have received the sacred herald [5] is to proclaim at
the Dionysia in the theatre the following proclam]ation 'The People of Chios
c[rowns Nikomedes, son of Aristandros, with a golden crown made from f]ifty
[Alexan]der [drachmas], and it will erect [a bronze statue of him in the marketplace. It also gives him prohedria i]n all of the contests that the city p[uts on,
because of his excellence and good will.'] The Agonothete [is to look after the
making of thi]s announcement. [A man] will be ch[osen to see to the preparation of the statue. The] first ambassadors whom the P[eople sends to Antigonos]
are to deliver [this [10] decree to Nikomedes …] and praise and crow[n him on
behalf of the People …] The […] will give to the amba[ss]adors the [money
for the c]rown that […] Kleandr[os, son of The]misti[os was chosen to see to
the preparation] of the statue.

4. Chian decree honouring Apollophanes, a judge sent by Ptolemy (Philadelphos?),
first half 3[rd] c. Chios was under Ptolemaic control in the 270s, possibly from 281
(Grainger 1990, 187). Bagnall (1976, 168): 'probably of the period 278–270'; Derow
(2015, 255): '?267–259'.

Stele of bluish marble, preserved on bottom and right, broken at top and right side.
0.585 × 0.41 m.
Removed from the Palaiokastro of Chios by Stephanou (1960, 140).
Chios Archaeological Museum inv. 1047 (Malouchou and Matthaiou 2006, 194 no. 7).
Stephanou 1960; Robert and Robert 1961, 208–9 no. 466; *SEG* 19, 569; *SEG* 20, 787; McCabe
and Brownson 1986, no. 13.
Text: based mainly on *SEG* 19, 569.
Photos: Stephanou 1960, pl. 1; Centre for the Study of Ancient Documents website www.csad.
ox.ac.uk/csad/Images/00/Image32.html (accessed Dec. 2016).

non-stoich.

[. . . . .^ca. 17. . . . . τ]ὰς ὑπ' αὐτ[οῦ . . . .^ca. 30. . . . .]

[. . . . . .^ca. 12. . . . . .]ΕΙΕΝ, οὐκ ὀλίγοις δὲ τῶν διᾳ[. . . . .^ca. 25. . . . .]

[. .^ca. 4. .]ως αἴτιος γέγονεν, εὐτάκτως δὲ πεποη[. . . . .^ca. 19. . . . . ἑαυ]-

[τὸν] ἀνέγκλητον παρεχόμενος πᾶσι τοῖς ἐν τῆι π[όλει . . . .^ca. 20. . . . .]

5 [τῶ]ν ἀρχόντων κατὰ τὸ ψήφισμα τοῦ δήμου ὅπως Ἀ[. . . . . . .^ca. 21. . . . .]

ιπεις δίκας συντελέσηι, ἠξίωκεν καὶ δεδέηται [ἀποστέλλεσθαι πρὸς τοὺς]

βασιλεῖς, φάσκων διὰ τὸ χρονιωτέραν αὐτῶι τὴν ἀποδη[μίαν κατασταθῆναι]

σπουδάζειν παραγενέσθαι πρὸς αὐτούς. δεδόχθαι τῶι [δήμωι ἐπαινέσαι]

[Ἀ]πολλοφάνην Ἀπολλοδώρου καὶ στεφανῶσαι χρυσῶι στεφά[νωι ἀρετῆς]

10 [ἕ]νεκα καὶ εὐνοίας τῆς εἰς τοὺς βασιλεῖς καὶ τὸν δῆμον καὶ ὅτ[ι καλῶς καὶ φιλο]-

τίμως συνετέλεσεν ἐφ' ἃ ἀπέστειλεν αὐτὸν ὁ βασιλεὺς Π[τολεμαῖος. ὅπως]

[δὲ] καὶ εἰδῶσι πάντες οἱ βουλόμενοι τὸν δῆμον εὐεργετε[ῖν ὅτι ὁ δῆμος]

ἐπίσταται τιμᾶν τοὺς ἀγαθοὺς ἄνδρας εἰς ἑαυτὸν γιν[ομένους, ἀνειπεῖν]

τὸν ἱεροκήρυκα Διονυσίοις ἐν τῶι θεάτρωι, ὅταν οἱ τῶν [παίδων χοροὶ μέλ]-

15 λωσιν ἀγωνίζεσθαι τόδε τὸ κήρυγμα. ὁ δῆμος ὁ Χίων στ[εφανοῖ Ἀπολλοφά]-

νην Ἀπολλοδώρου χρυσῶι στεφάνωι ἀρετῆς ἕνεκα κ[αὶ εὐνοίας τῆς εἰς ἑ]-

αυτὸν καὶ τοὺς βασιλεῖς καὶ ὅτι καλῶς καὶ φιλοτίμω[ς συνετέλεσεν ἐφ' ἃ]

ἀπέστειλεν αὐτὸν ὁ βασιλεὺς Πτολεμαῖος. τοῦ [δὲ κηρύγματος ἐπιμε]-

ληθῆναι τὸν ἀγωνοθέτην. ἵνα δὲ καὶ ἀποσταλῆι Ἀ[πολλοφάνης . . . .^ca. 8. . . .]

20 ται τοὺς πολεμάρχου<ς> καὶ τοὺς ἐξεταστὰς ἐπιμ[εληθῆναι ἵνα ἀποσ]-

ταλῆι Ἀπολλοφάνης ὡς κάλλιστα καὶ ἀσφαλ[έστατα· τὸ δὲ ψήφισμα τόδε]

ἀναγράψαι τὸν ἐπιμελητὴν τῆς εἰκόνος εἰστ[ήλην τὰς τιμὰς τὰς δεδο]-

[μ]ένας ὑπὸ τοῦ δήμου.

2 [. . . . . .]σι ἐν, οὐκ ὀλίγοις δὲ τῶν δι[καστηρίων Stephanou   2–3 δι[αφερομένων τῆς συλλύσε]ως J. and L. Robert   3 πεπόη[ται τὴν ἐπιδημίαν ἑαυ] J. and L. Robert   4 π[όλει, παρακληθεὶς δὲ ὑπὸ] J. and L. Robert   5–6 [ἀ|να]γεῖς Stephanou [ὑπο|λ]ιπεῖς ? Fraser   19–20 Ἀ[πολλοφάνης ὡς δεδέη]ται Klaffenbach ἀποσταλῆι [ἐπὶ τριήρους, ἐντέλλε]|ται McCabe and Brownson   21 ἀσφαλ[έστατα ἐπὶ τρήρους. καὶ] McCabe and Brownson

[…] under hi[m …] for many of those […] he was responsible, and in an orderly fashion he (?) did […] conducting [himsel]f in an irreproachable way to everyone in the c[ity. When summoned by? ⁵ th]e Archons in accordance with the decree of the People that A[pollophanes, son of Apollodoros?] complete the [rema]ining trials, thought it right and begged [to be allowed to return to the] Kings, urging that because his sojou[rn had been] very long he was eager to rejoin them. It is resolved by the [People to give praise to A]pollophanes, son of Apollodoros and to crown him with a gold crow[n b]ecause [of his excellence] ¹⁰ and good will to the Kings and the People and becau[se] he completed [well and zeal]ously the tasks for which King P[tolemy] sent him [and in order that] all who wish to serv[e] the People shall know [that the People] understands how to honour men who are good to it, it resolves that the sacred herald proclaim at the Dionysia in the theatre, whenever the [choruses of boys are ab]out [15] to compete the following proclamation: the People of Chios cr[owns Apollopha]-nes, son of Apollodoros with a gold crown on account of his excellence a[nd his good will to] it and the Kings and because [he completed] well and zeal-ousl[y the tasks] King Ptolemy sent him to do. The Agonothete is to see [to] the [proclamation]. And in order that A[pollophanes] be sent off [?on a trireme, the People ord]ers [20] the Polemarchs and the Auditors to see [to it that Apollophanes is sent] off in the best and saf[est] possible manner. The caretaker of the image will inscribe on a st[ele this decree, the honours giv]en by the People.

Dionysus was certainly a major deity in Chios by Classical times (Graf 1985, 74–97). Local tradition, attested as early as the fifth-century *Foundation of Chios* by Ion of Chios (*FGrH* 392 F 1; fr. 96 Leurini; fr. 29 W), made Oinopion the first settler (*oikistes*). Although Ion served Athenian imperial propaganda by making Theseus Oinopion's father (Herter 1939, 318; Olding 2007, 146–9), the tradition that Oinopion, with the significant name 'Wine-Drinker' or 'Wine-Face', was a son of Dionysus goes back at least as far as Hesiod fr. 238 (Ion's pro-Athenian sympathies are evident not only from his relationship with Cimon, but also the fact that the leader of the pro-Athenian democratic party in 411 was probably his son: Th. 8.38.3; Meiggs 1972, 362; Geddes 2007; Olding 2007, 149–54; Blanshard 2007). Theopompus, also a Chian, records that Oinopion first taught the islanders how to make wine, and that the Chians spread this wisdom to the rest of humanity (*FGrH* 115 F 276). A hero cult for Oinopion is well attested in Imperial times (Graf 1985, 125–6). By the first century coins from Chios are marked with Dionysian symbols (thyrsos, ivy crowns, and prizes at the Dionysia: see Robert 1935, 465 = *Op. Min.* I, 524). This special feeling of attachment to the wine god is likely to go back a long way: Chian wine was famous from the earliest Archaic period, when wine ampho-rae are found all over the Mediterranean. The cultic epikleseis for Dionysus of Omadios ('Raw Flesh Eater') and Phleus are attested for the island (Graf 1985, 74–80, 97).

Despite this, it is not until the fourth century that we have our first attestation of Chios' Dionysia (**1–3**). It included 'magnificent parades' (**1**) bringing sacrifices to an altar, appar-ently in the central marketplace. That the parade was characterised by the carnival licence elsewhere associated with Dionysian processions emerges from the extraordinary precau-tions taken by the Chians to guard against disorder (**1**), as well as a local myth about the Chian women succumbing to madness (παραφρονήσασαι) during the Dionysia and at-tacking their men (Harp. s.v. Ὁμηρίδαι): such myths are usually an aetiological licence for misbehaviour. Chios in the sixth century decorates drinking vessels with komast dancers who may have some connection with Dionysus, though the representations of their revels are more demure than we find in other regions (Smith 2010, 176–93).

Apart from the parade we only have evidence of a competition for boys' lyric choruses, and then only from around the mid third century (Ceccarelli 2010, 122 n. 72, 124 n. 79). The contest of the Dionysia where the herald is to make his proclamation in **4**, l. 14, is unfortunately lost ('men's', ἀνδρῶν would in principle fit as easily as 'boys'', παίδων, but both syntax and space preclude a reference to tragedy or comedy). It is perhaps significant

that the fourth-century decrees (**2–3**) mention no contest at all, but simply direct that honours be proclaimed 'at the Dionysia', though it is unclear what the failure to specify a
contest might mean at **2**, l. 22, **3**, l. 5 (?). Did a boys' choral competition not yet form part
of the programme of the Dionysia in the fourth century? The mention of an agonothete at **2**,
l. 29 and **3**, l. 8 would seem to imply some sort of competition, and it seems clear from the
fact that the agonothete is to take responsibility for the proclamation at the Dionysia (**2**, ll.
28–9, cf. **3**, ll. 7–8) that the Dionysia is part of his remit. Moreover, contests are mentioned
in the plural at **3**, l. 7 and restored at **2**, l. 15. From both **2** and **3** it is clear that at least some
of these contests belong to other festivals, so the fact that Chios had numerous contests
cannot exclude the possibility that the fourth-century Dionysia had only one (presumably
a contest for lyric boys' choruses), thus making specification of a contest unnecessary.
Conversely, the specification of the 'boys'' competition in the third-century decrees may,
but need not, imply that other contests had been introduced by this time.

The tradition of boys' lyric choruses on Chios certainly goes back to the very early
fifth century when we hear of a hundred boys being sent to perform in Delphi, probably in or shortly before 498 (Hdt. 6.27; Scott 2005, 145 *ad loc.*). In the Classical period
Chios produced a number of distinguished poets in dithyramb, including Licymnius (*PMG*
768–73, with Hordern 2002, 123), Demokritos (Ar. *PCG* F 930; Eup. *PCG* F 91; Power
2010, 186–7) and the very versatile Ion (*TrGF* 19) who, in addition to the history of Chios
mentioned above, wrote not only dithyrambs and other forms of poetry, but also tragedies.
Hornblower argues that Pindar wrote a dithyramb (frr. 71–4) for performance on the island
(2004, 145–56).

The practice that we find in the third century (and probably **4**) of making the boys' choral competitions the venue for the proclamation of honours might reflect a particular local
pride in the boys' choruses. Local evidence for a choregic system is limited to the funding
of boys' choruses (Wilson 2000, 309). In other Aegean festivals, tragic competitions are
more commonly specified as the preferred time for proclamations of honours (Le Guen
2001, 265). There are nonetheless parallels for the choice of a boys' competition in third/
second-century inscriptions from Delos (**Dvi**), and Minoa (*IG* XII 7, 228) and Arkesine (*IG*
XII 7, 32) on Amorgos (Ceccarelli 2010, 128–9, 145). But in the case of Delos, the evidence
comes from not the Dionysia, but the Apollonia, where there were no dramatic competitions and the only civically sponsored competition was for boys' choruses. This may have
been the case at Minoa as well, where it is the choregoi who are to effect the proclamation
of honours 'through the herald' before the boys' competition (*IG* XII 7, 228, ll. 5–9). These
parallels suggest that the boys' competition in Chios may have been chosen for honorary
proclamations because they were the only competition at the Dionysia, even, as suggested
above, in the third century and afterwards. We have as yet no direct evidence for men's
lyric choruses, let alone tragedy or comedy, at any time in antiquity. Moreover we know
the names of many distinguished musicians from Chios, but not a single actor. Ion in his
memoirs notes that Sophocles did visit Chios, but only on military duty (*FGrH* 392 F 6),
presumably in 440/39 at the time of the Samian revolt (Quinn 1981, 40; Scodel 2012, 33).

The earliest mention of the theatre in Chios is **4**, l. 14, but a reference to the theatre is re-
storable in **3**, l. 5 on the basis of the formulae used in **4**, ll. 13–15 and two mid third-century
Chian decrees found in Delphi (*FD* III 3, 214, ll. 23–4 and 215 = Nachtergael 1977, Actes

22, ll. 21–2). The theatre of Chios has not been found, but fragments of several stone theatre benches (labelled 'bathra') have been found including three with inscriptions that were
built into the Church of St. Nikolaos in Tourloti (a.k.a. Ἅγιος Νικόλαυς τοῦ Βουνοῦ). This
church is located at what is thought to be the western limit of Classical Chios (Tsardaka
2010–2013, 505; Hood et al. 1954, 125 fig. 1). One of the inscribed benches reads: [. . .
παί]δων χορηγίαν ἐν τῷ [...], 'a choregia for [bo]ys in the ...' (Studniczka 1888, 177 no.
23b; Zolotas 1923, 14). It is evidently of late date as it contains two ligatures. Another
inscribed bench, dated to the second century AD, is inscribed ΗΓΗΣΑΣΑΝ, probably from
the dedicatory formula χορηγήσας ἀνέθηκεν, '... after serving as choregos he dedicated
...' (Stephanou 1960, 144; Malouchou and Matthaiou 2006, 218 no. 180). It appears that in
Imperial times choregoi and other officials commemorated their public service by dedicating stone seating in the theatre (see also Stephanou 1960, 144 and pls. 3–4). The choregia
for the Dionysian competition however goes back at least to the third century (McCabe and
Brownson 1986, 213; Malouchou and Matthaiou 2006, 213 no. 132: [—]OEN[—] | [—]N
τὰς χορηγίας [—] | [—]νικήσας Διονυσ[—]). Also found at the same Church was a stone
frieze decorated with masks (Hood et al. 1954, 124).

Chios was one of the few members of the Delian League that provided ships and paid no
tribute, but the alliance was not an easy one and in 412 Chios went over to the Peloponnesian
side. As a non-tributary ally of the Delian League, Aristotle specifically says that Chios was
allowed to retain its constitution (*Ath.* 24.2), which appears to have been mildly oligarchic
(Rubinstein *IACP* 1067; Meiggs 1972, 208, 361–2; Quinn 1981, 39–49; O'Neil 1995, 39–
40) and this was replaced by a more narrowly oligarchic regime in 412 (Th. 8.38) which
probably lasted until at least 394. Aristotle tells us that an extreme oligarchic regime was
replaced, possibly at this time (*Pol.* 1306b3–6), but probably by a more moderate oligarchy
(Rubinstein *IACP* 1067). The regime is in any case still oligarchic in 355 (D. 15.19). We
do not know if Chios was ever a democracy during this time, but the evidence does suggest
a level of political instability that would justify the extraordinary vigilance attested in **1**.

Chios was a founding member of the Second Athenian Confederacy, but later formed
part of an anti-Athenian alliance backed by the Hecatomnids of Caria in 357 and then
fell under Hecatomnid domination by 346. The governing oligarchy sought Persian help
against Macedon. We have the 'letter' by which Alexander imposed a democracy on Chios
probably in 334 but not later than 332 (Heisserer 1980, 79–95; R-O II no. 84). This accounts for the prominence of the People in **2–4** in the distribution of honours in the theatre.
In particular the prescript of **2** shows that it belongs to the early years of the democracy,
but also the lettering style of the inscription, which is so close to Alexander's letter that
Heisserer (1980, 115) thinks **2** 'was inscribed ca. 320 by the same mason'.

The oligarchic government of Chios in the fifth and earlier fourth century may explain
why Chios seems to buck the trend towards the relatively early and full reception of an
Athenian model of Dionysia that we find in most other parts of the Aegean. As far as we can
tell Chios had no theatre before it became a democracy (**3**). Even then the only competition
attested for its Dionysia is boys' choruses with which it celebrated the Dionysia probably
since the sixth century. The Dionysia did have a procession, which probably also stems
from the earliest years of the settlement, but other Greeks found remarkable the anxiety with
which it was policed, and the same fear of revolution attested for the parade (**1**) doubtless

extended to all events of the Dionysia which involved large gatherings of citizens with low-ered inhibitions. It appears that the Dionysia in Chios remained undeveloped, despite the im-portance of Dionysus to the island, until the time of Chios' Hellenistic democracy, and even then it seems not to have admitted dramatic competitions (or even men's choruses). Chios' jittery ambivalence towards Dionysus found a fitting symbolic expression in the fact that the icon of the Chian Dionysus was bound in chains (Polemon *FHG* fr. 90; Graf 1985, 81–96).

Div: Cos. Antigonus of Carystus, *Collection of Marvellous Stories* 161 (= Call. fr. 407 xxxiii Pfeiffer; Eudoxus of Cnidus fr. 363 Lasserre). Antigonus probably wrote in the later 3ʳᵈ c. (Fraser 1972a II, 658 n. 62). He takes much of his material from Callimachus' *Collection of Marvels throughout the World by Location* (Krevans 2011, 124–6) and Callimachus in turn took much of his material from Eudoxus. Callimachus lived from ca. 305 to ca. 240. Eudoxus lived from ca. 390 to ca. 340: a philosopher, mathematician and astronomer, he also wrote descriptive geography. Text: Giannini.

> εἶναι δὲ παρὰ τοῖς Κῴοις καὶ ἄλλο τι ῥευμάτιον, ὃ πάντας τοὺς ὀχετούς, ὅθεν διαρρεῖ, λίθους πεποίηκεν. τοῦτο δὲ καὶ Εὔδοξος καὶ Καλλίμαχος παραλείπουσιν, ὅτι ἐκ τοῦδε τοῦ ὕδατος οἱ Κῷοι λίθους λατομήσαντες ᾠκοδόμησαν τὸ θέατρον· οὕτως ἰσχυρῶς ἀπολιθοῦται πᾶν γένος.

> The Coans have another stream which has made stones of all the channels that it flows through. Both Eudoxus and Callimachus say nothing about this because the Coans built their theatre after quarrying stones from this water. So powerfully are all things turned to stone.

Antigonus appears to refer to the ferruginous waters of Vourinna and Kokkinonero which still leave thick deposits of travertine around their springs (Gorceix 1876, 207–8; Poupaki 2004, 170 n. 81). This travertine stone was much used in construction in Cos from 366 to ca. 200, before it was exhausted (Livadiotti 1996, 121, 158).

The location of the Roman theatre at the south end of the ancient city is conspicuous on the flat plane of the city, and was always known. The theatre was partly excavated by the Italian School from 1922 to 1933 (for the remains, see Livadiotti 1996, 156–8). Herzog found a number of pre-Roman travertine benches in private properties in the area of the theatre and inferred that the Roman theatre had been built on top of the earlier theatre which has other-wise left no archaeological trace (1899, 187). Livadiotti notes that, given the generally flat topography of the city, the earlier theatre must have been in the same location (1996, 158).

Antigonus seems to argue that Eudoxus and Callimachus failed to mention the streams that produced stones because the Coans quarried the stone for their theatre and there were none left in the streams for them (or their sources) to notice and report upon. For Antigonus' logic to work, he must have supposed that the building of the theatre in the city of Cos preceded the writing of the book by Eudoxus to which he alludes. He therefore gives testimony for a theatre in Cos before 340 at the latest.

The city state of Cos was formed in 366, under a democratic constitution, by the synoe-cism of the previous settlements of Cos, Meropis and Astypalaia. The foundation, on a good harbour in the north-east corner of the island, was evidently designed to take full advantage of the flourishing north–south trade from the Black Sea to the Levant that ran along the coast of Asia Minor (Sherwin-White 1978, 225). If Antigonus was right in supposing that Eudoxus did not mention the travertine because it had already been removed for the theatre, then the theatre may have been part of the original design of the city or was at least built very soon after its foundation. The cult of Dionysus on Cos dates back at least to the synoecism (Paul 2013, 117–27). The earliest epigraphic evidence for the theatre comes from the late fourth century (306–301), but unfortunately in a massively reconstructed text, though Segre deemed his reconstructions 'sostanzialmente sicure' (1993, ED 71d A l. 5 = *IG* XII 4, 129, l. 71).

The first certain mention of the Coan theatre is 295–280, when money from the sale of priesthoods was diverted to the theatre, a clause that might be taken to suggest that some parts of it were still under construction (*IG* XII 4, 296, l. 24). A 'Dionysia' with competitions is attested from the same period (*IG* XII 4, 25, ll. 17–18) and later third-century inscriptions attest a full Dionysian programme with a parade, lyric choruses in the form of cyclic pyrrhiche, tragedy and comedy. Of particular interest is a fragmentary Dionysian victor list (*IG* XII 4, 451–2), of which survive the entries for 206/5–205/4 and ca. 190–180 (Ceccarelli 1995, 304, 305; Habicht 2004a, 64). They give evidence of a choregic system, overseen by an agonothete (Ceccarelli 1995; Wilson 2000, 289–90). In addition to choregoi for cyclic choruses and for tragedy, there were also competitions and choregoi for choruses of the Dionysian parade (*IG* XII 4, 451, ll. 6–7, with Ceccarelli 1995, 289, 291; Wilson 2000, 290). The victorious choruses are each named as belonging to one of the three traditional Doric tribes (Hylleis, Dumaneis, Pamphylloi) and we may suppose three for each category of competition. The fact that the lists name epimeletes, rather than choregoi, for comedy is odd but cannot be explained by the absence of a chorus or by exemption from the tribal organisation (Ceccarelli 1995, 290): *IG* XII 4, 452, ll. 60–2 reads 'the epimelete of the *komoidoi* of the tribe Hylleis', ἐπιμελητὰς κωμωιδῶν φυλᾶς Ὑλλέων, and it is very unlikely that *komoidoi* means 'comedy' rather than 'the comedians' (i.e. the comic chorus), especially as the proper term for 'comedy' follows immediately with reference to the victorious actor, ὑποκριτὰς κωμωιδίας (l. 63). The word order shows that it is the *komoidoi* who belong to the tribe, not necessarily the epimelete, and they could be nothing if not a chorus. Precisely this pattern is replicated in *IG* XII 4, 451, ll. 10–12. In addition to comic actors, the lists name victorious tragic actors. Tragedy continues to be performed at the Coan Dionysia until at least the first century (*IG* XII 4, 182, l. 12).

Another theatre, of Hellenistic date, has been excavated in the town of Astypalaia on the south end of the island (not to be confused with the island of Astypalaea, **Ev**) and in 1929 a further small theatre, probably of Roman date, was excavated at the foot of the acropolis of ancient Halasarna (Laurenzi 1931, 623–5).

Dv: Cythera. Aelian, *On the Nature of Animals* **11.19**. Written late 2nd or early 3rd c. AD. Pantakles was ephor in Sparta in 407 (X. *HG* 1.3.1, 2.3.10; Wilson 1999). Text: Hercher.

> χρῆται δὲ ἅμα ἐς τιμωρίαν τῶν ἀσεβῶν ἀνδρῶν ὑπηρέταις τοῖς ζῴοις ἡ Δίκη.
> καὶ τὸ μαρτύριον, Πανтακλῆς ὁ Λακεδαιμόνιος ἀναστείλας διὰ τῆς Σπάρτης
> ἐλθεῖν τοὺς ἐς Κύθηρα ἀπιόντας τῶν περὶ τὸν Διόνυσον τεχνιτῶν, εἶτα
> καθήμενος ἐν τῷ ἐφορείῳ ὑπὸ κυνῶν διεσπάσθη.

Justice at the same time uses animals as agents in the punishment of impious men. An indication of this is Pantakles the Lacedaemonian who prevented members of the Artists of Dionysus on their way to Cythera from passing through Sparta and then was torn apart by dogs while sitting on the ephor's throne.

Ripping apart by dogs is a stereotypical Dionysian punishment for any who offend Dionysus (and as 'poetic justice' for Dionysian poets: **VI Di 3**, **4**, **15**, **16**, **18**, **19**), and that may account for the presence of 'Artists of Dionysus' in this story, though the use of the term is certainly anachronistic in this passage. The text specifically imagines the destination of these performers to be Cythera, but there is no other evidence of theatrical activity there at this date. If this part of the story has any historicity, the performers may be using Cythera as an embarkation point to travel further east or west, though that is not the most natural inference from the text. Cythera did produce some famous musicians (Xenodamos in the seventh century, and the undated 'Alexander', Stefanis no. 105) and a choreut from the later third century (Stefanis no. 2308), but no known actors or poets.

Dvi: Delos

1. Thucydides, *History of the Peloponnesian War* 3.104. Referring to 426/5 and written soon after. The text of the *Homeric Hymn to Delian Apollo* (3.145–50, 165–72), as cited by Thucydides, is substantially different from the manuscripts of the *Hymn* and sometimes awkward Greek, though the differences do not affect his historical point. Text: Jones.

> τοῦ δ' αὐτοῦ χειμῶνος καὶ Δῆλον ἐκάθηραν Ἀθηναῖοι κατὰ χρησμὸν δή τινα. ἐκάθηρε μὲν γὰρ καὶ Πεισίστρατος ὁ τύραννος πρότερον αὐτήν, οὐχ ἅπασαν, ἀλλ' ὅσον ἀπὸ τοῦ ἱεροῦ ἐφεωρᾶτο τῆς νήσου· τότε δὲ πᾶσα ἐκαθάρθη τοιῷδε [104.2] τρόπῳ. θῆκαι ὅσαι ἦσαν τῶν τεθνεώτων ἐν Δήλῳ, πάσας ἀνεῖλον, καὶ τὸ λοιπὸν προεῖπον μήτε ἐναποθνήσκειν ἐν τῇ νήσῳ μήτε ἐντίκτειν, ἀλλ' ἐς τὴν Ῥήνειαν διακομίζεσθαι. ἀπέχει δὲ ἡ Ῥήνεια τῆς Δήλου οὕτως ὀλίγον ὥστε Πολυκράτης ὁ Σαμίων τύραννος ἰσχύσας τινὰ χρόνον ναυτικῷ καὶ τῶν τε ἄλλων νήσων ἄρξας καὶ τὴν Ῥήνειαν ἑλὼν ἀνέθηκε τῷ Ἀπόλλωνι τῷ Δηλίῳ ἁλύσει δήσας πρὸς τὴν Δῆλον. καὶ τὴν πεντετηρίδα τότε πρῶτον μετὰ τὴν κάθαρσιν [104.3] ἐποίησαν οἱ Ἀθηναῖοι τὰ Δήλια. ἦν δέ ποτε καὶ τὸ πάλαι μεγάλη ξύνοδος ἐς τὴν Δῆλον τῶν Ἰώνων τε καὶ περικτιόνων νησιωτῶν· ξύν τε γὰρ γυναιξὶ καὶ παισὶν ἐθεώρουν, ὥσπερ νῦν ἐς τὰ Ἐφέσια Ἴωνες, καὶ ἀγὼν ἐποιεῖτο αὐτόθι καὶ [104.4] γυμνικὸς καὶ μουσικός, χορούς τε ἀνῆγον αἱ πόλεις. δηλοῖ δὲ μάλιστα Ὅμηρος ὅτι τοιαῦτα ἦν ἐν τοῖς ἔπεσι τοῖσδε, ἅ ἐστιν ἐκ προοιμίου Ἀπόλλωνος·
>
>> ἀλλ' ὅτε Δήλῳ, Φοῖβε, μάλιστά γε θυμὸν ἐτέρφθης,
>> ἔνθα τοι ἑλκεχίτωνες Ἰάονες ἠγερέθονται
>> σὺν σφοῖσιν τεκέεσσι γυναιξί τε σὴν ἐς ἀγυιάν·
>> ἔνθα σε πυγμαχίῃ τε καὶ ὀρχηστυῖ καὶ ἀοιδῇ
>> μνησάμενοι τέρπουσιν, ὅταν καθέσωσιν ἀγῶνα.

[104.5] ὅτι δὲ καὶ μουσικῆς ἀγὼν ἦν καὶ ἀγωνιούμενοι ἐφοίτων ἐν τοῖσδε αὖ δηλοῖ,
ἅ ἐστιν ἐκ τοῦ αὐτοῦ προοιμίου· τὸν γὰρ Δηλιακὸν χορὸν τῶν γυναικῶν
ὑμνήσας ἐτελεύτα τοῦ ἐπαίνου ἐς τάδε τὰ ἔπη, ἐν οἷς καὶ ἑαυτοῦ ἐπεμνήσθη·

> ἀλλ᾽ ἄγεθ᾽, ἱλήκοι μὲν Ἀπόλλων Ἀρτέμιδι ξύν,
> χαίρετε δ᾽ ὑμεῖς πᾶσαι. ἐμεῖο δὲ καὶ μετόπισθε
> μνήσασθ᾽, ὁππότε κέν τις ἐπιχθονίων ἀνθρώπων
> ἐνθάδ᾽ ἀνείρηται ταλαπείριος ἄλλος ἐπελθών·
> ᾽ὦ κοῦραι, τίς δ᾽ ὔμμιν ἀνὴρ ἥδιστος ἀοιδῶν
> ἐνθάδε πωλεῖται, καὶ τέῳ τέρπεσθε μάλιστα;᾽
> ὑμεῖς δ᾽ εὖ μάλα πᾶσαι ὑποκρίνασθαι ἀφήμως·
> ᾽τυφλὸς ἀνήρ, οἰκεῖ δὲ Χίῳ ἔνι παιπαλοέσσῃ.᾽

[104.6] τοσαῦτα μὲν Ὅμηρος ἐτεκμηρίωσεν ὅτι ἦν καὶ τὸ πάλαι μεγάλη ξύνοδος
καὶ ἑορτὴ ἐν τῇ Δήλῳ· ὕστερον δὲ τοὺς μὲν χοροὺς οἱ νησιῶται καὶ οἱ Ἀθηναῖοι
μεθ᾽ ἱερῶν ἔπεμπον, τὰ δὲ περὶ τοὺς ἀγῶνας καὶ τὰ πλεῖστα κατελύθη ὑπὸ
ξυμφορῶν, ὡς εἰκός, πρὶν δὴ οἱ Ἀθηναῖοι τότε τὸν ἀγῶνα ἐποίησαν καὶ
ἱπποδρομίας, ὃ πρότερον οὐκ ἦν.

During the same winter (426/5) the Athenians purified Delos, no doubt in response to an oracle. Pisistratus the tyrant had previously purified the island
(ca. 543), though not all, but only the part of the island that is visible from
the sanctuary. At this time (426/5) the entire island was purified in this [104.2]
way. They removed the graves of all those who had died on Delos and they
proclaimed that no one was to die on the island nor give birth there, but be
taken to Rheneia. Rheneia is so close to Delos that Polycrates (ca. 523: West
1999b, 369–70 n. 17), the tyrant of Samos, who for some time had a powerful
navy and ruled the other islands, seized Rheneia, connected it to Delos with
a chain, and dedicated it to Delian Apollo. And the Athenians after the purification at this time (426/5) first [104.3] created the quadrennial festival called the
Delia. There was also once a long time ago a great gathering of the Ionians and
the neighbouring islanders in Delos. They travelled to the festival with their
wives and children, just as the Ionians do now at the Ephesia, and at that time
they also had both an [104.4] athletic and a musical contest, and the cities brought
along choruses. Homer especially shows that this was the case in these verses
that come from the proemium to Apollo: 'And when in Delos, Phoebus, you
feel delight in your heart most of all, then the Ionians with their trailing robes
are wont to gather with their children and wives into your broad street, when by
boxing, dance and song with you in mind they bring delight, whenever they set
up a competition.' [104.5] That there was also a musical competition and that they
kept coming with the intention of competing he once more makes clear in the
following verses from the same proemium. After singing a hymn to the Delian
chorus of the women he concludes his praises in these verses in which he also
mentions himself: 'But come, and may Apollo along with Artemis look kindly
upon you, and greetings to you (maidens) all. Remember me also in the future,

whenever any other man from among those who wander the earth, coming here travel-wearied, should ask "O maidens, who in your opinion is the most pleasant of all bards who have wandered here and in whom do you most delight?", then you, without naming names (?, see Burkert 1979, 61), all answer decisively: "The blind man, he who lives in rocky Chios".' [104.6] So much for the evidence Homer gives that in ancient times there was also a gathering and festival in Delos. Later the islanders and the Athenians kept sending their choruses along with sacrifices. But the competitions and most other things were discontinued doubtless because of misfortunes, until the Athenians at this time made a competition, including a horse (chariot) race which did not previously exist.

2. Dedication of the Athenian *Archetheoroi* at Delos, 426/5 (dated by reference to first penteteric festival, cf. **1**).

Two non-joining fragments of the upper part of a stele of white marble.
Fr. α: 0.24 × 0.16 × 0.09 m. Fr. β: 0.33 × 0.155 × 0.09 m.
Fr. α: broken on all sides, except for a small patch on top. Fr. β: preserves the upper right corner. Raised band above text. Back rough-picked.
Delos Museum A 1185 α, β.
Fr. α was perhaps found during excavations in the sanctuary of Apollo in 1887 (Homolle 1887, 410 no. 2). Fr. β found 16 July 1903 during excavations in a modern wall at the level of the Stoa of Philip at Delos.
Durrbach and Jardé 1905, no. 73; *ID* 43; Coupry 1954, 285–7; *IG* I³ 1468; Chankowski 2008, 92.
Text: *IG* I³ 1468.   Photo: Coupry 1954, 287 fig.1.

	α	β
	[οἵδε τῆς πρ]ώτης [πεντε]τηρίδος	non-stoich.
	[αἱρεθέντε]ς ἀρχε[θέωρ]οι ἀνέθεσ-	
	[αν τῶι Ἀπ]όλλωνι *vacat*	
	[—ᶜ·⁵— Πλ]ωθειεύς *vacat*	
5	[—ᶜ·⁵— -]ης ἐξ Οἴο *vacat*	
	[—ᶜ·⁵— -]χος Κυδαθ[ηναιε]ύς *vacat*	
	[—ᶜ·⁵—]Μελιτεύ[ς] *vacat*	
	[—ᶜ·⁵— -]έων Ἐλε[υσίνιος] *vacat*	
	[—ᶜ·⁵—]ατο[—⁹ ᵛᵉˡ ᵐⁱⁿ·—] *vacat*	
10	*vacat?*	

These men [chose]n as *arche[theor]oi* [of the fi]rst [quad]rennial embassy made this ded[ication to Ap]ollo: [… of Pl]otheia, […-]es of Oion, […-]chos of Kydath[ena]ion, […] of Melite, […-]eon of Ele[usis, …]ato[…]

3. Plutarch, *Life of Nicias* 3.5. Written ca. 114 AD (Angeli Bertinelli 1993, xxviii), and referring to an embassy that took place some time after 426 and no later than 415 when Nicias went on campaign to Sicily, where he died in 413: possible dates therefore, since the mention of a chorus indicates the penteteric Delia, are 425, 421 or 417. But Nicias,

who was of the deme Kydantidai, does not appear in **2**, eliminating 425. 417 makes better sense of Plutarch's claim that before Nicias, the choruses were disorganised, assuming this refers to the Delia: Hornblower 1991, 518. Chankowski (2008, 94) argues for 421, making the occasion the Peace of Nicias (cf. Plu. *Mor.* 724b which mentions a palm dedicated by Athens in commemoration of the Battle of Eurymedon). The statue known as the 'Colossus of the Naxians', mentioned by Plutarch, was a nine-metre image of Apollo, dedicated in the early sixth century, whose inscribed marble base, weighing about 32 tons, still sits by the Oikos of the Naxians. The base of the palm tree also survives. For the remains and their relation to the date of Nicias' embassy, see Bruneau 1995, 55–9. Text: Ziegler.

μνημονεύεται δ᾽ αὐτοῦ καὶ τὰ περὶ Δῆλον ὡς λαμπρὰ καὶ θεοπρεπῆ φιλοτιμήματα. τῶν γὰρ χορῶν, οὓς αἱ πόλεις ἔπεμπον ᾀσομένους τῷ θεῷ, προσπλεόντων μὲν ὡς ἔτυχεν, εὐθὺς δ᾽ ὄχλου πρὸς τὴν ναῦν [3.5.5] ἀπαντῶντος ᾄδειν κελευομένων κατ᾽ οὐδένα κόσμον, ἀλλ᾽ ὑπὸ σπουδῆς ἀσυντάκτως ἀποβαινόντων ἅμα καὶ στεφανουμένων καὶ μεταμφιεννυμένων, ἐκεῖνος ὅτε τὴν θεωρίαν ἦγεν, αὐτὸς μὲν εἰς Ῥήνειαν ἀπέβη, τὸν χορὸν ἔχων καὶ τὰ ἱερεῖα καὶ τὴν ἄλλην παρασκευήν, ζεῦγμα δὲ πεποιημένον [3.5.10] Ἀθήνησι πρὸς τὰ μέτρα καὶ κεκοσμημένον ἐκπρεπῶς χρυσώσεσι καὶ βαφαῖς καὶ στεφάνοις καὶ αὐλαίαις κομίζων, διὰ νυκτὸς ἐγεφύρωσε τὸν μεταξὺ Ῥηνείας καὶ [3.6.1] Δήλου πόρον, οὐκ ὄντα μέγαν· εἶθ᾽ ἅμ᾽ ἡμέρᾳ τήν τε πομπὴν τῷ θεῷ καὶ τὸν χορὸν ἄγων κεκοσμημένον πολυτελῶς [3.7.1] καὶ ᾄδοντα διὰ τῆς γεφύρας ἀπεβίβαζε. μετὰ δὲ τὴν θυσίαν καὶ τὸν ἀγῶνα καὶ τὰς ἑστιάσεις τόν τε φοίνικα τὸν χαλκοῦν ἔστησεν ἀνάθημα τῷ θεῷ, καὶ χωρίον μυρίων δραχμῶν πριάμενος καθιέρωσεν, οὗ τὰς προσόδους ἔδει [3.7.5] Δηλίους καταθύοντας ἑστιᾶσθαι, πολλὰ καὶ ἀγαθὰ Νικίᾳ παρὰ τῶν θεῶν αἰτουμένους· καὶ γὰρ τοῦτο τῇ στήλῃ <συν>ενέγραψεν. ἣν ὥσπερ φύλακα τῆς δωρεᾶς ἐν Δήλῳ κατέλιπεν. [3.8.1] ὁ δὲ φοῖνιξ ἐκεῖνος ὑπὸ τῶν πνευμάτων ἀποκλασθεὶς ἐνέπεσε τῷ Ναξίων ἀνδριάντι τῷ μεγάλῳ καὶ ἀνέτρεψε.

3.7.6–7 ἐνέγραψεν codd.   <συν>ενέγραψεν Kron.

Nicias' expenditures for Delos are also noted as brilliant and sure to please the god. The choruses that the cities used to send to sing for the god would put into harbour anyway they could. Great crowds would [3.5.5] greet the ships and ask the choruses to sing, not in any proper order, but tumultuously as they hurried to disembark while at the same time trying to tie on their garlands and put on their cloaks. But when he (Nicias) led the festival embassy, he disembarked with the chorus, the sacrificial animals, and the equipment at Rheneia. He brought along a bridge [3.5.10] that he had made to measure in Athens, magnificently fitted with gilding, colourful banners, garlands and tapestries, and during the night used it to link the strait between Rheneia and [3.6.1] Delos, which is not very wide. At dawn he led his chorus, lavishly costumed [3.7.1] and singing in procession for the god along the causeway and onto the island. After the sacrifice, the competition, and the banqueting, he erected the bronze palm tree as a dedication to the god, and he consecrated a tract of land that he purchased for ten thousand drachmas, stipulating that the revenues [3.7.5] were to serve as a contribution to the banquets of the Delians when they made sacrifice and called many blessings upon Nicias from the gods. And indeed this was written into the stele which he left on Delos as guardian of his benefaction. [3.8.1] That palm tree was blown down by the wind and fell upon the large statue dedicated by the Naxians and knocked it over.

4. **Xenophon, *Memorabila* 3.3.12–13**. Probably completed in the 350s with a dramatic date anywhere ca. 415–401. Though there are other possibilities for Athenian choruses performing on Delos (Rutherford 2004, 82–3; Rutherford 2013a, 305), the supplied 'the' in 'the chorus sent to Delos' presumably specifies the most important, namely the chorus for the Delia, and the context of choral rivalry would naturally suggest that festival's prize competition. In this passage Socrates speaks with a young man who has been chosen cavalry commander. He tries to establish that Athenians are superior performers because of their love of honour (*philotimia*). Text: Marchant.

> ἢ τόδε οὐκ ἐντεθύμησαι, ὡς, ὅταν γε χορὸς εἷς ἐκ τῆσδε τῆς πόλεως γίγνηται, ὥσπερ <ὁ> εἰς Δῆλον πεμπόμενος, οὐδεὶς ἄλλοθεν οὐδαμόθεν τούτῳ ἐφάμιλλος γίγνεται οὐδὲ εὐανδρία ἐν ἄλλῃ [3.13] πόλει ὁμοία τῇ ἐνθάδε συνάγεται;

> Or have you not considered the fact that whenever this city (Athens) produces a single chorus, such as <the> chorus sent to Delos, no other chorus from any other place can rival it, nor can any other [3.13] city assemble a display of manly excellence like that here?

5. **Acts of the Amphictyons of Athens (Sandwich Marble)**, accounting for the period from the start of 377/6 to the penultimate month, Thargelion, of 375/4, with the relevant expenses relating to the tenth penteteric festival of the Delia in 374 (Chankowski 2008, 110, 194).

Two fragments of an opisthographic stele of white marble.
a: 0.80 × 0.55 × 0.09 m; b: 0.72 × 0.36 × 0.09 m.
Fr. a was copied by A. Fourmont in Athens in the church of Ayios Elias before being brought to England. Fr. b was found near the Illisos in the vicinity of the Python.
Fr. a (covering lines 1–40 on Face A and 1–41 on Face B) is in the library of Trinity College, Cambridge. Fr. b (lines 41–111 on Face A and 42–53 on Face B): Epigraphical Museum, Athens, inv. 8022 a.
ID 98, Face A, frr. a–b, ll. 31–49; Prêtre 2002, 29–37; R-O II no. 28; Chankowski 2008, 417–20, no. 13A.
Text: Chankowski.

mostly stoich.

Aa 31 λήμματος κεφάλαιον ⌐ΤΤΤΧΧΧΧ⌐ΗΔΔΔΔΗΗΗΙΙϹ. ἀπὸ τότο
　　　　τάδε ἀνηλώθη· στέφανος ἀριστεῖον τῶι θεῶι καὶ τῶι ἐργασαμένω-
　　　　ι μισθός, ΧⲚ· τρίποδες νικητήρια τοῖς χοροῖς καὶ τῶι ἐργασαμέν-
　　　　ωι μισθός, Χ.· ἀρχεθεώροις Τ· εἰς κομιδὴν τῶν θεωρῶν καὶ τῶν χορῶ-

35 [ν] Ἀντιμάχωι Φίλωνος Ἑρμείωι τριηράρχωι ΤΧ. ἀριθμὸς βοῶν τῶν ε-
   [ἰς τὴ]ν ἑορτὴν ὠνηθέντων ΗΓΙΙΙΙ, τιμὴ τότων ΤΧΧΗΗΗΗΔΓΗΗΗ· πέταλ-
   [α χρυσ]ᾶ καὶ χρυσωτεῖ μισθός, ΗΔΔΓͰ· εἰς τὰ προθύματα τῆς ἑορτῆς
   [...· κομ]ιδὴ τῶν τριπόδων καὶ τῶν βοῶν [κα]ὶ πεντηκοστὴ καὶ τρο[φὴ]
   [τοῖς βοσ]ὶ καὶ ξύλων τιμὴ τῶν ἐπὶ τ[........¹⁶........ω]ν τιμ[ὴ ..]
40 [....⁸....] καταλλα[γὴ? — — — — — — — — — — — — — — — — —]
   [..............³¹................]Σ
Ab [..............²⁹................]ΣΑ
   [..............²⁹................]ΝΝΕ
   [..............²⁸................] κυλι[κ?—]
45 [........¹⁵.......]ΚΑ[......¹¹.....]ΑΛΑΙ
   [.......¹⁴........]ΑΙ[.....¹²......]ΙΗΡΑ
   [.....¹⁰.....]ς καὶ ΕΙ[......¹²......] τῶι χ —
   [.....⁹....]ι τὸν πελα[νὸν καὶ τὰ?] χορεῖα Τ — — — —

Total income: 8 talants, 4,644 drachmas, 2½ obols (52,644 drachmas, 2½
obols). From this the following was spent: for the crown, prize of excellence
for the god, and pay to the man who made it, payment 1,500 drachmas; for the
tripods that are victory prizes for the choruses, and pay to the man who made
them 1,000 (plus another lost figure representing a sum up to another 1,000)
drachmas; for the *archetheoroi* (leaders of the Athenian embassy: see below),
payment 1 talant (6,000 drachmas); for the transport of the *theoroi* (members
of the embassy) and the choruses [35] to the trierarch, Antimachos, son of Philon,
of Hermeios 1 talant, 1,000 drachmas (7,000 drachmas); the number of cattle
bought for the festival 109 (both Prêtre 2002, 33 and R-O II, 137 translate
'154', but see Coupry 1954, 290; R-O II, 145), their cost one talant 2,419
drachmas (8,419 drachmas); for the [gold l]eaves and pay to the gilder 126
drachmas; for the preliminary sacrifices at the festival [... trans]port of the
tripods and the cattle, [an]d the two-percent (export) tax, and fod[der for the
cattl]e, and the cost of wood for [((the altars?) ...] co[st [40] ...] exchan[ge] (the
following lines are too fragmentary to permit translation) [...[48] ...] the cak[e
and the equipment] for the choruses [...]

6. Aristotle, *Athenian Constitution* 56.3–4, written ca. 330. Aristotle discusses the duties of
the Archon Eponymous. Note that the responsibilities for Delos relate to two separate festivals (Chankowski 2008, 88, 93): the choregoi are for the Delia (they travel in a trireme
with a plurality of *archetheoroi*: cf. **2**) and the *archetheoros* (n.b. singular – there is no
room for Torr's supplement on the papyrus) and young men are for the Theseia, a separate
ritual commemoration of Theseus' visit to Delos (and they travel in a triakonter said to be
the same as the one Theseus himself travelled in). The word for 'youths' is an archaic one
that likely alludes to the traditional language of the myth of Theseus. Text: Oppermann.

κατίστησι δὲ καὶ εἰς Δῆλον χορηγοὺς καὶ ἀρχ[ι]θέω[ρον τ]ῷ τριακοντορίῳ
τῷ τοὺς ⁵⁶·⁴ ἠθέους ἄγοντι.

ἀρχ[ι]θέω[ρον] Lipsius   ἀρχ[ι]θέω[ρους] Torr

He also appoints choregoi for Delos and an arch[e]theo[ros] for [t]he triakonter which takes the youths.

7. Accounts of the *hieropoioi* with the earliest reference to the building of the theatre, 308–306 (letter forms, prosopography, lease variations). This is the earliest of many accounts recording expenditures on the Delian theatre and the only one likely to belong to the 4th c. For the others, see Fraisse and Moretti 2007, 155–202. The *hieropoioi* were overseers of the treasury of Apollo. They were assisted by a board, or several boards, of supervisors (*epimeletai*) who remained in office until the particular project, or projects, to which they were assigned was complete. Practical and technical issues relating to construction were the responsibility of an employee of the sanctuary, named the architekton (cf. **Aviii**; **I Bvi**), who held office for an indefinite period (Lacroix 1914; Vial 1984, 228–9). He seems to have combined the responsibilities of general manager, co-ordinator, foreman, critical-path programmer, building inspector, and possibly also designer. At the end of their term in office the *hieropoioi* published accounts, recording the sanctuary's income and expenses. The building accounts here, as at the Asclepieion at Epidaurus, are mainly concerned to list the jobs, the contractors, their guarantors, and monies paid. This series of accounts allows detailed glimpses of the construction phases of the Delian theatre over a period of one hundred and fifty years.

White marble block.
0.77 × 0.5 × 0.55 m.
Broken above and below, much damaged on surface, especially after line 20, but with right and left sides preserved.
Excavated in October 1907 from the northern part of the Agora of Theophrastos on Delos.
Durrbach 1911, 23–34, no. 6; *IG* XI 2, 142; Fraisse and Moretti 2007, 157–9.
Delos Museum inv. Γ 237.
IG XI 2, 142, ll. 22–48 with additions from Fraisse and Moretti 2007, 157.

ἀπὸ τούτου τάσδε δόσ[εις ἔδομεν —ca.18—]ΣΙΩΝΜΑΧ[......]
    ΝΑΡΧ . ΥΟΕ.[......] Στράτωνος
ἀρχιτέκτονος Καλλισθένους παρούσης [βουλῆς καὶ τῶ]ν γραμμ[ατέων —ca.12—
    ]ΚΑ [— ca.11 —]ΘΟΥΚΛΙ[...]Σ
τὴν ὀροφὴν ἐ[γλ]αβό[ντι ...]ΑΝΕ[..]ΟΥΤ[—ca.11—] Ἀπόλλωνος [—ca.13—
    Σμ]ερδ[ί]ωι τῷ[ι Λη]μνίω<ι> ἐγλαβόντ[ι....]
25 οἰκοδομῆσ[α]ι [τ.]ν ἐν τ[ῶι] Ἀσκληπιείω[ι ....]εξω[— —]Α[— — — —
    — — —] ΠΟΔ[..]ΧΩΙ τὴμ πρ[ώτην]
ἐδώκαμεν δόσιν · Δ[ΔΔ]ΓΗΗΗ[— — — — — — — — — — — —Α— — —
    ]ΟΝΗ · κε[λευ]όντων ἐπιστατ[ῶν]
καὶ [ἀρχιτέκτ]ονος· μι[σ]θωτοῖς τὰ ξύλα [ἐν]έγκα[σι —ca.22–4—]ΡΕΑ τὴν
    εἴσο[δον τὴ]ν τοῦ θεάτρου
[ἐ]δώ[κ]αμεν ·ΔΔΔΔ· τῶι τοὺς οἴκους [........]ΚΡΟ [— — — — — — —
    — — — — — —] μόλυ[βδ]ον. ΔΔΓ [κ]ελε[ύ]-

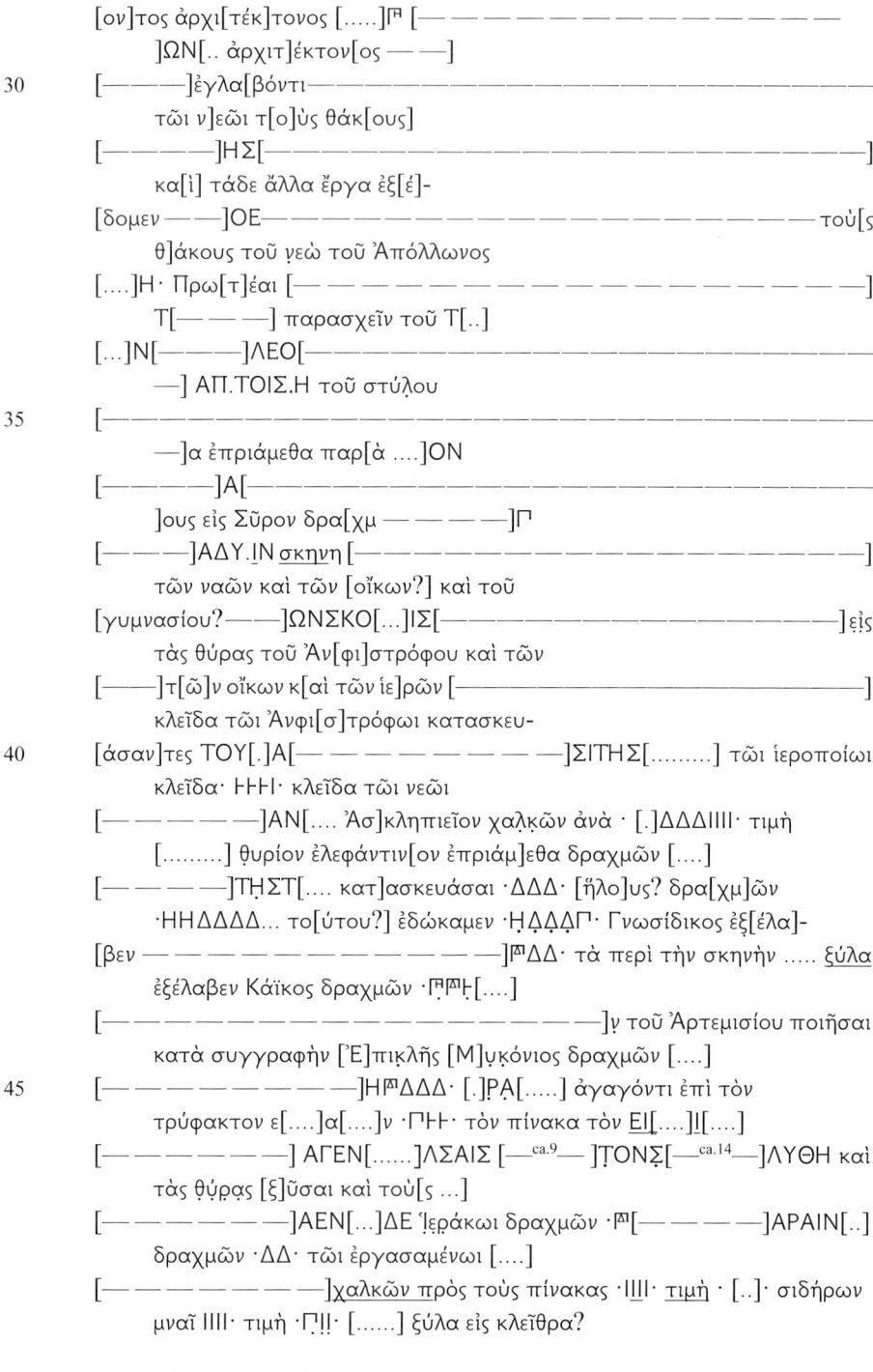

[ον]τος ἀρχι[τέκ]τονος [.....]⌐ [— — — — — — — — — — — — —

]ΩΝ[.. ἀρχιτ]έκτον[ος — —]

30 [— — — —]ἐγλα[βόντι— — — — — — — — — — — — — — — — — —

τῶι ν]εῶι τ[ο]ὺς θάκ[ους]

[— — — —]ΗΣ[— —]

κα[ὶ] τάδε ἄλλα ἔργα ἐξ[έ]-

[δομεν — — —]ΟΕ— — — — — — — — — — — — — — — — —τοὺ[ς

θ]άκους τοῦ νεὼ τοῦ Ἀπόλλωνος

[....]Η · Πρω[τ]έαι [— — — — — — — — — — — — — — — — — —]

Τ[— — —] παρασχεῖν τοῦ Τ[..]

[...]Ν[— — — — —]ΛΕΟ[— — — — — — — — — — — — — — — — —

—] ΑΠ.ΤΟΙΣ.Η τοῦ στύλου

35 [— —

—]α ἐπριάμεθα παρ[ὰ ....]ΟΝ

[— — — —]Α[— —

]ους εἰς Σῦρον δρα[χμ — — — —]⌐

[— — —]ΑΔΥ.ΙΝ σκηνη [— — — — — — — — — — — — — — — —]

τῶν ναῶν καὶ τῶν [οἴκων?] καὶ τοῦ

[γυμνασίου?— —]ΩΝΣΚΟ[...]ΙΣ[— — — — — — — — — — —]εἰς

τὰς θύρας τοῦ Ἀν[φι]στρόφου καὶ τῶν

[— —]τ[ῶ]ν οἴκων κ[αὶ τῶν ἱε]ρῶν [— — — — — — — — — —]

κλεῖδα τῶι Ἀνφι[σ]τρόφωι κατασκευ-

40 [άσαν]τες ΤΟΥ[.]Α[— — — — — — — —]ΣΙΤΗΣ[.........] τῶι ἱεροποίωι

κλεῖδα· ⊢⊢⊢· κλεῖδα τῶι νεῶι

[— — — — — —]ΑΝ[.... Ἀσ]κληπιεῖον χαλκῶν ἀνὰ · [.]ΔΔΔΙΙΙΙ· τιμή

[.........] θυρίον ἐλεφάντιν[ον ἐπριάμ]εθα δραχμῶν [....]

[— — — —]ΤΗΣΤ[.... κατ]ασκευάσαι ·ΔΔΔ· [ἥλο]υς? δρα[χμ]ῶν

·ΗΗΔΔΔΔ... το[ύτου?] ἐδώκαμεν ·ΗΔΔΔΓ· Γνωσίδικος ἐξ[έλα]-

[βεν — — — — — — — — — — —]⌐ΜΔΔ· τὰ περὶ τὴν σκηνὴν ..... ξύλα

ἐξέλαβεν Κάϊκος δραχμῶν ·⌐Μ⌐Μⱶ[....]

[— — — — — — — — — — — — — — — —]ν τοῦ Ἀρτεμισίου ποιῆσαι

κατὰ συγγραφὴν [Ἐ]πικλῆς [Μ]υκόνιος δραχμῶν [....]

45 [— — — — — — — —]Η⌐ΜΔΔΔ· [.]ΡΑ[.....] ἀγαγόντι ἐπὶ τὸν

τρύφακτον ε[....]α[....]ν ·⌐ⱶⱶ· τὸν πίνακα τὸν ΕΙ[....]Ι[....]

[— — — — — —] ΑΓΕΝ[......]ΛΣΑΙΣ [—ca.9—]ΤΟΝΣ[—ca.14—]ΛΥΘΗ καὶ

τὰς θύρας [ξ]ῦσαι καὶ τοὺ[ς ...]

[— — — — — —]ΑΕΝ[...]ΔΕ Ἱεράκωι δραχμῶν ·⌐Μ[— — — —]ΑΡΑΙΝ[..]

δραχμῶν ·ΔΔ· τῶι ἐργασαμένωι [....]

[— — — — — —]χαλκῶν πρὸς τοὺς πίνακας ·ΙΙΙΙ· τιμὴ · [..]· σιδήρων

μναῖ ΙΙΙΙ· τιμή ·⌐ΙΙ· [......] ξύλα εἰς κλεῖθρα?

27 'Pour les dimensions de la lacune, μι[σ]θωτοῖς τὰ ξύλα [ἐν]έγκα[σι εἰς τὸ θέατρον καὶ
ἐργασαμένοις] τὴν εἴσο[δον] conviendrait': Fraisse & Moretti   43 e.g. [ἐλάτινα] ξύλα

Fraisse & Moretti   45 ἐ[λεφ]α[ντινὴ]ν ? Hiller   45 conceivably τὸν πίνακα τὸν εἰ[ς
τὸ] τ[ροσκήνιον] Fraisse & Moretti (cf. *IG* XI 158 A lλ. 67–8).

From this sum [we made] the following expendit[ures …] Straton, son of
Kallisthenes the architekton in the presence of [the Council and th]e Secret[aries
…] to the c[on]tract[or (who …)] the roof […] of Apollo […] to [Sm]erd[i]os
th[e Le]mnian who contract[ed …] ²⁵ to buil[d th]e […] in the Asklepieio[n
…] we gave the fi[rst] instalment: 39 (+ ?) drachmas […] according to the
ins[truct]ions of the overse[ers] and the [architekt]on. To the hi[r]ed men who
broug[ht] the wood (into the theatre and built ?) the entrance[way] (paro[dos])
of the theatre we [g]a[v]e: 40 drachmas. To the man [who …] the buildings
[…] le[a]d: 25 drachmas on the [o]rde[rs] of the archi[tek]ton […] : 500 drachmas [… the archit]ekton [… ³⁰ …] who contr[acted … for the te]mple t[he]
benc[hes …] an[d] these other works [we] pa[id out …] th[e b]enches of the
temple of Apollo […]. To Proteas […] to provide […] of the […] of the column
³⁵ […] we bought from […] for Syros (:? and) five drachmas […] skene […]
of the temple and of the [buildings] and of the [gymnasium? …] for the doors
of the Amphistrophon and of the […] of t[h]e buildings a[nd of the sanc]tuar-
ies […] those who made the key for the Anti[s]trophon ⁴⁰ […] the key for the
hieropoios: 3 drachmas, 1 obol. The key for the temple [… As]klepieion: 43
(?) chalks per item: total price […] we [bought an] ivor[y] door for ? drachmas
[…] to [fur]nish: 30 drachmas. [Nai]ls?: 240(+ ?) dra[ch]mas [… for] th[is] we
gave: 135 drachmas. Gnosidikos [took] out the contract […] (something and ?)
70 drachmas. Kaikos took the contract for the (e.g. silver-fir) wood related to
the skene (or 'around the skene'): 551(+ ?) drachmas [… E]pikles of Myconos
(took the contract) to make the ? of the Artemision in accordance with the
specifications [… ⁴⁵ …]: (something and ?) 153 drachmas […] who brought the
? for the railing […]: 7 drachmas. The *pinax* (for the proskenion ??) […] and
finish the doors and th[e …] to Hierax: 50(+ ?) drachmas […]: 20 drachmas. To
the man who worked the […] of bronze for the pinakes: 4 : cost: […] of iron:
4 mnai: cost: 7. […] wood for bolts (?)

8. Accounts of the *hieropoioi* recording costs for the phallic procession of the Dionysia.
Month of Galaxion, 304? (Durrbach 1911, 21–3; Bruneau 1970, 312; letter forms,
prosopography, monetary symbol for talant).

Three joining fragments of a stele of bluish marble, inscribed on front, back and right side.
1.23 × 0.43 × 0.10 m.
Surface damage on both sides and cut in two places.
Two fragments found on 12 July 1905 near the Agora of the Compitaliastae, where they served
as threshold blocks for the Roman baths and the third fragment found on 31 July of the same year
built into a wall close by.
Delos, Museum inv. Γ 503, Α-Γ.
Schulhof 1908, 13–46 no. 3; *IG* XI 2, 144.
Text: *IG* XI 2, 144A, ll. 33–6.

μη[νὸ]ς Γαλαξιῶνος· ἐλαίου χοῦς ΗΗΗΙΙΙ·   τῶι Διονύσωι ἄγαλμα παρ᾽
    Ἀναξιθέμιδος Γ· Καΐκωι

ἐργασαμένωι ΓΗ· ξύλα εἰς τὸ φαλλαγωγεῖον παρ᾽ Εὐδιδάκτου ΓΗΗ· ποιήσαντι
    Καΐκωι τ[ὸ]

35   [φ]αλλαγωγεῖον Γ· Ναννάκωι γράψαντι τὸ ἄγαλμα ΔΗΗ· Καΐκωι στήσαντι τὸ
    ἄγαλμα καὶ

[ἀλεί]ψαντι ΗΗ· ἧλοι εἰς τὸ φαλλαγωγεῖον καὶ εἰς τὸ<μ> φαλλὸν ҺΙΙΙ· εἰς τὰ
    ἄ[λ]λα τὰ περὶ τὸ ἄγαλμα ΔΗΗ·

Month of Galaxion. A chous of oil: 4 drachmas, 3 obols; the icon (or 'image')
for Dionysus from Anaxithemis: 5 drachmas; to Kaikos who worked it: 6 drachmas; wood for the phallos-wagon from Eudidaktos: 8 drachmas; to Kaikos who
made t[he [35] ph]allos-wagon: 5 drachmas; to Nannakos who painted the icon
(or 'image'): 12 drachmas; to Kaikos who set up the statue and [put pla]ster on
it: 2 drachmas; bolts for the phallos-wagon and for th[e] phallos: 1 drachma, 3
obols; for the o[th]er expenditures on the icon (or 'image'): 12 drachmas.

9. Choregic dedication by Karystios, end of 4[th]–beginning of 3[rd] c. (letter forms and style
of relief). The stone phallos placed atop the base does not originally belong to it (see
below).

Rectangular marble base, probably for a votive statue, possibly of Dionysus.
1.29 × 0.53 × 0.405 m.
The Dionysus mentioned in *IG* XI 2, 219 A, l. 20 (272 or 271) and the Dionysus mentioned in
Bruneau 1970, 305, may refer to a statue of Dionysus that stood on this base (Moretti and Fincker
2008, 129, 135). The base is rough-picked at the back, with reliefs on the front and both sides. The
front shows a crowing cock with a phallic head (see further below). On the right side, a beardless
and, apart from a chlaina, naked Dionysus (centre) walks briskly between a satyr on his right and
a maenad with thyrsus on his left. He raises his right arm in the direction of the group's movement
and his left arm rests on the shoulder of the maenad who also has her right arm around the god's
neck. The bald and bearded satyr carries a krater in his left arm and raises his right arm straight
up 'dans un geste d'acclamation' (Bizard and Leroux 1907, 506). The left side is more heavily
damaged. Here Dionysus, right, walks forward with a maenad, who wears only a chiton, his left
hand holding her left hand and his right arm around her waist. In the maenad's right hand is a now
indistinct object. They are followed by a shorter figure with goat feet, presumably a Pan.
Found on the east side of the 'Rue du Péribole' or 'Rue de l'Est' that borders the peribolos wall
of the Sanctuary of Apollo at Delos. The votive was added to the south-east corner of a platform
(7.5 × 3.2 m), probably for an altar of Dionysus, ca. 280 (Bruneau and Ducat 2005, 256 no. 81;
Moretti and Fincker 2008).
Found in 1904 during the excavation of the altar.
In situ. The marble phallos that presently sits atop the base was found elsewhere on the site in
1886 and set upon the base by a Mr Stavropoullos (Bizard 1907, 499–500).
Bizard and Leroux 1907, 504–11; *IG* XI 4, 1148.

πᾶσι χορηγήσας καὶ νικήσας, Διονύσωι
εὐξάμενός με ἀνέθηκε Καρύστιος Ἀσβήλου παῖς.

πᾶσι stone   πα<ι>σὶ Wilhelm, Ieranò

He served as choregos for all (or reading with Wilhelm 'for boys') and won;
to Dionysus he dedicated me in fulfilment of his promise, Karystios, the son
of Asbelos.

10. Choregic dedication of Kritodemos, 300–250 (letter forms).

White marble votive choregic monument base.
1.00 × 0.40 × 0.35 m (Bruneau 1970, 318 n. 4).
Oval hole cut in top surface.
Reused in the 1st c. or later (Bruneau 1970, 318).
Found in 1882 in the north-east part of the Reservoir.
Delos Museum inv. E 500.
Reinach 1883, 370–1 no. 20; *IG* XI 4, 1149; Bruneau 1970, 318: Bruneau 1970, pl. 2.5 (detail).

πάντα χορηγήσας Πρεπεφύ[λ]ου π[α]ῖς Κριτόδημ[ος]
π[ά]ν[τ]α [δ]ὲ ν[ικ]ήσας Δι[ο]ν[ύσωι] τό[νδ]ε ἀν[έ]θ[η]κ[εν].

Kritodem[os], the s[o]n of Prepephy[l]os was choregos for all the contests,
[an]d w[in]ning a[l]l he de[d]i[c]a[ted] th[is to] Di[o]n[ysus]

11. Decree of Nesiotic League creating festival in honour of Demetrius, 306 or soon
after (prosopography), assuming that the reference is to Antigonus I and Demetrius the
Besieger; but Meadows (2013) argues that the Demetrius and Antigonus are Demetrius
II and Antigonus Gonatas, a position initially supported by Durrbach (1904), and that
the date is ca. 257 (Meadows' arguments are not accepted by Buraselis 2013, 175). The
League of Islanders, on the traditional view, was a confederacy of Cycladic islands,
set up ca. 314 as a protectorate by Antigonus and his son and co-regent Demetrius the
Besieger.

White marble stele.
1.02 × 0.54 × 0.175 m.
Cut on top and hollowed along the entire left side.
Found Sept. 1902 in the Baths where it was used as a threshold block.
Durrbach 1904, no. 1; Durrbach 1921–1923, no. 13.
Delos Museum inv. Δ 419.
Text: after *IG* XI 4, 1036 + *SEG* 15, 494.   Photo: Durrbach 1904, pl. 8.

```
         [— — — — διατελ]ε[ῖ] τ[ο]ὺς Ἕλληνας· [τιμῆσαι]
         [μὲν τὸ κοινὸν τῶν] νησιωτῶν ἀξίως κατὰ δύναμιν
         [Δημήτριον] ταῖς [πρεπ]ούσαις αὐτῶι τιμαῖς· ποῆ-
         [σαι δὲ αὐτοὺς ἐν] Δήλωι [τ]ὸ μὲν ἕτερον ἔτος τὴν π[α]-
   5     [νήγυριν τῶν Ἀν]τιγονε[ί]ων ἣν νῦν ποιοῦσιν, τὸ δ[ὲ]
         [ἕτερον θυσίαν] καὶ ἀγ[ῶ]νας καὶ σύνοδον ἐπονο-
         [μάσαντας Δημ]η[τρ]ίε[ι]α, καὶ συνέδρους ἀποστέλ-
         [λειν εἰς ταῦτ]α καθάπερ ἀποστέλλουσιν εἰς τὰ
         [Ἀντιγόνεια τήν τ]ε παρασκευὴν τῶν θυμάτων κα[ὶ]
  10     [τῶν ἀγώνων ποιεῖ]σθαι καὶ τὴν μίσθωσιν τῶν τεχν[ι]-
         [τῶν ....ca.9....]ντ....ΜΙΣ..ΟΙ.....Ν ἄθλων το[ῖς]
         [Δημητριείοι]ς [ἀπὸ τῶν κοιν]ῶν χρημάτων κατὰ
         [τὴν σύνταξιν] τὴν νῦν οὖσαν τοῖς νησιώταις ὑπ-
         [ὲρ τῶν Ἀντιγο]νείων καὶ ἐάν τινες τῶν νησιωτῶν
  15     [μὴ τελῶσιν ε]ἰς ταῦτα τὴν σύνταξιν τὴν ἐπιβ[άλ]-
         [λουσαν ....]ων χρημάτων .....ειανα....
         [..... ἐν ἐ]νδείαι τοῦ συντελεῖν, εἶναι λ
         [..... ca.10 .....]ταννη[..... ca.12 ......]μα[— — —]
         [..... ca.10 .....]λλον[... ca.6 ...]ε[— — — — — — —]
  20     [— — — — — — — το]ῦ ἐνιαυ[τοῦ — — —]
         [— — — — — — — — — — ]τὴν εὔνοιαν τ[ὴν]
         [.. ca.5 .. εἰς πάντ]α χρόνον ....ΝΙ ὄντα εὐε[ργ]-
         [έτην .... ca.8 ....] αὐτῶι καὶ λυ....Α.ΥΓΩΤΟΝ
         [..... ca.11 .....]ν ἣν ἔχουσι πρὸς αὐτὸν οἱ νησιῶτα[ι]
  25     [— — — —] ἀρ[γ]ύριον· ἐπιμέλειαν δὲ [.... ca.9 .....]
         [— — — — καθ]άπερ καὶ ΕΝΕ.ΓΟΡΕΝΙ[.... ca.7 ....]
         [— — — — — — — — — — —]ιον[— — — — —]
```

[— — — — — — — — — — — — — — — —]ν...
[— — — — — — — — —]οτη..... αὐτὸν ....
30 [— — — — — — — — — — —]τωι...αιτα..
[— — — — — — — —] ταῖς ἰδίαις πόλεσι[ν] ὅπω[ς]
[— — — — — ποή]σωνται τὰ αὐτά· τὰς δὲ .ο..
[— — — — — — — — —]καὶ κατατάξασθαι ὅπ[ως]
[— — — — — — — — — —]τὸς αἱ θυσίαι καὶ τὰ
35 [ἆθλα — — — — — — —]αι· ὅταν δὲ αἱ πόλε-
[ις ἕλωνται τοὺς συνέ]δ[ρους, τ]οὺς μὲν τοῦ εἰσιόν-
[τος ἔτους εἰς τ]ὰ Δημητρίεια παραγινομένους
[εἰσενεγκεῖν] χρήματα ὅσαπερ εἰς τὰ Ἀντιγόνε[ια]
[ἐτάχθη· φροντί]σαι δὲ καὶ σκέψασθαι ὅθεν ἔσται πα-
40 [ρέχεσθαι τὸ] ἀργύριον ἀφ’ οὗ τὰ Δημητρίεια ποιή-
[σουσι τὸν ὕσ]τερον χρόνον· καθ’ ὅ τι δ’ ἂν οἰκονο[μ]-
[ήσωσιν αὐτοί, τ]αῦτα κύρια εἶναι· τοὺς δὲ μετὰ τα[ῦ]-
[τα ἐξαποστ]ελλομένους, καθ’ ὅ τι ἂν συνταχθ[ῆι]
[ἐξ ἀρχῆς, τὰς εἰ]σφορὰ[ς] ποιεῖσθαι· ἀναγράψαι δὲ το[ὺς]
45 [συνέδρους τόδε] τὸ ψήφισμα καὶ στῆσαι παρὰ τὸν βω-
[ὸν τῶν Σωτήρω]ν.

[... continu]e[s to show benefaction to ?] the Greeks. [That the League of] Islanders honour to the best of its ability and according to his deserts [Demetrius] with honours [worth]y of him. That they prod[uce e]very second year the [5] f[estival] of the Antigone[i]a [in] Delos which they now celebrate and in [each following year sacrifice], con[t]ests and a gathering name[d the Dem]e[tr]ie[i]a, and sen[d] representatives [to the]m just as they send to the [Antigoneia and ma]ke provision for the sacrifices an[d [10] the contests] and [look a]fter the hiring of the perfor[mers ...] of prizes [for] the [Demetriei]a [from the com]mon funds in accordance with [the rate of contribution] that the Islanders presently make fo[r the Antigo]neia, and if any Islanders [15] [do not pay] their fa[ir] share [f]or these things [...] of money [... in d]efault of payment, let there be [... [20] ... with]in the yea[r ...] the good will t[hat ... for al]l time [...] since he is a bene[factor ...] for him [...] which the Islander[s] have towards him [25] [...] money. The responsibility [... jus]t as also [... [29] ...] him [... [31] ...] for the individual citie[s] so tha[t ...] they [do] the same things [...] and be allocated so [that ...] the sacrifices and the [35] [prizes ...]. Whenever the citi[es appoint their repr]es[entatives] for the coming [year] let them, when coming [to t]he Demetrieia, [bring] as much money as [they are assessed] to pay for the Antigone[ia and let them take thou]ght and consider from where they will be able to [40] pro[vide the] money with which they will prod[uce] the Demetrieia [in] time to c[ome]. Whatever arrangement [they] mak[e] let [t]his have the force of law. And those [sent ou]t afterwards are to make [their con]-tributions exactly as arrang[ed at the outset.] Th[e representatives] are to write up [45] this decree and place it beside the alt[ar of the Saviour]s.

For our purposes the history of Delos in the Classical period can be divided into three distinct periods: ca. 540–426; 425–314; and 314–166. Most of the first two periods is characterised by Athenian domination, the third by Delian independence. In the Hellenistic period, there followed after 166 a second period of Athenian control lasting until 88 (when the island was wasted by Mithridates). The important dates are:

540–528	Pisistratus purifies Delos
ca. 522	Polycrates holds 'Pythia and Delia' on Delos ?
477	Athens creates the Delian League
454	Athens transfers the treasury from Delos to Athens
426	Second purification of Delos by Athens
425	The first penteteric Delia
404	Athens cedes dominance over the Aegean to Sparta
394	Athens regains control of Delos
390	Athens resumes celebration of the Delia
377	Second Athenian Confederacy
314	Delian Independence

Given Athenian dominance of the island, and the leading role Athens played in the spread of theatre onto the Aegean islands, one might expect that Athens had simply transferred its theatre culture to Delos. The evidence however suggests a more complex history. In 425 Athens revived a festival of Apollo, the Delia, with lyric 'circular' choruses and equestrian competitions, but, though the choruses are competitive and sponsored by choregoi, they are perhaps best classified as 'cultic' rather than, strictly speaking, 'theatrical'. There is no evidence for a theatre nor for theatrical lyric or dramatic choruses in Delos until the time of its independence after 314.

Delos down to 426/5

Thucydides' history of Delos (**1**) is an excellent example of the kind of myth-historical bricolage indulged by Athenian politicians of the 420s to legitimate, with the help of an epic text and a few historical memories, an assertion of Athenian political and cultural hegemony over Ionia through the creation of the penteteric Delia. The new festival is presented as the restoration of something that existed from time immemorial, but had lapsed because of troubled times. It is framed as a regathering of the Ionian family, not merely official delegates, but wives and children, and emphatically all Ionians, including those of Asia Minor (like the Ephesia or the Panionia? – see Chankowski 2008, 17). The reference to Pisistratus' purification of the island suggests that the ancient gatherings also took place under Athenian tutelage.

Both the Ionian festival and Athenian hegemony over Delos appear to have been much more recent than **1** suggests. The gathering of the Ionians at Delos is indeed at least as old as the Homeric *Hymn to Apollo* (146–62). But though the hymn is variously dated from the seventh to late sixth century (Faulkner 2011, 11–12), the later date for the Delian portion is now widely accepted: it refers to the temple of Apollo in Delos (52, 56, 80) and so should postdate 540–530 (Burkert 1979, 62). The Homeric authorship of the *Hymn to Apollo* was already disputed in antiquity. The scholiast to Pindar *Nemean*

2.1 tells us that the late sixth-century poet Cynaethus of Chios, one of the Homeridae, composed the *Hymn to Apollo* and passed it off as Homer's (= *FGrH* 568 F 5). The *Hymn to Apollo* in fact stitches together two apparently self-standing hymns, probably of different dates, one to Pythian Apollo and one to Delian Apollo. Most scholars now accept Burkert's argument (1979) that the ideal time for a performance of this composite hymn would have been the festival of the 'Pythia and Delia' which Polycrates of Samos instituted on Delos at the time he dedicated the island of Rheneia (Zen. ms. 1.62 Miller, *CPG* 6.15; Phot. s.v. Πύθια καὶ Δήλια; Suda π 3128, τ 175; Apostol. 15.9; the ultimate source is thought by Crusius in *CPG* Suppl. II 147 to be the 4th-c. Atthidographer Damon). Thucydides (**1**) recalls Polycrates' dedication in the context of the early history of festivals in Delos.

West argued that the part of the *Hymn to Apollo* which is addressed to Delian Apollo is indeed by Cynaethus (1999b, 368–72). In West's view, Cynaethus combined his composition with an older Delphic hymn to Apollo to produce the *Hymn to Apollo* that has come down to us under the name of Homer (cf. Burkert 1979, 61). The Delian section of the *Hymn to Apollo* would accordingly have been composed shortly before Polycrates' death, either in 523 or 522 (West 1999b, 369–70 n. 17). If this is correct, then it is clear from the internal evidence of the hymn (cf. **1**) that musical competitions were held in Delos by ca. 522. But the poem itself speaks of festivals and competitions that were held in still earlier times. Should we accept this as testimony for festivals and musical competitions on Delos before ca. 522? Or, if the poem was written by Cynaethus and ascribed to Homer, are the earlier competitions mentioned in the poem a necessary part of the fiction of Homeric authorship? It is safest to suppose that the hymn provides an invented aetiology for Polycrates' festival, lending it authority on the pretext that it revived a timeless tradition. Later references to Homer on Delos (Hes. fr. dub. 357 M-W; *Certamen* 315–21) seem to depend upon the authority of the *Hymn*. The Delian hymn ascribed by Pausanias to the eighth-century (?) poet Eumelus (4.4.1) also shows signs of being a much later, in this case Classical, composition designed to claim a civic cultural identity for Messene stretching back to before the Messenian War (D'Alessio 2009, 137–45).

Polycrates' activity on the island apparently postdates Pisistratus' purification of the island (Pisistratus died in 527; **1**; Hdt. 1.64.2). It shows that Athens was just one of many foreign powers vying for influence on Delos in the sixth century. After the time of Polycrates we do have some evidence of Athenian activity on the island, but nothing to suggest a leading role in the organisation of any international festival (Chankowski 2008, 19–28). A small temple of Athenian stone and apparently Athenian construction was built on the island in the later sixth century (Parker 1996, 87). Solon's kyrbeis are said to have included regulations relating to the *Deliastai*, who were Athenian theoroi to Delos (Parker 2005, 82), and this is perhaps reflected in the 'Nicomachus Calendar' that regulates *theoria* and sacrifices to Delos (*SEG* 52, 49 fr. 8A col. 2, ll. 6–12; Lambert 2002, 382–3; Rutherford 2013a, 305), but recent scholarship takes this only to indicate that Athens sent delegations to Delos some time in the sixth century, dismissing any temporal, let alone authorial, connection with Solon (see e.g. Davis 2011).

Athenian activity in Delos in the early fifth century is attested by odd bits of evidence. Theophrastus tells us that the tragic poet Euripides was a Wine Steward for an upper-class association called the Dancers, who used to dance around the Temple of Apollo at Delos wearing Theran costume (fr. 576 Fortenbaugh: πυνθάνομαι δ' ἔγωγε καὶ Εὐριπίδην τὸν ποιητὴν οἰνοχοεῖν Ἀθήνησι τοῖς ὀρχησταῖς καλουμένοις· ὠρχοῦντο δ' οὗτοι περὶ τὸν τοῦ Ἀπόλλωνος νεὼν τοῦ Δηλίου τῶν πρῶτον ὄντες Ἀθηναίων καὶ κατεδύοντο ἱμάτια τῶν Θηραϊκῶν). The 'Dancers' have been tentatively connected with the Deliasts, and if the association is correct, it sheds some light on the cultic activities in which they were involved in the time of Euripides' youth, presumably the 470s or 460s (Parker 2005, 83). Another clue to Archaic Athenian activities on Delos is provided by the traditions surrounding the small triakonter (cf. **6** 'triakontorion') that supposedly carried the first Athenian chorus led by Theseus to Delos and continued to be used to carry theoroi to Delos until the time of Demetrius of Phaleron (Rutherford 2013a, 180). It is said to have been a very old and much repaired ship, so much so that philosophers made a celebrated ontological paradigm of it (was it Theseus' ship, despite every bit having been replaced at one time or another?). None of this evidence suggests that the Athenian rituals on the island formed part of an international festival.

There is also no evidence for any kind of competition on the island between ca. 522 and 427. The Homeric hymn mentions competitions of some sort, as well as boxing, dances and song (**1**, 104.4 ὀρχηστυῖ καὶ ἀοιδῇ). Presumably this describes the activities of Polycrates' Pythia and Delia. But the language does not necessarily imply choral competitions and the competition for 'song' may be the same as implied by the existence of the *Hymn to Apollo* itself, namely bardic hymns to Apollo, Artemis and Leto (l. 150: ὅταν στήσωνται ἀγῶνα, cf. **1**, 104.4). **1** asserts the existence of choral performances on Delos before 425: 'later (i.e. after Homer) the islanders and the Athenians used to send their choruses along with sacrifices'. But Thucydides' words also clearly indicate that these choruses did not compete in any prize-competition: the competitions were discontinued 'doubtless because of misfortunes' (**1**, 104.6).

Several surviving early to mid fifth-century lyric choruses, identified as paeans or dithyrambs, were probably written for performance on Delos: Pi. *Pae.* 5, 7b, 12 and possibly 4 (other possibilities in Kowalzig 2007, 57 nn. 6–7); Bacchylides' *Ode* 17 and fr. 65; other candidates are found among the fragments of Simonides' paeans (*PMG* 519 frr. 32, 41, 55, 84; cf. 519 frr. 37, 47, 70 with Rutherford 1990). Simonides is said to have written a whole book of dithyrambs called 'Delians' (Δηλιακά; see **Dii** and note Poltera 2005, who regards this as the corruption of an original reference to Semos' histories called *Deliaka*). The extant remains indicate that processional songs (in principle 'paeans') were written for choruses originating from Ceos (**Dii**), Naxos, Euboea, Athens, and probably elsewhere for performance in Delos (Kowalzig 2007, 56–128; Rutherford 2013a, 240–1). The remains probably date from the time when the Delian League was based in Delos (478–454). The Delian processional hymn (*prosodion*) composed by Pronomos (**V G**) for the Chalcidians is probably a little later (Paus. 9.12.6; Wilson 2010b, 191–6). The poetic remains indicate that the festival sometimes went beyond the function of maintaining connections between the (mainly Ionian) member states. Bacchylides 17 (which deals with Theseus and the Athenian youths and maidens encountering Minos in the mid Aegean) seems to offer ideological justification for the naval alliance under Athenian hegemony (see esp. Fearn 2013; cf. Rutherford 2004, 84–5 on Pi. *Pae.* 5). None of these remains indicate the existence of a prize competition (Kowalzig 2007, 88; Rutherford 2013a, 246). The odes appear to have been written for the cultic choruses that accompanied the sacrifices of the Athenian and other island embassies. These are surely the 'choruses with sacrifices' noted by Thucydides (**1**) that 'the islanders and the Athenians continued to send', despite the fact that 'the competitions and much else were discontinued'. It is worth stressing this point because many scholars assume that sending choruses also implied a competition at this time (Parker 1996, 150; Nagy 2011, 318).

Delos from 426/5–314

In 426/5 the Athenians purified Delos and established a penteteric festival on the island (**1–6**). An annual pilgrimage in the month of Thargelion seems already to have been an established Athenian tradition and is probably the festival referred to in **1**, 104.6 ('later the islanders and the Athenians kept sending their choruses along with sacrifice'). If so, the new initiative was confined to the aggrandisement of every fourth such festival occasion with choral and equestrian competitions. Both the annual and the penteteric events are referred to in our ancient sources as simply 'Delia' (cf. X. *Mem.* 4.8.2), with no evidence of a special terminology to distinguish the larger festival such as Great Delia *vel sim*. The stimulus for the new penteteric festival is said by Diodorus to have been the plague (12.58.6–7), but the religious reasons were doubtless aided by more strictly political concerns over secessionist tendencies among members of the League, combined with military concerns about the activity of an entirely unprecedented Spartan navy in the Aegean (Parker 1996, 150). The fact that Thucydides (**1**, 104) cites the Homeric hymn for evidence of an ancient pan-Ionian festival suggests that the penteteric Delia was self-consciously packaged as a revival of ancient custom, and that the existence of the supposed ancient custom was pressed into evidence for a time-honoured kinship between Athens, caretaker of Delos since Pisistratus, and its Ionian colonies (cf. Hornblower 1991, 521). It was at Apollo's own command that Athens once again purified the island and reassumed its responsibility and rights as the mother city of the Ionians and its role as primary caregiver to Apollo, divine ancestor of the Ionian race.

The order of events for the penteteric Delia is given in **3**: procession, sacrifice, contests and banquet. The choral competition at the Delia was probably a men's or boys' lyric, i.e. a 'circular', chorus. The primary evidence for this is the use of the tripod as a prize (**5**, ll. 33, 38). Some six tripod bases survive from the sanctuary of Apollo on Delos and another three from elsewhere on the island, and these suggest tripods of the same size and style as were given as prizes at the Thargelia in Athens (Amandry and Ducat 1973, esp. 40–1; Wilson 2007b, 176). The choral competitions may, therefore, to some extent have been modelled on the lyric performances by tribal men's and boys' choruses at the Athenian Dionysia, and more specifically the Thargelia, since they were for Apollo (Wilson 2007b, 175–82). A modelling of the Delia after the Thargelia is probably evident in other respects. The Delia was held in the month of Thargelion (as was the Athenian Thargelia) which fell in the same month in the calendars of both states, and which was, according to Athenian tradition, the birth month of Apollo (D.L. 2.44, 3.2; *Vita Plat.* 6 Didot; Chankowski 2008, 110–15), while in the period of Delian independence the Apollonia was in the Delian month of Hieros.

Another indication in favour of lyric 'circular choruses' forming the competition at the Delia is a cup by the Eretria Painter (Warsaw 142458), dated ca. 425–420, and therefore probably inspired by the creation of the Delia. It shows dancing satyrs and maenads with the inscribed names of Aegean islands, Lemnos, Delos, and Euboea (also a Tethys and in the tondo a Demon and Choro). This may be a forerunner of the conceit that the Cyclades (literally 'circlers') are themselves a 'circular chorus' dancing around Delos, a motif picked up by Callimachus (*Del.* 16–22; Kowalzig 2007, 85 n. 74; Heinemann 2013, 288–90).

There is an apparent inconsistency in the Athenian evidence relating to the number of choruses sent to Delos. **4**'s mention of 'a single chorus' might be read to mean that Athens sent only one chorus to the Delia (**3** also speaks of Nicias having a 'chorus' in the singular). In line with a single contest we might note that a contest for boy's choruses alone formed the musical competition of the post-independence Apollonia (see below). But **3** is focused on the cultic, not the competitive performance, while **4** most likely emphasises 'a single chorus' in the sense of one per competition category for the entire city (as opposed to e.g. one per tribe), and so is not inconsistent with there being different competitions for men's and boys' choruses. **5**, though it deals with a single Delia, speaks of prize tripods and also the transport of choruses in the plural; and **6** indicates a plurality of Athenian choregoi in a given year. It seems most likely therefore that at the Delia, as at the Thargelia and Dionysia, there were competitions both for men's and for boys' lyric ('circular') choruses.

The roles of *archetheoroi* (a.k.a. *architheoroi*) and choregoi must be carefully distinguished. The *archetheoroi*, of which there were five from Athens in 425 (**2**, cf. the plural in **5**), were the leaders of the festival delegation. Although *archetheoria* (payment for a religious embassy) could be a liturgy in Athens, it was not always, and **5** clearly shows that the *archetheoroi* were paid from public funds (Rutherford 2013a, 216–17). Choregoi, on the other hand, were always liturgists in Athens. *Archetheoroi* were well-known citizens, carefully selected for their trustworthiness and rectitude (Rutherford 2013a, 161–2), choregoi needed only to be wealthy and were appointed by a much more mechanical procedure. The *archetheoroi* had charge of the chorus that performed in the sacrificial procession (*pompe*) of the Delia (**3**), while the choregoi had charge of the chorus that competed for the prize in the contests that followed the sacrifice.

While these roles are clearly distinct, there is no reason why the persons could not on occasion be the same, such that an *archetheoros* might also perform as choregos. There is also no reason to exclude the possibility that the chorus that performed in the sacrificial procession was composed of the choruses that also competed in the contest, just as the men's and boys' lyric choruses performed both in the Parade and in the theatrical competitions of the Athenian Dionysia (**I Aiv 25**). Indeed there is some evidence to suggest this was the case in **3** when Nicias led the embassy to Delos. His organisation of his chorus relates to the orderly disembarkation of the processional chorus, but we know from Delian temple inventories that Nicias dedicated the golden ornaments (στλεγγίδες / στλιγγίδες) on the wreaths worn by his embassy (cf. Blech 1982, 35, 310): they numbered 103 (*ID* 104, ll. 113–14; *ID* 101, ll. 38–9; *ID* 104–11, B, ll. 12–13; *ID* 104–12, ll. 90–1; *ID* 104–30, ll. 11–12). The fact that Nicias dedicated them suggests that he also paid for them, but the number suggests that he himself sponsored both the boys' and the men's chorus (two lyric choruses of fifty, plus his own *stlengis* gives 101, possibly we are to reckon substitutes in case of illness, or a kanephoros and a piper in the same costume). The same inventories show that the super-wealthy Callias, son of Hipponikos, dedicated 119 *stlengides*, suggesting that he also sponsored two lyric choruses with an even larger accompaniment. No other such dedications appear in the inventories. Even if this interpretation of the dedications of Nicias and Callias is correct, **5** and **6** show that single sponsorship of both choruses, both for the procession and for the choral competition, was exceptional.

The suggestion has been made that only Athenian choruses participated in the competition (Chankowski 2008, 103), but this would hardly serve the festival's presumed bonding function between Athens and the other Ionian cities. It is also directly contradicted by **4** which envisages a single chorus from Athens (see above) in rivalry with those of other states, not to mention the tendency of **1** which treats the competitions as a revival of earlier pan-Ionian musical competitions. In addition to sending a theoric chorus for the procession (**3**), each participating state probably entered a chorus in one or both competitions. *IG* XII 4, 332b (Rutherford 2013a, 387–91 no. C7), l. 49, an inscription from Cos of the mid fourth century, is reconstructed to refer to the sending of a tribal chorus from Cos to the Delia, but the inscription is very fragmentary and even the reconstruction of the word 'chorus' is highly uncertain. A tribal chorus would go against the grain of the intercity competition suggested by **1** and **4**. Scholars are also tempted to draw some inference from the inscription of Karthaia in Ceos that honours Aristopeithes who led a boys' chorus to Delos (**Dii 2**), but the dating of the inscription suggests that it must relate to the period of Delian independence (Chankowski 2008, 103).

Chankowski's (2008, 225–6) reconstruction of the penteteric Delia argues regular celebrations every four years from 426/5 to 406/5 (in the same year as the Great Panathenaea) and then a resumption, following a gap of fifteen years after the Peloponnesian War, in 391/0 (no longer following the cycle of the Great Panathenaea). The annual Delia were not suspended after the Peloponnesian War, as is evident from the traditions relating to the delay of the execution of Socrates in 399 until after the return of the pilgrimage to Delos (Pl. *Phd.* 58a–c; X. *Mem.* 4.8.2; Chankowski 2008, 112–13). The evidence for the Delia after 333/2 is thin due to a gap in the epigraphic record. It appears however that Athens continued to control the island and to celebrate the Delia right down to 319/18 or 315/14 (Chankowski 2008, 220–1) when a dedicatory inscription from Eleusis made by soldiers in honour of Demetrius of Phaleron lists, among his accomplishments, a victory in the chariot race of the Delia (*IG* II² 2971).

Delos after 314

Our evidence for theatre and drama begins only in the period of independence. Independent Delos in fact offers the richest trove of evidence for post-Classical theatre history outside of Athens and Rome. In particular, two series of inscriptions, the *tabulae archontum* (*IG* XI 2, 105–33; Feyel 2000, 253–60; Prêtre 2000) and the accounts of the *hieropoioi* (*IG* XI 2, 134–289; *ID* 290–498; Vial 1984, 216–32) give an invaluable overview of festival structure and infrastructure on the island. The *tabulae archontum* begin ca. 300 and last until the end of the period of Delian independence. They record the names of people involved in the finance and performance of the festival competitions of the Apollonia and the Dionysia. The surviving accounts of the *hieropoioi* (here exemplified by **7** and **8**) span ca. 307 to the end of the period of Delian independence. They are the accounts of a board of two to four civic magistrates, the *hieropoioi*, appointed on an annual basis to oversee the treasury of Apollo and all other divine properties on the island. The inscriptions record the sanctuary's dedications, income and expenditures. The *hieropoioi* were also responsible for carrying out the decisions of the popular assembly relating to the construction and maintenance of buildings in Delos and so the inscriptions record the details of the provision of contracts, materials, and payments to contractors for all the building in the sanctuary.

The *tabulae archontum* ('Records of the Archons') give detailed evidence of a competition for a lyric boys' chorus at both the Apollonia and the Dionysia, and dramatic competitions, in both tragedy and comedy, at the Dionysia. From 284 four citizen choregoi are named for the boys' chorus at both the Apollonia and the Dionysia (*IG* XI 2, 105). The same inscription gives the names of four citizen choregoi and two metic choregoi for comedy at the Dionysia (in the order: 2 citizens + metic, 2 citizens + metic) and another four citizen and two metic choregoi for tragedy (and in the same peculiar order). The consistent appointment of four citizen choregoi in each category implies that each of the four Delian tribes put forward a choregos. The order for the Dionysia (boys' lyric, comedy, tragedy) probably follows the order of performance (cf. on the Law of Euegoros in **I Avi**). From 221 onwards the inscriptions identify the winning choregoi of both festivals by giving the names of two winners for each lyric competition, and the names of two citizen victors and one metic victor for each of the Dionysian dramatic competitions.

On this evidence Bruneau (1970, 319–21) and Vial (1984, 41–3) supposed that the competitions at the Delian Apollonia and Dionysia from ca. 300 to 167 generally had as many contestants as choregoi: namely four boys' choruses, plus, in the case of the Dionysia, six comedies and six tragedies. But on this theory it is difficult to understand why two citizens for each category and one metic for each dramatic competition are named as 'victors', since the verb νικᾶν is not used of second- or third-prize winners (see on the Dionysian Hypotheses in **I Avi**). Sifakis (1967, 31; 1968, 486–7), followed by Wilson (2000, 293) and Fraisse and Moretti (2007, 222–5), is surely right to see all the named winners for each category as participants in a *synchoregia* (though the term is not used): i.e. for each genre there were two citizens who shared a single choregia (as for the lyric choruses at the Athenian Thargelia, or for comedy at the Athenian Dionysia in the late fourth century), and in the case of the dramatic genres, one metic was added to the pair of citizen choregoi, so that the burden of sponsorship normally fell to three for each performance. Assuming such joint choregiai lie behind the puzzling wording of the *tabulae archontum*, the choral and dramatic contests of the Delian Apollonia and Dionysia each had only the minimum number of two contestants per competition. Even with the minimal number of competitions, the *tabulae archontum* indicate that contests were occasionally omitted: there was no contest for tragedy in 170 or 168 (*IG* XI 2, 133; Prêtre 2000, 267), and in *IG* XI 2, 112, l. 3 only one name seems to be given for tragic choregoi, which, unless the list is somehow defective (Fraisse and Moretti 2007, 225), suggests that in some circumstances tragedy could be performed without any real competition.

In general, the small number of contestants for each competition, and the use of metics to help supply a drama in each category, suggest that the wealthy elites of this small island nation were stretched to maintain a competition of international standing (Fraisse and Moretti 2007, 224–5). Further irregularity is shown by **9** and **10**, which appear to attest a single choregos taking on the expenses related to all the Dionysian competitions. This may, however, be an earlier arrangement than that attested in the *tabulae archontum*. An alternative solution, and perhaps the safer, is to assume that **9** and **10**'s references to service as choregoi in 'all genres' refers to service and victories one by one over a number of years (Sifakis 1967, 37; Fraisse and Moretti 2007, 223–4). A more ordinary form of choregic dedication may have been a stone phallos (such as that now arbitrarily placed on **9**). The dedication of stone phalloi was a common practice. Five or six were found at Delos (Moretti and Fincker 2008, 149). *IG* XI 2, 287 A, l. 119 refers to payment in 250 to a workman who 'moved the phalloi', a reference to votives (Vallois 1922, 101 n. 1; Bruneau 1970, 301 n. 1; Moretti and Fincker 2008, 150–1).

There is little in the *tabulae archontum* to suggest any additional competitions before 168, when we have some evidence for contests in 'men's and boys' Pythian *nomos*', and mixed choral-auletic performances (Prêtre 2000, 266–7, but see Fraisse and Moretti 2007, 217 n. 16). But the minimal offerings of the festival competitions were compensated by a usually large number of non-competitive performances. From the earliest surviving inscription (*IG* XI 2, 105 of 284) the *tabulae* name artists who 'gave shows for the god' (οἵδε ἐπεδείξαντο τῷ θεῷ). These include actors in tragedy and comedy and pipers, but also include artists of up to seventeen different performance genres. Some of these performers (harpists, magicians, mimes, pantomimes, magicians and puppeteers) are of a sort that are not included in competitions elsewhere in antiquity, and others not included in competitions until the late empire (Fraisse and Moretti 2007, 219), and indeed one is even female (*IG* XI 2, 110, l. 34; *IG* XI 2, 112, l. 22; *IG* XI 2, 113, l. 28). Even the actors, along with other performers, are frequently singled out as having performed 'twice', 'three times' or 'four times'. These facts suggest that much of this performance activity lay outside of the festival competitions (as did the old tragedies put on by the actors in Athens from 386), and possibly even outside of the regular programme of the festival itself. The expression 'gave shows for the god' (οἵδε ἐπεδείξαντο τῷ θεῷ) implies a voluntary performance dedicated to the god, though this should not exclude the likelihood of material rewards. The formula changes from ca. 236 to 'and these also contested/performed for the god' (καὶ οἵδε ἠγωνίσαντο τῷ θεῷ). *IG* XI 2, 107, ll. 24–5 (280) also names the 'poets of comedy' Philemon (thought to be Philemon the Younger in *PCG* VIII, T 3), Nikostratos (thought to be Nikostratos II in *PCG* VIII, T 4) and Ameinias, suggesting that they themselves were present to direct the comedies. 'Poet of tragedy', 'poet of dithyramb' and 'poet of comedy' appear in the list for 236 (*IG* XI 2, 120, ll. 50–3).

Although the lyric and dramatic competitions are only firmly attested from 284, they are reasonably assumed to begin sometime in the late fourth century. The Apollonia (Bruneau 1970, 69) and the Dionysia (**8**, **9**) both go back at least to ca. 304, and **7**, from 308–306, shows the Delians busy building up a theatre that is apparently already in a functional state (below). The earlier fifth-century lyric competitions of the Delia (above) seem not to have needed nor benefited from a theatrical space and probably took place in the sanctuary of

Apollo. The competitions of the Apollonia were, however, performed in the theatre probably from very soon after independence. Inscriptions, at least, show honours being announced in the theatre at the lyric competition at the Apollonia. The earliest certain use of
the full formula 'at the Apollonia in the theatre when the competition for boys' choruses
takes place' is only vaguely dated between 300 to 250 (*IG* XI 4, 600, ll. 8–12: στεφανῶσαι
αὐτὸν δάφνη[ς | στ]εφάνωι τοῖς Ἀπολλωνίοις | [ὅ]ταν ἦι τῶν παίδων ἀγὼν κα[ὶ | ἀν]
αγορεῦσαι τὸν ἱερο[κ]ήρυκα | [ἐν] τῶι θεάτρωι). But the details are probably intended
in inscriptions more securely dated to the earlier third century (*IG* XI 4, 514, ll. 20–1:
[ἀναγορεῦσαι] τοῖς Ἀπολλωνίο[ις]; *IG* XI 4, 542, ll. 29–30: ἀνειπεῖν δὲ τ[ὸν ἱεροκήρυκα
τὸν στέ]φανο[ν] Ἀπολλωνίοις [ἐν τῶι θεάτρωι]) and it is probably a safe assumption that
the preferred time and place for the announcement of crowns was the competition for boys'
choruses in the theatre from the beginning of the festival.

The evidence for the chronology of the theatre building comes, as stated above, from
the accounts of the *hieropoioi* (**7**, **8**). **7** is one of the earliest of the surviving accounts of
the *hieropoioi* (308/7). It describes construction of the entry and performance spaces of the
theatre; the theatron was not built for several decades (spectators sat on the bare hillside
until ca. 265). **7** specifically refers to construction of the entryway (l. 27; presumably into
the parodos: Fraisse and Moretti 2007, 158), the skene building (ll. 37, 43), and even the
pinakes (painted flats set in the intercolumniations of the proskenion, ll. 45, 48). Wood is
the principal building material at this stage (**7**, ll. 27, 43, 48; Fraisse and Moretti 2007, 233).
Long-range plans for a stone theatre probably existed from the beginning, though it is not
until 280 that work began on a permanent skene; the stone theatron, which would seat 6,500,
was not complete until after 246 (Fraisse and Moretti 2007, 233–7). The skene mentioned
in **7**, as well as the proskenion implied by mention of the pinakes, were doubtless temporary
buildings. The skene in fact had a short life: accounts show its disassembly and deposition in
the sanctuary of Apollo for four drachmas in 296 (*IG* XI 2, 154 A, l. 43) and the erection of a
new skene and proskenion (or reassembly of the old one) some time between 296 and 279 for
410 drachmas (*IG* XI 2, 153). The low price shows the latter must also have been of wood.

The earliest certain testimony for use of the theatre is ca. 280, an honorary decree stipulating that the herald is to announce the awarding of a golden crown 'in the theatre at
the Apollonia' (*IG* XI 4, 559, ll. 18–19); the formula is however restored in another honorary decree from closer to the beginning of the century (see *IG* XI 4, 542, l. 30, cited
just above). But it is above all the frequent reference to the preparation of pinakes (as in
7, ll. 45, 47) that shows the theatre is in active use before this time. The pinakes served
as decorative backdrops to the performance area, closing off the large intercolumniations
in the proskenion, and screening off what effectively became a backstage area (Moretti
1997). The pinakes were expensive to produce (1,430 drachmas, not counting the cost of
the wood, in 282: *IG* XI 2, 158, ll. 67–79), of very limited lifespan, and 'of little purpose
in a theatre that was not designed for immediate use' (Fraisse and Moretti 2007, 233, 237).

The Delian Dionysia probably goes back to the earliest years of Delian independence
(after 314), but no earlier. No space on the island sacred to Dionysus can be found before
this time (Moretti and Fincker 2008, 145). It appears, therefore, that the Dionysia was a
creation of independent Delos. Paradoxically, however, the Delian Dionysia seems closely
modelled upon the Athenian, including:

- Regular annual performance in the same month as at Athens (Galaxion, the equivalent of Athenian Elaphebolion: Trümpy 1997, 64, 70), and at the same time as the Athenian Dionysia (see next).
- A phallic parade, beginning of the Dionysia on Galaxion 12 (cf. the Athenian Parade on Elaphebolion 10: **I Ai 5**).
- Competitions in the same order as at Athens: lyric followed by comedy followed by tragedy (see on Law of Euegoros in **I Avi**).
- Competitions held in the theatre in the presence of the icon of Dionysus (see below), seated in a throne in the centre of the prohedria that was modelled upon that in the Lycurgan theatre (Fraisse and Moretti 2007, 74).
- A system of tribally based choregic funding. Note that Athens had extended the tribal model of joint choregoi adopted by Delos also to comedy after the middle of the fourth century.

The phallic parade in Delos is the best-attested Dionysian parade outside Athens. Its regular occurrence on 12 Galaxion is associated with expenses and preparations in the accounts of the *hieropoioi* that give us some indication of its route and contents. **8** is the earliest surviving mention of the phallos, but many of the later accounts are rich in interesting detail. Those of 269, for example, include the following expenses for Galaxion (*IG* XI 2, 203, ll. 36–9):

> Galaxion: a pig from Lampon to purify the sanctuary: 3 drachmas; a torch: 1 half-obol; wood for the image of Dionysus: 35 drachmas; to Aristothales who worked the image: 7 drachmas; to Naumakos who painted it: 7 drachmas; to Rhodon who made the road: 1 drachma, 2 obols; to Philokrates who cleaned up the river of the sanctuary of Leukothea and the sanctuary of Leukothea: 1 drachma; for the decoration of the image of Dionysus: 12 drachmas; to those who cleaned the skene in the theatre: 1 drachma, 1 obol; to the man who removed the dung from the sanctuary: 2 obols; for the sponges used for the decoration: 1 drachma; two choes of white oil: 3 drachmas, 1 obol; nitron: 3 obols, 2 half-obols; three half-kotyles of rose myrrh from Kombaris: 6 drachmas; etc.

Most of these are recurrent expense. There are some 25 references to the preparation of the phallos for the Dionysia in the Delian inscriptions (Vallois 1922; Bruneau 1970, 312–15). Each year a new phallos was made for the Dionysia. It is sometimes referred to as an 'image for Dionysus', sometimes an 'image of Dionysus', and sometimes simply referred to as 'the phallos' (**8**; *IG* XI 2, 154, ll. 43–4; *ID* 294, l. 7). One component of the 'image' is a *keraia* (a beam formed of a single timber: *IG* XI 2, 158A, l. 70; *IG* XI 2, 161, l. 90; *IG* XI 2, 179, l. 11; *IG* XI 2, 234, l. 8) forming the phallos pole. Another component, occasionally specified, is wooden wings (*ID* 372, l. 100; *ID* 440A, l. 32; *ID* 442A, l. 199 (restored); *ID* 444A, l. 29). The wings are fitted to the phallos pole by 'bolts, an axle and pins' (*ID* 440A, l. 32: ἧλοι καὶ ἄξων καὶ περ[όν]αι), the axle suggesting a moving part: possibly the wings were capable of flapping (Vallois 1922, 100). The phallos was therefore represented in the Delian parade as a phallos-bird. This is the phallos-cock that is represented on the front face of the base of the monument of Karystios (**9**), as Vallois argued (1922, 99). The cock on **9** has its 'neck' raised and its wings folded flat against its body in the position of a cock beginning to crow. If there were moving parts they were presumably deployed to emphasise the triumphant raising of the (phallic) head, rounding wings and body into a ball, and then crowing while flapping its wings (see Csapo 1993b for the cock as Dionysian victory symbol). The whole image was painted in encaustic (*ID* 290, l. 82; *ID* 372, l. 101) and then further decorated.

This 'image for/of Dionysus' is thought by some to be the icon of the god himself (Vallois 1922, 97; Detienne 1989). Frontisi-Ducroux (2015, 328–30) has recently rejected this interpretation, pointing out that the word here translated as 'image' (*agalma*) is not used of divine images or icons but only of objects dedicated to the god (Lanérès 2012b). One should point out that *the* icon of Dionysus in Athens is not equated with the phallos, but sits in the theatre watching the phallic procession (**I Aiii 3**), and the same might possibly be inferred for Delos from the existence of a late-Hellenistic statue of Dionysus seated in a replica of his prohedric throne (Hermary et al. 1996, 182–3; Cole 1993, 31). This should not mean, however, that the phallos cannot in some sense represent the god himself.

The phallos was mounted on a wagon (*IG* XI 2, 158A, l. 71; etc.), called the *phall-agogeion* in **8**. The wagon was stored in the treasury of the Naxians and, as the accounts show only trivial sums in connection with it (e.g. 5 obols for nails in *IG* XI 2, 158, l. 71), presumably for repairs, it appears that the same wagon did repeated annual service for many years. In addition to fixing the phallos on the wagon, the accounts show payments to workmen who carried lead to and from the wagon (*ID* 338 Aa, ll. 57–8; *ID* 440A, ll. 33–4; *ID* 442 A, l. 199; *ID* 444A, l. 30; *ID* 447, ll. 12–13). In one account this is combined with an entry for 'ballasting the wagon and unloading it' (*ID* 372 A, ll. 101–2: τοῖς τὴν ἄμαξαν ἑρματίσασιν καὶ ἀπαγαγοῦσ[ιν — · τ]ὸμ μόλυβδον ἐνέγκασιν καὶ ἀνενέγκασι ΓΗΗΙΙΙ), though it is unclear from the text if this is meant to be the same action. The word for 'ballasting' is often applied to ships, and some have therefore thought that the wagon must be a shipcart (**I Aiv 16–20**; Sifakis 1967, 10). This is not a natural inference from the use of the word, however, and there is nothing else to support the notion that this was meant to represent a Dionysian ship. The ballast is required, not for some symbolic need to treat the cart like a ship, but presumably to give the cart a low centre of gravity to keep the cart, with its upright and heavy image of Dionysus, from toppling over. This is especially necessary if the phallos had moveable parts. An inscribed relief from Edessa shows a phallos-bird on a wagon from the phallic parade of Emathia (Chamoux 1974; Nikolaou 1985; Csapo 1997, 283), but it lies flat, possibly because it has fallen over as a result of a collision with the pet pig that is the subject of the verse epitaph, but also possibly because it is meant to rise up dramatically and 'crow' at intervals during the procession. The smoothness of the route was, at all events, a matter of concern. Payments are made to those who clean the route and smooth the road by covering it with planking (*IG* XI 2, 203 A, l. 37; *IG* XI 2, 219A, l. 20 – cited below; *ID* 372A, ll. 101–2: τοῖς τὴν ὁδὸν στρώσασι τεῖ δωδεκάτει καὶ ξύλα ἐνέγκασιν καὶ ἀνενέγκασιν Δ). One should discard the fanciful theories that make the 'shipcart' float along the river running through the sanctuary of Leukothea (Sifakis 1967, 10–12), or make the phallos-bird seem to float upon it (Vallois 1922, 106). They are based on nothing more than a desire to turn the wagon somehow into a ship, and one should not have to point out that chickens do not swim.

The route implied by the cleaning operations that take place in Galaxion indicate something of the route taken by the phallic parade. *IG* XI 2, 203 (cited above) names the sanctuary of Leukothea (unfortunately of unknown location), as well as the skene of the theatre (supposed by Bruneau 1970, 317 to relate to the route of the parade rather than to the contests). *IG* XI 2, 219A, l. 20 adds a charge for a man 'who levelled the road leading to Dionysus' ([τὴν ὁδὸν στρώ]σαντι τὴν ἐπὶ Διόνυσον). This is taken by Bruneau to refer to the road leading to the altar of Dionysus (1970, 318; cf. on **9**). If this is correct, the information confirms that the parade included a passage through the theatre on its way to the sacrificial altar, as at Athens.

In addition to the Dionysia and Apollonia, Delos was the site, probably from soon after its independence, of a festival established by the League of Islanders (composed mainly of the Cycladic islands – Delos, though the meeting place of the League, may not have been a formal member: Buraselis 2013, 175). The Antigoneia was celebrated in honour of Antigonus Monophthalmos, who was responsible for 'liberating' the islands from Cassander. Our main information about the Antigoneia comes from **11**, a decree of the League of Islanders, which established a festival for Antigonus' son, Demetrius the Besieger, apparently on the same terms, and in alternating years with the Antigoneia. The occasion for the creation of the Demetrieia was probably the defeat by Demetrius of a Ptolemaic fleet at Salamis in Cyprus in 306, a victory that inspired Antigonus to claim kingship in both his and his son's names. **11** specifically names a sacrifice and contests, for which performers are to be hired and prizes given. The performers (*technitai*) could refer to musicians or actors, or both. The creation of the festival is in conformity with a pattern we find in other Greek states. Samos created an Antigoneia and Demetrieia at this time and a Demetrieia also seems likely for Sicyon (**Bv 7**). The Dionysia and Demetrieia in Athens and Euboea are about a decade later (see on **Dvii**). Most of these festivals (Athens, Euboea, Samos) demonstrably included tragic performances or dramatic competitions (**Dxiii 2**). The Delian account of the *hieropoioi* for 296 includes expenses for a chorus at the Antigoneia and the bringing of the skene into the sanctuary (*IG* XI 2, 154A, ll. 42–3). But the accoutrements of the chorus (δᾷδες εἰς τὸγ χορόν· ΓΗ[..]·ῥυμὸς καὶ ξύλα· Η) indicate that the Deliades, and therefore not a theatrical chorus, are meant (Sifakis 1967, 16; Bruneau 1970, 36–7). After the fall of Demetrius, the Antigoneia and Demetrieia were replaced around 280 by the Ptolemaia, a festival instituted by the League of Islanders in honour of Ptolemy Soter (Bruneau 1970, 516–45). These included tragic competitions (*IG* XI 4, 1043, ll. 14–16).

Delos leaves us with an interesting paradox. Athens evidently played a major role in the spread of theatre across the Aegean and beyond. Yet in Delos, the very heart of the Aegean, an island entirely under Athenian control for most of the Classical period, and an island reserved exclusively for functions connected to religious festivals, we have no trace of theatre until Delos became independent of Athens. Very soon after independence there is abundant evidence for theatre and theatre culture, and most of it very close to the Athenian model. One wonders if the Athenians deliberately avoided developing a Dionysia or Dionysian practices on the island, specifically so as to avoid any possible clash with its own Dionysia, which became the principal gathering of Athens' subjects and allies in and around the Aegean during its fifth- and fourth-century imperial adventures. The Delians, too, apparently realised the island's potential for developing a Dionysia that would have broad appeal throughout the region, and made the creation of a Dionysia, a theatre and dramatic competitions an immediate priority as soon as they were liberated from Athenian domination.

Dvii: Euboea: Eretria

1. **An agonistic, possibly choregic, dedication to (?) Dionysus with metrical inscription**, ca. 500 (by letter forms and orthography: Jeffery [*CEG* I, 321a]; Knoepfler 2010a, 229).

The upper part of a small greyish-white limestone column with a circular cavity in the top (D. 0.03 × diam. 0.035 m). The text is inscribed vertically on a band ca. 0.035 m high worked more smoothly.
0.50 × diam. 0.25–0.29 m.
Found in 1979 in secondary use in a Roman Imperial tomb south of the temple of Apollo.
Eretria Museum M 889.
Altherr-Charon and Lasserre 1981 (= *SEG* 31, 806); *CEG* I, 321a; Themelis 1987 (= *SEG* 36, 795). Photo: Altherr-Charon and Lasserre 1981, 26.

> Τιμοκράτες ἀνέθεκε Διο[νύσωι (??) τριποδίσκον]
> ἀνδρõν νικέρας, τõι χάριν ἀν[τιδιδούς].

1 Διο[νύσωι] Themelis   Διὸ[ς κοῦροι πένταθλον] Altherr-Charon and Lasserre   τὸν
ἀγõνα Hansen   Possibly [τριποδίσκον] *or* name of tribe in the dative   2
ΑΝΔΡΟΝΙΚΕΡΑΣ *lapis*   ἀν[τιδίδο] Hansen

Timokrates dedicated [(??) the little tripod to] Dio[nysus] after winning in the men's (sc. contest), [giving] him an offering in retu[rn.]

2. **Decree of the Council of Eretria awarding proxeny status and other honours, including prohedria, to Hegelochos of Taras**, 411. Probably the leader of a squadron of Tarantine ships that had assisted the Lacedaemonian naval commander Hagesandridas in 411 (Th. 8.91.2), Hegelochos is honoured for 'having contributed to the liberation of the city (of Eretria) from Athens' (ll. 8–10), doubtless in 411 (Knoepfler 2001a, 83). We excerpt the clause that reports the award of prohedria and the concluding statement of the grounds for the honours.

Two non-joining fragments of a stele of local marble (full description: Knoepfler 2001a, 77–82).
Original dimensions ca. 1.10 × 0.425–0.45 × 0.07 m.
Seen by Adolf Wilhelm in the town hall of Eretria in 1890.
Eretria Museum 1111.
Wilhelm 1890, 195–203; *IG* XII 9, 187A; Knoepfler 2001a, no. BII.
Text: based on Knoepfler 2001a.   Photos: Knoepfler 2001a, 79–80, figs. 11–12.

καὶ
προεδρίην ἐς τὸς ἀγῶνας, ὡς σ-
υνελευθερώραντι τὴμ πόλιν
10   ἀπ᾽ Ἀθηνάων.

… and prohedria at the contests, because he contributed to the liberation of the city ¹⁰ from Athens.

3. Decree of the People of Eretria awarding honours to Timotheos of Macedon, to be announced at the cyclic choral contest of the Dionysia, 319–318. Knoepfler (2001a, 181–4) argues that Timotheos is honoured for assisting in the restoration of democracy in Eretria at the behest of Philip III in 319 or 318. We excerpt the clause that mandates that his many honours – which include a gold crown, a bronze equestrian statue, *sitesis*, *ateleia*, and the gift of a house chosen from those that had belonged to banished exiles – be announced at the Dionysia.

Intact stele of local marble.
1.05 × 0.45 × 0.08 m.
Found during excavation of the sanctuary of Apollo in 1899.
Eretria Museum 1146.
Wilhelm 1909, 314; *IG* XII 9, 196; Knoepfler 2001a, no. BVII.
Text: based on Knoepfler 2001a.   Photos: Knoepfler 2001a, 176, fig. 38 (squeeze).

τὰς δὲ τιμὰς τὰς
15   δεδομένας αὐτῶι ἀνακηρῦξαι
τοὺς προβούλους τοῖς Διονυσίοις
ἐν τῶι ἀγῶνι τῶν κυκλίων χορῶν·

And the probouloi are to proclaim the honours granted to him at the Dionysia, at the contest of the cyclic choruses.

4. Fragment of a tripod base, a choregic dedication to Dionysus, 4ᵗʰ c. (by letter forms: Knoepfler 2010a, 226).

Central part of a triangular block of (possibly Attic) marble, with the remains of a circular mortice in the damaged upper surface to receive the supporting column for a tripod, while the lower surface, circular in shape (diam. 0.42 m) with a central rectangular mortice, is designed to sit above an unfluted column. The sides of the block are concave and all of the three points are broken off.
0.225 × 0.57 m.
Found during excavation in the west parodos of the theatre of Eretria in 1890.
Eretria Museum 1123.
Stavropoulos (1893 = *Athena* 5), 348 no. 3; *IG* XII 9, 273; Knoepfler 2010a, 225–7; cf. 110.
Text: based on Knoepfler 2010a.   Photo and drawings: Knoepfler 2010a, 110, 224–7.

[ὁ δεῖνα τοῦ δεῖνος ὑπὲρ *?* *name of tribe*]
 [καὶ - - - -ίδος φυ]λῆς παισὶ [χορηγῶν]
[*vacat ?* νικήσας ἀνέθ]ηκε Διονύσ[ωι. *vacat ?*]
  [*vacat ?* Καφισ]ίας Θηβαῖος *vacat*
5   [*vacat ?* η]ὔλει. *vacat*

2 [- - - ca. 10 - - -]λης Ziebarth *IG*   [- - - ca. 10 - - -]λὴς Roesch   4 [Καφισ]ίας
Roesch   [Καφισ?]ίας Knoepfler   Our reading based on the photograph at Knoepfler
2010a, 110

[*name and patronymic of dedicator, ?* on behalf of the tribe *name* and the tr]ibe
[*name* after winning as choregos] with the boys [dedic]ated this to Dionys[us.
? Kaphis]ias of Thebes [5] was the [p]iper.

5. Fragment of a probably choregic dedication, 4th c. (by letter forms).

Fragment of local bluish marble, broken on all sides, from the lower part of a quadrangular base.
0.27 × 0.17 × 0.80 m.
Found during excavation in the west parodos of the theatre of Eretria in 1890.
Eretria Museum. No inventory number.
Richardson 1890–1897, 132; *IG* XII 9, 274; Knoepfler 2010a, 227–8.
Text: based on Knoepfler 2010a.   Photo: Knoepfler 2010a, 228.

[- - - - - - - - - - - -] Πασιχ[αρίδας Βοιώτιος *?*]
       vacat ηὔλει. [*vacat ?*]

1 - - - - - - - - - - - πα<ι>σὶ χ[ορηγήσας Wilamowitz, Ziebarth

[…] Pasich[aridas *?* from Boeotia] was the piper.

6. Fragment of a tripod base, a choregic dedication to Dionysus, 4th c. (by letter forms
and prosopography).

Fragment from the left part of a triangular base with concave sides, made of grey-white marble.
Part of a circular mortice remains on the upper surface to receive the supporting column for a
tripod (diam. ca. 0.20 m). There is also a small rectangular mortice near the narrow point of the
stone for fixing one of the feet of the tripod (0.038 × 0.016 × 0.028 m). The lower surface, which is
more carefully worked, also has the remains of a circular mortice of the same diameter but slightly
greater depth, for the top of an unfluted column.
0.42 × 0.10 (original) × 0.27 m.
Found on 9 September 1973 (by Christine Dunant) in excavation in House I, just south of the
theatre in the west quarter by the city's western gate (Ducrey et al. 2004, 168–71) in reuse in a
2nd-c. phase of reconstruction.
Eretria Museum M 500.
Knoepfler 2010a, 219–23; cf. 104–9 (also mentioned at Knoepfler and Schefold 1976, 57).
Text: based on Knoepfler 2010a.   Photos and drawings: Knoepfler 2010a, 107, 220–2.

Τιμίας Λοφίτεω [παίδων χορηγῶν ? *name of tribe*]-
τίδι καὶ Ναρκιττ[ίδι φυλῆι νικήσας Διονύσωι ἀνέθη]-
κε, ηὔλει Χάρη[ς ? Βοιώτιος *or* Θηβαῖος ?].

3 Χάρη[ς] Knoepfler   Our reading based on the photograph at Knoepfler 2010a, 107, and
note that Knoepfler (2010a, 221) also airs Χαρικλῆς Χαιρίωνος Βοιώτιος (Stefanis no.
2611, 3ʳᵈ c.) as a possibility.

Timias son of Lophites [after winning as choregos in the boys with the tribe
…-]tis and [the tribe] Narkitt[is dedica]ted [this to Dionysus]; Chare[s of ?
Boeotia *or* Thebes] was the piper.

7. Fragment of a quadrangular base, probably a choregic dedication to Dionysus, 4ᵗʰ c. (by letter forms); possibly ca. 350–325 (by prosopography: see below on l. 5).

Fragment from the upper right-hand corner of a rectangular base of local marble; part of a circular
mortice on the upper surface to receive an unfluted column.
0.235 × 0.185 × 0.26 m.
Found on 3 July 1975 (by Denis Knoepfler) on the acropolis, having apparently been reused in
construction of a wall in late antiquity.
Eretria Museum M 564.
Knoepfler 2010a, 223–5; cf. 108–9 (also mentioned at Knoepfler and Schefold 1976, 57).
Text: based on Knoepfler 2010a (cf. *BE* 2011, 404). Photos and drawings: Knoepfler 2010a, 107,
223.

Ἀριστόβο[υλος τοῦ δεῖνος ὑπὲρ ?]
Ναρκιττίδ[ος καὶ *name of tribe*]
φυλῆς [e.g. παισὶ χορηγῶν ?]
νική[σας Διονύσωι ἀνέθηκε,]
5   Ἀλκ[- - - - - - - - - - - - - ηὔλει.]

5 Possibly Ἀλκάθους Σικυώνιος.

Aristobo[ulos son of *name*] after winn[ing as choregos in the boys ? on behalf of the tribe] Narkittis [and the] tribe [*name* dedicated this to Dionysus]; ⁵
Alk[-… of ? *place of origin* was the piper.]

8. Fragment of a probably choregic dedication to Dionysus, 4ᵗʰ c. (by letter forms).

Fragment from the right side of a probably quadrangular base.
0.23 × 0.16 × 0.09 m.
Found during excavation in front of the line of bases in the west parodos of the theatre of Eretria
in 1890.
Current whereabouts unknown.
Richardson 1890–1897, 132; *IG* XII 9, 275; Knoepfler 2010a, 228–9.
Text: based on Knoepfler 2010a.

[- - - - - - - - - - - - - - - νικήσα?]ς
[- - - - - - - - - - - - - - - ἀνέ]θηκε

[after winni]ng [... ded]icated this

9. Decree of the Council and People of Eretria providing for special celebrations for Dionysus in response to the liberation of the city and restoration of democracy during the parade for Dionysus, 308/7 or 285 (see below).

The inscription is known only from a copy of a transcript made by Cyriac of Ancona in April 1436, edited by Carlo Moroni in the 17th c. and by Ludovico Muratori in the 18th c. (see *IG*; Bodnar 1960, 74–87). Cyriac reported: 'in agro vinearum ubi templum Bacchi collapsum vetustate conspicitur in magno et ornatissimo marmore epigramma tale apparet'. 'Ornatissimo' suggests possible figure-work, or at least relief carving.

No recorded dimensions.

Cyriac identified the place where he saw the stone as a ruined temple of Dionysus, but Richardson (1890–1897, 128–9) notes that Cyriac identifies another inscription by its proximity to the theatre ('amphitheatrum') and suggests that he would likely have done the same if the ruined temple where he saw this inscription was the one near the theatre. The force of this argument is open to doubt, but the temple seen by Cyriac may not have belonged to Dionysus. His ascription may have been a deduction from the inscription itself. Cyriac's reference to grapevines sounds like an effort to convince his readers, or himself.

Current whereabouts unknown.

Moroni [Cyriac] ca. 1654, 36 no. 242; Muratori [Cyriac] 1739, 145; *CIG* 2144; *Syll.*[3] 323; *IG* XII 9, 192; Lewis 1990 (= *SEG* 40, 758); Knoepfler 2014, 87–90.

The disposition of the text is extremely uncertain. Cyriac's transcription, as reported by Moroni and Muratori, gave no good indication of where lines began or ended. The following is based largely on Knoepfler 2014 (except notably at ll. 5–6).

ὁ ἱερεὺς τοῦ Διονύσου Θεόδοτος Θεοδώρου
καὶ οἱ πολέμαρχοι Σ<ω>σίστρατος Πρωτομένου,
Αἰσχύλος Ἀντανδρίδου, Ἰθαιγένης Αἰσχύλου
εἶπα<ν>· ἐπειδὴ τῆι πομπῆι τῆι Διονύσου ἥ τε
5   φρου<ρ>ὰ ἀπῆλθεν ὅ τε δῆμος ἠλευθερώθη κ[ατ]ὰ
τοὺς ὕμνους καὶ τὴν δημοκρατίαν ἐκομίσατο·
ὅπως ὑπόμνημα τῆς ἡμέρας ταύτης ἦι, ἔδοξεν
τῆι βουλῆι καὶ τῶι δήμωι· στεφανηφορεῖν Ἐρε-
τριεῖς πάντας καὶ τοὺς ἐνοικοῦντας κιττ-
10   οῦ στέφανον τῆι πομπῆι τοῦ Διονύσου· τοὺς δὲ
π<ω>λ<η>τὰς ἀπομι<σ>θοῦν τε <τ>οὺς <σ>[τεφ]άνους·
ἐπάρχεσθαι δὲ καὶ τοὺς χ<ώ>ρους ἑκάστ<ου>ς τῶι
Διονύσωι οἶνον καταπεμπο[- - - - - - - - - - - -]
- -

2 ΣΟΣΙΣΤΡΑΤΟΣ Cyriac   5 ΦΡΟΥΤΑ Cyriac   5–6 κ[ατ]ὰ τοὺς ὕμνους
Boeckh   Κ . . . . Α. ΤΟΥΣ. ΗΜΝΟΥΣ Cyriac   κ[αὶ τοὺς π]ατ<ρί>ους <νόμ>ους

Dittenberger, Robert, Knoepfler   10–11 τοὺς δὲ πωλητὰς Robert   ΤΟΥΣ.
ΔΕ.ΠΟΛΙΤΑΣ Cyriac   τοὺς δὲ πολίτας [λαβεῖν τοὺς στεφάνους | ἀπὸ τοῦ δημοσίου]
Boeckh   11 Knoepfler   ΑΠΟΜΙΘΟΥΝΤΕ . . . ΑΝΟΥΣΙ . . . . . . ΑΝΟΥΣ Cyriac   [τὸν
ταμί]αν Dittenberger   12–13 τοὺς χ<ώ>ρους ἑκάστ<ου>ς τῶι Διονύσωι, οἶνον
καταπεμπομ[ένους] D. Lewis   τοὺς χοροὺς <χορ>είας τῶι Διονύσωι, οἶνον [δὲ . . . .]
Boeckh   ΤΟΥΣΧΟΡΟΥΣΕΙΑΣΤΑΣ Cyriac

The priest of Dionysus, Theodotos son of Theodoros and the polemarchs
Sosistratos son of Protomenes, Aischylos son of Antandrides, Ithaigenes son
of Aischylos, proposed: since on the occasion of the procession of Dionysus
the [5] garrison departed and the People was liberated in acc[ordance wi]th the
hymns (or 'd[urin]g the hymns') and rescued the democracy (or, rather than 'in
accordance with the hymns', perhaps 'and rescued the ancestral laws and the
democracy'); so that there might be a commemoration of this day, the Council
and the People decided that all Eretrians and inhabitants wear a crown [10] of ivy
at the procession of Dionysus. The *poletai* are to let the [cro]wns out for hire;
and (?) ea[ch] of the *chôroi* are to make an offering to Dionysus, send[ing]
down wine … (thus the text of D. Lewis; or with Boeckh: 'And the choruses
are to offer dances to Dionysus …')

10. Fragmentary (?) decree possibly relating to the leasing of the theatre in Eretria,
4th c. (by letter forms); perhaps ca. 308–304 (Holleaux 1897, 189).

Three small fragments.
No recorded dimensions.
'Found in the excavations about the stage in the theatre' (Richardson 1891, 253) in 1891.
Current whereabouts unknown.
Richardson 1891, 253; *IG* XII 9, 193.

```
        [- - - - - - - - - - - - - - - - - - -]Θ[- - - - - - - - - - - -]    ? stoich.
        [- - - - - - - - - -]ΑΝΔΕ . . . Ν[- - - - - - - - - - - -]
        [- - - - - - - - - -]ΤΩΝΔ . . ΔΙ[- - - - - - - - - - -]
        [- - - - - - - - - -] πολεμαρχ[- - - - - - - - - - - - -]
  5     [- - - - - - - - -]ḤΜΗΝΙΑΙΤ[- - - - - - - - - - - -]
        [- - - - - - - - - -] τὸ θέατρον [- - - - - - - - - - - -]
        [- - - - - - - - π]ωλεῖν ὥστ[ε - - - - - - - - - - - -]
        [- - - - - - - - - - -]ειν ἐς τὸ θ[έατρον - - - - - - - -]
        [- - - - - - - - - - - - π]ολεμ[αρχ- - - - - - - - - -]
  10    [- - - - - - - - - - - - -]ΟΥΝΤ[- - - - - - - - - - - - -]
        [- - - - - - - - - - - - - -]ΩΙΕ̣[- - - - - - - - - - - -]
```

8 perhaps [πωλ]εῖν Richardson

[(ll. 1–3 no complete word can be discerned) …] polemarch(?s) [… (l. 5: no
complete word can be discerned) …] the theatre […] to [s]ell so as t[o …]
for the th[eatre … p]olem[arch(?s) … (ll. 10–11 no complete word can be
discerned)]

The Theatre and Related Monuments

Overview of Eretria theatre and sanctuary from north-east. See also Colour Plate 15.

The theatre is situated south-west of the acropolis, within the Archaic city walls and near their western gate. A traveller approaching from that direction would be immediately struck by it on their left as they entered the city. Its site is very unusual as having not been selected for the ease provided by a natural slope for the rising of the seating. The choice may have been dictated by the prior existence of a sanctuary of Dionysus nearby (Fossum 1891, 257; Isler 2007, 17). The significant temple of Dionysus (12.25 × 23.05 m) that lies just 19 m from the south-west corner of the stage building can only be dated approximately to the middle of the fourth century or a little later. It may have been constructed at the same time as the first phase of the theatre (Isler 2007, 17 n. 31), though whether on the site of a pre-existing sanctuary or not cannot be said. At any rate by the end of the fourth century the sanctuary of Dionysus and the theatre were evidently conceived as a grand architectural unity, as in Athens (Richardson 1890–1897, 128–33; Auberson 1976, 59; Isler 2007, 17; further on the temple: Auberson and Schefold 1972, 46–56).

Despite a major recent study by the Swiss School in 1997–1998 (Isler 2007), following at some distance earlier excavation by the American School (between 1891 and 1895) and a detailed analysis by Fiechter (1937), the date and character of the earliest phase of this important theatre remain elusive. (See also Boukaras 2013, esp. 19–20 on the limited reports of early visitors.) The Swiss study concluded that the first phase of the skene is to be dated to the last quarter of the fourth century – perhaps around 320. This is based on the stratigraphical find of an Athenian coin dated 330–322/17 providing a *terminus post quem* and, somewhat less confidently, on the slender evidence of the polygonal masonry at the base of the stage area (Isler 2007, 20, 52). The date of a second phase is put at around 300 or soon after. This is confirmed by the placement of the dock, found *in situ*, for the stele with the Euboean law on the Artists of Dionysus at the inner corner of the eastern parodos (see below), for this law is certainly to be dated between 295 and 287 (Knoepfler 2007, 681–2). Major developments took place at this point, including the building up of a huge artificial mound for the theatron from soil, much of it excavated from the orchestra, the level of which was lowered by over 3 m, resulting in sloping parodoi and a skene building nearly 3.5 m above the level of the orchestra (Capps 1895, 341–3); and, further, the addition of a new stage front, with a two-storey skene. A third phase is dated approximately to sometime after the middle of the second century (Isler 2007, 52).

What remains entirely unclear is whether there is any evidence for the existence of a theatre prior to the first phase identified by the Swiss (the '320–' phase). Indications of an earlier construction under the skene may have been detected (Isler 2007, 52) and it is certain on other grounds that Eretria possessed a place for performance at its Dionysia prior to 320 (see further below on **1, 2**).

No evidence for the first phase identified by the Swiss (the '320–' phase) of the theatron – entirely overbuilt by the second – has survived. During the first phase the seating is very likely to have consisted of wooden stands erected on the flat ground in front of the orchestra (Dilke 1948, 150). The Swiss study, which focused particularly on the theatron, discovered that in its second phase this was rather larger than had been thought, extending to thirty rows of seats, with five or six more flattened rows at the summit suitable for standing (Isler 2007, 51). Its capacity has been estimated in the region of 6,000–6,400 spectators (Boukaras 2013, 24). It will have been in this theatre that the performances of tragedy, comedy and cyclic choruses mandated by the Euboean law of ca. 290 took place. In fact the stele-dock for the copy of this law to be erected in the parodos of the Eretrian theatre (*IG* XII 9, 207, ll. 55–6 ἀν[α]θεῖναι εἰς τὴν πάρ[οδον | τοῦ] θεάτρου) has been identified *in situ* on its eastern side, right at the corner formed by the retaining wall and the first row of seats (Knoepfler 1978; Isler 2007, pl. 14.5–6).

The second phase of construction also saw added to the theatre the highly unusual underground passage, over 13 m long, that leads from just behind the proskenion to the centre of the orchestra (Brownson 1891, 275–80; Dörpfeld and Reisch 1896, 112–17). This is probably an example of the 'steps of Charon' mentioned by Pollux (4.128, 132), thought to be designed for the subterranean appearance of ghosts and the like. On the other hand Capps (1895, 343–4) may well be right in thinking that it served rather (or perhaps it was also) as a ceremonial passageway for processions with priests, choregoi, officials, actors and choruses entering the theatre by this means after the sacrifices at the altar (see Green et al. 2015). The new orchestra of this phase was equipped with a semicircular channel around its outer edge that gathered rainwater and directed it through underground pipes and which was, remarkably, decorated on the plasterwork of its interior with ivy leaves and grape clusters.

It is possible that Menedemus of Eretria played an important part in promoting the energetic development of the theatre in this second phase. In addition to being a philosopher and politician, Menedemus was a devotee of dramatic poetry and poets. He is said to have quoted the Eretrian tragic poet Achaeus against his political opponents, and to have 'welcomed'

(D.L. 2.133 ἠσπάζετο) the tragic poet Lycophron of Chalcis (*TrGF* 100), despite the fact that the latter composed a satyr play named after him (the *Menedemus*) that ridiculed his eating habits. A fragment (*TrGF* 100 F 2) indicates that it included a speech by Silenos to his sons the satyrs, who in all likelihood served as a chorus (Xanthakis-Karamanos 1990–1996; Xanthakis-Karamanos 1997; Günther 1999; Sens 2010, 299). Menedemus was himself the son of an architect – or in fact a 'scene-painter' σκηνογράφος – and is reported as having learnt the latter trade himself (D.L. 2.125, 133).

The Americans mention having found fragments of throne-type prohedria of different periods in the region of the orchestra (Brownson 1891, 275), but they are poorly documented and the evidence apparently lost (cf. Knoepfler and Schefold 1976, 57, reporting the discovery of a support for a theatre seat in reuse on the Acropolis). The award of prohedria is attested from the fifth century (**2**), though it is rare before the very end of the fourth (Knoepfler 2001a, 86, 160–1 with n. 348). While the standard formula does not specify prohedria 'in the theatre' or 'at the Dionysia', but rather (in **2**) 'at the contests' or (in the later instances) 'at (all) the contests which the city (or People) runs' it is probable that this is a way of including events held at other sanctuaries, notably that of Artemis, and that it will nonetheless attest the existence of prohedria in the theatre as early as 411.

In the western parodos, a low retaining wall made of poros 1.20 m wide extended from the north-west corner of the stage building at an oblique angle for some 20 m, and was integral to its first (ca. 320–) phase (Capps 1895, 341–3; Isler 2007, 46–7, 52, pls. 31.2, 45.7–8, 46.3; see now the important pages of Knoepfler 2010a, 230–5 who rightly notes the general neglect of this significant feature and its monumental remains even by those who have studied the theatre building in detail). Fiechter (1937, 15) had proposed that there had been a similar wall with dedications on the eastern side of the stage building, but Isler (2007, 47) has rejected the idea. This helped to define the western parodos and to forge a closer physical connection with the temple of Dionysus that stood to the south of it. It also served as a lower foundation course or platform for the erection of various monuments, including choregic dedications, and thus helped to shape the western parodos as a monumental entranceway to the theatre that, like the eastern parodos and start of the Street of Tripods in Athens, gave full recognition to material (and other: see below on Menander) benefactors to the theatre.

On this platform there were found some eight uninscribed bases of local marble (and there will doubtless have been more originally), many (perhaps most or even all) of which were part of choregic monuments (**4** and **5** were found here). Six are quadrangular in shape (ca. 1.00 × 1.00 × 0.4 m), two with level upper surfaces designed to receive another block. **5, 7** and **8** were inscribed on quadrangular blocks. These may have rested directly on the retaining wall, like the quadrangular uninscribed blocks found *in situ* (Knoepfler 2010a, 230). Or they may have been set upon one or more uninscribed lower blocks, in step formation. The other four quadrangular bases found on the wall have a large circular cavity (diam. ca. 0.30 × D. 0.15 m) in their upper surface to receive a smooth column (see Knoepfler 2010a, 230–1, with the photograph at 231 showing the remains of one such column several metres in height; Isler 2007, 46–7, pls. 45.7–8, 46.1–4, 47.3). These columns evidently supported blocks inscribed with choregic dedications (as in **4, 6**) that in turn carried above them a tripod supported by a central column. Such dedications mounted on a substantial column were evidently a choregic norm in the Eretrian theatre. We might be tempted to compare those prominent above the theatron in the Athenian Theatre (**V F**), but there are regional models for the form closer to hand (see below on the parallel with Oropus).

At the eastern end of this wall, close to the stage building, there are the bases of two more, considerably larger, monuments, one square the other circular. The latter (diam. ca. 3.38 m²; 'E' on the Americans' plan at pl. 12, Capps 1895, 339; photo: Isler 2007, pl. 45.7) was found *in situ* in a kind of portico-like area formed by the two walls of the west wing of the skene after the addition of paraskenia in the theatre's second phase. To which phase this monument dates is unclear, but it seems *a priori* very much more likely to be the earlier phase (ca. 320–), since the addition of the paraskenia will have largely obscured it from the view of the theatron. It will originally have been a structure reminiscent of the monument of Lysikrates from Athens (**V F**), though without its high square base (Auberson and Schefold 1972, 48; image 4). A solid marble circular tholos-roof (Eretria Museum 1187; Themelis 1987, 121 and pl. 37) with Ionic entablature and leaf-shaped roof-'tiles', very like that of the Lysikrates monument, might possibly derive from this choregic monument, or another like it. Immediately to the west of this is the large square base 'F', formed by four blocks of neatly dressed black marble joined by Z clamps (diam. 1.97 m; Capps 1895, 339).

It is very likely that the statue of Menander, the base of which was discovered in 1896–1897 (0.46 × 1.08 × 0.72 m), was erected somewhere in this region. Inscribed simply with the poet's name, this was found near the theatre (no further specification in Kouroniotes 1897, 151 no. 4; *IG* XII 9, 280; now kept in the garden of the Eretria Museum). The block is broken to the left and the preparation of the upper surface shows that it carried another above it. The absence of any clamp marks at the rear suggests that the poet was represented in a standing position (unlike the seated Athenian version) while the fact that the lower part of the rear of the back has been chiselled more deeply and more roughly implies that it was set up before a wall where the lower stone projected somewhat, and the mason was required to shear off some of the lower rear surface to form a neat fit against the wall. The letter forms suggest a remarkably early date for this statue, as early as the late fourth or early third century – quite possibly in the lifetime of the poet, therefore, and substantially earlier than the statue in the Athenian Theatre. As Nervegna (2013, 37–8) remarks, such a memorial is suggestive of Menander having produced drama in person in Eretria as well as Athens.

In the early third century each of the other three confederated cities of Euboea party to the law concerning the organisation of the Dionysia and Demetrieia in each – namely Chalcis, Histiaea and Oreos – also had a theatre, for the law was to be inscribed on a stele 'and set up in the par[odos of the] theatre' *IG* XII 9, 207, ll. 54–6: τὰ δ[ὲ δό|ξαντ]α ἀναγράψαι τοὺς ἄρχοντας ἐν ἑκάστ[ηι] τῶν πόλεων ἐν στ[ή]ληι λιθίνηι καὶ ἀν[α]θεῖναι εἰς τὴν πάρ[οδον | τοῦ] θεάτρου.

The Dionysia

At least by the first half of the fourth century, the Dionysia of Eretria was one of the city's two most important festivals, along with the Artemisia in honour of the city's tutelary deity. They feature in the law against tyranny of ca. 340 as the occasions on which the city's priests and priestesses are to curse any who oppose the provisions of the law to safeguard democracy (*SEG* 51, 1105). That the Dionysia appears before the festival of Artemis (B l. 14: Διονυρίοις τε καὶ Ἀρτεμιρίοις: note the intervocalic rhotacism characteristic of Eretria, 'Dionyria'; cf. **1**, l. 2) should probably be taken to signify its calendrical priority rather than its greater importance, for we know that it fell upon 12 Lenaion (*IG* XII 9, 207, ll. 27–9) – towards the end of winter (February) – and Lenaion preceded Anthesterion, the month of the Artemisia (Knoepfler 2001b, 232).

The parade was an important element of the festival, and **9** may indicate, unsurprisingly, that hymns were sung to Dionysus during it (below). In the first century the parade was an occasion for the announcement of civic honours (*IG* XII 9, 236, ll. 44–5; *IG* XII 9, 237, ll. 21–3). These last two inscriptions also demonstrate the festival's longevity, and the theatre evidently remained in use into the Roman Imperial period. Drama is only securely attested from the early third century (*IG* XII 9, 207), but is very likely to have been part of the festival earlier. It is difficult to know whether the fact that Eretria produced a tragic poet of great note in the fifth century (Achaeus: *TrGF* 20), and Chalcis a tragic actor (Mynniskos: Stefanis no. 1757), points to a local theatrical tradition already by that date, or simply registers the magnetic orbit of nearby Athens (Wilson 2000, 283). The possible imposition of a cleruchy by Athens after a revolt from League membership in 446 (Moreno 2007, 80, 89–90, 99–100; cf. Bearzot 2013, 120 with earlier bibliography) might be important in this connection, although the evidence has been taken to suggest that the nature of Athenian land holding in Eretria was predominantly that of wealthy absentee landlords (for arguments the other way, see Green and Sinclair 1970). But as we shall see, the possibility of Athenian influence in the shaping of the Eretrian Dionysia may go back to a much earlier date, to the late sixth century. Purely choral contests feature prominently throughout the Classical period, from perhaps as early as the late sixth century (**1**). In the last quarter of the fourth century the contest of *kyklioi* was the moment chosen by the city to proclaim honours for its benefactors. The expression 'at the Dionysia, at the contest of the cyclic choruses' (**3**) is notably non-committal as to category – men or boys – and may imply the existence of both.

If, as seems most likely, **1** is to be interpreted as a dedication to Dionysus, a choral contest for men – and with it the Dionysia itself – are attested as early as the end of the sixth century. For while there is good evidence for the cult of Heracles, and athletic contests in his honour, in Eretria, Themelis and Knoepfler (Themelis 1987, 123) are surely right to interpret **1** as a dedication not to 'the son of Zeus', namely Heracles (see app. crit.), but to Dionysus. This may therefore be a very early memorial of a choral contest for Dionysus in Eretria – and the only surviving evidence for a men's event, which we might nonetheless have expected alongside that attested much later for boys (**4**). It would also be the earliest attested use of the expression (χορὸς) ἀνδρῶν from any site. For in a Dionysiac context the words ἀνδρῶν νικέρας (l. 2) are most probably a shorthand for 'having won in the choral contest of men', a type of idiom best known from Attica, though some two or three decades later (**Dxii 2**; *IG* I³ 833 bis: [νικέ]σας … [χο]ρõι ἀνδρõ[ν] in **V C**; *IG* II³ 4, 439 and the Atarbos Monument in **V F**; **III Bii**). **1** differs from the Attic type in its lack of a specific reference to 'the chorus' (unless one could be restored to the end of l. 1, but we cannot offer a suggestion), but χορῶι 'with a chorus' could be understood in this context. Alternatively one might restore an explicit reference to the contest – τὸν ἀγῶνα (Hansen) – at the end of l. 1, namely: 'Timokrates dedicated (sc. this) [to] Dio[nysus] after winning in the men's contest'. But it is probably preferable to reserve this place for the item dedicated: a 'small tripod' is plausible contextually and works metrically (**III Yi**). Small columns mounted on a base with a crowning block (certainly present in this case given the circular mortice in the top of the column) frequently served as the central support of tripods, notably for instance in those dedicated (ca. 530–450) to the hero Ptoios at Akraiphiai in nearby Boeotia (Guillon 1943 I, esp. 49 fig. 3; Papalexandrou 2008) and the dedication of a tripod mounted on a block itself set into a column is the best attested choregic form in fourth-century Eretria itself. (Rather less probably, the line might have ended with the name of the tribe for which Timokrates competed. If that were the case, we should have evidence for a choral contest among the tribes very close to the time at which the tribes themselves were introduced.)

The fact that Hypodikos of Chalcis was the first victor in the men's choral contest at the Athenian Dionysia in the late sixth century (*FGrH* 239 F A46: 509) and that that city produced the poet Tynnichos, who Plato says composed the finest paean (Pl. *Ion* 534d; *PMG* 707), further indicates that the cities of Euboea already had a highly sophisticated choral culture in the sixth century. Knoepfler has argued that there were six Eretrian tribes in all, rather than ten, despite the probable influence of the Attic system in their formulation, and that they were introduced at the end of the sixth century, in a kind of 'democratic revolution' akin to the one that took place in Attica at the same time, and directly linked to it. In 506 the Athenians – in response to an abortive attack by the Peloponnesians, Boeotians and Chalcidians that was at least in part aimed at defeating Cleisthenes and his proposed reforms – invaded and overcame Chalcis, confiscating land belonging to the oligarchic cavalry class and distributing it among 4,000 cleruchs (Hdt 5.77). Evidence for relations between Eretria and Athens at this date is virtually non-existent, but it appears from **1** that a tribal choral contest very like and probably modelled on the one introduced to the Athenian Dionysia in the last decade of the sixth century appeared in Eretria very soon after. Knoepfler (2001a, 177 n. 433) suggests that there were three choruses competing in each category (men and boys) and that the six tribes paired up to supply the choreuts and choregoi.

4–8 testify to an energetic tradition of choral performance, choregic service and dedication in the Eretrian theatre. **4** and **5** were both found in the western parodos of the theatre. **4** is a tripod base, a dedication by a choregos to Dionysus after a victory with the boys' chorus. Roesch (1982, 445) is confident that the musician in l. 3 is to be restored as Kaphisias, a famous piper who performed for Alexander at Susa in 324, doubtless named after the river Kephisos in Boeotia where the best reeds for pipes grew (Stefanis no. 1387; it is noteworthy, in light of the prominence of the hero Narcissus in Eretria – below – that in many traditions he was the son of the river Kephisos: Hyg. *Fab.* 271; Ov. *Met.* 3.3404; Stat. *Theb.* 7.340–2). Knoepfler (2010a, 227) notes that the even more famous Theban piper Ismenias is another possibility (Stefanis no. 1295). The former identification would put the date of the inscription into the latter decades of the century; the latter, probably a little earlier.

As it happens, no part of the verb χορηγεῖν or noun χορηγός survives in any Eretrian inscription. But there is no doubting the existence of choregia in the city and, though entirely restored, the verb χορηγήσας in l. 2 of **4** may be regarded as secure: the comparative evidence of Athenian (and other) choregic inscriptions urges it, as does the simple fact that these dedications commemorating victories (**7**) with choral performances in the Eretrian theatre were evidently made by individuals (**4, 6**) tasked by their tribes with the duty. That this is a choregic inscription is also indicated by the placement of the details of the piper at or near the end, as in Athenian choregic inscriptions (**V F**). Knoepfler's new supplements to and disposition of the text, which brings out the manner in which it was carefully centred on the stone, marks an important advance. He is confident that the genitive of the word 'tribe' preceded the word 'with the boys' in l. 2 ([φυ]λῆς; see app. crit.). The suggested use of ὑπέρ of the choregos' service 'on behalf of' his associated tribe or tribes (in the genitive) is to our knowledge unparalleled but nevertheless quite cogent, given the clear attestation of the word 'tribe' in the genitive in the newly published **7** (below). This entails that there was variation in this element of choregic dedicatory expression between ὑπέρ 'on behalf of' with the genitive and the simple dative (as in **6**).

Knoepfler's restorations to **5** are preferable to those of Wilamowitz, who assumed a stone-cutter's error in l. 1 (πασι for πα<ι>σί). Pasicharidas is a name attested in Thebes, and moreover in a family of actors of the late Hellenistic period (Stefanis no. 2016; cf. 1399). But there are other possibilities, such as Πασικλῆς, Πασιχάρης, Πασίχορος, Πάσιχος and Πασίων (see *LGPN* IIIB, s.v.; Knoepfler 2010a, 228).

6 and **7** are recent additions to the corpus of Eretrian choregic inscriptions. Both were found in reuse, though neither very far from the theatre. **6** certainly, and very probably also **7**, was part of a monument that took the form of a tripod dedication. In **6**'s case, the tripod was mounted on a central column inserted into the inscribed block. The combined block and column-mounted tripod are set in turn upon a smooth column, several examples of which survive in the immediate environs of the theatre. This larger smooth column was itself doubtless inserted into a larger base block of precisely the sort that survives in the western parodos of the theatre (below). Such a structure will have elevated the tripod imposingly above ground level (**4** was evidently from a similar monument). Knoepfler (2010a, 233–4) notes the general similarity of the type to those tripod bases preserved in somewhat better condition as dedicated prizes from the contest for the nymph Halia in Oropus (**Ci**), and suggests that the Oropians may have modelled the type of their choregic monuments on those of Eretria, with whom they had strong ancestral ties.

6 provides the first evidence that in Eretria the choral contest (or at least one of them) was organised like the Athenian Thargelia – and perhaps, as Knoepfler (1998, 106; cf. *BE* 2011, 405) argues, in direct imitation of it – with a single choregos leading two tribes and the victor describing himself as having won the contest 'with' the two tribes in question. This clear evidence of paired tribes in the competition justifies Knoepfler's approach to the reconstruction of **4** and **7**. **6** also newly supplies the name of one of these tribes, Narkittis (also in **7**) – named after the important local hero Narcissus the son of Amarynthos, closely associated with Artemis (Knoepfler 2010a, 101–26; at 1998, 107, Knoepfler suggests [Εὐρυ]τίδι or [Μηκι]τίδι as possible restorations for the first tribe in **6**). If the piper in **6** was indeed Chares he was quite possibly the Theban of that name who played at the Dionysia of Acharnae in the fourth century (**III Bii**).

In the second new inscription (**7**), the piper may have been the Alkathous from Sicyon who was part of the winning team with the boys at the Athenian Thargelia in 358 (*SEG* 27,

16), which would push the date of the monument up towards the middle of the fourth century, or its third quarter, a possibility viewed by Knoepfler as epigraphically plausible (pers. comm.), noting also the good relations between Eretria and Sicyon at this date demonstrated by a decree awarding citizenship to a Sicyonian (Knoepfler 2001a, no. 1). The fact that the tribe Narkittis seems to be first in its pair in this inscription, whereas it is certainly listed second in **6**, may suggest – what is in any case highly plausible – that the choregoi for the paired choral teams at the Eretrian Dionysia were selected by alternation between the two tribal members of each of the three pairs, since it is likely that the tribe to which the choregos belonged would be listed in first place (Wilson 2007b, 159). Denis Knoepfler also informs us that there is a further, unpublished fragment of a choregic base found in the American excavations in 1894, now lost, which mentions another tribe – 'Admetis' – a name attested in a third-century inscription listing donors to a sanctuary found by the Swiss in 2011 and recently published by Knoepfler and Ackermann (2012), with commentary on the role of the hero Admetus in Eretrian society.

Unlike their Athenian counterparts (**V F**), Eretrian choregoi for tribal choruses use the most traditional verb of dedication for a deity (ἀνέθηκε) and name the god. But as we have already noted, parallels with, perhaps direct imitations of, Athenian models are also evident, and suggested by what little can be deduced of the relevant historical context. In Eretria, we have solid evidence only for dedication by choregoi for choral contests, not drama. The fact that the contest of cyclic choruses is the event chosen for the announcement of honours, rather than a tragic agon as was most common in Athens, is also suggestive.

The intriguing decree **9**, known only from transcriptions of a copy made in 1436 by Cyriac of Ancona, has been placed as late as the Roman period, but Holleaux (1897) showed that the presence of a group of three polemarchs (ll. 2–5) with wide civic competence points to a period in which Eretria was a member of the Second Boeotian Confederacy, for the principal magistracy of Eretria was normally that of proboulos and membership of the Confederacy is otherwise associated with the prominent role of a college of polemarchs within member cities. Holleaux made a strong case for identifying this period as 308–304, for 308 marked the end of the control of the cities of Euboea by Polemaios, the general and nephew of Antigonus, with his assassination on Cos (cf. Bakhuizen 1970, 129). That would place the event described in **9**, and probably the decree itself, in 308/7. Knoepfler (1991, 197 n. 73) has however suggested that the period of Eretria's membership of the Confederacy began in 286/5, promising a fuller explanation as forthcoming. One of the proposing polemarchs, Aischylos son of Antandrides (ll. 3–4), is almost certainly to be identified with the prominent politician friendly to Demetrius and Antigonus and opposed to the philosopher-politician Menedemus (D.L. 2.141; Knoepfler 2001a, 257–9), but his attested dates could fit either alternative.

The decree establishes a special commemorative occasion at the city's Dionysia in response to a major event in Eretrian political history, the restoration of democracy after a period of military occupation (for a comparable Athenian example see *IG* II³ 4, 877, esp. ll. 43–5). And because that event took place, with a sense of the uncanny or of divine direction (Jacottet 1990, 153), during the procession of the city's Dionysia (l. 5), it is at the Dionysia that the commemoration is to take place. It is further specified that the garrison had departed κ[ατ]ὰ τοὺς ὕμνους (l. 7; Knoepfler 2014, 73–4 makes a robust case in favour of adopting a text here that refers to the restoration of the ancestral laws, along with democracy, but our text is closer to Cyriac's reported transcription). This may mean 'during the hymns', and reveal the (unexceptional) presence of such songs for the god in the course of the procession. But it is perhaps more likely to mean 'in accordance with the hymns', and be a reference to the answering of prayers for the liberation of the city that had been expressed in hymns to Dionysus, called upon as a saviour god (this is definitely preferable to the interpretation of Reinach, citing Hsch. υ 194: ὕμνος· χρησμός, as 'in accordance with the oracles': see Lewis 1990, 198–9). If the date of 308/7 is correct for this decree, the parallel is striking with the way in which, upon his arrival in Athens in 307 and more especially in 304, Demetrius the Besieger very deliberately styled himself as a saviour and restorer of democracy, modelling himself very directly on the god Dionysus. It is perhaps not impossible that **9** itself might date to 304, the year in which Demetrius the Besieger also 'liberated' Euboea from the domination of Cassander.

The inscription may have been rather lengthy – Cyriac noted that there had been other lines no longer legible ('diruta sequentia') – and much of the planned commemorative activity has probably been lost. What does survive is a direction that Eretrian citizens and residents are to wear an ivy crown at the (presumably next) procession of Dionysus. A popular interpretation of what follows (based on influential restorations of Boeckh and Dittenberger and taken further by Lewis 1990) maintains that the decree went on to stipulate that citizens were to wear these crowns at public expense, while by contrast non-citizens could hire them, but Robert's suggestion that the word in l. 14 should be *poletai* rather than 'citizens' (*politai*) is entirely compelling. This would remove the dichotomy between citizen and non-citizens in the rental of crowns. The rental of crowns itself may even be a mirage: the reported text at l. 16 (ΑΝΟΥΣΙ . . . . . . ΑΝΟΥΣ) requires considerable emendation and supplementation to make any sense at all. Following Knoepfler (2014), we have reduced the size of the imagined lacunae at this point, but it remains possible that the decree went on to outline the activity of *poletai* in some act of hiring, selling, or contracting quite distinct from what preceded (and note the collocation of renting and the theatre in **10**).

The fragmentary, poorly transcribed, final lines are the most important of all from our perspective. An offering to Dionysus of some sort is prescribed. Before the socio-political organisation of Eretria was better understood, this was generally thought to be an offering of choruses (ἐπάρχεσθαι δὲ καὶ τοὺς χορούς <χορ>είας τῶι Διονύσωι) but it is certain to be an injunction to the *chôroi* or 'districts' – an organisational element of Eretrian society below the level of the tribe and above that of the deme: there appear to have been five – to make a contribution to the event, probably the 'sending down' (from their regions in the hinterland) of wine. This interpretation goes back to D. Lewis (1962, 2) and is supported by L. Robert (*BE* 1964, 215, no. 406) and Knoepfler (1997, 429 n. 172; 2014). It is guaranteed by the parallel from the decree concerning the Eretrian Artemisia that makes the *chôroi* responsible for the provision of sacrificial victims at the festivals of Artemis and Hera in the fourth century (*IG* XII 9, 189, ll. 26–32). The text suggested by Lewis assumes an error of reading or transcription of an omicron for an omega (τοὺς χ<ώ>ρους), which is relatively easy, a clear case appearing in l. 2 (see app. crit.). Lewis construes the unintelligible sequence that follows – ΕΙΑΣΤΑΣ – as ἑκάστ<ου>ς 'each': 'And ea[ch] of the *chôroi* are to make an offering to Dionysus …'. Choruses thus disappear from the inscription, though it is entirely possible that some special form of performance was also to be staged at the Dionysia, the provisions for which are lost with the rest of the decree.

Ziebarth (*IG*) suggested that the decree of which **10** is a small fragment was concerned with the leasing out of the theatre in Eretria, but unfortunately little more than that bare possibility can be stated and it has not entered the recent discussion of this subject (e.g. Csapo 2007; Slater 2011; Carusi 2013). If the decree made reference to a college of polemarchs (ll. 4 and 9 are indeterminate as to number) it might date from the same period as **9**.

Dviii: Lemnos

1. Tragedy in Myrina, ca. 348 (historical and prosopographical reasons).

Decree of the Chalcidians living in Myrina, Lemnos, honouring the epimelete Theophilos, son of Meliton.
Marble stele, broken at top. A relief of a crown of olive appears below the text.
0.67 × 0.335 × 0.06 m.
Found in his fields on a peninsula north of Kastro (ancient Myrina) by M. J. Pantelidis, while ploughing.
Archaelogical Museum of Myrina 2049.
Cousin and Dürrbach (1885) 54–8, no. 3 (*ed. princ.*); *IG* XII 8, 4.
Text: *IG* XII 8, 4 and Cargill 1995, 233–4.

[. . . . . ¹⁶. . . . . ἐ]πειδὴ καὶ ὁ δῆ-   stoich. 28
[μος ὁ Ἀ]θ[ην]αίων ὁ ἐ[ν Μυρ]ίνει οἰκῶν ἔ-
[δ]ωκεν χωρίον τοῖς Χαλκιδεῦσιν, στῆσαι τὴν στήλην τὴν περὶ τοῦ ἐπιμε-
5   λητοῦ καὶ ἀνειπεῖν τὸν κήρυκα Διονυσίων τῶι ἀγῶνι τραγωιδοῖς ὅτι Χ-
αλκιδέες οἱ ἐν Μυρίνει οἰκοῦντες
στεφανοῦσι τῶιδε τῶι στεφάνωι τὸ-
ν ἐπιμελητὴν Θεόφιλον Μελίτωνο[ς]
10   Ἀλωπεκῆθεν ἀνδραγαθίας ἕνεκα κα-
ὶ δικαιοσύνης τῆς εἰς τοὺς Χαλκι[δ]-
έας τοὺς ἐν Μυρίνει οἰκοῦ<ν>τας.

[... s]ince also the de[mos of the A]th[en]ians dwelling i[n Myr]ine [g]ave land to the Chalcidians, to erect the stele concerning the epimelete ⁵ and that the herald announce at the tragic contest of the Dionysia that the Chalcidians living in Myrina crown with this crown the epimelete Theophilos, son of Meliton, ¹⁰ of Alopeke, for his rectitude and justice towards the Chalci[d]ians living in Myrina.

2. Tragedy in Hephaistia, unknown date, early 3ʳᵈ c.? (by letter forms).

The date can only be guessed on the precarious basis of the form of the sigmas as printed in the *editio princeps* (Cargill 1995, 65 n. 37).
Honorary decree of the Athenian cleruchs of Hephaistia, Lemnos.
Fragment of a marble stele, broken on all sides.
0.12 × 0.08 × 0.05 m.

Found ca. 1893 at Palaiopolis, near the gulf, at the house of Lascaris Kyriako. Palaiopolis is the peninsula that closed the north side of the harbour of ancient Hephaistia and apparently contained most of the settlement, including the theatre (see below), located on the Gulf side of the peninsula. One can guess that the inscription was originally erected in the theatre.
Current whereabouts unknown.
Ridder 1893, 128 no. 3; *IG* XII 8, 15.
Text: *IG* XII 8, 15.

[ἐπαινέσαι — —]ι̣ασιο— — — — — — — — — — — non-stoich.
[— — — — — —]ιον ἀρετῆς ἕν[εκεν καὶ εὐνοίας]
[ἧς ἔχων διατε]λεῖ π̣[ρ]ὸς τὸν [δῆμον τῶν Ἀθηναίων]
[τῶν ἐν Ἡφαιστίαι ἀ]νστελ[λ]οντ(?)— — — — — —
[— — — — — τ]ραγωιδ[ῶ]ν τ[ῶι ἀγῶνι ὅτι ὁ δῆμος]
[ὁ Ἡφαιστιέω]ν στεφανο[ῖ — — — — εὐνοίας]
[ἕνεκα, τὸ δὲ γε]νόμενον ἀν[άλωμα μερίσαι τὸν ταμίαν]·
[ὅπως οὖν καὶ ὑπ]όμνημα [ὑπάρχηι — — — αὐτῶι καὶ]
[τοῖς ἐκγόνοι]ς αὐ[τοῦ — — — — — — — — — — —].

[To praise …] on [acco]unt of the civic virtue [and kindness that he contin]ues [to show to]ward the [Athenian demos in Hephaistia … that the demos of the Hephaistia]ns crown [him for his kindness] at t[he contest of the t]ragedi[e]s. [The treasurer is to assign the re]sulting co[st. And so there should also be a me]morial [… to him and his descenda]nts.

Athenians probably settled in Lemnos in the late sixth to early fifth century (Graham 1983, 175), and certainly by ca. 480 (Marchiandi 2008, 12–13, 24–7). Settlement began in the area of Hephaistia and spread to other regions from there, but Myrina is listed as a separate community by 447/6 (*IG* I^3 265, ll. 111). The view that after ca. 450 the settlements were regarded as cleruchies, that is, as settlements of Athenian citizens who retained their citizen rights despite dwelling abroad (Meiggs 1972, 424–5; Figueira 1991, 12–13, 36–7, 253–5), is open to question (Moggi 2008; Marchiandi 2008; Ficuciello 2013, 199). The island was detached from Athens after its defeat in the Peloponnesian War, but was reattached in 394/3 (Aeschin. 2.76–7; And. 3.12–14) or 387/6 (Ficuciello 2010). Fourth-century inscriptions such as **1** and **2** make it clear that the settlers regarded themselves as Athenian citizens and were classified as 'cleruchs' in recognition of their Athenian citizen rights (Graham 1983, 176–84; Moggi 2008, 264–5; Clinton 2014).

The authors of **1**, who call themselves 'the Chalcidians living in Myrina', are probably refugees from Chalcidice expelled by Philip of Macedon (Cargill 1995, 69), although refugees from Chalcis are also possible. In 348 Philip destroyed Olynthus along with 'as many as thirty-two other settlements in Chalcidice' (Harding 1985, 105). We learn from lines 2–3 of the decree that 'the demos of the Athenians living in Myrina' granted land to the Chalcidians – not necessarily the initial grant (Cargill 1995, 69).

The nature of the office of epimelete (**1**, ll. 4–5) is unclear. Ficuciello suggests that the epimelete was an Athenian magistrate charged with supervising the local government and representing the authority of the metropolis (2013, 251). The only other Lemnian epimelete we hear of holds office in Hephaistia and Cargill warns that Theophilus 'is not necessarily *epimeletes* in Myrin[e] specifically' (1995, 94, cf. 153–4). Theophilus is probably the same man who gave evidence for Lykophron, the Hipparch for Lemnos, when tried in Athens on a charge of adultery in 333–330 (Hyp. *Lyc.* Ar. col. 16, l. 23 Jensen).

1 is the earliest certain indication we have on Lemnos for a Dionysia, for a competition in tragedy, and for the imitation of the Athenian practice of announcing honours granted by decree before the contest of the tragedies. A later fourth-century honorary decree from Myrina (*IG* XII 8, 7, ll. 15–16) can be restored with 'at the contest [of tragedies]' as easily as 'at the contest [of the Dionysia]' (Wilson 2010a, 38 n. 7). *IG* XII 8, 11, of uncertain date, attests choregiai in Myrina.

No theatre has yet been uncovered in Myrina, but archaeological research is limited because the site has been continuously occupied since antiquity and the modern city sits above the ancient. Ficuciello notes that the curvilinear form of Christodoulidi Street in modern Myrina seems to reproduce the shape of the upper part of a theatron, but that the area has never yet been investigated (2013, 253, pl. XV.11).

Though fragmentary, **2** attests a practice at Hephaistia of honorific announcements be-fore the contest of the tragedies. The reference to tragedy seems certain, and the formulaic nature of such decrees leaves little doubt about the general context. It is not impossible that the cleruchs intend that the announcement take place at the Dionysia in Athens (though in this case we might expect [ἐν Ἀθήναις Διονυσίων τῶν τ]ραγωιδ[ῶ]ν τ[ῶι ἀγῶνι in lines 4–5, for which there is insufficient space if the present restorations are correct). The later practice, not attested before the second century (*IG* II² 1223), was to announce special hon-ours at both the Athenian and the local Hephaistian Dionysia. Given **1**'s certain attestation of tragic performances on Lemnos by this date, we might guess that, if announcement at the Athenian Dionysia is involved in **2**, it is in combination with a local announcement at a parallel venue. The memorial mentioned in l. 8 is probably nothing more elaborate than the inscribed stele itself (*IG* II³ 1, 1078, l. 10; *IG* II² 637; *IG* II² 653, l. 50 etc.).

The colonies of Athens typically reproduce the political and religious institutions of the mother city in miniature (Parker 1994) and this is likely to have been the case from the time of the earliest Athenian settlement at Hephaistia in the late sixth or early fifth century. The existence of a theatre at Hephaistia, said in the most recent study to go back to precisely this date, makes it likely that drama was produced on Lemnos from the beginning.

The Early Hellenistic stone theatre of Hephaistia (Sear 2006, 341) is built on a hillside that had served as a cult centre from as early as the second half of the seventh century (cf. Correale 2008). Excavations from 2002 to 2004 beneath its central kerkis uncovered an earlier rectilinear space (21.5 × 13.5 m) delimited by parallel stone stairways and a narrow stone diadromos. Archontidou Argyri and Kokkinophorou (2004, 48–9) take these to be the remains of a wooden theatron dating back to the late sixth or early fifth century. If so, the theatre of Hephaistia may be nearly as old as the Theatre of Dionysus in Athens. No less astonishing, if true, is the claim that the earliest stone theatre dates to the late fifth or early fourth century (Archontidou Argyri and Kokkinophorou 2004, 48–9). But both of these datings seem impossibly early and, until the excavator's basis for dating these phases has been published, it is far more prudent to follow Greco and Voza in dating the wooden theatre from the end of the fifth or early fourth century, which is still very early, but in line with general patterns (Greco 2008, 19; Marchiandi 2008, 12; Greco and Voza 2010).

Underneath the theatre are the remains of an Archaic sanctuary which, as the remains clearly indicate, was used by the Lemnian population that was expelled by the Athenian settlers ca. 500 (Hdt. 1.57, 6.140; Th. 4.109.4; Str. 7, fr. 35; Ficuciello 2013, 156–9). Elsewhere on the island the Athenians respected the Lemnian sanctuaries but assimilated the rites to familiar forms; in Hephaistia and in Chloi, the Cabiric sanctuary under the control of Hephaistia, there is some indication that they transformed a native Lemnian mother-goddess rite into a worship of Cybele/Demeter with Eleusinian overtones (Greco and Ficuciello 2010; Ficuciello 2013, 232–42, 247–9) to which Dionysus probably bore some connection (Greco and Ficuciello 2010, 154, 157). In the later fifth century, around the time the Hephaistian theatre was built, Athenian poets were especially active building up Dionysus' links with both the Lemnian and Eleusinian goddesses (see below).

The possibility of performing or reperforming tragedy in Lemnos may be a factor in the sizeable number of fifth-century tragedies set in Lemnos. Aeschylus wrote four Lemnian plays that may have been a connected tetralogy (Deforge 1987). *Philoctetes* plays by Aeschylus, Sophocles, Euripides, Achaeus and Philocles are all set in Lemnos (Sophocles also wrote a *Philoctetes at Troy*). Lemnian history is also prominent in Euripides' *Hypsipyle* which draws a connection between the Euneidae, the Athenian priest-clan of Dionysus Melpomenos, and the royal succession in Lemnos going back to Dionysus (Burkert 1994). The god himself probably directed his grandson Euneus to settle in Athens and establish the cult, 'giving Athens a claim to religious and temporal authority in Lemnos' at a time when Athenian dominance of the North Aegean was under threat (Collard et al. 2004, 178; cf. Cropp 2003; Humphreys 2004, 238). *Hypsipyle* F 758a–b in particular seems to describe the Lemnian Dionysus with the language of the mysteries and probably in accord with Eleusinian ideas (Collard et al. 2004, 249–52, with Csapo 2017). Lemnos was in any case familiar to a great many Athenians from business and military service, because of its strategic and commercial location with respect to Athenian interests in Thrace and the Black Sea.

Dix: Lesbos

1. **Choregia in Mytilene: Antiphon, *On the Murder of Herodes* (5) 77**. The speech was delivered about ten years after the revolt of Mytilene from Athens in 427 (this is what 'these affairs' refers to), ca. 420–417. The choregia in question is likely to have antedated 427 (see commentary). It is a defence speech by a young citizen of Mytilene (named Euxitheos, according to Sopat. Rh. 4.316 Walz) on trial in Athens for the murder on Lesbos of an Athenian named Herodes. Here (74–9) the speaker attempts to defend his father's actions during and after the revolt. Text: Gagarin.

> ἐπεὶ δ' ὑμεῖς τοὺς αἰτίους τούτων ἐκολάσατε, ἐν οἷς οὐκ ἐφαίνετο ὢν ὁ ἐμὸς πατήρ, τοῖς δ' ἄλλοις Μυτιληναίοις ἄδειαν ἐδώκατε οἰκεῖν τὴν σφετέραν αὐτῶν, οὐκ ἔστιν ὅ τι ὕστερον αὐτῷ ἡμάρτηται, τῷ ἐμῷ πατρί, οὐδ' ὅ τι οὐ πεποίηται τῶν δεόντων, οὐδ' ἧς τινος λῃτουργίας ἡ πόλις ἐνδεὴς γεγένηται, οὔτε ἡ ὑμετέρα οὔτε ἡ Μυτιληναίων, ἀλλὰ καὶ χορηγίας ἐχορήγει καὶ τέλη κατατίθησιν.

χορηγεῖ Blass

But from the moment you punished those responsible for these affairs (my father was not found to be among their number) and you granted the rest of the Mytileneans an indemnity which allowed them to continue living on their own

land, he has not been guilty of a single fault, my father, and he has done absolutely everything required of him. The city has not been in need of any public
service (*leitourgia*) – neither your city nor that of the Mytileneans – but he was
performing choregiai and paid his dues.

2. **Preliminary decision of the Council (ll. 1–18) followed by confirmatory decree (ll. 19–28) of the People of Mytilene awarding proxeny and other honours to a man named Alexander**. Date: before 324/3 (Rhodes and Lewis 1997, 256–9 on the nature of the enactment formula). The fragmentary remains of ll. 2–5 make it clear that Alexander is being honoured for providing financial support to the city. Only ll. 5–18 quoted here.

Four joining fragments of the left-hand side of a marble stele. The surface of the front face is worn smooth on the right-hand side.
1.4 × 0.465 × 0.18 m.
Found in reuse built into the fort of Mytilene.
Mytilene Museum inv. no. 1087.
IG XII 2, 5 + Suppl.; see also *SEG* 26, 875; 38, 799.
Text: based on *IG* XII 2, 5 + Suppl.

5	[δέδοχθαι πρόξενον ἔμ]- μεναι Ἀλέξα[νδρον τᾶς πόλιος καὶ αὖτον] [κ]αὶ ἐκγόνοις· [— — — δὲ αὔτω — — — ὄ]- [π]οσα καὶ τοῖς ἄλ[λοισι εὐεργέταισι στε]- [φά]νωσθαι δὲ [καὶ αὖτον ἐν τοῖς Διονυσί]-	stoich.
10	[ο]ισι χρυσίω[ι στεφάνωι ἀρέτας ἔνεκα καὶ] εὐνοίας τᾶς εἰ[ς τὰν πόλιν· κάλεσσαι δὲ] [κ]αὶ εἰς [π]ροε[δρίαν αὖτον τοῖς ἀγωνοθέ]- [τα]ις· οἰ [δὲ ἐξέτασται ἐπιμελήθεντον ὄ]- [π]ως ἀναγ[ρ]α[φήσεται τὸ ψάφισμα τοῦτο]	
15	εἰς στάλαν λι[θίναν καὶ τεθήσεται εἰς] τὸ ἶρον τᾶς Ἀθά[νας. τὸ δ' ἀνάλωμα δότω ὀ] ταμίας ἐκ τῶν κ[ατ' ἔτος ἐγχερριζομένων] ἰς διοίκησιν.	

10 χρυσίω[ι στεφάνωι ἔνεκα] Hodot   χρυσίω [στεφάνω ἔννεκα] Paton

[It is decided that] Alexa[nder] be [proxenos of the city, both he himself a]nd his descendants. [… every]thing just as for the oth[er benefactors.] And that he be [cr]owned [at the Dionysi]a [10] with a gold [crown for his virtue and] good-will towar[ds the city. And] also [the agonothet]es [are to invite him] to [p]rohe[dria. The [auditors are to see to it th]at [this decree is] ins[cr]ibed [15] on a st[one] stele [and placed in] the sanctuary of Athe[na. The] treasurer [is to give the expense] from the a[nnual allocation] to the budget.

3. **Decree of the Council and People (*damos*) of Mytilene Honouring Atrometos, a Citizen of Magnesia on the Maeander**. Date: late 4th c. (Hodot 1976, 48, 52). The *Basileis* (securely) restored in l. 6 are a college of senior magistrates akin to the Archons at Athens. Their role here and in *IG* XII 2, 18 suggests they may have had overall

responsibility for the Dionysia of Mytilene (Labarre 1996, 166). Only ll. 1–11 quoted here. Traces remain below this decree of another that conferred further privileges on Atrometos and associates.

Stele of blue-grey marble, broken on all sides.
0.175 × 0.36 m.
Found in Mytilene.
Mytilene Museum inv. no. 1129.
IG XII Suppl. no. 2; *SEG* 26, 909 (Hodot).
Text: based on *SEG* 26, 909.

A — — — — — — — — — — — — — — —   stoich.
1 [δέδοχθαι] τᾶι βό[λλαι καὶ τῶι δάμωι· ἐπα]-
   [ίνεσαι τ]ε Ἀτρόμητο[ν . . . .⁸. . . . Μάγνητ]-
   [α εὐνοί]ας ἔνεκε τᾶς πρὸ[ς τὸν δᾶμον τῶν]
   [Μυτιλη]νάων καὶ στεφάν[ωσαι . . . .⁸. . . .]
5 [. τὰν π]όλιν χρυσίωι στε[φάνωι κατὰ τὸν]
   [νόμον κ]αὶ ὀγκάρυξαι τοῖς [βασίληας ἐν τ]-
   [οῖς Δι]ονυσίοισι, ὅτι στε[φάνοι ὁ δᾶμος]
   [ὁ Μυτι]ληνάων, Ἀτρόμητον [. . . . .¹¹. . . . .]
   [. . αὖτ]ον πρόξενογ καὶ εὐ[εργέταν . . . .]
10 [. Μυτιλ]ηνάων ἀνδραγαθί[ας ἔνεκε καὶ ε]-
   [ὐνοία]ς τᾶς πρὸς τὸν δᾶμο[ν — — — —]

[It is decided] by the Coun[cil and the Assembly: to praise] Atrometo[s ... of Magnesia] for his [good-will] toward[s the people of Mytile]ne and crow[n ... ⁵ the c]ity with a gold cro[wn according to the law a]nd the [*Basileis*] are to announce [at the Di]onysia that [the people of Mytil]ene crow[ns] Atrometos [... h]im a proxenos and ben[efactor ... of the ¹⁰ Mytil]eneans [for his] virtu[e and good-will] towards the peopl[e ...]

4. **Dionysia in Antissa: [Aristotle],** *Economics* **2.2.6 (1347a25–31)**. Written probably around the end of the 4ᵗʰ c. (Migeotte 2014, 34). Target date: 428–427, the period of defection from Athens, has been suggested (Van Groningen 1933, 82), but on the some-what slight grounds that this was probably a time when ready cash was tight. A date in the 4ᵗʰ c. is also possible. Philodemus attributed the *Economics*, transmitted under the name of Aristotle, to Theophrastus. Modern scholars tend to accept that attribution or suggest some other student or students of Aristotle (Pomeroy 1994, 68). The second book begins with a theoretical section that distinguishes four different types of econo-my, and is followed by a collection of historical examples of money-raising strategies adopted by cities (as here), governors, monarchs and military commanders. Sosipolis is not otherwise known. Text: van Groningen and Wartelle.

Σωσίπολις Ἀντισσαῖος, δεηθείσης τῆς πόλεως χρημάτων, εἰθισμένων δὲ αὐτῶν λαμπρῶς ἄγειν Διονύσια, ἐν οἷς ἄλλα τε πολλὰ ἀνήλισκον ἐξ ἐνιαυτοῦ παρασκευάζοντες καὶ ἱερεῖα πολυτελῆ, ὑπογύου δὲ οὔσης ταύτης τῆς ἑορτῆς, ἔπεισεν αὐτοὺς τῷ μὲν Διονύσῳ εὔξασθαι ἐς νέωτα ἀποδώσειν [30] διπλάσια, ταῦτα δὲ συναγαγόντας ἀποδόσθαι. συνελέγη οὖν αὐτοῖς χρήματα οὐκ ὀλίγα πρὸς τὴν χρείαν.

25 Σωσίπολις Γ (Γ = ancient Latin translation)   σῶμα ἡ πόλις Π²   σῶον τῇ πόλει
Π¹   27 ἐξ ἐνιαυτοῦ   *ab initio anni* Γ   28 ὑπογύου correction in M   ὑπεγγύου
Π¹   ὑπὸ ἐγγύου Π²   *transeunte* Γ   30 ἀποδόσθαι Groningen-Wartelle   ἀποδίδοσθαι
ἀποδεδόσθαι codd.   *in propinquas civitates* Γ

The city of Antissa was short of money, and its citizens were accustomed to conducting a lavish Dionysia at which they spent a lot of money in their preparations every year on a range of things, including expensive sacrifices. When this festival was imminent, Sosipolis of Antissa persuaded them to make a vow to Dionysus that they would render him twice as many offerings the following year, [30] and when they collected the offerings they sold them. And so in this way they realised a large sum of money to meet their need.

Mytilene was an original member of the Delian League, contributing ships rather than tribute and remaining *autonomoi* and *eleutheroi* until its revolt (in company with the other Lesbian cities except Methymna) against Athens in 428. At this time the city was an oligarchy (Th. 3.39.6). After the revolt was suppressed the (over 1,000) members of the oligarchic ruling class were sent to Athens, where they were executed as responsible (Th. 3.35.1) and the territory was divided into 3,000 lots, 300 of which were made sacred property. The remaining 2,700 were given to Athenian cleruchs, but the Athenians permitted the Mytileneans to rent back and work their own lands (Th. 3.50.2; **1**). The nature and duration of this cleruchy is debated. Gauthier (1966; Hornblower 1991, 440–1) argued from the fact that the rent was roughly the same as hoplite pay that the cleruchs were to form a resident garrison. Others interpret the decision to allow the Mytileneans to rent back and work their own lands to suggest that the Athenian cleruchs never formed anything like a permanent settlement on the island and were probably absentee rentiers (Mattingly 1996, 136; Labarre 1996, 17–18). We hear nothing of such a garrison from Thucydides (or any other source) and the destruction of the city's defences after the revolt probably rendered it unnecessary (Brunt 1993, 126–7). A highly fragmentary Athenian decree (*IG* I³ 66, possibly of 427/6 or 425/4) regulates relations with Mytilene and seems to assure the Mytileneans' *autonomia* (l. 11: αὐτο[νό]μος), but its fragmentary state leaves open the possibility that something more conditional was involved.

Euxitheos has phrased the account of his father's public service (**1**) in such a way as to imply that he performed 'liturgies' in Athens – 'your city' – as well as in his home of Mytilene. But it is clear that we should read the passage chiastically, with the choregiai being the liturgy (in the strict sense) undertaken in Mytilene, the *tele* the 'liturgy' undertaken for Athens, through a kind of euphemistic re-definition of the rents payable to the Athenian cleruchs or other entirely compulsory dues as 'liturgies' (Gagarin 1997, 213; Wilson 2000, 182). The alternative is to suppose that the Mytilenean had somehow attracted an obligation to perform choregiai in Athens, for which no good reason can be proffered.

On one interpretation, **1** only permits us to say that choregiai were operative in Mytilene *from* 427, since the claim appears to be that the speaker's father performed these duties in the period following the suppression of the Mytilene revolt: 'from the moment you punished those responsible ... he was performing choregiai'. But this is to press logic to a fault. It is in the speaker's interests to imply that his father's service did not date from the period of oligarchic dominance in Mytilene prior to the revolt, and while the introduction of Dionysia and choregia can sometimes be linked to the introduction of Athenian cleruchies, it is very unlikely that this was the case here, as there is no evidence that the Athenian cleruchs formed a settled community and some to suggest that they did not. It should also be noted that the imperfect tense χορηγίας ἐχορήγει (which Blass corrected to a present) could have a mildly continuative force 'he kept performing choregiai', suggesting a continuity in his actions before and after 427.

The choregiai in question will thus be for Mytilenean festivals. Which festival and what type of choral-based performances were supported is not known, but the existence of a prominent Dionysia in Mytilene in the next century (**2**) makes that one likely context. And even if the choregiai of Euxitheos' father were confined to the period following 427, the choregia itself will antedate 427 and will thus have been operative at a period when the city was an oligarchy. It is possible but far from certain that membership of the Delian League helped familiarise the city with the idea of liturgical choregia. A somewhat more likely influence from Athens is the practice of announcing crowns for benefactors at the city's Dionysia (**2, 3**).

The citation of past liturgic service to defend wealthy individuals whose actions may have compromised their standing is familiar from its frequent use by Athenians in democratic Athenian courts (Wilson 2000). **1** offers a fascinating insight into how a non-Athenian can rhetorically deploy choregic service abroad (under an oligarchy) in an Athenian court (cf. **Dxiv 1** for its use in a non-Athenian court).

Mytilene was a politically volatile state in the fourth century, experiencing shifts between democracy and oligarchy, as well as a period of tyranny. It was a founding member of the Second Athenian Confederacy and active militarily alongside Athens, serving as a base for naval operations (Brun 1988, 379–80), but left the Confederacy around 352 in the wake of an oligarchic coup. After the tyranny of Kammys that followed, Athenian ties were strong once more. Democracy was restored ca. 340–330 with some fanfare following the removal of the tyrant (*SEG* 36, 750; 752; Arr. *An*. 2.1.5) and there is evidence of vigorous public building (*IG* XII 2, 10; 11; 14). This is the likely historical context of **2**. Given the constraints of the stoichedon pattern, the recurrence of the Dionysia-announcement formula in **3** and later inscriptions (e.g. *IG* XII 2, 18, ll. 9–11, late 3rd c.: [καὶ | στεφάνω]σαι ἐν τοῖς Διονυσίοισι χρυσί[ω στεφ|άνω τῶ] καττὸν νόμον; *IG* XII 2, 15, ll. 29–30, ca. 214–213, Labarre 1996, 264: στεφάνωσαι αὔτοις ἐν τοῖς Διονυσίοισι χρυσ[ίω] | στεφάνω κατ' ὀνόματος; *IK Erythrai* 122 early 2nd c.) and the presence of invitation to prohedria among the honours awarded (ll. 11–12), although it is heavily restored (ll. 9–10), the Dionysia is almost certainly the festival at which a man named Alexander is honoured in **2**. And although also heavily restored, agonothetes (ll. 12–13) are almost certainly active in the conduct of the festival, implying the existence of contests at it (agonothetes remain active in Mytilene well into the Roman Imperial period).

On current evidence there is no direct attestation of dramatic performance at Mytilene. Notably, however, one of the first non-Athenian comic poets, Alcaeus, came from Mytilene, and was probably active in the last decades of the fifth century (unless Suda α 1274 is referring to or confusing Alcaeus with the lyric poet: see Storey 2011 I, 43 n. 1). Forms such as kitharody and dithyramb, closer to the old Aeolic musico-poetic traditions, are better attested. Mytilene produced a famous dithyrambic poet and kitharode in Phrynis, active throughout Greece in the second half of the fifth century (sources and chronology in Telò 2007, 28–33; **Axxvii**). A claim to a prominent place in the history of Dionysiac music and poetry was made for Lesbos through the figure of Arion of Methymna (in the north of the island), for he is credited with the invention of the dithyramb (Kowalzig 2013). Dionysus was one of the most important deities of Lesbos and, with Apollo and Artemis, at Mytilene itself (Shields 1917, 56–67; Casadio 1994, 29–36; Chaniotis 1997, 14 n. 22, notably on the plentiful evidence of theophoric names such as Bakchios, Bakchos, Dionysios, Dionysodoros). In the fourth century the evidence of Mytilenean coins shows a surge in the god's importance in that city (Shields 1917, 62). Comic figurines are produced in Mytilene from the middle of the fourth century (Acheilara 2000, 90–1, 240–1 nos. 197–200, 359–62 nos. 529–35).

The theatre of Mytilene lies on the side of a hill (Hag. Kyriakis) to the west of the city, its theatron dug into the natural slope, estimated to have a capacity of ca. 10,000 (Kourtzellis 2013, 24). Limited excavation took place in 1928, 1958 and 1967. In the last year Petrakos unearthed and studied the circular orchestra. His plan (1967, 450 fig. 3) remains the best available. The date of the theatre's first phase has not been ascertained, but is generally held to be late Classical or early Hellenistic (Isler in *TGR* II, 252; Hansen, Spencer, Williams in *IACP* 1029; Labarre 1996, 207; Olga Philaniotou, archaeologist reporting to Diazoma). It remained in use well into the Roman period (from which much of the visible structure dates: Sear 2006, 341–2), and there are numerous inscriptions of Imperial date (when a choregia is also attested: Labarre 1996, 185). The theatre is best known for having attracted the admiration of Pompey the Great, who arrived in Lesbos in 63 on his return from victory over Mithridates III of Pontus and 'being pleased with the theatre, he had sketches and plans of it made for him, that he might build one like it in Rome, only larger and more splendid' (Plu. *Pomp.* 42.4: ἡσθεὶς δὲ τῷ θεάτρῳ περιεγράψατο τὸ εἶδος αὐτοῦ καὶ τὸν τύπον, ὡς ὅμοιον ἀπεργασόμενος τὸ ἐν Ῥώμῃ, μεῖζον δὲ καὶ σεμνότερον).

The Mytilenean theatre has thus been accorded a place of importance in the history of theatre architecture in Rome (Tosi 2003 I, 666 for a survey of views). But if, as seems likely, Pompey's friend and associate Theophanes of Mytilene was the ultimate source for Plutarch's account, one may suspect the deviating effect of local pride in the claim. As Monterroso Checa (2010, 346–7) pertinently observes, it is extremely likely that Pompey will have been influenced by his extensive exposure to monumental theatre architecture across Asia Minor. Our recently improved knowledge of Pompey's theatre does little to suggest close affinity with its supposed Mytilenean model. Perhaps the most plausible similarity proposed is the existence of a sanctuary at the summit of the theatron in both cases – known for the theatre of Pompey and postulated for Mytilene (Gros 2009), but on the basis only of an unusual room with a double entrance at the bottom (not the top) of the western side of the theatron that may have served a cult purpose.

Elaborate Dionysia are attested elsewhere on Lesbos. **4** records a ruse devised by one Sosipolis (assuming this highly apposite name is indeed to be read: Van Groningen and Wartelle 1968, 55) to generate funds for the Dionysia at Antissa at a time of fiscal pressure. Much is unclear in this compressed account, but presumably what is implied is that Sosipolis extracted promises from the city's wealthy families of specially lavish donations at what seemed at the time like the safe distance of more than a year in the future. The vows were presumably to appease Dionysus with ample future recompense for the conversion of his already amassed store of offerings to cash to fund the immediately upcoming Dionysia.

The passage gives no explicit evidence for drama at the Antissans' Dionysia. However the emphasis on lavish expense, on advanced planning and the habitual inclusion of 'a range of things' in the festival, is consistent with a Dionysia that included dramatic performances.

The city of Antissa in the north-west of the island was, like Mytilene, a ship-contributing member of the Delian League. It too defected from Athens in 428, its territory sharing the same fate of division among Athenian cleruchs. And it too joined the Second Athenian Confederacy in ca. 375. Numismatic evidence in the form of a coin with reverse showing an archaic xoanon of Dionysus suggests the existence of an early (or at least an archaising) cult of Dionysus Phallen, which may have been in association with a cult of Orpheus (Shields 1917, 59; Lucian *Ind.* 109).

A Dionysia is also attested at Methymna and Eresus by the late third or early second centuries. Methymna also has a theatre, of uncertain date (Sear 2006, 341), and 'a scenic contest' at its Dionysia by the early second century (*IG* XII Suppl. 139, l. 54, before 167?: τοῖς Διονυσίοις τῶ ἄγωνι τῶ σκανίκω), though the cult of Dionysus in Methymna is considerably older (Shields 1917, 59–61). An inscription of ca. 200 also shows honours announced were to be 'at the Dionysia, before the carrying-around of the statue', *IG* XII 2, 503, ll. 9–10: ἐν τοῖς Διονυσί|οισι πρὸ τᾶς τῶ ἀγάλματος περιφόρας).

At Eresus the Dionysia had tragic contests probably by the early third century (depending on the substantial but plausible restoration of an honorific decree of that date honouring Samian judges *IG* XII 6, 1, 141, ll. 15–16 for which Hallof proposes e.g. [Διονυσίοισι τοῖς ἀγώνεσσι τοῖς τραγώ]|δοισι '[at the trag]ic [contests at the Dionysia]') and certainly by the early second century (*IG* XII Suppl. 121, ca. 200, ll. 32–3: ἐν τοῖς Διονυσίοισ[ι] τῶ ἄγωνι | [τ]ῶν τραγώιδων; *IG* XII 2, 527 Suppl. p. 33, ca. 250–200, l. 24: ἔν τε τοῖς Διονυσίοισι [τῶ ἄγωνι τῶν τραγώδων]; *IG* XII Suppl. 125, 2nd c., ll. 22–3: ἐγ τοῖς Διονυσίοισι τῶ ἄγωνι [τῶν | τραγώιδων]). Along with the gymnic contests of the Herakleia and of the Ptolemaia, this was the preferred venue for the announcement of honours. In the last of these inscriptions the honorand is described (ll. 15–16) as having 'been choragos from his own resources' (χορα|γήσαντα ἐκκ τῶν ἰδίων) but the context makes it virtually certain that the verb is used for 'financial provisioning' in general (the honorand is a market-warden who has ensured the supply of grain and other staples) and does not refer to choregia in the strict sense (*contra* Labarre 1996, 181).

The official tasked with the duty of making the announcement of awards at the Eresan Dionysia was however a *chorostatas* (*IG* XII 6, 1, 141, early 3rd c., l. 31: τὸν χοροστά[ταν]; *IG* XII Suppl. 121, ca. 200, l. 35: [ἐν] δὲ τοῖς Διονυσί[οισι] τὸν χορ[οσ]-

τάταον?; the word is securely restored from its appearance also in *IG* XII 2, 527 + Suppl. p. 33, ll. 32–3: τᾶς δὲ ἀγ[γελίας ἐπιμέλεσ|θαι ἐμ μ]ὲν τοῖς Διονυσίοισι τὸγ χοροστάταον). The name implies the continued importance of the chorus to the contests (Ceccarelli 2010, 139–40) – and the only attested type of performance at the festival is tragedy. It may be that the duties of this *chorostatas* involved the organisation of the contests of the festival, somewhat akin to the Athenian agonothete. In a decree of the second century that honours a judge and his secretary from Miletos we find the agonothete (rather than the *chorostatas*) responsible for making the announcement 'at the contest of boys at the nex[t D]ionysia' (ἐν τοῖς πρώ|[τοισι Δ]ιονυσίοισι τῶι ἄγωνι τῶν παίδων, *IG* XII Suppl. 140, ll. 10–11; also *IG* XII Suppl. 141, ll. 16–17, 2nd c.).

Dx: Naxos. Fragmentary inscription from Naxos possibly concerning a (?) chorus for Dionysus, (?) 5th c. (On the date, thus Savo 2004, 160, 246; Reger *IACP* 762: 'C4?'; Hiller: 'litterae optimae' – all without discussion. The letters of I appear from the squeeze kept in the Berlin Academy to be of Classical date.)

Two non-joining fragments possibly from the same stele of white marble: I from the left-hand side of the stele, left and upper edges apparently preserved, broken to the right; II a small fragment, broken at the top.
I: 0.47 × 0.19 × 0.08 m. II: dimensions not recorded.
I: found in the region known as Katachoria, in the Church of Hag. Georgios. II: found in the region known as Polichne in the south-west part of the island.
I: In 1892 kept in Naxos by M. Markopolis. II: After discovery kept in the house of S. Karegla in the nearby village known as Tripodes. I and II: current whereabouts unknown (Matthaiou).
Ridder 1897, 23 no. 8 (I); Markopolis 1892, 366; Ridder 1897, 20 no. 2 (II); *IG* XII 5, 45 (I + II; in *IG* Hiller mislabelled the fragments; corrected in *IG* XII 5, Part 2, Add. et Corr. p. 306 no. 45). Hiller and Ridder did not see II but worked from a copy provided by Markopolis.
Text: based on Ridder 1897.

<pre>
          I   II   stoich.
1   [-]υθυ [- - - - - - - (?) χ]-
     ορον [- - - - - -]οδ[- - - -]
     εσθα[ι - - (?) Δ]ιονύσ[ωι]
     κρον[- - - - - - -]ος
     vacat
</pre>

1–4 [ε]ὐθὺ[ς ἱστάναι χ]|ορὸν [καὶ] ὀ[λὰς θύ]|εσθα[ι Δ]ιονύσ[ωι] | Κρον[ιῶν]ος Hiller
2 Perhaps [τρίπ]οδ[α] ?   2–3 [- μὲ τίθ]|εσθα[ι] Matthaiou

(?? *Possibly the remains of a name*) … a (?) [ch]orus [… (??) trip]od […] to (*verb*) [… for D]ionysus (??) in the month Kronion (? *or some other dating formula* ?); (??) 'son of Kronion'

So prominent is Dionysus within the Naxian pantheon that he is thought to have been the island's principal protective deity (the evidence of the coins is especially clear: Reger in *IACP* 762). On the importance of his cults on the island, attested abundantly in literature and archaeology, see Savo 2004, ch. 2, esp. 147–61, 202–4. The major sanctuary at Hyria dating from ca. 570 has recently been identified as belonging to Dionysus and was probably the chief sanctuary of the island (Gruben 1997, 300). In the second century the eponymous official was it seems the priest of Dionysus (*IG* XII 5, 128, l. 23, Add. p. 308) but prior to that time Archons and *aisymnetai* appear in that capacity (Savo 2004, 200–1).

Athenian involvement dates from at least the middle of the sixth century, when Pisistratus supported the installation of Lygdamis as tyrant, granting effective Athenian control and leading to the settlement of Athenian colonists on the island (Hdt. 1.61, 64; 5.31.2; 8.46.3; Arist. *Ath.* 15.2–3; Ael. *VH* 8.5; Paus. 7.3.3). Naxos joined the Delian League in summer 477, but defected and was reduced by siege ca. 475–470. Some 500 Athenian cleruchs settled there in 453–448. Whether this history of close relations with the metropolis of drama played any part in its introduction to the island is unclear.

This inscription is an intriguing and neglected item of possible evidence for choral performance for Dionysus on Naxos in the Classical period. The larger fragment (I) was found near the sanctuary of Dionysus at Hyria. II was found some distance further to the south, in a region known as Polichne, near a village called in modern times Tripodes. This pattern is compatible with their having derived from a stele originally placed in the sanctuary of Dionysus at Hyria. Alternatively, it is perhaps just possible that the name of the village Tripodes preserves a memory of a site known for the dedication of tripods, like the street of that name in Athens. Perhaps the Church of the Virgin Mary Tripodiotissa in the town was so named for the remains of tripods, or images of them, built into it. It may be that this inscription records the dedication of one to Dionysus (see app. crit. l. 2).

Hiller is the only scholar to have devoted any serious attention to this important and relatively early evidence for the cult of Dionysus on Naxos (but see now Matthaiou 2013, 72–4). He offered no firm indication of date, but his 'litterae optimae' points to the fifth or fourth century, a judgement confirmed by his squeeze in the Berlin Academy. Hiller's reconstruction is free, even fanciful. He did not see II, but relied on a transcription provided by the local Naxian historian Markopolis, who had seen both fragments (and described the letters of II as 'ἀρχαϊκά'), and on the latter's belief that they were to be associated, to arrive at the conclusion that the two fragments came from the same stone. Evidently the lettering suggested a link. Ridder (1897, 20, following Markopolis), comments of II: 'Grosses lettres', while those of I are recorded as 0.027–0.03 m, which is certainly compatible with that description. We may perhaps guess that Markopolis had further reasons based on the physical characteristics of the stone. While the association may thus be regarded as at least plausible, a degree of healthy scepticism is in order (Matthaiou 2013, 73 argues against the association of the two fragments because of the distance between the findspots and the fact that neither Ridder nor Hiller saw II). We certainly cannot share Hiller's confidence that the line-length was 13 stoichoi. This was based on his restoration of ll. 2–4 as [θύ]‖εσθα[ι Δ]ιονύσ[ωι] | Κρον[ιῶν]ος, which is open to serious doubts: for instance, the article is more common with the name of the god in such contexts, and if it were included here l. 4 could no longer be the genitive of the month-name Kronion – otherwise unattested for Naxos, though known for Samos, Amorgos and Perinthos (Loukopoulou 1989, 111–12, 117, 408) – and Hiller's entire edifice starts to crumble.

That edifice is in any case rather over-elaborate. Hiller restored the text as some kind of sacred law that mandated the performance of a chorus and the offering of a sacrifice to

Dionysus at the start of the month Kronion. He extracts the dating formula and the instruction about the chorus from ll. 1–2, 4. But for the convoluted syntax of his own restored text (see app. crit. above) he must provide an explanatory gloss (*IG*): 'Accuratius dictum foret: Κρονιῶνος εὐθὺς ἱσταμένου ἱστάναι χορὸν καὶ οὐλὰς θύεσθαι Διονύσωι.' – namely 'At the start of Kronion, set up a chorus and sacrifice barley-groats for Dionysus'. In a preliminary discussion (1900, 340) he describes the dating formula as 'strange' ('befremdlich') and 'somewhat obscure' ('etwas versteckt'), but nonetheless regards it as a readily intelligible and a more impressive version of the usual participle ἱσταμένου with the month-name. He glides over the awkward fact that, even granted the displacement of the month-name at a distance from the (entirely restored) verb ἱστάναι, the verb must perform dual and very different service for the adverb before it – 'immediately' – and the noun that follows – '[ch]orus'.

The sacrifice of barley-groats is even more problematic. Hiller conjured this from ll. 2–3 by ignoring the delta reported clearly by Markopolis in l. 2 and replacing it with a lambda – ὀ[λάς] – a change Hiller unaccountably supposed (1900, 340) 'wird nicht als grosses Wagniss gelten'. Were it not for the fact that it was discovered many years later (July 1949), we might suspect that this fancy had been stimulated by the Dionysiac verses of Archilochus quoted in the Mnesiepes inscription from neighbouring Paros, in the section that treats the introduction of Dionysiac cult with iambic poetry to Paros by the poet. At l. 31 the word οὐλὰς 'barley groats' appears in a sequence of verse-line-beginnings, with 'Dionysus' in the preceding line and 'unripe grapes', 'bla[ck] figs' and 'The Fucker' in those that follow (*SEG* 15, 517, col. II, ll. 31–5 = Archil. fr. 251 W; Clay 2004, 16–22, 106–7). After οὐλὰς in l. 31 is a sequence of letters securely read by Kontoleon as ΤΥΑΖ, which he took as possibly hiding a reference to the 'sacrifice of barley-groats' to Dionysus (suggesting that τυάζ[εσθαι] might serve as an equivalent of θυάζ[εσθαι]: Kontoleon 1952, 78). But any influence was the other way round, for Kontoleon refers to the Naxian inscription as possible evidence for his interpretation, though he notes that Hiller's reconstruction was not secure. In any case there is no reason to suppose that the Naxian inscription referred to barley groats for Dionysus.

A more conservative approach still offers plenty of interest. If the two fragments do come from the same stele it is much more likely that we are dealing with a chorus (ll. 1–2: [χ]||ορὸν) or choruses ([χ]||ορõν) for Dionysus (l. 3) than, as one might otherwise have guessed, a *horos* (l. 2 OPON; Hiller 1900, 339–40; a *horos* could nonetheless make reference to a sanctuary or other property of Dionysus: **III Riii**; and note that Matthaiou 2013, 73 n. 4, airs a restoration for II as a *horos*: [hόρος τῆς ʸ| h]οδ[õ ἐς τὸ Δ]|ιονύσ[ιον ἀ|γ]όσ[ης]). Rather than being a sacred law of some sort it is perhaps more likely to be a dedication (although Matthaiou 2013, 74 notes that the thickness of II – 0.08 m – is more consistent with a stele and thinks of a sacred law from the sanctuary at Hyria). The first letters could be the remains of a name: *LGPN* I records Euthukarpides twice on Naxos, Euthymachos once. The absence of any good sense of line-length renders attempts at restoration futile, but in general terms the dedicant may have stated that he had 'led', set up or otherwise prepared a chorus and made a dedication (of a tripod? see above). Perhaps there then followed some such phrase as 'wishing to please Dionysus' or 'having vowed to offer to Dionysus'. A more plausible candidate for a middle or passive infinitive verb of dedication or offering in ll. 2–3 might be ἐπάρχεσθαι, for which note the parallel at Eretria in **Dvii 9**, l. 12. If the last line is not a reference to the month Kronion, it might all the same contain some sort of dating formula (an eponymous official?). A reference to Dionysus' father Zeus in the form Κρονίων might even be entertained.

The nature of any such chorus must be a matter of speculation. The only theatrical genre securely attested for Naxos is tragedy, with certainty from the late third and with some likelihood from the late fourth century (below), but it is tempting to associate this inscription with the tradition ultimately deriving from Pindar (in a *Hyporchema*: fr. 115 = Sch. Pi. *O.* 13.25 Drachmann) that 'dithyramb was first invented on Naxos'. Dionysus is also associated with dance and song in Naxian myth by Aglaosthenes (*FGrH* 499 F 3), a native of the island who may have lived early in the third century, in connection with his capture by the Tyrrhenian pirates. The god *iubet symphoniam canere*, at which the Tyrrhenians are seized with a dance frenzy, leap into the sea and turn into dolphins. Jacoby astutely noted the likely presence of the dithyramb behind the order *symphoniam canere*.

A theatre and tragedy at a Great Dionysia on Naxos are first clearly attested in a decree (found on Cos) dating to ca. 280, honouring the people of Cos and judges from Cos sent to settle disputed lawsuits (*SEG* 49, 1106). The city of Cos (**Div**) and each of its judges is to be crowned on Naxos with a gold crown, to be announced by the secretary of the Council 'in the theatre at the tragedies of the [Gre]at Dionysia' (ἐν τῶι θεάτρωι Διονυσίων | τῷ[ν μεγά]λων τραγωιδοῖς, ll. 16–17). Among other honours they are also 'to have prohedria in the [contests] which [the Peopl]e conducts' (ll. 26–7), implying that the Dionysia was not the only occasion for agones in the Naxian theatre. But 'pro[hedria at] the contests' (προ[ε]δρίαν ἐν] τοῖς ἀγῶσιν) is earlier attested by an honorific decree of the late fourth or early third century (*SEG* 33, 676, ll. 11–12; Matthaiou 1983), which probably suffices to push the date of the theatre and drama in it back that far. In another decree (*SEG* 25, 936, l.7, late 2nd – early 1st c.) one Anakleides is crowned 'with the sacred crown of Dionysus and another crown of gold, the largest according to the law' (ll. 3–5), and in addition to a bronze statue he is to be given 'prohedria in the contests and presence at the sacrifices which the city makes' (ll. 7–8). The importance attached here to the sacred crown of Dionysus may again suggest the primacy of his cult to the people of Naxos. The unknown recipient of another third-century honorific decree from Naxos is also awarded prohedria (*IG* XII 5, 35, ll. 4–5 [εἶναι δὲ αὐτῶι καὶ] | προεδρίαν ἐν τῶι [θεάτρωι ἐν τοῖς τῆς] πόλε[ως ἀγῶσιν]·). The restoration of 'in the [theatre]' here is virtually certain. The further clause '[at the contests of the cit]y', while extensively restored, has a parallel from Peparethos (*IG* XII 8, 640, ll. 25–6).

Does the epithet 'Great' (also attested for the Dionysia on neighbouring Paros in the late third and second centuries: *IMagn.* 50 + p. 295, ll. 41–2; *IG* XII 5, 129, l. 38) distinguish the event from lesser, local Dionysia, as is generally thought to be the rationale for the formula in Athenian usage? Does it imply imitation of an Athenian archetype? Fraisse and Moretti (2007, 25 n. 77, on the Parian case) are probably right to follow the suggestion of Gauthier (1999, 16) that the reference is to a grander event every two or four years, with a 'Small', less elaborate, Dionysia held in the other years. The Great Dionysia of Naxos seems to have a very long life: it surfaces again some 500 years later, in a second-century AD dedication by an agonothete after service for the festival. The recipient is Dionysus Mousagetes (*IG* XII 5, 46; Athens EM222; *SEG* 49, 1124). Whether that was the epithet of the god from the earliest days of the Naxian Dionysia is unclear. That it was probably so in the first century AD is clear from a dedication by an *epistates* who had been charged with the restoration of the proskenion of the theatre (*IG* XII 5, 52). The recipient is hidden in the fragmentary name Μουσ[-], restored by Hiller as 'to the Muses', but who also suggests 'to [Dionysus] Mous[agetes]' in his apparatus (cf. Savo 2004, 248).

The site of the theatre is unknown, and only the most modest architectural remains, found out of context, have been reported: two fragments of stone bench-seating, one in the area of the temple of Apollo (Touchais 1978, 738–9 with fig. 198; Gruben 1982, 165–6 with fig. 7 – listed, perhaps accidentally, under 'Archaische Bauten'; Fraisse and Moretti 2007, pl. 107, fig. 411); the other near the west entrance to the Kastro (Gruben 1999, 312). While this might conceivably come from an odeion, bouleuterion or any sort of structure with stepped seating, a theatre is very much the most likely, and further encouraged by the similarity of its profile with evidence from the Parian theatre (Müller 2003, 68 n. 214; Fraisse and Moretti 2007, pl. 107, fig. 410). Further, a single prohedric 'throne' seat was found in Naxos town (Metropolis) in reuse, and doubtless came from the theatre. This carries an inscription indicating that it was reserved for the high priest of imperial cult (Gruben 1999, 312, referring to advice from M. Wörrle; 317 pl. 5e; *IG* XII 5, 100; Fraisse and Moretti 2007, 258). Gruben speculates that the theatre was probably somewhere on the slope of the acropolis (modern Kastro). It at least seems clear that it was at Naxos city and not associated with the sanctuary of Dionysus at Hyria.

Dxi: Rhodes. Roman *Fasti*: Tragic actors' list. Dated by letter forms to 1ˢᵗ c. BC – 1ˢᵗ c. AD, referring to 4ᵗʰ c.

Eight fragments of Italian marble belonging to one or more marble slabs containing a Victors' List for Tragic Actors.

8: 0.28 × 0.21 m, letter size: 0.022 m. The lettering of the extant fragment appears similar in size and style to the Roman *Fasti* in **I Avi**.

Seven of these fragments (**1–7**) were first transcribed by Filippo Buonarroti (1661–1733), a celebrated Etruscologist, numismatist and epigrapher, secretary of Cardinal Gaspare Carpegna in Rome, later a civic official in Florence under Cosimo III, and, incidentally, great-grandnephew of Michelangelo. Buonarroti copied the inscriptions from the pavement of Saint Paul's Basilica in Rome, probably when they came to light in the course of rebuilding in the second half of the 17ᵗʰ c. (Moretti 1960, 269). For the original setting, see Roman *Fasti* in **I Avi**. Fragment **8** also originated in the pavement of Saint Paul's but was first published by Moretti 1960, 276.

8 is in the Lapidario Paolano. The fragments transcribed by Buonarroti (**1–7**) are lost, but Buonarroti's transcription is preserved in ms A 6 of the Biblioteca Marucelliana in Florence (copied in Moretti 1960, pl. 3). Beside the drawings Buonarroti wrote: 'these fragments are of a single stone and were not far separated from one another; moreover they were removed from the same place – the marble makes this clear – in such a way that they held letters within', '*haec fragmenta unius lapidis sunt nec longe inter se dissita, quaedam etiam ibidem (quod ex genere marmoris liquet) sic sunt deprompta ut litteras interius habeant*'. Kaibel took this to mean that Buonarroti had reason to believe that the marble was inscribed on the side or on the back of the blocks (1888, 268), but this is an unlikely interpretation of the Latin: for one thing there is only one fragment (**7**) which preserved so much as a tiny portion of the margin of the inscription. Buonarroti's words seem rather to suggest that the stones before removal from the paving of the church were located next to one another and that the inscribed surfaces faced downwards (*interius*), which explains why the lettering is so well preserved (Nocita 2013, 603). Another possibility is that he meant that the blocks were cut, for reuse, in such a way as to preserve the lines of letters within each segment, i.e. the original vertical and lateral breaks in the stone followed the orientation of the inscription (perhaps, if true, to serve as decorative inserts in a mediaeval building?).

Kaibel 1888; Wilhelm 1906, 205–8; Mette 1977, VI A–B; *IGUR* I 223–30.

Texts after *IGUR* with modifications.

Photos: Buonarroti's drawing and **8**: Moretti 1960, pl. 3 and pl. 2.2, *IGUR* I 194, 196; Nocita 2013.

1. *IGUR* I 223 (= fr. a on Buonarroti's drawing). It is not known which actor's record begins the list. We cannot be sure Aristomedes' name was in the nominative (which seems the normal way of beginning the list – see below on **2**). Aristomedes is not otherwise known (Stefanis no. 363), but Kleandros is known from *IG* II² 2318 as a victor at the Dionysia in 387 (where he performed tragedies of Sophocles the Younger) and from **Cvii**, a speech ascribed to Demosthenes and delivered around 345. Kleandros is said to have chanced upon the speaker's father in Leucas and restored him to his family in Athens. The father had been sold as a slave after 413 and remained in Leucas for 'many a year'. The meeting with Kleandros is unlikely to be later than about 380. In l. 5, Kleandros' name seems to reappear, this time, surprisingly, in the genitive: no Archon and no poet with the name Leandros or Kleandros is known. Thrasyboulos' name is in the nominative and so marks the beginning of a new list. The fact that a Lenaean victory is the first to be reported seems to indicate that he had no victories at the Athenian Dionysia. His Lenaean victory is also known from the Athenian Victor Lists (*IG* II² 2325H, l. 22 M-O). Thrasyboulos (Stefanis no. 1227) appears fourth on the Athenian list after Charidemos, whose first victory can be dated about 400, and tenth above Thettalos (Stefanis no. 1200), whose first Lenaean victory we can guess, on the basis of his earliest recorded Dionysian victory in 347, to be around 350. This should indicate a date for Thrasyboulos that is also not much later than the 380s. On Alkimachos (possible supplement to l. 6), see commentary below. Snell finds it unlikely that a new poet and tetralogy could be made to fit in the space between ll. 7 and 8 'even if we calculate a line of 60 letters' (1966, 21). Given that *Iberians* (l. 8) is not otherwise attested for Sophocles, Snell suggests that the tetralogy here listed belonged to Sophocles the Younger, grandson of the famous Sophocles. West (1999a) attributes a tragedy identified as the *Achilleu[s]* of Sophokl[es] on a 3ʳᵈ- or 2ⁿᵈ-c. Ashmolean papyrus to Sophocles the Younger (*DAGM* no. 5).

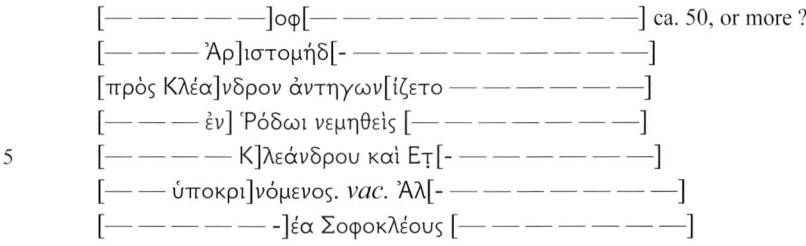

Buonarroti's drawing of fragments found in Saint Paul's Basilica, Rome

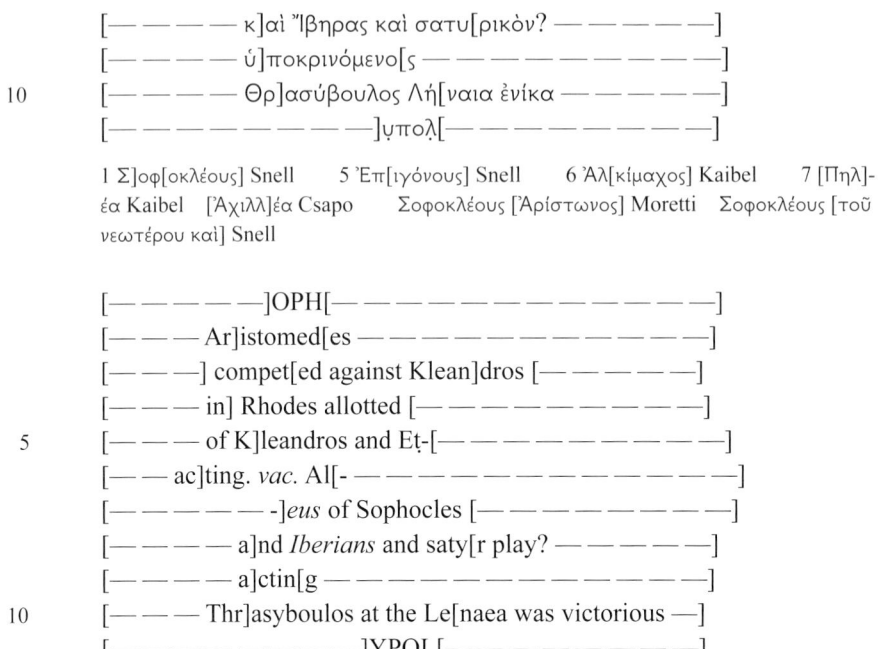

[— — — — κ]αὶ Ἴβηρας καὶ σατυ[ρικὸν? — — — — —]
[— — — — ὑ]ποκρινόμενο[ς — — — — — — — —]
[— — — — Θρ]ασύβουλος Λή[ναια ἐνίκα — — — — —]
[— — — — — — —]υπολ[— — — — — — —]

1 Σ]οφ[οκλέους] Snell   5 Ἐπ[ιγόνους] Snell   6 Ἀλ[κίμαχος] Kaibel   7 [Πηλ]-
έα Kaibel   [Ἀχιλλ]έα Csapo   Σοφοκλέους [Ἀρίστωνος] Moretti   Σοφοκλέους [τοῦ
νεωτέρου καὶ] Snell

[— — — — — —]OPH[— — — — — — — — — — —]
[— — — — Ar]istomed[es — — — — — — — — — —]
[— — — —] compet[ed against Klean]dros [— — — — — —]
[— — — — in] Rhodes allotted [— — — — — — — —]
[— — — — of K]leandros and Et-[— — — — — — — —]
[— — ac]ting. vac. Al[- — — — — — — — — — —]
[— — — — — -]eus of Sophocles [— — — — — — — —]
[— — — — — a]nd *Iberians* and saty[r play? — — — — —]
[— — — — a]ctin[g — — — — — — — — — — — —]
[— — — Thr]asyboulos at the Le[naea was victorious —]
[— — — — — — — —]YPOL[— — — — — — —]

2. *IGUR* I 224 (= fr. b on Buonarroti's drawing). Snell's supplement to l. 2 'a[t the City Dionysia]' may seem bold. It is based however on the observation that names in the nominative begin a new list (cf. **1**, l.10) and that the order is: firstly victories at the Athenian Dionysia, secondly victories at the Lenaea and thirdly victories in Rhodes. The epsilon could begin either 'i[n the city]', i.e. Athenian City Dionysia, or 'i[n Rhodes]'. The actor Mnesitheos (Stefanis no. 1723) is otherwise known only to have been victorious at the Dionysia some time around the mid fourth century (*IG* II² 2419, l. 10). A satyr play called *Students* (*Mathetai*) is known from the Athenian Victor List, referring to actors in the mid third century, where it may be an 'old satyr play'. Aristarchus of Tegea (Snell's supplement to l. 4) was a tragic poet and contemporary of Euripides.

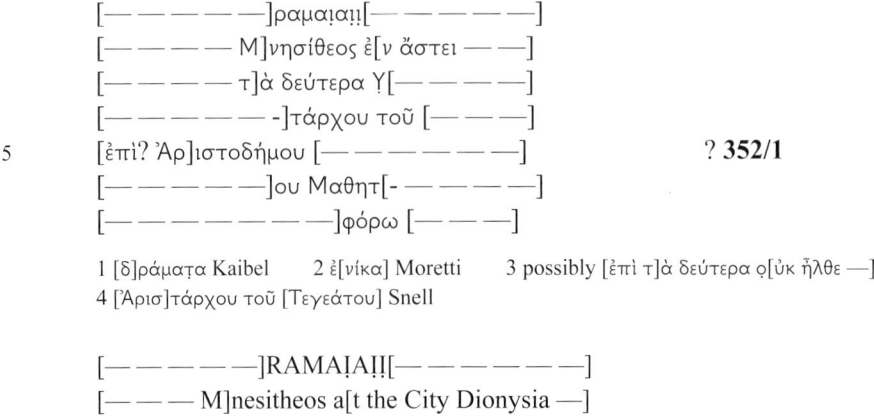

[— — — — —]ραμαιαι[— — — — —]
[— — — — M]νησίθεος ἐ[ν ἄστει — —]
[— — — — τ]ὰ δεύτερα Υ[— — — —]
[— — — — — -]τάρχου τοῦ [— — —]
[ἐπὶ? Ἀρ]ιστοδήμου [— — — — — —]   ? 352/1
[— — — — — —]ου Μαθητ[- — — — —]
[— — — — — — —]φόρω [— — —]

1 [δ]ράματα Kaibel   2 ἐ[νίκα] Moretti   3 possibly [ἐπὶ τ]ὰ δεύτερα ο[ὐκ ἦλθε —]
4 [Ἀρισ]τάρχου τοῦ [Τεγεάτου] Snell

[— — — — —]RAMAIAI[— — — — —]
[— — — — M]nesitheos a[t the City Dionysia —]

[— ?never came] second [— — — — — — —]
[— — — of ?Aris]tarchos of [Tegea? — — —]
5   [?in the Archonship of Ar]istodemos [— — —]   ? **352/1**
[— — — of — -]os *Studen*[*ts* — — — — — — —]
[— — — — — — —]PHORO [— — — — —]

3. *IGUR* I 225 (= fr. c in Buonarroti's drawing). This does not appear to be from the
body of an actors' victory list. It is possibly a section introduction or explanatory
addition (Snell 1966)? Given the likely supplements to l. 3, something is said about
things (presumably dramas) being written. If l. 4 refers to Sophocles (who is prominent in fr. **1**), it is possible that the stone here recorded literary historical information
about the authorship of plays directed by Sophocles the Younger. We know the titles
of no plays by Sophocles the Younger, but he appears to have directed some 40
(Suda σ 816), including the first Athenian production of his grandfather's *Oedipus at
Colonus* (see **V C** and **III J**). In Buonarroti's drawing the final letter in l. 6 is a vertical stroke with very slight thickening at the bottom which Moretti oddly transcribes
as 'L', hoping thereby to evince an epsilon (conjecturing Λην]αια ἐ[νίκα). But there is
no trace of the upper verticals required for an epsilon and the letter read and intended
by Buonarroti may be no other than 'I'.

[— — —]καιιτλλ[— — —]
[— — —]κασθαι λα[— —]
[— — — —]ραφηνα[— —]
[— — — —]κλεου[— — —]
5   [— — — — —]οπρε[— —]
[— — — — —]λιαι[— —]

2 [ἐνέγ]κασθαι Kaibel   3 [γ]ραφῆναι Kaibel   4 [Σοφο]κλέου[ς]   5 ? [Σοφοκλῆς]
ὁ πρε[σβύτερος] Snell   6 ? [ἐν ταῖς διδασκα]λίαι[ς Csapo

[— — —]and Ital?[— — —]
[— — to] win la[— — — —]
[— — — were w]ritten[— —]
[— — of ?Sopho]kles [— —]
5   [— — — — —]OPRE[— —]
[— — — — —]ĻIAI[— —]

4. *IGUR* I 226 (= fr. d in Buonarroti's drawing). There are no recognisable words in this
fragment.

[— —]εν μα[— — —]
[— —]πιομε![— — —]
[— —]ν καιναε[— —]
[— —]γεται δε[— —]
5   [— — — — —]τ[— —]

5. *IGUR* **I 227** (= fr. e in Buonarroti's drawing).

```
[— — — — —] καὶ Ὑπι[- — — — — — —]
[— — — — -]ιος ἐν Ῥόδ[ωι — — — — —]
[ἀντηγωνί]ζετο. vac. Γ[— — — — — —]
[— — — — —] Καιμειρίδι φυ-[— — — — —]
[— — — — —] Ληναίαι[— — — — — —]
[— — — — — —]κιλ[— — — — — — —]
```
(with line number 5 at left)

2 ἐν Ῥόδ[ωι νεμηθεὶς]   4 Κα{ι}μ{ε}ιρίδι φυ[λῆι] Kaibel, but Καμειρ- appears in Rhodian
inscriptions, e.g. *IG* XII 1, 701   5 Ληναίοι[Buonarroti   6 [Ἀλ]κίμ[αχος] Kaibel

```
[— — — — —] and Hypi[- — — — — — — —]
[— — — —]ios in Rhod[es — — — — — —]
[competed a]gainst. vac. G [- (or 3rd?) — — — — —]
[— in Rhodes allotted to the] Kamiran tr[ibe — —]
[— — — — —] at the Lenaea [— — — — — —]
[— — — — Al]kim[achos— — — — — — —]
```
(with line number 5 at left)

6. *IGUR* **I 228** (= fr. f in Buonarroti's drawing). This fragment may not belong to the list.
There is a combination of letters that might belong to the very rare name 'Chairebotos',
but in the dative. The name does not belong to any known poet or actor and the list has
no obvious place for dative forms other than in the formulae 'at the City Dionysia' (ἐν
ἄστει) or 'in Rhodes' (ἐν Ῥόδῳ).

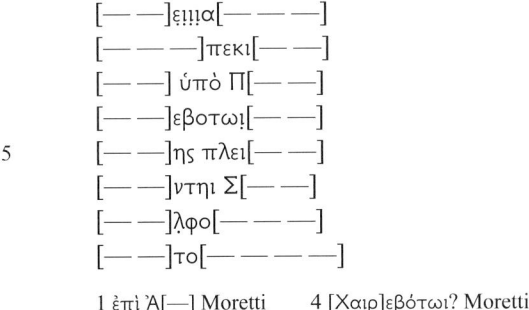

```
[— —]ε!!!α[— — —]
[— — —]πεκι[— —]
[— —] ὑπὸ Π[— —]
[— —]εβοτωι[— —]
[— —]ης πλει[— —]
[— —]ντηι Σ[— —]
[— —]λφο[— — —]
[— —]το[— — — —]
```
(with line number 5 at left)

1 ἐπὶ Ἀ[—] Moretti   4 [Χαιρ]εβότωι? Moretti

7. *IGUR* **I 229** (= fr. g on Buonarroti's drawing). Kaibel's attempt to join this fragment
to **1** (1888, 269) is firmly rejected by Wilhelm (1906, 205–6) and Moretti (1960, 271)
on the grounds that the recorded shape of the stones will not permit such a join and that
the left margin of **7** is clearly marked with a double line in Buonarroti's manuscript at
ll. 7–8. Nocita (2013), however, has recently argued in favour of the join. If Moretti
is right this would mean that the play titles listed here need have no connection with
Sophocles. Having said this, however, the fragments of play titles are not inconsistent with Sophocles' oeuvre. The Sophoclean title *Captive Women* (*Aichmalotides*) is
only evinced by a very invasive emendation by Snell, but two Sophoclean titles name
'Odysseus': *Mad Odysseus* (*Odysseus Mainomenos*) and *Odysseus Struck by a Sting*
(*Odysseus Akanthoplex*); and a Sophoclean Telephus trilogy or tetralogy is attested
by **III J** (Sienkewicz 1976). There are, however, Odysseus-plays by the early 4th-c.

tragedians Apollodoros (*TrGF* 64 T 1) and Chaeremon (*TrGF* 71 F 13) and Telephus-dramas by Iophon (Sophocles the Elder's son, *TrGF* 22 F 2c) and Cleophon (*TrGF* 77 F). The rare combination of letters in l. 1 is most likely to belong to the name Philotades, the name of a tragic actor, as reconstructed by Wilhelm at *IG* II² 2325, l. 270 (Stefanis no. 2654), who was winner of a sole victory at the Lenaea around 363.

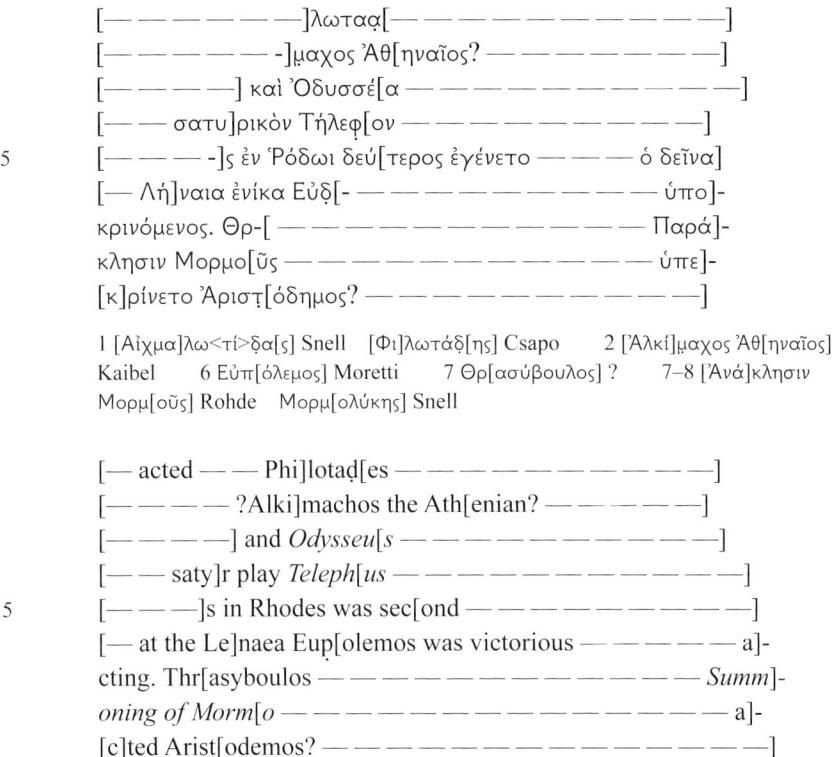

```
[— — — — — — —]λωταα[— — — — — — — — — — —]
[— — — — — -]μαχος Ἀθ[ηναῖος? — — — — — — — — —]
[— — — — —] καὶ Ὀδυσσέ[α — — — — — — — — — —]
[— — σατυ]ρικὸν Τήλεφ[ον — — — — — — — — —]
[— — — -]ς ἐν Ῥόδωι δεύ[τερος ἐγένετο — — — ὁ δεῖνα]
[— Λή]ναια ἐνίκα Εὐδ[- — — — — — — — — — — ὑπο]-
κρινόμενος. Θρ-[ — — — — — — — — — — Παρά]-
κλησιν Μορμο[ῦς — — — — — — — — — — ὑπε]-
[κ]ρίνετο Ἀριστ[όδημος? — — — — — — — — —]
```

1 [Αἰχμα]λω<τί>δα[ς] Snell   [Φι]λωτάδ[ης] Csapo   2 [Ἀλκί]μαχος Ἀθ[ηναῖος] Kaibel   6 Εὐπ[όλεμος] Moretti   7 Θρ[ασύβουλος] ?   7–8 [Ἀνά]κλησιν Μορμ[οῦς] Rohde   Μορμ[ολύκης] Snell

```
[— acted — — Phi]lotad[es — — — — — — — — —]
[— — — — — ?Alki]machos the Ath[enian? — — — — —]
[— — — — —] and Odysseu[s — — — — — — — — —]
[— — saty]r play Teleph[us — — — — — — — — —]
[— — — —]s in Rhodes was sec[ond — — — — — — — —]
[— at the Le]naea Eup[olemos was victorious — — — — — a]-
cting. Thr[asyboulos — — — — — — — — — — Summ]-
oning of Morm[o — — — — — — — — — — — a]-
[c]ted Arist[odemos? — — — — — — — — — — —]
```

8. *IGUR* I **230**. The name in l. 5 could be Euphron, Euthyphron, Polyphron or Thrasyphron. The genitive should indicate either an Archon or a tragic poet, but no known Athenian Archon or tragic poet has a name in -yphron. Moretti canvassed, but later doubted, the possibility of joining fragment **8** to **7**, which would at **7**, l. 5 and **8**, l. 3 allow the reading -]ς ἐν Ῥόδωι δεύτερος ἐγέν[ετο ('-s came second in Rhodes') and in the following lines allow the restoration of the names Eupolemos (**7**, l. 6 + **8**, l. 4) and Thrasyphron (**7**, l. 7 + **8**, l. 5). A tragic actor of the name Eupolemos (Stefanis no. 977) appears on the Athenian Victors' List for the Lenaea, early in the fourth century (just before the name of Thrasyboulos: see on **1** above). The principal obstruction to joining the fragments is the shape of **7** reported by Buonarroti which will not permit such a join. Moretti (1960, 273) hesitantly suggests: 'potrebbe però darsi che il Buonarroti non avesse disegnato esattamente la forma del fr. *g*'.

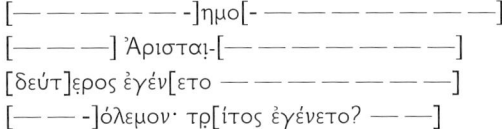

```
[— — — — — -]ημο[- — — — — — — —]
[— — —] Ἀρισται-[— — — — — — —]
[δεύτ]ερος ἐγέν[ετο — — — — — — —]
[— — -]όλεμον· τρ[ίτος ἐγένετο? — —]
```

5   [— — -]ύφρονος [— — — — — — — —]
       [— — — -]ος το[— — — — — — — — —]
       [— — — — -]ς ὑπο[κρι — — — — — — — —]

2 Ἀρισταρ[χου] cf. 2   4 [Εὐπ]όλεμον Moretti; if so, perhaps [ἀντηγωνίζετο πρὸς Εὐπ]-
όλεμον

       [— — — — — -]emo[- — — — — — — —]
       [— — —] Aristar[chos — — — — — — —]
       ca[me sec]ond [— — — — — — X competed]
       [against Eup]olemon; [he came] th[ird] ? — —]
5   [— of Thras?]yphron [— — — — — — —]
       [— — — -]os TO[— — — — — — — —]
       [— — — -]s act[ing — — — — — — —]

The evidence for drama in Rhodes shows how tenuous our information is for drama outside Attica in the Classical period. From Rhodes itself we have the remains of theatres at
Ialysos and Lindos. Neither can be precisely dated: the theatre in the sanctuary of Apollo
Erethymios at Ialysos has been dated as early as the fifth century (Jacopi 1932, 116), but
Arias dates it to the late fourth (1934, 128–31) and Isler (*TGR* II, 281) to the first half of
the third century; Arias (1934, 130) and Dyggve (1960, 406) date the Lindian theatre after
the mid fourth century, Moretti later (1991, 30), and Isler (*TGR* II, 279) after the third.
The epigraphic evidence is also predominantly late Hellenistic: we have evidence for both
tragedy and comedy by the second century (*Lindos* II 199; Hiller 1901, 440–3). But many
relevant inscriptions simply cannot be dated. Drama on the island is also indirectly attested
by the fame of Rhodian actors, poets and musicians or by actors' associations on the island
(*ATD* TE 78), but with the exception of Anaxandrides and Antiphanes (below), these are
only known from the third century onwards (Mygind 1999; Le Guen 2001, 280).

Given the dearth of early sources for the island, it is perhaps less surprising that firm evidence for drama in Classical Rhodes should come from elsewhere, though it is surprising
that it comes only from Imperial Rome. Most unexpectedly the Roman inscriptions give
evidence of a competition for actors performing tragedies by the second or third decade
of the fourth century. The Roman *Fasti* (**1–8**) list tragic actors who were victorious at the
Athenian Dionysia and Lenaea and/or the Rhodian Dionysia (there is no hint of any other
festival, though the inscription is very fragmentary). This fact suggests some preeminence
for the Rhodian festival, if only in the eyes of later antiquity.

If the pattern is the same as for the Comic Poets' Lists (Roman *Fasti* in **I Avi**; for the relationship, see below), the Actors' List represented by **1–8** listed tragic actors in the chronological order of their first entry into a competition, regardless of festival or ranking in the
competition. After the actor's name follow all the first-place finishes, then second-place
finishes, then third. No further sequencing rules are apparent from the Comic Poets' List,
though the Athenian Dionysia probably preceded the Lenaea (Roman *Fasti* in **I Avi**). It
is clear, however, that this list also provided some kinds of information not found in the
Comic Poets' List: **1** gives evidence of competitors (l. 3 'compet[ed against Klean]dros';
cf. **5**, l. 3); **1** and **5** name the Rhodian tribe to which the actor was allotted (see further
below).

The format of the inscription clearly indicates that Rhodes drew upon the same pool of actors who regularly performed and won prizes in Athens. Rhodes is only explicitly mentioned in **1**, **5** and **7** (cf. Moretti's supplement to **8**). This is as often as the name of the contest of the Athenian Lenaea appears (and there is no explicit reference to the Dionysia), so unless the remains are entirely misleading, Rhodes figured no less prominently on this part of the monument than the Athenian competitions. Unfortunately, given the great difference between the surviving and original length of the lines, we cannot connect any name or play with certainty to the Rhodian festival. **1** does however seem to include the mention of Rhodes within the list belonging to Kleandros, making it probable that the mention of Rhodes is in relation to Kleandros' performance at that festival. Other recognisable names in these fragments, save only that of Sophocles and possibly the Archon Aristodemos, all belong to tragic actors. [M]nesitheos and [Th]rasyboulos are certain supplements ([K]leandros virtually so: see the introductions to the fragments). All can be dated to the first half of the fourth century, with Kleandros and Thrasyboulos very early in the century. We can therefore infer that Rhodes was part of a regular festival circuit for top-ranking tragic performers.

The relationship between these fragments and the Comic Poet Didascalic Lists (**I Avi**) should not be doubted (see esp. Nocita 2013; *pace* Blum 1991, 138; see also **D Introduction**). The size and style of the letters is consistent. The formulae used appear to be the same, *mutatis mutandis*: name of contestant, contest, rank, Archon date (?), identification of tragedy by name and poet. Not enough remains to determine if the contests follow the same order (Dionysia, then Lenaea). The order does however seem to follow from first down to third prize, where relevant (see below). Moreover the language of the rankings (ἐνίκα for first, then ordinal adjectives) is paralleled by the Comic Poets' List, as is the terminology for the festivals (**1**, l. 10, **5**, l. 5 and **7**, l. 6 have Λήναια, 'at the Lenaea', and, much less certainly, **2**, l. 2 has ἐ[ν ἄστει], 'at the City Dionysia'). Fr. **2**, l. 3 seems also to reproduce the formula evident in the Comic Poet's List (Roman *Fasti* in **I Avi** document **a**, ll. 9 and 11) by which the absence of a ranking is noted: [ἐπὶ τ]ὰ δευτέρα ο[ὐκ ἦλθε].

Another stylistic feature shared with the Comic Poets' List (**I Avi**) is the use of a large space to introduce a new heading, either a new prize level (possibly **5**, l. 3) or a new name (**1**, l. 6). But unlike the Poets' List, numerals are not here conspicuous, while ordinal adjectives are, and it seems likely that **5**, l. 3 also introduces a new actor (Snell 1966, 16). Fr. **1**, l. 6, however, almost certainly introduces a new actor's name after the space. Though here we have only the first two letters, 'Al-', the information may be of some consequence. Wilhelm noted that the actors' names on our fr. **1** correspond closely with an unplaced fragment of the Athenian Victor Lists *IG* II² 2325 incerta fr. h', 1–5 M-O, which reads:

Θρασ[- — —
Πολυ[- — —
Ἀλκ[- — —
Κλε[- — —

As fr. **1** shows Kleandros and Thrasyboulos as immediate rivals, and very close in time with an actor whose name begins with 'Alk-', and is very possibly 'Alkimachos' (cf. **5**, l. 6; **7**, l. 2), it is tempting to complete the Athenian list as:

Θρασ[ύβουλος
Πολυ — —
Ἀλκ[ίμαχος
Κλέ[ανδρος

This is more convincing than Snell's attempt (*TrGF* I on DID A 3b) to restore the tragic poets to the fragment (Polychares, Alkimenes and Kleophon) for whom no evidence of contemporaneity exists, nor is it very clear that Polychares was a tragic poet (see **III Biii**) – Snell's alternatives Polyidus and Kleainetos are no better.

The prosopography (Thrasyboulos, Kleandros, Eupolemos) indicates that the performance dates recorded in this list began at least in the 380s. If the 'Sophocles' named in fr. **1** (cf. **3**, l. 4) is Sophocles the Younger, then a date in the 380s or 370s seems all the more probable as the Athenian *Fasti* show Sophocles the Younger winning the Dionysia in 387 (the year Kleandros won the actor's prize) and 375 (*IG* II^2 2318, ll. 1008 and 1153 M-O). Aristodemos' first victories were in the 370s (*IG* II^2 2325H, l. 23 M-O). The names Mnesitheos, Philotades (our supplement to fr. **7**, l. 1), and Aristodemos (if Archon) bring the list down to mid century (see introduction to **7**).

Despite its many uncertainties, this inscription gives clear testimony of tragic performances in Rhodes in the first decades of the fourth century. Rhodes was created by the synoecism in 408/7 of three cities: Kamiros, Ialysos and Lindos. The new city was divided into three tribes bearing the names of the original cities that had been united (Hansen 1995, 100; Papachristodoulou 1999, 29–30). There is ample epigraphic evidence, but nothing firmly datable before the second or first centuries, that tragedies and comedies at Rhodes were funded by three choregoi, one assigned by each of the tribes (see esp. Segre and Pugliese Carratelli 1949–1951, no. 63 [undated]). From frr. **1**, l. 4 and **5**, l. 4, where, it appears, actors were allotted by the city to the tribes (cf. **I Bi 12**), it seems that tribal funding, if not a choregic system, was in place by the early fourth century. Choregoi for boys' choruses are attested on Rhodes from ca. 330 (*Lindos* II 696) and for men's choruses from the third century (*IG* XII 1, 68). However, the choregia is not otherwise clearly attested for drama until the second century (*Lindos* II 199, dated to 165; ?*Lindos* II 233, dated 129; Hiller 1901, 440–3, 2nd c.; *Lindos* II 300, l. 8, dated 70; Maiuri 1925, nos. 21, 2nd/1st c., and 18, after ca. 88; *SEG* 39, 759, l. 17, after ca. 78; Pugliese Carratelli 1939–1940, 155, 1st c.; *IG* XII 1, 71 should be dated after ca. 156 – see Habicht 1970, 26–8). From the tribal allotment of actors in **1** and **5** we can infer that the Rhodian festival had three sets of tragic performers in competition with one another.

We cannot unfortunately infer from the mention of the poets whether or not they were present as disdaskaloi in Rhodes or if the actors took on the function of directing the plays. The possible mention of plays of Sophocles the Elder in **7**, or those of Aristarchus of Tegea (**2** and **8**), suggests the revival in competition of old plays, and indeed in Sophocles' case of a full tetralogy. If this is so, it is unique, excepting only the Rural Dionysia (**III J**), possible revivals of Aeschylus, and the very doubtful single reperformance of Teleclides' *Stiff Men* attested in document **a** of the Roman *Fasti* of **I Avi**. Nothing like the revival of a Sophoclean play, let alone a tetralogy, is attested for the competition of the Athenian Dionysia. The revivals attested for the Athenian Dionysia from 386 were single dramas (presumably either tragedy or satyr play) and not performed in competition (*IG* II^2 2318, ll.

1009–11 M–O; **I Avi**). The Athenian Lenaea also seems to be excluded on the basis of our present knowledge of the festival. On our evidence the Lenaea never had full tetralogies or revivals of any sort. If the plays listed in **7** are indeed by Sophocles the Elder, then we must infer that this section of the inscription refers to the Rhodian Dionysia and that there full tetralogies were revived by the actors as part of the competition. These tetralogies appear to have included a satyr play, something we might not have expected at this date. The Rhodian Dionysia may in this respect have been more conservative than the Athenian festivals.

It is impossible to say if the list included still other festivals. But even if this were so, the decision to include information about the Rhodian Dionysia seems extraordinary. This is especially so, since no information about non-Athenian festivals appears in the corresponding Victory Lists relating to Comic Poets, which also include the first half of the fourth century (see **I Avi**). Rhodes is the only dramatic festival in the Classical period that we know to have offered more than a single prize for actors. Perhaps its importance emerges from this singularity. Fr. **7**, l. 5 shows that there was at least a second prize and **5**, l. 3 and **8**, l. 4 seem to indicate a third prize, and it is possible that all the references to seconds and thirds are from the Rhodian festival. It is true that the Athenian *Fasti* do offer information about competing actors, but only for the Dionysia, and only after tragic actors began to be rotated between choregoi, possibly not before the second half of the fourth century. The information that 'X competed against Y' (**1**, l. 3, possibly **5**, l. 3 and **8**, l. 4) is also unique to this Actors' List.

A complete list of ranked prizes, first to third, would have provided ancient theatre antiquarians with an ideal means of reconstructing the real hierarchies and rivalries in the acting profession in the age of the classic greats. Other didascalic lists for the Athenian festivals, by contrast, mention nothing more than a first prize for tragic actors, and that was doubtless the case with the Athenian festivals in this list, since these festivals had only one tragic actors' prize. Without the Rhodian material, the actors' list might have seemed disappointingly spare and uninformative.

Perhaps there were other reasons contributing to the elevation of the Rhodian didascaliae. Rhodes had close political, cultural and commercial ties with the Ptolemaic empire: in particular Rhodes seems to have adopted a cult of Ptolemies from the time of Ptolemy Soter, whose epithet, Pausanias tells us (1.8.6; Segre 1941, 35–9), Rhodes first gave him. Someone working in the Museum at Alexandria may have had specifically regional motives for integrating the Rhodian material into the lists that served as a direct model for the Roman inscriptions (see **I Avi**). We thank Thomas Coward for the suggestion that this was the second-/first-century Rhodian scholar, Timachidas.

The Roman *Fasti* give no evidence of comedy in Rhodes, but we should probably infer the existence of comic competitions from the evidence that Anaxandrides, one of the most productive comic poets of the first half of the fourth century, was a Rhodian from Kamiros (*PCG* T 1–2), although the Suda (α 1982) admits that some claimed his birthplace was Colophon. The Suda also indicates that he was competing in Macedon (**VI F**) from at least the 101st Olympiad (376–372) and document **d** of the Roman *Fasti* in **I Avi** shows him competing at Athens from at least 374 and probably much earlier. The possibly still earlier and decidedly more prolific comic writer Antiphanes is said by 'Dionysios' to have been Rhodian, although others said he was from Kios (on the Propontis), Smyrna or Larissa (*PCG* T 1–2; the Dionysios in question is identified by *PCG* as the Hadrianic music historian from Halicarnassus).

Diodorus gives us our earliest literary evidence for Rhodian theatre: he mentions a Dionysion and a theatre in the city of Rhodes in connection with the devastating flood of 316 (19.45.5). This is presumably the Dionysion, located by the discovery of choregic monuments, beneath the Hospitaller Church of St. Demetrius of Piossasco (Maiuri 1928, 46; Karousos 1973, 67; Scaduto 2010, 92). Diodorus later mentions the theatre in connection with the siege of 305 (20.84.3, 20.93.1, 20.98.7). This theatre may have been built of wood (cf. D.S. 31.36) and in any case seems unrelated to the remains in the sanctuary of Apollo Erethymios (see above). Diodorus also names the theatrical festival a Dionysia (20.84.3 relating to 305) and this is confirmed by inscriptions from ca. 300 (Segre and Pugliese Carratelli 1949–1951, no. 106 = *SEG* 19, 317; *IG* XII 1, 6; cf. Ceccarelli 2010, 131). Drama was also performed in the second century at the Alexandreia (Pugliese Carratelli 1939–1940, 155 no. 16), a festival that may well go back to the time of Alexander (Habicht 1970, 27; Ferrandini Troisi 2005, 32), and at the Alexandreia and Dionysia (*IG* XII 1, 71; *Lindos* II 233; Maiuri 1925, no. 18; Pugliese Carratelli 1952–1954, no. 20; *SEG* 39, 759), a festival created out of the combination of the earlier separate festivals at some time between 156 and 129 (Segre 1941, 34–5; Habicht 1970, 27; Buraselis 2012, 254–5). The cult of Dionysus and the Muses, around which the Rhodian actors' association(s?) was organised, seems also to have been a third-century combination (Segre 1941, 33; *ATD* TE 78). Drama seems likely also for the Sminthia (for Dionysus Smintheus) at Lindos (*IG* XII 1, 762, an inscription of 23 AD according to Gabrielsen 2001, 233 but referring to 'ancient customs').

Athenian influence seems to have been strong in the period following the revolt against Sparta in 395, when Rhodes became a democracy and later (378/7) joined the Second Athenian Confederacy. The details of these inscriptions suggest that the Rhodian democracy adapted the Athenian format for their Dionysia and an Athenian-style model of funding. Three tragic competitors, probably each with a tragic tetralogy (three tragedies plus a satyr play), competed at the festival. Each was tribally organised (as were men's and boys' choruses, and by ca. 330 comedy, at the Athenian Dionysia). We may guess, from the distribution of actors to the tribe, both that actors were paid by the state, as at Athens, and that the tribal obligations fell to the lot of choregoi. We have abundant evidence for a choregia for tragedy and comedy from at least the second century, but also evidence for a choregos for boys' choruses probably around 330. Rhodian choregoi, like Athenian, set up choregic monuments for themselves, some of which included tripods (Wilson 2000, 290–2). In addition, Rhodes seems to have imitated some classic Athenian pre-performance rituals. Diodorus tells us that the Rhodians passed a decree that, among other social welfare provisions, required the Rhodian state to grant a panoply to the sons of the war dead in the theatre at the Dionysia when they had come of age (20.84.3). This provision directly copies a practice that existed in Athens but had been discontinued much earlier in the century (**I Av 5**).

Dxii: Salamis

An Athenian possession from the last decades of the sixth century, the island of Salamis was never incorporated into the Attic deme system, so the Dionysia held there was not a 'deme' Dionysia and, despite the close proximity to Attica, should properly be classified as a festival held by Athenians on overseas territory, akin to the Dionysia of Lemnos (**Dviii**;

Hansen in *IACP* 637–9 for the *status quaestionis* on Salamis and the 'Salaminioi'; Clinton 2014, 334–7, supporting the view of Salamis as a cleruchy). Consequently we have no good reason to assume (as most do, e.g., implicitly, *DFA*² 51) that it was celebrated at the time of deme Dionysia, in Posideon. The Athenians appointed an Archon for Salamis, as for other overseas possessions (Arist. *Ath.* 54.8 with Rhodes 1981, 611). His single most important duty was to 'run the Dionysia' τά τε Διονύσια ποιοῦσιν, including the appointment of its choregoi (to judge from the fact that it is the only duty mentioned in the *Athenaion Politeia*). The choregoi are likely to have been drawn from wealthy Athenian landowners (cleruchs and others) on Salamis (cf. Taylor 1997, 169). The status of the so-called 'Salaminioi', many of whom evidently lived not on Salamis but in Attica, is much debated; but if they were, or included, those who lived there prior to the Athenian take-over, it is unlikely (but not impossible) that they could have been required to help fund an essentially Athenian festival (Taylor 1997 *contra* argues that the Salaminioi are all Athenians). In the late second century *epimeletai* are found assisting with the manufacture and announcement of honorific crowns at the Dionysia (*IG* II² 1008, ll. 82–3; 1011, ll. 58–9), and *DFA*² 51 entertains the possibility that they similarly aided the Archon of Salamis with the festival in the earlier period. **2** shows that the Dionysia and its choregic structure were already in place by around 400, while **1** implies the same by ca. 420. How soon after Athenian occupation (ca. 525) it began can only be guessed, but the question is important not least because Salamis provides a very clear example of the transfer by the Athenians of the festival and associated choregic administrative practice beyond Attica (Wilson 2000, 245).

The Dionysia was one of the island's two major festivals, along with the Aianteia that commemorated the assistance given by Ajax at the battle of Salamis. It will have been among the most important occasions through which the Athenians resident on the island forged a sense of their rather special community identity, heavily influenced by their position slightly apart from Attica yet very close and belonging to it (Taylor 1997, 167). The fact that a purely choral contest is known for it in the Classical period hints at its pretensions to being a 'polis-grade' event (below).

Unlike the situation for most deme Dionysia, evidence for the life of the Dionysia of Salamis extends into the second century, when the island was once again in Athenian hands after the Macedonian dominion that began in 318, and 'the Salaminians engaged in a determined effort to revive their island's civic and religious life, with the active participation of the city of Athens' (Schmalz 2007–2008, 31). As it happens it is only in this later period that drama (tragedy only) is directly attested, but **1** almost certainly proves that it featured already in the fifth century. In 131/0 a gymnasiarch from Salamis is honoured with a gold crown to be announced 'at the tragedies of the Dionysia on Salamis, when it next takes place' Διονυσίων τῶν ἐν Σαλαμῖνι τραγωδοῖς, ὅταν | πρῶτον γίνηται (*IG* II² 1227, ll. 31–2). Rather than implying irregular periodicity (Nilsson 1900, 107–8; *DFA*² 51), the specification is more likely designed to ensure prompt enactment of the announcement at the next festival (Chaniotis 2007, 56). At a time when participation in the festival of Ajax on Salamis appears on the long list of activities expected of Athenian ephebes, late in the second century they and their *kosmetai* are awarded crowns 'at the Dionysia on Salamis, at the contest of tragedies' Διονυσίων [τ]ῶν ἐν Σαλαμῖνι τραγῳδῶν τῷ ἀγῶνι (*IG* II² 1008, l. 82, of 118/17; Mikalson 1998, 243–5; Perrin-Saminadayar 2007, 217–22).

In the somewhat later *IG* II² 1011, of 106/5, the event is further qualified – by highly plausible restoration – as 'the [new con]test of tragedies' (l. 58): Διονυσίων τῶν ἐν Σαλαμῖνι τραγωιδῶν τ[ῶι καινῶι ἀγ]ῶνι, an expression that almost certainly means 'at the contest for new tragedies', as opposed to an event for old – namely Classical – tragedy, suggesting that both featured at the festival at this date (Perrin 1997, 205–6).

A theatre is thus implied, and reports are now emerging of the discovery of a structure inside Ambelakia (ancient Salamis town). On the other hand, a 'garden' where 'dances and choral performances took place' is mentioned in the Augustan-era decree that restored ancient sanctuaries (*IG* II² 1035; as in *SEG* 26, 121, ll. 34–5: κῆπον ἐν κρ[- - - -|- - - - - - - ὅπου ὀρχή]σεις καὶ χορε[ῖ]αι ἐδρῶ[ντο]). This was probably just outside rather than in the city (Schmalz 2007–2008, 36 n. 124, notes that 'in Kr-' ἐν κρ[seems better suited to an extra-urban location) and has been proposed as a possible site for the Salaminian Dionysia (Schmalz 2007–2008, 36).

From at least some time in the Hellenistic period, Salamis – or the Athenians more generally – exploited a close association, real or imagined, with the poet Euripides, who was said to have been born there, and to have retreated thither to a cave overlooking the sea to muse and compose his poetry when disgruntled with his fellow Athenians (*TrGF* T Ea and 105). The so-called 'Cave of Euripides' at Peristeria on the southern tip of the island is now known to have been a site of heroic cult for the poet and touristic pilgrimage in Roman times (Lolos 2003; *AR* 44, 1997–1998, 16; Gell. 15.20.5). A late fifth- or early fourth-century black-glaze skyphos inscribed in the second or third century AD with the name of Euripides is the most spectacular evidence of the cult (*SEG* 47, 282 Εὐριππ[-), which may date back much further, perhaps indeed to the time when the island's Dionysia hosted old tragedy alongside new (above). Indeed its excavator has shown that a sanctuary on a terrace located below the cave was developed early in the third century. He argues that this was for the combined cult of the god and the tragic poet, and that it was transferred up to the cave only much later (2ⁿᵈ c. AD) when the latter became a tourist shrine (Lolos 2000; cf. *AR* 47, 2000–2001, 15–16). Evidence of Dionysian worship in the sanctuary includes a marble statue of the god and a fragment of a clay phallos (Lolos 2013, 81–3). The Euripidean associations claimed for the island may even be part of an explanation for the prominence of tragedy at Salamis at that date. Other, far mightier, centres made claims on the poet's heritage from the time of his death that suited their cultural aspirations: Macedon to be his resting-place (**VI Di 4, 7–8, 10–16, 18–19**); and Syracuse under Dionysius I – who acquired the poet's literary relics for dedication in the Syracusan theatre (**VI E; Axi**) – to be the new Hellenic centre of dramatic production. The story of Euripides' cave comes with the authority of Philochorus (*FGrH* 328 F 219, *pace* Scullion 2003, 391–2) and is more likely to be the result of a cult for the poet already in existence rather than the cause of it. The claims of Salamis(-Athens) to be the place of the poet's birth and poetic inspiration were part of a struggle over the legacy of the poet that began very early.

1. Tombstone with a relief showing the deceased as a tragic choreut, ca. 420–410 (by style).

Fragmentary stele of Pentelic marble with intact crowning pediment.
0.702 × 0.732 × 0.07–0.115 m.

Found in the necropolis of Ambelaki, site of the ancient city.
Piraeus Museum 4229 (ex Salamis Museum 74).
Tsirivakos 1974; Clairmont 1993–1995, 233–4, no. 1.075.
Photos: Tsirivakos 1974, pls. 48–51; Steinhauer 2001, ill. 447; Kattoula 2017. See also Colour
Plate 16.

Among the earliest 'Attic' tombstones, this fine fragmentary stele was found in the necropolis of ancient Salamis. Frel (1969, no. 94) thought it came from a workshop on the island.
Clairmont (1993–1995, 233) speculated (on the basis of the 'Ionian' features of style) that
it was by an Ionian in Athens working on the Parthenon. Wherever it was made, it will have
belonged to a local. A beardless young man gazes intently at a mask that he holds with his
right hand – perhaps by a strap, given the position of his fingers above the head (Slater
1985; Clairmont 1993–1995 thinks the hand too close to the head for this). The mask
is tragic, and almost certainly intended as that of a typical female chorus-member – the
preponderant gender for choral identities in Euripides (and perhaps not only in Euripides:
Foley 2003). We thus follow Green (1989, 37) in identifying the deceased as a choreut, represented thus in a familiar manner as recording a highlight of the civic and religious service
in the life of the deceased (who need not necessarily have died at the young age at which
he is depicted). This is on balance more likely than the alternative interpretations of him as
a poet (Slater 1985, 342) or actor (Tsirivakos 1974; Steinhauer 2001, 303). Indeed it conforms to a type of representation in funerary art for which we have three other examples.
A young man is similarly depicted with female mask and costume reaching to the ground

(the youth on the Salaminian monument may have been depicted wearing this also) in the choreut grave reliefs from Athens, Vari and Taras (Green 2012b; **V E**).

2. Choregic dedication, ca. 400–375 (by letter forms; use of o for ου and ε for ει).

> Three-sided marble base with concave sides, decorated with mouldings; four cavities in the upper surface for a tripod: one round, in the centre (0.2 m); the others rectangular, at the corners (0.17 × 0.14 m).
> 0.52 × 1.03 m.
> Found in a field near the town of Ambelaki, site of the ancient city.
> Current whereabouts unknown (cf. Amandry 1976, 22 n. 12).
> Monceaux 1882; *IG* II 1248; *IG* II² 3093; *IG* II³ 4, 499.
> Text: based on *IG* II³ 4, 499.

1	Διόδωρος Ἐξηκεστίδο	stoich.
	νικήσας χορῶι παίδων.	
	Παιδέας ἐδίδασκε.	non-stoich.
	Τηλεφάνης ηὖλε Μεγαρεύς.	
5	Φιλόμηλος ἦρχε.	

> Diodoros son of Exekestides, after a victory with a boys' chorus (sc. dedicated this); Paideas was the didaskalos; Telephanes of Megara was the piper. [5] Philomelos was Archon.

This choregic inscription is loosely modelled on an Athenian prototype from the choral contests of the City Dionysia (**V F**). Unlike them, it lacks a main verb (commonly ἐχορήγει 'was choregos', although when the verb of victory is, as here, applied to the choregos himself it is ἀνέθηκε 'dedicated': e.g. *IG* II³ 4, 467–8) and it makes no mention of a tribe (below), but the parallel extends to the object dedicated, and presumably awarded as prize in the contest, for this triangular base was designed to display a tripod. The letters of the first two lines are twice the height of the rest (0.04–0.02 m).

Philomelos was the Archon of Salamis who had organised the festival (Arist. *Ath.* 54.8). The choregos Diodoros was presumably a (cleruchic) resident of Salamis. The decision not to include his demotic may suggest that he wished to stress his membership of the local community (whence probably he derived his wealth) above the Attic deme in which he was formally registered. He may be a member of an Athenian family of liturgical status known to have property in Salamis. An Exekestides of Kothokidai served as syntrierach before 353/2 and his gravestone was found on Salamis (*APF* 176–7 does not mention our Diodoros as a potential member of the family in an earlier generation).

As it happens the boys' choral contest is the only one directly attested – an event normally organised by tribes in Athens. Such purely choral events are strikingly absent from the dossier of evidence for deme Dionysia (this may be why Makres *IG* II/III³ app. crit. believes the victory does not derive from a Dionysia). While we have no evidence that the demos of Athenians on Salamis was organised into tribes, as we know some other overseas Athenian cleruchies were (cf. *SEG* 45, 1162), some subdivision of the community for this agonistic purpose is implied. On the other hand, the fact that Diodoros the choregos is here described as the victor – '*with* a chorus' – might be taken to suggest that no formal civic subdivision was used to structure the contest but that choregoi simply conscripted their teams from the population (of Athenian settlers only?) as a whole. The existence of a choral contest normally reserved for Athenians in state-wide configuration is certainly consistent with the status of Salamis as a semi-autonomous cleruchy or (quasi)-polis (Hansen 2007, 322–3, explicitly describes cleruchies as '*poleis* of Athenians living abroad'). Such an event, even more than drama, will have focused on and helped to mould the identities of its participants as members of the community (Wilson 2000, 245).

Paideas is otherwise unknown. Telephanes is very probably the piper who helped Demosthenes out in his choregia for the City Dionysia of 348 by stepping in to take over the direction of the chorus when his chorodidaskalos had been 'corrupted'– something Telephanes himself supposedly detected and challenged (D. 21.17–18; **V G**). The fact that Demosthenes had won the right to choose the first piper by the fall of the lot (**I Bi 13a**) shows that Telephanes was the most attractive available in the pool of talent that year. He had evidently by that time achieved much of the fame that eventually saw him having his tomb built by a daughter of Philip on the road from Megara to Corinth (Paus. 1.44.6: for sources and argument that they reflect one rather than two pipers of the name see Stefanis no. 2408).

Dxiii: Samos

1. **Honorific decree of the Athenian cleruchy awarding a gold crown at the performance of tragedy**, ca. 350. (The date depends on the prosopography and chronology of events related to *IG* XII 6, 252, identified by Tracy ap. *IG* XII 6, 253 as by the same stonecutter – in particular, the theft from the sanctuary mentioned in *IG* XII 6, 252 apparently took place before the Heraion inventory of *IG* XII 6, 261 which is datable by Archon to 346/5.)

Two joining fragments of a stele of white marble.
0.225 × 0.36 × 0.065 m.
Fr. a found in the village of Kolonna in 1936; fr. b in a stone pile in the sanctuary of Hera in 1912.
Samos Museum Inv. Her. J 212 (fr. a); Inv. Her. M 169 (fr. b).
Fr. a: *SEG* 45, 1165; fr. b: Schede 1919, 3 no. 4 (= *SEG* 1, 349); fr. a + b: *IG* XII 6, 253.
Text: *IG* XII 6, 253.

```
        [— — — — — — — — — — — — — — —]
a       Σωσιγέν[ης — — — — — — — — — — —]
        εἶπεν : ἐψηφί[σ]θ[αι τῶι δ]ήμωι [:] τὰ μ[ὲν]     b
        ἄλλα καθάπερ τῆ[ι βουλ]ῆι : ἐπειδὴ δὲ
        Διότιμος : Νικοστρ[ά]του : Ἐλαιούσι-
5       ος : ἀνὴρ ἀγαθός ἐστ[ι]ν : καὶ νῦν : καὶ
        ἐν τῶι πρόσθεν χρόν[ωι] περὶ τὸν δῆμον
        τὸν ἐν Σάμωι, ἐπαινέσαι αὐτὸν καὶ στε-
        φανῶσαι χρυσῶι στεφάνωι ἀπὸ Ⲡ δρα-
        χμῶν ἀρετῆς ἕνεκ[α] καὶ δικαιοσύνης
```

10   [τῆ]ς εἰς τὸν δῆ[μον τ]ὸν ἐν Σάμωι καὶ
      [ἀνει]πεῖν Διονυ[σίων τ]οῖς τραγωιδοῖς : τ…
      [— — —]ΣΙΔΕΗ·[— — — —] τοὺς πρέσβει[ς — —]
      [— — — — —]ΗΜ^[— — — — — — — — — — — — —]
      [— — — — — — — — — — — — — — — — — — —]

11–12 [ἀνειπεῖν αὐτὸν τ]οῖς τραγωιδοῖς τ[ῶν | μεγάλων Διονυσίων] τοὺς πρέσβει[ς]
Schede

Sosigen[es …] proposed [that the P]eople vot[e] as did the [Counc]il. In addition, since Diotimos son of Nikostr[a]tos of the deme Elaious (an Attic deme) [5]
is a good man, both now and in the pas[t], towards the People in Samos, let us
praise him and crown him with a gold crown worth 500 drachmas for his virtue
and the fairness [10] he shows towards the Pe[ople] in Samos and [proc]laim it at
[t]he tragedies of the Diony[sia …] the ambassadors […]

2. Honorific decree of Samos for the tragic actor Polos of Aegina, making reference to the financial arrangements for his performance on Samos, soon after 306 (see on l. 7 below).

Intact stele of white marble with relief panel carrying an image, in a recessed rectangular panel, of the head of a young man with a club behind.
1.38 × 0.505–0.55 × 0.12 m.
Found in 1912 in part of the perimeter wall of the sanctuary of Hera facing north-east.
Archaeological Museum of Pythagoreion M 2793 (Inv. Her. M 190).
Schede 1919, 16 no. 7 (= SEG 1, 362); IG XII 6, 56.
Text: IG XII 6, 56.   Photos: Ghiron-Bistagne 1976, 165, 168 (figs. 62–3); Chatzidakis 2017.

1   Πώλωι Σωσιγένους Αἰγινήτηι·
            vacat 0.022
      ἔδοξε τῆι βουλῆι καὶ τῶι δήμωι, Δημά-
      ρετος Δημέου εἶπεν· ἐπειδὴ Πῶλος vac.
      Σωσιγένους Αἰγινήτης ἔν τε τοῖς πρότε-
5   ρον χρόνοις εὔνους καὶ πρόθυμος ὢν διε-
      τέλει περὶ τὴμ πόλιν καὶ νῦν τοῦ δήμου ψη-
      φισαμένου ἄγειν ἡμᾶς ἐπὶ τοῖς εὐαγγελίοις
      Ἀντιγόνεια καὶ Δημητρίεια καὶ τῶμ πρεσβευ-
      τῶμ παραγενομένωμ πρὸς αὐτὸν μισθῶν τε
10   ἐλασσόνων συνεχώρησεν ὑποκρινεῖσθαι τῶι
      δήμωι καὶ τὰ μὲν ἐκ τοῦ θεάτρου γενόμενα
      ἐκομίσατο, τὸ δὲ λοιπὸν ἐπέσχηκε τῆι πόλει
      καθότι ὁ δῆμος ἠξίωσεν αὐτόν, δεδόχθαι τῆ-
      [ι] βουλῆι καὶ τῶι δήμωι· ἐπηινῆσθαι μὲν Πῶλον
15   ἀρετῆς ἔνεκε καὶ προθυμίας ἣμ παρέσχηται τ-
      ῶι δήμωι, καὶ εἶναι αὐτῶι τῆς αὐτῆς ἐπιμελεία-
      ς τυγχάνειμ παρὰ τοῦ δήμου, δεδόσθαι δὲ αὐτῶι

καὶ πολιτείαν ἐφ᾽ ἴσηι καὶ ὁμοίαι καὶ ἐπικληρῶσα-
ι αὐτὸν ἐπὶ φυλὴν καὶ χιλιαστὺν καὶ ἑκατοστύ-
20 ν καὶ γένος καὶ ἀναγράψαι καθότι καὶ τοὺς ἄλλου-
ς Σαμίους, εἶναι δὲ αὐτὸν καὶ πρόξενον τοῦ
δήμου, εἶναι δὲ αὐτῶι καὶ εἴσπλουν καὶ ἔκπλου-
[ν] καὶ ἐμ πολέμωι καὶ ἐν εἰρήνηι ἀσυλεὶ καὶ ἀσπον-
δεί, ὑπάρχειν δὲ αὐτῶι καὶ ἔφοδον ἐπὶ τὴν βουλὴγ
25 [κ]αὶ τὸν δῆμον, ἄν του δέηται, πρώτωι μετὰ τὰ ἱερὰ κα-
[ὶ τ]ὰ βασιλικά, δεδόσθαι δὲ αὐτῶι καὶ προεδρίαν ἐν τ-
οῖς ἀγῶσιν οἷς ἂν ἡ πόλις ἄγηι πᾶσιν, εἶναι δὲ ταῦτα
καὶ αὐτῶι καὶ ἐκγόνοις, στεφανῶσαι δὲ Πῶλον θαλλοῦ στεφάνωι Διονυσίων τραγωιδοῖς, τῆς δὲ ἀναγ-
30 γελίας ἐπιμεληθῆναι τὸν ἀγωνοθέτην μετὰ τ-
οῦ δημιουργοῦ, τὸ δὲ ψήφισμα τόδε ἀναγράψαι εἰς
στήλην λιθίνην καὶ στῆσαι εἰς τὸ ἱερὸν τῆς Ἥρ-
ας, τῆς δὲ ἐπικληρώσεως καὶ τῆς ἀναγραφῆς ἐ-
πιμεληθῆναι τὸγ γραμματέα τῆς βουλῆς· *vac.*
35 ἔλαχε φυλὴν Χησιεῖς, χιλιαστὺς Οἴνωπες,
γένος καὶ ἑκατοστὺς Ἑλανδρίδαι.
            vacat 0.155

For Polos, son of Sosigenes, of Aegina.

The Council and the People decided; Demaretos son of Demeas made the proposal: since Polos son of Sosigenes of Aegina was in the [5] past consistently
well-disposed and energetic in respect of our city; and now, after the People
voted that we celebrate the Antigoneia and Demetrieia in response to the good
news and after the intervention of ambassadors, he has agreed to act for the
People for [10] lower fees and he has collected the takings from the theatre but
has presented the remainder to the city, as the People asked of him, the Council
and the People have decided that Polos be praised [15] for his virtue and the
energetic support which he has given to the People; that it should be possible
for him to experience the same show of concern from the People; that he be
granted citizenship on equal and shared terms; that he be allocated to a tribe
and a *chiliastys* ('division of 1000s') and a *hekatostys* ('division of 100s') [20]
and a *genos* and be registered in the same manner as the other Samians; he is
to be a proxenos of the People; he is to have free passage in and out by sea
both in time of war and peace, without fear of seizure and in the absence of a
treaty; he is to be accorded access to the Council [25] [a]nd the People, should he
need anything, in first place after the sacred and royal matters; he is also to be
granted prohedria in whatever contests the city holds; these privileges are to be
given both to him and to his descendants. It was decided to crown Polos with
an olive crown at the tragedies of the Dionysia; the [30] agonothete, with the *demiourgos*, is to take care of the announcement; this decree is to be inscribed on
a stone stele and erected in the sanctuary of Hera; the secretary of the Council
is to see to the allotment and the inscription. [35] The allotment assigned him

the tribe Chesieis, the *chiliastys* ('division of 1000s') Oinopes; the *genos* and *hekatostys* ('division of 100s') Elandridai.

1 is the earliest indication of the performance of any form of drama on the Ionian island of Samos – tragedy at the Dionysia. It is also the oldest honorific decree from the island. Another ten decrees, stretching from the end of the fourth century to the late second century, also require the announcement of a crown at the tragedies of the Dionysia (Ceccarelli 2010, 124–5). Of particular interest is *IG* XII 6, 150, ll. 2–4, of the late fourth century, in honour of judges from Cos, which requires 'the sacr[ed he]rald to announce each of them by name and patronymic in the theatre at the tragedies of the Dionysia'. We may however suspect that both the Dionysia and drama are older than the first direct evidence for them. It is not unlikely that drama was introduced as early as the fifth century.

The Dionysia at Samos may conform to a pattern that shows drama spreading with Athenian colonisation (**D Introduction**). The island spent much of the fifth century as a more or less autonomous ally of Athens and first received an Athenian cleruchy after the Samian revolt of 440, which lasted until the end of the Peloponnesian War. A second Athenian cleruchy, which involved the expulsion of the local population, dates from ca. 365 to 322 (Cargill 1995, 17–21), when the city had the same tribal subdivisions as in Attica. Remains of the ancient theatre (unexcavated and largely buried) can be found above modern Pithagorio, about 1.5 km north-east of the city. It was built into the natural slope, partly cut into the rock. The partially visible Greek phase of the theatron may, according to Isler, go back as far as the late fourth century (Isler in *TGR* II, 287). The theatre was in somewhat better condition when seen by Pococke in the eighteenth century (1745, 26–7; see also Fabricius 1884, 167–8).

What immediately followed the proclamation clause in **1** is unclear. The remains of ll. 11–12 may hint at a (?) further proclamation 'in [Athe]ns' (τ[οῖς | Ἀθήνη]σι ? Hallof app. crit.) by ambassadors (l. 12) of the Athenian cleruchs on Samos. The qualifier of 'Great' for the festival here, restored in older editions at ll. 11–12, can no longer stand.

Among the Arundel marbles taken to England in 1627 was a fragment of a victor-list from the Samian Dionysia, dated by Hallof to a little after the middle of the third century (*IG* XII 6, 176 with Hallof; note also *IG* XII 6, 177–8, 2nd c., with Hallof 1999). This lists for each year, underneath the names of the relevant eponymous official (*demiourgos* at this time in Samos: below) and of the agonothete, two choregoi for 'the boys' (this will mean a chorus of boys), followed by the winner and the piper; then the same for 'the men' (sc. chorus of men). Although the evidence for the dramatic contests is more fragmentary, it seems that they then followed, under the joint rubric 'tragedy and comedy' τραγωιδῶν καὶ κωμωιδῶν (restored at ll. 1, 18; cf. *IG* XII 6, 177, ll. 6, 15–16; *IG* XII 6, 178, l. 9). This too was followed by the names of two choregoi, and a winner. It thus seems that the same two men served for both dramatic genres. The binary structure of all these contests is, as Hallof (1999, 361) has noted, probably to be related to the two tribes into which the civic population of Samos was divided.

In at least one year recorded on *IG* XII 6, 176, the name of an actor (doubtless associated with the winning drama) appears. It is one Hermophantos (l. 5), probably the comic actor successful at the Athenian Lenaea ca. 240 (*IG* II² 2325F, l. 102 M-O; Stefanis no. 908;

Delcroix and Giannattasio Andria 1997). If the Hermophantos who had won high plaudits in the metropolis of theatre also appeared on Samos, we may deduce that Samian enthusiasm for high-quality drama was not confined to tragedy.

While we have firm evidence only for tragedy among these genres before the date of this victor-list, it is entirely possible and in fact quite likely that some or all of the boys, men and comedy also featured in the Samian Dionysia considerably earlier (that they shadow quite closely the core programme of the Athenian Dionysia is suggestive). The fact that **1** specifies the announcement of the crown 'at the tragedies of the Dionysia' might imply that there were other events at it by ca. 350.

2 honours one of the most famous actors of the fourth century, indeed of antiquity (Stefanis no. 2187; O'Connor 1966, 128–30; Ghiron-Bistagne 1976, 164–9; 354). Polos of Aegina may have been especially well known for his Sophoclean roles (Gell. 6.5; Stob. 4.28). Since at the date of this decree he is evidently already a great star to be courted we might guess that he was at least fifty, perhaps more (no evidentiary weight should be placed on the age of the young male in the image above the decree). That would put his birth around 360, making the stories of his association with the actor Archias of Thurii (Polos was said to be his 'student': Plu. *Mor.* 348e) and with Demosthenes at least possible, though he will have been some twenty years the junior of the orator (*Anon. Prolegom. Rhet.* 6.35, 27 Waltz; [Plu.] *Mor.* 848b; O'Connor 1966, 129 notes that if he had been a contemporary of Demosthenes the works of the latter are likely to have left some trace of him; the implication of Stob. 4.28 that he was a contemporary of Socrates must be dismissed). When Lucian (*Nec.* 16) writes of a famous tragic actor called Polos son of Charikles of the deme Sounion he may be fabricating a non-existent pastiche Polos, but equally he may be drawing on good sources, in which case we may deduce that the Aeginetan Polos was granted Athenian citizenship, as he was granted Samian by **2** (O'Connor 1966, 129. For honorific awards made by the Athenian People to actors and other theatre people in the 330s–320s see **I Aix 3**; **VI J**). That Plutarch lists him, along with Nikostratos, Kallippides, Mynniskos and Theodoros, among the glories of the Athenian stage also tends towards his having attained Athenian citizenship.

Polos is said on the authority of Eratosthenes and Philochorus to have been performing eight tragedies over four days shortly before his death at the age of 70 (*FGrH* 241 F 33; *FGrH* 328 F 222). If any credence can be put in the anecdote which reports that 'he could earn a talant for two days' performance' (δυσὶν ἡμέραις ἀγωνισάμενος τάλαντον λάβοι μισθόν [Plu.] *Mor.* 848b), this could have earnt him the vast sum of two talants. The anecdote can be traced back to the Peripatetic Critolaus (fr. 33 Wehrli), but the story also attaches to other actors, including Aristodemos of Metapontum (Gell. 11.9.2), who makes a better chronological fit. The good grace with which Polos is said in **2** to have 'agreed to act … for lower fees' (ll. 9–10) corroborates his potential to dictate the financial terms on which he performed at this time.

Samos had evidently achieved a coup by securing Polos for performance at a very special event, the festivals (with e.g. Habicht 1970, 62, we assume they are two, but it is possible that they are one: thus Ferguson 1948, 134–5) Antigoneia and Demetrieia, summoned into existence to honour the Antigonid 'saviours' of Greece, Antigonus I and his son Demetrius the Besieger, 'in response to the good news' (l. 7). The place in the calendar of these events is unclear, as is whether they were entirely new entities or replaced (or expanded) an existing major Samian festival. In 404 the Samian Heraia had been temporarily renamed or replaced by the Lysandreia in honour of Lysander, the first living man said to have received divine cult (Plu. *Lys.* 18.2–4; *IG* XII 6, 334; Habicht 1970, 3–6, 243–4), and during the final period of Demetrius' control of Athens the local Dionysia was restyled 'Dionysia and Demetrieia' (Parker 1996, 259; **VI L**). The Antigoneia and Demetrieia were at any rate quite distinct from the Samian Dionysia (l. 29).

The phrase 'the good news' helps to date the inscription with some precision, since it must refer to the news of the Antigonid victory over Ptolemy Soter off Cyprian Salamis in 306. Unless the formula that refers to the honorand's good service both 'in the past … and again now' is entirely empty (which is very unlikely) this was not the first occasion on which Polos had graced Samos with his professional presence. It is even possible (but there is no positive evidence to support the idea) that Polos' earlier services for Samos had extended beyond the theatre. As a well-connected actor he may have been in a position to assist the exiled Samians, who had only been returned to their home in 322 under the decree of Alexander (for the prominence of those who had helped Samians during their exile among the honorands of Samian decrees after 322 see Habicht 1957, 155).

The rewards Polos receives for his more recent generosity are very substantial – in addition to full civic rights, especially noteworthy are the assurance of safe passage and inviolability by sea, even in war time – particularly useful for the travelling professional, all the more so in this unsettled era – and prohedria 'in whatever contests the city holds' (ll. 26–7), implying a variety of agonistic contexts on Samos. The same clause appears in the late fourth-century Samian decrees *IG* XII 6, 38, ll. 21–3, and *IG* XII 6, 150, ll. 8–9, and with variations in several other later instances: the third-century *IG* XII 6, 112, ll. 7–9 has the additional clause '[and summon th]em to prohedria wi[th the other benefactors]'; while the honorand of *IG* XII 6, 119, of ca. 280–246, receives simply 'prohedria in the theatre' προεδρίαν ἐν τῶι θεάτρωι.

The odeion testified for the extra-urban Heraion in the fourth century (*IG* XII 6, 261) is very likely to have been the site of musical contests in honour of the goddess. By the second century the festival for Hera held there included actors' contests in old and new tragedy, as well as comedy; contests for poets of 'new' satyr play, 'new' tragedy and 'new' comedy, in addition to a contest for trumpeters and athletic events (*IG* XII 6, 173). It is not known when drama was added to this festival (and no weight can be put on the fact that decrees awarding a crown at the Dionysia were erected in the sanctuary of Hera when considering whether the Dionysia itself might have been held there rather than in the theatre, since all important inscribed public documents go in the Heraion).

2 is the only surviving example of a famous tragic actor having his crown announced 'at the tragedies of the Dionysia'. Perhaps Polos stayed in town until the next Dionysia to receive it. Presumably the agonothete and *demiourgos* (ll. 30–1), who are to see to the announcement of the crown at the Dionysia, together had general responsibility for the festival. The *demiourgos* is the eponymous official of Samos after 322 (under the cleruchy it was an Archon, in keeping with Athenian practice: Dmitriev 2005, 98). While we have no evidence for choregoi in the fourth century, the existence of an agonothete certainly does not rule out the possibility that a choregic system was already in operation by that time.

There will have been many more expenses other than a single actor's fees to cover. And it is striking that when evidence for choregoi appears in the third century (above; Wilson 2000, 286), agonothetes continue to operate (*IG* XII 6, 11; 156; 176; 177).

2 provides precious evidence for the contractual and financial practicalities required of a community to secure an actor for their festivals. Even though the event in question was evidently a special, one-off occasion and the individual in question a major star, we can assume that similar basic structures were used to secure actors for ordinary theatrical festivals at this time. Lines 8–13 are a summary of the main points of the contract which was brokered between 'the ambassadors' (ll. 8–9) of the People of Samos and Polos. It is important to recognise that these are quoted at some length because they present Polos in a flattering light. The city makes direct contact with the actor (why Slater 2011, 283 thinks this took place 'probably at Athens' is unclear).

The items from the agreement registered for honorific mention are: (1) Polos 'agreed to act for lower fees' (ll. 9–10). This will presumably be 'lower than his usual fees' rather than 'lower than he at first demanded', though the difference is perhaps nugatory. The point is that this was, to some extent, a 'charity' performance. 'Fees' (in the plural) might suggest appearances at two events – perhaps the Antigoneia *and* the Demetrieia, separately.

The second clause is much more difficult: (2) Polos 'collected the takings from the theatre but has presented the remainder to the city, as the People asked of him' (τὰ μὲν ἐκ τοῦ θεάτρου γενόμενα | ἐκομίσατο, τὸ δὲ λοιπὸν ἐπέσχηκε τῆι πόλει | καθότι ὁ δῆμος ἠξίωσεν αὐτόν ll. 11–13). For the middle of κομίζω in the sense of 'collect' when used in technical financial contexts see Palme (1987, 124). Our translation of this compressed clause takes it to mean that Polos collected his agreed – 'lower' – fees from the monies received 'from the theatre', probably 'at the gate'. The likely significance of this detail is that he did not insist on payment in advance, a considerable concession, especially to a city recovering its financial stability. τὰ … ἐκ τοῦ θεάτρου γενόμενα 'the takings from the theatre' refers to the monies generated in some way by the theatre. Slater (2011, 283) insists that this 'can only be the profits (*sic* – presumably he means simply 'income') from the admission fees to the performance put on by Polos'. (For a related but not identical expression see **III Bvi**.) While 'takings *at the gate*' is *prima facie* the most cogent interpretation, Slater is too quick to dismiss the possibility, accepted by Hallof (following Preuner in Schede 1919, 18), that what is meant is the income generated 'from the theatre' by a lease (**I E**; **III Bvi**; **III Vvi**). If the income had been generated by a lease, the sum would have been known in advance. Schede (1919, 18) thinks that this is precisely what happened, Polos receiving as his advance the reduced fee, taken from the theatre-lease. On the other hand, if 'the takings from the theatre' were sums generated by its rental to private entrepreneurs, it is more likely that these would have been paid (in part or full) up-front, thus removing or at least reducing the possibility that Polos had made a generous concession in waiting for the actual monies received at the gate.

The point about 'the remainder' (τὸ δὲ λοιπόν l. 12) is closely connected to and contrasted with (μέν - δέ) what precedes. The verb used here (ἐπέσχηκε) has been understood in a variety of ways (see Hallof app. crit.), but at least one of these can probably be ruled out by consideration of the honorific purpose of the document: namely that Polos 'postponed' payment of the remainder, for this seems like rather weak or ambivalent generosity. Slater

(2011, 283 n. 44) takes it thus, writing that Polos 'demanded and got not only all the takings but also even more money, for which the Samians had to request a delay of payment. Clearly they could make no profit on such an unusual contract.' It is however incomprehensible why the Samians would include such punishing terms in an honorific decree, and a much better interpretation of the verb ἐπέσχηκε is 'offered' (Croenert *SEG*; LSJ s.v. II). On this scenario, 'the remainder' is most likely a shortfall between the agreed fee and the income the theatre actually generated. Or perhaps it is 'the remainder' of what was taken at the gate, as a positive sum: we know that Polos had agreed to act for lower than his usual fees, and it is possible that the theatre generated more rather than less than this agreed, lower fee – generating a 'remainder' which Polos graciously agreed to give to the People, in keeping with their request. Alternatively it is just possible that 'the remainder' refers to the difference between his usual fees and the 'lower' ones for which he agreed in this instance to act.

Whatever the precise nature of the contract and its implementation, generosity publically acknowledged in offering his services will also have been in Polos' own best interests, for he is to be the star attraction of festivals in honour of the new power-brokers of the Aegean and beyond – in a city, moreover, that was to be an important base for the Antigonid fleet – or rather, to continue to be, since it had evidently served that role for some years before this date (O'Sullivan 1997, 110–14).

Schede (1919, 20) raised the possibility that the relief image represented Polos in a role for which he was famous, noting also the popularity of Euripides' *Heracles* in the Hellenistic period. Ghiron-Bistagne (1976, 168; also Meyer 1989, 154) concurs, thinking more specifically that this may have been a role he played for the Samians. Heracles certainly seems by far the most likely interpretation of the figure (Tagalidou 1993, 94 has some doubts) and the view that this was a role played by Polos for the Samians is entirely plausible. If Heracles was also intended to remind the viewer of the ancestry of the Macedonian monarchy (Ritti 1969, 309–10) that would certainly not rule out the possibility that Polos played Heracles on the Samian stage.

Dxiv: Siphnos

1. **Isocrates, *Aiginetikos* (19) 36**. Date: soon after the battle of Cnidus in 394 which marked the end of Spartan support for oligarchies in the Cyclades – perhaps 391 or 390. Isocrates wrote the *Aiginetikos* in support of an inheritance claim by the (unnamed) speaker, the adopted son of one Thrasylochos of Siphnos. Father and son were political refugees of aristocratic background from Siphnos who settled as metics in Aegina where the case was heard (hence the title given to the speech). In this passage the speaker defends his status as an appropriate adoptee of Thrasylochos. Text: Mandilaras.

> ἀλλὰ γὰρ ἴσως ἀνάξιος ἦν υἱὸς εἰσποιηθῆναι Θρασυλόχῳ καὶ λαβεῖν αὐτοῦ τὴν ἀδελφήν. ἀλλὰ πάντες ἂν μαρτυρήσειαν Σίφνιοι τοὺς προγόνους τοὺς ἐμοὺς καὶ γένει καὶ πλούτῳ καὶ δόξῃ καὶ τοῖς ἄλλοις ἅπασιν πρώτους εἶναι τῶν πολιτῶν. τίνες γὰρ ἢ μειζόνων ἀρχῶν ἠξιώθησαν ἢ πλείω χρήματ᾽ εἰσήνεγκαν ἢ κάλλιον ἐχορήγησαν ἢ μεγαλοπρεπέστερον τὰς ἄλλας λειτουργίας ἐλειτούργησαν; ἐκ ποίας δ᾽ οἰκίας τῶν ἐν Σίφνῳ πλείους βασιλεῖς γεγόνασιν;

Perhaps they will claim I was unworthy of being adopted as a son by Thrasylochos and of receiving his sister in marriage. But all the Siphnians would testify that my ancestors were foremost in birth, wealth, reputation and all else. For who were deemed worthy of higher office? Who made larger financial contributions? Who performed finer choregiai, or served more magnificently in the other liturgies? What house on Siphnos has produced more *Basileis*?

2. **Decree of the Council and People of Siphnos awarding honours to the piper Perigenes of Alexandria, including the proclamation of a gold crown in the theatre at the tragic contest of the Siphnian Dionysia**, probably 274–270. Perigenes had given a performance in Siphnos in commemoration of military successes of Ptolemy and Arsinoe (ll. 5–10). We follow Papazarkadas (2009, 86–7) who revives the view of Holleaux (1905) and Robert (1936) that the context is the First Syrian War (274–271) rather than the Battle of Raphia (June 217; for a restatement of this traditional dating, propounded by Hiller, see Nocita and Guizzi 2009, 136), and that the royals are therefore Ptolemy and Arsinoe Philadelphoi.

Stele of bluish-white local marble, broken at the top.
0.325 × 0.35 max. × 0.035 m.
Found in reuse in the wall of a house in Kastro and transferred to the Museum prior to 1902.
Kastro Museum Inv. no. 31 (*SEG* 55, 945).
IG XII 5, 481 (+ *add.* p. 317) (Hiller); *IG* XII Suppl. p. 111 (Klaffenbach).
Text: based on *IG* XII Suppl. p. 111. A new edition by Papazarkadas is in preparation.

```
       [— — ἀπαγγέλλει (or ἀπαγγελλοῦσι) τὴν ὑπάρχουσαν αὐτῶι]
       [πρὸς τὴν πόλι]ν ἡμῶν φιλί[αν διαφυλάσσειν τὸν]
       [βασιλέα Πτολεμ]αῖον, ὑγιαίνει[ν δὲ αὐτόν τε καὶ]
       [τὴν βασίλισσ]αν Ἀρσινόην καὶ τὰς δυν[άμεις],
  5    [συμπ]αρὼν δὲ καὶ Περιγένης Λεοντίσκου [Ἀλεξαν]-
       [δρεὺ]ς συνησθεὶ[ς] ἐπὶ τοῖς προσηγγελ[μ]ένοι[ς ἀγα]-
       [θοῖ]ς ἐπιδίδωσιν τεῖ πόλει, ὥστε αὐλῆσα[ι μ]όνο[ς]
       [ἐν] ἡμ<έ>ραις δυσίν, βουλόμενος ἀποδείκνυ[σ]θαι τὴ[ν]
       εὔνοιαν ἣν ἔχει εἴ[ς] τε τὸν βασιλέα καὶ τὴν [βασ]ίλι[σσαν]
 10    [κ]αὶ τὴν πόλιν τὴν ἡμετέραν· ὅπως οὖν καὶ [ἡμε]ῖς [φαινώ]-
       μεθα τιμῶντες τοὺς εὐχαριστοῦντας εἴς [τε] τὸν [βασι]-
       λέα Πτολεμαῖον καὶ εἰς τὴν βασίλισσαν καὶ ε[ἰς τὴ]ν [πό]-
       λιν τὴν ἡμετέραν, τύχει τεῖ ἀγαθεῖ δεδόχθ[αι τεῖ βουλεῖ]
       καὶ τῶι δήμωι· συνησθῆναι μὲν ἐπὶ τοῖς ἠγγελμένοι[ς ἀ]-
 15    [γ]αθοῖς, ἐπαινέσαι δὲ καὶ Περιγένην Λεοντί[σκου] Ἀλ[ε]-
       [ξ]ανδρῆ καὶ στεφανῶσαι χρυσῶι στεφάνωι ἀ[πὸ]
       [δ]ραχμῶν δισχιλίων ἀρετῆς ἕνεκεν καὶ φιλ[οτιμίας ἧς]
       [ἔ]χει περί τε τὸν βασιλέα καὶ τὴν βασίλισσαν κ[αὶ τὴν πό]-
       λιν τὴν ἡμετέραν, καὶ ἀνακηρῦξαι τὸν στέφανον ἐ[ν τῶι]
 20    θεάτρωι Δ[ιον]υ[σ]ί[ο]ις τραγωιδῶν τῶι ἀγῶνι· εἶναι δὲ Π[ερι]-
       γένην πρόξενον τῆς πόλεως ἡμῶν καὶ αὐτὸν καὶ
```

τοὺς ἐγγόνους αὐτοῦ, καὶ ὑπάρχειν αὐτοῖς εἴσπλουν καὶ ἔκπλουν καὶ πολέμου καὶ εἰρήνης καὶ
ἐν σύλοις ἀσυλίαν καὶ προεδρίαν ἐν τοῖς ἀγῶσιν
οἷς ἡ πόλις τίθησιν καὶ πρόσοδον πρὸς τὴν βουλὴν καὶ τὸν δῆμον, ἐάν του δέωνται, πρώτοις μετὰ τὰ ἱερά· ἀναγράψαι δὲ τόδε τὸ ψήφισμα τοὺς
πρυτάνεις εἰς τὸ περίφραγμα τοῦ Διονύσου.

25

7 [μ]όνο[ς] Wilson-Csapo   [μ]όνο[ν] Klaffenbach   7–8 ὥστε αὐλίσ[ασθαι αὐτόθι] |
[ἐν ἡ]μ[έ]ραις δυσί[ν] Hiller   8 start of line ΗΜΣ *lapis*

[? at the announcement of the news that King Ptolem]y is [carefully observing
the] friends[hip that he already has towards] our [cit]y, [and that both he and
Que]en Arsinoe and their for[ces] are in good health, [5] and being present [at the
same time], Perigenes son of Leontiskos [of Alexandri]a, rejoicing at the [goo]d
news, made a gift to the city, to the effect that he played the pipes [? s]olo
[? over the course of] two days, wishing to make a demonstration of the good will
he has towards the King and [Que]e[n] [10] and our city. Therefore, so that [w]e
too may [make it cl]ear that we honour those who bestow favour on [Kin]g
Ptolemy and the Queen and our city, with good fortune [the Council] and People
decided: to express our pleasure at the [g]ood news, [15] and to praise Perigenes
son of Leonti[skos] of Al[ex]andria and to crown him with a gold crown w[orth]
two thousand drachmas for his virtue and the am[bition which] he has towards
the King and Queen an[d] our city, and to proclaim the crown i[n the] [20] theatre
du[ring] the D[ion]y[s]i[a], at the tragic contest; and that P[eri]genes is to be a
proxenos of our city – both he himself and his offspring – and they are to have free
passage in and out in both war and peace, and inviolability for cargo seized and
prohedria at the contests [25] which the city holds and right of access to the Council
and People should he need anything, among the first after the sacrifices. The
Prytaneis are to inscribe this decree in the precinct (*periphragma*) of Dionysus.

1 provides clear evidence for the existence of a choregia in Siphnos in the fifth century
(and, incidentally, for the anticipated effectiveness of citing a record of choregiai in court
early in the fourth century, see **V F**; for Aeginetan non-dramatic choregiai as early as the
sixth century, see Wilson 2000, 281–2). The speaker refers to choregiai performed there
by his 'ancestors', not simply his (adopted) father, who may not have been very much
older than he (at §10 reference is made to their close affinity in childhood, having among
other things never 'celebrated any single festival except in one another's company'). We
can therefore be very confident that the choregia in Siphnos was operational by at least
ca. 420, and perhaps much earlier: if we take the implication of 'ancestors' seriously, we
would at a minimum be obliged to raise that date by another generation – say to ca. 440.
That the local Siphnian magistracies were known as *Basileis* (**1**) may suggest that the most
important civic offices remained, whether by law or practice, in the hands of aristocratic
families, despite the democratic constitution it apparently had throughout the fifth and
fourth centuries, apart from a likely period of oligarchic government from ca. 404 to ca.
394. It is possible that the Siphnian choregic system may have similarly been the privilege

of specific families rather than simply a duty on the rich. One of 'the other liturgies' mentioned is likely to have been the conduct of *theoriai*, to Delos and Delphi, perhaps among other sites. §10 also testifies to Siphnian *theoriai*, and we know that these delegations included choruses from the evidence of the third-century Delian accounts (*IG* XI 2, 287 A, ll. 76–7: λαμπάδες ὅτε ὁ χορὸς τοῖς Σιφνίων θε[ω]]ροῖς ἐγένετο ⊢⊢⊦ΙⲤ·).

Apart from the generalised reference to 'festivals' at Isoc. 19.10 (above), we currently have evidence, starting ca. 270 (**2**), for just a single Siphnian festival, the Dionysia. (The god's presence on the Siphnian treasury at Delphi ca. 525 may be indicative of his prominence in Siphnos at the time without constituting evidence for the festival by that date.) Note however the third-century decree honouring strategoi published by Papazarkadas (2013a, 185–8) which may mandate the announcement of their crowns at a festival other than the Dionysia: of the festival's name only a doubtful pi survives. Papazarkadas notes that 'at the P[tolemaieia]' is a possibility, but so too is 'at the ne[xt Dionysia]', τοῖς π[ρώτοις Διονυσίοις]. This increases the likelihood that the choregiai mentioned in **1** were associated with the choral events of the Siphnian Dionysia (further on Siphnian cults, for which the evidence is being increased notably by epigraphic finds, see Savo 2004, 261–95; Gorrini and Melfi 2005).

2 shows that the Siphnian Dionysia, held in a theatre, was the city's most important public occasion in the early decades of the third century, with its tragic contest the place for the announcement of honours, as in Athens (**I Av 4**). The award of prohedria (l. 24), while not specified as 'in the theatre', doubtless refers to performances in the theatre, even if it is not limited to them. The honorand is an Alexandrian piper (Stefanis no. 2045) who had performed on Siphnos in commemoration of the Ptolemaic masters of the Aegean. The (evidently solo) performance appears to have been presented as an offering made freely to the city (this will be the force of ἐπιδίδωσιν l. 7), but the honorific crown worth a very substantial 2,000 dr. probably served as a gently disguised form of payment.

The decree is to be erected in the place with the intriguing name of 'the *periphragma* of Dionysus' (ll. 27–8). Comparison with the limited usage of the term elsewhere suggests that this was some sort of hypaethral precinct of Dionysus, an open space with altar (Nocita and Guizzi 2009) rather than a civic archive (Savo 2004, 275). Nocita and Guizzi (2009, 138) plausibly suggest that the theatre was part of the same complex and that the expression may imply that the precinct was fenced with slabs of marble onto which decrees were inscribed. The evidence of newly published inscriptions shows that the sanctuary of Apollo Pythios was another (perhaps the most) important venue for the publication of Siphnian decrees, although the theatre remains the preeminent and perhaps only site for the public proclamation of honours (Papazarkadas 2007b and 2013b; Papadopoulou 2009; Papazarkadas and Papadopoulou 2010–2013).

A number of later decrees indicate that honours continued to be proclaimed at the tragic contest of the Siphnian Dionysia into the second century:

> *IG* XII 5, 482 (3rd–2nd c.; cf. Papadopoulou 2000, 441–2): the first decree on this stone mandates the announcement of a crown at the tragic contest of the Dionysia, with publication 'in the precinct (*periphragma*) of Dionysus' (with some safe restoration); a second decree is for a kitharode;

> *IG* XII 5, 471 with *SEG* 33, 680, second century: two decrees awarding crowns in the theatre at the tragic contest of the Dionysia, almost certainly correctly restored to include publication 'in the precinct (*periphragma*) of Dionysus';

Daux (1970, 70 no. 2), early second century: mandates the announcement of a crown at the tragic contest of the Dionysia, publication 'in the precinct (*periphragma*) of Dionysus' (heavily restored);

the small fragment in honour of strategoi published by Papazarkadas (2013a, 186) might be another (see above);

Papazarkadas and Papadopoulou 2010–2013 publish a proxeny decree which requires that the honorand be crowned in the theatre but the decree published in the Pythion (see also Papazarkadas 2013b).

It is difficult to assess the likely degree of influence, if any, of the seemingly close and stable relations between Athens and Siphnos (Papazarkadas 2007b, 144–5) on the introduction of theatre to the island. Even if the tradition reported by Herodotus (8.48) that Siphnos was founded by a colony of Ionians from Athens is more ideology than fact, it is telling as evidence of the wish to forge an early and intimate relationship. Siphnos was an early member of the Delian League and remained closely aligned with Athens during the Second Athenian Confederacy. The city was immensely rich from the Archaic period on from the exploitation of its mineral resources – silver and gold especially, but also marble – and was still named as the richest island ca. 525 (Hdt. 3.57–8, 8.46, 48). According to Herodotus (3.57.2) the productive income was distributed annually among the citizenry, possibly leading to a generally high level of median wealth rather than a very narrow concentration among mine-owners (see Neer 2001, 307–12 for a nuanced discussion) and explaining the ability of such a small state to sustain an extensive liturgical system.

Dxv: Tenos. Honorary Decree of the Patra of the Androkleidai for Theomnestos, late 4th or very beginning of 3rd c. (by letter forms).

Upper section of marble stele, including cornice.
0.287 × 0.34 × 0.05 m.
Found in 1971 during building works south of the Panagia Evanghelistria.
Zaphiropoulos 1971, 464; Étienne 1990, 37–9 no. 1.
Text: Étienne 1990, 37–8 (= *SEG* 40, 688).   Photo: Étienne 1990, pl. 12.2.

       ἔδοξεν Ἀνδρακλείδαις· Πεισαγόρας εἶ-
       πεν· ἐπειδὴ Θεόμνηστος Εὐκτ[ι]μένου
       ἀνὴρ ἀγαθός ἐστι περὶ τὴμ πάτραν καὶ ἐπε-
       μελήθη καλῶς καὶ δικαίως τῶγ κοινῶν
5   ὥστε γενέσθαι τῆι πάτραι εὐπορίαν χρη-
       μάτων καὶ διατελεῖ ἐπιμελόμενος
       τῶν τε ἄλλων κοινῶν τῆς πάτρας καὶ
       τῶν ἱερῶν· στεφανῶσαι αὐτὸν χρυσῶι στε-
       [φ]άνωι ἀπὸ ἑκατὸν δραχμῶν καὶ διμοιρί-
10   [αι] τῶν κοινῶν ἀρετῆς καὶ δικαιοσύνης
       [κα]ὶ ἐπιμελείας ἕνεκα τῆς περὶ τὴμ πά-
       [τ]ραν καὶ τὰ ἱερὰ καὶ ἀνακηρῦξαι Ποσιδεί-

[ω]ν τῶι ἀγῶνι ἐν τῶι θεάτρωι τόνδε τὸν
στέφανον· τὸ δὲ ψήφισμα τόδε ἀναγράψαι
15   [ἐν στή]ληι λιθίνηι καὶ στῆσαι ἐν τῶι ἱερῶι τῆς
[. . . . .]· τὸ δὲ ἀνάλωμα δοῦναι τοὺς ἄρχον-
[τας . . . . . .¹² . . . . . .]ου τῆς πάτρας.

The Andrakleidai decreed; Peisagoras proposed: as Theomnestos, son of
Eukt[i]menes is a good man in regards to the *patra* and oversaw the common
funds well and justly, ⁵ bringing the *patra*'s money to healthy abundance, and
because he continues to look after the common funds of the *patra* and especially the sacred fund, to crown him with a gold cro[w]n worth a hundred
drachmas and to give him double-portions ¹⁰ at common meals because of his
excellence, justice and care of the *patra* and its sacrifices, and to announce this
crown at the contest of the Posideia in the theatre, and to inscribe this decree ¹⁵
[on] a stone [ste]le and set it up in the sanctuary of the […]. The Archon[s] are
to furnish the expenditure […] of […] the *patra*.

Tenos was a faithful ally of Athens, probably from the beginning of the Delian League
down through the Second Athenian Confederacy (Reger *IACP* 777). It had a democratic
constitution, though in 411 it may have followed Athens' brief oligarchic revolution (Th.
8.69.3; Gehrke 1985, 159). Tenos is the last stepping-stone between Athens and Delos:
Nota Kourou describes it as 'of major importance to any city-state aspiring to the control
of the Cycladic islands' (2007, 19). This makes the island a likely candidate for the reception of Athenian theatrical culture, even though, surprisingly for an Aegean island, the
only fourth-century attestation of the theatre connects it with a festival for Poseidon, not
Dionysus.

   This is the earliest of a long series of Tenian decrees with provisions for proclaiming a
crown 'at the contest in the theatre'. Oddly, however, we have no other decree that places
the announcement 'at the contest of the Posideia in the theatre'. We have a Tenian decree
of ca. 278 (Étienne 1990, 95–6) that places the announcement simply 'at the contest of the
Posideia' (*IG* XII 5, 802, ll. 22–5); two third-century decrees that place the announcement
'at the contest of the tragedies of the Dionysia' (*IG* XII 5, 798, ll. 12–14; *IG* XII 5, 800,
ll. 8–10), and at least thirty decrees from the third and second centuries that call for an
announcement 'at the contest of the tragedies of the Posideia and Dionysia' (*IG* XII 5,
804, 813, 821, 822, 825, 828, 830–3, 835, 836, 838–43, 849–51, 855). From the end of
the second century we again have a reference to a Dionysia alone, but the announcements
are to take place not 'at the contest of the tragedies' but 'on the first day' (*IG* XII 5, 868,
ll. 59–61) or 'on the first day of the cyclic choruses' (*IG* XII Suppl. p. 135; Ceccarelli
2010, 127). Evidently the Posideia and the Dionysia had an independent existence until
some time in the (late?) third century. It is perhaps significant that the decrees that place
the announcement of honours at the Posideia do so at 'the contest in the theatre', or simply
'the contest', but those relating to the Dionysia or the combined Posideia and Dionysia are
explicit that announcements take place at 'the contest for tragedy'. Perhaps we are to infer
that the Posideian contest 'in the theatre' was not necessarily tragic.

   Dionysus is likely to have had a long-standing relationship with Tenos, as with the
neighbouring Cycladic islands (**Di**; **Dii**; **Diii**; **Dvi**; **Dx**; **Dxiv**). Grape-clusters, presumably

a symbol of Dionysus (shared with Ceos), appear on Tenian coinage from Archaic times (Artemis-Gyselen 1977). The Dionysia, accordingly, is likely to fit the pattern we find on the neighbouring islands where the Dionysia appear to date to the period of Athenian domination if not earlier. The Posideia, on the other hand, may not be much older than our decree, which first attests the festival's existence. Indeed, the evidence suggests that the sanctuary of Poseidon and Amphitrite was founded or developed only at the end of the fourth century (Schumacher 1993, 57; Kourou 2005, 97–8; Étienne et al. 2013, 136–42). The creation of a festival centred on the sanctuary was evidently part of a strategy to establish it as a place of pilgrimage and thereby boost the economy of the island. The strategy was successful and the sanctuary became the most important religious centre in the Aegean after Delos. We can guess that the merger of the Dionysia with the Posideia only took place when the Posideia had an established place in the international festival calendar and that the combination aimed at enhancing the more prestigious Posideia with the addition of pre-existing, but (for sea travel) less propitiously timed, tragic competitions.

Graindor (1907a, 36–9; 1907b, 113) thought he saw traces of the theatre just south-west of the church of Panagia Evanghelistria where a block thought to belong to the proskenion was found as well as one of the above-mentioned third-century stelai (*IG* XII 5, 798) which mention the contests of the Dionysia (cf. Étienne 1990, 23 and n. 43). Remnants of the foundations of what has been identified as a temple of Dionysus were found nearby underneath the foundations of the Panagia (Kourou 2005, 97). Neither the temple nor the theatre can be earlier than the mid fourth century, however. Tenos was enslaved by Alexander of Pherae in 362 (D. 50.4), and it was only when the island was repopulated after the middle of the fourth century that the urban centre was moved from its location on Xombourgo to the site of the present town (Étienne et al. 2013, 53).

The decree identifies the Androkleidai as a *patra*. *Patra* appears to be cognate or even an ancient spelling of φρατρία (= phratry: Roussel 1976, 5) and is a civic division possibly independent of the tribal and neighbourhood divisions of Tenos and 'may be seen as an aristocratic holdover' (Reger *IACP* 777–8). It is interesting to see that our first attested use of the theatre for the announcement of honours is not by the People of Tenos but by a social subdivision, even a subdivision of an exclusive sort (the *patrai* insist on legitimacy through the male line and restrict membership to men whose fathers have attained fifty years of age: Étienne 1990, 40–2 no. 2). The semi-private and non-democratic nature of the announcement may be a reason for placing it at the Posideia, rather than the Dionysia: the only other decree granting honours at the contest of the Posideia (*IG* XII 5, 802) is one that directly concerns the affairs of the sanctuary of Poseidon and Amphitrite. Similar announcements in the Theatre by social subdivisions at Athens seem to have been sponsored either by tribes, demes, or individuals (**I Av 4**).

Dxvi: Thasos

1. Fragmentary decree from Thasos concerning the end of oligarchy, late 5th or early 4th c. Grandjean and Salviat (1988) interpret as an Athenian decree imposing the restoration of democracy in 407 (by content and restored second, presumed Athenian, Archon at frag. B, l. 22). Picard (2000) interprets as a Thasian decree recording a reconciliation between two local parties on Thasos at the end of civil war in ca. 390 (by content and reference to the new monetary system at fr. B, ll. 9–12). Only ll. 12–19 of fr. A are quoted below: on either interpretation the immediate context is a set of sanctions imposed on opponents. Line 16 envisages the razing to the ground of their houses and l. 17 involves an announcement at a Dionysia.

Two non-joining fragments of a marble stele: A, from the top right-hand corner of the stele, has part of the triangular apex; B, from the lower right-hand corner, preserves part of the end of the text.
A: 0.26 × 0.175 × 0.10–11 m; B: 0.325 × 0.245 × 0.10–11 m.
A: found in 1980 in the north-east corner of the agora of Thasos; B: found built into a wall of the Church of St Nicholas, south of the agora.
A: Museum of Thasos inv. no. 3626; B inv. no. 1584.
IG XII 8, 262 and *Suppl.* 150 (B); Grandjean and Salviat 1988 (publish A + B) = *SEG* 38, 851.
Photos: Grandjean and Salviat 1988, 252; Picard 2000, 1060 (reconstruction).

```
12    [- - - - - - - - - - - - - - - - - - - - - - - - - - - ὅστις] ἂν μὴ ἕπηται, κατάρη[το]-
      [ς - - - - - - - - - - - - - - - - - - - - - - - - - - -]κται κατὰ τὰ γεγραμμ[έ]-
      [να - - - - - - - - - - - - - - - - - - - - - ἐς τὸν] ἀεὶ χρόνον, καὶ τὰ χρήμ[α]-
15    [τα δημόσια - - - - - - - - - - - - - - - - - - -] τῶν τε ἄλλων ἀφηγείσθω[ν]-
      [- - - - - - - - - - - - - - - - - - - - - - - - κ]ατασκαψάντων ἐς ἔδ[αφ]-
      [ος - - - - - - - - - - - - - - - - - - - - - Διονυ]σίοις ἐν τῶι ἀγῶνι ε Ι [. .]
      [- - - - - - - - - - - - - - - - - - - - - - - ἀνοι]κοδομῆσαι τὰς τούτω[ν ο]-
19    [ικίας- - - - - - - - - - - - - - - - - - - - - - -]λεσθωσι ἐν ὀλιγαρχ[ίηι]
```

12 ὅστις Picard   17 ἐν τῶι ἀγῶνι ε[Picard   Perhaps ἐν τῶι ἀγῶνι ἐγ [e.g. τῶι θεάτρωι] or ἐπ[ὶ *Archon's name*] Wilson

[… whoever] does not comply [is to be] curse[d …] according to what is written[n … for] all time, and his possess[ions (?) [15] become public property …] and of the others let them lead […] let them [r]aze to the gro[und …] at the [Diony]-sia at the contest (?) i[n … (?) re]build the [houses] of these men […] let them […] in oligarch[y] …

2. Hippocrates, *Epidemics* 1.20. Hippocrates resided on Thasos at some time during the 5th c. and recorded observations on patients he treated while there in *Epidemics* 1. His stay is traditionally dated to ca. 420–410. This is based on the (secure) identification of Antiphon son of Kritoboulos (1.18) with the *theoros* (magistrate) of that name in an inscribed list (*IG* XII 8, 277, l. 81), and a physical and chronological reconstruction of this list which fixes his tenure in the period 410–408 (Graham 2000, 319); he may have come to the island soon after the death of his patron Perdiccas II Macedon in 413 (Grandjean and Salviat 2012–2013). On the basis of an entirely new reconstruction of the list, endorsed by the late David Lewis, Robin Lane Fox will argue that *Epidemics* 1 was composed in the early 460s. Text: Littré.

οἷον οἱ δύο ἀδελφεοὶ, οἳ ἤρξαντο ὁμοῦ τὴν αὐτὴν ὥρην· κατέκειντο παρὰ τὸ θέατρον Ἐπιγένεος ἀδελφεοί· τουτέων τῷ πρεσβυτέρῳ ἔκρινεν ἕκτῃ· τῷ δὲ νεωτέρῳ, ἑβδόμη·

θέητρον C   θέρετρον A, Jones 1923 omitting ἀδελφεοί

For example two brothers, who became ill at the same hour – they were brothers of Epigenes, and lived near the theatre: of these the elder had a crisis on the sixth day; and the younger on the seventh.

3. **Monument in the sanctuary of Dionysus of Thasos commemorating performances in a range of theatrical genres**. Date: ca. 350–325 (by prosopography and style of sculpture).

Approached by a flight of ten steps leading up to a Doric portico with four columns, the monument (W. ca. 9 m × D. 10.5 m) was constructed, at its north and east sides, against the corner of the sanctuary wall, making use of the natural incline to support an elevated podium, with marble orthostates to the south and west and a krepis of four levels above. Inside, on the podium, was a semicircular exedra supporting free-standing sculpture: in central place, Dionysus (larger than the rest), with a range of 'genre' figures of diminishing size to the right (Montel 2008, 318–24 is the most complete discussion of the sculptural remains; the sculptures to the viewer's left are lost). Inscriptions on the front face of the blocks of the exedra (*IG* XII Suppl. 400) identify a number of the sculptures. Of the sculpture there has been found the head of Dionysus (Thasos Museum inv. 16; H. 0.60 m; Grandjean and Salviat 2000, fig. 192); the almost complete but headless female body of Comedy (Thasos Museum inv. 652; H. 1.71 m; Grandjean and Salviat 2000, fig. 191); and the upper part of a tragic mask of a bald and emaciated old man with associated drapery that suggests it was held by Tragedy (Thasos Museum inv. 17; H. 0.325 m; Grandjean and Salviat 2000, fig. 193).

Images: Grandjean and Salviat 2000, 92–3 with figs. 45 (plan of sanctuary), 46 (plan of monument), 47 (elevation).

Block a	Block b	Block c	Block d	Block e
Διόνυσος	Τραγωιδία	Κωμωιδία	Διθύραμβος	Νυκτερινός
	Θεόδωρος	Φιλήμων	Ἀρίστων	Βάταλος ηὔλει.
	ὑπεκρίνετο.	ὑπεκρίνετο.	Μιλήσιος ηὔλει.	
Dionysus	Tragedy.	Comedy.	Dithyramb.	Nykterinos.
	Theodoros was	Philemon	Ariston of Miletus	Batalos
	the actor.	was the actor.	was piper.	was piper.

4. **A decree of the People of Lampsacus honouring a Thasian named Nossikas**. Date: ca. 300 (by letter forms and prosopography: a Nossikas, grandfather of the honorand, was *theoros* on Thasos ca. 380: *IG* XII 8, 271, l. 98; the grandson himself was *theoros* ca. 320–300: *IG* XII 8, 284, l. 1; Picard and Avezou 1914, 304–5). A prominent Thasian named Nossikas is honoured for rescuing citizens of Lampsacus captured in a naval battle and paying for their return home (ll. 11–15). Only ll. 17–26 are quoted below. The break between fr. A and B occurs at ll. 22–3.

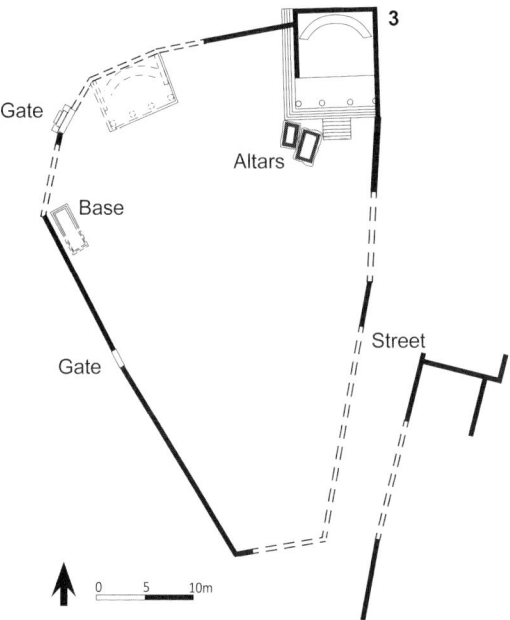

Site plan of sanctuary of Dionysus, Thasos

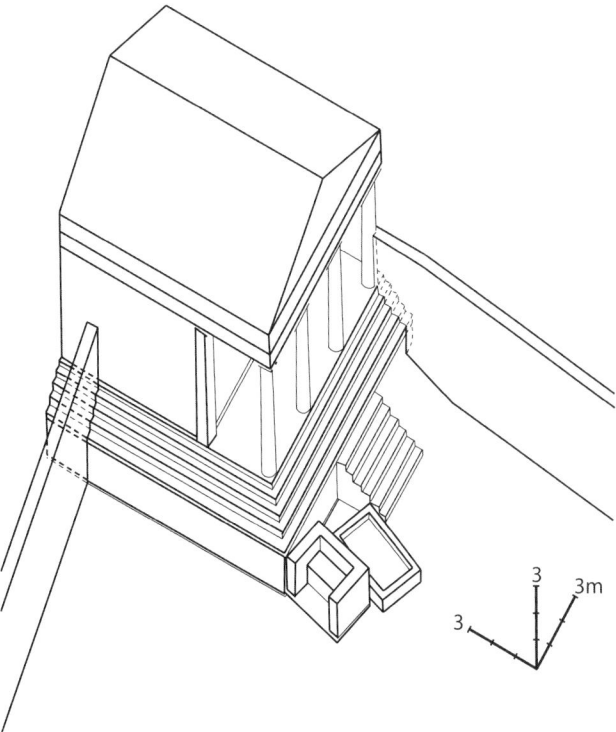

Reconstruction of monument in sanctuary of Dionysus, Thasos (at **3** above)

Four non-joining fragments of a stele of Thasian marble.

A, with pyramidal top of stele: 0.75 × 0.385–0.41 × 0.125 m; B, broken on all sides: 0.14 × 0.25 m;
C, right side only preserved: 0.12 × 0.185 m; D, bottom of stele: 0.60 × 0.424–0.433 × 0.15 m.

Found in June 1913 in a room north of the Prytaneion of Thasos.

Daux 1928, 46–50; *IG* XII Suppl. 354; *IK Lampsakos* 1.   Photo: Daux 1928, 46 (D only).

A   … δεδόχθαι τῆι βουλῆ[ι]·
           ἐπαινέσαι μὲν Νοσσικᾶν Ἡράδος [ἀ]ρε-
           τῆς ἕνεκεν καὶ εὐνοίας τῆς εἰς τὸν
20   [δ]ῆμον τὸν Λαμψακηνῶν καὶ στε[φα]-
           νῶσαι αὐτὸν ἐν Θάσωι ἐν τῶι θεά[τρωι]
           Διονυσί[οις τραγωιδῶν τῶι ἀγῶνι (?) - - - -]
B   [- - - - - - - - - - - - ποιουμένου τοῦ κήρυκος (?)]
           [τὴν ἀναγγελ]ίαν· ὁ δῆμος [ὁ Λαμψακηνῶν]
25   [στεφα]νοῖ Νοσσικᾶν Ἡρᾶδ[ος ἀρετῆς ἕνε]-
           [κεν καὶ εὐν]οίας τῆς εἰς αὐτόν … κτλ.

           22 Daux, also suggesting Διονυσί[οις τραγωιδοῖς].

… the Council decided: to praise Nossikas son of Heras for his [v]irtue and
good-will toward the [20] [P]eople of Lampsacus and to crow[n] him on Thasos
in the thea[tre] at the Dionysi[a, at the (?) contest of tragedies, with the herald
making the announcem]ent: 'The people [of Lampsacus [25] crow]n Nossikas
son of Heras [for his virtue and good]-will toward it' etc.

5. Commemoration of a victory in a contest, possibly in drama (?). Date: ca. 300 (by
letter forms: Daux 1928, 56); or possibly ca. 350 (by the use of o for false diphthong ου
l. 8, regarded by Daux as an anachronism).

Fragment of a base of non-Thasian marble, broken on all sides except possibly the left.
0.36 × 0.27 × 0.23 m.
Findspot not recorded.
Present location unknown.
Daux 1928, 55–6; *IG* XII Suppl. 357.

           ἐπὶ ἀρ[χόντων (?) {τοῦ δεῖνος τοῦ}]
           Πολυθροῦ, Βιτίω[νος {τοῦ δεῖνος}],
           Δαμασιστράτ[ο {τοῦ δεῖνος}]
           Σάτυρος τὴν Ο[- - - - - - - - - - - -]
5   ἐνίκησεν ἰδι[- - - - - - - - - - - - - - - -]
           ναι παρὰ τοῖς ἀ[- - - - (??) τραγωι]-
           δοῖς τοῖς μετὰ [(?) ἄρχοντος Φειδί]-
           ππο τõ Χρυσώρ[ο - - - - - - - - - - - -]
           ΟΡΠΟΣΑΝΟΔΩ[- - - - - - - - - - - - -]
10   δώτης Φιλ[- - - - - - - - - - - - - - - - - -]
                          vacat

6–7 [τραγωι]|δοῖς τοῖς μετὰ [(?) ἄρχοντος] Launey

In the ar[chonship of (?) *name*] son of Polythroos; of Bitio[n son of *name*]; of Damasistrat[os son of *name* ...] Satyros the [...] ⁵ was victorious [...] at the (??) c[ontests ...] in [the (??) trage]dies held in the [Archonship after Pheidi]-ppos son of Chrysor[os ... (no certain word or part-word in the remains of l. 9 can be distinguished) ...-]dotes Phil[- ... (these may be parts of two names)

6. A metrical funerary inscription for a choral poet, late 4ᵗʰ or early 3ʳᵈ c. (by letter forms).

Fragment of white marble broken on all sides except the bottom.
0.16 × 0.12 × 0.8 m.
Found in 1911 in the city of Thasos, in the region of the Panagia gate.
Thasos Museum inv. no. 516.
Pouilloux 1954b, 345–6 no. 130; *GVI* 1073a; *CEG* II, 675.   Photo: Pouilloux 1954b, pl. 37, 6.

    [− ⏑⏑] εἰμὶ . [⏑ −]
    [⏑⏑ −]ς βλάστη[μα]
    [⏑] . ιθου *vacat*
    [− πλεί]στους κυκλίο[υς]
5   [− ἐδί]δαξα χορού[ς].

1 [πάτριδος] εἰμὶ Θ[άσου Peek   2–3 βλάστη[μ᾽ Ἐπ|ιπ]ξίθου Peek   4 κυκλίο[υς] Pouilloux   5 [ἐδί]δαξα χορού[ς] Pouilloux   4–5 [ὃς πλεί]στους κυκλίο[υς | ζῶν ἐδί]-δαξα χορού[ς]. Peek

[...] I am [...] offspring of [*name ending in* -]ithos. [...] I t[rai]ned [very m]any cycli[c] choruse[s]

Prosperous from its mines and wine, Thasos joined the Delian League as a contributor of ships, but after revolting in 466/5 was forced to pay tribute (60 talants in 425/4: *IG* I³ 71, III, l. 155) and to cede its profitable possessions on the mainland. Some Athenians owned land on Thasos in the later fifth century (*IG* I³ 426, ll. 45, 144). An oligarchy was established in the wake of the revolution of the Four Hundred in Athens in 411, but not long after the island removed itself from the Athenian orbit altogether, restoring its walls, fleet and old institutions. In the spring of 407 the Athenians under Thrasybulus took the island again and restored democracy (X. *HG* 1.4.9; D.S. 13.72.1–2: below). In the early decades of the fourth century Thasos swung between Spartan and Athenian control, joining the Second Athenian Confederacy in 375.

If Grandjean and Salviat (1988) are correct to see in **1** the imposition by Athens of the terms of the restored democracy of 407, the Dionysia (l. 17) will be in Athens, not Thasos, and the clause will mandate the announcement, at the City Dionysia, of the treatment to be meted out to the rebellious Thasian oligarchs and their properties (Reger 1990 thinks that l. 16 refers rather to the demolition of fortifications built by the oligarchs in 408 and that the announcement in l. 17 was to the effect that the stipulations had already been carried out). Such an announcement would be consistent with known Athenian practice of using the City Dionysia as a context for making important (often highly ideologically charged) communications not only with the citizenry of Athens but also the subject states of the empire, whose delegates were all present with their tribute (**I Ai 3**). The festival in question would almost certainly be that of 406 (Grandjean and Salviat 1988, 263). Just three years earlier, in 409, the contest of the City Dionysia had been the momentous occasion for another set of highly political rituals, the taking of the oath of Demophantos against anti-democrats by the assembled citizenry and the announcement of honours for Thrasybulus of Calydon, the assassin of the oligarch Phrynichus, architect and leading agent of the anti-democratic revolution of 411. This was possibly the very first occasion on which benefactors were publically honoured at the festival in this way (**I Av 4a**; Wilson and Hartwig 2009; Wilson 2009). The Dionysia of 406 may similarly have been used in an attempt to shore up pro-Athenian sentiment and 'promote democracy' within the cities of the empire.

Given that rather less than a quarter of the whole inscription survives, and less than half the length of its extant lines (Picard 2000, 1060), it is possible that **1** specified that this announcement was (also?) to be made at the Thasian Dionysia, in which case it would be evidence for the festival on the island by the last decade of the fifth century. An Athenian decree of 307/6–304/3 (*IG* II² 555: **I Av 4m**) gives instructions to proclaim a crown both at the Dionysia in the theatre in the home city of its honorand, Byzantium (**Fi**), and also in Athens, 'at the tragic contest of the Great [Dionysia]' (ll. 6–7).

The existence of an active theatre on Thasos already in the latter decades of the fifth century is thus a distinct possibility. More evidence can be found in **2**, where Hippocrates, writing ca. 410, mentions two brothers said to have lived 'by the theatre' in Thasos. Some (e.g. Jones 1923; Graham 2000, 320, with the fundamental contribution of Littré 1840, 660–1) have argued that the correct reading is not 'theatre' but 'summer-house', the latter present in one manuscript (A). It is clear from Galen's commentary on the passage (Gal. *Hipp.Epid.* III, 17.1.197–8; Wenkebach 1936) that the textual mainstream of his day read 'theatre', but his commentary also shows that some texts read 'summer-house': 'some write not theatre (θέατρον), but *theratron* (θέρατρον), so that they are able to explain it as a place so named from the act of passing the summer (θερίζεσθαι)'. The meaningless θέρατρον (*theratron*) should clearly be θέρετρον *theretron* 'summer house'.

The word *theretron* also appears in Galen's glossary to Hippocrates: θέρετρον· τόπος ἐνδιατρίβειν θέρους ἐπιτήδειος· ἔνιοι δὲ θέντρον γράφουσι. '*Theretron*: a place suitable for passing the summer. Some write *thentron*' (Gal. *Gloss.* s.v.). The last word – θέντρον *thentron* – proffered by Galen as an alternative read by some for *theretron* ('summer-house') in the text of Hippocrates, is meaningless, and must be an error for θέατρον *theatron* 'theatre'. The glossary is based on the same passage of the *Epidemics* and shows that both textual variants were in circulation. Galen evidently regarded 'theatre' as the correct reading, or certainly the dominant one. One might, by the principle of *lectio difficilior*, opt for 'summer-house', but the word seems to be unattested outside this passage (and an entry *Et.Gud.* s.v. Πτολίεθρον that may derive from it), and on balance contextual considerations very much favour 'theatre': for how likely is it that a place called 'the summer-house' would become a notable landmark of Thasos? In order to overcome this last problem, editors are compelled to remove the word 'brothers', present in all manuscripts, from the phrase παρὰ τὸ θέατρον / θέρετρον Ἐπιγένεος ἀδελφεοί so as to render the genitive Ἐπιγένεος 'of Epigenes' available to indicate the owner of the summer-house.

The Thasian poet Hegemon, inventor of a form of epic parody (Arist. *Po.* 2.5, 1448a) and reported to be a practitioner of Old Comedy (on the authority of Chamaeleon of Pontus: Hegem. *PCG* T 4), was active in the later fifth century (Ath. 9.407a–b). The limited testimony to his career indicates success in Athens, probably at the Panathenaea, but some sort of training in a native tradition and practice is also implied (thus e.g. Grandjean and Salviat 2000, 105), in particular by the opening of the seemingly quasi- or pseudo-autobiographical long fragment of epic parody (Ath. 15.698d; Panomitros 2003) which is set on the speaker's return to Thasos, where 'the most disgusting of all men' πάντων ἀνδρῶν βδελυρώτατε is pelted with dung, apparently in a theatre, for 'mounting the fair platform with feet like that' καλὴν ἐς κρηπῖδα ποσὶν τοιοῖσδ' ἀναβῆναι, a reference to the 'inappropriate' end to which Hegemon put the noble metre of epic.

If, as seems increasingly likely, Picard (2000) is correct to interpret **1** as a Thasian decree recording a reconciliation between two local parties at the end of civil war and a later restoration of democracy in ca. 390, with no Athenian involvement whatsoever, we must assume that the reference in l. 17 is to an announcement of the terms of the accord at the festival of Dionysus on the island itself. It will thus be evidence for a Thasian Dionysia with a contest by ca. 390. Moreover the decision to schedule such a significant announcement at the Dionysia suggests that it had by that date established itself as the most important occasion on which large numbers of the populace gathered.

Material evidence for a flourishing theatre becomes more abundant around the middle or third quarter of the century, in the form of the impressive remains found in the (only partially excavated) Dionysion north-east of the agora (Grandjean and Salviat 2000, 92–4 with earlier bibliography). While no signs of earlier phases have as yet been uncovered in the rather limited excavations, the sanctuary is known, for the later fifth century, from its use as a topographical identifier by Hippocrates (*Epid.* 1.21: reference to a Pantakles 'who dwelt by the Dionysion'). Dionysus is identified, with Heracles, as a 'guardian of this city' in an inscription from the late sixth century (*IG* XII 8, 356) and his cult in the island will date from long before that time, especially in light of the city's Parian origins. Some time before ca. 340 a substantial peribolos wall was constructed (Bernard and Salviat 1959, 297) and the sanctuary became the site for the erection of a variety of monuments that indicate a competitive desire to commemorate theatrical events among the Thasians not unlike that known from the choregic monuments of Athens (Bernard and Salviat 1959, 329).

The best known of these is **3**, the large monument constructed against the north-east corner of the sanctuary wall. Over 9 m wide by 10.5 m deep, this was approached by a flight of some ten steps leading up to a Doric portico, and inside there was a semicircular exedra supporting lavish sculpture: in the central place, Dionysus (larger than the rest), with, to the right, personifications of Tragedy, Comedy, Dithyramb and the mysterious *Nykterinos* ('Serenade'?). Under each, the most important performer is recorded: 'Theodoros was the actor' for tragedy (Stefanis no. 1157); 'Philemon was the actor' for comedy (Stefanis no. 2485); 'Ariston the Milesian played the pipes' for dithyramb (Stefanis no. 381); and 'Batalos was the piper' for the *nykterinos* (Stefanis no. 519).

A number of small fragments from the plinth of the god's statue show that Dionysus wore *endromides* and carried a thyrsus in his left hand, from which it has been deduced that he was dressed as a hunter in a short *chiton*, a type (Dionysus Hope) that became popular in the Roman period and which featured on a metope of the theatre's proskenion in the Imperial period (Montel 2008, 321). The bases to the other side of Dionysus do not survive, but symmetry demands that there will have been more figures there. Proposals include lesser divinities like Pan, or the Muses; or possibly even the dedicants of the complex (Daux 1926, 236). Given that, so far as one can tell, the monument commemorates a single event, it seems unlikely that further genres appeared on that side.

A higher date of the middle or third quarter of the century is now favoured (Salviat 1979; Grandjean and Salviat 2000, 93; it had been put as late as mid third century: Bernard and Salviat 1959, 333) encouraging us to see here some of the great stars of the later Classical age – including the Athenian celebrity Theodoros, not touring the provinces close to retirement but at the very peak of his fame. It also shows a very energetic and healthy investment in the Thasian theatre around the middle of the century. Recent study of the sculpture (Holtzmann 2005; cf. Croissant 2011–2012) argues that it represents the best pioneering trends of the period after ca. 350 as exemplified by Attic artists, and may in fact have been the work of a commissioned Attic master (the mask of Tragedy and the body of Comedy are said to be of Pentelic marble).

Along with another base excavated in the Dionysion that also carried sculptures (Bernard and Salviat 1959, 288, 298–300 with earlier bibliography), this structure has often been assumed to be a choregic dedication (Borbein 1973, 48–55; Agelidis 2009, 71–5, 270–3; *contra*: Holtzmann 2005, 175; Kreeb 2010, 1214–15). A choregia is not attested for Thasos, though the existence of one is far from unlikely (Wilson 2000, 295). But there is no reason to describe the Thasian monument as 'choregic'. The dedicatory inscription that would illuminate the question will have been on the architrave of the building's façade, none of which has been found. Bernard and Salviat (1959, 328–9) note that the multiplicity of events commemorated – at least four – renders it very unlike the type of Classical choregic dedication known from Athens, and they plausibly think instead of a dedication by a magistrate of a sort akin to the Athenian agonothete. The fact that, for the dramatic genres, only actors are mentioned, and no poets, has been taken to imply that the works performed were not new productions, but classics (Salviat 1979, 166). Nor is there any indication that there had been a contest. This major monument was more probably designed to commemorate a very special, one-off event. It has the appearance of deriving from an especially significant celebration, on which little expense was spared to have stars of the stage appear and all the Dionysian genres represented in their finest form. The event, and its lavish commemorative monument, will in all probability have been funded by a number of local worthies (whether serving in an official capacity or not), perhaps with public or sanctuary funds in addition. There is no reason to suppose (as Sismondo Ridgway 1990, 50 does) that the performers themselves made the dedication. Such a dedication by performers is entirely unparalleled.

The theatre itself was around 200 m further to the north-east of the Dionysion, set directly against the north-west city wall and built into a natural depression in the side of a hill (Bonias 2012; Grandjean and Salviat 2000, 105–9 with earlier bibliography). Sufficient remains of an elegant Doric proskenion survive to enable a reconstruction (Grandjean and

Salviat 2000, 105, 107–8 with fig. 62). This was dedicated to Dionysus by a Thasian worthy named Lysistratos son of Kodis (*IG* XII Suppl. 399), doubtless the person of the same – extremely rare – name who was a magistrate (*theoros*) on Thasos in the mid fourth century (*IG* XII Suppl. 278). The earliest phase of the excavated remains of the theatre is dated to the late fourth century, but it is increasingly clear from recent excavation, the publication of which is still underway, that the theatre occupied the same site before that date. That there was an earlier monumental phase has been suggested by the discovery of two long terraced retaining walls beneath the stage building, following exactly the same course as the later structure above, and of monumental remains of high quality beneath the proskenion (Bonias and Marc 1996, 883–4; Bonias 2012). Many seats in the theatre were inscribed with the names of individuals or families for whom they were reserved (Grandjean and Salviat 2000, 107).

A further concentration of evidence appears at the end of the century. A law listing the major festivals of Thasos in calendrical order shows at least three in honour of Dionysus (*SEG* 17, 415, ll. 1–2): the Anthesteria (February–March), the Dionysia (March–April) and the Choreia (May–June), this last otherwise unattested but certainly a 'festival of choruses': a Dionysus Chore[os] is known from the mother-city of Thasos, Paros (Salviat 1958, 237–9). The festivals were much older than the law that mentions them. **4**, a decree of the People of Lampsacus, found on Thasos and made of local stone, awards honours to a prominent Thasian named Nossikas and specifies that he be crowned 'in the thea[tre] at Thasos, during the Dionysi[a, (?) at the tragic contest]'; or perhaps just 'at the tragedies'. It is clear that particular prestige was to be had for Nossikas to receive his awards in the theatre of his home city, so that arrangements were made to permit the Lampsacians to have the honours announced there, and the decree erected on Thasos. Crowns were still awarded at the tragedies of the Thasian Dionysia in the second century (*IG* XII Suppl. 361, ll. 8–9, 20–1: the reading of τραγωιδ[οῖς] 'at the tragedies' at l. 21 might encourage its restoration in **4**; although if **1**, l. 17 refers to the Thasian rather than Athenian Dionysia, it might on the other hand incline us towards the inclusion of the words τῶι ἀγῶνι 'at the contest').

Another inscription (**5**), also dated by its first editor to around 300, though possibly as much as fifty years older (see above), presents many problems of interpretation but appears, after a standard Archon-dating formula (ll. 1–4), to have reported a victory ἐνίκησεν ἰδι[- - -] 'was victorious …' (l. 5), perhaps 'at the (??) c[ontests …]' παρὰ τοῖς ἀ[γῶσι - - -] (l. 6; Daux 1928, 56) of some festival. The latter part of the same line may hint at the Dionysia, for a possible restoration is 'at/in [the trage]dies held in the [Archonship after Pheidi]ppos son of Chrysor[os …]' [(??) τοῖς τραγωι]|δοῖς τοῖς μετὰ [(?) ἄρχοντος (Launey 1937, 384) Φειδί]|ππο τõ Χρυσώρ[ο - - -]: for the word ending -|δοῖς Daux also canvassed the possibilities of comedy, kitharody and aulody. However the possibility that the 'victory' in question was in a legal trial cannot be ruled out entirely (cf. the language of e.g. *IG* XII 8, 267, l. 16: καὶ ἂν ὁ ἰδιώτης νικήσηι κτλ; on the other hand the traces following ἰδι[- - -] in *IG* XII Suppl. 357 appear to be incompatible with an omega: Daux 1928, 56). Satyros (l. 4) is doubtless the victor. None of the performers by that name known to Stefanis are certainly Thasian (the piper Satyros seen at the Samian Dionysia around the middle of the third century, Stefanis no. 2236, will surely be too late: *IG* XII 6, 176, l. 12).

The name is very well attested on Thasos (*LGPN* I has some 47 entries and gives a floruit for our Satyros – no. 91 – of ca. 360).

Finally **6** is the remains of a funerary inscription in the form of an elegiac couplet; perhaps inscribed on a column (Peek); and probably from the Thasian necropolis (Pouilloux 1954b, 345). Lines 1–3 declare the identity and parentage of the deceased trainer-poet (didaskalos). He was probably a Thasian, and ll. 4–5 proudly assert that he trained many cyclic choruses. (Peek restored l. 1 as a declaration of his Thasian origins, but Hansen's objection that that would be unlikely in Thasos itself has some force.) The epigram shares a number of features with the early fifth-century dedication by a poet from the Athenian Acropolis (*IG* I³ 833 bis in **V C**), most notably its emphasis on the 'very many choruses' trained over a career. The term 'cyclic' common already in fourth-century Athens for the choruses of men and boys at the City Dionysia might suggest performances at the Thasian Dionysia but need not be so restrictive. It is noteworthy that the cultic term 'dithyramb' appears in Thasos for a performance commemorated in the Dionysion (above).

E │ Asia Minor

Introduction

A survey of archaeologically attested theatres across the vast region of Asia Minor was conducted in the 1960s and 1970s (Bernardi Ferrero 1966–1974) and there has been some important high-quality work undertaken at a number of sites since, but a lack of systematic investigation and publication devoted to individual theatres, already remarked upon by Moretti over twenty-five years ago (1992a, 9), remains a serious problem.

The established view that theatre came to Asia only with Alexander the Great, and that the construction of permanent theatres began only in the third century (Bernardi Ferrero 1966–1974 IV, 94; Moretti 1992a, 11) now requires qualification. It is true that Alexander the Great defined Macedonian imperial culture as Greek and put theatre at its centre (**VI G**); and that he had learnt from, and developed, the example of his father and of Archelaus before him as to how theatre could be used as a tool of diplomacy and propaganda. But we should not overstate the direct influence of Alexander for the spread of theatre in this large and complex region. As far as we know, the various theatrical performances set up by Alexander on campaign in the east were uniformly of an *ad hoc* nature, largely designed to celebrate and advertise major victories or other events of great significance to his empire, such as the conquest of Egypt in 331 or the mass dynastic wedding celebrations held in the old centre of Achaemenid power, Susa, in 324. In no case can we be certain that the associated theatres or performance contexts were intended to persist beyond the particular occasion, nor is there any compelling evidence that these events led to the establishment of a theatrical culture in the places in question.

The one site where this question remains open is Babylon (see also **Eii**). It has been suggested that it was in Babylon that the mass entourage of Artists from Greece performed for the celebration of Hephaestion's funeral in 324 (Le Guen 2014, 259, 266, on Arr. *An.* 7.14.10; **VI G**) and there is a possibility that the first phase of the theatre at Babylon dates to the early Hellenistic period. There is a certain plausibility in the idea that the construction of such a significant monument on the urban landscape of the city would pre-date the foundation of Seleucia on the Tigris as the royal capital around 306, for this to some extent had the effect of undermining the *raison d'être* of Babylon from the point of view of the Macedonian conquerors (Plin. *HN* 6.30; De Giorgi 2016, 46). Thus some (Michel 2011; cf. Moretti 2014a, 111) confidently place the theatre's construction under Alexander, or at least prior to ca. 306, while others (Le Guen 2014, 258) are more circumspect, noting that all claims made on the archaeological evidence are based on the assertions of Wetzel et al. (1957, 19) who, writing half a century after the excavation of the site by Koldewey in 1904, placed the first phase at the very beginning of the Hellenistic period, but without providing the full archaeological evidence. More recently it has become clear that under

Antiochus IV (reigned 175–163), the Greek population of Babylon grew considerably (Van der Spek 2005; Van der Spek 2009). The theatre was very probably modified at this time, with the addition of a raised stage building likely dated to this era and – as we learn from the Babylonian Astronomical Diaries – it was used as a political meeting place for the Greek population, where letters from the kings were read aloud to the assembled citizens (Van der Spek 2001: the Greek word *theatron* appears in cuneiform texts as *bīt tamarti*, 'house of observation'; Potts 2011).

On the other hand, a number of places reveal theatrical activity long before the arrival of Alexander. Recent evidence from the Ionian cities of Erythrae (**Evi**) and Phocaea (**Ev**) in particular demands a qualification of the accepted position and raises questions about the possible influence of the self-styled metropolis of Ionia, Athens, in this region (Cyme may be another case: **Eiv**). Moreover a sound literary tradition attests the composition of tragedy for the Hellenised Carian Hecatomnid dynasty of Halicarnassus by around 350 (**Eix**). Influence here (if a direct influence be needed) is rather the model offered by Alexander's late fifth-century predecessor, Archelaus (**VI D**), or his father Philip II (**VI F**). Further south, new excavation in the theatre of Caunus (the publication of which appeared too late to permit inclusion on our map at p. 774 and Plate 5) proposes to raise the date of that theatre by over two centuries, with a first phase already in the first half of the fourth century and a stage building equipped with *periaktoi* in a second, early Hellenistic, phase (below).

Our survey of the evidence for theatre in Asia Minor follows an approximately north to south direction, moving from the Troad to Caria. The Troad gives us two virtually certain instances of permanent theatres built before the end of the fourth century, Ilium (**Eii**) and Scepsis (**Eiii**), with a third quite likely in the important Hellespontine port city of Abydos (**Ei**). There are two further somewhat ambiguous cases, Neandreia to the south-west and Assos on the southern coast of the Troad, facing Lesbos. Preliminary archaeological evidence of a partially excavated theatre in the civic centre of Neandreia suggests the presence of a rectilinear orchestra, and hence the possibility of a relatively early date (Trunk 1994, 95–6). The first phase of the theatre of Assos has customarily been assigned to ca. 200 (Sear 2006, 330) with Attalid influence detected, but recently Arslan (2016, 93–4) has argued, on the basis of new soundings, that substantial civic construction took place in the city ca. 300, notably of the bouleuterion, and he would place the theatre in this context, putting its first phase around the last quarter of the fourth century. A Late Classical tomb has revealed, among a rich array of over 60 artefacts, a set of terracottas that include various seated female musicians, a poet and comic actors, the costumes of the latter implying a local take on the Attic norm (Ağtürk and Arslan 2015; a Dionysia with a competition of pipers is attested in the city for the late second century, *IK Assos* 7, l. 8).

Abydos, Neandreia and Assos are among cities in Asia Minor whose close involvement with Athens for much of the second half of the fifth century as tribute-paying members of the Delian League means that at the very least their ambassadors will have been exposed to theatre at the Athenian Dionysia, though in the case of Abydos there is some reason to believe that theatre was more probably introduced by the local tyrant or oligarchy in the second half of the fourth century. Assos was ruled by tyrants in the fourth century, notably Hermias, a pupil of Plato's Academy (Str. 13.1.57; Theopomp. *FGrH* 115 F 250) and eventual father-in-law to Aristotle, who in 347 founded a philosophical school in Assos after the death of Plato and remained there for three years under the patronage of Hermias

(Ford 2011). The cultural prominence of the city under the Athenian-educated tyrant in the middle of the fourth century is suggestive.

The two more secure cases, Ilium and Scepsis, are interesting examples of the part that relations with the new Macedonian masters played in stimulating construction of monumental theatres and enthusiastic adoption of theatre culture in Asia Minor. As already noted, it is a remote possibility that the theatre at Ilium was the direct result of the intervention of Alexander the Great, who famously visited the city in 334 and vowed to make the once mighty city of Homeric epic, now little more than a village, great once more, presenting himself at the same time as a new Achilles come to liberate the Greek cities of Asia from barbarian rule. The Ilium theatre is however more likely to date from the period (from 315) during which Antigonus was lord of Asia and highly active in the Troad. Around 310 he created a new League of cities in the area that was centred on the cult of Athena Ilias in Ilium and it is in connection with her cult that the Ilium theatre appears to have been constructed and drama performed at her Panathenaea. Further inland, on the upper reaches of the Scamander, Scepsis differs from Ilium in having had close contact with Athens during the fifth century as a member of the Delian League, and being for much of the period a democracy. This might be part of the explanation for its relatively early construction of a theatre, but the city shares with Ilium close involvement with Antigonus and the possibility remains that the Scepsians used, if they did not also build, their theatre late in the fourth century, as a way to honour and otherwise establish good relations with him.

The latest work on the archaeological remains of the theatre in the harbour city of Cyme in Aeolis suggests a date for its first phase in the second half of the fourth century (**Eiv**), while **Eiv 1–2** are evidence both of an appetite for tragic theatre in the wider region of Aeolis by the start of the fourth century and for the organisation of one-off theatrical events by military commanders in the field, in this case with an eye to personal enrichment or perhaps campaign funding.

On current evidence, some four Ionian cities may have had theatre with contests at regular Dionysia by the end of the fourth century – Phocaea, Erythrae, Ephesus and Priene (on Miletus see below). In the case of Phocaea and (less certainly) Priene, tragedy is attested by ca. 300. At Erythrae and Priene there is evidence for a cult of Dionysus in close association with the theatre. In all four cities the Dionysia is used as a site for important proclamations of civic honours. It is possible that the close historical and cultural ties to Athens that existed or were asserted by many Ionian cities, and at times by Athens itself, played some part in their adoption of theatre. All were also members of the Delian League. For instance, in the period during which Priene was being refounded, the city strategically deployed its colonial relationship with Athens, granting the Athenians en masse 'prohedria at the contests' in Priene as part of the process (**Evii 1**). This suggests that such concrete festival exchange formed part of the ongoing relation between (putative) metropolis and colony.

The discovery in 1991 of the stone theatre of Phocaea datable to ca. 340–330 marks a significant event in the history of the theatre in East Greece, for it is the most important evidence to set against the established view that theatre came to Asia Minor only in the wake of Alexander's conquest. In fact the retaining walls of this theatre may date to around 400 or even earlier, making it entirely possible that wooden seating was used on the slope of the hill from around 400, with construction of the stone seating following that of the retaining walls by some decades (a situation for which other theatres, including the Athenian Theatre of Dionysus, offer direct parallels). **Ev 1** shows that the Phocaeans held a Dionysia with tragedy by around 290, and perhaps as early as 330. The fact that a colony founded by Phocaea in Southern Italy – Elea (Hyele) – certainly had a theatre by ca. 300 and may already have done so by as early as the middle of the fifth century (**A Introduction**), hints at a long-standing predilection for drama.

The reference in **Evi 1** of 394 to the award of prohedria, with no further qualification – such as 'in the theatre' or 'at the festivals the city holds' – may be sufficient to deduce the existence of a theatre in Erythrae by the early fourth century, although it will be an earlier phase than the one whose remains survive on the northern slope of the city's acropolis. The earliest surviving archaeological remains have been dated to the last quarter of the fourth century, but it is entirely possible – not least given the fact that the stage building continued to be made of wood even when the theatron had been built in stone – that in an earlier phase the natural slope of the acropolis had afforded spectators a place to watch, with wooden seats constructed for the purpose, and with some form of prohedric seating erected at the front. By around 333 the Erythraeans announce honours for important benefactors at their Dionysia, which was run by an agonothete, showing that it had contests (**Evi 2**). Although we have no explicit indication that these were dramatic, the fact that the city held a Dionysia in a theatre with a stage building points in that direction. Like many other cities in the region and beyond, Erythrae associated its Dionysia with worship of the relevant power brokers during the period of the Successors. It may have been associated with a festival for Alexander already by the late fourth, and it was certainly associated with one for Seleucus early in the third century.

Ephesus presents a somewhat ambiguous case. The earliest archaeological remains of the city's large theatre are now definitively dated to the second quarter of the second century, although the decisions as to its site and design are sometimes associated with the refoundation of the city by Lysimachus ca. 290 (Ruggendorfer and Krinzinger 2017, 129, 523). Yet we know from inscriptions that Ephesus already had a theatre at least by the closing years of the fourth century, when honours were announced (among them 'prohedria at the contests') for the Macedonian general and relative of Demetrius the Besieger, Archestratos, 'at the Dionysia, in the theatre' (*IK Ephesos* 1452, ll. 3–4, of 302/1; also *IK Ephesos* 1457, ll. 3–4, for a Theban, 4th/3rd c.). How long this theatre had been in existence we cannot say, and our further knowledge depends on the dating of a number of inscriptions with similar clauses, which at present tend to be placed merely in the 'early Hellenistic' period (e.g. *IK Ephesos* 1408, 1411, 1440, ca. 306–289; *IK Ephesos* 2003, ca. 300); another of around the same period bestows 'prohedria at all the contests which the city holds' (*Suppl. Ephes.* 126, 2, ll. 7, 10); while another informs us that at around 300 the pan-Ionian festival of the Ephesia was also held in the theatre (*IK Ephesos* 1453, l. 10 of ca. 300; Hornblower 1982c on Th. 3.104; Kowalzig 2007, 103–10).

Whether and when drama featured at the Ephesian Dionysia (or for that matter, at the Ephesia) we cannot say. Some form of theatrical or at least choral contest is likely to have formed part of the fourth-century Dionysia, but explicit evidence for drama is again absent: a men's contest, probably choral, is attested in an inscription of 'Hellenistic' date (*IK Ephesos* 1390, ll. 5–7; and *IK Ephesos* 1470 honours a Boeotian piper; Ceccarelli 2010,

133–4). An agonothete is active in connection with the Dionysia by the early Hellenistic period (*IK Ephesos* 1452, l. 3; *Suppl. Ephes.* 126, 2, l. 7). The antiquity of the city's cult and festival for Dionysus is guaranteed: Heraclitus F 15 D-K is good evidence for an Ephesian Dionysia, with prominent phallic parade, in the late sixth to early fifth centuries: εἰ μὴ γὰρ Διονύσωι πομπὴν ἐποιοῦντο καὶ ὕμνεον ᾆσμα αἰδοίοισιν, ἀναιδέστατα εἴργαστ' ἄν· ὡυτὸς δὲ Ἀίδης καὶ Διόνυσος, ὅτεωι μαίνονται καὶ ληναΐζουσιν. 'If it were not for Dionysus that they were making a parade and singing hymns to sexual organs, their action would be most shameful. Hades and Dionysus are the same, for whom they rave and rage.' (The identification of Dionysus with Hades here is very probably the philosopher's own 'idiosyncratic and provocative' interpretation: Wildberg 2011, 207.) There is a clear continuity between the festival known to Heraclitus and the Ephesian festival for Dionysus (also called the Katagogia) which had a prominent phallic parade, that is attested many centuries later (*Acta S. Timothei.* p. II.1 Usener; Plu. *Ant.* 24.3; *IK Ephesos* 661, 2nd c. AD; further evidence for public cults and more restricted associations of Dionysus in Ephesus from the 4th c. to the 2nd c. AD: Jacottet 2003 II, 229–43).

With the city of Priene much depends again on the uncertain dating of inscriptions, which show the existence of a Dionysia, tragic performances and a theatre (closely associated with Dionysus) across a chronological span of uncertainty ca. 340–322 (**Evii**).

The question of whether the great Ionian city of Miletus had theatre culture by the end of the fourth century cannot at present be answered. Sacked by the Persians in 494, reconstituted in 479 and a member of the Delian League from 478, Miletus seems thereafter to have had a moderate oligarchy that was backed by Athens against the demos in a period of civil unrest in the fifth century ([X.] *Ath.* 3.11). But a democracy heavily influenced by the Athenian model was introduced by the 430s (Herrmann 1970) and is visible in the city again by 380, though later in the fourth century Miletus was ruled by the Hecatomnids until its capture by Alexander in 334. By 300 the city certainly had a Dionysia. In 300/299, among many other benefactions, the city granted Antiochus, son of Seleucus I '[prohedria in Miletus] at the Dionysia and in Didyma [at the Didymeia, at] the circular contests' (*IDidyma* 479, ll. 36–8: εἰσκαλεῖσθαι δὲ αὐτὸν [εἰς προεδρίαν ἐν Μιλήτωι] | τοῖς Διονυσίοις καὶ ἐν Διδύμο[ις τοῖς Διδυμείοις ἐν] | τοῖς κυκλίοις ἀγῶσιν). The most likely interpretation of this unusual phrase is that 'circular contests' (itself an unusual way of saying contests of circular choruses) featured at both festivals, the Dionysia and the Didymeia for Apollo (Ceccarelli 2013b, 165). This may be a case of the term being applied to describe non-cultic, theatrical lyric choral performances, and in a pattern (almost certainly derived from Athens, and observable at Delphi: **Cvi**) where such choral contests formed part of the festivals of Apollo as well as Dionysus.

As for the archaeological evidence, the dating of the (much smaller) Greek predecessor to the great theatre of Miletus is hotly disputed and suggestions range from the fourth century (Lauter 1976) to the third quarter of the third (Bernardi Ferrero 1966–1974 III, 92). We follow Moretti (1992a, 11) in endorsing the date of ca. 300 proposed by Gerkan (1935, 107), although the fact that the theatre, on the south-west slope of the hill between the Lion and Theatre harbours, was not incorporated into Hippodamus' grid plan in the fifth century is suggestive of an older and more provisional site (Krauss 1973, 2–3). The excavated fourth-century temple for Dionysus, not far from the theatre, certainly had sixth- and fifth-century predecessors (Gorman 2001, 174 with further evidence on the god's well-attested cult). A (probably healing) sanctuary inside a cave underneath the theatre, centred on a natural spring, appears to have been set up in conjunction with the Hellenistic phase of the theatre's construction (Niewöhner 2016). In the fourth century, Miletus produced the piper Ariston, remembered on the elaborate monument in the Dionysion of Thasos (**Dxvi 3**) for having accompanied a dithyramb (Stefanis no. 381) and in the late third century the Milesian comic actor Nikophon (Stefanis no. 1871) was honoured by the Samians living at Minoa on Amorgos for 'arriving at their harbour … and announc[ing] he would perform three dramas for the god over three days' (*IG* XII 7, 226, ll. 1–6). By the second century the Milesian Dionysia saw the performance of tragedies and the significance of the event is marked by the fact that it was the occasion for the award of public honours (*IG* XII 4, 3870, ll. 3–4; cf. *IG* XII 4, 3895, ll. 24–5).

The strong association between eastern potentates and tragedy finds another expression in the Carian city of Halicarnassus (**Eix**). A tradition concerning Mausolus, the highly Hellenised ruler of Caria (377–353) who made Halicarnassus the capital of the Hecatomnid dynasty founded by his father, reports that, on his death in 353, his sister and widow Artemisia set up a funeral contest in praise of the dead king with valuable monetary and other prizes. It was either for this event or a separate but related occasion that the orator and tragedian Theodectes of Phaselis composed his *Mausolus*, which is likely to have broadcast from the tragic stage the divine ancestry and status of Mausolus as the founder of a new Carian state. There is a strong possibility that the first phase of the great theatre in Halicarnassus was integral to Mausolus' original urban plan and dates to his reign; and good evidence that theatre continued to thrive in Halicarnassus after the end of the Hecatomnid dynasty. **Eviii** further shows us the strategic use, by a Macedonian satrap in Caria in the 320s, of a choregic system in association with a Dionysia to generate funds from the local élite.

Elsewhere in Caria, we have abundant evidence for an energetic theatre culture in the coastal city of Iasus, with a distinctive choregic system that is well documented by a series of inscriptions placed on the parodos wall and gateway to the theatre through which spectators entered (Migeotte 1993; Crowther 2007; Maddoli 2007, 352–61). The city had been a member of the Delian League and maintained close contacts with Athens throughout the fifth century. By the middle of the fourth century it was part of the Hecatomnid Empire and after that, changed hands between the Ptolemies, the Macedonians (227) and the Seleucids (197) until liberated a few years later thanks to Roman intervention.

The Iasians took great care permanently to record those who contributed to their theatre and it is a sobering thought that many other cities which were less careful may well have had equally lively theatre cultures, all trace of which is lost to us. However virtually all of this epigraphic evidence dates to the (early) second century, which is also the period to which the remains of the theatre itself are ascribed (Sear 2006, 339). The theatre was in part funded by contributions from ex-choregoi (*IK Iasos* 164, 179, 180, 182, 182; Maddoli 2007, 352–61). The second century is also the era of the Iasian poet of tragedy Dymas, who was lavishly recompensed by the people of Samothrace for his services as a poet, having composed a drama *Dardanus* about the hero who went from the island to Asia, founding Dardanus and Troy (*TrGF* 130; Rutherford 2007). In mid century we find the Iasians, in bad economic times, drawing upon their 'friendship from ancient times toward' the Artists of Dionysus in Ionia and the Hellespont in their request for help with their Dionysia (*ATD* TE 53, ll. 4–5, 14;

Aneziri 2003, 392 D13). The Association responded by sending a group of its members at no charge, including two tragedians, two comedians, two pipers, a kitharode and a kitharist.

This evidence falls outside our period and would not merit mention were it not for the possibility that this rich theatrical culture and economy we see in second-century Iasus had considerably older roots. An honorific decree recently dated by Fabiani to ca. 300–285 (Fabiani 2015, 259 on *IK Iasos* 43) envisages the crowning of its honorand, a citizen named Hermophantos (Fabiani 2015, 224) 'in the theatre at the Diony[sian contest]' ἐν τῶι θεάτρωι τῶι Διονυ[σιακῶι ἀγῶνι] (l. 5) and proclamation 'whenev[er the city first] conducts its choruses' ὅτα[ν ἡ πόλις πρῶτον] | χορούς ἄγηι (ll. 6–7). Hermophantos is also granted 'prohedria at the Dionysian contest' [προεδρίαν] | ἐν τῶι Διονυσιακῶι ἀγῶνι (ll. 9–10). It follows that Iasus did in fact have a theatre more than a century earlier than the dated remains, and that a Dionysia was held in it by the start of the third century. The (partially restored) expression 'whenev[er the city first] conducts its choruses' will not refer to the first ever such occasion but to the *next* occasion on which the choral contest is held and thus, in effect, means simply the next Dionysia (Chaniotis 2007, 56; Fabiani 2015, 105 airs the possibility that it is a vaguer way of expressing 'on the first day' of the choral contest, as in *IK Iasos* 82, l. 20, dated to the 150s, κυκλίων τῆι πρώτηι, which incidentally shows that by that date the contest of cyclic choruses at the Dionysia lasted for more than one day).

While not explicitly mentioning dramatic genres, the expressions used in *IK Iasos* 43 – notably 'Dionysiac contest', and even the phrase 'the city … conducts choruses' – could encompass drama. We thus find a Dionysia held in the Iasus theatre, very possibly with drama, by the period of Ptolemaic rule of the city (early third century). It is also worth noting that prohedria was one of the earliest, most prestigious and most long-lasting civic honours conferred by decree in Iasus (Fabiani 2014, 111). It is already attested by the late fifth century (Maddoli 2007, 216, no. 1.3: [prohe]dria awarded to an Argive and his descendants ca. 412–394) and through the fourth (e.g. *SEG* 36, 982B, l. 8, 360s: Fabiani 2015, 13–14), when it develops into 'prohedria at the contests' (e.g. *IK Iasos* 42, l. 7, ? 4th to 3rd c.; Fabiani 2015, 78–80 for further developments in the formula). While there is no corroborative evidence to suggest that the prohedria awarded in the fifth and fourth centuries was at a Dionysia or in a theatre, that must at least remain a possibility.

Further south, beyond the Cnidian peninsula and close to Lycia, the small but prosperous Carian harbour city of Caunus is yielding tantalising new evidence to suggest that it too may have had theatre culture well before 300. As an illustration of the Sicilians' love of Euripides, Plutarch reports a story (**Axi 5**) that some Caunians, pursued by pirates off the coast of Sicily, were only admitted to harbour (Syracuse is doubtless intended) when they assured the Sicilians that they could teach them songs they knew by the tragic poet. Until recently the choice of Caunus in this anecdote would have been naturally interpreted as a more or less random fabrication designed to show how a peripheral and only partially Hellenised city like Caunus gave the Athenian poet greater honour than his own birthplace. It is now more likely that Caunus was chosen precisely because, although almost as distant to the east from Athens as Syracuse to the west, it did in fact already have a theatrical culture by the fourth century (and the fact that Caunians are known to have exported figs to Italy at the very least adds plausibility to Plutarch's account: Marek and Frei 2016, 401). Although the sources of the anecdote are unknown (Philochorus has been supposed an intermediary:

Axi 5) and while little probative weight can be placed upon it, it is striking that the reference to the songs of Euripides (ᾄσματα τῶν Εὐριπίδου) suggests that the Caunians' acquaintance derived from their direct participation in choruses performing Euripides' works.

The city's status as a tributary member of the Delian League from 453/2 may be relevant, while in the fourth century – the period of Caunus' major expansion and prosperity – it was part of the satrapy of Caria under Hecatomnus and his highly Hellenised son Mausolus. Towards the end of Hecatomnid control we find the Carian language replaced in Caunus by the Attic koine (*SEG* 47, 1568). In 333 it came under Macedonian rule; in 313 it was taken by Antigonus, from whom it was captured four years later, in 309, by Ptolemy I. After the victory of Demetrius and Antigonus at Salamis in 306 Caunus reverted to their control. Around 190 it became a possession of Rhodes. The city's strategic location on an important trade route from the Aegean to the eastern Mediterranean and its proximity to Rhodes (to whose elaborate Dionysia famous tragic and comic actors were drawn by at least the 380s: **Dxi**) made it very attractive to a series of powerful overlords. The same features probably encouraged and aided its adoption of theatre.

The theatre itself, one of the best preserved in Asia Minor, lies on the rather steep north-western slopes of the city's 'Great' acropolis, 152 m high (so called to distinguish it from an adjacent, lower acropolis). Its capacity in its largest, Roman, phase was ca. 5,000 (little is known as yet of the theatron in its earlier phases). The stage building was constructed directly on the bedrock, with some terracing at its northern side to produce a level surface. The theatre has long been dated to the second century, but soundings taken in 2005–2007 permitted its excavator to identify five phases of the stage building (Varkıvanç 2017), and to place the first of these some two centuries earlier than previously thought. Varkıvanç dates the first phase by ceramic finds (yet to be published) to the first half of the fourth century (2016, 920). This structure was narrower than its successors, some 18.90 m wide, with paraskenia (13.30 m between the paraskenia). A depth of ca. 6.5 m has been proposed, on a somewhat hypothetical reconstruction (Varkıvanç 2016, 921). Varkıvanç would restore four columns *in antis* at the front of the stage building between the paraskenia, and a flat, possibly tiled, roof (2016, 925, figs. 6–7). This earliest phase is now represented by a row of travertine blocks at the front of both parodoi and extending into the orchestra, as well as holes cut into the bedrock for them, which Varkıvanç suggests served as the support for a stage building above, constructed in timber and mudbrick (2017, 284, fig. 4). He also identified a block with a large circular hole in it as the base for a timber post of the Classical stage building (Varkıvanç 2016, 921 with figs. 6, 10).

Varkıvanç dates a second phase to the early Hellenistic period. The stage building continues to be made of timber and mudbrick. A very striking feature reconstructed for this phase is *periaktoi*, a pair of revolving triangular plinths placed at each end of the stage building that pivot on a central axis, used to indicate a change of scene (**Gi 2**). Varkıvanç (2015) plausibly identifies these from the remains of two circular foundations (2.10 m diam.) in front of the theatre's skene to the south and north, made up of small blocks around a central large block with a hole for a dowel in its upper surface (0.10 × 0.10 × 0.03 m). These would constitute the lower course of the *periaktoi*, and traces of abrasion on the central blocks show that they had clearly been in use as the axis for a larger, mobile structure above. This is the only instance of archaeologically attested *periaktoi* found in place in an orchestra.

Numerous marble and limestone elements found in the theatre, some reflecting Doric and Corinthian architectural forms, derive from the three later phases, starting with the first fully stone stage building in the Doric order in the third phase (Varkıvanç 2015, 189; 2017), dated to around the mid-second century, at which point the theatron may also have been constructed in stone (see also Say Özer and Oğuz Özer 2016). A circular structure, excavated near the theatre, has revealed the names of two tribes, Rhadamanthis and Kranais, inscribed above bronze rings to tether sacrificial victims (Ehrhardt 1997). This is likely to suggest publicly sponsored communal feasting (Ma 2000, 108; *IKaunos* 64, 2nd or 1st c.) in some connection with the theatre. Chaniotis (2007, 60) associates it with tribally organised seating in the theatre (**Eii**).

Confirmation of the fourth-century and Hellenistic phases of the Caunus theatre must await full publication of the material. If proved correct, the existence of a stage building with paraskenia in the first half of the fourth century would strongly imply that dramatic performances took place in the theatre at that date. A theatre with *periaktoi* is one for which the ability to change scenes is paramount, so that, if Varkıvanç's interpretation stands, drama will certainly have featured at Caunus by this second, early Hellenistic, period. The oblique evidence of Plutarch aside, explicit reference to drama appears only much later, although the visit reported by Strabo (14.2.3) of the famous kitharist, kitharode and wit Stratonicus (cf. **Fiii 4**) implies the existence of musical contests in the fourth century (a *mousikos agon* is attested in the 2nd c: *IKaunos* 19, ll. 91–3). A highly fragmentary inscription of probably second-century date comes from a victor-list at a local festival (possibly the Ptolemaia of l. 13), where pipers, actors and choregoi all feature (*IKaunos* 37). And some time after 167 (*IKaunos* 62) the probably local tragic poet Polyxenos son of Philagros (Stefanis no. 2112) had a statue of himself erected in the city centre to record his 'victory, twice, over the poets of tragedies at the penteteric contests for Leto and the goddess Rome established by the People' (νικήσας τοὺς ποιητὰς | τῶν τραγῳδιῶν δὶς | ἐν τοῖς τιθεμένοις ὑπὸ | τοῦ δήμου Λητοῖ καὶ Ῥώμηι | πενταετηρικοῖς ἀγῶσιν. ll. 2–6).

The painter and sculptor Protogenes, rival of Apelles, was one of Caunus' most famous sons. Around 300 he erected a significant family monument in the centre of his home town that consisted of five bronze statues on bases inscribed with epigrams, set on a semi-circular plinth forming an exedra (Isik and Marek 1997). The statues were of himself, his parents and two companions (*hetairoi*). Protogenes and his monument have a number of intriguing Dionysian and theatrical associations: among the artist's works was an *Alexander and Pan* (Pl. *HN* 35.106), a portrait that according to Isik and Marek (1997, 68) will have depicted the Macedonian as a New Dionysus (but for other interpretations of Alexander's association with Pan see Pollit 1986, 305 n. 23). There was another portrait of King Antigonus – perhaps the founder of the dynasty, but the son of Demetrius the Besieger is more likely – although we are not told in this instance whether this drew on Dionysiac imagery. He also painted the tragic poet Philiscus, deep in thought (*Philiscum tragoediarum scriptorem meditantem*: Pl. *HN* 35.106). Philiscus was intimately involved with the Association of *Technitai* in Egypt set up under and in support of Ptolemy (**G Introduction**). Protogenes' acknowledged masterpiece, the painting of Ialysos, mythical founder of the city of Ialysos, was made for the Dionysion of Rhodes, and had been famously spared by Demetrius, who was besieging the city in 305 as it was being completed

(Plin. *HN* 35.101–6; Plu. *Demetr.* 22; Suda π 2963). His *Satyr* was also in Rhodes, proba- bly likewise in the Dionysion (Str. 14.2.5; Isik and Marek 1997, 67–8). Protogenes' mother had the Dionysian name of Euanthis (*IKaunos* 51; Euanthes was a son of Dionysus and Ariadne and an epithet of the god himself: Hom. *Od.* 9.197; Ath. 11.465a). The Lysias honoured on the Caunian monument – probably, along with [Ky]dias (*IKaunos*, 52), one of the 'affectionate companions' of Protogenes, ἀσπασίων τ' ἐτάρων (*IKaunos* 49, l. 2) – had had some form of significant involvement in Dionysian cult in the past ('You plucked the flourishing ivy from mature [leaves] and placed it on top of your blonde [curls]' [ἀ]μφιθαλῆ μὲν ἔθου ξανθοῖς ἐπύπ[ερθε πλοκοῖσι | [κ]ισσὸν ἀπ' ὡραίων δρεψάμενος π[ετάλων], *IKaunos* 53, ll. 1–2). The Caunians now praise him for his public service as Prytanis, and either dedicate his statue directly to Dionysus, invoked as 'Lord of the choruses', or simply enact their praise before the god (πρύτανιν δέ σε πα[τρίδος αἴης] | ἤινεσε μητίσας λαὸς ἄνακτι χορῶν, ll. 3–4; on the difficult text and expression see Merkelbach and Stauber 1998, 30; Isik and Marek 1997, 56). Isik and Marek (1997, 61 n. 58) state that the cult of Dionysus and the Prytanis were linked in Caunus, though the evidence they offer is far from conclusive. But this somewhat mysterious sketch of Lysias at least attests to an at- tachment to choral culture of a Dionysian stamp and could perhaps be pressed to imply the existence of a cult in Caunus that included choral performance by 300.

The theatre at New Paphos in Cyprus should be mentioned here. Its first phase is dated to around the end of the fourth or start of the third century (Green and Stennett 2002; Green 2007; Green et al. 2015, 323 for the epigraphic evidence for this date, a few letters of an inscription from the bedrock of the upper theatron dated by M. Osborne within a couple of decades either side of 300). The city of New Paphos itself was founded around 320 by the last king of Cyprus, Nikokles. The island became the object of military conflict between Ptolemy and Antigonus and his son Demetrius, not least since it occupied a crucial strategic position for trade between the Eastern Mediterranean and the Aegean. It came definitively under Ptolemaic control in 294 and it may be to this period of thoroughgoing Hellenisation that the construction of the theatre should be dated (Papantoniou 2012, 155). The impor- tant early Hellenistic writer of parodic *phlyakes* Sopater was born in Cyprus around 320 and may have begun his dramatic career on the island before moving to Alexandria (Favi 2017d, 264–469). The Ptolemies thought of Dionysus as the protector of their dynasty (Tondriau 1950). A Synodos of Artists of Dionysus appears in Cyprus in the second cen- tury (Aneziri 1994; Aneziri 2003, 119–20), when close connection with the cult of the Ptolemies is clear. But it is striking that when Alexander the Great set up elaborate tragic and dithyrambic contests, as well as comedy, at Tyre in the spring of 331 in the wake of his conquest of Egypt, he appointed the kings of Cyprus as his choregoi (Plu. *Alex.* 29.5; *Mor.* 334e), which suggests that these kings were already predisposed to drama, if not entirely familiar with it. At the very least it shows that they were aware of the great prestige they could derive from association with such an occasion.

If Alexander the Great has been decentred from the account of the spread of theatre in Asia Minor, the importance of the model of autocratic theatre sponsorship, and of the Macedonian kings in particular, remains and gains a sharper focus. The successful propa- gandistic use of drama and theatre by Archelaus and Philip may lie behind its adoption by the Hecatomnid dynasty of Caria by 350, unless we should think of an even more widely diffused model of autocratic theatre that includes familiarity with the Western Greek tradition of the Deinomenids and Dionysii of Syracuse (**A Introduction**; **VI A**; **VI E**): there can be little doubt that Macedonian and Sicilian autocrats were acutely aware of each others' theatrical ambitions. The picture also presents the very earliest example of *ad hoc* theatrical performances organised by a military commander (in this case a Greek named Alexander: **Eiv**), decades before the Macedonians recognised the potential of this format. And around the end of the fourth century and beyond, the Macedonian overlords who dominated the region provided an added stimulus to theatre as an institution and to theatrical festivals that included drama, when these proved to be an effective means for cities to manage relations with them, as had also been the case in Athens from at least the time of Demetrius the Besieger (**VI L**).

The direct or indirect influence of Athens on theatrical culture in the region appears to be strong. A number of cities that had adopted theatre before the appearance of the Macedonians on the scene had had political and cultural associations with Athens since at least the fifth century – not only the Ionians, but several others – notably through membership of the Delian League and its successor Confederacy. And the practices of theatre culture across the region show broad consistencies with the Athenian model: the context of performance is, in the great majority of known cases, a Dionysia; the format is competitive; tragedy is the preponderant genre, while lyric/cyclic choruses probably akin to those at the Athenian Dionysia or Thargelia feature in a number of places (it is striking that there is no sign of comedy, the case of Alexander at Tyre in 331 aside). The theatre and its festivals also serve as an important medium for distributing civic honours both to local and external benefactors, as had long been the case at Athens. The very limited evidence for choregic systems does not point to direct adoption or close imitation of the Athenian model.

Ei: Abydos. Pseudo-Aristotle, *Marvels Heard* **832b17–21.** Internal references to Agathocles and Cleonymus indicate that the work could not have been compiled before ca. 270, but it is collected mainly from 4th-c. writers (Priestley 2014, 77–8). The main sources of the *Marvels Heard* (*Mirabiles Auscultationes*) are the ninth book of Aristotle's *History of Animals*, Theophrastus, and Timaeus (Flashar 1972, 40–1, although the Aristotelian authorship of *History of Animals* 9 is questioned by Balme 1991, 9–10), while the only citations are from the 5th- and 4th-century authors Hanno, Xenophanes, Polykritos, Callisthenes and Eudoxus. This story is therefore likely to have been taken from a 4th-century source. Text: Westermann.

> λέγεται δέ τινα ἐν Ἀβύδῳ παρακόψαντα τῇ διανοίᾳ καὶ εἰς τὸ θέατρον ἐρχόμενον ἐπὶ πολλὰς ἡμέρας θεωρεῖν, ὡς ὑποκρινομένων τινῶν, καὶ ἐπισημαίνεσθαι· καὶ ὡς κατέστη τῆς παρακοπῆς, ἔφησεν ἐκεῖνον αὑτῷ τὸν χρόνον ἥδιστα βεβιῶσθαι.

> It is reported that a man in Abydos who had gone mad went to the theatre and sat in the auditorium for many days, as if some actors were performing, and his symptoms were evident. But, when he recovered from his insanity, he maintained that it had been one of the happiest experiences of his life.

Abydos was a tributary of Athens until 411. Its oligarchic constitution (Arist. *Pol.* 1305b33) possibly dates from this time, though this was replaced by a tyranny under Iphiades ca. 360 (Arist. *Pol.* 1306a26–31; *IK Knidos* 603; Mitchell *IACP* 1003). It would therefore be unsafe to infer any connection between the theatre here and Athens or democracy; it was more probably introduced by the local tyrant or oligarchy in the second half of the fourth century, supposing that Pseudo-Aristotle is copying a fourth-century source.

An inscription from Ilium indicates a 'Dionysia and Xenia' and a theatre in Abydos in the last third of the third century (*IK Ilion* 2; cf. Robert 1966, 25–30), and in any case no later than 200 (Habicht 2004b, 91). Until that time Abydos was a member of the Confederation (koinon) of the sanctuary of Athena Ilias, apparently created some time before 306 (Boehm 2011, 66–7), which shared responsibility for the Panathenaea at Ilium and which, the same inscription shows, included a tragic competition (**Eii**).

There are no physical traces of a theatre nor any other significant archaeological remains from this very important Hellespontine port city. The only other indication of theatrical activity is from the third century: a comic choreut and kitharode from Abydos (Stefanis nos. 803, 2897). Note that Pseudo-Aristotle reports acting in the theatre in such a way as to allow that it may have been a delusion on the part of the subject in this specific instance, but this implies nothing about its general plausibility.

Eii: Ilium. A set of five or six recommendations (*gnomai*) of the Council of the Confederation (koinon) of Athena Ilias, three of which (**1**, **2**, **4**) are resolved as honorific decrees, acknowledging the financial generosity of Malousios of Gargara, including the gift of funds and credit to build a theatre in Ilium (**6** is the start of a new proposal or an amendment to **5**: Migeotte 1984, 265), ca. 306 or possibly 334. The inscription is usually dated to around 306: e.g. Frisch, *IK Ilion*. This is based on the assumption that the inscribed order reflects the order of their passing and, since Antigonus is mentioned in **1** by name (l. 9) and in **2** as 'the king' (l. 24), **1** is thought to date to soon before, **2** to soon after 306, the year he assumed the royal title. However, Frisch (*IK Ilion*, 6) had doubts about the order and suggested that the last, **6**, may be the earliest. Verkinderen (1987) argues that **1** is the chronologically latest of a group of three decisions to honour Malousios. On this view, **4** is the resolution that follows the proposal of **6**, which was publicised according to **5**; **3** presents new grounds for honour and thus for a new resolution, of which **2** is the official version; while **1** adds the new honour of tax exemption on the basis of the honorand's most recent benefactions. According to Verkinderen 'the king' of l. 24 is Alexander, while Antigonus in ll. 8–9 will be acting in his role as Alexander's 'general of the allies'. Verkinderen notes various elements that accord with the literary tradition about Alexander's actions in Ilium in 334. He was met on his way to the city by a delegation offering him a gold crown (Arr. 1.12.1). He gave the village the title of city, adorned the temple of Athena with offerings, ordering those in charge to start a programme of building and promising to make a great city of it (Str. 13.1.26; Plu. *Alex.* 15). Gauthier (*BE* 1988 no. 419) points to problems with Verkinderen's interpretation, and the traditional dating is probably correct. **5** appears to be designed to assemble a dossier made up of **1–4**, perhaps on the motion of **6**, the ensemble to be inscribed in the member states of the Confederation, not in Ilion (as had been the case with **1**, **2**, **4**).

Marble stele, broken at bottom.

1.10 × 0.53 × 0.16 m.

Found in 1873 in a field belonging to Calvert near Hisarlik (the site of Troy and Ilium), immediately south of the cistern in the temple of Athena: Hirschfeld 1875, 154.

Çannakale Museum.

Hirschfeld 1875, 151; Schliemann 1885, 821–3 (text of Koumanoudes from squeeze of Calvert); *IK Ilion* 1; Migeotte 1984 no. 79 (decrees **1–3**); Meier 2012 no. 45 (decrees **1–3**).

Text: *IK Ilion* 1.   Photos: *IK Ilion* Taf. 1–2.

1.

      [γνώμη τῶν συνέδρω]ν· ἐπειδὴ Μαλούσιος Βακχίο[υ]
      [Γαργαρεὺς ἀνὴρ ἀγ]αθὸς ὢν διατελεῖ περὶ τὸ ἱερὸν τῆς Ἀθ-
      [ηνᾶς τῆς Ἰλιάδος] καὶ περὶ τὰς πόλεις, καὶ πρότερόν τε πολλὰ χρήσι-
      [μος ἐγένετο τῶι] συνεδρίωι καὶ ταῖς πόλεσιν, εἴς τε τὰ κατασκευάσμα-
5   [τα τοῦ ἱεροῦ καὶ τῆ]ς πανηγύρεως καὶ εἰς τὰς πρεσβείας τὰς ἀποστελ-
      [λομένας καὶ ὑπὲρ] τῶν ἄλλων τῶν συμφερόντων τῆι πανηγύρει χρήματ[α]
      [δοὺς ἄτο]κα, καὶ τὴν ἄλλην προθυμίαν ἐμ πᾶσιν τοῖς καιροῖς παρεχόμε-
      [νος μετὰ] πολλῆς εὐνοίας, καὶ νῦν εἴς τε τὴν πρεσβείαν τὴν ὕστερον ἀποσ-
      [τελλομέ]νην πρὸς Ἀντίγονον ἔδωκεν χρυσοὺς διακοσίους ἀτόκους καὶ εἰς
10 [τὴν το]ῦ θεάτρου κατασκευὴν χρήματα κομίσας εἰς Ἴλιον ἔδωκεν τοῖς ἐπ[ι]-
      [στ]άταις, ὅσον ἐδέοντο, χρυσοῦς χιλίους τετρακοσίους πεντήκοντα
      ἀτόκους· ἐπειδὴ Μαλούσιος διατελεῖ πράττων καὶ λέγων ἀπροφα-
      σίστως ἐμ πᾶσι τοῖς καιροῖς τὰ συμφέροντα τῆι θεῶι καὶ ταῖς πόλεσιν,
      ἀγαθῆι τύχηι, δεδόχθαι τοῖς συνέδροις, ἐπαινέσαι Μαλούσιον
15 [Β]ακχίου Γαργαρέα καὶ στεφανῶσαι αὐτὸν ἐν τῶι γυμνικῶι ἀγῶνι
      χρυσῶι στεφάνωι ἀπὸ δραχμῶν χιλίων ἀρετῆς ἕνεκεν τῆς περ[ὶ]
      τὸ ἱερὸν καὶ τὴν πανήγυριν καὶ τὸ κοινὸν τῶν πόλεων, δεδόσθαι δὲ
      αὐτῶι μὲν τὴν ἀτέλειαν καθάπερ δέδοται, δεδόσθαι δὲ καὶ τοῖς ἐκ-
      γόνοις αὐτοῦ τὴν ἀτέλειαν, ὅ τι ἂν πωλῶσιν ἢ ἀγοράσωσιν· τὸ δὲ ψή-
20 φισμα τόδε ἀναγράψαντας εἰς στήλην θεῖναι εἰς τὸ ἱερὸν τῆς
      Ἀθηνᾶς, ἐπιμεληθῆναι δὲ τοὺς Γαργαρεῖς, ὅπως ἂν εἰδῶσιν ἅπα[ντες]
      ὅτι ἐπίσταται τὸ κοινὸν τῶν πόλεων τοῖς οὖσιν ἀγαθοῖς ἀνδράσιν εἰς
      αὐτοὺς χάριν ἀποδιδόναι·

2.

                   γνώμη τῶν συνέδρων· ἐπειδὴ Μαλούσι[ος]
      ἀποστελλόντων τῶν συνέδρων πρέσβεις πρὸς τὸν βασιλέα ὑ[πὲρ]
25 τῆς ἐλευθερίας καὶ αὐτονομίας τῶν πόλεων τῶν κοινονουσ[ῶν τοῦ]
      ἱεροῦ καὶ τῆς πανηγύρεως ἔδωκεν ἄτοκα χρήματα τοῖς ἀποστε[λλο]-
      μένοις ἀγγέλοις, ὅσα ἐκέλευον οἱ σύνεδροι, παρεσκεύασεν δὲ καὶ τὰ π[ρὸς]
      σκηνὴν ἄτοκα χρήματα, καὶ τἆλλα δὲ προθύμως ὑπηρετε[ῖ ε]ὶς ὅ τι ἂ[ν πα]-
      ρακαλῆι τὸ συνέδριον, ἀγαθῆι τύχηι, δεδόχθαι τοῖς συνέδροις, ἐπα[ι]-
30 νέσαι τε Μαλούσιον Βακχίου Γαργαρέα, ὅτι ἀνὴρ ἀγαθός ἐστιν περ[ὶ τὸ]
      ἱερὸν τῆς Ἀθηνᾶς καὶ τὴν πανήγυριν καὶ τὸ κοινὸν τῶν πόλεων, καὶ στ[ε]-
      φανῶσαι αὐτὸν χρυσῶι στεφάνωι ἀπὸ δραχμῶν χιλίων ἐν τῶι γυ-
      μνικῶι ἀγῶνι· ἀναγράψαι δὲ τὸ ψήφισμα τόδε εἰς στήλην τὴν ὑπὲ[ρ]

τῶν συνεδριῶν τῶν Μαλουσίου μέλλουσ(α)ν ἀνατεθήσεσθαι εἰς τὸ ἱερό[ν]·
35   ἐπιμεληθῆναι δὲ τοὺς Γαργαρεῖς, ὅπως ἂν εἰδῶσιν ἅπαντες ὅτ[ι]
ἐπίσταται τὸ κοινὸν τῶν πόλεων τοῖς οὖσιν ἀγαθοῖς ἀνδράσιν εἰς αὐτοὺς χάριν ἀποδιδόναι·

3.

γνώμη τῶν συνέδρων· ἐπειδὴ Μαλούσιος κε-
λεύει ἐπαγγεῖλαι αὐτῶι ἤδη τὸ συνέδριον, πόσων δεῖται παρ᾽ αὐτοῦ χρημάτων εἴς τε τὸ θέατρον καὶ εἰς τἆλλα κατασσκευάσματα καὶ εἰς τ[ὰ]
40   ἱερὰ καὶ εἰς τὴν πρεσβείαν, καί φησι θέλειν παρόντων τῶν συ[ν]-
έδρων ἤδη δοῦναι πάντα, ἀγαθῆι τύχηι, δεδό[χθαι] τοῖς συ[ν]-
έδροις ἐπαγγεῖλαι Μαλουσίωι δοῦναι τοῖς ἀγωνοθέταις χρ[υσοῦς]
τρισχιλίους καὶ πεντακοσίους σὺν τοῖς πέρυσι ὀφειλο[μέ]νοις ἀ[τόκους],
τοὺς δὲ ἀγωνοθέτας, οἷς μὲν ἂν αὐτοὶ χρήσων[ται, τ]ὰ δὲ ἄ[λλα χρή]-
45   ματα θεῖναι [εἰ]ς τὸ ἱερ[ό]ν· ἂν δέ τι περιγένηται ἐ[κ]δοθέντ[ων τῶν]
ἔργων, ἀποδοῦναι Μ[αλο]υσίωι·

4.

γνώμη τῶν συνέδρων· [ἐπειδὴ Μα]-
λούσιος [Βακ]χίου Γαργαρεὺς ἀνὴρ ἀγαθὸς ὢν διατελ[εῖ περὶ τὸ]
ἱερὸν τῆς Ἀθ[ην]ᾶς τῆς Ἰλιάδος καὶ τὸ συνέδριον, δ[εδόχθαι]
τοῖς συνέδρ[οι]ς, στεφανῶσαι Μαλούσιον χρυσῶι στ[εφάνωι ἀπὸ]
50   χρυσῶ[ν] τρι[άκο]ντα· καλεῖν δὲ α[ὐτὸν καὶ] εἰς προεδρί[αν Παναθηναί]-
οις ἐν τοῖς ἀγῶσιν ὀνομασ[τεί· δια]μεῖναι δὲ [τὴν προεδρίαν]
καὶ αὐτῶι καὶ ἐγγόνοις· τὸ δὲ ψήφ[ισμα τόδε] ἀναγράψαντα[ς τοὺς ἀγωνο]-
θέτας εἰς στήλην θεῖναι εἰς τὸ [ἱ]ερὸν τῆς Ἀθηνᾶς·

5.

[γνώμη τῶν συν]-
έδρων· ἐπειδὴ Μαλούσιος ἀνὴρ ἀγαθὸς ὢν διατ[ελεῖ περὶ τὸ ἱερὸν]
55   τῆς Ἀθηνᾶς τῆς Ἰλιά[δος] καὶ τὸ κοινὸν τῶν πόλεω[ν καὶ τὴν πανήγυριν],
ἀγαθῆι τύχηι, δεδόχ[θαι τοῖ]ς συνέδροις, αἷς τιμαῖς [τετίμηται Μαλού]-
σιος ὑπὸ τοῦ συνε[δρ]ίου, ἀναγράψαι ἑκά[στη]ν [τῶν πόλεων τῶν κοινωνου]-
σῶν τοῦ ἱεροῦ κ[αὶ τῆ]ς πανηγύρεως, καὶ θεῖν[αι τὴν στήλην ὅπου ἑκάσ]-
τηι νόμος ἐστ[ίν]·

6.   (or amendment to **5**)

Σίμαλος Λαμψακην[ὸς εἶπεν· ἐπειδὴ Μαλούσιος]
60   ὁ Γαργαρεὺς ἐ[πιμ]ελεῖται προθύ[μως — — — — — — — — — — — —]
τὰ ἀναλώμ[ατα —]
πόλεσιν [— —]
ὅτι προθυ[μ— —]
στεφα[ν— —]
65   φαν[— —]

7 δοὺς Migeotte   ἔδωκεν Hirschfeld, Frisch   34 συνεδριῶν Migeotte
(*lapis*) συνεδρ<ε>ιῶν Dittenberger   43 ἀ[τόκους] Migeotte   ἀ[τόκοις] others

1.

[Recommendation of the Council membe]rs: since Malousios son of Bakchios [of Gargara] continues to be a [go]od [man] to the sanctuary of Ath[ena Ilias] and the surrounding cities, and was in former times often helpf[ul to the] Council and the cities, [having given interest]-free funds both for the building[s [5] of the sanctuary and] *panegyris* and for the embassies sen[t and in the furtherance of] other advantages for the *panegyris*; and otherwise offeri[ng] ready support on every occasion [with] much goodwill, and now has given two hundred gold (sc. staters) interest-free for the latest embassy s[en]t to Antigonus and he has given to the *ep[ist]atai* and delivered to Ilium funds for [10] [the] construction of [th]e theatre, as much as they needed – 1,450 gold (sc. staters) interest-free. Since Malousios continues without hesitation on every occasion to do and say what is advantageous to the goddess and the cities: with good fortune, the Council members have decided to praise Malousios son of [15] [B]akchios of Gargara, and to crown him at the gymnic contest with a gold crown worth a thousand drachmas for his excellence toward[s] the sanctuary and the *panegyris* and Confederation of cities, and give him freedom from taxes, as has been given, and to give freedom from taxes also to his descendants, on any purchases or sale. The Gargarians are to oversee the inscription of this [20] decree on a stele and its erection in the sanctuary of Athena, so that a[ll] may know that the Confederation of cities knows how to return gratitude to those who are good men towards them.

2.

Recommendation of the Council members: since, when the Council members were dispatching ambassadors to the king o[n behalf of] [25] the freedom and autonomy of the cities who are members of the Confederation [of the] sanctuary and *panegyris*, Malousios gave funds interest-free to the messengers se[n]t – as much as the Council members requested – and also provided funds interest-free for the stage building, and furthermore provide[s] eager assistance in any matter for which the Council mig[ht c]all upon him: with good fortune, the Council members have decided to pr[a]ise [30] Malousios son of Bakchios of Gargara because he is a good man in respect [of the] sanctuary of Athena and the *panegyris* and the Confederation of cities, and to c[r]own him with a gold crown worth one thousand drachmas at the gymnic contest. This decree is to be inscribed on the stone stele that is to be erected in the sanctuar[y] on the subject of the *synedriai* (service as his city's representative on the *synedrion*, Council) of Malousios. [35] The Gargarians are to take care of it, so that everyone may know that the Confederation of cities knows how to return gratitude to those who are good men towards them.

3.

Recommendation of the Council members: since Malousios already bids the Council inform him how much money it needs from him for the theatre, the other structures, th[e] [40] sacred matters and the embassy, and says in the presence of the Cou[n]cil members he is willing to give further everything: with good fortune, the Council members have decided to inform Malousios to give the agonothetes three thousand five hundred go[ld (sc. staters)] interest-[free], along with those ow[e]d from last year, and the agonothetes should us[e] some themselves, and put [t]he r[est of the fu]nds [45] [i]n the temp[l]e. And if any is left over when [the] works [have] been put out to c[o]ntract, it is to be returned to M[alo]usios.

4.

Recommendation of the Council members: [since Ma]lousios, son of [Bak]-chios of Gargara continu[es] to be a good man [in respect of the] sanctuary of Ath[en]a Ilias and the Council, the Council memb[er]s [have deci]ded to crown Malousios with a gold cr[own worth] [50] thir[t]y gold (sc. staters); and [further] to invite h[im] by nam[e] to a seat of honou[r] at the [Panathenae]a, at the contests; and to [all]ocate [the seat of honour], both to him and his descendants. [The agono]thetes are to inscribe [this] dec[ree] and erect it in the [sa]nctuary of Athena.

5.

[Recommendation of the Coun]cil members: since Malousios contin[ues] to be a good man [in respect of the sanctuary] [55] of Athena Ilia[s] and the Confederation of citie[s and the *panegyris*]: with good fortune, [th]e Council members have decid[ed]: e[ac]h [of the cities who are members of the C]onfederation of the sanctuary a[nd th]e *panegyris* is to inscribe the honours with which [Malou]sios [has been honoured] by the Coun[ci]l and erec[t the stele where] the law states for [eac]h.

6.

(or amendment to **5**)
Simalos of Lampsak[os proposed: since Malousios] [60] of Gargara enthusiast[ically] o[ver]sees […] the expenses […] for the cities […] in order that enthusias[tic …] crow[n …]

This is the earliest evidence for the Confederation (koinon) of Athena Ilias, a political and cultic league of cities centred upon the sanctuary of Athena Ilias in Ilium. One dating of these inscriptions (above) places them in 334, making Malousios' generosity the direct result of the stimulus of Alexander and placing the start of the construction of the theatre of Ilium as early as 334. However the dominant and more likely interpretation puts the dossier in the period (from 315) during which Antigonus Monophthalmos was lord of Asia and highly active in the Troad (**Eiii**). The creation of the Confederation is generally credited to Antigonus some time before 306, largely on the basis of the traditional dating of these inscriptions and in particular the implication of **1** that he is not yet king at the time of its passing (above); and on the assumption that the energetic building programme to which they testify should date from the early years of the Confederation's existence. This building programme – with a theatre as its centrepiece – was heavily funded by an extremely wealthy individual, Malousios of Gargara, a city on the south-western coast of the Troad. It is safe to assume that the tax exemptions granted to Malousios and his descendants (on both sale and purchase: l. 19) within the wide geographical framework of the Confederation will have represented a real commercial benefit to his family.

In **1** Malousios is thanked (*inter alia*) for having just recently (perhaps around 308?) supplied the huge sum of 1,450 gold (sc. staters) interest-free 'for [the] construction of [th]e theatre (theatron)'. This was delivered to *epistatai* (ll. 10–11) – probably (Migeotte 1984, 266) a special commission charged with the construction is meant, though the agonothetes are also involved (below). Migeotte also draws attention to the detail that Malousios has ensured the delivery of this huge amount of money which, given its weight and value, would pose significant issues of logistics and security. The 'gymnic contest' at which he is to receive a gold crown will doubtless have been at the Panathenaea.

In **2**, perhaps soon after 306, Malousios gave further funds interest-free for the theatre's stage-building. No sum is specified: rather than being an editorial omission, this seems to reflect a situation in which Malousios has established a more or less open line of credit for the construction of the theatre. The fact that **1** spoke of 'the construction of the theatron' (l. 10) and **2** of the stage building (ll. 27–8) probably reflects the actual stages in the progress of the works, and suggests that by *theatron* was meant the seating and its supporting auditorium. **3** (ll. 45–6) makes it clear that the construction works were to be put out to contractors rather than conducted directly by the city of Ilium or the Confederation. It also shows the extent to which Malousios has opened his pockets, with its reference to his request to be told by the Council 'how much money it needs from him for the theatre, the other structures, the sacred matters and the embassy', and his statement 'in the presence of the Council members [that] he is willing to give further everything' (ll. 38–41). The sum thus requested was 3,500 staters (ll. 42–3). This was not it seems meant entirely for the theatre – in addition to the costs of an embassy it is also to be applied to 'other structures and the sacred matters'. These might but need not be closely related to the theatre works. Migeotte (1984, 266) notes that τὰ ἱερά 'sacred matters' (ll. 39–40) does not mean 'sacrificial victims', as some have taken it, but is a broad term for cult expenses in general.

Even though the two stated sums of interest-free credit (totalling 4,950 staters) are directed at more than the construction of the theatre, it is clear that other, unspecified, funds were sought and received for the theatre project. We can thus conclude that more than 18 talants or 108,000 dr. were spent on the Ilium theatre in the late fourth century (the sum assumes a value of ca. 22 dr. per stater at this date: Rose 2014, 167). The fact that the funds are interest-free implies that they are credit rather than an outright gift, though we might doubt whether repayment was very seriously anticipated. If it was, income from the theatre itself may have played a part in generating the requisite funds.

The funds are in any case to be managed by agonothetes (ll. 42, 44, 54), who are to disburse them on the works and guard the remainder in the temple of Athena. The Confederation's agonothetes seem to have consisted of a board of five, delegates of the five cities of the Confederation representing five geographical sectors, and responsible for the organisation of the annual Small Panathenaea, as well as a penteteric Great festival, as at Athens (Knoepfler 2010b). They are also to ensure the inscription of **4**, which grants Malousios and his descendants prohedria at the contests of a festival which, though heavily restored, will certainly be the Panathenaea (ll. 50–3).

The construction of a stage building suggests without definitively proving that the theatre was to host drama. An inscription from the last third of the third century (*IK Ilion* 2, ll. 40–2) directs the agonothetes to proclaim honours 'at the contest of tragedies and at the gymnic contest', evidently of the Panathenaea. The cultic gravity of Athena was so strong here that drama was performed at her Panathenaea, and not for Dionysus. The suggestion that it might have focused on Homeric subjects (Rose 2014, 167) that could be made to serve the propagandistic needs of the city, the new Confederation and its overlords, might be dismissed as a pleasing fancy, were it not that the audience sat in the theatre in blocks named after local civic tribes, which were themselves named after Homeric heroes such as Deiphobus, Panthoos, Assarakos (grandfather of Anchises) and Alexander (Paris) (Rose 2014, 105, 159, 167, 241 on the balustrade inscribed with these names; *SEG* 44, 982). The glory of Homeric tradition was one of the new Confederation's great resources, and the 'theatre of Troy' may well have been designed as a place to celebrate and communicate its power.

On the remains of the theatre, which had a capacity of around 10,000 (Sear 2006, 356) see Rose (2014, 163–7).

Eiii: Scepsis. A decree concerning the funding of performances for Dionysus and of repairs to the theatre, ca. 300 (Wilhelm 1900, 57 placed the inscription by its letter forms no later than the 3rd c., and considered a 4th-c. date possible; the name Leukios, l. 5, led Schliemann and Judeich to put it in the 2nd–1st c., but this argument has no force as the name is attested in a number of Greek cities from the 6th c.).

Small slab of white marble, probably part of a stele (below on l. 1).
Found in Scepsis (modern Kursunlu Tepe): Schliemann 1884, 262.
Presumed to be in the Çannakale Museum as part of the Calvert donation.
Schliemann 1884, 262–3 no. 24 (from a squeeze provided by Calvert); Judeich 1898, 236; Wilhelm 1900, 54–8 (from squeezes provided by Reichel and Calvert, in whose house in the Dardanelles the stone was kept at that time); a new edition is in progress.
Text: based on Wilhelm 1900.

        ἱερὰ Διονύσου·
    [φ]ρατρίου τριακάδι· ἐπρυτάνευον Σκα-
    μάνδριος Ἡρακλείδου, Διονύσιος Βάκχο-
    υ, Μιλήσιος Ἀνδρηράτου, Ἡρακλείδης Ἀπ[ε]-
5   λλικῶντος· ἐπεστάτει Λεύκιος Μιλησί[ου],
    ἐγραμμάτευε Σιμίας Σιμίου· ἐβασίλευε Μη[τ]-
    ρόδωρος Μίμαντος· Ἡρακλείδης Ἄβαντος [εἶ]-
    πεν· ἀγαθῆι τύχηι συντετάχθαι περὶ τῶν χορ[ῶ]-

[ν] ὅπως καθ᾽ ἕκαστον ἔτος ἡ πόλις ποῆι τῶι Διον-

10 [ύ]σωι θέαν· τὸ δὲ ἀργύριον εἶναι τὸ εἰς τὴν θέαν

τὸ περιγιγνόμενον ἀπὸ τῶν ἱερείων ἑκάστου ἔτ[ο]-

[υ]ς στατῆρας διακοσίους· κατασκευάσαι δὲ κα[ὶ τ]-

[ὸ] θέατρον καὶ ἀνελεῖν τοὺς ἀρχαίους βασμοὺς

καὶ ἀναχῶσαι ὡς κάλλιστα· καὶ ὅσος μὲν ἂν το[ῦ]

15 ὑπάρχοντος λίθου χρήσιμος ἦι εἰς τοὺς βασμο[ὺ]-

ς καὶ τἄλλα, τούτωι χρήσασθαι. τὸ δὲ λοιπὸν ἐπιτ[ε]-

λεῖν καθ᾽ ἕκαστον ἔτος ἀπὸ τοῦ ἀργυρίου τοῦ περ[ι]-

[γ]ινομένου ἀπὸ τῆς θέας. κατασκευάσαι δὲ καὶ τ[ὸ]

[πρ]οσκήνιον ὡς ἂν δοκῇι τοῖς ἀποδειχθεῖσι· οἰκο[δο]-

20 μῆσαι δὲ καὶ τὸ τειχίον τὸ ἐπάνω τοῦ θεάτρου ἀπ[ὸ]

τοῦ πύργου ἕως τῶν Σκαμανδρίου οἰκιῶν καὶ ν-

ῆσαι τετράπηχυ καὶ γεῖσον εἶναι. τὸ δὲ πέρ[υ]-

σι καὶ τὸ τρίτον ἔτος περιγενόμενον ἀργύριον ἀ-

πὸ τῶν ἱερείων ἀναλίσκειν εἴς τε τὴν ἀνά[χωσι]-

25 ν τοῦ θεάτρου καὶ τὴν ἄλλην ἐπισκευήν· ἂν δέ [τι]

ἐλλείπηι, διδόναι τὸν ταμίαν· μὴ ἐξεῖ[ναι δὲ τοῦτ]-

ο τἀργύριον εἰς μηθὲν ἄλλο κατ[αναλίσκειν ἢ καθ]-

άπερ συντέτα{τα}κται· ἂν δέ [τίς . . . . παρὰ]

τὰ γεγραμμένα ΟΙ . [. . . . .]

30 [. . . . . .]ήκοντα [. . . . .]

1–2 Wilhelm   ἱερὰ Διονύσου· μηνὸς [   ]|βατρίου τριακάδι Judeich   3–4
Wilhelm   Βάκο|υ Judeich   4 end Wilhelm   Ἀ<π>ε- Judeich   5 end
Judeich   ΜΙΛΗΣΙ[ΟΣ] Schliemann   7–8 Wilhelm   [ἔλε]|ξεν Judeich   20–1
Wilhelm   <κ>αὶ | [τ]οῦ Judeich   24–6 Wilhelm   εἴς τε τὴν ἀναχρ[είαν] | τοῦ θεάτρου
καὶ εἰς ἄλλην ἐπισκευὴν ἂν [τι] | ἐλλείπηι διδόναι τὸν ταμίαν· Judeich

(The stele is) sacred to Dionysus. On the thirtieth of the (month) Phratrios; the
prytaneis were Skamandrios son of Herakleides; Dionysios son of Bakchos;
Milesios son of Andreratos; Herakleides son of [5] Ap[e]llikon; the *epistates* was
Leukios son of Miles[ios]; the secretary was Simias son of Simias; the *basileus*
was Me[t]rodoros son of Mimas; Herakleides son of Abas [made the pr]oposal:
with good fortune, arrangements have been made concerning the chor[uses],
so that each year the city should hold a show for [10] Dion[y]sus. The money for
the show is to be revenue from the sacrifices, each y[e]ar two hundred staters.
And furth[er the] theatron is to be refurbished, the old steps taken up and in-
filled as well as possible. Any of th[e] [15] existing stone that might be useful for
the steps and the rest is to be used. Henceforward it is to be accomplished each
year from the money coming in from the show. And further th[e pr]oskenion is
to be refurbished as seems appropriate to those who are appointed. And [20] further the wall above the theatron is to be built, fro[m] the tower to the buildings

of Skamandrios, and it is to be built up to a height of four cubits and to have
a coping. The money from the sacrifices of last year and the year before is to
be spent on the in[fillin]g [25] of the theatron and the other repair work. If there
is [any] shortfall, the treasurer is to give it. It is not allow[ed] to s[pend thi]s
money on anything [other than] as has been specified. If [anyone … against]
what has been written […]

Scepsis was a city in the interior of the north-west region of the Troad, on the site of a
large hill (modern Kursunlu Tepe) at the foothills of Mt Ida, from whose pines the city may
have derived much wealth. It had an extensive territory in the plain around the basin of
the upper Scamander River. The people of Scepsis are said to have moved to this site at an
unknown date from an 'old Scepsis' in the highest parts of Ida (Str. 13.1.51–52, writing on
the authority of the local Demetrius of Scepsis, 2nd c.). The arrival of Milesians to join the
city (probably after 494) seems to have been treated as a refoundation, and after this date
the city was, according to Strabo, a democracy (13.1.52; traces of the Milesian element can
be seen in the names of two men in the decree, ll. 4–5). From at least 453/2 to 441/0 – and
probably rather later – Scepsis was a tribute-paying member of the Delian League, and
intermittently from the late fifth into the fourth century under Persian control.

  The first line was apparently inscribed in slightly larger letters (Wilhelm 1900, 55) and
serves as a heading for the whole. The word 'stele' is almost certainly to be understood –
giving us an idea of the original form of the stone, the whereabouts of which are not
known. The phrase '(The stele is) sacred to Dionysus' consecrates the stone to the god
whose cult is its concern, and has a striking parallel from fifth-century Ikarion (**III Miii**),
where financial and administrative matters to do with the theatrical festival of Dionysus
are also at issue. Although there is no formal statement to the effect (such as 'the People
decided'), it is abundantly clear from the presence of the full panoply of civic officials in
the preamble (ll. 2–7) that this inscription is a decree of the People of Scepsis, based on the
proposal of Herakleides son of Abas (l. 7; whether he bears any relation to the two other
Herakleideis mentioned in the prescript cannot be determined).

  The decree treats the funding of an annual 'show for Dionysus', and of fairly extensive repair works to the theatre; perhaps also of ongoing maintenance. Its telegraphic style
leaves quite a lot unclear. The first part seems to indicate that the city had at some time in
the past made arrangements for holding an annual 'show for Dionysus' (ll. 8–10). This is
how we interpret the force of the perfect tense συντετάχθαι 'arrangements have been made'
(though Meier 2012, 328 argues that the reference is not to a pre-existing law but to a draft
resolution of this decree). These arrangements were apparently in a 'law concerning choruses' (συντάσσω is often used of prescriptions encoded in law: e.g. *Milet* I 3, 145, ll. 79–80).
The language might imply purely choral performances were it not for the fact that the theatre had a stage building, so the festival probably included drama (Slater 2011, 284). The
existence of such a law puts the date at which Scepsis held a Dionysia with a 'show' back
some years before the (uncertain) date of this decree. It also indicates that arrangements
were in place to cover the organisation, including presumably the cost, of choruses. It follows as very likely that the choruses at the Scepsis Dionysia were made up of locals (**V E**).

That the cult of Dionysus was prominent in Scepsis is further clear from contemporary coins (Judeich 1898, 235) and perhaps incidentally from the name of one of the prytaneis of our decree, Dionysios son of Bakchos (ll. 3–4). It certainly remained important in the second century, which is the (uncertain) date given to a decree regulating the sale of the priesthood of Dionysos (?) Bambyleios (*SEG* 26, 1334): the priest is to wear an ivy crown on (among other occasions) the first of the month of Lenaion and 'at all the publically funded festivals' (ll. 8–10). The Dionysia will be one such festival, for the present decree shows that it falls into that category. The priest is also permitted 'to wear a golden crown and purple robes and shoes matching his clothes' (ll. 10–12), which may reflect the privileges or simply the habits of the *Technitai* of Dionysus (Artem. 2.3). The later inscription also shows that the theatre remained operative in the second century, for the priest of Dionysus in Scepsis is to have 'a seat set for [h]im in the theatre and he shall sit in [prohed]ria at the triennial festivals and at the panegyris' (ll. 14–17 τίθεσθαι δ[ὲ | αὐ]τῷ καὶ θρόνον ἐν τῷ θεάτρῳ καὶ καθῆσθαι αὐτὸν ἐν | [προεδ]ρίᾳ ἔν τε ταῖς τριετηρίσιν καὶ ἐν τῇ πανηγύρει ἡ σ[υν|τελεῖται]). Even though the reference is to prohedria and thus not easily generalisable to the rest of the theatre, the fact that a seat needs to be placed for the priest (physical placement rather than notional 'setting aside' seems to be implied) suggests that there was no permanent prohedria and offers some support for the view that the *basmoi* mentioned in our decree are foundation blocks or low steps upon which benchwork or cushions were placed, rather than 'seats' as such.

The decree proper begins by indicating how the show for Dionysus is to be funded: from a sum of 200 staters (perhaps around 4,400 dr.) generated each year 'from the *hiera*' (ll. 10–12 τὸ περιγιγνόμενον ἀπὸ τῶν ἱερείων), a phrase that most probably refers to the sale of sacrificial meat and hides (Migeotte 1995, 84; Slater 2011, 284; parallels for the expression: Meier 2012, 330). Slater would confine the sacrifices to those for Dionysus, meaning that 'the theatre improvement was meant to be self-funding', but that probably imposes an overly ambitious target and it is more likely that the funding of the festival is produced by income derived from a variety of cults. What items are meant to be covered by this money is unclear. We might guess at choruses, actors and perhaps more sacrificial victims. And the show itself is to generate an income, for the Scepsians charge money for it (ll. 17–18). There is no indication that this is a novel feature introduced by this decree. The fundamental funding model for the Scepsian Dionysia thus seems to be based on the provision of the necessary up-front funds 'from the *hiera*' with an income anticipated 'from the show' (note the parallel budgetary description for the latter of τὸ περιγιγνόμενον ἀπὸ τῆς θέας).

This decree is principally concerned with works needed on the theatre (below). These are to be funded from an accumulation of two years of income from the *hiera* (ll. 22–5), though if this is inadequate, public funds are to make up the deficiency (ll. 25–6). And it appears that some work is to be achieved with income 'from the show', too (ll. 16–17). Given that the works are substantial, it is probable that the two years of funds earmarked for them are not capped by the 200 stater annual allocation. And the fact that this accumulated income is available at all indicates that the festival – or at least its 'show' element – has almost certainly not been held for the last two years. Whether that is because the theatre was in no state to be used, perhaps because of earthquake damage or general neglect, or for some other reason entirely (below), is unclear. Whatever the reason, it appears that there has been a period during which the Scepsians have not been able to fulfil their own requirement to have a choral show for Dionysus each year, and that this decree remedies the situation.

Some 17 lines (ll. 12–28) are occupied with instructions for the works to be completed on the theatre and their financing. The fact that the (stone) theatre is in need of repair shows that it was far from new at the time the decree was passed (or damaged by earthquake). The verb κατασκευάσαι must mean 'refurbish' in l. 12 (but see below on its use in l. 18), since this is not construction *de novo* as old *basmoi* are being replaced, and ἐπισκευή (l. 25) is often used for repair work on sanctuaries, statues and the like.

The areas of work are the theatron (ll. 12–18) the proskenion (ll. 18–19) and a wall above the theatre (ll. 19–22). The work on the theatron involves the removal of 'the old *basmoi*', consolidation of their earthen support and construction of new *basmoi*, using where possible the stone from the old. We are left to deduce that new *basmoi* are to be built from the instructions about the reuse of the stone 'for the *basmoi* and the rest' (ll. 15–16; Meier 2012, 96–9 on the phenomenon of recycling building materials in Greek public building; **Ci**). These *basmoi* are evidently the stone 'steps' of the theatron (Hellmann 1992, 68 on the term, used from the early Hellenistic period for the steps of a building's foundation, and of an independent step or set of steps). It is hard to judge whether they are what we would call the 'seats' of the theatre or, more probably, as Slater (2011, 284) has convincingly argued, the low foundation blocks or revetments placed into an earthen slope upon which wooden seats, benchwork or cushions were to be set. Nor is it clear whether the entire theatron is affected, or just part. The directive in l. 13 could be to remove *all* the old seating of the theatre, or just a particular set – 'the old ones'. Given that the reason for the renovation seems to be subsidence or erosion of the earth below the theatron, the latter seems more likely. The fact that ἀρχαῖος can mean 'worn out' (LSJ s.v. I 4) makes it virtually certain. The action of 'infilling' or 'piling up' (l. 14 ἀναχῶσαι; restored with some hesitation by Wilhelm in ll. 24–5 ἀνά[χωσι]|ν; Hellmann 1992, 437 on the term) refers to the business of consolidating the earth (Slater 2011, 284–5). This may have been necessitated by ordinary geomorphological processes or by more radical damage such as that caused by earthquake (common in the region) or flooding. Our translation of ll. 16–18 'Henceforward it is to be accomplished each year from the money coming in from the show' understands this as a reference to the completion of the work on the theatron, or more probably – given the reference to 'each year' – to its ongoing maintenance, from a different funding source, namely the show itself.

The verb κατασκευάσαι used in the sense of 'refurbish' in l. 12 appears again in l. 18 with reference to the proskenion. It seems *prima facie* likely that it would have the same meaning so soon after, in which case the theatre was not being furnished with a proskenion anew but having its existing one refurbished or repaired. But the work involved was certainly significant and there is some reason to think that this may be entirely new construction. It is clear at any rate that the technical work associated with the proskenion is to be assigned to a special commission of men who are separately tasked with making all the necessary decisions in regard to it (l.19). This further shows that the present document is the general enabling decree, not the detailed contract of works (cf.

III Wvi). Slater (2011, 284) is probably right to suggest that all the work was given out to contractors.

The final item of works is the construction of a wall 'above the theatre'. This is once again perhaps more likely to be a rebuild rather than a completely new construction, despite the use of the simple verb 'build' (οἰκο[δο]μῆσαι ll. 19–20). The use of the article ('*the* wall' τὸ τειχίον l. 20) suggests a wall already known. It may have suffered the same fate of neglect or ruin that affected the adjacent theatre. Given our ignorance of the topography of the ancient city we cannot say anything with confidence about the size or function of this wall. But it will not, as Meier (2012, 328) suggests, be integral with the proskenion, for 'above the theatron' means at the high point above the back of the theatre, not near the stage (thus Slater 2011, 284). The description of the wall as extending from 'the tower to the buildings of Skamandrios' might imply a wall between a defensive tower (perhaps itself part of the city walls?) and some well-known feature of the urban environment, 'the buildings of Skamandrios'. It seems a plausible guess from its location above the theatre and its association with the other works that the wall played some structural role in relation to the theatre – perhaps as part of or in association with a retaining wall. The addition of a coping (*geison*) suggests it was on show. It would be interesting to know whether the Skamandrios in question was the same as one of the three prytaneis (ll. 2–3) under whose leadership this scheme took shape.

Although we know so little about the history of Scepsis, one possible historical context in which the renovation of the city's theatre and dramatic festival makes sense is the period during which the whole area of the Troad, Scepsis included, was seeking to establish relations with Antigonus Monophthalmos, the new superpower of the early Hellenistic period. For a similar possible context for the construction of a theatre in another city in the area see **Eii**. An inscribed letter from Antigonus found in Scepsis announces the conclusion of peace between himself and Cassander, Ptolemy and Lysimachus in 311 (*OGIS* 5) and in the same year the People of Scepsis respond by honouring Antigonus, resolving among other things to set up a sanctuary, altar, statue and annual festival for him, 'just as it was even formerly carried out' (*OGIS* 6). Perhaps they planned to add honours for Antigonus to their Dionysia. Alternatively, the city of Scepsis was probably abandoned during the period from ca. 306–301 when it was part of the city Antigoneia (later, Alexandreia Troas) formed by Antigonus through synoecism of a number of cities in the region (Str. 13.1.33; Cohen 1995, 145–6). Perhaps this is the explanation of the need to refurbish the theatre and plan for the future funding of its dramatic performances.

Eiv: Aeolis (Region) and Cyme

1. **Polyaenus, *Strategems* 6.10**. Written early 160s AD, referring to an event in (probably) 399 or (less likely) 391. The likely context is the first mission of the Spartan general Thibron in Asia Minor, sent in 399 to aid the Ionian Greeks against Tissaphernes. Two features of this campaign suggest its relevance: it involved a number of Aeolian cities (X. *HG* 3.1.4–7); and Xenophon, whose veterans of the march of the 10,000 joined Thibron, says that Thibron allowed his army to plunder the allies (*HG* 3.1–2). Thibron

was sent to Asia Minor a second time (summer 391) to pursue hostilities against the satrap of Ionia, Strouthas (see **2**). Text: Melber and Woelfflin.

Ἀλέξανδρος φρούραρχος τῶν περὶ τὴν Αἰολίδα χωρίων, μισθωσάμενος τῶν ἀπ' Ἰωνίας τοὺς ἀρίστους ἀγωνιστάς, αὐλητὰς μὲν Θέρσανδρον καὶ Φιλόξενον, ὑποκριτὰς δὲ Καλλιππίδην καὶ Νικόστρατον, θέαν ἐπήγγειλε. πρὸς μὲν τὴν δόξαν τῶν ἀγωνιστῶν συνέδραμον ἐκ τῶν πλησίον πόλεων ἅπαντες. ἐπεὶ δὲ πλῆρες τὸ θέατρον ἦν, περιστήσας τοὺς στρατιώτας καὶ τοὺς βαρβάρους, μεθ' ὧν ἐφρούρει τὰ χωρία, πάντας τοὺς θεατὰς συλλαβὼν αὐτοῖς παισὶ καὶ γυναιξὶ, λύτρα μεγάλα λαβὼν τοὺς μὲν ἀπέλυσεν, αὐτὸς δὲ τὰ χωρία Θίβρωνι παραδοὺς ἀπηλλάγη.

Alexander, a garrison commander of the territories in Aeolis, proclaimed a show, hiring the best performers from among those from Ionia – the pipers Thersandros and Philoxenos, and the actors Kallippides and Nikostratos. The eminence of the performers drew the entire populace from the cities nearby. When the theatre was full, Alexander surrounded it with his own soldiers and the barbarians with whom he guarded the region, and seized the spectators, along with their children and wives. After receiving large sums in ransom he released them, and he himself handed over the region to Thibron and departed.

2. Xenophon, *Hellenica* 4.8.18–19. Written perhaps in the 350s, referring to persons and events in 391 of which Xenophon had close personal knowledge. Text: Marchant.

προϊόντος δὲ τοῦ χρόνου κατανοήσας ὁ Στρούθας ὅτι Θίβρων βοηθοίη ἑκάστοτε ἀτάκτως καὶ καταφρονητικῶς, ἔπεμψεν ἱππέας εἰς τὸ πεδίον καὶ καταδραμόντας ἐκέλευσε περιβαλλομένους ἐλαύνειν ὅ τι δύναιντο. ὁ δὲ Θίβρων ἐτύγχανεν ἐξ ἀρίστου διασκηνῶν μετὰ Θερσάνδρου τοῦ αὐλητοῦ. ἦν γὰρ ὁ Θέρσανδρος οὐ μόνον αὐλητὴς ἀγαθός, [19] ἀλλὰ καὶ ἀλκῆς [ἰσχύος], ἄτε λακωνίζων, ἀντεποιεῖτο. ὁ δὲ Στρούθας, ἰδὼν ἀτάκτως τε βοηθοῦντας καὶ ὀλίγους τοὺς πρώτους, ἐπιφαίνεται πολλούς τε ἔχων καὶ συντεταγμένους ἱππέας. καὶ Θίβρωνα μὲν καὶ Θέρσανδρον πρώτους ἀπέκτειναν·

διασκηνῶν codd.   δισκεύων Riekher

But as time went on, Strouthas, who had observed that each of Thibron's military efforts was carried out in a disorderly and disdainful manner, sent cavalry to the plain and ordered them to rush upon the enemy and surround and carry off whatever they could. It happened that Thibron was retiring in his tent (or with Riekher's emendation 'was engaged in throwing the discus') after the morning meal with Thersandros the piper. For Thersandros was not only a good piper, [19] but also made some claim to prowess as the active partner in anal sex (or ' but also laid claim to physical strength, inasmuch as he was an imitator of things Lacedaemonian'). Strouthas, seeing that the enemy was making

> its sortie in disorder, and that the foremost of them were few in number, ap-
> peared upon the scene with a large force of cavalry, drawn up in good order.
> And the first they killed were Thibron and Thersandros.

The identity of the Alexander in **1** is unknown, but the story recorded of him is more plausible than might at first appear. The line between brigandage and legitimate fiscal activity
was sometimes fine and the historical record attests to the particular difficulties faced by
Greek commanders in raising money for their armies in this field of action at this period
(Azoulay 2004, 208; **Eviii** reports a not dissimilar fund-raising strategy adopted by the
Macedonian satrap of Caria). Under these circumstances, the idea of investing in a costly
theatrical performance that would attract the interest of many from local cities in the neighbourhood of the garrison in order to extort under threat of force an extraordinary 'payment'
for the show does not ring entirely untrue.

Historical veracity is also urged by the association between Thibron and one of the
performers, Thersandros the piper (Stefanis no. 1193), attested by Xenophon (**2**), who was
close to the events and their principals. In 391 Thersandros is found in the company of
Thibron in the region of Ephesus just prior to the failure of his second mission to Asia and
death. If **1** is to be placed in 391, it seems likely that Thibron took the piper with him when
the region around Aeolis was handed over to him by Alexander (Aneziri 2003, 257 suggests that the piper was also subject to capture and ransom, but **1** is explicit on the point that
it was the spectators, not the performers, who were detained). But on the more likely dating
of **1** to 399 in the context of Thibron's first Asian campaign, the fact that the 'Ionian' piper
and the Spartan general are found together eight years earlier still provides some context
for this later familiarity. (The alternative – that the story in **1** was invented to explain the
relationship attested by Xenophon – can probably be dismissed.)

2 has various problems of text and interpretation, but Hindley (1994) has very plausibly
resolved these, most importantly by defending the transmitted διασκηνῶν 'retiring in his
tent' over Riekher's emendation δισκεύων 'throwing the discus' (there is no obvious irregularity in the manuscripts). The result is a report that 'Thibron was retiring in his tent after the
morning meal with Thersandros the piper. For Thersandros was not only a good piper, but
also made some claim to prowess as the active partner in anal sex' (taking λακωνίζων in this
sense, paralleled, if infrequently, in Classical texts, and attributed to it by lexicographers).
Xenophon's wider moral point is that his lack of self-control led to Thibron's downfall. The
fact that the piper Thersandros – apparently a 'soft' Ionian – was in the sexually domineer-
ing position over a male Spartiate adds further bite to the sketch (Azoulay 2004, 382).

There are a number of remarkable features about the theatrical event organised by
Alexander. Although it attracted spectators from neighbouring cities, it seems to have
been designed (also) for Alexander's own troops – a 'mixed' population of Greeks and
non-Greeks, it is worth noting. This makes it a precursor by some decades of the habit
attested with Philip (**VI F**) of providing theatrical entertainments to his troops. It is also
quite early evidence for the practice of hiring a theatrical 'troupe' entirely from an external provider. The performance may have consisted primarily or solely of tragedy, the two
pipers Thersandros and Philoxenos (Stefanis no. 2539) perhaps engaged to provide musical support to the tragedies acted by the celebrities Kallippides (Stefanis no. 1348) and

Nikostratos (Stefanis no. 1861; Braund 2000; Csapo 2002). The involvement of supporting actors (in the employ of the protagonists?) or of choruses can only be guessed at.

Kallippides and Nikostratos were two of the most successful and celebrated tragic actors of their day, the last decades of the fifth and the early years of the fourth century. Kallippides was victorious five times at the Athenian Lenaea (*IG* II² 2325H, l. 7 M-O), one of them in 418 (*IG* II² 2319 col. 3, ll. 16–17 M-O). Nikostratos, perhaps slightly younger than Kallippides, is probably to be restored among the victors in tragic acting at the Great Dionysia recorded in the Athenian Victors' Lists (*IG* II² 2325B col. 2, l. 22 M-O) and appears to have won at least one victory at the Lenaea around the mid 410s (*IG* II² 2325H, l. 8 M-O; Millis and Olson 2012, 154). He was also the likely victor at the Athenian Dionysia in the year 399 (*IG* II² 2318, l. 864 M-O), which will have made him particularly sought after at the time of **1** and provide a *terminus post quem* for the event in Aeolis, spring 399.

Kallippides and Nikostratos were recognised by Philodemus as 'everything in tragedy' (*Rh.* col. 15a, 3–10). The fact that Philodemus treated them as a pair is suggestive, in light of their appearance together in **1**. Perhaps this is evidence of a more regular practice of combining their professional skills to offer theatrical services. (On the other hand, Philodemus' words may suggest that they were the stereotypical tragic superstars of their age, and so their paired presence in **1** could be the result of little or nothing more than such received tradition, thus diminishing rather than enhancing the plausibility of the account.)

The expression used of the performers at Alexander's event, describing them as 'from among those from Ionia' τῶν ἀπ' Ἰωνίας τοὺς ἀρίστους ἀγωνιστάς, has some affinity with the nomenclature of the 'koinon of the Artists of Dionysus in Ionia and the Hellespont' κοινὸν τῶν περὶ τὸν Διόνυσον τεχνιτῶν ἐπ' Ἰωνίας καὶ Ἑλλησπόντου, whose activities are first attested over a century later, in the second half of the third century (*ATD* I, 199–291). The affinity persists, despite **1**'s use of the phrase '*from* Ionia' ἀπ' Ἰωνίας rather than the later Union's '*in* Ionia' ἐπ' Ἰωνίας. It might be explained by anachronistic contamination in Polyaenus' source(s) (and in support of such an argument one might also point to the expression θέαν ἐπήγγειλε 'proclaimed a show', a quasi-technical term for the proclamation of games by sending of ambassadors that becomes common only from the third century). But it is perhaps more likely to reflect the inherent unity of 'Ionia' as a geographical and organisational term. At any rate it provides a broad ethnic identity to these four performers, whose home cities are not otherwise attested.

The site of the performance was evidently the non-urban garrison, and the 'theatre' in question ('when the theatre was full' ἐπεὶ δὲ πλῆρες τὸ θέατρον ἦν) will hardly have been a permanent structure, just as the performance itself, so far as we can tell, was an *ad hoc* event, not part of a cyclical festival, or indeed of any festival at all. But a large city in the south of Aeolis – Cyme – and Phocaea, not far distant in Ionia (**Ev**), seem to have had permanent theatres in the fourth century. The important coastal city of Cyme had been a dependent polis in the Persian Empire and subsequently a member of the Delian League, and had a democratic constitution at least for some of the fifth century (Arist. *Pol.* 1304b39–5a1). Preliminary excavation under the Roman theatre has found evidence of a Hellenistic phase thought to date to the second half of the fourth century, notably in the form of a wall that marks the curve of the orchestra; part of the eastern retaining wall; and part of the central theatron (some eleven steps). Architectural fragments found nearby derive from an architrave decorated with Dionysiac and theatrical motifs – masks and heads of silens (Lagona 1993, 278–80; 2007, 10). Inscriptions dating to around 275 allude to the exist-ence of a combined Dionysia and Antiocheia in honour of the god and monarch, which is likely to have involved theatrical performances (Manganaro 2000; Le Guen 2010, 507). A decree from Bargylia mandates the proclamation of honours for a judge from Cyme at the Cyme Dionysia at the beginning of the third (Reinach) or in the second (Pappadopoulos-Kerameus) century (*IK Kyme* 2, l. 17; see also *IK Kyme* 89) and in the mid third century prohedria is one of the suite of awards on offer to benefactors (*IK Kyme* 4, l. 6).

Ev: Phocaea

1. Honorary decree of the Council and People of Priene for judges from Phocaea, Nisyros and Astypalaea. Hiller (*IPriene* 14; cf. 308) argued for a likely (earliest) date of ca. 328/7 by prosopographical links to other early plausibly datable decrees and letter forms. Crowther (1996) has persuasively argued for the end of the year 286/5 on the grounds of the very expansive chancellery style, the apicated lettering and a revision of the dates of known eponyms. He places it in a context following the incursions made into Ionia by Demetrius the Besieger and suggests that the juridical services provided by the other cities for Priene may have treated claims arising from the disruptions by warfare of normal credit relations. Blümel and Merkelbach in *IK Priene* suggest ca. 330–300 or 286/5. Each of the judges and each of their home cities are to be awarded a gold crown (ll. 25–6). Our first excerpt (ll. 26–9) gives directions for the announcement of the crowns at the tragic contest of the Dionysia in Priene (**Evii**); while the second (ll. 43–52) gives directions for the delivery of the crowns to the home cities of the judges and their an-nouncement at the tragic contest of those cities' respective Dionysia (**D Introduction**). At l. 35 the judges are among other honours granted 'prohedr[i]a at the contes[t]s' in Priene.

Two large contiguous fragments (A: upper + B: lower) of a marble stele.
A: 0.515 × 0.52 × 0.05 m; B: 0.55 × 1.30 × 0.15 m.
A: found in the temple of Asclepius at Priene; B: found on a street of stairs leading up to the west from the Athena terrace.
In situ in September 1990 (Crowther 1996, 234); Priene Inv. 163 (A); 234 (B).
IPriene 8 + p. 308; (cf. *SEG* 4, 471); Crowther 1996, 234–8 = *SEG* 46, 1481; *IK Priene* 107.
Text: *IK Priene* 107.   Photos: Crowther 1996, pls. 5ac (squeezes).

26   [τῆς δὲ ἀναγγε]-
λίας τοῦ στεφάνου τὴν ἐπιμέλειαμ ποιήσασθαι [τὸν ἀγωνο]-
θέτην τοῖς πρώτ[οι]ς Δ[ιο]υσίοις τραγωιδῶ[ν τ]ῶ[ι ἀγῶνι, δη]-
λοῦντα διὰ τῆς ἀναγ[γελ]ίας τὰς αἰτίας [δι'] ἃ[ς στεφανοῦνται]·

43   ἑλέσθαι δὲ
καὶ πρεσβευτὴν ἐξ ἁπάντων τῶμ πολιτῶν εἰς ἑκάστη[ν]
45   πόλιν ἄνδρα ἕνα, ὅστις παραγενόμενος οὖ ἂν αἱρεθῆι τό
τε ψήφισμα ἀποδώσει καὶ τὸν στέφανον τῶι δικαστηρίω[ι]
καὶ αἰτήσεται τὴμ βουλὴγ καὶ τ[ὸ]ν δῆμον ἀναγγελίαν τοῦ
στεφάνου δοῦναι Διον[υ]σίοις ἐν τῶι ἀγ[ῶ]νι τῶν τραγωιδ[ῶ]ν,

καθότι καὶ Πριηνεῖς παρ᾽ αὐτοῖς ἐψηφι[σμ]έ[ν]ọι εἰσίν· καὶ τὸ [ψή]-
50   φισμα τόδε ἀναγράψαι εἰς ọτήλ[η]ν λ[ιθί]νην κạὶ στῆσαι εἰς [τὸ]
ἱερόν, οὗ ἂν τῶι δήμωι τῶι ἀποστείλαντι [τ]ọὺ[ς] δικαστὰς ἐπ[ι]-
τήδειον εἶναι φαίνηται·

[26] … [the agonothe]te is to take care of [the announce]ment of the crown at
the firs[t] (= 'next') D[io]nysia, [at t]h[e contest] of the tragedies, mak[ing c]
lear by means of the announ[cem]ent the grounds [for] wh[ich they are being
crowned].

[43] … And also to elect an ambassador from all the citizens – one man for
each [45] city – who, when he arrives at whichever place for which he has been
selected, shall hand over both the decree and the crown to the court, and ask
the Co[u]ncil and t[h]e People to make the announcement of the crown at the
Dion[y]sia, during the con[t]est of tragedies, just as the Prienians had also voted among themselves; and to inscribe [50] this [de]cree on a st[on]e [s]tel[e] and
set it in [the] sanctuary, wherever seems fitting to the people who dispatched
[t]he judges.

2. An inscription from the theatre of Phocaea indicating tribal seating, 'Hellenistic' date (Özyiğit 1993, 3); 2nd c. (Ma 2000, 116).

Inscribed over three stone blocks in front of a passageway (diazoma) in the theatron uncovered
in excavation in 1991.
In situ (Ma 2000, 116).
Özyiğit 1993, 3; *SEG* 43, 873.
Text: *SEG* 43, 873.   Photos: Özyiğit 1993, photos 6–7.

φυλὴ [Τ]ευθα[δέων]

ΦΥΛΗ ΕΥΘΑ[........] Özyiğit

Tribe of [T]eutha[deis]

The discovery of the theatre of Phocaea of ca. 340–330 by Ömer Özyiğit in 1991 marks an
extremely important event in the history of the theatre in East Greece, for it further erodes
the established view that theatre came to Asia Minor only in the wake of Alexander's conquest (**E Introduction**). Just before an apartment development was to be constructed on
the spot, Özyiğit uncovered the remains of a heavily damaged stone theatre on the north-
west slope of the Değirmenli hill to the east of Foça (ancient Phocaea). He had already
made the dramatic discovery of some 5 km of the course of the great Archaic city walls,
including a city gate that showed all the devastation wrought on it by the Persian attack of
546 (and in it, the most ancient catapult stone whose date is known: Özyiğit 2003, 116). He
correctly concluded that the site of the Değirmenli hill within the walls was the likely place
to find a theatre and proceeded to conduct excavation in two distinct areas, the theatron and
the northern analemma wall.

In the theatron several rows of seats were uncovered, as well as an access staircase ca. 0.95 m wide and part of an associated diazoma some 1.47 m wide (Özyiğit 1993, 2–4 with photos 2–7). The seats had been fitted onto the carved bedrock and, though not in good condition, provided examples with a sufficiently clear profile to demonstrate considerable similarity to that of seating from the Erythraean theatre (Özyiğit 1993, 7 with figs. 1–2). The inscription **2** was found extending over three blocks of an area in front of a walkway between sections of seats (diazoma). Özyiğit (1993, 3) describes the inscription as of 'Hellenistic' date, while Ma (2000, 116) after autopsy inspection declares it to be second century. It thus seems not to be contemporary with the main construction of the theatron (below), but indicates that at least by the second century the Phocaeans sat in their theatre in tribal formation (the tribe Teuthadeis was already attested by *CIG* 3415).

Separate excavation exposed a 5.10 m long stretch of the analemma wall to the north, 2.10 m in width (Özyiğit 1993, figs. 3–6, photos 9–12). A possible side entrance that had been closed at a later date was identified in this wall. The ceramic remains found in the wall included a majority of sixth-century Orientalising and East Greek-style skyphoi, oinochoai and plates, along with some Attic, Corinthian and Chian materials of the same period. In the original fill of the wall were found some sixth- but mostly fifth-century pottery fragments. A single piece of ca. 400 was the latest in date to be found, implying to the excavator that the construction of the analemma wall must date after ca. 400. One might however consider the possibility that this single late fifth-century sherd is an outrider and that the weight of this evidence in fact tends towards a somewhat earlier fifth-century date for the wall, and thus for the first shaped theatron. The use of quite small stones for the construction of the wall also suggested an early date to Özyiğit.

It would be entirely in keeping with what is known of theatre construction if the building of the stone seating followed that of the analemma walls by a considerable period, with wooden seating used on the (perhaps already shaped) slope of the hill in the meantime. A number of coins of ca. 350–300 were found in the original fill under the seats. Comparison of the seating profile with that from the theatre of Erythrae leads Özyiğit to believe that the Phocaean theatre is the older. He would date the Erythraean theatre to possibly the last quarter of the fourth century, and the Phocaean somewhat earlier in the same century (Özyiğit 1993, 7; 2006, 21–2). It should be noted however that he regards *IK Erythrai* 24, of ca. 277–275, as the earliest inscription giving evidence for the theatre in Erythrae. While it is the first explicitly to refer to the theatre, there is good reason to believe that there was some form of theatre in Erythrae from as early as the early fourth century (**Evi**).

1 shows that by as early as around 290 or somewhat earlier the Phocaeans held a Dionysia (doubtless in the theatre, though that is not made explicit) and that it had a tragic agon (Graf 1985, 418 for other limited evidence for the cult of Dionysus in Phocaea: it can be hoped that recent and future excavation will bring more to light). It is also important evidence not only that this event was a major occasion upon which civic honours were proclaimed in Phocaea but that a group of cities associated in a network of civic and political communality might expect to use the Dionysia of their cities to advertise the associations that linked them. Crowther (1996, 228) notes that as a member of the Ionian koinon it is no surprise to find Phocaea assisting Priene in this capacity, but that we might expect Nisyros and Astypalaea to have been Ptolemaic by a date in the mid 280s, though we cannot be sure they were so by the time this decree was passed.

Phocaea was a member of the Delian League from at least 453/2 (in the Ionian district). It was also an energetic coloniser: with Lampsacus in 654/3 and Massalia ca. 600. And, somewhat closer in time to be relevant to our concerns, the Phocaeans who failed in the venture of Alalie in Corsica in ca. 560 moved on ca. 540 to found Elea (Hyele). It is a strong possibility that Elea had a theatre dating to the middle of the fifth century (**A Introduction**).

Evi: Erythrae

1. Honorary decree of the Council and People of Erythrae for Conon. Date: 394. Conon led a victorious Athenian and Persian fleet at Cnidus in 394 that ended Sparta's aspiration for naval supremacy. Erythrae was one of several cities that hastened to honour the Athenian.

Upper right part of a stele.
Found in the Church of the Theotokos, 30 minutes south of Erythrae (Ma 2006).
Current whereabouts unknown.
Le Bas 1856, 3–4 no. 2; Tod 1948, no. 106; *IK Erythrai* 6; R-O II no. 8.
Text: based on R-O II no. 8.   Photo: *IK Erythrai* Taf. III (squeeze).

1	[ἔδοξεν] τῆ βουλῆ καὶ τῶι	stoich. 17–20
	[δήμωι· Κ]όνωνα ἀναγράψαι	
	[εὐεργ]έτην Ἐρυθραίων	
	[καὶ π]ρόξενον, καὶ προε-	
5	[δρί]ην αὐτῶι ἔναι ἐν Ἐρυ-	
	[θρ]ῆισιν καὶ ἀτέλειαν	
	[π]άντων χρημάτων καὶ	
	[ἐ]σαγωγῆς καὶ ἐξαγωγῆς	
	[κ]αὶ πολέμο καὶ εἰρήνης·	
10	[κα]ὶ Ἐρυθραῖον εἶναι	
	[ἢν] βούληται· εἶναι δὲ	
	[ταῦ]τα καὶ αὐτῶι καὶ ἐκ-	
	[γόνοι]ς· ποήσασθαι δὲ	
	[αὐτοῦ ε]ἰκόνα χαλκῆν	
15	[? ἐπίχρυσον] καὶ στῆσαι	
	[ὅπο ἂν δόξηι] Κόνωνι·	
	[.....11.....]ι καὶ [- - -]	

15 [ἐπίχρυσον] Le Bas   Ma 2006 notes the precarious grounds for this restoration, without proposing another.

The Council and [People decided:] to inscribe [C]onon as a [benef]actor [and p]roxenos of the Erythraeans, and that [5] he should have prohe[dri]e at Ery[thr]-ae and immunity (*ateleia*) for [a]ll commodities, both of [i]mport and export [a]nd during war and peace; [10] [an]d he is to be an Erythraean [if] he wishes. [Thes]e things are to be both for him and for his des[cendan]ts. And a [? gild-ed] bronze [l]ikeness [of him] is to be made [15] and erected [wherever] Conon [decides]. […] and […].

2. **Honorary decree of the Council and People of Erythrae for a civic benefactor**.
Date: probably soon after 323. For the date, based on historical context and reference to 'Philippic' staters, see Varınlıoğlu et al. 1990, 78. Phanes had apparently assisted in removing a (probably Persian) occupying force from the city.

Stele of white marble.
0.60 × 0.45 × 0.16 m.
Found at Erythrae.
Kept after discovery in the Museum of the Evangelical School at Smyrna.
Fontrier 1878, 58 no. 139; *SEG* 19, 696; *IK Erythrai* 21.
Text: *IK Erythrai* 21 with *SEG* 19, 696.   Photo: *IK Erythrai* Taf. IV (squeeze).

1	[ἔδ]οξ[ε]ν [τῆι] βουλῆι καὶ τῶι δήμωι·	stoich.
	[πρυτάν]εων, στρατηγῶν, ἐξεταστῶ-	
	ν γ[νώ]μη· ἐπειδὴ Φανῆς Μνησιθέου	
	[ἀ]νὴ[ρ] ἀγαθὸς ὢν καὶ εὔνους διατε-	
5	[λ]εῖ εἰς τὸν δῆμον τὸν Ἐρυθραίων	
	[π]ᾶσαν προθυμίαν ἐνδεικνύμενο-	
	[ς], χρήματά τε ἐσήν[ε]γκεν ἄτοκα κα-	
	[ὶ] εἰς τὴν ἔκπεμψι[ν τ]ῶν στρατιωτ-	
	[ῶν] καὶ τῆς ἀκροπόλεως τὴν κατα[σ]-	
10	[κα]φήν, δεδόχθαι τῆι β[ο]υλῆι, στε[φ]-	
	[α]νῶσαι Φανῆν Μνησιθέου χρυσῶι	
	[σ]τεφάνωι στατήρων Φιλιππείων	
	[π]εντήκοντα, καὶ ἀναγγεῖλαι τοῖ-	
	[ς] Διονυσίοις· ὅπως δὲ ἀναγγελθή-	
15	σεται, ἐπιμεληθῆναι Ζηνόδοτον	
	τὸν ἀγωνοθέτην· δεδόσθαι δὲ αὐτ-	
	ῶι καὶ ἐμ πρυτανείωι σίτησιν· ἀν-	
	αγράψαι δὲ τὸ ψήφισμα τόδε εἰς σ-	
	τήλας δύο, καὶ θεῖναι μίαμ μὲν εἰ-	
20	ς τὸ Ἀθήναιον, μίαν δὲ εἰς τὸ Ἡράκ-	
	λεον, ἵνα ἅπαντες εἰδῶσιν ὅτι ἐπ-	
	ίσταται ὁ δῆμος χάριτας ἀποδιδ-	
	όναι κατ' ἀξίαν τῶν εἰς αὐτὸν εὐ[ε]-	
	ργετημάτων.	

[The] Council and people [de]cid[e]d; the op[ini]on of the [prytan]eis, the generals, the auditors (*exetastai*): since Phanes son of Mnesitheos, being a good [m]a[n] and well-disposed, continu[e]s [5] to demonstrate his [c]omplete enthusiasm for the People of the Erythraeans, and has contr[i]buted money without interest bot[h] for the sending ou[t] of [t]he soldie[rs] and the dest[ru]ction of the acropolis, [10] the [Co]uncil decided to cr[o]wn Phanes son of Mnesitheos with a gold [c]rown worth [f]ifty Philippic staters, and to proclaim it at th[e] Dionysia. [15] Zenodotos the agonothete is to make sure that it will be announced. And he is also to be given dining rights in the prytaneion. And this decree is to be inscribed on two stelai: one to be placed in [20] the sanctuary of Athena, and one in the sanctuary of Heracles, so that everyone may know that the People returns favours commensurate to the ben[e]factions it receives.

3. Altar in the orchestra of the theatre dedicated to Dionysus and Demos, 'Hellenistic' (Varınlıoğlu 1981, by letter forms); probably Augustan era (Moretti 2009, 45).

A cylindrical monolith marble altar on a plinth with moulding at top and bottom. The shaft is decorated with a garland suspended from four rams' heads. The inscription begins under the moulding over the ram's head facing the orchestra. Part of the upper moulding and a few letters of l. 2 broken off.

H. 1.00; diam. 0.72 m.

Found '*in situ* right before the front seats in the orchestra' of the theatre (Varınlıoğlu 1981, 47). Apparently *in situ*.

Varınlıoğlu 1981, 47–8 no. 2 = *SEG* 31, 971; Graf 1985, 465 IE suppl. 5.

Text: based on Varınlıoğlu 1981.   Photo: Varınlıoğlu 1981, Taf. V no. 2.

1   Σύμμαχος Ζηνοδότου
     ἀγων[. .]ήσας τὸν βῶμον
     Διονύσωι καὶ τῶι Δήμωι.

     2 Varınlıoğlu: probably ἀγων[οθε]τήσας

Symmachos son of Zenodotos after serving as agon[othet]e (sc. dedicated) the altar to Dionysus and Demos.

Rhodes and Osborne (R-O II, 45) are surely right to understand the award of prohedria at Erythrae to the victorious Athenian general Conon (**1**) as evidence for the existence of a theatre in the city by 394. We might reasonably deduce that Erythrae already had a theatre by the early fourth century, although it will be an earlier phase than the one whose remains survive (below) and was probably largely of wooden construction. In the 350s another honorific decree, for the Carian satrap Mausolus (**Eix**), likewise awards prohedria *simpliciter* (*IK Erythrai* 8, l. 10, ca. 357–355; and *IK Erythrai* 12, l. 7 is another example, dated 'well before 340'), while a short time later, perhaps in a period of non-democratic rule (Varınlıoğlu 1981, 47), the Carian dynast Idrieus of Mylasa is awarded 'prohedria at the contests' (προεδρίην ἐν τοῖς ἀγῶσι: Varınlıoğlu 1981, 45–7 no. 1, l. 11 = *SEG* 31,

969, prob. 351–344: Pleket, *SEG*). The first explicit surviving (and at least approximately datable) reference to the theatre itself is in a decree of ca. 277–275, which mandates the announcement of honours by '[the] agonothetes [at the Dionysia and Seleukeia in the] theatre, whe[n they conduct the contests.]' (*IK Erythrai* 24, ll. 30–2).

2 of ca. 333 shows Erythrae engaging in the habit, energetically pursued at this time by Athens and many other cities, of announcing honours for important benefactors at the Dionysia, for which festival it also provides our first explicit reference. The Dionysia was doubtless the (or at least one) occasion with agones at which those honoured with pro-hedria in the earlier decrees were to enjoy it (for a full survey of the rich suite of other cults known for Erythrae see Graf 1985, 147–375). The fact that the festival was under the direction of an agonothete certainly indicates the centrality of the agones to it. While we find no reference to theatrical contests or any event more specific than 'agones' it is highly likely that the agones of the Erythraean Dionysia included theatrical and/or choral events. A choregia is not attested.

Like a number of other cities (e.g. **Dvi**; **Dxi**; **Dxiii**; **VI L**), Erythrae associated its Dionysia with worship of the relevant power brokers in its region during the period of the Successors. Already by the late fourth or early third century (*IK Erythrai* 13), honours are to be announced at the Dionysia, along with one or more other (restored) festivals, for which Engelmann and Merkelbach (*IK Erythrai* I, 68) suggest *inter alia* the Alexandreia or Seleukeia. From soon after 280 the Dionysia seems to be regularly combined with the Seleukeia (*IK Erythrai* 27, restored; *IK Erythrai* 24, l. 31, restored; *IK Erythrai* 119, ll. 3–4, ca. 280; *IK Erythrai* 35, l. 13, ca. 260; *IK Erythrai* 36, l. 13, mid 3rd c.). Noting that in (only) *IK Erythrai* 119 the article is not applied to the Seleukeia in the phrase τῶν Διονυσίων καὶ Σε|λευκε[ίω]ν, and that 'the Dionysia and Seleukeia' appear to be admin-istered by a board of agonothetes, Buraselis (2012, 251) argues that this may represent a 'possible development from a form of dynastic festival appended to but distinct from the Dionysia of Erythrae, to a unified festival in which the appended part no longer needed to be distinguished by a definite article'. At some point this combination was dissolved: in *IK Erythrai* 115, described simply as of 'Hellenistic' date, we find the Dionysia alone as the site for the announcement of honours, a habit that continues into the second cen-tury (*IK Erythrai* 111, ll. 29–32, ca. 160). The theatre is still active as late as the second century AD, although in repurposed form, for it was modified among other ways by the transformation of the orchestra into an arena, possibly on the occasion of the visit to the city by Hadrian in 124 AD (for the involvement in which by the 'thymelic association' see *IK Erythrai* 60).

It is particularly unfortunate that the excavations conducted under Ekrem Akurgal have not been published, for the theatre at Erythrae is one of the oldest in Asia Minor and is noteworthy as having existed well before the conquest of Alexander, thereby undermining the established view that theatre came to Asia Minor only in his wake (Bernardi Ferrero 1966–1974 IV, 76; cf. Moretti 1992a, 11). It currently shares this status with perhaps only Caunus (**E Introduction**) and Phocaea (**Ev**). This may have something to do with the close relations between Erythrae and Athens in the fifth century. An Athenian decree of (probably) the mid 450s (*IG* I³ 14) appears to be a response to Erythrae's defection from the Delian League at that time. The decree enforces a democratic constitution on the city, which was possibly to be safeguarded with a garrison (cf. *IG* I³ 15), and the defection may have taken place during and been driven by a pro-Persian tyranny or oligarchy. The same decree (ll. 2–4) begins with a requirement to bring grain to the Great Panathenaea in Athens, to be distributed to those Erythraeans present. Very little of the further provisions concerning participation in the festival (ll. 5–9) can be read, but sacrificial meat may also be mentioned (l. 8). It is possible, though far from certain, that Erythrae may have been imagined (at least by Athens) as an Ionian 'colony' of Athens, and that the mandated involvement in the Great Panathenaea in some way reflects such a view (**I Aiv 9**). At any rate it is clear that at least by the middle of the fifth century the Erythraeans were intimately familiar with Athenian festival culture. At a date closer to our first surviving evidence for theatre, Erythrae joined with the Lacedaemonians against Athens (413/12), though as **1** shows, they allied themselves again with Athens in 394 after the naval victory at Cnidus.

Made of local marble and limestone, the theatron whose remains survive was built into the side of the northern slope of the acropolis, on top of which sat the temple of Athena (cf. **2**, ll. 19–20). The stage building was of rectangular shape, divided internally into four rooms. Excavations undertaken in 1982 showed from the evidence of holes cut into the rock in the region of the stage building that it was a temporary or demountable structure, presumably made of wood (Özyiğit 1993, 7). The radius of the orchestra is said to be ca. 9.5 m. The profile of the surviving seats (Bernardi Ferrero 1966–1974 IV, 82 fig. 116) is quite similar to that of some surviving seats in the theatre of Phocaea (Özyiğit 2003, 118). Özyiğit (1993, 7) would date the stone Erythraean theatre to possibly the last quarter of the fourth century, while placing the Phocaean earlier in the century, on the basis of more solid stratigraphic finds (**Ev**). His argument rests on a comparison of the seat profiles and other features of the construction of these two theatres, and also relies on the epigraphic evidence mentioned above – namely the first explicit reference to the theatre in a decree of ca. 277–275 (*IK Erythrai* 24). He presumably either discounts (as not being explicit with regard to a theatre) or neglects the possible value of **1**, **2** and the related inscriptions cited above. It seems entirely possible – not least given the fact that the stage building continued to be wooden even when the theatron had been built in stone – that in an earlier phase the natural slope of the acropolis had afforded spectators a place to watch, possibly with wooden seats constructed for the purpose, and with some form of prohedric seating erected at the front (**1**).

3 is an altar dedicated to Dionysus and Demos found *in situ* in the orchestra of the Erythraean theatre in front of the front seats. The inscription indicates it was dedicated by one Symmachos, son of Zenodotos, probably after especially lavish service as agonothete (note the highly probable restoration of l. 2 suggested by Varınlıoğlu 1981, 48). It thus offers further clear evidence for the association of the cult of Dionysus with the theatre (for the cult of Dionysus in Erythrae more generally see Graf 1985, 283–95). The fact that the altar was dedicated 'to Dionysus' without further epithet (some four are known for Dionysus in Erythrae) parallels the situation in Athens, where there is virtually no Classical evidence that an epithet (viz. Eleuthereus) was commonly applied to the god worshipped on the south slope of the Acropolis (**I Aiii 4**).

For the minimal published evidence for the theatre see Bernardi Ferrero 1966–1974
IV, 10 fig. 1; 81–2 with figs. 114–16; Isler in *TGR* III, 451; Özyiğit 2003, 118; Sear 2006,
336–7.

Evii: Priene

1. Decree of the Council and People of Priene honouring Athens, mandating Prienian participation in the Great Panathenaea at Athens, ca. 330 (on prosopographical and contextual grounds: Shear 2001, 190; cf. *IPriene* 8, 10; Blümel and Merkelbach in *IK Priene* 5: shortly before 326/5).

Five joining fragments of a marble stele; right and left sides intact, broken at top and bottom.
0.78 × 0.82 × 0.24 m.
All fragments found together in later additions to the upper gymnasium.
Pergamon Museum Berlin, Priene Inv. 208.
IPriene 5; *IK Priene* 5.
Text: *IK Priene* 5.   Photo: *IPriene*, p. 9.

(faint traces of a few lines)

[. . . .].Α.Ο[. . . . .]Ν· ἔ[δοξε τῆι βουλῆι καὶ]
τῶι δήμωι· τῆι Ἀθηνᾶι τῆι Πολιάδι καθ᾽ ἑ[κ]άστην
πεντετηρίδα τοῖς Παναθηναίοις τοῖς μεγάλοις
πομπὴν καὶ πανοπλίαν εἰς Ἀθήνας ἀποστέλλε[ιν]
5   μνημεῖον τῆς ἐξ ἀρχῆς συγγενείας καὶ φιλίας
ἡμῖν ὑπαρχούσης πρὸς αὐτούς· εἶναι δὲ Ἀθη[ναίοις]
ἅπασι καθάπερ καὶ πρότερον ὑπῆρχεν αὐτοῖς [καὶ]
πολιτείαν ἐμ Πριήνηι καὶ ἰσοτέλ[ε]ιαν καὶ προεδ[ρίαν]
ἐν τοῖς ἀγῶσι, καὶ εἰσκηρύσσεσθ[αι] αὐτοὺς καθά[περ]
10   τοὺς εὐεργέτας· αἱρεῖσθαι δὲ τ̣[ὸν δῆ]μον θεωρο̣[ὺς]
δύο τοὺς τὰς ἀπαρχὰς ἀπ[ο]ί̣[σοντας καὶ τ]ὰ ἱερὰ
ποιήσοντας τῆι Ἀθηνᾶι τῆι Πολιάδι κα[θ᾽ ἑκάστην]
πεντετηρίδα· τοὺς δὲ νῦν αἱρεθέντας με[τὰ τῶν]
ἱερῶν καὶ τὸ ψήφισμα φέρειν καὶ ἀποδοῦν[αι τῆι]
15   βουλῆι καὶ τῶι δήμωι τῶι Ἀθηναίων, ἵνα εἰδῶσ[ι τὴν]
τῶν Πριηνέω̣ν εἰς τὸν δῆμον τὸν τῶν Ἀθηνα[ίων]
εὔνοιαν· ἐ[πα]γγεῖλαι δὲ τῶι δήμωι τῶι Ἀθηνα[ίων]
καὶ ὑπὲ[ρ Δι]φίλου τοῦ ἐς Σάμωι στρατηγοῦ, ὅτ[ι]
ἐσ[τὶν εὔνου]ς περὶ τὸν δῆμον τὸν Πριηνέων καὶ [ἐπι]-
20   [μελεῖται καθὼ]ς προσῆκόν ἐστιν τῶν ἐξ ἀρχῆ[ς συγ]-
[γενῶν καὶ συμμάχων] γεγενημένων παρὰ πάν[τα τὸν]
[χρόνον, ὅπως καὶ εἰς τ]ὸ̣ν ἄλλον χρόνον τοῖς [. . . . . .]
[   ] π[ρο . . . .]

[… *name* propose]d; [the Council and] People de[cided: to] dispatch to Athens a processional escort and a panoply to the Great Panathenaea as [5] a memorial of the ancestral kinship and friendship that exists between us; that all the Athe[nians] should have citizenship in Priene just as formerly belonged to them, equal t[a]x status and prohed[ria] at the contests; and that they are to be proclaimed by herald as [10] benefactors. T[he Pe]ople is to elect two theoroi [to con]vey the first fruits [and] to make [t]he offerings to Athena Polias at [each] quadrennial celebration, and those presently elected are to take alon[g with the] sacred offerings the decree and to hand it over [to the] [15] Council and People of the Athenians, so that they may know [the] goodwill of the Prienians towards the People of the Atheni[ans]; and to r[ep]ort to the People of the Atheni[ans] also concern[ing Di]philos the general on Samos, th[at] he [is well-dispo]sed towards the People of the Prienians and [20] [takes care a]s is fitting of those who have long been his ancestra[l kinsmen and allies] across all [time, so that also for t]he future […]

2. Honorary decree of the Council and People of Priene for Megabyxos of Ephesus, 334–323 (Blümel and Merkelbach); 296/5 (Crowther 1996); ca. 334 (*IPriene*, p. 6). Crowther 1996 offers a detailed response to Hiller's dating of this and **3** on a wide range of grounds and proposes a precise dating of **2** by reference to known eponymous office-holders. Megabyxos was a *neokoros* of Artemis in Ephesus and is honoured for his efforts in helping with the construction of the temple of Athena in Priene. The base of the statue awarded by this decree (ll. 9, 16–24c) has survived: *IK Priene* 150 = *IPriene* 231. Blümel and Merkelbach support their dating on the grounds that a formula used in the decree is documented in Priene in the period ca. 330–300, and because they identify Megabyxos with the man of that name associated with Alexander in his lifetime (Plin. *HN* 35.93; Plu. *Alex.* 42.1). We excerpt only the clause mandating the proclamation of the awards.

Marble stele broken to the right.
1.62 × 0.60 × 0.19 m.
Found in the pavement of the main Byzantine church.
Pergamon Museum Berlin, Priene Inv. 52.
IPriene 3; Crowther 1996 = *SEG* 46, 1479; *IK Priene* 16.
Text: *IK Priene* 16.

τὰς δὲ δω[ρεὰς]

25 τὰς δεδομένας αὐτῶι ἀνα[γγ]εῖλαι τὸγ κήρυ[κα τοῖς]
Διονυσίοις, ὅπως εἰδῶσι πά[ντ]ες ὅτι δύναται ὁ [δῆμος]
ὁ Πριηνέων ἀπο[δ]ιδόναι χάρι[τας] τοῖς εὖ ποιοῦσιν [αὐτόν]·

And the hera[ld] is to ann[oun]ce the aw[ards] granted to him at [the] Dionysia, so that ever[yon]e may know that the Prienian [People] is able to re[t]urn fav[ours] to those who treat [it] well.

3. Honorary decree of the Council and People of Priene for Apellis for service as state

secretary, ca. 330–300 (Blümel and Merkelbach: a formula used at ll. 3–4 is documented in Priene during this period); 293/2 (Crowther 1996: see on **2**); ca. 338–332 (*IPriene*,
p. 8). The decree commemorates the career of Apellis, lasting some 20 years in the elected office of secretary (*grammateus*). Apellis was honoured by another decree, passed a
few years later and inscribed on the same stele, which also mandates that the agonothete
is to oversee proclamation of his honours 'at the Dionysia in the theatre' (*IK Priene* 20,
ll. 5–7 = *IPriene* 4b, ll. 54–6). We excerpt only the clause mandating the proclamation
of the awards and the grant of prohedria.

Marble stele broken into two pieces, worn in the middle of the inscribed surface.
1.72 × 0.64–0.67 × 0.14 m.
Found in the pavement of the main Byzantine church.
Pergamon Museum Berlin, Priene Inv. 49.
IPriene 4a; cf. Crowther 1996 = *SEG* 46, 1479; *IK Priene* 19.
Text: *IK Priene* 19.

καὶ ἀναγγεῖλαι τοῖς
[πρ]ώτο[ις] Διον[υσ]ίο[ις ἐ]ν τῶι [θε]άτ[ρ]ωι τόν τε στέφανον καὶ
τὰς ἄλλας τιμὰ[ς] ạ[ἶς τ]ε[τ]ί[μη]κεν αὐτὸ[ν] ὁ δῆμος· τῆς δὲ
ἀναγγελίας ἐ[π]ι[μελε]ῖ[σ]θαι τὸ[ν] ἀγωνοθέτην· δεδόσ-

35   [θαι δ]ὲ αὐτῶι κ[αὶ προε]δ[ρ]ίαν ἐν τοῖς ἀγῶσι …

… and to announce the crown and the other honour[s with] whi[ch] the People
has [h]o[n]o[ur]ed him at the [fi]rst (= 'next') Dion[ys]ia [i]n the [the]at[r]e;
the agonothete is to take [care] of the announcement; and to gran[t] him fu[rther
prohe]d[r]ia at the contests …

If the redating by Crowther of **3** to 292 rather than ca. 330 is correct, the only explicit
textual evidence for a fourth-century theatre in Priene disappears. But in their recent edition, Blümel and Merkelbach do not accept Crowther's redating, and opt for a range over
the last three decades of the fourth century. Although it does not mention the theatre, **2**
shows that a Dionysia at which honours were announced had existed by 334–323 (Blümel
and Merkelbach) or by 296/5 (on Crowther's redating). It is important to note that the
absence of reference to a theatre in decrees mandating the announcement of awards at a
Dionysia does not necessarily entail the absence of a theatre in fact. Thus for instance in
a decree of ca. 262 – at a time when Priene certainly had a theatre – one Nymphon is to
be honoured 'at the trag[ic] contest [at the next Diony]sia' [τοῖς πρώτοις Διον]υσίοις τῶι
ἀγῶνι τῶν τραγω[ι|δῶν] (*IK Priene* 23 = *IPriene* 22, ll. 16–17). This makes the business
of identifying the first evidence for a theatre from the epigraphic record somewhat less
straightforward.

Sometimes other evidence, such as the award of prohedria, might point to the existence
of a theatre (**Ev**). This is at issue here, for in ll. 8–10 of **1**, dated to ca. 330, the Athenians
are granted, *en masse*, 'prohed[ria] at the contests' in Priene, and we may assume that the

earlier clause 'just as formerly belonged to them' (l. 7) extends to the right of prohedria. Even if the antiquity of these prohedric rights is little more than a fiction born of the hopeful and strategic assertion by Priene of a colonial relationship with Athens, the existence of the right to prohedria for Athenians at contests at Priene at least by ca. 330 should not be doubted. The phrase seems deliberately open-ended and probably implies a multiplicity of festival contexts and, correspondingly, a multiplicity of physical contexts in which prohedria existed or could be erected. A Dionysia is likely. The festival of the city's principal divinity, Athena Polias, is another probable candidate. And another possibility, given the importance of the claim to shared Ionian ethnicity that undergirds the Prienians' rhetoric in **1**, is the festival of the Ionian League, the Panionia, once again in Prienian control from (probably) 373 (Stylianou 1983).

The meeting place of the League at this date was in a sanctuary of Poseidon on the northern slope of Mt Mycale, on the top of a low hill called Otomatik Tepe near Güzelçamlı. The assembly building dated to the mid fourth century found here has the form of a small theatre with an overall diameter of ca. 31.8 m. Rough-hewn blocks of limestone supported benches for prohedria around the orchestra and the excavators found a series of raised plinths to support five single prohedric seats (they posited an original total of nine), while most of the remaining ten rows of seats above were carved directly from the rock (Kleiner et al. 1967; Hansen and Fischer-Hansen 1994, 67–9; Isler in *TGR* III, 446; some parallels in construction with the theatre in Priene have been identified). Cities of the League were required to participate in the sacrifices here with choruses ([θύ]ειν δὲ] τῶι Διὶ τῶι Βουλα[ίωι τοῖς τε ἄλλοις θε]οῖς, οἷς] ἐν χόρωι θύειν δεῖ [κατὰ τὸν ἱερὸν νόμον]; Kleiner et al. 1967, 45–63, ll. 9–11; Kowalzig 2005, 46–56).

3 shows that the Dionysia was run by an agonothete by the start of the third century (no choregia is attested). Tragedy is first found at the Priene Dionysia by ca. 300 or a little later (**Ev 1**) and remains the event at which honours are announced (*IK Priene* 28 = *IPriene* 17, ll. 41–3, soon after 278; *IK Priene* 29 = *IPriene* 18, ll. 8–10, ca. 270–262; *IK Priene* 24 = *IPriene* 23, ll. 13–15, 3rd c.) until the appearance around 266 of 'the first contest of the pipers' (i.e. a contest of choruses accompanied by pipers: *IK Priene* 22, ll. 10–12 = *IPriene* 21, ll. 18–20), although the same man is honoured soon after at the tragic contest (*IK Priene* 23 = *IPriene* 22, ll. 16–17). By the middle of the third century announcements are timetabled 'at the next Dionysia, at the boys' choral contest accompanied by pipers' (*IK Priene* 25 = *IPriene* 19, ll. 53–6 ἐν τοῖς πρώτοις | [Δ]ιονυσίοις αὐλητῶν τῶ[ι] ἀγῶνι τῶι παιδικῶ[ι]) and choral contests, especially that for boys, remain prominent throughout the second century (on these developments and likely implications for the changing importance of the events see Ceccarelli 2010, 135–6). The evidence of various dedications to Dionysus from the theatre, found in the area of the prohedria (*IK Priene* 180–3 = *IPriene* 175–8; cf. 144 = 174, 3rd–2nd c.) confirms the close association of the building with the god's cult.

The archaeological evidence for the first built theatre in Priene, which is known to have had several phases extending over a number of centuries, is controversial (Bernardi Ferrero 1966–1974 III, 9–20 with figs. 1–13, tav. 1–2 with previous bibliography; Isler in *TGR* III, 441–2; Sear 2006, 349–50). The main conclusion of the study by Gogos (1998) was that the existence of an entire structure cannot be confirmed prior to the third century, but the view of Dörpfeld (1924) that the construction in stone of the seating area might date to ca. 340, while the stage building was still made of timber, remains a strong possibility. This would place the first phase of the theatre in the period immediately following the likely re-foundation of the city and situate its commencement within the first phase of the construction of the new city's public buildings (see Rubinstein *IACP* 1092–3 for a summary of the much-debated questions as to whether and when Priene was refounded, and if so whether it was on the same site as the Archaic and Classical city). That refoundation is likely to have included the involvement of Athens, given the efforts evidenced by **1** on the part of the Prienians to invoke a colonial connection to Athens at this time (Shear 2001, 191).

Eviii: Caria. [Aristotle], *Economics* **2.2.31 (1351b36–1352a8).** Written probably around the end of the 4th c. (Migeotte 2014, 34). Target date: ca. 326–323. Philodemus attributed the *Economics*, transmitted under the name of Aristotle, to Theophrastus. Modern scholars tend to accept that attribution or suggest some other student or students of Aristotle (Pomeroy 1994, 68). The second book begins with a theoretical section that distinguishes four different types of economy, and is followed by a collection of historical examples of money-raising strategies adopted by cities, governors, monarchs and military commanders. Text: van Groningen and Wartelle[2].

Φιλόξενός τις Μακεδὼν Καρίας σατραπεύων δεηθεὶς χρημάτων Διονύσια ἔφασκε μέλλειν ἄγειν καὶ χοραγοὺς [1352a] προέγραψε τῶν Καρῶν τοὺς εὐπορωτάτους καὶ προσέταττεν αὐτοῖς ἃ δεῖ παρασκευάζειν. ὁρῶν δ' αὐτοὺς δυσχεραίνοντας ὑποπέμπων τινὰς ἠρώτα τί βούλονται δόντες ἀπαλλαγῆναι τῆς λειτουργίας. οἳ δὲ πολλῷ πλέον ἢ ὅσον ᾤοντο ἀναλώσειν ἔφασαν δώσειν τοῦ μὴ ὀχλεῖσθαι καὶ ἀπὸ τῶν ἰδίων ἀπεῖναι. ὃ δὲ παρὰ τούτων λαβὼν ὃ ἐδίδοσαν, ἑτέρους κατέγραψεν, ἕως ἔλαβε παρὰ τοῦτο, ὃ ἠβούλετο, καὶ προσόν. † παρ' ἑκάστης †

τοῦτο, ὃ corr. van Groningen   τούτων codd.   καὶ προσόν †παρ' ἑκάστης† omitted in the old Latin translation (*translatio vetus*)

A Macedonian named Philoxenos, who was satrap of Caria, being in need of funds declared that he intended to hold a Dionysia and [1352a] publically appointed as choragoi the wealthiest Carians and told them what they were required to prepare. Seeing that they were annoyed, Philoxenos sent people to them privately and asked what they would be willing to give to be relieved of the liturgy. They told him that they would give much more than they expected to spend in order to avoid the trouble and the interruption of their private affairs. He accepted what they were offering him, and enrolled others, until he received beside this amount, which he wanted, even further income.

It is widely agreed that the *Economics* is the product of sound Peripatetic research of the period following Aristotle's death. The information concerning this scheme to generate income devised by the Macedonian satrap of Caria, Philoxenos, is thus quite credible. And the language used uniformly indicates familiarity with the practice and terminology of choregic systems of the period. The use of the Doric form χοραγός is especially noteworthy (χοραγοὺς is 'normalised' to the Attic χορηγοὺς in a number of manuscripts, no doubt wrongly). We might expect to find the form χοραγός in use in Macedonian circles, but its presence here could equally be explained by reference to the cultural position of Carian Halicarnassus in particular, an original member of the Dorian Hexapolis (Hdt. 1.144) with ongoing intimate relations to Rhodes, an island with an energetic choragic system and a flourishing theatre in the fourth century (**Dxi**).

Philoxenos was probably appointed as the first Macedonian satrap of Caria after the death of Ada, Queen of the Carians, in 326. When he entered Caria in 334 Alexander permitted Ada to adopt him as her son (Arr. *An*. 1.23.8) and she thus secured her position as Queen of Caria for the period 334–326. Arrian evidently refers to Philoxenos acting as satrap of Caria in 324/3 (*An*. 7.23.1; cf. 7.24.1), while in 323 he was succeeded by Asander and may have gone on to receive the satrapy of Cilicia from Perdiccas in 321 (Just. *Epit*. 13.6.16; Wilcken 1901, 191–2). Wilcken (1901, 191) disassociates him from the Philoxenos involved in the Harpalos affair, said to have seized Harpalos' treasurer in Rhodes (Paus. 2.33.4–5), and from the Philoxenos who was Alexander's tax collector in Asia (Arr. *An*. 3.6.4), but the thread of fiscal acuity that runs through all these testimonia is suggestive.

Philoxenos' strategic use of a Dionysia to generate funds beyond what might be termed a normative expectation of a financial return on a festival is paralleled by another Greek military commander operating in Asia earlier in the century – the Alexander who extracted money from a literally captive theatre audience in Aeolis (**Eiv 1**). Philoxenos' plan does not rely on brute force but may instead exploit cultural unfamiliarity with the principle and practices of choregic liturgy among the local Carian elite, who had a tradition of raising tribute owed to Susa, but very probably not of civic euergetism of the choregic type. For it is clear that the proposed service of choragia was of the 'hands on' type, requiring its holder to perform and organise a range of cultural activities and not simply to 'sign a cheque': as much is clear from the fact that Philoxenos' ruse is precisely to offer the option of signing a cheque to his disgruntled appointees, and from the use of the verb 'prepare' παρασκευάζειν rather than simply 'provide' (sc. funds) to describe the initial obligation ('[he] told them what they were required to prepare' προσέταττεν αὐτοῖς ἃ δεῖ παρασκευάζειν). For a possible more formal example of the monetisation of choregic obligation see **III Yii** on the 'sale' of choregiai in the Attic deme of Thorikos.

When Caria fell under Macedonian control in 334/3 the new overlords seem to have employed a form of satrapal administration that displayed considerable continuity with the Achaemenid era (Briant 1985). Action such as that undertaken by Philoxenos shows however that the new overlords could be innovative in their fiscal endeavours. Alexander himself may have set a relevant precedent with his application of an Athenian-type choregia to the tragic and dithyrambic contests he set up in Tyre in 331, for which he appointed the kings of Cyprus as choregoi (**E Introduction**).

We are not given any indication of the location of Philoxenos' planned Dionysia. But the choragoi were apparently drawn from across all of Caria and not confined to one sub-region or city (might the corrupt final phrase conceal a reference to regional divisions of Caria from which Philoxenos had drawn his choragoi: †παρ᾽ ἑκάστης† 'from each …'?). It is a likely guess, however, that the old Hecatomnid capital of Halicarnassus (still such as recently as 334) was to be the site of the Dionysia. The city had already witnessed the work of at least one Greek tragedian and may have had a theatre by this date (**Eix**). The close relationship between the last of the Hecatomnids, Ada, and Alexander the Great in the governance of Caria from 334 may also be part of the relevant context, given the propagandistic value that Alexander derived from theatre. While theatrical performances are not explicitly mentioned, it is inherently more likely that a Macedonian overlord in the tradition of Alexander would propose a Dionysia that included drama rather than one with purely choral events.

Eix: Halicarnassus

1. **Aulus Gellius,** *Attic Nights* **10.18.5–7 (=** *TrGF* **I, 72 T 6)**. Aulus Gellius wrote his miscellany *Attic Nights* in Athens and Rome in the second half of the 2nd c. AD. Text: Marshall.

> *id monumentum Artemisia cum dis manibus sacris Mausoli dicaret, agona, id est certamen laudibus eius dicundis, facit ponitque praemia pecuniae aliarumque rerum bonarum amplissima.* [6] *ad eas laudes decertandas venisse dicuntur viri nobiles ingenio atque lingua praestabili, Theopompus, Theodectes, Naucrates; sunt etiam qui Isocratem ipsum cum his certavisse memoriae mandaverint. sed eo certamine vicisse Theopompum iudicatum est. is fuit Isocratis discipulus.* [7] *exstat nunc quoque Theodecti tragoedia, quae inscribitur Mausolus; in qua eum magis quam in prosa placuisse Hyginus in exemplis refert.*

When Artemisia dedicated this monument, consecrated to the deified shades of Mausolus, she instituted an agon, that is to say, a contest in enunciating his praises, and she offered very substantial prizes of money and other valuables. [6] Men distinguished for their eminent talent and eloquence are said to have come to contend in this eulogy – Theopompus, Theodectes and Naukrates; some have even written that Isocrates himself competed with them. But Theopompus was adjudged the winner in that contest. He was a pupil of Isocrates. [7] The tragedy of Theodectes, entitled *Mausolus*, is still extant today; and Hyginus in his *Examples* reports that in it Theodectes was more pleasing than in his prose work.

2. **Suda s.v. Θεοδέκτης ('Theodectes', θ 138) (=** *TrGF* **I, 72 T 1)**. Compiled ca. 1000 AD. Text: Adler with modification.

> Θεοδέκτης, Ἀριστάνδρου, Φασηλίτης ἐκ Λυκίας, ῥήτωρ, τραπεὶς δὲ ἐπὶ τραγῳδίας, μαθητὴς Πλάτωνος καὶ Ἰσοκράτους καὶ Ἀριστοτέλους. οὗτος

καὶ ὁ Ἐρυθραῖος Ναυκράτης καὶ Ἰσοκράτης ὁ ῥήτωρ, ὁ Ἀπολλωνιάτης, καὶ Θεόπομπος, ἐπὶ τῆς ϛς´ ὀλυμπιάδος εἶπον ἐπιτάφιον ἐπὶ Μαυσώλῳ, Ἀρτεμισίας τῆς γυναικὸς αὐτοῦ προτρεψαμένης. καὶ ἐνίκησε μάλιστα εὐδοκιμήσας ἐν ᾗ εἶπε τραγῳδίᾳ. ἄλλοι δέ φασι Θεόπομπον ἔχειν τὰ πρωτεῖα. δράματα δὲ ἐδίδαξε ν´. τελευτᾷ δὲ ἐν Ἀθήναις ἐτῶν ἑνὸς καὶ μ´, ἔτι τοῦ πατρὸς αὐτοῦ περιόντος. ἔγραψε δὲ καὶ τέχνην ῥητορικὴν ἐν μέτρῳ, καὶ ἄλλα τινα καταλογάδην.

ϛς´ Jacoby *FGrH* 115 T 6a (D.S. 16.36.2)   ργ´ codd., Adler   ρζ´ Clinton

'Theodectes': son of Aristandros, from Phaselis in Lycia; an orator, he turned to tragedy. A pupil of Plato, Isocrates and Aristotle. This man, along with Naukrates of Erythrae, the orator Isokrates of Apollonia and Theopompus delivered, in the 106th Olympiad (= 356/5–353/2), a funeral speech for Mausolus at the instigation of his wife Artemisia. And he won, gaining great approval for the tragedy in which he spoke; but others say that Theopompus took first place. He produced 50 plays. He died in Athens at the age of 41, when his father was still alive. He also wrote an art of rhetoric in verse; and other works in prose.

3. Suda s.v. Ἰσοκράτης ('Isokrates', ι 653) (= *TrGF* I, 72 T 5). Compiled ca. 1000 AD. Text: Adler.

Ἰσοκράτης, Ἀμύκλα τοῦ φιλοσόφου, Ἀπολλωνίας τῆς ἐν τῷ Πόντῳ, ἢ Ἡρακλείας, ὡς Καλλίστρατος ὁ ῥήτωρ· μαθητὴς καὶ διάδοχος τοῦ μεγάλου Ἰσοκράτους, διακούσας δὲ καὶ Πλάτωνος τοῦ φιλοσόφου. οὗτος δὲ ὁ Ἰσοκράτης καὶ Θεοδέκτῃ τῷ ῥήτορι καὶ τραγῳδιοποιῷ καὶ Θεοπόμπῳ τῷ Χίῳ, ἅμα τῷ Ἐρυθραίῳ Ναυκράτῃ διηγωνίσατο περὶ λόγων εἰς τὸν ἐπιτάφιον Μαυσώλου τοῦ βασιλέως Ἁλικαρνασσοῦ. καὶ λόγοι αὐτοῦ ε´· Ἀμφικτυωνικός, Προτρεπτικός, Περὶ τοῦ τάφου μὴ ποιῆσαι Φιλίππῳ, Περὶ τοῦ μετοικισθῆναι, Περὶ τῆς ἑαυτοῦ πολιτείας.

Ναυκράτῃ Meursius   Ναυκρατίτῃ codd.

'Isokrates': son of Amyklas the philosopher, of Apollonia in Pontus or, according to Callistratus, of Heraclea – the orator; a pupil and successor of the great Isocrates; he also studied with Plato the philosopher. This Isokrates took part in a rhetorical contest with Theodectes, the orator and tragic poet; with Theopompus of Chios; and also with Naukrates of Erythrae, in the matter of the funeral oration for Mausolus, the king of Halicarnassus. His speeches are five: *Amphictyonic Speech*; *Protreptic*; *On Not Making a Tomb for Philip*; *On Being Resettled*; *On the Constitution of His Own City*.

From the early fourth century, but especially under Mausolus, the highly Hellenised ruler of Caria (377–353), the Hecatomnids engaged in an energetic centralisation and transformation of the Carian economy into a major commercial maritime centre of the eastern Aegean, undertaking a huge programme of urban development. Mausolus rebuilt the city of Halicarnassus as the new capital of the synoecised Hecatomnid dynasty, as well as developing various other maritime cities and cult centres (Hornblower 1982a, 333–41; Caliò 2005). The extent to which Greek cultural and technical skills were central to this enterprise is clear. Like Archelaus a few decades earlier (**VI D**), Mausolus invited numerous Greek intellectuals, artists and craftsmen to his court, among them the astronomer and mathematician Eudoxus of Cnidus (D.L. 8.87) and the Athenian orator – and actor – Aeschines (Philostr. *VS* 1.482 with Hornblower 1982a, 337). Some of the finest Greek architects and sculptors of the day were extensively employed at many sites, including the dynasty's great sanctuary at Labraunda, which was equipped with a state-of-the-art monumental stadium (Hornblower 1982a, 333–41; Roos 2011).

'The high point of Hekatomnid patronage was reached on a day in the year 353 BC, when Artemisia staged a funeral contest or ἀγών for her dead husband and brother Mausolus' (Hornblower 1982a, 333). This event is attested by a sound literary tradition (**1–3**) which makes it clear that, also like Archelaus, the Hecatomnids employed a Greek tragedian in their efforts of self-representation, for among those who competed was Theodectes of Phaselis, orator and tragedian (*TrGF* 72). It is very possible, though not directly provable, that Mausolus had drawn on the cultural and political possibilities offered by theatre while alive: the theatre of Halicarnassus may have been integral to Mausolus' design of the city and may date to his reign (below). And it has been plausibly argued that Theodectes might have helped Mausolus' cause diplomatically at an earlier time, in return for the satrap's patronage, by encouraging his home city of Phaselis to adopt a policy of conciliation towards him (see below on the political efforts of the Halicarnassian tragic poet Zenodotus at a later time). This would certainly explain how Phaselis managed to broker an advantageous agreement with the satrap that permitted it to maintain its independence (Hornblower 1982a, 122–3, 367).

The evidence for the precise nature of this funeral contest is ambiguous. **1** inspires most confidence, with telling detail and terminology (such as *agona … facit*) that suggests it drew on well-informed Greek sources. The contest was evidently associated with the dedication of the Mausoleum – a one-off event is thus most likely, though the intention of a periodic celebration cannot be ruled out. The mention of substantial prizes is striking, and is evidence for the direct application of the concentrated wealth of the dynasty in a manner that is lacking but may be assumed for other dramatic commissions by potentates. What the 'other valuables' on offer might be can only be guessed – land, tax breaks or other perks? It looks like the prizes served to advertise the event and attract talent and thus that the funeral contest was open to all-comers, rather than that Artemisia hand-picked and effectively commissioned the competing performers, indicating to this degree a model not altogether unlike that of the Athenian Dionysia. However it seems that the circumstances surrounding the tragedy composed by Theodectes were different from that of the funeral contest proper.

The sources are consistent in reporting the names of the four Greek men of eloquence who contended in their eulogies for the dead Mausolus – Theopompus (the historian from Chios), Theodectes, Naukrates and Isokrates. The tradition reported by **1** that this was 'the' Isocrates is clearly an instance of the common confusion between these homonyms (Flower 1994, 56–7), compounded by the Isocratean associations of all four contenders. A copy of Theopompus' encomium appears to have been held in a library in second-century Rhodes, an island that had been annexed by Mausolus in the 350s. An inscribed library catalogue includes Θεοπ[όμ]που … [Μαύσ]σωλος '[*Maus*]*solos* of Theop[om]pus' (Maiuri 1925, no. 11, ll. 13, 15; the preceding entries are the *Techne* of Theodectes in four books and his *Amphictyonic Speech*; Rosamilia 2014). Elsewhere Theopompus characterised the satrap as a man who would do anything for money (*FGrH* 115 F 229).

It is clear from **1** that Hyginus had both a prose work and a tragedy of Theodectes on Mausolus before him (Gellius himself seems only to have had access to the tragedy). It follows as likely that Theodectes composed two works for the Hecatomnids. The most economical explanation is that Artemisia's contest was in prose eulogy and that the tragedy was a somewhat separate affair (Zwierlein 1966, 154; Snell *TrGF* I airs the possibility that the tragedy was performed in Athens, but there are no grounds for the suggestion). No other tragedian is mentioned in connection with the dedication of the Mausoleum, and **2**'s identification of the *epitaphion* of Theodectes with the tragedy, and its odd expression 'the tragedy in which he spoke' (ἐν ᾗ εἶπε τραγῳδίᾳ), are best understood as a maladroit attempt to reconcile misunderstood evidence for the existence of both a prose and a dramatic *Mausolus* by Theodectes rather than reporting the genuine existence of a new mixed genre of 'tragic funeral oration' or the like. The expression in **2** is thus no solid ground on which to build a theory that the *Mausolus* was a kind of monodrama recited by Theodectes (Ribbeck 1875, 146).

Many have nonetheless thought that there was a separate tragic contest at Artemisia's ceremonies (*FHG* I, lxvii n. 3; Hornblower 1982a, 334; Flower 1994, 57) but the evidence does not favour it. **2**'s claim that Theodectes won with his tragedy is compromised by its attendant confusion. From **1** we might best deduce that Theodectes did not win in the prose eulogy and that his tragedy was 'more pleasing' than his prose contribution. That tells us nothing about the context in which the tragedy pleased its audience. The likelihood favours a performance of the tragedy that was entirely separate from the competition in prose eulogy at the funeral. It has been suggested that the tragedy might have been performed while Mausolus was still alive, to commemorate the synoecism of Halicarnassus (Jeppesen and Luttrell 1986, 107), but this is to wander too far away from what little evidence we have. More plausible is a performance at a subsequent memorial festival in honour of Mausolus, rather than at the funeral itself (Hornblower 1982a, 258–61 for the possibility that Mausolus was awarded heroic honours). Such a configuration would find a direct and contemporary parallel in Pontic Heraclea, where the death of the son and successor – Timotheos – of the founding tyrant, Klearchos, was celebrated with 'not only equestrian but also dramatic, musical and gymnic competitions, some at the funeral and others yet more splendid later on' (**Fiv 1**). The last clause suggests that commemorative competitions were held, possibly a year after his death, or even annually for some time. Although no source directly says as much, something of the sort may well have taken place for Mausolus, and would go some way towards explaining the confusion in the accounts of the funeral honours.

Hornblower is surely right to suggest that Theodectes' *Mausolus* will have served the Carian in much the same way as Euripides' *Archelaus* served its homonymous commissioner (**VI D**). He argues that Theodectes gave Mausolus divine ancestry from a mythical homonym who was a son of Apollo Helios and who gave his name to a river that was later called the Indos (Ps.-Plu. *Fluv.* 25.1: ἐκαλεῖτο δὲ πρότερον Μαυσωλὸς ἀπὸ Μαυσωλοῦ τοῦ Ἡλίου; Hornblower 1982a, 261, 271, 335–6). Jeppesen and Luttrell (1986, 107) *contra* postulate that Mausolus' descent in the play was drawn from Theseus (the great synoecist of Attica) and Heracles and, drawing on a suggestion that goes back to Ribbeck (1875), supposes that the *Mausolus* presented Mausolus as synoecist and founder of a Carian state. Hornblower (1982a, 333) also thinks that heroic honours for Mausolus as the second founder, through synoecism, of Halicarnassus is likely 'in a tomb designed and decorated by Greeks and overlooked by a theatre where perhaps Theodektes' new tragedy, the *Mausolus*, and Isokratean panegyrics of the dead satrap, had just been recited'. The iconography of the Mausoleum is adduced in support of these various interpretations (Jeppesen 2004, 90 argues against the prominence of the iconography of Apollo/the sun-god on the Mausoleum and Hecatomnid coinage asserted by Hornblower).

The identification of Mausolus as the offspring of Apollo would be confirmed if the 'son of Phoibos' (Φοιβήιος ἶνις l. 35) in a fragmentary section of the Salmakis inscription from Halicarnassus (late 2nd c.) does indeed refer to Mausolus, as its first editor proposed (Isager 1998, 15). Some reference to the founder of the synoecised city in this poetic expression of 'the pride of Halicarnassus' might well be expected (D'Alessio 2004, 48; *contra*: Jeppesen 2004). Any such forms of mythic propaganda may have continued to serve the dynasty after the death of Mausolus, for it persisted until 335, with four more children of Hecatomnus following Mausolus (himself a son of Hecatomnus) in succession. (For the period after Alexander's arrival in 334 see **Eviii**.)

It is striking that, though he was 'an important member of the fourth-century Athenian literary scene' (Bollansée 1999, 395) and very active in Athens in the 370s, winning his first of seven victories at the Dionysia soon after 372 (*IG* II² 2325A, l. 45 M-O; Webster 1954, 303 put it in around 368), Theodectes hailed from neighbouring Lycia rather than Athens. The Phaselites erected a statue of him in their agora (around which Alexander revelled in 334 and which he crowned: Plu. *Alex.* 17.9), a very early attestation of a statue honouring a tragic poet, including in Athens (Ma 2013, 76; it has been argued that the statue was of Theodectes' son, also Theodectes: Weißenberger *BNP* s.v. 'Theodectes'). Its presence in the agora suggests that for all his time abroad Theodectes remained a figure of great importance to his home city. (The importance of theatre to the Phaselites in later years, including dithyramb, satyr play and very probably tragedy, is attested by *SEG* 55, 1466, 2nd/1st c.) Another, albeit oblique, association between Theodectes and Caria is the reference to the difficulty of understanding 'the craft (*techne*) of Theodectes' in Antiphanes' comedy *Carians* (*PCG* F 111), but this is perhaps more likely to refer to his rhetorical rather than his tragic craft (above). Theodectes' homonymous son combined some of his father's generic diversity (though there is no evidence for tragedy), composing among other works an art of rhetoric and an encomium for a potentate – in his case Alexander of Epirus (Suda θ 139). That the

Hecatomnids were known for an attachment to theatre and tragedy in particular is suggested by Alexander the Great's choice of the famous tragic actor Thettalos as an emissary to
Mausolus' brother Pixodarus (Plu. *Alex.* 10.2–3) at a delicate moment in 337/6 'because his
profession made him peculiarly acceptable at Halikarnassos – either that, or he was bound
for Karia anyway, which is no less culturally significant' (Hornblower 1982a, 337).

The existence of a vigorous theatrical culture in Halicarnassus by the later fourth century
is further suggested by the existence of a number of Halicarnassian tragic and comic poets,
and a marked concern on the part of their home city to recognise their achievements and
to remember them long after. Phanostratos was a notable tragic poet from Halicarnassus
(*TrGF* I, 94; Kotlińska-Toma 2015, 161–2) who won at the Athenian Dionysia or Lenaea
(or both?) in 306 (**V I** on *IG* II³ 4, 518). The event was significant within Athens as the first
held under the restored democracy, and Phanostratos' fellow citizens went to the effort and
expense of arranging for the dedication of a statue of their successful son on the Athenian
Acropolis, probably to commemorate his role in it. Its inscribed base was found on the
slope above the Odeon of Herodes (*IG* II² 2794, ca. 307/6 Φανόστρατον Ἡρακλείδου | ὁ
δῆμος ὁ Ἁλικαρνασσέων | ἀνέθηκεν. 'The People of Halicarnassus dedicated (sc. this statue
of) Phanostratos son of Herakleides'). Phanostratos was also made proxenos on Delos (*IG*
XI 4, 528) and remembered in Halicarnassus over a century and a half later in the Salmakis
inscription (*SEG* 48, 1330, ll. 50–1) as a 'servant of Dionysus, a poet splendid at the sa-
cred crowns of the sons of Kekrops' (δμῶα Διωνύσου Φανόστρατον ἀοιδόν | Κεκροπιδῶν
ἱεροῖς ἁβρὸν ἐνὶ στεφάνοις). The language suggests that the memory of Phanostratos' success in Athens lived long in his homeland.

Two other famous sons of Halicarnassus recorded in the Salmakis inscription were probably comic poets of the late fourth or early third centuries: the Menestheus 'excelling in the
realm of the Muses' (*SEG* 48, 1330, l. 47) may be the comic poet of that name victorious
at the Lenaea (*IG* II² 2325E, l. 100 M-O; Isager 1998, 17); and the comic poet Dionysios
(*SEG* 48, 1330, l. 49) may also be the comic poet of that (not uncommon) name victorious
at the Lenaea in Athens in (probably) the second century (*IG* II² 2325E, l. 185 M-O; Millis
and Olson 2012, 179; Lloyd-Jones 1999, 11).

By the early decades of the third century at the latest, Halicarnassus had its own Dionysia,
with a prominent 'choral contest' at which honours were announced (*SEG* 28, 837, ll. 5–8:
στε[φανῶσαι — καὶ | ἀναγγεῖλα]ι ἐν τῶι χο[ρικ]ῶι ἀ[γῶνι — | — τοῖς Διο]νυσίοις ὅτι
ὁ δῆμ[ος — | —]ν χρυσῶι στεφ[άνωι —] 'to cr[own … and announc]e at the cho[ra]l
co[ntest …] at the [Dio]nysia that the Peop[le … crown …] with a gold crow[n …]). It
is difficult to say whether an event so described might have included drama (Ceccarelli
2010, 137 airs the possibility). The city became part of the Ptolemaic dominions from
280, but despite the manner in which the Ptolemies energetically promoted an association
of their power with the god Dionysus, creating an Association of Artists the more effectively to do so, there is no evidence to suggest that they actually introduced the festival
to the city. (Ptolemy II features prominently in *SEG* 28, 837, which is dated as a consequence to 281–266. Its honorand is an Athenian, perhaps Kallias of Sphettos, who served
Ptolemy II as a mercenary commander in Halicarnassus from 270/69: Shear 1978, 44–5.)
Reference to 'the day when the choruses perform' (*GIBM* 890, l. 2: [— ἡ]μέραι ὅτα[ν οἱ
χοροὶ συντελῶνται]) was (heavily) restored by Robert (1937, 150) to another fragmentary

decree from Halicarnassus, thought to date to the fourth century. The tantalising [-]υσω[-] '-*yso*-' in the previous line might conceal a reference to Dion*ysus*, and so indicate a Dionysia already in the fourth century, though a gold (χρυσῶι) ? crown is at least as likely in the context.

The tradition continued into the later Hellenistic period. The Salmakis inscription gives a homeland in Halicarnassus (l. 50) to the tragic poet Zenodotus hitherto known by a single fragment (*TrGF* I, 215). It also probably gives us his patronymic, since he has been plausibly identified as the Zenodotus son of Baukideus who received honours at Troezen, redoubled by honours from his home city of Halicarnassus, for having come to help expel an occupying garrison in Troezen during their struggle for freedom. Although in neither the Troezenian nor Halicarnassian case does the (fragmentary) decree refer to Zenodotus' career as a tragic poet, Jameson (2004, 97–8) seems confident of the identification. It is further possible that this tragic poet is, as Snell (*TrGF* I, 325) proposed, also to be identified with the Z[eno]do[tus] (Ma 2007, 229 = *SEG* 57, 1136) who had a victory in a contest of satyr play at Teos.

The Greek theatre of Halicarnassus was excavated in the 1970s and 1980s under the direction of Omit Serdaroğlu but never published. Substantial restoration work and some additional excavation took place from 2002 to 2006. This was a large theatre – close in size and form to that of Epidaurus, with a capacity of ca. 10,000 – and lay behind and beyond the agora and Mausoleum, viewed from arrival in the harbour. As Hornblower (1982a, 301) notes, 'conversely the seaward view from a seat in the theatre was interrupted by the Mausoleum on its enormous podium'.

Pedersen and Isager (2015) review the state of the archaeological evidence and publish some inscriptions from the theatre for the first time. One of these (2015, 310) is a dedication to Dionysus by an agonothete of the western gateway (πυλών), probably of second-century date, demonstrating that Dionysus was the deity associated with the Halicarnassian theatre and that by that date an agonothesia was in operation in connection with it. Its earliest phase has been variously dated in the mid fourth, the first half of the third, or the second century (*TGR* III, 402; Sear 2006, 337; Caliò 2005, 58: ca. 350). Its excavator (Serdaroğlu 1982, 355) was convinced of a mid fourth-century date under Mausolus for its first phase, citing but not describing architectural finds from the stage building ('architektonischen Fundstücken von der Skene'). Pedersen and Isager (2015, 306–7) note the weight of circumstantial evidence for such a date, including the existence, around 360–350, of both a need for a theatre and the financial resources to construct one. They suggest that the circle-based form of the Halicarnassian theatre may be another instance of the rapid transfer of architectural innovation from the Greek mainland to a receptive Caria. The theatre was extensively developed in the Hellenistic and Roman periods. There is evidence for prohedria in the 'early Hellenistic' period (Pedersen and Isager 2015, 310). It appears that there was an altar near the northern edge of the orchestra, off the central axis to the east, described by Pedersen (2004, 149) as 'of Dionysos'.

The city's strong affinity with Athens in the fifth century, implied by membership of the Delian League and service as a naval base after the allied revolt of 412 – combined with the desire of the Hecatomnids to legitimate and advertise their rule through a popular medium – made the adoption of theatre and tragedy in particular a highly attractive prospect.

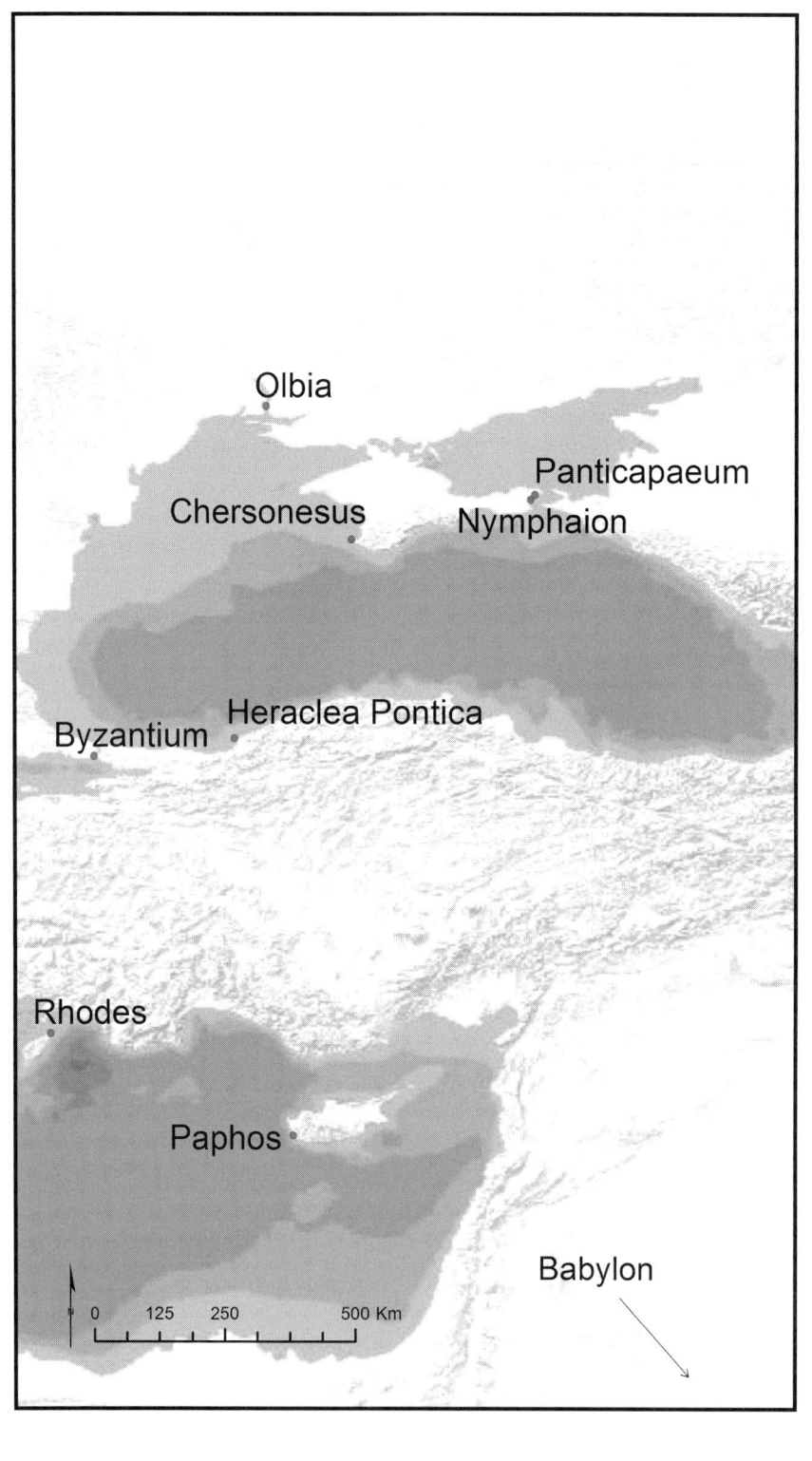

Olbia

Panticapaeum

Chersonesus

Nymphaion

Heraclea Pontica

Byzantium

Rhodes

Paphos

Babylon

0   125   250   500 Km

F | Black Sea

Introduction

Theatre culture is attested in many Black Sea locations by the second half of the fourth century and is certainly widespread throughout the region by the third. There are intimations in places that it may have been earlier. Readily discernible are two patterns of reception, already familiar from other parts of Greece.

1. The many Greek cities of the Black Sea coast were politically and culturally dominated by Athens, as was the Aegean, from about 437 and they were brought by various means into its empire (Braund 2005). One means was to establish democratic regimes (as in Cyzicus, Istros or Sinope), or support already established democratic regimes (Byzantium). These regimes seem to have embraced not only Athenian forms of government but also Athenian cultural forms, among them a theatre culture, as far as we can tell, upon the Athenian model (in this case a preference for Dionysia – even an Anthesteria and Thargelia – dramatic contests, public or choregic funding, ceremonial announcements of honours, international stars, etc.). The evidence is, however, regrettably thin and late.
2. There were also tyrants and kings who, as in Sicily, Macedon, and elsewhere, found theatre a useful instrument of public relations, as in the Cimmerian Bosporos (**Fiii**) and Heraclea (**Fiv**).

The Black Sea area also gives us some of our best evidence for a third factor that enhanced theatre's allure, particularly for autocrats. By the fourth century, and perhaps particularly for states on the 'barbarian' fringe, theatre culture signified both Greekness and, in an oddly contradictory way, internationalism. In some of the Pontic cities, at least, we have evidence that autocrats used theatre to advertise their personal ability to make and maintain cultural and political links with the wider world, and particularly the Greek world, which provided the main market for the Black Sea's abundant grain, slaves, fish and raw materials.

The Democratic Cities (**Fi–Fii**)

Byzantium (**Fi**) was probably an original member of the Delian League and remained an ally of Athens for most of the fifth century and during the Second Athenian Confederacy in the fourth. It seems also to have been a democracy for most of this time, and when it lapsed, Athenian intervention more than once saw to the restoration of a democratic constitution (Loukopoulou and Laitar *IACP* 916). It also contained a large population of resident Athenians by ca. 390 (X. *HG* 4.8.27). The city depended, therefore, for security and no doubt much income, on Athens and its Black Sea trade, until it became subject to Philip II of Macedon in the second half of the fourth century. It would not therefore be surprising to find that Byzantium, like the Aegean Islands, was an early recipient of Athenian theatre culture. It is however not until 306–303 that we can be sure that Byzantium had a Dionysia, a theatre, and an unspecified contest (probably tragedy) in the theatre: an Athenian decree honouring Asklepiades of Byzantium and making provision for an announcement of honours in his home city 'in the theatre [at the contest] of the Dionysia' (**Fi**). So little information comes from local sources that we can infer nothing from silence. Byzantium probably had theatre from a much earlier date.

The silence of our sources makes it impossible to judge the time of the earliest reception of theatre in the region stretching from the Propontis to the eastern shores of the Black Sea. Many of the cities shared a similar history of Athenian and then Macedonian domination. From the earliest years of the third century inscriptions reveal theatres and (mainly) Dionysia throughout the region. On the Phrygian shore of the Propontis, Cyzicus was an early member of the Delian League, and, probably with Athenian aid, overthrew an oligarchic regime to become a democracy with administrative structures remarkably close to the Athenian model (Arist. *Oec.*1347b30–4; Avram *IACP* 984). The city continued to be dominated by Athens in the fourth century when it joined the Second Athenian Confederacy (Avram *IACP* 984–5). An honorific inscription of the earliest years of the third century shows Cyzicus in possession of a Dionysia, an Anthesteria, and a theatre (Michel 1900, no. 534 = *IMT Kyz Kapu Dağ* 1437, ll. 12, 20–1), all certainly in place from at least the fourth century (cf. Avram *IACP* 985).

On the Thracian side of the Propontis, Perinthus, like Byzantium, with which it had a sympoliteia for some time in the fourth century, was also a member of both Athenian confederacies, before coming under the domination of Philip II. A third-century inscription records honours proposed by an agonothete for a visiting *tragoidos* who competed well in the local competition (Sayar 1998, no. 2). No archaeological evidence helps us say how far back its theatre goes. Though the theatron is easily visible on the southern slope of Perinthus' acropolis, it has never been excavated (Loukopoulou and Laitar *IACP* 921).

North of Byzantium, on the west coast of the Black Sea, Apollonia too was dominated by Athenian economic interests for most of the Classical period and was a member of the Delian League. The city has yielded a large number of comic figurines that were imported from Athens from the early to mid fourth century (*MMC³* AT 15d, 36c, 69c, 74e). More remarkably, Apollonia appears to have produced its own imitations of Attic comic figurines in the same period (*MMC³* XT 1–10, with many as yet unpublished examples from the site: J. R. Green *pers. comm.*). The chances that it had theatre by the fourth century are therefore good, but it is again not until the third century that we have a firm epigraphic record of the theatre as well as the Dionysia at Apollonia (*SEG* 52, 658; cf. *IScM* I 64, l. 36; *SEG* 52, 661).

Moving further north, the cities of Mesembria, Kallatis and Istros were probably all part of the Athenian Empire and members of the Delian League. Istros indeed seems to have owed its democratic constitution to Athenian intervention (Arist. *Pol.* 1305b1–12; Plu. *Per.* 20; *IACP* 933). Third-century inscriptions reveal a Dionysia, theatre and contests at Mesembria (*IGBulg* I² 307, 308(2), 308(3)); a Dionysia and a theatre at Kallatis (*IScM* III 3, cf. *IScM* III 5); and a Thargelia, contests and multiple theatres at Istros (*IScM* I 8, l. 16:

ἐμ πᾶσι τοῖς θεάτροις; *IScM* I 1, l. 12; 12, l. 17; *IScM* I 25; *IScM* I 65, 30; *SEG* 51, 933).
Reports of remains of a theatre at Dionysopolis were made in 1968 but remain unconfirmed
and the alleged inscriptions with musical notation found in it are also in doubt (cf. West
1992, 283: 'must be treated as highly suspect').

The time and social circumstances of Olbia's reception of theatre culture are unclear (**Fii**). In the fifth century there are indications that the city was ruled by a tyranny from ca. 480 and it is widely believed that Olbia was at this time a 'protectorate'
of Scythian kings, who probably exercised power through the tyrants (Avram, Hind
and Tsetskhladze in *IACP* 938; Burstein 2006, 141–3; Müller 2013, 48; but vigorously
disputed by Kryzhitskiy 2005). Olbia seems to have joined the Delian League after
Pericles took his fleet to the Black Sea ca. 437 (Braund 2005, 85, but disputed by Lewis
1997, 120). Possibly Olbia also adopted a democratic constitution at this time, though
the evidence is vague (Vinogradov 1981b; Robinson 2011, 162–4). If Athens offered
a political and cultural alternative to tyranny and/or Scythian domination this might to
some extent explain Olbia's early local interest in theatre. It is from this time (430–420)
that our first clear evocation of theatre appears in the Black Sea, three joining fragments
of an Attic bell krater showing two tragic choreuts dancing together with a piper and
his assistant (**V E**). This of course proves nothing about contemporary performance in
Olbia, but it does suggest interest in and knowledge of dramatic performance, as do the
Attic comic terracotta figurines that were imported to Olbia from at least the second
quarter of the fourth century and a statue of an actor as Papposilenos from the late
fourth or early third century. It is however not until ca. 325 that an Olbian inscription,
associated with the onset of a radical phase of the democracy, gives firm proof of the
existence of a theatre and a Dionysia (**Fii**). The theatre has probably been located, but
was so thoroughly robbed of its stones in antiquity that it is unlikely to yield much
information.

Some 300 km by sea south-east of Olbia, the city of Chersonesus seems to have maintained a democratic constitution, even receiving democratic exiles from Heraclea in the
time of Klearchos (Zolotaryov 2005, 151). Chersonesus has the only fully excavated theatre in the region. Stratigraphy shows it to be late fourth or more probably third century,
a time when a Dionysia appears to be independently attested (*IosPE* I² 344; Dana 2011,
57). An earlier theatre is likely: Braund and Hall feel 'we may be sure that the city enjoyed
theatrical performances in the two centuries and more before the stone theatre was constructed' (2014, 386).

Almost directly south of Chersonesus, on the south coast of the Black Sea and 500 km
to the east of Heraclea, Sinope is specifically mentioned by Plutarch as an object of
Athenian imperial interests. At the time of Pericles' expedition, probably ca. 437,
Athenian forces expelled the tyrant Timoleos and established a democratic constitution,
and even planted 600 Athenian colonists in the city (Plu. *Per.* 20; Vinogradov 1981a;
Braund 2005). It probably also acquired a theatre by the fourth century, though the evidence is only indirect. No less than four dramatic poets, both tragic (Diogenes) and
comic (a different Diogenes, Diodorus, and Diphilus), came from fourth-century Sinope
(Taplin *forthcoming*). For the region's later importance for drama, dance, mime and pantomime see Dana 2011, 60–7.

Black Sea Tyrants (**Fiii**–**Fiv**)

In the north-eastern regions of the Black Sea, specifically in the Cimmerian Bosporus, evidence of theatres and theatre culture is no earlier than the fourth-century Spartocid kings (**Fiii**). Despite the region's long history of autocracy, Athens was probably a factor in theatre's reception. Close economic and cultural ties date from the time of Satyros (433–389), the founder of the Bosporan dynasty (**Fiii 1**). As Athens controlled the sea routes from the Black Sea, the Spartocids controlled the grain, and this mutual dependence only grew as Athens' need for grain increased in the fourth century. Good relations with Athens thus enabled the Spartocids, a Greco-Scythian aristocratic family from Panticapaeum, to acquire and maintain their rule (Moreno 2007, 144–208). Athens, for its part, was willing to indulge their seizure of its garrison at Nymphaion (Moreno 2007, 166, 174–5, 189), sometimes gave the Spartocids military aid (R-O II no. 64 with comm. p. 324), and even helped them suppress internal dissent (Isoc. 17.5). Control over the grain trade also meant control over the distribution of wealth within and beyond the kingdom. The Spartocids added to their own internal security both by creating a wealthy merchant class to counterbalance the power of rival aristocrats and by ensuring that these aristocrats, as well as rival Scythian kings in the grain-producing hinterland, were bound to support Spartocid interests if they wished to acquire a personal share in the economic benefits. From Athens the Spartocids received prestige as well as wealth: in return for securing Athens' grain they received Athenian citizenship, tax exemption (*ateleia*) and other honours (*IG* II³ 1, 298).

We can guess that the ties between Athens and the Spartocids politicised cultural affiliation within this mixed Greek and Scythian region. Athenian culture became a prestige culture for élites in sympathy with the Spartocid *status quo*. Elite Bosporan families sent their sons to study in Athens, especially it seems in the school of Isocrates, in the hope they would acquire Athenian culture and form networks with the Athenian élite (**Fiii 1**; Isoc. 15.224, 17.3–4; Moreno 2007, 175, 177; cf. on **Fiv**). At the same time it appears that many rival aristocratic families, disenchanted with the Spartocid stranglehold on political and economic power, reaffirmed and indeed reinvented their Scythianness (Moreno 2007, 193–206).

Indirect evidence of theatre in the Cimmerian Bosporus comes as early as the first years of the fourth century, in the form of visits by Athenian theatre people (**Fiii 1**) and the importation of comic vases and figurines. This is soon followed by direct evidence in the form of an inscribed architrave of a propylon for the theatre at Nymphaion (**Fiii 3**), datable to 389–349, which also attests the presence of an agonothete (an office attested elsewhere in the realm) and Dionysus' proprietorship of the theatre. By the mid fourth century we have our earliest reference to (multiple) theatres in the kingdom, and sojourns at court by international stars (**Fiii 2**; **Fiii 3**), in both cases kitharodes. Comedy, however, is assured by what appears to be a pair of choregic dedicatory reliefs datable to the second half of the fourth century (**I Aviii 1d**). Traces of a theatre have been found at Panticapaeum including a marble throne of the fourth century that is thought to be from (the prohedria of?) the theatre.

Klearchos, the founder of the tyranny in Heraclea Pontica in 365, studied with Plato and Isocrates (**Fiv**). Here as in the Cimmerian Bosporus, an Athenian education appears to have been *de rigueur* for local elites. Most famous among them were Klearchos' countrymen Heraclides, one time Deputy Head of Plato's Academy (361/0), and Chamaeleon (ca. 350–after 281). None of them seems to have shared Plato's disapproval of the theatre. Between them Heraclides and Chamaeleon wrote several books on the Athenian dramatists, including all three of the great fifth-century tragedians, on comedy, on satyr play and even forged tragedies by Thespis. Klearchos himself was highly cultivated, and is said to be the first tyrant to have amassed a large library, which he did probably in imitation of those of the Academy and presumably Isocrates' school (Pinto 2013, 94–5). It was almost certainly a personal library, but was doubtless shared with other former students of the Athenian masters. This fact strongly suggests that an openness to Panhellenic and especially Athenian culture was official policy, though we have no direct evidence that theatre formed a part. His enthusiasm for Plato and Athens entailed certain risks, it seems, as a group of conspirators, chief among them Chion, who had acquired a hatred of tyrants while studying at the Academy, ambushed and murdered Klearchos at the Dionysia in 353 while he was 'walking to a spectacle', probably to lead the Dionysian parade (see on **Fiv**). The first attested drama in the region was in the context of a funeral in 338 sponsored by Klearchos' son (perhaps significantly named) Dionysius, for his more popular brother, Klearchos' immediate successor (**Fiv 1**). From about the same time (330s–320s) we have our earliest reference to the theatre building in Heraclea where the scholar Heraclides was crowned (**Fiv 2**).

Fi: Byzantium. Athenian decree honouring Asklepiades of Byzantium, 306–303 (reference to Antigonus and Demetrius as 'Kings' at the beginning of the decree and lack of standard reference to the law of 303 limiting the value of honorary crowns; the reference to 'the other Greeks' in l. 5 makes 304/3 probable, as this was the time of Demetrius' second expedition to Greece: Billows 1997, 376). Asklepiades appears to have played some role in the 'liberation' of the Greeks by Antigonus and Demetrius. The section of the decree reproduced here follows directly upon **I Av 4m**, which relates to the awarding of a crown at the Athenian Dionysia.

Fragment of a marble stele.
0.5 × 0.42 × 0.13 m.
Found on the Acropolis.
IG II 5, 251c; *IG* II² 555.
Text: Based on *IG* II² 555, ll. 16–38.

```
            ὅπως δ᾽ ἂν ὅ τε στέφανος ἀναγορε-        stoich. 34
            [υθεῖ] ἐν Βυζαντίωι καὶ ἡ εἰκὼν σταθεῖ ἡ Ἀσκ-
            [ληπι]άδου χειροτονῆσαι τὸν δῆμον τρεῖς ἄ-
            [νδρα]ς ἐξ Ἀθηναίων ἁπάντων, οἵτινες ἀφικό-
    20      [μενοι] εἰς Βυζάντιον ἀξιώσουσιν τὸν δῆμο-
            [ν τὸν Βυ]ζαντίων ψηφίσασθαι τὸν στέφανον
            [ἀναγορε]ῦσαι ἐν τῶι θεάτρωι Διονυσίων [τῶ]-
            [ι ἀγῶνι κ]αὶ τὴν εἰκόνα στῆσαι τὴν Ἀσκλη[πι]-
            [άδου ἐν τ]εῖ ἀγορᾶι ἣν ὁ δῆμος ὁ Ἀθηναίων . .
    25      [. . . ⁷ . . .]ν αὐτοῦ καὶ διδάσκειν αὐτοὺς [ὅτι]
            [ταῦτα πρ]άττοντες χαριοῦνται τῶι [δήμωι, τ]-
```

[ἧς δὲ ποι]ήσεως τοῦ στεφάνου καὶ τ[ῆς εἰκόν]-
[ος ἐπιμε]λη[θ]ῆναι τὸν ἐπὶ τεῖ διο[ικήσει με]-
[τὰ τῶν αἱ]ρεθέντων πρέσβεων· δο[ῦναι δ᾽ ἑκάσ]-
30   [τωι τῶν α]ἱρεθέντων πρέσβεω[ν ἐφόδιον τὸν]
[ταμίαν τ]οῦ δήμου πεντήκον[τα δραχμὰς ἐκ τ]-
[ῶν εἰς τὰ] κατὰ ψηφίσματα [ἀναλισκομένων τ]-
[ῶι δήμωι]. ἀναγράψαι [δ]ὲ τ[όδε τὸ ψήφισμα τὸν]
[γραμματ]έα τὸν κατ[ὰ πρυτανείαν ἐν στήλει]
35   [λιθίνει] καὶ στῆσ[αι ἐν ἀκροπόλει, εἰς δὲ τὴ]-
[ν ἀναγρα]φὴν τῆς [στήλης δοῦναι τὸν ταμίαν]
[τοῦ δήμο]υ τρι[άκοντα δραχμὰς ἐκ τῶν εἰς τὰ]
[κατὰ ψηφ]ίσμ[ατα ἀναλισκομένων τῶι δήμωι].
vacat 0.015

And so that the crown might [be] announced in Byzantium and the statue of Asklepiades erected, the People is to elect three m[en] from all the Athenians who are to g[o] [20] to Byzantium and ensure that the [By]zantine People vote to [annou]nce the crown in the theatre [at the contest] of the Dionysia [a]nd erect the statue of Askle[piades in th]e agora which the Athenian People [25] […] and to instruct them [that by d]oing [this] they will show favour to the [People]. The chief finan[cial officer along with the ch]osen ambassadors is to [loo]k a[f]ter the [const]ruction of the crown and t[he statue], and the People's [treas-urer] is to gi[ve each] [30] of the chosen ambassado[rs a travel allowance] of fift[y drachmas from the money spent by the People] on decrees. [The secretar]y of the [prytany] is to have t[his decree] written [on a [35] stone stele] and set u[p on the Acropolis; the People]'s [treasurer is to give] thi[rty drachmas for the inscri]bing of the [stele from the money spent by the People on de]cr[ees].

This is our only reference to a theatre in Byzantium and the first of only two ancient referenc-es to a Dionysia there. The second, *IK Byzantion 2*, is much later (ca. 150) and refers to the 'announcement of crowns at the contest of the Dionysia' (ll. 23–5). The lack of specificity, shown by both inscriptions, about the nature of the contest, permits no inferences about the existence or non-existence of drama or any genre of drama (see commentary on **I Av 4m**).

Braund and Hall point out that Dionysus cult, though of limited importance in many Dorian states, was of great importance to Megara (**Bi; I Aiii 4**) and to cities that traced their origins to Megara (2014, 378–9). Megarian foundations include Megara Hyblaea (**Aiii**) and Selinus (**Axiv**) in the west, Heraclea Pontica (**Fiv**) and Kallatis (**F Introduction**) on the Black Sea, and Byzantium. Indirect evidence for theatre in fourth-century Byzantium may come from Athenaeus' claim that Python, the possible author of the satyric *Agen,* produced 326–324 (Le Guen 2014), may have been from Byzantium: but Catane is named first as a possibility, and Athenaeus also suggests that Alexander himself may have written *Agen* (Ath. 2.50f, 13.586d, 13.595d). Archaeological evidence for the Byzantine theatre comes only from much later. Imperial Byzantium had as many as four theatres (Sear 2006, 421). The *Theatrum Maius*, reputed to be the oldest, is said by the *Chronicon*

Paschale (495.4 Dindorf) to have been built by Septimius Severus, but Dio (74.12.4) already attests a plurality of theatres at the time of the siege of Byzantium by Severus in 193–195 AD.

In the third century we also have epigraphic evidence of two kitharodes and a boy choreut from Byzantium (Stefanis nos. 87, 2616, 2817).

Fii: Olbia. Decree honouring Kallinikos, son of Euxenos, ca. 325 (letter forms and historical context: see below). On the College of the Seven, attested from 330–200 and mentioned in the prescript, see Dubois 1996, 139–40.

Three joining fragments of a marble base for a bronze statue (cuttings for feet visible), parts of all sides of front preserved.

Fr. a: 0.21 × 0.22 × 0.07 m. Fr. b–c (*IosPE* I² 25): 0.355 × 0.74 × 0.58 m.

Fragment a (*IosPE* I² 31) preserved at top, broken on all other sides. Fragments b–c, apparently joined when found, preserve the parts of the left, right and bottom of the front of the base.

Fragment a found 1900 in the ruins of ancient Olbia and given in the same year to the Odessa Museum; Fragments b–c found in walls of Olbia in 1848; in Odessa Museum for 'more than 75 years' in 1983.

Odessa Archaeological Museum.

Ouvaroff 1855, 55–7, pl. 24.2; *IosPE* I² 25 + 31; Vinogradov and Karyshkovsky 1982 and 1983 (= *SEG* 32, 794).

Text: based on *SEG* 32, 794; cf. *BE* 1990, no. 536.

Photos: Vinogradov and Karyshkovsky 1982, fig. 1; Nikolayev 2013, fig. 3 (parts of last five lines).

[ἔδοξε βουλῆι καὶ δήμωι, οἱ ἄρχοντες καὶ οἱ ἑ]πτὰ εἶπαν· ἐπειδὴ Καλ[λίνικος]
[Εὐξένου ἀνὴρ καλὸς κἀγαθὸς ὢν διατελεῖ(?) τὰ] βέλτιστα τῶι δήμωι κα[τεργα]-
[ζόμενος(?) — — — — — — — — — τῆι] πόλει παρὰ τὴν ἔγδοσι[ν . . ⁵ . .]
[— — — — — — — — — — — — — —]ου τάς τε προσόδους συ[ναυξ . . ⁵ . .]
5   [— — — — ἐπεὶ (e.g.) αἴτιος γέγο]νεν τοῦ τὸν δῆμον κατα[στῆναι]
[εἰς εἰρήνην, αὐτὸς οὔτε (e.g.) φοβούμενος ὅ τι ἐμ]ποδὼν οὔτε φιλίαν περ[ὶ πλείονος]
[ποιούμενος σπεύδων τε τοὺς διαφερομένους] ἐν τῆι πόλει εἰς ὁμόγ[οιαν κα]-
[ταστῆσαι, τὴν ἀποκοπὴν τῶν] χρεῶν ε[ἰσήνεγ]κεν, ὅ τε δῆμος ἐστεφα[νωκὼς δια]-
[σώισ]αντος αὐτοῦ χ[ρήμα]σι καὶ ἀνδριάν[τι τ]ά τε τέλη τὰ ἐπιβεβλη[μένα οἷς]
10 [πάν]τες ἐβλάπτοντο ἀφείρηκεν καὶ τὴν κοπὴ[ν το]ῦ χαλκοῦ κατὰ λ[όγον ἦχεν(?)· ἵνα]
[καὶ] οἱ ἄλλοι φιλοτιμότερον ἔχωσι πρὸς τὸ κα[ὶ λ]έγειν καὶ πρά[ττειν τὰ βέλτιστα]
[εἰ]δότες, ὅτι τιμῆς καὶ δωρεᾶς ἀξίας ἕκαστο[ι τε]ύξονται παρὰ το[ῦ δή]μο[υ τῶν]
εὐεργετημάτων, δεδόχθαι τῶι δήμωι· ἐπαι[νέσαι Κ]αλλίνικον Εὐξέν[ου]

ἀρετῆς ἕνεκεν καὶ εὐεργεσίας τῆς εἰς τὸ[ν δ]ῆμον καὶ στεφανωθῆνα[ι]
15   αὐτὸν χρυσοῖς χιλίοις καὶ ἀνδριάντι τὸν δ[ὲ] στέφανον ἀναγορευθῆναι τοῖς
Διονυσίοις ἐν τῶι θεάτρωι.

ὁ δῆμος Διὶ Σωτῆρι.

5 ἐπεὶ (e.g.) ὁ κίνδυνος αἴτιος γέγο]νεν τοῦ τὸν δῆμον κατα[στῆναι εἰς διαφοράν]
Vinogradov and Karyshkovsky

[The Council and the People decreed, the Archons and the S]even spoke.
Kal[linikos the son of Euxenos, a true gentleman, has in the past] per[formed
the] greatest benefits for the People [and continues to do so …] for the city
beyond the letting ou[t …] and in[creased] the income [⁵ … (e.g.) he was
responsible for] brin[ging] the People [to a peaceful settlement] (or e.g. '[and
when the danger arose that] cau[sed division among] the People, he') [fearing
no ob]stacle, [and putting aside] partisan sympathy, [and making every effort
to bring the opposed parties] in the city to an underst[anding], he int[roduced
legislat]ion [to cancel] debts, and the People, because he [sav]ed them, gar-
landed with m[one]y and a statu[e] (the text cannot be right here: even if we
accept the doubtful 'garland with money' the direct object cannot be in the genitive absolute) and he did away with the impo[sed] taxes [by which ¹⁰ they al]l
suffered harm and he [ratio]nalised (?) the mintin[g] of [th]e copper coin. [So]
others [also] become more ambitious in bo[th s]peaking and act[ing in the best
interests of the city in the kn]owledge that each man will [re]ceive honours
and gifts from th[e Pe]op[le] in exchange for [their] benefactions, it is decreed
by the People: to pra[ise K]allinikos son of Euxen[os] for his excellence and
benefaction to t[he P]eople and to have him crown[ed] ¹⁵ with (a crown of)
one thousand gold staters (= 20,000 Attic drachmas or 3⅓ talants) and a statue
a[nd] to have the crown announced at the Dionysia in the theatre.

The People for Zeus the Saviour.

The inscription is connected to radical social reforms attested by Macrobius (*Sat.* 1.11.33):
'And lest you think such things happen only in our republic, the Borysthenites (i.e. Olbians)
when besieged by Zopyrion, were able to withstand the enemy once the slaves were liberated, the foreign residents were given citizenship, and debts were cancelled.' The siege
of Olbia by Zopyrion, the Macedonian governor of Thrace, is dated by most historians to
331–330 (e.g. Vinogradov and Kryžickij 1995, 135; Dubois 1996, 47), but some favour a
later date, 328–326 (Atkinson and Yardley 2009, 104), or even 326–325 (Niese 1893, 499;
Ehrhardt 1987, 100 n. 161). Zopyrion may have died in the winter of 325/4 (Atkinson and
Yardley 2009, 104).

 At the beginning of the fourth century Olbia became a moderate democracy, but a
more radical democratic revolution was triggered by the siege of Olbia. Vinogradov and
Kryžickij (1995, 136) reconstruct the history by bringing the evidence of this document
together with the evidence from Macrobius:

The crisis created by Zopyrion's siege of Olbia aggravated various social and economic contradictions, and in particular tensions between creditors and debtors made worse by the imposition of the direct war tax. The danger threatened to deliver the city to the enemy. Kallinikos succeeded: in getting the Assembly to pass a bill concerning the payment of debts; in settling the differences; in restoring civic unity; and in mobilising the city to defend itself. A major contribution to the latter effort was the freeing of slaves and the extension of citizen rights to foreigners. Invigorated by the defeat of the enemy, Olbia undertook a series of democratic reforms, abolishing direct taxation and minting an obol – the Borysthenites – that made it easier for less well-off inhabitants to pay off their debts. (trans. Csapo)

There are various bits of evidence that can be brought to support this portrait of social revolution. The bronze obols minted by the city were soon after 330 replaced by copper coins of reduced weight known as 'borysthens' and it is to this innovation that Vinogradov and Karyshkovsky (1982) refer Kallinikos' reform of the coinage mentioned in l. 10. A mass burial of 52 men and children, evidently killed by stoning, and among whom two were found in fetters, also belongs to this period of social upheaval (Vinogradov and Kryžickij 1995, 136; cf. Karjaka 2008). Vinogradov and Golovačeva (1990, 15–30) argue that an ostrakon addressed to Zopyrion (*SEG* 42, 711) was sent to the Macedonian general by a member of a fifth column inside the city ('[Ni]kophanas, son of Adrastos, gave a horse to Zopyrion. Let him send it back to the city to me and let him give [h]im the lette[rs]'). Dubois more soberly draws attention to the unexceptional character of the name Zopyrion in the region (1996, 49). As another index of social trauma, Nikolayev (2013, 68) observes that the dedication of the decree to Zeus the Saviour is characteristic of decrees of the years 328–320 immediately following the siege of Olbia. On the connection between the siege and the cult of Zeus the Saviour, see Vinogradov and Kryžickij 1995, 112.

Though the cult of Dionysus in Olbia is well attested (Vinogradov and Kryžickij 1995, 116–17; Dubois 1996, 128–9, 145–6, 154–5; Feraru 2004–2005; Braund 2008), this is the earliest firm evidence we have for the existence of a Dionysia and a theatre in Olbia. There is no mention of any particular contest and we may infer only that the time reserved for such announcements was invariable. The two other Olbian inscriptions that mention the theatre, both honorific decrees of the third century, seem to offer the same formula 'to be announced at the Dionysia in the theatre' (*SEG* 34, 758, ll. 48–50: [τὸν δὲ σ]τέφανον ἀναγορε[υθῆναι τοῖς Διονυσίοις ἐ]ν τῷ[ι] θεάτρωι ὑπ[ὸ τοῦ κήρυκος]; *SEG* 39, 702, ll. 15–16: ἀναγγελθῆναι δ[ὲ τὸν στέφανον Διονυσίοις ἐν τῶι θεά]τρωι).

The theatre of Olbia has been located in an 'amphitheatre shaped' terrain in the lower town, close to the marketplace: archaeological sondages in this terrain revealed a 'staircase configuration' in the soil, which led Karasev and Levi (1958, 137) to infer that the stone theatre had been robbed of its stones at some time of need in antiquity (cf. Wasowicz 1975, 95–6; Dana 2011, 57).

Olbian interest in tragedy by about 425 is attested by the imported Attic red-figured vase fragment showing a chorus in performance (**V E**). Olbia was also an importer of

Attic comic terracotta figurines throughout the fourth century with locally produced copies from at least the second quarter of the century (*MMC*³ AT 60c, AT 89, AT 115a, XT 15; Koshelenko 1984, pl. 118 no. 1; Green 2009, 256–7 no. 112; *MNC*³ 1AT 56a–b, 1DT 12). An Olbian 'agonothete' may be attested in a letter of ca. 500 (Ceccarelli 2013a, 338–9; cf. **Fiii 3** and commentary).

Fiii: Cimmerian Bosporus

1. **Isocrates, *Trapeziticus* 17.52**. Delivered ca. 393 (the collapse of Spartan maritime hegemony is referred to at 17.36, so the speech must have been delivered after the Battle of Cnidus in August 394 and before the death of Satyros I, which D.S. 14.93.1 puts in 393 but which was probably ca. 389: see Werner 1955). D.H. *Isoc.* 18.23–4 identifies the young Bosporan who delivers this speech as one of Isocrates' foreign students (ὃν ἔγραψε ξένῳ τινὶ τῶν μαθητῶν; cf. Trevett 1990, 25–6). The passage is of interest for its mention of Xenotimos, son of Carcinus, travelling from Satyros' court to Athens (Stefanis no. 1910). This is clearly the son of the tragedian Carcinus I (see **Ax**). For Xenotimos, see commentary below. The passage is from the prosecution of the banker Pasion for refusing to return money deposited with him by the speaker, who is a citizen of the Cimmerian Bosporus. It is of some interest that the money in question is, by the prosecutor's own admission, money that was hidden from Satyros in the guise of a loan from Pasion at a time when the prosecutor's father had been arrested by Satyros and the prosecutor feared the money would be confiscated. The father was subsequently acquitted of all charges and restored to the tyrant's favour. The passage refers to a failed attempt by the prosecutor and a spokesman of Pasion to have Satyros arbitrate the dispute. The text of the letter is not preserved, but it was apparently read out in the trial by the court clerk. Text: Mathieu and Brémond.

> ἀκούσας δὲ Σάτυρος ἀμφοτέρων ἡμῶν δικάζειν μὲν οὐκ ἠξίου περὶ τῶν ἐνθάδε γενομένων συμβολαίων, ἄλλως τε καὶ μὴ παρόντος τούτου μηδὲ μέλλοντος ποιήσειν ἃ ἐκεῖνος δικάσειεν· οὕτω δὲ σφόδρ' ἐνόμιζεν ἀδικεῖσθαί με ὥστε συγκαλέσας τοὺς ναυκλήρους ἐδεῖτ' αὐτῶν βοηθεῖν ἐμοὶ καὶ μὴ περιορᾶν ἀδικούμενον, καὶ πρὸς τὴν πόλιν συγγράψας ἐπιστολὴν ἔδωκε φέρειν Ξενοτίμῳ τῷ Καρκίνου.

> When Satyros had listened to both of us he did not wish to make a ruling over contracts formed here (in Athens), especially as this man was not present and unlikely to comply with whatever judgement he might give. But so strongly did he feel the injury done to me that he summoned the ship owners and asked them to assist me and not to ignore the injury done to me and he composed a letter to the city (Athens) and gave it to Xenotimos the son of Carcinus to deliver.

2. **Polyaenus, *Stratagems* 5.44.1.1–10**. Written: early 160s AD, referring to an event in 353. Although the work is generally known as the Στρατηγήματα, the title is probably

rather *The Art of Generalship*, Στρατηγικά (Wheeler 2010, 34–6). Memnon was a Rhodian military commander in the service of the Persian satrap Artabazus (ca. 380–333). Leucon was king of the Cimmerian Bosporus from 389 to 349. His capital was Panticapaeum, but the anecdote seems to embrace theatres throughout the region. Text: Melber with emendation.

Μέμνων ἐπιτιθέμενος Λεύκωνι τῷ Βοσπόρου τυράννῳ, βουλόμενος καταμαθεῖν τὰ μεγέθη τῶν πολεμίων [πόλεων] καὶ τὰ πλήθη τῶν ἐνοικούντων ἔπεμψεν Ἀρχιβιάδην Βυζάντιον ἐπὶ τριήρους πρεσβευτὴν πρὸς ⁵ Λεύκωνα ὡς ὑπὲρ φιλίας καὶ ξενίας διαλεξόμενον. συνέπεμψε δὲ αὐτῷ καὶ Ὀλύνθιον κιθαρῳδὸν Ἀριστόνικον, εὐδοκιμοῦντα μάλιστα δὴ πάντων τότε παρὰ τοῖς Ἕλλησιν, ὅπως ἐν τῷ παράπλῳ προσορμιζομένων, ἐπιδεικνυμένου τοῦ κιθαρῳδοῦ, τῶν ἐνοικούντων εἰς ¹⁰ τὰ θέατρα σπουδῇ συνιόντων τὸ πλῆθος τῶν ἀνθρώπων κατάδηλον τῷ πρεσβευτῇ γένοιτο.

Ἀριστόνικον codd.   Στρατόνικον Braund and Hall

When Memnon was planning to attack Leucon the tyrant of the Bosporus and wanted to ascertain the size of the enemy['s cities] and their population he sent Archibiades of Byzantium in a trireme as an ambassador to ⁵ Leucon on the pretext of discussions about friendship and alliance. Along with him he sent the Olynthian kitharode Aristonikos, a man who was extremely famous throughout all Greece, so that while sailing past they could come to anchor, the kitharode could give a performance, the inhabitants would hurry to ¹⁰ the theatres and the size of the population could be made clear to the ambassador.

3. **Inscribed architrave of a propylon thought to be for the theatre or sanctuary of Dionysus at Nymphaion**. Date: 389–349 (letter forms; reference to Leucon).

Inscribed architrave block, one of many fragments of a monumental propylon excavated in 2000 on a terrace on the southern slope of the plateau of Nymphaion, 14 km south of Panticapaeum on the Kerch Strait. Blue, red and yellow paint appear in the decoration of the cornice, and blue and red on the monument's ionic capitals, thought by Bujskikh (2007, 135) to be the earliest example of a local North-Pontic architectural style. The inscription is aligned to the left and still contains red paint, designed to make the letters stand out against a white background.
3.53 × 0.565 m.
SEG 52, 741.
Sokolova 2000–2001; Sokolova and Pavilchenko 2002; Sokolova 2007; Braund and Hall 2014, 383–4.
Text: *SEG* 52, 741.   Photos and reconstruction of propylon: Sokolova and Pavilchenko 2002.

Θεοπροπίδης Μεγακλέος τὴν εἴσοδον ἀνέθηκεν Διονύσωι
ἀγωνοθετέων, Λεόκωνος ἄρχοντος Βοσπόρο καὶ Θεοδοσίης
καὶ τῆς Σινδικῆς πάσης καὶ Τορετέων καὶ Δανδαρίων καὶ Ψησσῶν.

Theopropides, Son of Megakles, dedicated the entrance (or 'the eisodos') to Dionysus, while agonothete, at the time that Leucon was ruling the Bosporus and Theodosia and the whole of Sindike and the Toretai, the Dandarioi and the Psessoi.

4. Machon, *Sayings* fr. 11.141–7 (Gow). Machon's *Sayings* (Χρεῖαι) were written in Alexandria in the 3rd c. The date of the supposed visit of Stratonicus to Pairisades (if that is who is meant: see below) must be after 348, the beginning of a five-year period of joint rule between Pairisades I and his brother, Spartokos II, or afterwards during the long period of sole rule by Pairisades (344–310). Stratonicus is the famous wit and kitharist/kitharode (Stefanis no. 2310). Text: Gow.

> Στρατόνικος ὁ κιθαρῳδὸς ὡς Βηρισάδην
> ἔπλευσεν εἰς τὸν Πόντον ὄντα βασιλέα.
> πολλοῦ χρόνου δ᾽ ἤδη γεγονότος ἀποτρέχειν
> ἠβούλετο Στρατόνικος εἰς τὴν Ἑλλάδα.
> 145   ὡς δ᾽ αὐτὸν ὡς ἔοικεν οὐ προσίετο
> τοῦτ᾽ ἀποκριθῆναί φασι τῷ Βηρισάδῃ,
> σὺ γὰρ διανοεῖ, φησίν, αὐτοῦ καταμένειν;

Stratonicus the kitharode sailed to the Black Sea to the court of Berisades who was king and when he had been there a long time Stratonicus wanted to get away to Greece. [145] But as he (Berisades) apparently would not give him leave they say he gave this response to Berisades, 'So do you intend to remain here?'

The kingdom had close ties with Athens, because it was Athens' principal supplier of grain, delivering 400,000 medimnoi in 355/4, 'as much as from all other sources put together' (D. 20.31–2). From the time of Satyros (433–389), the Spartocid kings charged no export tax on grain shipped to Athens and in return received Athenian citizenship, tax exemption (*ateleia*) and other honours (*IG* II³ 1, 298 = R-O II no. 64; D. 20.29–40; [D]. 34.36). These ties may have contributed to the dynasty's receptivity to theatre.

That Satyros himself took an interest in theatre is suggested by his connection with Xenotimos, son of Carcinus (**1**). Carcinus combined a successful career as a tragic poet with a political and military career (Th. 2.23.2; *IG* I³ 365, ll. 36–9; *IG* I³ 874; Harp. s.v. Καρκίνος), but his three (or four) sons were remembered only for their theatrical interests (**IV Ax**; *APF* no. 8254; Sutton 1987, 18; Stewart 2016). Xenotimos is identified as a tragic choreut in Sch.^{VG} Ar. *Peace* 778 (cf. Sch.^{VAld} Ar. *Wasps* 1502), and as an actor (Sch. Ar. *Frogs* 86a). Aristophanes probably refers to him at *Wasps* 1505 with the ambiguous word *tragoidos*, which could mean 'tragic choreut' or 'actor', though here apparently not 'tragic poet' as 1511 refers to another member of the family who 'writes the tragedies'. The manner of Xenotimos' appearance in *Wasps* does not help resolve whether we are to think of him as a choreut or an actor for although the sons were well known for energetic and innovative tragic dancing, the manner of their appearance in *Peace* also implies that they performed independently of the chorus. Carcinus and his sons probably regularly worked together as a troupe (Stewart 2016) and each of the sons was trained in many if not all facets of tragic production (one of Carcinus' sons, Xenocles, gained success as a tragic poet). It is a reasonable, though not secure, inference that professional interests lay behind Xenotimos' visit to the Cimmerian Bosporus (**1**). Xenotimos is nowhere else mentioned in the speech and the fact that the man who delivered the letter is mentioned at all and by name implies that he was well known to the Athenian public and that his presence in the Cimmerian Bosporus was thought to require no explanation. This suggests that he was an actor or at least known to be active as a didaskalos or chorodidaskalos. There is, despite the scholia mentioned above, no evidence for the existence of a tragic choreutic profession at this time.

2–3 attest multiple theatre buildings and theatrical competitions (indicated by **3**'s mention of an agonothete) in the Bosporan Kingdom before the middle of the fourth century. **3**'s dedication to Dionysus implies that at Nymphaion Dionysus was the patron of the theatre and competitions. The office of agonothete is attested at Hermonassa (part of the Bosporan Kingdom, just across the Strait from Nymphaion) in the second half of the fourth century (*CIRB* 1039), but in this case in a dedication to Apollo. An agonothete may also be attested at Olbia (see on **Fii**). The office of agonothete may have been different from that later attested for Athens where dedications while in office (implied by **3**'s use of the present participle ἀγωνοθετέων) are not found.

Mere traces of a theatre have been found at Panticapaeum. Most significantly a marble throne of the fourth century that is thought to be from (the prohedria of?) the theatre, and a relief of a Silenos from the same period thought possibly to be from the theatre (Braund and Hall 2014, 382). The Cimmerian Bosporus imported Attic figurines of comic actors from the early fourth century (Dana 2011, 58; from Great Bliznitza *MMC*³ AT 9d, 10h, 20c, 21c, 23c, 74a, 89a, 91, 92a, 93–5, 97; from Taman *MMC*³ AT 21e; from Chersonesus *MMC*³ AT 26q; from Panticapaeum *MMC*³ AT 60b, 96, 119; from Kerch *MMC*³ AT 29a?, 46f, 89b–c, 105, XT 15; from Crimea *MMC*³ AT 26e). Two probably choregic reliefs, one from Kepoi (also part of Leucon's empire on the Taman Peninsula: **I Aviii 1d**) and another of local but unknown provenance (see commentary on **I Aviii 1**), attest to theatrical activity in the broader region in the second half of the fourth century. An Attic chous, found at Phanagoria (*MMC*³ AV 8), seems to indicate a knowledge and interest in comedy in the region ca. 400.

The Black Sea certainly features prominently in the travels of Stratonicus (**Fiv**) and **4** appears to attest a stay by Stratonicus in the Bosporan Kingdom. The testimony is problematised by the name 'Berisades' used by Machon, and by Stratonicus' dates. Berisades is the name of a short-lived king (ca. 358–356) of the Odrysae, a Thracian tribe dwelling in the plain of the river Hebrus. 'Birisades' is however a form of the name 'Pairisades' used by Dinarchus (*Against Demosthenes* 43) with reference to the king of the Cimmerian Bosporus. Since **4** refers to Stratonicus sailing to the Black Sea, not a possible route for reaching the Hebrus valley, the Thracian Berisades would have been excluded from consideration were it not for a general belief that Stratonicus was dead before Pairisades became king. This belief is based on Phaenias' claim that Stratonicus had been executed by Nikokles the king of Cyprus for making one wisecrack too many (Ath. 8.352d) and, as Nikokles was assassinated sometime before 354/3, Stratonicus' death, on this account, must have been earlier. But as Gilula (2000, 425) points out, this version of Stratonicus' death belongs to a type of anecdote, much loved in the fourth century, that thematises the death or punishment of culture heroes, especially theatre stars, who misjudge the degree of freedom of speech they can use in the court of a tyrant (cf. **VI E**). It would be hazardous to put much stress on this report of the death of an archetypal high-society joker, especially as we have another incompatible version of his death, by Machon himself, at the hands of a different tyrant, Nikokreon of Salamis in Cyprus, for quite a different witticism.

If we follow Machon's version, the death of Stratonicus was more than two decades later, as Nikokreon came to the throne in 332 (Gow 1965, 90–1). There are other indications that Stratonicus lived to the mid fourth century or beyond (Gow 1965, 81; Zhmud 2012, 133 n. 130). Unfortunately, the variant traditions of his death merely demonstrate the unreliability of the circumstantial detail attached to any of the anecdotes, even though many of the witticisms were collected by a contemporary, Callisthenes of Olynthus (*FGrH* 124 F 5), beyond perhaps the mere fact of his many travels and possibly their general geographical range. We cannot therefore say more than that Stratonicus might have visited Panticapaeum in the 340s or later. If **4** has any substrate in fact, it would seem to attest to an attempt by the Black Sea tyrants to emulate the attempts of the Macedonian and Syracusan tyrants to add brilliance to the life of the court by importing and retaining famous entertainers (**VI A; VI D–G**).

Braund and Hall's suggestion that we should read the name Stratonicus rather than Aristonikos in **2** is unfounded (2014, 382–3). Apart from the fact that Stratonicus, the famous wit and kitharist/kitharode, is identified by Phaenias (Ath. 8.352c–d) as an Athenian, not an Olynthian, the kitharode Aristonikos is mentioned by Theopompus (*FGrH* 115 F 236 = Ath. 10.435b), Arrian (*An.* 4.16.6–7) and Plutarch (*Mor.* 334f). He performed in Macedon at Philip's celebration of his victory at Chaeronea in 338. Arrian and Plutarch both attest that he died fighting as a soldier (οὐ κατὰ κιθαρῳδόν) in the battle of Zaraspia in 328. He was a friend of Alexander and Alexander erected in his memory a bronze statue at Delphi of him with his kithara (see Stefanis no. 367; Power 2010, 159–60).

Fiv: Heraclea Pontica

1. **Photius' Summary of Memnon's *History of Heraclea*, Books 9–10 (= *FGrH* 434 F 1.3.2–3)**. Target date: 338. Photius' *Library* (written 9th c. AD) summarises the ninth to sixteenth books of Memnon's history (probably 2nd c. AD) of his native city of Heraclea Pontica from the tyranny of Klearchos (365–353) to the time of Julius Caesar (100–44). Memnon may have used Nymphis' 13-volume history of Heraclea as a source (3rd c.). The cited segment deals with Klearchos' sons, Timotheos, who ruled Heraclea 353–338, and Dionysius, who ruled 338–306. Text: Jacoby.

> διὸ σφόδρα μὲν περιὼν τοῖς πολεμίοις μὲν φοβερὸς ἦν, καὶ πάντες αὐτὸν
> κατωρρώδουν, ἐπειδὰν ἀπεχθάνοιτο, τοῖς δ' ἀρχομένοις γλυκύς τε καὶ
> ἥμερος, ἔνθεν καὶ τελευτῶν πόθον αὐτοῦ κατέλιπε πολύν, καὶ πένθος ἤγειρε
> τῷ πόθῳ ἐνάμιλλον· ὁ δὲ τούτου ἀδελφὸς Διονύσιος καίει μὲν τὸ σῶμα

πολυτελῶς, σπένδει δὲ αὐτῷ καὶ τὰ ἀπὸ βλεφάρων δάκρυα καὶ τὰς ἀπὸ τῶν σπλάγχνων οἰμωγάς, ἐπιτελεῖ δὲ καὶ ἀγῶνας ἱππικούς, οὐχ ἱππικοὺς δὲ μόνον ἀλλὰ καὶ σκηνικοὺς καὶ θυμελικοὺς καὶ γυμνικούς· τοὺς μὲν αὐτίκα, τοὺς δὲ λαμπροτέρους καὶ ὕστερον.

Therefore while he (Timotheos) lived he was a terror to his enemies, and all loathed him, but to his subjects he was sweet and mild. As a result when he died he left behind much longing for himself and roused a grief that matched the longing. His brother Dionysius burned his body in a lavish way, poured out tears from his eyes and groans from his heart, and incurred the expense of equestrian competitions, and not only equestrian but also dramatic, musical and gymnic competitions, some at the funeral and others yet more splendid later on.

2. **Hermippus in Diogenes Laertius,** *Lives of the Philosophers* **5.91 (=** *FHG* **III, 46).**
Target date: ca. 338–ca. 322. Hermippus of Smyrna was a grammarian and a biographer of the 3rd c. He is notorious for luridly sensationalistic death scenes. The philosopher Heraclides of Pontus, born in Heraclea ca. 390, was Deputy Head of Plato's Academy during Plato's third Sicilian voyage (361/0) but left the Academy to return to Heraclea sometime after the death of Speusippus (339/8), when Xenocrates was preferred as Head. The events recounted here, if they have any historical foundation, must have taken place between his return and his death after 322. Text: Long.

Ἕρμιππος δὲ λιμοῦ κατασχόντος τὴν χώραν φησὶν αἰτεῖν τοὺς Ἡρακλεώτας τὴν Πυθίαν λύσιν. τὸν δὲ Ἡρακλείδην διαφθεῖραι χρήμασι τούς τε θεωροὺς καὶ τὴν προειρημένην, ὥστ' ἀνειπεῖν ἀπαλλαγήσεσθαι τοῦ κακοῦ, εἰ ζῶν μὲν Ἡρακλείδης ὁ Εὐθύφρονος χρυσῷ στεφάνῳ στεφανωθείη πρὸς αὐτῶν, ἀποθανὼν δὲ ὡς ἥρως τιμῷτο. ἐκομίσθη ὁ δῆθεν χρησμὸς καὶ οὐδὲν ὤναντο οἱ πλάσαντες αὐτόν. αὐτίκα γὰρ ἐν τῷ θεάτρῳ στεφανούμενος ὁ Ἡρακλείδης ἀπόπληκτος ἐγένετο, οἵ τε θεωροὶ καταλευσθέντες διεφθάρησαν. ἀλλὰ καὶ ἡ Πυθία τὴν αὐτὴν ὥραν κατιοῦσα ἐς τὸ ἄδυτον καὶ ἐπιστᾶσα ἑνὶ τῶν δρακόντων δηχθεῖσα παραχρῆμα ἀπέπνευσε. καὶ τὰ μὲν περὶ τὸν θάνατον αὐτοῦ τοσαῦτα.

Hermippus says that at a time when famine gripped the country the people of Heraclea asked the Pythia for a solution. He says Heraclides bribed the ambassadors and the Pythia to announce that they would rid themselves of their trouble if Heraclides, son of Euthyphron, were crowned by them with a gold crown while he lived, and if he were honoured as a hero when dead. This response was brought home and its forgers derived no benefit. For Heraclides, while he was being crowned in the theatre, immediately became apoplectic, the ambassadors died when they were stoned, and the Pythia at the same time had gone into the inner sanctum of the temple and stepping upon one of the snakes was bitten and died at once.

Heraclea Pontica, a Megarian colony founded ca. 560, was the largest city on the south coast of the Black Sea between Byzantium and Sinope. The founder of the tyranny in Heraclea Pontica, Klearchos, had an Athenian education and studied with Plato and Isocrates (Memn. *FGrH* 434 F 1.1.1; Isoc. *Ep.* 7.12). This may have made him something of a cultural Athenophile. He was in any case bookish and is said to have been the first tyrant to amass a large library (*FGrH* 434 F 1.1.2; Pinto 2013, 94–5). Other prominent Heracleots had links with Athens and especially the Academy. This is especially true of Heraclides (**2**), whose interest in Athenian drama is indicated by his authorship of three books *On the [Myths, Songs?] of Euripides and Sophocles*, and a book *On the Three Tragedians* (D.L. 5.87–8). He is also credited with forging tragedies under Thespis' name (Aristox. fr. 114 W).

A Dionysia with an elaborate parade is attested for Heraclea in 353 since our sources (save Trogus in Just. *ep. Trog.* 16.12–16) indicate that Klearchos was assassinated at the Dionysia. Diodorus says he was killed 'during the Dionysia while walking to a spectacle' (16.36.3). But the spectacle was probably not drama but the Dionysian parade. A more de-tailed account appears in a fictional letter supposedly written by another student of Plato's, Chion of Heraclea, to Plato himself (the forgery is generally thought to date to the 1st–2nd c. AD) in which 'Chion' explains his intention to murder the tyrant at the parade because he is likely to have fewer bodyguards (17.1.5–7). Memnon merely reports that he was intending to perform a public sacrifice when Chion stabbed him, which is at least consistent with his presiding over the Dionysian parade (*FGrH* 434 F 1.1.3). Co-conspirators of Chion also are said to have connections with the Academy (Just. *ep. Trog.* 16).

The only direct evidence for drama in Heraclea Pontica is the funerary and commemora-tive competitions held for Timotheos in and after 338 (**1**). More regular theatrical activity is implied by the existence of crowning ceremonies in the theatre, attested by the crowning of the prominent Academician, Heraclides (**2**), and may also be suggested by the report of a visit by the kitharode Stratonicus, presumably on a professional voyage anytime between 370 and ca. 340 (Ath. 8.351c–d). The tragic poet Spintharus, active in the last quarter of the fifth century, is said by Suda (σ 945) to be from Heraclea, though it is not clear which Heraclea (we know about a dozen ancient cities of this name). Aristophanes mocks Spintharus (*Birds* 762–3), if he is referring to this same Spintharus (which is doubtful, see Dunbar 1995, 471 *ad loc.*), as a Phrygian, which, assuming only a limited degree of comic distortion, still leaves a few options that are closer to Phrygia than Heraclea Pontica.

Diphilus, said to be from Sinope, wrote a comedy called *Amastris* which many have thought to refer to Amastris the wife of Dionysius of Heraclea (Phot. α 466 = Suda α 729; Meineke 1839, 450–1) though this is far from certain (Webster 1970, 153). A comedy rid-iculing the wife of the tyrant doubtless had local appeal, though, if it was ever performed in Heraclea, it seems unlikely, given the subject matter, to have been performed before Dionysius' death in 306.

G | Africa

Introduction

Africa provides a surprisingly early chapter in the history of Greek theatre. The city of Cyrene had long been known to have a large theatre in a central urban setting, at the western end of the great sanctuary of the city's founding god Apollo, on the 'Myrtousa' terrace. But recent archaeological study suggests that the first phase of this theatre should be placed in the first half of the fifth century. This implies that the theatre culture that is known, above all from a series of financial inscriptions (**Gi 2–4**), to have flourished in fourth-century Cyrene and that certainly featured tragedy and dithyramb (with choruses) may have been introduced by Arcesilas IV rather than the 'democracy' that followed the kings' fall. In 2002 a second Greek theatre was discovered in Cyrene in the sprawling sanctuary of Demeter and Kore that lay outside the city wall to the south, on a vast terraced site established in the sixth century. The likelihood that this was used for dramatic performances in the fifth century (as well as for rituals more closely tied to the cult of Demeter and Kore) is much increased in light of the publication of what may be a graffito *kalos* acclamation for an actor inside the theatre (**Gi 1**).

A small number of other sites are potential candidates for theatre culture in our period. Cyrene's harbour town of Apollonia has a Roman theatre with a Greek phase below it of uncertain date (**Gi**). More significantly, in neighbouring Egypt, Alexandria under the Ptolemies evidently had a 'great' theatre in the early third century (the qualifier implying perhaps the existence of more than one), though it has not been located archaeologically (Ath. 14.620d). And the city had a flourishing tradition of dramatic poetry and festivals (Hunter 2003, 182–3 on Theoc. 17.112–14).

It is highly likely that by 280 Egypt had an Association of *Technitai* sponsored by the Ptolemies, possibly the very first such Association, older even than the Athenian. The Corcyrean tragic poet Philiscus (*TrGF* 104, *pace TrGF* I 89; Kotlińska-Toma 2015, 66–74) featured prominently in the great Dionysiac procession of Ptolemy II in Alexandria ca. 280–270 (Ath. 5.196a, 198c; Suda φ 358), processing – behind satyrs wearing gold ivy crowns and dark red cloaks – in the capacity of poet and priest of Dionysus, and in company with 'all the *Technitai* associated with Dionysus' (Φιλίσκος ὁ ποιητὴς ἱερεὺς ὢν Διονύσου καὶ πάντες οἱ περὶ τὸν Διόνυσον τεχνῖται Ath. 5.198c). This priesthood, held by a tragic poet who was a member of the Alexandrian Pleiad, will represent the eponymous magistracy of an Association of *Technitai*, making this evidence for the existence of an Egyptian corporation at this early date (Le Guen 1997, 86; Aneziri 2003, 111; *ATD* I, 295, 346–7). The festival to which this great procession was the prelude will surely have featured dramatic performances. By some time between 269 and 246, and perhaps as early as 279, another probably local branch Association of these *Technitai* was well established further south at Ptolemais Hermiou in Egypt, under the double patronage of Dionysus and the 'Theoi Adelphoi' (deified Ptolemy II and his sister Arsinoe). To judge by the list of specialisms in one of their decrees (*ATD* TE 61) Ptolemais' vigorous Dionysia included performances of tragedy, comedy, epic, kitharody and kithara playing (*ATD* TE 60–1; Favi 2017d, 273–7 further on the theatre culture of Alexandria in the early Hellenistic period).

Gi: Cyrene

1. (?) *Kalos* **inscription from the theatre in the extramural sanctuary of Demeter in Cyrene**, late 5th or very early 4th c. (by letter forms, and use of E for H, O for Ω).

Roughly inscribed graffito on the front of the fourteenth row of seats (counting from the bottom) in the eastern part of the theatre. The surface of local limestone on which it is inscribed is corroded and scratched.

W: 0.65 m.

Height of letters: 0.125–0.14 m.

Found by M. Luni between 2003 and 2005 during excavation in the theatre by the Missione Italiana dell'Università di Urbino.

In situ.

Inglese 2011 (*SEG* 61, 1556); *IGCyr* 116100.

Text: based on Inglese 2011. Photos: Inglese 2011, 274 fig. 15; Inglese 2013, 238–9, 436 with fig. 18.

> [(?) -]ΓΕΤΟΡ ΚΑΛΟ[- (?)]

Inglese suggests as a less likely alternative [(?) -]ΛΕΤΟΡ ΚΑΛΟ[- (?)]. On this reading the first word must be older than the second, since an archaic lambda would be used.

[*start of a name, possibly* Hag]etor is beauti[ful!]

2. Public accounts mentioning expenditure on tragic and dithyrambic choruses, ca. 335 (by letter forms and use of numeric symbols that reflect a reform to the Cyrenean monetary system of ca. 335: Laronde 1987, 121, 244). One of some 38 inscribed accounts of officials known as *damiergoi*, which range in date from the end of the 5th to the 2nd century (on the series as a whole see Chamoux 1988). After a heading naming the eponymous priest of Apollo and the three *damiergoi* in office these accounts generally list: a valuation (τίμασις) of the price of a variety of agricultural produce; total annual revenue (τὸ πᾶν ἐσιὸν τῶ ἐνιαυτῶ); annual expenses (ἐξιόν); the difference between the two (λοιπόν); the sum to be paid to the *damiergoi* as allowance (παρόρεγμα). **2, 3** and **4** differ from the rest by the inclusion of a detailed list of expenditures on various religious activities (note also the extremely fragmentary *SEG* 9, 18, which makes reference to 'dress' (l. 3) as in **2**, l. 15, **3**, l. 18; to 'guards' (l. 4) as in **2**, l. 16, **3**, l. 19; and possibly a piper (ll. 5–6 [αὐλ]|ητᾶι) as in **2**, l. 16, **3**, ll. 20–1).

One of five texts (*SEG* 9, 11–15) inscribed on a single quadrangular stone of white marble: 11 and 12 on the left side, 13 (= **2**) on the front, 14 and 15 on the right side; the fourth side was not prepared for inscription and must have been set against a wall (Oliverio 1933, 85).

0.78 × 0.59 × 0.56 m.

Found in 1929 during excavation in the temple of Apollo (Chamoux 1988, 144) in the agora of Cyrene.

Kept on site in the *strategeion* in the sanctuary of Apollo (Laronde 1987, 241).

Oliverio 1933, 88 no. 12 (= *SEG* 9, 13); Dobias-Lalou 1993 (= *SEG* 43, 1186); see also *SEG* 57, 1994; *IGCyr* 11600.

Text: based on *SEG* 9, 13.   Photo: Ceccarelli and Milanezi 2007, 188.

non-stoich.

Θ[εοί].
Ἱαρεὺς τῶ Ἀπόλ[λων]ος Εὐκλείδας Παραιβάτα,
δαμιεργοὶ Λῦσι[ς] Ἀνδροκλεῦς, Τιμῶναξ Πρώρω,
Ἀντίμαχος Δαιλέ[ο]ντος. Καρπῶ τίμασις· κριθαὶ
5   ἂν Ζ >, σπυροὶ ἂν Ζ [>] > > >, ὄσπρια ἂν Ζ > >, κάρφη ἤμερα
ἂν Ϡ Ϡ Ϡ, ἄγρια ἂν Ϡ Ϡ, ἄχυρα ἂν Ϡ Ϡ, σπυραμινὰ ἂν Ϡ Ϲ,
σταφυλὰ ψυθία ἔνδος τᾶς προκλησίας ἂν Ϡ Ζ, ἔξος
ἂν Ϡ, μέλαινα ἔνδος τᾶς προκλησίας ἂν Ϡ, ἔξος
ἂν Ϲ Ζ > > –, σταφὶς ἂν Ζ >, σῦκα ἂν > > > >, ἐλαῖαι ἂν Ζ,
10   ἔλαιον ἂν Ϡ Ϡ, κύμινον ἂν Ϡ >. τὸ πᾶν ἐσιὸν τῶ
ἐνιαυτῶ Μ Ϡ Ϲ Γ = – Χ Χ Χ Ϡ Ϡ Ϲ Ζ > Δ Δ, ἐξιὸν ἱαροθυσίας,
ἄρκωι τροφᾶς, Ἀρτάμιτι Καταγωγίδι ἐς τὰ ἱαρ[ά, ἱ]αρέαι
Ἀ⟨θ⟩αναίας τροφά, περιακτριαι ἐ[ς τὸ]ν κόσμον, χοροῖς
τραγικοῖς τρισὶ ἑκάστωι βοῦς, διθυραμ[βικ]ῶι χορῶι
15   βοῦς, ἐξάρχοις, κάρυξι τρισὶ ἐς ἡμάτ[ια κ]αὶ ἐς τρο-
φάν, αὐλητᾶι, γροφεῖ, ταμίαι, μαγίρω[ι, π]ρωροῖς, λυ-
χνοκαίᾳ Ἰατρῶι ποθ' ἑσπέραν· ἐπισκ[ευᾶ]ς τῶν μη-
ρῶν τῶν βοέων, εὑρόντων ἂν τρισκ[αίδε]κα στατῆρας
ἑκάστω βοὸς τῶν μηρῶν· τὸ πᾶν ἐξ[ι]ὸν τῶ ἐνιαυτῶ
20   σὺν ἱαροθυσίαις Μ Ϡ Γ – Χ Χ Χ Ϡ Ϡ Ζ > > – Δ Δ, λοιπὸν
Μ Ϲ = Ϡ Ζ > > > Δ Δ Δ Δ. παρόρεγμα δαμιεργοῖς : Μ = –

12 Oliverio   ἄρκωι τροφᾶς Ἀρτάμιτι Καταγωγίδι ἐς τὰ ἱαρ[ά] Dobias-Lalou
16–17 Dobias-Lalou   [π]ρωροῖς, λυ|χνοκαιία, ᵛ ἰατρῶι πο(θ)' ἑσπέραν, ἐπισκ[όποι]ς
Oliverio   [π]ρωροῖς, λυ|χνοκαιίαι, ἰατρῶι, ποθ' ἑσπέραν ἐπισκ[όποι]ς Chamoux 1988

Gods. Priest of Apollo: Eukleidas son of Paraibatas; *damiergoi*: Lysis son of Androkles, Timonax son of Proros, Antimachos son of Daïleon. Valuation of the agricultural produce: barley [5] at 1 dr. and 1 ob.; wheat at 1 dr. and 4 ob.; pulse at 1 dr. and 2 ob.; cultivated hay at 12 dr.; wild hay at 8 dr.; straw at 8 dr.; wheat flour at 6 dr.; early grapes among the choice ones at 5 dr.; outside the choice ones at 4 dr.; black grapes among the choice ones at 4 dr.; outside the choice ones at 3 dr., 2 ob. and a dichalcous; raisins at 1 dr. and 1 ob.; figs at 4 ob.; olives at 1 dr.; [10] olive oil 8 dr.; cumin at 4 dr. and 1 ob. Total revenue for the year: 308 minae (= 30,800 dr.) and 75 dr., 1 ob. and 2/10. Expenditure: for the sacrifice; to the bear (*or* 'the Bear') for maintenance; to Artemis Katagogis for the ceremon[ies]; to the [p]riestess of Athena maintenance; ?(to the) *periaktriai*? fo[r th]e decoration; to each of the three tragic choruses an ox; to the dithyram[bic] chorus [15] an ox; to the *exarchoi*; to the three heralds for dres[s a]nd maintenance; to the piper; to the secretary; to the treasurer; to the butcher / cook; to the [g]uards; illumination for Iatros towards the evening; for the prepar[atio]n of the thighs of the oxen, having been evaluated at thir[tee]n staters for the thighs of each ox. Total expenditure for the year, [20] sacrifices included, 20,669 dr., 2 ob. and 7/10. The difference: 10,205 dr., 3 ob. and 4/10. Contribution to the *damiergoi*: 300 dr.

3. Public accounts mentioning expenditure on tragic and dithyrambic choruses, ca. 335 (by letter forms: see on **2**). See **2**. Unlike **2** the expenditure recorded in this list is further divided into subsections: ll. 8–22 on choruses and other ritual activities, excluding the *hiarothusia*; ll. 23–4 on the *hiarothusia*; ll. 25–6 giving the total sum. Unlike **2**, **3** also records the individual sums spent on each item.

Two adjoining fragments (a, b) of a marble panel broken on all sides except the left. The fragments join at l. 17.
0.31 × 0.16 m.
Fr. a found before 1933, fr. b in 1966 during excavation by the Missione Archeologica Italiana in the agora of Cyrene.
Cyrene Museum 161 (fr. b); storeroom of the Italian missions, unknown inv. number (fr. a).
a: Marengo and Paci 1998 (= *SEG* 48, 2052); see also *SEG* 57, 1994; b: Oliverio 1933, 91 no. 17 (= *SEG* 9, 18); a+b: *SEG* 48, 2052; *IGCyr* 88200.
Text: based on *SEG* 48, 2052.   Photo: Ceccarelli and Milanezi 2007, 194.

```
            - - - -                              non-stoich. ca. 22
       [ἀχύρ]ων ῥῖπο[ς sum σταφυλά]
       [ψυθί]α ἔνδος τᾶ[ς προκλησίας]
       [sum] : μέλαινα ἔ[νδος τᾶς πρ]-
       [οκλ]ησίας ⊏ Ζ > > – [ψυθία ἔξος]
 5     [τᾶς] προκλησία[ς sum μέλαινα]
       [ἔξ]ος τᾶς προκλ[ησίας sum]
       [ἔλ]αιον Ʒ Ʒ Ζ : ἐλ[αίαι sum]
       τὸ πᾶν ἐσιόν : Μ : Ʒ [- - - ἐξιόν(?)]
       τάδε ἔξος ἱαρο[θυσίας : - - -]-
 10    οιδικῶν χορῶν [- - - -]
       Μ : - Ʒ Ʒ ⊏ : ἐπιθεν[- - - : Μ : (?)]
       Χ Χ Χ Χ Ʒ Ʒ ⊏ : διθυ[ραμβικῶν]
       χορῶν τῶι : νικ[- - : Μ : - - -]
       τᾶι ἄρκωι τροφ[ά - - -]-
 15    θρα : Μ = Χ Χ : τᾶι [ἱαρέαι τᾶς Ἀθ]-
       αναίας : Μ : = : τ[οῖς ἐξάρχοι]-
       ς : Μ = Χ : κάρυξ[ι τρισὶ ἐς τροφά]-
       ν καὶ ἡμάτια [: Μ : - - -(?)]
       πρωροῖς τρι[σί : Μ : - - - τα]-
```

20   μίαι : Μ : Π = = 𐅂 [- - - αὐλ]-

ητᾶι : Μ : = = Χ[- - -]

τὸ πᾶν : Μ : > [- - -]

τὸ πᾶν ἰαρ[οθυσίας - - -(?) περ]-

ὶ τὸ τιμαχ[εῖον - - -(?) : Μ : - - -]

25   = Χ Χ 𐅂 𐅂 ⊏ [- - - τὸ πᾶν ἐξιόν]

τῶ ἐνι[αυτῶ - - -(?) : Μ : - - -]

Π = – Χ Χ [- - -]

λοιπ[όν : Μ : - - -]

[Ζ] > > [- - -(?)]

30   - - - -

4 [ψυθία ἔνδος] Marengo and Paci   9–10 [τραγ]οιδικῶν Marengo and Paci   (?)
[κωμ]οιδικῶν   10 [τῶι νικάθρωι?] Marengo and Paci   11 ? ἐπιθέν[τος + *official*
cf. Marengo and Paci 1998, 383   13 νικ[άθρωι] Marengo and Paci   τῶι : νικ[ῶντι]
suggested as a possibility by Ceccarelli and Milanezi   14–15 τᾶι ἄρκωι τροφ[ὰ καὶ ἐς
τὰ γεῖ]θρα, τᾶι ἄρκωι τροφ[ὰ καὶ ἐς τὰ κύρι]θρα suggested as possibilities by Ceccarelli
and Milanezi   17–30 = Oliverio no. 17, *SEG* 9, 18   23–4 [περ]ὶ suggested as a
possibility by Marengo and Paci   [κα]ὶ Oliverio

… bundle of [str]aw at [*sum*; early grapes] am[ong the choice ones at *sum*];
black a[mong the ch]oice ones at 3 dr., 2 ob. and a half; [early grapes out-
side] [5] the choice ones at [*sum*; black out]side the choic[e ones at *sum*; ol]ive
oil at 9 dr.; oliv[es at *sum*]. Total of the revenue 200 minae (20,000 dr.) and
[…]. [Expenditure?]: the following without the sac[rifice:] [prize?] for the [(?)
trag][10]edic (or possibly '[com]edic') choruses 110 dr.; with the further addition
[? by … of minae ?- …] 90 dr.; the pri[ze? …] for the dithy[rambic] choruses
[*sum*]; maintenan[ce] for the bear (fem.) (or 'the Bear' (*fem.*)) […] [15] ?-*thra*
2 minae and 40 dr.; to the [priestess of Ath]ena, 2 minae; to th[e *exarcho*]*i* 2
minae and 20 dr.; to the [three?] heralds [for maintenan]ce and dress [*sum*;
something else ?]; to the thre[e] guards [*sum* …; to the trea][20]surer 9 minae and
4 dr.; [… to the pi]per 4 minae and 20 dr.; [something else]; total, minae [10+];
total of the sacr[ifice … ? in respect o]f the *timach*[*eion*] (some sort of public
building), [25] 2 minae and 50 dr. [… Total expenditure] for the year [? minae];
differen[ce, minae …].

4. Public accounts mentioning *exarchoi*, 4th c. (by letter forms). A fragment from another
set of accounts of *damiergoi*, which like **2** and **3** provided more detail on the rituals upon
which expenses were made.

Fragment from a large marble panel, broken on all sides.
0.13 × 0.14 × 0.04 m.
Found before 1929 during excavation in the agora of Cyrene.
Cyrene Museum 443.
Oliverio 1933, 92 no. 20 (= *SEG* 9, 21); *IGCyr* 12300.
Text: *SEG* 9, 21.   Photo: Oliverio 1933, pl. 13, fig. 22.

- -] καλλιστήια τ[- -
- -]Ϡ Ϡ : ἐξάρχοις [- -
- - Ἀ]θαναίας ἱαρέα[ι τροφά, - -
- -] ⊏ ⊏ Χ Ϡ Ϡ Ϡ Ζ[- -
5   - -]Χ Χ[- -

1 Dobias-Lalou   - - καλλιστήιαις - - Oliverio   ΚΑΛΛΙΣΤΗΙΑΤ *lapis*

[…] *kallisteia* ('beauty contest' or perhaps 'prize') [(?) for …], 8 dr.; for the *exarchoi* […]; for the priestes[s] of Athena [maintenance, …] 433 dr. […] 40 dr. […]

The city of Cyrene in North Africa (ancient Libya), traditionally founded in the seventh century by Dorian Greeks of Thera (itself a Spartan foundation) and, by the fourth, one of the largest of all Greek cities, came in time to have some five theatres, though three of these date to the Roman period and seem to be successive replacements following earthquake damage (Chamoux 1998, 138–9; Ensoli 2010b, 117). The city's harbour town of Apollonia, ca. 18 km distant, had another, though its first phase, which lies beneath major Roman rebuilding, has proven difficult to date. Goodchild (1971, 189) placed it loosely in the Hellenistic period; Stucchi (1975, 136) at the end of the fourth or early in the third century; while Harrison (1975, 164) argued it was contemporary with the city wall, whose line it respects – dated by White (1976, 141) to the first two decades of the third century.

Aristotle described the Cyrenean constitution that followed the end of the monarchy around the middle of the fifth century as a 'democracy' (*Pol.* 1319b15–27; fr. 611 Rose), though modern scholars tend to regard it as having a republican character dominated by a wealthy aristocracy (Laronde 1987, 129–36). Wealthy Cyrenean citizens were ambitious and successful competitors on the Panhellenic athletic circuit throughout the fifth century, as were its aristocracy and royalty in its first half, with Telesikrates in 474 commissioning the only Pindaric ode to celebrate victory in the hoplite race (Pi. *P.* 9) and Arcesilas IV commissioning *Pythian* 4 (the longest of all Pindaric odes) and 5 following his victory in the chariot race in 462. All three odes were probably performed at the Carneia in honour of Apollo and testify to a familiarity in the city with choral culture at its most sophisticated. The evidence for the importance of theatre in the life of the city is extensive and begins early, with two theatres having been found, both with first phases dated to the fifth century (below). Theatre was energetically promoted in Cyrene at a time when it was ruled by kings.

2–4 are fragments from a series of inscribed annual accounts maintained by the main officials of Cyrene, the *damiergoi*. They come from different years but appear to be close in time. These accounts were displayed in the agora, in or near the sanctuary of Apollo, Cyrene's leading deity. They list the values of a variety of annual agricultural produce – the city's main source of wealth – and provide a total annual revenue, followed by a statement of annual expenses and a calculation of the difference between the two. **2–4** differ from the rest of the corpus by the detail they provide on the expenditure side. **3** and **4** differ from **2** in that they further record the individual sums spent on each item. The objects of expenditure are a series of religious activities.

The elliptical nature of the documents leaves much unclear. Their syntax is not always self-evident nor is it in each case clear where breaks between entries should be placed. The documents raise many questions without providing sufficient evidence for secure answers (for the best discussion see Ceccarelli and Milanezi 2007, on which we draw extensively). Does the list of expenditures follow a particular sequence – say that of the Cyrenean religious calendar? Why do these expenses – and only these in the Cyrenean cultic calendar – come under the competence of the *damiergoi*? Why do the entries vary from year to year? Not surely because each cult was celebrated with an irregular frequency; more likely perhaps that the expenses only fell to the *damiergoi* under certain circumstances. Did the more generic officials such as the secretary, treasurer, piper and guards serve one specific cult or a range (further on this below)?

The documents establish a direct connection between income from agricultural production administered by the *damiergoi* and ritual expense, but it is not clear which productive lands are in question. Laronde (1987, 156–7, 325–34) suggests the lands that had belonged to the old Cyrenean monarchy which had been quite recently made into public property; Dobias-Lalou (1993, 25) thinks of property belonging to Apollo (*contra* Marengo and Paci 1998, 387–8, noting the persistent absence of any reference to the cult of Apollo in the new fragments they publish); Chamoux (1988, 147–8) also thinks of the properties of Apollo – once administered by the kings – with the addition of the latter's personal properties; while Migeotte (2014, 165) cautiously assumes that the divine proprietors were those listed in the accounts – Artemis, Athena and Iatros. Nor is it clear what percentage of gross annual productive capacity is represented by the listed annual total incomes, for Laronde (1987, 331) has cogently argued that those totals represent only a surplus that was put to sale. He notes that while it appears that the lands in question were used to raise livestock (hence the oxen that could be assigned to the choruses), no livestock are listed as sold and so presumably they were not (Chamoux 1988, 150–1, by contrast, thinks livestock are absent because the *damiergoi* did not exploit the lands directly, but rented them out to others to do so in return for fixed returns for the agricultural produce, while the business of raising and selling animals on the lands rested with those who rented them).

But perhaps a more likely explanation of the careful recording of individual prices for various agricultural items alongside expenditure on cult activity is that they reflect a situation in which the *damiergoi* regulated a market in produce that was associated with a major festival. It implies that they may have required producers to pay a market (sales) tax on their goods, doubtless a percentage of these fixed prices (and whether or not the sellers achieved the fixed price). The listed annual incomes may then represent the total of the taxes received on the sales. At a minimum it appears that we are dealing with a form of 'central' funding for (aspects of) a range of cults, rather than a situation in which each cult provided for all its cultic purposes from its own resources.

As far as theatre is concerned, a number of things emerge with certainty: **2** and **3** record expenses on tragic and dithyrambic choruses. And, since the first part of [τραγ]οιδικῶν '[trag]edic' in **3**, ll. 9–10 is restored, it is also possible that **3** recorded expenditure on comedy rather than tragedy: '[com]edic' [κωμ]οιδικῶν. While [τραγ]οιδικῶν '[trag]edic' would maintain the reference to tragedy attested in **2**, at the same time it introduces, somewhat awkwardly, an alternative designation for the genre that in **2** (ll. 13–14) was described with the more expected 'tragic', χοροῖς τραγικοῖς. For evidence of interest in comedy in Cyrene from the fifth century, see below.

The oxen in **2** (ll. 14–15) for 'each of the three tragic choruses' and for 'the dithy-ram[bic] chorus' will be prizes. Or perhaps, at least in the case of tragedy, since each chorus (note the emphatic 'each' in a document not prone to elaboration) appears to re-ceive its own sacrificial beast, we should rather describe the oxen as symbolic rewards for performance. (The fact that only one dithyrambic chorus is mentioned in **2** need not nec-essarily imply that there was only one in the festival: perhaps only one received a prize; and note the plurality of dithyrambic choruses in **3**.) **3** does not mention these oxen, but it evidently specifies a 'prize' or 'winner' explicitly: the letters τῶι : νικ[- at the start of the entry for the dithyrambic choruses in **3**, l. 13 were convincingly construed by Marengo and Paci as the start of τῶι νικάθρωι – and they restore the same expression in full for the '[trag]edic' choruses in **3**, l. 10. νίκαθρον *nikathron* is a word attested by a Spartan inscription where it is used of a thank offering for victory (*IG* V 1, 267, l. 10). Like its Attic equivalent νικητήριον, νίκαθρον could evidently be used both for a variety of prize that was to be shared collectively and for its eventual dedication by the winner (Hsch. ν 564: νίκαθρον· ἔπαθλον, ἐπινίκιον). Another possibility, adumbrated by Ceccarelli and Milanezi (2007, 206 n. 48), is to restore τῶι : νικ[ῶντι] at **3**, l. 13 'for the winn[er]'. Perhaps the most economical conclusion to draw is that the *damiergoi* of **3**'s year have adopted a slightly different official style, whether or not it reflects some actual practical difference: instead of budgeting specifically for oxen for the choruses they have budgeted a sum for a 'prize'. (That the author of **3** had somewhat different linguistic habits from that of **2** is also nicely illustrated by the presumably inconsequential variation between the adjectives 'tragic': τραγικοῖς **2**, l. 14, and – if the restoration is correct – '[trag]edic': [τραγ]οιδικῶν χορῶν **3**, ll. 9–10, to qualify these choruses.) That the 'prize' in **3** was all the same an ox is very likely, since as Marengo and Paci (1998, 384) point out, the sum of 110 dr. allocated to the '[trag]edic' or '[com]edic' choruses is roughly twice the 52 dr. budgeted in **2** (l. 18) for a single ox. This in turn suggests that there were two '[trag]edic' or '[com]edic' choruses in the year of **3**. There had been three tragic choruses in **2**. If the choruses in **2** are '[trag]edic' an explanation is needed for the change in number. There would however be no such need if these choruses are '[com]edic': instead, we might deduce that there were either – perhaps in alternate years – three tragic or two comic choruses at the festival in question.

As for dithyramb, **2**, l. 14 can be taken to imply a single chorus, whereas there is cer-tainly a plurality in **3**. But **2** could also be consistent with a plurality, since the matter is 'an ox for the (sc. winning) dithyrambic chorus'. We may be faced with a situation somewhat the reverse of the case in Athens, in which the tragic choruses were organised on the basis of the three tribes of Cyrene (and so each was given a collective 'prize'), while the dith-yrambic choruses were not (and so only one of them was awarded a prize). The oxen for the choruses will have been sacrificed and consumed by the – presumably local – choral teams: as much is clear not only from the terminology (see on νίκαθρον = Attic νικητήριον above) but also from the fact that **2**, ll. 16–19 provides for a butcher/cook and, more spe-cifically, for the preparation of the thighs of the oxen for consumption. It is very likely that the victorious lyric choruses at the Athenian Dionysia received oxen as *niketeria* (**I Avii 1**). The winners in the contests that were reserved for citizens at the Panathenaea certainly did (*IG* II² 2311, ll. 83–93 with Shear 2003b, 93). As Ceccarelli and Milanezi (2007, 206) note, the fact that both types of chorus receive the same beast for sacrificial consumption implies that they may have been of roughly the same size – a notable difference from the situation in Athens.

The intriguing entry in **3** following the one for '[trag]edic' or '[com]edic' choruses indicates some further budget item for that genre beyond the 'standard' one of money for prizes: 'with the further addition [? by *official* ..., minae ? ...] 90 dr.' (? ἐπιθέν[τος + *official* - - - : Μ : ?]|Χ Χ Χ Χ ϟ ϟ Ϲ : ll. 11–12). Ceccarelli and Milanezi (2007, 207) air a number of possibilities for this extra expenditure: a further prize? the hire of the costumes? For the latter they compare the use of another compound of the same verb – κατατίθημι – by the Delian Archon who chose to note in his accounts that he 'did not register the cost of hiring the costumes for the Dionysia', having paid for it himself (*IG* XI 110, ll. 17–18, of 268: καὶ τῶν ἱματίων τοὺς μισθοὺς οὐ κατεθέμην | τῶν εἰς τὰ Διονύσια). The 'official' hypothesised on the interpretation of this entry by Marengo and Paci (1998, 383) may have been the treasurer (below).

Right before the tragic choruses in **2** is a very difficult entry that some take to refer to expenditure on a form of revolving stage machinery known from later literary sources as *periaktoi* and named here *periaktria(i)* (a *hapax*, which can be construed as either a dative singular or nominative plural): l. 13 περιακτριαι ἐ[ς τὸ]ν κόσμον. This would imply a high degree of technical innovation on the part of the Cyrenean theatre. Two alternative interpretations have however been offered: the *periaktria* is a female officiant tasked with adorning a statue; or – perhaps most plausibly – a female leader of processions around an object or site. The position of the entry does not much help in settling the question, coming as it does after the priestess of Athena and before the tragic choruses. It might go with either, or even relate to a different cult. In general the case for the theatrical interpretation seems weak, but cannot be ruled out. Ceccarelli and Milanezi (2007, 190–1) review the evidence carefully and are sympathetic without being committed to the theatrical interpretation.

We have left our translation neutral '?(to the) *periaktriai*? fo[r th]e adornment'. The case for interpreting this as an alternative word for *periaktoi*, a pair of revolving (apparently three-sided) machines that pivot on a central axis used to indicate a change of scene and placed at each end of the stage building, was apparently initiated by Paul Maas (Dobias-Lalou 2000, 238), who in the 1940 *addenda* to LSJ glossed it as '= μηχανὴ ἀπὸ σκηνῆς περίακτος', no doubt with (unacknowledged) reference to Plutarch (*Mor.* 348e). In that passage Plutarch evokes the grand entry, as if in procession, of all the masters of Athenian drama and the instruments of their craft, among which are μηχανὰς ἀπὸ σκηνῆς περιάκτους 'revolving machines from the stage building'. Some editors, following Pantazides (1898, 15), add a καὶ 'and' before περιάκτους to isolate the term as a separate noun, *periaktoi*. The other relevant ancient evidence from the literary tradition for *periaktoi* used as a stand-alone term is Vitr. 5.6.8 and Poll. 4.126, on which see Poe 1993. The fact that Plutarch is imagining the Athenian theatre of the Classical period is suggestive, but little more, since it is possible to point to many anachronistic details in his depiction.

Few today place much faith in the existence of these devices in the fifth-century theatre, though there is some acceptance that they may have come into use in the fourth century or early Hellenistic period (thus e.g. Meineck in *EGT*, 1346 s.v. 'Stage Set'). Bieber (1961, 75–7) was the most energetic proponent of the view that they went back to the Classical period, but some of the evidence relating to the Theatre of Dionysus in Athens to which she alludes, in the form of large stones with rounded central holes for the insertion and turning of a pole, has been shown to have served for the mechane (Papastamati-von Moock 2014, 65–71; **V B**). The leading contemporary experts in the architecture of the Greek theatre find no material evidence for the existence of *periaktoi* in the Classical and Hellenistic theatre (but note the new evidence from Caunus, **E Introduction**) and think those mentioned by Pollux and Vitruvius belong in Italian theatres of the late Republic and Empire (Fraisse and Moretti 2007, 167–9). It is possible that the question will be illuminated with better archaeological knowledge of the relevant Cyrenean theatre. Already in the fifth century the theatre in the sanctuary of Apollo had various cuttings in the rock floor of its orchestra, one of which (1.70 × 0.81 m) was probably used for staging apparitions from underground (Stucchi 1975, 36; Ensoli 2010a, 124–5 with fig. 10; below). If true, the existence of such an element of stage architecture at such an early date suggests an interest in technical innovation that would be consistent with the introduction of *periaktoi* by the fourth century. Finally, in response to the objection of Dobias-Lalou (1993, 29) that the relationship between *periaktriai* in a theatrical sense and the qualifying phrase ἐ[ς τὸ]ν κόσμον is unsatisfactorily explained, Ceccarelli and Milanezi (2007, 191) rightly point to the use by Vitruvius of the equivalent Latin word *ornatus* (twice) and the phrase *speciem ornationis* in the very same paragraph (5.6.8) in which he mentions *periaktoi*. There is little problem in supposing that κόσμος could have been used in a Greek context for the 'embellishment' or 'ordered decoration' of a theatre. *Eukosmia* εὐκοσμία appears in connection with the Theatre of Dionysus in 342, apparently as an ideal of its orderly operation (**I Bii**).

Oliverio (1933, 119) offers some plausible *comparanda* for his view of the *periaktria* as a female priestess or officiant tasked with adorning a statue to be used in a cult procession (though he neglects to specify to which cult he thinks it belongs – we may guess that of Athena which precedes). Dobias-Lalou (2000, 239; 1993, 29; accepted by Migeotte 2014, 361) makes the case for the (in our view) most compelling interpretation – *periaktria* as a female leader of processions around (the force of the περι- compound) an altar, temple, even the city itself, in a sacred procession, composed of humans and sacrificial animals. Such female leaders of processions are known to have been elaborately dressed, hence the need for expenditure on *kosmos*: 'for the woman who leads the procession, for her adornment'. But a problem with this interpretation as Dobias-Lalou puts it is that she requires the cultic context to be the same as that of the tragic and dithyrambic choruses that follow, which she says do not suggest a theatrical representation but 'a sung and danced procession'. The grounds for such an assertion are weak, although one might be tempted to situate at least the dithyramb in the context of such a procession, given the highly unusual use of the 'cultic' name for the genre in these inscriptions (below). All the same, the 'female leader of processions' interpretation could still stand if we were willing to place the procession in some other relationship to the subsequent tragic and dithyrambic choral performances (perhaps if the choruses were in honour of Demeter a female procession leader would be expected to begin a festival that included them) or to suppose the procession in question belonged to Athena.

Exarchoi appear in **2** (l. 15) after the ox for dithyramb and before the heralds; in **3** (by a cogent restoration at l. 16) after the priestess of Athena and before the heralds; and in **4** (l. 2) after the *kallisteia* and before the priestess of Athena, but the length of the intervening gaps cannot be determined. Given the prominence of the term in literary texts to describe choral leaders, and especially those 'leaders of the dithyramb' in whose actions Aristotle saw the origins of tragedy (*Po.* 1449a9: τῶν ἐξαρχόντων τὸν διθύραμβον; cf. Archil. frr. 120–1 with Ieranò 1997, 175–85; E. *Ba.* 141; D. 18.260), there is good reason to suppose that these Cyrenean *exarchoi* may be connected to the choruses (Chamoux 1988, 152–3; Dobias-Lalou 1993, 30). Ceccarelli and Milanezi (2007, 211) note the value of the evidence of the third-century Cyrenean scholar Eratosthenes, which shows that he associated *exarchoi* with choral performance in a general way. In a passage preserved as a scholion to Pi. *O.* 9.1 (*FGrH* 241 F 44) Eratosthenes defines the role of the *exarchos* in relation to the chorus, the piper and the player of the kithara. He writes that in the absence of one of these musicians the *exarchos* would step in and deliver the *tenella* outside the song, while the chorus of komasts would contribute the *kallinike*. The discussion concerns the traditional victory cry that greeted athletic victors and which was adapted into increasingly formal choral performance. It is therefore clear that for Eratosthenes the *exarchos* is not associated specifically with dithyramb. He may however have seen the *exarchos* as a figure associated only with more narrowly cultic choral types, and those in processional form – which is to say, not with the choruses of drama.

The evidence of **2** is ambiguous on this issue: for while on one view there may only be a single dithyrambic chorus in the festival envisioned there, there is certainly a multiplicity of *exarchoi*, suggesting that the tragic choruses were also provided with *exarchoi* (Ceccarelli and Milanezi 2007, 212). The alternative however is that the reference in **2** is to a victorious dithyrambic chorus from a competing multiplicity (see above) and further that the *exarchoi* are perhaps to be associated only with the cultic, processional dithyramb (the brevity of **4** precludes any firm conclusions, and Ceccarelli and Milanezi 2007, 212 plausibly suggest that the *kallisteia* may in any case be some sort of beauty contest that involved choruses; as less likely alternatives they suggest it could be a prize for the best chorus or the finest offering for a sacrifice).

The placement of *exarchoi* in the lists seems at any event to be determined in large part by a decision to categorise them along with a number of other 'generic', technical experts. This is the case in **2**, where they come first, before heralds, a piper, a secretary, a treasurer, a butcher/cook and guards; and similarly in **3**, where the *exarchoi* stand at the head of a slightly shorter list, followed by heralds, guards, a treasurer and a piper. Thus, although in **3** the *exarchoi* are separated from the choral prizes by a number of entries relating to other cults – expenses for the bear/Bear (Artemis) and for the priestess of Athena – they are, as in **2**, associated as a group with these other generic officials. As Ceccarelli and Milanezi (2007, 211) very plausibly argue, this list of technical staff appears to have been formed in this way because they were the necessary personnel for the organisation and conduct of a particular festival. And further, since it is most likely that the *exarchoi* are to be associated with the (tragic and) dithyrambic choruses, as their leaders, it follows that we would thus be presented with the technical *équipe* necessary to run the festival which included tragedy and dithyramb in Cyrene.

It is thus very likely that the *exarchoi* are leaders of the dithyrambic choruses (whether they are to be associated with the doubtless non-processional tragic choruses must remain an open question). They are presumably experts in choral technique (dance and song), and doubtless participants in the event rather than off-stage trainers. We might suppose that they led choruses made up of locals (as much is implied by the nature of the sacrificial prize oxen: above), but were not themselves necessarily local. The very existence of their role implies a specific need and a demand that would have encouraged use of experts from anywhere. If this is so it is interesting that the obligation to fund the *exarchoi* was taken on by the city and not by choregoi (who are not in fact attested).

Some further illumination can be gleaned from the sums allocated to various officials in **3**: the *exarchoi* receive 220 dr. The number is divisible by 2, 4 and 5 and the evidence of **2** suggests that 4 may be the most likely candidate, since it implies the existence of 3 tragic and 1 (but see above) dithyrambic choruses. That means that each *exarchos* received 55 dr. It is impossible to say whether they may have received more remuneration in coin or kind from other sources (such as choregoi) and it is difficult to gauge whether the sum is generous (it is at least enough to buy an ox in Cyrene, and the cost of staples like wheat was much lower in Cyrene than Attica: Migeotte 2014, 163). We can compare it to the 240 dr. paid to the Bear (very probably an individual in the cult of Artemis) for maintenance (and something else, probably some kind of dress or masks: see Ceccarelli and Milanezi 2007, 213 on **3**, ll. 14–15); the 200 dr. received by the priestess of Athena; the 420 dr. received by the piper and the 904 dr. for the treasurer (**3**, ll. 19–20).

That the treasurer was by a very long way the best remunerated is noteworthy. In **3**, where this sum is recorded, the secretary, his natural assistant, does not appear. Perhaps the treasurer was now expected to provide his own from the sum allocated to him. Perhaps also some of these funds were to be disbursed by him on other matters within his competence (none of these sums are specified as 'pay' e.g. μισθός and so may be more general budget allocations). We might for instance suppose the treasurer to be the official tasked to supply the 'extra' funds for tragedy at **3**, l. 11: ἐπιθέν[τος τοῦ ταμίου …] 'with the further addition [by the treasurer of *sum*]'. The piper's sum, while low by Panhellenic standards of the Hellenistic period (**V G**), is more than seven times greater than that received by an *exarchos*. It seems virtually certain that the one piper played for all the choruses at the festival. What the heralds received is not preserved but it is noteworthy that it is targeted at their maintenance and dress. The term for the latter, a Doric form of *himation*, will refer to an outer garment. Why three heralds rather than one are needed for what we have taken to be a single (if elaborate) festival is not clear. Perhaps the job was a taxing one and a different man took the role on successive days. Given that there are only three of them (**3**, l. 19) the guards, as Ceccarelli and Milanezi (2007, 211) astutely note, are more likely to be some kind of official escorts of the procession rather than enforcers of security in the face of serious threats.

It is clear that these documents provide only part of the picture of the finances of Cyrenean drama. There is no evidence to date for the existence of a choregia to support the choruses themselves in training, but it would be no surprise to learn of one. Liturgies of unspecified nature are attested in the first century from a town some 14 km to the east of Cyrene, Mgarnes (*SEG* 9, 354, ll. 10–14 with Laronde 1987, 334–6); and, in the Augustan era, more generally in the Cyrenaica (*SEG* 9, 8, ll. 57, 104, 114–15, 136 with Ceccarelli and Milanezi 2007, 208). The precise provision by the *damiergoi* of funds for (sacrificial) prizes; for *exarchoi*; for some sort of 'extra' for tragedy (in **3**); for a piper, heralds, guards and other technical support, suggests a division of responsibility with another entity or individuals. How actors and poets were funded remains unclear. **2–4** offer no hint, unless the 'extra' funds for tragedy (or comedy) at **3**, l. 11 were intended for that purpose. The extent to which the city invested in theatrical infrastructure is however manifest.

2 and **3** provide no internal evidence as to the divine recipient or festival of their tragic and dithyrambic choruses. But the use of the word 'dithyrambic' itself (**2**, l. 14; **3**, l. 12) is very striking. The term is extremely rare in inscriptions, and virtually absent even where we might most expect it, to describe the men's and boys' choruses that performed at the Athenian Dionysia (Fearn 2007; Ceccarelli 2010; D'Alessio 2013, 113–18). The intimate association between dithyramb and Dionysus (and for that matter, tragedy) naturally encourages us to look for a cult of Dionysus in which to locate these Cyrenean dithyrambic and tragic choruses, but to date only modest evidence has emerged. There are two likely contenders for the context in which these choruses performed in Cyrene, reflecting in turn the existence of two large fifth-century Greek theatres in the city, neither of which was however connected (primarily) to a cult of Dionysus.

The first is situated to the north-north-east of the acropolis of Cyrene, at the western end of the great sanctuary of the city's founding and protecting god Apollo, on the 'Myrtousa' terrace, built directly into the hillside. It was excavated before the Second World War but the results were never properly published (Stucchi 1975, 34–7, 68–70, 208–10, 286, figs. 115, 209, 291–2; Goodchild 1971, 125–9, fig. 15; Chamoux 1998). In expeditions led by the Missione Archeologica Italiana a Cirene in 2005 and 2006 a project was devoted to this theatre under the leadership of Serenella Ensoli, with financial support from the Global Heritage Fund (preliminary findings reported in Ensoli 2010a; Ensoli 2010b, 116–17; Ensoli 2011; Ensoli 2012; http://ghn.globalheritagefund.org/uploads/library/doc_443.pdf). These campaigns will, when their results are fully published, arrive at a much improved understanding of the many phases of this major Greek theatre that was later transformed into a Roman amphitheatre.

There are at least four distinct phases in the life of the building as a Greek theatre. The clearest evidence for the earliest two phases consists of a series of cuttings made in the rock in the orchestra and the area of the stage building and parodoi, including a set in three parallel lines in the area of the stage building designed to receive timber members. These had been seen but not properly recorded in the 1930s and were rediscovered in the recent studies, along with others not previously noted (Ensoli 2010a, 122–4). Some had been concealed with lime-fillers in subsequent ancient works designed to regularise the rocky ground level. The cuttings indicate the existence of two phases of stage buildings made of timber, the second much larger (8.288 × 3.552 m) than the first (Stucchi 1975, 34–7). As there was no sign of work for a theatron in these phases, it was assumed by Stucchi (1975, 34, endorsed by Ensoli) that the audience at this period probably sat directly on the slope of the acropolis.

Prior to the recent work, the dating of the first two phases had relied heavily on Anti's hypothesis (1947, 90, 123–5) that the first stage building had been structurally analogous to the first trapezoidal theatre of Syracuse, thought by Anti to date soon after 500. The dating of the Syracusan theatre is itself a matter of ongoing controversy (**Ai**), but a fifth-century phase remains virtually certain. Anti's conclusion was followed in large part by Stucchi

(1975, 35) and the present director of excavations appears to concur. Ensoli (2010a, 124–5) alludes to recent discoveries (whose precise nature is as yet unclear) that confirm a high date and believes that the first two phases are both to be placed in the era of the Battiads, namely the first half of the fifth century (Ensoli 2011, 80 with fig. 4; 2012, 113 with fig. 3; 2012, 111: the middle of the 5th c. or even 475–450). The principal evidence is the discovery of a foundation wall of the stage building made of regular courses of stone that can be dated to around the middle of the fifth century. It would appear that already at this time the theatre was furnished with a stage building made in part at least of stone rather than entirely of timber. Ensoli believes this theatre served religious functions related to the adjacent major civic cults (Apollo and Artemis; the oracular grotto and the two springs of Apollo and Kyra on the higher terraces) and that it probably came also to serve as a place of gathering for the community, as well as for theatre proper under patronage of Apollo and in the context of his major festival, the Carneia.

The third phase shows a marked increase in the monumentalisation of the theatre, with considerably greater use of stone, notably for its new stage building and the large retaining wall of the (somewhat less than semicircular) theatron, considerable stretches of the eastern part of which survive. There are also significant traces of the foundations of the new stage building (17.76 × 3.25 m), which was in simple rectangular form without paraskenia; and cuttings in the ground rock to receive timbers for the proskenion. The seats were probably rock-cut into the natural slope in this period, and perhaps already divided into seven blocks (Ensoli 2010a, 126). And there was already at this date, as in later phases, an entrance to the theatre at the south, from the slope of the acropolis. In general many analogies were identified with the first circular theatre of Syracuse and the theatre at Iasus, with the analemma walls converging towards the orchestra. Stucchi (1975, 69–70) dated this third phase to the second half of the fourth century, and hence the era of **2–4** (these documents are themselves sometimes adduced to assist with the dating of this phase: Ensoli 2010a, 127). In further support of such a date Ensoli (2010a, 127) refers to the discovery of fragments of capitals from the Archaic Apollonion that had apparently been reused in building the third phase. Since we know that the new temple of Apollo dates to before 308, perhaps some time before, it follows as likely that the third phase is to be associated in time with the rebuilding of this temple.

A fourth major phase, in which the seating capacity may have reached over 14,000 (Chamoux 1998, 136), has been dated to the Ptolemaic period, and indeed associated more specifically with the enthusiasm of the Ptolemies for the cult of Dionysus and theatrical activity, notably that of Ptolemy II Philadelphus in Alexandria (Ensoli 2010a, 128–30; below); a fifth phase followed in the first half of the first century AD; and finally two major rebuilding events in the second century AD saw the theatre's transformation into an amphitheatre.

Ceccarelli and Milanezi (2007) raise various possibilities for the festival context of Cyrenean tragedy and dithyramb but tend to favour this theatre, supposing that the performances took place at the Carneia for Apollo and that Dionysiac dithyrambs were incorporated into the celebrations for Apollo, noting the presence of circular choruses for Apollo at the Athenian Thargelia and the fact that the theatre on Delos was built in the sanctuary of Apollo. Ensoli is preparing a full publication of the frontal decoration of the temple of Apollo (Ensoli 2010b, 123) and has intimated that Dionysus featured in this decoration in the late Classical period (Ensoli 2002, 196).

Following Chamoux (1953, 271–2), Ensoli (2002, 195–6; 2010a, 128; 2012, 118–20) also believes that the hitherto unidentified deity to whom the small temple immediately to the east of the theatre (Stucchi 1975, 53–4) was dedicated was Dionysus. She proposes as a further possibility to the Carneia that the theatrical performances may have taken place in honour of Dionysus and the Nymphs (his nurses) in the context of the festival Theodaisia known from an entry in the Suda to have been celebrated by the Libyans (Cyrene will certainly have been intended) in their honour (Ensoli 2002, 195; Nilsson 1906, 115–16, 279–80). The Suda entry reads as follows: (α 4266) Ἀστυδρόμια· παρὰ Λίβυσιν οἰονεὶ τῆς πόλεως γενέθλια, καὶ Θεοδαίσια ἑορτὴ, ἐν ᾗ ἐτίμων Διόνυσον καὶ τὰς Νύμφας· ἐμοὶ δοκεῖν, νηφάλιόν τε καὶ τὴν ἀγαθὴν κρᾶσιν αἰνιττόμενοι. 'Astydromia: among Libyans (this is) like a birthday celebration of the city, and a Theodaisia festival, in which they used to honour Dionysus and the Nymphs; it seems to me they are hinting at both unmixed [wine] and the good mixture' (the meaning of the latter gloss is obscure). A relief found in the sanctuary of Apollo of ca. 300 (Edinburgh Nat. Mus. Scotland inv. 1956.364; *LIMC* IV, 870 no. 308) has been thought to depict Demeter and Kore with Dionysus, but its interpretation is disputed and the male figure is often regarded instead as Pluto.

The nature of the (unpublished) inscriptions on the front of the seats in the 'Myrtousa' theatre is unclear. They are described as 'abbreviations' and reported without further detail at http://ghn.globalheritagefund.org/uploads/library/doc_443.pdf (3.6), where the existence of a longer inscription on one of the seats of the theatron is also mentioned. One of the fragments photographed in the report and described as part of a base from near the great dedicatory monument of the second century AD that consists of a flight of steps surmounted by a structure with three (lost) statues appears to show the enticing combination ΘΕΑ- (in Classical or early Hellenistic letters).

The second theatre is in the sanctuary of Demeter and Kore which lay outside the city wall to the south, on a vast terraced site (some 5 ha: Luni 2013, 204), established in the sixth century and in continuous use well into Roman times. This was discovered in 2002 by the Missione Italiana dell'Università di Urbino (Luni 2006a, 2186–91, figs. 10–11; 2006b, 153–5; 2010, figs. 1–2; 2011; 2013, 222–5, 434 with fig. 15). The theatre was built in the middle of the sanctuary, along the route taken by the processions in honour of Demeter. It was mostly directly cut from the rock, with some 21 rows and apparently a single central access staircase, thought by the excavator to suggest a design aimed more at the linear flow of individuals rather than convenient mass entrance. Recent excavations reveal that the stage building was of a non-canonical type (Luni 2013, 222, 434 with fig. 15). The theatron has affinities with a number of Hellenistic theatres, including the one at nearby Apollonia, but there are signs that this reflects a redevelopment (including an expansion) of the older Classical structure, which may have had a rectangular form (Luni 2013, 224–5). A fragment of a small marble base inscribed with a dedication to Dionysus was found in a worked natural rock cavity immediately adjacent to the orchestra (to the west), and had probably originally been set into one of the several niches inside it (*IGCyr* 113800; Luni 2013, 222–3, 435 with fig. 16; dated by Marengo 2010, 144–6 to around the middle of the 2nd c.). While inside a somewhat larger cavity in the rock to the east side of the orchestra was found the basin of a fountain inscribed as belonging to the Nymphs (Luni 2013, 223, 435 with fig. 17, dated 2nd–3rd c. AD). It looks likely that Dionysus and the Nymphs played a part in the cult of the theatre.

D'Alessio (2013, 131) supports the case for this being the theatre in which dithyramb and tragedy were performed. He points to the analogy of the Eleusinia in honour of Demeter in Sparta, held in her extramural sanctuary on the slopes of Mt Taygetus, in the context of which it has plausibly been argued that dithyrambs were performed (D'Alessio 2013, 130–1). In both the Spartan and the Cyrenean context, Demeter appears to have to some extent shared her cult with Dionysus, an association that can be identified at many other sites, such as Eleusis and Corinth. And in Cyrene, evidence has recently emerged that Dionysus had a place within Demeter's large sanctuary – along with other deities, including the Nymphs (but the basis upon which Luni 2011, 235 describes this as 'le théâtre de Dionysos' is not entirely clear). On a large terraced area to the west of the theatre a series of small structures were found disposed along processional routes, many cut or built into the rock walls. In one of these was found part of a small second-century marble relief inscribed, according to a plausible restoration, as a dedication to Dionysus (Marengo 2010, 144–6). A statue and temple were consecrated in the first century AD (*CIG* 5139; *SEG* 9, 163–4; Callot 1999, 94, 142, 258–9) and some of the pottery from the sanctuary shows Dionysiac subjects already by the Archaic period (Ceccarelli and Milanezi 2007, 199). Further evidence that Dionysus shared the sanctuary with Demeter comes from the western edge of the sanctuary site, where a statue of the god in the form of a herm (H. 1.6 m) was found in a zone of cultic grottoes, carved niches and natural springs (Luni 2013, 227–8). The close association between Dionysus and Demeter in Callimachus' *Hymn to Demeter* (6.70) may reflect a Cyrenean cultic context, though the identity of the deity honoured by the festival in the Hymn is debated (Hopkinson 1984, 35–9).

1 was carved directly onto the front of one of the upper rows of seats in the theatre in the sanctuary of Demeter. Its early date, at the end of the fifth century or – at the latest – very early in the fourth, seems to be secure on the basis of its letter forms and the evident use of pre-Ionic script (E for Η, O for Ω). This would provide a *terminus ante quem* of ca. 410 for the construction of the upper theatron. While necessarily somewhat speculative, the interpretation of its first editor as a *kalos* acclamation for a man whose name ends in -etor is compelling (Inglese 2011, 279–81; 2013, 238–9; Luni 2013, 224 airs the possibility that the name was that of a theatre benefactor). She suggests as a possible candidate Hagetor (Ἁγήτωρ), a name attested from the fourth century as current in a well-known Cyrenean family (*LGPN* I, s.v.; *SEG* 46, 2198, l. 121). Inglese compares the inscription ΕΥΑΙΩΝ ΚΑΛΟΣ ΑΙΣΧΥΛΟ 'Euaion son of Aeschylus is beautiful!' that appears on a number of Attic vases of ca. 440 with clear reference to the son of Aeschylus in his role as a tragic actor (e.g. *ARV²* 1017.53; 1020.92; **Aix**), and suggests that the person thus acclaimed in the Cyrenean theatre may likewise have had some connection with the theatre.

While such a thing is unparalleled at this early date (compare the much later evidence from Aphrodisias and Ephesus: Roueché 1993; 2002), its likelihood is increased by the growing understanding that such *kalos* acclamations are not confined to inscriptions on pots from the elite world of the Attic symposium and the sons of notable families (Shapiro 1987) but were also applied to participants in a range of agonistic undertakings, and inscribed as graffiti on a variety of architectural and rupestral sites, in many places (Langdon 1985, 266–9 on Attic and Thasian rupestral evidence; Shear 1984, 14–15 for two examples from the euthynteria of the Stoa Poikile in Athens; *IG* XII 3, 536–553 for a set from the gymnasium on Thera). A good parallel is offered by the many graffiti inscriptions found in the tunnel of the stadium at Nemea, dating in the earliest cases from the fourth century, that acclaim athletic contestants – such as 'Akrotatos is beautiful'– alongside other claims such as 'I win!' (νικῶ: the writer's name was included but only the initial kappa is legible: Miller 2001, 84–9; 311–66; *SEG* 51, 364, 369, 371, 373, 375–8, 381, 387). A similar combination of support for (in this case choral) victory and erotic attachment is to be found in the curse-tablet from Sicily (probably Gela) dated to ca. 470–450 (**Avii**).

It is therefore all the more intriguing that a tragic actor by the name of (H)agetor is recorded as victor in the tragic actors' competition at the Athenian Lenaea ca. 310 (*IG* II² 2325H, l. 64 M-O; Millis and Olson 2012, 208 on the date; Stefanis no. 38). Nothing else is known of this man, but he is very unlikely to be a native Athenian. *LGPN* II register him as the only known Athenian Hagetor, but the doubt which they attach to the assignation (with a '?') is insufficient, for there are no positive grounds for believing he was an Athenian. The (Doric) name is otherwise not attested in Attica, with a single somewhat dubious exception (*SEG* 50, 168 B, l. 50; Lambert 2000, 64; *Addenda* to *LGPN* II, s.v., 4th c.). In addition to Cyrene, the name is predominantly found in Rhodes and a few neighbouring islands, as well as Delphi and Thessaly. It is at least possible, given the extent to which acting was a family tradition, that the Hagetor in the Cyrenean theatre was a forefather on the stage of the tragic actor successful nearly a century later in Athens, and likely that both were from one of the Dorian locales in which their name is attested, quite possibly Cyrene itself.

Evidence for a tradition of comic performance (see above), or rather of an appreciation of comedy, begins as early as the last decade of the fifth century. This is at least the date of production of the Attic chous (Louvre N3408; *ARV²* 1335.34; *MMC³* AV 6) depicting Heracles accompanied by a Nike on a chariot drawn by centaurs and led by a dancing male figure in the costume of a comic actor (wearing comic tights as well as a phallos), though it is impossible to say at what point it made its way to Cyrene. While its precise degree of referentiality to a specific comedy is debated, there is no doubt that it takes pains to render realistic production details of comedy (Revermann 2006, 145–6; Csapo 2010, 27–8). The importation of considerable amounts of Attic pottery already attested for the Archaic period continued into and beyond the fifth century. The local manufacture of comic figurines in the first half of the fourth century suggests a high degree of local engagement. That several examples, including the two best-preserved (*MMC³* AT 10e = Paris Louvre inv. MN642; *MMC³* AT 70a = Paris Louvre inv. MN638: an hetaira raising a himation before her face as if to hide; and an old woman, probably a brothel keeper), are instances of Attic types suggests that interest in Athenian comedy had permeated to Cyrene by this date and met with a certain level of sophistication in interpretation (Green 2008, 215; Green 2014a, 333–5 with figs. 13.2–3).

The choice made by Diphilus (active 2nd half of 4th c.) to set the play on which Plautus' *Rudens* was based in Cyrene (*Rud.* 32–3; Diph. *PCG* T 11), and to populate it with Athenians in exile, is suggestive. It has been argued (on the basis of Alciphr. 4.18) that the comic poet Philemon spent time at the court of Ptolemy Philadelphus in Alexandria, and perhaps performed his plays there (Bruzzese 2011, 18–22). Alexandria appears to have had a 'great' theatre by the early third century, but its location has not been found (Ath. 14.620d; Theoc. *Id.* 17.112–14). The story told in Plutarch (*Mor.* 458a) of Philemon's shipwreck on the

African coast and subsequent treatment by the regent and (from ca. 300) king of Cyrene, Magas, is understandably given less credence, seen to be a likely product of themes reworked from his own plays (Bruzzese 2011, 17–19). But it is clear that Philemon had ridiculed Magas in one of his comedies (F 132) and although that comedy is unlikely to have been performed in Cyrene itself, the implication of Plutarch that Magas was aware of its public performance is unexceptionable (δημοσίᾳ γὰρ ὑπ' αὐτοῦ κωμῳδηθεὶς ἐν θεάτρῳ 'ridiculed in a comedy by him publicly in a theatre'). Perhaps the performance took place at the court of his half-brother and rival Ptolemy Philadelphos.

In the third century Cyrene itself produced a comic actor who was active on the international circuit – one Polyaratos son of Eudoxos, who performed at Delphi ca. 260 and Oropus, where he and his descendants were granted a range of rights (Stefanis no. 2090; in *IOrop*. 25, ll. 2–3 he is described simply as ὁ ὑποκριτὴς 'the actor'; **Ci**).

The persistence of a keen interest in Greek drama well into the Roman period is attested not only by the continued construction of theatres (above) but by the evidence of wall painting in tombs, in particular a second-century AD frieze from the North cemetery that depicts a series of musical and dramatic performances, framed by scenes from comedy and tragedy. The comic scene shows a Youth gesturing towards a Leading Slave with worried pose, left hand to chin. They stand before a door above which is an iambic inscription that indicates a knocking at the door and the arrival of the father (*PCG* adesp. F 1107); all of which suggests that a particular scene from a particular comedy is intended (Bacchielli 1993, 86–95; Bacchielli 2002; Perusino 1993 on the inscription).

The issue of whether and to what extent Cyrenean theatrical culture was influenced by the Athenian model has been assessed by Ceccarelli and Milanezi (2007, 201–4, 214), who very plausibly conclude that while the cultural and economic prominence of Athens in the Aegean will have played its part, direct and systematic influence was highly unlikely in the Classical period, and a range of other factors need to be taken into account: the Spartan (and more generally Dorian) traditions of Cyrene; the Arcadian strand dating from the constitutional reforms of Demonax ca. 550; the relationship with Delphi from the city's origins, and of continued importance in the fourth century; as well as a variety of epichoric traditions. One of the prize items in support of a direct Athenian influence is the two large reliefs, dated to the last quarter of the fifth century and worked in local limestone (Cyrene museum inv. 15003), found in the city's eastern necropolis and depicting Heracles leading Alcestis to the Underworld and a young man exhorting a reluctant old man. Both have been associated specifically with scenes from Euripides' *Alcestis* of 438 and encouraged a belief that that tragedy was performed in Cyrene very soon after its first production in Athens (Laronde 1987, 140; Chamoux 1998, 134). Ceccarelli and Milanezi (2007, 201–3) successfully dismiss these large claims, demonstrating that the story was equally at home at the Spartan Carneia (cf. E. *Alc*. 445–51), and is more likely to reflect local traditions than Athenian influence.

Bibliography

Abbreviations

AEMΘ	*Αρχαιολογικό Έργο στη Μακεδονία και στη Θράκη*
Agora	*The Athenian Agora: Results of Excavations Conducted by the American School of Classical Studies at Athens.* 1953– . Princeton.
APF	Davies, J. K. 1971. *Athenian Propertied Families 600–300 B.C.* Oxford.
ARV²	Beazley, J. D. 1963. *Attic Red-Figure Vase-Painters².* Oxford.
ATD	Le Guen, B. 2001. *Les associations de Technites dionysiaques à l'époque hellénistique,* 2 vols. Nancy.
BE	*Bulletin épigraphique*
BNJ	Worthington, I. ed. 2007–. *Brill's New Jacoby.* Brill Online Reference. Leiden.
BNP	Cancik, H., Schneider, H. and Landfester, M. eds. 1996–. *Brill's New Pauly: Encyclopaedia of the Ancient World.* Leiden and Boston.
CA	Powell, J. U. 1925. *Collectanea Alexandrina.* Oxford.
CAG	*Commentaria in Aristotelem Graeca,* 23 vols. 1882–1909. Berlin.
CEG	Hansen, P. A. 1983–1989. *Carmina epigraphica graeca,* vol. 1: *Saeculorum VIII–V a. Chr. n.,* vol. 2: *Saeculi IV a. Chr. n.* Berlin and New York.
CFST	Todisco, L. ed. 2003. *La ceramica figurata a soggetto tragico in Magna Grecia e in Sicilia.* Archaeologica 140. Rome.
CID	Rougement, G., Bousquet, J., Bélis, A. and Lefèvre, F. eds. 1977–. *Corpus des inscriptions de Delphes.* Paris.
CIG	Boeckh, A. 1828–1877. *Corpus inscriptionum graecarum,* 4 vols. Berlin.
CIRB	Struve, V. 1965. *Corpus Inscriptionum Regni Bosporani.* Moscow.
CLGP	Bastianini, G., Haslam, M., Maehler, H., Montanari, F., and Römer, C. E. 2004–. *Commentaria et lexica Graeca in papyris reperta,* multiple volumes. Munich and Leipzig
CNS	Calciati, R. 1983–1987. *Corpus Nummorum Siculorum: The Bronze Coinage.* Milan.
Corinth 8.1	Meritt, B. D. 1931. *Corinth VIII.1: Greek Inscriptions, 1896–1927.* Cambridge, MA.
Corinth 8.3	Kent, J. H. 1966. *Corinth VIII.3: The Inscriptions, 1926–1950.* Princeton.
CPG	Leutsch, E. L. and Schneidewin, F. G. 1839–1851. *Corpus Paroemiographorum Graecorum,* 2 vols. Reprinted, Hildesheim 1961. Göttingen.
CVA	*Corpus Vasorum Antiquorum.* 1922–. Paris et al.
DAGM	Pöhlmann, E. and West, M. L. 2001. *Documents of Ancient Greek Music: The Extant Melodies and Fragments Edited and Transcribed with Commentary.* Oxford.
DFA²	Pickard-Cambridge, A. W. 1988. *The Dramatic Festivals of Athens²,* revised with addenda by J. Gould and D. Lewis. Oxford.
D-K	Diels, H. and Kranz, W. 1951–1952. *Die Fragmente der Vorsokratiker,* 3 vols. Berlin.
DTC²	Pickard-Cambridge, A. W. 1962. *Dithyramb, Tragedy, and Comedy²,* revised by T. B. L. Webster. Oxford.
EGM	Fowler, R. 2000. *Early Greek Mythography,* vol. 1: *Text and Introduction.* Oxford.
EGT	Roisman, H. M., ed. 2013. *The Encyclopedia of Greek Tragedy,* 3 vols. Chichester, Malden, MA and Oxford.

EKM 1   Beroia Gounaropoulou, L. and Hatzopoulos, M. B. 1998. *Επιγραφές Κάτω Μακεδονίας: μεταξύ του Βερμίου όρους και του Αξιού ποταμού. Τεύχος Α΄: Επιγραφές Βέροιας.* Athens.

FD II   Bousquet, J. 1952. *Le Trésor de Cyrène: Fouilles de Delphes*, II: *Topographie et Architecture*. Paris.

FD III   Bourguet, E., et al. 1929–. *Fouilles de Delphes*, III: *Épigraphie*. Paris.

FGE   Page, D. L. 1981. *Further Greek Epigrams*. Cambridge.

FGrH   Jacoby, F. et al. 1923– . *Die Fragmente der griechischen Historiker*. Berlin and Leiden.

FHG   Müller, K. O. 1841–1883. *Fragmenta Historicorum Graecorum*, 5 vols. Paris.

GAI I   Threatte, L. 1980. *The Grammar of Attic Inscriptions*, vol. 1: *Phonology*. Berlin.

GIBM   Hicks, E. L., Hirschfeld, G., Marshall, F. H. and Newton, C. T. 1874–1916. *The Collection of Greek Inscriptions in the British Museum*, 4 vols. in 6. London.

GVI   Peek, W. 1955. *Griechische Vers-Inschriften*. Berlin.

IACP   Hansen, M. H. and Nielsen, T. H., eds. 2004. *An Inventory of Archaic and Classical Poleis*. Oxford.

ID   Durrbach, F., et al. 1926–1972. *Inscriptions de Délos*, 7 vols. Paris.

IDidyma   Rehm, A. 1958. *Didyma, II: Die Inschriften*. Berlin.

IE   Clinton, K. 2005. *Eleusis: The Inscriptions on Stone: Documents of the Sanctuary of the Two Goddesses and Public Documents of the Deme*, vol. 1. Athens.

IEG   West, M. L. 1989–1992. *Iambi et elegi Graeci ante Alexandrum cantati*[2]. Oxford.

IG   *Inscriptiones Graecae*. 1873– . Berlin.

IGASMG II[2]   Arena, R. 2002. *Iscrizioni greche arcaiche di Sicilia e Magna Grecia. Iscrizioni di Sicilia*, vol. 2: *Iscrizioni di Gela e Agrigento*[2]. Alessandria.

IGBulg I[2]   Mihailov, G. 1970. *Inscriptiones graecae in Bulgaria repertae*[2], vol. 1: *Inscriptiones orae Ponti Euxini*. Sofia.

IGCyr   Dobias-Lalou, C. ed. 2017. *Inscriptions of Greek Cyrenaica*, in collaboration with Alice Bencivenni and Hugues Berthelot with help from Simona Antolini, Silvia Maria Marengo and Emilio Rosamilia. Bologna. http://doi.org/10.6092/UNIBO/IGCYRGVCYR

IGDS   Dubois, L. 1989. *Inscriptions grecques dialectales de Sicile*. Paris and Rome.

IGR I   Cagnat, R. 1911–1927. *Inscriptiones graecae ad res romanas pertinentes*, 3 vols. Paris.

IGUR   Moretti, L. 1968. *Inscriptiones Graecae Urbis Romae*. Rome.

IK Assos   Merkelbach, R. 1976. *Die Inschriften von Assos*. Inschriften griechischer Städte aus Kleinasien, vol. 4. Bonn.

IKaunos   Marek, C. 2006. *Die Inschriften von Kaunos*. Vestigia: Beiträge zur Alten Geschichte 55. Munich.

IK Byzantion   Łajtar, A. 2000. *Die Inschriften von Byzantion*. Inschriften griechischer Städte aus Kleinasien, vol. 58. Bonn.

IK Ephesos   Börker, C., Engelmann, H., Knibbe, D., Meriç, R., Merkelbach, R., Nollé, J., Şahin, S. and Wankel, H. 1979–1984. *Die Inschriften von Ephesos*, 7 vols. Inschriften griechischer Städte aus Kleinasien, vols. 11–17. Bonn.

IK Erythrai   Engelmann, H. and Merkelbach, R. 1972–1973. *Die Inschriften von Erythrai und Klazomenai*. Inschriften griechischer Städte aus Kleinasien, vols. 1 and 2. Bonn.

IK Iasos   Blümel, W. 1985. *Die Inschriften von Iasos*, 2 vols. Inschriften griechischer Städte aus Kleinasien, vol. 28. Bonn.

IK Ilion   Frisch, P. 1975. *Die Inschriften von Ilion*. Inschriften griechischer Städte aus Kleinasien, vol. 3. Bonn.

IK Iznik Şahin, S. 1979, 1981–1982. *Katalog der antiken Inschriften des Museums von Iznik (Nikaia)*. Inschriften griechischer Städte aus Kleinasien, vols. 9 and 10. Bonn.

IK Knidos Blümel, W. 1992. *Die Inschriften von Knidos I*. Inschriften griechischer Städte aus Kleinasien, vol. 41. Bonn.

IK Kyme Engelmann, H. 1976. *Die Inschriften von Kyme*. Inschriften griechischer Städte aus Kleinasien, vol. 5. Bonn.

IK Lampsakos Frisch, P. 1978. *Die Inschriften von Lampsakos*. Inschriften griechischer Städte aus Kleinasien, vol. 6. Bonn.

IK Priene Blümel, W. and Merkelbach, R. 2014. *Die Inschriften von Priene*. Inschriften griechischer Städte aus Kleinasien, vol. 69. Bonn.

ILS Dessau, H. 1892–1916. *Inscriptiones Latinae Selectae*, 3 vols. Berlin.

IMagn. Kern, O. 1900. *Die Inschriften von Magnesia am Mäander*. Berlin.

IMT Kyz Kapu Dağ Barth, M. and Stauber, J. (eds.), 1996. *Inschriften Mysia & Troas: Kyzikene, Kapu Dağ*. Munich.

IOrop. Petrakos, B. C. 1997. Οἱ ἐπιγραφὲς τοῦ Ὠρωποῦ. Athens.

IosPE I² Latyshev, V. 1916. *Inscriptiones antiquae orae septentrionalis Ponti Euxini graecae et latinae*, vol. 1: *Inscriptiones Tyriae, Olbiae, Chersonesi Tauricae*². St. Petersburg.

IPriene Hiller von Gaertringen, F. 1906. *Inschriften von Priene*. Berlin.

IRhamn. Petrakos, B. C. 1999. Ο δήμος του Ραμνούντος. Σύνοψη των ανασκαφών και των ερευνών (1813–1998), II. Οἱ ἐπιγραφές. Athens.

ISamos McCabe, D. F., Brownson, J. V. and Ehrman, B. D. 1986. *Samos Inscriptions: Texts and List*. Princeton.

IScM I Pippidi, D. M. 1983. *Inscriptiones Scythiae Minoris graecae et latinae*, vol. 1: *Inscriptiones Histriae et viciniae*. Inscriptiones Daciae et Scythiae Minoris antiquae. Bucharest.

IScM III Avram, A. 2000. *Inscriptiones Scythiae Minoris graecae et latinae*, vol. 3: *Callatis et territorium*. Inscriptiones Daciae et Scythiae Minoris antiquae. Bucharest.

IThesp. Roesch, P. 2007–2009. *Les Inscriptions de Thespies*. Lyon.

IThrAeg Loukopoulou, L. D., Parissaaki, M. G., Psoma, S. and Zournatzi, A. 2005. Ἐπιγραφὲς τῆς Θράκης τοῦ Αἰγαίου μεταξὺ τῶν ποταμῶν Νέστου καὶ Ἕβρου (Νομοὶ Ξάνθης, Ῥοδόπης καὶ Ἕβρου). Athens.

IvO Dittenberger, W. and Purgold, K. 1896. *Die Inschriften von Olympia*. Berlin.

LCS Trendall, A. D. 1967. *The Red-Figured Vases of Lucania, Campania and Sicily*, 2 vols. Oxford.

LCS Suppl. 3 Trendall, A. D. 1983. *The Red-Figured Vases of Lucania, Campania and Sicily: Third Supplement*. Oxford.

LGPN *Lexicon of Greek Personal Names*. 1987– . Oxford.

LIMC *Lexicon Iconographicum Mythologiae Classicae*. 1981–1999. Zurich.

Lindos II Blinkenberg, C. 1941. *Lindos: Fouilles et recherches, 1902–1914*, vol. 2: *Inscriptions*. Copenhagen and Berlin.

LSJ Liddell, H. G. and Scott, R. 1940. *A Greek–English Lexicon*, revised and augmented by Sir Henry Stuart Jones. Oxford.

Milet I 3 Kawerau, G. and Rehm, A. 1914. *Milet: Ergebnisse der Ausgrabungen und Untersuchungen seit dem Jahr 1899*, vol. 1.3: *Das Delphinion in Milet*. Berlin.

*MMC*² Webster, T. B. L. 1969. *Monuments Illustrating Old and Middle Comedy*². BICS Supplement 23. London.

*MMC*³ Webster, T. B. L. 1978. *Monuments Illustrating Old and Middle Comedy*³, revised and enlarged by J. R. Green. BICS Supplement 39. London.

MNC[2]	Webster, T. B. L. 1969. *Monuments Illustrating New Comedy*[2]. BICS Supplement 24. London.
MNC[3]	Webster, T. B. L. 1995. *Monuments Illustrating New Comedy*[3], revised and enlarged by J. R. Green and A. Seeberg. BICS Supplement 50. London.
M-O	Millis, B. W. and Olson, S. D. 2012. *Inscriptional Records for the Dramatic Festivals in Athens*. Leiden.
OCD[3]	Hornblower, S. and Spawforth, A. eds. 2003. *The Oxford Classical Dictionary*[3]. Oxford.
O.Edfu	Michałowski, K. 1974. *Od Edfu do Faras*. Warsaw.
OGIS	Dittenberger, W. 1903. *Orientis Graeci Inscriptiones Selectae*. Leipzig.
OLD	Glare, P. G. W. 2012. *Oxford Latin Dictionary*[2]. Oxford.
PAA	Traill, J. S. 1994– . *Persons of Ancient Athens*. Toronto.
PAdd	Trendall, A. D. 1959. 'Paestan Addenda', *PBSR* 27: 1–37.
PCG	Kassel, R. and Austin, C. 1983–2001. *Poetae Comici Graeci*, 8 vols. Berlin and New York.
PhV[2]	Trendall, A. D. 1967. *Phlyax Vases*[2]. BICS Supplement 19. London.
PMG	Page, D. L. 1962. *Poetae Melici Graeci*. Oxford.
RE	Wissowa, G., Kroll, W., Mittelhaus, K., Ziegler, K. and Gärtner, H. eds. 1893–1980. *Paulys Realencyclopädie der classischen Altertumswissenschaft*. Stuttgart.
R-O II	Rhodes, P. J. and Osborne, R. G. 2003. *Greek Historical Inscriptions*, vol. 2: *404–323 BC*. Oxford.
RVAp	Trendall, A. D. and Cambitoglou, A. 1978–1982. *The Red-Figured Vases of Apulia*, 2 vols. Oxford.
RVP	Trendall, A. D. 1987. *The Red-Figured Vases of Paestum*. London.
RVSIS	Trendall, A. D. 1989. *Red Figure Vases of South Italy and Sicily*. London.
SEG	*Supplementum Epigraphicum Graecum*. 1923– . Leiden.
SGDI	Collitz, H. and Bechtel, F. eds. 1884–1915. *Sammlung der griechischen Dialekt-Inschriften*, 4 vols. Göttingen.
SH	Lloyd-Jones, H. and Parsons, P. J. 1983. *Supplementum Hellenisticum*. Berlin and New York.
SSH	Lloyd-Jones, H. 2005. *Supplementum Supplementi Hellenistici*. Berlin and New York.
Stefanis	Stefanis, I. E. 1988. *Διονυσιακοὶ Τεχνῖται*. Herakleion.
Suppl. Ephes.	Alpers, M., Halfmann, H., Mansfield, J. and Schäfer, C. 1995. *Supplementum Ephesium*. Hamburg.
Syll.[1]	Dittenberger, W. 1883. *Sylloge Inscriptionum Graecarum*. Leipzig.
Syll.[2]	Dittenberger, W. 1898–1901. *Sylloge Inscriptionum Graecarum*[2]. Leipzig.
Syll.[3]	Dittenberger, W. 1915–1924. *Sylloge Inscriptionum Graecarum*[3], 4 vols. Leipzig.
TGR	Ciancio Rossetto, P. and Pisani Sartorio, G. eds. 1994–1996. *Teatri greci e romani: Alle origini del linguaggio rappresentato*, 3 vols. Rome.
TrGF	Kannicht, R., Radt, S. and Snell, B. eds. 1971–2004. *Tragicorum Graecorum Fragmenta*, 5 vols. Göttingen.

Acheilara, L. 2000. *Η κοροπλαστική της Λέσβου*. PhD Diss. Thessaloniki.

Ackermann, D. 2011. 'Un nouveau type de communauté en Attique: Les pentékostyes du dème d'Aixone', in N. Badoud, ed. *Philologos Dionysos: mélanges offerts au professeur Denis Knoepfler*. Geneva. 39–78.

2018. *Une microhistoire d'Athènes: Le dème d'Aixône dans l'Antiquité*. BÉFAR 379. Athens.

Adam-Veleni, P. 2010. *Θέατρο και θέαμα στην αρχαία Μακεδονία*. Thessaloniki.

2012. 'Τὸ θέατρο στη Μακεδονία', in P. Adam-Veleni, ed. *Αρχαία Θέατρα της Μακεδονίας*. Diazoma 3. Athens. 19–34.

Adrimi-Sismani, V. 2011. 'Τὸ αρχαίο θέατρο των Φθιωτίδων Θηβών', in V. Adrimi-Sismani, ed. *Αρχαία Θέατρα στη Θεσσαλία*. Diazoma 5. Athens. 49–66.

Agelidis, S. 2009. *Choregische Weihgeschenke in Griechenland*. Bonn.

Ağtürk, T. and Arslan, N. 2015. *A Terracotta Treasure at Assos*. Istanbul.

Ahrens, H. L. 1839–1843. *De Graecae Linguae Dialectis*, 2 vols. Göttingen.

Alcock, S. E. 2002. *Archaeologies of the Greek Past: Landscape, Monuments, and Memories*. Cambridge.

Alexander, J. A. 1970. 'Cassandreia during the Macedonian Period: An Epigraphical Commentary', in B. Laourdas and C. Makaronas, eds. *Ἀρχαία Μακεδονία Ι ἀνακοινώσεις κατὰ τὸ πρῶτον διεθνὲς συμπόσιον 26–28 Αὐγούστου 1968*. Thessaloniki. 127–46.

Alipheri, S. 2009. 'The Eleusinian Decrees *REG* 91 (1978) 289–306 Reconsidered', in A. A. Themos and N. Papazarkadas, eds. *Ἀττικὰ ἐπιγραφικά. Μελέτες πρὸς τιμὴν τοῦ Christian Habicht*. Athens. 183–92.

2010–2013. 'Στοιχεῖα Διονυσιακῆς λατρείας σὲ ψήφισμα τῶν Ἰκαριέων', *Horos* 22–25: 145–53.

Allamani-Souri, V., Karadedos, G., Misaplidou, V. and Poulakakis, N. 2012. 'Τὸ αρχαίο θέατρο της Μιέζας', in P. Adam-Veleni, ed. *Αρχαία Θέατρα της Μακεδονίας*. Diazoma 3. Athens. 129–43.

Allan, W. 2000. *The 'Andromache' and Euripidean Tragedy*. Oxford.

2001. 'Euripides in Megale Hellas: Some Aspects of the Early Reception of Tragedy', *G&R* 48: 67–86.

Altherr-Charon, A. and Lasserre, F. 1981. 'Héraclès à Erétrie. Une nouvelle inscription agonistique archaïque', *Etudes de lettres* 189: 25–36.

Álvarez Salas, O. 2007a. 'Pseudepicharmea: Alle origini di un corpus pseudepigrafo', *Nova Tellus* 25.1: 117–53.

2007b. 'Epicarmo e Senofane: Tessere di una polemica', *Nova Tellus* 25.2: 85–136.

2016. 'From Epicharmus' Theatrics to Zeno's Paradoxical "Drama"', in H. Reid and D. Tanasi, eds. *Philosopher Kings and Tragic Heroes: Essays on Images and Ideas from Western Greece*. Iowa. 25–44.

Amandry, P. 1976. 'Trépieds d'Athènes: I. Dionysies', *BCH* 100: 15–93.

1980. 'Sur les concours argiens', *Études argiennes*. BCH Supplement 6: 211–53.

1983. 'Le bouclier d'Argos (Note complémentaire)', *BCH* 107: 627–34.

Amandry, P. and Ducat, J. 1973. 'Trépieds déliens', *BCH* Supplement 1: 17–64.

Amandry, P. and Spyropoulos, T. 1974. 'Monuments chorégiques d'Orchomène de Béotie', *BCH* 98: 171–246.

Amit, M. 1973. *Great and Small Poleis: A Study in the Relations between the Great Powers and the Small Cities in Ancient Greece*. Brussels.

Ampolo, C. 1981. 'Tra finanza e politica: carriera e affari del signor Moirokles', *RivFil* 109: 187–204.

Amyx, D. A. 1988. *Corinthian Vase-Painting of the Archaic Period*, 3 vols. Berkeley.

Andreou, I. 1976. '"Ηπειρος, Ἀνασκαφικὲς ἐργασίες. Ἄρτα', *ArchDelt* 31 B: 199–201.

1983. 'Τὸ μικρὸ θέατρο της Αμβρακίας', *Ηπειρωτικά Χρονικά* 25: 9–23.

1994. 'Ὁ δῆμος των Αιξωνίδων Αλών', in W. Coulson, O. Palagia, T. Shear, H. Shapiro and F. Frost, eds. *The Archaeology of Athens and Attica under the Democracy*. Oxford. 191–209.

Aneziri, S. 1994. 'Zwischen Musen und Hof: Die dionysischen Techniten auf Zypern', *ZPE* 104: 179–98.

2003. *Die Vereine der dionysischen Techniten im Kontext der hellenistischen Gesellschaft: Untersuchungen zur Geschichte, Organisation und Wirkung der hellenistischen Technitenvereine*. Historia Einzelschriften 163. Stuttgart.

2007. 'The Organisation of Musical Contests in the Hellenistic Period and Artists' Participation: An Attempt at Classification', in P. Wilson, ed. *The Greek Theatre and Festivals: Documentary Studies.* Oxford. 67–84.

2011. 'World Travellers: The Associations of Artists of Dionysus', in R. Hunter and I. Rutherford, eds. *Wandering Poets in Ancient Greek Culture.* Cambridge. 217–36.

Angeli Bertinelli, M. G. 1993. *Le vite di Nicia e di Crasso: Plutarco.* Verona.

Angiolillo, S. 1981. 'La visita di Dioniso a Ikarios nella ceramica attica: Appunti sulla politica culturale pisistratea', *DialArch* 3: 13–22.

1997. *Arte e cultura nell'Atene di Pisistrato e dei Pisistratidi.* Bari.

Anti, C. 1947. *Teatri greci arcaici da Minosse a Pericle.* Padua.

Anti, C. and Polacco, L. 1969. *Nuove ricerche sui teatri greci arcaici.* Padua.

Antoniou, G. P. 2015. 'The Theatre of Dodona: New Observations on the Architecture of the Cavea', in R. Frederiksen, E. R. Gebhard and A. Sokolicek, eds. *The Architecture of the Ancient Greek Theatre: Acts of an International Conference at the Danish Institute at Athens 27–30 January 2012.* Monographs of the Danish Institute at Athens 17. Aarhus. 177–91.

Aravantinos, V. 1998. 'Θήβα', *ArchDelt* 53 B: 355.

Archontidou Argyri, A. and Kokkinophorou, M., eds. 2004. *Archaio Theatro Ephaistias.* Lemnos.

Arena, R. 1994. 'Le iscrizioni antiche di Gela e Agrigento', *Acme* 47.2: 11–14.

2002. *Iscrizioni greche arcaiche di Sicilia e Magna Grecia*, vol. 2: *Iscrizioni di Gela e di Agrigento²*. Alessandria.

Arias, P. E. 1934. *Il teatro greco fuori di Atene.* Florence.

Arnott, W. G. 1968. 'Studies in Comedy, I: Alexis and the Parasite's Name', *GRBS* 9: 161–8.

1996. *Alexis: The Fragments. A Commentary.* Cambridge.

2000. *Menander*, vol. 3. Cambridge, MA and London.

Arrighetti, G. 1964. *Satiro: Vita di Euripide.* Pisa.

Arslan, N. 2016. 'Neue Forschungen zur Agora von Assos', in N. Arslan, E.-M. Mohr and K. Rheidt, eds. *Assos: Neue Forschungsergebnisse zur Baugeschichte und Archäologie der südlichen Troas.* Asia Minor Studien 78. Bonn. 85–106.

Artemis-Gyselen, L. 1977. 'Les monnaies archaïques de Ténos', *RBN* 123: 5–15.

Asheri, D., Lloyd, A. and Corcella, A. 2007. *A Commentary on Herodotus Books I–IV.* Oxford.

Atkinson, J. E. and Yardley, J. C. 2009. *Curtius Rufus: Histories of Alexander the Great, Book 10.* Oxford.

Auberson, P. 1976. 'Le temple de Dionysos', in *Eretria: Ausgrabungen und Forschungen*, vol. 5. Bern. 59–67.

Auberson, P. and Schefold, K. 1972. *Führer durch Eretria.* Bern.

Aupert, P. 1979. *Fouilles de Delphes II, Le Stade.* Paris.

Austin, C. and Olson, S. D. 2004. *Aristophanes: Thesmophoriazusae.* Oxford.

Avronidaki, C. 2007. *Ο Ζωγράφος του Άργου· Συμβολή στην έρευνα της βοιωτικής ερυθρόμορφης κεραμικής στο β' μισό του 5ου αιώνα π.Χ.* Athens.

Azoulay, V. 2004. *Xenophon et les grâces du pouvoir: De la charis au charisme.* Paris.

Bacci, G. and Spigo, U. 1991. 'Archeologia urbana. Messina riscoperta', *Archeo* 75: 115–16.

Bacchielli, L. 1993. 'Pittura funeraria antica in Cirenaica', *LibSt* 24: 77–116.

2002. 'La "Tomba dei Ludi" a Cirene: Dai viaggiatori dell'Ottocento alla riscoperta', *QAL* 16: 285–312.

Baçe, A. 2002–2003. 'Griechische Theater des 5. bis 3. Jahrhundert in Illyrien und Epirus', *BJb* 202/3: 365–511.

Bacilieri, C. 2001. *La rappresentazione dell'edificio teatrale nella ceramica italiota.* Oxford.

Bagnall, R. S. 1976. *The Administration of the Ptolemaic Possessions Outside Egypt.* Leiden.

Bagordo, A. 2014. *Alkimenes - Kantharos: Einleitung, Übersetzung, Kommentar.* Fragmenta Comica 1.1. Heidelberg.

Baiter, G. and Sauppe, H. 1850. *Oratores Attici*, vol. 2. Zurich.

Bakhuizen, S. C. 1970. *Salganeus and the Fortifications on its Mountains*. Groningen.

Bakola, E. 2010. *Cratinus and the Art of Comedy.* Oxford.

Balme, D. M. 1991. *Aristotle: History of Animals. Books 7–10.* Cambridge, MA.

Barbantani, S. 2000. 'Competizioni poetiche tespiesi e mecenatismo tolemaico: Un gemellaggio tra l'antica e la nuova sede delle Muse nella seconda metà del III secolo a.C. Ipotesi su *SH* 959', *Lexis* 18: 127–72.

   2010. *Three Burials (Ibycus, Stesichorus, Simonides): Facts and Fiction about Lyric Poets in Magna Graecia in the Epigrams of the Greek Anthology.* Alessandria.

Bardane, V. 1992–1998. 'Δημοτικὸ ψήφισμα Ἁλαιέων', *Horos* 10–12: 53–60.

Baron, C. A. 2013. *Timaeus of Tauromenium and Hellenistic Historiography.* Cambridge.

Barra Bagnasco M. 2005. 'Locri Epizefirii tra i due Dionigi', in R. Gigli, ed. *Megalai Nesoi: Studi in onore di Giovanni Rizza per il suo ottantesimo compleanno.* Catania. 79–89.

Barracco, G., Helbig, W. and Bruckmann, F. 1892. *La Collection Barracco, publiée par Frédéric Bruckmann, d'après la classification et avec le texte de Giovanni Barracco et Wolfgang Helbig*, 2 vols. Munich and Rome.

Barresi, S. 2002. 'Ceramica figurata siceliota dalla città e dalla chora di Adranon', *MÉFRA* 114: 611–53.

Bathrellou, E. 2012. 'Menander's *Epitrepontes* and the Festival of the Tauropolia', *CA* 31: 151–92.

Battezzato, L. 2008. 'Pythagorean Comedies from Epicharmus to Alexis', *Aevum Antiquum* 8: 139–64.

   2013. 'Dithyramb and Greek Tragedy', in B. Kowalzig and P. Wilson, eds. *Dithyramb in Context.* Oxford. 93–110.

Bearzot, C. 2013. 'Da isolani a continentali. L'Eubea tra la fine del VI e la fine del V secolo a.C.', in C. Bearzot and F. Landucci, eds. *Tra mare e continente: L'isola d'Eubea.* Milan. 105–35.

Beazley, J. D. 1952. 'The New York "Phlyax-Vase"', *AJA* 56: 193–5.

Bechtel, F. 1921. *Die griechischen Dialekte*, vol. 1. Berlin.

Beck, M. 2002. 'Plutarch to Trajan: The Dedicatory Letter and the Apophthegmata Collection', in P. Stadter and L. Van der Stockt, eds. *Sage and Emperor: Plutarch, Greek Intellectuals, and Roman Power in the Time of Trajan (98–117 AD).* Leuven. 163–89.

Bedigan, K. M. 2006. 'Changed Appearances: The Use of Masks on the Ceramics from the Theban Kabeirion in Greece', *eSharp* 8: 1–23.

   2008. *Boeotian Kabeiric Ware: The Significance of the Ceramic Offering at the Theban Kabeirion in Boeotia.* PhD Diss. Glasgow.

Beekes, R. S. P. 2004. 'The Origin of the Kabeiroi', *Mnemosyne* 57: 465–77.

Behrend, D. 1970. *Attische Pachturkunden.* Vestigia 12. Munich.

Beister, H. 1970. *Untersuchungen zu der Zeit der thebanischen Hegemonie.* Munich.

Belinger, A. 1963. *Essays on the Coinage of Alexander the Great.* New York.

Bélis, A. 2004. 'Un papyrus musical inédit au Louvre', *CRAI*: 1305–29.

Bell, M. 1988. 'Excavations at Morgantina, 1980–1985: Preliminary Report XII', *AJA* 92: 313–42.

   2012. 'Spazio e istituzioni nell'agora greca di Morgantina', in C. Ampolo, ed. *Agora greca e agorai di Sicilia.* Pisa. 111–18.

Bencivenga Trillmich, C. 1994. 'Il teatro sull'acropoli di Velia. Rendiconto dello scavo ed alcune considerazioni sulle fasi edilizie ed urbanistiche', in F. Krinzinger and G. Greco, eds. *Velia: Studi e ricerche.* Modena. 87–96.

Benos, S. 2009. *Περιόδεια του Προέδρου του Διαζώματος κ. Σταύρου Μπένου στα αρχαία θέατρα του Νομου Αργολίδας*. Athens.

Bentley, R. 1699. *A Dissertation upon the Epistles of Phalaris. With an Answer to the Objections of the Honourable Charles Boyle, Esquire*. London.

Berk, L. 1964. *Epicharmus*. Groningen.

Berlinzani, F. 2008. 'Teleste di Selinunte il ditirambografo', *Aristonothos* 2: 109–40.

Bernabò Brea, L. 1964–1965. 'Due secoli di studi, scavi e restauri del teatro greco di Tindari', *RivIstArch* 13–14: 99–144.

   1967. 'Studi sul teatro greco di Siracusa', *Palladio* 17: 97–154.

   1973. 'Attività della Soprintendenza alle Antichità per la Sicilia Orientale', *Kokalos* 18–19: 161–92.

   1981. *Menandro e il teatro greco nelle terrecotte liparesi*. Genoa.

   1994. *Meligunìs Lipára*, vol. 7: *Lipari, Contrada Diana: Scavo XXXVI in proprietà Zagami (1975–1984)*. Palermo.

   2001. *Maschere e personaggi del teatro greco nelle terrecotte liparesi*. Rome.

Bernabò Brea, L. and Cavalier, M. 1965. *Meligunìs Lipára*, vol. 2: *La necropoli greca e romana nella Contrada Diana*. Palermo.

   2000. 'Il ritratto di Euripide nella coroplastica liparese', in I. Berlingò, ed. *Damarato: Studi di antichità classica offerti a Paola Pelagatti*. Milan. 261–4.

   2002. *Terracotte teatrali e buffonesche della Sicilia Orientale e Centrale*. Palermo.

Bernard, P. and Salviat, F. 1959. 'Nouvelles découvertes au Dionysion de Thasos', *BCH* 83: 228–335.

Bernardi Ferrero, D. de, 1966–1974. *Teatri classici in Asia Minore*, 4 vols. Rome.

Bevan, E. 1986. *Representations of Animals in Sanctuaries of Artemis and Other Olympian Deities*, 2 vols. Oxford.

Bieber, M. 1920. *Die Denkmäler zum Theaterwesen im Altertum*. Berlin and Leipzig.

   1961. *The History of the Greek and Roman Theatre*[2]. Princeton.

Bierl, A. 2009. *Ritual and Performativity: The Chorus in Old Comedy*. Washington, DC.

Biers, W. R. 1971. 'Excavations at Phlious, 1970', *Hesperia* 40: 424–47.

   1973. 'Excavations at Phlious, 1972', *Hesperia* 42: 102–20.

   1975. 'Excavations at Phlious, 1973', *Hesperia* 44: 51–68.

Biers, W. R. and Boyd, T. D. 1982. 'Ikarion in Attica: 1888–1981', *Hesperia* 51: 1–18.

Biles, Z. 2006–2007. 'Aeschylus' Afterlife: Reperformance by Decree in 5th C. Athens?', *ICS* 31–2: 206–42.

Biles, Z. and Olson, S. D. 2015. *Aristophanes: Wasps*. Oxford.

Billows, R. A. 1997. *Antigonus the One-Eyed and the Creation of the Hellenistic State*. Berkeley and Los Angeles.

Bing, P. 1988. 'Theocritus' Epigrams on the Statues of Ancient Poets', *A&A* 34.1: 17–123.

Bingen, J. 1982. 'Epigraphica (Thrace, Rhodes)', *ZPE* 46: 183–4.

   1984. 'Inscriptions (III)', in H. F. Mussche, J. Bingen, J. Servais and P. Spitaels, *Thorikos VIII: 1972/1976*. Brussels. 175–9.

   1990. 'Inscriptions (IV)', in H. F. Mussche, J. Bingen, J. E. Jones and M. Waelkens, *Thorikos IX. 1977/1982*. Brussels. 144–53.

   1991. *Pages d'épigraphie grecque: Attique – Égypte (1952–1982)*. Brussels.

Bintliff, J., Slapšak, B., Noordervliet, B., Van Zwienen, J., Uytterhoeven, I., Sarri, K., Van der Enden, M., Shiel, R. and Piccoli, C. 2012. 'The Leiden-Ljubljana Ancient Cities of Boeotia Project 2009 Seasons', *Pharos* 17.2: 1–63.

Bizard, L. 1907. 'Fouilles de Délos, exécutées aux frais de M. le Duc de Loubat (1904–1907): Le côté oriental du téménos d'Apollon, I. Description des ruines', *BCH* 31: 471–503.

Bizard, L. and Leroux, G. 1907. 'Fouilles de Délos, exécutées aux frais de M. le Duc de Loubat (1904–1907): Le côté oriental du téménos d'Apollon, II. Monuments de sculpture', *BCH* 31: 504–25.

Blakely, S. 2006. *Myth, Ritual, and Metallurgy in Ancient Greece and Recent Africa.* Cambridge.

Blanshard, A. 2007. 'Trapped between Athens and Chios: A Relationship in Fragments', in V. Jennings and A. Katsaros, eds. *The World of Ion of Chios.* Leiden. 155–75.

Blech, M. 1982. *Studien zum Kranz bei den Griechen.* Berlin and New York.

Blok, J. 2010. 'Deme Accounts and the Meaning of *hosios* Money in Fifth-Century Athens', *Mnemosyne* 63: 61–93.

Blum, G. and Plassart, A. 1914. 'Orchomène d'Arcadie. Fouilles de 1913. Topographie, architecture, sculpture, menus objets', *BCH* 38: 71–88.

Blum, R. 1991. *Kallimachos: The Alexandrian Library and the Origins of Bibliography.* Madison.

Blume, H. 1978. *Einführung in das antike Theaterwesen.* Darmstadt.

Bodnar, E. 1960. *Cyriacus of Ancona and Athens.* Brussels.

Boeckh, A. 1874. *Gesammelte Kleine Schriften*, vol. 4. Leipzig.

Boehm, R. A. 2011. *Synoikism, Urbanization, and Empire in the Early Hellenistic Period.* PhD Diss. University of California at Berkeley.

  2015. 'Alexander, "Whose Courage Was Great": Cult, Power, and Commemoration in Classical and Hellenistic Thessaly', *CA* 34: 209–51.

Boethius, A. 1918. *Die Pythais: Studien zur Geschichte der Verbindungen zwischen Athen und Delphi.* Uppsala.

Böhr E. and Böhr, H.-J. 2009. 'Rehwild oder Damwild oder Rotwild? Zur Darstellung von Cerviden auf griechischen Vasen und zu deren Vorkommen im antiken Griechenland', in E. M. Moormann and V. V. Stissi, eds. *Shapes and Images: Studies on Attic Black Figure and Related Topics in Honour of Herman A.G. Brijder.* BABesch Supplement 14. Leuven. 137–44.

Bollansée, J. 1999. *Hermippos of Smyrna.* Die Fragmente der griechischen Historiker Continued, IV A: *Biography.* Fasc. 3. Leiden.

Bommelaer, J.-F. 1996. 'Autour de l'orchestra du théâtre de Delphes', *Ktema* 21: 273–94.

  2002. 'Sur la localisation des concours musicaux de Delphes avant la construction du théâtre actuel', *Ktema* 27: 119–30.

  2008. 'Pergame et le Théâtre de Delphes', in M. Kohl, ed. *Pergame: Histoire et archéologie d'un centre urbain depuis ses origines jusqu'à la fin de l'antiquité: Actes du collogue du 8–9 décembre 2000.* Lille.

  2010. 'Ce que j'ai appris au contact des architectes danois', in E. Hallager and D. Mulliez, eds. *The French Connection: 100 Years with Danish Architects at l'École française d'Athènes. Acts of a Symposium held in Athens and Copenhagen 2008 with l'École française d'Athènes.* Monographs of the Danish Institute at Athens 13. Athens. 55–68.

Bonanno, D. 2010. *Ierone il Dinomenide: Storia e rappresentazione.* Pisa and Rome.

Bonanno, M. 1972. *Studi su Cratete comico.* Padua.

Bonias, Z. 2012. 'Το αρχαίο θέατρο της Θάσου', in P. Adam-Veleni, ed. *Αρχαία θέατρα της Μακεδονίας.* Diazoma 3. Athens. 225–44.

Bonias, Z. and Marc J.-Y. 1996. 'Chroniques et rapports. Thasos. 2: Théâtre', *BCH* 120: 883–8.

Borbein, A. 1973. 'Die griechische Statue des 4. Jahrhunderts v. Chr. Formanalytische Untersuchungen zur Kunst der Nachklassik', *JdI* 88: 43–212.

Boring, T. 1979. *Literacy in Ancient Sparta.* Leiden.

Bosanquet, R. C. 1905–1906. 'Laconia II. Excavations at Sparta, 1906. §7. The Cult of Orthia as Illustrated by the Finds', *BSA* 12: 331–43.

Bosher, K. 2012. 'Hieron's Aeschylus', in K. Bosher, ed. *Theater Outside Athens: Drama in Greek Sicily and South Italy*. Cambridge. 97–111.

2013. 'Problems in Non-Athenian Drama: Some Questions about South Italy and Sicily', *Ramus* 42: 89–103.

2014. 'Epicharmus and Early Sicilian Comedy', in M. Revermann, ed. *The Cambridge Companion to Greek Comedy*. Cambridge. 79–94.

Bottin, C. 1930. 'Étude sur la chorégie dithyrambique en Attique jusqu'à l'époque de Démétrius de Phalère (308 avant J.-C.)', *RBPhil* 9: 749–82.

Boukaras, C. 2013. 'Το αρχαίο θέατρο της Ερέτριας', in R. Kolonia, ed. *Αρχαία θέατρα της Στερεάς Ελλάδος*. Diazoma 7. Athens. 19–30.

Bourguet, E. 1900. 'Inscriptions de Delphes. Les comptes sous Caphis et sous Théon. La chronologie delphique sous Alexandre', *BCH* 24: 463–509.

1905. *De rebus delphicis imperatoriae aetatis capita duo*. Montpellier.

Bousquet, J. 1988a. 'Delphes et les "Pythioniques" d'Aristote', *RÉG* 97: 374–80.

1988b. *Études sur les comptes de Delphes*. BÉFAR 267. Paris.

Bowie, E. L. 1974. 'Greeks and their Past in the Second Sophistic', in M. I. Finley, ed. *Studies in Ancient Society*. London. 166–209.

Branciforti, M. G. 2010. 'Da Katane a Catina', in M. G. Branciforti and V. La Rosa, eds. *Tra lava e mare: Contributi all'archailoghia di Catania: Atti del convegno, Catania, ex Monastero dei Benedettini, novembre 2007*. Catania. 135–258.

Braun, K. and Haevernick, T. E. 1981. *Bemalte Keramik und Glas aus dem Kabirenheiligtum bei Theben*. Das Kabirenheiligtum bei Theben 4. Berlin.

Braund, D. 2000. 'Strattis' *Kallippides*: The Pompous Actor from Scythia?', in D. Harvey and J. Wilkins, eds. *The Rivals of Aristophanes: Studies in Athenian Old Comedy*. Swansea. 151–8.

2005. 'Pericles, Cleon and the Pontus: The Black Sea in Athens c. 440–421', in D. Braund, ed. *Scythians and Greeks: Cultural Interactions in Scythia, Athens and the Early Roman Empire (sixth century BC – first century AD)*. Exeter. 80–99.

2008. 'Scythian Laughter: Conversations in the Northern Black Sea Region in the 5th Century BC', in P. Guldager Bilde and J. Hjarl Petersen, eds. *Meetings of Cultures in the Black Sea Region: Between Conflict and Coexistence*. Black Sea Studies 8. Aarhus. 347–68.

Braund, D. and Hall, E. 2014. 'Theatre in the Fourth-Century Black Sea Region', in E. Csapo, H.-R. Goette, J. R. Green and P. Wilson, eds. *Greek Theatre in the Fourth Century B.C.* Berlin and Boston. 371–90.

Breitholz, L. 1960. *Die dorische Farce im griechischen Mutterland vor dem 5. Jahrhundert. Hypothese oder Realität?* Stockholm, Göteburg and Uppsala.

Bremmer, J. M. 2014. *Initiation into the Mysteries of the Ancient World*. Berlin.

Brenk, F. E. 1998. *Relighting the Souls: Studies in Plutarch, in Greek Literature, Religion and Philosophy, and in the New Testament Background*. Stuttgart.

Bressan, M. 2009. *Il Teatro in Attica e Peloponneso tra età greca ed età romana: Morfologie, politiche edilizie e contesti culturali*. Padua.

Briant P. 1985. 'Les Iraniens d'Asie Mineure après la chute de l'Empire achéménide. À propos de l'inscription d'Amyzon', *DHA* 11: 166–95.

Brienza, E., Caliò, L. and Lippolis, E. 2011. 'Castiglione di Paludi: nuove ricerche nel sito della città antica', in G. De Sensi Sestito and S. Mancuso, eds. *Enotri e Brettii in Magna Grecia: modi e forme di interazione culturale. Società antiche: storia, culture, territori*. Soveria Mannelli. 235–86.

Brilliant, R. 1995. 'Kirke's Men: Swine and Sweethearts', in B. Cohen, ed. *The Distaff Side: Representing the Female in Homer's Odyssey*. Oxford. 165–74.

Brinck, A. 1886. *Inscriptiones graecae ad choregiam pertinentes.* Diss. Halle.

  1906. *De choregia quaestiones epigraphicae.* Kiel.

Brønsted, P. 1826. *Reisen und Untersuchungen in Griechenland.* Paris.

Brown, P. G. McC. 2005. 'The Legal and Social Framework of Plautus' *Cistellaria*', in F. Cairns, ed. *Papers of the Langford Latin Seminar*, vol. 12: *Greek and Roman Poetry, Greek and Roman Historiography.* Cambridge. 53–70.

Brownson, C. 1891. 'The Theatre at Eretria. Orchestra and Cavea', *The American Journal of Archaeology and of the History of the Fine Arts* 7: 266–80.

Brulé, P. 1987. *La Fille d'Athènes: la religion des filles à Athènes à l'époque classique. Mythes, cultes et société.* Paris.

Brun, P. 1988. 'Mytilène et Athènes au IVᵉ siècle av. J.-C.', *RÉA* 90: 373–84.

  1989. 'L'île de Kéos et ses cités au IVᵉ siècle av J.C.', *ZPE* 76: 128–38.

  2000. *L'orateur Démade: Essai d'histoire et d'historiographie.* Bordeaux.

Bruneau, P. 1970. *Recherches sur les cultes de Délos à l'époque hellénistique et à l'époque impériale.* BÉFAR 217. Paris.

  1995. '*Deliaca* X', *BCH* 119: 35–62.

Bruneau, P. and Ducat, J. 2005. *Guide de Délos*⁴. Paris.

Brunt, P. 1993. *Studies in Greek History and Thought.* Oxford.

Bruzzese, L. 2011. *Studi su Filemone comico.* Lecce.

Buchholz, H. 1963. 'Ein Friedhof im Gebiet des attischen Demos Kephale', *AA*: 455–98.

Buck, C. D. 1892. 'Discoveries in the Attic Deme of Ikaria, 1888', *Papers of the American School of Classical Studies* 5 (1886–1890): 43–134.

  1955. *The Greek Dialects*². Chicago.

Buckler, J. 1978. 'Plutarch on the Trials of Pelopidas and Epameinondas (369 B.C.)', *CP* 73: 36–42.

Buda, G. 2015. 'Teatro antico di Catania: Lavori tra il 2014 e il 2015', in F. Nicoletti, ed. *Catania Antica: Nuove prospettive di ricerca.* Palermo. 247–79.

Budelmann, F. 2012. 'Epinician and the Symposion: A Comparison with the Enkomia', in C. Agócs, C. Carey and R. Rawles, eds. *Reading the Victory Ode.* Cambridge. 173–90.

Budelmann, F. and Power, T. 2015. 'Another Look at Female Choruses in Classical Athens', *ClAnt* 34: 252–95.

Buitron-Oliver, D. and Cohen, B. 1995. 'Between Skylla and Penelope: Female Characters of the *Odyssey* in Archaic and Classical Greek Art', in B. Cohen, ed. *The Distaff Side: Representing the Female in Homer's Odyssey.* Oxford. 29–58.

Bujskikh, A. 2007. 'The North-Pontic Architectural School: Problems of Genesis', in A. Bresson, A. Ivntchik and J.-L. Ferrary, eds. *Une koinè pontique: Cités grecques, sociétés indigènes et empires mondiaux sur le littoral nord de la Mer Noire (VIIᵉ s. a.C.–IIIᵉ s. p. C.).* Bordeaux. 133–9.

Bulle, H. 1928. *Untersuchungen an griechischen Theatern.* Munich.

Bultrighini, I. 2013. '"Twin Inscriptions" from the Attic Deme of Myrrhinous', *ZPE* 186: 141–51.

  2015. *Demi attici della Paralia.* Lanciano.

Buraselis, K. 2012. 'Appended Festivals: The Coordination and Combination of Traditional Civic and Ruler Cult Festivals in the Hellenistic and Roman East', in J. R. Brandt and J. W. Iddeng, eds. *Greek and Roman Festivals: Content, Meaning, and Practice.* Oxford. 247–65.

  2013. 'Confederacies, Royal Policies and Sanctuaries in the Hellenistic Aegean: The Cases of Nesiotai, Lesbioi and Kretaieis', in P. Funke and M. Haake, eds. *Greek Federal States and their Sanctuaries: Identity and Integration. Proceedings of an International Conference of the Cluster of Excellence 'Religion and Politics' Held in Münster, 17.06. – 19.06.2010.* Stuttgart. 173–84.

Burford, A. 1966. 'Notes on the Epidaurian Building Inscriptions', *BSA* 61: 254–323.

    1969. *The Greek Temple Builders at Epidauros.* Liverpool.

Burkert, W. 1979. 'Kynaithos, Polycrates and the Homeric Hymn to Apollo', in G. W. Bowersock, W. Burkert and M. C. J. Putnam, eds. *Arktouros: Hellenic Studies Presented to Bernard M. W. Knox on the Occasion of his 65th Birthday.* Berlin and New York. 53–62.

    1983. *Homo Necans: The Anthropology of Ancient Greek Sacrificial Ritual and Myth.* Berkeley and Los Angeles.

    1985. *Greek Religion.* Cambridge, MA.

    1994. 'Orpheus, Dionysos und die Euneiden in Athen: Das Zeugnis von Euripides' *Hyspipyle'*, in A. Bierl and P. von Möllendorff, eds. *Orchestra: Drama, Mythos, Bühne. Festschrift für Hellmut Flashar anlässlich seines 65. Geburtstages.* Stuttgart and Leipzig. 44–9.

Burmeister, E. 2006. *Antike griechische und römische Theater.* Darmstadt.

Burstein, S. M. 2006. 'The Greek Cities of the Black Sea', in K. H. Kinzl, ed. *A Companion to the Classical Greek World.* Oxford. 137–52.

Butrica, J. 2001. 'Democrates and Euripides' Andromache (Σ Andr. 445 = Callimachus fr. 451 Pfeiffer)', *Hermes* 129: 188–97.

Bywater, I. 1909. *Aristotle On the Art of Poetry.* Oxford.

Cabanes, P. 1974. 'Les inscriptions du théâtre de Bouthrôtos', in *Actes du colloque 1972 sur l'esclavage.* Annales littéraires de l'Université de Besançon 163. Paris. 105–209.

    1976. *L'Épire de la mort de Pyrrhos à la conquête romaine (272–167 av. J.C.).* Centre de Recherches d'Histoire Ancienne 19. Paris.

Cagnazzi, S. 1993. 'Notizie sulla partecipazione di Euripide alla vita pubblica ateniese', *Athenaeum* 81: 165–75.

Calame, C. 1997. *Choruses of Young Women in Ancient Greece: Their Morphology, Religious Role, and Social Functions.* Lanham.

    2009. 'Apollo in Delphi and Delos: Poetic Performance between Paean and Dithyramb', in L. Athanassaki, R. Martin and J. F. Miller, eds. *Apolline Politics and Poetics.* Athens. 169–97.

Caliò, L. 2005. 'Theatri curvaturae similis. Note sull'urbanistica delle città a forma di teatro', *ArchCl* 56: 49–130.

Callot, J. 1999. *Recherches sur les cultes en Cyrénaïque durant le Haut-Empire romain.* Nancy.

Cameron, A. 1995. *Callimachus and His Critics.* Princeton.

Campagna, L. 2004. 'Architettura e ideologia della basilica a Siracusa nell'età di Ierone II', in M. Caccamo Caltabiano, A. Campagna and L. Pinzone eds. *Nuove prospettive della ricerca sulla Sicilia del III sec. a.C.* Messina. 151–90.

    2006. 'L'architettura di età ellenistica in Sicilia: Per una rilettura del quadro generale', in M. Osanna and M. Torelli, eds. *Sicilia ellenistica, consuetudo italica: Alle origini dell'architettura ellenistica d'Occidente. Spoleto, Complesso monumentale di S. Nicolò, 5–7 novembre 2004.* Rome. 15–34.

    2011. 'L'archeologia dei teatri nella Sicilia ellenistica tra tradizione e nuove prospettive di ricerca', in D. Tomasello, ed. *La scena dell'isola: Turismo, cultura e spettacolo in Sicilia.* Rome. 41–57.

Cantarella, R. 1949. *Aristophanis comoediae quae exstant*, vol. 1. Milan.

    1970. *Scritti minori sul teatro Greco.* Brescia.

Capps, E. 1895. 'Excavations in the Eretrian Theatre in 1894', *The American Journal of Archaeology and of the History of the Fine Arts* 10: 338–46.

    1943. 'A New Fragment of the List of Victors at the City Dionysia', *Hesperia* 12: 1–11.

Carey, C. 2016. 'Mapping Iambos: Mining the Minor Talents', in L. Swift and C. Carey, eds. *Iambus and Elegy: New Approaches.* Oxford. 122–39.

Cargill, J. 1981. *The Second Athenian League: Empire or Free Alliance?* Berkeley and Los Angeles.

    1995. *Athenian Settlements of the Fourth Century B.C.* Leiden.

Carpenter, T. H. 1986. *Dionysian Imagery in Archaic Greek Art.* Oxford.

2014. 'A Case for Greek Tragedy in Italic Settlements in 4th Century BC Apulia', in T. H. Carpenter, K. M. Lynch and E. G. D. Robinson, eds. *The Italic People of Ancient Apulia: New Evidence from Pottery for Workshops, Markets, and Customs.* Cambridge. 265–80.

2016. 'Some Observations on Apulian Vase-Inscriptions with a Particular Focus on the Darius Painter', in D. Yatromanolakis, ed. *Epigraphy of Art: Ancient Greek Vase-Inscriptions and Vase-Paintings.* Oxford. 135–44.

Carrara, P. 2008. *Il testo di Euripide nell'antichità. Ricerche sulla tradizione testuale euripidea antica (sec. IV a.C. – sec. VIII d.C.).* Florence.

Carter, D. M. 2004. 'Was Attic Tragedy Democratic?', *Polis* 21: 1–25.

Carter, D. M. ed. 2010. *Why Athens? A Reappraisal of Tragic Politics.* Oxford.

Carter, J. B. 1987. 'The Masks of Ortheia', *AJA* 91: 355–83.

Cartledge, P. 2016. *Democracy: A Life.* Oxford.

Cartledge, P. and Spawforth, A. 2002. *Hellenistic and Roman Sparta: A Tale of Two Cities*[2]. London and New York.

Carusi, C. 2006. 'Alcune considerazioni sulle *syngraphai* ateniesi del v e del iv secolo a. C.', *ASAA* s. III 6: 11–35.

2013. 'The Lease of the Piraeus Theatre and the Lease Terminology in Classical Athens', *ZPE* 188: 111–35.

Caruso, A. 2016. *Mouseia: Tipologie, contesti, significati culturali di un'istituzione sacra (VII–I sec. a.C.).* Rome.

Cary, M. 1924. 'The Trial of Epaminondas', *CQ* 18: 182–4.

Casadio, G. 1994. *Storia del Culto di Dioniso in Argolide.* Rome.

1999. *Il vino dell'anima: Storia del culto di Dioniso a Corinto, Sicione, Trezene.* Rome.

Casevitz, M., Pouilloux, J. and Jacquemin, A. 1999. *Pausanias, Description de la Grèce Tome V: Livre V, L'Élide (I).* Paris.

Caskey, J. L. 1964. 'Excavations in Ceos, 1963', *Hesperia* 33: 314–35.

Caskey, M. E. 1971. *Keos II: The Temple at Ayia Irini: Part I: The Statues.* Princeton.

1980. 'Dionysos in the Temple of Ayia Irini', *AJA* 84: 200.

2009. 'Dionysos in the Temple at Ayia Irini, Kea', in D. Danielidou, ed. *ΔΩΡΟΝ: Τιμητικός τόμος για τον Καθηγητή Σπύρο Ιακωβίδη.* Athens. 143–63.

Casolari, F. 2003. *Die Mythentravestie in der griechischen Komödie.* Münster.

Cassio, A. C. 1985. 'Two Studies on Epicharmus and His Influence', *HSCP* 89: 37–51.

2000. 'Un epigramma votivo spartano per Atena Alea', *RivFil* 128: 129–34.

Catucci, M. 2003. 'Tempi e modi di diffusione di temi teatrali in Italia attraverso la ceramica di importazione', in *CFST.* 1–97.

Cawkwell, G. 2010. 'Between Athens, Sparta, and Persia: The Historical Significance of the Liberation of Thebes in 379', in H.-G. Nesselrath, ed. *Plutarch On the Daimonion of Socrates: Human Liberation, Divine Guidance and Philosophy.* Tübingen. 101–9.

Ceccarelli, P. 1995. 'Le dithyrambe et la pyrrhique: À propos de la nouvelle liste de vainqueurs aux Dionysies de Cos (Segre, ED 234)', *ZPE* 108: 287–305.

1998. *La pirrica nell'antichità Greco-romana: Studi sulla danza armata.* Pisa and Rome.

2004. 'Dancing the Pyrriche in Athens', in P. Murray and P. Wilson, eds. *Music and the Muses: The Culture of Mousike in the Classical Athenian City.* Oxford. 91–117.

2010. 'Changing Contexts: Tragedy in the Civic and Cultural Life of Hellenistic City-States', in I. Gildenhard and M. Revermann, eds. *Beyond the Fifth Century: Interactions with Greek Tragedy from the Fourth Century BCE to the Middle Ages.* Berlin and New York. 99–150.

2013a. *Ancient Greek Letter Writing: A Cultural History (600–150 BC)*. Oxford.

2013b. 'Circular Choruses and the Dithyramb in the Classical and Hellenistic Period', in B. Kowalzig and P. Wilson, eds. *Dithyramb in Context*. Oxford. 153–70.

Ceccarelli, P. and Milanezi, S. 2007. 'Dithyramb, Tragedy – and Cyrene', in P. Wilson, ed. *The Greek Theatre and Festivals: Documentary Studies*. Oxford. 185–214.

Ceka, N. 1987. 'Mbishkrime Byline', *Iliria* 17: 49–121.

Chamoux, F. 1953. *Cyrène sous la monarchie des Battiades*. Paris.

1974. 'L'épitaphe du cochon d'Édesse', in *Mélanges de philosophie, de littérature, et d'histoire ancienne offerts à Pierre Boyancé*. Rome. 1953–62.

1988. 'Les comptes des démiurges à Cyrène', in D. Knoepfler, ed. *Comptes et inventaires dans la cité grecque: Actes du colloque international d'épigraphie tenu à Neuchâtel du 23 au 26 septembre 1986 en l'honneur de Jacques Tréheux*. Neuchâtel and Geneva. 143–54.

1998. 'Le théâtre grec en Libye', in J. Leclant and J. Jouanna, eds. *Le théâtre grec antique: La tragédie. Actes du 8ème colloque de la Villa Kérylos*. Paris. 129–42.

Champlin, E. 1981. 'Serenus Sammonicus', *HSCP* 85: 189–212.

Chandler, R. 1774. *Inscriptiones Antiquae, pleraeque nondum editae: In Asia Minori et Graecia, praesertim Athenis*. Oxford.

1776. *Travels in Greece: or an Account of a Tour Made at the Expense of the Society of Dilettanti*. Oxford.

1825. *Travels in Asia Minor and Greece*, vol. 2. *A New Edition, with Corrections and Remarks by Nicholas Revett, Esq*. Oxford.

Chaniotis, A. 1988a. *Historie und Historiker in den griechischen Inschriften: Epigraphische Beiträge zur griechischen Historiographie*. Stuttgart.

1988b. 'Als die Diplomaten noch tanzten und sangen: Zu zwei Dekreten kretischer Städte in Mylasa', *ZPE* 71: 154–6.

1997. 'New Inscriptions from Old Books: Inscriptions of Aigion, Delphi and Lesbos copied by Nicholas Biddle and Stavros Táxis', *Tekmeria* 3: 7–21.

2007. 'Theatre Rituals', in P. Wilson, ed. *The Greek Theatre and Festivals: Documentary Studies*. Oxford. 48–66.

Chankowski, V. 2008. *Athènes et Délos à l'Époque classique: Recherches sur l'administration du sanctuaire d'Apollon délien*. BÉFAR 331. Paris.

Chantraine, P. 1968–1980. *Dictionnaire étymologique de la langue grecque: Histoire des mots*, 4 vols. Paris.

Charami, A. 2013. 'Τὸ αρχαίο θέατρο της Τανάγρας', in R. Kolonia, ed. *Αρχαία θέατρα της Στερεάς Ελλάδας*. Diazoma 7. Athens. 43–50.

Charami, C. and Bardani, V. 2011. 'New Fragment from the Altar of Apollo Pythios', *Deltion of the Greek Epigraphic Society*, www.greekepigraphicsociety.org.gr/newsletter_05–2011. aspx?menu=10.

Charami, A. and Jeammet, V. 2015. 'Les figurines de la tome B1 158 de Thèbes: Tanagréennes ou Thébaines?', in A. Muller and E. Laflı, eds. *Figurines de terre cuite en Méditerranée grecque et romaine*. Iconographie et contextes 2. Villeneuve d'Ascq. 296–331.

Chasapi-Christodoulou, E. 1991–1992. 'Πήλινα θεατρικά ειδώλια από τη Μακεδονία και τη Θράκη. Πέλλα, Αμφίπολη, Ἄβδηρα', *Makedonika* 28: 268–323.

Chatzidakis, P. J. 2017. 'Honorary Stele for the Actor Polos, Son of Sosigenes', in A. Chaniotis, N. Kaltsas and I. Mylonopoulos, eds. *A World of Emotions*: *Ancient Greece, 700 BC–200 AD*. New York.

Cherry, J., Davis, J. and Mantzourani, E. eds. 1991. *Landscape Archaeology as Long-Term History: Northern Keos in the Cycladic Islands from Earliest Settlement until Modern Times.* Monumenta Archaeologica 16. Los Angeles.

Chiarini, S. 2018. *The So-called Nonsense Inscriptions on Ancient Greek Vases: Between Paideia and Paidiá.* Brill Studies in Greek and Roman Epigraphy 10. Leiden and Boston.

Chiavetta, A. 2015. 'Aspetti geologici, morfologici e idrologici dell'area del teatro antico di Catania', in F. Nicoletti, ed. *Catania Antica: Nuove prospettive di ricerca.* Palermo. 23–32.

Christesen, P. 2007. *Olympic Victor Lists and Ancient Greek History.* Cambridge.

Chryssanthaki-Nagle, K. 2007. *L'Histoire monétaire d'Abdère en Thrace (VIᵉ s. av. J.-C. – IIᵉ s. ap. J.-C.).* Meletemata 51. Athens.

Cinaglia, N. 2012. 'Immaginario di un compagno di giochi e di vita: Il cane di razza maltese', *Ostraka* 21: 109–36.

Cipolla, P. 2009. 'Due *testimonia* relativi a Pratina di Fliunte (Dioscoride, *AP* 7.707; *Pap. Petrie* 2.49 (B). 20–24', in P. Mureddu, G. F. Nieddu and S. Novelli, eds. *Tragico e Comico nel dramma attico e oltre: Intersezioni e sviluppi parateatrali (Cagliari, 4–5 febbraio 2009).* Amsterdam. 51–75.

Ciurcina, C. 2014. 'Culti a Siracusa in età ellenistica: Il contributo da un'area sacra prossima al complesso monumentale della Neapolis', in T. Alfieri Tonini and S. Struffolino, eds. *Dinamiche culturali ed etniche nella Sicilia orientale dall'età classica all'epoca ellenistica.* Aristonothos Quaderni 4. Trento. 35–53.

Clairmont, C. W. 1993–1995. *Classical Attic Tombstones*, 9 vols. Kilchberg.

Clarke, E. 1818. *Travels in Various Countries of Europe, Asia, and Africa*, vol. 6: *Greece, Egypt and the Holy Landᴵᴵ.* London.

Clay, D. 2004. *Archilochos Heros: the Cult of Poets in the Greek Polis.* Cambridge, MA.

Clayman, D. L. 2009. *Timon of Phlius: Pyrrhonism into Poetry.* Berlin.

Clear, R. 2013. 'Family, Duty and Expectation: A Case for the Joint Performance of Pindar's *Isthmian* 2 and *Pythian* 6', *Mnemosyne* 66: 31–53.

Clinton, K. 1992. *Myth and Cult: The Iconography of the Eleusinian Mysteries.* Stockholm.

    1996. 'The Thesmophorion in Central Athens and the Celebration of the Thesmophoria in Attica', in R. Hägg, ed. *The Role of Religion in the Early Greek Polis.* Stockholm. 111–25.

    2005. *Eleusis: The Inscriptions on Stone: Documents of the Sanctuary of the Two Goddesses and Public Documents of the Deme*, vol. 1. Athens.

    2008. *Eleusis: The Inscriptions on Stone: Documents of the Sanctuary of the Two Goddesses and Public Documents of the Deme*, vol. 2. Athens.

    2014. 'The Athenian Cleruchy on Lemnos', in A. P. Matthaiou, R. K. Pitt and H. B. Mattingly, eds. *ΑΘΗΝΑΙΩΝ ΕΠΙΣΚΟΠΟΣ: Studies in Honour of Harold B. Mattingly.* Athens. 327–37.

Cohen, G. 1995. *The Hellenistic Settlements in Europe, the Islands, and Asia Minor.* Hellenistic Culture and Society 17. Berkeley.

Cohn, M. 2016. 'Sicyonian Comedy', *CJ* 112: 1–24.

Cole, S. G. 1993. 'Procession and Celebration at the Dionysia', in R. Scodel, ed. *Theater and Society in the Classical World.* Ann Arbor. 25–38.

Collard, C. 2004. 'Antiope', in C. Collard, M. J. Cropp and J. Gibert, *Euripides: Selected Fragmentary Plays*, vol. 2. Oxford. 259–325.

Collard, C., Cropp, M. J. and Gibert, J. 2004. *Euripides: Selected Fragmentary Plays*, vol. 2. Oxford.

Collard, C., Cropp, M. J. and Lee, K. H. 1995. *Euripides: Selected Fragmentary Plays*, vol. 1. Warminster.

Collin Bouffier, S. 2011. 'Diodore de Sicile témoin du Ve siècle av. J.-C.: Un âge d'or pour la Sicile?', *DHA Supplément* 6: 71–112.

Condoléon, N. M. 1949. 'Inscriptions de Chios', *RPhil* 23: 1–13.

Constantakopoulou, K. 2005. 'Proud to be an Islander: Island Identity in Multi-Polis Islands in the Classical and Hellenistic Aegean', *MHR* 20: 1–34.

Constantinidou, S. 1998. 'Dionysiac Elements in Spartan Cult Dances', *Phoenix* 52: 15–30.

Conti Bizzarro, F. 1994. 'Note ai comici greci', *MCr* 29: 155–60.

  1999. *Poetica e critica letteraria nei frammenti dei poeti comici greci.* Naples.

Cooper, C. 2008. 'Hypereides, Aristophon, and the Settlement of Keos', in C. Cooper, ed. *Epigraphy and the Greek Historian.* Phoenix Supplementary Volume 47. Toronto. 31–56.

Cooper, F. A. and Morris, S. 1990. 'Dining in Round Buildings', in O. Murray, ed. *Sympotica: A Symposium on the Symposium.* Oxford. 66–85.

Cope, E. M. 1877. *The Rhetoric of Aristotle with a Commentary*, vol. 2. Cambridge.

Cordano, F. 1980. 'I Messeni dello stretto di Pausania', *PP* 35: 436–40.

  1992. *Le tessere pubbliche dal tempio di Atena a Camarina.* Rome.

  1994. 'La città di Camarina e le corde della lira', *PP* 49: 418–26.

Cornford, F. M. 1914. *The Origin of Attic Comedy.* London.

Correale, A. 2008. 'Lo scavo all'esterno della cortina muraria: Un nuovo santuario ad Efestia', in E. Greco and E. Papi, eds. *Hephestia 2000–2006: Atti del Seminario, Siena-Certosa di Pontignano, 28–29 maggio 2007.* Paestum and Athens. 75–91.

Corsaro, M. 1987. 'Crasto', in G. Nenci and G. Vallet, eds. *Bibliografia topografica della colonizzazione greca in Italia e nelle isole tirreniche*, vol. 5. Pisa. 457–8.

Corso, A. 2004. *The Art of Praxiteles: The Development of Praxiteles' Workshop and its Cultural Tradition until the Sculptor's Acme (364–1 BC).* Rome.

Costabile, F. ed. 1992. *Polis ed Olympieion a Locri Epizefiri: Costituzione, economia e finanze di una città della Magna Grecia. Editio altera e traduzione delle tabelle locresi.* Soveria Mannelli.

Coulton, J. 1977. *Greek Architects at Work: Problems of Structure and Design.* London.

Coupry, J. 1954. 'ΑΡΧΕΘΕΩΡΟΙ ΕΙΣ ΔΗΛΟΝ', *BCH* 78: 285–94.

Cousin, G. and Dürrbach, F. 1885. 'Inscriptions de Lemnos', *BCH* 9: 45–64.

Couvenhes, J.-C. and Moretti, J.-Ch. 2003. Review of B. Petrakos 1999, Ὁ δῆμος τοῦ Ραμνοῦντος, *Topoi* 11: 767–84.

Croissant, F. 2003. *Fouilles de Delphes* IV, *Monument figurés, Sculptures* 7: *Les frontons du temples du IVe siècle.* Paris.

  2011–2012. 'Deux sculpteurs athéniens du milieu du IVe siècle: Praxias père et fils', *RA* 52: 309–22.

Cropp, M. J. 1995. 'Telephus', in C. Collard, M. J. Cropp and K. H. Lee, eds. *Euripides: Selected Fragmentary Plays*, vol. 1. Warminster. 17–52.

  2003. 'Hypsipyle and Athens', in E. Csapo and M. Miller, eds. *Poetry, Theory, Praxis: The Social Life of Myth, Word and Image in Ancient Greece.* Oxford. 129–45.

Cropp, M. J. and Fick, G. 1985. *Resolutions and Chronology in Euripides: The Fragmentary Tragedies.* BICS Supplement 43. London.

Crowther, C. 1996. '*I.Priene* 8 and the History of Priene in the Early Hellenistic Period', *Chiron* 26: 195–250.

  2007. 'The Dionysia at Iasos: Its Artists, Patrons, and Audience', in P. Wilson, ed. *The Greek Theatre and Festivals: Documentary Studies.* Oxford. 294–334.

Cruccas, E. 2007. 'Odisseo e i Grandi Dei di Samotracia. Reminescenze cultuali e questioni iconografiche', in S. Angiolillo and M. Giuman, eds. *Il vasaio e le sue storie: giornata di studi sulla ceramica attica in onore di Mario Torelli per i suoi settanta anni.* Cagliari. 61–74.

2014. *Gli dei senza nome: Sincretismi, ritualità e iconografia dei Cabiri e dei Grandi Dei tra Grecia e Asia minore.* Rahden.

Crusius, O. 1891–1893. 'Epicharm bei den Paroemiographen', *Philologus Suppl.* 6: 281–94.

1893. 'Aristophanes von Byzanz bei Zenobius und der Vers des Maison (189)', in *CPG* Supplement 4. 275–80.

Csapo, E. 1993a. 'A Case Study in the Use of Theatre Iconography as Evidence for Ancient Acting', *AK* 36: 41–58.

1993b. 'Deep Ambivalence: Notes on a Greek Cockfight (Part I)', *Phoenix* 47: 1–28.

1997. 'Riding the Phallus for Dionysus: Iconology, Ritual and Gender-Role De/construction', *Phoenix* 51: 253–95.

2002. 'Kallippides on the Floor-Sweepings: The Limits of Realism in Classical Acting and Performance Styles', in P. Easterling and E. Hall, eds. *Greek and Roman Actors: Aspects of an Ancient Profession.* Cambridge. 127–47.

2003. 'The Dolphins of Dionysus', in E. Csapo and M. Miller, eds. *Poetry, Theory, Praxis: The Social Life of Myth, Word and Image in Ancient Greece.* Oxford. 69–98.

2004. 'Some Social and Economic Conditions behind the Rise of the Acting Profession in the Fifth and Fourth Centuries B.C.', in C. Hugoniot, F. Hurlet and S. Milanezi, eds. *Le statut de l'acteur dans l'Antiquité grecque et romaine.* Tours. 53–76.

2005. *Theories of Mythology.* Chichester.

2007. 'The Men Who Built the Theatres', in P. Wilson, ed. *The Greek Theatre and Festivals: Documentary Studies.* Oxford. 87–115.

2010. *Actors and Icons of the Ancient Theater.* Chichester.

2013. 'Comedy and the *Pompe*: Dionysian Genre-Crossing', in E. Bakola, L. Prauscello and M. Telò, eds. *Greek Comedy and the Discourse of Genres.* Cambridge. 40–80.

2015. 'The Earliest Phase of "Comic" Choral Entertainments in Athens. The Dionysian Pompe and the "Birth" of Comedy', in S. Chronopoulos and C. Orth, eds. *Fragmente einer Geschichte der griechischen Komödie.* Studia Comica 5. Heidelberg. 66–108.

2017. 'Imagining the Shape of Choral Dance and Inventing the Cultic in Euripides' Later Tragedies', in L. Gianvittorio, ed. *Choreutika: Performing Dance in Archaic and Classical Greece.* Biblioteca dei Quaderni Urbinati di Cultura Classica. Pisa. 111–48.

Csapo, E. and Miller, M. C. 2007. 'General Introduction', in E. Csapo and M. C. Miller, eds. *The Origins of Theater in Ancient Greece and Beyond: From Ritual to Drama.* Cambridge. 1–38.

Csapo, E. and Wilson, P. 2014. 'The Finance and Organisation of the Athenian Theatre in the Time of Eubulus and Lycurgus', in E. Csapo, H.-R. Goette, J. R. Green and P. Wilson, eds. *Greek Theatre in the Fourth Century B.C.* Berlin and Boston. 393–424.

2015. 'Drama Outside Athens in the Fifth and Fourth Centuries BC', in A. Lamari, ed. *Reperformances of Drama in the Fifth and Fourth centuries BC.* Trends in Classics 7.2. Berlin. 316–95.

Cuff, P. 1954. 'The Trials of Epaminondas – A Note', *Athenaeum* 32: 259–64.

Currie, B. 2005. *Pindar and the Cult of Heroes.* Oxford.

Curtius, E. and Kaupert, J. A. 1881. *Karten von Attika. Heft I. Erläuternder Text: Athen und Peiraieus.* Berlin.

1904. *Karten von Attika.* Berlin.

Cushing, W. L. 1888. 'The Theatre of Thoricus, Supplementary Report', *Papers of the American School of Classical Studies at Athens* 4 (1885–1886): 23–34.

Dakaris, S. I. 1964. *Οἱ γενεολογικοὶ μῦθοι τῶν Μολοσσῶν.* Athens.

D'Alessio, G. B. 1996. *Callimaco: Inni; Epigrammi; Ecale; Aitia; Giambi e altri frammenti*, 2 vols. Rome.

2004. 'Some Notes on the Salmakis Inscription', in S. Isager and P. Pedersen, eds. *The Salmakis Inscription and Hellenistic Halikarnassos*. Aarhus. 43–57.

2007. '῍Ην ἰδού: Ecce satyri (Pratina, *PMG* 708 = *TrGF* 4 F 3): Alcune considerazioni sull'uso della deissi nei testi lirici e teatrali', in F. Perusino and M. Colantonio, eds. *Dalla lirica corale alla poesia drammatica: Forme e funzioni del canto corale nella tragedia e nella commedia greca*. Pisa. 95–128.

2009. 'Defining Local Identities in Greek Lyric Poetry', in R. Hunter and I. Rutherford, eds. *Wandering Poets in Ancient Greek Culture: Travel, Locality and Pan-Hellenism*. Cambridge. 137–67.

2013. 'The Name of the Dithyramb: Diachronic and Diatopic Variations', in B. Kowalzig and P. Wilson, eds. *Dithyramb in Context*. Oxford. 113–32.

Dana, M. 2011. *Culture et mobilité dans le Pont-Euxin*. Bordeaux.

D'Andria, F. 1997. 'Ricerche archeologiche sul teatro di Segesta', in *Seconde giornate internazionali di studi sull'area elima (Gibellina, 22–26 ottobre 1994)*. Pisa and Gibellina. 429–50.

D'Angour, A. 1997. 'How the Dithyramb Got Its Shape', *JHS* 47: 331–51.

Daniel, R. 1996. 'Epicharmus in Trier: A Note on the Monnus-Mosaic', *ZPE* 114: 30–6.

Daumas, M. 1998. *Cabiriaca: Recherches sur l'iconographie du culte des Cabires*. Paris.

Daux, G. 1926. 'Nouvelles inscriptions de Thasos (1921–1924)', *BCH* 50: 213–49.

1928. 'Inscriptions de Thasos', *BCH* 52: 45–65.

1970. 'Deux fragments de décrets à Siphnos', *Klio* 52: 67–72.

1983. 'Le calendrier de Thorikos au Musée J. Paul Getty', *AntCl* 52: 150–74.

David, E. 1989. 'Laughter in Spartan Society', in A. Powell, ed. *Classical Sparta: Techniques Behind her Success*. London. 1–25.

Davies, J. K. 1967. 'Demosthenes on Liturgies: A Note', *JHS* 87: 33–40.

Davies, M. 1987. 'The Ancient Greeks on Why Mankind Does Not Live Forever', *MusHelv* 44: 65–75.

Davies, M. and Finglass, P. 2014. *Stesichorus: The Poems*. Cambridge.

Davis, G. 2011. '*Axones* and *Kurbeis*: A New Answer to an Old Problem', *Historia* 60: 1–35.

Davison, J. A. 1959. 'Dieuchidas of Megara', *CQ* 9: 216–22.

1968. *From Archilochus to Pindar: Papers on Greek Literature of the Archaic Period*. London.

De Angelis, F. 1996. 'La Battaglia di Maratona nella Stoa Poikile', *AnnPisa* 1: 119–71.

2006. 'Going Against the Grain in Sicilian Greek Economics', *G&R* 53: 29–47.

2016. *Archaic and Classical Greek Sicily: A Social and Economic History*. Oxford.

De Bernardi, A. 2000. 'Considerazioni sui risultati finora raggiunti nello studio e nel rilevamento del teatro di Segesta', in *Terze giornate internazionali di studi sull'area elima (Gibellina – Erice – Contessa Entellina, 23–26 ottobre 1997)*. Pisa. 369–81.

De Bernardi, M. L. 2000. 'Analisi della anomalie architettoniche dell'attuale cavea del teatro di Segesta', in *Terze giornate internazionali di studi sull'area elima (Gibellina – Erice – Contessa Entellina, 23–26 ottobre 1997)*. Pisa. 383–7.

De Cesare, M. 1992. 'Alkmena ad Entella: Ceramografi sicelioti e campani nel IV secolo a.C.', *AnnPisa* 22: 979–83.

De Cremoux, A. 2011. 'La maxime chez Epicharme et la naissance de la comédie: Problèmes de méthode et pistes de réflexion', in C. Mauduit and P. Paré-Rey, eds. *Les maximes théâtrales en Grèce et à Rome: Transferts, réécritures, remplois*. Lyon. 55–68.

Dederich, A. 1855. *Sex. Iulii Frontini Strategematicon libri quattuor*. Leipzig.

Deforge, B. 1987. 'Éschyle et la légende des Argonautes', *RÉG* 100: 30–44.

De Giorgi, A. 2016. *Ancient Antioch: From the Seleucid Era to the Islamic Conquest*. Cambridge.

Delcroix, K. and Giannattasio Andria, R. 1997. 'Herodotos Recited in the Alexandrian Theatre?: A Puzzling Page on Hellenistic Performance (Athen. XIV 620D)', *AncSoc* 28: 121–47.

Delneri, F. 2006. *I culti misterici stranieri nei frammenti della commedia attica antica.* Eikasmos Studi 13. Bologna.

Demand, N. 1971. 'Epicharmus and Gorgias', *AJP* 92: 453–63.

1982. *Thebes in the Fifth Century: Heracles Resurgent.* London.

De Miro, E. 2006. 'Agrigento in età ellenistica: Aspetti di architettura', in M. Osanna and M. Torelli, eds. *Sicilia ellenistica, consuetudo italica: Alle origini dell'architettura ellenistica d'Occidente. Spoleto, Complesso monumentale di S. Nicolò, 5–7 novembre 2004.* Rome. 69–81.

2012. 'Agorai e *forum* in Agrigento', in C. Ampolo, ed. *Agora greca e agorai di Sicilia.* Pisa. 101–10.

2014. *Heraclea Minoa: Mezzo secolo di ricerche.* Pisa and Rome.

2016. 'Il teatro di Morgantina. A proposito di una recente pubblicazione', *Sicilia Antiqua* 12: 83–6.

Denoyelle, M. and Silvestrelli, F. 2013. 'From Tarporley to Dolon: The Reattribution of the Early South Italian "New York Goose Vase"', *Metropolitan Museum Journal* 48: 59–71.

Derow, P. 2015. *Rome, Polybius, and the East.* Oxford.

De Sensi Sestito, G. 2014. 'Siracusa, le guerre di confine fra Locri e Reggio e il "trattato" di Eliano', *Aionos* 17: 17–48.

Despinis, G. I. 2002. 'Il relievo votivo di Aristonike ad Artemis Brauronia', in B. Gentili and F. Perusino, eds. *Le orse di Brauron: Un rituale di iniziazione femminile nel santuario di Artemide.* Pisa. 153–65.

2003. *Hochrelieffriese des 2. Jahrhunderts n. Chr. aus Athen.* Munich.

2004a. 'Der Dionysos-Altar in Brauron', *JdI* 119: 41–65.

2004b. 'Die Kultstatuen der Artemis in Brauron', *AM* 119: 261–315.

2007. 'Neues zu der spätarchaischen Statue des Dionysos aus Ikaria', *AM* 122: 103–37.

2010. Ἄρτεμις Βραυρωνία: Λατρευτικά ἀγάλματα καί ἀναθήματα ἀπό τά ἱερά τῆς θεᾶς στή Βραυρῶνα καί τήν Ἀκρόπολη τῆς Ἀθήνας. Athens.

Detienne, M. 1989. 'Un phallus pour Dionysos', in M. Detienne and G. Sissa, eds. *La vie quotidienne des dieux grecs.* Paris. 253–64.

Deubner, L. 1932. *Attische Feste.* Berlin.

1966. *Attische Feste².* Berlin.

Develin, R. 1989. *Athenian Officials 684–321 BC.* Cambridge.

De Vincenzo, S. 2013. *Tra Cartagine e Roma: I centri urbani dell'eparchia punica di Sicilia tra VI e I sec. a.C.* Berlin and Boston.

Dickey, E. 2007. *Ancient Greek Scholarship: A Guide to Finding, Reading, and Understanding Scholia, Commentaries, Lexica and Grammatical Treatises, from their Beginnings to the Byzantine Period.* London and New York.

Dickins, G. 1905–1906. 'Excavations at Sparta, 1906: 10. The Theatre', *BSA* 12: 394–406.

Dickins, J. P. 1929. 'Terracotta Masks', in R. M. Dawkins, ed. *The Sanctuary of Artemis Orthia in Sparta.* JHS Supplement 5. London. 163–86.

Di Clemente, P. 2008. 'Sparta ridente. Le maschere di Orthia e le origini della farsa dorica', in O. Menozzi, M. L. Di Marzio and D. Fossataro, eds. *SOMA 2005: Proceedings of the IX Symposium on Mediterranean Archaeology, Chieti (Italy), 24–26 February 2005.* Oxford. 183–5.

Dilke, O. A. W. 1948. 'The Greek Theatre Cavea', *BSA* 43: 125–92.

1950. 'Details and Chronology of Greek Theatre Caveas', *BSA* 45: 21–62.

Dillon, J. and Hershbell, J. 1991. *Iamblichus, On the Pythagorean Way of Life: Text, Translation, and Notes.* Atlanta.

Dilthey, K. 1878. 'Schleifung der Dirke', *AZ* 36: 43–54.

Dimadis, K. A. 1974. 'Le Théâtre d'Abdera (données archéologiques)', *BalkSt* 15: 308–21.

Dimartino, A. 2006. 'Per una revisione dei documenti epigrafici siracusani pertinenti al regno di Ierone II', in C. Ampolo, ed. *Guerra e pace in Sicilia e nel Mediterraneo antico (VIII–III sec. a.C.): Arte, prassi e teoria della pace e della guerra*, vol. 2. Pisa. 703–17.

　　2009. 'Ierone II, Filistide e il teatro greco di Taormina. Note in margine a *IG* XIV, 437', in C. Ampolo, ed. *Immagine e immagini della Sicilia e di altere isole del Mediterraneo antico*, vol. 2. Pisa. 721–6.

　　2011. 'Siracusa. A. Fonti epigrafiche', in C. Ampolo, ed. *Siracusa*. Pisa. 59–132.

　　forthcoming. 'Politica, religione, società: Le iscrizioni greche "teatrali" di Sicilia', in *Giornate Messinesi dei dottorandi e dei giovani ricercatori in Scienze dell'Antichità*.

Di Stefano, G. 1996. 'La Sicilia dalla basileía di Agatocle alla fine del Regno di Gerone II. Riflessioni sull'ellenismo in Sicilia in margine alla mostra "I Greci in Occidente"', *Quaderni del Museo Archeologico Regionale 'Antonio Salinas'* 2: 143–54.

　　2013. 'Camarina. Terrecotte di argomento teatrale', *Sicilia antiqua* 10: 169–78.

Dmitriev, S. 2005. *City Government in Hellenistic and Roman Asia Minor*. Oxford.

Dobias-Lalou, C. 1993. 'Les dépenses engagées par les démiurges de Cyrène pour les cultes', *RÉG* 106: 24–38.

　　2000. *Le dialecte des inscriptions grecques de Cyrène*. Paris.

Dobrov, G. 2010. 'Comedy and Her Critics', in G. Dobrov, ed. *Brill's Companion to the Study of Greek Comedy*. Boston and Leiden. 3–33.

Doepner, D. 2002. *Steine und Pfeiler für die Götter: Weihgeschenkgattungen in westgriechischen Stadtheiligtumern*. Wiesbaden.

Dörpfeld, W. 1922. 'Alte und neue Ausgrabungen in Griechenland', *AM* 47: 25–47.

　　1924. 'Das Theater von Priene und die griechische Bühne', *AM* 49: 50–101.

Dörpfeld, W., Goessler, P., van Hille, E., von Seidlitz, W. and Uhde, R. 1927. *Alt-Ithaka: Ein Beitrag zur Homer-Frage. Studien und Ausgrabungen auf der Insel Leukas-Ithaka*. Munich.

Dörpfeld, W. and Reisch, E. 1896. *Das griechische Theater: Beiträge zur Geschichte des Dionysos-Theaters in Athen und anderer griechischer Theater*. Athens.

Dougherty, C. 1993. *The Poetics of Colonization: From City to Text in Archaic Greece*. Oxford.

Doulgeri-Intzesiloglou, A. 2011. 'Στα ίχνη του αρχαίου θεάτρου των Φερών', in V. Adrimi-Sismani, ed. *Αρχαία Θέατρα στη Θεσσαλία*. Diazoma 5. Athens. 67–73.

Dova, A. 2013. 'Επιγραφή υποθήκης από τη βασιλική Ολύμπου Καλυβίων Αττικής', in A. Stefanis, ed. *Πρακτικά ΙΔ΄ Επιστημονικής Συνάντησης ΝΑ. Αττικής: Καλύβια Θορικού Αττικής, 6–9 Οκτωβρίου 2011*. Kalyvia Thorikou. 59–68.

Dow, S. 1963. 'The Attic Demes OA and OE', *AJP* 84: 166–81.

　　1965. 'The Greater Demarkhia of Erchia', *BCH* 89: 180–210.

Dowden, K. 1989. *Death and the Maiden: Girls' Initiation Rites in Greek Mythology*. London.

　　2006. *Zeus*. London.

Dragatsis, I. C. 1879. 'Τὸ θέατρον τὸ πρὸς τῇ Μουνιχίαι', *Parnassos* 3: 577–8.

　　1881a. '῎Ανδρου ἀρχαιολογήματα', *Parnassos* 3: 781–801.

　　1881b. 'Ἀνάγλυφον τοῦ εἴδους τῶν νεκροδείπνων ἐκ τῶν ἁλῶν', *Parnassos* 5: 1095–6.

Drerup, E. 1901. 'Das griechische Theater in Sirakus', *AM* 26: 9–32.

Drougou, S. 1997. 'Das antike Theater von Vergina. Bemerkungen zu Gestalt und Funktion des Theaters in der antiken Hauptstadt Makedoniens', *AM* 112: 281–305.

　　2012. 'Βεργίνα: το αρχαίο θέατρο', in P. Adam-Veleni, ed. *Αρχαία Θέατρα της Μακεδονίας*. Diazoma 3. Athens. 45–56.

Dubbini, R. 2010. '*Agones* on the Greek *Agora* between Ritual and Spectacle: Some Examples from the Peloponnese', in A. Chaniotis, S. Leopold, H. Schulze, E. Venbrux, T. Quartier, J. Wojtkowiak, J. Weinhold and G. Samuel, eds. *Ritual Dynamics and the Science of Ritual*, vol. 2: *Body, Performance, Agency and Experience*. Wiesbaden. 157–81.

Dubois, L. 1989. *Inscriptions grecques dialectales de Sicile*. Paris and Rome.

  1996. *Inscriptions grecques dialectales d'Olbia du Pont*. Geneva.

Ducat, J. 2006. *Spartan Education: Youth and Society in the Classical Period*. Swansea.

  2007. 'Une cabane pour Dionysos', in D. Berranger-Auserve, ed. *Épire, Illyrie, Macédoine: mélanges offerts au professeur Pierre Cabanes*. ERGA recherches sur l'antiquité 10. Clermont-Ferrand. 113–23.

Ducrey, P., Fachard, S., Knoepfler, D., Theurillat, T., Wagner, D. and Zannis, A. G. eds. 2004. *Eretria: a Guide to the Ancient City*. Gollion.

Dunbar, N. 1995. *Aristophanes: Birds*. Oxford.

Dunst, G. 1959. 'Ein neues chiisches Dekret aus Kos', *Klio* 37: 63–8.

  1960. 'Bemerkungen zu griechischen Inschriften', *SBBerl* 1. Berlin.

Duplouy, A. 2015. 'Genealogical and Dynastic Behavior in Archaic and Classical Greece: Two Gentilician Strategies', in N. Fisher and H. van Wees, eds. *'Aristocracy' in Antiquity: Redefining Greek and Roman Elites*. Swansea. 59–84.

Durrbach, F. 1904. 'Fouilles de Délos (1902), Inscriptions', *BCH* 28: 93–188.

  1911. 'Fouilles de Délos, exécutées aux frais de M. le Duc de Loubat, inscriptions financières (1906–1909)', *BCH* 35: 5–86.

  1921–1923. *Choix d'inscriptions de Délos*. Paris.

Durrbach, F. and Jardé, A. 1905. 'Fouilles de Délos, exécutées aux frais de M. le Duc de Loubat (1903), Inscriptions (*Suite*)', *BCH* 29: 169–257.

Dyggve, E. 1960. *Lindos: Fouilles de l'Acropole 1902–1914 et 1952*, III: *Le sanctuaire d'Athena Lindia et l'architecture lindienne*, vol. 2. Berlin and Copenhagen.

Easterling, P. E. 1994. 'Euripides Outside Athens: A Speculative Note', *ICS* 19: 73–80.

Eckstein, F. 1969. *ΑΝΑΘΗΜΑΤΑ: Studien zu den Weihgeschenken strengen Stils im Heiligtum von Olympia*. Berlin.

Edelstein, L. and Edelstein, E. J. 1945. *Asclepius: Collection and Interpretation of the Testimonies*, 2 vols. Baltimore.

Edwards, A. T. 2004. *Hesiod's Ascra*. Berkeley.

Ehrhardt, N. 1987. 'Die politischen Beziehungen zwischen den griechischen Schwarzmeergründungen und ihren Mutterstädten. Ein Beitrag zur Bedeutung von Kolonialverhältnissen in Griechenland', in *Acta Centri Historiae Terra Antiqua Balcanica 2. IXᵉ Congrès international d'épigraphie grecque et latine*. Sofia. 78–117.

  1997. 'Die Phyleninschriften vom Rundbau am Theater in Kaunos', *AA*: 45–50.

Eickstedt, K.-V. von, 1991. *Beiträge zur Topographie des antiken Piräus*. Athens.

Eidinow, E. 2007. *Oracles, Curses, and Risk Among the Ancient Greeks*. Oxford.

Ekroth, G. 2002. *The Sacrificial Rituals of Greek Hero-Cults in the Archaic to the Early Hellenistic Periods*. Liège.

Elia, D. 2014. 'Local Production of Red-figure Pottery at Locri Epizephyrii: A Synthesis on the Last Decade of Studies', in S. Schierup and V. Sabetai, eds. *The Regional Production of Red-Figure Pottery: Greece, Magna Graecia and Etruria*. Aarhus. 279–90.

Eliot, C. W. J. 1962. *Coastal Demes of Attika: A Study of the Policy of Kleisthenes*. Toronto.

Else, G. E. 1957. *Aristotle's Poetics: The Argument*. Cambridge, MA.

Enríquez de Salamanca Alcón, M. 2015. 'La culture théâtrale à Mégara Hyblaea: Premières hypothèses', in M. Mastelloni, ed. *Lípara ed il teatro in età tardoclassica ed ellenistica*. Palermo. 76–82.

Ensoli, S. 2002. 'Il vaso Portland e Cirene', *QAL* 16: 165–260.

    2010a. 'Il Teatro-Anfiteatro del Santuario di Apollo a Cirene', in M. Luni, ed. *Cirene e la Cirenaica nell'Antichità: Cirene 'Atene d'Africa' III*. Rome. 117–45.

    2010b. 'Cirene 1998–2008', *Libya Antiqua* 5: 115–45.

    2011. 'I lavori di documentazione per lo studio e il restauro del Teatro-Anfiteatro di Cirene', *KGS Forum* 18: 77–86.

    2012. 'L'attività della Missione Archeologica Italiana a Cirene (MAIC) della Seconda Università degli Studi di Napoli (SUN). Le ricerche svolte nel 2009 e 2010 in collaborazione con il Dipartimento alle Antichità (DoA) di Cirene: strategie e prospettive future', in S. Ensoli, ed. *For the Preservation of the Cultural Heritage in Libya: A Dialogue among Institutions*. Pisa and Rome. 111–38.

Erler, M. and Ungern-Sternberg, J. von, 1987. 'Κακὸν γυναῖκες. Griechisches zu der Rede des Metellus Macedonicus "De prole augenda"', *MusHelv* 44: 254–6.

Étienne, R. 1990. *Ténos II: Ténos et les cyclades du milieu du IV*^{e} *siècle av. J.-C. au milieu du III*^{e} *siècle ap. J.-C.* BÉFAR 263. Paris.

Étienne, R., Kourou, N. and Simantoni-Bournia, E. 2013. *Η αρχαία Τήνος*. Athens.

Fabiani, R. 2014. 'Gli onori dei prosseni a Iasos', in J. Fischer, ed. *Der Beitrag Kleinasiens zur Kultur-und Geistesgeschichte der griechisch-römischen Antike, Akten des internationalen Kolloquiums, Wien, 3.–5. November 2010*. Vienna. 99–123.

    2015. *I decreti onorari di Iasos: Cronologia e storia*. Munich.

Fabricius, E. 1884. 'Alterthümer auf der Insel Samos', *AM* 9: 163–97.

    1903. 'Demokopos', *RE* 5.1: 133.

Falco, G. 1997. 'Due gruppi fittili di soggetto teatrale da Centuripe e da Adrano e una maschera marmorea da Tindari: Ipotesi per l'identificazione delle maschere di Tiresia, Edipo e Fineo', *MÉFRA* 109: 813–31.

Fantuzzi, M. 2007. 'Dioscoride e la storia del teatro', in R. Pretagostini, ed. *La cultura letteraria ellenistica: Persistenza, innovazione, trasmissione. Atti del Convegno COFIN 2005, Università di Roma 'Tor Vergata', 19–21 settembre 2005*. Rome. 105–23.

Faraguna, M. 2006. 'La città di Atene e l'amministrazione delle miniere del Laurion', in H.-A. Rupprecht, ed. *Symposion 2003: Vorträge zur griechischen und hellenistischen Rechtsgeschichte (Rauischholzhausen, 30. September – 3. Oktober 2003)*. Vienna. 141–60.

Faulkner, A. 2011. 'Modern Scholarship on the Homeric Hymns: Foundational Issues', in A. Faulkner, ed. *The Homeric Hymns: Interpretive Essays*. Oxford. 1–25.

Favaloro, G. 1922. *Agyrion: Memorie storiche ed archeologiche*. Catania.

Favi, F. 2017a. 'Lo Ὀδυσσεὺς αὐτόμολος di Epicarmo', *ZPE* 201: 17–31.

    2017b. 'La più antica testimonianza sul teatro a Siracusa? Nota a Diom. *GL* I p. 486, 27–31 Keil e [prob.] *Comm. in Verg. Buc. et Georg.* p. 324, 23–325, 3 Hagen', *RivFil* 145: 106–25.

    2017c. *Epicarmo e pseudo-Epicarmo: Commento a [Epich.] frr. 240–295 K.-A.* PhD Diss. Scuola Normale Superiore, Pisa.

    2017d. *Fliaci: Testimonianze e Frammenti*. Studia Comica 7. Heidelberg.

Fazello, T. 1560. *De rebus Siculis decades duae*^{2}. Palermo.

Fearn, D. W. 2003. 'Mapping Phleious: Politics and Myth-Making in Bacchylides 9', *CQ* 53: 347–67.

    2007. *Bacchylides: Politics, Performance, Poetic Tradition*. Oxford.

    2011. 'The Keians and their Choral Lyric: Athenian, Epichoric, and Panhellenic Perspectives', in L. Athanassaki and E. Bowie, eds. *Archaic and Classical Greek Song*. Berlin. 207–34.

2013. 'Athens and the Empire: The Contextual Flexibility of Dithyramb, and its Imperialist Ramifications', in B. Kowalzig and P. Wilson, eds. *Dithyramb in Context*. Oxford. 133–52.

Felsch, R. C. S. 2001. 'Opferhandlungen des Alltagslebens im Heiligtum der Artemis Elaphebolos von Hyampolis in den Phasen SH IIIC-spätgeometrisch', in R. Laffineur and R. Hägg, eds. *Potnia: Deities and Religion in the Aegean Bronze Age. Proceedings of the 8th International Aegean Conference Göteborg, Göteborg University, 12–15 April 2000*. Aegaeum 22. Liège and Austin. 193–9.

Feraru, R. M. 2004–2005. 'Sărbători dionysiace în cetățile grecești din Pontul Stâng', *Pontica* 37–8: 239–52.

Ferguson, W. S. 1948. 'Demetrius Poliorcetes and the Hellenic League', *Hesperia* 17: 112–36.

Ferrandini Troisi, F. 2005. 'La divinizzazione di Alessandro Magno. Testimonianze epigrafiche', *Epigraphica* 67: 23–34.

Feyel, C. 2000. 'Inscriptions inédites du Prytanée délien: Dédicaces et actes d'archontes', *BCH* 124: 247–57.

Feyel, M. 1942. *Contribution à l'épigraphie béotienne*. Le Puy.

Ficuciello, L. 2008. *Le strade di Atene*. Studi di Archeologia e di Topografia di Atene e dell'Attica 4. Athens and Paestum.

2010. 'Il territorio di Myrina (Lemno): Indizi sull'occupazione e sullo sfruttamento delle risorse', *ASAtene* 88: 237–70.

2013. *Lemnos: Cultura, storia, archeologia, topografia di un'isola del nord-Egeo*. Lemno 1.1, Monografie della Scuola archeologica di Atene e delle missioni italiane in oriente 20.1.1. Athens.

Fiechter, E. 1930. *Das Theater in Oropos*. Stuttgart.

1931. *Das Theater in Sikyon*. Stuttgart.

1937. *Das Theater in Eretria*. Stuttgart.

Fiedler, M. 2014. 'Aspekte der städtebaulichen Entwicklung Apollonias. Die deutsch-albanischen Forschungen 2006–2013', in L. Përzhita, I. Gjipali, G. Hoxha and B. Muka, eds. *Proceedings of the International Congress of Albanian Archaeological Studies: 65th Anniversary of Albanian Archaeology (21–22 November, Tirana 2013)*. Tirana. 253–65.

Fiedler, M., Franz, S., Gjongecaj, S., Hesberg, H., Hinz, V., Lahi, B., Quantin, F., Shehi, E., Shkodra-Rrugia, B. 2011. 'Neue Forschungen zum hellenistisch-römischen Theater von Apollonia (Albanien)', *RömMitt* 117: 55–200.

Fiedler, M. and Hermanns, M. H. 2011. 'Die hellenistische Brücke über die Meeresenge von Leukas (Akarnanien): Die längste Steinbrücke des antiken Griechenlands', in Bayerische Gesellschaft für Unterwasserarchäologie, ed. *Archäologie der Brücken: Vorgeschichte, Antike, Mittelalter, Neuzeit*. Regensburg. 48–52.

Figueira, T. J. 1991. *Athens and Aegina in the Age of Imperial Colonization*. Baltimore.

Finglass, P. 2013. 'How Stesichorus Began his *Sack of Troy*', *ZPE* 185: 1–17.

Finley, M. 1952. *Studies in Land and Credit in Ancient Athens, 500–200 B.C.* New Brunswick and New Jersey.

Fiorelli, G. 1884. 'Notizie degli scavi: XXVII. Catania', in *Notizie degli Scavi di Antichità*. Rome. 433–4.

Fisher, N. 2001. *Aeschines: Against Timarchos*. Oxford.

2003. '"Let Envy Be Absent": Envy, Liturgies and Reciprocity in Athens', in D. Konstan and N. Rutter, eds. *Envy, Spite and Jealousy: the Rivalrous Emotions in Ancient Greece*. Edinburgh. 181–215.

Flashar, H. 1972. *Aristoteles: Mirabilia*. Aristoteles Werke in deutscher Übersetzung 18.2. Darmstadt.

Flower, M. 1994. *Theopompus of Chios: History and Rhetoric in the Fourth Century B.C.* Oxford.

Foley, H. 2003. 'Choral Identity in Greek Tragedy', *CP* 98: 1–30.

Fontrier, A. 1878. Ἐπιγραφαὶ ἐναποκείμεναι ἐν τῷ Μουσείῳ', *Μουσείον καὶ Βιβλιοθήκη τῆς Εὐαγγελικῆς Σχολῆς* 2, 2–3: 58–64.

Ford, A. 2011. *Aristotle as Poet: The Song for Hermias and Its Contexts*. Oxford.

Forsdyke, S. 2005. *Exile, Ostracism, and Democracy: The Politics of Expulsion in Ancient Greece.* Princeton.

Forsén, G. 2000. 'Population and Political Strength of some South-eastern Arkadian *Poleis*', in P. Flensted-Jensen, ed. *Further Studies in the Ancient Greek Polis.* Historia Einzelschriften 138. Stuttgart. 35–56.

Fossey, J. M. 1988. *Topography and Population of Ancient Boiotia*, vol. 1. Chicago.

 1991. *Epigraphica Boeotica I: Studies in Boiotian Inscriptions.* Amsterdam.

Fossum, A. 1891. 'The Stage-Building of the Theatre of Eretria', *The American Journal of Archaeology and of the History of the Fine Arts* 7: 257–66.

 1905. 'The Theatre at Sikyon', *AJA* 9: 263–76.

Foucart, P. 1893. 'Inscriptions d'Éleusis', *RÉG* 6: 322–42.

 1895. 'Dédicace de deux chorèges', *RPh* 19: 119–22.

 1904. *Le culte de Dionysos en Attique.* Paris.

 1906. 'Documents pour l'histoire du théâtre athénien', *JSav* 5: 590–602.

Fougères, G. 1890. 'Fouilles de Mantinée (1887–1888) II. Topographie intérieure', *BCH* 14: 245–75.

 1898. *Mantinée et l'Arcadie orientale.* Paris.

Fowler, R. 2013. *Early Greek Mythography. II: Commentary*. Oxford.

Fraenkel, E. 1954. 'Vermutungen zum Aetna-Festspiel des Aeschylus', *Eranos* 52: 61–75.

Fraisse, P. and Moretti, J.-Ch. 2007. *Le Théâtre*, 2 vols. Exploration archéologique de Délos 42. Paris.

Franco, A. 2010. 'Filisto e la *mesogheia* di Sicilia nella *Suda*', in G. Vanotti, ed. *Il lessico Suda e gli storici Greci in frammenti.* Tivoli. 191–205.

Franklin, J. C. 2012. 'The Lesbian Singers: Towards a Reconstruction of Hellanicus' *Karneian Victors*', in D. Castaldo, F. G. Giannachi and A. Manieri, eds. *Poesia, musica e agoni nella Grecia antica: Atti del IV convegno internazionale di ΜΟΙΣΑ, Lecce, 28–30 ottobre 2010.* Rudiae. Ricerche sul mondo classico 22–23. Galatina. 719–64.

 2013. '"Songbenders of Circular Choruses": Dithyramb and the "Demise of Music"', in B. Kowalzig and P. Wilson, eds. *Dithyramb in Context.* Oxford. 213–36.

Franz, S. and Hinz, V. 2015. 'The Architecture of the Greek Theatre of Apollonia in Illyria (Albania) and its Transformation in Roman Times', in R. Frederiksen, E. R. Gebhard and A. Sokolicek, eds. *The Architecture of the Ancient Greek Theatre: Acts of an International Conference at the Danish Institute at Athens 27–30 January 2012.* Monographs of the Danish Institute at Athens 17. Aarhus. 335–49.

Fraser, P. M. 1972a. *Ptolemaic Alexandria.* 3 vols. Oxford.

 1972b. 'Notes on Two Rhodian Institutions', *BSA* 67: 113–24.

Frazer, J. G. 1898. *Pausanias's Description of Greece*, vol. 5: *Commentary on Books IX, X, Addenda.* London.

Frederiksen, R. 2002. 'The Greek Theatre. A Typical Building in the Urban Centre of the Polis?', in T. H. Nielsen, ed. *Even More Studies in the Ancient Greek Polis.* Historia Einzelschriften 162. Stuttgart. 65–124.

 2015. 'Early Greek Theatre Architecture: Monumentalised Koila Before and After the Invention of the Semicircular Design', in R. Frederiksen, E. R. Gebhard and A. Sokolicek, eds. *The Architecture of the Ancient Greek Theatre: Acts of an International Conference at the Danish Institute at Athens 27–30 January 2012.* Monographs of the Danish Institute at Athens 17. Aarhus. 81–104.

Freitag, K. 1994. 'Oiniadai als Hafenstadt – Einige historisch-topographische Überlegungen', *Klio* 76: 212–38.

Frel, F. 1969. *Les sculpteurs attiques anonymes, 430–300.* Prague.

Frey, H. 1919–1920. *Der ΒΙΟΣ ΕΥΡΙΠΙΔΟΥ des Satyros und seine literaturgeschichtliche Bedeutung.* Diss. Zurich.

Frickenhaus, A. 1911. 'Das Herakleion von Melite', *AM* 36: 113–44.

Frisk, H. 1960. *Griechisches etymologisches Wörterbuch.* Heidelberg.

Froehner, W. 1892. *Collection van Branteghem.* Brussels.

Frohberger, H. 1880. *Ausgewählte Reden des Lysias für den Schulgebrauch.* Leipzig.

Fronda, M. 2010. *Between Rome and Carthage: Southern Italy during the Second Punic War.* Cambridge.

Froning, H. 2002. 'Bauformen – Von Holzgerüst zum Theater von Epidauros', in S. Moraw and E. Nölle, eds. *Die Geburt des Theaters in der griechischen Antike.* Mainz. 31–59.

    2014. 'Comedy and Parody: Some Reflections on the "Perseus Jug" of the Vlastos Collection', in P. Valavanis and E. Manakidou, eds. *Essays on Greek Pottery and Iconography in Honour of Professor Michalis Tiverios.* Thessaloniki. 303–20.

Frontisi-Ducroux, F. 1995. *Du masque au visage: Aspects de l'identité en Grèce ancienne.* Paris.

    2015. '"Images" de Dionysos? Le dieu masque et son phallos', in S. Estienne, V. Huet, F. Lissarrague and F. Prost, eds. *Figures de dieux: Construire le divin en images.* Rennes. 319–36.

Furley, W. D. and Bremer, J. M. 2001. *Greek Hymns*, 2 vols. Studien und Texte zu Antike und Christentum 10. Tübingen.

Furtwängler, A. 1895. *Masterpieces of Greek Sculpture: A Series of Essays on the History of Art.* London.

Gabričević, B. 1981a. 'Neka Razmišljanja o Teatru u Issi', in D. Rnjak, *Antički Teatar na tlu Jugoslavije: Saopštenja sa naučnog skupa 14.–17. april 1980.* Novi Sad. 67–72.

    1981b. 'Epigraphica Quaedam', in D. Rnjak, *Antički Teatar na tlu Jugoslavije: Saopštenja sa naučnog skupa 14.–17. april 1980.* Novi Sad. 147–54.

Gabrielsen, V. 2001. 'The Rhodian Associations and Economic Activity', in Z. H. Archibald, J. Davies, V. Gabrielsen and G. J. Oliver, eds. *Hellenistic Economies.* London. 215–44.

Gagarin, M. 1997. *Antiphon: The Speeches.* Cambridge.

Gaiser, K. 1973. 'Die Platon-Referate des Alkimos bei Diogenes Laertios (III 9–17)', in *Zetesis: Album amicorum daor vrienden en collega's aangeboden aan Prof Dr. E. de Strycker.* Antwerp and Utrecht. 61–79.

Galinski, G. K. 1972. *The Herakles Theme: The Adaptations of the Hero in Literature from Homer to the Twentieth Century.* Oxford.

Gallavotti, C. 1978. 'Le copie di Pausania e gli originali di alcune iscrizioni di Olimpia', *BollClass* 26: 3–27.

Gallo, L. 2003. 'I teatri delle poleis siciliane: Funzione politica e implicazioni demografiche', in A. Corretti, ed. *Atti delle quarte Giornate Internazionali di studi sull'area elima*, vol. 2. Pisa. 537–48.

Gantz, T. 1993. *Early Greek Myth.* Baltimore.

Gardiner, E. A., Loring, W., Richards, G. C., Woodhouse, W. J. and Schultz, R. V. 1892. *Excavations at Megalopolis 1890–1891.* JHS Supplement 1. London.

Gardiner, P. 1893. *Catalogue of the Greek Vases of the Ashmolean Museum.* Oxford.

Garland, R. 1987. *The Piraeus: From the Fifth to the First Century B.C.* London.

Gassner, V. 2016. 'Velia. Fortifications and Urban Design. The Development of the Town from the Late 6th to the 3rd c. BC', *Empuries* 56: 75–100.

Gauss, W., Smetana, R., Dorner, J., Eitzinger, P., Lätzer-Lasar, A., Leibetseder, M. and Trapichler, M. 2015. 'Old and New Observations from the Theatre at Aigeira', in R. Frederiksen, E. R. Gebhard and A. Sokolicek, eds. *The Architecture of the Ancient Greek Theatre: Acts of an International Conference at the Danish Institute at Athens 27–30 January 2012*. Monographs of the Danish Institute at Athens 17. Aarhus. 267–77.

Gauthier, P. 1966. 'Les clérouques de Lesbos et la colonisation athénienne au Ve siècle', *RÉG* 79: 64–88.

1979. 'La réunification d'Athènes en 281 et les deux archontes Nicias', *RÉG* 92: 348–99.

1999. 'Nouvelles inscriptions de Claros: Décrets d'Aigai et de Mylasa pour des juges colophoniens', *RÉG* 112: 1–36.

Gebhard, E. R. 1973. *The Theater at Isthmia*. Chicago.

1974. 'The Form of the Orchestra in the Early Greek Theater', *Hesperia* 43: 428–40.

2015. 'The Sunken Orchestra: Its Effects on Greek Theatre Design', in R. Frederiksen, E. R. Gebhard and A. Sokolicek, eds. *The Architecture of the Ancient Greek Theatre: Acts of an International Conference at the Danish Institute at Athens 27–30 January 2012*. Monographs of the Danish Institute at Athens 17. Aarhus. 105–17.

Geddes, A. 2007. 'Ion of Chios and Politics', in V. Jennings and A. Katsaros, eds. *The World of Ion of Chios*. Leiden. 110–38.

Gehrke, H.-J. 1985. *Stasis: Untersuchungen zu den inneren Kriegen in den griechischen Staaten des 5. und 4. Jahrhunderts v.Chr.* Munich.

Geissler, P. 1969. *Chronologie der altattischen Komödie*^{2}. Dublin and Zurich.

Gentili, B., Angeli-Bernardini, P., Cingano, E. and Giannini, P. eds. 1995. *Pindaro: Le Pitiche*. Milan.

Gentili, G. 1952. 'Nuovo esempio di "theatron" con gradinata rettilinea a Siracusa', *Dioniso* 15: 122–30.

Georgiadou, A. 1997. *Plutarch's Pelopidas: A Historical and Philological Commentary*. Stuttgart.

Gerkan, A. von 1935. *Milet 2.3: Die Stadtmauern*. Berlin.

Gerkan, A. von and Müller-Wiener, W. 1961. *Das Theater von Epidauros*. Stuttgart.

Germani, M. 2012. 'Tebe. Nèos Synoikismòs. Gli scavi archeologici dal 1967 al 1997. Il teatro antico e la sua ricostruzione', *Αρχαιολογικό Έργο Θεσσαλίας και Στερεάς Ελλάδα* 3 [2009]: 985–98.

2014. 'Il teatro di Orchomenos in Beozia: Vecchi e nuovi scavi', *Notiziario della Scuola Archeologica Italiana di Atene* 11–12: 31–2.

2015a. 'Dal teatro greco al teatro romano: Il caso di Orchomenos in Beozia, Osservazioni preliminari', *Αρχαιολογικό Έργο Θεσσαλίας και Στερεάς Ελλάδας* 4 [2012]: 789–94.

2015b. 'Boeotian Theatres: An Overview of the Regional Architecture', in R. Frederiksen, E. R. Gebhard and A. Sokolicek, eds. *The Architecture of the Ancient Greek Theatre: Acts of an International Conference at the Danish Institute at Athens 27–30 January 2012*. Monographs of the Danish Institute at Athens 17. Aarhus. 351–63.

Geus, K. 2002. *Eratosthenes von Kyrene*. Munich.

Ghiron-Bistagne, P. 1976. *Recherches sur les acteurs dans la Grèce antique*. Paris.

Giamalide, M. and Daifa, C. 2013. 'Νέα στοιχεία στην τοπογραφία του αρχαίου δήμου των Αλών Αιξωνίδων από την περιοχή της Βούλας', in A. Stefanis, ed. *Πρακτικά ΙΔ΄ Επιστημονικής Συνάντησης ΝΑ. Αττικής: Καλύβια Θορικού Αττικής, 6–9 Οκτωβρίου 2011*. Kalyvia Thorikou. 113–26.

Giannopoulos, N. I. 1902. 'Ἔκθεσεις ἀρχαιολογικῆς ἐκδρομῆς ἀνὰ τὸν δῆμον Σκοτούσης', *Ἁρμονία* 3: 427–32.

Giannopoulou-Konsolaki, H. 1990. *Γλυφάδα: Ἱστορικὸ παρελθὸν καὶ μνημεῖα*. Athens.

Giannou, T. 2016. 'Theatre and Music in Classical and Hellenistic Macedonia', *Logeion* 6: 30–92.

Gigante, M. 1971a. *Rintone e il teatro in Magna Grecia*. Naples.

　1971b. 'Testimonianze di Filodemo su Maison', *CronErcol* 1: 65–8.

Gilkes, O. ed. 2003. *The Theater at Butrint: Luigi Maria Ugolini's Excavations at Butrint (1928–1932)*. BSA Supplement 35. London.

Gill, D. 1991. *Greek Cult Tables*. New York.

　2006. 'Hippodamus and the Piraeus', *Historia* 55: 1–15.

Gilula, D. 2000. 'Stratonikos, the Witty Harpist', in D. Braund and J. Wilkins, eds. *Athenaeus and His World*. Exeter. 423–33.

Ginouvès, R. 1972. *Le théâtron à gradins droits et l'odéon d'Argos*. Études péloponnésiennes 6. Paris.

Giordano, D. 1990. *Chamaeleontis Heracleotae fragmenta*. Bologna.

Goette, H.-R. 1992–1998. 'Ο ΔΗΜΟΣ ΤΗΣ ΠΑΛΛΗΝΗΣ', *Horos* 10–12: 105–18.

　1995a. 'Griechische Theatrebauten der Klassik – Forschungsstand und Fragestellungen', in E. Pöhlmann, ed. *Studien zur Bühnendichtung und zum Theaterbau der Antike*. Studien zur klassischen Philologie 93. Frankfurt. 9–48.

　1995b. 'Studien zur historischen Landeskunde Attikas IV. Der Hügel der Panagia Thiti bei Vari unde seine Inschriften', *AM* 110: 235–46.

　1995c. 'Studien zur historischen Landeskunde Attikas V. Beobachtungen im Theater des Amphiareion von Oropos', *AM* 110: 253–60.

　2001. *Athens, Attica and the Megarid*. London and New York.

　2007. 'Choregic Monuments and the Athenian Democracy', in P. Wilson, ed. *The Greek Theatre and Festivals: Documentary Studies*. Oxford. 122–49.

　2014. 'The Archaeology of the "Rural" Dionysia in Attica', in E. Csapo, H.-R. Goette, J. R. Green and P. Wilson, eds. *Greek Theatre in the Fourth Century B.C.* Berlin and Boston. 77–105.

Goette, H.-R. and Hammerstädt, J. 2004. *Das antike Athen: Ein literarischer Stadtführer*. Munich.

Goette, H.-R. and Weber, T. M. 2004. *Marathon: Siedlungskammer und Schlachtfeld – Sommerfrische und Olympische Wettkampfstätte*. Mainz.

Goette, H.-R. and Wilson, P. *forthcoming*. 'A Double-Sided Relief from Ikarion: Dionysus or Apollo?'.

Gogos, S. 1998. 'Bemerkungen zu den Theatern von Priene und Epidauros sowie zum Dionysostheater in Athen', *ÖJhBeibl* 67: 66–106.

　2004. *Το αρχαίο θέατρο των Οινιαδών*. Athens.

　2011. *Das Theater von Epidauros*. Vienna.

Goldberg, S. 1998. 'Plautus on the Palatine', *JHS* 88: 1–20.

Gondicas, D. 1990. 'Ikarios I', *LIMC* V: 645–7.

González, J. A., Arteaga, C., Arteaga-Manjón-Cabeza, F. and García, R. 2013. 'The Natural Landscape of Epicnemidian Locris: The Historical Conditions of its Physical Environment', in J. Pascual and M.-F. Papakonstantinou, eds. *Topography and History of Ancient Epicnemidian Locris*. Leiden. 9–61.

Goodchild, R. 1971. *Kyrene und Apollonia*. Zurich.

Gorceix, H. 1876. 'Aperçu géologique sur l'île de Cos', *Annales scientifiques de l'École Normale Supérieure*, 2nd series 5: 205–16.

Gorman, V. 2001. *Miletos, the Ornament of Ionia: A History of the City to 400 B.C.E.* Ann Arbor.

Gorogianni, E. 2011. 'Goddess, Lost Ancestors, and Dolls: A Cultural Biography of the Ayia Irini Terracotta Statues', *Hesperia* 80: 635–55.

Gorrini, M. E. and Melfi, M. 2005. 'Siphnos: Some Notes on the Reconstruction of the Pantheon', in *Πρακτικά Β΄ διεθνούς Σιφναϊκού συμποσίου: Σίφνος 27–30 Ιουνίου 2002: εἰς μνήμην Νικολάου Βερνίκου-Ευγενίδη*. Athens. 215–26.

Gow, A. S. F. 1952. *Theocritus: Edited with a Translation and Commentary*², 2 vols. Cambridge.

1965. *Machon: The Fragments*. Cambridge.

Graf, F. 1974. *Eleusis und die orphische Dichtung Athens in vorhellenistischer Zeit*. Berlin.

1985. *Nordionische Kulte: Religionsgeschichtliche und epigraphische Untersuchungen zu den Kulten von Chios, Erythrai, Klazomenai und Phokaia*. Rome.

Graham, A. J. 1983. *Colony and Mother City in Ancient Greece*. Manchester.

2000. 'Thasos: The Topography of the Ancient City', *BSA* 95: 301–27.

Graham, J. W. 1972. 'Notes on Housing and Housing-Districts at Abdera and Himera', *AJA* 76: 295–301.

Graindor, P. 1907a. 'Les fouilles de Tenos en 1905', *MusB* 11: 1–51.

1907b. 'Inscriptions des Cyclades', *MusB* 11: 97–113.

Grainger, J. D. 1990. *Seleukos Nikator: Constructing a Hellenistic Kingdom*. Abingdon and New York.

Grandjean, C. 1995. 'Les comptes de Pompidas (*IG* VII 2426). Drachmes d'argent symmachique et drachmes de bronzes', *BCH* 119: 1–26.

Grandjean, Y. and Salviat, F. 1988. 'Décret d'Athènes, restaurant la démocratie à Thasos en 407 av. J.-C.: *IG* XII 8, 262 complété', *BCH* 112: 249–78.

2000. *Guide de Thasos*². Paris and Athens.

2012–2013. 'Hippocrate et le Sanctuaire de la Délienne à Thasos', *BCH* 136–137: 215–23.

Gras, H., Tréziny, H. and Broise, H. 2004. *Mégara Hyblaea*, vol. 5: *La ville archaïque*. Paris.

Greco, E. 2008. 'Indigeni e Greci ad Efestia. Per una classificazione preliminare degli indicatori archeologici', in E. Greco and E. Papi, eds. *Hephestia 2000–2006: Atti del Seminario, Siena-Certosa di Pontignano, 28–29 maggio 2007*. Paestum and Athens. 15–27.

2011. 'Alla ricerca dell'Agora di Sparta', *ASAtene* 89: 53–77.

Greco, E. and Ficuciello, L. 2010. 'Cesure e continuità: Lemno, dai "Tirreni" agli Ateniesi', *ASAtene* 88: 149–68.

Greco, E. and Voza, O. 2010. 'Osservazioni sulle fasi cronologiche del teatro di Efestia', *ASAtene* 88: 99–102.

Green, J. R. 1982. 'Dedication of Masks', *RA*: 237–48.

1989. 'Theatre Production: 1971–1986', *Lustrum* 31: 7–96, 273–78.

1994. *Theatre in Ancient Greek Society*. London and New York.

1999. 'Tragedy and the Spectacle of the Mind: Messenger Speeches, Actors, Narrative and Audience Imagination in Fourth-Century BCE Vase Painting', in B. Bergmann and C. Kondoleon, eds. *The Art of Ancient Spectacle*. Washington. 37–63.

2003. 'Smart and Stupid: the Evolution of Some Masks and Characters in Fourth-Century Comedy', in J. Davidson and A. Pomeroy, eds. *Theatres of Action: Papers for Chris Dearden*. Auckland. 118–32.

2007. 'Paphos and the World of the Theatre', in P. Flourentzos, ed. *From Evagoras to the Ptolemies*. Proceedings of the International Archaeological Conference, Nicosia, 29–30 November 2002. Nicosia. 3–16.

2008. 'Theatre Production: 1996–2006', *Lustrum* 50: 7–391.

2009. *The Logie Collection: a Catalogue of the James Logie Memorial Collection of Classical Antiquities at the University of Canterbury, Christchurch*. Christchurch.

2010. 'The Material Evidence', in G. Dobrov, ed. *Brill's Companion to the Study of Greek Comedy*. Boston and Leiden. 71–102.

2012a. 'Comic Vases in South Italy: Continuity and Innovation in the Development of a Figurative Language', in K. Bosher, ed. *Theater Outside Athens: Drama in Greek Sicily and South Italy*. Cambridge. 289–342.

2012b. 'Tragic Chorusmen in Taranto and Athens', *Ostraka* 21: 155–64.

2014a. 'Regional Theatre in the Fourth Century', in E. Csapo, H.-R. Goette, J. R. Green and P. Wilson, eds. *Greek Theatre in the Fourth Century B.C.* Berlin and Boston. 333–69.

2014b. 'Two Phaedras: Euripides and Aristophanes?', in S. D. Olson, ed. *Ancient Comedy and Reception: Essays in Honor of Jeffrey Henderson.* Berlin and Boston. 94–131.

Green, J. R., Barker, C. and Stennett, G. 2015. 'The Hellenistic Phases of the Theatre at Nea Paphos in Cyprus: The Evidence from the Australian Excavations', in R. Frederiksen, E. R. Gebhard and A. Sokolicek, eds. *The Architecture of the Ancient Greek Theatre: Acts of an International Conference at the Danish Institute at Athens 27–30 January 2012.* Monographs of the Danish Institute at Athens 17. Aarhus. 319–34.

Green, J. R. and Sinclair, R. 1970. 'Athenians in Eretria', *Historia* 19: 515–27.

Green, J. R. and Stennett, G. H. 2002. 'The Architecture of the Ancient Theatre at Nea Pafos: A Preliminary Report', in *Report of the Department of Antiquities Cyprus.* 155–88.

Griffin, A. 1982. *Sikyon.* Oxford.

Griffith, M. 1978. 'Aeschylus, Sicily and Prometheus', in R. Dawe, ed. *Dionysiaca: Nine Studies in Greek Poetry by Former Pupils Presented to Sir Denys Page on his Seventieth Birthday.* Cambridge. 105–39.

2006. 'Horsepower and Donkeywork: Equids and the Ancient Greek Imagination', *CP* 101: 185–246.

2013. 'Satyr-Play, Dithyramb, and the Geopolitics of Dionysian Style in Fifth-Century Athens', in B. Kowalzig and P. Wilson, eds. *Dithyramb in Context.* Oxford. 257–81.

Griffo, P. 1987. 'Cratere attico a fondo bianco con Perseo ed Andromeda del Museo Regionale di Agrigento', *Quaderni di archeologia: Università di Messina* 2: 91–104.

Grimaldi, W. M. A. 1988. *Aristotle, Rhetoric II: A Commentary.* New York.

Grimes, B. 2002. '*IG* II^2 1198: Money Awarded by Attic Demes for the Purpose of Sacrifice', *ZPE* 140: 80.

Gros, P. 2009. 'Les sanctuaires in summa cavea. L'enseignement des recherches récentes sur le théâtre de Pompée à Rome', in J.-C. Moretti, ed. *Fronts de scène et lieux de culte dans le théâtre antique.* Travaux de la Maison de l'Orient 52. Lyon. 52–64.

Gruben, G. 1982. 'Naxos und Paros. Vierter vorläufiger Bericht über die Forschungskampagnen 1972–1980. I. Archaische Bauten', *AA*: 159–95.

1997. 'Naxos und Delos: Studien zur archaischen Architektur der Kykladen', *JdI* 112: 261–416.

1999. 'Wandernde Saulen auf Naxos', in N. Stampolides, ed. *Φως Κυκλαδικόν. Τιμητικός τόμος στη μνήμη του Ν. Ζαφειρόπουλου.* Athens. 296–317.

Guardì, T. 1980. 'L'attività teatrale nella Siracusa di Gerone I', *Dioniso* 51: 25–47.

Guarducci, M. 1967–1978. *Epigrafia greca,* 4 vols. Rome.

1987. *L'epigrafia greca dalle origini al tardo Impero.* Rome.

Gudeman, A. 1929. 'Stephanos 13', *RE* 3 A: 2399–401.

1934. *Aristoteles Περὶ ποιητικῆς.* Leipzig.

Guerrera, V. 2013. *Orcomeno Minia in età arcaica.* Diss. Naples.

Guillon, P. 1943. *Les trépieds du Ptoion I–II.* Paris.

Günther, T. 1999. 'Lykophron', in R. Krumeich, N. Pechstein, B. Seidensticker, eds. *Das griechische Satyrspiel.* Darmstadt. 617–23.

Gutas, D. 2012. 'The *Poetics* in Syriac and Arabic Transmission', in L. Tarán and D. Gutas, *Aristotle: 'Poetics'.* Leiden and Boston. 77–128.

Habash, M. 1995. 'Two Complementary Festivals in Aristophanes' *Acharnians*', *AJP* 116: 559–77.

Habicht, C. 1957. 'Samische Volksbeschlüsse der hellenistischen Zeit', *AM* 72: 152–274.

1970. *Gottmenschentum der griechischen Städte^2.* Munich.

2004a. 'The Dating of the Koan Monarchoi', in K. Höghammar, ed. *The Hellenic Polis of Kos: State, Economy and Culture*. Uppsala. 61–7.

2004b. 'Ein neuer Gymnasiarch am Fest der Athena Ilias', *EpigAnat* 37: 91–4.

Hackens, T. 1967. 'Le théâtre', in *Thorikos III, 1965*. Brussels. 74–96.

Hagel, S. 2009. *Ancient Greek Music: A New Technical History*. Cambridge.

Hall, E. 1989. *Inventing the Barbarian: Greek Self-Definition through Tragedy*. Oxford.

2006. *The Theatrical Cast of Athens*. Oxford.

Hall, J. M. 1995. 'How Argive was the "Argive" Heraion? The Political and Cultic Geography of the Argive Plain, 900–400 B.C.', *AJA* 99: 577–613.

Halliwell, S. 2008. *Greek Laughter: A Study of Cultural Psychology from Homer to Early Christianity*. Cambridge.

Hallof, K. 1999. 'Choregenliste aus Samos', *Philologus* 143: 359–62.

Hamilton, R. 1992. *Choes and Anthesteria: Athenian Iconography and Ritual*. Ann Arbor.

Hammond, N. G. L. 1967. *Epirus: The Geography, the Ancient Remains, the History and the Topography of Epirus and Adjacent Areas*. Oxford.

Hammond, N. G. L. and Griffith, G. T. 1979. *A History of Macedonia*, vol. 2: *550–336 B.C.* Oxford.

Handley, E. 1997. 'Some Thoughts on New Comedy and Its Public', *Pallas* 47: 185–200.

2003. 'Theocritus on Epicharmus', in J. Davidson and A. Pomeroy, eds. *Theatres of Action*. Auckland. 142–8.

Hansen, M. H. ed. 1995. *Sources for the Ancient Greek City-State: Symposium August 24–27 1994*. Acts of the Copenhagen Polis Centre 2. Copenhagen.

2007. 'A Comment on the Review Article of the Publications of the Copenhagen Polis Centre in *AWE* 5', *AWE* 6: 321–7.

Hansen, M. H. and Fischer-Hansen, T. 1994. 'Monumental Political Architecture in Archaic and Classical Greek *Poleis*: Evidence and Historical Significance', in D. Whitehead, ed. *From Political Architecture to Stephanus Byzantius: Sources for the Ancient Greek Polis*. Historia Einzelschriften 87. Stuttgart. 23–90.

Hanslik, R. 1931. 'Menekles 2', *RE* 15.1: 796–7.

Harder, A. 1985. *Euripides' Kresphontes and Archelaos*. Leiden.

2012. *Callimachus: Aetia*, 2 vols. Oxford.

Hardie, A. 1997. 'Philitas and the Plane Tree', *ZPE* 119: 21–36.

Harding, P. 1985. *From the End of the Peloponnesian War to the Battle of Ipsus*. Cambridge.

Harris, E. M. 1993. '*Apotimema*: Athenian Terminology for Real Security in Leases and Dowry Agreements', *CQ* 43: 73–95.

Harrison, R. 1975. 'The Theater', in R. Goodchild, J. Pedley and D. White, eds. *Apollonia, the Port of Cyrene: Excavations by the University of Michigan 1965–1967, Supplement to Libya Antiqua IV*. Tripoli. 163–74.

Hartwig, A. 2014. 'The Evolution of Comedy in the Fourth Century', in E. Csapo, H.-R. Goette, J. R. Green and P. Wilson, eds. *Greek Theatre in the Fourth Century B.C.* Berlin and Boston. 207–27.

Harvey, D. 2000. 'Phrynichos and his Muses', in D. Harvey and J. Wilkins, eds. *The Rivals of Aristophanes: Studies in Athenian Old Comedy*. London. 91–134.

Hatzfield, J. 1907. 'Bas-relief des Pythaistes', *MÉFR* 27: 137–42.

Hatzopoulos, M. B. 1996. *Macedonian Institutions under the Kings*, vol. 2: *Epigraphic Appendix*. Meletemata 22. Athens.

Haverfield, F. J. 1913. *Ancient Town-Planning*. Oxford.

Hayward, C. and Lolos, Y. 2015. 'Building the Early Hellenistic Theatre at Sikyon', in R. Frederiksen, E. R. Gebhard and A. Sokolicek, eds. *The Architecture of the Ancient Greek Theatre: Acts of an International Conference at the Danish Institute at Athens 27–30 January 2012*. Monographs of the Danish Institute at Athens 17. Aarhus. 161–76.

Heath, M. 1990. 'Aristophanes and his Rivals', *G&R* 37: 143–58.

2013. 'Aristotle *On Poets*: A Critical Evaluation of Richard Janko's Edition of the Fragments', *Studia Humaniora Tartuensia* 14: 1–27.

Heimberg, U. 1982. *Die Keramik des Kabirions.* Das Kabirenheiligtum bei Theben 3. Berlin.

Heinemann, A. 2013. *Der Gott des Gelages: Dionysos, Satyrn und Mänaden auf attischem Trinkgeschirr des 5. Jahrhunderts v. Chr*. Berlin.

Heisserer, A. J. 1980. *Alexander the Great and the Greeks: The Epigraphic Evidence.* Norman.

Hellmann, M.-C. 1992. *Recherches sur le vocabulaire de l'architecture grecque d'après les inscriptions de Délos.* BÉFAR 278. Athens and Paris.

1999. *Choix d'inscriptions architecturales grecques, traduites et commentées.* Lyons.

Henderson, J. 1991. *The Maculate Muse: Obscene Language in Attic Comedy.* Oxford.

Henrichs, A. 1990. 'Between Country and City: Cultic Dimensions of Dionysos in Athens and Attica', in M. Griffith and D. J. Mastronarde, eds. *Cabinet of the Muses: Essays on Classical and Comparative Literature in Honor of Thomas G. Rosenmeyer.* Atlanta. 257–77.

Herington, C. J. 1967. 'Aeschylus in Sicily', *JHS* 87: 74–85.

Hermann, G. 1839. *Opuscula*, vol. 7. Leipzig.

Hermary, A., Jockey, P., Queyrel, F. and Marcadé, J. 1996. *Sculptures déliennes.* Paris.

Herrmann, P. 1970. 'Zu den Beziehungen zwischen Athen und Milet im 5. Jahrhundert', *Klio* 52: 163–73.

Herter, H. 1939. 'Theseus der Athener', *RhM* 88: 244–86, 289–326.

Herzog, R. 1899. *Koische Forschungen und Funde.* Leipzig.

Hesberg, H. von, 1994. *Formen privater Repräsentation in der Baukunst des 2. und 1. Jahrhunderts v. Chr.* Cologne.

Hesberg, H. von, and Eck, W. 2008. 'Reliefs, Skulpturen und Inschriften aus dem Theater von Apollonia (Albanien)', *RömMitt* 114: 31–97.

Hilgard, A. ed. 1901. *Grammatici Graeci* 1.3. Leipzig.

Hiller von Gaertringen, F. 1900. 'Dionysosinschrift aus Naxos', *Hermes* 35: 339–40.

1901. 'Inschriften von Rhodos und Thera', *Hermes* 36: 440–7.

Hindley, C. 1994. '*Eros* and Military Command in Xenophon', *CQ* 44: 347–66.

Hinrichs, G. 1883. 'Philologische Paralipomena Bergks', *Hermes* 18: 481–520.

Hirschfeld, G. 1875. 'Inschriften von Novum-Ilium (Hissarlyk)', *AZ* 32: 151–6.

Hobhouse, J. C. 1813. *A Journey through Albania, and Other Provinces of Turkey in Europe and Asia, to Constantinople During the Years 1809 and 1810*, vol. 1. London.

Hodkinson, S. and Hodkinson, H. 1981. 'Mantineia and the Mantinike: Settlement and Society in a Greek Polis', *BSA* 76: 239–96.

Hodot, R. 1976. 'Notes critiques sur le corpus epigraphique de Lesbos', *Etudes d'Archéologie Classique* 5: 17–81.

Hoffmann, A. 2002. *Grabritual und Gesellschaft: Gefäßformen, Bildthemen und Funktionen unteritalisch-rotfiguriger Keramik aus der Nekropole von Tarent.* Leidorf.

Holford-Strevens, L. 2009. 'Selinus or Athens?', *CQ* 59: 624–6.

Holleaux, M. 1897. 'Note sur un décret d'Érétrie', *RÉG* 10: 157–89.

1905. 'Sur une inscription de Siphnos', *BCH* 29: 319–28.

Hollinshead, M. 2015. *Shaping Ceremony: Monumental Steps in Greek Architecture.* Madison.

Hollis, A. 1992. 'Attica in Hellenistic Poetry', *ZPE* 93: 1–15.

Holtzmann, B. 2005. 'Praxias et Fils: Un atelier de sculpture attique actif à Thasos durant la seconde moitié du IVe siècle av. J.-C.', in V. M. Strocka, ed. *Meisterwerke: Internationales Symposion anlässlich des 150. Geburtstages von Adolf Furtwängler. Freiburg im Breisgau, 30 Juni-3 Juli 2003*. Munich. 169–78.

Homolle, T. 1887. 'Rapport sur une mission archéologique dans l'île de Délos', *Archives des missions scientifiques et littéraires* ser. 3, 13: 389–435.

1898. 'Inscription de Delphes', *BCH* 22: 260–70.

1899. 'Le gymnase de Delphes', *BCH* 23: 560–83.

Hondius, J. 1919–1921. 'A New Inscription of the Deme Halimous', *BSA* 24: 151–60.

Hood, M. S. F., Boardman, J. and Anderson, J. K. 1954. 'Excavation on the Kofinà Ridge, Chios', *BSA* 49: 123–82.

Hoover, O. 2012. *Handbook of Coins of Sicily (Including Lipara)*. Lancaster.

Hopkinson, N. 1984. *Callimachus: Hymn to Demeter*. Cambridge.

Hordern, J. H. 2002. *The Fragments of Timotheus of Miletus*. Oxford.

2004. *Sophron's Mimes: Text, Translation, and Commentary*. Oxford.

Horky, P. 2013. *Plato and Pythagoreanism*. Oxford.

Hornblower, S. 1982a. *Mausolus*. Oxford.

1982b. 'The Second Athenian Confederacy', *CR* 32: 235–9.

1982c. 'Thucydides, the Panionian Festival, and the Ephesia (III 104)', *Historia* 31: 241–5.

1990. 'When Was Megalopolis Founded?', *BSA* 85: 71–7.

1991. *A Commentary on Thucydides*, vol. 1: *Books I–III*. Oxford.

2004. *Thucydides and Pindar: Historical Narrative and the World of Epinikian Poetry*. Oxford.

2008. *A Commentary on Thucydides*, vol. 3: *Books V.25–VIII.109*. Oxford.

Hubbard, T. 2011. 'The Dissemination of Pindar's Non-Epinician Choral Lyric', in L. Athanassaki and E. Bowie, eds. *Archaic and Classical Choral Song: Performance, Politics and Dissemination*. Trends in Classics Supplement 10. Berlin. 347–64.

Huffman, C. 2005. *Archytas of Tarentum: Pythagorean, Philosopher and Mathematician King*. Cambridge.

Hug, A. 1877. *Aeneas von Stymphalos*. Gratulationsschrift der Universität Zürich an die Universität Tübingen zu deren Vierhundertjähriger Stiftungsfeier von VIII.–XI. August MDCCCLXXVII. Zurich.

Hughes, A. 2003. 'Comedy in Paestan Vase Painting', *OJA* 22: 281–301.

2006. 'The "Perseus Dance" Vase Revisited', *OJA* 25: 413–33.

Hulot, J. and Fougères, G. 1910. *Sélinonte: la ville, l'acropole et les temples*. Paris.

Humphreys, S. C. 2004. *The Strangeness of Gods: Historical Perspectives on the Interpretation of Athenian Religion*. Oxford.

2018. *Kinship in Ancient Athens: An Anthropological Analysis*. Oxford.

Hunt, W. S. 1940–1945. 'An Archaeological Survey of the Classical Antiquities of the Island of Chios Carried out between the Months of March and July 1938', *BSA* 41: 29–52.

Hunter, R. L. 1983. *Eubulus: The Fragments*. Cambridge.

2003. *Theocritus: Encomium of Ptolemy Philadelphus*. Berkeley.

Huxley, G. 1978. 'Simonides and his World', *Proceedings of the Royal Irish Academy* 78: 231–47.

Iannucci, A. 2010. 'Il tempio E della collina orientale di Selinunte: Ipotesi per un' identificazione del culto', in E. Acquaro, P. De Vita and A. Iannucci, eds. *Selinunte si racconta: CAM, 5 Maggio 2010*. Messina. 18–22.

Ieranò, G. 1992. 'Apollo Pizio e Dioniso Ikarios', *QS* 36: 171–80.

1997. *Il Ditirambo di Dioniso: Le testimonianze Antiche*. Pisa and Rome.

2013. '"One Who is Fought Over by All the Tribes": The Dithyrambic Poet and the City of Athens', in B. Kowalzig and P. Wilson, eds. *Dithyramb in Context*. Oxford. 368–86.

Inglese, A. 2011. 'Inscription inédite du théâtre du sanctuaire de Déméter', *CRAI*: 273–81.

2013. 'Il santuario di Demetra a Cirene. Le iscrizioni', in A. Inglese, *Epigrammata 2: Definire, descrivere, proteggere lo spazio. In ricordo di André Laronde*. Tivoli. 231–51, 436–9.

Intzesiloglou, B. G. 2011. 'Τὸ αρχαίο θέατρο Δημητριάδος', in V. Adrimi-Sismani, ed. *Αρχαία Θέατρα στη Θεσσαλία*. Diazoma 5. Athens. 33–48.

Irigoin, J. 1986. 'Le catalogue de Lamprias: Tradition manuscrite et éditions imprimées', *RÉG* 99: 318–31.

Isager, S. 1998. 'The Pride of Halikarnassos. Editio Princeps of an Inscription from Salmakis', *ZPE* 123: 1–23.

Isik, C. and Marek, C. 1997. *Das Monument des Protogenes in Kaunos*. Bonn.

Isler, H. P. 1981. 'Contributi per una storia del teatro antico: il teatro greco di Iaitas e il teatro di Segesta', *NumAntCl* 10: 131–64.

2000a. 'Il teatro greco di Iaitas', *SicArch* 98: 201–20.

2000b. 'Monte Iato: scavi 1995-1997', in *Terze giornate internazionali di studi sull'area elima (Gibellina – Erice – Contessa Entellina, 23–26 ottobre 1997)*. Pisa and Gibellina. 715–29.

2003. 'Il teatro greco di Iaitas', *Dioniso* 2: 276–91.

2007. *Eretria XVIII: Das Theater, Grabungen 1997 und 1998*. Gollion.

2011. Review of S. Gogos, 2009, *Das antike Theater von Oiniadai*, *MusHelv* 68: 104.

Ismard, P. 2010. *La cité des réseaux: Athènes et ses associations, VIᵉ–Iᵉʳ siècle av. J.-C.* Paris.

Jacoby, F. 1912. 'Harmodios von Lepreon', *RE* 7: 2379.

Jacopi, G. 1932. 'Il tempio e il teatro di Apollo Eretimio', *ClRh* 2: 77–116.

Jacottet, A.-F. 1990. 'Le lierre de la liberté', *ZPE* 80: 150–6.

2003. *Choisir Dionysos: Les associations dionysiaques ou la face cachée du dionysisme*, 2 vols. Zurich.

Jacquemin, A. 1999. *Offrandes monumentales à Delphes*. BÉFAR 304. Paris.

2007. 'Étoliens, Antigonides et Attalides à Delphes. De l'utilité de l'histoire et du mythe quand il s'agit d'occuper l'espace et d'affirmer son pouvoir', in F.-H. Massa-Pairault and G. Sauron, eds. *Images et modernité hellénistiques*. Collection de l'École française de Rome 390. Rome. 103–11.

Jacquemin, A., Mulliez, D. and Rougemont, G. 2012. *Choix d'inscriptions de Delphes, traduites et commentées*. Études Épigraphiques 5. Athens.

Jameson, M. 1971. 'Sophocles and the Four Hundred', *Historia* 20: 541–68.

1982. 'The Leasing of Land in Rhamnous', in *Studies in Attic Epigraphy, History and Topography: Presented to Eugene Vanderpool*. Hesperia Supplement 19. 66–74.

2004. 'Troizen and Halikarnassos in the Hellenistic Era', in S. Isager and P. Pedersen, eds. *The Salmakis Inscription and Hellenistic Halikarnassos*. Aarhus. 93–107.

2014. *Cults and Rites in Ancient Greece: Essays on Religion and Society*. Cambridge.

Jameson, M., Jordan, D. and Kotansky, R. 1993. *A Lex Sacra from Selinous*. Durham.

Jamot, P. 1895. 'Fouilles de Thespies', *BCH* 19: 311–85.

Janko, R. 2011. *Philodemus, On Poems, Books 3–4, with the Fragments of Aristotle, On Poets*. Oxford.

Jeammet, V. 2010. 'Origin and Diffusion of the Tanagra Figurines', in V. Jeammet, ed. *Tanagras: Figurines for Life and Eternity. The Musée du Louvre's Collection of Greek Figurines*. Valencia. 4–11.

Jebb, R. 1905. *Bacchylides: the Poems and Fragments*. Cambridge.

Jeffery, L. H. 1990. *The Local Scripts of Archaic Greece: A Study of the Origin of the Greek Alphabet and Its Development from the Eighth to the Fifth Centuries BC.* 2nd edn with supplement by A. W. Johnston. Oxford.

Jeppesen, K. 2004. 'À propos of the List of Colonizers in the Salmakis Inscription: Was Maussollos or his Mythological Namesake Referred to in Lines 35–36?', in S. Isager and P. Pedersen, eds. *The Salmakis Inscription and Hellenistic Halikarnassos.* Aarhus. 89–91.

Jeppesen, K. and Luttrell, A. 1986. *The Mausolleion at Halikarnassos*, vol. 2: *The Written Sources and their Archaeological Background.* Aarhus.

Johnston, S. I. 1999. *Restless Dead: Encounters Between the Living and the Dead in Ancient Greece.* Berkeley.

Jones, C. P. 1966. 'Towards a Chronology of Plutarch's Works', *JRS* 56: 61–74.

1999. *Kinship Diplomacy in the Ancient World.* Cambridge, MA.

Jones, N. F. 1987. *Public Organization in Ancient Greece: A Documentary Study.* Philadelphia.

1999. *The Associations of Classical Athens: The Responses to Democracy.* New York and Oxford.

2004. *Rural Athens Under the Democracy.* Philadelphia.

Jones, W. H. S. 1923. *Hippocrates*, vol. 1. Cambridge, MA and London.

Jordan, D. 1985. 'A Survey of Greek *Defixiones* Not Included in the Special *Corpora*', *GRBS* 26: 151–97.

2007. 'An Opisthographic Lead Tablet from Sicily with a Financial Document and a Curse Concerning *Choregoi*', in P. Wilson, ed. *The Greek Theatre and Festivals: Documentary Studies.* Oxford. 335–50.

Jordan, D. and Curbera, J. 2008. 'A Lead Curse Tablet in the National Archaeological Museum, Athens', *ZPE* 166: 135–50.

Jost, M. 1985. *Sanctuaires et cultes d'Arcadie.* Paris.

Joyce, L. B. 2001. 'Dirce Disrobed', *CA* 20: 221–38.

Jucker, I. 1963. 'Frauenfest in Korinth', *AntK* 6: 47–61.

Judeich, W. 1898. 'Skepsis', in *Beiträge zur alten Geschichte und Geographie: Festschrift für Heinrich Kiepert.* Berlin. 225–40.

1931. *Topographie von Athen*[2]. Munich.

Jurriaans-Helle, G. 1986. 'Apollo and the Deer on Attic Black-Figure Vases', in H. A. G. Brijder, A. A. Drukker and C. W. Neeft, eds. *Enthousiasmos: Essays on Greek and Related Pottery Presented to J. M. Hemelrijk.* Amsterdam. 111–20.

Kaibel, G. 1878. *Epigrammata Graeca ex lapidibus conlecta.* Berlin.

1888. 'Scenische Aufführungen in Rhodos', *Hermes* 23: 268–78.

1899. *Comicorum Graecorum Fragmenta* I.1. Berlin.

1907. 'Epicharmos 2', *RE* 6.1: 34–41.

Kakavogianni, O. ed. 2003. *Αρχαιολογικές έρευνες στην Μερέντα Μαρκοπούλου, στον χώρο κατασκευής του νέου Ιπποδρόμου και του Ολυμπιακού Ιππικού Κέντρου.* Athens.

2009a. 'Τοπογραφία του αρχαίου δήμου Μυρρινούντος', in V. Vassilopoulou and S. Katsarou-Tzeveleki, eds. *Από τα Μεσόγεια στον Αργοσαρωνικό: Β' Εφορεία Προϊστορικών και Κλασικών Αρχαιοτήτων, το έργο μιας δεκαετίας 1994–2003. Proceedings of the Symposium, Athens, 18–20 December 2003.* Athens and Markopoulo. 47–78.

2009b. 'Αρχαίες οδοί στα νότια και δυτικά Μεσόγεια και τη Λαυρεωτική', in M. Korres, ed. *Αττικής οδοί: Αρχαίοι δρόμοι της Αττικής.* Athens. 182–97.

Kakavogianni, O. and Anetakis, M. 2012. 'Les agoras commerciales des dèmes antiques de la Mésogée et de la région du Laurion', in V. Chankowski and P. Karvonis, eds. *Tout vendre, tout acheter: Structures et équipements des marchés antiques.* Bordeaux and Athens. 185–99.

Kakavogianni, O., Argyropoulos, B., Anetakis, M., Kontopanagou, M. and Sklavos, M. 2009. 'Δημόσια κτίρια, μικρά ιερά και οδοί πέριξ του αρχαίου ναού στη Μερέντα', in V. Vassilopoulou and S. Katsarou-Tzeveleki, eds. *Από τα Μεσόγεια στον Αργοσαρωνικό. Β΄ Εφορεία Προϊστορικών και Κλασικών Αρχαιοτήτων. Το έργο μιας δεκαετίας 1994–2003. Proceedings of the Symposium, Athens, 18–20 December 2003*. Athens and Markopoulo. 103–26.

Kakavogianni, O. and Galiatsatou, P. 2009. 'Από τα αρχαία νεκροταφεία στα Μεσόγεια. Ο αρχαίος δήμος της Όης. Αττική κεραμική από το νεκροταφείο της Όης στο Κορωπί: οικόπ. Κ. Τούλα', in V. Vassilopoulou and S. Katsarou-Tzeveleki, eds. *Από τα Μεσόγεια στον Αργοσαρωνικό. Β΄ Εφορεία Προϊστορικών και Κλασικών Αρχαιοτήτων. Το έργο μιας δεκαετίας 1994–2003. Proceedings of the Symposium, Athens, 18–20 December 2003*. Athens and Markopoulo. 399–406.

Kalogeropoulos, K. 2013. *Το Ιερό της Αρτέμιδος Ταυροπόλου στις Αλές Αραφηνίδες (Λούτσα)*, 2 vols. Athens.

Kalogeropoulou, A. 1986. 'Fragment from a Decree of an Attic Deme', *AW* 13: 3–5.

Kaltsas, N. 2001. *Εθνικό Αρχαιολογικό Μουσείο. Τα Γλυπτά*. Athens.

    2004. *ΑΓΩΝ. Κατάλογος έκθεσης στο Εθνικό Αρχαιολογικό Μουσείο 15 Ιουλίου - 31 Οκτωβρίου 2004*. Athens.

Kapetanios, A. *forthcoming*. '"Thorikos" Theatre: Retaining Walls – Retaining Chronologies?', in *Proceedings of the Symposium Thorikos 1963–2013: 50 Years of Belgian Excavations: Evaluation and Perspectives, Athens 7–8 October 2013*.

Kapparis, K. 1999. *Apollodoros 'Against Neaira' [D. 59]*. Berlin and New York.

Käppel, L. 1989. 'Das Theater von Epidauros. Die mathematische Grundidee des Gesamtentwurfs und ihr möglicher Sinn', *JdI* 104: 83–106.

    1992. *Paian: Studien zur Geschichte einer Gattung*. Berlin and New York.

Karadedos, G. 1986. 'Τὸ Ἑλληνιστικὸ θέατρο τοῦ Δίου', in *Ancient Macedonia IV: Papers Read at the Fourth International Symposium held in Thessaloniki, September 21–25, 1983*. Thessaloniki. 325–40.

    2005. 'Ένα αυτοματοποιημένο θέατρο στην υπερεσία των θεατρικών αγώνων στο Δίον', *ΑΕΜΘ* 19: 381–90.

    2012a. 'Το στάδιο του αρχαίου Δίου', in P. Adam-Veleni, ed. *Αρχαία Θέατρα της Μακεδονίας*. Diazoma 3. Athens. 63–72.

    2012b. 'Το ελληνιστικό θέατρο του Δίου', in P. Adam-Veleni, ed. *Αρχαία Θέατρα της Μακεδονίας*. Diazoma 3. Athens. 73–89.

Karadima, C., Zambas, C., Chatzidakis, N., Thomas, G. and Doudoumi, E. 2015. 'The Ancient Theatre at Maroneia', in R. Frederiksen, E. Gebhard and A. Sokolicek, eds. *The Architecture of the Ancient Greek Theatre*. Athens. 253–64.

Karapanagiotou, A. B. 2001. 'Ανασκαφικές εργασίες στο αρχαίο θέατρο Μεγαλόπολης 1995–1997: πρώτες επιτιμήσεις', in V. Mitsopoulos-Leon, C. Schauer and W. Gauss, eds. *Forschungen in der Peloponnese. Akten des Symposions anlässlich der Feier "100 Jahre Österreichisches Archäologisches Institut Athen." Athen 5.3–7.3.1998*. Athens. 331–42.

Karasev, A. and Levi, O. 1958. 'Ольвийская Агора (по раскопкам 1946–1947 гг.)', *SA* 4: 127–43.

Karassava-Tsilingiri, F. D. 2007. 'Παρατηρήσεις στο Χορηγικό Μνημείο του Αγνία στο Ικάριον Αττικής', delivered at the: Ανακοίνωση στο Α΄ Διεπιστημονικό Συνέδριο για την ιστορία των Δομικών Κατασκευών (Ξάνθη 29 Νοεμβρίου – 1η Δεκεμβρίου 2007).

Karatzeni, P. 1982. 'Οδός Τσακάλωφ (οικόπεδο Λιόγκα-Μηλιώνη)', *ArchDelt* 37 B: 263.

Karjaka, A. V. 2008. 'The Defense Wall in the Northern Part of the Lower City of Olbia Pontike', in P. G. Bilde and J. H. Petersen, eds. *Meetings of Cultures in the Black Sea Region: Between Conflict and Coexistence*. Aarhus. 163–80.

Karlsson, I. 1996. 'The Altar of Hieron at Syracuse. A Discussion of its Function', *OpRom* 21: 83–7.

Karousos, C. 1973. *Rhodos: History, Monuments, Art.* Athens.

Karouzou, S. 1968. *National Archaeology Museum: Collection of Sculpture.* Athens.

Kassel, R. 1973. 'Kritische und exegetische Kleinigkeiten IV', *RhM* 116: 97–112.

Kaster, R. 1988. *Guardians of Language: The Grammarian and Society in Late Antiquity.* Berkeley, Los Angeles and London.

Kattoula, T. 2017. 'Funerary Stele of an Actor Holding a Mask', in A. Chaniotis, N. Kaltsas and I. Mylonopoulos, eds. *A World of Emotions*: *Ancient Greece, 700 BC-200 AD.* New York.

Kaza-Papageorgiou, C. 1993. 'Οδός Ρώμα, πάροδος Ηγησιπύλης (οικόπεδο Αφών Ν. Λουράντου, Ο.Τ. 272)', *ArchDelt* 48 B: 67–70.

　2005. 'Άλιμος: Συμβολή των οδών Κυθηρίων, Ρόδων, Κυβέλης, και Χλόης (Ο.Τ. 236Α, οικόπεδο Γ. Βλάχου)', *ArchDelt* 60 B 2: 245.

　2006. *Alimos: A Greek–English Edition of the City's History.* Athens.

　2016. *The Ancient City Road and the Metro Beneath Vouliagmenis Avenue.* Athens.

Keaney, J. 1967. 'New Fragments of Greek Authors in Codex Marc. Gr. 444', *TAPA* 98: 205–19.

Kearns, E. 1989. *The Heroes of Attica.* BICS Supplement 57. London.

Keller, D. R. and Wallace, M. B. 1988. 'The Canadian Karystia Project: Two Classical Farmsteads', *EchCl* 32: 151–7.

Kellogg, D. L. 2013. *Marathon Fighters and Men of Maple: Ancient Acharnai.* Oxford.

Kennell, N. M. 1995. *The Gymnasium of Virtue: Education and Culture in Ancient Sparta.* Chapel Hill and London.

Kenzler, U. 1999. *Studien zur Entwicklung und Struktur der griechischen Agora in archaischer und klassischer Zeit.* Frankfurt.

Kerkhecker, A. 1991. 'Zum neuen hellenistischen Weihepigramm aus Pergamon', *ZPE* 86: 27–34.

　1999. *Callimachus' Book of Iambi.* Oxford.

Kerkhof, R. 2001. *Dorische Posse, Epicharm und attische Komödie.* Munich and Leipzig.

Kern, O. 1890. 'Die boiotische Kabiren', *Hermes* 25: 1–16.

Kimmel-Clauzet, F. 2013. *Morts, tombeaux et cultes des poètes grecs.* Bordeaux.

Kirigin, B., Johnston, A., Vucetic, M. and Lusic, Z. 2009. 'Palagruza – The Island of Diomedes – and Notes on Ancient Greek Navigation in the Adriatic', in S. Forenbaher, ed. *A Connecting Sea: Maritime Interaction in Adriatic Prehistory.* Oxford. 137–54.

Kleiner, G., Hommel, P. and Müller-Wiener, W. 1967. *Panionion und Melie.* Berlin.

Klimek-Winter, R. 1993. *Andromedatragödien: Sophokles, Euripides, Livius Andronikos, Ennius, Accius.* Stuttgart.

Knoepfler, D. 1978. 'Epigraphisch-topographische Arbeiten', *ArchDelt* 33 B: 130.

　1991. *La vie de Ménédème d'Erétrie de Diogène Laërce: Contribution à l'histoire et la critique du texte des 'Vies des philosophes'.* Basel.

　1992. 'Sept années de recherche sur l'épigraphie de la Béotie (1985–1991)', *Chiron* 22: 411–503.

　1995. 'Les relations des cités eubéennes avec Antigone Gonatas et la chronologie delphique au début de l'époque étolienne', *BCH* 119: 137–59.

　1997. 'Le territoire d'Erétrie et l'organisation politique de la cité (*dêmoi, chôroi, phylai*)', in M. H. Hansen, ed. *The Polis as an Urban Centre and as a Political Community.* Copenhagen. 352–449.

　1998. 'Le héros Narkittos et le système tribal d'Erétrie', in M. Bats and B. d'Agostino, eds. *Euboica: L'Eubea e la presenza euboica in Chalcidica e in Occidente. Atti del Convegno Internazionale di Napoli 13–16 novembre 1996.* Centre Jean Bérard vol. 16. *AION ArchStAnt* 12. Naples. 105–8.

2001a. *Décrets érétriens de proxénie et de citoyenneté*. Lausanne.

2001b. 'Loi d'Erétrie contre la tyrannie et l'oligarchie (1ère partie)', *BCH* 125: 195–238.

2007. 'Béotie-Eubée', *RÉG (BE)* 120: 665–86.

2010a. *La patrie de Narcisse: Un héros mythique enraciné dans le sol et dans l'histoire d'une cité grecque*. Paris.

2010b. 'Les agonothètes de la Confédération d'Athéna Ilias. Une interprétation nouvelle des données épigraphiques et ses conséquences pour la chronologie des émissions monétaires du Koinon', *Studi ellenistici* 24: 33–62.

2014. 'ΕΧΘΟΝΔΕ ΤΑΣ ΒΟΙΩΤΙΑΣ: The Expansion of the Boeotian Koinon towards Central Euboia in the Early Third Century BC', in N. Papazarkadas, ed. *The Epigraphy and History of Boeotia: New Finds, New Prospects*. Leiden. 68–94.

Knoepfler, D. and Ackermann, G. 2012. '*Phulè Admètis*: Un nouveau document sur les institutions et les cultes de l'Éretriade trouvé dans les fouilles de l'École Suisse d'Archéologie en Grèce', *CRAI*: 905–49.

Knoepfler, D. and Schefold, K. 1976. 'Forschungen in Eretria 1974 und 1975', *AntK* 19: 51–8.

Köhler, U. 1872. 'Der Areopag in Athen', *Hermes* 6: 92–112.

Kolb, F. 1981. *Agora und Theater, Volks- und Festversammlung*. Berlin.

Kolonas, D. L., Stavropoulou-Gatsi, M., and Stamatis, G. 2009. *Τα αρχαία θέατρα της Αιτωλοακαρνανίας*. Diazoma 2. Athens.

Kolonia, R. 2013a. 'Μουσικά και θεατρικά δρώμενα στους Δελφούς', in R. Kolonia, ed. *Αρχαία θέατρα της Στερεάς Ελλάδας*. Diazoma 7. Athens. 113–30.

2013b. 'Η κατασκευή του θεάτρου', in R. Kolonia, ed. *Αρχαία θέατρα της Στερεάς Ελλάδας*. Diazoma 7. Athens. 131–45.

Konecny, A. L., Aravantinos, V. and Marchese, R. 2013. *Plataiai: Archäologie und Geschichte einer boiotischen Polis*. Österreichisches Archäologisches Institut, Sonderschriften 48. Vienna.

Konecny, A. L., Boyd, M. J., Marchese, R. T. and Aravantinos, V. 2008. 'Plataiai in Boiotia: A Preliminary Report on Geophysical and Field Surveys Conducted in 2002–2005', *Hesperia* 77: 43–71.

2012. 'The Urban Scheme of Plataiai in Boiotia: Report on the Geophysical Survey, 2005–2009', *Hesperia* 81: 93–140.

Konecny, A. L., Boyd, M. J. and Whitbread, I. 1999. 'Der Plataiai Survey: Die Kampagne 1998', *ÖJh* 67: 41–52.

Konstan, D., Clay, D., Glad, C. E., Thom, J. C. and Ware, J. 1998. *Philodemus On Frank Criticism*. Atlanta.

Konstantakos, I. M. 2011. 'Ephippos' *Geryones*: A Comedy between Myth and Folklore', *ActaArchHung* 51: 223–46.

2012. '*"My Kids for Sale"*: The Megarian's Scene in Aristophanes' *Acharnians* (729–835) and Megarian Comedy', *Logeion* 2: 121–66.

2015. 'Tendencies and Variety in Middle Comedy', in S. Chronopoulos and C. Orth, eds. *Fragmente einer Geschichte der griechischen Komödie*. Studia Comica 5. Heidelberg. 159–98.

Kontoleon, N. 1952. 'Νέαι ἐπιγραφαὶ περὶ τοῦ Ἀρχιλόχου ἐκ Πάρου', *ArchEph* 91: 32–95.

Korres, C. J. and Tomlinson, R. A. 2002. 'Sphettia Hodos. Part of the Road to Kephale and Sounion', in H.-R. Goette, ed. *Ancient Roads in Greece: Proceedings of a Symposium Organized by the Cultural Association Aigeas (Athens) and the German Archaeological Institute (Athens) with the Support of the German School at Athens, November 23, 1998*. Hamburg. 43–60.

Korres, M. ed. 2009. *Αττικής οδοί. Αρχαίοι δρόμοι της Αττικής*. Athens.

Körte, A. 1893. 'Archäologische Studien zur alten Komödie', *JdI* 8: 61–93.

1894. 'Eine böotsche Vase mit burkesker Darstellung', *AM* 19: 346–50.

1902. 'Ein Gesetz des Redners Lykurgos', *RhM* 57: 625–7.

1921. 'Komödie', *RE* 11: 1207–75.

1928. 'Maison', *RE* 13.1: 609.

1931. 'Susarion', *RE* 4 A: 973–4.

1935. Review of J. Kirchner, *Inscriptiones Graecae II, III. Editio minor*, *Gnomon* 11: 625–41.

1937. 'Tolynos', *RE* 29: 1694.

1941. 'Phormis', *RE* 20: 540–1.

Koshelenko, G. A. 1984. *Античные Государства Северного Причерноморья.* Moscow.

Kossatz-Deissmann, A. 1978. *Dramen des Aischylos auf westgriechischen Vasen.* Mainz am Rhein.

1980. 'Telephus travestitus', in H. A. Cahn and E. Simon, eds. *Tainia: Festschrift für Roland Hampe*, 2 vols. Mainz. 281–90.

Koster, W. J. W. 1975. *Prolegomena de Comoedia.* Scholia in Aristophanem, Part I, fasc. I A. Groningen.

Kotlińska-Toma, A. 2015. *Hellenistic Tragedy: Texts, Translations and a Critical Survey.* Bloomsbury Classical Studies Monographs. London.

Koukouli-Chrysanthaki, C. and Karadedos, G. 2012. 'Το αρχαίο θέατρο των Φιλίππων', in P. Adam-Veleni, ed. *Αρχαία Θέατρα της Μακεδονίας.* Diazoma 3. Athens. 193–217.

Koumanoudes, S. A. 1874. 'Ἐπιγραφὴ Ἀττικῆς ἀνέκδοτος', *Athenaion* 3: 687–90.

1877a. 'Ἄλλαι ἐπιγραφαί', *Athenaion* 6: 157–60.

1877b. 'Ἐπιγαφαί εκ του Ασκληπιείου και των πέριξ τόπων', *Athenaion* 6: 127–48, 265–82, 367–85, 474–91.

Kourinou, E. 2000. *Σπάρτη. Συμβολή στην μνημειακή τοπογραφία της.* Athens.

Kourinou-Pikoula, E. 1992–1998. 'Μνᾶμα γεροντείας', *Horos* 10–12: 259–76.

Kouroniotes, K. 1897. 'Ἐπιγραφαί Ἐρετρίας', *ArchEph*: 143–63.

Kourou, N. 2005. *Τήνος, ιστορία και πολιτισμός.* Tenos.

2007. 'Archaeological Foreword', in L. M. Castelnuovo, *Tenos in epoca arcaica e classica.* Macerata. 17–31.

Kourtzellis, I. 2013. 'The Ancient Theatre', in Z. Myroyianni, ed. *Mytilene: Unique Approaches.* Lesbos. 22–5.

Koutsogiannis, D. 1984. *Παληά Βουλιαγμένη.* Vouliagmeni.

Kowalzig, B. 2005. 'Mapping out *Communitas*: Performances of *Theoria* in their Sacred and Political Context', in J. Elsner and I. Rutherford, eds. *Pilgrimage in Graeco-Roman and Early Christian Antiquity: Seeing the Gods.* Oxford. 41–72.

2007. *Singing for the Gods: Performances of Myth and Ritual in Archaic and Classical Greece.* Oxford.

2008. 'Nothing to Do With Demeter? Theatre and Society in the Greek West', in M. Revermann and P. Wilson, eds. *Performance, Iconography, Reception: Studies in Honour of Oliver Taplin.* Oxford. 128–57.

2013. 'Dancing Dolphins on the Wine-Dark Sea: Dithyramb and Social Change in the Archaic Mediterranean', in B. Kowalzig and P. Wilson, eds. *Dithyramb in Context.* Oxford. 31–58.

Krauss, F. 1973. *Das Theater von Milet: Das hellenistische Theater. Der römische Zuschauerbau, Milet IV, 1.* Berlin.

Krausskopf, I. 2012. 'Bilder griechischer Feste', *ThesCRA* 7: 78–125.

Kreeb, M. 2010. Review of S. Agelidis 2009, *Choregische Weihgeschenke*, *GFA* 13: 1205–29.

Krevans, N. 2011. 'Callimachus' Philology', in B. Acosta-Hughes, L. Lehnus and S. Stephens, eds. *Brill's Companion to Callimachus.* Leiden. 118–33.

Krinzinger, F. 2003. 'Il teatro di Velia', in G. Greco, ed. *Elea-Velia: Le nuove ricerche*. Naples. 21–27.
2006. 'Velia. Architettura e urbanistica', *Atti Taranto* 45: 157–92.

Krinzinger, F. and Gassner, V. 1997. 'Velia – neue Forschungen auf der Akropolis', *ÖJh* 66: 229–52.

Kroll, J. H. 1972. *Athenian Bronze Allotment Plates*. Cambridge, MA.

Kroll, W. 1919. 'Kallisthenes 2', *RE* 10: 1674–726.

Kromayer, J. 1907. *Antike Schlachtfelder in Griechenland: Bausteine zu einer antiken Kriegs-geschichte*, vol. 2: *Die hellenistisch-römische Periode: von Kynoskephalae bis Pharsalos*. Berlin.

Krumeich, R. 2002. '"Euaion ist schön". Zur Rühmung eines zeitgenössischen Schauspielers auf attischen Symposiengefäßen', in S. Moraw and E. Nölle, eds. *Die Geburt des Theaters in der griechischen Antike*. Mainz. 141–5.

Kryzhitskiy, S. D. 2005. 'Olbia and the Scythians in the Fifth Century BC: The Scythian "Protector-ate"', in D. Braund, ed. *Scythians and Greeks: Cultural Interactions in Scythia, Athens and the Early Roman Empire (sixth century BC – first century AD)*. Exeter. 123–30.

Kühner, R. and Blass, F. 1892. *Ausführliche Grammatik der griechischen Sprache*[3], vol. 1 part 2. Hannover.

Kuiper, W. E. J. 1936. *Grieksche Origineelen en Latijnsche Navolgingen zes Komedies van Menander bij Terentius en Plautus*. Amsterdam.

Kurke, L. 2005. 'Choral Lyric as "Ritualisation": Poetic Sacrifice and the Poetic *Ego* in Pindar's Sixth Paean', *CA* 24: 81–130.

Kussmaul, P. 1969. *Synthekai: Beiträge zur Geschichte des attischen Obligationenrechts*. Diss. Basel.

Kyle, D. G. 1993. *Athletics in Ancient Athens*[2]. Leiden.
2015. *Sport and Spectacle in the Ancient World*[2]. Chichester.

Kyparissis, N. and Peek, W. 1941. 'Attische Urkunden', *AM* 66: 218–39.

Kyriazi, O. 2013. 'Αρχαίο θέατρο της Χαιρώνειας', in R. Kolonia, ed. *Αρχαία θέατρα της Στερεάς Ελλάδας*. Diazoma 7. Athens. 69–78.

Kyriazi, O., Kitsou, G. and Bilis, T. 2013. 'Το αρχαίο θέατρο Ορχομενού Βοιωτίας', in R. Kolonia, ed. *Αρχαία θέατρα της Στερεάς Ελλάδας*. Diazoma 7. Athens. 79–91.

Labarre, G. 1996. *Les Cités de Lesbos aux époques hellénistique et impériale*. Paris.

Lacroix, M. 1914. 'Les Architectes et les entrepreneurs à Délos de 314 à 240', *RPhil* 38: 303–26.

Lagona, S. 1993. 'Kyme Eolica', in G. Pugliese Caratelli, ed. *Arslantepe, Hierapolis, Iasos, Kyme: scavi archeologici italiani in Turchia*. Venice. 248–301.
2007. 'Kyme 2004', *Kazı Sonuçları Toplantısı* 28.1: 9–14.

Lalonde, G. 2006. '*IG* I[3] 1055 B and the Boundary of Melite and Kollytos', *Hesperia* 75: 83–119.

Lamagna, G. 2000. 'Terracotte di argomento teatrale da Adrano', *SicArch* 98: 221–46.

Lamb, W. 1924. *Plato*, vol. 2: *Laches. Protagoras. Meno. Euthydemus*. Cambridge, MA and London.

Lambert, S. D. 1993. *The Phratries of Attica*. Ann Arbor.
1997. *Rationes Centesimarum: Sales of Public Land in Lykourgan Athens*. Archaia Hellas 3. Amsterdam.
1998. *The Phratries of Attica*[2]. Ann Arbor.
2000. 'The Sacrificial Calendar of the Marathonian Tetrapolis', *ZPE* 130: 43–70.
2002. 'The Sacrificial Calendar of Athens', *BSA* 97: 353–99.
2003. '*IG* II[2] 410: An Erasure Reconsidered', in D. Jordan and J. Traill, eds. *Lettered Attica: A Day of Attic Epigraphy*. Athens and Toronto. 56–67.
2004. 'Athenian State Laws and Decrees, 352/1–322/1: I. Decrees Honouring Athenians', *ZPE* 150: 85–120.

2008. 'Polis and Theatre in Lykourgan Athens: The Honorific Decrees', in A. P. Matthaiou and I. Polinskaya, eds. *Μικρὸς ἱερομνήμων. Μελέτες εἰς μνήμην Michael H. Jameson*. Athens. 53–85.

2010. 'A Polis and its Priests: Athenian Priesthoods Before and After Pericles' Citizenship Law', *Historia* 59: 143–75.

2014. 'Notes on Inscriptions of the Marathonian Tetrapolis', *AIO Papers* no. 1: 1–11.

Lambert, S. D. and Blok, J. 2009. 'The Appointment of Priests in Attic Gene', *ZPE* 169: 95–121.

Lambrinoudakis, V. K. and Kazolias, E. 2006. 'Το έργο της Επιτροπής Συντήρησης Μνημείων Επιδαύρου στο θέατρο της αρχαίας Πόλης της Επιδαύρου', in V. K. Lambrinoudakis, L. Kolonas and D. Hardy, eds. *Το Έργο των Επιστημονικών Επιτροπών Αναστήλωσης. Συντήρησης και Ανάδειξης Μνημείων*. Athens. 59–69.

Lampaki, A. 2012. *Τα αρχαία ελληνικά θέατρα ως χώρος ίδρυσης γλυπτών και επιγραφών*. PhD Diss. University of Ioannina.

2015. 'Εικόνες Διονύσου και θεατρικός χώρος στα κλασικά και ελληνιστικά χρόνια', in C. Kyriakos, ed. *Το αρχαίο ελληνικό θέατρο και η πρόσληψή του Πρακτικά του Δ΄ Πανελλήνιου Θεατρολογικού Συνεδρίου*. Patras. 71–92.

Lanérès, N. 2012a. 'La dédicace du "trone" d'Aléa *SEG* 46, 400, nouvelle lecture', *RÉG* 125: 715–25.

2012b. 'La notion de l'ἄγαλμα dans les inscriptions grecques, des origines à la fin du classicisme', *Métis* 10: 137–73.

Langdon, M. 1985. 'Hymettiana I', *Hesperia* 54: 257–70.

2000. 'The Quarries of Peiraieus', *ArchDelt* 55 A: 235–50.

Laqueur, W. 1927. 'Sosibios 2', *RE* 3 A: 1146–9.

Laronde, A. 1987. *Cyrène et la Libye hellénistique: Libykai Historiai*. Paris.

Larson, J. 2017. 'Venison for Artemis? The Problem of Deer Sacrifice', in S. Hitch and I. Rutherford, eds. *Animal Sacrifice in Ancient Greece*. Cambridge. 48–62.

Larson, S. L. 2007. *Tales of Epic Ancestry: Boiotian Collective Identity in the Late Archaic and Early Classical Periods*. Historia Einzelschriften 197. Stuttgart.

Lasagni, C. 2004. 'I decreti onorifici dei demi attici a la prassi politica delle realtà locali', in E. Culasso Gastaldi, ed. *La prassi della democrazia ad Atene: Voci di un seminario*. Alessandria. 92–128.

La Torre, G. 2004. 'Il processo di "romanizzazione" della Sicilia: Il caso di Tindari', *Sicilia Antiqua* 1: 111–46.

2006. 'Urbanistica e architettura ellenistica a Tindari, Eraclea Minoa e Finziade: Nuovi dati e prospettive di ricerca', in M. Osanna and M. Torelli, eds. *Sicilia ellenistica, consuetudo italica: Alle origini dell'architettura ellenistica d'Occidente. Spoleto, Complesso monumentale di S. Nicolò, 5–7 novembre 2004*. Rome. 83–95.

Latte, K. 1913. *De saltationibus Graecorum*. Giessen.

1957. 'ΑΣΚΩΛΙΑΣΜΟΣ', *Hermes* 85: 385–91.

Lattermann, H. 1906. 'Inschrift aus Eleusis', *Klio* 6: 140–68.

Lauffer, S. 1959. 'Die Diodordublette XV 38–50 über die Friedenschlusse zu Sparta 374 und 371', *Historia* 8: 315–48.

1976. 'Inschriften aus Boiotien (I)', *Chiron* 6: 11–51.

1980. 'Inschriften aus Boiotien (II)', *Chiron* 10: 161–82.

Launey, M. 1937. 'Le verger d'Héraklès à Thasos', *BCH* 61: 380–409.

Laurenzi, L. 1931. 'Nuovi contributi alla topografia storico-archeologica di Coo', *Historia: Studi storiche per antichità classica* 5: 603–26.

Lauter, H. 1976. Review of F. Krauss 1973, *Das Theater von Milet: Das hellenistische Theater. Der römische Zuschauerbau, Milet IV, 1*, *Gnomon* 48: 57–63.

1993. *Attische Landgemeinden in klassischer Zeit.* Attische Forschungen 4. Marburg.

Lauter, H. and Lauter-Bufe, H. 2004. 'Thersilion und Theater in Megalopolis. Das Bauensemble im Licht neuer Forschungen', *AA*: 135–76.

Lauter-Bufe, H. 1979. 'Das Wehrdorf Lathouresa bei Vari. Ein Beitrag zum Dekeleischen Krieg', *AM* 94: 161–92.

Lavecchia, S. 2000. *Pindari Dithyramborum Fragmenta.* Rome and Pisa.

Lawton, C. L. 1995. *Attic Document Reliefs: Art and Politics in Ancient Athens.* Oxford.

2007. 'Children in Classical Attic Votive Reliefs', in A. Cohen and J. Rutter, eds. *Constructions of Childhood in Ancient Greece and Italy.* Hesperia Supplement 41. Princeton. 41–60.

Lazaridis, D. 1952. 'Ἀνασκαφαὶ καὶ ἔρευναι ἐν Ἀβδήροις', *Prakt*: 260–78.

1960. *Πήλινα εἰδώλια Ἀβδήρων.* Athens.

1966. 'Ἀρχαιότητες καὶ μνημεῖα Ἀνατολικῆς Μακεδονίας', *ArchDelt* 21 B 2: 359–65.

1971. *Ἄβδηρα καὶ Δίκαια.* Ancient Greek Cities 6. Athens.

Leake, W. M. 1835. *Travels in Northern Greece*, 4 vols. London.

1841. *The Topography of Athens with Some Remarks on its Antiquities*[2]. London.

Le Bas, P. 1847. *Voyage archéologique en Grèce et en Asie Mineure: Fait par ordre du Gouvernement Français pendant les années 1843 et 1844*, vol. 2. Paris.

1856. 'Décades épigraphiques', *RA* 13: 1–11.

Lebek, W. D. 1990. 'Neue Phalaikeen aus Pergamon', *ZPE* 82: 297–8.

Lefèvre, E. 1991. 'Curculio oder der Triumph der Edazität', in E. Lefèvre, E. Stärk and G. Vogt-Spira, *Plautus barbarus: Sechs Kapitel zur Originalität des Plautus.* Tübingen. 71–106.

Lefkowitz, M. 1981. *Lives of the Greek Poets.* London.

1991. *First-Person Fictions: Pindar's Poetic 'I'.* Oxford.

Legrand, P. E. 1917. *The New Greek Comedy.* Translated by J. Loeb. London.

Le Guen, B. 1997. 'Tribulations d'artistes pergaméniens en 129 av. J.-C.', in B. Le Guen, ed. *De la scène aux gradins: Théâtre et représentations dramatiques après Alexandre le Grand.* Pallas 47. Toulouse. 73–96.

2001. 'L'Activité dramatique dans les îles grecques à l'époque hellénistique', *RÉA* 103: 261–98.

2004. 'Le statut professionnel des acteurs grecs à l'époque Hellénistique', in C. Hugoniot, F. Hurlet, and S. Milanezi, eds. *Le statut de l'acteur dans l'Antiquité grecque et romaine.* Tours. 77–106.

2010. 'Les fêtes du théâtre grec à l'époque hellénistique', *RÉG* 123: 495–520.

2014. 'Theatre, Religion, and Politics at Alexander's Travelling Royal Court', in E. Csapo, H.-R. Goette, J. R. Green and P. Wilson, eds. *Greek Theatre in the Fourth Century B.C.* Berlin and Boston. 249–74.

Lehmler, C. 2005. *Syrakus unter Agathokles und Hieron II: Die Verbindung von Kultur und Macht in einer hellenistischen Metropole.* Frankfurt am Main.

Leigh, M. 1998. 'Sophocles at Patavium (fr. 137 Radt)', *JHS* 118: 82–100.

Lennartz, K. 2010. *Iambos: Philologische Untersuchungen zur Geschichte einer Gattung in der Antike.* Wiesbaden.

Lenormant, F. 1862. *Recherches archéologiques à Éleusis: Exécutées dans le cours de l'année 1860 sous les auspices des ministères de l'instruction publique et d'état: Recueil des inscriptions.* Paris.

Leo, F. 1901. *Die griechisch-römische Biographie nach ihrer literarischen Form.* Leipzig.

Leprohon, R. 2007. 'Ritual Drama in Ancient Egypt', in E. Csapo and M. C. Miller, eds. *The Origins of Theater in Ancient Greece and Beyond: From Ritual to Drama.* Cambridge. 259–92.

Lesi, R. 1975–1977. 'Note ad Epicarmo', *MCr* 10–12: 83–90.

Lesky, A. 1972. *Die tragische Dichtung der Hellenen*³. Göttingen.

Le Ven, P. 2014. *The Many-Headed Muse: Tradition and Innovation in Late Classical Greek Lyric Poetry*. Cambridge.

Lewis, D. M. 1962. 'The Federal Constitution of Keos', *BSA* 57: 1–4.

    1984. 'Further Notes on Page, *Further Greek Epigrams*', *JHS* 104: 179–80.

    1985. 'A New Athenian Decree', *ZPE* 60: 108.

    1997. *Selected Papers in Greek and Near Eastern History*. Cambridge.

Lewis, N. 1990. 'The "Ivy of Liberation" Inscription', *GRBS* 31: 197–202.

Libertini, G. 1929. 'I principali problemi intorno all'antico Teatro di Catania', in *Catania: Rivista del Comune* I, no. 2: 9–18.

Lionis, D. 2005. 'Αρχαίες αγροικές στα Μεσόγεια', in G. Steinhauer, O. Apostolopoulou-Kakavogi- anni, M. Platonos-Yiota, D. Skilarnti, A. Pantelidou-Alexiadou, D. Christodoulou, M. Stathi, P. Nezeri, E. Mauromathi and D. Lionis. *Αττικής οδού περιήγηση*. Athens. 191–2.

Lippolis, E., Garaffo, S. and Nafissi, M. 1995. *Taranto: Culti greci in Occidente*, vol. 1. Taranto.

Littré, E. ed. 1840. *Oeuvres complètes d'Hippocrate*, vol. 2. Paris.

Livadiotti, M. 1996. 'Il teatro', in M. Livadiotti and G. Rocco, eds. *La presenza italiana nel Dode- caneso tra il 1912 e il 1948. La ricerca archeologica, la conservazione, le scelte progettuali*. Catania. 156–8.

Livadiotti, M., Caminneci, V. and Caliò, L. 2017. *Agrigento: Nuove ricerche sull'area pubblica centrale*, Rome.

Lloyd-Jones, H. 1999. 'The Pride of Halicarnassus', *ZPE* 124: 1–14.

Lobel, E. 1959. 'List of Plays by Epicharmus', *POxy.* 25: 1–2.

Lohmann, H. 1993. *Atene: Forschungen zu Siedlungs- und Wirtschaftsstruktur des klassischen Atti- ka*, vol. 1. Vienna.

    1998. 'Zur baugeschichtlichen Entwicklung des antiken Theaters: Ein Überblick', in G. Binder, ed. *Das antike Theater: Aspekte seiner Geschichte, Rezeption und Aktualität*. Trier. 191–249.

Lolling, H. G. 1879. 'Inschriften aus Nordgriechenland', *AM* 4: 193–227.

    1889. 'Ἐπιγραφαὶ ἐκ τῆς Ἀκροπόλεως', *ArchDelt* 5: 86–96.

Lolos, G. 2000. 'Σαλαμινιακές έρευνες, 1998–2000. Μέρος Α΄. Το ιερό του Διονύσου υπό το σπήλαιο του Ευριπίδη', *Dodone* 29: 113–65.

    2003. 'Το Σπήλαιο του Ευριπίδη στη Σαλαμίνα: Η προϊστορία του χώρου', in E. Konsola- ki-Giannopoulou, ed. *Αργοσαρωνικός. Πρακτικά 1ου Διεθνούς Συνεδρίου Ιστορίας και Αρχαιολογίας του Αργοσαρωνικού, Πόρος, 26–29 Ιουνίου 1998*. Athens. 85–101.

    2013. 'Νεώτερα πορίσματα από την εξέλιξη της πανεπιστημιακής ανασκαφής Σαλαμίνος', in M. Donka-Toli and S. Oikonomou, eds. *Αρχαιολογικές συμβολές, τόμος Α: Αττική*. Athens. 81–91.

Lolos, Y. 2011. *Land of Sikyon: Archaeology and History of a Greek City-State*. Hesperia Supple- ment 39. Princeton.

    2013. 'Αρχαιολογική έρευνα επιφανείας στην περιοχή της Σικυωνίας', in K. Kissas and W.- D. Niemeier, eds. *The Corinthia and the North-east Peloponnese: Topography and History from Prehistoric Times until the End of Antiquity. Proceedings of the International Conference Organized by the Directorate of Prehistoric and Classical Antiquities, the LZ' Ephorate of Prehistoric and Classical Antiquities and the German Archaeological Institute, Athens, Held at Loutraki, March 26–29, 2009*. Athenaia 4. Munich. 469–78.

Lolos, Y. and Gourley, B. 2011. 'The Town Planning of Hellenistic Sikyon', *AA:* 87–140.

Lomas, K. 1993. *Rome and the Western Greeks, 350 BC–AD 200: Conquest and Acculturation in Southern Italy*. London.

Loomis, W. 1998. *Wages, Welfare Costs, and Inflation in Classical Athens*. Ann Arbor.

Lo Porto, F. 1964. 'Satyrion (Taranto): Scavi e scoperte nel luogo del più antico insediamento laconico in Puglia', *NSc* 18: 177–279.

Lorenz, A. 1864. *Leben und Schriften des Koers Epicharmos: nebst Fragmentensammlung.* Berlin.

Loukopoulou, L. D. 1989. *Contribution à l'histoire de la Thrace propontique.* Athens.

Loukopoulou, L. D., Parissaki, M. G., Psoma, S. and Zournatzi, A. 2005. Ἐπιγραφὲς τῆς Θράκης τοῦ Αἰγαίου μεταξὺ τῶν ποταμῶν Νέστου καὶ Ἕβρου (Νομοὶ Χάνθης, Ῥοδόπης καὶ Ἕβρου). Athens.

Lowe, N. 1998. 'Thesmophoria and Haloa: Myth, Physics and Mysteries', in S. Blundell and M. Williamson, eds. *The Sacred and the Feminine in Ancient Greece.* London and New York. 149–73.

  2007. *Comedy.* Greece and Rome New Surveys in the Classics 37. Cambridge.

  2013. 'Comedy and the Pleiad: Alexandrian Tragedians and the Birth of Comic Scholarship', in E. Bakola, L. Prauscello and M. Telò eds. *Greek Comedy and the Discourse of Genres.* Cambridge. 343–56.

Ludwig, W. 1970. 'Die plautinische Cistellaria und das Verhältnis von Gott und Handlung bei Menander', in E. G. Turner, ed. *Ménandre.* Entretiens sur l'Antiquité Classique 16. Vandoeuvres. 43–110.

Luni, M. 2006a. 'Un demi-siècle de recherches archéologiques à Cyrène', *CRAI*: 2173–98.

  2006b. *Cirene: Atene d'Africa.* Monografie di archeologia libica 28. Rome.

  2010. 'La scoperta a Cirene di un nuovo teatro greco', *Mare Internum* 2: 57–61.

  2011. 'Le nouveau sanctuaire de Déméter et la "Ceinture sacrée" à Cyrène à l'époque royale', *CRAI*: 221–87.

  2013. 'Definire lo spazio sacro a Cirene. L'area del santuario extra-urbano di Demetra', in A. Inglese, ed. *Epigrammata 2: Definire, descrivere, proteggere lo spazio. In ricordo di André Laronde.* Tivoli. 197–230, 424–39.

Luppe, W. 1969. 'Zu einer Choregeninschrift aus ΑΙΞΩΝΑΙ (IG II/III² 3091)', *APF* 19: 147–51.

  1974. 'Nochmals zur Choregeninschrift IG II/III² 3091', *APF* 22: 211–12.

Luraghi, N. 1994. *Tirannidi arcaiche in Sicilia e Magna Grecia da Panezio di Leontini alla caduta dei Dinomenidi.* Florence.

Ma, J. 1997. 'Thémistocle entre cité et empire', *Mètis* 12: 269–93.

  2000. 'The Epigraphy of Hellenistic Asia Minor: A Survey of Recent Research', *AJA* 194: 95–121.

  2006. 'A Gilt Statue for Konon at Erythrai?', *ZPE* 157: 124–6.

  2007. 'A *Horse* from Teos: Epigraphical Notes on the Ionian–Hellespontine Association of Dionysiac Artists', in P. Wilson, ed. *The Greek Theatre and Festivals: Documentary Studies.* Oxford. 215–45.

  2013. *Statues and Cities: Honorific Portraits and Civic Identity in the Hellenistic World.* Oxford.

Maaß, E. 1883. *Analecta Eratosthenica.* Philologische Untersuchungen 6. Berlin.

MacDowell, D. M. 1971. *Aristophanes: Wasps.* Oxford.

  1985. 'Athenian Laws about Choruses', in F. Nieto, ed. *Symposion 1982: Vorträge zur griechischen und hellenistischen Rechtsgeschichte.* Cologne. 65–77.

  2000. *Demosthenes: On the False Embassy (Oration 19).* Oxford.

Mac Góráin, F. 2014. 'The Mixed Blessings of Bacchus in Virgil's Georgics', *Dictynna* 11.

Macgregor Morris, I. 2009. 'Liars, Eccentrics and Visionaries: Early Travellers to Sparta and the Birth of Laconian Archaeology', in W. G. Cavanagh, C. Gallou and M. Georgiadis, eds. *Sparta and Laconia: From Prehistory to Pre-Modern.* British School at Athens Studies 16. London. 387–95.

Mack, W. 2015. *Proxeny and Polis: Institutional Networks in the Ancient Greek World.* Oxford.

Mackil, E. 2014. 'Creating a Common Polity in Boeotia', in N. Papazarkadas, ed. *The Epigraphy and History of Boeotia: New Finds, New Prospects.* Leiden. 45–67.

Maddoli, G. 2007. 'Epigrafi di Iasos. Nuovi supplementi I', *PP* 62: 193–372.

Madella, P. 2015. 'Le rappresentazioni a soggetto teatrale nella ceramica siceliota a figure rosse da Lipari', in M. A. Mastelloni, ed. *Lipára ed il teatro in età tardoclassica ed ellenistica*. Palermo. 5–12.

Magnolo, E. 1995. 'Notazioni numerali nel teatro di Metaponto: Un restauro antico?', *Studi di Antichità* 8.1: 77–90.

Maiuri, A. 1925. *Nuova silloge epigrafica di Rodi e Cos*. Florence.

   1928. 'Topografia monumentale di Rodi', *ClRh* 1: 44–55.

Makres, A. 1992–1998. 'Χορηγικὴ ἐπιγραφὴ Διονυσίων καὶ ἄγνωστη ἀναγραφὴ στὴν ΕΜ 10301 (*IG* II² 3092)', *Horos* 10–12: 61–70.

   1994. *The Institution of the 'Choregia' in Classical Athens*. Diss. Oxford.

   2004. 'The Rediscovery of IG I³ 253–4', in A. P. Matthaiou and G. E. Malouchou, eds. Ἀττικαὶ Ἐπιγραφαί: *Πρακτικὰ συμποσίου εἰς μνήμην Adolf Wilhelm (1864–1950)*. Athens. 123–40.

   2004–2009. 'Ἀναθηματικὴ ἐπιγραφὴ ἀπὸ τὶς Ἀχαρνές', *Horos* 17–21: 143–6.

Makres, A. and Sakka, N. 2010–2013. 'Χορηγικὴ ἐπιγραφὴ Θαργηλίων', *Horos* 22–25: 155–62.

Malkin, I. 1987. *Religion and Colonization in Ancient Greece*. Leiden.

Malouchou, G. E. 2015. 'Τῶν σκηνῶν καὶ τῶν ἐδάφων: Νέα Ἀττικὴ ἐπιγραφὴ τοῦ 4ου αἰ. π.Χ.', in A. Matthaiou and N. Papazarkadas, eds. *ΑΖΩΝ: Studies in Honor of Ronald S. Stroud*. Athens. 187–204.

Malouchou, G. E. and Matthaiou, A. P. 2006. 'Συνοπτικὸς κατάλογος τῶν ἐπιγραφῶν τοῦ Μουσείου Χίου', in G. E. Malouchou and A. P. Matthaiou, eds. *Χιακὸν Συμπόσιον εἰς μνήμην W. G. Forrest*. Athens. 185–252.

Manganaro, G. 2000. 'Kyme e il dinasta Philetairos', *Chiron* 30: 403–14.

Manieri, A. 2009. *Agoni poetico-musicali nella Grecia antica. 1. Beozia*. Testi e commenti 25. Certamina musica graeca 1. Pisa and Rome.

   2015. 'Gare corali ai *Pythia* di Delfi: Filippo di Macedonia e l'agonistica greca', *RCCM* 57: 25–41.

   2016. 'I Soteria di Delfi e gli agoni drammatici in età ellenistica', *QUCC* 113: 65–91.

Manni Piraino, M. 1967. 'Note di epigrafia siceliota', *Kokalos* 13: 194–201.

Mantzourani, E. 1991. 'Coins and Commentary', in J. Cherry, J. Davis and E. Mantzourani, eds. *Landscape Archaeology as Long-Term History: Northern Keos in the Cycladic Islands from Earliest Settlement until Modern Times*. Monumenta Archaeologica 16. Los Angeles. 157–9.

Marchetti, P. 1977. 'À propos de l'archonte delphien de 344/3', *BCH* Supplement 4: 67–89.

Marchiandi, D. 2008. 'Riflessioni in merito allo statuto giuridico di Lemno nel V secolo a.C.', *ASAtene* 86: 11–39.

   2011. *I periboli funerari nell'Attica classica: Lo specchio di una 'borghesia'*. Studi di Archeologia e di Topografia di Atene e dell'Attica 3. Athens and Paestum.

Marconi, C. 2005. 'I *Theoroi* di Eschilo e le antefisse sileniche siceliote', *Sicilia Antiqua* 2: 75–93.

   2012. 'Between Performance and Identity: The Social Context of Stone Theaters in Late Classical and Hellenistic Sicily', in K. Bosher, ed. *Theater Outside Athens: Drama in Greek Sicily and South Italy*. Cambridge. 175–207.

   2014. 'Two New Aulos Fragments from Selinunte: Cult, Music and Spectacle in the Main Urban Sanctuary of a Greek Colony in the West', in A. Bellia, ed. *Musica, culti e riti nell'Occidente Greco*. Pisa and Rome. 105–16.

Marconi, C. and Scahill, D. 2015. 'The "South Building" in the Main Urban Sanctuary of Selinunte: A Theatral Structure?', in R. Frederiksen, E. R. Gebhard and A. Sokolicek, eds. *The Architec-

ture of the Ancient Greek Theatre: Acts of an International Conference at the Danish Institute at Athens 27–30 January 2012. Monographs of the Danish Institute at Athens 17. Aarhus. 279–92.

Marek, C. and Frei, P. 2016. *In the Land of a Thousand Gods: A History of Asia Minor in the Ancient World.* Princeton.

Marengo, S. 2010. 'Iscrizioni da nuovi scavi a Cirene', in M. Luni, ed. *Cirene nell'antichità: Atene d'Africa II.* Monografie di archeologia libica 29. Rome. 139–56.

Marengo, S. and Paci, G. 1998. 'Nuovi frammenti dei conti dei damiurghi', in E. Catani and S. Marengo, eds. *La Cirenaica in età antica: Atti del convegno internazionale di studi, Macerata 18–20 Maggio 1995.* Pisa and Rome. 373–92.

Marginesu, G. 2012. 'χρῆσθαι λίθοις καὶ γῆι in un decreto del demo del Pireo (*SEG* 33.143.1–7)', *ZPE* 180: 153–7.

Mari, M. 1998. 'Le Olimpie Macedoni di Dion tra Archelao e l'età romana', *RivFil* 126: 137–69.

Marino, S. 2010. *Copia/Thurii: Aspetti topografici e urbanistici di una città romana della Magna Grecia.* Paestum.

Markopolis, M. 1892. 'Ἐπιγραφαὶ ἐκ Νάξου', *Ἑστία* 10: 366.

Marshall, C. W. 2001. 'A Gander at the Goose Play', *Theatre Journal* 53: 53–71.

Martano, A. 2012. 'Chamaeleon of Heraclea Pontica: The Sources, Text and Translation', in A. Martano, E. Matelli and D. Mirhady, eds. *Praxiphanes of Mytilene and Chamaeleon of Heraclea: Text, Translation and Discussion.* New Brunswick and London. 157–337.

Martin, R. 1951. *Recherches sur l'agora grecque.* Paris.

Martinelli, M. 2010. 'Una nuova Medea in musica: *P.Louvre* inv. E 10534 e la *Medea* di Carcino', in M. Celentano, ed. *Ricerche di metrica e musica greca per Roberto Pretagostini.* Alessandria. 61–76.

Martorano, F. 1985. 'Il porto e l'*ekklesiasterion* di Reggio nel 344 a.C.: Ricerche di topografia e di architettura antica su una *polis* italiota', *Rivista storica Calabrese* 6: 231–57.

Massaro, F. 2018. *Agoni poetico-musicali nella Grecia antica. 3. Sparta.* Testi e commenti 31. Certamina musica graeca 1. Pisa and Rome.

Mastrokostas, E. 1958. 'Ἀνασκαφὴ τάφων ἐν Ῥαμνοῦντι', *Prakt*: 28–37.

   1961. 'Ἐπιτύμβιοι στῆλαι καὶ ἀνάγλυφα ἐξ Ἀττικῆς καὶ Σαλαμῖνος', *ArchEph*: 9–24.

Mastromarco, G. 2006. 'La paratragodia, il libro, la memoria', in E. Medda, M. Mirto, M. Pattoni, eds. *ΚΩΜΩΔΟΤΡΑΓΩΔΙΑ: Intersezioni del tragico e del comico nel teatro del V secolo.* Pisa. 137–91.

Mastronarde, D. J. 2002. *Euripides: Medea.* Cambridge.

Matthaiou, A. P. 1983. 'Τιμητικὸ Ψήφισμα τοῦ Δήμου τῶν Ναξίων', *Horos* 1: 39–44.

   1990–1991. 'Σῶν', *Horos* 8–9: 179–82.

   1992–1998. 'Αἰξωνικά', *Horos* 10–12: 133–69.

   2009. 'Attic Public Inscriptions of the Fifth Century BC in Ionic Script', in L. Mitchell and L. Rubinstein, eds. *Greek History and Epigraphy: Essays in Honour of P. J. Rhodes.* Swansea. 201–12.

   2013. 'Ναξιακὰ ἐπιγραφικὰ σημειώματα', *Grammateion* 2: 71–80.

Mattingly, H. B. 1990. 'Some Fifth-Century Epigraphical Hands', *ZPE* 83: 110–22.

   1996. *The Athenian Empire Restored: Epigraphic and Historical Studies.* Ann Arbor.

Mayor, A., Colarusso, J. and Saunders, D. 2014. 'Making Sense of Nonsense Inscriptions Associated with Amazons and Scythians on Athenian Vases', *Hesperia* 83: 447–93.

McCabe, D. F. and Brownson, J. V. 1986. *Chios Inscriptions: Texts and Lists.* Princeton.

McCredie, J. R. 1971. 'Hippodamos of Miletos', in D. G. Mitten, J. G. Pedley and J. A. Scott, eds. *Studies Presented to George M. A. Hanfmann*. Mainz. 95–100.

McDonald, W. 1943. *The Political Meeting Places of the Greeks*. Baltimore.

McPhee, I. 2004. 'Classical Pottery from Ancient Corinth: The A.D. Trendall Memorial Lecture 2003', *BICS* 47: 1–21.

Meadows, A. 2013. 'The Ptolemaic League of Islanders', in K. Buraselis, M. Stefanou and D. J. Thompson, eds. *The Ptolemies, the Sea and the Nile: Studies in Waterborne Power*. Cambridge. 19–38.

Meier, L. 2012. *Die Finanzierung öffentlicher Bauten in der hellenistischen Polis*. Berlin.

Meiggs, R. 1963. 'The Crisis of Athenian Imperialism', *HSCP* 67: 1–35.

1972. *The Athenian Empire*. Oxford.

Meineke, A. 1839. *Fragmenta comicorum graecorum*, vol. 1: *Historia critica comicorum Graecorum*. Berlin.

Mendoni, L. 1985–1986. 'Ἀρχαιολογικές ἔρευνες στήν Κέα: Ἀρχαία Καρθαία', *Archaiognosia* 4: 149–84.

1989. 'More Inscriptions from Keos', *ABSA* 84: 289–96.

1990. 'Addenda et corrigenda ad inscriptiones Ceae', in *Ποικίλα*. Meletemata 10. Athens. 287–305.

2009. 'Τιμητικό ψήφισμα από την Καρθαία', in S. Drougou, D. Evgenidou, C. Kritzas, N. Kaltsas, B. Penna, I. Tsourti, M. Galani-Krikou and E. Ralli, eds. *Κερμάτια Φιλίας: Studies in Honour of Ioannis Touratsoglou*, vol. 2. Athens. 71–9.

Meriani, A. 2003. *Sulla musica greca antica: Studi e ricerche*. Naples.

Meritt, B. D. 1936. 'Greek Inscriptions', *Hesperia* 5: 355–430.

1960. 'Greek Inscriptions', *Hesperia* 29: 1–77.

1963. 'Greek Inscriptions', *Hesperia* 32: 1–56.

Meritt, B. D., Wade-Gery, H. T. and McGregor, M. F. 1950. *The Athenian Tribute Lists*, vol. 3. Princeton.

Merkelbach, R. and Stauber, J. 1998. *Steinepigramme aus dem griechischen Osten*, vol. 1: *Die Westküste Kleinasiens von Knidos bis Ilion*. Stuttgart and Leipzig.

Merkouri, C. 2012. 'Η Αμβρακία του Πύρρου και τα θέατρα της Αμβρακίας', in K. I. Soueref, ed. *Αρχαία θέατρα της Ηπείρου*. Diazoma 6. Athens. 144–55.

Merlino, R. and La Mattina, D. 2008. 'Teatro di Heloros (Eloro)', in *Studio tematico della Carta del Rischio del Patrimonio Culturale della Regione Siciliana. I. Parte. Architetture teatrali siciliane di età antica: fase della conoscenza*. Palermo. 127–30.

Merriam, A. 1889. 'Report of Professor Merriam', *Seventh Annual Report of the Management Committee of the American School of Classical Studies at Athens, 1887–1888*. 25–101.

Mertens, D. 1984. Review of L. Polacco and C. Anti 1981, *Il teatro di Siracusa*, *Gymnasium* 91: 263–4.

2004. 'Siracusa e l'architettura del potere. Un schizzo', *Sicilia Antiqua* 1: 29–34.

2006. *Città e monumenti dei Greci d'Occidente*. Rome.

Mertens, D. and De Siena, A. 1982. 'Metaponto: Il teatro–ekklesiasterion', *BdA* 16: 1–60.

Mette, H. J. 1977. *Urkunden dramatischer Aufführungen in Griechenland*. Berlin.

Meyer, E. 1938. 'Phigaleia', *RE* 19: 2065–85.

1939. *Geschichte des Altertums*[3], vol. 4. Stuttgart.

1941. 'Phleius', *RE* 20.1: 269–90.

Meyer, M. 1989. *Die griechischen Urkundenreliefs*. Berlin.

Michel, C. 1900. *Recueil d'Inscriptions Grecques*. Brussels.

Michel, P. 2011. 'Le théâtre de Babylone: Nouveauté urbaine et néologisme en Mésopotamie', in M. Fuchs and B. Dubosson, eds. *Theatra et spectacula: Les grands monuments des jeux dans l'Antiquité*. Études de lettres 1–2. Lausanne. 153–70.

Micheli, M. E. 1987. 'Su di un gruppo di troni con decorazione vegetale', *Boreas* 10: 63–80.

Michelini, A. N. 1989. 'Neophron and Euripides' *Medea* 1056–80', *TAPA* 119: 115–35.

Migeotte, L. 1984. *L'emprunt public dans les cités grecques: Recueil des documents et analyse critique*. Quebec and Paris.

   1992. *Les souscriptions publiques dans les cités grecques*. Geneva.

   1993. 'De la liturgie à la contribution obligatoire: Le financement des Dionysies et les travaux du théâtre à Iasos au IIe siècle avant J.-C.', *Chiron* 23: 269–94.

   1995. 'Finances et constructions publiques', in M. Wörrle and P. Zanker, eds. *Stadtbild und Bürgerbild im Hellenismus: Kolloquium München 24 bis 26 Juni 1993*. Munich. 79–86.

   2010. 'La fondation d'Aristoménès et de Psylla à Corcyre: Dispositions administratives et financières', *Studi ellenistici* 24: 63–9.

   2011. 'Pratiques financières dans un dème attique à la période classique: L'inscription de Plôtheia *IG* I³, 258', in G. Thür, ed. *Symposion 2009: Vorträge zur griechischen und hellenistischen Rechtsgeschichte (Seggau, 25.–30. August 2009)*. Akten der Gesellschaft für Griechische und Hellenistische Rechtsgeschichte 21. Vienna. 53–66.

   2014. *Les Finances des cités grecques aux périodes classique et hellénistique*. Paris.

Mikalson, J. D. 1975. *The Sacred and Civil Calendar of the Athenian Year*. Princeton.

   1977. 'Religion in the Attic Demes', *AJP* 98: 424–35.

   1998. *Religion in Hellenistic Athens*. Berkeley.

Milanezi, S. 2004. *Mémoire civique et comique des concours en l'honneur de Dionysos à Athènes (Vᵉ–IIIᵉ siècles av. J.-C.)*, vol. 1: *Synthèse*, vol. 2: *Choix de documents*. Diss. Paris.

   2007. 'Les Icariens et le dème des Icariens (*IG* II² 1178): À propos de l'identité politique dans un dème attique', in J.-C. Couvenhes and S. Milanezi, eds. *Individus, groupes et politique à Athènes de Solon à Mithradate*. Tours. 241–72.

Milchhöfer, A. 1883. *Erläuterungen zu den Karten von Attika*, vol. 2: *Erläuternder Text*. Berlin.

   1887a. 'Das Heiligtum des Dionysos in Ikaria', *BPW* 7: 770–2.

   1887b. 'Antikenbericht aus Attika', *AM* 12: 81–104, 277–330.

   1888. 'Antikenbericht aus Attika', *AM* 13: 337–62.

   1907. 'Euonymon', *RE* 6.1: 1156–8.

Miles, M. 2015. 'The Vanishing Double Stoa at Thorikos and its Afterlives', in M. Miller, ed. *Autopsy in Athens: Recent Archaeological Research on Athens and Attica*. Oxford. 163–80.

Miller, A. 1973. *Studies in Early Sicilian Epigraphy: An Opisthographic Lead Tablet*. PhD Diss. North Carolina.

Miller, S. G. 1978. 'The Date of the First Pythiad', *CSCA* 11: 127–58.

   2001. *Excavations at Nemea* II: *The Early Hellenistic Stadium*. Berkeley and Los Angeles.

   2004. *Ancient Greek Athletics*. New Haven.

Miller, W. 1888. 'The Theatre of Thoricus, Preliminary Report', *Papers of the American School of Classical Studies at Athens* 4 (1885–1886): 1–10.

Millett, P. 1991. *Lending and Borrowing in Ancient Athens*. Cambridge.

Millino, G. 2000. 'Epicarmo e i Pigmei', *Anemos* 1: 113–50.

   2001. 'Considerazioni sulla monetazione di Anassilao', in L. Braccesi, ed. *Hesperìa 14, Studi sulla grecità di Occidente*. Rome. 105–40.

Millis, B. W. 2014. 'Inscribed Public Records of the Dramatic Contests at Athens: IG II² 2318–2323a and IG II² 2325', in E. Csapo, H.-R. Goette, J. R. Green and P. Wilson, eds. *Greek Theatre in the Fourth Century B.C.* Berlin and Boston. 425–45.

2015. 'Out of Athens: Greek Comedy at the Rural Dionysia and Elsewhere', in S. Chronopoulos and C. Orth, eds. *Fragmente einer Geschichte der griechischen Komödie*. Studia Comica 5. Heidelberg. 228–49.

Millis, B. W. and Olson, S. D. 2012. *Inscriptional Records for the Dramatic Festivals in Athens*. Leiden.

Minì, A. 1979. *Monete di bronzo della Sicilia antica*. Palermo.

Mirone, S. 1918. 'Le monete dell'antica Catana', *RIN* 31: 9–76.

Missalidou-Despotidou, V. 1993. 'A Hellenistic Inscription from Skotoussa (Thessaly) and the Fortifications of the City', *BSA* 88: 187–217.

Mitchell, A. G. 2009. *Greek Vase Painting and the Origins of Visual Humour*. Cambridge.

Mitchell-Boyask, R. 2008. *Plague and the Athenian Imagination: Drama, History, and the Cult of Asclepius*. Cambridge.

Mitsos, M. 1965. 'Χορηγικὴ ἐπιγραφὴ ἐκ Βαρκίζης', *ArchEph* 104: 163–7.

Moggi, M. 2008. 'Fra *apoikia* e *klerouchia*: Il caso di Lemno', in E. Greco and E. Papi, eds. *Hephestia 2000–2006: Atti del Seminario, Siena-Certosa di Pontignano, 28–29 maggio 2007*. Paestum and Athens. 259–70.

Möllendorff, P. von. 2001. 'Frigid Enthusiasts: Lucian on Writing History', *PCPS* 47: 117–40.

Möller, A. 2001. 'The Beginning of Chronography: Hellanicus' *Hiereiai*', in N. Luraghi, ed. *The Historian's Craft in the Age of Herodotus*. Oxford. 241–62.

Molyneux, J. 1992. *Simonides: A Historical Study*. Wauconda.

Mommsen, A. 1878. *Delphika*. Leipzig.

Monceaux, P. 1882. 'Inscriptiones de Salamine', *BCH* 6: 521–53.

Montana, F. 2015. 'Hellenistic Scholarship', in F. Montanari, S. Matthaios and A. Rengakos, eds. *Brill's Companion to Ancient Greek Scholarship*, vol. 1: *History, Disciplinary Profiles*. Leiden and Boston. 60–183.

Montanaro, A. C. 2007. *Ruvo di Puglia e il suo territorio, le necropoli: I corredi funerari tra la documentazione del XIX secolo e gli scavi moderni*. Rome.

Montel, S. 2008. *Recherches sur la présentation architecturale des groupes sculptés en Grèce antique*. Diss. Université de Paris X – Nanterre.

Monterroso Checa, A. 2010. *Theatrum Pompei: Forma y arquitectura de la génesis del modelo teatral de Roma*. Madrid.

Moraux, P. 1984. *Der Aristotelismus bei den Griechen*, vol. 2. Berlin.

Moraw, S. and Nölle, E. eds. 2002. *Die Geburt des Theaters in der griechischen Antike*. Mainz. 70–95.

Moreno, A. 2007. *Feeding the Democracy: The Athenian Grain Supply in the Fifth and Fourth Centuries BC*. Oxford.

Moret, J.-M. 1975. *L'Ilioupersis dans la céramique italiote: Les mythes et leur expression figurée au IVᵉ siècle*. Geneva.

Moretti, J.-Ch. 1991. 'L'Architecture des théâtres en Grèce (1980–1989)', *Topoi* 1: 7–38.

1992a. 'L'Architecture des théâtres en Asie Mineure (1980–1989)', *Topoi* 2: 9–32.

1992b. 'Les entrées en scène dans le théâtre grec: L'apport de l'archéologie', *Pallas* 38: 79–107.

1993. *Théâtres d'Argos*. Sites et Monuments 10. Paris.

1997. 'Formes et destinations du *proskènion* dans les théâtres hellénistiques de Grèce', *Pallas* 47: 13–39.

1999–2000. 'The Theater and Sanctuary of Dionysus Eleuthereus in Late Fifth-Century Athens', *ICS* 24–25: 377–98.

2001. *Théâtre et Société dans la Grèce antique: Une archéologie des pratiques théâtrales*. Paris.

2009. 'Les lieux de culte dans le théâtre grec', in J.-Ch. Moretti, ed. *Fronts de scène et lieux de culte dans le théâtre antique*. Lyon. 23–52.

2010. 'Le coût et le financement des théâtres grecs', in B. Le Guen, ed. *L'Argent dans les concours du monde grec*. Vincennes. 147–87.

2014a. 'The Evolution of Theatre Architecture Outside Athens in the Fourth Century', in E. Csapo, H.-R. Goette, J. R. Green and P. Wilson, eds. *Greek Theatre in the Fourth Century B.C.* Berlin and Boston. 107–37.

2014b. 'L'architecture des théâtres en Grèce antique avant l'époque impériale: Un point de vue sur les études publiées entre 1994 et 2014', *Perspective* 2: 195–223.

Moretti, J.-Ch. and Fincker, M. 2008. 'Un autel de Dionysos à Délos', *BCH* 132: 115–52.

Moretti, L. 1953. *Iscrizioni agonistiche greche*. Rome.

1960. 'Sulle didascalie del teatro attico rinvenute a Roma', *Athenaeum* 38: 263–82.

1968. *Inscriptiones Graecae urbis Romae*, vol. 1. Rome.

Morgan, K. A. 2012. 'A Prolegomenon to Performance in the West', in K. Bosher, ed. *Theater Outside Athens: Drama in Greek Sicily and South Italy*. Cambridge. 35–55.

2015. *Pindar and the Construction of Syracusan Monarchy in the Fifth Century*. Oxford and New York.

Morpurgo Davies, A. 1965. 'A Note on Thessalian', *Glotta* 43: 235–51.

Morrison, A. 2007. *Performances and Audiences in Pindar's Sicilian Victory Odes*. London.

Morrow, G. R. 1960. *Plato's Cretan City: A Historical Interpretation of the Laws.* Princeton.

Morton, J. 2001. *The Role of the Physical Environment in Ancient Greek Seafaring.* Leiden.

Mosshammer, A. A. 1982. 'The Date of the First Pythiad – Again', *GRBS* 23: 15–30.

Mossman, J. 2011. *Euripides: Medea.* Oxford.

Muccioli, F. 1990. 'Osservazioni sull'uso di Timonide nella Vita di Dione di Plutarco', *AncSoc* 21: 167–87.

Müller, C. 2011. 'Évergétisme et pratiques financières dans les cités de la Grèce hellénistique', *RÉA* 113: 345–63.

2013. 'Mobility and Belonging in Antiquity: Greeks and Barbarians on the Move in the Northern Black Sea Region', in U. Bosma, G. Kessler and L. Lucassen, eds. *Migration and Membership Regimes in Global and Historical Perspective.* Leiden. 23–50.

Müller, H. 1989. 'Ein neues hellenistisches Weihepigramm aus Pergamon', *Chiron* 19: 499–553.

Müller, K. 2003. *Hellenistische Architektur auf Paros*. Berlin.

Mulliez, D. 1998. 'La chronologie de la prêtrisse IV (170/69–158/7) et la date de la mort d'Eumène II', *Topoi* 18: 231–41.

2013. 'Οι πυθικοὶ ἀγώνες. Οι μαρτυρίες των επιγραφών', in R. Kolonia, ed. *Αρχαία θέατρα της Στερεάς Ελλάδας*. Diazoma 7. Athens. 147–53.

Murray, P. 2004. 'The Muses and their Arts', in P. Murray and P. Wilson, eds. *Music and the Muses: The Culture of Mousike in the Classical Athenian City.* Oxford. 363–89.

2013. '*Paides Malakon Mouson*: Tragedy in Plato's *Laws*', in A. Peponi, ed. *Performance and Culture in Plato's Laws.* Cambridge. 294–312.

Mussche, H. F. ed. 1994. *Studies in South Attica II*. Ghent.

1998. *Thorikos: A Mining Town in Ancient Attika*. Ghent.

Musti, D. 2005. 'Tindari: La città dei gemelli', *Sicilia Antiqua* 2: 141–3.

Mygind, B. 1999. 'Intellectuals in Rhodes', in V. Gabrielsen, P. Bilde, T. Engberg-Pedersen, L. Hannestadt and J. Zahle, eds. *Hellenistic Rhodes: Politics, Culture and Society.* Studies in Hellenistic Civilization 9. Aarhus. 247–93.

Mylonas, G. E. 1960. 'Ελευσίς καὶ Διόνυσος', *ArchEph*: 68–115.

Nachtergael, G. 1977. *Les Galates en Grèce et les Sôtéria de Delphes: Recherches d'histoire et d'épigraphie hellénistiques.* Brussels.

Nafissi, M. 1997. 'Atene e Metaponto: Ancora sulla *Melanippe Desmotis* e i Neleidi', *Ostraka* 6: 337–57.

Nagy, G. 2011. 'The Earliest Phases in the Reception of the Homeric Hymns', in A. Faulkner, ed. *The Homeric Hymns: Interpretive Essays.* Oxford. 280–333.

Nails, D. 1998. 'The Dramatic Date of Plato's Republic', *CJ* 93: 383–96.

 2002. *The People of Plato: A Prosopography of Plato and Other Socratics.* Indianapolis.

Napolitano, F. 1979. 'Il teatro di Sositeo', *RAAN* 54: 65–92.

Nauck, A. 1903. *Euripidis Tragoediae*³, vol. 1. Leipzig.

Naudet, J. 1845. *Théâtre de Plaute*², 2 vols. Paris.

Neer, R. 2001. 'Framing the Gift: the Politics of the Siphnian Treasury at Delphi', *CA* 20: 273–344.

Nemes, Z. 1984. 'Some Observations on the Publications of the Attic Deme-Inscriptions', *ACD* 20: 3–10.

 1987. 'On the EM 7748 (*IG* II² 1206)', *ACD* 23: 19–26.

Nervegna, S. 2013. *Menander in Antiquity: The Contexts of Reception.* Cambridge.

 2014. 'Performing Classics: The Tragic Canon in the Fourth Century and Beyond', in E. Csapo, H.-R. Goette, J. R. Green and P. Wilson, eds. *Greek Theatre in the Fourth Century B.C.* Berlin and Boston. 157–87.

Nesselrath, H.-G. 1990. *Die attische Mittlere Komödie: Ihre Stellung in der antiken Literaturkritik und Literaturgeschichte.* Berlin and New York.

 2016. 'A Minor but Not Uninteresting Poet of Athenian Middle Comedy: Epicrates of Ambracia', *Logeion* 6: 231–44.

Neutsch, B. 1954. 'Archäologische Grabungen und Funde im Beriech der Soprintendenzen von Sizilien (1949–1954)', *JdI* 69: 465–706.

Nicholson, N. 2016. *The Poetics of Victory in the Greek West: Epinician, Oral Tradition, and the Deinomenid Empire.* Greeks Overseas. Oxford.

Nicolucci, V. 2003. 'Il dramma satiresco alla corte di Attalo I: fonti letterarie e documenti archeologici', in A. Martina, ed. *Teatro greco postclassico e teatro latino, teorie e prassi drammatica: Atti del convegno internazionale, Roma, 16–18 ottobre 2001.* Rome. 325–42.

Nielsen, I. 2002. *Cultic Theatres and Ritual Drama: A Study in Regional Development and Religious Interchange between East and West in Antiquity.* Aarhus.

Nielsen, T. H. 1999. 'The Concept of Arcadia – the People, their Land and their Organisation', in T. H. Nielsen and J. Roy, eds. *Defining Ancient Arkadia.* Acts of the Copenhagen Polis Centre 6. Copenhagen. 16–79.

 2000. 'Epiknemidian, Hypoknemidian, and Opountian Lokrians. Reflections on the Political Organisation of East Lokris in the Classical Period', in P. Flensted-Jensen, ed. *Further Studies in the Ancient Greek Polis.* Stuttgart. 91–120.

Niese, B. 1893. *Geschichte der griechischen und makedonischen Staaten seit der Schlacht bei Chaeronea I: Geschichte Alexanders des grossen und seiner Nachfolger und der Westhellenen bis zum Jahre 281 v. Chr.* Gotha.

Nieswandt, H.-H. 1984. 'No. 58', in K. Stähler, ed. *Griechische Vasen aus westfälischen Sammlungen.* Münster. 159–60.

Niewöhner, P. 2016. 'An Ancient Cave Sanctuary underneath the Theatre of Miletus, Beauty, Mutilation, and Burial of Ancient Sculpture in Late Antiquity, and the History of the Seaward Defences', *AA*: 67–156.

Nikolaou, N. 1985. 'Le cochon d'Édesse', *RÉG* 98: 147–52.

Nikolayev, N. I. 2013. 'Νέα ανάγνωση της επιγραφής *IosPE* Ι² 161 από την Ολβία', *Grammateion* 2: 67–70.

Nilsson, M. P. 1900. *Studia de Dionysiis Atticis.* Lund.

    1906. *Griechische Feste von religiöser Bedeutung mit Ausschluss der Attischen.* Leipzig. (Reissued Darmstadt 1957.)

Noack, F. 1927. *Eleusis: Die baugeschichtliche Entwicklung des Heiligtumes.* Berlin.

Nobili, C. 2016. 'Iambi in Sparta', *Greek and Roman Musical Studies* 4: 38–50.

Nocita, M. 2012. *Italiotai e Italikoi: Le testimonianze greche nel Mediterraneo orientale.* Hesperìa 28. Rome.

    2013. 'Qualche nota epigrafica su Roma: Didascalie sceniche del Campo Marzio', *Mediterraneo Antico* 16: 597–608.

Nocita, M. and Guizzi, F. 2009. 'At the Periphragma of Dionysos', in *Πρακτικά Γ΄διεθνούς Σιφναϊκού συμποσίου: Σίφνος 29 Ιουνίου - 2 Ιουλίου 2006.* Athens. 135–40.

Ober, J. 2008. *Democracy and Knowledge: Innovation and Learning in Classical Athens.* Princeton.

O'Connor, J. B. 1966. *Chapters in the History of Actors and Acting in Ancient Greece: Together with a Prosopographia Histrionum Graecorum.* New York.

Oetjen, R. 2014. *Athen im dritten Jahrhundert v. Chr.: Politik unde Gesellschaft in den Garnisonsdemen auf der Grundlage der inschriftlichen Überlieferung.* Düsseldorf.

Oikonomou, D. 2013. 'Θέατρο Θήβας', in R. Kolonia, ed. *Αρχαία θέατρα της Στερεάς Ελλάδας.* Diazoma 7. Athens. 51–4.

Olding, G. 2007. 'On the Wineman: The Manipulation of Myth', in V. Jennings and A. Katsaros, eds. *The World of Ion of Chios.* Leiden. 139–54.

Oliverio, A. 1933. *I conti dei demiurgi.* Documenti antichi dell'Africa italiana II. Bergamo.

    1946. *Frammenti della commedia greca e del mimo nella Sicilia e nella Magna Grecia².* Naples.

Olivieri, O. 2009. 'Zeus, Opora … e Dioniso: Considerazioni su una epiclesis di Zeus e Dioniso a Tebe', *SIFC* 102: 233–40.

    2011. *Miti e Culti Tebani nella Poesia di Pindaro.* Rome.

Ollà, A., Sardella, A., Spigo, U., Martinelli, M. and Giordano, L. 2018. 'Nuovi dati e materiali dalla necropoli di Lipari: La campagna di scavo 2012–2013', in S. Bonomi and C. Malacrino, eds. *Ollus leto datus est: Architettura, topografia e rituali funerari nelle necropoli dell'Italia meridionale e della Sicilia fra antichità e medioevo. Atti del Convegno Reggio Calabria, 22–25 ottobre,* vol. 1: *Dalla preistoria all'ellenismo.* 387–98.

Olson, S. D. 1998. *Aristophanes: Peace.* Oxford.

    2001. 'We Didn't Know Whether to Laugh or Cry: The Case of Karkinos I of Athens', in D. Harvey and J. Wilkins, eds. *The Rivals of Aristophanes.* London. 65–74.

    2002. *Aristophanes: Acharnians.* Oxford.

    2007. *Broken Laughter: Select Fragments of Greek Comedy.* Oxford.

    2014. *Eupolis frr. 326–497: Fragmenta incertarum fabularum.* Fragmenta Comica 8.3. Heidelberg.

O'Neil, J. 1995. *The Origins and Development of Ancient Greek Democracy.* Lanham.

Orlandos, A. K. and Travlos, I. N. 1986. *Λεξικὸν ἀρχαίων ἀρχιτεκτονικῶν ὅρων.* Athens.

Ornaghi, M. 2010. 'Sincronismi giambici: Archiloco, Ipponatte e lo smembramento di Semonide', *Annali Online di Lettere – Ferrara* 2: 18–88.

    2016. *Dare un padre alla commedia: Susarione e le tradizioni megaresi.* Alessandria.

Osanna, M. 2008. 'EPTAPYLOI THEBAI. Le mura tebane da Omero a Pausania', in S. Angiolillo et al., eds. *Le perle e il filo: A Mario Torelli per i suoi settanta anni.* Venosa. 243–60.

Osborne, R. 1985. *Demos: The Discovery of Classical Attika.* Cambridge.

1988. 'Social and Economic Implications of the Leasing of Land and Property in Classical and Hellenistic Greece', *Chiron* 18: 225–70, 279–323.

2019. 'Euergetism and the Public Economy of Athens: the Initiative of the Deme', in Z. Archibald and J. Haywood, eds. *The Power of the Individual and Community in Ancient Athens and Beyond: Essays in Honour of J. K. Davies.* Stuttgart. 147–62.

Ostwald, M. 1992. 'Athens as a Cultural Centre', in D. M. Lewis, J. Boardman, J. K. Davies and M. Ostwald, eds. *The Cambridge Ancient History*[2], vol. 5. Cambridge. 306–69.

O'Sullivan, L. 1997. 'Asander, Athens and *IG* II[2] 450: A New Interpretation', *ZPE* 119: 107–16.

Otranto, R. 2000. *Antiche liste di libri su papiro.* Rome.

Ouvaroff, A. 1855. *Recherches sur les antiquités de la Russie méridionale et des côtes de la Mer Noire.* Paris.

Owens, E. J. 1983. 'The Koprologoi at Athens in the Fifth and Fourth Centuries B.C.', *CQ* 33: 44–50.

Özyiğit, Ö. 1993. '1991 Yılı Phokaia Kazı Çalışmaları', *Kazı Sonuçları Toplantısı* 14.2: 1–22.

2003. 'Recent Work at Phokaia in the Light of Akurgal's Excavations', *Anadolu / Anatolia* 25: 109–29.

2006. 'Nouvelles recherches archéologiques à Phocée', in *Velia: Atti del quarantacinquesimo convegno di studi sulla Magna Grecia, Taranto-Marina di Ascea 21–25 settembre 2005.* Taranto. 9–22.

Padgett, J. M. 2004. 'Priam or Icarius?', *MeditArch* 17: 65–70.

Padgett, J. M., Comstock, M. B., Hermann, J. J. and Vermeule, C. C. eds. 1993. *Vase-Painting in Italy: Red-Figure and Related Works in the Museum of Fine Arts, Boston.* Boston.

Paga, J. 2010. 'Deme Theaters in Attica and the Trittys System', *Hesperia* 79: 351–84.

Page, D. L. 1936. 'The Elegiacs in Euripides' *Andromache*', in C. Bailey, ed. *Greek Poetry and Life: Essays Presented to Gilbert Murray on his Seventieth Birthday.* Oxford. 206–30.

Palagia, O. 1994. 'No Demokratia', in O. Palagia, W. D. E. Coulson, T. L. Shear Jr., H. A. Shapiro and F. J. Frost, eds. *The Archaeology of Athens and Attica Under the Democracy: Proceedings of an International Conference Celebrating 2500 years Since the Birth of Democracy in Greece, Held at the American School of Classical Studies at Athens, December 4–6, 1992.* Oxford. 113–22.

Palaiokrassa-Kopitsa, L. 1996. *Παλαιόπολις Ἄνδρου I, Τα οικοδομικά, Από την προανασκαφική έρευνα.* Andros.

ed. 2007. *Παλαιόπολη Ἄνδρου, Είκοσι χρόνια ανασκαφικής έρευνας.* Athens.

2009. 'Πυθώνυμος Νικοκράτους, ένας επιφανής Ἄνδριος', in D. Kyrtatas, L. Palaiokrassa-Kopitsa and M. Tiverios, eds. *Εύανδρος, Τόμος εις μνήμην Δημητρίου Ι. Πολέμη.* Andros. 33–50.

Palles, G. 2000–2003. 'Εἰς *IG* II[2] 3057', *Horos* 14–16: 95–7.

Palme, B. 1987. 'Ein attischer Prospektorenvertrag? *IG* II[2] 411', *Tyche* 2: 113–39.

Palyvou, C. 2001. 'Notes on the Geometry of the Ancient Theatre of Thorikos', *AA*: 45–58.

Panagou, T. 2010–2012. 'Το αρχαίο θέατρο της Καρθαίας στην Κέα: Έκθεση εργασιών έτους 2011', *Archaiognosia* 16: 343–76.

Pandermalis, D. 1997. *Dion: The Archaeological Site and the Museum.* Athens.

2002. 'New Discoveries at Dion', in M. Stamatopoulou and M. Yeroulanou, eds. *Excavating Classical Culture: Recent Archaeological Discoveries in Greece.* Oxford. 99–107.

Panofka, T. 1849. 'Komödienscenen auf Thongefäßen', *AZ* 7: 18–21, 33–44.

Panomitros, D. 2003. 'Hegemon, the Lentil Soup: His Literary Evolution in Relation to Arist. *Poet.* 1449a and his Influence on Comedy', *Parnassos* 45: 145–62.

Pantazides, I. 1898. 'Κριτικαί παρατηρήσεις εις τα Ηθικά του Πλουτάρχου', *Parnassos* 2: 1–16.

Panvini, R. 2005. *La ceramiche attiche figurate del museo archeologico di Caltanissetta.* Bari.

Panvini, R. and Giudice, F. eds. 2003. *TA ATTIKA*: *Veder Greco a Gela. Ceramiche attiche figurate dall'antica colonia*. Rome.

Papachristodoulou, I. 1999. 'The Rhodian Demes within the Framework of the Function of the Rhodian State', in V. Gabrielsen, P. Bilde, T. Engberg-Pedersen, L. Hannestad and J. Zahle, eds. *Hellenistic Rhodes: Politics, Culture and Society*. Studies in Hellenistic Civilization 9. Aarhus. 27–44.

Papadopoulou, C. 2016. 'Aixone: Insights into an Athenian Deme', *AR* 62: 103–10.

Papadopoulou, Z. 2000. 'Dionysiac Artists in Siphnos during the Classical and Hellenistic Periods', in *Πρακτικά Α΄ διεθνούς Σιφναϊκού συμποσίου: Σίφνος 25–28 Ιουνίου 1998*. Athens. 437–48.

———. 2009. 'Νέα στοιχεία για την ακρόπολη του αρχαίου άστεως της Σίφνου', in *Πρακτικά Γ΄ διεθνούς Σιφναϊκού συμποσίου: Σίφνος 29 Ιουνίου - 2 Ιουλίου 2006*. Athens. 41–56.

Papagiannopoulos-Palaios, A. 1929a. 'Ἀττικαὶ ἐπιγραφαί', *Polemon* 1: 161–73.

———. 1929b. 'Ἀττικαὶ ἐπιγραφαί Ι: Ξυπεταίονες νικηταὶ κώμαρχοι κωμασταί', *Polemon* 1: 44–52, 107–9, 232–7.

———. 1929c. 'Ἀνάθεσις τῷ Διονύσῳ ὑπὸ στεφανωθέντων Ἐλευσινίων', *Polemon* 1: 237–40.

———. 1949–1951. 'Ἀττικά: τὸ θέατρον Αἰξωνῆσιν', *Polemon* 4: 138.

Papalexandrou, N. 2008. 'Boiotian Tripods: The Tenacity of a Panhellenic Symbol in a Regional Context', *Hesperia* 77: 251–82.

Papantoniou, G. 2012. *Religion and Social Transformations in Cyprus: From the Cypriot Basileis to the Hellenistic Strategos*. Boston and Leiden.

Papastamati-von Moock, C. 2014. 'The Theatre of Dionysus Eleuthereus in Athens: New Data and Observations on its "Lycurgan" Phase', in E. Csapo, H.-R. Goette, J. R. Green and P. Wilson, eds. *Greek Theatre in the Fourth Century B.C.* Berlin and Boston. 15–76.

———. 2015. 'The Wooden Theatre of Dionysos Eleuthereus in Athens: Old Issues, New Research', in R. Frederiksen, E. R. Gebhard and A. Sokolicek, eds. *The Architecture of the Ancient Greek Theatre: Acts of an International Conference at the Danish Institute at Athens 27–30 January 2012*. Monographs of the Danish Institute at Athens 17. Aarhus. 39–80.

Papazarkadas, N. 2004–2009. 'Ἀττικὰ ἐπιγραφικὰ σημειώματα', *Horos* 17–21: 91–109.

———. 2007a. 'Four Attic Deme Documents Revisited', *ZPE* 159: 155–78.

———. 2007b. 'An Honorific Decree from Classical Siphnos', *RÉA* 109: 137–46.

———. 2007c. '*IG* II² 2490, the Epakreis and the Pre-Cleisthenic Trittyes', *CQ* 57: 22–32.

———. 2009. 'Οἱ ἐπιγραφὲς τῆς Σίφνου', in *Πρακτικά Γ΄ διεθνούς Σιφναϊκού συμποσίου, Σίφνος 29 Ιουνίου - 2 Ιουλίου 2006: εἰς μνήμην Νικολάου Βερνίκου-Ευγενίδη*. Athens. 85–94.

———. 2011. *Sacred and Public Land in Ancient Athens*. Oxford.

———. 2013a. 'The Epigraphy of Honours at Siphnos: New Evidence', in P. Martzavou and N. Papazarkadas, eds. *Epigraphical Approaches to the Post-Classical Polis: Fourth Century BC to Second Century AD*. Oxford. 181–98.

———. 2013b. 'Δύο ἀνέκδοτα προξενικὰ ψηφίσματα τῆς Σίφνου', in *Πρακτικά Δ΄ διεθνούς Σιφναϊκού συμποσίου, Σίφνος 25–26 Ιουνίου 2010*. Athens. 99–110.

Papazarkadas, N. and Papadopoulou, Z. 2010–2013. 'Σιφναϊκὸ ψήφισμα ὑπὲρ Ἀμφιχάρους Σεριφίου', *Horos* 22–25: 453–80.

Parke, H. W. 1977. *Festivals of the Athenians*. Ithaca.

Parker, L. P. E. 1997. *The Songs of Aristophanes*. Oxford.

Parker, R. 1989. 'Spartan Religion', in A. Powell, ed. *Classical Sparta: Techniques Behind her Success*. London. 142–72.

———. 1994. 'Athenian Religion Abroad', in R. Osborne and S. Hornblower, eds. *Ritual, Finance, Politics: Athenian Democratic Accounts Presented to David Lewis*. Oxford. 339–46.

1996. *Athenian Religion: A History.* Oxford.

2005. *Polytheism and Society at Athens.* Oxford.

2010a. 'Agesilaus and the Bones of Alcmena', in H.-G. Nesselrath, ed. *Plutarch On the Daimonion of Socrates: Human Liberation, Divine Guidance and Philosophy.* Tübingen. 129–37.

2010b. 'New Problems in Athenian Religion: The "Sacred Law" from Aixone', in J. Dijkstra, J. Kroesen and Y. Kuiper, eds. *Myths, Martyrs, and Modernity: Studies in the History of Religions in Honour of Jan N. Bremmer.* Leiden. 193–208.

Parra, M. C. 1998. 'Il teatro di Locri tra spettacolo e culto: Per una revisione dei dati', *AnnPisa* 3: 303–22.

Paschidis, P. 2008. *Between City and King: Prosopographical Studies on the Intermediaries Between the Cities of the Greek Mainland and the Aegean and the Royal Courts in the Hellenistic Period (322–190 BC).* Meletemata 59. Athens.

Pascual, J. 2013. 'The Ancient Topography of the Epicnemidian Locris', in J. Pascual and M.-F. Papakonstantinou, eds. *Topography and History of Ancient Epicnemidian Locris.* Leiden. 65–200.

Patanè, R. 1992. 'Timoleonte a Centuripe e ad Agira', *CronCatania* 31: 67–82.

Patterson, L. E. 2010. *Kinship Myth in Ancient Greece.* Austin.

Paul, S. 2013. *Cultes et sanctuaires de l'île de Cos.* Liège.

Pautasso, A. 2010. 'Santuari lungo le rotte: Per una storicizzazione della stipe votive di piazza S. Francesco', in M. G. Branciforti and V. La Rosa, eds. *Tra lava e mare: Contributi all'archaiologhia di Catania: Atti del convegno, Catania, ex Monastero dei Benedettini, novembre 2007.* Catania. 109–18.

Pavlou, M. 2012. 'Fathers in Absentia in Pindar's Epinician Poetry', *GRBS* 52: 57–88.

Pearson, L. 1960. *The Lost Histories of Alexander the Great.* New York.

Pedersen, P. 2004. 'Halikarnassos and the Ptolemies II. The Architecture of Hellenistic Halikarnassos', in S. Isager and P. Pedersen, eds. *The Salmakis Inscription and Hellenistic Halikarnassos.* Aarhus. 145–64.

Pedersen, P. and Isager, S. 2015. 'The Theatre at Halikarnassos – and Some Thoughts on the Origin of the Semicircular Greek Theatre. With an Appendix "The Inscriptions from the Theatre at Halikarnassos"', in R. Frederiksen, E. Gebhard and A. Sokolicek, eds. *The Architecture of the Ancient Greek Theatre: Acts of an International Conference at Athens 27–30 January 2012.* Monographs of the Danish Institute at Athens 17. Aarhus. 293–317.

Peek, W. 1969a. 'Inschriften aus dem Asklepieion von Epidauros', *AbhLeip* 60.2. Berlin.

1969b. 'Inschriften von den dorischen Inseln', *AbhLeip* 62.1. Berlin.

1972. 'Neue Inschriften aus Epidauros', *AbhLeip* 63.5. Berlin.

1977. 'Ein neues Euripides-Fragment?', *Philologus* 121: 306–7.

Pelagatti, P. and Voza, G. 1976. 'L'attività della Soprintendenza alle Antichità della Sicilia Orientale', *Kokalos* 22: 519–85.

Pelling, C. 2002. *Plutarch and History: Eighteen Studies.* London.

Peper, L. 1912. *De Plutarchi 'Epaminonda'.* Diss. Jena.

Peristeri, K. 2012. 'Το αρχαίο θέατρο της Αμφίπολης' in P. Adam-Veleni, ed. *Αρχαία Θέατρα της Μακεδονίας.* Diazoma 3. Athens. 191–2.

Pernice, E. 1893. 'Inschriften aus Andros und Paros', *AM* 18: 7–20.

Perrier, A. 2013. 'Το στάδιο των Δελφών', in R. Kolonia, ed. *Αρχαία θέατρα της Στερεάς Ελλάδας.* Diazoma 7. Athens. 155–63.

Perrin, E. 1997. 'Propagande et culture théatrales à Athènes à l'époque hellénistique', in B. Le Guen, ed. *De la scène aux gradins: Théâtre et représentations dramatiques après Alexandre le Grand.* Pallas 47. Toulouse. 201–18.

Perrin-Saminadayar, E. 2007. *Éducation, culture et société à Athènes: Les acteurs de la vie culturelle athénienne (229–88): Un tout petit monde*. Paris.

Perusino, F. 1993. 'Commedia nuova a Cirene', in R. Pretagostini, ed. *Tradizione e innovazione nella cultura greca da Omero all'età ellenistica: Scritti in onore di Bruno Gentili*, vol. 2. Rome. 735–40.

Petrakos, V. C. 1967. Ἀρχαιότητες καὶ μνημεῖα Νησιῶν Αἰγαίου', *ArchDelt* 22 B 2: 445–62.

    1968. Ὁ Ὠρωπὸς καὶ τὸ ἱερὸν τοῦ Ἀμφιαράου. Athens.

    1979. 'Νέες ἔρευνες στὸν Ῥαμνούντα', *ArchEph*: 1–81.

    1991. *Rhamnous*. Athens.

    1994. Ἀνασκαφή Ραμνούντος', *Prakt*: 1–44.

    1995. *The Amphiareion of Oropos*. Athens.

    1997. Οἱ Ἐπιγραφὲς τοῦ Ὠρωποῦ. Athens.

    1998. Ἀνασκαφές', *Ergon* 45: 11–67.

    1999. Ὁ δῆμος τοῦ Ῥαμνοῦντος. Σύνοψη τῶν ἀνασκαφῶν καὶ τῶν ἐρευνῶν (1813–1998). Ι. Τοπογραφία. ΙΙ. Οἱ ἐπιγραφές. Athens.

    2017. 'Θουρία', *Ergon* 64: 14–15.

Petrides, A. 2003. 'Talking (from) Baskets: Epicharmus fr. 123 K.-A.', *Eikasmos* 14: 75–86.

Petrounakos, S. 2015. Οι επιγραφές του θεάτρου της πόλης της Αρχαίας Επιδαύρου. Athens.

Pettersson, M. 1992. *Cults of Apollo at Sparta: The Hyakinthia, the Gymnopaidiai and the Karneia*. Stockholm.

Pfeiffer, R. 1968. *History of Classical Scholarship: From the Beginnings to the End of the Hellenistic Age*. Oxford.

Pfister, F. 1913. 'Die Lokalhistorie von Sikyon bei Menaichmos, Pausanias und den Chronographen', *RhM* 68: 529–37.

Philios, D. 1881. Ἔκθεσις περὶ τῶν ἐν Πειραίει νασκαφῶν', *Prakt* 10–12: 47–61.

    1887. Ἐπιγραφαὶ ἐξ Ἐλευσῖνος', *ArchEph*: 171–96.

    1890. Ἐπιγραφαὶ ἐξ Ἐλευσῖνος (Συνέχεια)', *ArchEph*: 69–102.

    1894. Ἐπιγραφαὶ ἐξ Ἐλευσῖνος', *AM* 19: 163–93.

Picard, C. 1944. 'Un type méconnu de lieu-saint dionysiaque: le *stibadeion*', *CRAI* 88: 127–57.

Picard, C. and Avezou, C. 1914. 'Les fouilles de Thasos (1913)', *CRAI* 3: 276–305.

Picard, O. 2000. 'Le retour des émigrés et le monnayage de Thasos (390)', *CRAI* 144: 1057–84.

Piccirilli, L. 1974. 'Susarione e la rivendicazione megarese dell'origine della commedia greca (Arist., *Poet*. 3, p. 1448a29–48b2)', *AnnPisa* 4: 1289–99.

    1975. *Megarika: Testimonianze e frammenti*. Pisa.

Pickard-Cambridge, A. W. 1927. *Dithyramb, Tragedy and Comedy*. Oxford.

Piérart, M. 1996. 'Le Culte de Dionysos à Argos', *Kernos* 9: 423–9.

Pinto, P. M. 2013. 'Men and Books in Fourth-Century BC Athens', in J. König, K. Oikonomopoulou and G. Woolf, eds. *Ancient Libraries*. Cambridge. 85–95.

Pipili, M. 1987. *Laconian Iconography of the Sixth Century B.C.* Oxford.

    2000. 'Wearing an Other Hat: Workmen in Town and Country', in B. Cohen, ed. *Not the Classical Ideal: Athens and the Construction of the Other in Greek Art*. Leiden. 153–79.

Piqueux, A. 2006. 'Quelques réflexions à propos du cratère en cloche d'Astéas "Phrynis et Pyronidès"', *Apollo* 22: 3–10.

Pirenne Delforge, V. 2016. 'Teletê peut-elle être déesse? Note épigraphique (*SEG* 50, 168)', *Métis* 14: 35–48.

Pisani, M. 2008. *Camarina. Le terrecotte figurate e la ceramica da una fornace di V e IV secolo a.C.* Studia Archaeologica 164. Rome.

Pitt, R. 2008. Review of P. Wilson, ed. 2007, *The Greek Theatre and Festivals: Documentary Studies*, *JHS* 128: 222.

Pittakys (a.k.a. Pittakis, Pittakes), K. S. 1835. *L'ancienne Athènes, ou La description des antiquités d'Athènes et de ses environs*. Athens.

Piva, G. 2011. 'Le vicende di Eracle nel teatro di Epicarmo: Osservazioni sul fr. 92 K.-A.', in A. Andrisano, ed. *Ritmo, parola, immagine: Il teatro classico e la sua tradizione*. Palermo. 103–13.

Plassart, A. 1928. *Exploration archéologique de Délos faite par l'École Française d'Athènes: Les Sanctuaires et les cultes du Mont Cynthe*. Délos XI. Paris.

Platonos-Yiota, M. 2004. Αχαρναί: Ιστορική και τοπογραφική επισκόπηση των αρχαίων Αχαρνών, των γειτονικών δήμων και των οχυρώσεων της Πάρνηθας. Acharnai.

2007. 'ΔΗΜΟΣ ΑΧΑΡΝΩΝ', *ArchDelt* 62: 164–201.

2013. 'Οἱ αρχαιότητες του Δήμου των αρχαίων Αχαρνών και η αποκάλυψη του θεάτρου', in M. Donka-Toli and S. Oikonomou, eds. Αρχαιολογικές συμβολές. Τόμος Α: Αττική. Athens. 137–52.

Plepelits, K. 1970. *Die Fragmente der Demen des Eupolis*. Vienna.

Pliakou, G. 1997. 'Νέα στοιχεία για το αρχαίο θέατρο της Λευκάδας. Μια τοπογραφική προσέγγιση', *Epirotika Chronika* 32: 37–42.

Pliakou, G. and Smyris, G. 2012. 'Το θέατρο, το βουλευτήριο και το στάδιο της Δωδώνης', in K. I. Soueref, ed. Αρχαία θέατρα της Ηπείρου. Diazoma 6. Athens. 62–100.

Poccetti, P. 1989. 'Le popolazioni anelleniche d'Italia tra Sicilia e Magna Grecia nel IV sec. a.C.: Forme di contatto linguistico e di interazione culturale', in A. Cassio and D. Musti, eds. *Tra Sicilia e Magna Grecia: Aspetti di interazione culturale nel IV sec. a.C. Atti del convegno (Napoli, 19–20 marzo 1987)*. AION 11. Pisa. 97–135.

2012. 'Language Relations in Sicily: Evidence for the Speech of the Σικανοί, the Σικελοί and Others', in O. Tribulato, ed. *Language and Linguistic Contact in Ancient Sicily*. Cambridge. 49–94.

Pococke, R. 1745. *A Description of the East and Some Other Countries*, vol. 2, part 2. London.

Podlecki, A. 1981. 'Some Early Athenian Commemorations of Choral Victories', in G. S. Shrimpton and D. J. McCargar, eds. *Classical Contributions: Studies in Honour of Malcolm Francis McGregor*. Locust Valley, NY. 95–101.

Poe, J. P. 1993. 'The Περίακτοι and Actors' Entrances', *Hermes* 121: 377–82.

Pohlenz, M. 1927. 'Das Satyrspiel und Pratinas von Phleius', *NAkG*: 298–321.

1954. *Die griechische Tragödie*, 2 vols. Göttingen.

Pöhlmann, E. 1995a. 'Die Proedrie des Dionysos-Theaters im 5. Jh. und das Bühnenspiel der Klassik', in E. Pöhlmann, ed. *Studien zur Bühnendichtung und zum Theaterbau der Antike*. Frankfurt. 49–62.

1995b. 'Zur Bühnentechnik im Dionysos-Theater des 4. Jh.', in E. Pöhlmann, ed. *Studien zur Bühnendichtung und zum Theaterbau der Antike*. Frankfurt. 155–64.

2015. 'Epicharmus and Aeschylus on Stage in Syracuse in the 5th Century', *Greek and Roman Musical Studies* 3: 137–66.

Polacco, L. 1982. 'La posizione del teatro di Siracusa nel quadro dell'architettura teatrale greca in Sicilia', in M. Gualandi, L. Massei and S. Settis, eds. *APARCHAI: Nuove ricerche e studi sulla Magna Grecia e la Sicilia antica in onore di Paolo Enrico Arias*. Pisa. 431–43.

1990. 'Témenos e *teatro*', in L. Polacco, ed. *Il Teatro di Siracusa: Pars altera*. Padua. 117–59.

Polacco, L. and Anti, C. 1981. *Il teatro di Siracusa*. Rimini.

Polacco, L. Trojani, M. and Scolari, A. 1989. *Il santuario di Cerere e Libera ad summam Neapolin di Siracusa*. Venice.

Polinskaya, I. 2006. 'Lack of Boundaries, Absence of Oppositions: The City-Countryside Continuum of a Greek Pantheon', in R. Rosen and I. Sluiter, eds. *City, Countryside and the Spatial Organization of Value in Classical Antiquity.* Mnemosyne Supplement 279. Leiden. 61–92.

Poli Palladini, L. 2013. *Aeschylus at Gela: An Integrated Approach.* Hellenica 47. Alessandria.

Pollitt, J. 1986. *Art in the Hellenistic Age.* Cambridge.

Poltera, O. 2005. 'Deliaka (Sim. PMG 539): Zu einer vermeintlichen Gedichtsammlung', *StIt* 98: 183–7.

    2008. *Simonides lyricus, Testimonia und Fragmente: Einleitung, kritische Ausgabe, Übersetzung und Kommentar.* Basle.

Pomeroy, S. 1994. *Xenophon: Oeconomicus: A Social and Historical Commentary.* Oxford.

Portale, E. 2015. 'Un confronto: La Sicilia nel III secolo', in *La Magna Grecia da Pirro ad Annibale: Atti del cinquantaduesimo convegno di studi sulla Magna Grecia, Taranto, 27–30 settembre 2012.* Taranto. 697–736.

Potts, D. 2011. 'The *Politai* and the *bīt tāmartu*: The Seleucid and Parthian Theatres of the Greek Citizens of Babylon', in E. Cancik-Kirschbaum, M. van Ess and J. Marzahn, eds. *Babylon: Wissenskultur in Orient und Okzident.* Topoi: Berlin Studies of the Ancient World 1. Berlin. 239–51.

Pouilloux, J. 1954a. *La forteresse de Rhamnonte.* Paris.

    1954b. *Recherches sur l'histoire et les cultes de Thasos I: De la fondation de la cité à 196 avant J.-C.* Études Thasiennes 3. Paris.

    1977. 'Travaux à Delphes à l'occasion des Pythia: Les comptes de Dion 347/6?', *BCH* Supplement 4: 103–23.

Poulsen, F. 1920. *Delphi.* London.

Poupaki, E. 2004. 'Quarries of the Hellenistic Age on the Island of Kos: Possible Uses of the Stones Extracted', in K. Höghammar, ed. *The Hellenistic Polis of Kos: State, Economy and Culture. Proceedings of an International Seminar Organized by the Department of Archaeology and Ancient History, Uppsala University, 11–13 May, 2000.* Boreas 28. Uppsala. 165–79.

Power, T. 2010. *The Culture of Kitharoidia.* Cambridge, MA.

    2011. 'Cyberchorus: Pindar's Κηληδόνες and the Aura of the Artificial', in L. Athanassaki and E. Bowie, eds. *Archaic and Classical Choral Song: Performance, Politics and Dissemination.* Trends in Classics Supplement 10. Berlin. 67–114.

Prandi, L. 1985. *Callistene: Uno storico tra Aristotele e i re macedoni.* Milan.

Prauscello, L. 2006. *Singing Alexandria: Music Between Practice and Textual Transmission.* Leiden and Boston.

    2009. 'Wandering Poetry, "Travelling" Music: Timotheus' Muse and Some Case-Studies of Shifting Cultural Identities', in R. Hunter and I. Rutherford, eds. *Wandering Poets in Ancient Greek Culture: Travel, Locality and Pan-Hellenism.* Cambridge. 168–94.

    2013. 'Comedy and Comic Discourse in Plato's *Laws*', in E. Bakola, L. Prauscello and M. Telò, eds. *Greek Comedy and the Discourse of Genres.* Cambridge. 319–42.

Preger, T. 1891. *Inscriptiones graecae metricae ex scriptoribus praeter Anthologiam collectae.* Leipzig.

Preiser, C. 2000. *Euripides: Telephos.* Spudasmata 78. Zurich and New York.

Preka-Alexandri, K. 2012. 'Το θέατρο των Γιτάνων (προκαταρκτική έρευνα)', in K. I. Soueref, ed. *Αρχαία θέατρα της Ηπείρου.* Diazoma 6. Athens. 109–16.

Preller, L. 1838. *Polemonis Periegetae Fragmenta.* Leipzig.

Prêtre, C. 2000. 'La *Tabula* délienne de 168 av. J.-C.', *BCH* 124: 261–71.

    2002. *Nouveau choix d'inscriptions de Délos: Lois, comptes et inventaires.* Études épigraphiques 4. Athens.

Preuner, E. 1924. 'Aus alten Papieren', *AM* 49: 102–52.

Preuss, E. 1879. *Quaestiones Boeoticae*. Programm des Nicolaigymnasiums. Leipzig.

Priestley, J. 2014. *Herodotus and Hellenistic Culture: Literary Studies in the Reception of the Histories*. Oxford.

Pritchett, W. K. 1969. *Studies in Ancient Greek Topography II*. University of California Publications: Classical Studies 4. Berkeley and Los Angeles.

Privitera, G. A. 1980. 'La politica religiosa dei Dinomenidi e l'ideologia dell'*optimus rex*', in *Perennitas: Studi in onore di Angelo Brelich*. Rome. 393–411.

Privitera, S. 2009. 'Lo sviluppo urbano di Catania dalla fondazione dell'apoikia alla fine del V secolo d.C.', in L. Scalisi, ed. *Catania: L'identità urbana dall'antichità al settecento*. Catania. 37–71.

Pugliese Carratelli, G. 1939–1940. 'Per la storia delle associazioni in Rodi antica', *ASAtene* n.s. 1–2: 145–200.

    1952–1954. 'Supplemento Epigrafico Rodio', *ASAtene* n.s. 14–16: 247–316.

Quinn, T. J. 1981. *Athens and Samos, Lesbos and Chios 478–404 B.C.* Manchester.

Raccuia, C. 1995. 'Una iscrizione selinuntina di V sec. a.C. ed il problema della patria di Epicarmo', *Archivio Storico Messinese* 70: 157–64.

Rawles, R. 2012. 'Early Epinician: Ibycus and Simonides', in P. Agócs, C. Carey and R. Rawles, eds. *Reading the Victory Ode*. Cambridge. 3–27.

Rea, J. 1968. 'List of Comic Poets and their Plays', *POxy.* 33: 70–6.

Reger, G. 1990. 'Some Remarks on "*IG* XII 8, 262 complété" and the Restoration of Thasian Democracy', *Klio* 72: 396–401.

    1994. 'The Date and Historical Significance of *IG* XII v 714 of Andros', *Hesperia* 63: 309–21.

Reger, G. and Risser, M. 1991. 'Coinage and Federation in Hellenistic Keos', in J. Cherry, J. Davis and E. Mantzourani, eds. 1991. *Landscape Archaeology as Long-Term History: Northern Keos in the Cycladic Islands from Earliest Settlement until Modern Times*. Monumenta Archaeologica 16. Los Angeles. 305–15.

Reich, H. 1903. *Der Mimus: Ein literar-entwicklungsgeschichtlicher Versuch*. Berlin.

Reichert-Südbeck, P. 2000. *Kulte von Korinth und Syrakus: Vergleich zwischen einer Metropolis und ihrer Apoikia*. Würzburger Studien zur Sprache und Kultur 4. Dettelbach.

Reinach, S. 1883. 'Fouilles de Délos (L'Inopus et le sanctuaire des Cabires)', *BCH* 7: 329–73.

Reinhardt, U. 1996. 'Zu den Anfängen der Mythenburleske: Griechische Mythen in den Komödien Epicharms und bei Stesichoros, auf Caeretaner Hydrien und anderen westgriechischen Sagenbildern', *Thetis* 3: 21–42.

Reisch, E. 1885. *De musicis Graecorum certaminibus*. Vienna.

    1899a. 'Chor', *RE* 3.2: 2373–404.

    1899b. 'Χορηγία', *RE* 3.2: 2409–22.

Reitzenstein, R. 1893. *Epigramm und Skolion: Ein Beitrag zur Geschichte der Alexandrinischen Dichtung*. Giessen.

Revermann, M. 2006. *Comic Business: Theatricality, Dramatic Technique, and Performance Contexts of Aristophanic Comedy*. Oxford.

Rhodes, P. J. 1981. *A Commentary on the Aristotelian Athenaion Politeia*. Oxford.

    2010. *A History of the Classical World 478–323 BC*². Chichester.

Rhodes, P. J. and Lewis, D. M. 1997. *The Decrees of the Greek States*. Oxford.

Rhodes, P. J. and Osborne, R. 2003. *Greek Historical Inscriptions 404–323 BC*. Oxford.

Ribbeck, O. 1875. 'Über einige historische Dramen', *RhM* 30: 145–61.

Richardson, R. 1890–1897. 'A Temple in Eretria', *Papers of the American School of Classical Studies at Athens* 6: 123–34.

1891. 'Inscriptions Discovered at Eretria, 1891', *The American Journal of Archaeology and of the History of the Fine Arts* 7: 246–53.

Richer, N. 2012. *La religion des Spartiates: Croyances et cultes dans l'antiquité*. Paris.

Richter, O. 1885. *Über antike Steinmetzzeichen*. Berlin.

Ridder, A. de. 1893. 'Inscriptions de Thasos et Lemnos', *BCH* 17: 125–8.

1897. 'Inscriptions de Paros et de Naxos', *BCH* 21: 16–25.

1922. 'Fouilles de Thespies et de l'Hiéron des Muses de l'Hélicon: Monuments Figurés', *BCH* 46: 217–306.

Ridgeway, W. 1915. *The Dramas and Dramatic Dances of Non-European Races in Special Reference to the Origin of Greek Tragedy with an Appendix on the Origin of Greek Comedy.* Cambridge.

Ridgway, B. S. 1997. *Fourth-Century Styles in Greek Sculpture*. Madison and London.

Riginos, G. 2012. 'Το θέατρο και το βουλευτήριο της Κασσώπης', in K. I. Soueref, ed. *Αρχαία θέατρα της Ηπείρου*. Diazoma 6. Athens. 132–43.

Rigsby, K. J. 1996. *Asylia.* Berkeley and Los Angeles.

Ritter, F. 1845. *Didymi Chalcenteri opuscula.* Cologne.

Ritti, T. 1969. 'Sigle ed emblemi sui decreti onorari greci', *MemLinc* 14: 259–360.

Riu, X. 2011. 'La storia del teatro secondo Aristotele e la questione del coro in Epicarmo', in A. Andrisano, ed. *Ritmo, parola, immagine: Il teatro classico e la sua tradizione*. Dionysus ex Machina. Palermo. 115–38.

Rizza, G. 2008. 'Demetra a Catania', in C. Di Stefano, ed. *Demetra: I santuari, il culto, la leggenda.* Rome and Pisa. 187–92.

Rizza, S. 2000. *Studi sulle fortificazioni greche di Leontini.* Catania.

Rizzo, G. 1923. *Il teatro greco di Siracusa.* Milan.

Robert, J. and Robert, L. 1961. 'Bulletin Épigraphique', *RÉG* 74: 119–268.

1974. 'Bulletin Épigraphique', *RÉG* 87: 186–340.

1978. 'Bulletin Épigraphique', *RÉG* 91: 385–510.

Robert, L. 1935. 'Sur les inscriptions de Chios', *BCH* 59: 453–70.

1936. 'Notes d'épigraphie hellénistique', *BCH* 60: 184–9.

1937. *Études anatoliennes: Recherches sur les inscriptions grecques de l'Asie Mineure*. Paris.

1938. 'Inscriptions du dème d'Acharnai', in *Études épigraphiques et philologiques*. Paris. 293–316. Reprinted in *Choix d'Écrits*, ed. D. Rousset. Paris 2007.

1966. *Les monnaies antiques en Troade.* Geneva.

1990. *Opera Minora Selecta: Epigraphie et antiquités grecques*, vol. 7. Amsterdam.

Robertson, D. S. 1923. 'Euripides and Tharyps', *CR* 37: 58–60.

Robertson, M. 1986. 'Two Pelikai by the Pan Painter', *Greek Vases in the J. Paul Getty Museum* 3: 71–90.

Robertson, N. 1978. 'The Myth of the First Sacred War', *CQ* 28: 38–73.

1993. 'Athens' Festival of the New Wine', *HSCP* 95: 197–250.

2010. *Religion and Reconciliation in Greek Cities: The Sacred Laws of Selinus and Cyrene*. Oxford and New York.

Robinson, D. M. 1930. *Excavations at Olynthus II: Architecture and Sculpture: Houses and Other Buildings*. Baltimore.

1938. 'Inscriptions from Macedonia', *TAPA* 69: 43–76.

1948. 'Three New Inscriptions from the Deme of Ikaria', *Hesperia* 17: 141–3.

Robinson, E. G. D. 2004 [2006]. 'Reception of Comic Theatre amongst the Indigenous South Italians', *MeditArch* 17: 193–212.

2014. 'Greek Theatre in Non-Greek Apulia', in E. Csapo, H.-R. Goette, J. R. Green and P. Wilson, eds. *Greek Theatre in the Fourth Century BC*. Berlin. 319–32.

Robinson, E. W. 1997. *The First Democracies: Early Popular Government Outside Athens*. Historia Einzelschriften 107. Stuttgart.

2011. *Democracy Beyond Athens: Popular Government in the Greek Classical Age*. Cambridge.

Rodríguez-Noriega Guillén, L. 1994. 'Plutarco y Epicarmo', in M. García Valdés, ed. *Estudios sobre Plutarco: Ideas Religiosas, Actas del III Symposion Internacional sobre Plutarco*. Madrid. 659–69.

1996. *Epicarmo de Siracusa: Testimonios y Fragmentos. Edición crítica bilingüe*. Oviedo.

2012. 'On Epicharmus' Literary and Philosophic Background', in K. Bosher, ed. *Theater Outside Athens: Drama in Greek Sicily and South Italy*. Cambridge. 76–96.

Roesch, P. 1980. *Teiresias: Appendix Epigraphica* 9: 1–17.

1982. *Études béotiennes*. Paris.

Rohde, E. 1878. 'Γέγονε in den Biographica des Suidas', *RhM*: 161–220.

Romano, I. B. 1982. 'The Archaic Statue of Dionysos from Ikarion', *Hesperia* 51: 398–409.

Roos, P. 2011. 'The Stadion at Labraunda', in L. Karlsson and S. Carlsson, eds. *Labraunda and Karia: Proceedings of the International Symposium Commemorating Sixty Years of Swedish Archaeological Work in Labraunda*. Uppsala. 257–66.

Rosamilia, E. 2014. 'Biblioteche a Rodi all'epoca di Timachidas', *AnnPisa* 6: 325–444.

Rose, C. 2014. *The Archaeology of Greek and Roman Troy*. Cambridge.

Rosen, R. M. 1992. 'Mixing of Genres and Literary Program in Herodas 8', *HCSP* 94: 205–16.

Rosenberg, J. L. 2015. 'Masks of Orthia: Form, Function and the Origins of Theatre', *BSA* 110: 247–61.

Rosokoki, A. 1995. *Die Erigone des Eratosthenes*. Heidelberg.

Ross, L. 1855. *Archäologische Aufsätze*, Band 1: *Griechische Gräber. Ausgrabungsberichte aus Athen. Zur Kunstgeschichte und Topographie von Athen und Attika*. Leipzig.

Rossi, L. 2001. *The Epigrams Ascribed to Theocritus: A Method of Approach*. Louvain.

Rossignoli, B. 2004. *L'Adriatico greco: Culti e miti minori*. Rome.

Rothwell, K. 1992. 'The Continuity of the Chorus in Fourth-Century Attic Comedy', *GRBS* 33: 209–25. Reprinted in G. W. Dobrov, ed. 1995. *Beyond Aristophanes: Transition and Diversity in Greek Comedy*. Atlanta. 99–118.

1994. 'Was Carcinus I a Tragic Playwright?', *CP* 89: 241–5.

Rotstein, A. 2009. *The Idea of Iambos*. Oxford.

Roueché, C. 1993. *Performers and Partisans at Aphrodisias in the Roman and Late Roman Period: A Study Based on Inscriptions from the Current Excavations at Aphrodisias in Caria*. JRS Monograph 6. London.

2002. 'Images of Performance: New Evidence from Ephesus', in P. Easterling and E. Hall, eds. *Greek and Roman Actors: Aspects of an Ancient Profession*. Cambridge. 254–81.

Rousopoulos, A. 1864. 'Scavi attici di Aixone', *BdI*: 129–32.

Roussel, D. 1976. *Tribu et cité: Études sur les groupes sociaux dans les cités grecques aux époques archaïques et classiques*. Annales littéraires de l'Université de Besançon. Centre de recherches d'histoire ancienne 23. Paris.

Roux, G. 1954. 'Le Val des Muses, et les Muses chez les auteurs anciens', *BCH* 78: 22–48.

1961. *L'architecture de l'Argolide aux IVe et IIIe siècles av. J. C.* BÉFAR 199, 2 vols. Paris.

Roy, J. 1973. 'Diodorus Siculus XV 40 – The Peloponnesian Revolutions of 374 BC', *Klio* 55: 135–9.

2000. 'Problems of Democracy in the Arcadian Confederacy 370–362 BC', in R. Brock and S. Hodkinson, eds. *Alternatives to Athens: Varieties of Political Organization and Community in Ancient Greece*. Oxford. 308–36.

Rozokoki, A. 2017. 'Eratosthenes' *Erigone* fr. 4 Rosokoki (= 22 Powell)', *Mnemosyne* 70: 939–57.

Rubinstein, L. 2000. *Litigation and Cooperation: Supporting Speakers in the Courts of Classical Athens*. Stuttgart.

Ruggendorfer, P. and Krinzinger, F. 2017. *Das Theater von Ephesos: Archäologischer Befund, Funde und Chronologie*. Vienna.

Ruhnken, D. 1768. *P. Rutilii Lupi de figuris sententiarum et elocutionis libri duo*. Leiden.
    1823. *Opuscula, varii argumenti, Oratoria, Historica Critica²*. Leiden.

Ruschenbusch, E. 1982. 'Eine Bürgerliste von Iulis und Koresia auf Keos', *ZPE* 48: 175–88.

Rusten, J. 2006. 'Who "Invented" Comedy? The Ancient Candidates for the Origins of Comedy and the Visual Evidence', *AJP* 127: 37–66.

Rutherford, I. C. 1990. 'Paeans by Simonides', *HSCP* 93: 169–209.
    1995. 'Apollo in Ivy: The Tragic Paean', *Arion* 3: 112–35.
    2000. 'Keos or Delos? State-Pilgrimage and the Performance of *Paean* 4', in M. Cannatà Fera and S. Grandolini, eds. *Poesia e religione in Grecia: Studi in onore di G. Aurelio Privitera*, vol. 2. Naples. 605–12.
    2001. *Pindar's Paeans: A Reading of the Fragments with a Survey of the Genre*. Oxford.
    2004. 'χορὸς εἷς ἐκ τῆσδε τῆς πόλεως (Xen. *Mem.* 3.3.12): Song-Dance and State-Pilgrimage at Athens', in P. Murray and P. Wilson, eds. *Music and the Muses: The Culture of Mousike in the Classical Athenian City*. Oxford. 67–90.
    2007. 'Theoria and Theatre in Samothrace. The Dardanos by Dymas of Iasos', in P. Wilson, ed. *The Greek Theatre and Festivals: Documentary Studies*. Oxford. 279–93.
    2013a. *State Pilgrims and Sacred Observers in Ancient Greece: A Study of Theoria and Theoroi*. Cambridge.
    2013b. '*Dithyrambos, Thriambos, Triumphus*: Dionysia Discourse at Rome', in B. Kowalzig and P. Wilson, eds. *Dithyramb in Context*. Oxford. 409–23.

Rutter, K. 2000. 'Syracusan Democracy: Most Like the Athenian?', in R. Brock and S. Hodkinson, eds. *Alternatives to Athens: Varieties of Political Organization and Community in Ancient Greece*. Oxford. 137–51.

Saatsoglou-Paliadeli, C. 2002. 'Βεργίνα 2000–2003, Ἀνασκαφή στο ιερό της Εὔκλειας', *AEMΘ* 16: 479–88.

Saflund, G. 1937. 'Unveröffentlichte antike Steinmetzzeichen und Monogramme aus Unter-italien und Sizilien mit besonderer Berücksichtigung der Stadtmauer von Tyndaris', in R. Paribeni, ed. *Scritti in onore di Bartolomeo Nogara: raccolti in occasione del suo LXX anno*. Vatican City. 409–20.

Salapata, G. 2001. Review of E. Kourinou 2000, *Σπάρτη. Συμβολή στὴν μνημειακή τοπογραφία της*, *BMCR* 2001.08.11.

Salviat, F. 1958. 'Une nouvelle loi thasienne: Institutions judiciaires et fêtes religieuses à la fin du IVᵉ siècle av. J.-C.', *BCH* 82: 193–267.
    1979. 'Vedettes de la scène en province: Signification et date des monuments chorégiques de Thasos', in *Thasiaca*. BCH Supplement 5. Paris. 155–67.

Sanders, G. D. R. 2009. 'Platanistas, the Course and Carneus: Their Places in the Topography of Sparta', in W. G. Cavanagh, C. Gallou and M. Georgiadis, eds. *Sparta and Laconia from Pre-history to Pre-Modern*. British School at Athens Studies 16. London. 195–203.

Sanders, L. J. 2008. *The Legend of Dion*. Toronto.

Sandys, J. E. 1908. *A History of Classical Scholarship*, vol. 3: *The Eighteenth Century in Germany and the Nineteenth Century in Europe and the United States of America*. Cambridge.

Sansone, D. 2016. 'The Size of the Tragic Chorus', *Phoenix* 70: 233–54.

Sauciuc, T. 1911. 'Zum Ehrendecret von Andros IG XII 5, 714', *AM* 36: 1–20.

1914. *Andros: Untersuchungen zur Geschichte und Topographie der Insel.* Vienna.

Savo, M. B. 2004. *Culti, sacerdozi e feste delle Cicladi dall'età arcaica all'età romana.* Rome.

Say Özer, Y. and Oğuz Özer, N. 2016. 'Kaunos Tiyatrosu'nun Biçimsel Analizi ve Temel Mimari Karakteri', in A. Diler, S. Özen, U. Çörtük, M. Doyran, B. Özen-Kleine, S. Akerdem, N. Oğuz Özer and Y. Say Özer, eds. 2016. *Basileus – 50. Yılında Kaunos / Kbid.* Ankara. 111–22.

Sayar, M. H. 1998. *Perinthos-Herakleia (Marmara Ereğlisi) und Umgebung: Geschichte, Testimonien, griechische und lateinische Inschriften.* Vienna.

Scaduto, R. 2010. *Il ritorno dei Cavalieri: Aspetti della tutela e del restauro dei monumenti a Rodi tra il 1912 e il 1945.* Palermo.

Scafuro, A. 2009. 'The Crowning of Amphiaraos', in L. Mitchell and L. Rubinstein, eds. *Greek History and Epigraphy: Essays in Honour of P. J. Rhodes.* Swansea. 59–86.

Scahill, D. 2015. 'The Hellenistic Theatre at Corinth: New Implications from Recent Excavations', in R. Frederiksen, E. R. Gebhard and A. Sokolicek, eds. *The Architecture of the Ancient Greek Theatre: Acts of an International Conference at the Danish Institute at Athens 27–30 January 2012.* Monographs of the Danish Institute at Athens 17. Aarhus. 193–202.

Schachter, A. 1981. *Cults of Boiotia 1: Acheloos to Hera.* BICS Supplement 38.1. London.

1986. *Cults of Boiotia 2: Heracles to Poseidon.* BICS Supplement 38.2. London.

1994. *Cults of Boiotia 3: Potnia to Zeus, Cults of Deities Unspecified by Name.* BICS Supplement 38.3. London.

2016a. *Boiotia in Antiquity: Selected Papers.* Cambridge.

2016b. 'Evolutions of a Mystery Cult: The Theban Kabiroi', in A. Schachter, *Boiotia in Antiquity: Selected Papers.* Cambridge. 315–43. = 'Evolutions of a Mystery Cult: The Theban Kabiroi', in M. B. Cosmopoulos, ed. 2003. *Greek Mysteries: The Archaeology and Ritual of Ancient Greek Secret Cults.* London. 112–42.

Schachter, A. and Slater, W. J. 2007. 'A Proxeny Decree from Koroneia, Boeotia, in Honour of Zotion, Son of Zotion, of Ephesos', *ZPE* 163: 81–95.

Schede, M. 1919. 'Aus dem Heraion von Samos', *AM* 44: 1–46.

Schiassi, G. 1955. 'I Prospalti di Eupoli', *PP* 40: 295–306.

Schiesaro, A. 2016. 'Bacchus in Roman Drama', in S. Frangoulidis, S. J. Harrison and G. Manuwald, eds. *Roman Drama and its Contexts.* Trends in Classics – Supplementary Volumes 34. Berlin. 25–42.

Schliemann, H. 1884. *Troja.* Leipzig.

1885. *Ilios, ville et pays des Troyens: Résultat des fouilles sur l'emplacement de Troie et des explorations faites en Troade de 1871 à 1882.* Paris.

Schmaltz, B. 1974. *Terrakotten aus dem Kabirenheiligtum bei Theben: Menschenähnliche Figuren, menschliche Figuren und Gerät.* Das Kabirenheiligtum bei Theben 5. Berlin.

Schmalz, G. C. R. 2007–2008. 'Inscribing a Ritualized Past: The Attic Restoration Decree *IG* II² 1035 and Cultural Memory in Augustan Athens', *Eulimene* 8–9: 9–46.

Schmid, W. 1912. *Wilhelm von Christs Geschichte der griechischen Litteratur*⁶. Munich.

1946. *Geschichte der griechischen Literatur*, vol. 1.4. Munich.

Schmidt, M. 1998. 'Komische Teufel und andere Gesellen auf der griechischen Komödienbühne', *AntK* 41: 17–32.

Schnabel, H. 1910. *Kordax: Archäologische Studien zur Geschichte eines antiken Tanzes und zum Ursprung der griechischen Komödie.* Munich.

Schnapp, A. 2011. 'The "Antiquitates" of the Greco-Roman World and their Effect on Antiquarian Thought in Europe from the Renaissance to the Early Nineteenth Century', in G. Klanicazy, M. Werner and O. Gecser, eds. *Multiple Antiquities – Multiple Modernities: Ancient Histories in Nineteenth Century European Cultures.* Frankfurt and New York. 279–304.

Schneidewin, F. M. 1833. *Ibyci Rhegini Carminum Reliquiae*. Göttingen.

    1837a. *Eustathii prooemium commentariorum Pindaricorum*. Göttingen.

    1837b. '86. 87. Stück', *GGA* 99: 849–59.

Scholl, A. 1994. 'Πολυτάλαντα μνημεῖα. Zur literarischen und monumentalen Überlieferung aufwendiger Grabmäler im spätklassischen Athen', *JdI* 109: 239–71.

    2002. 'Denkmäler der Choregen, Dichter und Schauspieler des athenischen Theaters', in W. D. Heilmeyer and M. Maischberger, eds. *Die griechisch Klassik: Idee oder Wirklichkeit*. Exhibition catalogue. Mainz. 546–54.

Schorn, S. 2004. *Satyros aus Kallatis: Sammlung der Fragmente mit Kommentar*. Basel.

    2007. '"Periegetische Biographie" – "Historische Biographie": Neanthes von Kyzikos (FgrHist 84) als Biograph', in M. Ehrler and S. Schorn, eds. *Die griechische Biographie in hellenistischer Zeit*. Berlin. 115–56.

    2012. 'Chamaeleon: Biography and Literature *Peri tou deina*', in A. Martano, E. Matelli and D. Mirhady, eds. *Praxiphanes of Mytilene and Chamaeleon of Heraclea: Text, Translation, and Discussion*. New Brunswick and London. 411–44.

Schörner, G. and Goette, H.-R. 2004. *Die Pan-Grotte von Vari*. Mainz.

Schulhof, E. 1908. 'Fouilles de Délos exécutées aux frais de M. le Duc de Loubat: Inscriptions financières (1904 et 1905)', *BCH* 32: 5–132.

Schultz, P. and Wickkiser, B. L. 2010. 'Communicating with the Gods in Ancient Greece: The Design and Functions of the "Thymele" at Epidauros', *International Journal of Technology, Knowledge & Society* 6: 143–63.

Schultz, P., Wickkiser, B. L., Hinge, G., Kanellopoulos, C. and Franklin, J. 2017. *The Thymele of Epidauros: Healing Space, and Musical Performance in Late Classical Greece*. Fargo, ND.

Schumacher, R. W. M. 1993. 'Three Related Sanctuaries of Poseidon: Geraistos, Kalaureia and Tainaron', in N. Marinatos and R. Hägg, eds. *Greek Sanctuaries: New Approaches*. London. 51–69.

Schwandner, E.-L. 2006. 'Die Ausgrabung in der antiken Stadt Stratos (Aitoloakarnania) und der Survey des Staatsgebietes "Stratike"', in *Α΄ Αρχαιολογική Σύνοδος Νότιας και Δυτικής Ελλάδος, ΣΤ Εφορεία Προϊστορικών και Κλασικών Αρχαιοτήτων, 6η Εφορεία Βυζαντινών Αρχαιοτήτων. Πρακτικά, Πάτρα 9–12 Ιουνίου 1996*. Athens. 531–40.

Schwarzmaier, A. 2011. *Die Masken aus der Nekropole von Lipari*. Wiesbaden.

Schwenk, C. J. 1985. *Athens in the Age of Alexander: The Dated Laws and Decrees of 'The Lykourgan Era' 338 – 322 B.C.* Chicago.

Schwyzer, E. 1923. *Dialectorum graecarum exempla epigraphica potiora*. Leipzig.

Scodel, R. 2003. '"Young Men of Sidon", Aeschylus' Epitaph, and Canons', *CML* 23: 129–41.

    2012. 'Sophocles' Biography', in K. Ormand, ed. *A Companion to Sophocles*. Chichester. 25–37.

Scott, L. 2005. *Historical Commentary on Herodotus Book 6*. Mnemosyne Supplement 268. Leiden and Boston.

Scott, W. 1885. *Fragmenta Herculanensia: A Descriptive Catalogue of the Oxford Copies of the Herculanean Rolls*. Oxford.

Scullion, S. 2002a. 'Tragic Dates', *CQ* 52: 81–101.

    2002b. 'Nothing to Do with Dionysus: Tragedy Misconceived as Ritual', *CQ* 52: 102–37.

    2003. 'Euripides and Macedon, or the Silence of the *Frogs*', *CQ* 53: 389–400.

Sear, F. 2003. 'The Theatre at Butrint: Parallels and Function', in O. Gilkes, ed. *The Theater at Butrint: Luigi Maria Ugolini's Excavations at Butrint (1928–1932)*. BSA Supplement 35. London. 181–94.

Sear, F. 2003. 'The Theatre at Butrint: Parallels and Function', in O. Gilkes, ed. *The Theater at Butrint: Luigi Maria Ugolini's Excavations at Butrint (1928–1932)*. BSA Supplement 35. London. 181–94.

2006. *Roman Theatres: An Architectural Study*. Oxford.

Séchan, L. 1926. *Études sur la tragédie grecque*. Paris.

Seeberg, A. 1965. 'Hephaistos Rides Again', *JHS* 85: 101–9.

1995. 'From Padded Dancers to Comedy', in A. Griffiths, ed. *Stage Directions: Essays in Ancient Drama in Honour of E. W. Handley*. BICS Supplement 66. London. 1–12.

Seelinger, R. A. 1998. 'The Dionysiac Context of the Cult of Melikertes/Palaimon at the Isthmian Sanctuary of Poseidon', *Maia* 50: 271–80.

Segre, M. 1941. 'Epigraphica VII: Il culto rodio di Alessandro e dei Tolomei', *BSRAA* 34: 29–39.

1993. *Iscrizioni di Cos*. Rome.

Segre, M. and Pugliese Carratelli, G. 1949–1951. 'Tituli Camirenses', *ASAtene* 27–29: 141–318.

Sens, A. 2010. 'Hellenistic Tragedy and Lycophron's *Alexandra*', in J. J. Clauss and M. Cuypers, eds. *A Companion to Hellenistic Literature*. Chichester and Malden. 297–313.

Serdaroğlu, U. 1982. 'Bautätigkeit in Anatolien unter der persischen Herrschaft', in D. Papenfuss and V. Strocka, eds. *Palast und Hütte: Beiträge zum Bauen und Wohnen im Altertum von Archäologen, Vor- und Frühgeschichtlern*. Mainz. 347–56.

Sestieri, P. C. 1960. 'Vasi pestani di Pontecagnano', *ArchCl* 12: 155–69.

Sève, M. 1993. 'Les concours d'Epidaure', *RÉG* 106: 303–28.

Shapiro, H. A. 1987. 'Kalos-Inscriptions with Patronymic', *ZPE* 68: 107–18.

1989. *Art and Cult under the Tyrants in Athens*. Mainz.

1995. *Art and Cult under the Tyrants in Athens: Supplement*. Mainz.

Shaw, C. 2014. *Satyric Play: The Evolution of Greek Comedy and Satyr Drama*. Oxford.

Shear, J. L. 2001. *Polis and Panathenaia: The History and Development of Athena's Festival*. PhD Diss. Pennsylvania.

2003a. 'Atarbos' Base and the Panathenaia', *JHS* 123: 164–80.

2003b. 'Prizes from Athens: The List of Panathenaic Prizes and the Sacred Oil', *ZPE* 142: 87–108.

Shear, T. L. 1928. 'Excavations in the Theatre District and Tombs of Corinth in 1928', *AJA* 32: 474–95.

1929. 'Excavations in the Theatre District and Tombs of Corinth in 1929', *AJA* 33: 515–46.

1978. *Kallias of Sphettos and the Revolt of Athens in 286 B.C.* Hesperia Supplement 17. Princeton.

1984. 'The Athenian Agora: Excavations of 1980–1982', *Hesperia* 53: 1–57.

Sherk, R. K. 1991. 'The Eponymous Officials of Greek Cities III', *ZPE* 88: 225–60.

Sherwin-White, S. M. 1978. *Ancient Cos: An Historical Study from the Dorian Settlement to the Imperial Period*. Hypomnemata 51. Göttingen.

Shields, E. 1917. *The Cults of Lesbos*. Wisconsin.

Shipley, G. 2005. 'Little Boxes on the Hillside: Greek Town Planning, Hippodamos, and Polis Ideology', in M. H. Hansen, ed. *The Imaginary Polis. Symposium, January 7–10, 2004*. Acts of the Copenhagen Polis Centre 7. Copenhagen. 335–403.

Sickinger, J. P. 1999. *Public Records and Archives in Classical Athens*. Chapel Hill and London.

Sidwell, K. 2009. *Aristophanes the Democrat: The Politics of Satirical Comedy During the Peloponnesian War*. Cambridge.

Sienkewicz, T. J. 1976. 'Sophokles' *Telepheia*', *ZPE* 20: 109–12.

Sifakis, G. M. 1967. *Studies in the History of Hellenistic Drama*. London.

1968. 'Notes on Delian Inscriptions', *BCH* 92: 486–92.

1971. 'Aristotle, *E.N.* IV, 2, 1123a 19–24, and the Comic Chorus in the Fourth Century', *AJP* 92: 410–32.

Simantoni-Bournia, E., Panagou, T. and Mavrokordatou, D. 2015. *Αρχαίο θέατρο Καρθαίας, Πρόταση για τη δημιουργία χορηγικού φακέλου από το Σωματείο ΔΙΑΖΩΜΑ*. Athens.

Simon, E. 1985. 'Hekate in Athen', *AM* 100: 271–84.

Sinopoli, G. 1929–1933. *Agyrium. Memorie Storiche* or *Storia di Agira*. Unpublished manuscript, Biblioteca Comunale, Agira. (accessed from www.agira.org/Pubblicazioni_Sinopoli/Agyrium/index.html).

Sismondo Ridgway, B. 1990. *Hellenistic Sculpture: The Styles of ca. 331–200 BC*. Wisconsin.

Sisto, M. A. 2003. 'Le forme dei vasi italioti e sicelioti a soggetto tragico', in *CFST*, 99–132.

Sjöqvist, E. 1962. 'Excavations at Morgantina (Serra Orlando) 1961: Preliminary Report VI', *AJA* 66: 135–43.

Skalet, C. H. 1928. *Ancient Sicyon with a Prosopographia Sicyonia*. Baltimore.

Skias, A.N. 1896. 'Ἐπιγραφαὶ Ἐλευσῖνος', *ArchEph*: 23–56.

1897. 'Ἐπιγραφαὶ Ἐλευσῖνος', *ArchEph*: 32–66.

Slapšak, B. 2007. 'The Leiden-Ljubljana Ancient Cities of Boeotia Project 2006', *Teiresias* 37.2: 11–20.

Slater, N. W. 1985. 'Vanished Players: Two Classical Reliefs and Theater History', *GRBS* 26: 333–44.

Slater, W. J. 1995. 'The Pantomime Tiberius Claudius Apolaustus', *GRBS* 36: 263–92.

1997. 'L'hégemôn dans les fêtes hellénistiques', *Pallas* 47: 97–106.

2011. 'Theatres for Hire', *Philologus* 155: 272–91.

Small, J. P. 2003. *The Parallel Worlds of Classical Art and Text*. Cambridge.

Smith, D. 2018. 'The Reception of Aeschylus in Sicily', in R. Kennedy, ed. *Brill's Companion to the Reception of Aeschylus*. Leiden and Boston. 9–53.

Smith, T. J. 1998. 'Dances, Drinks and Dedications: the Archaic Komos in Laconia', in W. G. Cavanagh and S. E. C. Walker, eds. *Sparta in Laconia*. London. 75–81.

2010. *Komast Dancers in Archaic Greek Art*. Oxford.

Snell, B. 1938. 'Identifikationen von Pindarbruchstücken', *Hermes* 73: 424–39.

1966. *Zu den Urkunden dramatischer Aufführungen*. Nachrichten der Akademie der Wissenschaften in Göttingen, Philologisch-Historische Klasse. Göttingen.

Sofia, A. 2003. 'Influssi egizi in Sicilia e in Magna Grecia. Testimonianze nella commedia dorica, nel mimo e nella farsa fliacica', *Aegyptus* 83: 133–61.

Sokolova, O. Y. 2000–2001. 'New Material from the Excavation of Nymphaeum', *Talanta* 32/3: 81–90.

2007. 'City of Nymphaeum: Excavation Results (1991–2000)', in S. L. Solovyov, ed. *Greeks and Natives in the Cimmerian Bosporos 7th–1st Centuries BC: Proceedings of the International Conference October 2000, Taman Russia*. BAR International Series 1729. Oxford. 113–16.

Sokolova, O. Y. and Pavilchenko, N. A. 2002. 'Новая посвятительная надпись из Нимфея', *Hyperboreus* 8: 99–121.

Sokolowski, F. 1936. 'Sur le péan de Philodamos', *BCH* 60: 135–43.

Solders, S. 1931. *Die ausserstädtischen Kulte und die Einigung Attikas*. Lund.

Solmsen, F. 1947, 'Eratosthenes' *Erigone*: A Reconstruction', *TAPA* 78: 252–75.

Sommerstein, A. H. 1996a. *Aristophanes: Frogs*. Warminster.

1996b. 'Aeschylus' Epitaph', *MCr* 30/31: 111–17.

2001. *Aristophanes: Wealth*. Warminster.

Sonnino, M. 2014. 'Comedy Outside the Canon: From Ritual Slapstick to Hellenistic Mime', in G. Colesanti and M. Giordano, eds. *Submerged Literature in Ancient Greek Culture.* Berlin and Boston. 128–50.

Sordi, M. 1992. *La dynasteia in Occidente (Studi su Diogini I).* Padua.

Sosin, J. D. 2002. 'Grain for Andros', *Hermes* 130: 131–45.

Soueref, K. I. 2012. 'Μεταξύ Πίνδου και Ιονίου', in K. I. Soueref, ed. *Αρχαία θέατρα της Ηπείρου.* Diazoma 6. Athens. 9–20.

Sourvinou-Inwood, C. 2003. *Tragedy and Athenian Religion.* Oxford and Lanham.

Sparkes, B. 1967. 'The Taste of the Boeotian Pig', *JHS* 87: 116–30.

    1975. 'Illustrating Aristophanes', *JHS* 95: 122–35.

Spigo, U. 1992–1993. 'Nuovi rinvenimenti di ceramica a figure rosse di fabbrica Siceliota ed Italiota da Lipara e dalla provincia di Messina', *MeditArch* 5–6: 32–47.

    2003. 'Rinvenimenti di ceramica siceliota dalla provincia di Messina: Breve nota di aggiornamento', in G. M. Bacci and M. C. Martinelli, eds. *Studi classici in onore di Luigi Bernabò Brea.* Palermo. 103–20.

    2006. 'Tindari. Considerazioni sull'impianto urbano e notizie preliminari sulle recenti campagne di scavo nel settore occidentale', in M. Osanna and M. Torelli, eds. *Sicilia ellenistica, consuetudo italica: Alle origini dell'architettura ellenistica d'Occidente. Spoleto, Complesso monumentale di S. Nicolò, 5–7 novembre 2004.* Rome. 97–105.

Spineto, N. 2005. *Dionysos a teatro. Il contesto festivo del dramma greco.* Rome.

Sposito, A. 2011. *Morgantina: Il teatro ellenistico. Storia e restauri.* Rome.

Stadter, P. A. 2014. *Plutarch and his Roman Readers.* Oxford.

Stählin, F. 1924. *Das hellenische Thessalien – Landeskundliche und geschichtliche Beschreibung Thessaliens in der hellenischen und römischen Zeit.* Stuttgart.

Stais, B. 1891. 'Ἀνασκαφὴ Ραμνοῦντος', *Prakt*: 13–18.

Stama, F. 2014. *Frinico: Introduzione, Traduzione e Commento.* Fragmenta Comica 7. Heidelberg.

Stamatopoulou, Z. 2014. 'Inscribing Performances in Pindar's Olympian 6', *TAPA* 144: 1–17.

Stanzel, M. 1991. *Die Tierreste aus dem Artemis-Apollon Heiligtum bei Kalapodi in Boötien/Griechenland.* Diss. Munich.

Stavropoulos, D. 1893. 'Ἐρετρικαί ἐπιγραφαί Ἀνέκδοτοι', *Athena* 5: 345–70, 551–2.

Steinhauer, G. 1973–1974. 'Ἀρχαιότητες καὶ μνημεῖα Λακωνίας-Ἀρκαδίας 1973–1974', *ArchDelt* 29 B 2: 283–301.

    1992. 'Δύο δημοτικὰ ψηφίσματα τῶν Ἀχαρνέων', *ArchEph* 131: 179–93.

    2001. *The Archaeological Museum of Piraeus.* Athens.

    2002. 'The Classical Mesogaia (5th–4th century BC)', in *Mesogaia: History and Culture of Mesogeia in Attica.* Athens. 81–147.

    2004–2009. 'Ἕνα νέο δημοτικὸ ψήφισμα τῶν Ἀλῶν Αἰξωνίδων', *Horos* 17–21: 69–72.

    2007. 'Δημοτικὸ ψήφισμα ἀπὸ τὸ θέατρο τοῦ Εὐωνύμου', *ArchEph* 146: 43–7.

    2009. 'Οδικό δίκτυο τῆς Αττικῆς', in M. Korres, ed. *Αττικῆς οδοί: Αρχαίοι δρόμοι της Αττικῆς.* Athens. 34–73.

Stephanou, A. P. 1960. 'Ψήφισμα τοῦ Δήμου Χίων', in M. Myrtides, ed. *Εἰς μνήμην Κ. Ἀμάντου (1874–1960).* Athens. 140–6.

Steskal, M. 2002. 'Das Theater von Velia. Bericht über die Ausgrabungen 2001', *ÖJh* 71: 267–84.

Stevens, P. T. 1956. 'Euripides and the Athenians', *JHS* 76: 87–94.

Stewart, E. 2016. 'An Ancient Theatre Dynasty: The Elder Carcinus, the Young Xenocles and the Sons of Carcinus in Aristophanes', *Philologus* 160: 1–18.

    2017. *Greek Tragedy on the Move: The Birth of a Panhellenic Art Form c. 500–300 BC.* Oxford.

Stibbe, C. M. 1991. 'Dionysos in Sparta', *BABesch* 66: 1–44.

   1992. 'Dionysos mit einer Kithara?', in H. Froning, T. Hölscher and H. Mielsch, eds. *Kotinos: Festschrift für Erika Simon.* Mainz. 139–45.

Stillwell, R. 1952. *Corinth II: The Theater.* Princeton.

Stiros, S., Psimoulis, P. and Kolonas, C. 2005. 'The Theatre of Aitolian Makyneia', *BSA* 100: 299–313.

Stockert, W. 2012. *T. Maccius Plautus, Cistellaria: Einleitung, Text und Kommentar.* Munich.

Stone, S. 2014. *Morgantina Studies*, vol. 6f: *The Hellenistic and Roman Fine Pottery.* Princeton.

Storey, I. C. 2003. *Eupolis: Poet of Old Comedy.* Oxford.

   2011. *Fragments of Old Comedy*, 3 vols. Vol. 1: *Alcaeus to Diocles*, vol. 2: *Diopeithes to Phere-crates*, vol. 3: *Philonicus to Xenophon – Adespota.* Cambridge, MA and London.

Strauss-Clay, J. 1996. 'Fusing the Boundaries: Apollo and Dionysos at Delphi', *Mètis* 11: 83–100.

Stroud, R. S. 1974. 'Three Attic Decrees', *CSCA* 7: 279–98.

   1998. *The Athenian Grain-Tax Law of 374/3 BC.* Hesperia Supplement 29. Princeton.

   2013. *Corinth XVIII.6: The Sanctuary of Demeter and Kore. The Inscriptions.* Princeton.

Stucchi, S. 1952. 'Scavo di un santuario presso il teatro greco', *FA* 7: no. 1605.

   1954. 'Syracuse, Siracusa', *FA* 7: 136–7.

   1975. *Architettura cirenaica.* Roma.

Studniczka, F. 1888. 'Aus Chios', *MdI* 13: 160–201.

Sturgeon, M. C. 2004. *Corinth IX 3: Sculpture; The Assemblage from the Theater.* Princeton.

Stylianou, P. J. 1983. 'Thucydides, the Panionian Festival and the Ephesia (III 104), Again', *Historia* 32: 245–9.

   1998. *A Historical Commentary on Diodorus Siculus, Book 15.* Oxford.

Summa, D. 2004. 'Una dedica coregica inedita', *ZPE* 150: 147–8.

   2006. 'Attori e coreghi in Attica: Iscrizioni dal teatro di Thorikos', *ZPE* 157: 77–86.

   2010. 'Ricerche sulla vita teatrale e il suo finanziamento in Locride', in B. Le Guen, ed. *L'argent dans les concours du monde grec.* Vincennes. 107–25.

Süss, W. 1905. *De personarum antiquae comoediae Atticae usu atque origine.* Bonn.

   1938. 'Nochmals zur Cistellaria des Plautus', *RhM* 87: 97–141.

Sutton, D. F. 1987. 'The Theatrical Families of Athens', *AJP* 108: 9–26.

   1989. *Dithyrambographi Graeci.* Hildesheim.

Svenshon, H. 2012. 'Vermessen(d)e Planung – Babylonische Mathematik, Heron von Alexandria und das Theater in Epidauros', in H. Svenshon, M. Boos and F. Lang, eds. *Werkraum Antike, Beiträge zur Archäologie und antiken Baugeschichte.* Darmstadt. 83–102.

Svoronos, J. N. 1900. 'Τὰ πηλινὰ εἰσιτήρια τοῦ θεάτρου τῆς Μαντινείας', *JIAN* 3: 197–228.

Svoronos, J. N. and Barth, W. 1937. *Das Athener Nationalmuseum*, vol. 3. Athens.

Symeonoglou, S. 1985. *The Topography of Thebes from the Bronze Age to Modern Times.* Princeton.

Syropoulos, G. 2013. 'Ἀνασκάπτοντας στην οδό Πειραιῶς', in M. Donka-Toli and S. Oikonomou, eds. *Ἀρχαιολογικές Συμβολές. Τόμος Α: Ἀττική, ΚΣΤ και Β´ Ἐφορείες Προϊστορικῶν και Κλασικῶν Ἀρχαιοτήτων.* Athens. 57–65.

Tagalidou, E. 1993. *Weihreliefs an Herakles aus klassischer Zeit.* Jonsered.

Takeuchi, K. 2010–2013. 'Ten Notes on Inscriptions from the Attic Demes', *Horos* 22–25: 85–106.

   2011. 'EM 7709 (*IG* II² 1161) and the Proclamation at the Dionysia of Lamptrai', *Kobe University Yearbook of History* 26: 1–24.

   2018. *Land, Meat, and Gold: The Cults of Dionysos in the Attic Demes.* PhD Diss. National and Kapodistrian University of Athens.

forthcoming '*IG* I³ 250, the Eleusinian Cults and Zeus Herkeios', in *Proceedings of the Second North American Congress of Greek and Latin Epigraphy (2016)*. Leiden.

Takeuchi, K. and Wilson, P. 2014. 'Dionysos and Theatre in Sphettos', *Logeion* 4: 40–69.

Talbert, R. 1975. *Timoleon and the Revival of Greek Sicily 344–317 B.C.* Cambridge.

Taormina, A. 2015. 'Nuove ricerche archeologiche nel teatro antico di Catania', in F. Nicoletti, ed. *Catania Antica: Nuove prospettive di ricerca*. Palermo. 281–349.

Taplin, O. 1977. *The Stagecraft of Aeschylus: The Dramatic Use of Exits and Entrances in Greek Tragedy*. Oxford.

1987. 'Phallology, Phlyakes, Iconography and Aristophanes', *PCPS* 33: 92–104.

1993. *Comic Angels: And Other Approaches to Greek Drama Through Vase-painting.* Oxford.

1998. 'Narrative Variation in Vase-painting and Tragedy: The Example of Dirke', *AntK* 41: 33–57.

1999. 'Spreading the Word through Performance', in S. Goldhill and R. Osborne, eds. *Performance Culture and Athenian Democracy.* Cambridge. 33–57.

2007. *Pots & Plays: Interactions Between Tragedy and Greek Vase-painting of the Fourth Century B.C.* Los Angeles.

2010. 'A Curtain Call?', in O. Taplin and R. Wyles, eds. *The Pronomos Vase and its Context.* Oxford. 255–64.

2012. 'How was Athenian Tragedy Played in the Greek West?', in K. Bosher, ed. *Theater Outside Athens: Drama in Greek Sicily and South Italy.* Cambridge. 226–50.

forthcoming. 'The Spread of Greek Theatre to the West – and to the North-East?', in D. Braund, E. Hall and R. Wyles, eds. *Ancient Theatre and Performance Culture around the Ancient Black Sea.* Cambridge.

Taplin, O. and Wyles, R. eds. 2010. *The Pronomos Vase and its Context.* Oxford.

Tarán, L. and Gutas, D. 2012. *Aristotle: 'Poetics'.* Leiden and Boston.

Taylor, M. 1997. *Salamis and the Salaminioi: The History of an Unofficial Athenian Demos.* Amsterdam.

Televantou, C. A. 1996. *Ἄνδρος. Τὰ Μνημεῖα καὶ τὸ Ἀρχαιολογικὸ Μουσεῖο.* Athens.

2002. *Αρχαιολογικὸ Μουσείο Παλαιοπόλεως η αρχαία πόλις της Ἄνδρου.* Athens.

Telò, M. 2007. *Eupolidis Demi.* Florence.

Telò, M. and Porciani, L. 2002. 'Un'alternativa per la datazione dei *Demi* di Eupoli', *QUCC* 72: 23–40.

Te Riele, G. J. M. J. 1976. 'Charitésia', in J. M. Bremer, S. L. Radt and C. J. Ruijgh, eds. *Miscellanea tragica in honorem J. C. Kamerbeek.* Amsterdam. 285–91.

Themelis, P. 1987. 'Ερετριακές λατρείες', in *Φίλια Ἔπη to George E. Mylonas to Commemorate his Sixty Years as an Excavator*, vol. 3. Athens. 106–25.

2010. *Τα θέατρα της Μεσσήνης.* Diazoma 4. Athens.

Themelis, P. and Sidiropoulos, K. 2015. 'The Theatre at Messene: Building Phases and Mason's Marks', in R. Frederiksen, E. R. Gebhard and A. Sokolicek, eds. *The Architecture of the Ancient Greek Theatre: Acts of an International Conference at the Danish Institute at Athens 27–30 January 2012.* Monographs of the Danish Institute at Athens 17. Aarhus. 203–31.

Thompson, H. A. 1950. 'Excavations in the Athenian Agora', *Hesperia* 19: 313–37.

Threpsiades, J. 1939. 'Decree in Honour of Euthydemos of Eleusis', *Hesperia* 8: 177–80.

Tiverios, M. A. 1993. 'Από την οχύρωση της αρχαίας Ἄνδρου', in *Πρακτικά του Α΄ Κυκλαδολογικού Συνεδρίου. Τα περί Ἄνδρου, Ἄνδρος 5–9 Σεπτεμβρίου 1991. Ανδριακά Χρονικά* 21: 209–31.

Tod, M. N. 1948. *A Selection of Greek Historical Inscriptions*, vol. 2: *From 403 to 323 B.C.* Oxford.

Todisco, L. 2002. *Teatro e spettacolo in Magna Grecia e in Sicilia: Testi, immagini, architettura.* Milan.

    ed. 2006. *Pittura e ceramica figurata tra Grecia, Magna Grecia e Sicilia.* Bari.

    2012. 'Il vaso di New York MMA 24.97.104 e le *Tesmoforiazuse* di Aristofane', *Ostraka* 21: 187–98.

    2015. 'Noterella sull'ubicazione del teatro Greco di Taranto', *RendLinc* ser. 9, 26: 57–70.

Tomlinson, R. A. 1983. *Epidauros.* London.

Tondriau, J. 1950. 'La Dynastie Ptolémaïque et la Religion Dionysiaque', *ChrÉg* 25 no. 50: 283–316.

Tortorici, E. 2008. 'Osservazioni e ipotesi sulla topografia di Catania antica', in L. Quilici and S. Quilici Gigli, eds. *Edilizia pubblica e privata nelle città romane.* Rome. 91–124.

    2010. 'Ulteriori osservazioni sulla topografia di Catania Antica', in M. G. Branciforti and V. La Rosa, eds. *Tra lava e mare: Contributi all'archaiologhia di Catania: atti del convegno, Catania, ex Monastero dei Benedettini, novembre 2007.* Catania. 319–37.

Tosi, G. 2003. *Gli edifici per spettacoli nell'Italia romana.* Rome.

Touchais, G. 1978. 'Chronique des fouilles et découvertes archéologiques en Grèce en 1977', *BCH* 102: 641–770.

    1998. 'Chronique des fouilles et découvertes archéologiques en Grèce en 1996 et 1997', *BCH* 122: 705–988.

    1999. 'Chronique des fouilles et découvertes archéologiques en Grèce en 1998', *BCH* 123: 655–6.

Tozzi, G. 2016. *Assemblee politiche e spazio teatrale ad Atene.* Padua.

Tracy, S. V. 1995. *Athenian Democracy in Transition: Attic Letter-Cutters of 340 to 290 B.C.* Berkeley.

Traill, J. S. 1975. *The Political Organization of Attica: A Study of Demes, Trittys, and Phylai and their Representation in the Athenian Council.* Princeton.

    1986. *Demos and Trittys: Epigraphical and Topographical Studies in the Organization of Attica.* Toronto.

Travlos, J. 1988. *Bildlexicon zur Topographie der antiken Attika.* Tübingen.

Trendall, A. D. and Webster, T. B. L. 1971. *Illustrations of Greek Drama.* London.

Trevett, J. C. 1990. 'P.Oxy. 2537 and Isocrates' *Trapeziticus*', *ZPE* 81: 22–6.

Tréziny, H. 2012. 'L'agora de Mégara Hyblaea', in C. Ampolo, ed. *Agorai di Sicilia, agorai d'Occidente: Atti del seminario du Studio, Pisa, 30 giugno–2 luglio 2008.* Pisa. 119–23.

Triandaphyllos, D. 1984. 'Άβδηρα Ίστορικά στοιχεία', *Άρχαιολογία* 13: 27–34.

Trümpy, C. 1997. *Untersuchungen zu den altgriechischen Monatsnamen und Monatsfolgen.* Heidelberg.

Trunk, M. 1994. 'Das Theater von Neandria? Vorbericht zu einer Stufenanlage im Stadtzentrum', in E. Schwertheim and H. Wiegartz, eds. *Neue Forschungen zu Neandria und Alexandria Troas.* Asia Minor Studien 11. Bonn. 91–100.

Tsardaka, D. A. 2010–2013. 'Συμβολή στην ιστορική τοπογραφία της αρχαίας πόλεως Χῖου', *Horos* 22–25: 481–517.

Tschiedel, H. J. 1986. 'Hic Abdera. Gedanken zur Narrheit eines Gemeinwesens im Altertum—oder : Wie dumm waren die Abderiten?', in P. Krafft and H. J. Tschiedel, eds. *Concentus hexachordus: Beiträge zum 10. Symposion der bayerischen Hochschullehrer für Klassische Philologie in Eichstätt (24.–25. Februar 1984).* Eichstätter Beiträge 13. Regensburg. 169–95.

Tsingarida, A. 2002. '"Nul ne sait qui n'essaye". Alphonse van Branteghem et sa collection de vases grecs', in D. C. Kurtz and A. Tsingarida, eds. *Appropriating Antiquity/Saisir l'Antique: Collections et collectionneurs d'antiques en Belgique et en Grande Bretagne au XIXe siècle.* Brussels. 245–73.

2014. 'The Search for the Artist. The van Branteghem and Bourguignon Collections and the Con-
noisseurship of Greek Vases', in S. Schmidt and M. Steinhart, eds. *Sammeln und Erforschen:
Griechische Vasen in neuzeitlichen Sammlungen.* Munich. 115–21.

Tsirivakos, E. 1974. Ἡνίοχος τέχνης τραγικῆς', *ArchDelt* 29 A: 88–94.

Tsountas, C. 1884. Ἐπιγραφὴ ἐξ Ἐλευσῖνος', *ArchEph* 3: 69–74.

Tzachou-Alexandri, O. 1980. Ἀνασκαφή θεάτρου στούς Τράχωνες Ἀττικῆς', *Prakt*: 64–7.

1999. 'The Original Plan of the Greek Theater Reconsidered: the Theater at Evonymon of Attica',
in *Proceedings of the XVth International Congress of Classical Archaeology, Amsterdam, July
12–17, 1998: Classical Archaeology towards the Third Millennium, Reflections and Perspectives.* Amsterdam. 420–3.

2007. Ἀρχαιστικὰ ἀγάλματα Διονύσου ἀπὸ τὸ θέατρο τοῦ Εὐωνύμου', *ArchEph* 146:
1–42.

Tziafalias, A. 2011. Ἀποκάλυψη αρχαίων θεάτρων Λάρισας', in V. Adrimi-Sismani, ed. *Αρχαία
Θέατρα στη Θεσσαλία.* Diazoma 5. Athens. 23–32.

Ugarković, M. 2016. 'Trouble in Paradise? Among the Last Comedy Scenes in Red-figure: An Oinochoe from Issa and its Cultural Context', *Vjesnik za arheologiju i povijest dalmatinsku* 109:
57–98.

Ugolini, L. M. 1931–1932. 'Un interessante teatro greco-romano che sta per venir alla luce a But-
trinto', *Dioniso* 3: 7–12.

Ussing, J. 1854. *Graeske og latinske indskrifter i København.* Copenhagen.

Vahtikari, V. 2014. *Tragedy Performances Outside Athens in the Late Fifth and the Fourth Centuries
BC.* Papers and Monographs of the Finnish Institute of Athens 20. Helsinki.

Vaillant, A. 1927. 'Sur un fragment d'Epicharme', *RPhil* 1: 327.

Valavanis, P. 2007. Κιονωτό επιτύμβιο μνημείο στο Ικάριον Αττικῆς', in E. Simantoni-Bournia,
A. A. Laimou, L. G. Mendoni and N. Kourou, eds. Ἀμύμονα ἔργα. Τιμητικός τόμος γιὰ τόν
καθηγητὴ Βασίλη Κ. Λαμπρινουδάκη. Athens. 281–96.

Valente, S. 2015. *The Antiatticist: Introduction and Critical Edition.* Berlin and Boston.

Vallet, G. 1973. 'Megara Hyblaea', in P. Pelagatti and G. Voza, eds. *Archeologia nella Sicilia sud-ori-
entale.* Naples. 159–71.

1993. 'Chronique, Mégara Hyblaea', *MÉFRA* 105: 462–70.

Vallois, R. 1922. 'L' "Agalma" des Dionysies de Délos', *BCH* 46: 94–112.

1926. 'Le théâtre de Tégée', *BCH* 50: 135–73.

Vamvouri Ruffy, M. 2004. *La fabrique du divin: Les Hymnes de Callimaque à la lumière des Hymnes
homériques et des Hymnes épigraphes.* Kernos Supplement 14. Liège.

Vanderpool. E. 1979. 'The Genos Theoinidai Honors a Priestess of Nymphe', *AJP* 100: 213–16.

Van der Spek, R. 2001. 'The Theatre of Babylon in Cuneiform', in W. H. van Soldt, J. G. Dercksen,
N. J. C. Kouwenberg and T. J. H. Krispijn, eds. *Studies Presented to Klaas R. Veenhof on the
Occasion of his Sixty-Fifth Birthday.* Leiden. 445–56.

2005. 'Ethnic Segregation in Hellenistic Babylon', in W. H. van Soldt, R. Kalvelagen and D. Katz,
eds. *Ethnicity in Ancient Mesopotamia: Papers Read at the 48th Rencontre Assyriologique In-
ternationale. Leiden, 1–4 July 2002.* Leiden. 393–408.

2009. 'Multi-Ethnicity and Ethnic Segregation in Hellenistic Babylon', in T. Derks and N. Roy-
mans, eds. *Ethnic Constructs in Antiquity: The Role of Power and Tradition.* Amsterdam.
101–15.

Van Dijk, G.-J. 1997. *Ainoi, Logoi, Mythoi: Fables in Archaic, Classical, and Hellenistic Greek Literature.* Leiden, New York and Cologne.

Vandlik, K. 2002. 'Phrynis', *BMusHongr* 97: 21–32.

Van Groningen, B. 1933. *Aristote: Le Second Livre de l'Économique*. Leiden.

Van Groningen, B. and Wartelle, A. 1968. *Aristote Économique.* Paris.

Van Looy, H. 1994. 'Le théâtre de Thorikos et les représentations dramatiques', in H. Mussche, ed. *Studies in South Attica II*. Ghent. 9–25.

Van Straten, F. T. 1995. *Hiera Kala: Images of Sacrifice in Archaic and Classical Greece.* Leiden.

Van Wees, H. 2013. *Ships and Silver, Taxes and Tribute: A Fiscal History of Archaic Athens*. London and New York.

Varınlıoğlu, E. 1981. 'Inscriptions from Erythrae', *ZPE* 44: 45–50.

Varınlıoğlu, E., Bresson, A., Brun, P., Debord, P. and Descat, R. 1990. 'Une inscription de Pladasa en Carie', *REA* 92: 59–78.

Various Authors 2012. *Υπουργείο Πολιτισμού και Τουρισμού Γενική Διεύθυνση Αρχαιοτήτων και Πολιτιστικής Κληρονομιάς 2000–2010 από το Ανασκαφικό Έργο των Εφορείων Αρχαιοτήτων*. Athens. www.yppo.gr/0/anaskafes/pdfs/B_EPKA.pdf

Varkıvanç, B. 2015. 'Periaktoi at the Theatre of Kaunos', *Adalya* 18: 181–202.

2016. 'Kaunos Tiyatrosu Klasik Dönem Sahne Binası', in Y. Hazırlayanlar, B. Takmer, E. Akdoğu Arca and N. Gökalp Özdil, eds. *Vir doctus anatolicus: Studies in Memory of Sencer Şahin*. Istanbul. 915–25.

2017. 'The Stone Architecture of the Proskene of the Theater in Kaunos', *Adalya* 20: 267–89.

Vassallo, S. 2012. 'The Theater of Montagna dei Cavalli-Hippana', in K. Bosher, ed. *Theater Outside Athens: Drama in Greek Sicily and South Italy*. Cambridge. 208–25.

Vassallo, S. and Zirone, D. 2012. 'Il teatro alto-ellenistico di Montagna dei Cavalli / Ippana', in C. Ampolo, ed. *Sicilia Occidentale: Studi, rassegne, ricerche*. Pisa. 105–12.

Vatin, C. 1964. 'Pharsaliens à Delphes', *BCH* 88: 446–54.

Vela Tejada, J. and Martín García, F. 1991. *Eneas el Táctico: Poliorcética. Polieno: Estratagemas.* Madrid.

Velenis, G. 2012. 'Αντερεισματικοί τοίχοι των πρώιμων ελληνιστικών χρόνων στα θέατρα των Φιλίππων και των Αιγών', in P. Adam-Veleni, ed. *Αρχαία Θέατρα της Μακεδονίας*. Diazoma 3. Athens. 35–44.

Veligianni-Terzi, C. 1997. *Wertbegriffe in den attischen Ehrendekreten der Klassischen Zeit*. Heidelberger Althistorische Beiträge und Epigraphische Studien 25. Stuttgart.

Verkinderen, F. 1987. 'The Honorary Decree for Malousios of Gargara and the κοινόν of Athena Ilias', *Tyche* 2: 247–69.

Vermeule, C. C. 1970. 'Greek Vases in Boston: Important Recent Acquisitions', *BurlMag* 112: 624–31.

Versnel, H. 1993. *Transition and Reversal in Myth and Ritual: Inconsistencies in Greek and Roman Religion II*. Leiden.

Vial, C. 1984. *Délos indépendante (314–167 avant J.-C.): Étude d'une communauté civique et de ses institutions*. BCH Supplement 10. Paris.

Vickers, M. 1999. *Ancient Greek Pottery*. Oxford.

Vierneisel, K. and Scholl, A. 2002. 'Reliefdenkmäler dramatischer Choregen im klassischen Athen: das Münchner Maskenrelief für Artemis und Dionysos', *MüJb* 53: 7–55.

Vikatou, O., Frederiksen, R. and Handberg, S. 2014. 'The Danish-Greek Excavations at Kalydon, Aitolia: The Theatre. Preliminary Report from the 2011 and 2012 Campaigns', *Proceedings of the Danish Institute at Athens* 7: 221–34.

Villard, F. 2013. 'Epicharme ou la richesse de la vie culturelle à Mégara Hyblaea', in S. Bouffier, ed. *L'occident grec: De Marseille à Mégara Hyblaea*. Bibliothèque d'Archéologie Méditerranéenne et Africaine 13. Paris. 171–6.

Vinogradov, J. G. 1981a. 'Синопа и Ольвия в V в. до н.э.: Проблема политического устройства I', *VDI* 156: 65–90.

1981b. 'Синопа и Ольвия в V в. до н.э.: Проблема политического устройства II', *VDI* 157: 49–75.

Vinogradov, J. G. and Golovačeva, I. V. 1990. 'Новый источник о походе Зопириона', in V. L. Janin, ed. *Нумизматические исследования по истории юго-восточной Европы*. Kisiniev. 15–29.

Vinogradov, J. G. and Karyshkovsky, P. O. 1982. 'Каллиник, Сын Евксена. Проблемы политической и социально-экономической истории Ольвии второй половины IV в. до н.э. I', *VDI* 162: 26–46.

1983. 'Каллиник, Сын Евксена. Проблемы политической и социально-экономической истории Ольвии второй половины IV в. до н.э. II', *VDI* 163: 21–39.

Vinogradov, J. G. and Kryžickij, S. D. 1995. *Olbia: Eine altgriechische Stadt im nordwestlichen Schwarzmeerraum*. Mnemosyne Supplement 149. Leiden.

Viola, G. 2008. 'I teatri di Akrai, Eloro, Eraclea Minoa, Monte Iato, Montagna dei Cavalli, Montagna di Marzo, Morgantina, Solunto', in *Studio tematico della Carta del Rischio del Patrimonio Culturale della Regione Siciliana. I. Parte. Architetture teatrali siciliane di età antica: Fase della conoscenza*. Palermo. 105–10.

Vitucci, G. 1939. 'Le rappresentazioni drammatiche nei demi attici: Studiate su alcune testi epigrafici', *Dioniso* 7: 210–25.

Vivliodetis, E. 2005. Ὁ Δῆμος τοῦ Μυρρινοῦντος: Ἡ ὀργάνωση καὶ ἡ ἱστορία τοῦ. *ArchEph* 144. Athens.

Vollgraff, G. 1919. 'Novae inscriptiones Argivae', *Mnemosyne* 47: 252–70.

Vollgraff, W. 1927. 'Le péan à Dionysos (suite)', *BCH* 51: 423–68.

Voutiras, E. 1982. 'Λ Dedication of the *Hebdomastai* to the Pythian Apollo', *AJA* 86: 229–33.

Voza, G. 1993–1994. 'Attività archeologica della Soprintendenza di Siracusa e Ragusa', *Kokalos* 39–40: 1281–94.

2001. 'Nuove ricerche sul teatro greco di Siracusa', in C. Basile and A. Di Natale, eds. *La Sicilia antica nei rapporti con l'Egitto: Atti del Convegno internazionale, Siracusa, 17–18 settembre 1999*. Syracuse. 207–10.

2007. 'Teatro greco di Siracusa: stato delle conoscenze', in G. Meli, ed. *Teatri antichi nell'area del Mediterraneo: Atti del II convegno internazionale di studi 'La materia e i segni della storia', Siracusa, 13.–17. ottobre 2004*. Palermo. 72–80.

2008. 'Siracusa – Teatro Greco: L'eccezionalità', in *Numero Unico XLIV Ciclo Spettacoli Classici*. Fondazione INDA. Syracuse. (www.indafondazione.org/senza-categoria/siracusa---teatro-greco-l'eccezionalita/)

2014. 'Teatro Greco a Siracusa, la solitudine dei numeri primi', in F. Granata, L. Godart, G. Voza, G. Di Rauso and M. Centanni, eds. *Siracusa: Capitale del teatro*. Pachino. 18–49.

Wachter, R. 2001. *Non-Attic Greek Vase Inscriptions*. Oxford.

Walbank, F. W. 1957. *A Historical Commentary on Polybius*, vol. 1: *Commentary on Books i–vi*. Oxford.

1967. *A Historical Commentary on Polybius*, vol. 2: *Commentary on Books vii–xviii*. Oxford.

Walbank, M. B. 1982. 'Regulations for an Athenian Festival', Hesperia Supplement 19: 173–82.

1991. 'Leases of Public Lands', in G. Lalonde, M. Langdon and M. Walbank, eds. *The Athenian Agora*, vol. 19: *Inscriptions: Horoi, Poletai Records, and Leases of Public Lands*. Princeton. 149–207.

Wallace, R. W. 2007. 'Revolutions and a New Order in Solonian Athens and Archaic Greece', in K. A. Raaflaub, K. Ober and R. W. Wallace, eds. *Origins of Democracy in Ancient Greece.* Berkeley and Los Angeles. 49–82.

Walsh, D. 2009. *Distorted Ideals in Greek Vase-Painting.* Cambridge.

Walters, H. B. 1892–1893. 'Odysseus and Kirke on a Boeotian Vase', *JHS* 13: 77–87.

Wankel, H. 1976. *Demosthenes: Rede für Ktesiphon über den Kranz*, 2 vols. Heidelberg.

Wasowicz, A. 1975. *Olbia pontique et son territoire: L'aménagement de l'espace.* Centre de recherches d'histoire ancienne 13, Annales littéraires de l'université de Besançon 168. Paris.

Waywell, G. B. 1999. 'Sparta and its Topography', *BICS* 43: 1–24.

    2002. 'New Discoveries at the Ancient Theatre of Sparta', in M. Stamatopoulou and M. Yeroulanou, eds. *Excavating Classical Culture: Recent Archaeological Discoveries in Greece.* Oxford. 245–53.

Waywell, G. B. and Wilkes, J. J. 1994. 'Excavations at Sparta: The Roman Stoa, 1988–91, Part 2', *BSA* 89: 377–432.

Weber, L. 1887. *Quaestionum Laconicarum Capita Duo.* Diss. Göttingen.

Webster, T. B. L. 1948. 'South Italian Vases and Attic Drama', *CQ* 42: 15–27.

    1951. 'Masks on Gnathia Vases', *JHS* 71: 222–32.

    1953–1954. 'Attic Comic Costume: A Re-Examination', *ArchEph*: 192–201.

    1954. 'Fourth Century Tragedy and the *Poetics*', *Hermes* 82: 294–308.

    1961. Review of L. Breitholz 1960, *Die dorische Farce im griechischen Mutterland vor dem 5. Jahrhundert*, *Gnomon* 33: 452–6.

    1967. *The Tragedies of Euripides.* London.

    1970. *Studies in Later Greek Comedy*². Manchester.

    1974. *An Introduction to Menander.* Manchester.

Wehrli, F. 1967. *Aristoxenos*². Die Schule des Aristoteles. Basle and Stuttgart.

Weil, H. 1895. 'Le péan delphique à Dionysos: Supplément', *BCH* 19: 343–418.

    1897. 'Le péan delphique à Dionysos: Supplément', *BCH* 21: 510–13.

Weil, R. 1876. 'Von den griechischen Inseln. Reisebericht', *AM* 1: 235–52.

Wenkebach, E. ed. 1936. *Galeni in Hippocratis Epidemiarum librum III commentarii I–III. CMG* V 10, 2, 1. Leipzig.

Werner, R. 1955. 'Die Dynastie der Spartokiden', *Historia* 4: 412–44.

West, M. L. 1974. *Studies in Greek Elegy and Iambus.* Berlin and New York.

    1975. 'Cynaethus' Hymn to Apollo', *CQ* 25: 161–70.

    1978. 'An Unrecognized Fragment of Archilochus?', *ZPE* 32: 1–5.

    1982. 'Stesichorus' Horse', *ZPE* 48: 86.

    1989. 'The Early Chronology of Attic Tragedy', *CQ* 39: 251–4.

    1992. *Ancient Greek Music.* Oxford.

    1999a. 'Sophocles with Music (?): Ptolemaic Music Fragments and Remains of Sophocles (Junior?)', *ZPE* 126: 43–65.

    1999b. 'The Invention of Homer', *CQ* 49: 364–82.

    2007. 'A New Musical Papyrus: Carcinus, *Medea*', *ZPE* 161: 1–10.

    2010. 'Rhapsodes at Festivals', *ZPE* 173: 1–13.

Westlake, H. 1938. 'The Sources of Plutarch's Timoleon', *CQ* 32: 65–74.

Wetzel, F. von, Schmidt, E., and Mallwitz, A. eds. 1957. *Das Babylon der Spätzeit.* Berlin.

Wheeler, E. L. 1988. *Stratagem and the Vocabulary of Military Trickery.* Leiden.

    2010. 'Polyaenus: *Scriptor Militaris*', in K. Brodersen, ed. *Polyainos: Neue Studien. / Polyaenus: New Studies.* Berlin. 7–54.

Wheler, G. 1682. *A Journey into Greece by George Wheler, Esq., in Company of Doctor Spon of Lyons*. London.

White, D. 1964. 'Demeter's Sicilian Cult as a Political Instrument', *GRBS* 5: 261–79.

1976. 'The City Defenses of Apollonia', in J. H. Humphrey, ed. *Apollonia, the Port of Cyrene: Excavations by the University of Michigan 1965–1967*. Libya Antiqua Supplement 4. Tripoli. 85–155.

White, S. A. 1995. 'Thrasymachus the Diplomat', *CP* 90: 307–27.

Whitehead, D. 1977. *The Ideology of the Athenian Metic*. Cambridge.

1983. 'Competitive Outlay and Community Profit: Φιλοτιμία in Democratic Athens', *ClMed* 34: 55–74.

1986a. *The Demes of Attica 508/7 – ca. 250 B.C.: A Political and Social Study*. Princeton.

1986b. 'Festival Liturgies in Thorikos', *ZPE* 62: 213–20.

1993. 'Cardinal Virtues: The Language of Public Approbation in Democratic Athens', *ClMed* 44: 37–75.

Wide, S. 1901. 'Ἀναθηματικὸν ἀνάγλυφον ἐξ Αἰγίνης', *ArchEph*: 113–20.

Wilamowitz-Möllendorff, U. von, 1875. 'Die megarische Komödie', *Hermes* 9: 319–41.

1880. 'Excurse zu Euripides Medeia', *Hermes* 15: 481–523.

1886. *Isyllos von Epidauros*. Berlin.

1898. 'Lesefrüchte', *Hermes* 33: 513–33.

1899. 'Lesefrüchte', *Hermes* 34: 601–39.

1905. *Bucolici Graeci*. Oxford.

1906. Review of A. Wilhelm 1906, *Urkunden dramatischer Aufführungen in Athen*, *GGA* 168: 611–40.

1907. *Einleitung in die griechische Tragödie*. Berlin.

1914. *Aeschyli tragoediae*. Berlin.

1922. *Pindaros*. Berlin.

1930. 'Lesefrüchte', *Hermes* 65: 241–58.

Wilcken, U. 1901. 'Zu den pseudo-aristotelischen Oeconomica', *Hermes* 36: 187–200.

Wildberg, C. 2011. 'Dionysos in the Mirror of Philosophy: Heraclitus, Plato, and Plotinus', in R. Schlesier, ed. *A Different God? Dionysos and Ancient Polytheism*. Berlin and Boston. 205–32.

Wiles, D. 1997. *Tragedy in Athens: Performance Space and Theatrical Meaning*. Cambridge.

Wilhelm, A. 1890. 'Ψηφίσματα ἐξ Ἐρετρίας', *ArchEph*: 195–206.

1900. 'Nachlese zu griechischen Inschriften', *ÖJh* 3: 40–62.

1906. *Urkunden dramatischer Aufführungen in Athen*. Vienna.

1909. *Beiträge zur griechischen Inschriftenkunde mit einem Anhange über die öffentliche Aufzeichung von Urkunden*. Vienna.

1940. 'Themis und Nemesis in Rhamnus', *ÖJh* 32: 200–9.

1943–1947. 'Διόνυσος Ἐλευθερεύς', *WS* 51: 162–6.

Willi, A. 2008. *Sikelismos: Sprache, Literatur und Gesellschaft im griechischen Sizilien (8.–5. Jh. v. Chr.)*. Basel.

2012. 'Challenging Authority: Epicharmus between Epic and Rhetoric', in K. Bosher, ed. *Theater Outside Athens: Drama in Greek Sicily and South Italy*. Cambridge. 56–75.

2015. 'Epicharmus, the Pseudepicharmeia, and the Origins of Attic Drama', in S. Chronopoulos and C. Orth, eds. *Fragmente einer Geschichte der griechischen Komödie*. Studia Comica 5. Heidelberg. 109–45.

Williams, C. 2013. 'Corinth 2011: Investigation of the West Hall of the Theater', *Hesperia* 82: 487–549.

Williams, C. and Zervos, O. H. 1989. 'Corinth, 1988: East of the Theater', *Hesperia* 58: 1–50.

Williams, H. 2005. 'The Exploration of Ancient Stymphalos, 1982–2002', in E. Østby, ed. *Ancient Arcadia: Papers from the Third International Seminar on Ancient Arcadia held at the Norwegian Institute at Athens, 7–10 May 2002.* Athens. 397–405.

Williams, H., Schaus, G., Gourley, B., Cronkite-Price, S.-M., Sherwood, K. D. and Lolos, Y. 2002. 'Excavations at Ancient Stymphalos, 1999–2002', *Mouseion* 2: 135–87.

Wilson, N. G. 1997. *Aelian: Historical Miscellany.* Cambridge, MA.

  1999. 'Travelling Actors in the Fifth Century?', *CQ* 49: 625.

Wilson, P. 1997. 'Amymon of Sikyon: A First Victory in Athens and a First Tragic Khoregic Dedication in the City? (*SEG* 23, 103b)', *ZPE* 118: 174–8.

  2000. *The Athenian Institution of the Khoregia: The Chorus, The City and the Stage.* Cambridge.

  2002. 'The Musicians among the Actors', in P. Easterling and E. Hall, eds. *Greek and Roman Actors: Aspects of an Ancient Profession.* Cambridge. 39–68.

  2007a. 'Choruses for Sale in Thorikos? A Speculative Note on *SEG* 34, 107', *ZPE* 161: 125–32.

  2007b. 'Performance in the Pythion: The Athenian Thargelia', in P. Wilson, ed. *The Greek Theatre and Festivals: Documentary Studies.* Oxford. 150–82.

  2007c. 'Sicilian Choruses', in P. Wilson, ed. *The Greek Theatre and Festivals: Documentary Studies.* Oxford. 351–77.

  2008. 'Costing the Dionysia', in P. Wilson and M. Revermann, eds. *Performance, Reception, Iconography.* Oxford. 88–127.

  2009. 'Tragic Honours and Democracy: Neglected Evidence for the Politics of the Athenian Dionysia', *CQ* 59: 8–29.

  2010a. 'How Did the Athenian Demes Fund their Theatre?', in B. Le Guen, ed. *L'argent dans les concours du monde grec.* Vincennes. 37–82.

  2010b. 'The Man and the Music (and the Choregos?)', in O. Taplin and R. Wyles, eds. *The Pronomos Vase and its Context.* Oxford. 181–212.

  2011a. 'The Glue of Democracy: Tragedy, Structure, and Finance', in D. M. Carter, ed. *Why Athens? A Reappraisal of Tragic Politics.* Oxford. 19–43.

  2011b. 'Dionysos in Hagnous', *ZPE* 177: 79–89.

  2013. 'The Decree of Teleas from the Theatre of Thorikos, Revisited', *ZPE* 184: 159–64.

  2015. 'The Festival of Dionysos in Ikarion: A New Study of *IG* I³ 254', *Hesperia* 84: 97–147.

  2017a. 'A Potted Political History of the Sicilian Theater (to ca. 300)', in H. Reid, D. Tanasi and S. Kimbell, eds. *Politics and Performance in Western Greece: Proceedings of the Second Interdisciplinary Symposium on the Heritage of Western Greece.* Sioux City, IA. 1–32.

  2017b. 'The Theatres and Dionysia of Attica', in A. Kavoulaki, ed. *Πλειών: Papers in Memory of Christiane Sourvinou-Inwood.* Ariadne Supplement 1. Rethymno. 99–146.

Wilson, P. and Csapo, E. 2012. 'From Choregia to Agonothesia: Evidence for the Administration and Finance of the Athenian Theatre in the Late Fourth Century BC', in D. Rosenbloom and J. Davidson, eds. *Greek Drama IV: Texts, Contexts, Performance.* Oxford. 300–21.

Wilson, P. and Favi, F. 2017. 'Choragic Spells in Gela: A Textual and Exegetical Note on Apellis' *Defixio, SEG* LVII 905B', *ZPE* 204: 138–40.

Wilson, P. and Hartwig, A. 2009. '*IG* I³ 102 and the Tradition of Announcing Honours at the Tragic *Agon* of the Athenian City Dionysia', *ZPE* 169: 17–27.

Wilson, R. 1988. 'Archaeology in Sicily', *AR* 34: 105–50.

Winkler, J. J. 1990. 'The Ephebes' Song: *Tragoidia* and *Polis*', in J. J. Winkler and F. I. Zeitlin, eds. *Nothing to Do with Dionysos? Athenian Drama in its Social Context.* Princeton. 20–62.

Wolf, S. 1998. 'Unter dem Einfluß des Dionysos', *JdI* 113: 49–90.

Wolters, P. and Bruns, G. 1940. *Das Kabirenheiligtum bei Theben*, vol. 1. Berlin.

Woodhead, A. G. 1997. *The Athenian Agora*, vol. 16: *Inscriptions: The Decrees*. Princeton.

Woodward, L. H. 2010. *Diogenes of Babylon: A Stoic on Music and Ethics*. MPhil. Thesis. University College London.

Woytek, E. 2004. 'Zur Datierung der Cistellaria', in R. Hartkamp and F. Hurka, eds. *Studien zu Plautus' Cistellaria*. Tübingen. 281–94.

Wuilleumier, P. 1939. *Tarente, des origines à la conquête romaine*. Paris.

Wulfmeier, J.-C. 2005. *Griechische Doppelreliefs*. Münster.

Wycherley, R. E. 1957. *The Athenian Agora*, vol. 3: *Literary and Epigraphical Testimonia*. Princeton.

Xanthakis-Karamanos, G. 1990–1996. 'The *Menedemus* of Lycophron', *Athena* 81: 339–65.

    1997. 'Echoes of Earlier Drama in Sositheus' *Daphnis* and Lycophron's *Menedemus*', *AC* 66: 121–43.

Young, R. 1951. 'An Industrial District of Ancient Athens', *Hesperia* 20: 135–288.

Ypsilanti, M. 2006. 'Laïs and her Mirror', *BICS* 49: 193–213.

Yunis, H. 2001. *Demosthenes: On the Crown*. Cambridge.

Zabbou, E. 1997. 'Μεγαλόπολη', *ArchDelt* 52 B 1: 200–6.

Zanker, P. 1995. *The Mask of Socrates: the Image of the Intellectual in Antiquity*. Berkeley and Los Angeles.

Zaphiropoulos, N. 1971. 'Χρονικά: Κυκλάδες', *ArchDelt* 26: 463–7.

Zaphiropoulou, F. 1977. 'Ἀρχαιότητες καὶ Μνημεῖα Κυκλάδων', *ArchDelt* 32 B 2: 308–11.

Zecchini, G. 1989. *La cultura storica di Ateneo*. Milan.

Zhmud, L. 2012. *Pythagoras and the Early Pythagoreans*. Oxford.

Ziebarth, E. 1934. 'Neue Verfluchungstafeln aus Attika, Boiotien und Euboia', *SBBerl* 33: 1022–50.

Ziehen, L. 1939. 'Olympia', *RE* 18.1: 1–71.

Zielinski, T. 1887. *Quaestiones comicae*. St. Petersburg.

Zimmermann, B. 1992. *Antike Dramentheorien und ihre Rezeption*. Stuttgart.

    1993. *Dithyrambos, Geschichte einer Gattung*. Hypomnemata 98. Göttingen.

Zirone, D. 2005. 'Storia della Ricerca Archeologica', *Bibliografia Topografica della Colonizzazione Greca in Italia e nelle Isole Tirreniche* 19: 145–386.

Zizza, C. 2006. *Le iscrizioni nella Periegesi di Pausania: Commento ai testi epigrafici*. Pisa.

Zolotaryov, M. I. 2005. 'The Civic Frontiers of Tauric Chersonesus in the Fourth Century BC', in D. Braund, ed. *Scythians and Greeks: Cultural Interactions in Scythia, Athens and the Early Roman Empire (sixth century BC - first century AD)*. Exeter. 148–52.

Zolotas, G. I. 1923. *Ἱστορία τῆς Χίου*, vol. 1: *Ἱστορικὴ τοπογραφία καὶ γενεαλογία*, pt. 2: *Τοπογραφία πόλεως Χίου γενεαλογία*. Athens.

Zoumpakes, S. 1987. 'Θεατρικὰ προσωπεῖα τοῦ Ἐθνικοῦ Ἀρχαιολογικοῦ Μουσείου', *ArchDelt* 42 A: 35–65.

Zunino, M. 1997. *Hiera Messeniaka: La storia religiosa della Messenia dall'età micenea all'età ellenistica*. Udine.

Zwierlein, O. 1966. *Die Rezitationsdramen Senecas*. Meisenheim-am-Glan.

General Index

Museum Index

Agrigento
  Museo Archeologico Regionale

AG 7	white-ground calyx krater	363

Andros
  Archaeological Museum

82	honorific decree	**IV Di**
185	statue base	614

Athens
  Agora Museum

P 23985	polychrome oinochoe	428

  Epigraphical Museum

139	deme decree	**III Di**
4213	honorific decree	**III Wvi**
7239	polis decree	**III Viii**
7693	tribal decree	190
7709	tribal decree	**III P**
7719	deme decree	**III Vvi**
7744	deme decree	**III Rii**
7745	deme decree	**III Rii**
7748	deme decree	**III Bvi**
8022	Amphictyonic accounts	**IV Dvi 5**
8188	tragic victor list	**IV Bvi 5**
10301	choregic monument	**III Biii**
10670	choregic monument	**III C**
12667	deme decree	**III Dii**
12693	choregic monument	**III J**
13180	choregic monument	**III Ei**
13262	deme decree	**III Div**
13315	votive dedication	**III Mxii**
13316	choregic monument	**III Miv**
13319	deme decree	**III Mx**
13446	deme decree	**III Vvi**
13447	deme decree	**III Vvi**
13537	sacrificial calendar	256
—	deme decree	**III Iii**
—	polis decree	**III Viv**

  National Archaeological Museum

BΣ 518	Perseus Dancer Vase	256, 415, 443

Athens (cont.)

231	statue of Themis	**III Wiii**
1500	choregic relief	183, 208
1733	Bryaxis base	205
2328	statue of Dionysus	237
2400	choregic relief	11, 16, 247, 252
3064	tragic female mask	142
3072	statue of Dionysus	**III Mi**
3073	statue of Dionysus	**III Mi**
3074	statue of Dionysus	**III Mi**
3078	relief with gods, chorus, goat	**III Mxi**
3897	statue of Dionysus	**III Mi**
4531	choregic monument	**III Mv**
4833 (face A)	deme accounts	**III Mii**
4833 (face B)	Dionysia regulations	**III Miii**
4880	deme decree	**III Mvi**
4884	deme decree	138
4888	statue canopy	**III Mi**
Kar. 1205	deme decree	**III Dv**
10426	Cabiric vase	551–2
12507	statue inscription	**III Mi**
12556	figurine woman with skyphos	433
14470	curse tablet	271
—	terracotta tesserae	**IV Bxi**

Berlin

Pergamon Museum

Priene Inv. 49	honorific decree	**IV Evii 3**
Priene Inv. 52	honorific decree	**IV Evii 2**
Priene Inv. 208	honorific decree	**IV Evii 1**

Staatliche Museen, Antikensammlung

F 3046	rf bell krater (now lost)	**IV Axxiii**
F 3296	rf calyx krater	**IV Axviii**

Boston

Museum of Fine Art

69.695	rf bell krater	**IV Axxiv**, 415

Brauron

Archaeological Museum

BE 848	deme decree	**III X**
BE 2925	deme decree	**III Ki**
NE 1177	altar with reliefs	85

Caltanissetta

Museo Archeologico

1301bis	rf calyx krater	**IV Axx**, 399

Cambridge
  Trinity College Library
    —   Amphictyonic accounts   **IV Dvi 5**

Çannakale
  Archaeological Museum
    —   administrative decree   **IV Eii**
    —   administrative decree   **IV Eiii**
Chapel Hill
  University of North Carolina Library, Rare Book Room
    —   lead curse tablet   **IV Avii**
Chios
  Archaeological Museum
    652   honorific decree   **IV Diii 2**
    1047   honorific decree   **IV Diii 4**
Copenhagen
  National Museum
    ABb. 255   deme decree   **III Bi**
Corinth
  Excavations
    2435   inscribed theatre seat   **IV Biv 7**
    2437   inscribed theatre seat   **IV Biv 7**
    2438   inscribed theatre seat   **IV Biv 5**
    2439   inscribed theatre seat   **IV Biv 6**
    2440   inscribed theatre seat   **IV Biv 4**
    2441   inscribed theatre seat   **IV Biv 3**
    2447   inscribed theatre seat foundation **IV Biv 8**
Cos
  Castle Museum
    619   honorific decree   **IV Diii 3**
Cyrene
  Archaeological Museum
    161   public accounts   **IV Gi 3**
    443   public accounts   **IV Gi 4**
    15003   limestone reliefs   808

Delos
  Archaeological Museum
    A 1185   votive dedication   **IV Dvi 2**
    Γ 237   treasury accounts   **IV Dvi 7**
    Γ 503   treasury accounts   **IV Dvi 8**
    Δ 419   Nesiotic League decree   **IV Dvi 11**
    E 500   choregic monument   **IV Dvi 10**

Ikarion
 Excavations
  in situ   choregic monument   **III Mix**

Kastro
 Archaeological Museum
  31   honorific decree   **IV Dxiv 2**

Lavrion
 Archaeological Museum
  591   record of choregoi   **III Yv**
  593   votive dedication   **III Yi**
  TE 83.02   deme decree   **III Yii**
  TE 83.03   choregic monument   **III Yiv**
  TE 85.105   deme decree   **III Yiii**

London
 British Museum
  1785,0527.7   deme decree   **III Vv**
  inscription 12   deme decree   **III Vvi**

Malibu
 J. Paul Getty Museum
  83.AE.41   white-ground lekythos   363–4

Marathon
 Archaeological Museum
  Λ 125   statue canopy   **III Mi**

Milan
 Museo Civico Archeologico
  AO.9.284   rf bell krater   420

Moscow
 State Historical Museum
  Б 2691   choregic comic relief   **I Aviii 1d**, 778, 787

Munich
 Staatliche Antikensammlungen und Glyptothek
  552   votive relief   **III Kii**

Myrina
 Archaeological Museum
  2049   honorific decree   **IV Dviii**

Mytilene
 Archaeological Museum
  1087   honorific decree   **IV Dix 2**
  1129   honorific decree   **IV Dix 3**

Naples
 Museo Archeologico Nazionale
  Stg 368   relief guttus   **IV Axxvi**

Index Locorum

Aelian
    NA 6.51: **IV Av 2**, 338, 343, 344
    NA 11.19: **IV Dv**
    VH 2.13: **III Vi**
    VH 14.40: **IV Cx 3**, 587–8
Aeneas Tacticus
    17.5: **IV Diii 1**, 611, 628, 630–1
Aeschines
    1.157: **III Oi**
    3.41–8: **I Av 4g**, 190
Aeschylus
    Eu. 9–14: 580
    TrGF F 231: 364
    TrGF F 233: 357
    TrGF F 261: 357
    TrGF F 365: 364
    TrGF F 382: 30, 31
    TrGF T 1.35–47: **IV Aix 2**, 358, 359–61
    TrGF T 3: **IV Aix 1**, 358
    TrGF T 86: 355
    TrGF T 162: 359
Aglaosthenes
    FGrH 499 F 3
Alciphron
    3.12: 534
    4.18: 807
Alexis
    PCG F 146: 504–5
    PCG T 1: 288
Amphion of Thespiae
    FGrH 387 F 1: **IV Cv 3**, 564–5
Anaxandrides
    PCG T 1: 697
    PCG T 2: 697
Androtion
    FGrH 324 F 38: 77
Anonymous
    De com. 1–7: **I Avii 3d**, 453
    De com. 9: **IV Aiii 8**, 317–18, 328, 343

    De com. 32: **IV Avi**
    Vit. Aesch. 10–11: **IV Aix 2**, 358, 359–61
    Vit. Aeschin. 1.7: **III Oiv**
    Vit. Eurip. 6: **IV Cix 1**, 536, 584–5
    Vit. Soph. 55–8: **IV Cviii**
    Vit. Soph. 78–9: **IV Bvi 6**
Anthologia Graeca
    7.21: 37
    7.37: **IV Bvi 8**, 432, 480–1
    7.82: 482
    7.125: **IV Aiii 7**, 318, 319
    7.707: **IV Bvi 9**, 432, 480–1, 482
    7.708: 481
    9.600: **IV Aiii 6**
    11.32: **IV Bv 5**, 432, 471
    13.28: 261
Antiatticist
    π 34: 344
Antigonus of Carystus
    Mir. 161: **IV Div**
Antiphanes
    PCG F 111: 334, 771
    PCG F 145: 272
    PCG T 1: 697
    PCG T 2: 697
Antiphon
    5.77: **IV Dix 1**, 606, 679–80
Apollodorus
    Neaer. 59.78: 31
Apollophanes
    PCG F 9: 343
Apostolius
    15.9: 647
Archilochus
    fr. 251 West: 685
Arion
    PMG 939: 214
Ariphron
    PMG 813: 47

Epigraphical Index